The **Rough Guide** to

Southwest USA

written and researched by

Greg Ward

D0108997

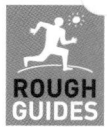

ROUGH GUIDES

NEW YORK · LONDON · DELHI

www.roughguides.com

Contents

Native peoples insert
following p.184

**On location in the
Southwest** insert
following p.440

◄◄ Wigwam Motel, Holbrook, Arizona ◄ North Window, Arches National Park

Introduction to

Southwest USA

The Southwest is the most extraordinary and spectacular region of the United States. The splendor and scale of its scenery consistently defies belief – a glorious panoply of cliffs and canyons, buttes and mesas, carved from rocks of every imaginable color, and enriched here by groves of shimmering cottonwoods and aspens, there by cactuses and agaves. In addition, the Southwest is unique in being the only part of the United States whose original inhabitants remain in residence. Though century after century has brought fresh waves of intruders, somehow none has entirely succeeded in displacing its predecessors, leaving all to co-exist in an intriguing blend of cultures and traditions.

The area covered by this book roughly corresponds to the former Spanish colony of **New Mexico**, which has belonged to the US for little more than 150 years, and is now divided between the modern states of New Mexico, Arizona, Utah, Colorado, and Nevada. Though rainfall is scarce everywhere, not all the region is **desert**; indeed, the popular image of the Southwest as consisting of scrubby hillsides studded with many-armed saguaro cactuses is true only of the Sonoran Desert of southern Arizona. Towering snow-capped **mountains** rise not only in southern Colorado and northern New Mexico, at the tail-end of the Rockies, but are scattered across Utah and Arizona as well, while dense **pine forests** cloak much of northern Arizona.

Where to go

The most dramatic landscapes in the Southwest stretch along the **Colorado Plateau**, an arid mile-high tableland, roughly the size of California, that extends across the **Four Corners** region of Arizona, Utah, Colorado, and New Mexico. Atop the main body of the plateau, layers of rock are piled level upon level, creating a "**Grand Staircase**" of successive cliffs and plateaus. During the last dozen or so million years, the entire complex has been pushed steadily upwards by subterranean forces. As it has risen, the earth has cracked, warped, buckled and split, and endless quantities of crumbling sandstone have been washed away by the Colorado River and its tributaries. The **Grand Canyon** is simply the most famous of hundreds of dramatic **canyons**, its vastness a challenge to human comprehension. Sheer weirdness overwhelms in **southern Utah** – the red rocks of **Monument Valley**, the fiery sandstone pinnacles of **Bryce Canyon**, the endless expanses of **Canyonlands**.

◀ Harris hawk, Arizona-Sonora Desert Museum, Tucson

5

Reminders of the Southwest's remarkable **history** are everywhere you look. Ancient archeological sites abound, ranging from the free-standing pueblos of Chaco Canyon and the cliff dwellings of Mesa Verde to the artificial caves of Bandelier and the haunting rock art of Horseshoe Canyon, while the flourishing **Navajo** and **Apache** lands are merely the largest of around fifty modern-day Indian reservations. The **Spanish** too have been a presence for almost five hundred years; exquisite eighteenth-century missions survive at San Xavier and Tumacácori in southern Arizona, while northern New Mexico holds stunning adobe churches such as San Francisco de Asis at Taos,

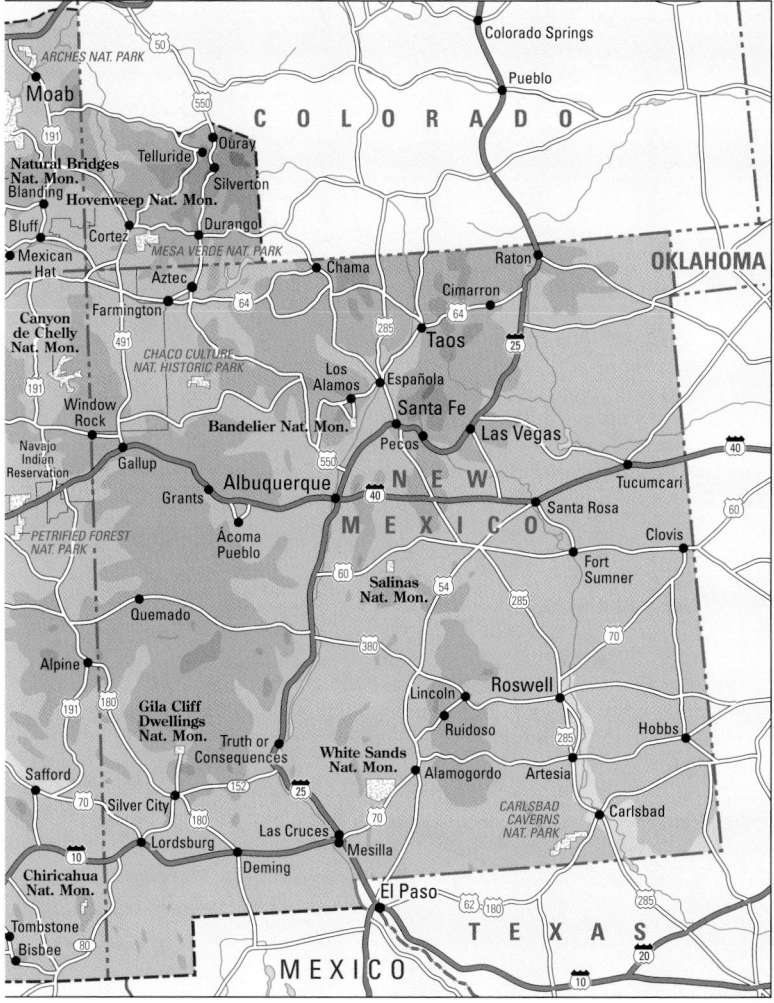

and the humbler but still ravishing shrine at Chimayó. The first Americans to arrive after the Spaniards were the **Mormons**, a religious sect who through utter determination and communal effort colonized Utah in the nineteenth century. **American settlers** arrived soon after and swiftly outnumbered everyone else.

In the early years of US rule, the Southwest was very much the **Wild West**. That era is now recalled in towns like **Lincoln**, New Mexico, where Billy the Kid blazed his way out of jail, and **Tombstone**, Arizona, where the Earps and the Clantons fought it out at the OK Corral.

Route 66

If you do ever plan to motor west, there's still one definitive highway that's the best. Eighty years since it was first completed, seventy since John Steinbeck called it "the mother road, the road of flight" in *The Grapes of Wrath*, and sixty since songwriter Bobby Troup set it all down in rhyme, what better reason to visit the Southwest could there be than to get hip to this timely tip, and get your kicks on **Route 66**?

The heyday of Route 66 as the nation's premier cross-country route – winding from Chicago to LA – lasted barely twenty years, from its being paved in 1937 until it began to be superceded by freeways in 1957. It was officially rendered defunct in 1984, when Williams, Arizona, became the last town to be bypassed. Nonetheless, substantial stretches of the original Route 66 survive, complete with the motels and drive-ins that became icons of vernacular American architecture. Restored 1950s roadsters and the latest Harley Davidsons to cruise along the atmospheric, neon-lit frontages of towns such as Albuquerque and

▲ Vintage sign on former Route 66, Albuquerque

Flagstaff, or through such empty desertscapes as those between Grants and Gallup in New Mexico, or Seligman and Kingman in Arizona.

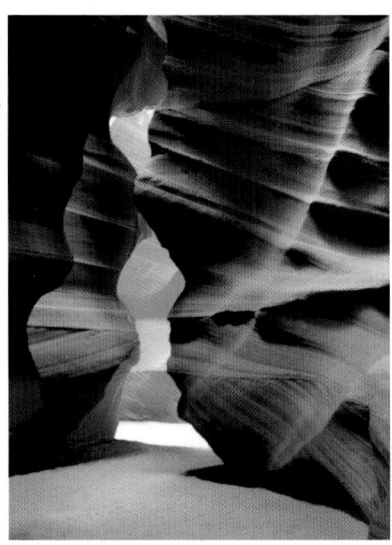

▲ Antelope Canyon

The century since Utah, Arizona, and New Mexico achieved statehood has been characterized by attempts to transform the landscape on an unprecedented – not to say unnatural, let alone unsustainable – scale. A series of monumental **water** projects, including the construction of **Hoover Dam**, the damming of Utah's Glen Canyon to form **Lake Powell**, and the creation of a network of canals across hundreds of miles of the Arizona desert, has brought the region prosperity as the **Sunbelt**.

▶ Saguaro cactus

While the proximity of the wilderness remains the supreme attraction for most visitors, certain Southwestern **cities** make worthwhile destinations in their own right. **Santa Fe** is the best example, with its 400-year history, top-quality museums and galleries, and superb array of hotels and restaurants; **Tucson** holds an enjoyable combination of desert parks, Hispanic history, restaurants, and ranch resorts; and **Las Vegas**, entirely and quintessentially a product of the modern era – it was only founded in 1905 – is far too amazing to miss. **Phoenix**, on the other hand, is one to avoid; it's possible to have a good time there, but it isn't worth a stop unless you have a *very* long vacation.

Though most of the region's **smaller towns** are best treated as overnight pit-stops, some

Fact file

• **New Mexico** covers 121,599 square miles – which makes it the fifth largest state in the Union – and has a population of 1,903,289, just under ten percent of whom are of Native American descent. The state holds 22 reservations, comprising 19 separate pueblos plus the Jicarilla and Mescalero Apache lands and part of the Navajo Nation. New Mexico became the 47th state on January 6, 1912; its capital is Santa Fe.

• **Arizona**, with an area of 113,635 square miles, is the sixth largest state. Around five percent of its 5,743,834 population are of Native American descent; its 21 Indian reservations include the homelands of the Navajo, the Hopi, the Havasupai, the Hualapai, the 'O'odham and the San Carlos, and Tonto and White Mountain Apache. With Phoenix as its capital, it achieved statehood on February 14, 1912, as the last of the "lower 48."

• **Utah** comprises 84,916 square miles – 65 percent is owned by the federal government – and has a population of 2,389,039, over 70 percent of which are Mormons. This book covers the state's southern desert areas, where around 170,000 people are spread across 27,000 square miles. Utah became the 45th state on January 4, 1896.

• The portion of southwest **Colorado** described in this book represents about 5000 of the state's 103,730 square miles and holds about 38,000 of its total population of 4,601,403. Colorado was the 38th state to join the Union, on August 1, 1876.

• Finally, this book also includes a chapter on **Las Vegas** in southern Nevada. Las Vegas is in Clark County, which takes up just 7,910 of the state's 109,826 square miles, but holds almost two thirds of its 2,334,771 population. It's not the capital however– Carson City is. Nevada became the 36th state on October 31, 1864.

Native Americans

Although the Southwestern terrain may appear inhospitable in the extreme, it has been home to **Native Americans** for over ten thousand years. The fifty distinct reservations in the region range in size from tiny **pueblo** villages in New Mexico to the largest reservation in the United States, the **"Navajo Nation,"** which covers 27,000 square miles and takes up much of the Colorado Plateau. For the most part, tribes continue to occupy the homelands of their ancestors, as opposed to the pattern elsewhere in the US, where Native Americans were forcibly displaced onto poorer lands with which they lack any spiritual connection.

Nonetheless, considerable bitterness still surrounds the allocation of reservations. The Navajo themselves only arrived in the Southwest shortly before the Spaniards, for example, and encroached upon the Hopi, so the fact that their reservation now surrounds and constricts the Hopi's remains a source of ongoing contention. What's more, US law dictates that reservations can only consist of lands where a single tribe can prove it had exclusive use, so traditionally shared hunting grounds were excluded from the reservations and left open to exploitation by Anglo settlers.

Much more detail can be found in the *Native peoples of the Southwest* color section near the middle of the guide.

have blossomed into appealing bases. **Moab** and **Springdale** make welcome exceptions to the typical monotony of southern Utah farming communities; the college town of **Flagstaff** is a lively enclave within easy reach of the Grand Canyon; and **Taos** still has the feel of the artists' colony that attracted Georgia O'Keeffe and D. H. Lawrence.

The only practical way to explore the Southwest in any detail is to **drive** yourself around; the very limited public transport options are outlined on p.28 and p.44. However long your vacation may be, aim to spend most of your time on the Colorado Plateau, seeing as much as possible of the Four Corners region and southern Utah.

What airport you land at will largely dictate a **one-week itinerary**. From **Las Vegas**, loop around the Colorado River to Grand Canyon, Zion and possibly Bryce Canyon national parks; from **Phoenix**, head to Canyon de Chelly, Monument Valley, and the Grand Canyon; **Albuquerque** is a gateway to Santa Fe, Taos, and Ácoma Pueblo; from **Salt Lake City** you can head south to make a lightning tour of all of Utah's national parks.

With **two weeks**, you can extend any of the aforementioned itineraries to cover most of the Colorado Plateau, making sure you get to Canyon de Chelly, Monument Valley, and Mesa Verde. If you want to do any major hiking – for example into the stunning Havasupai Indian Reservation, or down to *Phantom Ranch* in the Grand Canyon – it's possible on a one-week trip, but you'll limit the scope of the region you can cover.

When to go

ummer is the peak tourist season for most of the Southwest, though temperatures in excess of 100°F render cities such as Phoenix and Tucson all but unbearable, and make it an ordeal even to get out of your car in many of the national parks. Hikers, bikers, and rafters would do better to come either between mid-September and late October, when the crowds are gone and dazzling fall colors

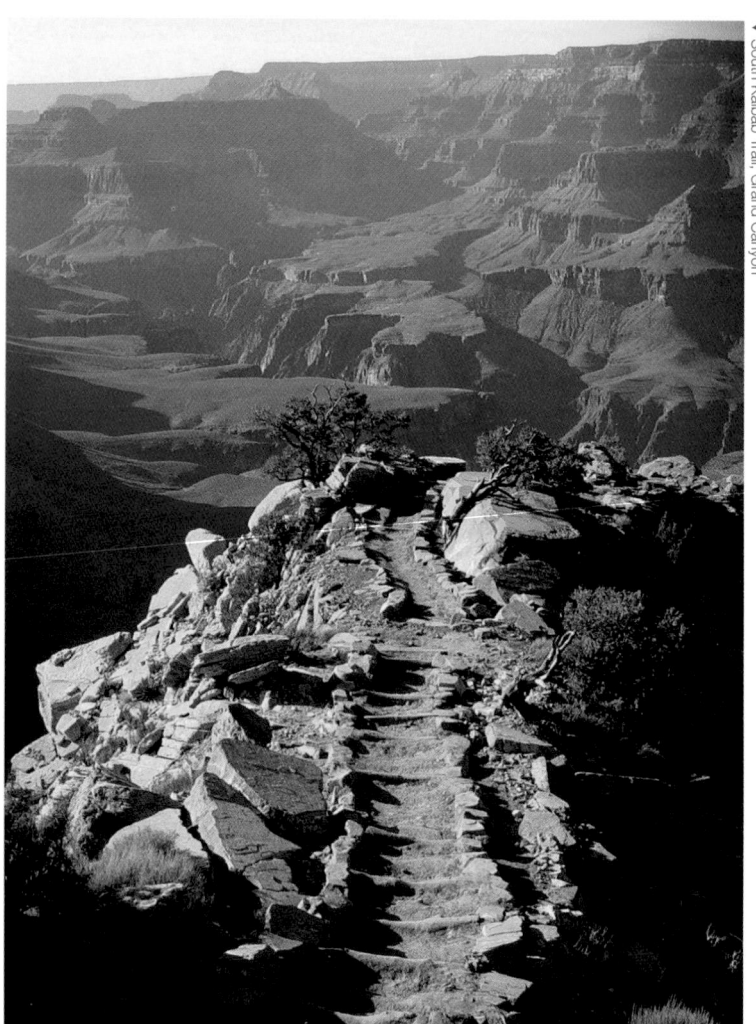

brighten the canyons, or in April and May, when wildflowers bloom in the desert.

If your schedule isn't flexible, however, don't worry. It's always possible to escape the heat – the thermometer drops by 3°F for every thousand feet above sea level, so Santa Fe, for example, is always relatively cool – and the summer is also the peak period for the region's festivals, as detailed on p.53.

Winters can be seriously cold, and snowfalls close down certain areas altogether – don't reckon on seeing Mesa Verde, or the North Rim of the Grand Canyon, between October and April. Those parks that remain open are often at their most beautiful when frosted with snow, however – Bryce Canyon is quite magical – while ski resorts like Telluride and Taos are in full swing, and Tucson and Phoenix fill up with sun-seeking "snowbirds" from colder states. The major drawback to winter is that there are significantly fewer hours of daylight, which makes it much harder to both cover great distances by road and enjoy your destination once you arrive.

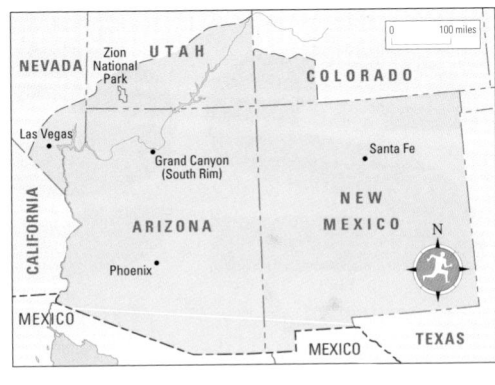

Average temperatures and rainfall

	Jan	Feb	Mar	Apr	May	Jun	Jul	Aug	Sep	Oct	Nov	Dec
Grand Canyon (South Rim)												
Av High °F	41	45	51	60	70	81	84	82	76	65	52	43
Av Low °F	18	21	25	32	39	47	54	53	47	36	27	20
Rainfall (in)	1.3	1.5	1.4	0.9	0.7	0.4	1.8	2.3	1.6	1.1	0.9	1.6
Las Vegas, NV												
Av High °F	56	67	68	77	87	98	104	101	94	81	66	57
Av Low °F	33	37	42	49	59	68	75	73	65	53	41	33
Rainfall (in)	0.5	0.5	0.4	0.2	0.2	0.1	0.5	0.5	0.3	0.3	0.4	0.3
Phoenix, AZ												
Av High °F	65	69	75	84	93	102	105	102	98	88	75	66
Av Low °F	38	41	45	52	60	68	78	76	69	57	45	39
Rainfall (in)	0.8	0.8	0.8	0.5	0.3	0.3	0.7	0.9	0.6	0.6	0.6	0.8
Santa Fe, NM												
Av High °F	40	44	51	60	69	79	82	80	74	63	50	41
Av Low °F	19	22	28	35	43	52	57	56	49	38	27	20
Rainfall (in)	0.6	0.8	0.8	0.9	1.2	1.1	2.4	2.3	1.7	1.1	0.7	0.7
Zion National Park												
Av High °F	52	57	63	73	83	93	100	97	91	78	63	53
Av Low °F	29	31	36	43	52	60	68	66	60	49	37	30
Rainfall (in)	1.6	1.6	1.7	1.3	0.7	0.6	0.8	1.6	0.8	1.0	1.2	1.5

To convert Fahrenheit to Celsius, subtract 32, multiply by 5, and divide by 9.
To convert inches to millimeters, multiply by 25.4

29

things not to miss

It's not possible to see everything that the Southwest has to offer in one trip – and we don't suggest you try. What follows is a selective and subjective taste of the region's highlights: spectacular national parks, unforgettable outdoor activities, Wild West towns, and Las Vegas glitz. They're arranged in five color-coded categories to help you find the very best things to see, do, and experience. All entries have a page reference to take you straight into the guide, where you can find out more.

01 **Ácoma Pueblo** Page **122** • The Ácomans defied the Spaniards from this stunning cliff-top village five centuries ago, and they're still here.

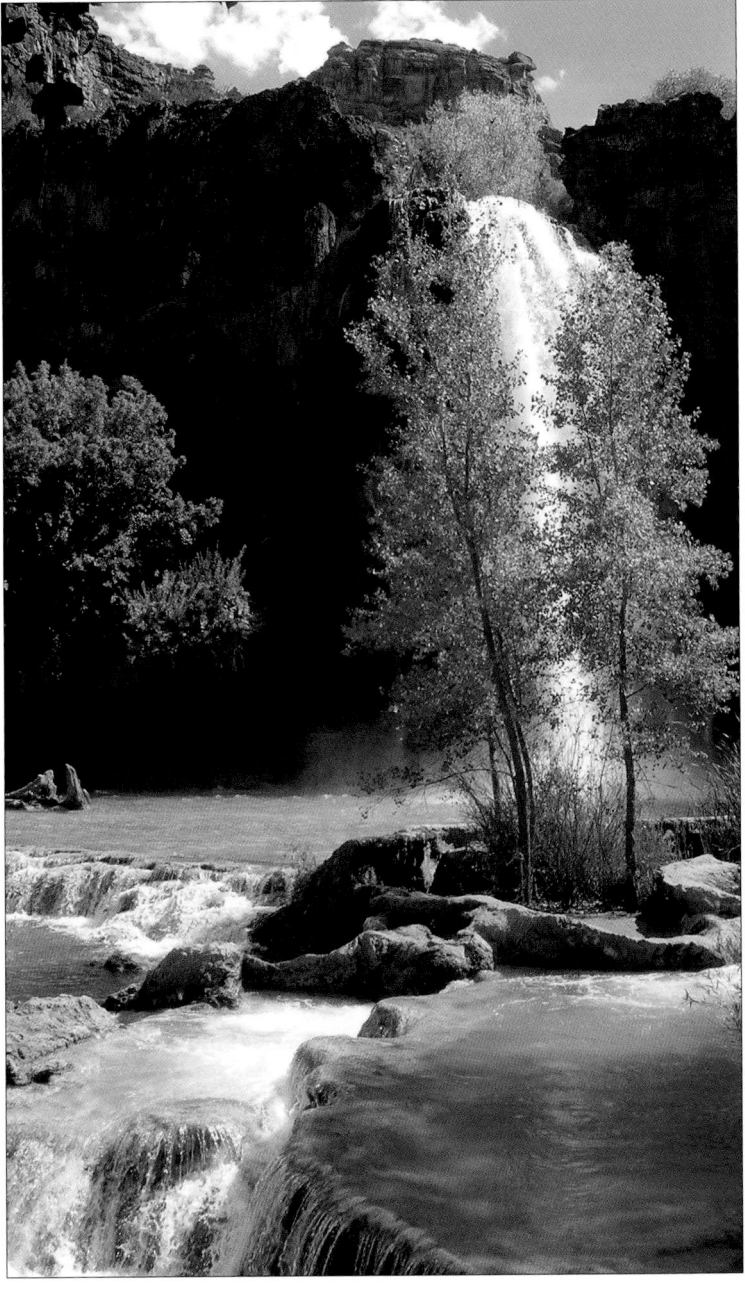

02 Havasu Falls Page **396** • These lush turquoise waterfalls turn the Havasupai Reservation into an amazing Grand-Canyon oasis.

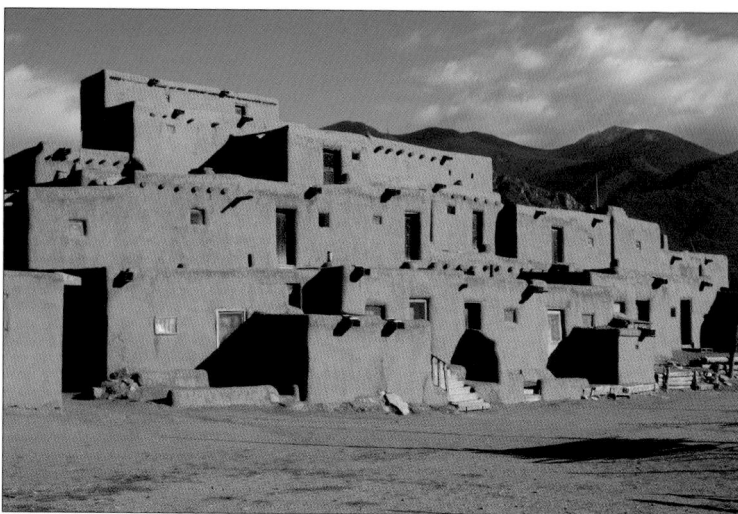

03 **Taos Pueblo** Page **187** • The most famous of the modern Pueblos makes a dramatic sight at the foot of the Sangre de Cristo mountains.

05 **Delicate Arch** Page **515** • The trail up to Utah's state symbol, an extraordinary free-standing natural arch, epitomizes the wonder of Utah's wilderness parks.

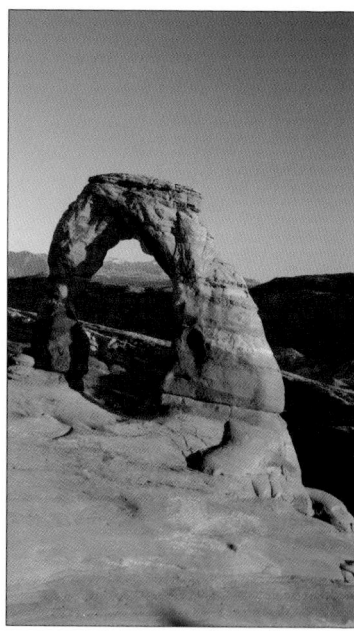

04 **Native American crafts** Page **50** • From silver and turquoise jewelry and Hopi kachinas or fine Pueblo ceramics, the Southwest is renowned for its locally produced craftworks and souvenirs.

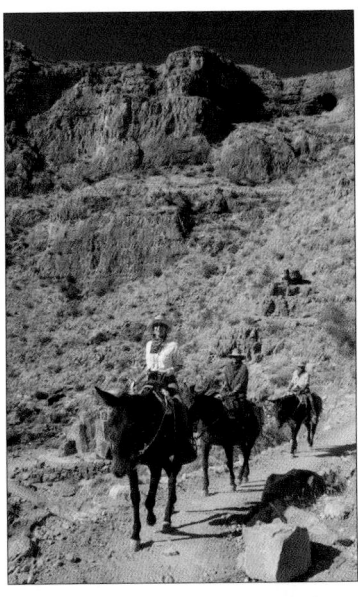

06 **Calf Creek Falls** Page **468** • Not far off the highway in the heart of southern Utah, this glorious waterfall is the highlight of Grand Staircase-Escalante National Monument.

08 **La Fonda de Santa Fe** Page **136** • Historic Western hotels don't come any more atmospheric than this beauty at the end of the Santa Fe Trail.

I ACTIVITIES I CONSUME I EVENTS I NATURE I SIGHTS I

09 **The buffets of Las Vegas** Page **566** • Las Vegas' all you-can-eat buffets
have long been a byword for value; these days the food itself can be great too.

10 **Saguaro National Park** Page **281** • The saguaro cactuses, spreading
in majestic abundance through the deserts of southern Arizona, are one of the
quintessential symbols of the Southwest.

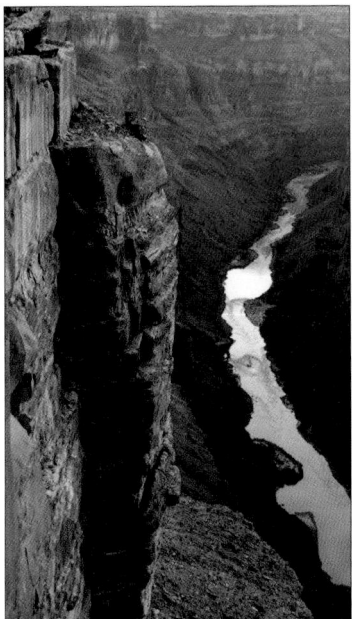

12 **Mesa Verde** Page **94** • If you've never understood all the fuss about "cliff dwellings," the ancient remains hidden in these Colorado canyons should make their appeal abundantly clear.

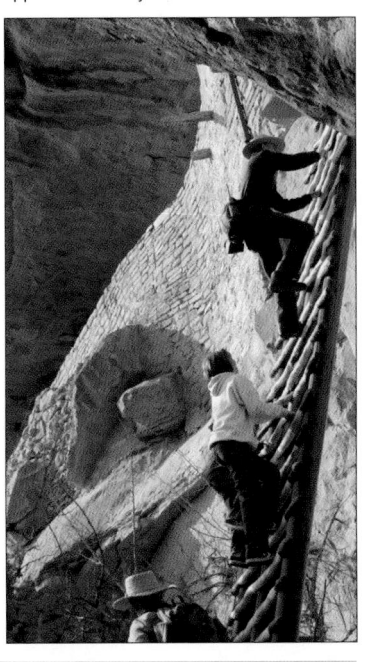

11 **Toroweap Point** Page **410** • At times the Grand Canyon can seem too vast to comprehend, but this unique canyon overlook, above a 3000-foot drop to the river, has an immediate visceral impact.

13 **Albuquerque International Balloon Festival** Page **208** • The early-morning mass ascents of hundreds of colorful hot-air balloons during Albuquerque's October showcase are an utterly breathtaking sight.

14 **Cirque de Soleil** Page **560** • Staging two of the finest shows the city has to offer, the Canadian circus troupe has transformed Las Vegas' entertainment scene.

15 **Canyon de Chelly** Page **75** • Perhaps the most beautiful canyon in the Southwest, rendered all the more magical by its magnificent Ancestral Puebloan ruins.

17 Monument Valley Page 69 • You may have seen them a thousand times in the movies, but your first real-life glimpse of the silhouetted buttes of Monument Valley is a guaranteed heart-stopping moment.

16 The Great Gallery Page 505 • The most fascinating and mysterious ancient rock art in the Southwest, only accessible via a long desert hike into a remote region of Utah's Canyonlands.

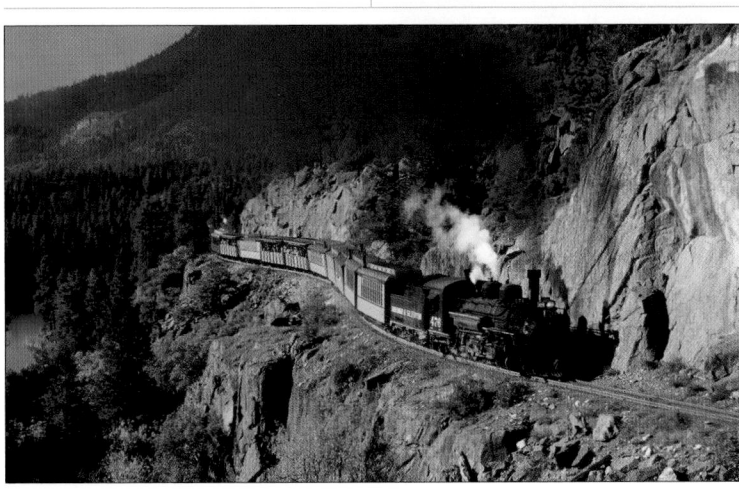

18 Ride the Durango & Silverton Railroad Page 102 • Taking a steam train up to the old Colorado mining town of Silverton is the perfect way to spend a day in the Rockies.

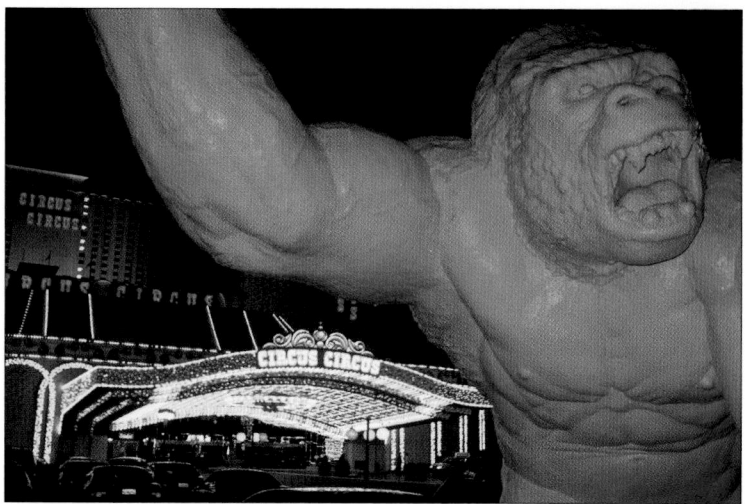

19 Las Vegas at night Page **548** • The blazing neon along the Strip, with its volcanoes, pyramids, and battling pirates, is an all-out assault on the senses.

20 San Xavier del Bac Page **286** • Mission churches throughout the Southwest bear witness to the region's Hispanic heritage, but none is more exquisite than the "White Dove of the Desert" outside Tucson.

21 The Inter-Tribal Indian Ceremonial
Page **116** • The classic Route 66 town of Gallup, New Mexico, comes alive in August for this annual Navajo fair.

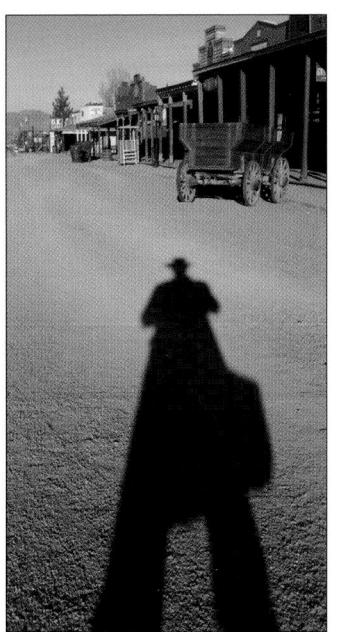

22 Tombstone
Page **296** • With hourly Wild West shoot-outs on the streets outside the OK Corral, Tombstone loves to ham up its past, but it's still great fun to visit.

23 White Sands National Monument
Page **229** • This dazzling sandscape of snow-white dunes amply rewards the long drive across southern New Mexico.

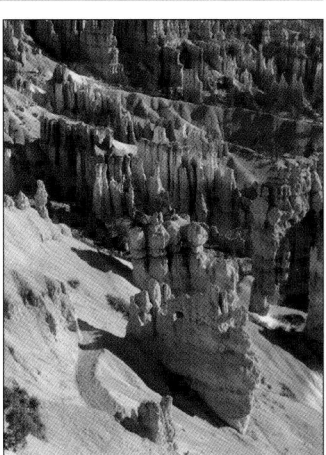

24 Bryce Canyon
Page **450** • An utterly unforgettable landscape, where the earth peels back to reveal a rainbow-hued forest of towering sandstone pinnacles.

25 Zion Canyon Page **425** • Carved by the Virgin River into the red-rock hills of southern Utah, Zion makes a lovely refuge as you escape the mayhem of Las Vegas.

26 Rafting in Canyonlands Page **524** • Whether you choose a gentle float or a multi-day whitewater epic, Canyonlands National Park makes a fabulous destination for a raft trip.

27 Lincoln Page **221** • The town that witnessed some of Billy the Kid's most legendary exploits still feels like a lonesome frontier outpost.

29 La Posada Page **325** • This enormous, rambling, and irresistible former railroad hotel, now lovingly restored, is an unexpected gem in the Route 66 outpost of Winslow.

28 Hiking in the Grand Canyon Page **384** • Explore the innermost secrets of the Grand Canyon on one of its many superb hiking trails.

Basics

Basics

Getting there

For US and Canadian travelers who live too far from the Southwest simply to drive there, and for international travelers, the most cost-effective way to visit Southwest USA is to fly to one of the three major cities described in this book, rent a car there, make a loop tour, and fly home from the same airport.

Las Vegas, Nevada, is probably the best bet, as it offers low air fares and rental-car rates, welcomes more direct flights from overseas than its rivals, and makes an exhilarating starting point for tours to the Grand Canyon and the national parks of southern Utah. Sky Harbor International Airport in **Phoenix**, Arizona, is equally well served by the major domestic carriers, and although Phoenix itself is a less appealing destination it's convenient for both the Grand Canyon and the deserts of southern Arizona. New Mexico's principal airport, in **Albuquerque**, receives fewer long-distance flights, but it's the obvious point of arrival if you want to see Santa Fe and Taos, and it's also the closest airport to the Four Corners region.

If Utah is your prime destination, it's also worth considering flying to **Salt Lake City**. Although the state capital lies in Utah's mountainous northwest corner and is therefore outside the area covered in this guide, it's little more than half a day's drive from adventure-driven Moab and national parks such as Canyonlands and Arches.

The kind of fares you can expect to pay to reach the region from different parts of the world are outlined in the sections that follow. Note that fares also vary widely according to how far in advance you make a reservation. **Finding the best price** of course involves shopping around; any travel agent should be prepared to check with several different airlines, and it's easy to do so yourself on the Internet.

Booking flights online

Good deals can often be found through discount or auction sites, as well as through airlines' own websites. These online services avoid the costs of agents and middlemen.

Online booking agents and general travel sites

ⓦ **www.cheapflights.com** (US), ⓦ **www.cheapflights.co.uk** (UK), ⓦ **www.cheapflights.ca** (Canada), ⓦ **www.cheapflights.com.au** (Australia). Flight deals, travel agents, plus links to other travel sites.
ⓦ **www.cheaptickets.com** Discount flight specialists (US only).
ⓦ **www.ebookers.com** Efficient, easy-to-use flight finder, with competitive fares.
ⓦ **www.expedia.co.uk** (UK), ⓦ **www.expedia .com** (US), ⓦ **www.expedia.ca** (Canada). Discount airfares, all-airline search engine and daily deals.
ⓦ **www.flyaow.com** "Airlines of the Web" – online air travel info and reservations.
ⓦ **www.hotwire.com** Bookings from the US only. Last-minute savings of up to forty percent on regular published fares. Travelers must be at least 18 and there are no refunds, transfers or changes allowed. Log-in required.
ⓦ **www.lastminute.com** (UK), ⓦ **www.lastminute.com.au** (Australia), ⓦ **www.lastminute.co.nz** (New Zealand), ⓦ **www.site59.com** (US). Good last-minute holiday package and flight-only deals.
ⓦ **www.orbitz.com** Comprehensive web travel source, with the usual flight, car hire and hotel deals but also great follow-up customer service.
ⓦ **www.priceline.com** (US), ⓦ **www.priceline .co.uk** (UK). Name-your-own-price website that has deals at around forty percent off standard fares.
ⓦ **www.qixo.com** Flight finder for online airfares.
ⓦ **www.travelocity.com** (US), ⓦ **www .travelocity.co.uk** (UK), ⓦ **www.travelocity .ca** (Canada), ⓦ **www.zuji.com.au** (Australia). Destination guides, hot fares and great deals for car rental, accommodation and lodging.
ⓦ **www.travelshop.com.au** Australian site offering discounted flights, packages, insurance, and online bookings.

From North America

North American travelers can drive to the Southwest or reach it by air, by rail, and by bus. As is made clear in the **Getting Around** section, which starts on p.41, however, it's not practical to tour the region using public transport; if you don't arrive by car, plan to rent one once you're there.

By air

Flights to the Southwest are at their most expensive in summer, which despite soaring temperatures is the **peak season** for travel. Prices drop during the **"shoulder"** seasons – September to shortly before Christmas, and March through May – and are cheapest during the **low** season, from January to February. Note also that flying on weekends, to Las Vegas in particular, can add a hefty premium to fares; price ranges quoted below assume midweek travel.

In general, the best bargains tend to be on flights to **Las Vegas;** JetBlue, for example, offers round-trip fares from New York for around $200. It should be possible to find fares to Las Vegas for around $100 from Los Angeles, $200 from Seattle, and $300 from New York; even a two-week **fly-drive** trip from New York to Las Vegas should cost well under $500 per person.

A high-season round-trip from New York to **Phoenix** should cost about $300–350; equivalent figures for Chicago might be $250–300, and for Los Angeles, just under $100. Sample fares from Montréal to Phoenix start from CAN$600, and from Vancouver CAN$350. Fares to **Albuquerque** are similar, with a round-trip from New York or Chicago costing approximately $350; a round-trip between New York and **Salt Lake City** starts at about $300.

A good first call is to contact Southwest Airlines, which in recent years has set out to establish itself as the lowest-price carrier to the region, traveling to Phoenix, Las Vegas, Tucson, Salt Lake City, and Albuquerque from around fifty other US cities. While regular fares are competitive, travelers who plan in advance can take advantage of special promotions, such as sixty percent off published fares, with no fare

higher than $99 one way. Check for online promotions.

Commuter airlines connect each of the Southwest's major airports with smaller communities in the region. Thus several airlines link **Phoenix** with towns such as Durango, Flagstaff, Lake Havasu City, Telluride, Tucson, and Yuma – America West has the most extensive service – while **Salt Lake City** is connected with airports in southern Utah such as Moab and St George. Mesa Airlines, which operates America West Express, uses **Albuquerque** as its hub for flights to destinations including Carlsbad, Durango, Farmington, Roswell, and Silver City. **Las Vegas** has the best connections of all, including direct flights to (and over) the Grand Canyon; operators are detailed on p.29.

Few of these flights are particularly suited to the needs of tourists, however. The cheapest fares tend to be on the scale of $75–150 for a one-way trip, and it's far easier to drive from place to place than to have to rent another car every few days.

The best plan if you need to get somewhere that only has a minor airport is to fly to the Southwest with a specialist **regional carrier** that will also fly you to your ultimate destination for a small additional cost. America West serves all four principal regional airports, and if you fly into Phoenix with them it can cost under $50 extra to continue to Tucson, whereas an ordinary round-trip flight between Phoenix and Tucson can cost a ludicrous $500. Similarly, Skywest, Delta's regional commuter airline, flies into Albuquerque and Salt Lake City and has connections for Cedar City, Durango, St George, and Yuma.

By rail

Amtrak **rail service** to and within the Southwest is restricted to three completely separate east–west routes, two of which pass through Arizona and New Mexico on the way to and from Los Angeles, while the other crosses northern Utah.

The daily Southwest Chief originates in Chicago and crosses from Colorado into northern New Mexico near Raton, passing close to Santa Fe (connected by a bus service from tiny Lamy) and through

Airlines

	US	UK	Australia	
Aer Lingus		☏0845/084444		ⓦ www.aerlingus.ie
Air Canada	☏1-888/247-2262			ⓦ www.aircanada.ca
Air New Zealand		☏0800/028 4149	☏13 2476	ⓦ www.airnewzealand.com
Alaska Airlines	☏1-800/252-7522			ⓦ www.alaska-air.com
America West	☏1-800/235-9292	☏02/9267 2138		ⓦ www.americawest.com
American Airlines	☏1-800/433-7300	☏0845/778 9789	☏1300/130 757	ⓦ www.aa.com
American Trans Air	☏1-800/435-9282			ⓦ www.ata.com
British Airways	☏0845/773 3377	☏1300/767 177		ⓦ www.ba.com
Continental Airlines	☏1-800/523-3273	☏0800/776464		ⓦ www.continental.com
Delta Air Lines	☏1-800/221-1212	☏0800/414767	☏02/9251 3211	ⓦ www.delta.com
Frontier Airlines	☏1-800/432-1359			ⓦ www.flyfrontier.com
Hawaiian Airlines	☏1-800/367-5320			ⓦ www.hawaiianair.com
Japan Airlines			☏02/9272 1111	ⓦ www.japanair.com
JetBlue	☏1-800/538-2583			ⓦ www.jetblue.com
Mesa Airlines	☏1-800/637-2247			ⓦ www.mesa-air.com
Northwest/KLM	☏1-800/225-2525	☏0870/507 4074		ⓦ www.nwa.com
Qantas			☏13 1313	ⓦ www.qantas.com.au
Salmon Air	☏1-800/448-3413			ⓦ www.salmonair.com
Scenic Airlines	☏1-800/634-6801			ⓦ www.scenic.com
Skywest	☏1-800/453-9417			ⓦ www.skywest.com
Southwest	☏1-800/435-9792			ⓦ www.southwest.com
United Airlines	☏1-800/241-6522	☏0845/844 4777	☏13 1777	ⓦ www.ual.com
US Airways	☏1-800/428-4322			ⓦ www.usair.com
Virgin Atlantic		☏01293/747747		ⓦ www.virgin-atlantic.com

Albuquerque before heading west via **Gallup**, **Flagstaff** – where connecting buses run north to the Grand Canyon – and **Williams**, the home of the entirely distinct Grand Canyon Railway (see p.371). Between Albuquerque and Gallup, an onboard Native American guide describes natural and Native American sites, speaking over the intercom system. The thrice-weekly Sunset Limited from New Orleans reaches southern New Mexico via El Paso, Texas, then calls at Deming, Lordsburg, before hitting Arizona towns Benson, **Tucson,** and Yuma. There is no longer any rail service to **Phoenix**, or to **Las Vegas**, which is linked by bus with Barstow, California, a stop on the Southwest Chief route. It is possible to reach **Green River** in Utah by rail, on the daily California Zephyr between Chicago and San Francisco, which also calls at Denver and Salt Lake City.

For fares and schedules, call ☏1-800/872-2745 or visit ⓦwww.amtrak.com; do not contact individual stations.

Fly less – stay longer! Travel and climate change

Climate change is a serious threat to the ecosystems that humans rely upon, and air travel is the fastest-growing contributor to the problem. Rough Guides regards travel, overall, as a global benefit, and feel strongly that the advantages to developing economies are important, as is the opportunity of greater contact and awareness among peoples. But we all have a responsibility to limit our personal impact on global warming, and that means giving thought to how often we fly, and what we can do to redress the harm that our trips create.

Flying and climate change

Pretty much every form of motorized travel generates CO_2 (the main cause of human-induced climate change) but planes are far and away the worst offenders, not just because of the sheer distances they allow us to travel, but because they release a selection of greenhouse gases high into the atmosphere. The statistics are frightening: two people taking a return flight between Europe and the US will contribute as much to climate change as an average household's gas and electricity over a whole year.

Fuel-cell and other less harmful types of plane may emerge eventually. But until then, there are really just two options for concerned travellers: to reduce the amount we travel by air (take fewer trips – stay for longer!), and to make the trips we do take "climate neutral" via a carbon offset scheme.

Carbon offset schemes

Offset schemes run by climatecare.org, carbonneutral.com and others allow you to make up for some or all of the greenhouse gases that you are responsible for releasing. To do this, they provide "carbon calculators" for working out the global-warming contribution of a specific flight (or even your entire existence), and then let you contribute an appropriate amount of money to fund offsetting measures. These include rainforest and other indigenous reforestation, and initiatives to reduce future energy demand – often run in conjunction with sustainable development schemes.

Rough Guides, together with Lonely Planet and other concerned partners in the travel industry, are supporting a carbon offset scheme run by climatecare.org. Please take the time to view our website and see how you can help to make your trip climate neutral.

www.roughguides.com/climatechange

By bus

If you're happy to sit on a **bus** for days on end, Greyhound usually offers the cheapest possible way to get to the Southwest. A one-way trip to **Albuquerque** from Los Angeles takes around twenty hours and costs $67 if booked a week in advance, or $76 on the day of travel; the ride from Milwaukee takes a day and a half and costs $79 or $156, respectively; and the two-day cross-country trek from New York costs $103 or $170.

For full details of routes and fares, and to make reservations, contact Greyhound on ☎1-800/231-2222 or ⓦwww.greyhound.com.

Southwest tour operators

Backroads, Inc ☎1-800/462-2848, ⓦwww.backroads.com. Hiking or biking tours covering New Mexico, Arizona, and southern Utah; eight nights in Zion, the Grand Canyon, and Bryce costs around $2200 if you're camping, $2800 if you stay in hotels.
Canyonlands Field Institute ☎435/259-7750 or 1-800/860-5262, ⓦwww.canyonlandsfieldinst.org. NPS-authorized adult and family wilderness expeditions, not exclusively in Canyonlands; $1125 for a five-night hike to remote Rainbow Bridge, $900 for a six-day canoeing and hiking trip along the Green River.
Delta Vacations ☎1-800/654-6559, ⓦwww.deltavacations.com. Flight and hotel packages, especially to Las Vegas.

GORP ☎ 1-877/440-4677, ⊛ www.gorptravel
.com. The Great Outdoors Recreation Pages website
carries a tantalizing collection of energetic Southwest
expeditions, like a week's backpacking along Utah's
Escalante River or in New Mexico's Gila Wilderness, or
a week-long biking and rafting jaunt in Canyonlands,
all priced at around $1500.

Grand Canyon Field Institute ☎ 928/638-2485
or 1-866/471-4435, ⊛ www.grandcanyon
.org/fieldinstitute. Park-sponsored program of hikes
and educational expeditions in the Grand Canyon;
typical prices include $375 for a three-night hike
down into the canyon; $535 for a four-night rim-
to-rim backpacking trip, including shuttle service;
and $495 for a six-night off-trail adventure in the
wilderness of the western canyon.

Green Tortoise ☎ 1-800/867-8647, ⊛ www
.greentortoise.com. California-based, youth-oriented
bus tours; the nine-day "Canyons of the West" tour
from San Francisco costs around $600 including
food kitty.

Museum of Northern Arizona ☎ 928/774-5213,
⊛ www.musnaz.org. The prestigious Flagstaff
museum runs an extensive program of tours and
excursions in the Four Corners region.

REI Adventures ☎ 1-800/622-2236, ⊛ www
.rei.com/travel. Small-group hiking trips in Utah,
Arizona and New Mexico; a six-night trip, with
accommodation, typically costs around $1600.

Sierra Club Outings ☎ 415/977-5522, ⊛ www
.sierraclub.org/outings. The environmental activist
group offers some fabulous opportunities to come
to grips with the landscapes and resources of the
Southwest, such as a week of mapping archeological
sites in Grand Canyon-Parashant National Monument
for $495, or a week's hiking in the Canyon de Chelly
with Navajo guides for $825.

Smithsonian Journeys ☎ 1-800/258-5885,
⊛ www.smithsonianjourneys.org. An extensive
program of Southwest guided tours, using upscale
hotel accommodation and ranging from four nights at
the opera in Santa Fe for $2395 to six days at Chaco
Canyon and Mesa Verde for $2255.

Southwest Ed-ventures ☎ 435/587-2156 or 1-
800/525-4456, ⊛ www.sw-adventures.org. Hiking,
backpacking and rafting trips for all ages on the
Colorado Plateau, with a strong educational element;
three days rafting on the San Juan costs $545, a
week with archeologists in Chaco Canyon $2570.

Suntrek ☎ 1-800/292-9696, ⊛ www.suntrek
.com. Three-week camping adventure tour of
the Southwest, starting from San Francisco;
$1300–1500.

TrekAmerica/Footloose ☎ 1-800/221-0596,
⊛ www.trekamerica.com or ⊛ www.footloose.com.
Active tours and treks for 18- to 38-year-olds,
including transportation by small van, guide services,
and park and attraction entrance fees. Some, like
the ten-day, $1078 "National Parks Walk" tour, are
predominantly camping; others, such as the seven-
day, $1032 "Canyons and Indian Lands" trip, use
motels and lodges.

From Britain and Ireland

There are only two direct, nonstop flights
from Britain or Ireland to any of the cities
covered in this book: British Airways flies
from London Heathrow to Phoenix daily
except Wednesdays, while Virgin Atlantic
flies from London Gatwick to Las Vegas daily
except Saturdays. Typical round-trip fares
range from around £335 in winter up to more
like £550 in summer.

Most other transatlantic carriers can get
you to Phoenix, Las Vegas, or Albuquerque
for similar or slightly lower fares, but all
require at least one stop en route. From
Britain, you can either fly nonstop to the
West Coast and then double back toward
the Southwest, or touch down on the East
Coast and then fly west; time-wise, it makes
little difference. If you'd rather keep your
flying time to a minimum, it's also worth
considering flying nonstop to California and
driving to the Southwest from there, taking
advantage of the state's low rental-car rates.
Both British Airways and Virgin fly twice daily
from London to Los Angeles, while American, United, and Air New Zealand fly once
daily. A flight to San Diego will leave you just
as close to the Southwest as one to Los
Angeles.

From Ireland, Aer Lingus flies from Dublin
or Shannon to Boston, Chicago, Los Angeles, New York, and Washington, and Delta
from Dublin and Shannon to Atlanta. Alternatively, you can fly to London and take your
pick of transatlantic routes.

Packages

Packages can work out cheaper than
arranging the same trip yourself, especially
for a short-term stay. **Fly-drive** deals, which
give cut-rate (sometimes free) car rental
when buying a transatlantic ticket from an
airline or tour operator, are always cheaper
than renting on the spot and give great value
if you intend to do a lot of driving. On the
other hand, you'll probably have to pay more

for the flight than if you booked it through a discount agent.

Several of the operators listed below go one stage further and book accommodation for **self-drive tours**; some travelers consider having their itineraries planned and booked by experts to be a real boon. Bon Voyage, for example, arranges tailor-made packages in the Southwest; the cost of twelve nights in Arizona, Utah, and Nevada, flying into Las Vegas and out from Phoenix, and staying in standard hotels, ranges from around £1300 per person in low season up to more like £1700 in high season (you're paying a premium of perhaps 25 to 30 percent for accommodation). Schemes under which you buy **pre-paid hotel vouchers** in advance, and then have to seek out hotels that will accept them, tend to be more bother than they're worth, and seldom save any money.

Companies such as TrekAmerica organize **camping tours** of the Southwest, usually starting in California or Las Vegas and circling through Utah's national parks and the Grand Canyon. Typical trips range in price – excluding flights – from £500 for a week in low season up to around £850 in mid-summer. TrekAmerica also offer some trips that use hotel accommodation, like the six-night "Footloose Canyons & Indian Lands" tours, which starts at £613.

Tour operators

American Holidays Northern Ireland ☎028/9031 0000, Republic of Ireland ☎01/673 3840 ⓦwww .american-holidays.com
Bon Voyage UK ☎0800/316 0194, ⓦwww .bon-voyage.co.uk

British Airways Holidays UK ☎0870/850 9850, ⓦwww.baholidays.co.uk
Exodus UK ☎020/8675 5550, ⓦwww.exodus .co.uk
Explore Worldwide UK ☎0870/333 4001, ⓦwww.explore.co.uk
Jetsave UK ☎0870/162 3502, ⓦwww.jetsave .co.uk
North America Travel Service UK ☎020/7499 7299, ⓦwww.northamericatravelservice.co.uk
Saddle Skedaddle UK ☎0191/265 1110, ⓦwww.skedaddle.co.uk

Visa requirements for foreign travelers

Under the **visa waiver scheme**, passport-holders from Britain, Ireland, Australia, New Zealand, and most European countries do not require visas for trips to the United States, including Hawaii, so long as they stay less than ninety days in the US, and have an onward or return ticket. Instead you simply fill in the visa waiver form handed out on incoming planes. Immigration control takes place at your point of arrival on US soil.

For you to be eligible for the visa waiver scheme, your passport must be machine-readable (with a barcode-style number). All children need to have their own individual passports. Holders of older nonreadable passports should therefore either obtain new ones or apply for visas prior to travel. For full details, visit ⓦhttp://travel .state.gov/vwp.

Titan HiTours UK ℡01293/455345, ⓦwww
.titantravel.co.uk
Travelsphere UK ℡0870/240 2426, ⓦwww
.travelsphere.co.uk
TrekAmerica UK ℡0870/444 8735, ⓦwww
.trekamerica.co.uk

From Australia and New Zealand

There are no direct flights from Australia or New Zealand to any of the Southwestern cities, so you'll have to fly to one of the main US gateway airports and pick up onward connections – or a rental car – from there.

The cheapest route, and the one with the most frequent services from Australia and New Zealand, is to **Los Angeles**, which also has plenty of onward flights to Albuquerque, Las Vegas, and Phoenix. Air New Zealand and Qantas/American fly to LA at least twice daily, while United flies once a day; other airlines that serve LA include Japan Airlines and Singapore Airlines.

Packages and tours

Package deals available to travelers in Australia and New Zealand range from fly-drive deals to fully escorted bus tours and camping treks, and can work out significantly cheaper than making the same arrangements yourself; some of the no-frills flight and car-rental packages, for example, can cost less than a flight alone. You can also add on whatever extra tours you choose; by way of example, Adventure World offers trips from LA like the ten-day "Western Wonders" that starts at A\$1627, or a seven-day jaunt to the Grand Canyon, Zion, and Las Vegas for A\$821.

Specialist **hotel** and **camping tours** for small groups can get you further off the beaten track. TrekAmerica, for example, which can be booked through STA, offers several itineraries ranging from one to three weeks; for more details, see p.31.

Specialist agents

Adventure World Australia ℡02/8913 0755, ⓦwww.adventureworld.com.au, New Zealand ℡09/524 5118, ⓦwww.adventureworld.co.nz
Sydney Travel Australia ℡02/9220 9230, ⓦwww.sydneytravel.com
travel.com.au Australia ℡1300/130 482, ⓦwww.travel.com.au
travel.co.nz New Zealand ℡0800/468 332, ⓦwww.travel.co.nz

Health and insurance

In view of the high cost of medical care in the US, all travelers visiting the US from overseas should be sure to buy some form of travel insurance. American and Canadian citizens should check that you're not already covered – some homeowners' or renters' policies are valid on vacation, and credit cards such as American Express often include some medical or other insurance, while most Canadians are covered for medical mishaps overseas by their provincial health plans. If you only need trip cancellation/interruption coverage (to supplement your existing plan), this is generally available at about \$6 per \$100.

Health

The major health and safety issues facing Southwest travelers are coping with **desert** conditions. For anyone unused to dealing with extremes of heat and cold and the sheer inhospitality of this kind of terrain, it's essential to take precautions. In addition, you may remember reports of the "mystery illness" that

Rough Guides travel insurance

Rough Guides has teamed up with Columbus Direct to offer travel insurance that can be tailored to suit your needs.

Readers can choose from many different travel insurance products, including a low-cost backpacker option for long stays or a typical holiday package. There are also annual multi-trip policies for those who travel regularly, with variable levels of cover available. Different sports and activities (trekking, skiing, etc) can be covered if required on most policies.

Rough Guides travel insurance is available to the residents of 36 countries with different language options to choose from via our website – ⓦ**www.roughguidesin-surance.com** – where you can also purchase the insurance.

Alternatively, UK residents should call ☎0800 083 9507; US citizens should call ☎1-800/749-4922; Australians should call ☎1 300 669 999. All other nationalities should call ☎+44 870 890 2843.

killed around fifty people in the Four Corners region in 1993. It was eventually traced to a hantavirus spread by the droppings of deer mice. Such viruses remain present in the region, so backpackers should take care to avoid camping near rodent nests (take note of tell-tale droppings).

Desert survival

If you plan to go **hiking in the desert**, it's crucial to plan ahead. Tell somebody where you are going and write down all pertinent information, including your expected time of return. Keep in mind that cell phones are unlikely to provide coverage in many of the remote regions described in this book. Carry an extra two days' food and water and never go anywhere without a map. Try to cover most of your ground in early morning: the midday heat is too debilitating, and you shouldn't even think about it when the mercury goes over 90°F.

Stick to official trails in the national parks, as described throughout this book, and you shouldn't face any serious **technical difficulties**. Many trails are marked only by occasional stone cairns, however, and if your concentration starts to wander your feet may do so too. If you do get lost, try your utmost to retrace your steps; if that fails, find some shade and wait. As long as you've registered, the rangers will eventually come and fetch you. If you attempt to scramble out of a pinch on your own, you may risk becoming **rim-rocked**; picking your way across even a shallow gully, it's much easier to climb up

than down, and you may well find yourself stuck above a drop you're unable to negotiate.

Whatever experience you may have had anywhere else, hiking in **canyons** is different. Most hikers are far more familiar with walking up hills and mountains, where it's the initial climb that's most demanding, and if your energy levels start to flag you can simply turn around and walk back to base. Canyon hiking is deceptively seductive. The descent seems easy, and your progress quick. Eventually, however, you have to pay: start the climb back out when you're already tired and the midday heat has set in, and you're in for a murderously long haul. Turn back after a third of your allotted time; if you plan a six-hour hike, reckon on two hours hiking down and four hours to hike up.

To stay cool during the day, wear full-length sleeves and trousers. Shorts and a T-shirt will expose you to far too much sun – something you won't be aware of until it's too late. A wide-brimmed hat and a pair of good sunglasses will spare you the blinding headaches that can result from the desert light.

You may also have to contend with **flash floods**, which can appear from nowhere: One innocent-looking dark cloud can turn a dry wash into a raging river. In fact, you may be looking at a merely overcast sky, but a rainstorm somewhere else could cause your area to receive an oncoming flash flood. Never camp in a dry wash, and don't attempt to cross flooded areas until the water has receded.

Bear in mind, too, that much of the Southwest – such as the Colorado Plateau, home to the Grand Canyon and Utah's national parks – is more than a mile above sea level, and the **altitude** alone can impose severe demands on even the fittest of athletes. Before arriving at these altitudes, consider taking low doses of aspirin a day in advance. Be prepared for below-freezing temperatures at high elevations at night.

Water

It's essential to carry – and **drink** – large quantities of liquid in the desert. An eight-hour hike in typical summer temperatures of more than 100°F would require you to drink a phenomenal **thirty pints** of water. Loss of appetite and thirst are early symptoms of heat exhaustion, so it's possible to become seriously dehydrated without feeling thirsty. Watch out for signs of dizziness or nausea, and if you feel weak and stop sweating, it's time to get to the doctor. You should always know whether water will be available on your chosen trail – park rangers keep abreast of the latest conditions – and carry at least two pints per person even if you expect to be able to pick up more en route. Just to confuse things, there's also the risk of **hyponatremia**, or **water intoxication**, which in its first stages closely resembles heat exhaustion, and happens if you drink too much without eating. As hikers can burn up to a thousand calories per hour, expect to eat at least twice as much **food** as normal, both during your hike and also, ideally, before it. Salty snacks such as cookies, crackers, and trail mix are recommended, as well as jerky or salami and dried ready-made meals. Finally, it's easy to forget that at the end of a long hike there may be no facilities at the trailhead. Don't forget to leave some food and water in your vehicle as well.

Backpackers should never drink from rivers and streams, however clear and inviting they may look; you never know what unspeakable acts people – or animals – have performed further upstream. **Giardia** – a water-borne bacteria that causes an intestinal disease, characterized by chronic diarrhea, abdominal cramps, fatigue, and weight loss – is a serious problem. Water that doesn't come from a faucet should be boiled for at least five minutes or cleansed with an iodine-based purifier (such as Potable Aqua) or a giardia-rated filter, available from any camping or sports store.

Insects and allergies

Mosquitoes and biting insects are rarely a problem in the Southwest, though in spring-time you may encounter them near rivers in parks such as Zion. Avon Skin-so-soft hand-cream or anything containing DEET are fairly reliable repellents. **Ticks** – tiny beetles that plunge their heads into your skin and swell up with your blood – can be a hazard. If you pluck them off you can sometimes leave their heads inside, causing blood clots or infections, so get advice from a park ranger if you've been bitten.

Beware, too, of **poison oak**, an allergenic shrub that grows all over the western states, usually among oak trees. Its leaves come in groups of three and are distinguished by prominent veins and shiny surfaces. If you come into contact, wash your skin (with soap and cold water) and clothes as soon as possible – and don't scratch. In serious cases, hospital emergency rooms can give antihistamine or adrenaline jabs.

Snakes and creepy-crawlies

Though the Southwestern deserts are home to an assortment of **poisonous creatures**, these are rarely aggressive toward humans. By observing obvious **precautions**, you should be able to avoid trouble. Don't attempt to handle wildlife; keep your eyes open as you walk, and watch where you put your hands when scrambling over obstacles; shake out shoes, clothing, and bedding before use; and back off if you do spot a creature, to give it room to escape.

If you are **bitten** or stung, current medical thinking rejects the concept of cutting yourself open and attempting to suck out the venom; whether snake, scorpion, or spider is responsible, apply a cold compress to the wound, constrict the area with a tourniquet to prevent the spread of venom, drink lots of water, and bring your temperature down by resting in a shady area. Stay as calm as possible and seek medical help immediately.

Information, maps, and websites

There's no single perfect source for information on the entire Southwest; that's the point of this book, after all. Each of the states covered here has its own tourist office, accessible via a website as well as by phone, which in addition to providing copious information online can also mail prospective visitors a colossal range of free maps, leaflets, and brochures. In addition, the region includes ten national parks, as well as dozens of other federally managed national monuments, national forests and the like, and fifty or so Indian reservations, each of which attempts to meet the needs of visitors in its own way.

Local information

Visitor centers in most towns – often known as the "Convention and Visitors Bureau," or CVB, and listed throughout this book – provide details on the area. Almost all also have their own Web presence, usually with extensive links to local businesses and attractions. In cities such as Las Vegas, Phoenix, and Santa Fe, **free newspapers** carry dining and entertainment listings. In addition, you're likely to come across the useful **Welcome Centers** along the interstates close to the state borders, which dispense maps and information on the entire state. For details on national and state parks, and other public lands, see p.46.

State tourist offices

Arizona Office of Tourism ☎602/364-3700 or 1-866/275-5816, ⓦ www.arizonaguide.com
Colorado Travel and Tourism Authority ☎303/832-6171 or 1-800/265-6723, ⓦ www.colorado.com
Nevada Commission on Tourism ☎702/687-4322 or 1-800/638-2328, ⓦ www.travelnevada.com
New Mexico State Tourism ☎505/827-4000 or 1-800/733-6396, ⓦ www.newmexico.org
Utah Travel Council ☎801/538-1030 or 1-800/200-1160, ⓦ www.utah.com

Maps

The best general-purpose **road map** for the principal areas covered in this book is the *Guide to Indian Country*, available free to members of the American Automobile Association and sold throughout the Southwest for $4.95. It focuses on the Four Corners region, however, and does not extend into southern Arizona, southern New Mexico, or Nevada, and furthermore it's not reliable for dirt roads and backcountry routes. Each individual state also issues a free **highway map**, which is fine for general driving and route planning and can be obtained either direct from the tourist office or from local visitor centers. In addition, Rand McNally (see below) produces good **regional maps** – bound together in their *Rand McNally Road Atlas*, or printed separately for each state – while free **town maps** are generally available at local visitor centers.

All **national parks**, and most state parks, national forests, and the like – as detailed on pp.44–45 – provide reasonable maps to visitors. Both these, and the maps throughout this book, are adequate for day-hikes on the most popular trails. Serious hikers and backpackers, however, should equip themselves with detailed **topographical maps**. Among the best are the waterproof and tearproof maps of individual national parks published by National Geographic–Trails Illustrated (ⓦ maps.nationalgeographic.com/trails), which also produces state maps of Colorado, New Mexico, and Utah.

Useful Southwest websites

Websites for regional and local tourism information, activity operators, hotels and accommodation options, parklands, and other attractions are listed throughout this book. In addition, the following more general sites may be of interest.

Americansouthwest.net @www .americansouthwest.net. Privately-run fan site devoted to the national parks and wilderness areas of the desert Southwest, featuring great photos, masses of links, and a copious section on slot canyons.

Discover Navajo @www.discovernavajo.com. The official tourism website of the Navajo Nation is packed with useful information for travelers planning a visit to the Four Corners.

GORP @www.gorp.com. The Great Outdoors Recreation Pages website is especially strong in its home territory of the US, offering step-by-step practical guides to all the major national parks and wilderness areas as well as selling its own program of adventurous tours; see p.31.

High Country News @www.hcn.org. Biweekly newspaper devoted to environmental issues in the West as a whole, with special reference to national parks and public lands, and a useful online archive.

Las Vegas Review-Journal @www.lvrj.com. The online version of Las Vegas's daily newspaper provides news on the West as well as up-to-date listings of what's happening in the city.

National Park Service @www.nps.gov. This invaluable website covers every component of the national park system, with full practical details for the whole gamut of monuments and recreation areas as well as for the parks themselves. For big names, such as the Grand Canyon, the range of information is breathtaking, covering camping, hiking, wildlife, and lodging, with links to accommodation options and activity operators in the vicinity.

National Scenic Byways Online @www .byways.org. Sponsored by the Federal Highway Administration, this luscious site honors America's most beautiful driving routes.

Sierra Club @www.sierraclub.org. The veteran environmental organization uses its website to promote awareness of issues and events throughout the US, with links to "chapters" in each individual state for coverage of local activities. For travelers, however, its most useful feature is the "Outings" section, which details the club's lengthy list of adventure-travel expeditions; see p.31.

Costs and money

This book contains detailed price information for lodging and eating throughout the Southwest. Accommodation rates are coded according to the system explained on p.39, which excludes any local taxes that may apply, while restaurant prices include food only and not drinks or tip. For museums and similar attractions, the entrance fees quoted are for adults; unless specified otherwise, assume that children get in half-price. Naturally, costs will increase slightly overall during the life of this edition.

Costs

North American travelers find **prices** in the Southwest broadly similar to the rest of the US, with food and lodging generally cheaper than in major US cities and tourist regions, and gas and groceries, especially in out-of-the-way places, a little more expensive. Most visitors from Europe and Australasia feel that their money goes further in the US than it does at home. However, if you're used to traveling in the less expensive countries of Europe, let alone in the rest of the world, you can't expect to scrape by on the same minuscule budget in the US.

As explained on p.41, the only way to reach most of the places described in this book is to drive. If you can't bring your own vehicle, your least avoidable major expense will be **car rental**, at around $150 per week. What you spend on **accommodation** is more flexible. For most of the year, in most places, you should have no problem getting a motel room for under $60, though even the cheapest peak-season rates in or near certain national parks, or in downtown Santa Fe, are more like $80. Although **hostels** offering dorm beds – usually for $12 to $20 – are reasonably common, they're by no means everywhere, and in any case they save little money for two or more people traveling together. **Camping** is not only cheap, with federal and state park campgrounds ranging from free to perhaps $16 per night, in many wilderness areas it's the only option.

As for **food**, $20 per day is enough to get an adequate life-support diet, consisting of perhaps one full-scale meal in a local diner supplemented by a stash of groceries, while for a daily total of around $30 you can eat pretty well. If you're visiting a significant number of **national parks** and monuments, buy a National Parks pass (see p.45); the $50 fee covers all passengers in your vehicle. You'll probably also spend another $5 or $10 a day on admissions to state parks, museums, and the like.

The most economical possible vacation, therefore, with two people sharing a rental car, camping in state and federal parks most nights, and eating one restaurant meal per day, will work out at a minimum of $300 per person per week.

For advice on **tipping** and **taxes**, see pp.54–55.

Cash, cards, and checks

Expect to pay most of your major expenses by **credit or debit card**; hotels and car rental agencies usually demand a credit card imprint as security, even if you intend to settle the bill in cash, and you'll be at a serious disadvantage if you don't have one. Visa, MasterCard, Diners Club, American Express, and Discover are the most widely used.

You'll also need to carry a certain amount of **cash**. If you have a MasterCard or Visa, or a cash-dispensing card linked to an international network such as Cirrus or Plus – check with your home bank before you set off – you can withdraw cash from appropriate automatic teller machines (**ATMs**). Also consider carrying US dollar travelers' checks, which offer the security of knowing that lost or stolen checks will be replaced. Checks issued by American Express, Visa, and Thomas Cook are universally accepted as cash in shops, restaurants, and gas stations, and change from your transactions will be rendered in hard currency. Carry plenty of $10 and $20 denominations, and don't be put off by "no checks" signs, which only refer to personal checks. Foreign travelers should *not* bring travelers' checks issued in their own currencies; it can be hard to find a bank prepared to change them, and no other business is likely to accept them.

Accommodation

On the whole, accommodation in the Southwest is relatively inexpensive. Most travelers simply want a bed for the night before moving on the next day, so motels everywhere provide clean, no-frills places to sleep without bothering to offer additional amenities. Basic room rates in rural areas start as low as $30 per night, while prices along the principal highways and interstates tend to start at $45. Only in the most popular summer destinations – cities such as Santa Fe, or "gateway" towns near the major national parks – will you find it hard to get a room for under $80. If you prefer a bit more comfort, it's almost always available; in most areas covered by this book you can get a room in a top-class hotel for under $100.

At the lower end of the spectrum, a fair number of budget **hostels** are scattered across the region, though with a single dorm bed usually costing between $12 and $20, groups of two or more will find them little cheaper than motels. Many motel rooms

Accommodation price codes

Throughout this book, **room rates** in hotels, motels, and B&Bs are indicated with the symbols below, according to the cost of their least expensive double rooms, **excluding taxes**, which can add between five and fifteen percent. Significant seasonal variations are indicated as appropriate, as are establishments that hold rooms at widely differing prices. The cheapest price code, ❶, is also used to indicate hostels which offer individual dorm beds, in which cases specific rates are also included.

❶ up to $30   ❹ $60–80   ❼ $130–175
❷ $30–45   ❺ $80–100 ❽ $175–250
❸ $45–60   ❻ $100–130 ❾ $250+

hold two double beds and will accommodate three or four guests for slightly over the normal two-person rate. On the other hand, the lone traveler has a hard time of it: a "single" room is just a double at a fractionally reduced rate.

Wherever you stay, you'll be expected to pay in advance, at least for the first night and perhaps for further nights too. Most places ask for a credit card imprint when you arrive, but they'll also accept cash or dollar travelers' checks. Reservations – essential in busy areas in summer – are only held until 5pm or 6pm unless you've warned the hotel you'll be arriving late.

For advice on **camping**, see the "Outdoors" section beginning on p.44.

Hotels and motels

It's easy to find a basic **motel** room in the Southwest. Drivers approaching any significant town pass lines of motels along the highway, while the choice along major cross-country routes is phenomenal. Most of the towns mentioned in this book hold more motels than there's room to review; the very few that have none at all are clearly indicated.

For the most part, **hotels** and **motels** are essentially the same thing, although motels tend to be located beside main roads away from city centers, and thus are much more accessible to drivers. The budget ones are pretty basic affairs, but in general there's a uniform standard of comfort everywhere – each room comes with a double bed, a TV, a phone to which it's usually possible to hook up a computer, and an attached bathroom – and you don't get a much better deal by

paying, say, $75 instead of $50. Over $75 or so, the room and its fittings simply get bigger and more luxurious, and there'll probably be a swimming pool which guests can use for free.

The very cheapest properties tend to be family-run, independent motels, but there's a lot to be said for paying a few dollars more to stay in motels belonging to the national **chains**. After a few days on the road, you should find that a particular chain consistently suits your requirements and budget (Super 8 is a personal recommendation). You can then use its central reservation number or website, listed overleaf, to book ahead, and possibly obtain discounts as a regular guest. Not many budget hotels or motels bother to compete with the ubiquitous diners and offer **breakfast**, although many provide free self-service coffee and sticky buns.

During off-peak periods many motels and hotels struggle to fill their rooms, so it's worth haggling to get a few dollars off the asking price. Travelers who belong to the American Automobile Association can usually get a discount of around ten percent, as can members of equivalent foreign organizations such as Britain's AA. Staying in the same place for more than one night may bring further reductions. Additionally, look out for **discount coupons**, especially in the free magazines distributed by local visitor centers and interstate welcome centers. These can offer amazing value – $30 for a double room in a comfortable mid-range chain – but read the small print, as rates are often limited to midweek.

Mention should also be made of the fact that many towns throughout the Southwest still hold **historic hotels**, whether dating from the arrival of the railroads a century ago or from the heyday of Route 66 in the 1940s and 1950s. So long as you accept that not all will have up-to-date facilities to match their period charm, these can make wonderfully characterful places to spend a night or two. Those that are exceptionally well preserved or restored may charge up to $200 per room, but a more typical rate for a not overly luxurious but atmospheric, antique-furnished room would be more like $100. Prime examples include *La Fonda* in Santa Fe (see p.136); the *Historic Taos Inn* in Taos (p.183); the *Strater Hotel* in Durango (p.103); *La Posada* in Albuquerque (p.209); and the fabulous *La Posada* in Winslow (p.325). Occasionally, venerable Western hotels have been refitted to serve as budget-oriented accommodation options, as with Tucson's *Hotel Congress* (p.277) and Flagstaff's *Monte Vista* and *Weatherford* (p.329).

In addition, several **national parks** feature long-established and architecturally distinguished hotels, traditionally known as **lodges**, that can be real bargains thanks to their federally controlled rates. The only drawback is that all rooms tend to be reserved far in advance. Among the best are *El Tovar* and *Grand Canyon Lodge* on the south and north rims, respectively, of the Grand Canyon, and *Zion Lodge* in Zion Canyon.

Hotel, hostel, and motel chains

Best Western (❸–❻) ☎ 1-800/780-7234, ⓦ www.bestwestern.com
Comfort Inns (❸–❺) ☎ 1-877/424-6423, ⓦ www.choicehotels.com
Days Inn (❸–❺) ☎ 1-800/329-7466, ⓦ www.daysinn.com
Econolodge (❷–❹) ☎ 1-877/424-6423, ⓦ www.choicehotels.com
Fairfield Inns (❹–❺) ☎ 1-800/228-2800, ⓦ www.marriott.com
Hampton Inns (❹–❺) ☎ 1-800/426-7866, ⓦ www.hampton-inn.com
Hilton Hotels (❺ and up) ☎ 1-800/445-8667, ⓦ www.hilton.com
Holiday Inn (❹ and up) ☎ 1-800/465-4329, ⓦ www.ichotelsgroup.com
Hosteling International – American Youth Hostels (❶) ⓦ www.hiayh.org
Howard Johnson (❸–❹) ☎ 1-800/446-4656, ⓦ www.hojo.com

La Quinta Inns (❹) ☎ 1-866/725-1661, ⓦ www.lq.com
Marriott Hotels (❺ and up) ☎ 1-888/236-2427, ⓦ www.marriott.com
Motel 6 (❷) ☎ 1-800/466-8356, ⓦ www.motel6.com
Quality Inns (❸–❹) ☎ 1-877/424-6423, ⓦ www.choicehotels.com
Ramada Inns (❹ and up) ☎ 1-800/272-6232, ⓦ www.ramada.com
Sleep Inn (❸–❹) ☎ 1-877/424-6423, ⓦ www.choicehotels.com
Super 8 (❷–❹) ☎ 1-800/800-8000, ⓦ www.super8.com
Travelodge (❸–❹) ☎ 1-800/578-7878, ⓦ www.travelodge.com

Bed and breakfasts

Bed and breakfast has become an ever more popular option, often as a luxurious – if not necessarily any more expensive – alternative to conventional hotels. Some B&Bs consist of no more than a couple of furnished rooms in someone's home. Even the larger establishments tend to have no more than ten rooms, without TV and phone but often laden with flowers, stuffed cushions, and an almost over-contrived cozy atmosphere.

The price you pay for a B&B – which typically varies from around $75 to $150 – always includes a huge and wholesome breakfast. The crucial determining factor in price is whether or not your room has an ensuite bathroom; providing private bath facilities can damage the authenticity of a fine old house. Those that do provide an ensuite bath tend to be more expensive. At the top end of the price spectrum are "bed and breakfast inns" that may appear no different than a hotel to the traveler but are called such because the property is owned by a private individual rather than a chain.

In many areas, B&Bs have grouped together to form central **booking agencies**, making it much easier to find a room at short notice; we've given addresses and numbers for these where appropriate. Statewide organizations include the Arizona Association of B&B Inns (ⓦ www.arizona-bed-breakfast.com); B&B Inns of Utah (ⓦ www.bbiu.org); B&B Innkeepers of Colorado (☎ 1-800/265-7696, ⓦ www.innsofcolorado.org); and the New Mexico B&B Association (☎ 505/766-5380 or

1-800/661-6649, ⓦwww.nmbba.org). In addition, almost every B&B has its own Website; simple searches will usually throw up a myriad of possibilities.

Hostels

Around twenty **hostels** provide accommodation for backpackers and budget travelers in the Southwest. For two people traveling together, most work out little cheaper than motels, so there's not much point staying in hostels unless you prefer their youthful ambience and sociability. Note also that many are not accessible on public transport, or particularly convenient for sightseeing in the towns and cities, let alone in rural areas.

These days, most hostels are independent, with no affiliation to HI-AYH (Hosteling International–American Youth Hostels) network. Many are no more than converted motels, where the "dorms" consist of a couple of sets of bunkbeds in a musty room, which is also let out as a private unit on demand; others may be purpose-built rural properties, or at least converted and modernized to a high standard. Those few hostels that do belong to HI-AYH – currently only those in Phoenix and Taos – tend to impose curfews and limit daytime access hours, and segregate dormitories by sex. Most expect guests to bring sheets or sleeping bags. Rates range from $12 to about $17 for HI members; non-members generally pay an additional $3 per night.

Especially in high season, it's advisable to **reserve ahead**, by phone or email. The maximum stay is often restricted to three nights, though this rule tends to be ignored if there's space. Few hostels provide meals but most have cooking facilities.

Keep in mind that youth hostels are often shoestring organizations, prone to changing address or closing down altogether. Similarly, new ones appear each year; check the notice boards of other hostels for news.

Getting around

Attempting to tour the Southwest by public transport is an extremely bad idea. While buses and planes – and trains to a much lesser extent – connect the major urban areas, the national parks and wide-open landscapes that are the region's greatest attractions simply cannot be explored without your own vehicle. Even public transport within the cities is minimal. Unless you're an *extremely* energetic cyclist, therefore, you'll need a motorbike or car.

If you can't drive, the only itinerary that makes much sense is to cross northern Arizona and northern New Mexico by bus or train, flying in or out of **Albuquerque** in the east or **Las Vegas** in the west. Obvious stops would include **Flagstaff**, with a side-trip by bus to the Grand Canyon, and **Santa Fe**, the only city small enough to be seen on foot. Phoenix and Tucson are no fun at all without a car, while what little public transport exists in southern Utah is no use for seeing the parks. **Hitchhiking** is not recommended under any circumstances.

Commuter flights within the Southwest are detailed on p.28.

By car

To **rent** a car, you're supposed to have held your license for at least one year; drivers under 25 years old may encounter problems and have to pay higher than normal insurance premiums. Rental companies expect customers to have credit cards; if you don't, they may let you leave a cash deposit (at least $200), but don't count on it.

All the major rental companies have outlets at the main regional airports. Reservations are handled centrally rather than locally, so the best way to shop around for **rates is either online, or by** calling their national toll-free numbers. Potential variations are endless; certain cities and states are consistently cheaper than others, while individual travelers may be eligible for corporate, frequent-flier, or AAA discounts. In low season, you might find a tiny car (a "subcompact") for as little as $100 per week, but a typical budget rate would be more like $35–40 per day, and $150 per week, including taxes. A car rented in Las Vegas, Nevada, can easily cost $100 less per week than one rented in Colorado, and prices in Arizona, New Mexico, and Utah are ranged between the two.

Don't automatically go for the cheapest rate. Little-known local rental companies may offer appealing prices, but if you break down several hundred miles from their offices it may be hard to get assistance. Even between the major operators, there can be a big difference in the quality of cars. Industry leaders like Hertz and Avis tend to have newer, lower-mileage cars, often with air-conditioning and high-quality sound systems as standard equipment – no small consideration on a 3000-mile desert drive. Always be sure to get free **unlimited mileage**, and remember that leaving the car in a different city to the one where you rent it can

incur a drop-off charge of as much as $200.

When you rent a car, read the small print carefully for details on **Collision Damage Waiver** (CDW), sometimes called Liability Damage Waiver (LDW), a form of insurance that often isn't included in the initial rental charge but is well worth considering. This specifically covers the car that you are driving yourself; you are in any case insured for damage to other vehicles. At $10–15 a day, it can add substantially to the total cost, but without it you're liable for every scratch to the car – even those that aren't your fault. Some credit card companies offer automatic CDW coverage to anyone using their card; contact your issuing company for details.

Your rental papers should include an emergency number to call in case of breakdown or accident; contact the rental company before you arrange, or pay, for any repairs. If you don't have one already, you should also consider renting a **mobile telephone** with your car – you often only have to pay a nominal amount until you actually use it, and it can be a lifesaver should something go terribly wrong.

The **American Automobile Association**, or AAA (☎1-800/222-4357, ⓦwww.aaa .com), provides free maps and assistance to its members and to members of affiliated associations overseas, such as the British AA and RAC.

Car rental companies

Alamo	ⓦwww.alamo.com
Avis	ⓦwww.avis.com
Budget	ⓦwww.budgetrentacar.com
Dollar	ⓦwww.dollar.com
Enterprise	ⓦwww.enterprise.com
Hertz	ⓦwww.hertz.com
Holiday Autos	ⓦwww.holidayautos.com
National	ⓦwww.nationalcar.com
Thrifty	ⓦwww.thrifty.com

Renting an RV

RVs – Recreational Vehicles – can be rented at prices which start at around $600 per week (plus mileage charges) for a basic camper on the back of a pickup truck, with sleeping room for two adults. If you're looking for one of those huge juggernauts that rumble down the highway complete with multiple bedrooms, bathrooms, and kitchens, you'll have to pay at least double that rate. Though good for groups or families traveling together, RVs can be unwieldy on the road, and as people tend to own their own, rental outlets are not as common as you might expect. On top of rental fees, you'll also have to take into account the cost of gas (some RVs do twelve miles to the gallon or less) and any drop-off charges. It's rarely legal simply to pull up in an RV and spend the night at the roadside; you are expected to stay in designated parks that cost $20–30 per night.

The Recreational Vehicle Rental Association (☎703/591-7130 or 1-800/336-0355, ⓦwww.rvra.org) maintains a searchable online directory of rental firms. Among the larger companies offering RV rentals are Cruise America (☎1-800/327-7799, ⓦwww.cruiseamerica.com) and Moturis (☎1-877/668-8747, ⓦwww.moturis.com).

Driving for foreigners

Foreign nationals from English-speaking countries – which obviously includes UK, Irish, Australian, and New Zealand citizens – can drive in the US using their full domestic **driving licenses.** (International Driving Permits are not always regarded as sufficient.) Fly-drive deals are good value if you want to rent a car (see p.31 and p.33), though you can save up to sixty percent simply by booking in advance with a major firm. If you choose not to pay until you arrive, be sure you take a written confirmation of the price with you. Remember that most standard rental cars have automatic transmissions, and that it's safer not to drive immediately after a long transatlantic flight.

It's also easier and cheaper to book **RVs** in advance from Britain. Most travel agents who specialize in the US can arrange RV rental, and usually do it cheaper if you book

---

For up-to-date information on current road conditions on major highways – which is essential if you're driving in the Four Corners region in winter – call the following numbers:
Arizona ☎1-888/411-7623
Colorado ☎1-877/315-7623
New Mexico ☎1-800/432-4269
Utah ☎1-801/964-6000

---

a flight through them as well. A price of £500 for a five-berth van for two weeks is fairly typical.

Buying a **secondhand car** and selling it at the end of your trip might sound like a money-saving idea, but registering and insuring it is a complicated and expensive business. Each state has different regulations; contact the AAA for details.

Desert driving

Whenever you **drive** in the desert, be sure to have two gallons of water per person in the car. You should also carry flares, matches, a first-aid kit, and a compass, plus a shovel, air pump, and extra gas. If the car's engine **overheats**, don't turn it off; instead, try to cool the engine quickly by turning the front end toward the wind. Carefully pour some water on the front of the radiator, and turn the air-conditioning off and heating up full blast. In an emergency, never panic and leave the car: you'll be harder to find wandering around alone.

By bike

Although riding a bike in the Southwest can be absolutely exhilarating, long-distance cyclists face a fearsome challenge, above all in the heat of summer. Neighboring towns can be as much as a hundred miles apart, along desert highways that offer no food, water, or shade. Quite apart from the high mountains and deep canyons, most areas covered in this book are a mile or more above sea level, so the altitude alone can be a real problem. The only road from A to B may well turn out to be a major interstate; when there's no alternative, cyclists are generally allowed to ride on interstate shoulders, but they have to battle the slipstream of mighty trucks.

If you have a good bike and know how to maintain it, however, and time your trip for the cooler months, it is feasible to explore the Southwest by bike. Specific regions that lend themselves to **cycle touring** are north-central New Mexico, where countless routes radiate from Santa Fe; the vicinity of Flagstaff and Sedona in Arizona; and southwest Utah, around Zion National Park. Other areas have seen a recent boom in **mountain-biking,** such as Moab, Utah – home of the grueling Slickrock Bike Trail (see p.524) – and Durango, Colorado.

For general **information** and advice, contact the New Mexico Touring Society (☎505/237-9700, ⓦwww.nmts.org), the Arizona Bicycle Club (☎602/264-5478, ⓦwww.azbikeclub.com), or Bicycle Utah (ⓦwww.bicycleutah.com). The national, nonprofit **Adventure Cycling Association** (formerly Bikecentennial; ☎1-800/755-2453, ⓦwww.adv-cycling.org) publishes maps ($10.50 each) of several 400-mile routes, including the *Grand Canyon Connector* and the *Utah Cliffs Loop*, detailing campgrounds, motels, restaurants, bike shops, and sites of interest. Backroads Bicycle Tours (☎1-800/462-2848, ⓦwww.backroads.com) and the HI-AYH hosteling group (see p.40) also arrange group tours.

Greyhound, Amtrak, and major airlines all carry passengers' bicycles – dismantled and packed into a box – for a small additional fee.

By train

Details of the very limited Amtrak **rail service** to and across the Southwest appear on p.28. There are also a number of **historic** and **scenic railroads** in the region – some of them steam-powered or running along narrow-gauge mining tracks – including the Cumbres & Toltec line in northern New Mexico (see p.194); the Grand Canyon Railway between Williams and the Grand Canyon in northern Arizona (see p.371); the Verde Canyon Railroad in northern Arizona (see p.345); and the Durango & Silverton Narrow Gauge Railroad in Colorado (see p.102).

By bus

Greyhound buses link all major cities and many smaller towns in the Southwest; for fares, schedules, and reservations, call ☎1-800/231-2222, or access the website at ⓦwww.greyhound.com. Routes that are particularly useful for tourists – as well as services offered by other operators – are detailed at the relevant points in this book.

While scheduled buses can get you from city to city, they're of no use when it comes to enjoying the great outdoors. **Tour buses**, however, do set off into the wilderness from most major towns; they, too, are detailed throughout this book.

The outdoors

Cut by deep canyons, coated by dense forests, and capped by great mountains, the Southwest glories in some of the most fabulous wilderness areas in the United States.

By far the easiest way for visitors to enjoy this natural wonderland is to plot an itinerary that samples the countless **national, state, and county parks**. Although these are not invariably the most beautiful places of all – after all, some are simply lands that pioneer farmers, Indian tribes, and mining corporations never bothered or managed to grab – they do offer the campgrounds and hiking trails that make backcountry exploration possible even for the least experienced tourists.

National parks and monuments

The **National Park Service** administers both national parks and national monuments. It's sadly underfunded, however: the NPS doesn't even automatically get to keep park entrance fees, which are absorbed into the general Federal treasury. In style and design, many of its visitor centers and other facilities still date conspicuously from the 1950s. Nonetheless, park rangers do a superb job of providing information and advice to visitors, maintaining trails, and organizing such activities as free guided hikes and campfire talks.

In principle, the point of a **national park** is to preserve an area of outstanding natural beauty, which encompasses a wide range of terrain as well as sites of historic interest. There are also several lesser federal designations, such as **national monuments**. Traditionally, these are much smaller, focusing perhaps on just one archeological site or geological phenomenon and thus holding a narrower appeal for tourists. In practice, however, the distinction between parks and monuments is somewhat blurred in the Southwest. Most of the parks cover desert regions that have barely known human occupation and thus boast little historic significance, and while the Grand Canyon, Zion and Canyonlands are huge and very varied, parks such as Bryce Canyon and Carlsbad are essentially one-trick wonders. Mesa Verde is unique in having become a national park solely on account of its ancient cliff dwellings.

While many of the national monuments do consist of a single Indian ruin or nineteenth-century fort, several more are as diverse and spectacular as the parks – Arizona's **Canyon de Chelly**, for example, would surely be a national park were it not on the Navajo reservation. There's also been a recent trend to create vast new national monuments in areas that need extra federal protection but are not intended to become major tourist destinations. **Grand Staircase-Escalante** monument in Utah, the best-known example, is larger than any of the national parks covered in this book; others include the even newer **Grand Canyon-Parashant** and **Vermilion Cliffs** national monuments.

Fees and passes

Most national parks and monuments charge an admission fee of between $4 and $20, which covers a vehicle and all its occupants for up to a week. For anyone on a touring vacation, it will almost certainly make more sense to buy one of the various passes that are sold at all federal parks and monuments. The annual National Parks Pass ($50) grants unrestricted access to the bearer, and any accompanying passengers, to all national parks and monuments for a year from the date of purchase. When parks list a "per person" charge, the pass still covers any accompanying immediate relatives.

You can also pay an additional $15 to affix a Golden Eagle hologram to your National Parks Pass, which extends its cover to sites managed by the US Fish and Wildlife Service, the Forest Service, and the Bureau of Land Management. You can buy the hologram at any time, but it only lasts for the lifetime of the pass to which it is attached. In any case, typical first-time visitors to the Southwest tend not to visit such sites, so the extra $15 is probably not worth paying. As a rule, neither pass covers or reduces such additional park fees as charges for camping in official park campgrounds or permits for backcountry hiking or rafting.

Two additional passes grant free access for life to all national parks and monuments, again to the holder and any accompanying passengers, and also provide a fifty percent discount on camping fees. The Golden Age Passport is available to any US citizen or permanent resident aged 62 or older for a one-time processing charge of $10, while the Golden Access Passport is issued free to blind or permanently disabled US citizens or permanent residents.

Park facilities

National parks don't necessarily hold many **facilities** for tourists. All have at least one visitor center, staffed by expert rangers who can advise on tours and activities as well as local history, geology, and wildlife. Only four of the Southwest parks hold hotel-style lodges – the Grand Canyon, Zion, Bryce, and Mesa Verde – and several don't offer restaurants or cafeterias either. It's almost always possible to camp, often in lovely and well-equipped campgrounds like those in Zion and Capitol Reef, but in certain parks only backcountry camping is permitted, in leave-no-trace spots that offer no water, let alone restrooms or showers. Whether or not food and lodging are available in the parks themselves, "gateway towns" nearby cater to the basic needs of tourists. Some, like Springdale near Zion, and Moab near Arches and Canyonlands, are appealing destinations in their own right, and offer a range of adventure sports and activities that may not be permitted within the actual parks.

Other public lands

National parks and monuments are often surrounded by tracts of **national forest**, which are also federally administered but are much less protected. While these too tend to hold appealing rural campgrounds, each is, in the words of the slogan, a "Land of Many Uses," and usually allows some limited logging and other land-based industry – ski resorts more often than strip mines, fortunately.

Further government departments administer a whole range of wildlife refuges, national scenic rivers, recreation areas, and the like – such administration consisting basically of leaving the natural landscape alone. The **Bureau of Land Management** (BLM) has the largest holdings of all, most of it open rangeland, such as in Utah, but also including some enticingly out-of-the-way reaches.

State parks and state monuments are a mirror-image of the national system, preserving sites of more limited, local significance. Many are explicitly designed for recreational use and thus hold better campgrounds than their federal equivalents.

Information resources

For up-to-the-minute information on the national park system, access the official National Park Service **website** at Ⓦwww .nps.gov. It features full details of national parks and monuments, including opening hours, the best times to visit, admission fees, hiking trails, and visitor facilities.

Websites for individual **national parks** are given throughout this book. For more general maps, and information on camping on public lands, try the **Public Lands Information Center** website, Ⓦwww.publiclands.org, which contains information on both BLM and forest-service lands, or the **state parks** office for **Arizona** (☎602/542-4174, Ⓦwww .pr.state .az.us); **Colorado** (☎303/866-3437, Ⓦwww.coloradoparks.org); **New Mexico** (☎1-888/667-2757, Ⓦwww.emnrd.state. nm.us); or **Utah** (☎801/538-7220, Ⓦwww .stateparks.utah.gov).

Camping and backpacking

The ideal way to see the Southwest – especially if you're on a low budget – is to tour the region by car and **camp** at night in state and federal campgrounds. These may lack the amenities of the commercially run campgrounds, found in abundance near the larger towns, but they tend to be far more peaceful, far more scenic, and far better positioned for days of hiking and canyoneering. Typical public campgrounds range in **price** from free (usually when there's no water available, which may be seasonal) to around $15 per night; commercial fees are more like $15–25, for campgrounds that can be more like open-air hotels, with shops, restaurants, and washing facilities.

There may be plenty of campgrounds, but there are also plenty of people who want to use them: if you're camping during public holidays or the high season, you should either reserve in advance or avoid the most popular areas. By contrast, basic campgrounds in isolated areas may well be completely empty whatever time of year you're there, and if there's any charge at all you'll be expected to pay by leaving the money in the bin provided.

Backcountry camping in the national parks is usually by permit and may be free or

Adventure travel

The opportunities for active traveling in the Southwest are all but endless. In the last twenty years, the former uranium mining town of **Moab**, Utah, has grown to become the region's major base for adventure travel of all kinds. Mountain biking is its specialty, with rafting and four-wheel-driving (universally abbreviated to 4WD) as close rivals; full listings can be found on p.524. Other towns popular with energetic visitors include **Durango**, Colorado (see p.100), and **Sedona**, Arizona (see p.337); guides, outfitters, and local tour operators are recommended throughout this book.

cost a few dollars per night. Before you set off on anything more than a half-day hike, and whenever you're headed for anywhere at all isolated, be sure to inform a ranger of your plans and ask about weather conditions and specific local tips. Carry sufficient food and drink to cover emergencies, as well as all the necessary equipment and maps. In summer in the national parks, you have to carry so much water – see p.35 – that you'll need to lighten your load as much as possible, perhaps by sleeping in a lightweight sack rather than a sleeping bag.

When camping rough, check that **fires** are permitted before you start one; even if they are, try to use a camp stove instead of local materials – in some places firewood is scarce, although you may be allowed to use deadwood. In wilderness areas, try to camp on previously used sites. Where there are no toilets, bury human waste at least six inches into the ground and a hundred feet from the nearest water supply and campground. Burn what trash you can and take the rest away.

Flora and fauna

Though the popular conception of the Southwest sees the region as an arid wasteland, in fact it holds a broad spectrum of plant and animal life. Scientists divide the earth into "**life zones**" according to climate and distance from the equator, each of which holds a different assortment of species. In the Southwest, altitude substitutes for latitude; the higher the elevation, the cooler the temperature. Within the Grand Canyon alone, the range of habitat is equivalent to that experienced in a trip from the deserts of Mexico to the forests of the Canadian mountains. Wherever you may be hiking, do not blaze your own trail or you may damage the environment. What looks like a faint coating of dead moss on a sandy surface is **cryptobiotic crust** – the building block on which all desert life depends, and merely treading on it has serious ecological consequences.

Of the Southwest's zones, it's the lowest, hottest level, the **Lower Sonoran** zone, that's home to the rattlesnakes and cactuses you're probably expecting. Southern Arizona is the obvious example, with its dramatic saguaro and organ-pipe cactuses, but a similar ecosystem can be found in the depths of the Grand Canyon.

By the time you reach a mile above sea level – the height of most of Utah's national parks – you're in the **Upper Sonoran** zone. This is characterized by smaller prickly pear cactuses and sagebrush, animals such as rabbits and prairie dogs, and predators like coyotes and mountain lions (not that tourists are at all likely to encounter lions). Low rainfall results in a "pigmy forest" where gnarled, long-lived trees such as the piñon (also spelled pinyon) pine and Utah juniper grow to a maximum height of little more than twenty feet.

Around ten thousand feet up in the mountains of southern Colorado, northern New Mexico, and central-southern Utah, the **Canadian** zone is even more densely forested, with Douglas firs joining the aspen and ponderosa, and bighorn sheep making an appearance in remoter areas. The Colorado Rockies and Utah's Henry and La Sal ranges rise higher still into the **Hudsonian** zone, between eleven and twelve thousand feet. Before the tree cover gives out altogether, ultra-resilient species such as the bristlecone pine, which can live for literally thousands of years, cling to the slopes.

The highest summits in the Southwest – places like the San Francisco Peaks (12,633ft) near Flagstaff, Arizona, Wheeler Peak (13,161ft) near Taos, New Mexico, and Uncompahgre Peak (14,309ft) near Ouray, Colorado – belong to the **Arctic** or **Alpine** zone, where the occasional tiny mammal scuttles through the tundra-like grasses and mosses.

Wherever and whenever **water** is abundant, however, the picture changes. Southwestern riverbeds are lined with magnificent **cottonwood** and **aspen** trees, so many a canyon buried deep in the desert still manages a superb display of fall colors, while spring snowmelts help bring the mountain hillsides and the meadows of Zion alive with wild flowers.

Food and drink

The short-lived international craze for contemporary Southwestern cuisine did little to turn the Southwest itself into a gourmet's paradise. However, in Santa Fe, dozens of top-class restaurants have followed in the footsteps of Mark Miller's trail-blazing *Coyote Café*, while the upscale resorts of Phoenix, Tucson, Taos, and Sedona – as well of course as Las Vegas – all offer opportunities for fine dining.

Out there on the road, the great American **diner** still holds sway. Southern Utah, for example, is the last place to go if lingering over an exquisite meal in atmospheric surroundings ranks high on your vacation wish list. With a typical meal in a diner starting well below $10, travelers happy to eat the same old steak or chicken, with baked potato and salad bar, can get excellent value for money. Vegetarians are in for a rough ride, unless a buffet's macaroni strips with jello bits consistently hit your spot.

The **Hispanic** regions of New Mexico and southern Arizona do at least have their own indigenous cuisine, broadly similar to **Mexican** food but influenced by the Pueblo Indians. The essential ingredient is the **chile,** technically the "fruit" of the pepper plant. (New Mexicans insist it should never be spelled *chili* or *chilli*, which indicates the Texas-style stew made with ground beef and tomato sauce.) You'll soon become familiar with the bright-red *ristras* – strings of dried peppers that adorn the region's doorways and restaurant entrances, celebrating the fiery delights that lie within. In principle the red pepper is the mature version of the green, but confronted with a plateful there's no guarantee which will be the hotter variety. They in turn go to make spicy **salsa**, which at its most basic is simply dried peppers mixed with water, but more usually contains tomato and onion, cilantro (coriander) and other herbs, oil and lemon juice, plus other secret ingredients. If it's too hot for you, the best remedy is to drink milk.

A basic meal in a New Mexican café or diner is broadly similar to what you'd eat south of the border, though it may make more use of fresh meats and vegetables. The essentials are: lots of rice and pinto beans, often served refried as *frijoles* (ie boiled, mashed, and fried), with variations on the **tortilla**, a very thin cornmeal or flour pancake that can be wrapped around the food and eaten by hand (a burrito); folded, fried, and filled (a taco); rolled, filled, and baked in sauce (an enchilada); or fried flat and topped with a stack of filling (a *tostada*). Meals are usually served with complimentary nachos (chips) and salsa dip, or with *sopaipillas*, deep-fried air-filled pastry "pillows," often sweetened with honey. The *chile relleno* is a good vegetarian option – a green pepper stuffed with cheese, dipped in egg batter and fried.

Here and there, you'll also find **Native American** restaurants, both on and off the reservations. The most ubiquitous dish, generally known as a **Navajo taco**, consists of a piece of **fry-bread** – a puffy deep-fried slab of bread – smothered with beans, lettuce, and cheese. A Hopi taco, an Apache taco, and a Pueblo taco are all surprisingly similar. **Corn** or maize, the first crop cultivated in the Americas, comes in some amazing multicolored varieties. Blue corn chips have spread beyond the Southwest, but you may also encounter blue cornflakes and wafer-thin *piki* or *piiki* bread made with blue cornflour.

Drinking

In general, to buy and consume **alcohol** in the US, you must be aged 21 or over; you may be asked for ID even if you look much older. In **New Mexico** and **Arizona**, most restaurants have liquor licenses, and it's always easy to find a drink. In Mormon-dominated **Utah** – whose drinking laws are outlined on p.418 – things are a bit more complicated, though it's not quite the "dry" state of popular legend. Most small towns have at least one restaurant licensed to sell beer or wine to diners.

On **Indian reservations**, however, alcohol is prohibited altogether; you can't have beer in your car, let alone in your motel room.

Communications

Telephones

It's usually easy to find a public **payphone** in the Southwest. As a rule, local calls cost 35¢, but you may have to feed in nine or ten quarters just to call the next town down the highway, and long-distance calls can cost far more. Some budget **motels** offer guests free local calls, but in general calls from **motel rooms** are even more expensive.

To save money on calls when you're on the road, it's well worth buying a **prepaid phone card**, available in various denominations from gas stations, supermarkets, and other outlets. These offer sizable savings on conventional phone rates – not least because they're normally accessed via a toll-free number that incurs no additional charge when called from a motel room.

US mail

Post offices in the Southwest are usually open Monday to Friday from 9am until 5pm, and Saturday from 9am to noon, and there are blue mailboxes on many street corners. Ordinary mail within the US costs 39¢ for a letter weighing up to an ounce. Airmail between the US and Europe or Australia

Useful numbers

Emergencies ☏911; ask for the appropriate emergency service: fire, police, or ambulance
Directory information ☏411
Long-distance directory information ☏1-(area code)/555-1212
Directory enquiries for toll-free numbers ☏1-800/555-1212

International telephone calls

The telephone code to dial **TO THE US** from the outside world (excluding Canada) is 1.
To make international calls **FROM THE US**, dial 011 followed by the country code:
Australia 61   **Ireland** 353
New Zealand 64   **UK** 44

costs 75¢ for postcards or aerograms, 84¢ for letters weighing up to one ounce (two single thin sheets), and generally takes about a week.

Internet access

Public **Internet access** is not as widely available in the Southwest as you might expect. Most public and university libraries offer free access; hostels that cater to international travelers tend to have a computer or two where guests can send and pick up email; and here and there a self-styled "alternative" café lets customers go online. On the road, however, it's not always easy to stay in touch.

If you're carrying a Wi-Fi–equipped laptop computer, you could simply cruise the streets looking for access, while those dependent on modems can usually plug in at even the cheapest motel (though you may have to shift that supposedly immovable bed to reach the socket). A greater concern among international travelers is whether one's Internet service provider is reachable via a toll-free or at least local call in the US, rather than having to make an international call just to log on – rarely an issue with larger ISPs, such as AOL. The useful website Ⓦwww.kropla.com explains how to plug in your laptop while traveling and provides phone country codes and information about electrical systems worldwide.

Traveling in Indian country

There are around fifty separate Indian reservations in the Southwest, ranging in size from the vast Navajo reservation (or "Navajo Nation"), which extends across three states in the Four Corners region, to the nineteen autonomous pueblos of New Mexico, many of which consist of one single village.

Some reservations make no effort to attract or inform visitors; some do the bare minimum to sate tourists' curiosity; some eagerly encourage paying guests to stay in tribal-run motels and campgrounds. Among the most compelling attractions on Native American soil are **Monument Valley**, **Canyon de Chelly**, and **Navajo national monuments**, all on the Navajo reservation; the stupendous waterfalls of the **Havasupai reservation**, deep in the Grand Canyon; and the adobe pueblos of **Taos** and **Ácoma** ("Sky City") in New Mexico.

Many outsiders – Americans and non-Americans alike – feel uncomfortable about entering Native land, but so long as you behave with due **cultural sensitivity** you will almost always be made to feel welcome. In particular, travelers in "Indian Country" should respect the laws that bar the sale, possession, and consumption of **alcohol** on the reservations. Always request permission before **photographing** (or even drawing) people or personal property, and accept that you may be asked for a fee. As well as obeying explicit signs that ask you not to enter specific areas, such as shrines or *kivas*, you should also be aware that **off-road driving** and **off-trail hiking** or **climbing** is forbidden. If you have to drive up to someone's home or *hogan*, stay in your car and wait to be approached, rather than blundering in.

On a more general note, attempts to make friends may run contrary to what Native Americans regard as good **manners**. In the words of a leaflet issued by the Navajo, "the general exuberance many cultures define as friendliness is not considered such by the American Indians." Most Southwestern Indians regard **eye contact** as rude and will avoid meeting your eye; they may also prefer not to shake hands. Your **clothing** may also be an issue; the Hopi, for example, request that visitors not wear shorts or hats, or use umbrellas. Persistent, intrusive questioning is obviously liable to offend. In Pueblo communities especially, don't ask about religious matters when children are present, as children are only initiated into religious secrets at the appropriate age.

Buying Indian crafts

For many tourists, the quest to buy **Indian crafts** becomes a major focus of their visit to the Southwest. Museums and galleries throughout the region display beautiful Pueblo pots, Navajo rugs, Apache baskets, and silver and turquoise jewelry of all kinds, stimulating a desire for affordable gifts and souvenirs that stores everywhere can barely keep up with.

Much of what's widely seen as traditional Indian craftwork has in fact only developed in the last hundred years or so. The collapse of traditional tribal economies coincided with the nineteenth-century arrival of the railroads, and with them the Southwest's first wave of tourists. Enterprising traders encouraged Indians to adapt or learn craft techniques to make souvenirs; as one anthropologist put it, the resultant hybrid was "the Indian's idea of the trader's idea of what the white man thought was Indian design."

To ensure good prices and good quality, you should ideally buy specific Indian crafts as near as possible to where they're made. On the Navajo reservation, head for the **Hubbell Trading Post** (see p.81); on the Hopi reservation, try the **Hopi Cultural Center** and the nearby stores; **Ácoma**, **Taos**, and **San Ildefonso** pueblos are also good bets. More accessibly, the Indian traders in front of the Palace of the Governors in **Santa Fe** are a reliable source, while that city's summer **Indian Market** is a showcase for the entire region. In addition, the Museum of Northern Arizona in Flagstaff, the Heard museum in Phoenix, and the Millicent Rogers museum in Taos all have excellent stores.

If you want to be sure that whatever you're buying was individually crafted by a Southwestern Indian, you're entitled to ask the vendor for a written Certificate of Authenticity. Only the phrase "Authentic Indian handmade" has any legal force. "Indian handmade" means that the object was designed and assembled by American Indians; "Indian crafted" means that American Indians had a hand in the process; and words such as "real" and "genuine" mean nothing. The **Indian Arts & Crafts Association** (☎505/265-9149, ⊛www.iaca.com) can provide further detailed advice, and publishes lists of recommended crafts workers and retail outlets on its website.

Jewelry

Jewelry is perhaps the oldest Southwestern craft of all. The Ancestral Puebloans made necklaces of disks cut from seashells; a single specimen unearthed near Kayenta

---

Another Hopi specialty, the carving of the wooden statuettes known as *kachina* dolls, is described on p.85.

---

was 36 feet long and held over fifteen thousand beads. Such necklaces are now known as *heishi* and are the specialty of New Mexico's Santo Domingo Pueblo.

Turquoise has always been prized by Southwestern Indians; the prehistoric city at Chaco Canyon (see p.112) was probably founded on the proceeds of the turquoise trade, while to this day the Navajo see the greenish-blue, semiprecious stone as symbolizing the state of harmony and beauty known as *hozho*. Necklaces of raw and polished turquoise beads are widely available; the stone also adds color and character to the **silver** jewelry made by the Hopi, Zuni, and Navajo in particular.

Silversmithing is a relatively recent tradition, probably introduced from Mexico in the mid-nineteenth century. For many years, acquiring chunky silver bracelets or belts studded with solid-silver conches was the standard Navajo way of accumulating wealth. Such items could be pawned for cash at trading posts on the reservation and then redeemed when times got easier; now known as pawn jewelry, they count as valuable collectors' pieces. Casual buyers tend to prefer – and to be more able to afford – the more delicate **overlay** style, in which a stenciled design is cut from a thin sheet of silver then soldered onto a solid backing sheet. This technique originated in 1947, when returning Hopi servicemen were trained in the technique as a means of earning a living, and the Hopi remain its finest exponents. Overlay designs can be seen on earrings, belt buckles, rings, and, especially, the clasps of *bola*, or bootlace, ties.

Weaving

The best **weavers** in the Southwest are generally acknowledged to be the Navajo. In legend, they acquired the craft from Spider Woman, who lives atop Spider Rock in the Canyon de Chelly; in fact, they were probably taught by the Pueblo peoples after the Pueblo Revolt of 1680. That was also when they began to raise sheep, which had been introduced by the Spanish a century earlier.

Originally, the Navajo wove blankets and clothing; **Navajo rugs** were the brainchild of nineteenth-century traders, who also suggested that using "earth" colors such as brown would appeal to tourists expecting a "natural" look. Many individual Navajo communities or families weave designs named for their own area, such as Teec Nos Pos, Ganado, or Two Gray Hills. As a rule, the patterns have no religious significance, but most include an "escape route" or "spirit line," a line that runs to the very edge of the rug and ensures that the weaver's spirit is not trapped within it. Traditional rugs also have a hole in the center, as in a spider's web.

Authentic Navajo rugs take months to create and sell for thousands of dollars; anything you see cheaper is probably a mass-produced Mexican imitation. The monthly Navajo Rug Auction at Crownpoint in New Mexico (see p.115) is the best opportunity to pick up a genuine bargain.

Pottery

Spanish explorers in 1540 spoke of Pueblo women as making "jars of extraordinary labor and workmanship, which were worth seeing." The **ceramic** tradition of northern New Mexico's pueblos remains as strong as ever, having been revitalized in the twentieth century by the San Ildefonso potter **Maria Martinez**. Although she consciously modeled her earlier work on designs found in ancient archeological sites, the black-on-black museum pieces for which she became famous are a far cry from the popular conception of Native American crafts. Many tourists prefer either the straightforward pots and jars, painted with rectilinear "pueblo motifs," created at Ácoma Pueblo, or the ubiquitous "**storyteller**" figures, showing a mother surrounded by children, that were first created at Cochiti Pueblo. A representative cross-section of styles can be seen at the roadside store run by **Pojoaque Pueblo**, twelve miles north of Santa Fe (see p.168).

Festivals and public holidays

The box opposite lists the Southwest's major annual festivals. Specific annual events are described in the relevant town accounts, and you'll also find a full calendar of events in the pueblos of New Mexico on p.171. In addition, tourist offices for each state (see p.36) can provide full lists, or you can call local visitor centers ahead of your arrival and ask what's coming up. As a rule, only the Indian Market in Santa Fe and the Balloon Festival in Albuquerque attract large enough crowds to place a serious strain on accommodation and other facilities.

Public holidays

On national **public holidays** listed below, shops, banks, and offices are liable to be closed all day. The traditional **summer season** for tourism runs from Memorial Day, in late May, to Labor Day, in early September; some tourist attractions are only open during that period.

Jan 1	New Year's Day
Jan 15	Martin Luther King Jr's Birthday
3rd Mon in Feb	Presidents' Day
Last Mon in May	Memorial Day
July 4	Independence Day
1st Mon in Sept	Labor Day
2nd Mon in Oct	Columbus Day
Nov 11	Veterans' Day
Last Thurs in Nov	Thanksgiving Day
Dec 25	Christmas Day

Annual festivals and events

Jan to mid-Feb	Gem & Mineral Show	Quartzsite, AZ
Early Feb	Festival of the Arts	Tubac, AZ
April & May	World Series of Poker	Las Vegas, NV
Mid-May	Waila ("chicken scratch") Festival	Tucson, AZ
Late May	Iron Horse Bicycle Classic	Durango, CO
Mid-June	Bluegrass Festival	Telluride, CO
Late June	New Mexico Arts & Crafts Fair	Albuquerque, NM
Late June to mid-Oct	Utah Shakespeare Festival	Cedar City, UT
Late June to Aug	Santa Fe Opera	Santa Fe, NM
Early July	Hopi Marketplace	Flagstaff, AZ
July 4	Nambe Falls Celebration	Nambe Pueblo, NM
July (second week)	Taos Pueblo Powwow	Taos Pueblo, NM
July (last week)	Spanish Market	Santa Fe, NM
Early Aug	Navajo Marketplace	Flagstaff, AZ
Early Aug	Jazz Festival	Telluride, CO
Aug (first week)	Old Lincoln Days	Lincoln, NM
Aug (second week)	Inter-Tribal Indian Ceremonial	Gallup, NM
Aug (third week)	Indian Market	Santa Fe, NM
Aug (third week)	Zuni Fair	Zuni Pueblo, NM
Late Aug	Central Navajo Fair	Chinle, AZ
Sept 2	San Esteban Feast Day	Ácoma Pueblo, NM
Labor Day (first Mon in Sept)	All-American Futurity (horse race)	Ruidoso, NM
Early Sept	New Mexico State Fair	Albuquerque, NM
Early Sept	Hatch Chile Festival	Hatch, NM
Early Sept	Film Festival	Telluride, CO
Sept (second week)	Fiestas de Santa Fe	Santa Fe, NM
Sept (second week)	Navajo Nation Fair	Window Rock, AZ
Early Oct	International Balloon Fiesta	Albuquerque, NM
Early Oct	Northern Navajo Fair	Shiprock, NM
Mid-Oct	Western Navajo Fair	Tuba City, AZ
Late Oct	Arizona State Fair	Phoenix, AZ
Oct (third week)	Helldorado Days	Tombstone, AZ
Late Oct	Halloween Bike Fest	Moab, UT
Early Dec	National Finals Rodeo	Las Vegas, NV
Early Dec	Shalako ceremony	Zuni Pueblo, NM

Directory

Airport tax This is invariably included in the price of your ticket.

Banks As explained on p.38, if you carry an ATM card and/or US dollar travelers' checks, you won't need to visit a bank in the Southwest. However, normal banking hours are from 9am or 10am until 3pm or 4pm Monday to Thursday, and slightly longer on Friday.

Disabled travelers For information on specific states, contact the tourism departments listed on p.36; New Mexico, for example, produces the free *Access New Mexico* guide (☎505/827-6328,

ⓦ www.state.nm.us/gcch/accessnm.htm). SATH (☏ 212/447-7284, ⓦ www.sath.org) is a nonprofit travel-industry referral service that passes queries on to its members as appropriate; allow plenty of time for a response. Mobility International USA (☏ 541/343-1284, ⓦ www.miusa.org) offers travel tips to members ($35 a year) and operates an exchange program for disabled people. The Golden Access Passport, issued without charge to permanently disabled US citizens, gives free lifetime admission to all national parks. *Easy Access to National Parks*, published by the Sierra Club, details access facilities in every national park for people with disabilities, senior citizens, and families with children. Various other useful publications are produced and/or distributed by Twin Peaks Press (☏ 360/694-2462).

Electricity The US electricity supply is 110 volts AC. Plugs are standard two-pins – foreign visitors will need an adapter and voltage converter for their own electrical appliances.

Emergencies Dial ☏ 911.

Floors The first floor of a building in the US is what would be the ground floor in Britain; the second floor would be the first floor, and so on.

Gay and lesbian travelers Resources for gay and lesbian travelers in the Southwest include the Gay and Lesbian Community Center, 24 W Camelback Rd, suite C, Phoenix (☏ 602/234-2752, ⓦ www.phxcenter. org); Wingspan, 425 E Seventh St, Tucson; (☏ 520/624-1779, ⓦ www.wingspan.org); and the Gay and Lesbian Community Center of Southern Nevada, 953 E Sahara Ave, Las Vegas (☏ 702/733-9800, ⓦ www .thecenter-lasvegas.com). Websites catering to visitors to, and residents of, Arizona include ⓦ www.visitgayarizona.com, which is run by the Greater Phoenix Gay and Lesbian Chamber of Commerce, while ⓦ www.gaynm.com and ⓦ www.abqpride. com are equivalents for New Mexico. The Gay Las Vegas website, ⓦ www.gayvegas. com, can tell you all you need to know about Sin City.

ID You should carry ID at all times. Two pieces should suffice, one of which should have a photo: A passport and credit card(s) are your best bets. Not having your license with you while driving is an arrestable offense.

Measurements and sizes US measurements are Imperial, though American pints and gallons are about four-fifths of Imperial ones. Clothing sizes are two figures less than in the UK – a British women's size 12 is a US size 10 – while British shoe sizes are half below American ones for women, and one size below for men.

Senior travelers Anyone over the age of 62, who can produce suitable ID, can enjoy certain discounts. Amtrak and Greyhound, for example, offer (smallish) percentage reductions on fares to older passengers. US residents aged 50 or over can join the American Association of Retired Persons, 601 E St NW, Washington DC 20049 (☏ 202/434-2277 or 1-800/424-3410, ⓦ www.aarp.org), which organizes group travel for senior citizens and can provide discounts on accommodation and vehicle rental. Elderhostel, 75 Federal St, Boston, MA 02110 (☏ 1-877/426-8056, ⓦ www .elderhostel.org) runs educational and activity programs in the Southwest for persons aged 60 and over and their companions. For details of Golden Age Passports, which allow free admission to national parks for US citizens or residents aged 62 or older, see p.45.

Tax Sales tax is added to virtually everything you buy in a shop, but isn't included in the marked price. The actual rate varies from place to place, but in the states covered in this book it ranges between around five and seven percent – except on Indian reservations, which do not levy sales tax. Most towns also charge lodging taxes of between five and fifteen percent.

Temperatures Always given in Fahrenheit.

Time zones New Mexico, Utah, Colorado, and Arizona all operate on **Mountain Standard Time**, which is two hours behind Eastern Standard Time and seven hours behind Greenwich Mean Time, so 2pm in Santa Fe is 4pm in New York City and 9pm in London. Nevada and California are on **Pacific Standard Time**, another hour behind. An Energy Policy Act passed in 2005 has set new start and end dates for **Daylight Savings Time**: beginning in 2007, between the second Sunday in March and the first Sunday in November, New Mexico, Utah, Colorado, and Nevada advance their clocks by one hour. Arizona, however, does not, so in summer it joins Nevada in being an hour behind New Mexico and Utah. Confusingly, the **Navajo Nation** in northeast Arizona does shift to Daylight Savings Time, making it one hour later than the rest of Arizona in summer, while the Hopi reservation, entirely surrounded by the Navajo Nation, stays put. The time in the part-Navajo, part-Hopi town of Tuba City, Arizona – see p.65 – varies from street to street.

Tipping For wait staff in restaurants fifteen to twenty percent is the standard rate. Ten percent would be more usual for bar staff.

Guide

Guide

The Four Corners

CHAPTER 1 # Highlights

* **Hiking to Betatakin** Beautiful ranger-led hike to one of the Southwest's most spectacular ancient ruins, in Navajo National Monument. **See p.67**

* **Monument Valley** Where the West was won, in the movies at any rate; nowhere in the world can match it. **See p.69**

* **White House Trail** Everything about the Canyon de Chelly is magnificent, but the one free-access trail down into it is absolutely unmissable. **See p.79**

* **The Hopi Mesas** These unbelievably remote and isolated desert fastnesses hold the oldest communities in North America. **See p.87**

* **Mesa Verde** Perhaps the most photogenic of all the Southwest's ancient cliff dwellings, tucked into the hillsides of southwestern Colorado. **See p.94**

* **Durango & Silverton Railroad** Ride a steam train through the majestic Colorado Rockies. **See p.102**

* **Silverton** Former mining town, high in the Rockies, that oozes Wild West romance from its every dirt-packed street. **See p.103**

* **Ácoma Pueblo** With the most dramatic setting of any Pueblo community, "Sky City" has occupied a sheer-sided butte for almost a thousand years. **See p.122**

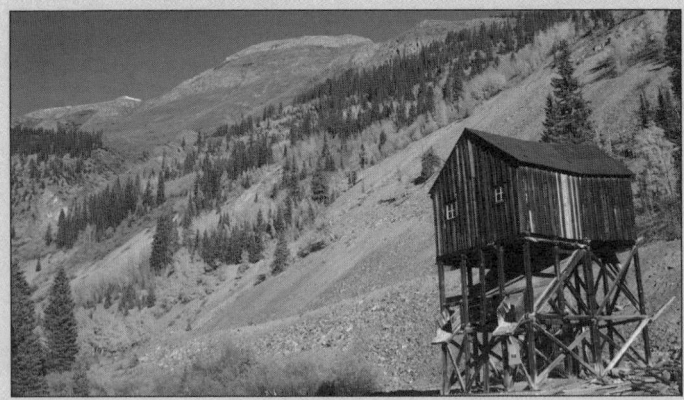

△ Abandoned mine workings on the San Juan Skyway, CO

The Four Corners

The **Four Corners** region is the heartland of the Southwest, not because the states of Arizona, Utah, Colorado, and New Mexico happen to meet here, but because it remains dominated by **Native American** cultures to an extent that's unique in the modern United States.

The region centers on the **Colorado Plateau**, which is said to be the highest inhabited plateau in the world, bar Tibet. These dramatic and hauntingly beautiful uplands may have had a larger population a thousand years ago. At that time, the people now known to historians as the **Ancestral Puebloans** occupied settlements scattered throughout the region. Although they're chiefly remembered for their fabulous "**cliff dwellings**," which cling like eagle nests to the walls of soaring red-rock canyons, in fact they lived everywhere, from the valley floors to the mesa tops. Seven centuries ago, the Ancestral Puebloans moved away from the plateau, for reasons that have yet to be fully explained, and at some point thereafter the nomadic **Navajo** took their place. Now over 300,000 strong, the Navajo are the largest single Native American group in the United States, and their reservation occupies the bulk of the Four Corners area. Contrary to popular legend, however, the Ancestral Puebloans did not vanish completely. Some of their descendants still live nearby, in the **Hopi** villages of Arizona and the pueblos of **Zuni** and **Ácoma**, across the border in New Mexico. Still more migrated further west, to the valley of the Rio Grande.

The ruins left by the Ancestral Puebloans have become the Four Corners' prime tourist destinations. Among the most significant are those at **Mesa Verde National Park** in southwest Colorado, where dozens of graceful pueblo complexes are tucked into high rocky alcoves, and the fully fledged cities of New Mexico's remote **Chaco Canyon**, where Ancestral Puebloan civilization reached its peak. For sheer beauty, however, **Canyon de Chelly National Monument** in Arizona, where Navajo farmers live alongside the ancient remains, far surpasses both. Elsewhere, the main appeal is the **scenery**, which ranges from the Western-movie deserts epitomized by **Monument Valley**, via lone outcrops such as **Shiprock**, to the snow-capped peaks of southwest Colorado.

Planning a Four Corners itinerary can be hard work. The real attractions are far-flung and the towns in between are nothing special. Apart from a handful of expensive motels near Canyon de Chelly and Monument Valley, **accommodation** tends to be concentrated around the region's fringes. "Edge-of-the-res" towns like Gallup and Farmington may no longer be the alcohol-fueled hellholes of yesteryear, but they're basically characterless, concrete conglomerations, and you'd do better to stay slightly further afield, in places like **Durango**, Colorado, or **Flagstaff**, Arizona (covered in Chapter Five).

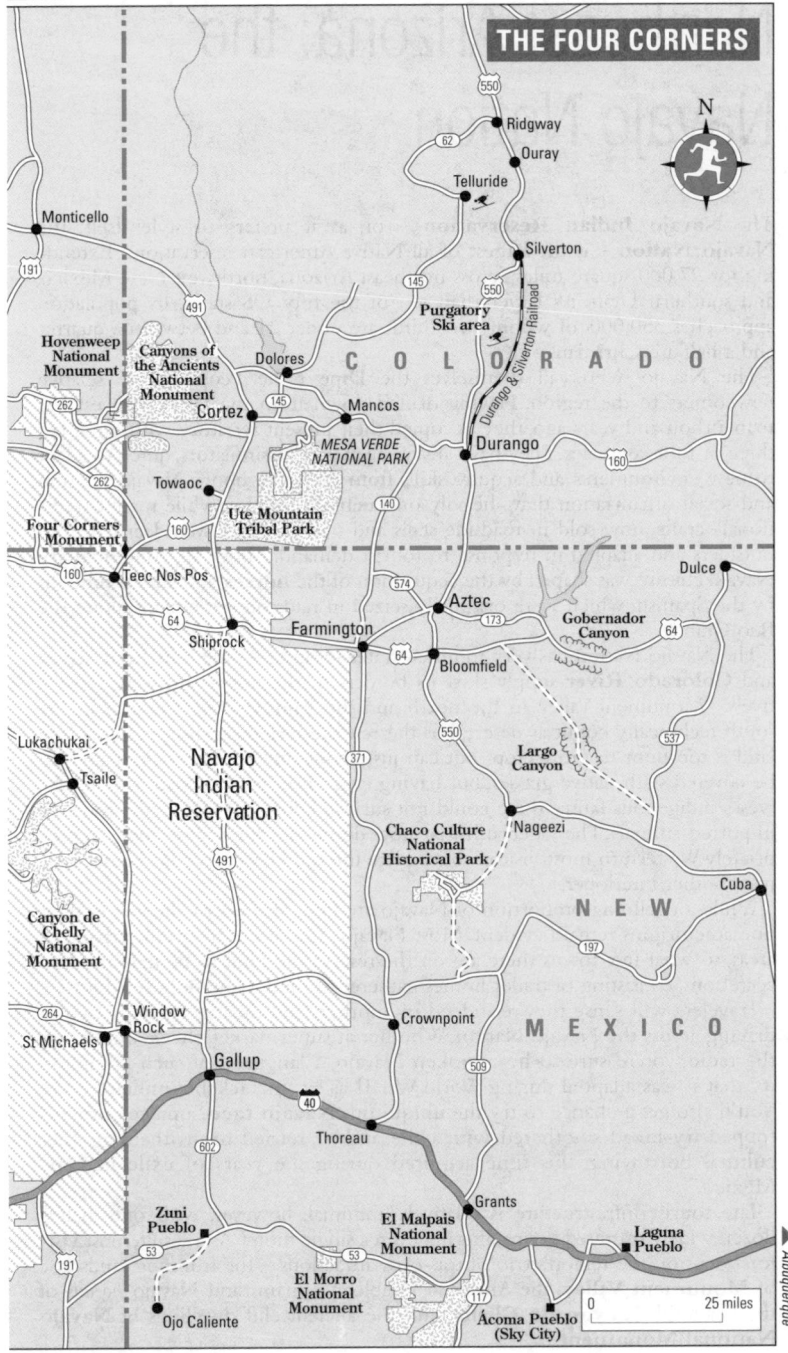

▲ Moab

THE FOUR CORNERS

N

Monticello

191

Ridgway
62
Ouray
Telluride
Silverton
550
145
Purgatory Ski area

Hovenweep National Monument
Canyons of the Ancients National Monument
Dolores
C O L O R A D O
262
Cortez
145
Mancos
MESA VERDE NATIONAL PARK
Durango
160

Durango & Silverton Railroad

Towaoc
Ute Mountain Tribal Park
140

Four Corners Monument
160
Teec Nos Pos
574
Aztec
Dulce
64
Gobernador Canyon
173
Farmington
64
Shiprock
Bloomfield
550

Lukachukai
Tsaile
491
371
Largo Canyon
537

Navajo Indian Reservation
Chaco Culture National Historical Park
Nageezi
Cuba
197

Canyon de Chelly National Monument
N E W

Window Rock
Crownpoint
M E X I C O
264
St Michaels
509
Gallup
40
602
Thoreau

Zuni Pueblo
Grants
El Malpais National Monument
Laguna Pueblo
53
53
117
El Morro National Monument
191
Ojo Caliente
Ácoma Pueblo (Sky City)

▲ Albuquerque

0   25 miles

Northeast Arizona: the Navajo Nation

The **Navajo Indian Reservation** – or, as it prefers to style itself, the **Navajo Nation** – is the largest of all Native American reservations. Extending for 27,000 square miles across northeast Arizona, northwest New Mexico, and southern Utah, it's larger than ten of the fifty US states. Its population approaches 350,000, of whom two-thirds are under 21 and between a quarter and a half are Christians.

The Navajo, who call themselves the Diné ("the People"), are relative newcomers to the region. Having drifted down from the far Northwest less than a thousand years ago, they occupied their present territory within the last three or four centuries. They have always been great assimilators, quick to adapt to new environments and acquire skills from their neighbors. Navajo religion and social organization draw heavily on Pueblo examples, while many "traditional" crafts, now sold in roadside stalls and trading posts, were learned from outsiders and adapted in response to tourist demand. Above all, contemporary Navajo culture was shaped by the acquisition of the **horses** and **sheep** brought by the Spanish, which were originally seized in raids on settlements along the Rio Grande.

The Navajo Nation has very minimal water resources – the **San Juan River** and **Colorado River** simply skirt its borders to the north and west, respectively. Monument Valley in the north and the Painted Desert region in the south technically count as desert, but the rest the terrain is **steppe**, where the land is too poor to grow crops but can just about support livestock. It used to be covered with native grasses, but having evolved in tandem with the Southwest's indigenous fauna, these could not survive being gnawed to the roots by imported animals. The sagebrush that now dominates the region looks appropriately Western to most visitors, but is, like the tumbleweed or Russian thistle, just another interloper.

While a declining proportion of Navajo are now farmers or shepherds, their nomadic origins remain evident. Most Navajo choose not to live in urbanized areas, so what few towns there are on the reservation tend to be ugly modern accretions, consisting of trailer homes gathered around a few disheveled lots.

Travelers will sense they're indeed in another land during a day or two of driving across the Navajo Nation. Whether at supermarket check-outs or on the radio, you're sure to hear spoken Navajo, a language of such complexity that it was adapted during World War II as an uncrackable military code. You'll also get a chance to try the ubiquitous **Navajo taco**, a piece of open-topped fry-bread smothered with chile and/or refried beans that's another cultural borrowing, this time acquired during the years of exile in New Mexico.

The tourist infrastructure is relatively minimal, however, with only half a dozen widely scattered towns offering even a single motel. As a result, most visitors focus on the region's trio of top-class attractions – the stunning sandscape of **Monument Valley**, the Ancestral Puebloan remains and Navajo *hogans* of the beautiful **Canyon de Chelly**, and the ancient cliff dwellings of **Navajo National Monument**.

Note that between early April and late October, when the Navajo Nation joins Utah and New Mexico on **Daylight Savings Time**, it's **one hour later** than the rest of Arizona, including the Hopi Reservation.

For more information on visiting the Navajo Nation, and a schedule of upcoming events, check out the official Navajo **website**, Ⓦwww.discovernavajo.com.

Tuba City

Though it's the largest community on the western side of the Navajo Nation, you're only likely to stop at **TUBA CITY** if you're too tired to drive any further. It stands on US-160 ten miles northeast of US-89, just under eighty miles north of Flagstaff and the same distance east of the Grand Canyon's South Rim; if you're feeling weary, spare a thought for the Hopi runner reported as having *run* to Flagstaff and back from Tuba City in under 24 hours. The town owes its unusual name to a distortion of "Tuuvi," a Hopi from nearby Moenkopi who, upon converting to Mormonism in 1877, invited a group of Mormon families to settle here. Soon, however, the Mormons were monopolizing the site's precious springs, fed by an aquifer that reaches to Monument Valley. As a result, they were forced to move out when the area was added to Navajo lands in 1903.

Tuba City has two unusual claims to fame. The first is a set of petrified **dinosaur tracks**, near the highway five miles southwest of town. These widely spaced 65-million-year-old sandstone imprints were left by a ten-foot creature known as Dilophosaurus. They were hugely significant in proving that dinosaurs could run, but there's no evidence to support the suggestion in *Jurassic Park* that Dilophosaurus also spat venom. It's hard to spot the tracks on your own – in truth, they're not all that riveting – but waiting Navajo guides can lead you to them for a small donation. Secondly, Tuba City straddles two separate **time zones**. Most businesses along the highway, such as Basha's supermarket, operate on Mountain Standard Time, while clocks in the town proper, a block or two uphill to the north, are set in summer to Daylight Savings Time, an hour later. Previous editions of this book included a rather lame joke to the effect that you shouldn't expect to see any **brass bands** in Tuba City, but strangely enough that's no longer quite true. Since 2002, the town has intermittently played host to an annual **TubaChristmas** event, in which tuba players descend from all over the country to play an ear-blasting December concert; similar TubaChristmases take place in many other cities, but naturally the one in Tuba City has an extra resonance. For current schedules, access Ⓦwww.tubachristmas.com. More in keeping with its heritage, Tuba City also stages the three-day **Western Navajo Fair** in mid-October each year.

Practicalities

In the center of Tuba City, a climb of a mile north from the US-160/Hwy-264 intersection, a complex of buildings around the *hogan*-shaped Tuba City Trading Post services most visitor needs. The large, attractively maintained *Quality Inn* here (Ⓣ928/283-4545 or 1-800/644-8383; Ⓦwww.qualityinnnavajonation .com; winter ❺, summer ❻) has pricey but acceptable rooms, with RV spaces also available. Alongside, the *Hogan Restaurant* (Ⓣ928/283-5260) features a long, inexpensive Mexican-American menu – the lunch buffet is truly atrocious, but if you order from the menu the food is OK – and a gift store sells rugs, jewelry, books, and groceries.

There are two other accommodations in town. The recently renovated *Diné Inn Motel*, on US-160 to the east (☎928/283-6107; ❹), is a simple but very acceptable budget motel, while students at **Grey Hills High School** operate part of the school complex as the *Grey Hills Inn,* left off US-160, half a mile northeast of town (☎928/283-6271; ❸). The thirty basic twin-bedded rooms share bathrooms. Back at the intersection of US-160 and Hwy-264, the *Tuba City Truck Stop Cafe* (☎928/283-4975) is renowned for its cheese-and-chile-topped Navajo tacos, and you'll also find a *KFC*, a *Taco Bell*, and a *McDonalds* in the vicinity.

Navajo National Monument

Despite its name, **NAVAJO NATIONAL MONUMENT** has little to do with the Navajo. Instead, it's among the most beautiful Ancestral Puebloan sites in the Southwest, though visitors should bear in mind that it can only be fully appreciated when its hiking trails are open. It's reached via a ten-mile spur road that runs north from US-160 fifty miles northeast of Tuba City and twenty miles southwest of Kayenta.

Each of the monument's three separate parcels preserves a long-lost Ancestral Puebloan **cliff dwelling**. Set in an enormous rocky alcove, **Betatakin** can be admired from an overlook near the visitor center, or accessed via a six-hour, ranger-led hike. The even larger **Keet Seel** is a seventeen-mile round-trip hike from the road, and thus it's only seen by a dedicated few. Finally, fragile **Inscription House** – named not for ancient petroglyphs, but for the date "1661" carved on a wall, suggesting that some seventeenth-century Spaniard passed this way – has been closed to visitors for over forty years.

Archeologists divide the Ancestral Puebloans of the Four Corners into three subgroups. One centered on Mesa Verde (see p.94) and another on Chaco Canyon (see p.112); the focus of Navajo National Monument, **Tsegi Canyon**, is the definitive **Kayenta** site. Its inhabitants are seen as conservative, in that they still lived in pithouses long after the people of Chaco and Mesa Verde started to construct sophisticated pueblos. They were fine potters, however, and Kayenta ceramics are now much-prized museum pieces. Tree-ring dating pinpoints their move into the alcoves of Tsegi Canyon to around 1250 AD. The first three of the still-standing dwellings in Betatakin were erected in 1267; another was added in 1268, and a further ten or more, plus a *kiva* (see p.604), in 1275. By 1300 AD, intensive irrigation had lowered the water table and rendered farming impossible, and the canyon had been abandoned.

What became of the Kayenta people is no mystery. According to the Navajo, Keet Seel was built by settlers from Navajo Mountain, and Betatakin by a group from Chaco. That dovetails with the **Hopi** legend that as many as eight of their clans lived here for around fifty years, just before their migrations ended at the Hopi Mesas, fifty miles south. A pictograph at Betatakin – consisting of a bird-like figure within a large white circle – shows Masaw, the symbol of the Hopi Fire Clan. Hopis regularly return for ceremonies honouring their ancestors, and at the time of the Oraibi dispute, in 1906 (see p.588), the breakaway Hopi faction that eventually founded Hotevilla seriously considered resettling here.

Navajo National Monument was established in 1909, after Navajo guides led members of the Wetherill family (of Mesa Verde fame; see p.96) to Keet Seel. Betatakin was "discovered" a year or two later, by chance already within the monument boundaries.

Practicalities

The paved section of Hwy-564 ends ten miles north of US-160, at the monument's **visitor center** (daily 8am–5pm; ☎928/672-2700, ⓦwww.nps .gov/nava; no admission charge). Ordinary vehicles should not continue any further along Hwy-564's unpaved extension. You can't see the ruins from the visitor center, but interesting displays include a mock-up of three rooms from Betatakin, assorted artifacts from the site, and a traditional Navajo forked-stick male *hogan* (see p.80) in the forest at the back.

The lovely little **campground** nearby is open year-round, and all its first-come first-served sites are free; there are no hook-ups for RVs. In summer, visitors who arrive after the campground is full are accommodated in a more primitive campground a mile north. The closest **motel** is the 57-room *Anasazi Inn* (☎928/697-3793, ⓦwww.anasaziinn.com; winter ❸, summer ❹), whose turquoise-roofed cabins are located in the town of **TSEGI** on US-160 ten miles northeast of the turn-off, halfway to Kayenta. It has a small restaurant and no neighbors apart from its derelict predecessor.

The Sandal Trail

If you only have time for a brief visit, all you can do is gaze across the canyon to **Betatakin** from the end of the **Sandal Trail**. This easy, paved one-mile round-trip hike, which doubles as a nature trail, runs partly on a boardwalk and partly over level open rock.

The view at the end, where a sumptuous orange recess in the canyon wall arches above the 135-room cluster of dwellings, is quite amazing, and especially so in late afternoon, when direct sunlight penetrates the alcove. Their straight walls rise in tiers from a ledge above the canyon floor; hence the Navajo name Betatakin, or "house on ledges." It's all in such good condition – everything you see is original, except for the ladders and a few of the roof beams – that it's hard to believe the 120 or so inhabitants left not seven years but seven centuries ago.

Hiking to Betatakin

While it's worth visiting the monument for the long-distance view alone, to get any closer to Betatakin you have to join a free, ranger-guided **hike**, which is also a great opportunity to learn more about the land and its history. Schedules vary according to staffing and budget levels, so it's worth calling the visitor center to check the current situation, but in recent years two hikes have departed daily in summer, between Memorial Day and Labor Day, at 8.30am and 11am, while during the rest of the year there has been one daily hike at 10am. Advance reservations are not accepted; only the first 25 people who register at the visitor center for each tour, on that same day, get to go. Remember the time difference if you're hurrying here from beyond the Navajo Nation; the monument is an hour ahead of other Arizona locations, like the Grand Canyon or Flagstaff, during Daylight Savings Time.

All hikers are expected to bring enough food and water (at least half a gallon) to last the six-hour round-trip. Although you rendezvous for a briefing at the visitor center, the hike actually starts a mile or two's drive away, along a trail that drops steeply into the canyon from the top of Skeleton Mesa. Betatakin itself only comes into sight right at the end, as you head up a steadily narrowing side canyon, filled with delicate aspens that turn a gorgeous yellow in the fall. The closer you approach, the more overwhelming the awesome dimensions of the alcove become; it's 452ft high, 370ft wide, and 135ft deep. Until 2000, groups used to climb right up into the plaza of the ancient pueblo, but that is no longer permitted, due to the danger of rocks flaking from the ceiling above. Now you have to content yourself with admiring and photographing them from a discreet distance.

Keet Seel

Getting all the way to **Keet Seel** – Arizona's largest cliff dwelling – is a major undertaking. The grueling seventeen-mile, self-guided round-trip **hike** is generally considered too much to attempt in a single day, so most hikers spend the night at the primitive campground near the ruin. There's no drinkable water en route, though you may well have to wade through muddy streams.

Unlike for Betatakin, all hikers *must* make reservations through the visitor center, anywhere from one day to five months in advance. The trail is only open in summer, when up to twenty (free) permits per day are issued, on condition that you attend a briefing session, held daily at 8.15am and 4pm. To allow enough time for the long, tiring hike, you therefore have to attend the briefing the day before. In addition, a free ranger-guided day hike is offered once every two weeks or so, to no fixed schedule; call ahead to check.

Visitors to Keet Seel can only enter the ruins with the ranger stationed nearby. The village reaches deep back into the hillside, so well sheltered that its 150-plus rooms have barely deteriorated. No more than half a dozen are *kivas* – the Kayenta were not such relentless builders of these ceremonial chambers as their neighbors at Mesa Verde. Keet Seel was a longer-lasting and more dynamic settlement than Betatakin; its cliff dwellings date from the same era, but people

Hard Times At Black Mesa

Immediately opposite the Navajo National Monument turn-off, a broad but poorly surfaced road sets off south to climb **Black Mesa**. Only 4WD vehicles can get more than a mile or two along here, so few tourists see the gaping **strip mines** where the Peabody Western Coal Company has long extracted the prodigious coal deposits for which the mesa is named.

The future of these mines is uncertain and surrounded by controversy. **Black Mesa Mine** itself, which supplied coal to the Mohave Power Plant in Laughlin, Nevada, closed down on January 1, 2006. Amazingly enough, the coal was transported on its 265-mile, three-day trip around the Grand Canyon by **pipeline**. In the only such operation in the US, crushed coal was slurried in a 50:50 mixture using an extravagant 1.3 billion gallons of pure water per year, pumped from the Navajo Aquifer. When springs and water sources, many of which were considered sacred, started to run dry across the Hopi and Navajo reservations, many tribal members called for Peabody's leases to be discontinued, or at least renegotiated. Peabody's two thousand Native American employees, on the other hand, some of whom earned $80,000 per year – ten times the average local family income – spoke of economic devastation should the mines shut down.

Black Mesa Mine closed not because of local activism, but because the Mohave Power Plant ceased operations in the face of lawsuits from the Sierra Club and other environmental groups. It could not afford to reduce its sulfur dioxide emissions to the levels necessary to end air pollution in the Grand Canyon region. For the moment, the nearby **Kayenta Mine** continues to function; you may well pass one of the endless trains that ferry coal from it up to the Navajo Generating Station at Page (see p.481).

lived in the vicinity from around 950 AD, and migrating groups came and went for the next few hundred years. Little now survives of the large free-standing pueblo that stood on the valley floor not far away.

Kayenta

KAYENTA, where US-160 meets US-163 twenty miles northeast of Navajo National Monument, is not in any sense an historic town. Having begun life in the 1950s as a dormitory community for workers in the uranium mines to the north, it later became the main base for the miners of Black Mesa. Just twenty miles south of Monument Valley, it now also caters to ever-increasing numbers of tourists, but remains little more than a conglomeration of trailer homes, with barely a two-story building to its name.

Practicalities

Kayenta's *hogan*-shaped **visitor center**, at the highway intersection (hours vary; daily 10am–9pm in summer; ℡928/697-3572), carries information on the whole Navajo Nation, holds several crafts stalls, and stages Navajo dances on summer Tuesdays (from 8pm). The *Burger King* next door (℡928/697-3534) has a large display on the wartime Navajo Code Talkers, as seen in the 2002 movie *Windtalkers*.

Kayenta is also home to three upscale **motels**. Immediately south of the junction, facing drivers arriving from Monument Valley, the large *Holiday Inn–Kayenta* (℡928/697-3221 or 1-800/465-4329, Ⓦwww.ichotelsgroup .com; winter ❺, summer ❻), houses the distinctive and good-value *Wagon Wheel* **restaurant**, as well as its own pool. A little to the west, beyond the *Burger King*, the *Hampton Inn–Navajo Nation* (℡928/697-3170 or 1-800/426-7866, Ⓦwww .hamptoninn.com; winter ❸, summer ❺) is not only the smartest in town but also, just, the cheapest, again with a pool and a restaurant. The *Best Western Wetherill Inn*, a mile north on US-163 (℡928/697-3231 or 1-800/780-7234, Ⓦwww.gouldings.com; winter ❸, summer ❻), is less fancy, but the fact that it's run by the same people as *Goulding's* in Monument Valley makes it handy for arranging tours. The routine *Golden Sands Cafe* stands alongside (℡928/697-3684), while the Mexican food at the *Amigo Cafe* (℡928/697-8448), a little further north, is deservedly popular. There's also a reasonable deli counter at the central *Basha's* supermarket.

Monument Valley

The classic Wild West landscape of stark sandstone buttes and forbidding pinnacles of rock, poking from an endless expanse of drifting red sands, has become an archetypal image. Only when you arrive at **MONUMENT VALLEY** do you realize how much your perception of the West has in fact been shaped by this one spot. Such scenery does exist elsewhere, of course, but nowhere is it so perfectly concentrated and distilled. While movie-makers have flocked here since the early days of Hollywood, the sheer majesty of the place still takes your breath away. Add the fact that it remains a stronghold of **Navajo** culture, surprisingly little affected by tourism, and Monument Valley may well prove to be the absolute highlight of your trip to the Southwest.

△ Monument Valley at dawn

Monument Valley Navajo Tribal Park straddles the Arizona–Utah state line, 24 miles north of Kayenta and 25 miles southwest of Mexican Hat. Although you can see the buttes for free – silhouetted on the skyline from anything up to fifty miles away, and towering alongside US-163 – the four-mile detour to enter the park is rewarded with much closer views, while the tours beyond the end of the road are unforgettable.

A history of Monument Valley

Monument Valley is not really a valley. There's no permanent stream, nor higher ground to either side, and no valley has buttes along its floor. This whole

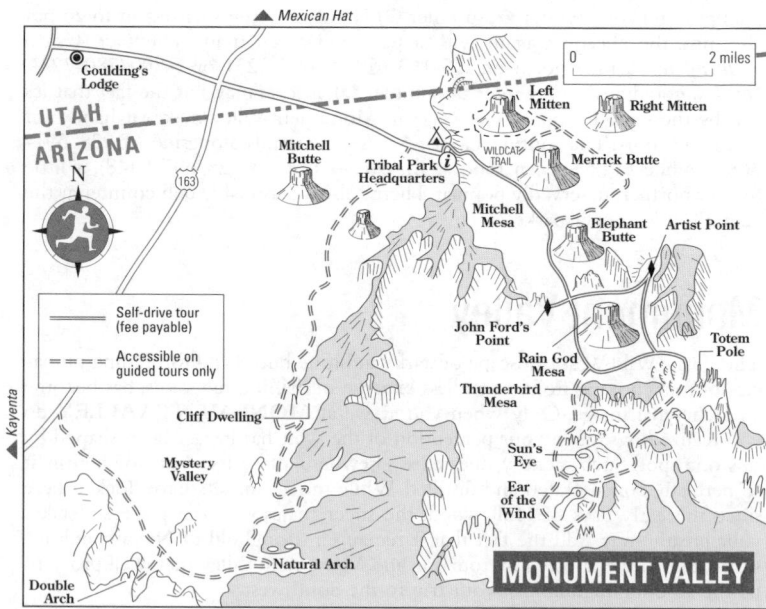

region was once a flat plain, concealing the top of what are now the tallest "monuments." In the past ten million years, the Monument Uplift – part of the general upthrust of the Colorado Plateau – has pushed that plain up from below, bulging to create cracks that have since eroded to leave only isolated nuggets of harder rock.

On the surface, thanks to annual rainfall of under ten inches, this looks like an unpromising region in which to live. However, sand dunes are surprisingly efficient at conserving moisture, and a huge aquifer deeper down stretches all the way to Tuba City. Beneath the small **cliff dwellings** that burrow into the rocks, the slopes are littered with ancient potsherds, indicating an Ancestral Puebloan presence that lasted until around 1300 AD. After that, the area may have remained unoccupied until a band of Navajo retreated here to avoid Kit Carson's round-up in 1864 (see p.77). Their leader, **Hoskinnini**, is said to have discovered silver nearby. Two white prospectors sneaked some of the metal away in 1880, but were killed – by passing Paiutes, according to the Navajo – when they returned, at the bases of **Mitchell Mesa** and **Merrick Butte** respectively.

The Navajo, who named Monument Valley *Tse 'bii'ndisgaii'*, or "there is a treeless area amid the rocks," see the whole place as a *hogan*, with its "door" facing

Valley Tours

In the parking lot, among the crafts stalls, several Navajo-run outfits tout for takers on their valley tours, by jeep or horse. These are very highly recommended; all can be booked in advance, but it's usually easy to turn up and get on a tour straight away. Shop around, as prices can vary enormously for substantially the same experience. Only you can decide whether it's worth paying extra for a "private" tour for your own group, rather than joining with other visitors.

Horseback tours

Horseback tours generally work out cheaper if you book in advance rather than arranging them with the outfitters waiting in the parking lot. That said, if you're happy to take a chance, the best option of all is to drive down to the stables at John Ford's Point on the valley floor, where it's often possible to saddle up on the spur of the moment for a good price, and you don't have to pay for the extra riding time to and from the valley proper. To be totally sure of a ride, however, reserve in advance with operators like Roy Black's or Sacred Monument, both listed below; their rates range around $40 for 1hr 30min, $60 for 2hr 30min, and upwards from $150 for the whole day. Sacred Monument also offers **guided hikes** at similar rates.

Jeep tours

Typical rates for guided jeep tours, whether on the spot or reserved in advance, range from $25–45 per person for 1hr 30min, $30–60 for 3hr, and $90–160 for an all-day tour. Operators include Simpson's Trailhandler Tours (☏435/727-3362 or 435/727-3255 ⓦwww.trailhandlertours.com), which is generally among the cheapest; Totem Pole Tours (☏435/727-3313; ⓦwww.totempoletour.com); Sacred Monument Tours (☏435/727-3218; ⓦwww.monumentvalley.net); and Roy Black's Jeep & Horse Tours (☏928/309-8834 or evenings 435/739-4205; ⓦwww.blacksmonumentvalleytours.com).

In addition, *Goulding's Lodge* and the associated *Wetherill Inn* in Kayenta offer jeep tours from farther afield. Call ahead for the latest schedules, but as a guideline, all-day trips (adult $75.50, under-8s $57) start from *Goulding's Lodge* daily at 9am; half-day tours (3hr 30min; adult $42.50, under-8s $27) leave daily at 9am and at some point in the afternoon, depending on the season; and shorter 2hr 30min tours (adult $33, under-8s $26) leave daily at 1.30pm.

east at the visitor center, and the butte behind *Goulding's Lodge* as its central hearth. They say the whole area has become drier during the past century, perhaps because the spirit of the Totem Pole formation, which was regarded as a line of prayersticks capable of granting rain, was offended when it was climbed during the filming of *The Eiger Sanction* (see p.74).

Park practicalities

The approach road to the tribal park ends four miles east of US-163, at a large raised parking lot where a booth collects the **admission fee** of $5. A terrace alongside offers a superb panorama of Monument Valley, while the **visitor center** (daily: hours vary from 7am–7pm in summer down to 8am–5pm in winter; Thanksgiving 8am–noon; closed Christmas Day and New Year's Day; ☎435/727-5870; ⊛www.navajonationparks.org) in the adjoining building holds displays on Navajo culture and history, including the story of the wartime Code Talkers, as well as on the valley itself. It also stages Navajo **dances** on summer evenings, from 8pm.

The same large complex holds an appropriately named **restaurant**, *The View* (daily: Oct–March 8am–6pm; April–Sept 6am–10pm; ☎435/727-3312), which serves lunchtime burgers and sandwiches ($7–8) named for film stars such as John Wayne and Shirley Temple, as well as fried chicken for $10 and Navajo fry-bread for $8. The Navajo Park Trading *Post* sells a wide range of souvenirs.

Although the only hotel accommodation in the vicinity is six miles away, at *Goulding's Lodge* (see p.73), you can **camp** a short walk from the visitor center. The exposed *Mitten View* campground operates on a first-come, first-served basis, with sites costing $10 in summer and $5 in winter, when the shower facilities are closed.

Seeing the valley

The most prominent of the buttes visible from outside the visitor center are the pair known as **The Mittens**, which consist logically enough of the Left or West Mitten and the Right or East Mitten. Rising a thousand feet from the desert floor, each has a distinct "thumb" that splinters off from its bulkier central section. Alongside them stands **Merrick Butte**, completing a trio that's illuminated a glowing red at sunset.

A rough, **unpaved road** drops from the western end of the visitor center parking lot to run through Monument Valley. Taking a guided tour is preferable, but the 17-mile loop marked as the **self-drive** route (daily: summer 8am–6pm; winter 8am–4.30pm) makes a bearable if bumpy, hour-plus ride in an ordinary vehicle. You're allowed to stop en route to stretch your legs, but not to hike for any distance. At the main halt, **John Ford's Point**, you can enjoy the classic wide-screen valley panorama and also browse a few jewelry stalls. A Navajo man normally poses on horseback at the tip of the nearby promontory, while closer at hand, children in traditional dress invite you to photograph them for a dollar or two. The road goes on to pass near the **Totem Pole** before heading back via **Artist Point** to the visitor center.

Guided tours follow the same route, but they also take visitors "behind the scenes" beyond the main road and offer a fascinating Navajo perspective on the place (for tour operators, see p.71). Likely stops on longer tours include the **Sun's Eye** – a high natural arch, with petroglyphs of bighorn sheep at its base – and the similar, even more dramatic **Ear of the Wind**, as well as an obligatory visit to a *hogan* for a weaving demonstration. The most striking **Ancestral**

Monument Valley and the Mythic West

The real star of my Westerns has always been the land ... My favorite location is Monument Valley. It has rivers, mountains, plains, desert, everything that land can offer ... I consider this the most complete, beautiful, and peaceful place on earth.

John Ford, *Cosmopolitan*, March 1964

In 1937, Harry Goulding, the owner of *Goulding's Lodge*, heard talk that Hollywood producers were planning to shoot Western-themed movies in the Southwest. Although Monument Valley had featured in a 1925 silent, George B Seitz's *The Vanishing American*, its splendors remained largely unknown. Armed with a portfolio of photographs, Goulding set off for California and started knocking on doors. Within a year, **John Ford** had brought a crew to Goulding's remote desert outpost and was filming *Stagecoach*.

From their first moment on screen, Monument Valley's emblematic buttes served as a visual shorthand for the Wild West. The geographical reality was irrelevant. *Stagecoach* supposedly followed a coach heading through Apache territory from Tonto in southern Arizona to Lordsburg in New Mexico. In fact, it did no more than duck in and out of Monument Valley; as John Wayne put it, "there's some things a man just can't run away from." Wayne was at it again in *The Searchers* (1956), when he spent five years scouring Texas for Scar's band of Comanche, although in reality both he and they were within the same five-mile radius of the Mittens all along. In *My Darling Clementine* (1946), Henry Fonda as Wyatt Earp drove his cattle across the floor of Monument Valley and into Tombstone, somehow transplanted from southern Arizona complete with (potted) saguaro cactuses; the OK Corral perched on a mesa nearby. Monument Valley consistently symbolized the untamed wilderness that lay beyond the ramshackle towns, beleaguered forts, isolated cabins, or crude fences of the West's earliest white pioneers.

In total, John Ford made seven movies in Monument Valley, including his "cavalry trilogy" of *Fort Apache* (1948), *She Wore A Yellow Ribbon* (1949), and *Rio Grande* (1950). Both Wayne and Fonda played opposite the adult Shirley Temple in *Fort Apache*. Ford worked closely with the Navajo, who featured as all-purpose Indians whenever necessary, camping out in wigwams in *The Searchers*, for example, at what's now known as John Ford's Point. Medicine man Hosteen Tso is said to have been kept on hand to control the weather, and is credited with producing a snow-storm and a sandstorm to order for *Stagecoach*. The construction of Monument Valley's first road, in the 1950s, spoiled Ford's hitherto pristine landscape, but he carried on filming here until *Cheyenne Autumn* (1963). He died shortly after announcing plans to make *Appointment at Precedence* in the valley, in 1972.

The spectacle of Henry Fonda's son smoking marijuana in Monument Valley, in *Easy Rider* (1969), may have marked an end to the days of the classic Western, but the valley itself has remained in demand. Clint Eastwood had some perilous moments on top of the Totem Pole in *The Eiger Sanction* (1975), and Michael J. Fox's souped-up DeLorean outgunned pursuing Indian warriors in *Back to the Future III* (1989). Other visitors have included Mick Jagger in *Freejack* (1992) and Tom Hanks in *Forrest Gump* (1994), while in Mario van Peebles' hip-hop *Western Posse* (1993), Monument Valley was almost bursting with Sioux Indians, gold mines, railroads, and buffalo soldiers.

Monument Valley's starring role as the setting for many Roadrunner **cartoons** probably stems from its appearances in the wildly popular Krazy Kat syndicated comic strip of the 1920s and 1930s. Learned critics such as e e cummings, who referred to the strip's "strictly irrational landscape," and Umberto Eco, who spoke of "surrealistic inventions, especially in the improbable lunar landscapes," clearly were oblivious to the fact that artist **George Herriman** was a regular visitor to *Goulding's Lodge*. The adventures of Krazy Kat and Ignatz Mouse – set in Coconino County – were played out against a backdrop of realistic depictions of Monument Valley formations.

Puebloan remains are in adjacent **Mystery Valley**, which you'll probably only visit if you take a full-day tour.

It's now also possible to **hike** into the valley without a guide, so long as you stick to the 3.3-mile loop of the **Wildcat Trail**. Starting from a primitive campground just under half a mile down from the visitor center, this circles the Left Mitten butte. Assorted plants used by the Navajo are labeled along the way, but the real glory of the hike is the chance to be alone in such an overwhelming landscape, dwarfed beneath the mighty rock formations. Expect to take over two hours to complete the circuit. Wear sunscreen, carry plenty of water, and be prepared for a tiring climb back up at the end.

Goulding's Lodge

The only **accommodation** within twenty miles of Monument Valley is two miles west of US-163, along a road that starts immediately opposite the park approach road. *Goulding's Monument Valley Lodge* (☎435/727-3231; ⓦwww .gouldings.com; Jan to mid-March ❹, second fortnight of March and mid-Oct to Dec ❻, April to mid-Oct ❼,) rises in tiers at the foot of a large sandstone bluff, with superb views across the valley. It began life as a 1920s trading post, opened by Harry Goulding and his wife "Mike," and has expanded to incorporate an upscale motel, a restaurant, an indoor pool, a general store, and a gas station. All the motel rooms have balconies, as well as VCRs to watch the *Lodge's* library of westerns. The adequate but unexceptional dinners at the *Stagecoach Dining Room* (daily 6.30am–9pm) will set you back up to $20. As always on the reservation, no alcohol is served; the bafflement of European tourists confronted by a "wine list" of alcohol-free wines is a joy to behold. There's also a **campground** (☎435/727-3235; mid-March to mid-Oct $32, mid-Oct to mid-March $18), which opens its pool in summer but offers only minimal facilities in winter.

The original lodge building has been preserved much as the Gouldings left it and holds a small, but entertaining **movie museum** (April–Nov Mon–Fri 7.30am–9pm, Sat & Sun 8am–9pm), where visitors are invited to make a $2 donation towards scholarships for Navajo students. Behind it stands the cabin used by John Wayne, as Captain Nathan Brittles, in *She Wore A Yellow Ribbon*. The nearby store, incidentally, sells John Wayne Toilet Tissue: "It's rough, it's tough, and it doesn't take crap off anyone."

From Monument Valley to Canyon de Chelly

The most direct – and also the most scenic – route between the Navajo Nation's two major tourist attractions, Monument Valley and Canyon de Chelly, is **Arrowhead Hwy-59**. This gorgeous drive heads south off US-160 eight miles east of Kayenta, and then spends almost fifty miles skirting the northern flanks of Black Mesa.

For most of the way, it runs across flat desert grasslands, like a slightly more fertile version of Monument Valley, with cracks in the plains to either side hinting at unfathomable canyons. Occasionally, off to the south, villages such as **Chilchinbito** and **Rough Rock** nestle against the mesa, but the road ignores them. When it finally drops down **Carson Mesa** to reach Chinle Valley, you're confronted by the unlikely waters of **Many Farms Lake**. The road meets US-191 at the community of **Many Rivers**, fourteen miles north of Chinle.

Canyon de Chelly

A short way east of **Chinle**, twin sandstone walls emerge abruptly from the desert floor, then climb with phenomenal speed to become the thousand-foot cliffs of **CANYON DE CHELLY NATIONAL MONUMENT**. Between these sheer sides, the cottonwood-fringed Chinle Wash meanders through an idyllic oasis of meadows and planted fields. Here and there, a *hogan* stands in a grove of fruit trees, a straggle of sheep is penned in by a crude wooden fence, and ponies drink at the water's edge. And everywhere, perched above the valley

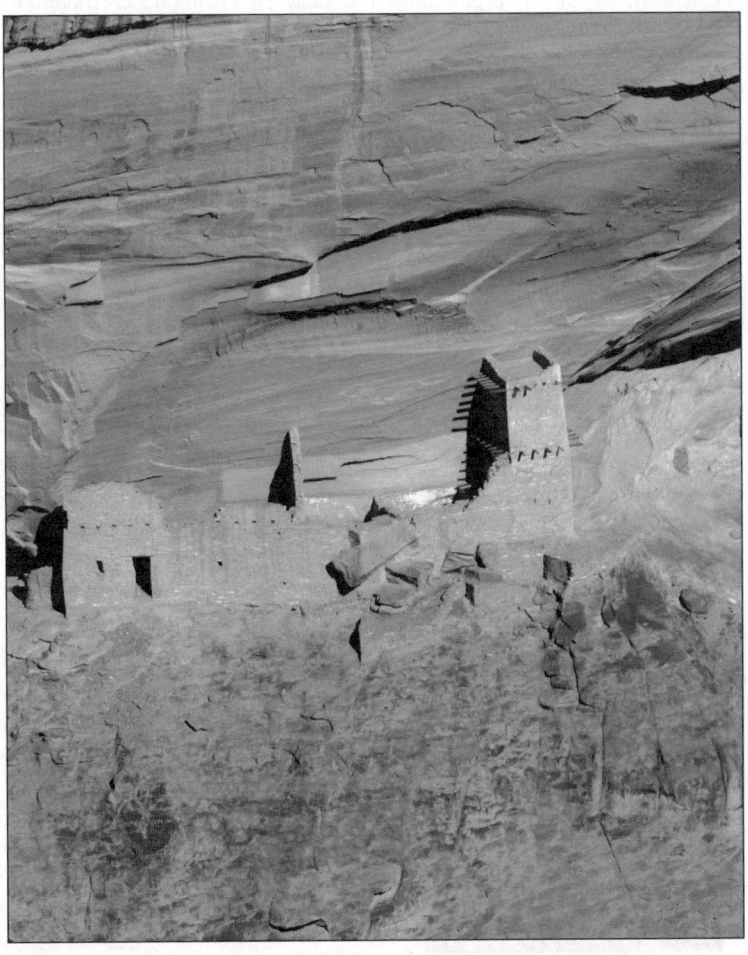

△ Antelope House Ruin, Canyon del Muerto

on ledges in the canyon walls and dwarfed by the towering cliffs, are the long-abandoned stone and adobe dwellings left by the **Ancestral Puebloans**.

The monument in fact holds two main canyons, which branch apart a few miles upstream: **Canyon de Chelly** to the south and **Canyon del Muerto** to the north. Each twists and turns in all directions, scattered with immense rock monoliths, while several smaller canyons break away. The whole labyrinth threads its way upwards for thirty miles into the Chuska Mountains.

Canyon de Chelly is a magnificent place, easily on a par with any of the Southwest's national parks. Its relative lack of fame owes much to the continuing presence of the **Navajo**, for whom the canyon retains enormous symbolic significance, despite the fact that they did not themselves construct its cliff dwellings. Casual visitors are restricted to peering into the canyon from above, from overlooks along the two "**rim drives**". There's no road in, and apart from one short but superb hike, you can only enter the canyons with a Navajo guide. Incidentally, "de Chelly" is pronounced "de shay"; the name is a corruption of the Navajo *tségi*, meaning "rock canyon."

A history of Canyon de Chelly

Ancestral Puebloan Basketmakers first occupied Canyon de Chelly around 200 AD, digging primitive pithouses into the valley floor. Over the next thousand years, their descendants moved first into free-standing "pueblo" apartment-style blocks (from 750 AD), and then into elegant cliff dwellings, starting in 1100 AD. Virtually all these canyon-wall complexes face south to catch the sun, with cooler storage chambers set in deep recesses. Many now look more inaccessible than they actually were, thanks to rock falls and the erosion of toe- and hand-holds in the soft sandstone. The valley's population peaked at roughly one thousand, shortly before drought drove the Ancestral Puebloans out around 1300 AD.

For the next few centuries, **Hopis** from the west farmed the canyon floor in summer, but no permanent inhabitants returned before the Pueblo Revolt of 1680 (see p.575). As the Spanish reasserted control over New Mexico, the first **Navajo** arrived in the region, quite possibly accompanied by Pueblo refugees. From then on, the Navajo and Spanish were locked in a bloody cycle of armed clashes and slave raids. As the "stronghold of the Navajo," Canyon de Chelly became the target of punitive **Spanish** expeditions. In 1805, Lieutenant Antonio Narbona's party gunned down over a hundred Navajo in the Canyon del Muerto. According to the Spanish, ninety of them were warriors; the Navajo say that the warriors were away at the time, and that all the dead were women, children, and elders.

After the Yankees took over in Santa Fe, the US Army in turn set about dislodging the Navajo. The process culminated in 1864, when General Carleton's men despatched all the Navajo they could round up on the "**Long Walk**" to Fort Sumner (see p.217). In Canyon de Chelly, **Kit Carson** starved the last Navajo warriors down from the natural Navajo Fortress and destroyed their homes, livestock, and beloved peach orchards. Within a few years, however, Congress allowed the Navajo to return from their barbaric imprisonment. To this day, 25 Navajo families still farm the Canyon de Chelly in summer, the land having passed down from mother to daughter – as is usual for the Navajo – from the women between whom it was reapportioned in the 1870s.

Arrival and information

No **entrance fee** is charged at Canyon de Chelly. The monument's **visitor center** is a little over two miles east of Chinle and US-191 (daily: May–Sept 8am–6pm; Oct–April 8am–5pm; ☎928/674-5500, ⬤www.nps.gov/cach). Set on the mound where Kit Carson signed the "treaty" that ended his siege of the canyon in 1864, it holds useful displays and is the place to arrange hiking or motorized expeditions (see p.79). No **public transport** runs closer to the canyon than the Greyhound buses and Amtrak trains that ply the I-40 corridor to the south.

Accommodation and eating

Although Canyon de Chelly remains remarkably unspoiled, nearby facilities are overstretched in summer, so it's essential to book **accommodation** well in advance. None of the three options could be considered cheap. The closest to the canyon is *Thunderbird Lodge*, reached by turning right just past the visitor center (☎928/674-5841 or 1-800/679-2473, ⬤www.tbirdlodge.com; mid-Nov to March ❹, April to mid-Nov ❻). Its conventional motel rooms surround a century-old trading post, which houses a large and reasonably priced self-service **cafeteria** (daily 6.30am–9pm), which is an utterly ordinary setting except for the fact that it's full of Navajo. The consistently boring food is made no better by the prohibition of alcohol. The dining room is festooned with rugs from the **giftshop** next door, which also stocks a wide range of books, crafts, and souvenirs (daily 7.30am–9pm). If you take a *Thunderbird* sightseeing tour on the day you leave, check out of your room first; they charge you for another day after 11am.

The former **Garcia Trading Post**, half a mile short of the monument entrance, holds a somewhat fancier lodging option, in the shape of the adobe-fied *Chinle Holiday Inn* (☎928/674-5000 or 1-800/465-4329, ⓦwww.holiday-inn.com/chinle-garcia; winter ❺, summer ❻). This comfortable hundred-room complex adjoins *Garcia's Restaurant*, which serves a breakfast buffet, full lunches (Mon–Fri only), and good-quality dinners. The *Best Western Canyon de Chelly*, just east of the US-191 intersection in Chinle (☎928/674-5875 or 1-800/327-0354, ⓦwww.canyondechelly.com; winter ❹, summer ❺), is an adequate but somewhat characterless alternative, again with its own restaurant.

Chinle itself is a brief nondescript straggle on the highway, with gas stations, *Taco Bell*, *KFC*, a post office, and a laundromat. In late August, it hosts the **Central Navajo Fair.**

No **camping** is permitted in the canyons. However, the first-come first-served *Cottonwood Campground* spreads among the trees beside *Thunderbird Lodge*. All sites are free, with a five-day maximum stay, and RVs are welcome, but there are no showers, and when the water is cut off, as it often is between November and March, no restrooms either. The equally primitive and much less convenient Navajo-owned *Spider Rock RV & Campground* (☎928/674-8261 or 1-877/910-2267; ⓦhome.earthlink.net/~spiderrock/; $10–15, cash only) is near the end of South Rim Drive. It also holds a couple of traditional *hogans* that can be rented at $25 per night and upwards.

The view from above: the rim drives

The monument's two rim drives are equally superb. The dead-end **South Rim Drive** traces the south rim of the Canyon de Chelly, while the **North Rim Drive** follows the north rim of the Canyon del Muerto and then heads off to the northeast. Each involves a round-trip drive of roughly forty miles from the visitor center, punctuated by overlooks where short walks across the mesa-top lead to views of natural or archeological wonders. Even if you don't stop at every overlook, each drive takes around half a day; for the best **photographs**, tour the North Rim in the morning and the South Rim in the afternoon. Thefts from cars have been a major problem, so follow the prominent warnings.

The South Rim Drive

The first stop along the South Rim Drive – **Tunnel Overlook**, two miles from the visitor center – is a trailhead for guided hikes; unaccompanied travelers have no reason to stop. **Tsegi Overlook**, just beyond, stands high above a sweeping curve in the canyon. Though the wash itself is seldom more than a trickle, its broad sandy floor clears a wide gap between the fringe of cottonwoods. Behind the *hogan* near the stream, fields and paddocks reach to the cliffs.

By now, as you look back west, Chinle is visible spreading across the valley, with the full stretch of Black Mesa beyond. Four miles further, **Junction Overlook** marks the meeting of the two main canyons. Canyon de Chelly narrows off to the right, behind a large monolith, while Canyon del Muerto to the left is much less conspicuous. Two tiny ruins indent the base of the canyon walls opposite.

At **White House Overlook**, six miles from the visitor center, Canyon de Chelly is 550ft deep, with its rim topped by strange whorls of slickrock. Pale and majestic, the cliff that drops on the far side of the wash forms a stupendous backdrop for the photogenic **White House Ruin**. Squeezed into a tiny recess,

Canyon de Chelly tours

With the exception of the White House Trail (see below), taking a **guided tour** is the only way to get a close-up view of Canyon de Chelly's amazing Ancestral Puebloan remains or to see the rock art that lines its walls. It's also unforgettable for the scenery alone, with the glorious, glowing cliffs towering far above you, and tranquil Navajo farms to either side.

The most popular are the **4WD** trips organized by *Thunderbird Lodge* (see p.77), which zigzag into either or both canyons following the washes, which vary from two or three feet deep during the spring thaw to completely dry in summer. For most of the year, these "shake'n'bake" tours are in open-top flatbed trucks, lurching over the rutted riverbed, and the heat can be incredible; in winter they carry on in glass-roofed army vehicles with caterpillar tracks. A **half-day** trip (daily: summer 9am & 2pm, winter 9am & 1pm; adults $40, under-13s $30.50) enables you to see a wide variety of sites and terrain, but to reach as far as Spider Rock, you have to take the **full-day** tour (late spring to early fall only, daily 9am; $65, no reductions).

Other companies offering **jeep tours**, with Navajo guides, include De Chelly Tours (☎928/674-3772, ⊚www.dechellytours.com) and Canyon de Chelly Unimog Tours (☎928/674-5433, ⊚www.canyondechellytours.com), which charge a typical fee of around $125 for two to three passengers for a three-hour jaunt, and $30 for each additional hour. The latter also offers three-hour tours to White House Ruin, leaving the *Chinle Holiday Inn* daily at 9am and 1pm (adults $50, under-13s $30). If you have your own 4WD vehicle, you can also hire a Navajo guide at the visitor center to accompany you for around $15 per hour.

In addition, the visitor center arranges highly recommended 4.5-mile, four-hour **group hikes** into the canyon, at a cost of $15 per person. The precise schedule varies, but for most of the year there's usually a morning hike each day, starting at 9am, which heads down the White House Trail and back up to Tunnel Overlook, and an afternoon trip at 1pm into the Canyon del Muerto. Separate **night hikes** last just two hours but cost slightly more. A fuller but much more expensive hiking experience of the canyon is offered by Footpath Journeys (☎928/724-3366, ⊚www.footpathjourneys.com). They arrange five-day, four-night trips, usually to coincide with the full moon, during which you camp on family land close to the canyon at night and take different hikes each day, at a cost of from $685 up to $835.

Totsonii Ranch, located a mile along a dirt road from the end of the paved South Rim Drive (☎928/755-6209, ⊚www.totsoniiranch.com) organizes **horseback** trips into remote parts of the Canyon de Chelly, including Spider Rock, for $15 per person per hour, plus $15 an hour for a guide. They too offer multi-day trips, with a three-day, two-night option costing $515 per person.

---

well above the fields, this cluster of rooms originally stood above a larger pueblo on the valley floor, roughly half of which has now eroded away; it was probably reached by ladders on the roofs of the topmost towers.

The **White House Trail**, to the right of the viewing area, offers the sole opportunity for visitors to hike alone into the canyon. As such, it's one of the major highlights of any Southwest itinerary. A beautiful if slightly precarious walk – some of it runs along ledges chiseled into the rock – reaches the canyon floor through a tunnel that perfectly frames a Navajo *hogan* and its glowing attendant cottonwood. Thus far the ruin has been hidden from view, but once across the wooden footbridge that spans the wash you can admire it close up, separated only by a protective fence. Sixty feet above you, the ancient dwelling appears to be in almost perfect condition, still with the dazzling coat of plaster that gave it its name. Navajo traders nearby sell sodas and trinkets while keeping an eye out for hikers tempted to wander any further than the permitted hundred yards in either direction. Allow at least two hours for the 2.5-mile round-trip hike back up to the overlook: 30 to 45 minutes to get down, and a good hour to climb up again.

From **Sliding House Overlook** – separated from the road by a couple of hundred yards of cairned slickrock, twelve miles along – the **Sliding House Ruin** appears to be tucked into the slenderest of crevices in the cliff face. It's now steadily slipping down toward the ploughed Navajo fields below.

South Rim Drive ends after roughly twenty miles at the astonishing double monolith of **Spider Rock**, where Monument and Bat canyons split away from Canyon de Chelly. These eight-hundred-foot twin pinnacles of rock soar to within two hundred feet of the canyon rim and are said by the Navajo to be home to Spider Woman. She taught them the art of weaving, but also steals misbehaving children; their bleached, gnawed bones lie strewn across the top.

The North Rim Drive

Although the **Ledge Ruin Overlook**, five miles along the North Rim Drive, does not rank among the monument's more significant moments, both the viewpoints at **Antelope House Overlook**, five miles beyond that, are well worth seeing. The first faces across to **Navajo Fortress**, at the tip of the mesa that divides Canyon del Muerto from Black Rock Canyon. It took Kit Carson's besieging forces three months, from December 1863 onwards, to starve down a group of defiant Navajo warriors who had reached the summit of this solitary tower of rock by means of ladders which they then drew up behind them.

The Navajo *hogan*

The traditional dwelling known as a *hogan* (pronounced *ho-wun*), as seen throughout Canyon de Chelly, is the focus of Navajo life and the venue for all sacred ceremonies. These days, few Navajo actually live in a *hogan* year-round, but every family owns at least one, and those who still farm and raise sheep in the backcountry are likely to have several.

The earliest *hogans*, described by the Spanish in the sixteenth century and still widely used until the 1940s, were known as "**male**" *hogans*. They consisted of three vertical forked sticks propped against each other, aligned to the north, south, and west, covered with logs, brush, and mud, and with a door that faced east to greet the rising sun.

Virtually all the *hogans* on the reservation today are "**female**," larger six- or eight-sided structures made of cribbed horizontal logs and once again covered with mud. These became more popular at the end of the nineteenth century, with the advent of steel saws to cut the timber and wagons to haul it; in fact many were made from salvaged railroad ties. The doorway still faces **east**, with a floor of hard-packed dirt to provide contact with the earth and a smoke hole in the center of the domed roof for access to the sky. Each area of the *hogan* has a particular significance; the south side "belongs" to the women and the north to the men, while the male head of the household sits to the west. Food is prepared and stored on the northeast side; the southwest is the sleeping area.

Since the 1970s, more and more Navajo have chosen to live in trailers rather than face the labor of constantly renewing a *hogan*'s protective mud coating. Navajo custom dictates than when death occurs within a dwelling place, it must be abandoned. Since many Navajo now die in a hospital, there's less of a deterrent to building elaborate homes.

The other viewpoint looks down on **Antelope House Ruin**, at the base of a huge white overhang in a separate twist of Canyon del Muerto. This site was first occupied in 693, and grew to comprise two square towers to the rear, plus a central plaza that held half a dozen dwellings. It's named after an antelope pictograph painted by the Navajo artist Dibé Yazhi, or Little Sheep, in the 1830s. He was also responsible for the "Spanish Mural" a little further along, which shows a Spanish lieutenant, priest, and troops advancing through the canyon. Across the wash, in the **Tomb of the Weaver**, the embalmed body of an old man was found wrapped in golden eagle feathers.

The next, final spur road off the North Rim Drive splits to reach two separate overlooks. To the south, **Mummy Cave Overlook** offers a clear view of the single most striking ruin in the monument – **Mummy Cave Ruin**, which the Navajo call **House Under The Rock**. Inhabited for over a thousand years, from 300 until 1300, it consists of two pueblo complexes deep in the shade of adjacent alcoves, with a prominent **Central Tower** on the spur in between. As the masonry of the tower is more sophisticated than the rest, and its construction has been dated to 1284, archeologists believe it may have been built by migrants from Mesa Verde.

In the "cave" visible from **Massacre Cave Overlook**, to the north, Narbona's expedition of 1805 killed more than a hundred Navajo (see p.591). It's less of a cave than a pitifully exposed ledge, far above the canyon floor, on which the huddled group were easily picked off by the Spanish, using ricochets off the overhang above. A short walk away – there's no sign to guide you there, but you can't fail to spot the protective wall built around the tip of the outcrop, lower down to your right – you can also see **Yucca House Ruin**, which unlike the rest of the monument's Ancestral Puebloan sites is very near the mesa-top. It's an amazing location, set in a hollow in the rock above a sheer drop, with no conceivable way down to the valley floor, but almost none of the buildings survive.

As Hwy-64, the North Rim Drive continues for fifteen more miles to meet Arrowhead Hwy-12 in the small town of **TSAILE**. The upper floors of Diné College here hold the stimulating **Ned Hatathli Museum** of Navajo history (Mon–Fri 8.30am–4.30pm; free), which also sells craft items. It's possible to hike into Canyon del Muerto from this end, with a guide hired in Chinle.

Ganado and the Hubbell Trading Post

The village of **GANADO**, halfway between Chinle and I-40 to the south and thirty miles west of Window Rock, was named after Chief Ganado Mucho ("Won a lot"), one of the twelve signatories of the 1868 treaty that ended the Navajo's imprisonment at Fort Sumner.

After the Navajo returned from New Mexico, independent white entrepreneurs set up trading posts at the edge of the reservation, supplying the Indians with goods from the world beyond in return for craft items such as blankets and jewelry. One such merchant, John Hubbell (1853–1930) established more than thirty trading posts during his long career. His original base, founded a mile west of Ganado in the early 1870s, still functions today, run by the Park Service as the **Hubbell Trading Post** (daily: summer 8am–6pm; winter 8am–5pm; ☎928/755-3475, ⓦ www.nps.gov/hutr). Located at the end of a tree-lined avenue beside the Pueblo Colorado Wash, it's a fascinating living museum, where you can watch Navajo weavers at work and wander out to the old stables, piled with hay and filled with venerable wooden wagons. Serious collectors pay premium prices for the best rugs and silverwork, but the groceries in the general store – pretty historic themselves – make less expensive souvenirs. There's no admission charge, though a $2 donation is asked of visitors who join the regular tours of the fascinating Hubbell family home, behind the store.

Ganado has no **motels**, but the *Cafe Sage* (☎928/755-3411) makes a good lunchtime stop. To the east, Hwy-264 climbs onto the thickly wooded Defiance Plateau and heads for Window Rock, while US-191 undulates for forty miles due south, through more forests, to Chambers on I-40.

Window Rock

The capital of the Navajo Nation, **WINDOW ROCK** sits on the Arizona–New Mexico border 25 miles northwest of Gallup. It only became capital in the 1930s, and remains much more of an administrative headquarters than a lively town. Most casual visitors simply pass through on Hwy-264 and spot a few malls and gas stations plus the showpiece *Quality Inn Navajo Nation Capital*. Technically, if you do that, you're not in Window Rock at all; you also won't see the rock itself.

Both "town" and rock are a mile or two north on Arrowhead Hwy-12. The **Window Rock**, an impressive, almost circular hole in a golden sandstone cliff, used to surmount a spring where water was collected for the Water Way ceremony. With the spring now dry, it has become the focus of a landscaped area with picnic tables, dedicated as the Navajo Nation Veterans Memorial in November 1995. A statue of a crouching Navajo soldier, complete with walkie-talkie, commemorates the work of the Code Talkers during World War II. Nearby stands the octagonal **Council Chamber** where the **Navajo Tribal Council** meets at least four times yearly.

Back on Hwy-264, the large **Navajo Nation Museum and Visitor Center** (☎928/871-7941; summer Mon & Sat 8am–5pm, Tues–Fri 8am–8pm; winter Mon–Fri 8am–5pm; donation) stands a short distance east of the *Navajo Nation Inn*. This is a good spot to pick up tourist information and ask any questions you may have about the Navajo themselves, but surprisingly enough, it doesn't hold permanent displays covering Navajo history and culture. Most of its exhibitions are temporary and well conceived, but it's impossible to say whether there will be anything to capture your interest. Tucked among the rocky outcrops across the parking lot, a small **zoo** (daily 8am–5pm; free) holds specimens of local wildlife, including a bald eagle and a growling cougar that endlessly eyes the neighboring elk. The captions are in Navajo, so visits double as language lessons.

Window Rock is otherwise chiefly of interest for hosting the annual five-day **Navajo Nation Fair** (☎928/871-6478), held in September beginning the Wednesday after Labor Day.

Practicalities

Regular **buses**, run by the Navajo Transit System (☎928/729-5449), connect Window Rock with Gallup, New Mexico (see p.116) as well as Tuba City and the Hopi mesas. The **Navajoland Tourism** office, in the Economic Development Building on Hwy-264 a couple of miles west of town, can supply general information on the region (PO Box 663; Mon–Fri

8am–5pm; ☎928/871-6436; ⓦ www .discovernavajo.com).

Much of the Navajo's day-to-day business is conducted in the **restaurant** and coffee shop of the *Quality Inn Navajo Nation Capital*, at 48 W Hwy-264 (☎928/871-4108 or 1-800/662-6189; ⓦ www.navajonationinn.com; ❹), which is open for all meals daily. Ask at the desk for details of their program of local **tours**, which can incorporate pretty much anything you're interested in doing, but start at an expensive $100 per day. The rooms are good value, although they can be hard to come by in summer; if you're stuck, continue two miles west to the *Navajoland Days Inn* in St Michaels (☎928/871-5690; ❹), which is, if anything, a bit smarter and has an indoor pool.

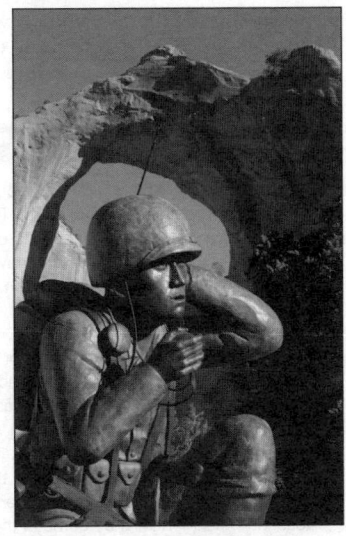

△ Navajo Code Talker, Window Rock

The Hopi Indian reservation

The ten thousand inhabitants of the **Hopi Indian reservation** can trace their ancestry back well over a thousand years, to the **Ancestral Puebloan** people who formerly dominated the entire Four Corners region. What's more, almost uniquely in the United States, the Hopi have occupied the same spot for at least eight hundred years. A detailed history of the Hopi appears in Contexts, on p.585.

To outsiders, it's not obvious why, with the whole Southwest to pick from, the Hopi should have chosen to live on three barren and unprepossessing fingers of rock, poking from the southern flanks of **Black Mesa** in the depths of northeast Arizona. There are two simple answers. The first lies within the mesa itself: although it has no perennial streams, its subterranean rocks are tilted at just the correct angle to deliver a tiny but dependable trickle of water, while the "black" in its name comes from the coal that gives the Hopi limitless reserves of fuel. The second is that the Hopi used to farm and hunt across a much wider area and have only been restricted to their mesa-top villages by the steady encroachment of their Navajo neighbors. Although the Hopi are celebrated for their skill at "**dry farming**," managing to preserve enough precious liquid to grow corn, beans, and squash on hand-tilled terraces laid out beneath the villages, this precarious and difficult way of life has nonetheless been forced upon them.

The Hopi **language**, Hopic, belongs to the Uto-Aztecan group of languages, and is spoken in different dialects on each of the three mesas. Although it bears similarities to the Ute and Paiute languages, the Hopi themselves have little in common with either tribe. Their culture and beliefs are instead closely related to those of the Pueblo peoples of New Mexico, to the east. Until the 1920s, the Hopi were generally known by a name coined

Hopi religion: The *Kachinas*

The Hopi feel neither the urge nor the obligation to divulge details of their **religious beliefs** and practices to outsiders. To that end, they have resisted attempts to make Hopic a written language, or to expose it to scrutiny by teaching it in schools. Missionaries and anthropologists have gleaned what they can, but well-known accounts of Hopi spirituality, such as Frank Waters' *Book of the Hopi*, are based on the reports of informants not themselves initiated into the innermost secrets of the *kiva*. Inevitably, Hopi spirituality has been repeatedly misrepresented to the world, whether as barbarous devil-worship or New Age guff.

There is in any case no single unified Hopi religion; ceremonials vary from clan to clan and village to village. The most basic common element is the role of the *kachina* (often spelled *katsina*, with the plural *katsinum*). These "spirit messengers," which may represent the spirits of the dead, live in the San Francisco peaks north of Flagstaff, and return to the Hopi mesas in the form of rain-bearing clouds.

There are over three hundred different *kachinas*. At one time, they visited the mesas in person; now they come in the form of masked dancers. Not every village follows the same **ceremonial calendar**, but in general the *kachinas* arrive each year in early February for the *Powamuya* ceremony, or **Bean Dance**. Each matriarch receives a bundle of fresh bean sprouts to plant for the coming year, and the *so'so'yoktu* ogres that threaten to eat disobedient (*ka-hopi*) children are placated by gifts of food from their parents. The *kachinas* continue to visit throughout the growing season, before returning home after the *Niman* ceremony or **Home Dance** in July.

The Hopi do not worship the *kachinas*; their main significance is as examples and allegories for the children. All Hopi babies receive a *tihu* – what outsiders know as a kachina **doll** – at their first *Niman* ceremony, and the girls receive further dolls at each *Powamuya* and *Niman* ceremony thereafter. Most boys and girls alike are initiated into a kachina **society** at around the age of ten, when they discover that the *kachina* dancers are their own relatives, and begin to participate themselves.

All the Southwestern pueblos had some form of *kachina* cult, which is occasionally suggested to have arisen as a post-Hispanic mimicry of Catholicism. However, pottery, murals, and rock carvings point to an earlier origin, around 1300 AD. Anthropologists have tended to argue that it spread east from the Hopi mesas or Zuni Pueblo rather than west from the Rio Grande, though the *kachina* cult's virtual disappearance along the Rio Grande is probably due to vigorous Spanish attempts to stamp it out. In fact, it seems to have reached both regions from the **Mimbres** culture to the south, and to have developed in **Mexico**.

The role and iconography of specific Hopi *kachinas* strongly echo **Aztec** deities such as **Tlaloc**, the god of rain, and **Quetzalcoatl**, the plumed serpent, who was also the bringer of rain and corn. For the Aztec preoccupation with death, blood, and human sacrifice, however, the Hopi and other Southwestern people substituted an obsessive focus on **rain**.

Attending Hopi ceremonies

For much of the twentieth century, the Hopi promoted their ceremonies as tourist attractions. Even after cameras were banned in 1916, occasions such as the **Snake Dance**, when members of the Snake clan dance with live snakes between their teeth, drew as many as 2500 observers. More recently, however, the Hopi have moved toward the **exclusion** of non-Indians. By 1989, Second Mesa had closed all its cereby the people of Ácoma: **Moki**, or Moqui. Because that sounded too much like a Hopic word meaning "to have died," they then changed to *Hopi*, which means "well-behaved."

monies to outsiders, and it was joined by all the First Mesa villages in 1992 after the publication of a *Marvel* comic that characterized the *kachinas* as violent avengers.

While spectators are now very unlikely to be allowed at any *kachina* dances, some **social dances**, held between August and January when the *kachinas* are away from the mesas, may still be "open." Held in the village plazas, these usually take place at the weekend, so that Hopi who live off the reservation can return. Specific timings tend not to be announced until a few days in advance; for information, ask at the Cultural Center (see p.86) or call ☎928/734-2244. If you do get the chance to attend a ceremony, wear clothing that fully covers your body, keep your distance, and do not photograph, sketch, or question either dancers or audience.

Kachina dolls

Kachina **masks**, as worn by ceremonial dancers, are sacred objects, and the Hopi have successfully petitioned to remove them from museum displays. However, because a "*kachina* doll" or *tihu* (the plural is *ti'tihu*) is just an instructional tool, it has become acceptable for them to be sold to outsiders as collectors' items.

The *ti'tihu* given to Hopi children were originally flat dolls that were intended to hang from beams or walls within the home. Made from kaolin clay, and thus white in color, the basic shape was painted to show a head, plus a pair of arms folded over a kilt that represented rain. Local trading posts stocked these simple dolls in the 1890s, and by 1900 they were being made specifically for sale.

Since then, they have acquired a much greater complexity of form and color, as well as feet to enable them to stand. Most are carved from cottonwood roots; the carving is seen as a prayer for water, symbolizing the root's own search for water. The artists themselves – who thanks to the art market's desire for signed pieces are no longer anonymous – became more interested in representing human anatomy, and also began to tailor their designs to suit the tastes of white collectors. Strictly speaking, only men should carve *ti'tihu*, but the rewards are great enough that some women make them now as well.

Not all *ti'tihu* represent *kachinas*. Some of the most popular designs depict the clowns who also appear during ceremonies, such as the black-and-white-striped *koshares*, and the knobbed "mudheads" or *koyemsi*. Just as the clowns may devise costumes to mock tourists, for example, certain *ti'tihu* are caricatures of recognizable figures, like basketball players or anthropologists.

The Hopi do, however, draw the line at attempts by others to cash in on the commercial success of the *kachina*-doll business. During the 1960s, the tribal council failed in a bid to copyright the word "*kachina*" and thus stop Navajo and other non-Indian copyists from using the name. Genuine hand-carved dolls are both exquisite and expensive, and a top-class carver will produce fewer than fifty per year, while fake *kachinas* are mass-produced in New Mexico at the rate of over 100,000 per year. People from Ácoma Pueblo have acceded to a Hopi request to stop working in one such factory, but the Navajo have refused to do so.

Good places to buy a *kachina* doll include the Hopi Cultural Center on Second Mesa, the Museum of Northern Arizona in Flagstaff (see p.330), and the Indian Pueblo Cultural Center in Albuquerque (see p.212), though it's hard to find a reasonable-sized piece for under $300. The best bet of all is to come to the reservation, and either call in at stores like Tsakurashovi on Second Mesa (☎928/734-2478) or the Monongya Gallery at Oraibi (☎928/734-2344), or simply take a tour of Walpi and see what you're offered.

The Hopi are a matriarchal society, with homes, land, and clan affiliation passing down the female line. They are not a united people; each of the thirteen villages or settlements, which belong to five main clusters, is an independent entity. Although there is a Hopi Tribal Council, as required by federal law, it's currently recognized by the religious leaders of only two of the villages.

By their very survival, not to mention the persistence of their ancient beliefs and ceremonies in the heart of modern Arizona, the Hopi have long been a source of fascination to outsiders. Visitors are welcomed, but the Hopi have no desire to turn themselves into a tourist attraction. A motel makes it possible to stay on the reservation, and stores and galleries provide plenty of opportunity to buy much-prized Hopi **crafts** such as pottery, basketwork, silver overlay jewelry, and hand-carved *kachina* dolls. However, tourists who arrive in the hope of extensive sightseeing – let alone spiritual revelations – are likely to leave disappointed and quite possibly dismayed by what they perceive as conspicuous poverty.

Since 1986, when increased mining revenues finally placed the tribal economy on a relatively secure footing, non-Indians have been barred from almost all Hopi ceremonies. These days, the easiest way for visitors to get a sense of traditional Hopi life is to take a guided tour of the magnificently situated village of **Walpi**, on First Mesa.

Arrival and information

The Hopi mesas – three distinct spurs along a 25-mile stretch of Black Mesa, numbered from east to west as **First**, **Second**, and **Third** mesas – are roughly fifty miles north of I-40, fifty miles east of Tuba City, and ninety miles southwest of Canyon de Chelly.

Both the roads from the interstate up to the mesas, **Hwy-87** from Winslow and **Hwy-77** from Holbrook, run through a superbly desolate butte-studded segment of the Navajo reservation, on the western fringes of the Painted Desert. If you're coming from the Grand Canyon, take **Hwy-264** east from US-160. Once beyond the Hopi outpost of **Moenkopi**, just outside Tuba City (see p.65), this traverses some rugged canyonlands and then climbs onto Third Mesa after around fifty miles.

Advance **information** for tourists planning to visit the Hopi reservation can be obtained from either the Hopi Tribal Council (℡928/734-3000, Ⓦwww .hopi.nsn.us) or the Hopi Cultural Preservation Office (℡928/734-3612, Ⓦwww.nau.edu/~hcpo-p/). Once you arrive, the essential first stop is the roadside **Hopi Cultural Center,** below Second Mesa, which serves as motel and restaurant – see p.88 – as well as gift store and information center. If any forthcoming events are open to tourists, the friendly staff should be able to tell you about them. Otherwise, check out the wide-ranging historical exhibits and the choice displays of Hopi arts and crafts, in the adjoining **museum** (summer Mon–Sat 8am–5pm, Sun 9am–4pm; winter Mon–Fri 8am–5pm; $3; (℡928/734-6650). The large single-story shop next door is particularly good for silver.

Touring the Hopi mesas

Each of the mesa-top Hopi villages centers around a **plaza**, where successive generations have built new houses on top of the old ones as they crumble into sand. Often the main entrance is via the roof, itself reached by a wooden ladder. A few buildings are now constructed of gray concrete blocks, but they still blend almost imperceptibly with the ruins that trail away down the slopes. Several villages stand on open seams of coal, and large chunks of coal lie scattered around. Outhouses are dotted across the hillsides; all waste was traditionally thrown over the edge of the mesa to tumble down and fertilize the terraces. That conservationist policy works less well now that refrigerators and old bedsteads are being thrown over too.

The only village that offers **guided tours** is the most impressive one, **WALPI** (daily: winter 10am–4pm, summer 9.30am–6pm; adults $8, ages 5–17 $5; ☏928/737-2262). By Hopi standards, Walpi is not in fact that old; it was hastily thrown together in the immediate aftermath of the Pueblo Revolt of 1680, when the people of First Mesa decided to move to a more secure site in the face of possible Spanish or Navajo attack (see p.586). The spot they chose is absolutely stunning, standing alone at the narrow southernmost tip of the mesa, and connected to the other First Mesa villages by the merest slender neck of stone, with a drop of three hundred feet to either side. It now serves as a permanent home to just three people, who live without electricity or running water. Others return to their family homes for special events, or come up each day to sell crafts.

To see Walpi, take Hwy-264 to modern **POLACCA**, at the foot of First Mesa, then drive a mile up the twisting paved road until it ends in **SICHOMOVI**. Although you can't tell where one village stops and the next begins, you've just passed through **HANO**. Its inhabitants arrived during the Pueblo Revolt to offer their services as the defenders of First Mesa and still speak the Tewa language.

The tours assemble in Sichomovi's small Ponsi Hall Community Center, setting off at regular intervals for a half-hour walk to and around Walpi. Depending on the time of year, you'll either be in a group of twenty or so, or on your own, but either way there's plenty of opportunity to ask questions and to buy pottery, *kachina* dolls, and fresh-baked *piiki*, a flatbread made with blue cornflour.

Elsewhere on the reservation, signs beside the highway will point you toward shops and stalls selling Hopi handicrafts of all kinds. At some point down any side road you choose to follow, as you approach a village, you'll come to a large notice forbidding you to drive any further, but possibly allowing you to walk within a specified area. Once you've seen Walpi, the most intriguing destination on the other mesas has to be **ORAIBI** on Third Mesa, which is regarded as the oldest Hopi settlement of all. No scheduled tours can guide you around, but there are normally one or two stores open and eager for your business. It's also possible to join a Hopi guide for your own private **tour**, which will show you far more of the reservation than you can see alone. Both Gary Tso of the Left-Handed Tour Co (☏928/734-2567, ✉lhhunter58@hotmail.com) and Bertram Tsavadawa of Ancient Pathways Tours (☏928/734-9231 or 306-7849; ✉ancientpathways4@hotmail.com) take visitors around Old Oraibi and to little-known petroglyph sites, as well as visiting craftspeople and local galleries. Rates depend on how many members there are in your party; if there are just two of you, expect to pay from around $65 per person for a three-hour tour, up to $150 per person for a full day.

Accommodation and eating

The only place to **stay** on the Hopi reservation is below Second Mesa, in the modern, mock-Pueblo *Hopi Cultural Center Motel* (☏928/734-2401,

Ⓦwww.hopiculturalcenter.com; mid–Oct to mid–March ❹, mid–March to mid–Oct ❺); in summer, its plain but acceptable rooms are usually booked solid a week or more in advance. The cafeteria serves good, substantial meals, including local delicacy *noqkwivi*, lamb stewed with hominy, but be warned that there's precious little to do between the time it closes, at 9pm (or 8pm in winter), and 7am the next morning, when you can indulge your curiosity by having blue cornflakes for breakfast.

Southwest Colorado

In ancient times, of course, the straight-line boundaries that divide the states of Arizona, New Mexico, Utah, and Colorado – and mark the northeastern limits of the Navajo Nation – did not exist. As a result, although Colorado might not spring to mind as a "Southwestern" state, its far southwest corner holds some of the region's most fascinating archeological sites. **Mesa Verde National Park** is absolutely unmissable, and **Ute Mountain Tribal Park** offers adventurous travelers an even more exhilarating sense of discovery.

Once you've crossed the border into Colorado, it's hard to resist the lure of the Rockies, looming along the skyline to the north. There's no scope in this book to do more than sketch out a brief tour, looping up the **San Juan Skyway** from lively **Durango** to historic mining towns such as **Silverton** and **Ouray**.

Four Corners Monument Navajo Tribal Park

The **Four Corners Monument Navajo Tribal Park** (daily: May to early Sept 7am–8pm, early Sept to April 8am–5pm; $3), reached by a short spur road half a mile northeast of US-160, is the only place in the United States where four states meet at a single point. However exciting you may find the concept, the reality is bleak and dull. A steady stream of visitors mooch around the pivotal brass plaque, contorting a limb into each state for demeaning photographs. Navajo stalls on all sides sell crafts, T-shirts, and fry-bread.

Ute Mountain Tribal Park

For a couple of centuries after **Ute Indians** acquired horses from the Spanish, their hunting territory extended east from Utah as far as what's now Nebraska. As miners pushed the Victorian-era frontier westwards, however, the Ute were confined to ever decreasing areas of poorer land. The creation of reservations split them into three separate groups: the **Northern Utes**, who now live in the mountains near Utah's border with Wyoming; the **Southern Utes**, who occupy a strip of southern Colorado south of Durango; and the **Ute Mountain Utes**.

The two-thousand-strong band of Ute Mountain Utes take their name from a long, low mountain ridge in Colorado's far southwestern corner, known to outsiders as **Sleeping Ute Mountain** because of its uncanny resemblance, when seen from the east, to a slumbering warrior. Also known as the Weeminuche, they have long ranked among the Southwest's poorest peoples, and draw their income these days from mineral leases and a large **casino** near the main settlement of **Towaoc**, which offers hotel accommodation and a cheap restaurant (T970/565-8800 or 1-800/258-8007; W www.utemountaincasino .com; ❹).

The Ute Mountain Utes are chiefly of interest to visitors because they run the inaccessible but utterly enthralling **Ute Mountain Tribal Park**, which abuts against Mesa Verde National Park and preserves an equally extraordinary but far less visited assortment of ancient **Ancestral Puebloan** remains. The only way to see the park is to join a **Ute-guided tour**. In principle, these leave at 8.30am daily from the tribe's **visitor center**-cum-museum (April–Oct daily 8am–3pm, but hours subject to fluctuation; T970/749-1452, W www.utemountainute .com), housed in a former gas station at the intersection of US-160 and US-491, twenty miles up from the Four Corners Monument. That schedule varies according to demand, however, and while in season it's usually possible to take the tour by turning up at the meeting point around 8am, it's much safer to arrange things in advance (T970/565-3751 ext 330 or 1-800/847-5485, W www.utemountainute.com).

If you don't have the time to take a full-day tour, which costs $42 and gets you back to the highway around 4pm, the half-day tour at $22 makes a very poor alternative. On the half-day trip, you simply leave the group at the end of the morning, having seen a couple of potsherd-scattered mounds, concealing ancient surface-level pueblos, at the foot of the cliffs. On the full-day tour, you continue along a remote and circuitous dirt road to the top of the mesa, and then inch down a succession of ladders onto a three-mile ledge footpath skirting **Lion Canyon**. This leads to three beautifully preserved **cliff dwellings**, built at the same time as those on Mesa Verde: Tree House Ruin, the eighty-room Lion House, and the precarious Eagle's Nest, perched in a colossal natural alcove. The whole expedition demands a fair amount of walking and something of a head for heights, but only the final ascent to Eagle's Nest is difficult for vertigo sufferers – you can admire it from below if you prefer.

Visitors are expected to drive their own sturdy vehicles on the tour and to bring food and drink for the day. However, the tour leader's van will accommodate half a dozen passengers; if there's room, you're welcome to pay an extra $8 to ride along, which means you get the benefit of that much more informed commentary on what you're seeing. For $12 per vehicle, you can stay overnight at a primitive **campground** close to the main highway.

On special request, it's also possible to arrange trips to more remote areas of the park, which involve significantly more **hiking**; groups have to consist of four or more members, each of whom pays $60.

Hovenweep National Monument

Hidden in the fifty-mile-wide swathe of no-man's-land that straddles the Utah–Colorado border, the Ancestral Puebloan ruins at **HOVENWEEP**

NATIONAL MONUMENT lack the scale and setting of the Mesa Verde cliff dwellings or similar Four Corners sites. Instead, sprouting from the rims of shallow desert canyons and dwarfed by the distant mountains, they offer a haunting sense of timeless isolation. They also have one distinctive and unusual feature, in the shape of the tall **towers** that many archeologists regard as early astronomical observatories.

Whatever most tourist maps may suggest, almost all the roads that lead to Hovenweep have now been paved, thanks largely to companies such as Mobil drilling for oil and gas around Aneth. The monument is best reached by driving 35 miles due **west** from Cortez along County Road G, which leaves US-160 near the airport at the south end of town, or 25 miles **east** from US-191 via Hwy-262, which branches off halfway between Bluff and Blanding in Utah; when conditions are dry, it's also possible to follow a dirt road **southwest** from Pleasant View in Colorado through the new Canyons of the Ancients National Monument (see overleaf).

The monument includes five abandoned villages –the name Hovenweep comes from a Ute word meaning "deserted valley" – located in four distinct parcels a few miles apart. Easy public access, however, is restricted to **Little Ruin Canyon**, which lies just behind the smart **visitor center** (daily: March– Oct 8am–6pm, Nov–Feb 8am–5pm; ☎970/562-4282, ⊛ www.nps.gov/hove; $6 per vehicle, or $3 per person). Until a few years ago, it was possible to walk among and even into the structures ranged above and below the rim of this shallow cleft, known collectively as the **Square Tower Unit**, but now a single trail simply loops around the edge, keeping visitors at a safe distance.

A complete circuit of the trail, which is open daily from sunrise until sunset, takes just under an hour. The trail first meets the canyon close to the fortress-like **Stronghold House**, then heads to the right, past the prosaically named

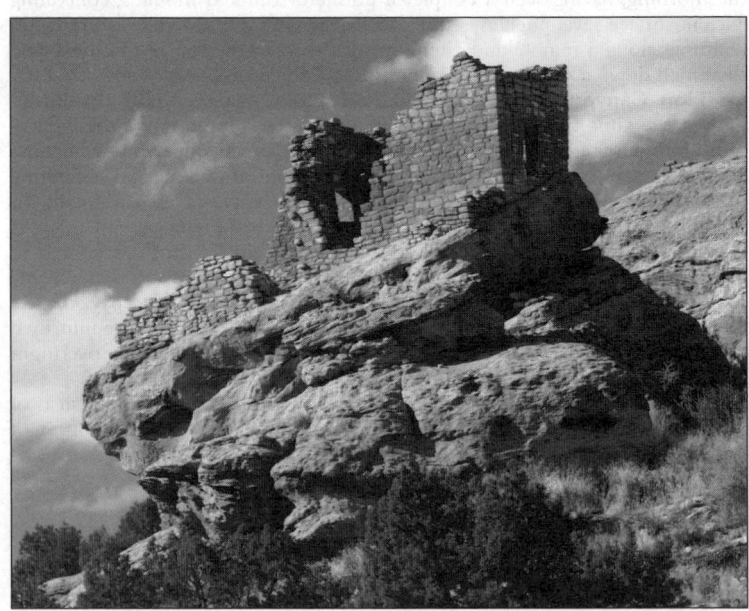

△ Hovenweep National Monument

Unit-type House, where niches in the walls appear to line up with the angle of the sun at the summer and winter solstices. **Hovenweep Castle**, a four-square building five minutes' walk farther on at the head of the canyon, was constructed around 1200 AD. It may well have stood guard over a much larger pueblo complex that nestled on the sandy canyon floor a mere thirty feet below, clustered around the perennial spring that was the site's only source of water. Of that whole complex, only **Square Tower Ruin** can still be discerned, while up above Hovenweep Castle has endured, a perfect illustration of the Biblical admonition that only a house built on rock shall stand. It takes another ten minutes to reach the final significant ruin, the **Twin Towers**. Doubling back on yourself at that point, rather than completing the loop, will spare you the final steep dip and climb through the middle of the canyon, but saves no time overall.

No accommodation, gasoline, or food is available at or anywhere near Hovenweep, but a 31-site **campground** near the visitor center remains open all year ($10; no reservations).

Cortez

The town of **CORTEZ**, twenty miles north of the US-160/US-491 intersection, consists of little more than a long curve of over-developed highway. Were it not so close to Mesa Verde National Park, there would be no reason to visit; as it is, Cortez offers a large, if not exactly broad, selection of roadside motels and diners.

Cortez's well-stocked **visitor center**, on the edge of City Park at 928 E Main St (daily: summer 8am–6pm, winter 8am–5pm; ℡970/565-3414 or 1-800/253-1616, ⓦwww.swcolo.org and ⓦwww.mesaverdecountry.com), doubles as a Colorado Welcome Center, and thus has information on the entire state.

Accommodation

In the past few years, a few of the big-name chains have joined the couple of dozen similar **motels** that line the main strip of Cortez, meaning that it's now possible to get a higher standard of accommodation if you don't mind spending $80 rather than $50 per night.

Aneth Lodge 645 E Main St ℡970/565-3453 or 1-877/263-8454 ⓔ anethlodge@hubwest.com. The good-sized rooms here are more kitsch than fancy, but they're clean, cheap, and close to Cortez's pulsating heart. Winter ❷, summer ❹

Best Western Turquoise Inn & Suites 535 E Main St ℡970/565-3778 or 1-800/547-3376, ⓦwww.bestwesternmesaverde.com. Central two-story motel that's the smartest option in Cortez, with a small outdoor pool open in summer only and an indoor one for the winter. Winter ❸, summer ❻

Budget Host Inn Bel Rau Lodge 2040 E Main St ℡970/565-3738 or 1-888/677-3738, ⓦwww.budgethostmesaverde.com. The "budget" tag doesn't quite do justice to this comfortable and nicely presented motel, with pool and hot tub, a short way out toward Mesa Verde. Winter ❷, summer ❸

Kelly's Place 14663 County Rd G ℡970/565-3125, ⓦwww.kellyplace.com. Truly exceptional B&B ranch, tucked away amid the peach orchards of McElmo Canyon, ten miles west of Cortez en route toward Hovenweep. Accommodation, all en-suite, is in seven comfortable lodge rooms or two separate cabins, and meals are served in the central dining room. Staff-led hikes to Ancestral Puebloan ruins –several are on site – cost $125 for a group of up to four for half a day, or $195 for a full day; it's also possible to ride horses or to take an overnight covered-wagon trip. Rooms ❹, cabins ❼

Super 8 505 E Main St ℡970/565-8888 or 1-800/800-8000, ⓦwww.super8.com. Comfortable, inexpensive three-story motel next to the *Turquoise Inn* in central Cortez, with a good free breakfast bar. Winter ❷, summer ❹

Eating

With so many visitors passing through, Cortez is bursting with **restaurants**, including all the usual fast-food options as well as the home-grown alternatives listed below.

Dry Dock 200 W Main St ☎970/564-9404. Unquestionably the best restaurant in town, serving delicious seafood specialties – they even have fresh oysters – in a garden decorated with underwater-themed murals..There's also steaks, fajitas, and burritos. Typical entrees cost $13–15. Daily 5–10pm.

Main Book Co 34 W Main St ☎970/565-8158. Part cafe, part book and antiques store, part wine bar, housed in a former post office. Coffee and pastries for breakfast, sandwiches and salads for lunch, but in the evening only cheese and hors d'oeuvres are served with the selection of wines. Daily 8.30am–8pm.

Francisca's 125 E Main St ☎970/565-4093. Cheap but pretty good Mexican food: only the most lavish of the fajitas cost over $10, so it's no wonder it's usually crowded. Tues & Sat 4–9pm, Wed–Fri 11am–9pm.

Homesteaders 45 E Main St ☎970/565-6253. Old-time Western diner, piling up plates full of deep-fried fish and chicken, as well as barbecued meats and big steaks – and don't imagine that the Mexican platters are lighter options. Mon–Sat 11am–10pm; in summer also Sun 5–10pm.

Main Street Brewery 21 E Main St ☎970/564-9112. Colorful central brewpub with a pressed tin ceiling, a wide range of microbrews, as well as list, and a full menu of pizzas, burgers, snacks, and steaks. Daily 3pm–midnight.

Silver Bean 410 W Main St ☎970/946-4404. This eye-catching, old-fashioned silver trailer just west of downtown serves espresso coffees, chais, and smoothies as well as burritos and pastries; drive-through customers welcome. Mon–Fri 6.30am–3pm, Sat 7.30am–1pm.

Canyons of the Ancients National Monument

Cortez is very much the largest town in **Montezuma Valley** these days, but a thousand years ago the entire valley was densely populated. In fact, it's said to contain the highest density of archeological sites of anywhere in the United States, which explains why the great bulk of it was designated in 2000 as the **Canyons of the Ancients National Monument**. For the moment, however, the new monument largely consists of several pre-existing small museums and lesser-known sites dotted around the valley. Its creation attracted considerable local opposition, because the economy in these parts has long been based on extracting gas, oil, and minerals from the canyons all around. As 85 percent of the monument is already covered by leases that will still be allowed to be exploited, fears that livelihoods are in danger seem somewhat misplaced.

Incidentally, romantic notions that Montezuma Valley was in ancient times a peaceful agricultural community have been dashed by recent archeological research, which as well as uncovering evidence of warfare and wholesale slaughter has even provided the first conclusive proof of ancient **cannibalism** in the Southwest. Human excrement discovered alongside the butchered remains of 23 Ancestral Puebloans in Cowboy Wash was found to contain proteins that could only have come from eating their flesh.

Dolores

The national monument headquarters is located in what, despite the general trend toward using the term "Ancestral Puebloan," is still called the **Anasazi Heritage Center**, three miles west of **DOLORES** and six miles due north of

Cortez (daily: March–Oct 9am–5pm, Nov–Feb 9am–4pm; ☎970/882-5600, ⓦwww.co.blm.gov/canm).This centers on a couple of twelfth-century pueblos, which were excavated and stabilized during the construction of nearby McPhee Dam – which was responsible for turning the Dolores River into a broad lake at this point.The pueblos were named after the eighteenth-century Spanish friars Domínguez and Escalante, who first noted the traces of prehistoric Indians in the area. Admission to a well-equipped **museum of Pueblo life** costs $3, but access to the trail around the ruins themselves is free (daily 8am–5.30pm).

Dolores holds a couple of **accommodation** options.The *Rio Grande Southern B&B*, 101 S Fifth St (☎970/882-7527 or 1-800/258-0434; closed Dec–Feb; ❹), is an inexpensive, charming B&B, replete with period furnishings, while *Dolores Mountain Inn*, 701 Railroad Ave (☎970/882-7203 or 1-800-842-8113; winter ❸ summer ❹) offers decent motel rooms.

Lowry Pueblo

From **Pleasant View**, fourteen miles northwest of Dolores on US-491, the undulating but straight County Road CC leads a further nine miles west to **Lowry Pueblo Ruins** (no fixed hours; free).There's not a tremendous amount to see at this free-standing pueblo, but in summer, it's noteworthy as one of the few sites where at least part of an **Ancestral Puebloan mural** remains in place on the walls of a "Great Kiva" (see p.110). In winter, the mural is taken away for preservation, and the gravel surface of the approach road's last four miles is often impassable to vehicles.

Crow Canyon Archeological Center and Sand Canyon

Each summer, **Crow Canyon Archeological Center**, five miles northwest of Cortez at 23390 County Rd K (☎970/565-8975 or 1-800/422-8975; ⓦwww .crowcanyon.org), runs day programs for amateur archeologists (June–Aug Wed & Thurs 9am; $50) and week-long residential courses for more serious students of Southwestern prehistory ($995). Both provide the chance to assist on digs at Ancestral Puebloan sites in the valley, such as the 1800-room **Yellow Jacket**, and **Sand Canyon Pueblo**, a walled city that once covered the cliff-tops at Crow Canyon, further south.

It's also possible to make your own free, unguided visit to Sand Canyon Pueblo at any time. Signs on the spot explain how the 420-room pueblo may once have looked, but there are no facilities of any kind. Either drive straight there along county roads P and N, which leave US-491 northwest of Cortez, or take County Road G off US-491 south of Cortez, which is also the main route to Hovenweep, and **hike** to the pueblo along the rough, six-mile **Sand Canyon Trail**.

Mancos

Fourteen miles east of Cortez, and seven miles east of the foot of the approach road that climbs up into Mesa Verde, the compact and attractive little community of **MANCOS** is almost exclusively devoted to catering to visitors to the national park. To that end, it holds several **accommodation** options, including the comfortable *Mesa Verde Motel*, 191 Railroad Ave (☎970/533-7741 or 1-800/825-6372; ⓦwww.mesaverdemotel.com; winter ❷, summer ❸), which has its own restaurant, and the atmospheric *Old Mancos Inn*, 200 W Grand Ave

(☎970/533-9019; ⓦ www.oldmancosinn.com; ❷—❸), where the cheaper rooms share bathrooms. The *Absolute Bakery & Cafe*, 110 S Main St (☎970/533-1200), serves coffees and fresh breads plus breakfast and lunch daily; it also doubles as a bookstore.

Mesa Verde National Park

MESA VERDE NATIONAL PARK, the only national park in the US to be exclusively devoted to archeological remains, is set high in the plateaus of southwest Colorado, off US-160 halfway between Cortez and Mancos. It's an astonishing place, so far off the beaten track that its extensive **Ancestral Puebloan ruins** remained unseen by outsiders until late in the nineteenth century.

Mesa Verde itself – the "green table" – is a densely wooded sandstone plateau, cut at its southern edge by sheer canyons that divide the land into narrow fingers. Hundreds of natural alcoves, eaten high into the canyon walls by seeping water, served as homes for over seven hundred years; by the time they were abandoned, around 1300, several held multistory **cliff dwellings** that have remained virtually intact to this day.

By Southwestern standards, the mesa is not especially pretty, and it doesn't offer the same **hiking** opportunities as the region's other national parks. The relics, however, are compelling enough to make Mesa Verde an essential stop on any Four Corners itinerary; it was even voted as the world's top tourist attraction by readers of *Condé Nast Traveler*. As things can get very crowded in summer, the **best months** to visit are in May, September, and October. The 8000ft elevation means that most of the sights become inaccessible in **winter**, though the park itself, its main museum, and one ruin – Spruce Tree House – remain open all year round. **Concessions** such as gas, food, and lodging only operate between late March and early November.

A history of Mesa Verde

Although Archaic sites in Montezuma Valley down below date back to 5500 BC, no earlier trace of humans on Mesa Verde has been found than an Ancestral Puebloan Modified Basketmaker pithouse from 550 AD. People first moved to the mesa, therefore, at around the time they acquired the skill of pottery. They were not so much farmers as gardeners, who continued to gather wild plants and hunt deer and rabbits as well as grow small fields of corn and own domesticated dogs and turkeys. For five hundred years, they lived in pithouses dug into the floors of sheltered caves; then, around 1100, they congregated in walled villages up on the mesa tops. A century later, they returned to the canyon-side alcoves to build the "palaces" for which Mesa Verde is now famous. No one has lived here since the end of the thirteenth century.

Archeologists believe that each settlement held significantly fewer people than it did rooms, as many rooms were exclusively used for storage. They suggest the largest Cliff Palace housed a population of around 120. Two or three people may have slept in a typical living room, measuring six feet by eight feet, while each family had its own *kiva* – see p.604 – which when not in ceremonial use was used for weaving and other domestic activities. No rigid social hierarchy is indicated either in the architecture, or the relatively few burials that have been found – some in sealed chambers, and some simply, if reverentially, in the trash heaps. Mesa Verde may well have been a **peripheral community**. While its population is thought to have peaked at around 2500, in the middle of the thirteenth century, there were at least eight larger surface pueblos down in Montezuma Valley, whose inhabitants are thought to have been generally hostile to the Mesa Verdeans.

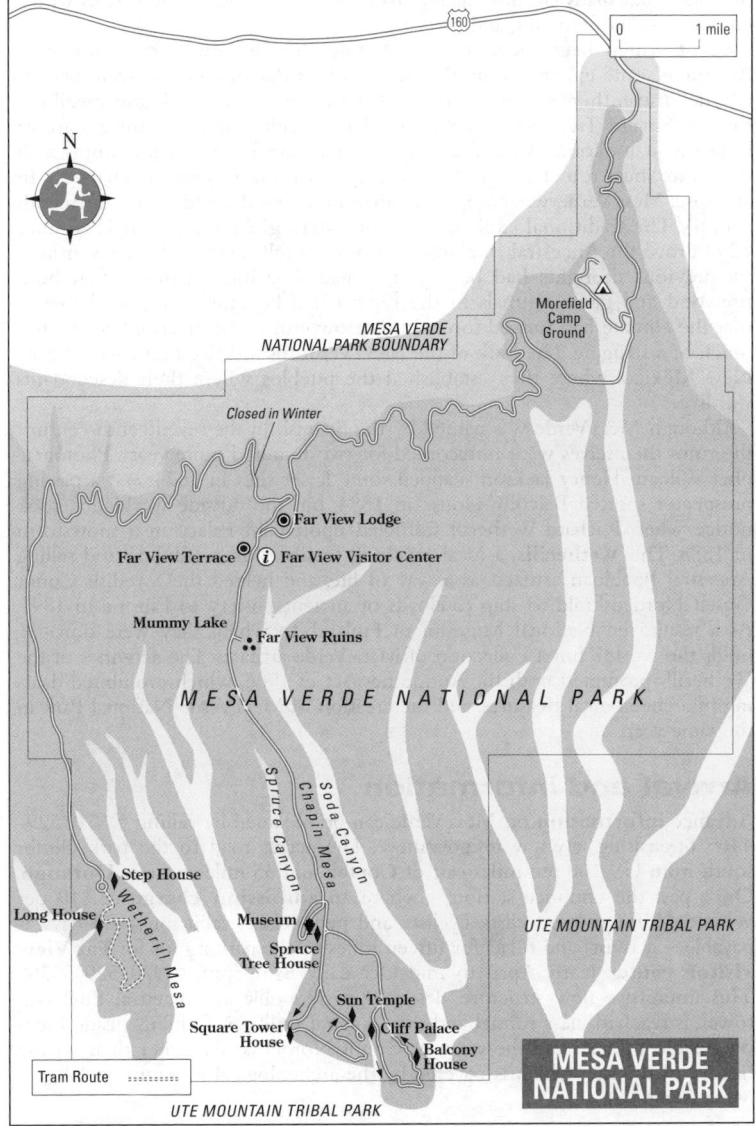

Ironically, archeologists regard the cliff dwellings that seem so elegant to modern visitors as signs of a declining culture. They say the mesa-top pueblos were more sophisticated in both design and construction, while the alcove complexes are haphazard accretions, forced into contortions by the constraints of the rock and characterized by inferior craftsmanship. These were not ideal homes; older members of the community must have found it impossible to get in or out, while children lived in constant peril of fatal falls. In theory, each complex got its water from the seep or spring that had created its alcove in the first place, but many of those springs had run dry, leaving the occupants with a constant cycle of fetching and carrying.

All of which begs the question of why the cliff dwellings were built. Although some experts argue that sites such as Balcony House were primarily defensive, there's little evidence that they were attacked, and dwellings such as Spruce Tree House lie exposed to assault, while the towers are of little use as lookouts. Agricultural space may have been at a premium, with the entire mesa top crisscrossed by dams, terraces, and irrigation channels. In any case, Mesa Verde was completely abandoned by the end of the thirteenth century. The traditional explanation, that a **drought** lasting from 1276 until 1299 drove the Ancestral Puebloans away, only tells part of the story, in that six previous droughts had been just as bad. The likely truth is that both firewood and game animals in the region had become seriously depleted, that the climate had turned too cold to grow crops, and survival became too much of a struggle. The bulk of the Mesa Verdeans migrated into what's now New Mexico, where they established the pueblos where their descendants still live.

Although Mesa Verde was named by the Spanish in the seventeenth century, the ruins themselves went unrecorded for two hundred more years. Photographer William Henry Jackson snapped some lesser sites in 1874, and a passing prospector spotted Balcony House in 1884, but the outside world first took notice when Richard Wetherill stumbled upon Cliff Palace in a snowstorm in 1888. The **Wetherills**, a local ranching family, took to finding and selling Ancestral Puebloan artifacts as a way of life, and helped the Swedish Count Gustaf Nordenskïold to ship caseloads of ancient pottery to Europe in 1891. As a result, the National Museum of Finland, to which they were donated, holds the world's finest collection of Mesa Verde artifacts. The activities of the Wetherills prompted both the Antiquities Act of 1906, which prohibited dealing in archeological treasures, and the creation of Mesa Verde National Park in the same year.

Arrival and information

Advance **information** on Mesa Verde can be obtained by calling ☏970/529-4465 or visiting ⓦwww.nps.gov/meve. The access road to the park climbs south from US-160 ten miles east of **Cortez** and 35 miles west of **Durango**. Once past the entrance station – where an **admission charge** of $10 per vehicle, $5 for motorcyclists, cyclists, and pedestrians, valid for seven days, is payable – it twists and turns for fifteen miles to the parking lot for **Far View visitor center** (early April to mid-Oct daily 8am–5pm; ☏970/529-5036). This impressive new structure, designed to resemble an Ancestral Puebloan tower, is reached via a tunnel and then a spiral walkway. Exhibits inside focus on Pueblo pottery and the story of Count Nordenskïold rather than on the history of the site, which is covered by the archeological museum on Chapin Mesa (see p.98).

Half-day **bus tours** of the park start from the nearby *Far View Terrace* restaurant at 9am and 1pm daily between late April and late October, costing $39 for adults and $28 for ages 5–17; call ☎ 1-800/449-2288 for reservations. Taking a tour can ease the laborious business of driving around Mesa Verde, and of queuing for tickets, but the sheer cost makes it hard to recommend them for family groups. Day-trips to Mesa Verde that start from **Durango** are listed on p.100.

Immediately beyond the visitor center, the road divides to the two main constellations of remains: Chapin Mesa to the south, and Wetherill Mesa to the west.

Accommodation and eating

The only **rooms** at Mesa Verde are in the *Far View Motor Lodge*, near the visitor center (☎ 970/564-4300 or 1-800/449-2288; ⓦ www.visitmesaverde.com; closed late Oct to late April; ⓞ). It's a peaceful place, away from the bustle of the park; guestrooms, which lack phones or TVs, are in two-story units dotted around the mesa-top. The sweeping views reach into the Rockies to the north, but no archeological sites are visible. The *Metate Room*, in the mock-adobe main lodge, is a pretty good restaurant that's open daily for dinner only; entrees such as elk tenderloin are priced at up to $30.

Mesa Verde Tours and Tickets

The three major ruins in Mesa Verde National Park can only be visited on guided tours, though it is possible to see Cliff Palace and Long House from nearby overlooks. To take a tour, you must first buy **tickets** at the visitor center. The exact seasons and times of the tours vary according to both funding and climate; each costs **$2.75**, with tickets valid for one specific time only. Allow several hours between tours on Chapin and Wetherill mesas. After the visitor center closes in late fall, tour tickets are sold at the museum on Chapin Mesa (see overleaf). On **Chapin Mesa**, during the busiest months, you may well not be allowed to tour Balcony House and Cliff Palace on the same day (though many couples circumvent the regulations by queuing separately for tickets). If you're forced to choose, Cliff Palace can at least be seen from a distance without joining a tour, but on the other hand, the Cliff Palace tours are much less strenuous than those of Balcony House. On days when they let you tour both, **photographers** should visit Balcony House first, for the best light. For most of the rest of the ruins, the best time for photography is late afternoon.

	daily hours	tour times
Cliff Palace on Chapin Mesa		
Early April to mid-May	9am–5pm	hourly
2nd two weeks of May	9am–5pm	half-hourly
June to early Sept	9am–6pm	half-hourly
Early Sept to mid-Oct	9am–5pm	half-hourly
Mid-Oct to early Nov	9am–4pm	hourly
Balcony House on Chapin Mesa		
1st two weeks of May	9am–5pm	9.30am, noon, 2pm, 3.30pm
2nd two weeks of May	9am–5pm	hourly
June to early Sept	9am–5.30pm	half-hourly
Early Sept to mid-Oct	9am–5pm	hourly
Long House on Wetherill Mesa		
late May to early Sept	9am–4pm	hourly

The park's official **campground** – the very large and almost never full *Morefield Campground* (early May to mid-Oct; ☎970/564-4300 or 1-800/449-2288; ⓦwww.visitmesaverde.com) – is four miles up from the entrance, and thus a long way from the ruins. No reservations are necessary; a site for one or two vehicles costs $20, or $25 with hook-ups.

Food is also available in season at the *Far View Terrace* (early May to mid-Oct daily 7am–8pm), across from the visitor center – which serves espresso coffees and has a gas station – and all year round at *Spruce Tree Terrace* (daily, summer 10am–7pm, winter 10am–5pm), near the Chapin Mesa museum, which has a pleasant shaded terrace. Light snacks are sold at the end of the road on Wetherill Mesa.

Chapin Mesa

A couple of miles from the visitor center toward **Chapin Mesa**, you reach **Far View** itself, a mesa-top pueblo abandoned early in the thirteenth century. Thanks to the coal-burning power plants that dominate the middle distance, it seldom lives up to its name these days. Archeologists speculate that a large open area nearby doubled as both an open-air plaza and a reservoir, which has been dubbed **Mummy Lake** and was capable of holding half a million gallons. It has even been suggested that the rhythmic shuffling feet of ceremonial dancers were deliberately choreographed to wear grooves in the rock along which rainwater would flow to be collected.

Another four miles on, **Chapin Mesa Museum** (daily: mid-April to mid-Oct 8am–6.30pm, mid-Oct to mid-April 8am–5pm) contains the park's best displays on the Ancestral Puebloans, including several dioramas made in the 1930s. Hikers can register at the adjacent **park headquarters** for a couple of unremarkable two- to three-mile nature trails.

The museum is also the starting point for the short, steep hike down to **Spruce Tree House**, the only ruin that can be seen in winter. Consisting of several well-preserved three-story structures, snugly molded into the recesses of a rocky alcove and fronted by open plazas, the neat little village was occupied from 1200 AD until 1276 AD. One of its *kivas* has been re-roofed, and visitors can enter the dusty, unadorned interior by way of a ladder. Between early November and early March, Spruce Tree House can only be seen on free guided tours, which set off from the museum daily at 10am, 1pm and 3.30pm. For the rest of the year, the trail is open for free self-guided visits; hours vary from 8.30am–6.30pm in summer down to 9am–5pm in spring and fall.

Ruins Road, beyond the museum area, is only open between April and early November, from 8am until sunset daily. It has two one-way, six-mile loops, but if you're pressed for time, skip the western one, even though its overlooks are still interesting. The western loop's first stop is **Square Tower House**. A 500-foot stroll is rewarded by views of an eighty-room alcove complex, focused around the four-story Square Tower – at 26 feet, the tallest tower in the park. **Sun Point Overlook** looks across Spruce Canyon to as many as twelve distinct cliff dwellings, including Cliff Palace, making it clear just how crowded the canyon was in its heyday. Unlike the alcove sites, the mesa-top **Sun Temple**, next, was built to a premeditated design, and may have been a ceremonial center for the whole community. It was never finished, however, and its shape and function can only really be appreciated from aerial photos; walking around its walls is not very thrilling.

The first stop on the eastern portion of Ruins Road, **Cliff Palace** is the largest Ancestral Puebloan cliff dwelling to survive anywhere. Tucked a hundred feet below an overhanging ledge of pale rock, it holds 217 rooms and 23 *kivas*, each of which is thought to have belonged to a separate family or clan. Archeologists have recently downgraded their estimates of its former population, as it's now thought this may have been a ceremonial or storage center rather than simply a communal habitation. Cliff Palace may have been home to around 120 people.

If you haven't managed to get a ticket for a tour of Cliff Palace (see p.97), you can still get a great view from the promontory where the tour groups gather, just below the parking lot. However, walking through the empty plazas and peering down into the mysterious *kivas*, especially on a quieter day, provides a haunting evocation of a lost and little-known world. Fading murals can still be discerned inside some of the structures. As you leave, climbing an unalarming metal stairway through a narrow crevice, you may spot the original toe- and footholds used by the Ancestral Puebloans.

Technically, Ruins Road passes out of the national park just beyond Cliff Palace and briefly enters **Ute Mountain Tribal Park**, where you can pick up information on tours (see p.89). It then arrives at **Balcony House**. This is one of the few Mesa Verde complexes that was clearly geared toward defense. Built around 1240, it was remodeled during the 1270s to make it even more impregnable; access is very difficult, and it's not visible from above. Guided tours involve scrambling up three hair-raising ladders and crawling through a narrow tunnel, above a steep drop into Soda Canyon. Those who don't share the fearless Ancestral Puebloan attitude to heights should give it a miss, but if you do have the stomach it's a spectacular site, with two circular *kivas* standing side by side in a commanding central position.

Distant views of Balcony House can be had from three-quarters of a mile along the forested **Soda Canyon Overlook Trail**, which starts a short way further around Ruins Road.

Wetherill Mesa

The tortuous twelve-mile drive onto **Wetherill Mesa** from the visitor center is usually open from late May until early September. Access is then permitted between 9.15am and 4.30pm daily, though motorcycles and large vehicles such as RVs are always banned.

From the parking lot at the far end of the road, where there's a ranger station and snack kiosk, a free **miniature train** loops around the tip of the mesa. Priority is given to visitors with tickets for the timed Long House tours (see p.97). Any time spent waiting can be occupied by walking down to examine nearby **Step House**, where a single alcove contains a restored pithouse, dating to 626, as well as a pueblo from 1226.

The mini-train stops at various trailheads from which hikers can walk to early mesa-top sites or alcove overlooks, but its principal destination is the **Long House**. The park's second largest ruin is set in its largest cave; hour-long tours descend sixty or so steps to reach its central plaza, then scramble around its 150 rooms and 21 *kivas*. These ruins are said to be especially authentic, having been "restabilized" in recent years, rather than subjected to the same extensive rebuilding as the better-known sites were in the first part of last century. Excavations here uncovered a number of unburied bodies, some of whom had clearly met violent deaths.

Durango

Named after Durango, Mexico, and also twinned with it, **DURANGO** was founded in 1880 as a rail junction for the Gold Rush community of Silverton, 45 miles further north. **Steam trains** still run the same high-mountain route, through the Animas Valley, and are the foundation of the local tourist economy. In addition, Durango has become a new-style Wild West boomtown, attracting a large influx of computerized teleworkers. Combine them with outdoors enthusiasts, who come to ride their **mountain bikes** on the grueling back roads nearby, and in the morning at least the place has a youthful, energetic buzz. By the evening, most people seem too wiped out to do anything much.

Despite such developments as the construction of the huge Durango Mall at the town's southern end, the **downtown** district, located along Main Avenue between 7th and 11th streets, remains the liveliest urban area in the Four Corners and is worth an hour or two of anyone's time. As well as the outdoors outfitters you might expect, it's packed with funky and upmarket fashion and home furnishing stores.

Arrival and information

Durango's **visitor center** is a block or two south of downtown, near the train station at 111 S. Camino del Rio (June–Sept Mon–Sat 8am–5pm, Sun 10am–4pm; Oct–May Mon–Fri 8am–5pm; ☎970/247-0312 or 1-800/525-8855; ⓦwww.durango.org). Greyhound (TMN & O) **buses** between Denver and Albuquerque call in at 275 E Eighth Ave (☎970/259-2755).

Mountain bikes can be rented for around $30 per day from Mountain Bike Specialists, 949 Main Ave (☎970/247-4066), and Southwest Adventures, 12th St and Camino del Rio (☎970/259-0370 or 1-800/642-5389, ⓦwww .mtnguide.net) – who also run guided biking tours for $60–125 per day. The cheapest **4WD rentals** are from RentAWreck, 21698 US-160W (☎970/259-5858 or 1-800/682-5858; ⓦwww.rentawreck.com; closed Sun). Mesa Verde Guided Tours (☎970/533-1944 or 1-800/449-2288) pick up from local motels at around 8am daily for $65 **Mesa Verde bus tours**.

The visitor center can also supply details of the many operators that run **river-rafting** excursions on the Animas River. Full-day expeditions with Mountain Waters Rafting (☎970/259-4191 or 1-800/585-8243, ⓦwww .mtnh2o.com) or Mild to Wild Rafting (☎970/247-4789 or 1-800/567-6745, ⓦwww.mild2wildrafting.com), for example, cost from around $70 upwards, and it's even possible to combine a day's rafting with a ride home on the steam train. If you just want a taster, brief float trips with Flexible Flyers (☎970/247-4628 or 1-800/346-7741, ⓦwww.flexibleflyersrafting.com) cost from as little as $12, while a one-hour ride through the nearest set of rapids is just $14.

Accommodation

Only a handful of **accommodation** options are to be found in downtown Durango, including a couple of fancy but expensive historic hotels. If you're having problems finding a room, the local visitor center offers a reservations hotline on ☎1-800/463-8726.

Most of the **motels**, including all of the budget ones, are located well to the north, on the farther reaches of the forty-block Main Avenue, which is served by a frequent and inexpensive **trolley** (Mon–Sat 6.45am–6.15pm; 75¢). The trolley also passes by the best place to **camp** near town, the

DURANGO

| 0 | 500 yards |

Silverton ▲

A

Vallecita Reservoir ▶

Animas

JUNCTION CREEK ROAD

Mesa Verde & Cortez ◀

Forest Service
& BLM offices

Mercy
Medical
Center

Durango
Public
Library

Fort Lewis
College

Durango & Silverton
Railroad Depot

Bus
Station

B

Visitor Center

N

ACCOMMODATION

Adobe Inn	B
Durango Lodge	E
General Palmer Hotel	D
Siesta	A
Strater Hotel	C

EATING

Carver's Bakery & Brewpub	1
East by Southwest	7
Jean Pierre Bakery	6
Ken & Sue's	5
Seasons Rotisserie & Grill	4
Steaming Bean Co.	2
Steamworks Brewing Co.	3

▼ *Airport & Pagosa Springs*

The Durango & Silverton Railroad

Between mid-May and late October, the **Durango & Silverton Narrow Gauge Railroad** operates up to four daily return trips along a spectacular route through the mountains that parallels the gorgeous San Juan Skyway. Opened in July 1882, the track took just nine months to construct. Its photogenic steam trains have been featured in around twenty Hollywood movies, most memorably being blown up in *Butch Cassidy and the Sundance Kid* in 1969.

Precise schedules vary, but all trains leave **Durango** early in the morning, from the depot at 479 Main Ave at the south end of town, and allow time for lunch in **Silverton** at the far end. The journey takes 3hr 30min in each direction, at a maximum speed of 18mph. No trains run between late October and late November, but between late November and early May, when the higher mountain reaches are closed by snow, shorter excursions operate on the most scenic section only, as far as Cascade Canyon. In the weeks leading up to Christmas, the Polar Express service offers hour-long trips to the "North Pole." Reservations should be made at least two weeks in advance, via ☎970/247-2733, 1-877/872-4607, or ⊛www.durangotrain.com.

Departures from Durango

early Jan to early March	10am (Wed–Sat)*
early March to early May	10am*
early May to mid-May	8.15am*
mid-May to early June	8.15am, 9am*
early June to late June	8.15am, 9am*, 9.45am
late June to early Aug	7.30am (Mon–Thurs), 8.15am, 9am*, 9.45am
early Aug to mid-Aug	8.15am, 9am*, 9.45am
mid-Aug to mid-Oct	8.15am, 9am*
mid-Oct to late Oct	8.15am*
late Nov to Dec	10am*, 5.10pm[a]

All departures are daily unless otherwise stated

Fares

early May to late Oct	adults $62, ages 5–11 $31
late Nov to early May	adults $45, ages 5–11 $22

* First Class Parlor available, adults only; summer $109, winter $89.
[a] Polar Express; adults $24, ages 3–11 $16

riverside United Campground, 1322 Animas View Drive (☎970/247-3853 ⊛www.unitedcampground.com), where the well-shaded tent sites cost $23.

Adobe Inn 2178 Main Ave ☎970/247-2743 or 1-877/247-9615. Reasonable cheap motel, not too far north of downtown, with a hot tub and coffee bar. Winter ❷ summer ❹

Country View Lodge 28925 Hwy-160 E ☎970/247-5701. Large, friendly, and well-maintained hostel, six miles east of Durango, which offers dorm beds for $15 and private double cabins for $40, together with a kitchen, lounge, and laundry. You can also camp for $10 per night on the streamside lawns behind. ❶/❷

Durango Lodge 150 East Fifth St ☎970/247-0955, ⊛www.durangolodge.com Small, not particularly attractive but very convenient central motel, close to the railroad station. Spacious rooms plus a pool. Winter ❸, summer ❻

General Palmer Hotel 567 Main Ave ☎970/247-4747 or 1-800/523-3358, ⊛www.generalpalmer.com. Very smart, old historic hotel, close to the railroad depot, that's perhaps slightly more chintzy than the similar *Strater* on the next block, but still provides an enjoyable taste of old-Western style. Lower-priced rooms face inward rather than out on the street. Winter ❺, summer ❻ inside, ❼ outside.

Siesta 3475 Main Ave ☎970/247-0741. Very inexpensive motel, at the curve in the highway well north of the center; all rooms have phone and TV, but little more. Winter ❷, summer ❸

Strater Hotel 699 Main Ave ☎970/247-4431 or 1-800/247-4431, ⊛www.strater.com. Major downtown landmark that's bursting with frontier elegance and offers almost a hundred mostly small but appealingly antique-furnished rooms. Great buffet breakfasts, a reasonable restaurant, and frequent performances of theatrical melodramas. Winter ⑥, summer ⑦

Eating

Main Avenue downtown, and the streets to either side of it, are filled with places to **eat** and **drink**, some with their sights set on affluent train passengers, others aimed at young mountain bikers. There's at least one **espresso bar** on every block.

Carver's Bakery & Brewpub 1022 Main Ave ☎970/259-2545. Bustling brewpub, with a good menu of big breakfasts and grilled specials such as "two skewers of bison brats" for $15. Mon–Sat 6.30am–10pm, Sun 6.30am–1pm.

East by Southwest 160 E College Drive ☎970/247-5533. Ravishing "pan-Asian bistro" a block up from Main Avenue in the heart of downtown, serving a wide array of delicious Thai, Vietnamese, Indonesian, and above all, Japanese dishes. Typical Thai entrees cost $10–15, while sushi or sashimi platters for two are around $30. Mon–Fri 11am–3pm & 5–10pm, Sat & Sun 5–10pm.

Jean-Pierre Bakery & Cafe 601 Main Ave ☎970/385-0122. It may be a little incongruous in this historic Wild-West building, but this classic French bakery offers utterly exquisite breads and pastries, plus sandwiches, salads, and quiches for $7–10. Daily 7am–9.30pm.

Ken and Sue's 636 Main Ave ☎970/385-1810. Hip, stylish little downtown restaurant specializing in Southwestern cooking with a slight but definite Asian twist; cilantro-crusted halibut, for example, costs $17. Mon–Fri 11am–2.30pm & 5pm until late, Sat & Sun 5pm until late.

Seasons Rotisserie & Grill 764 Main Ave ☎970/382-9790. Smart modern bistro with a New Orleans feel but contemporary Southwestern cuisine, with sandwiches and pasta for lunch and $15–30 dinner entrees such as pan-seared salmon trout or braised lamb shank. Mon–Fri 11.30am–2.30pm & 5.30–9.30pm, Sat 5.30–9.30pm.

Steaming Bean Co 915 Main Ave ☎970/385-7901. Early-morning espressos and pastries, as well as specialty drinks, sandwiches, and live music later on. Internet access is also available. Mon–Sat 6.30am–9pm, Sun 7am–8pm.

Steamworks Brewing Co 801 E Second Ave ☎970/259-9200. Large brewpub just off Main Avenue, where in summer you can enjoy wood-fired pizzas served on a sunny open-air patio and in winter you can drink vast quantities of home-brewed beer. Daily 11am until late.

Silverton

North of Durango, the **San Juan Skyway** sets off to loop over two hundred miles through the Rockies, up US-550 and then back via Hwy-62, Hwy-145, and US-160. Its first stretch, across invigorating high passes, is known as the **Million Dollar Highway**, for the amount of gold in the ore-bearing gravel that was used in its construction. As you skirt around the bald, red-striped **Engineer Mountain**, just beyond the Purgatory Ski Area, the views are totally spectacular.

The first town along the way, **SILVERTON**, spreads across a small flat valley in the heart of the mountains fifty miles up, and marks journey's end for the narrow-gauge railroad from Durango. It's one of Colorado's most atmospheric mountain towns, with wide dirt-packed streets leading off toward the hills to either side of the one main road. Silverton's zinc- and copper-mining days only came to an end in 1991; the population has dropped since then, but those that remain have resisted suggestions that its future lies in legalizing gambling to draw in tourists. Meanwhile, the false-front stores along "Notorious Blair Street," paralleling the main drag, recall the days when legendary gunslinger

Bat Masterson was the city marshal – and are the scene of a daily shoot-out at 5.30pm.

Without a 4WD vehicle, it's hard to explore the mountains away from the main highway, but it's possible to continue several miles beyond Silverton in an ordinary car if you simply keep going beyond the end of the main street along the Animas River. The dirt road usually starts to get difficult around the ruins of **EUREKA**, seven miles along, which make a good starting point for hikes to nearby waterfalls. The crest of the mountain ridge to the east marks the Continental Divide, with the source of the Rio Grande on the far side.

Practicalities

Silverton is heavily dependent on tourism, which makes it pretty quiet in off season. It's also geared more toward day-trippers than overnight guests, so to spend a night here is to step back a century. For local information, call in at the helpful **visitor center** close to the highway at the southern edge of town (daily: July–Sept 9am–6pm, May–June & Oct 9am–5pm, Nov–April 9am–4pm; ☎970/387-5654 or 1-800/752-4494, ⓦwww.silvertoncolorado .com).

Bargain **accommodation** is to be had in the tin-walled *Silverton Hostel*, 1025 Blair St (check–in daily 8–10am & 4–10pm; ☎970/387-0015; ❶/❷), which offers $11 dorm beds as well as a few plain, inexpensive, private doubles, or at the ugly but well-maintained *Triangle Motel*, 864 Greene St (☎970/387-5780, ⓦwww.trianglemotel.com; winter ❸, summer ❹), at the south end of town, which also offers good-value two-room suites and jeep rental. The central *Grand Imperial Hotel*, 1219 Greene St (☎970/387-5527 or 1-800/341-3340, ⓦwww.grandimperialhotel.com; winter ❸, summer ❺), has far more historic ambience without being much more expensive, though its old-style rooms are not exactly opulent. You can get a bit more comfort at the *Teller House Hotel*, across the road at 1250 Greene St (☎970/387-5423 or 1-800/342-4338, ⓦwww. tellerhousehotel.com; winter ❸, summer ❹), where some of the rooms share bathrooms, and the *French Bakery* downstairs (☎970/387-5976; closed Nov–Feb) serves **food** from sandwiches to full meals. In addition to the Western-style steakhouses in the heart of downtown, *Romero's*, at 1151 Greene St (☎970/387-5501), is an enjoyable Mexican *cantina*, while *Avalanche Coffee House*, 1067 Blair St (☎970/387-5282), is a friendly hangout offering fresh coffee, pastries, and snacks.

Ouray

The equally attractive mining community of **OURAY** lies 23 miles north of Silverton, on the far side of 11,018-foot **Red Mountain Pass**, where the bare rock beneath the snow really is red, thanks to mineral deposits. The Million Dollar Highway twists and turns, passing abandoned mine workings and rusting machinery in the most unlikely and inaccessible spots; back roads into the mountains offer rich pickings for hikers or 4WD drivers.

Ouray itself squeezes into an impossibly slender verdant valley at the head of the Uncompahgre River, with the commercially-run **Ouray Hot Springs** ranged alongside the river at the north end of town. A mile or so south, a one-way loop dirt road leads to **Box Cañon Falls Park** (daily 8am–dusk; $3), where a straightforward 500-foot trail, partly along a swaying wooden parapet, leads into the dark, narrow Box Cañon. At the far end, the falls thunder through a tiny cleft in the mountain.

Practicalities

Ouray's **visitor center** is outside the hot springs (summer daily 8am–6pm, winter Wed–Sun 8am–6pm; ☎970/325-4746 or 1-800/228-1876, ⓦwww .ouraycolorado.com). Switzerland of America, 226 Seventh Ave (☎970/325-4484 or 1-800/432-5337, ⓦwww.soajeep.com) rents **4WD vehicles** and also offers guided jeep tours.

At *Box Canyon Lodge*, an old-style timber **motel** below the park at 45 Third Ave (☎970/325-4981 or 1-800/327-5080, ⓦwww.boxcanyonouray.com; ❹), you can bathe in natural hot tubs. The luxurious *St Elmo Hotel* **B&B**, 426 Main St (☎970/325-4951 or 1-866/243-1502; ⓦwww.stelmohotel.com; ❺), adjoins the good *Bon Ton* **restaurant**, where Cajun-tinged Italian entrees cost $14–22. The central *Backstreet Bagel & Deli*, 524 Main St (☎970/325-0550), serves sandwiches and smoothies.

Ridgway

As you head north beyond Ouray, the scenery makes an abrupt change, with the canyon of the Uncompahgre characterized by red rocks and sparse sagebrush. To complete the loop of the San Juan Skyway, turn west on Hwy-62 after eight miles at **RIDGWAY**. This enables you to circle around the northern limits of the San Juan Mountains, which stand as a magnificent serrated ridge along the southern skyline.

While there's no great reason to stop in Ridgway, it did serve as a pivotal location for the movie *True Grit*, filmed here in fall 1968. The 62-year-old **John Wayne**, who won his first Oscar as one-eyed Marshal Rooster Cogburn, met his young sidekick, played by Kim Darby, outside the town courthouse, while their subsequent adventures were played out against the magnificent backdrop of the **Wilson Peaks**, which you'll see if you continue west on the San Juan Skyway.

Telluride

As Hwy-62, the San Juan Skyway meets Hwy-145 23 miles southwest of Ridgway, and then turns sharply back eastward on Hwy-145 along the pretty, well-wooded valley of the San Miguel River. The former mining village of **TELLURIDE** is a total drive of 74 miles from Silverton, even though as the crow flies, straight across the mountains, the two towns are barely ten miles apart.

In the 1880s, Telluride was briefly home to the young Butch Cassidy, who robbed his first bank here in 1889. These days it's better known as a **ski resort**, rivaling Aspen and Vail as a winter destination for the stars. Telluride has, however, achieved this status without losing its character – the wide main street, a National Historic District with low-slung buildings on either side, still heads directly up toward one of the most stupendous mountain views in the Rockies. Healthy young bohemians with few visible means of support but top-notch ski equipment form the bulk of the 1200 citizens, while most of the glitzy visitors

△ Telluride, CO

hang out two miles above the town in **Mountain Village**, which is reached by a free year-round gondola service.

Telluride's winter season, which starts as the fall colors fade, usually in late November, continues until early April. Prospective **skiers** should contact the Telluride Reservations Center (℗970/728-3041 or 1-888/339-2664, Ⓦwww .telluride.com), which coordinates lodging and package deals, and provides free lift tickets for the first month of the season for guests in certain lodges. Alternatively, skiing comes half-price if you stay in any of seven neighboring towns; otherwise a full-price lift ticket costs a hefty $76 per day.

In recent years, the town has also become a premier **snowboarding** destination and regularly holds the US national championships; it has also hosted the world championships as well. Many former ski trails are now reserved exclusively for snowboarders, and expert instruction is available from the Telluride Ski and Snowboard School (℗970/728-7507 or 1-800/778-8581, Ⓦwww .tellurideskiresort.com). Over a dozen operators rent out ski and snowboarding equipment, with the largest being Telluride Sports (℗970/728-4477 or 1-800/828-7547, Ⓦwww.rentskis.com).

In summer, the **hiking** opportunities are excellent. One three-mile round-trip walk, which also makes a great if grueling bike ride, switchbacks up a bumpy 4WD road from the head of the valley to reach Colorado's highest waterfalls, the 365-foot **Bridal Veil Falls**. To take the hike, simply follow the main highway all the way through town, park where it ends at Pioneer Mill, and set off uphill. Don't expect to be able to cool off with a swim in the falls, however; it's far too perilous a spot for that.

Practicalities

Telluride's **visitor center** is on the edge of downtown at 630 W Colorado Ave (daily 9am–6pm; ℗970/728-3401 or 1-888/355-8743, Ⓦwww.visittelluride.com).

Accommodation is much less expensive in summer than during ski season, though prices do go up for the Bluegrass Festival in mid-June (ⓦwww.bluegrass .com), the Jazz Festival at the beginning of August (ⓦwww.telluridejazz.com), and the Film Festival at the start of September (ⓦwww.telluridefilmfestival.com).The Telluride Reservations Center, detailed above, can help you find a room.

Of specific places to stay, the 1895 *New Sheridan Hotel*, 231 W Colorado Ave (ⓣ970/728-4351 or 1-800/200-1891, ⓦwww.newsheridan.com; winter ❺, summer ❹), offers some bargain rooms with shared bath, while the *Victorian Inn*, 401 W Pacific Ave (ⓣ970/728-6601 or 1-800/611-9893, ⓦwww.tellurideinn .com; winter ❼, summer ❻), is an upscale motel with very smart doubles and its own sauna.

At the dinner-only *Cosmopolitan*, 300 W San Juan Ave (ⓣ970/728-1292), the fanciest **restaurant** in town, the contemporary Southwestern entrees are priced at $20 and up, while *Smugglers Brewpub and Grille*, at San Juan and Pine (ⓣ970/728-0919), is a lively evening hangout with a wide-ranging menu. *Baked in Telluride*, 127 S Fir St (ⓣ970/728-4705), is good for morning espressos and pastries, with a nice little terrace where you can enjoy soup, sandwiches, or pizza.

Northwest New Mexico

Although **northwest New Mexico** formed the heart of the Dinetah, the Navajo's original homeland in the Southwest, the Navajo territories here are now less visited than their more scenic equivalents in Arizona. Archeology buffs are drawn to **Chaco Canyon** and **Aztec Ruins**, but although these rank among the most significant Ancestral Puebloan sites anywhere, they are – unfortunately for casual tourists – less photogenic than their better-known rivals. None of the towns nearby, whether on or off the reservation, holds any lasting interest.

Instead the region is notorious as the home of the **Four Corners Power Plant**, near Farmington. After this coal-fired generating station opened in the 1960s, it was said to be the single greatest source of pollution in the United States, emitting more noxious gases than either New York City or Los Angeles. Regulations have been tightened since then, but with the **Navajo Mine**, the largest open-pit coal mine in the West, just a mile away, and several other generating plants in the immediate neighborhood, there's no incentive for outsiders to linger. For the Navajo, of course, who provide much of the industry's workforce, it's a different story.

Shiprock

By far the most striking landmark in the dusty red plains of New Mexico's far northwestern corner is the craggy monolith known as **Shiprock**. In Navajo legend, as *Tsé bit'a'i* or "Rock Wing," this awesome 1500-foot peak was home to one or two monstrous birds, which were either killed by the hero Monster

Slayer or turned into an eagle and an owl. To Anglo eyes, it resembled instead a mighty ocean-going ship. Navajo medicine men continued to use it in sacred ceremonies until 1939, when Sierra Club members including David Brower – the "Arch-Druid" who later founded Friends of the Earth (see p.482) – defiled Shiprock by climbing it.

You can spot it from a distance of 60 miles, but **US-491** runs within a few miles of Shiprock's vast, eerie bulk, and signs at a roadside pull-out explain that the mountain is a volcanic plug, the hard central core of a volcano that has itself eroded away. There's no point trying to approach it any closer; these days you can't even walk up to the base, let alone climb it. Neither is it worth stopping at the sprawling mining town six miles north, also known as **SHIPROCK**, other than in early October, when it hosts the **Northern Navajo Fair**.

Farmington

FARMINGTON, the largest town in northwestern New Mexico, lies roughly fifty miles east of the Four Corners Monument and fifty miles southwest of

The Beast Is Dead

Here is wisdom. Let him who has understanding calculate the Number of the Beast, for it is the number of a man: His number is 666.

Revelation 13:18

Until 2003, 666 was not merely the Number of the Beast, and the number of a man; it was also the number of the main highway north through the Navajo Nation from Gallup to Shiprock. **US-666** was assigned the dreaded "666" in 1942, on account of being the sixth major road to branch off Route 66, and swiftly acquired such nicknames as the "Devil's Highway" and the "Highway to Hell." Although for the most part it's very straight, and was doubtless paved with good intentions, it became renowned for an appalling accident record. *USA Today* rated it as the most dangerous highway in the country, while in 1995 the *Wall Street Journal* ran an article headlined "Beast of a Highway: Does Asphalt Stretch Have Biblical Curse?".

Prompted by state governor Bill Richardson, New Mexico's House and Senate passed a Joint Resolution in 2003 that declared:

WHEREAS, people living near the road already live under the cloud of opprobrium created by having a road that many believe is cursed running near their homes and through their homeland; and

WHEREAS, the number 666 carries the stigma of being the mark of the beast, the mark of the devil, which was described in the book of Revelation in the Bible; and

WHEREAS, there are people who refuse to travel the road, not because of the issue of safety, but because of the fear that the devil controls events along United States route 666; and

WHEREAS, the economy in the area is greatly depressed when compared with many parts of the United States, and the infamy brought by the inopportune naming of the road will only make development in the area more difficult.

. . . the number of the road should be changed as soon as possible. A state highway official was reported as having no preference concerning the new designation: "As long as it's not 666 and it's nothing satanic, that's OK." The former US-666 therefore duly became US-491 on May 31, 2003.

Durango, Colorado. Once you know that it was founded as "Farmingtown," in 1876, you know enough of its past; now that it's a mere ten miles west of both the Navajo Mine and the Four Corners Power Plant, you can imagine its present.

As the mineral boom got going in the 1950s, Farmington acquired a dreadful reputation as a definitive "edge-of-the-res" community, rife with racism and violence. Over the years, it cleaned itself up and prospered accordingly. Having a mall suggests the epitome of contentment and the **Animas Valley Mall**, 4601 E Main St, is the principal business center of a wide area.

Farmington's principal concession to tourism is its **museum**, in the Gateway Park on the northeast edge of town at 3041 E Main St (Mon–Sat 9am–5pm; free), which traces town history from the geological "New Mexico Seacoast" up to trading-post times; it also has extensive displays on local mining and refining.

The **Bisti/De-Na-Zin Wilderness**, thirty miles due south of Farmington on Hwy-371, is an area of weirdly eroded desert **badlands** overseen by the Bureau of Land Management (℡505/599-8900). You can camp here, but there are no facilities and campfires are forbidden. It's worth a hike to see its petrified logs and strange rock formations known as "hoodoos."

Practicalities

The local **visitor center** is in the museum at 3041 E Main St (same hours; ℡505/326-7602 or 1-800/448-1240, ⓦwww.farmingtonnm.org). TNM&O Coaches, 101 E Animas St (℡505/325-1009), run **buses** to Durango, Denver, and Albuquerque, while the Four Corners Airport, west of town, has **flights** to Albuquerque (Mesa Airlines ℡505/326-3338 or 1-800/637-2247), Denver (Great Lakes Airlines 1-800/554-5111, ⓦwww.greatlakesav.com), and Phoenix (America West Express ℡505/326-4494 or 1-800/235-9292).

You may not set out with the intention of spending a night in Farmington, but if you have to, there are over twenty **motels** to choose from. The best budget choice is the *Super 8*, southeast on US-64 at E Broadway (℡505/325-1813 or 1-800/800-8000; ❷). Upscale options include *La Quinta*, 675 Scott Ave (℡505/327-4706 or 1-800/531-5900; ❹), and the large nearby *Best Western Inn at Farmington*, 700 Scott Ave (℡505/327-5221 or 1-800/780-7234; ❺), which is arranged around an appealing courtyard and holds a reasonable, if predictable, **restaurant**. There's a quite extraordinary alternative three miles out of town at 3204 Crestridge Drive, in the shape of *Kokopelli's Cave*, which is a genuine **cave dwelling** hollowed out 75 feet below ground level but opening onto a cliff-face balcony hundreds of feet above the La Plata River. It's rented out as a B&B apartment to groups of up to four people (℡505/326-2461, ⓦwww .bbonline.com/nm/kokopelli; ❽).

Back in town, *Clancy's Pub*, 2703 E 20th St (℡505/325-8176), is a youth-oriented pseudo-Irish **bar** that serves simple meals. There's slightly better food at the *Three Rivers Eatery and Brewhouse*, 101 E Main St (℡505/324-2187), while the *Main Street Bistro*, 122 N Main St (℡505/334-0109), offers good coffee and pastries.

Aztec

The town of **AZTEC**, fourteen miles northeast of Farmington, is the county seat of San Juan County and a lower-key and more enjoyable place than

Farmington. On its leafy central thoroughfare, the quaint **Aztec Museum**, 125 N Main Ave (summer Mon–Sat 9am–5pm; winter Mon–Sat 10am–4pm; $2), incorporates a mock-up pioneer village peopled by life-size mannequins, who hang out in frontier-style buildings such as a schoolhouse, a jail, and a bank.

The main reason anyone comes to Aztec, however, is to see **Aztec Ruins National Monument**, across the Animas River a mile north of town (daily: summer 8am–6pm; winter 8am–5pm; $4 per person; ☎505/334-6174, Ⓦwww.nps.gov/azru). This preserves an **Ancestral Puebloan pueblo** erroneously attributed by early Anglo settlers to ancient Mexicans. In fact, it's a large "outlier" settlement, built from 1111 onwards by people from the Chaco culture (see p.114), and connected with Chaco Canyon, 64 miles south, by a die-straight road now only visible from the air. Aztec stands halfway between Chaco and Mesa Verde, and is thought to have been remodeled by a new wave of settlers from Mesa Verde around 1225.

From the visitor center, which holds a handful of interesting ancient artifacts, a short trail leads around and through the **West Ruin,** the only part of the site to have been excavated. This 500-room E-shaped structure held only one entrance and was entirely walled. The trail leads through room after room (you'll have to stoop to get through the succession of low doorways) before culminating in the awesome **Great Kiva** – the technical term for a *kiva* used by an entire community rather than an individual clan or family. Reconstructed in 1934, this is the only Great Kiva in the Southwest that can be seen in anything approaching its original state. Aspects of the restoration remain conjectural, but there's no disputing the circular chamber's sheer size, which measured fifty feet across. Its 95-ton roof was supported by four pillars that rested on four 375-pound limestone disks, carried here from forty miles away. Archeologists say that the *kiva* may have been in use when the *kachina* religion was first being developed, and that the fifteen side rooms, now connected with the main chamber by ladders, may have served as changing rooms from which masked figures would emerge during ceremonies. An informative trail guide, written by an Indian from Santa Clara Pueblo quite possibly descended from the site's original inhabitants, explains much of what you see. A corresponding East Ruin lurks mysteriously beneath shapeless hillocks.

Practicalities

Aztec's well-stocked **visitor center**, east of the river at 110 N Ash St (Mon–Fri 9am–noon & 1–5pm; ☎505/334-9951, Ⓦwww.aztecnm.com), even sells an *Aztecopoly* board game.

Only two of the local **motels** are worth considering. Despite external appearances, the shiny modern *Step Back Inn*, where US-550 meets Main Avenue at 103 W Aztec Blvd (☎505/334-1200 or 1-800/334-1255; ❹), has rooms furnished with Victorian antiques. The smaller *Enchantment Lodge*, 1800 W Aztec Blvd (☎505/334-6143 or 1-800/847-2194, Ⓦwww.enchantmentlodge .com; ❸), is an old-fashioned, no-frills alternative. There's also a tiny and slightly twee B&B, *Miss Gail's Inn*, 300 S Main Ave (☎505/334-3452 or 1-888/334-3452; ❹), which has its own **restaurant**, *Giovanni's*, which serves tasteful, lighter midday meals. The *Aztec Restaurant*, 107 W Aztec Blvd (☎505/334-9586), is a venerable steak-and-pancake **diner** opposite the *Step Back*.

The Pueblitos of Dinétah

Although they lie beyond the present-day boundaries of the Navajo Nation, the remote Largo and Gobernador canyons to the southeast of Farmington and Aztec were the original cradles of the **Dinétah**, the traditional Navajo homeland. The earliest known trace of a Navajo presence is a *hogan* in Gobernador Canyon that has been tree-ring dated to 1541, but the most significant era in its history followed the Pueblo Revolt of 1680. Refugees from the Rio Grande pueblos fled west during the immediate aftermath of the revolt, to be joined by further waves of migrants when the Spaniards returned to reconquer New Mexico from 1692 onwards.

Between 1680 and 1750, Navajo and Pueblo Indians combined to build around 130 stone fortresses in the region, known as the **Pueblitos of Dinétah**. Perched on high eminences close to the canyon rims, or tucked into alcoves just below them, these "little pueblos" are clearly reminiscent of older Ancestral Puebloan sites such as those at Hovenweep (see p.90). Most were too small to house an entire community for any length of time; instead they were intended as lookouts, retreats for elders and religious leaders, and, above all, as shelters during raids. The Spaniards sent punitive expeditions into the area every summer between 1705 and 1716, while from the 1720s Ute war parties threatened Navajo and Spaniard alike.

The real importance of the pueblitos, however, was their role in forging a new synthesis of Navajo and Pueblo cultures. Many of the modern hallmarks of Navajo identity, both in terms of practical skills such as rug-weaving and sheep-herding, and of religious beliefs, were acquired during this period. The main agent in the process seems to have been the intermarriage of Navajo men with women from the pueblo of Jemez. Their union created the **Coyote Pass People**, still one of the most prominent Navajo clans. Influences were also absorbed from further afield. Not only were Spanish metal-working techniques introduced, but in Three Corn Pueblito, which was abandoned in the 1750s, archeologists have even unearthed a Qing dynasty plate from China.

It's possible to drive into both Largo and Gobernador canyons, along good-quality dirt roads maintained by the companies who drill there for natural gas, but without expert assistance you'll have no chance of reaching or even spotting the pueblitos themselves. The Bureau of Land Management office at 1235 La Plata Hwy in Farmington (☎505/599-8900) can provide detailed directions to sites located on BLM lands. A better idea is to join an **organized tour** with either the archeologists at Salmon Ruins (☎505/632-2013, ⓦwww.salmonruins.com), who charge $275 for an all-day 4WD trip for up to four people, or Aztec Archaeological Consultants (☎505/334-6675, ⓦwww.aztecarcheology.com), which offers half-day trips for one or two people for $110 and full-day trips for $230.

Bloomfield

BLOOMFIELD, eight miles south of Aztec and twelve miles east of Farmington, is an unattractive little desert crossroads notable only for its **Salmon Ruins**, two miles west (May–Oct Mon–Fri 8am–5pm, Sat & Sun 9am–5pm; Nov–April Mon–Fri 8am–5pm, Sat 9am–5pm, Sun noon–5pm; $3; ☎505/632-2013, ⓦwww.salmonruins.com). This outlying Chacoan pueblo was constructed between 1088 and 1094, roughly twenty years before its neighbor at Aztec. Salmon Ruins may mark the first attempt to build a "new Chaco," which failed when the San Juan River proved too unruly to tame at this point, whereupon Aztec was built as a replacement. Salmon Ruins went through a similar cycle of abandonment and reoccupation by migrants from Mesa Verde, as did Aztec.

Homesteader George Salmon discovered the ruin on his land during the 1880s, and his family spared it the usual looting until they sold it to the county in 1979. Excavations since then have unearthed well over a million artifacts, the finest of which are displayed, together with reconstructed dwellings, in the on-site museum.

Practicalities

If you find yourself in Bloomfield for the night, the best of its few **motels** is the *Super 8*, at 505 W Broadway (☎505/632-2113 or 1-800/800-8000; ❷). The *Triangle Cafe*, across the highway at 506 W Broadway (☎505/632-9918), is a traditional, friendly **diner**.

Chaco Canyon

Although the **Ancestral Puebloan ruins** of **CHACO CANYON** form the **largest pre-Columbian city** in North America, for sheer beauty and drama they can't compete with lesser settlements such as Canyon de Chelly. The low-walled canyon itself, now protected as **Chaco Culture National Historical Park**, is a mere scratch in the scrubby high-desert plains, and the Chaco Wash that runs through it is often completely dry. Add the fact that the site is a long, bumpy, twenty-mile ride off the nearest paved road, and more than double that from any significant town or facilities, and it's no wonder that visitors on tight itineraries often decide it's more bother than it's worth.

Once you accept that you won't have amazing photos to show the folks back home, however, there's still plenty about Chaco to take your breath away. Over 3600 separate sites have been logged in the canyon, of which the thirteen principal ones are open to visitors. Six of these, arrayed along the canyon's north wall, are what's known as **Great Houses** – self-contained pueblos, three or four stories high, whose fortress-like walls concealed up to eight hundred rooms. The largest, **Pueblo Bonito**, is claimed to have been the largest single building in America until structural steel was developed in 1898.

Arrival and information

Both **routes to Chaco Canyon** entail driving twenty miles over rough but passable dirt roads. They remain open all year, but should not be attempted during, or within a day of, a rainstorm. This situation may change, as federal money was earmarked in 2005 to pave the two roads, but locals believe it may still be several years before any concrete action takes place.

To approach from the **south**, leave I-40 at Thoreau, 28 miles northwest of Grants; follow Hwy-57 north for another 28 miles, beyond **Crownpoint**, then turn right onto Arrowhead Hwy-9 for 13 miles to **Seven Lakes**, at which point the dirt road to Chaco itself branches off to the left. Coming from the **north** or **east**, turn off US-550 (still shown on some maps as NM Hwy-44) at Nageezi, 36 miles south of **Bloomfield**.

The two routes meet inside the park on its eastern side at the **visitor center** (daily: summer 8am–6pm; winter 8am–5pm; ☎505/786-7014, ⓦ www.nps.gov/chcu). That's where the park **admission fee** of $8 per vehicle is payable, and you can also pick up maps and brochures, plus schedules of summer-only ranger-led tours. Rangers in the center show videos such as *Sundagger*, which explains how carefully sited rocks and petroglyphs atop nearby **Fajada Butte** plotted not only the annual solstices, but also the moon's 18.5-year cycle. The center is close to the start of the one-way loop road that provides the only access to the ruins themselves.

The basic first-come, first-served *Gallo* **campground** ($10), a short way east of the visitor center, is the only visitor facility the park has to offer; from April to October it's usually full by 3pm. Bring any firewood you require. Backcountry camping is forbidden.

Seeing the park

The gates of the canyon's eight-mile one-way **loop road** are immediately north of the visitor center, and open the same hours. The major stop is at the far end, where **Pueblo Bonito** ("beautiful town" in Spanish), can be explored on an easy half-mile trail. Work on this four-story D-shaped structure, which is almost perfectly aligned east–west, started in 850 and continued for around three hundred years. Speculation that hordes of slaves were forced to build it have been deflated by precise dating of its parts; even during its busiest era, a workforce of just thirty men, cutting and hauling trees for a full month each year, and quarrying and shaping stone for four months every two years, could have done the job.

The trail leads around the back of Pueblo Bonito, passing the spot where Threatening Rock, a colossal boulder whose collapse the ancient inhabitants staved off with prayer sticks and supporting walls, finally destroyed thirty rooms in 1941. Entering the ruin via its lowest levels, the path reaches its central plaza, which held at least three **Great Kivas** of the kind restored at Aztec (see p.110). From there, you can walk through the passageways and chambers of the pueblo proper, where the rows of neatly finished doorways, each framed by the next, are Chaco's most photographed feature.

A separate trail from the same parking lot heads to the smaller complex of **Chetro Ketl**, a quarter of a mile to the east. Constructed over the course of a century, from 1010 onwards, this shows Chacoan masonry at its most sophisticated – or as some archeologists put it, at its most obviously influenced by MesoAmerican models. Its horizontal rows of large, squared-off stones are chinked with smaller, flatter stones and set into a bed of adobe mortar with a mosaic-like precision. Many of the original beams (*vigas*) remain in place, and a vivid fragment of an ancient mural is protected behind a glass panel.

Pueblo del Arroyo, the next stop along the loop road, is the only Great House to stand right beside Chaco Wash. Although it rarely holds much water, the stream channel is much deeper and broader than it was in Ancestral Puebloan days, thanks to erosion of its bank caused by over-grazing. The pueblo, raised on a small hillock, was occupied between 1070 and 1105. Only half of it has been excavated. The road turns back here, but if you have time you can follow hiking trails up to 3.6 miles further along the wash, to reach assorted further pueblos and petroglyph sites.

Casa Rinconada, perched on another mound as the road heads back down the canyon, is the canyon's largest **Great Kiva**, at 62 feet across. It now lies open to the sun, the subtleties of its precise astronomical alignments lost but its central features still clearly identifiable. Archeologists are unsure whether the two large vaults in the *kiva* floor served as foot drums, or to propagate seedlings; both usages are suggested by modern Pueblo and especially Hopi practices. Minor house sites and unexcavated mounds are scattered on the canyon floor nearby.

To archeologists, Chaco Canyon represents the apogee of Ancestral Puebloan achievement. However, what they call the **Chaco phenomenon** remains one of the Southwest's greatest puzzles. How can the canyon's apparent unsuitability for large-scale occupation – if anything, it was slightly drier in Ancestral Puebloan times than it is today – be reconciled with its massive structures and demonstrable influence over an "empire" that covered at least 25,000 square miles?

Pithouses built by early Ancestral Puebloan Basketmakers are scattered around the canyon, but Chaco's surface pueblos began to appear during the ninth century. Sophisticated masonry techniques were either developed or brought here by migrants from the Mesa Verde region, around 1000, enabling the construction of larger multistory apartments. The canyon's heyday was between around 1050 and 1125; its last definite tree-ring date is 1132, and by 1200 it was abandoned altogether. A prodigious amount of work went into its construction. Upwards of 200,000 tree trunks, mostly ponderosa pines and corkbark fir, were carried here from hillsides fifty or more miles away, without the use of animals or the wheel.

When Chaco became a national monument in 1907, archeologists estimated that it was once home to twenty thousand people. That figure was later revised to five thousand, based on the number of rooms in the pueblos. Now, in view of the low number of burials that have been found, the lack of signs that the upper floors were ever inhabited, and the canyon's poor soil, modern theories suggest that Chaco never held more than two thousand inhabitants. By that reckoning, the Great Houses were not homes, but some combination of warehouses, temples, and palaces.

Thus Chaco was not a residential community so much as a **ceremonial center**. Huge quantities of **turquoise** have been discovered – harvester ants, who for some reason collect blue and green turquoise to adorn their nests, scavenged fifty thousand pieces in Pueblo Bonito alone. Turquoise, still precious to contemporary Indian cultures, was the most valuable trading commodity in the ancient Southwest. The Chacoans acquired raw turquoise from distant mines – mostly to the east, in the Cerrillos region (see p.156) – and crafted it into sacred and ornamental objects. Ultimately, turquoise from Chaco passed from hand to hand down trading networks into the heart of Mexico; thus ninety percent of the turquoise found in the Aztec capital of Tenochtitlan was of Southwestern origin. Similarly, the parrots and scarlet macaws whose skeletons have been found here must have come from southern Mexico or beyond.

Chaco's primary significance, however, was much more local. Having started as a small settlement that specialized in trading turquoise, it probably became a place of pilgrimage, where individuals came, with appropriate rituals, to obtain the sacred

Crownpoint

CROWNPOINT, almost forty miles southwest of Chaco Canyon and 24 miles north of the I-40 town of **Thoreau**, is the principal town along the eastern flank of the Navajo Nation. Its only conceivable appeal for tourists is as the site of the **Navajo Rug Auction**, held usually but not always on the third Friday of each month, at Crownpoint Elementary School. Viewing is from 4pm until 6pm, with the auction at 7pm, and prices range from $100 up to perhaps $3000 (no credit cards). For more details, contact Crownpoint Rug Weavers (℡505/786-7386, ⓦwww.crownpointrugauction.com).

stone. From there, it's a small step to picture regional **festivals**, held at regular intervals, when large crowds would assemble for public ceremonies. For most of the year, Chaco held a relatively small, high-caste population, and the upper floors of its pueblos were empty or used for storage; at festival times, they accommodated a large influx of temporary guests.

Evidence for this ceremonial role includes the extraordinary 450-mile network of **roads** that link Chaco with around 75 **"outlier"** communities. Averaging thirty feet in width, they were far wider than ordinary human foot-traffic could require; in fact they were often more like causeways, built of hard-packed stone and running arrow-straight across cliffs, mesas, and canyons. Most are now only visible from the air. The longest to have been identified stretched all the way to Aztec Ruins, 64 miles north (see p.110), but if that same line is extended *south*, it makes a virtually perfect alignment with the site known as either **Casas Grandes** or **Paquimé**, over 300 miles away in Mexico. Roadside beacons may have been lit to summon pilgrims to major festivals.

Navajo legends relate that Chaco was ruled by the despotic **Great Gambler**, who was born to a poor Chacoan woman, taught to gamble by his father, the Sun, and won control over the canyon and all it held. When he was eventually defeated, he was shot into the sky, where he once more accumulated great wealth and returned to the region in the shape of the Spaniards. Meanwhile, freed of their oppressor, the people of Chaco had dispersed.

Recently, ferocious archeological debate has focused on explaining the signs of large-scale **violence** at Chaco. Human remains found in two thirds of the Great Houses appear to have been mutilated in a manner that suggests **cannibalism**. In the absence of evidence of warfare, they're seen as possible victims of ritual slaughter. The leading exponent of this theory, Christy Turner III, has even argued that a wandering group of Toltec refugees entered the region from the south around 900, and established a reign of terror at Chaco by introducing the bloodthirsty Mexican practice of **human sacrifice**.

Trying to guess why the Chacoans left the canyon when they did – from 1230 onwards – is probably futile, although only a tiny reduction in rainfall might have been enough to drive them out. **Where** they went, however, is no great mystery. Both Aztec, at its peak between 1110 and 1275, and Casas Grandes, an even richer commercial center occupied from 1250 to 1500, can be seen as successive "capital cities" of the same cultural tradition.

Ácoma Pueblo (see p.122) is just one of many modern pueblos that show a clear continuity with Chacoan culture. At least nine Hopi clans trace their origins back to what they remember as "the place beyond the horizon," while the Zuni say a medicine society known as the Sword Swallowers joined them from Chaco.

Western New Mexico

Although the reality of today's **I-40** may not match the romance of its predecessor, **Route 66**, crossing **western New Mexico** still has its rewards. The interstate passes through some memorable desert scenery, while successive detours to the south lead to crucial sites in Southwestern history. At **Zuni Pueblo**, Spanish conquistadors first encountered the region's indigenous inhabitants, and

El Morro National Monument records centuries of further incursions. Above all, **Ácoma Pueblo**, the superbly sited "Sky City," makes it worth spending a night in the dreary interstate towns of **Gallup** or **Grants**.

Gallup

As the largest town in I-40's 300-mile run between Albuquerque and Flagstaff, the famous Route 66 stop of **GALLUP**, 25 miles from the Arizona state line, might be expected to offer a diverting break in a long day's drive. Don't get your hopes up; cheap motels make it a handy overnight pit stop, but there's nothing to hold your interest.

Gallup sprang into being when the railroad arrived in 1881, and its role as the major railhead for the Navajo Nation has since been augmented by the construction of first Route 66, and later I-40. The interstate and the railroad tracks still run east–west through the heart of town, paralleled by a ten-mile stretch of the former Route 66 that's lined with endless budget motels and fast-food outlets.

In the week leading up to the second weekend in August, the Navajo and other local Native Americans come together in Gallup for the **Inter-Tribal Indian Ceremonial**, a six-day extravaganza centered on Red Rock State Park, four miles east of town. A two-day powwow is followed by four days of rodeo, craft shows, and dancing, culminating in a Saturday morning parade through town (information and tickets ☎505/863-3896 or 1-888/685-2564; ⓦwww .indianceremonial.com). Be sure to make motel reservations well in advance.

During the rest of the year, Gallup remains a major commercial center for the Navajo. An estimated eighty percent of all **silver jewelry** sold in the Southwest passes through the hands of traders like Shush Yaz, 1304 W Lincoln Ave (☎505/722-0130, ⓦwww.shushyaz.com), Richardson's Trading Company, 222 W 66 Ave (☎505/722-4762, ⓦwww.richardsonstrading.com), and Perry Null Trading Company, 1710 S Second St (☎505/722-3806, ⓦwww.pntrader.com). For more mundane shopping, head to the **Rio West Mall**, near exit 20 off I-40, which has the usual mall stores and a movie theater.

Practicalities

The Amtrak station at 201 E 66 Ave has one daily **train** to Flagstaff (7.08pm) and one to Albuquerque (8.45am). **Buses** along I-40 call in at the Greyhound station at 200 E 66 Ave (☎505/863-3761), which is also used by Navajo Transit System (☎505/729-4005) services to Window Rock, Arizona (see p.82). Gallup's **visitor center** is in the adjoining Gallup Multi-Cultural Center, 201 E 66 Ave (summer daily 8am–5pm; winter Mon–Fri 8am–5pm; ☎505/863-3841 or 1-800/242-4282; ⓦwww.gallupnm.org and ⓦwww.indiancountrynm.org).

Absolutely *the* place to **stay** is *El Rancho Hotel and Motel*, 1000 E 66 Ave (☍ ☎505/863-9311 or 1-800/543-6351, ⓦwww.elranchohotel.com; ❹), built in 1937 by the brother of movie mogul D.W. Griffith. From the murals in its opulent Spanish Revival lobby to the gallery of signed photos of celebrity Hollywood guests – John Wayne, Humphrey Bogart, and Ronald Reagan among them – this sumptuous Route 66 roadhouse is bursting with atmosphere. As its original slogan, still proudly displayed above the door, put it, it combined "The Charm of Yesterday and the Convenience of Tomorrow." Its decorative **restaurant** serves burgers named after Wayne and Bogart, plus (separate) Lucille Ball and Errol Flynn sandwiches, and the usual range of

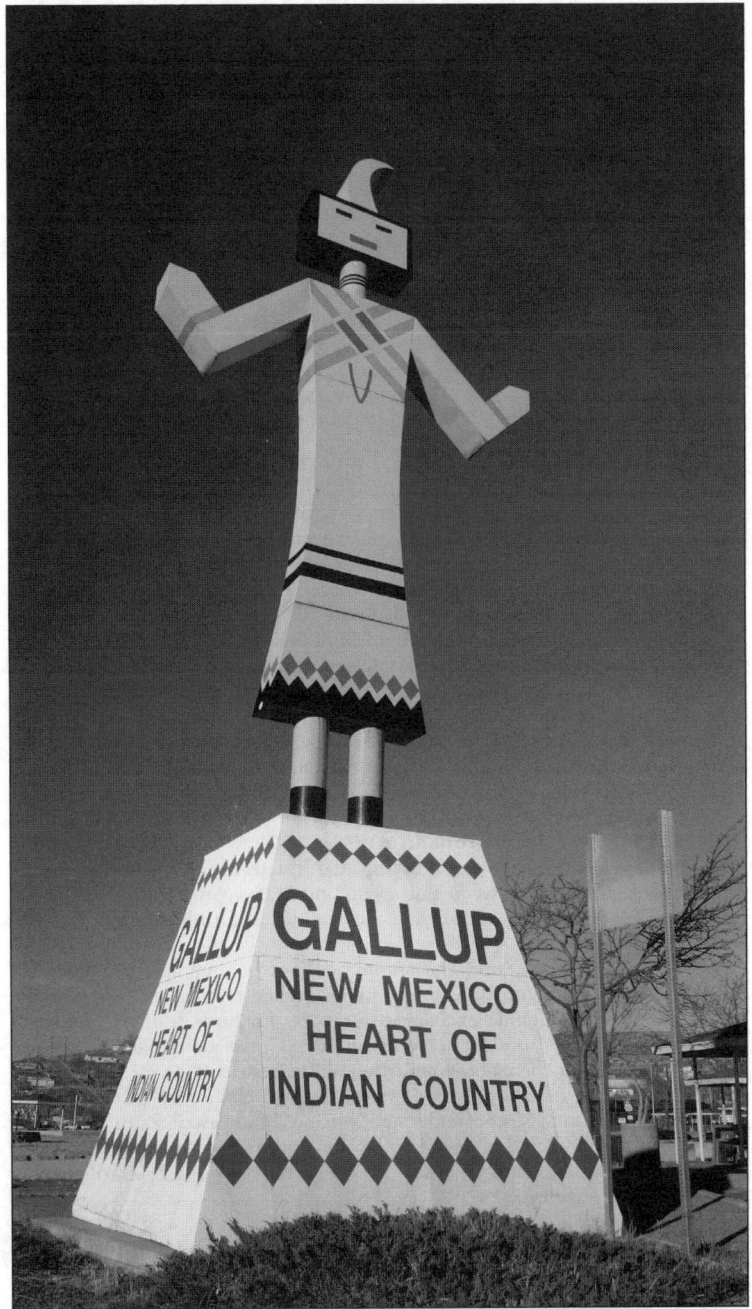

△ Roadside sign, Gallup, NM

barbecue, steaks, and shrimp priced at around $13. There's also a bar and a gift store. Some guest rooms are in the original ranchhouse, the rest in a less characterful two-story motel building alongside.

You can pay under $30 per night and still manage to avoid the dingiest of Gallup's other 2000 rooms by staying at places like the *Colonial*, 1007 W Coal Ave (☎505/863-6821; ❶). The *Super 8*, 1715 W Hwy-66 (☎505/722-5300 or 1-800/800-8000; winter ❷, summer ❸), is not quite up to the chain's usual standards, but it's still reliable. The best place to **camp** is Red Rock State Park – see p.116 – where a fully equipped site costs $10 (☎505/863-9330, ✉rrsp@ci.gallup.nm.us). *Earl's Restaurant*, 1400 E 66 Ave (☎505/863-4201), is an inexpensive diner on the east side of town, which serves plenty of chile-rich New Mexican specialties and is usually bustling with Navajo crafts sellers, while the *Oasis*, 100 E 66 Ave (☎505/722-9572), offers tasty, healthy Mediterranean specialties. If all you want is a **snack** or a cappuccino, head instead for the lively, arty *Coffee House*, in the heart of town at 203 W Coal Ave (☎505/726-0291).

Zuni Pueblo

Although few tourists make the effort to visit the remote and, superficially, unenthralling **ZUNI PUEBLO**, 35 miles south of Gallup and a short way west of Hwy-602, it occupies a pivotal role in Southwestern history. Here, in 1539, the black African **Esteban** became the first outsider to enter the Pueblo world, and was promptly killed and cut into strips by the Zuni. Fray Marcos de Niza, following close behind him, fled for his life back to Mexico, to report "this land …is the greatest and best of all that have been discovered." The Zuni call themselves *A:shiwi*, "the flesh," and their country *Shi:wona*, "the land that produces flesh." Fray Marcos, who garbled that name into Cíbola, announced that the six Zuni towns were the **Seven Cities of Cíbola**. Spanish conquistadors had long sought the legendary Seven Cities of Antilla, founded by bishops who sailed west to escape the Moorish invasion of Portugal in 714 AD and said to be rich in **gold**. In 1540, therefore, a Spanish expedition led by Francisco Vásquez de **Coronado** returned to Zuni. Turned back from the now-vanished town of Hawikku, the Spaniards defeated its inhabitants in the first battle ever fought between Europeans and Native Americans. For the full tale of the Coronado expedition, and more about Esteban's extraordinary life, see Contexts on p.572.

There was no gold at Zuni. The region had by that time been occupied for eight hundred years and had become a major Pueblo trading center, where the peoples of the Rio Grande exchanged turquoise for birds, feathers, and shells brought up from the south. Life went on after Coronado departed, but, like the Hopi, the Zuni thereafter found themselves restricted to an ever smaller area by Navajo, Apache, Spanish, and Anglo newcomers. Today's **Zuni Indian reservation** encompasses around three percent of ancestral Zuni lands and, with agriculture rendered marginal by erosion and over-grazing, the Zuni now depend for most of their livelihood on the recently acquired skill of making **silver overlay jewelry**.

Visiting Zuni Pueblo

The dominant feature on the Zuni reservation is the red-and-white-striped mesa of **Towayalane** or **Corn Mountain**, which has long served as a refuge for the Zuni people in times of trouble. Immediately below, straddling

Hwy-53 three miles west of Hwy-602, stands the main **village**. Now invariably known as **ZUNI**, it was founded as *Halona Idiwan'a*, or "Middle Place of the World," around 1700, when the Zuni came down from Corn Mountain after the Pueblo Revolt.

Simply driving along Hwy-53 through Zuni, it looks like just another rundown desert community. Almost none of the architecture is at all distinctive, though several buildings hold jewelry outlets, crafts shops, and simple diners. As even those structures used for ceremonial purposes are built to resemble new houses, you get little sense that the traditional life of the pueblo is continuing.

In recent years, however, the Zuni have made a concerted attempt to make their culture more accessible to visitors. Head three blocks south from the highway at the only stoplight in town, along Pia Mesa Road, and just across the Zuni River, facing the *Halona Plaza* supermarket, you'll come to the **A:shiwi A:wan Museum and Heritage Center** (summer Mon–Sat 9am–5.30pm, winter Mon–Fri 9am–5.30pm; donations welcome; ☏505/782-4403). A former trading post that has been refitted as an excellent modern museum, it sets out to document Zuni history for tribal members as well as for tourists, and centers on a remarkable collection of artifacts that were excavated from the long-abandoned site of **Hawikku** during the 1920s, and only returned by the Smithsonian Institution in 2001. Enthusiastic staff are happy to talk you through the displays and also provide local information of all kinds.

Not far to the east, north of the river but still south of the main road, the adobe **Our Lady of Guadalupe Mission Church**, erected by the Spanish in 1629, has been restored to more or less its original appearance. In line with historical accounts, the interior once more holds "life-size" murals of Zuni *kachinas* (Mon–Fri 8am–4.30pm; for a guide, call Zuni Tourism, below; donation). An ancient five-story "apartment block," like the two at Taos Pueblo (see p.187), still stands nearby, but the bottom floors are now underground, while the upper levels are concealed beneath modern accretions; the only traditional pueblo structures you'll see are the beehive-shaped bread ovens scattered around the plaza.

On a typical day, few visitors make it to Zuni, and even fewer stay very long. Special events can draw crowds, however, most notably the **Zuni Tribal Fair** in late August and the all-night **Shalako** dance, held in late November or early December. Anthropologists believe that this winter-solstice celebration, in which the *kachina* cult appears to blend with Aztec elements, was introduced by Mexican Indians left behind by Coronado.

As for **Hawikku** itself, the mound that conceals its ruins is roughly twelve miles southeast of Zuni, just west of the dirt road leading to the agricultural community of **Ojo Caliente**. You're only allowed to visit with permission from, and a guide supplied by, the Heritage Center. There's precious little to see, apart from multicolored potsherds poking from the rubble, but once you know the history it's an extraordinarily evocative site. Standing at the edge of the Pueblo world, you get a real sense of what a shock it must have been when first Esteban, and later Coronado, appeared across the infinite grasslands from the west.

Practicalities

For advance information on the Zuni, contact Zuni Tourism (☏505/782-4403, ⓦwww.experiencezuni.com). While there are no **motels** on the reservation, it does hold a superb **B&B**. Spending a night at the *Inn at Halona*, tucked out of sight behind the *Halona Plaza* supermarket at 23 B Pia Mesa Rd (✦ PO Box

446, Zuni, NM 87327; ☎505/782-4547 or 1-800/752-3278, ⓦwww.halona .com; ⑤), is a memorable, indeed unmissable, experience for anyone with an interest in Zuni life. Eight charming and individually styled guest rooms, almost all en-suite and sharing use of sitting rooms as well as a patio and an extensive library, are located in two separate buildings. The very hospitable owners, who are not themselves Zuni but whose roots here go back over a century, provide excellent breakfasts, and are a mine of information. The inn does not serve dinner, but simple restaurants along the highway include *Chuh-Chu's Pizzeria*, 1242 B Hwy-53 (☎505/782-2100), and *Route 53 Café*, near the stop sign at 1169 Hwy-53 (☎505/782-4404).

El Morro National Monument

Hidden away on Hwy-53 south of the Zuni mountains, 25 miles east of Zuni Pueblo and 42 miles west of Grants, **EL MORRO NATIONAL MONU-MENT** feels as far off the beaten track as it's possible to be in the modern United States. It seems incredible, therefore, that this sheer sandstone cliff was a regular rest stop for international travelers before the Pilgrims landed at Plymouth Rock. The evidence is plain to see, however. It was first recorded by Spanish explorers in 1583 – *el morro* means "the headland" – and in 1605, **Don Juan de Onate**, the founder of New Mexico, carved the first of the many messages that earned it the American name of **Inscription Rock**.

Translations and explanations of El Morro's graffiti are displayed in the **visitor center** (daily: summer 9am–7pm; winter 9am–5pm; ☎505/783-4226, ⓦwww .nps.gov/elmo; admission $3 per person). You can see the real thing on a half-mile **trail**, which stays open until an hour before the visitor center closes.

El Morro is technically a *cuesta*, a long sloping mesa terminating in an abrupt bluff. The trail's first stop is the reason so many people passed this way: a cool, perennial pool of **water**, collected beneath a waterfall that tumbles through a cleft in the pale pink cliffs. In such a self-evidently sacred spot, it's no surprise to see ancient **petroglyphs** scraped into the desert varnish there.

Not far beyond, Don Juan's chiseled signature celebrates "the discovery of the South Sea"; he was returning from an expedition that had taken him all the way to the mouth of the Colorado. Further inscriptions follow thick and fast, some detailing the minutiae of minor campaigns on the Spanish frontier, others recording moments such as the Reconquest after the Pueblo Revolt. Many inscriptions from later years were removed by national park employees when the monument was first created, for not being historic enough, but surviving oddities include the autograph of P. Gilmer Breckenridge, who led a caravan of 25 **camels** past El Morro in 1857.

An optional and much more demanding two-mile hike climbs the cliff beyond the last of the inscriptions to see the recently excavated **A'ts'ina Ruins**, up on top. Its builders, who abandoned it in 1350 AD, were among the ancestors of the modern Zuni.

El Malpais National Monument

If you had to pick one national site in the Southwest *not* to visit, **EL MALPAIS NATIONAL MONUMENT** would be the obvious choice. There was more than a whiff of the pork-barrel about its creation in the 1980s, which was bitterly opposed by neighboring Ácoma Indians. They lost, in part, because they preferred not to reveal the locations of shrines they wanted to remain inviolate. For tourists, however, the problem with El Malpais is more basic: it's **dull**.

El Malpais is Spanish for "the **Badlands**," and it preserves a tract of territory covered by **lava flows** from a volcanic eruption two or three thousand years ago – recent enough for the landscape to remain blackened and barren. Spelunkers delight in underground "lava tubes" up to seventeen miles long, but hiking any distance across the rough rock above is a pretty miserable business.

The map of El Malpais is a peculiar patchwork of desolate lava interspersed with pockets of grassland that the eruption somehow missed. Confusingly, only the lava areas belong to the **national monument**, which is run by the National Park Service and served by a **visitor center** twenty miles east of El Morro on Hwy-53 (daily 8.30am–4.30pm; ☎505/783-4774, Ⓦwww.nps .gov/elma; admission free). The rest is administered as a **National Conservation Area** by the Bureau of Land Management, which has a **ranger station** on Hwy-17, nine miles south of I-40 exit 89 (daily 8am–4.30pm; ☎505/240-0300). Each of those roads skirts the periphery of the badlands; in an ordinary vehicle you can only get from one to the other via Grants.

On **Hwy-17**, the more interesting drive of the two, **Sandstone Bluffs Overlook** near the ranger station commands views westwards across the flatlands to the jagged peaks of the **Cerritos de Jaspe** and north to Mount Taylor. Displays at the viewpoint illustrate the difference between the two main kinds of lava, known to geologists the world over by their Hawaiian names of *aa* and *pahoehoe*. Not far beyond, **La Ventana Arch** is a chunky natural window three-quarters of the way up a cliff face east of the highway.

Grants

In general, **GRANTS**, sixty miles east of Gallup on I-40, looks a lot better by night than it does by day. Daylight exposes an air of dereliction along its old Route 66 frontage that's concealed when the neon signs come on after dark. Even so, Grants has more character than Gallup and is a handy base for detours off the interstate.

Like Gallup, Grants started out as a railroad town. In the 1950s, just as a half-hearted **carrot** boom fizzled out, it struck it rich in a rather less wholesome way. A Navajo shepherd, Paddy Martinez, picked up some yellow rocks on nearby Haystack Mountain, and Grants found itself sitting on half the US's reserves of **uranium**. Both the Anaconda mining company, which opened an enormous mine, and the Santa Fe Railroad, which owned the land, made a fortune; Martinez got a monthly pension and the title "official uranium scout."

Grants' uranium years have receded into history, but they're enjoyably recalled in the **New Mexico Museum of Mining** at 100 N Iron Ave (Mon–Sat 9am–4pm; $3). Visits consist of a faked descent into a mock-up mine, where you can poke around with no fear of radiation.

Practicalities

Grants' own **visitor center** (☎505/287-4802 or 1-800/748-2142 ext 32, Ⓦwww.grants.org), in the same building as the mining museum (see above), opens during the same hours. At the east end of town, just south of I-40 exit 85 at 1900 E Santa Fe Ave, the **Northwest New Mexico Visitor Center** is a "multi-agency" resource offering information on all the region's public lands (daily 8am–5pm; ☏505/876-2783).

Most of the town's more salubrious **motels** – the ones that charge by the night, not the hour – congregate east of downtown, across the railroad near exit 85 off the interstate. These include a good *Super 8*, 1604 E Santa Fe Ave (☏505/287-8811 or 1-800/800-8000; ❸), and a slightly more upmarket *Holiday Inn Express*, 1496 E Santa Fe Ave (☏505/285-4676 or 1-800/465-4329; ❺). Back in town, the *Sands Motel*, 112 McArthur Ave (☏505/287-2996 or 1-800/424-7679; ❷) is a decent budget option.

The most popular place to **eat** is *La Ventana*, 110 Geis St in the Hillcrest Center (☏505/287-9393; closed Sun), which offers pretty much everything from steaks to fajitas, plus lighter sandwich lunches. In the heart of town, the *Mission at Riverwalk*, 422 W Santa Fe Ave (☏505/285-4632, ☏www.grantsmission.com; ❻), is an appealing converted church that now doubles as a community theater and healthy café, serving sandwiches, smoothies, and coffee; it also has a separate guest house for rent. The tiny *Uranium Cafe*, 519 W Santa Fe Ave (☏505/287-7540; closed Sun), is a vintage diner opposite the mining museum, open for breakfast and lunch only.

Ácoma Pueblo

The amazing **ÁCOMA PUEBLO**, south of I-40 fifteen miles east of Grants and fifty miles west of Albuquerque, encapsulates a thousand years of Native American history. Focused around the ancient village known as "**Sky City**," atop a magnificent mesa, it has adapted to repeated waves of invaders while retaining its own strong identity. The Acomans have long been happy to take the tourist dollar – they run a large casino beside the interstate and have hosted the Miss America swimsuit pageant – so visitors seldom feel the awkwardness possible at other Pueblo communities. Nonetheless, Ácoma is the real thing, and its sense of unbroken tradition can reduce even the least culturally sensitive traveler to awestruck silence.

A history of Ácoma Pueblo

Only certain Hopi villages (see p.87) can rival Sky City's claim to be the **oldest inhabited settlement** in the United States. This isolated mesa, 367ft high and 7000ft above sea level, was probably first occupied by Chacoan migrants at some point between 1100 and 1200, when the great pueblos of Chaco Canyon were still in use. The name Ácoma means "people of the white rock"; by the start of the sixteenth century, it's thought to have held around six thousand inhabitants, living in five hundred or so three- to four-story houses.

The **Coronado** expedition of 1540 described the Acomans as "robbers, feared by the whole country round about." Noting the mesa's redoubtable defenses – it could only be reached by climbing ladders through a narrow crevice – the Spaniards commented that "no army could possibly be strong enough to capture the village."

In October 1598, Don Juan de **Oñate** visited Ácoma in peace, while exploring his recently proclaimed colony of New Mexico. A month later, however, his nephew Juan de **Zaldívar**, following with reinforcements, arrived at the foot of the mesa, demanded food, and was rejected. Depending on which version you believe, the Spaniards either tricked their way onto the mesa, or the Acomans invited them up and then ambushed them. In the ensuing fight, all the Spaniards were killed, save four who survived being hurled off.

When a punitive Spanish force of seventy men, equipped with cannons, stormed into the village in January 1599, over eight hundred Acomans died in a three-day house-to-house battle. Five hundred women and children and eighty men were taken prisoner. All were sentenced to twenty years of penal servitude, and each man had a foot publicly chopped off, in the plazas of the Rio Grande pueblos. Bitterness persists among the Pueblo peoples to this day; a statue of Oñate erected in Alcalde, New Mexico, in 1999 had its right foot disappear within days.

Oñate was eventually called back to Mexico City and removed from office, in punishment for his savagery. By 1629, Ácoma had a resident Spanish friar – Fray Juan Ramírez is said to have been accepted after he caught a child who fell off the mesa – and the Acomans were hard at work building a huge mission church. Ramírez's successors were driven out during the Pueblo Revolt, and a tyrannical eighteenth-century priest was thrown to his death, but in theory the pueblo was permanently converted to Catholicism.

The people of Ácoma clearly never felt inclined to follow the architectural example of the mission, whose mighty beams were carried 25 miles from Mount Taylor without once being permitted to touch the ground. Instead, they went on constructing the same multistory stone and adobe houses that can still be seen today.

Five hundred years since the Spanish arrived, the **Ácoma Indian Reservation** still has a population of six thousand. Most of those live in three communities that were originally sited for their proximity to fresh water but now stand conveniently close to I-40 – **ACOMITA**, **McCARTYS,** and **ANZAC**. Only thirteen families, forty people in all, live on the mesa itself, but others make daily trips to sell pottery or fry-bread, and many more return to their ancestral homes for feast days and other ceremonies. Eighty percent of Acomans call themselves Catholic, but the old religion endures; there are fourteen separate clans, and the Antelope Clan is still, as it has always been, in charge of everything. Even today, the priest that serves the community, who is not himself an Indian, is only permitted to visit the mesa once a week, on Wednesdays.

Arrival and information

Sky City is twelve miles south of the interstate, via any of three connecting roads. For the most dramatic approach, come in from the **west**, leaving I-40 at exit 102. When the mesa comes into view, glowing in the sunlight as you drop down a hillside roughly three miles distant, you'll understand why the first Spanish explorers spoke of cities of gold.

Before you take any photographs, however, you must first pay the relevant fees at the **Sky City Cultural Center**, at road's end below the mesa. You can only see Sky City itself on an hour-long **tour**; buses take groups up at regular intervals (daily: May–Oct 8am–7pm; Nov–April 8am–4pm; last tour leaves one hour before closing; admission $10, plus $10 for photo permit, no camcorders or video; ☏505/470-0181 or 1-800/747-0181, ⓦwww.skycity.com). For several years, since the previous visitor center burned down, the tribal offices here were housed in temporary structures, but by the time you read this, the replacement should finally be open, and incorporate the promised **Haak'u Museum** of

Ácoma history. Note that Ácoma is **closed to all visitors** on June 24, June 29, July 10–13, July 25, during the first and/or second weekend in October, and the first Saturday of December.

Accommodation at Ácoma is only available up by the interstate, in the large, comfortable, and stylish *Sky City Hotel*, adjoining the casino (☎505/552-6123 or 1-888/759-2489, ⓦwww.skycityhotel.com; ❹). The casino holds the *Huwaka'a* **restaurant**, offering cheap buffets as well as a full menu, and coffee bar, while the new visitor center should have its own snack bar.

Sky City

While the original walls of **Sky City**'s oldest houses lie concealed beneath several centuries of replastering, the overall appearance of the village changed little in the last millennium. The high windowless wall of the main pueblo, at the northern edge of the mesa, protected its inhabitants against both the chill north wind and potential invaders. Three or four stories of terraced "apartments" face south to maximize the winter sun. Just one room still has its original tiny "windowpane" of translucent mica. Digging *kivas* down into the sandstone requires too much labor, so seven of the above-ground rooms are *kivas*, each shared by two clans and entered by a tall ladder pointing to the north. Ácoma's sparse rainfall collects in natural depressions in the rock; beside the largest of these cisterns is the mesa's only tree, a slender cotton-wood.

Tour groups stroll more or less at will around the mesa-top, with plenty of opportunities to buy handmade pottery or ears of multicolored corn. Don't expect to enter any individual dwellings, however. The main stop is the still-active mission church of **San Esteban del Rey**, which measures 120ft long by 40ft wide, with seventy-foot-high walls that taper from 10ft thick at the base to 6ft at the top. The floor is made of hard-packed earth, while the whitewashed interior walls are decorated with a mixture of Christian images and Pueblo motifs. Ácoma's greatest treasure hangs above the altar – a painting of **St Joseph**, said to answer prayers for rain, which was borrowed by Laguna Pueblo in 1800 and only returned after the Acomans took Laguna all the way to the US Supreme Court. As no photography is permitted within the church, no pre-existing, postcard image prepares you for the sublime view as you turn around from the altar and look back across the cavernous space to the glorious New Mexican light that streams in through the doorway.

There's no soil on the mesa-top, so all the adobe bricks of the church were made with mud carried up from below, and its **cemetery** was filled with endless basket-loads of sand. Only honoured elders can now be buried here – not in coffins, but "replanted," facing east. At first, the churchyard wall looks crenellated, but in fact the bumps are "warriors," placed to guard the dead.

Legend has it that the forbidding **Enchanted Mesa**, visible to the east, once held its own Pueblo community. The only access to the top was via a spider's-web of ropes strung between the mesa itself and an adjoining rock pillar. When that pillar collapsed one day while the men were away from the village, two women and a child on top were left stranded, their cries for help fading as they starved.

If you prefer, you can walk rather than ride back down from Sky City, following the ancient footpath through clefts in the rock.

Laguna Pueblo

LAGUNA PUEBLO (☎505/552-6654 ⓦwww.lagunapueblo.org), just north of the interstate six miles east of Ácoma and 44 miles west of Albuquerque, is the **youngest** of the New Mexican pueblos. It was established in 1698 by refugees from several different pueblos, driven here by the disruption of the Pueblo Revolt and the increasing threat of Navajo and Apache raids. It's also the **richest** pueblo, thanks to the presence of the world's largest **uranium mine**, Anaconda's Jackpile mine. That closed in 1982, after operating for thirty years, but the Laguna people are still living off the royalties, and they've also opened two separate **casinos**, off I-40 at exits 108 and 140. On the down side, they're having to cope with the **pollution** caused by the uranium mining, which burrowed its way under the main Pueblo village; birth defects and cancer have become major problems.

All of Laguna Pueblo, including its **San José Mission Church**, is visible from a **rest stop** on the west-bound side of the interstate halfway between the two casinos, where traders sell crafts. There's no reason to explore any further.

Santa Fe and
northern New Mexico

CHAPTER 2 **Highlights**

* **La Fonda de Santa Fe** Splendidly atmospheric old hotel that once marked the end of the Santa Fe Trail. **See p.136**

* **The Palace of the Governors** The oldest public building in the country flew the flags of three other nations before the Americans moved in. **See p.140**

* **Museum of International Folk Art** The most enjoyable of Santa Fe's many fine museums; a wonderland of folk art objects from around the globe. **See p.144**

* **Coronado State Monument** When the fall colors are at their peak, the sunsets at this historic Pueblo settlement, beside the Rio Grande, are out of this world. **See p.154**

* **Bandelier National Monument** New Mexico's most appealing ancient site, where the ancestors of today's Pueblo peoples carved their homes into soft volcanic rock. **See p.160**

* **Santuario de Chimayó** Exquisite little adobe pilgrimage church beside the mountainous High Road from Santa Fe to Taos. **See p.174**

* **Millicent Rogers Museum** Stunning Native American and Spanish Colonial artifacts make this Taos museum an absolute must-see. **See p.187**

* **Taos Pueblo** The multistory adobe dwellings of Taos are a living legacy of New Mexico's extraordinary history. **See p.187**

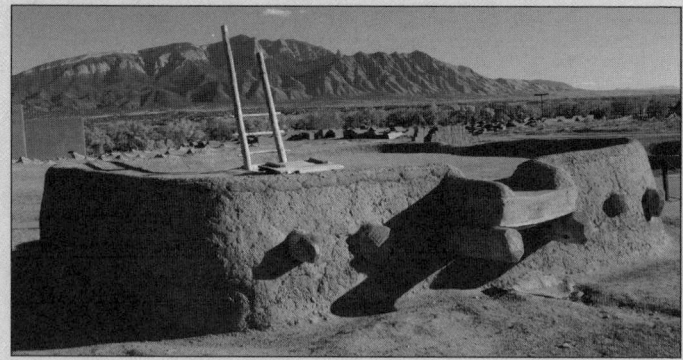

△ *Kiva*, Coronado State Monument

Santa Fe and northern New Mexico

B
asking in the magical "**light**" that artists – and tourist boards – rave about, and stretching beneath the flame-red peaks of the Sangre de Cristo mountains, **northern New Mexico** is the New Mexico of popular imagination, with its pastel colors, vivid desert landscape, and adobe architecture. Quite apart from its ravishing **beauty**, nowhere else in North America can boast such a sense of unbroken **history**. Native American pueblos and Hispanic colonial settlements have stood side by side along the Rio Grande for four hundred years, and the Yankees who arrived on the Santa Fe Trail still seem like relative newcomers.

State capital **Santa Fe**, the only city in the region, more than lives up to its high-profile image as the epitome of Southwestern style, bursting with top-class museums, galleries, and restaurants. Nonetheless, it remains less than

Adobe

For many visitors, the defining feature of New Mexico is its **adobe architecture**, as seen in homes, churches, and even shopping malls and motels. While ancient pueblo villages were constructed using blocks of mud, cut from the riverbeds and mixed with grass, it was early Franciscan missionaries who introduced molded adobe **bricks**. The Spaniards had themselves learned the technique – in which a mixture of earth, sand, charcoal, and chopped grass or straw is left to bake in the sun in a wooden frame known as an *adobero* – from the Arabs. Built into walls, the bricks are set with a mortar of much the same composition, and then plastered over with mud and straw. The color of the soil used dictates the color of the final building, and thus subtle variations can be seen all across the state. However, adobe is far from being a convenient material: it needs replastering every few years and turns to mud when water seeps up from the ground, so that many buildings must be sporadically raised and bolstered by the insertion of rocks at their base.

These days, most of what looks like adobe is actually painted cement or concrete, but even this looks attractive enough in its own semi-kitsch way. Superb old adobes include the remote **Santuario de Chimayó** (see p.175) on the High Road between Santa Fe and Taos, the formidable church of **San Francisco de Asis** (see p.190) in Ranchos de Taos, and the multitiered dwellings of **Taos Pueblo** (see p.189).

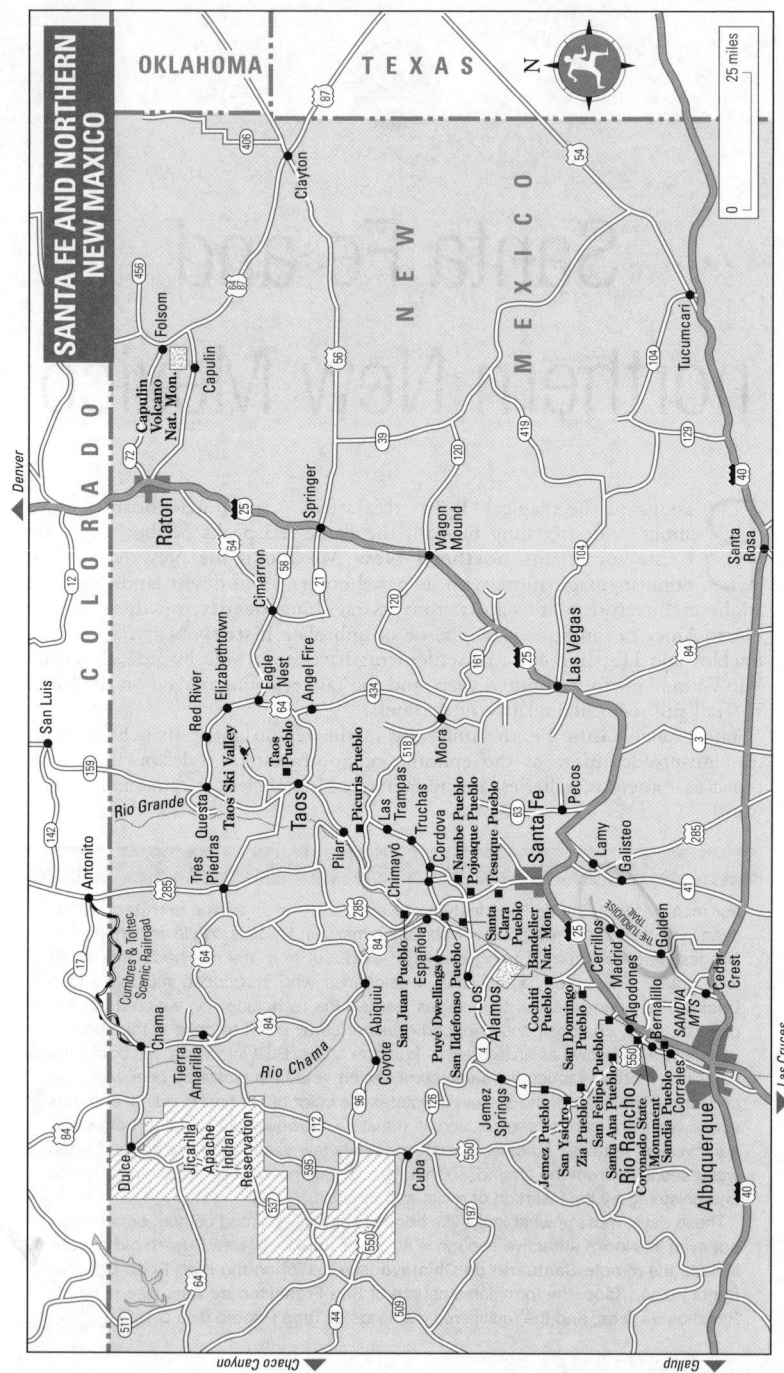

SANTA FE AND NORTHERN
NEW MEXICO

OKLAHOMA   TEXAS   N

25 miles

0

Denver

COLORADO

San Luis

Antonito

Cumbres & Toltec Scenic Railroad

Chama

Dulce

Jicarilla Apache Indian Reservation

Tierra Amarilla

Rio Chama

Abiquiu

Coyote

Cuba

Jemez Springs

San Ysidro

Jemez Pueblo

Zia Pueblo

Rio Grande

Tres Piedras

Questa

Red River

Taos Ski Valley

Taos Pueblo

Taos

Pilar

Picuris Pueblo

Las Trampas

Truchas

Chimayó

Cordova

Nambe Pueblo

Pojoaque Pueblo

Tesuque Pueblo

Santa Fe

Española

San Juan Pueblo

San Ildefonso Pueblo

Puyé Dwellings

Los Alamos

Santa Clara Pueblo

Bandelier Nat. Mon.

Cochiti Pueblo

San Domingo Pueblo

San Felipe Pueblo

Santa Ana Pueblo

Sandia Pueblo

Coronado State Monument

Rio Rancho

Corrales

Algodones

Bernalillo

SANDIA MTS

Cedar Crest

Golden

Madrid

Cerrillos

THE TURQUOISE TRAIL

Albuquerque

Las Cruces

COLORADO

Raton

Capulin Volcano Nat. Mon.

Capulin

Folsom

Clayton

Springer

Cimarron

Elizabethtown

Eagle Nest

Angel Fire

Wagon Mound

Las Vegas

Mora

Pecos

Lamy

Galisteo

N E W   M E X I C O

Santa Rosa

Tucumcari

Gallup

Chaco Canyon

a tenth of the size of Albuquerque, and its central plaza is still recognizable as the frontier marketplace that welcomed trade caravans from Mexico and the Mississippi. **Taos**, 75 miles northeast and even smaller, has become almost equally celebrated thanks to a remarkable twentieth-century influx of artists and writers such as **Georgia O'Keeffe** and **D.H. Lawrence**. It too has its share of museums and amenities and is a near neighbor to the most striking of the Rio Grande pueblos, multistory **Taos Pueblo**.

Both Taos and Santa Fe are surrounded by spectacular scenery, and detours away from the Rio Grande and into the mountains are rewarded with glimpses of countless fascinating communities. These range from the ancient **cliff dwellings** of **Bandelier National Monument** on the Pajarito Plateau west of the river to Hispanic villages such as **Chimayó** on the **High Road** to the east, Wild-West towns like **Las Vegas**, and even the high-tech home of the H-Bomb, **Los Alamos**.

Santa Fe

Since the early 1980s, **SANTA FE** has ranked among the most chic destinations in the US, repeatedly voted the country's most popular city with upmarket travelers. That appeal rests on a very solid basis; it's one of America's **oldest** and most **beautiful** cities, founded by Spanish adventurers and missionaries a decade before the Pilgrims reached Plymouth Rock. Spread across a high plateau at the foot of the stunning **Sangre de Cristo** mountains, New Mexico's capital still glories in the adobe houses and baroque churches of its original architects, and they're now joined by museums and galleries that attract art-lovers from all over the world. The busiest season is **summer**, when temperatures usually reach into the eighties Fahrenheit; in winter, the average daytime high is a mere 42°F, though with snow on the mountains the city looks more ravishing than ever.

With upwards of a million and a half tourists every year – not to mention twenty thousand daily commuters from Albuquerque – descending upon a town of fewer than seventy thousand inhabitants, Santa Fe has inevitably grown somewhat overblown. Long-term residents bemoan what's been lost, while first-time visitors are inclined to wonder how anyone could complain about such a charming city. The urban sprawl as you approach town from the interstate does make a lousy introduction, while the rigorous insistence that every downtown building should look like a seventeenth-century Spanish colonial palace takes a bit of getting used to. This is the only city in the world where what on first glance appears to be a perfectly preserved ancient adobe turns out to be a multi-story parking lot, and it would be illegal to build a gas station that didn't resemble an Indian prayer chamber.

There's still a lot to like about Santa Fe, however. Despite the summer crowds, the downtown area – clustered around its venerable **plaza** – still has the peaceful ambience of a small country town, and it's rare indeed for it to be such fun simply to stroll around a Southwestern city. "Santa Fe style" may have become something of a cliché, but even the clichés change over time; the pastel-painted **wooden coyotes** that were once the obligatory souvenir have been replaced

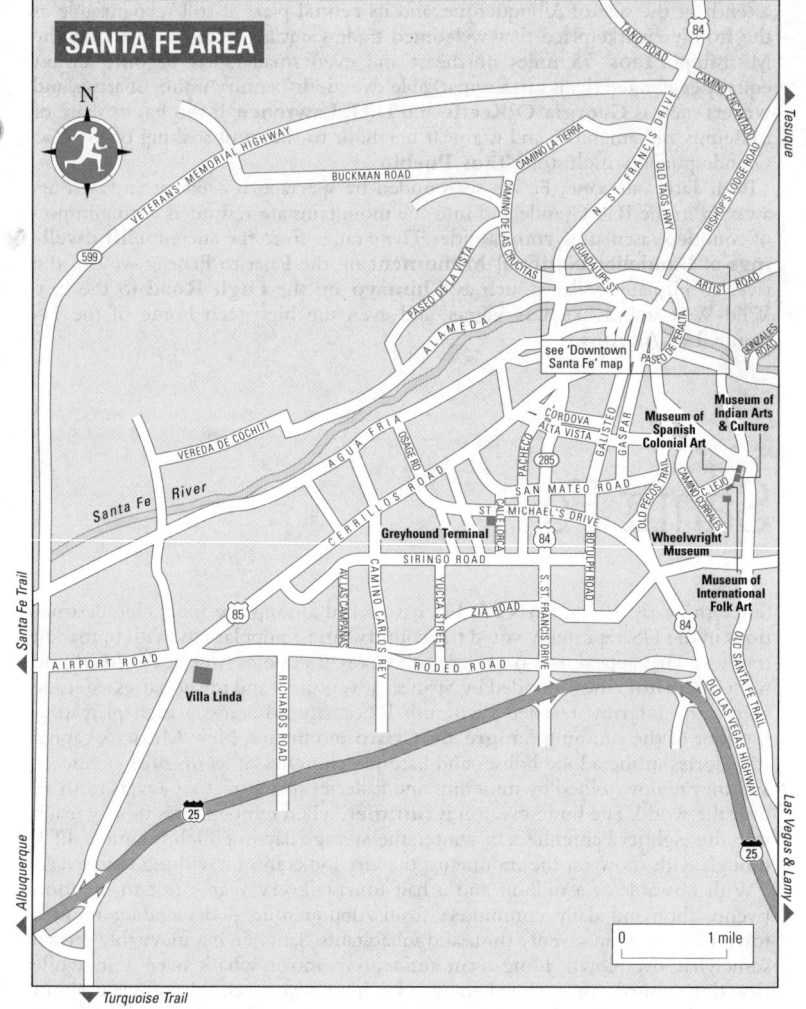

Taos ▲

SANTA FE AREA

N

see 'Downtown
Santa Fe' map

Museum of
Indian Arts
& Culture

Museum of
Spanish
Colonial Art

Santa Fe River

Greyhound Terminal

Wheelwright
Museum

Museum of
International
Folk Art

Santa Fe Trail ▲

Villa Linda

Albuquerque ▲

Las Vegas & Lamy ▶

0   1 mile

▼ Turquoise Trail

by cast-iron sculptures of Kokopelli, the hunch-backed Ancestral Puebloan flute-player. In a town where the *Yellow Pages* list over 250 art galleries – more than half of them along a single mile of **Canyon Road** – you'll get plenty of opportunities to buy one.

A history of Santa Fe

The first homes of **La Villa de Santa Fe** were erected on the ruins of an abandoned Native American pueblo in around 1604. In 1610, after previous Spanish settlements to the northwest had been deemed unsuitable, it became the third capital of the infant colony of **New Mexico**. Its name, "Holy Faith," was taken from the camp outside Granada where Spanish monarchs Ferdinand and Isabella made their base before the assault that drove the Moors from Spain in 1492. Santa Fe was laid out as an imposing administrative city; as the **Palace of the Governors**, the *casas reales* or "royal houses" that commanded its parade-ground plaza went on to house Spanish, Pueblo, Mexican, and American rulers.

Santa Fe was the base from which horses, introduced to North America by the Spanish, spread across the continent and were acquired by Native American peoples. During its first two centuries the city presented an inviting target for mounted Apache, Ute, and Comanche raiders. Relations with the **Pueblo** peoples whom the Spaniards had come to convert were initially stable, but growing antagonism led to the **Pueblo Revolt** of 1680, when Santa Fe was besieged and conquered by an alliance of many different Indian groups. One thousand Spaniards fled south and lived in exile for twelve years at El Paso before returning under a new governor, **Don Diego de Vargas**. Their fight to regain control of the city is still celebrated in the annual **Fiestas de Santa Fe**.

Santa Fe was always a neglected outpost of the Spanish empire; at the time of Mexican independence in 1821, its garrison was so poorly supplied as to be armed with bows and arrows. Attempts to improve the economy thereafter focused on the ever-expanding United States, and the dispatch of a trade delegation to St Louis in 1824 resulted in the opening of the **Santa Fe Trail** across the plains. Although American goods poured in, US citizens were forbidden to settle in the city, in a bid to avoid a repetition of the Yankee takeover of Texas. In 1843, the Mexican president ordered that the Santa Fe Trail be closed altogether, but a mere three years later New Mexico passed into American hands. A discreet payment of $50,000 to Governor Armijo ensured that there was no opposition to the entry of the US Army on **August 18, 1846**.

Although the Yankees set about transforming the squat, dusty Mexican town into something more conspicuously American, building in wood rather than adobe, Santa Fe remained largely unchanged for the rest of the nineteenth century. What's more, no sooner did the old buildings start to disappear than the city was seized by the conviction that the only way to retain its identity was to turn the clock back again – ironically the campaign was largely inspired by Anglo newcomers with their own romantic visions of how Santa Fe ought to look. Since the 1930s, city mandates have ensured that almost every structure within sight of the plaza has been designed or redecorated to suit the **Pueblo Revival** mode. As a result, Santa Fe today – at least at its core – looks much more like its original Spanish self than it did a hundred years ago.

Arrival

Santa Fe is surprisingly far off the beaten path. Most out-of-state visitors **fly** into Albuquerque – see p.205 – and either rent a vehicle at the airport for the hour's drive up I-25 to Santa Fe, or catch one of the many **shuttle buses**, which typically cost $20–25 one way, offered by companies such as Santa Fe Shuttle (☎505/243-2300 or 1-888/833-2300, ⊛www.santafeshuttle.com), Twin Hearts Express (☎505/751-1201 or 1-800/654-9456, ⊛www.twinheartsexpress.com), or Sandia Shuttle Express (☎505/474-5696 or 1-888/775-5696, ⊛www .sandiashuttle.com). Santa Fe's **municipal airport**, ten miles southwest of town, is served only by commuter planes, including flights from Denver on United Express (☎505/473-4118 or 1-800/242-6522).

Buses from all over the Southwest call at the Greyhound terminal at 858 St Michael's Drive (☏505/471-0008), a long way from the plaza. These include four daily buses to and from Albuquerque, which cost $13. There's no direct **rail** link. Amtrak trains arrive every afternoon at **Lamy**, seventeen miles southeast, from Albuquerque and Chicago – to be met by Lamy Shuttle vans ($16 one-way; ☏505/982-8829).

Information

The downtown office of Santa Fe's **Convention & Visitors Bureau**, two blocks northwest of the plaza in the lobby of the Convention Center, 201 W Marcy St (Mon–Fri 8am–5pm; ☏505/955-6200 or 1-800/777-2489, ⓦwww.santafe.org), stocks a very limited selection of brochures, but there's a larger **visitor center** at Santa Fe Premium Outlets, 830 Cerrillos Rd (Mon–Sat 10am–8pm, Sun 11am–6pm). In addition, the **New Mexico Department of Tourism**, in the Lamy Building at 491 Old Santa Fe Trail (summer daily 8am–7pm, winter daily 8am–5pm; ☏505/827-4000 or 1-800/545-2040, ⓦwww.newmexico.org), has racks of material on the whole state, and in summer, there's a small information kiosk in the plaza itself. The **Public Lands Information Center**, 1474 Rodeo Rd (Mon–Fri 8am–5pm; ☏505/438-7542, ⓦwww.publiclands.org), carries details on all public lands in New Mexico, including maps and brochures for state and national parks.

The main **post office** is also northwest of the plaza, at 120 S Federal Place (Mon–Fri 7.30am–5.30pm, Sat 9am–1pm; ☏505/988-6351).

Getting around

Most of what there is to see in Santa Fe lies within walking distance of the central plaza, but to get there from your hotel, or to see the farther-flung attractions, you may need to use the Santa Fe Trails **bus service**. All nine routes start from the **Sheridan Transit Center**, a block northwest of the plaza on Sandoval Street (Mon–Fri 6am–11pm, Sat 8am–8pm, Sun 10am–7.45pm; ☏505/955-2001), with a standard adult fare of $1, one-day passes for $2, and monthly passes for $20. The most useful for visitors are route #2, which runs up **Cerrillos Road** at half-hourly intervals, and route #M, which loops between the plaza and the **outlying museums**, again roughly every half-hour.

The only **taxi** company in town is Capital City Cabs (☏505/438-0000), while **bikes** can be rented at Sun Mountain Bike Company, 102 E Water St (☏505/982-8986, ⓦwww.sunmountainbikeco.com).

Tours and excursions

Two-hour **walking tours** of town are conducted by various companies. The Friends of the Palace of the Governors sets off from the Palace's blue gate on Lincoln Avenue (May–Oct Mon–Sat 10.15am; $10; ☏505/476-5109). Aboot About conducts similar tours (daily 9.30am & 1.30pm from *Eldorado Hotel* or 9.45am & 1.45pm from *Hotel St Francis*; $10; ☏505/988-2774, ⓦwww.abootabout.com). Walk Through Time Tours, based at the *Inn at Loretto*, 211 Old Santa Fe Trail (daily 10am & 2pm; $10; ☏505/231-2770) also operates Loretto Line bus tours.

Excursion trains down to Lamy, drawn by diesel, not steam, leave from the old Santa Fe Southern Railway depot at 410 S Guadalupe St (April Tues–Thurs, & Sat 10.30am; Fri noon; Sun 2pm; May same as April, plus Mon 10.30am; June–Oct Mon, Wed & Fri 1pm; Tues, Thurs, & Sat 10.30am; Sun 2pm; Nov–March Thurs & Sat 11am, Sun 2pm; round-trip $28–55; ☎505/989-8600 or 1-888/989-8600, ☯www.sfsr.com). The schedule given here should be regarded as a general guide only; extra excursion trains are often added. Prices vary slightly according to which of the three classes of coach you choose to ride and to the length of the trip – departures after 1pm don't go all the way to Lamy.

Accommodation

Even in winter, you won't find a room within walking distance of downtown Santa Fe for under $60, and in summer – when every bed in town is frequently taken – there's little under $100. **Cerrillos Road** (US-85), the main road in from I-25, holds most of Santa Fe's **motels** and its one **hostel**. Everything gets more expensive as you approach the center, though **B&Bs** make an attractive alternative to paying the sky-high prices demanded by the plush plaza-area hotels. If you get stuck, contact All Santa Fe Reservations (☎505/474-5557 or 1-877/737-7366, ☯www.all-santafe.com).

Commercial **campgrounds** in the Santa Fe area include *Los Campos RV Resort*, 3574 Cerrillos Rd (mid-May to Sept; ☎505/473-1949 or 1-800/852-8160), which does not accept tenters, and the *KOA*, further east at I-25 exit 290 (March–Oct; ☎505/466-1419, ☯www.santafekoa.com). Camping nearby in the **Santa Fe National Forest** (☎505/753-7331, ☯www.fs.fed.us/r3/sfe) is a cheaper and much more appealing prospect. The *Black Canyon* campground (☎1-877/444-6777, ☯www.reserveusa.com; $10), which holds just under fifty tent sites and is unusual in offering advance reservations, is seven miles up Hwy-475, northeast of town, and is only open between April and November. Two much smaller sites lie further on: *Big Tesuque* (year-round; free) is five miles beyond *Black Canyon*, and *Aspen Basin* (year-round; free) is another three miles beyond that, at the ski area (see p.146). Both have toilet facilities, but no showers. For more information, contact the Public Lands Information Center (see opposite).

Inexpensive

Santa Fe International Hostel 1412 Cerrillos Rd at Alta Vista ☎505/988-1153, ☯www.users.qwest.net/~epreston1/. This old-fashioned HI-AYH hostel, housed in a ramshackle former motel a couple of miles southwest of the plaza, is one of those love-it-or-hate-it places. Some travelers find the staff unfriendly, the owner a control freak, and the rooms poorly furnished and dirty; others seem totally satisfied, say there's a good atmosphere, and don't mind the compulsory chores. Dorms beds cost $15, or you can get a room to yourself for $33 single, $43 double. In winter the whole place can be pretty damp and cold. ❶/❷

Silver Saddle 2810 Cerrillos Rd at Siler Rd ☎505/471-7663, ☯www.motelsantafe.com. Busy, down-to-earth but surprisingly characterful motel, well out from downtown. Winter ❸, summer ❹

Super 8 3358 Cerrillos Rd at Richards Ave ☎505/471-8811 or 1-800/800-8000, ☯www.super8.com. Thanks to its half-hearted adobe exterior, this hundred-room chain motel, four miles from downtown, looks pretty strange, but it's a dependable bargain. Winter ❸, summer ❹

Western Scene Motel 1608 Cerrillos Rd at Cochiti ☎505/983-7484. Presentable two-story adobe motel, a short way south of the hostel. Winter ❸, summer ❹

Mid-range

El Rey Inn 1862 Cerrillos Rd at St Michael's Drive ☎505/982-1931 or 1-800/521-1349, ☯www.elreyinnsantafe.com. This white-painted adobe, here since the 1930s, has the most character and best value of the Cerrillos Road motels, with surprisingly stylish and distinctive Southwestern rooms adorned with Art Deco tiles, some nice suites, complimentary breakfasts, a pool, and a large garden. ⑥

Garrett's Desert Inn 311 Old Santa Fe Trail ☎505/982-1851 or 1-800/888-2145, ⓦwww .garrettsdesertinn.com. Large, rather dull-looking two-story motel, but the rooms are well equipped and reasonably appealing, and the rates are good for such a convenient location. On-site pool and café, Nov–April ⑤, May–Oct ⑥

Hotel Santa Fe 1501 Paseo de Peralta at Cerrillos Rd ☎505/982-1200 or 1-800/825-9876, ⓦwww .hotelsantafe.com. Run by Picuris Pueblo (see p.177), this attractive, very comfortable adobe hotel on the edge of downtown is just within walking distance of the plaza, has its own good restaurant, *Amaya*, and stages free lectures by local experts. ⑥

Hotel St Francis 210 Don Gaspar Ave ☎505/983-5700 or 1-800/529-5700, ⓦwww.hotelstfrancis .com. Very tasteful hotel in the center of town, where the ambience is deliberately European rather than Southwestern, with individually themed, antique-furnished rooms that go for bargain rates at quieter times. The cheapest of all are rather too small, but a "standard" size room costs only a few dollars extra. Winter ⑤, summer ⑥

Old Santa Fe Inn 320 Galisteo St ☎505/995-0800 or 1-800/745-9910, ⓦwww.oldsantafeinn .com. This former Route 66 motor court has been totally revamped to become an appealing mid-range inn; many of its tasteful, Mexican-themed rooms have their own gas fireplaces. Breakfast included. Winter ⑤, summer ⑥

🏃 **Santa Fe Motel & Inn** 510 Cerrillos Rd ☎505/982-1039 or 1-800/930-5002, ⓦwww.santafemotel.com. To call this delightfully stylish yet inexpensive little adobe complex a "motel" barely does it justice; even its most conventional rooms are appealingly furnished, and some have their own kitchens, while there are also several gorgeous little casitas. The staff are very friendly, and the rates, which are great for such a quiet, central location, include a full cooked breakfast. Winter ⑤, summer ⑥

Santa Fe Sage Inn 725 Cerrillos Rd at Don Diego; ☎505/982-5952 or 1-866/433-0355, ⓦwww .santafesageinn.com. The most centrally located of the chain motels; large, clean, functional if not inspiring, and a mile or so from the plaza. Winter ④, summer ⑤

Expensive

Eldorado Hotel & Spa 309 W San Francisco St ☎505/988-4455 or 1-800/955-4455,

ⓦwww.eldoradohotel.com. Consummately stylish, tastefully tiled upmarket hotel, a very short walk west of the plaza, offering spacious, well-appointed rooms – many with wood-burning *kiva* fireplaces – plus a rooftop swimming pool, spa with massage therapies, espresso bar, top-flight restaurant, and gym. Winter ⑦, summer ⑨

Hilton of Santa Fe 100 Sandoval St ☎505/988-2811 or 1-800/336-3676, ⓦwww.hiltonofsantafe.com. Attractive luxury hotel, a short walk west of the plaza, which incorporates three rooms of the 250-year-old adobe Casa de Ortiz as B&B-style honeymoon suites; there's also a good restaurant and the airy *Chamisa Courtyard* cafe. Winter ⑦, summer ⑧; suites ⑨

Inn of the Anasazi 113 Washington Ave ☎505/988-3030 or 1-800/688-8100, ⓦwww .innoftheanasazi.com. No-expense-spared hotel just north of the plaza, with its interior modeled on an ancient cliff-dwelling and featuring a superb restaurant. It's a luxurious place to stay, although most rooms offer no views to speak of. Winter ⑧, summer ⑨

Inn & Spa at Loretto 211 Old Santa Fe Trail ☎505/988-5531 or 1-800/727-5531, ⓦwww .innatloretto.com. This upmarket hotel rising between the plaza and the river is an extraordinary spectacle, with its seven tiers, designed to resemble Taos Pueblo. Besides its opulent rooms and public spaces, the high-class *Baleen* restaurant, and the adjoining Loretto Chapel, it hosts one of the town's finest spas. ⑧

🏃 **La Fonda de Santa Fe** 100 E San Francisco St; ☎505/982-5511 or 1-800/523-5002, ⓦwww.lafondasantafe.com. Gorgeous old inn on the southeast corner of the plaza, marking the end of the Santa Fe Trail; guests have ranged from Kit Carson to John F. Kennedy. Built in 1920 to replace the century-old original, it features hand-painted murals and stained glass throughout and plenty of nooks and crannies where you can sit and soak up the atmosphere. Each lavishly furnished room is different, with some lovely suites in the newer *La Terrazza* section, and there's a good restaurant plus the *Bell Tower* rooftop bar. ⑨

La Posada de Santa Fe Resort & Spa 330 E Palace Ave ☎505/986-0000 or 1-800/727-5276, ⓦwww.laposadadesantafe.com. Downtown's most peaceful option, with individual adobe *casitas* (cottages) set in spacious gardens as well as ultra-modern spa rooms. Sizes and furnishings vary, but the smaller cottages offer excellent value. Winter ⑧, summer ⑨

B&Bs

Adobe Abode 202 Chapelle St ☎505/983-3133, ⓦwww.adobeabode.com. Small, playfully themed and very central B&B, with assorted folk-art-filled rooms both in a century-old house and in a separate newer building. **❼**

Alexander's Inn 529 E Palace Ave ☎505/986-1431 or 1-888/321-5123, ⓦwww.alexanders-inn.com. Romantic Victorian inn with barely a Southwestern touch in sight, offering ten rooms, not quite all of which are en-suite, plus five guest cottages which have their own separate kitchens and living rooms. Winter **❺**, summer **❻**

El Paradero 220 W Manhattan Ave ☎505/988-1177, ⓦwww.elparadero.com. Converted Spanish-era farmhouse near Guadalupe Street. The rooms, especially those that open onto the central courtyard, are relatively plain and simple and furnished with folk art; twelve are en-suite, while two share baths. Winter **❹**, summer **❺**

The Galisteo Inn 9 La Vega, Galisteo ☎505/466-8200 or 1-866/404-8200, ⓦwww.galisteoinn.com. This 300-year-old adobe hacienda, twenty miles south of central Santa Fe in the peaceful, historic Galisteo Basin, has been colorfully refurbished to become a high-end B&B inn. The two cheapest of its eleven rooms share a bathroom, the rest range up to considerable levels of opulence. The on-site *La Mancha* restaurant serves Mediterranean and Mexican flavored dinners Tues–Sat only. **❺–❾**

The Madeleine, 106 Faithway St ☎505/986-1431 or 1-888/321-5123, ⓦwww.madeleineinn.com. Large Queen Anne inn with a peaceful garden setting behind the cathedral. The mixture of rooms (not all en-suite) and cottages are all furnished with Pueblo and Mexican artworks. Shared bath **❹**, en-suite **❼**

The City

Although it can be almost impossible to distinguish genuine historic buildings from modern counterfeits, there's a definite, romantic continuity between today's Santa Fe and the Spanish settlement of four hundred years ago. The most enjoyable way to start a visit is just to wander the narrow streets of the old town. Before long you'll find plenty of specific diversions to capture your interest.

Once you've got your bearings in the **plaza**, the best places to get a sense of local history and culture are the four components of the Museum of New Mexico: the **Palace of the Governors** and the **Museum of Fine Arts** downtown, and the museums of **Indian Arts and Culture** and **Folk Art** a couple of miles southeast. There are also worthwhile private museums, in the form of the **Museum of Spanish Colonial Art** and the **Georgia O'Keeffe Museum**. Alternatively, set about exploring Santa Fe's distinct neighborhoods, such as the old **Barrio Analco** just southeast of downtown, home to the **San Miguel Mission**; the **Canyon Road** arts district, just beyond; and the funkier **Guadalupe Street** district to the west.

Santa Fe festivals

The first of the three major events in Santa Fe's annual calendar is **Spanish Market** (ⓦwww.spanishmarket.org), held during the last week in July, when examples of the traditional folk arts of Hispanic New Mexico are sold on the plaza and contemporary works are on sale in the Palace of the Governors.

Indian Market (ⓦwww.swaia.org) fills the plaza on the weekend after the third Thursday in August, attracting over 100,000 buyers and craftspeople from all over the world for the premier showcase of Southwestern Native American arts and crafts.

September's **Fiestas de Santa Fe** (☎505/988-7575, ⓦwww.santafefiesta.org), which take place over the weekend after Labor Day, have been held annually since 1712 to celebrate the Spaniards' return after the Pueblo Revolt. The ceremonial burning of *Zozobra* ("Old Man Gloom") in Fort Marcy Park on the Thursday prior, which kicks off the parades and processions, is not a Catholic tradition; it was invented in the 1920s by atheist American intellectuals.

▼ Albuquerque, Turquoise Trail & other Cerrillos Road motels

ACCOMMODATION

Adobe Abode	A
Alexander's Inn	I
El Paradero	N
Eldorado Hotel & Spa	B
Garrett's Desert Inn	L
Hilton of Santa Fe	D
Hotel Santa Fe	O
Hotel St Francis	G
Inn & Spa at Loretto	J
Inn of the Anasazi	C
La Fonda de Santa Fe	F
La Posada de Santa Fe	
Resort & Spa	H
Old Santa Fe Inn	K
Santa Fe Motel & Inn	M
Santa Fe Sage Inn	P
The Madeleine	E

The plaza

Santa Fe's central **plaza** has been the heart of the city since 1610, though the original rectangular parade ground of the Spanish garrison was twice as large as the neat, leafy square of today. As well as witnessing many turning points in New Mexican history – from the public hanging of three Indian "witchdoctors"

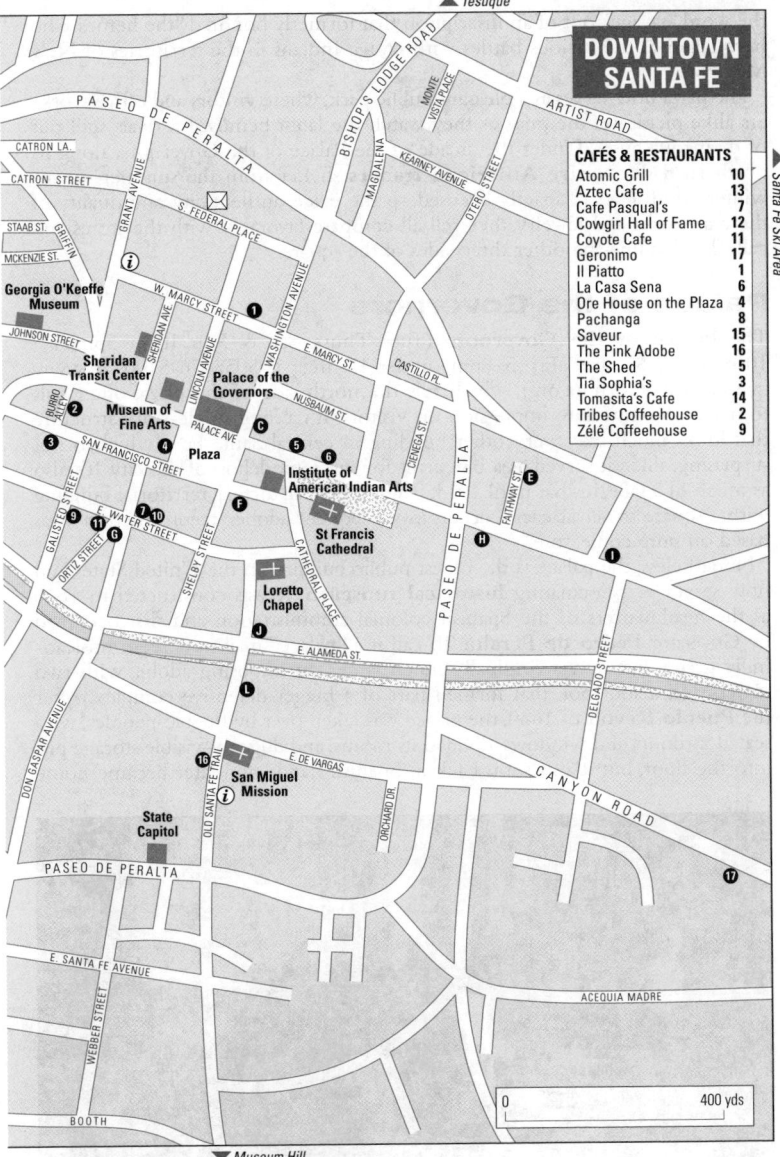

DOWNTOWN
SANTA FE

CAFÉS & RESTAURANTS

Atomic Grill	10
Aztec Cafe	13
Cafe Pasqual's	7
Cowgirl Hall of Fame	12
Coyote Cafe	11
Geronimo	17
Il Piatto	1
La Casa Sena	6
Ore House on the Plaza	4
Pachanga	8
Saveur	15
The Pink Adobe	16
The Shed	5
Tia Sophia's	3
Tomasita's Cafe	14
Tribes Coffeehouse	2
Zélé Coffeehouse	9

Georgia O'Keeffe Museum

Sheridan Transit Center

Museum of Fine Arts

Palace of the Governors

Plaza

Institute of American Indian Arts

St Francis Cathedral

Loretto Chapel

San Miguel Mission

State Capitol

▼ Museum Hill

in 1675 (which helped to trigger the Pueblo Revolt five years later, when Pueblo Indians filled the plaza to lay siege to the Palace of the Governors), to the nineteenth-century celebrations of Mexican independence and annexation by the United States – it served as journey's end for countless weary travelers on the Santa Fe Trail. Just how contentious the city's history remains is illustrated by the **obelisk** at the center of the plaza, where unknown hands have chiseled the word "savage" out of an inscription that formerly honored "the heroes who have fallen in the various battles with savage Indians in the territories of New Mexico."

The plaza now serves as a pleasant public park, where visitors and office workers alike picnic on the grass as they watch the latest bemused arrivals spill out of their tour buses. Under the arcade of the Palace of the Governors, along its northern flank, **Native American traders** shelter from the summer sun or winter wind. They're strictly licensed, so the price, authenticity, and quality of the craftworks and jewelry they sell all compare favorably with the stores and galleries that line the other three sides of the square.

Palace of the Governors

The **Palace of the Governors** (Tues–Thurs, Sat, & Sun 10am–5pm, Fri 10am–8pm; $7, free Fri 5–8pm; under-17 free; ☎505/476-5100, ⓦwww .palaceofthegovernors.org), which fills the north side of the plaza, often fails to make an immediate impression on visitors. It's a long single-story structure that looks much like every other building in central Santa Fe – which is not surprising, since it served as a blueprint for the remodeling of the city. It's also as much of a fake, in that until 1913, it was a typical, formal, territorial building with a square tower at each corner; its subsequent adobe "reconstruction" was based on pure conjecture.

Nonetheless, the palace is the oldest public building in the United States and now serves as a fascinating **historical museum**. It was constructed in 1610 as the headquarters of the Spanish colonial administration and first occupied by Governor **Pedro de Peralta**. To call it a "palace" may now seem misleadingly grand, but it was originally much larger, an imposing adobe, with two towers and a sod roof, that formed part of a bigger defensive complex. After the **Pueblo Revolt** of 1680, the palace was taken over by Pueblo peoples, who sealed its doors and windows, divided its rooms, and dug still-visible storage pits into the floor, but it was soon back in Spanish hands, and later became home

△ Native American crafts sellers outside the Palace of the Governors, Santa Fe

to first Mexican, and then American, governors of New Mexico. The American governor **Lew Wallace** wrote part of *Ben Hur* here during his term of office from 1878 to 1881. By then, the palace had turned Victorian, but its balustrades, elaborate windows, and wallpaper were removed after it ceased to be the official Governor's residence in 1909, when it was restored as part of the **Museum of New Mexico**.

Displays in its well-preserved interior are especially strong on Hispanic New Mexico, featuring a reproduction nineteenth-century chapel with a genuine 1830 altarpiece. Starting with the sixteenth-century Spanish *entrada* into the Southwest, the exhibits also convey that the frontier experience of New Mexico lasted for three centuries, far longer than anywhere else in the United States. In addition, the sensational Art of Ancient America collection boasts some wonderful Maya and Olmec artifacts as well as fascinating figures and urns from the lesser-known Nayarit culture, which if you didn't know better could easily convince you that the Chinese beat Columbus to central America by a millennium. Be sure to visit the well-stocked bookstore (which you can also access without paying admission), and to wander into the peaceful open-air courtyard beyond, where the restrooms still have their antique fittings, and the Palace Print Shop sells handprinted cards and booklets (daily 9am–4.30pm).

At the time of writing, construction work on a large extension, wrapped around the back of the palace complex, had been completed, but plans to use the new addition to expand the museum's displays had yet to bear fruit.

Museum of Fine Arts

On the northwest corner of the plaza at 107 E Palace Ave, Santa Fe's **Museum of Fine Arts** (Tues–Thurs, Sat, & Sun 10am–5pm, Fri 10am–8pm; $7, free Fri 5–8pm, under-17 free; ☎505/476-5072, Ⓦ www.museumofnewmexico .org) is housed in a particularly attractive adobe, with ornamental beams and a cool central courtyard. Erected in 1917, this was Santa Fe's first example of the "Pueblo Revival" school of architecture and remains unsurpassed to this day. It was also one of the few major art museums to be established by artists rather than educators or collectors, and it continues to concentrate on painting and sculpture by local artists. Since the opening of the separate Georgia O'Keeffe Museum, the Fine Arts Museum has focused more than ever on changing exhibits of contemporary work, though intriguing older pieces in the selections from the permanent collection displayed upstairs usually include an O'Keeffe or two. Once again, there's also a good shop selling Southwestern prints.

Georgia O'Keeffe Museum

Santa Fe's showpiece **Georgia O'Keeffe Museum** is a block northwest of the Museum of Fine Arts at 217 Johnson St (July–Oct Mon–Thurs, Sat, & Sun 10am–5pm, Fri 10am–8pm; Nov–March Mon, Tues, Thurs, Sat, & Sun 10am–5pm, Fri 10am–8pm; $8, free Fri 5–8pm; under-16 free; ☎505/946-1000, Ⓦ www.okeeffemuseum.org). Its ten galleries house the world's largest collection of O'Keeffe's work, including many of the desert landscapes she painted near **Abiquiu**, forty miles northwest of Santa Fe (see p.172), where she lived from 1946 until her death in 1986. In its permanent collection, housed in the first two galleries, some New York cityscapes make a surprising contrast among the more familiar sun-bleached skulls and iconic flowers. There's such an abundance of material that entire rooms can be set aside to concentrate on paintings of particular motifs, be it flowers or pink seashells, all characterized by O'Keefe's trademark close focus and voluptuousness. Most of the museum is given over to touring exhibitions devoted to differing aspects of O'Keeffe's work, typically on show for three to four months, so there's little guarantee as to which pieces may be displayed at any one time.

St Francis Cathedral

Santa Fe only acquired its first Catholic bishop in 1851, after New Mexico joined the United States and ceased to belong to the Mexican diocese of Durango. As described in Willa Cather's novel *Death Comes for the Archbishop*, the arrival of **Jean Baptiste Lamy** – a Frenchman, previously resident in Kentucky – threw the overwhelmingly Hispanic church in New Mexico into turmoil.

Lamy's most lasting achievement, **St Francis Cathedral**, now makes an unlikely spectacle, looming at the top of San Francisco Street two blocks east of the plaza. Eschewing adobe, the first church west of the Mississippi to be designated a cathedral was built of solid stone, between 1869 and 1886, in the formal – and, frankly, dreary – Romanesque style of France. To enable services to continue during construction, its walls rose over and around those of its eighteenth-century predecessor, which was progressively removed as rubble. The only part of that structure to survive, the side chapel of **Our Lady of the Rosary**, gives pride of place to a statue of the Virgin known as **La Conquistadora**. Originally brought from Mexico in 1625, she was credited by the Hispanic population of Santa Fe with facilitating both their escape from the Pueblo Revolt in 1680 and their subsequent reconquest of the province. The statue itself looks more like a Victorian doll than a venerated religious artifact – an effect enhanced by the practice of dressing it in different clothes at different times of the year. She is still paraded through the city each June, on the Sunday after Corpus Christi.

Institute of American Indian Arts Museum

The stimulating **Institute of American Indian Arts Museum,** 108 Cathedral Place (June–Sept daily 9am–5pm; Oct–May Mon–Sat 10am–5pm, Sun noon–5pm; $4, under-16 free; ☎505/983-8900, ⓦwww.iaiancad.org) is housed in a modern building – which naturally looks like adobe – facing the cathedral. Don't confuse it with the Museum of Indian Arts and Culture on the edge of town (see p.144); as they insist on telling you before you come in, "we're contemporary, not historical," and most of the artwork exhibited is likely to be less than a year old. Encompassing paintings, installations, collages, and mixed-media pieces, it's all a long way from the usual stereotyped images of Native American art. The sculpture garden is especially recommended.

Loretto Chapel

A block away from the plaza at the start of Old Santa Fe Trail, the **Loretto Chapel** (winter Mon–Sat 9am–5pm, Sun 10.30am–5pm; summer Mon–Sat 9am–6pm, Sun 10.30am–5pm; ⓦwww.lorettochapel.com, $2.50, ages 7–12 $2) was built for the Sisters of Loretto convent under the auspices of Archbishop

Lamy. Work was directed from 1873 onwards by Projectus Mouly, the 18-year-old son of the French architect responsible for St Francis Cathedral. In different accounts, he either drank himself to death, unable to take criticism of his design, or was killed by Lamy's cousin. Either way, when the chapel was completed it lacked any means of reaching the choir loft, twenty feet above the nave. Hence the legend of its **Miraculous Staircase**, an elegant wooden spiral – more of a spring, in a sense – which makes two complete 360° turns as it rises and was built without a single nail or any support at either the center or the sides. It's said to be the work of a mysterious carpenter who arrived in answer to the nuns' prayers and disappeared without demanding payment.

The story is more entertaining than the reality, however. The chapel is now deconsecrated and belongs to the upmarket *Inn at Loretto*, with direct access from the hotel, so it's always packed with irreverent tourists. What's more, the nuns found the staircase too frightening to climb, so they disfigured it by adding banisters. The whole thing is now propped up with a metal brace.

San Miguel Mission

Two blocks south of the Loretto Chapel, across the river along Old Santa Fe Trail, **San Miguel Mission** (Mon–Sat 9am–5pm, Sun 1.30–4pm; Mass on Sun at 5pm; $1, under-7 free) is said to be the oldest church in the United States to have remained in continuous use. The site is known to have been occupied in 1300 AD, while the church was built by Tlaxcalan Indians from central Mexico, who accompanied New Mexico's earliest Spanish settlers in 1610. Although its roof was destroyed during the 1680 Pueblo Revolt, parts of its graceful, sloping adobe walls survived. That said, before the church was "restored" to its current appearance in the nineteenth century, its external lines were much sharper than they are today; its rounded adobe look is not necessarily authentic.

Once inside, a hole in the floor beneath the altar reveals the foundations of an ancient pueblo, as well as the original steps of the sanctuary, while the pale green reredos, or altarpiece, above was painted in 1798 to frame a statue of San Miguel brought by missionaries from Mexico. The mission also holds a buffalo hide and a deerskin, painted with depictions of Jesus on the cross, which date from around 1630. In addition, its gift shop contains what's said to be the oldest bell in the US, cast in Spain in 1356.

The claims of a nearby adobe to be the **oldest house in the United States** are generally dismissed, though it too probably stands on the ruins of the former pueblo. This whole district, the **Barrio de Analco**, is now an appealing residential neighborhood, abounding in two-hundred-year-old houses.

Guadalupe Street

A few blocks southwest of the plaza, the stretch of **Guadalupe Street** that runs south from the tiny Santa Fe River has become the focus of one of Santa Fe's most characterful little districts, catering more to local students and artists than passing tourists. It centers around the small **Santuario de Guadalupe** at Guadalupe and Agua Fria (May–Oct Mon–Sat 9am–4pm, Nov–April Mon–Fri 9am–4pm; donation), a shrine built between 1776 and 1795 to mark the end of the Camino Real highway from Mexico City. Remodeling in the 1880s added an incongruous New England-style spire and tall windows, and the church was further restored to become a small museum of its own history to mark its (and the nation's) bicentennial in 1976. Since then it has hosted regular dance and music performances, with Mass celebrated only on the 12th of each month, but it's expected to revert to a more exclusively religious role in the near future.

In the late nineteenth century, the surrounding neighborhood became the point of arrival into Santa Fe for trains on the Atchison, Topeka & Santa Fe, and Denver & Rio Grande railroads. Old warehouses and small factory premises nearby have been converted to house stores such as a large branch of Borders, as well as art galleries and restaurants.

Canyon Road and Acequia Madre

Before Santa Fe ever existed, **Canyon Road**, which climbs a steady but shallow incline east from Paseo de Peralta, a few hundred yards east of San Miguel Mission, was an Indian trail that led to the pueblo at Pecos. Later it was the main route by which firewood from the mountains was brought to the city. Since the 1920s, however, it has been famous as the center of Santa Fe's **art colony**. It's now dominated by galleries and high-class stores – some of which are reviewed on p.151 – but even if you don't plan to buy anything it makes for an intriguing half-day stroll out from downtown.

At Canyon Road's far eastern end, the 1940 **Cristo Rey** church is the largest adobe building in the US and holds a huge carved-stone altarpiece from the long-demolished La Castrense chapel that once stood on the plaza. It's over three miles out, however, and most walkers prefer either to double back along Canyon Road at some earlier point, or return to town via **Acequia Madre**, one block south. The name of this ancient unpaved street literally means the "mother ditch"; following the course of the city's first irrigation canal, it's lined with beautiful adobe homes.

Museum of Indian Arts and Culture

The excellent **Museum of Indian Arts and Culture** (daily except Mon 10am–5pm; $7, under-17 free; ⊺505/827-6344, ⓦwww.miaclab.org) is on a raised plateau known as **Museum Hill**, two miles southeast of downtown, with extensive views of the hills and mountains that almost surround the city. It stands at the northern end of **Milner Plaza**, a tranquil landscaped area that also holds a good café (see p.148) and a giant bronze statue of an Apache Mountain Spirit Dancer.

The centerpiece of the museum, a permanent exhibition entitled **Here, Now, and Always**, provides comprehensive coverage of all the major Southwest tribes, including the 'O'odham, Navajo, Apache, Pai, Ute, and Pueblo peoples. It's intended as much for Native Americans themselves as for tourists – hence the taped messages at the start of the Ancestors section, which warn Navajo and Tewa visitors to proceed no further in order to avoid religiously proscribed contact with the world of their dead forebears. Myth and history are explained in copious detail, while contemporary realities are acknowledged in such forms as the inclusion of computer games, alongside music, architecture, and language, in the exhibit on the modern Apache way of life. Different parts of the exhibit focus on the topography of the Southwest, explaining how native peoples have thrived in such differing terrains as canyons, river basins, mesas, and deserts.

The museum also boasts a superb array of Native American pottery, from pristine thousand-year-old Ancestral Puebloan and Mimbres pieces up to the works of twentieth-century revivalists. María Martínez of San Ildefonso (see p.168) gets her own special section, Touched By Fire.

Museum of International Folk Art

The delightful **Museum of International Folk Art** (daily except Mon 10am–5pm; $7, under-17 free; ⊺505/827-6344, ⓦwww.moifa.org), across

Milner Plaza from the Indian Arts and Culture Museum, centers on the huge **Girard Collection** of paintings, textiles, and, especially, **clay figurines**, gathered from all over the world. These are arranged in colorful dioramas that include a Pueblo Feast Day, complete with dancing *kachinas* and camera-clicking tourists, and street scenes from countries such as Poland, Peru, Portugal, and Ethiopia featuring fabulously ornate churches and cathedrals. The sheer scale of the place has to be seen to be believed.

An equally eclectic array of folk art objects is on display in the Neutrogena Collection, where the specific artifacts displayed tend to change each year, but the emphasis is usually on textiles, ranging from an amazing leather fireman's jacket from nineteenth-century Japan to a Peruvian cloth fragment from 600 AD with uncannily contemporary designs. Pottery styles from all over the world are illuminated in the Cerámica y Cultura section, which traces Chinese influences on Mexican ceramics, Italian influences on Spanish pieces, and all sorts of other interesting combinations.

The traditional New Mexican crafts in the **Hispanic Heritage Wing** are also fascinating, and easily the match of anything in the new Museum of Spanish Colonial Art (see below). Alongside the expected *santos* (religious depictions of saints, whether carved figures or painted panels of wood), you'll encounter eerie skeletal wooden figures of "Death Personified," associated with the Penitente brotherhoods (see p.175). Excellent temporary exhibitions focus on more recent works such as *paños* – handkerchiefs decorated with religious and secular images in magic marker or pencil by often-anonymous prison inmates.

Be sure to call in at the museum **gift store**, which stocks some of the best souvenirs in town.

Museum of Spanish Colonial Art

Traditional Hispanic religious artworks like *retablos* (often-naïve painted images) and *bultos* (carved wooden statues of saints) are so pervasive in the iconography of Santa Fe that the creation of the **Museum of Spanish Colonial Art** (Tues–Sun 10am–5pm; $6, under-16 free; ☎505/982-2226, ⓦwww.spanishcolonial.org), in 2002 was long overdue. Immediately north of the museums on Milner Plaza, it makes a valiant attempt toward placing colonial art in a global context. Statuettes in its World of Art room are drawn from as far afield as Goa and Guatemala, with prime specimens including a figure of San (Saint) Roque daintily exposing his knee. Showcasing work by contemporary New Mexican schoolchildren, another gallery, El Futuro, shows that local traditions are in no danger of dying out. The whole collection is appealingly laid out in a former private home, one room of which replicates the living room of an eighteenth-century Spanish captain in New Mexico (see p.146) and reveals so-called "Santa Fe style" is more than a mere home decorating invention.

Sadly, however, given the abundance of Hispanic colonial art on display throughout Santa Fe, and in particular the superior exhibits in the neighboring folk art museum (see opposite), there may well be little here that isn't already familiar to you. In addition, being by definition largely vernacular, the pieces tend not to be of such exceptional quality as to merit a special trip.

Wheelwright Museum of the American Indian

The large, private **Wheelwright Museum of the American Indian** (Mon–Sat 10am–5pm, Sun 1–5pm; $2 donation; ☎505/982-4636, ⓦwww .wheelwright.org), the last of the four museums on Museum Hill, stands down a short slope behind the folk art museum. Designed to resemble a Navajo *hogan* or dwelling place (see p.80), its original purpose was to record Navajo sand paintings and ceremonials. These days, however, its permanent collection is seldom on show, and it concentrates instead on changing exhibitions, usually of contemporary art that's similar to what you'll see in the galleries in town. The Case Trading Post downstairs sells jewelry, rugs, and *kachinas* of very high quality, at very high prices.

Rancho de las Golondrinas

The **Rancho de las Golondrinas** (June–Sept Wed–Sun 10am–4pm; guided tours available by reservation, also in April, May, & Oct; $5, ages 13–18 $4, under-13 $2; ℡505/471-2261, ⓦwww.golondrinas.org), fifteen miles south of Santa Fe, was once a fortified *paraje* (or stopping place) on the Camino Real and is now run as a living history museum. To reach it, turn right onto Hwy-599 from exit 276 on I-25, then left onto Frontage Road, and then right onto Los Pinos Road, which you follow for three more miles.

The adobe farmstead at the center of the "Ranch of the Swallows" is thought to have welcomed the governor of New Mexico in 1698 and strongly resembles Pueblo architecture of the period. As La Cienaga Ranch, it belonged in the eighteenth century to Captain Manuel Delgado, whose living room is reproduced in the Spanish colonial art museum (see p.145), and who was wealthy enough to own a wardrobe of thirteen velvet, cashmere, and silk suits. Topped by a tall *torreon* or watchtower, the 200-acre farmstead incorporates a covered well and plenty of stables and livestock pens within its strongly defensive walls, while planted fields reach down to the river beyond. Other early Hispanic structures – many of them brought from elsewhere in New Mexico – include a watermill, a replica Penitente *morada* or chapel (see p.175), a smithy, and smaller farmhouses. The whole place is staffed by well-informed but unobtrusive "villagers" in period costume, with different sections maintained in the style of the seventeenth, eighteenth, and nineteenth centuries. On top of all that, it's an absolutely lovely spot in its own right, ranged across the meadows and woodland to either side of the river and bursting with wild flowers and sweet-smelling herbs.

The best time to visit Las Golondrinas is during one of the **theme** or **festival weekends** ($7), held on the first weekend of each month in summer and also on several other weekends as well. Festival season starts with the Spring Festival in June and ends with October's Harvest Festival. Whenever you come, however, the ranch provides an authentic evocation of New Mexico's early days.

Santa Fe ski area

Santa Fe's **ski area**, located within the Santa Fe National Forest, is just sixteen miles northeast of the city, off the winding and very scenic Hwy-475. Boasting a 12,053ft summit and 1703ft of vertical skiing, its 44 runs are usually open from late November until early April (daily lift tickets $49 full-day, $36 half-day; information on ℡505/982-4429 or ⓦwww.skisantafe.com). Skiing is suitable for all levels, and there is a ski/snowboard school as well as multiday programs and workshops for both children and adults. Equipment can be rented on site, but **no resort facilities** exist as such, although a café and a grill provide soups, burgers, sandwiches, and the like for hungry riders.

Pecos National Historical Park

A short way north of I-25, twenty-five miles east of Santa Fe, a long, low ridge in the heart of the Sangre de Cristo mountains served for over a thousand years as one of the most significant cultural rendezvous in the Southwest. Excavations during the 1920s so precisely chronicled changes in pottery and architecture as to become the model for all other such digs, and **PECOS NATIONAL HISTORICAL PARK** is thus famed as the "birthplace of Southwestern archeology."

Ninth-century Basketmakers (see p.566) were the first to inhabit this spot, but between 1450 and 1550, as the pueblo of **Cicuyé**, it was home to over two thousand people, including five hundred warriors. Protected behind four-story walls, it was a major **trading center**, where Pueblo peoples exchanged turquoise, axes, and shells from as far west as the Pacific for bison meat, hides, and wood for bows brought by plains nomads who camped outside the walls. As described on p.573, **Coronado** stayed here in 1541 and met a captive from the plains who lured his expedition east in search of the nonexistent gold of Quivira.

After Franciscan missionaries built a church alongside what they called **Pecos Pueblo** sixty years later, Spaniards too came to trade, but Apache and Comanche raids eventually forced Pecos into decline. Its last twenty survivors migrated 65 miles west to join Jemez Pueblo in 1838. Their descendants continue to elect a governor of Pecos Pueblo, and return for ceremonies. One such occasion took the form of a mass reburial in May 1999, after Jemez Pueblo had successfully campaigned that over two thousand skeletons be repatriated from Massachusetts, where they'd languished in Harvard's Peabody Museum and the Phillips Academy.

The whole Pecos story is well told in the **visitor center** (daily: summer 8am–6pm, winter 8am–5pm; ℡505/757-6414, Ⓦwww.nps.gov/peco; $3 per person), from where a mile-long trail loops onto the ridge itself. Much of the former pueblo area remains unexcavated, though some walls are exposed, and large buried structures are obvious everywhere. Beyond it, the trail leads around and through the high roofless walls of the **mission church**, stark in the bright sunlight and surrounded by the ruined *convento* buildings where its priests once lived. The *kiva* in the heart of the church was dug as a deliberate act of sacrilege during the Pueblo Revolt. Note that if you're pressed for time, you can park close to the church, and spare yourself the hike from the visitor center, by following the signs off the approach road to the "picnic area." Two additional parcels of the park, not currently open to visitors, incorporate the site of the **Battle of Glorieta Pass**. Fought on March 28, 1862, it was the turning point of the **Civil War** in the Southwest, when four thousand Union soldiers repelled three thousand Confederate invaders who had already briefly occupied Santa Fe.

Eating

Santa Fe has been renowned as one of America's most exciting places to **eat** since the early 1980s, when a stupendous feat of marketing managed to make dishes such as banana-crusted sea bass seem quintessentially Southwestern. There are scores of good restaurants to choose from – but that doesn't make it any easier to get a reservation at the latest hotspot in summer. In addition, the presence of so many tourists and the fact that their clientele is constantly changing make it hard for restaurants to develop much character. Nonetheless, there's some memorable dining to be had, and it doesn't have to be wallet-busting. The sheer inventiveness of the city's menus makes up for its shortage of ethnic alternatives (though you will find the odd adobe sushi bar here and there). Note that while most of the restaurants popular with tourists lie within easy walking distance of the plaza, there's a separate concentration of largely cheaper and more varied alternatives on and around **Guadalupe Street** to the southwest.

The **Santa Fe School of Cooking**, in the Plaza Mercado at 116 W San Francisco St (℡ 505/983-4511 or 1-800/892-4688, ⓦ www.santafeschoolofcooking .com), offers lunchtime classes in preparing Southwestern specialties, culminating in the opportunity to eat the lot (2hr 30min; $35–75 depending on ingredients).

Cafés and coffeehouses

Aztec Cafe 317 Aztec St ℡ 505/820-0025. Counterculture hangout in the Galisteo Street district, offering a travelers' notice board and a nice patio, as well as coffees, pastries, smoothies, light meals, and occasional live music. Mon–Sat 7am–7pm, Sun 8am–7pm.

Tribes Coffeehouse 139 W San Francisco St ℡ 505/982-7948. Spacious downtown gallery inside a mall that also serves espresso coffees, plus soup, salad, and sandwich lunches. Mon–Fri 7am–5pm, Sat & Sun 8am–3pm.

Zélé Coffeehouse 201 Galisteo St ℡ 505/982-7835. Central, roomy downtown spot that's a popular local rendezvous, serving pastries, omelets, sandwiches, and killer granola, plus great juices and smoothies, with some seating out on the sidewalk. Mon & Sun 7am–6.30pm, Tues–Sat 7am–10pm.

Inexpensive

Atomic Grill 103 E Water St ℡ 505/820-2866. Snack-oriented restaurant, with patio seating, one block south of the plaza, that squeezes burgers, sandwiches, and some reasonable pizzas for under $10 onto a menu that holds over fifty microbrews. Breakfasts such as *huevos rancheros* are served all day. Mon–Fri 7am–3am, Sat 9am–3am, Sun 9am–midnight.

mu du noodles 1494 Cerrillos Rd ℡ 505/983-1411. Largely, but not exclusively, vegetarian place near the hostel. Its Asian-flavored menu may not always be authentic, but its coconut-rich noodle dishes are invariably tasty. Dinner entrees cost $10–15. Daily except Sun 5.30–9pm.

Museum Hill Café 705 Camino Lejo ℡ 505/820-1776. Spacious cafe, poised on the plaza between the folk art and Indian arts museums southeast of town and featuring fabulous mountain views from its open-air terrace. Inexpensive but good sandwiches, burgers, pasta specials, and salads, and a large brunch on Sundays. Daily except Mon 9am–3pm.

Saveur 204 Montezuma St ℡ 505/989-4200. High quality cafe-cum-salad bar not far west of the State Capitol building, serving delicious cooked and raw specialties by the pound, and offering major discounts after 3pm. Mon–Sat 8am–4pm.

The Shed 113 E Palace Ave ℡ 505/982-9030. Typical Mexican-flavored local restaurant in a pleasant garden courtyard not far northeast of the plaza, which serves a steady diet of chile enchiladas, blue-corn tortillas, and even low-fat specialties. There's nothing over $9 on the lunch menu, but dinner is a little more expensive. Mon–Sat 11am–2.30pm & 5.30–9pm.

Tecolote Cafe 1203 Cerrillos Rd at Cordova ℡ 505/988-1362. This inconspicuous joint, a couple of miles south of downtown, is renowned for magnificent breakfasts – burritos, *huevos rancheros*, creamy eggs benedict, or shirred eggs (poached on a bed of chicken livers). Daily except Mon 7am–2pm.

Tia Sophia's 210 W San Francisco St ℡ 505/983-9880. Spicy, very inexpensive Mexican diner, a block or two west of the plaza. It's so popular with lunching locals that you can expect to have to wait in line. Daily breakfast specials available. Mon–Sat 7am–2pm.

Tomasita's Cafe 500 S Guadalupe St ℡ 505/983-5721. Lively, unpretentious place cranking out quick-fire platefuls of tasty Mexican food for under $12, plus margaritas by the pitcher, in the old railroad station. Mon–Sat 11am–10pm.

Moderate

Cowgirl Hall of Fame 319 S Guadalupe St ℡ 505/982-2565. Probably the liveliest restaurant in town, with lots of well-priced barbecued or grilled meat dishes – many of them costing under $10 – plus Mexican specialties and cookhouse-style stews. There's lashings of beer for adults and a play area for kids, plus live music most nights. Mon–Fri 11am–midnight, Sat 8.30am–midnight, Sun 8am–11pm.

Il Piatto 95 W Marcy St ℡ 505/984-1091. Reasonably priced and very good Italian restaurant, festooned with cooking utensils and serving pasta galore, such as a calamari spaghetti for $12, plus specials like grilled duckling for $15. Mon–Fri 11.30am–2pm & 5.30–9pm, Sat & Sun 5.30–9pm.

La Plazuela *La Fonda de Santa Fe*, 100 E San Francisco St ☏ 505/982-5511. Delightful, beautifully furnished and decorated Mexican restaurant in the heart of *La Fonda*, which feels like an open-air courtyard even though it's covered by a glass ceiling. All the usual Mexican dishes are on offer at reasonable prices, as well as some more expensive dinner entrees such as filet mignon, costing up to $35. The cooking is well above average. Mon–Fri 7–10.45am, 11.30am–2pm, & 5.30–10pm, Sat & Sun 7–10.45am, 11.45am–3pm, & 5.30–10pm.

Ore House on the Plaza 50 Lincoln Ave ☏ 505/983-8687. "Nueva Latina" restaurant whose menu ranges from $5 green chile stews or an $8 *ceviche* up to elaborate $28 dinner entrees such as rack of lamb. The location is unbeatable: from the tiled tables on its *ristra*-garlanded balcony, on the southwest corner of the plaza, you can watch all the life of the city. Daily 11.30am–10pm.

Pachanga 416 Agua Fria ☏ 505/988-5991. Very good, very stylish Mexican restaurant – far from an ordinary *cantina* – that's housed in the former convent of the Santuario de Guadalupe. Unusual and delicious specialties include an appetizer of spiced corn truffles with cheese for $10, and pit roasted lamb, or *barbacoa*, as an entree for $12; more conventional Mexican dishes, like *queso fundido* or *chimichangas*, cost under $10. Mon–Wed 5–9pm, Thurs–Sat 5pm–1am, plus lunch daily in summer only.

The Pink Adobe 406 Old Santa Fe Trail ☏ 505/983-7712. This 300-year-old adobe provides a deeply romantic setting for a hybrid New Mexican/Cajun menu that's not wildly inspiring. Open for lunch on weekdays only, with salads and sandwiches for around $9, and dinner nightly, when entrees such as *poulet Marengo Pink Adobe* – a half chicken cooked in wine and brandy – cost just over $20. Mon–Fri 11.30am–2pm & 5.30–10pm, Sat & Sun 5.30–10pm.

Expensive

The Anasazi Restaurant *Inn of the Anasazi*, 113 Washington Ave ☏ 505/988-3236. Very plush Pueblo-style hotel dining room, with an emphasis on organic ingredients. The eclectic dinner menu features entrees such as filet mignon encrusted with chiles and halibut with plantain, many of them priced at around $30; lunchtime specials serve as cheaper samplers. Daily 7–10.30am, 11.30am–2.30pm, & 5.30–10pm.

Cafe Pasqual's 121 Don Gaspar Ave ☏ 505/983-9340. Lovely, lively, and ever-innovative Old/New Mexican restaurant that serves top-quality food in an attractive tiled dining room, a block from the plaza. Among entrees like vegetarian *enchiladas* ($19) or chile-rubbed filet mignon ($34) are less orthodox specials such as black mussels steamed with lemongrass ($24). Appetizers include spicy Vietnamese squid ($12) and the delicious Pigs and Figs salad, made with bacon, figs, and mozzarella ($14). They also serve tasty (and large) breakfasts. Mon–Thurs 7am–3pm & 6–9.30pm, Fri & Sat 7am–3pm & 6–10pm, Sun 8am–2pm & 6–9.30pm.

Coyote Cafe 132 W Water St ☏ 505/983-1615. Celebrity chef Mark Miller's showcase restaurant, just off the plaza, remains as super-trendy as ever, though local gourmands feel the establishment's tendency to rest on its laurels has allowed previously high standards to drop significantly. The à la carte prices can be ferocious, with entrees like fried red-banana-crusted sea bass or cumin roasted duck breast at $26–40, though $10 for an appetizer like venison carpaccio with ahi tuna sashimi is not unreasonable. Lunch, especially at the rooftop *cantina* upstairs, is a better deal, while at times they also serve a prix-fixe set dinner for around $40. It's possible to plot a vegetarian course through the menu, if a *polenta torta* is worth $42 to you and you can cope with the cowhide seats. Daily 11.30am–9pm.

Geronimo 724 Canyon Rd ☏ 505/982-1500. With its separate small dining rooms, this converted ancient adobe is Santa Fe's most intimate upmarket restaurant, with a streetfront patio and a cool inner courtyard. The menu is mostly contemporary fusion with the odd Mexican touch, with dinner entrees consistently priced at over $20, but the $12 blue-cheese buffalo burger, topped with sensational spiced fries, makes a great lunch. Mon 6–9.30pm, Tues–Sun 11.30am–2pm & 6–9.30pm; closed for lunch in winter.

La Casa Sena 125 E Palace Ave ☏ 505/988-9232. Lovely courtyard restaurant, a block from the plaza; zestful Southwestern lunches, with entrees priced at $11–15, are the best deal – the $12 Sena Sampler plate is great value – though the $42 set dinners are consistently good. *La Cantina*, adjoining, is a little cheaper and its staff perform Broadway show tunes as they work. Mon–Sat 11.30am–3pm & 5.30–10pm, Sun 11am–3pm & 5.30–10pm.

The Old House *Eldorado Hotel*, 309 W San Francisco St ☏ 505/988-4455. The *Eldorado*'s signature restaurant unquestionably serves some of the finest food in town, a rich, meaty blend of Mediterranean and New Mexican traditions. Entrees like mustard-crusted rack of lamb cost around $30. The decor is elegantly Southwestern, though it's a bit too brightly lit to call romantic. Daily 5.30–10pm.

Nightlife and entertainment

Santa Fe has the range of **nightlife** you'd expect in a small city, though its **cultural scene** livens up during the summer tourist season. For full **listings** of what's going on, check the free weekly *Reporter* (Ⓦhttp://sfreporter.com) or the *Pasatiempo* section of Friday's *New Mexican*. The city runs its own ticket agency for local events (℡505/988-1234, Ⓦhttp://ticketssantafe.org).

Year round, musical and theatrical performances – by touring artists as well as local groups – are hosted downtown at the **Lensic Performing Arts Center**, a strikingly converted former movie theater at 211 W San Francisco St (℡505/988-7050, Ⓦwww.lensic.com). The much-anticipated **Santa Fe Opera** season runs from late June through August in a magnificent amphitheater seven miles north of town on US-84 (℡505/986-5900 or 1-800/280-4654, Ⓦwww.santafeopera.org); tickets are sold in the *Eldorado Hotel*, 309 W San Francisco St. July and August is also the time to catch the six-week **Santa Fe Chamber Music Festival** (℡505/983-2075 or 982-1890, Ⓦwww.santafechambermusic.org) and the **Shakespeare in Santa Fe** season, which for its first weekend takes place in the Lensic Center (see above), and then for three subsequent weekends is held alfresco in the courtyard of St John's College, 1160 Camino de la Cruz Blanca (℡505/982-2910). The Jean Cocteau Cinema, in the Guadalupe Street district at 418 Montezuma St (℡505/988-2711), shows interesting repertory **movies** and offers the best prospect in Santa Fe of finding fellow Bohemians to admire your beret.

Some of the most atmospheric places to **drink** in town are in the old hotels – the downstairs *La Fiesta* lounge and rooftop bar in *La Fonda* on the plaza are good bets – but otherwise conventional bars are surprisingly few and far between.

Bars and clubs

Catamount Bar 125 E Water St ℡505/988-7222. Downtown bar with plenty of microbrews on tap and live rock or blues most nights.

El Farol 808 Canyon Rd ℡505/983-9912, Ⓦwww.elfarolsf.com. Historic bar-cum-restaurant that serves Spanish tapas to a musical accompaniment ranging from blues to flamenco.

Evangelo's 200 W San Francisco St ℡505/982-9014. The only good bare-bones bar in easy walking range of the plaza, with a pool table and a jukebox, plus occasional live music.

Second Street Brewery 1814 Second St ℡505/982-3030. This lively brewpub is too far from the center to attract many tourists, which is half the reason it's so popular with young locals; there's also live music several nights a week.

Swig 135 W Palace Ave ℡505/955-0400. Very classy and expensive downtown DJs-and-martinis bar that also serves tasty Asian-style tapas.

WilLee's Blues Club 401 S Guadalupe St ℡505/982-0117, Ⓦwww.willees.com. Busy nightclub in the Guadalupe Street district that's open for live blues and jazz nightly.

Shopping

Secure in the knowledge that many visitors come specifically to **shop**, central Santa Fe is bursting with (generally high-priced) stores and galleries. The galleries alone turn over more than $200 million each year. The city remains largely the preserve of independents, however; few of the international names that move in seem to last long. Don't expect to make an early start; most stores and galleries don't open until 10am.

Almost everyone agrees that the best place to buy **Indian crafts**, such as silver and turquoise **jewelry**, is from the Native American sellers outside the Palace of the Governors, ideally during August's Indian Market (see p.137). If you're interested in **Hispanic folk art**, take a look at the gift store in the Museum of International Folk Art before you shop downtown.

The two main **malls**, neither of which is particularly large or interesting, are the **Villa Linda Mall**, southwest at 4250 Cerrillos Rd, and the **De Vargas Mall**, ten minutes' walk northwest of the plaza at N Guadalupe Street and Paseo de Peralta; there's also a large Borders **bookstore** at 500 Montezuma in the Guadalupe Street District.

Central Santa Fe

Andrea Fisher Fine Pottery 100 W San Francisco St ☎505-986-1234. Museum-like gallery, a block west of the plaza, that specializes in Native American pottery and boasts one of the nation's largest selections of Maria Martinez pieces.

Artesanos 222 Galisteo St ☎505/983-1743. Lots of tin mirrors and glassware, toys and *piñatas*, *ristras* (strung chiles), furniture, Mexican ceramics, and a room filled with tiles of all sizes.

Collected Works Bookstore 208B W San Francisco St ☎505/988-4226. Very central bookstore that's a great source for books on New Mexican history and culture.

Design Warehouse 101 W Marcy St ☎505/988-1555. For a change from *ristras* and Mexican tin, browse through this funky colorful assortment of stuff from soap to notebooks to lamps – all the best in contemporary design, at affordable prices.

Jackalope 2820 Cerrillos Road ☎505/471-8539. A Southwestern legend for its pile-'em-high philosophy, this sprawling complex, centered on a disused church well out from downtown, completely takes the mystique out of purchasing folk art. However, the rock-bottom prices for its mostly Mexican and Peruvian arts, crafts, and downright junk make it the ideal spot to pick up inexpensive souvenirs.

Mira 101A W Marcy St; ☎505/988-3585. Tongue-in-cheek religious kitsch (Virgin Mary snow globes and the like), plus antique clothing and oddities, at very inexpensive prices. One block north of the plaza.

Móntez Gallery 125 E Palace Ave ☎505/982-1828. Friendly little store near the plaza, specializing in good-quality antique Hispanic religious art, plus attractive and very inexpensive reproductions.

Posters of Santa Fe 111 E Palace Ave ☎505/982-6645 or 1-800/827-6745, ⊛www.postersofsantafe.com. *The* place to find the perfect visual image of Santa Fe, whether it's a fine-art print by Gustave Baumann or Georgia O'Keeffe,

a vintage cowboy or rodeo girl illustration, or a simple card or notebook.

Canyon Road

Hahn Ross Gallery 409 Canyon Rd ☎505/984-8434, ⊛www.hahnross.com. Enjoyable fine art gallery, run by a children's book illustrator and specializing in very bright paintings that blend the fantastic with the naïve.

Judy's Unique Apparel 714 Canyon Rd ☎505/988-5746. Theatrical, feminine clothing store, where cowboy style meets vintage boudoir, with lots of opulent velvets and silks and also antique jewelry.

Kania-Ferrin Gallery 662 Canyon Rd ☎505/982-8767. Native American antiques such as baskets and rugs, antique Mexican *ex-votos*, and even carved canoe prows from New Guinea, all at prices that run into thousands of dollars.

Kevin O'Farrell Hats 725 Canyon Rd ☎505/989-9666. A great array of Western hats, some adorned with fancy trimmings, some plain and understated.

Nambe Showroom 924 Paseo de Peralta ☎505/988-5528. Factory outlet at the foot of Canyon Road with a large stock of Nambe ware – shiny, futuristic table- and ovenware made from a local alloy that looks like silver but has unique heat-retaining properties.

Nathalie 503 Canyon Rd ☎505/982-1021, ⊛www.nathaliesantafe.com. Little of the Western wear here would be at home on the range – it's all a little too chic and decorative for life on horseback – but it'll still look great when you wear it back home.

Pachamama 223 Canyon Rd ☎505/983-4020. Unusually cheap Hispanic crafts, mainly from Mexico, including *retablos*, statues, and lots of tin.

Silver Sun 656 Canyon Rd ☎505/983-8743, ⊛www.silversun-sf.com. Native American arts and crafts, with a stand-out collection of beautiful turquoise jewelry.

South to Albuquerque

Travelers embarking on the sixty-mile drive southwest from Santa Fe to Albuquerque have a choice of two routes. The **interstate**, I-25, is fast and reasonably scenic, but for atmosphere and Old West charm it doesn't begin to match the **Turquoise Trail**, which squeezes between the Sandia and Ortiz mountains to the east.

The interstate route

Commuters may not give it a second thought, but the hour-long journey from Santa Fe to Albuquerque on **I-25** represents a major transition. When it drops down the escarpment known as **La Bajada**, twenty miles from downtown Santa Fe, the interstate leaves the Rocky Mountains and enters the desert. To the north of La Bajada, the Rio Grande was traditionally known as the **Rio Arriba**, or Upper River, and cuts through a deep rocky gorge; to the south, the **Rio Abajo** or Lower River meanders across a broad floodplain.

La Bajada also marks the dividing line between the northern and southern **pueblos**. Below it, the interstate runs through three separate Indian reservations. In 1996, when state legislators seemed poised to outlaw the Indian gaming that has finally brought the pueblos a degree of prosperity, pueblo authorities retaliated by threatening to place **toll-gates** on the interstate at every boundary.

Cochiti Pueblo

COCHITI PUEBLO, ten miles west of the interstate on Hwy-16, at the foot of La Bajada – and a total distance of around 24 miles from Santa Fe – is home to a thousand Keresan-speaking Indians who trace their ancestry back to the cliff dwellers of Bandelier (see p.160). In the Keresan language, its name is *Kotyete*, meaning "stone *kiva*." Visitors have free access to the pueblo in daylight hours, and while you may find some residents selling crafts outside their houses, there are no formal stores. The mission church of **San Buenaventura** still incorporates vestiges of its original adobe form, as built in 1628, but it has been greatly modified over the years, and the contemporary frescoes within are not all that enthralling.

A Cochiti potter, Helen Cordero, fashioned the first ceramic "**storyteller**" here in 1946. Each depicting a mother with up to thirty children, these rank among New Mexico's best-selling souvenirs and are made by over two hundred Indians, including around fifty Cochiti.

In the 1970s, the tribe leased part of its land to the federal government to create **Cochiti Lake**, by constructing what was then the world's largest earthen dam across the Rio Grande. Though the dam itself is something of an eyesore, the lake now attracts a million recreational users each year and has a campground as well as a small **visitor center** (Mon–Fri 8.30am–3.30pm, Sat 10am–2pm, Sun noon–4pm; ☎505/465-0307). A planned residential community went bankrupt, however, and the loss of Cochiti agricultural land has left the pueblo skeptical about further "developments."

Kasha-Katuwe Tent Rocks National Monument

What was previously a little-known corner of Cochiti Pueblo was designated in 2001 as New Mexico's newest national monument, **KASHA-KATUWE TENT ROCKS NATIONAL MONUMENT** (daily April–Oct 7am–7pm, Nov–March 8am–5pm; $5 per vehicle, national park passes accepted; ☏505/761-8768, Ⓦ www.nm.blm.gov), jointly administered by the Bureau of Land Management and the pueblo. Kasha-Katuwe means "white cliffs" in Keresan and erosion in the remarkable landscape has sculpted a canyon wall of pale, soft volcanic rock into cone-like shapes that range out to almost one hundred feet tall. Only a few are free-standing pinnacles; most are "hoodoos" that poke from the hillside. It's nothing like as dramatic as, say, Utah's Bryce Canyon (see p.450), but it makes an interesting half-day venture off the interstate.

To reach the monument, follow signs off the interstate for Cochiti Pueblo. Just after a left turn signed to the actual pueblo, turn right at a painted water tower, onto Tribal Route 92, which becomes Forest Service Road 266. A 4.5-mile, unpaved spur road dead-ends at a parking lot, from which the easy two-mile **Cave Loop Trail** circles Peralta Canyon to pass the main formations. While it's not quite long or hard enough to count as a hike, take it seriously enough to wear decent shoes and carry water. If you want more exercise, follow the **Canyon Trail** at the furthest point of the loop, which climbs steeply through a narrow slot canyon for another mile to reach Vista Point, which grants an overview of the whole ensemble.

Santo Domingo Pueblo

Six miles south of Cochiti, **SANTO DOMINGO PUEBLO** is the largest Keresan pueblo, with a population approaching five thousand. For many centuries, its people have been renowned for their **jewelry-making**, and especially necklaces of delicate shell and turquoise *heishi* beads. By some accounts, Santo

△ Kasha-Katuwe Tent Rocks National Monument

Domingans taught the art of silversmithing to the Navajo in the nineteenth century, and they're now prominent among the Native American vendors in Santa Fe.

Santo Domingo doesn't have a visitor center or formal opening hours, but as well as a adobe church with a lovely painted facade, its central plaza holds several stores selling jewelry, pottery, and other crafts, and also a simple café, *Rosetta's Trading Post* (☎505/465-2504).

San Felipe Pueblo

SAN FELIPE PUEBLO, the next of the southern pueblos, stands another six miles downriver from Santo Domingo. Until 1250 AD, the San Felipeans were a single tribe with their fellow Keresan speakers now known as the Cochiti. Their subsequent migrations only ended in 1693, when they settled here for good after the Pueblo Revolt.

Daytime visits are always permitted here, but photography is not. On the pueblo's **feast day**, May 1, its plaza, worn down over the generations into a bowl-shaped depression, is thronged with dancers performing a day-long corn dance. The tribe runs a large **casino** and **travel center** both of which house restaurants, at exit 252 off the interstate.

Algodones

Stretching languidly beside the river five miles southwest of San Felipe, the village of **ALGODONES** makes a tranquil base for visits to both Santa Fe and Albuquerque. *Hacienda Vargas*, 1431 El Camino Real (☎505/867-9115 or 1-800/261-0006, ⑭www.haciendavargas.com; ⑤), is one of New Mexico's most relaxing rural **B&B**s, set in a lovely adobe trading post. All of its seven separate rooms have en-suite facilities, in some cases including hot tubs.

Bernalillo and Coronado State Monument

BERNALILLO, five miles south of Algodones, is an unexciting satellite community at the edge of Albuquerque's urban sprawl, principally noteworthy as the site of **CORONADO STATE MONUMENT** (daily except Tues 8.30am–5pm; $3; ☎505/867-5351). In a spectacular setting a mile west of the interstate, on the west bank of the Rio Grande and with fabulous views of the Sandia Mountains to the east, the monument preserves what remains of the ancient pueblo of **Kuaua**. The Spaniards knew this region as **Tigüex**, and described it as a "broad valley planted with fields of maize and dotted with cottonwood groves"; Francisco de Coronado spent the winter of 1540 in the vicinity, though there's no evidence it was at this precise spot. Kuaua was then a thriving community of well over a thousand rooms; now it's a ruin, of which a few eroded adobe walls have been exposed by archeologists. The central feature is a restored *kiva*, decorated with vivid reproductions of its multicolored **murals**. The faded originals, preserved in the visitor center, include scenes of a rabbit hunt – the animals are still abundant in the undergrowth by the river. In Pueblo art, rabbits often represent the **moon**, as Pueblo peoples see a "rabbit in the moon" rather than a "man in the moon." The monument is especially ravishing from late October onwards, when the fall colors along the riverbank are unbelievable.

While Bernalillo itself holds no **accommodation** options, the state's largest and most luxurious resort, the *Hyatt Regency Tamaya*, is just six miles up Hwy-44 (US-550) at Santa Ana Pueblo; for a full review, see p.166. Otherwise, the state maintains a large but attractive riverfront **campground** near the monument entrance (℡505/867-5589; $8-11), where rates depend on what degree of comfort you require.

Bernalillo does boast one of New Mexico's finest **restaurants**. At the south end of town, east of the river – and, being close to exit 240 off I-25, an easy evening excursion from Albuquerque – the *Range Cafe*, 925 Camino del Pueblo (Sun–Thurs 7.30am–9pm, Fri & Sat 7.30am–9.30pm; ℡505/867-1700), is a brightly decorated hall that serves three meals daily. Huge Mexican-style appetizers like *chimichangas* cost $9 or less and strongly chile-flavored main dishes, like the fabulous quesadillas garnished with blue-corn chips, cost a little more. It's a very popular spot, and since reservations are only accepted for large parties, you can expect a wait. Another top-quality restaurant, the *Prairie Star*, stands only a mile or so northwest of the monument on Santa Ana Pueblo lands; see review on p.166.

Across the Rio Grande, just downhill from the monument entrance, the enormous Jackalope outlet (℡505/867-9813) is utterly unabashed about selling "Folk Art by the Truckload"; if you're looking for a large, cheap **souvenir**, and you haven't already sampled their Santa Fe store (see p.151), this is the place to come.

Rio Rancho

If you're unpleasantly surprised by the volume of traffic climbing US-550 past Coronado State Monument, that's probably because you've never heard of **RIO RANCHO**, reached via a turn-off a short way further up the hill. This ever-expanding community was founded in the early 1960s, after the AMREP Corporation purchased the Koontz cattle ranch for residential development. Rio Rancho's population has mushroomed since it was incorporated as a city in 1980, with retirees being joined by Albuquerque commuters, and Intel making it the site of the world's largest chip-manufacturing plant. Rio Rancho has even overtaken Santa Fe to become New Mexico's third largest city, with a population now exceeding seventy thousand. Although it holds half a dozen chain motels, however, there's no reason for tourists to visit.

Sandia Pueblo

SANDIA PUEBLO, between Bernalillo and Albuquerque, dates back to around 1300 AD and was visited by Coronado in 1540. *Sandía* is the Spanish word for watermelon; differing stories have it either that the Spaniards mistook the squashes they saw growing here for watermelons, or they thought that at sunset the mountains to the east resembled segments of pink watermelon. The village's Tiwa name – **Nafiat**, meaning "dry or sandy place" – seems more appropriate to its dusty central plaza. After it was destroyed in 1692 by Spaniards returning after the Pueblo Revolt, many of its inhabitants took refuge with the Hopi, far to the west, and the settlement was not rebuilt for fifty years.

Today the main preoccupation of the three-hundred Sandians is protecting their sacred sites in the nearby mountains from blundering hikers. Being so close to Albuquerque, they're also among the chief beneficiaries of the legalization of Indian gaming. The success of the 24-hour **Sandia Casino**, alongside the interstate, has enabled the tribe to open the striking **Sandia Resort** (℡505/798-3930 or 1-877/272-9199; ⑥), a luxury hotel and conference center with five restaurants and full spa facilities.

Other Sandia concerns include the *Bien Mur Trading Post* **crafts center** and **restaurant**, on Tramway Road (Mon–Sat 9am–5.30pm, Sun 11am–5pm;

505/821-5400 or 1-800/365-5400, Ⓦ www.bienmur.com), which commands views of a **buffalo preserve** that holds the tribe's herd of buffalo.

❷ The Turquoise Trail

The **Turquoise Trail** – less glamorously known as **Hwy-14** – is a modern name for what may be one of the oldest thoroughfares in North America. It connects **mines** along the eastern flanks of the Sandia Mountains with the settlements of the Rio Grande Valley. In the last two hundred years, these mines have yielded considerable quantities of copper, coal, and even gold, but **turquoise** production dates back perhaps ten times as far. Long before the coming of the Spaniards, traders carried local stone all over the Southwest and down into Mexico, and wealthy pueblos lined the nearby streams.

Until the recent influx of artists, craftworkers, and small-scale entrepreneurs, communities along the trail had dwindled to become little more than **ghost towns**, but now funky **Madrid**, in particular, makes an appealing day-trip destination for visitors to Santa Fe.

Cerrillos

The northernmost Turquoise Trail town, **CERRILLOS**, is just over twenty miles south of Santa Fe, reached simply by continuing south on Cerrillos Road, which becomes Hwy-14, for fifteen miles beyond its intersection with I-25. The dusty rolling hillocks that surround it – the "little hills" of its name – hold one of the world's greatest concentrations of **turquoise**.

Archeologists have estimated that ninety percent of the fabled turquoise treasures seized by the Spaniards from the Aztec capital of Tenochtitlán were crafted using stone from this unprepossessing spot. With basic tools, prehistoric miners scooped a hundred thousand tons of rock from **Mount Chalchihuitl**, two miles northeast, leaving a cavern 300 feet wide and 200 feet deep. Early Spanish settlers may have forced the Indians to work for them; it's said that a mine collapse around 1680, which killed up to eighty Indians, helped to precipitate the Pueblo Revolt. By the time the Spaniards returned, the Indians had deliberately hidden many of the shafts, and tales of fabulously wealthy "**lost mines**" still abound.

Today's Cerrillos, nestled amid the giant cottonwoods along the bank of the broad but usually dry Galisteo River, has changed little since its last boom in the 1890s. Mining not only turquoise but gold, silver, copper, and lead, it was briefly rich enough to support eight daily newspapers and numerous hotels and saloons. In 1988, its unpaved streets and falsefront wooden buildings made it an ideal location for the bratpack Western flick *Young Guns*.

There's still a bit of life in the old town; as recently as 1983, robbers made off with $500,000 worth of gold from the nearby Ortiz Mines. Tourists, however, have to content themselves with the **Casa Grande Trading Post, Turquoise Mining Museum, and Petting Zoo** (daily 9am–5pm; $2; Ⓣ505/438-3008), an endearing shop-cum-museum that offers a random assortment of old bills and letters, porcupine quills, rattlesnake skins, and petrified wood, plus the chance to pet a llama or pull on a string to make a plaster Indian hammer on a rock.

Madrid

Between 1869 and 1959, the village of **MADRID** (pronounced *MAD-rid*), three miles south of Cerrillos, made a good living from mining **coal**. The hills here are unusual in that they hold deposits of both bituminous (soft) and anthracite (hard) coal, which in the early days was hauled by wagon as far as St Louis and later was consumed in vast quantities by the Santa Fe Railroad. Tunnels ran directly beneath the main street, while a mine shaft that burrows straight into the hillside can now be seen in the **Old Coal Mine Museum** at the south end of town (daily: May–Sept 9am–5.30pm, Oct–April 9.30am–4.30pm; $4). The rest of the museum consists of several barns stuffed with ancient junk like obsolete X-ray machines and decrepit Model "T" Ford trucks, plus the Engine House Theater, which stages the moustache-twirling **Madrid Melodrama** on summer weekends (performances May–Sept Sat 3pm & 7pm, Sun & holiday Mondays 3pm; Oct Sat & Sun 3pm; $10; ☎505/435-3780, ⓦwww.madridmelodrama.com).

After the mine closed down, the whole town was auctioned off piecemeal, and the straggle of wooden cottages to either side of the narrow highway have progressively been taken over by New-Agey newcomers. Several hold genuinely interesting crafts and antiques stores; if you're close enough to home to carry **furniture**, there are some real bargains to be had.

One attractive old mining home, *Java Junction* (☎505/438-2772, ⓦwww .java-junction.com; ❹), houses a **coffeeshop** downstairs, serving a limited array of bagels and pastries, and a **B&B** apartment upstairs, with kitchen and bathroom. *Mama Lisa's Ghost Town Kitchen* (☎505/471-5769) serves good salads and daily specials, while the lively *Mine Shaft Tavern*, in front of the museum (☎505/473-0743), claims to have the longest **bar** in New Mexico and stays open late every night, with live **music** on weekends. Burgers, fajitas, and the like are available at lunchtime daily and until 8pm on Friday and Saturday.

Golden

In 1825, **GOLDEN**, fifteen miles south of Madrid, was the site of the Wild West's first-ever gold rush. It has yet to revitalize to any great extent, and you might hardly notice that it's there as the highway races down its former main street. Look out, however, for the tumbledown **adobe church** on the hill at the north edge of town, which served the mining camp of **Tuerto** and has preserved its pioneer graveyard.

Sandia Crest and Cedar Crest

Ten miles south of Golden, the **Sandia Crest Scenic Byway** branches west from Hwy-14, to climb for eight tortuous miles up to the razorback ridge atop the Sandia Mountains. From the mile-high **observation deck** at road's end, you can survey the sprawling city of **Albuquerque**, with the Rio Grande flowing in from the north, and also look east across the endless plains, beyond the Ortiz Mountains. The adjacent *Sandia House* sells tasteless snacks and useless gifts. A fee of $3 is charged for day-use of the nearby trails, but most visitors stay for barely ten minutes before heading back down the hill; there's no through route to Albuquerque.

In winter, **skiers** exploring the eastern Sandia slopes base themselves down below, in **CEDAR CREST** at the foot of the Scenic Byway. *Elaine's*, 72 Snowline Estates (☎505/281-2467 or 1-800/821-3092, ⓦwww.elainesbnb .com; ❺), is a very comfortable B&B set in spacious grounds, while the *Sandia Mountain Hostel* (☎505/281-4117; ❶) offers dorm **accommodation** at $14 per bed, and *Kokopelli's Kafe* (☎505/281-2002) serves all **meals**. The Turquoise Trail ends six miles south at the intersection with I-40, which sweeps the final dozen miles west to Albuquerque through **Tijeras** – "Scissors" – **Canyon**.

West of Santa Fe

The **Jemez Mountain Trail**, which loops through the mountains west of Santa Fe, can be enjoyed as a long day's excursion or a roundabout route down to Albuquerque. Communities along the way range from modern **Los Alamos** – the top-secret "town that never was" – to the ancient dwellings of **Bandelier National Monument**; the scenery encompasses mountain meadows and desert canyons.

The **Pajarito Plateau**, the dominant feature of the landscape, was created just over a million years ago, when colossal **volcanic eruptions** buried four hundred square miles of land beneath a thousand feet of ash. This solidified into the easily eroded rock known as **tuff**, which has been eaten away by wind and rain ever since to form an intricate tangle of deep gorges and forested mesas. "Pajarito" means "little bird" in Spanish; it's a direct translation of the Tewa *tsirege*, the name of an abandoned local pueblo. Only one road climbs onto the plateau, **Hwy-502**, which branches west from US-84 near Pojoaque Pueblo, fifteen miles north of Santa Fe.

Visitors to both Los Alamos and Bandelier should take care to avoid the **rush-hour** traffic that heads up Hwy-502 until around 9am and comes back down again from 3pm onwards.

Los Alamos

The wealthy enclave of **LOS ALAMOS**, eighteen miles up Hwy-502, is not so much a town as the overgrown campus of the **Los Alamos National Laboratory**. Home during World War II to the **Manhattan Project**, which first developed the atomic bomb, it has remained the leading US center for the research and development of nuclear weapons and is now run by the University of California.

Although many homes and other facilities were destroyed by the Cerro Grande **forest fire** in 2000, casual tourists will barely spot a trace of the damage. Nonetheless, it remains a confusing place to visit. The layout – sprawling along several "fingers" at the edge of the Pajarito Plateau, separated by deep canyons – is bizarre in the extreme, and the fact that most of the complex is off-limits to the public doesn't help. Most visitors call in at one of the two local **museums**, then head on to Bandelier.

The **Bradbury Science Museum**, at Central Avenue and 15th Street (Tues–Fri 9am–5pm, Sat–Mon 1–5pm; free), presents the authorized version of the laboratory's history. Opponents of nuclear proliferation are given space to state their case – there are forcefully argued rival displays on the decision to drop atomic bombs on Japan – but overall the line is extremely gung-ho. In the section entitled "Strengthening Global Security," you're invited to press buttons to light up those countries on a world map that "might pose a threat to stability." The central exhibits are full-sized 1940s replicas of "Little Boy," which devastated Hiroshima, and "Fat Man," dropped on Nagasaki. The **visitors' book** is fascinating enough to have been published, while the excellent Otowi Station **bookstore**, alongside, is open daily for varying but consistently longer hours than the museum.

Los Alamos Historical Museum, close to the visitor center at 1921 Juniper St (winter Mon–Sat 10am–4pm, Sun 1–4pm; summer Mon–Sat 9.30am–4.30pm, Sun 11am–5pm; free), is housed in the former dining hall of Los Alamos Ranch School. As well as displays on the school and local geology and prehistory, it too covers the bomb in some detail. Exhibits range from a 360° aerial photo of Hiroshima to classic examples of atomic kitsch, such as a picture of the commander of the 1946 tests at Bikini cutting a mushroom-cloud shaped cake, some earrings made with "atomsite" fused glass from the Trinity site, and an A-bomb-shaped lamp.

Practicalities

Los Alamos' **visitor center** is a couple of blocks west of the Bradbury Museum, at 2132 Central Ave (Mon–Fri 9am–5pm, Sat 9am–4pm, Sun 10–3pm; ☎505/662-8105 or 1-800/444-0707, ⓦ www.visit.losalamos.com).

> ### The Town That Never Was: Los Alamos and the Bomb
>
> In 1942, the American and British governments decided to amalgamate the nine research efforts then racing to build the **atomic bomb**. Albert Einstein had suggested the idea to President Roosevelt three years earlier, and a team led by Enrico Fermi was achieving promising results in a laboratory beneath a disused football stadium in Chicago. The search was on for a suitable location in a sparsely populated area, away from the sea, with a reasonable year-round climate. **J. Robert Oppenheimer**, the scientific chief of the **Manhattan Project**, had backpacked before the war in New Mexico. He recommended the Los Alamos Ranch School, an exclusive private school on the Pajarito Plateau, and the site was duly bought out. When its final class graduated in February 1943, the scientists moved in.
>
> Working in the utmost secrecy – the words "Los Alamos" were forbidden, and newcomers were told merely to report to 109 Palace Avenue in Santa Fe – scientists made the bomb a reality in just over two years. The first successful test took place at the **Trinity Site**, two hundred miles south (see p.221), on July 16, 1945. Three weeks later, bombs were dropped on the cities of **Hiroshima**, on August 6, and **Nagasaki**, August 9; a complete Japanese surrender followed immediately.
>
> For Oppenheimer, who described the development of the bomb with a quotation from the *Bhagavad Gita*, "I am become Death, the shatterer of Worlds," Los Alamos had served its purpose, and the laboratory could now close. Instead, as the Cold War set in, its energies were devoted toward the construction of the **H-Bomb**. Though security was more paramount than ever, ideologically motivated spies such as **Klaus Fuchs** and **David Greenglass** (whose sister and her husband, **Ethel** and **Julius Rosenberg**, were later executed) soon betrayed Los Alamos' secrets to the Russians. Paranoia grew to the point that employees were instructed to "Watch Your Liberal Friends," and Oppenheimer himself was barred by his successor Edward Teller from access to privileged information.
>
> The gatehouse on the road up from Santa Fe that denied outsiders access to Los Alamos was finally removed in 1957, and the ownership of private property on the plateau was allowed in 1962. The laboratory business is still booming, spending well over half its billion-dollar annual budget on the research and development of nuclear weapons. While the lab has also drilled a 12,000-foot hole to "mine" heat from hot rocks deep in the earth and worked on the Human Genome Project, which aims to map the entire DNA structure of human beings, its public image remains firmly linked with nuclear experimentation – recent revelations concerning spies operating on behalf of China have hardly helped. Constantly changing plans for the disposal of its radioactive waste are among New Mexico's hottest political issues.

As well as a couple of upmarket **motels** that cater largely to visiting scientists – the *Best Western Hilltop House*, 400 Trinity Drive (☎505/662-2441 or 1-800/462-0936, @www.bestwesternlosalamos.com; ➎), and *Holiday Inn Express*, 2455 Trinity Drive (☎505/661-1110; ➍) – the town has a handful of **B&Bs**, such as *Adobe Pines B&B*, 3496 Orange St (☎505/661-8828, @www.losalamoslodging.com; ➍). The *Blue Window Bistro*, 813 Central Ave (☎505/662-6305), is the best-value place to **eat** in town, with sandwich lunches and tasty dinner entrees for under $15, while the *Cafe Allegro*, 800 Trinity Drive (☎505/662-4040; closed Sun), serves a mean espresso.

Bandelier National Monument

Long before the scientists descended upon Los Alamos, the "finger canyons" of the Pajarito Plateau were home to Native Americans. At **BANDELIER NATIONAL MONUMENT** (daily: winter 8am–4.30pm; summer 8am–6pm; $10 per vehicle; ☎505/672-3861, @www.nps.gov/band), ten miles south of Los Alamos – a fifty-mile drive from Santa Fe – **Ancestral Puebloans** enlarged natural cavities in the soft volcanic rock to create **cliff dwellings**, and also built free-standing pueblo communities beside the streams on the valley floors. Set amid delightful woodlands and framed against the rose-pink canyon walls, Bandelier's intriguing remains provide an ideal introduction to New Mexico's prehistoric roots. The **visitor center**, at the bottom of a narrow switchback road down from Hwy-4, gives an excellent overview of the monument, with displays of pottery and jewelry, models of the ruins, full-scale reconstructions of pueblo interiors, and century-old photographs of Indian life.

Although the Ancestral Puebloans are often said to have "disappeared" around 1300 AD, there's little mystery about where they went. Bandelier is a "missing link," occupied between roughly 1150, at the time the Four Corners region was being abandoned, and 1550, when many of today's pueblos were established. As successive itinerant groups streamed in, perhaps fleeing drought or invasion, they may have merged here to create the modern Pueblo culture. The peoples of **Cochiti** and **San Ildefonso** in particular trace their ancestry back via Bandelier to Mesa Verde, and it was a Cochiti guide who led amateur archeologist **Adolph Bandelier** to this site in 1880.

Frijoles Canyon

The monument's major sights are concentrated along a 1.5-mile loop trail through **Frijoles Canyon**, which remains open daily from dawn to dusk. From the visitor center, the trail leads swiftly to the remains of **Tyuonyi** on the canyon floor, a circular, multistory village of four hundred rooms, of which only the ground floor and foundations survive. Its name means "place of agreement," and it's seen as a center for trade and storage, common to the **Keresan**-speaking peoples, whose pueblos lay to the south, and the **Tewa** speakers to the north. Despite the apparently large number of dwellings, the total population in the canyon is estimated to have reached a maximum of between five and seven hundred. Local obsidian was traded as far as the Dakotas and the Mississippi. Tyuonyi may have still been in use when Coronado's soldiers became the first Spaniards to penetrate the Southwest (see p.572), though they didn't reach this far.

A side path from Tyuonyi leads up to dozens of **cave dwellings**, their rounded chambers scooped into the warmer, south-facing wall of the canyon.

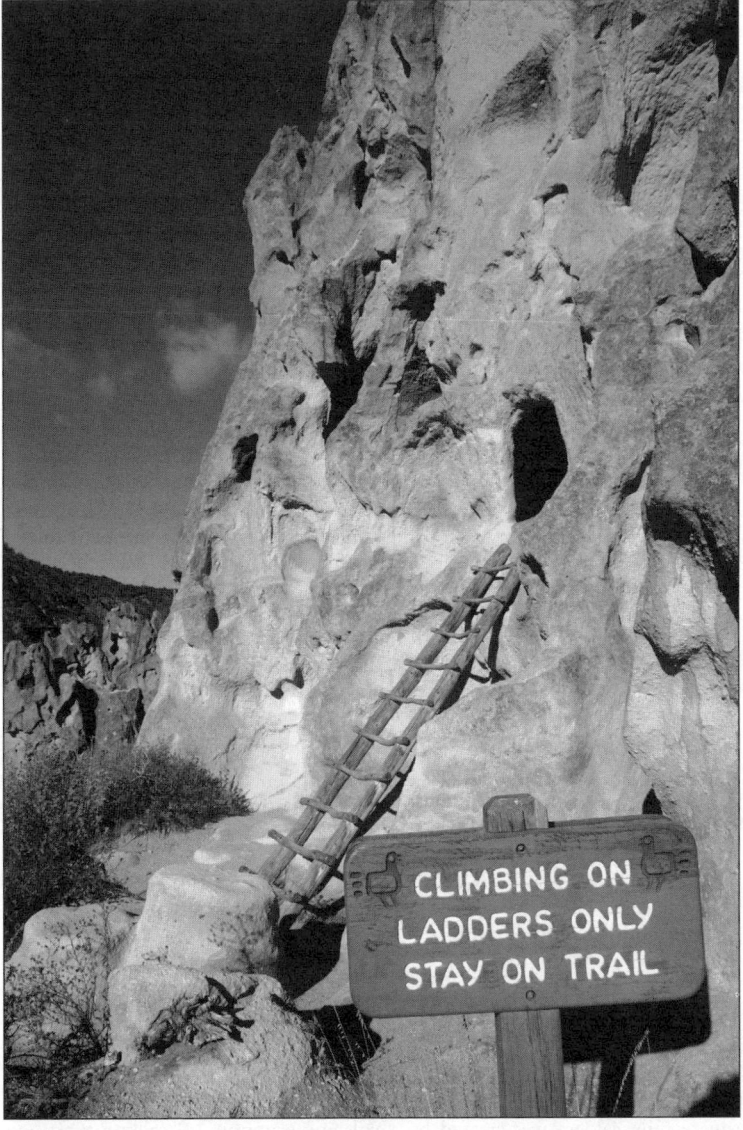

△ Cave dwellings at Bandelier National Monument

(As artificial creations, technically these are "cavates" rather than caves.) Ladders and walkways mean visitors can scramble up to, and even enter, some of them, to peer out across the valley.

The main trail continues to the **Long House**, an 800ft-long series of two- and three-story houses built side by side against the cliffs. Though most of the upper stories have collapsed to expose the plastered walls, you can still see the mortised holes that held up their pine roof beams or *vigas*. Above these are rows of petroglyphs and pictographs, mostly depicting figures and abstract symbols.

Though the main trail doubles back to the visitor center, keen hikers can follow the stream for another half-mile, to the point where **Alcove House** nestles in a rocky overhang 150 feet above the canyon floor. Reaching it entails climbing three hair-raising ladders, as well as steep stairways hacked into the crumbling rock. At the top, you can see by the *viga*-holes that the cave once held several structures, but it is now bare except for a reconstructed *kiva*, set down in its sloping sandy floor, and entered by ladder.

Another trail drops south from the visitor center, coming out after a mile and a half at the **Lower Falls** – at their best in late spring – and then reaches the Rio Grande in another ten minutes. It's also possible to hike up into the backcountry above Frijoles Canyon; a very demanding trek of 6.5 miles each way leads to two very weathered but still remarkable **stone mountain lions**, carved by ancient sculptors. The trail begins at the visitor center.

Tsankawi

The small, separate **Tsankawi** section of Bandelier lies a dozen miles northeast of the monument visitor center, just off Hwy-502 as it climbs from the Rio Grande valley up to Los Alamos. Visits consist of an hour-long loop hike onto and around an isolated mesa-top that holds the almost indiscernible ruins of an ancient pueblo. If the site itself is disappointing, however, the trail is not; following the same route once used by the Ancestral Puebloans, it's worn waist-deep into the soft tuff in places, and includes a number of prehistoric "stairways." Assuming you're happy to negotiate a couple of short ladders, you're also rewarded with lovely views down into the valley, as well as glimpses of the mysterious Los Alamos laboratories closer at hand.

Practicalities

Snacks and sodas are available at the monument visitor center, but there's no **accommodation** at Bandelier itself apart from the very pleasant *Juniper Campground*, just off Hwy-4 up on Frijoles Mesa (first-come, first-served; $10; information on T505/672-3861, ext 517). Tsankawi, however, stands close to the tiny community of White Rock, which holds the gleaming white *Hampton Inn*, 124 Hwy-4 (T505/672-3838 or 1-888/813-0912, Wwww .hamptoninnlosalamos.com; ❹).

Valles Caldera National Preserve

Hwy-4 climbs west of Bandelier and Los Alamos, bursting unexpectedly out of the forests to skirt the long rim of **Valle Grande**. This 500-foot-deep, 176-square-mile caldera was created by a volcanic eruption 1.2 million years ago, and is still considered active. Its wide meadows form a lush counterpoint to the dry-as-dust terrain of most of New Mexico, and the basin was much prized by ancient peoples both as prime hunting territory and as a source of obsidian, a volcanic glass that can be chipped to form ultra-sharp blades.

The national government purchased the huge Baca Ranch here for $101 million in 2000, in what Bill Clinton called "one of the most significant federal land acquisitions in recent history," to create the 89,000-acre **VALLES CALDERA NATIONAL PRESERVE**. The basic aim is to run it as a self-sustaining wildlife reserve – it's home to a large elk herd in summer, as well as several rare bird species – funded through commercial activities. You don't need a permit to walk the one-mile trail that leads from a roadside pullout on Hwy-4, but to take a longer hike, you have to reserve and pay a $10 fee at least 24 hours in advance (☎1–877/851-8946, ⓦwww.vallescaldera.gov). The altitude of 8750 feet makes all physical activity demanding, and lightning strikes are such a constant threat, thanks to the almost daily afternoon thunderstorms, that all hikers are advised to leave the area by 2pm. In practice, the preserve remains primarily a drive-through experience.

Spence's Hot Spring

Perhaps the most obvious vestiges of the volcanic past in the vicinity of Valles Caldera are the numerous **hot springs** that bubble from beneath the ground. Among the most irresistible is **SPENCE'S HOT SPRING**, on a promontory above the Jemez River between mileposts 24 and 25 on Hwy-4, half an hour out of Los Alamos. Half a dozen waterfall-connected pools provide a range of temperatures to suit anybody, from the high 90°sF in the lower pools to a blissful 104°F at the top; local custom calls for bathing suits on weekend nights, otherwise it's clothing optional. To get there, cross the river over a fallen tree and then climb up the canyon, keeping to the left for about a ten-minute walk uphill.

Cuba

When Hwy-4 dips south, Rte-126 continues a northwest way to the lonely farming community of **CUBA**, but the road is actually a dirt mountain one that can close in winter. Cuba is good for an overnight pitstop if you're on your way to Mesa Verde (p.94) or Chaco Canyon (p.112), but you're best off approaching it from the south, via US-550 (sometimes still referred to as Hwy-44). Of the three **motels**, the *Frontier* (☎505/289-3474; ❶), at the north end of town across the Rio Puerco, is the most salubrious. Alongside it, the friendly *Frontier Cafe*, 6478 US-550 (☎505/289-3130), is smarter than it looks from the outside and makes an excellent stop for a Mexican lunch or dinner: a delicious *posole* stew, with chile and *sopaipillas*, costs under $5. Set in the hills five miles out of town, the appealing *Circle A Ranch* **hostel** (PO Box 2142, Cuba, NM 87013; May to mid-Oct; ☎505/289-3350, ⓦwww.circlearanch.info; ❶–❸), is an adobe *hacienda* that offers dorm beds for $20 as well as private rooms with and without baths.

Jemez Springs

Five miles downhill from Spence's Hot Spring, Hwy-4 runs past the bizarre (and very smelly) **Soda Dam**, where calcified deposits all but block the Jemez River, to enter **JEMEZ SPRINGS**. This appealing hamlet, where the river is lined by glowing cottonwoods and flows between high canyon walls that flame gold and red, was once the site of the Towa-speaking pueblo of **Giusewa**, the "Place of the Boiling Waters." The most active of its hot mineral springs was enclosed in the 1870s by a **bath house**, where you can enjoy a thirty-minute soak for $10, or a massage for $37 (℡505/829-3303 or 1-866/204-8303, ⓦwww.jemezspringsbathhouse.com).

The substantial shell of the mission church of **San Jose de los Jemez**, built by Franciscans in 1621 only to be destroyed almost immediately by Navajo raiders, is now preserved in **Jemez State Monument** (daily 8.30am–5pm; April–Oct $3, Nov–March $2). Walls that once held bright frescoes are now just stumps, but the principal doorway has been reconstructed. Most of the ruins that surround it were convent outbuildings rather than pueblo dwellings, although you can still spot the locations of several subterranean *kivas*. Jemez Springs' religious tradition continues to this day, as it's home to large Christian monasteries as well as a Zen center.

Practicalities

Jemez Springs offers several small-scale **accommodation** options, including the beautiful river-view *Dancing Bear B&B*, 314 San Diego Drive (℡505/829-3336 or 1-800/422-3271, ⓦwww.dancingbearbandb.com; ➎–➏), and the equally lovely *Cañon del Rio–Riverside Inn*, 16445 Hwy-4 (℡505/829-4377, ⓦwww.canondelrio.com; ➏), which has an outdoor hot tub. The *Laughing Lizard Cafe* (℡505/829-3108, ⓦwww.thelaughinglizard.com; ➍) serves coffee and full meals on a nice terrace above both highway and river, and offers four inexpensive motel-style rooms, while the late-opening *Los Ojos Restaurant and Saloon* (℡505/829-3547) has food, pool tables, and cheap beer.

Jemez Pueblo

After Giusewa Pueblo was abandoned in 1630, its inhabitants built **JEMEZ PUEBLO**, fifteen miles downstream of Jemez Springs. There they participated in the Pueblo Revolt of 1680, sacking their church and killing its priest; when the Spaniards returned, they briefly retreated northwest, establishing cultural and family links with the Navajo that endure to this day. They also assimilated the last twenty survivors of Pecos Pueblo in 1838 (see p.147). Jemez now has a population of around 3000 and is the only surviving Towa-speaking pueblo. Its people successfully resisted plans to develop a geothermal power plant in the Jemez mountains in 1982.

Home for the Jemez Indians is a gorgeous, lush canyon floor, surrounded by low cliffs of rich red rock. In honor of that scenery, they call themselves **Walatowa**, "people of the canyon," and that's also the name of their village. The pueblo itself is only open to visitors on feast days such as August 2, November 12, and December 12. An impressive **visitor center**, three miles north on Hwy-4 at **Red Rock** holds displays on their history, can arrange group tours, and sells a wide range of crafts (daily 8am–5pm; ℡505/834-7235 or 1-877/733-5687, ⓦwww.jemezpueblo.org). On weekends between April and mid-October, the **Jemez Pueblo Open Air Market**, also at Red Rock, sells food and artwork.

Zia Pueblo

Hwy-4 ends at US-550 at San Ysidro. Just to the south, reached by a short spur road, is little **ZIA PUEBLO**, best known for the **sun symbol** that features on

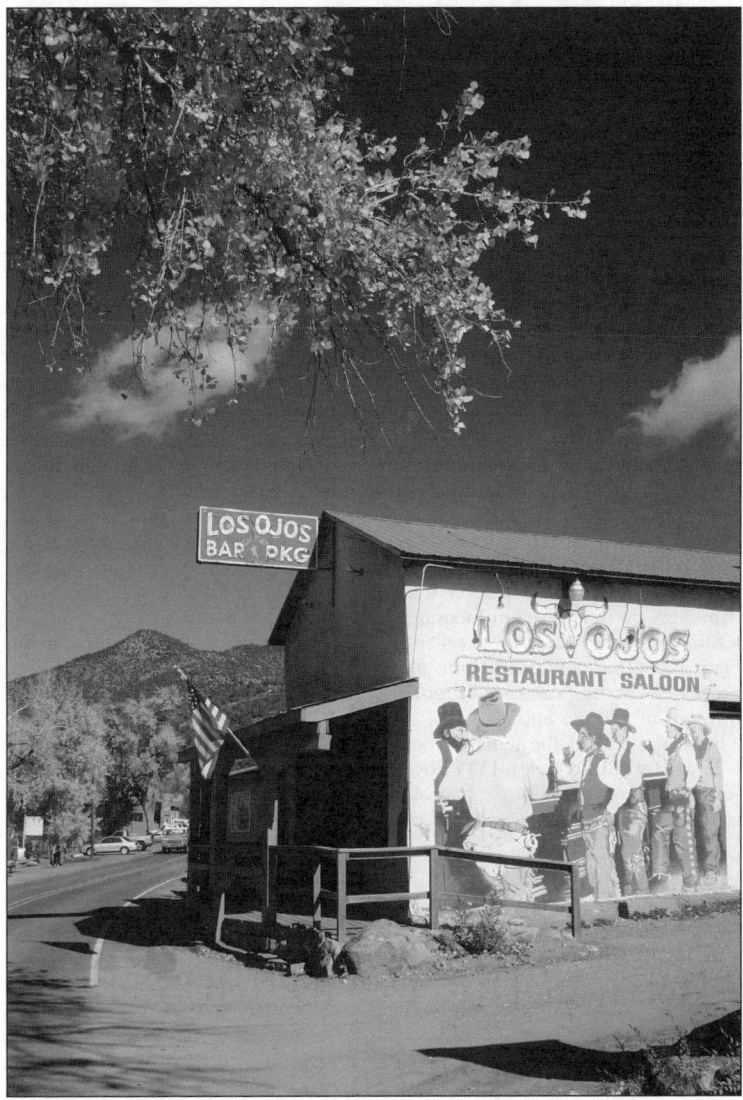

△ Saloon in Jemez Springs

New Mexico's flag and license plates. Now 750 strong, the Zia Indians have occupied this spot since the sixteenth century, when they were visited by early Spanish explorers; they've long been campaigning to receive royalties for the use of their sun symbol, but so far with no luck. They have, however, earned money in recent years from allowing movie crews to shoot on their land; both *All The Pretty Horses* and *Ghosts of Mars* were filmed here. The pueblo overlooks the Jemez River a dozen miles further downstream.

There's little reason for outsiders to visit Zia, but the tribe does maintain a small **visitor center** not far off the highway (Mon–Fri 8am–noon & 1–5pm; free; ℡505/867-3304).

Santa Ana Pueblo

Zia's closest neighbors, at the equally small **SANTA ANA PUEBLO**, eight miles southeast along US-550, are also Keresan speakers, who moved in after the Pueblo Revolt. Until the 1990s, they were relatively reclusive and did little to welcome visitors, but since the advent of Indian gaming they've experienced an extraordinary transformation. Profits from the successful **Santa Ana Star Casino** (Ⓦ www.santaanastar.com), beside the highway not far north of Coronado State Monument (see p.154), which holds four restaurants and a large bowling center, have enabled the tribe to branch out in several new directions. These include two top-quality golf courses, 22 soccer fields, and several crafts outlets.

The most conspicuous development of all, however, has been the creation of New Mexico's most prestigious **luxury resort**, built as a joint venture between the pueblo and the Hyatt Corporation. As well as 350 opulent rooms and suites, the *Hyatt Regency Tamaya Resort & Spa*, at 1300 Tuyuna Trail (℡505/867-1234, Ⓦ www.hyatt.com; May–Oct ❽, Nov–April ❼), features three swimming pools, a fitness center and spa, four restaurants, a championship golf course, and its own stables and hot-air balloon. It also holds the Tamaya Cultural Center (daily 9am–5pm), a free museum focusing on the people of Santa Ana.

Also on Pueblo land, the excellent *Prairie Star* restaurant, 1000 Jemez Canyon Dam Rd (Tues–Sun 5.30–9pm; ℡505/867-3327) resides in an adobe home northwest of the casino and offers contemporary Southwestern cuisine at upwards of $20 per entree.

From the end of the Jemez Mountain Trail, when US-550 (Hwy-44) meets I-25 at **Bernalillo** (see p.154), downtown Albuquerque is a sixteen-mile drive south – though the suburbs start almost immediately – while Santa Fe is forty miles northeast, a drive described on p.152 onwards.

From Santa Fe to Taos: the northern pueblos

The quickest route between Santa Fe and Taos follows **US-84** as far as the Rio Grande, then continues northeast beside the river on **Hwy-68** – not that the switch from one road to the other, at **Española**, is discernible to the naked eye. US-84 passes through the heartland of the **northern pueblos**, a cluster of tiny Tewa-speaking villages that have survived for over five hundred years. The most interesting for casual visitors are **Nambe**, near the impressive **Nambe Falls**, and **Pojoaque** beside the highway, where a museum and visitor center

provide a quick taste of Pueblo culture. Serious collectors can head instead for
San Ildefonso and its famous pottery.

Tesuque Pueblo

Nine miles north of Santa Fe, west of US-84, and overlooked by the remarkable
Camel Rock, the traditional community of **TESUQUE PUEBLO** studiously
turns its back on the city. Its name means "place of the cottonwood trees,"
and its people were the first to strike against the Spaniards during the Pueblo
Revolt. There's no visitor center, but the tribe operates the **Camel Rock
Casino** (℡505/984-8414 or 1-877/989-3600, Ⓦwww.camelrockcasino.com),
which has a good buffet restaurant, and also holds an open-air colorful weekend
flea market, selling everything from clothing to furniture to hot sauce (March
to late-Nov Fri–Sun).

▲ Chama

THE PUEBLOS AND THE HIGH ROAD

0   10 miles

Taos Pueblo

Taos

Ghost Ranch

Ojo Caliente

Orilla Verde Recreation Area

Pilar

Picuris Pueblo

Embudo

Abiquiu

Las Trampas

Sipapu ski area

Alcalde
San Juan Pueblo

THE HIGH ROAD

Española   Chimayó   Truchas

Cordova

Santa Clara Pueblo

Puyé Cliff Dwellings

Pojoaque Pueblo

Los Alamos   San Ildefonso Pueblo   Nambe Pueblo

Tsankawi   Nambe Falls

Valle Grande

Santa Fe ski area

Tesuque Pueblo

Bandelier National Monument

Rio Grande

Cochiti Dam

Santa Fe

Kasha-Katuwe Tent Rocks National Monument

Cochiti Pueblo

Rancho de las Golondrinas

Pecos

Pecos National Historical Park

▼ Albuquerque   ▼ Turquoise Trail   ▼ Las Vegas

Pojoaque Pueblo

POJOAQUE PUEBLO, twelve miles out of Santa Fe on US-84, was once one of the largest pueblos, but its original settlement was abandoned after a smallpox epidemic in 1895, and in terms of land it's now the smallest in the state. Though some ceremonial activities have resumed in the last twenty years, most of the tribe's attention is devoted to running a busy roadside complex just east of US-84. Its **visitor center** covers the history and culture of all the Tewa peoples (Jan–March Mon–Sat 9am–5.30pm, Sun 10am–4pm, April–Dec Mon–Sat 9am–6pm, Sun 9am–4pm; ℡505/455-3460) and sells a wide range of Native American artifacts. The **Poeh Museum** (Tues–Sat 9am–5pm, ⓦwww .poehmuseum.com; $1) concentrates on craftworks from the northern pueblos. Displays are little different from those in the visitor center's store. On summer Saturdays and Sundays, the museum is the venue for **dance** performances at 11am and 1pm. The complex includes the *O Eating House* restaurant.

The Cities of Gold **casino**, alongside the museum (℡505/455-3313, ⓦwww .citiesofgold.com), which contains another restaurant, has proved so lucrative that the tribe was able to buy the nearby Santa Fe Downs racetrack, adjoining the pueblo, in order to close it down. Across from the casino, the *Cities of Gold* **hotel** offers 124 comfortable but unexciting rooms (℡505/455-0515 or 1-877/455-0515; ⑥).

Nambe Pueblo

The most beautifully sited of the northern pueblos is **NAMBE PUEBLO**, reached by turning right on Hwy-503 just beyond Pojoaque. Keep going up the hillside beyond the Sacred Heart church, and after a total of three verdant miles, you'll come to a turn on the right. Three road signs in quick succession here suggest that Nambe lies five miles, six miles, and eight miles further on. In fact, the actual pueblo is 1.5 miles along and is not visible from the road; in any case, apart from a large *kiva*, not much remains in its old plaza area. The signs actually refer, respectively, to a tribal ranger station that controls access to the triple-decker **Nambe Falls**; to the falls themselves; and to the reservoir that stands above them, reached by a separate fork of the road.

Seeing Nambe Falls requires a steep five-minute hike from the far end of the picnic area and campground just beyond the ranger station; the admission fee is $5, while a still photography permit costs $10 extra (daily March, Sept, & Oct 7am–7pm; April and May 7am–8pm; June–Aug 6am–8pm). At the top of the climb, you can admire the waters as they tumble through a jagged cleft in the surrounding red rocks, but the view is somewhat marred by the colossal concrete dam that towers above. There's no way to reach the foot of the falls, let alone swim there. **Camping** back at the picnic area (March–Sept only) costs $20 per night.

San Ildefonso Pueblo

Five miles west of Pojoaque, before Hwy-502 crosses the Rio Grande and climbs up to Los Alamos, **SAN ILDEFONSO PUEBLO** is best known as the former home of potter **María Martínez**. From 1919 onwards, together with her husband Julian, she was responsible for revitalizing the Pueblo ceramic tradition; the finest collection of the pair's work is in Taos' Millicent Rogers Museum (see p.187).

The people of San Ildefonso trace their ancestry back to Mesa Verde, by way of the Pajarito Plateau. In 1694, when the Spaniards returned after the Pueblo Revolt, refugees from San Ildefonso and its neighbors held out on a nearby mesa, **Black Rock**, until they were starved down.

San Ildefonso now consists of two plazas, one of which holds a replica of its original mission church. Individual artisans sell pottery from their own homes – look out for signs – or you can buy from the selection in the **Tewa Visitor Center** when you pay your pueblo admission fee (Feb–Oct daily 8am–5pm; Nov–Jan Mon–Fri 8am–5pm; ☏505/455-3549; $3 per vehicle, plus 50¢ per person; $10 photo permit, $20 video). The nearby **Tribal Museum** (Mon–Fri 8am–4pm; no additional charge) holds some of Martinez's original works.

Santa Clara Pueblo and Puyé Cliff Dwellings

Five miles north of San Ildefonso, or five miles west of Española, **SANTA CLARA PUEBLO** is known to its 1500 inhabitants as Kapo, "where the roses grow near the water." They're thought to have migrated here during the sixteenth century from their previous home in Santa Clara Canyon, eleven miles west. There they inhabited two tiers of cliffside "apartments," plus a large mesa-top pueblo, at the edge of the Pajarito Plateau. That ancient settlement remains remarkably well preserved, and closely resembles the better-known ruins at Bandelier National Monument (see p.160), which makes it plausible that the Santa Clarans descended from the builders of Mesa Verde. Until 2000, the site was open to visitors as **PUYÉ CLIFF DWELLINGS**. It was then closed in the wake of severe forest fires, and the pueblo has shown no sign of reopening it, quite possibly because of a new source of income. The successful Big Rock Casino in Española (𝕎www.bigrockcasino.com) means there's no longer an economic incentive to allow outsiders into such a revered ancestral site. Call ahead to the tribal headquarters on ☏505/753-7326 to check on the cliff dwellings' current situation.

Assuming Puyé is still off-limits, the only activity for visitors to the pueblo is to shop for pottery from outlets around the main plaza; the visitor center here can tell you which ones are open (Mon–Fri 8am–4.30pm).

Española

The only sizeable Hispanic settlement between Santa Fe and Taos is **ESPAÑOLA**, roughly halfway between the two and immediately south of the confluence of the Rio Chama and the Rio Grande. While most highway traffic continues northeast at this point toward Taos on Hwy-68, US-84 veers west across the river toward Chama (see p.194) and Colorado.

Other than watching the local youth cruising the streets in their customized "low-riders" or joining them in one of the dozens of neighborhood fast-food joints, Española has little to offer tourists. However it can make an inexpensive alternative base to Santa Fe or Taos, with a strip of budget **motels** that includes

Visiting the Rio Grande pueblos

In 1540, the first Spaniards to explore what is now New Mexico encountered a settled population of around a hundred thousand people, living in a hundred or so villages and towns. They named the inhabitants **Pueblo Indians**, *pueblo* being the Spanish for "village." Smallpox, war, and general disruption took their toll, but New Mexico is still home to around forty thousand Pueblo Indians, who live in nineteen autonomous pueblos, each with its own laws and system of government.

Fifteen of those pueblos are concentrated along the Rio Grande north of Albuquerque. There's a long-standing division between the seven southern pueblos, south of Santa Fe, most of which speak Keresan, and the eight to the north, which mostly speak Tewa (pronounced *tay-wah*). The remaining four pueblos lie further afield. All jointly promote themselves through Albuquerque's **Indian Pueblo Cultural Center**, described on p.212, which serves as a general information resource on Pueblo culture (℗505/843-7270 or 1-800/766-4405, ⓦwww.indianpueblo.org).

Despite their fascinating history – outlined on p.567 – most pueblos aren't really the tourist attractions they're often touted to be. The best-known, **Taos** and **Ácoma**, retain their ancient defensive architecture, but the rest tend to be dusty adobe hamlets scattered around a windblown plaza. All the pueblos have to some extent incorporated **Catholicism**, as introduced by the Spanish, into their religious beliefs, and thus the villages tend to center on an old adobe mission church. Rarely, however, does Christianity amount to more than a syncretic imposition upon more fundamental traditional beliefs, and you'll also see *kivas*, or prayer chambers, nearby. That so many Pueblo Indians have Spanish surnames is due to their baptism into the Catholic Church rather than any mixed ancestry; most also have names in their own languages.

If you can time your visit to coincide with one of the feast days listed opposite, a trip to a pueblo is an extraordinary experience. The spectacle of hundreds of costumed, body-painted tribal members of all ages, drawn from other pueblos as well as the host village, performing elaborate dances in such timeless surroundings, seems like a genuine glimpse of the ancient life of the continent. You won't be allowed to photograph or even sketch the ceremonies, but stalls selling food, jewelry, ceramics and other Pueblo crafts make it possible to take something away with you.

Otherwise, unless you are a knowledgeable shopper in search of Pueblo arts and crafts – most pueblos have their own specialties – visits can be disappointing. In addition, you'll certainly be made to feel unwelcome if you fail to behave respectfully – don't "explore" places that are off-limits to outsiders, such as shrines, *kivas*, or private homes.

Visitors to each pueblo are required to register at a visitor center; some charge an admission fee of $3 to $10, and those that permit such activities at all charge additional fees of about $5 for still photography, $10–15 for video cameras, and up to $100 for sketching. The recent explosion of Native American gaming has seen many pueblos open their own casinos, usually along the major highways, well away from residential areas.

Southern pueblos

Cochiti; p.152	℗505/465-2244	ⓦwww.pueblodecochiti.org
Jemez; p.164	℗505/834-7235	ⓦwww.jemezpueblo.org
San Felipe; p.154	℗505/867-4706	ⓦwww.sanfelipecasino.com
Sandia; p.155	℗505/867-3317	ⓦwww.sandiapueblo.nsn.us
Santa Ana; p.166	℗505/867-3301	ⓦwww.santaana.org
Santo Domingo; p.153	℗505/465-2214	
Zia; p.164	℗505/867-3304	

Northern pueblos

Nambe; p.168	℗505/455-2036	
Picuris; p.177	℗505/587-2519	
Pojoaque; p.168	℗505/455-3334	ⓦwww.citiesofgold.com

San Ildefonso; p.168	℡ 505/455-3549	
San Juan; p.172	℡ 505/852-4400	
Santa Clara; p.169	℡ 505/753-7326	
Taos; p.187	℡ 505/758-1028	ⓦ www.taospueblo.com
Tesuque; p.167	℡ 505/983-2667	

Pueblos further afield

Ácoma; p.122	℡ 505/470-0181 or 1-800/747-0181	ⓦ www.skycity.com
Isleta; p.237	℡ 505/869-3111	ⓦ www.isletapueblo.com
Laguna; p.124	℡ 505/552-6654	ⓦ www.lagunapueblo.org
Zuni; p.118	℡ 505/782-4403	ⓦ www.experiencezuni.com

A pueblo calendar

Jan 1	Turtle Dance	Taos
Jan 1	Corn Dance	Santo Domingo
Jan 1	Cloud or Basket Dance	San Juan
Jan 6	Three Kings Day	Most pueblos
Jan 22–23	San Ildefonso Pueblo Feast Day	San Ildefonso
Jan 25	St Paul's Feast Day	Picuris
Feb 2	Candelaria Day	Picuris, San Felipe
March 19	St Joseph's Feast Day	Laguna
Easter	Dances	Nambe, San Ildefonso, Zia
May 1	San Felipe Feast Day	San Felipe
May 3	Santa Cruz Feast Day	Taos
June 13	San Antonio Feast Day	Most pueblos
June 24	San Juan Pueblo Feast Day	San Juan, Taos
June 29	San Pedro Feast Day	Santa Ana
July 4	Nambe Falls Celebration	Nambe
July 14	San Buenaventura	Cochiti
July (2nd wk)	Taos Pueblo Pow-wow	Taos
July (3rd wk)	Northern Pueblo Artist & Craftsman Show	varying northern pueblos
July 25	Corn Dances	Taos & others
July 26	Santa Ana Feast Day	Laguna, Santa Ana
Aug 2	Santa Persingula Feast Day	Jemez
Aug 4	Santo Domingo Feast Day	Santo Domingo
Aug 10	San Lorenzo Feast Day	Ácoma, Picuris
Aug 12	Santa Clara Feast Day	Santa Clara
Aug 15	Assumption	Laguna, Zia
Aug (3rd wk)	Indian Market	Santa Fe
Aug (3rd wk)	Zuni Tribal Fair	Zuni
Aug 28	San Augustine Feast Day	Isleta
Sept 2	San Esteban Feast Day	Ácoma
Sept 4	Isleta Pueblo Feast Day	Isleta
Sept 8	Corn Dances	Laguna, San Ildefonso
Sept 19	Laguna Pueblo Feast Day	Laguna
Sept 29–30	Feast of San Gerónimo	Taos
Oct 3–4	San Francisco Feast Day	Nambe
Nov 12	San Diego Feast Day	Jemez, Tesuque
Early Dec	Shalako ceremony	Zuni
Dec 12	Guadalupe Feast Day	Pojoaque
Dec 25	Matachina Dance	most pueblos
Dec 26	Turtle Dance	San Juan
Dec 26	Children's Dances	Picuris, Santa Clara

a *Super 8*, 298 S Riverside Drive (☎505/753-5374 or 1-800/800-8000, ⓦwww.super8.com; winter ➋, summer ➌). Typical New Mexican **restaurants** in town include *Angelina's*, 1226 N Railroad Ave (☎505/753-8543), and *La Paragua*, where Hwy-76 meets US-285 (☎505/753-3211).

Abiquiu and Ghost Ranch

Twenty miles up US-84 from Española, the landscape erupts into a riot of red-rock splendor. Cliffs and mesas of Chinle, Entrada, and Windgate sandstone soar above corrugated hillocks of gray, brown, and red clays, all strongly reminiscent of southern Utah and the Navajo badlands of northeast Arizona. Surprisingly few visitors pass this way, but it's hardly little-known. If it now appears definitively Southwestern, that's largely because the paintings of Georgia O'Keeffe have done so much to shape contemporary notions of the Southwest – and it was this very terrain that inspired those paintings. Of one peak near Abiquiu, the **Pedernal**, O'Keeffe said, "God told me if I painted that mountain enough, I could have it."

From 1946 until she died, at age 98, in 1986, O'Keeffe lived and worked in the pretty adobe village of **ABIQUIU**, originally a settlement of *genízaros* (the Christianized descendants of Plains peoples captured by eighteenth-century Spaniards). Her former home, perched on a hilltop south of the highway, is not currently open to the public, but you can stay nearby at the *Abiquiu Inn* (☎505/685-4378 or 1-888/735-2902, ⓦwww.abiquiuinn.com; ➏), which has nineteen comfortable guestrooms and a good restaurant, and arranges local tours.

The village itself was a trading center on par with Taos in the late eighteenth and early nineteenth centuries, and grew to become, briefly, New Mexico's third largest town. These days, it consists of little more than a small plaza, surrounded by tumbledown adobes and centered by the beautiful, restored church of **Santo Tomás**; photography is not permitted.

Several religious groups have established retreats in the Abiquiu (pronounced *a-beh-cue*) region, including the international Muslim community that erected the **Dar al-Islam mosque** on the mesa above the village; the Presbyterian ministry at **Ghost Ranch**, fourteen miles north – where there are also **museums** of local anthropology and paleontology (Tues–Sat 9am–noon & 1–5pm; $3); and the Benedictine **Monastery of Christ in the Desert** (ⓦwww.christdesert.org), thirteen miles west of Ghost Ranch.

A few miles north of Abiquiu, Hwy-96 leads west, making a good route if you're driving between Santa Fe and either Durango or Chaco. West of **Coyote**, the route takes you through the truly spectacular ranching country, where the highway is paralleled to the north by a magnificent escarpment of striated red rock.

San Juan Pueblo

SAN JUAN PUEBLO, the largest of the Tewa pueblos, is set amid the cottonwoods on the east bank of the Rio Grande off Hwy-68, five miles north of Española. It's the third of three villages to have stood in this area since 1250, all of which have been called **O'ke**, meaning "we are the brothers." The first two capitals of the colony of New Mexico were also built here in 1598. Before they relocated to Santa Fe in 1610, the Spanish started out by taking over O'ke and calling it **San Juan**, and then occupied nearby Yunge and renamed it **San Gabriel**. Later that century, San Juan was the birthplace of **Po'pay**, the medicine man who led the Pueblo Revolt.

The centerpiece of the plaza is the much-restored **mission church**, which was the first building in the Southwest to be made with adobe bricks as opposed to simple chunks of mud. It's flanked by two rectangular *kivas*, as well as a smaller Catholic chapel. Admission is free in daylight hours, but photography is by permission only.

Next to the **Ohkay Casino**, on Hwy-68 just outside Española, the *Best Western Ohkay Resort* (T505/747-1668 or 1-877/829-2865, Wwww.ohkay.com; rooms ④, suites ⑥) offers one hundred conventional motel **rooms** and twenty more luxurious suites.

Alcalde

The previously low-profile community of **ALCALDE**, a couple of miles further up the Rio Grande from San Juan Pueblo, hit the local headlines in 1999. Shortly after the unveiling of a statue of New Mexico's first governor, Don Juan de Oñate, unknown assailants amputated its right foot – an obvious reference to the barbaric punishment Oñate meted out to the defeated menfolk of Ácoma Pueblo in 1599 (see p.123).

Embudo

Another half-dozen miles on from Alcalde, the funky little village of **EMBUDO** has in recent years become something of an alternative artists' colony. Its handful of crafts and oddities stores include Gasoline Alley, whose forecourt display of 1950s' gas pumps is a great little slice of Americana. Inside, you'll find what its owner calls the "shiny stuff", largely consisting of assorted neon and glass advertising signs from the Route 66 era. Open to no fixed hours, it's more of a museum than a shop, though around ten percent of the stock is for sale.

Just across the Rio Grande nearby, *Embudo Station* is a **brewpub** and **restaurant** housed in a former railroad station (April–Oct daily except Mon 11.30am–9pm, Nov–March Sat & Sun 11.30am–9pm; T505/852-4707, Wwww.embudostation.com; ④). Commanding a lovely spot beside a bend in the river, its patio garden makes a great place to sit out on a summer's evening, and there are also a couple of rental cabins if you fancy lingering longer.

Pilar and the Orilla Verde Recreation Area

PILAR, perched above the Rio Grande fifteen miles southwest of Taos, started out as a Jicarilla Apache farming village. On May 30, 1854, around two or three hundred Jicarilla defeated sixty US dragoons nearby in the Battle of Cieneguilla, and it took several more years of fighting before they signed a treaty that confined them to their current reservation to the west (see p.195). These days,

Pilar is a base for summer **rafting** trips run by the operators listed on p.182. Sadly, its roadside *Rio Grande Gorge Hostel* has closed down, but it's still possible to buy basic meals at the tiny *Pilar Cafe*.

The main objective of the Bureau of Land Management **visitor center**, on the east side of Hwy-68 in Pilar (daily 8.30am–5pm; ℡505/751-4899), is to inform travelers about the **Orilla Verde Recreation Area** located just to the northeast. Reached by a minor road across from the visitor center, this consists of a stretch of publicly owned land that runs to either side of the southern end of the **Upper Rio Grande Gorge**. Six miles along, there's a developed riverside **campground** charging $7 per vehicle.

Whatever your map may suggest, landslides have long since precluded continuing toward Taos at this level, along the east bank of the river. However, it's possible to meet up with US-285 by following the dirt road that crosses the river beyond the campground. More to the point, the **Vista Verde Trail** shortly after the bridge is an enjoyable 1.25-mile hiking trail that leads across the sagebrush-topped west-bank mesa to an overlook above the Rio Grande Gorge. There's also a longer trail, slightly further up the hillside, that runs all the way to the Rio Grande Gorge Bridge (described on p.194); at around seven miles one way, it's better tackled on a bike or a horse than on foot.

The High Road

Though the most direct route from Santa Fe to Taos heads straight up the Rio Grande Valley – see p.166 – the **"High Road"** over the forested Sangre de Cristo Mountains to the east makes a rewarding alternative if you have a couple of hours to spare. Winding its way through timeless **Hispanic villages**, the road passes some splendid old **adobe churches** and offers good opportunities to buy locally produced folk art or sample traditional New Mexican food.

Chimayó

The first and most famous of the High Road towns, **CHIMAYÓ** is 25 miles north of Santa Fe, eight miles northeast of **Pojoaque Pueblo** via Hwy-592 and Hwy-503, or eight miles east of **Española** on Hwy-76. Stretching luxuriantly through the fertile upland meadows that line the Santa Cruz River, and backed by scrubby red-tinged hills, it feels more part of the Rio Grande Valley below than part of the mountains to the east.

Chimayó was founded in 1740 as a sort of penal colony for Hispanic troublemakers. In Tewa, the word *tsimayo* means "good flaking stone," and Indians from San Juan Pueblo quarried obsidian here, which they chipped to form sharp blades. They held a nearby dried-up hot spring sacred, claiming that the mud from around it, when eaten, had healing properties. Within the *barrio* (neighborhood) at Chimayó's southern end known as **El Potrero**, that spring is now the site of a spell-binding colonial chapel, the **Santuario de Chimayó** (daily May–Sept 9am–6pm; Oct–April 9am–4pm).

The church was built between 1813 and 1816, after the landowner, **Bernardo Abeyta**, was told by a visiting priest about the shrine at Esquipulas in Guatemala, which had arisen at a similar spring venerated by Guatemalan Indians. As a

The Penitentes

During the nineteenth century, the remote hills above Chimayó were renowned as the heartland of the mysterious Hispanic Catholic sect known as the **Penitentes**. Anglo newcomers claimed to have glimpsed hooded figures filing along the ridges at dawn, **whipping** themselves as they went.

A large grain of truth lay beneath the lurid speculation. Self-mortification – the infliction of pain in order to share the suffering of Christ – was widespread in medieval Europe. The Spanish expedition that founded New Mexico performed public self-flagellation on Good Friday 1598, as it marched up through Mexico, and similar acts by early Franciscan missionaries attracted Pueblo Indian scorn. The Penitentes as such, however, emerged after Mexico achieved independence in 1821. Cut off from Spanish funding, the Franciscans vanished from New Mexico within twenty years, leaving the region almost devoid of priests. Hispanic Catholics formed **lay brotherhoods** to keep their faith alive.

The Penitentes – **Los Hermanos de Nuestro Padre Jesús Nazareno**, or the Brothers of Our Father Jesus of Nazareth – may well have modeled themselves on a Guatemalan example, introduced at the same time as the Guatemalan-influenced pilgrimages to Chimayó. From an initial emphasis on individual prayer and penance, they extended to develop a complex system of rituals. They never administered the sacraments, but brought solace to Catholics forced to live – and die – in the absence of priests. The Penitente brotherhood in each village soon became a mutual-aid society for the community, a cultural and political force as well as a spiritual one.

After the American takeover of New Mexico in 1846, the Penitentes were suddenly outsiders not only in their own country but even in their own church. The first Catholic bishop of Santa Fe, Jean Baptiste **Lamy** (see p.142), had little sympathy for the unorthodoxies of his Hispanic flock, and denied the sacraments to their most prominent spokesman, Father **Martínez** of Taos (see p.179). The Penitentes were forced into **secrecy** and began to gather at night in remote spots. Denied access to official church property, they met instead in plain adobe structures known as *moradas* – not necessarily distinguished with crosses or towers, but adorned with the hand-made sacred images known as **santos**.

The focus of ritual activity was **Lent**, when all Catholics practice some form of self-denial, and the Penitentes attempted to experience the passion and death of Christ. For processions, they divided into *Los Hermanos de Luz* – the **Brothers of Light**, responsible for the candles and music – and *Los Hermanos de Sangre*, the **Brothers of Blood**, who scourged themselves with yucca whips or carried giant wooden crosses. Participants were hooded to ensure humility. Some re-enacted the **crucifixion**, though tied rather than nailed to the cross, while others dragged a **Death Cart** – a wooden wagon holding an effigy of Death, armed with a bow and arrow – laden with stones. The Death Cart also figured in the Penitentes' elaborate **funeral** processions. The wayside stone cairns, topped with crosses, seen throughout the High Country are not graves, as outsiders supposed, but *descansos* – places where the coffin-bearers would pause to rest.

A century of conflict ended in 1947, when the Penitentes were officially recognized by the Bishop of Santa Fe. Those that remain now regard themselves as members of the **Third Order of St Francis**, a lay branch of the Franciscan monastic order, and the most lasting Penitente legacy in New Mexico is the *santero* tradition of religious folk art.

result, Abeyta's church also centered on a crucifix known as **Nuestro Señor de Esquipulas**, supposedly found locally in 1810 (conceivably it had been buried during the Pueblo Revolt).

The church, the crucifix, and the still-exposed *posito*, or dust pit, swiftly became the focus of **pilgrimages** not only by Hispanic peasants but also by Pueblo Indians, for whom the sacred hole in the earth clearly echoed the ancient concept of the *sipapu* (see p.567). To this day, it remains the "**Lourdes of America**." Devout New Mexican Catholics resent state advertising campaigns that seem to reduce festivals – such as the Good Friday ceremonies, and the re-enactment of the conquest of Spain by Santiago Matamoros (Saint James the Moor-killer), held during the fourth weekend in July – to the status of picturesque tourist attractions.

However, the Santuario is an undeniable delight to visit, a ravishing little round-shouldered, twin-towered, tin-roofed adobe beauty set in a walled churchyard beneath the rolling Sangre de Cristo foothills. At the heart of the altar within, the crucifix is framed by a gorgeous reredos painted by the nineteenth-century *santero* Molleno, with a small equestrian statue of Santiago to the right. Two smaller **side chapels** are filled with a mind-boggling array of votive offerings – paintings, photographs, statues, press cuttings, even discarded crutches. The hole containing the "Holy Dirt" is in the floor at the rear; pilgrims are allowed to take a scoop, as it's replenished regularly with earth from the hills. **Mass** is celebrated at noon on Sundays, and on all other days at 11am in summer, 7am in winter.

The smaller and more ramshackle **Santo Niño Chapel** (same hours), across the plaza, contains a diminutive statue of Santo Niño, the Holy Child – more of a doll, if truth be told – to whom expectant mothers bring offerings such as tiny pairs of shoes.

Chimayó has specialized in **weaving** since 1805, when two weavers sent as teachers from Spain chose to live here in preference to Santa Fe. Outlets scattered through the village sell hand-woven goods; other galleries concentrate on wood-carving and religious art. The High Road Marketplace, very close to the Santuario, is a community craft store stocking work by several local artists (closed Jan–March; ☎505/351-1078).

Practicalities

Two properties make Chimayó an appealing overnight destination. The ⚐ *Rancho de Chimayó*, Hwy-503 (closed Mon Nov–April; ☎505/351-4444; ❺), must be the best traditional New Mexican **restaurant** in the state, serving superb *flautas* and a mouthwatering *sopaipilla*, stuffed with meat and chiles, on a lovely sun-drenched outdoor patio. The *Rancho* offers some reasonable **rooms** in a separate building across the highway, but there's an even more tasteful **B&B** on the edge of town in the shape of *Casa Escondida* (☎505/351-4805 or 1-800/643-7201, ⓦwww.casaescondida.com; ❺). Its eight comfortable rooms feature *viga* ceilings, tiled floors, and *kiva* fireplaces, and all have their own private bathrooms.

Truchas

By the time you reach **TRUCHAS**, eight miles northeast of Chimayó on Hwy-76, you're well into the mountains; the views from the highway down and across the Río Grande Valley are tremendous. Villagers from Las Trampas, further up, were granted permission to establish Truchas in 1754, on condition that it was enclosed within a walled square, to defend against Comanche attacks.

The settlement took on its present form almost immediately, however, consisting of separate individual farms arrayed along a high ridge above the Río de las Truchas, or "river of trout." As one of New Mexico's least changed Hispanic communities, it served in 1987 as the location for Robert Redford's film adaptation of John Nichol's *Milagro Beanfield War* (see p.603).

Hwy-76 makes a right-angle bend to avoid Truchas, but a detour east onto the minor road up the valley takes you along a narrow street of adobe homes and barns – interspersed with the odd incongruous art gallery – and past the fields toward the 13,103-foot **Truchas Peak**.

Las Trampas

Truchas' parent community, the quiet hamlet of **LAS TRAMPAS**, is another eight miles along Hwy-76. It started life as an outpost used by fur-trappers pursuing beaver – hence its name, "the traps" – which by attracting Comanche raids doubled as an early-warning system for Santa Fe. Though no longer walled, its dusty central plaza, right alongside the highway, still holds the powerfully evocative adobe church of **San Jose de Gracia** (daily 10am–4pm). Built in 1760, it features a choir loft that extends both inside and out, so that singers could accompany ceremonies on the square as well as in the church. Note the unattached *morada* – Penitente meeting place (see p.175) – beside the cemetery to the east. Las Trampas holds a couple of gift stores, plus a hideous auto scrapyard, but nowhere to eat or sleep.

Five miles on from Las Trampas, Hwy-76 meets Hwy-75 ten miles west of Hwy-68 and the Rio Grande. The quickest route to Taos, twenty miles north, is via Hwy-73 to the east, and then Hwy-518 to the north; more Hispanic villages line the way, but none is of interest to tourists.

Picuris Pueblo

Turn left at the junction where Hwy-76 meets Hwy-75, and half a mile toward the Rio Grande you'll come to tiny **PICURIS PUEBLO**. Tucked away in a side valley, this was the last pueblo to be "discovered" by the Spanish, and proudly insists that it has never signed a treaty with any government, the US included. Its population has never risen much above two hundred, and Picuris remains no more than a cluster of adobe houses spreading across the hillside around a whitewashed church. The best-known tribal enterprise is the excellent *Hotel Santa Fe* in Santa Fe, reviewed on p.136.

There's a model of the pueblo and a reconstructed *kiva* in the village **museum** (daily 9am–5pm; $3 suggested donation). The same building also holds a gift store and the *Hidden Valley Restaurant*, a snack bar with views over a small blue lake. A self-guided **pueblo tour**, which leads past a few active *kivas* – including an unusual 500-year-old tower *kiva* – costs $5, plus another $6 for a photo permit.

Sipapu

Turning right off Hwy-76 onto Hwy-75 brings you to Hwy-518, the final leg of the High Road to Taos. Pass Hwy-518 and in a couple of miles you'll enter the tiny **ski resort** of **SIPAPU**, tucked into the pretty mountain valley known as **Tres Ritos Canyon**. *Sipapu Lodge*, along the highway to either side of the Rio Pueblo (Route Box 29, Vadito, NM 87579; ☎505/587-2240 or 1-800/587-2240, ⓦ www.sipapunm.com; ❶–❺), offers every possible grade of accommodation, from dorm beds ($19 in summer, $24 in winter) through private camping cabins, motel rooms, and luxury duplexes. Lift tickets in season, which generally runs mid-December through March, cost $38. Taos is just 22 miles away.

Taos

Part Spanish colonial outpost, part hangout for bohemian artists and New Age dropouts, and home to one of the oldest Native American communities in the United States, tiny **TAOS** has become famous out of all proportion to its size. Just six thousand people live in its three component parts: **Taos** itself, around the old plaza; sprawling **Ranchos de Taos** three miles south; and the Indian village of **Taos Pueblo** two miles north.

Like Santa Fe, Taos – the name rhymes with "house" – stretches languidly across a glorious high-desert plateau. The approach from the south is especially spectacular, as you cross a final bluff on Hwy-68 to be confronted by the pine-forested Sangre de Cristo mountains soaring above the sun-bleached foothills. This far up, the **Rio Grande** is not yet meandering through a well-watered valley but lies deep in a craggy canyon west of town, occasionally glimpsed as a crack in the plateau.

Beyond the usual unsightly highway sprawl, Taos is a delight to visit. As well as museums, galleries, and stores to match Santa Fe, it still offers the unhurried pace and charm, and the sense of a meeting place between Pueblo, Hispanic, and American cultures, that attracted figures such as Georgia O'Keeffe and D.H. Lawrence.

A history of Taos

As detailed on p.187, **Taos Pueblo** is around a thousand years old. Its first Franciscan mission was established in 1598. However, the modern town of Taos dates from the 1630s, when an uprising at the pueblo induced Spanish colonists to found the separate community of **Fernando de Taos** a few judicious miles south. Although its early history was dogged by Pueblo rebellions, the Spaniards and Pueblos eventually united to resist raids by "horse Indians" such as the Apache and Comanche. In the early nineteenth century, despite attempts by the Mexican authorities in Santa Fe to restrict contact with the outside world, Taos became the venue for annual **rendezvous**, at which "mountain men" and trappers from the Rockies traded with Indians from the pueblos and plains, and New Mexican merchants.

After the US takeover of New Mexico, Taos' Hispanic and Pueblo citizens once more found common cause. In **1847**, the territory's first American governor,

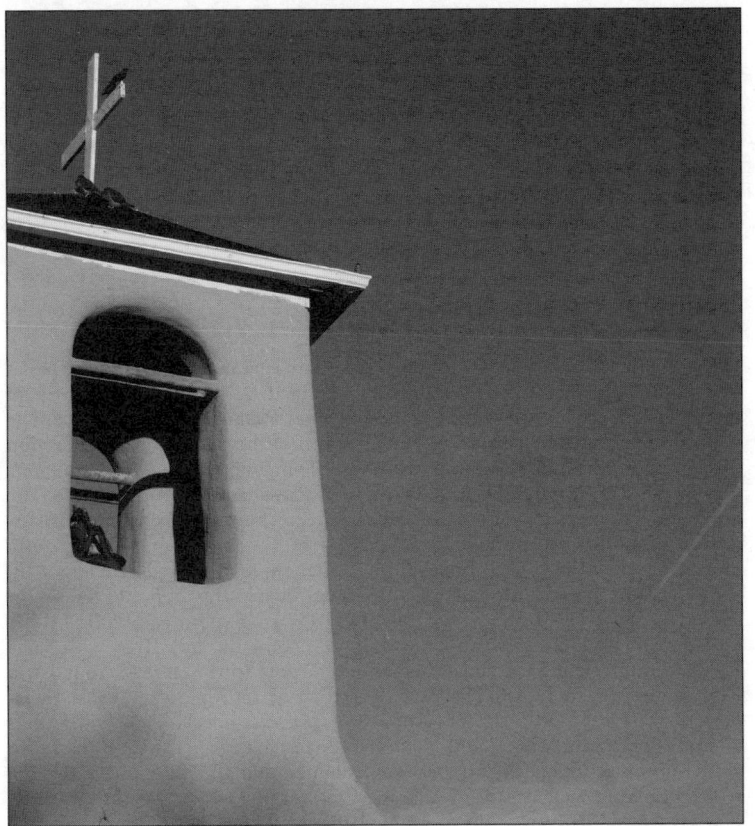

△ San Francisco de Asis church, Ranchos de Taos

Charles Bent, was killed in his Taos home, but the revolt failed to spread to Santa Fe, and the US Army launched an assault on the Pueblo that succeeded in suppressing further resistance. Long after that defeat, local priest **Antonio José Martínez** – sometimes alleged to have been complicit in the uprising, and the villain of Willa Cather's *Death Comes for the Archbishop* – continued to champion the rights of the Hispanic population.

Taos' reputation as an **arts colony** began at the end of the nineteenth century, with the arrival of the painter Joseph Henry Sharp. He was soon joined by two young New York artists, Bert Phillips and Ernest L. Blumenschein; legend has it that their wagon lost a wheel outside of Taos as they headed for Mexico in 1898, and they liked the place so much they never got around to leaving. The three men formed the nucleus of the **Taos Society of Artists**, established in 1915. Soon afterwards, society heiress and arts patron Mabel Dodge arrived and married an Indian from the Pueblo to become **Mabel Dodge Luhan**; she later speculated that perhaps "Taos" was the plural of "tao." In turn, she also wrote a fan letter to English novelist **D.H. Lawrence**, who visited three times in the early 1920s; his widow **Frieda** made her home in Taos after his death. New generations of artists and writers have "discovered" Taos ever since, but the most famous of all was

Georgia O'Keeffe, who stayed for a few years at the end of the 1920s before moving to Abiquiu (see p.172). Her renditions of the church at Ranchos de Taos in particular were a major influence on contemporary Southwestern art.

An influx of hippies converged upon Taos in the late 1960s, to be followed in subsequent decades by art-loving tourists, gallery-owning entrepreneurs, and, it would seem, wealthy divorcées. Even as the urban area has grown, however, the population has remained minimal, though the opening of a Wal-Mart store in 1999 was seen as a shocking warning that commercialization might finally start to change the place for the worse.

Arrival and information

Hwy-68, the main route up to Taos from Santa Fe and Albuquerque, passes first through Ranchos de Taos and is then lined by an uninspiring strip of motels as it approaches downtown and becomes **Paseo del Pueblo Sur**. The well-equipped **visitor center**, two miles south of the plaza at the intersection of highways 68 and 585 (summer daily 9am–5pm, winter Mon–Sat 9am–5pm; ☎505/758-3873 or 1-800/732-8267, ⓦwww.taoschamber.com), stocks all the brochures and maps you could possibly require, including valuable **accommodation discount coupons**.

Greyhound and TNM&O **buses** from Albuquerque ($28) and Santa Fe ($18) arrive at **Taos Bus Center**, at 1386 Paseo del Pueblo Sur, opposite the visitor center on Hwy-68 (☎505/758-1144). Twin Hearts Express (☎505/751-1201 or 1-800/654-9456, ⓦwww.twinheartsexpress.com) also links Taos with Santa Fe ($30, round-trip $55) and Albuquerque airport (one-way $45, round-trip $85; connection to Taos Ski Valley costs a total of $50 one-way). Faust Transportation (☎505/758-3410 or 1-888/830-3410) connects Taos with Albuquerque for a similar fare, and also offers local taxi service within Taos. No airline currently offers **flights** between Albuquerque and Taos, but it may be worth checking with Westward Airways (☎505/242-1178 or 1-877/435-9742, ⓦwww.westwardairways.com or ⓦwww.iflyrga.com) to see whether they have resumed their previous service.

Taos' **post office** is not far north of the plaza at 318 Paseo del Pueblo Norte (Mon–Fri 8am–4pm, Sat 9am–1pm; ☎505/758-2081), while **internet access** is available at *Island Coffees and Hawaiian Grill*, 1032 Paseo del Pueblo Sur (☎505/758-7777, ⓦwww.islandcoffees.com; closed Sun), and the *Wired Coffee Shop*, 705 Felicidad Lane (☎505/751-9473, ⓦwww.wiredcoffeeshop.com), both of which are near the visitor center.

Getting around

Walking is the best way to get around the compact center of Taos, though a public **bus** service, the Chile Line (☎505/751-4459), covers the greater urban area. The hourly Red Chile bus runs along a twelve-mile stretch of Hwy-68, between Ranchos de Taos and Taos Pueblo, with a loop around the plaza in the middle (Mon–Sat 7am–6pm, Sun 8am–5pm; 50¢ one-way, $1 for an all-day pass); the Green Chile bus, which circles the residential districts, is less of use for sightseeing, while a separate Ski Valley line runs in winter only. Another option is to rent a **bike** from Gearing Up, 129 Paseo del Pueblo Sur (☎505/751-0365, ⓦwww.gearingupbikes.com).

Taos Ski Valley

Colorado

Rio Grande

522
150
64

TAOS AREA

Taos Pueblo

Millicent
Rogers
Museum

MILLICENT ROGERS ROAD

64

PASEO DEL PUEBLO NORTE

CAMINO DEL PUEBLO

BLUEBERRY HILL ROAD

UPPER RANCHITOS ROAD

N

Taos

CAMINO DE LA PLAZA

VALVERDE

Plaza

KIT CARSON ROAD

Martínez
Hacienda

LOWER RANCHITOS ROAD

240
RANCHITOS ROAD

see 'Downtown
Taos' map

CAMINO DEL MEDIO

CALLEJON

CAMINO DE LA MERCED

SALAZAR ROAD

PASEO DEL PUEBLO SUR

64

Angel Fire

PASEO DEL CAÑON

585

SANTE FE ROAD

RANCHOS
DE TAOS

San
Francisco
de Asis

68

518
ESPINOSA ROAD

0   800 yds

Santa Fe   Las Vegas

Tours and excursions

Several of Taos' lodging options serve as bases for **guided walks** around town, with regular two-hour tours leaving from *La Fonda*, on the plaza, for example (late May to early Sept Mon, Wed, & Fri 10am; ☎505/758-2211; $15). In summer, open-air **trolley tours** visit the main attractions (Historic Taos Trolley Tours; May–Oct daily 10.30am and 2pm from visitor center, 10.45am and 2.15pm at plaza; ☎505/751-0366, ⓦwww.taostrolleytours.com; $33, including entry fees). All the tours include a visit to Taos Pueblo, except for those on Sundays and Monday afternoons, which go to the Millicent Rogers Museum and the Martínez Hacienda instead.

Out of ski season, between mid-April and mid-July, many visitors go **white-water rafting** instead, through the Taos Box Canyon of the Rio Grande, which offers rapids up to Class V. Operators based at Pilar, south of town – see p.173 – include Far Flung Adventures (one-day trips Mon–Fri $100, Sat & Sun $115; ☎505/758-2628 or 1-800/359-2627, ⓦwww.farflung.com), and Cottam's Rio Grande River Trips (half-day $50, full-day $95; ☎505/758-2822 or 1-800/322-8267, ⓦwww.cottamsoutdoor.com).

Taos Indian Horse Ranch (☎505/758-3212) runs **horseback** excursions on Pueblo lands, under the slogan "discover the Indian in your cupboard"; short beginners' rides cost from $45 to $110, while longer rides can take you into areas up in the mountains that you'd never be able to see otherwise. Rafting, biking, hiking, and, in winter, snowmobiling can also be arranged through Native Sons Adventures, 1033-A Paseo del Pueblo Sur (☎505/758-9342 or 1-800/753-7559, ⓦwww.nativesonsadventures.com). The Pueblo Balloon Company (☎505/751-9877, ⓦwww.puebloballoon.com) offers **hot-air balloon rides** over the Rio Grande gorge, at a cost of $225 for adults, $100 for ages 6-12.

Accommodation

Taos has **accommodation** to meet all needs, at prices well below those of Santa Fe. However, midwinter rates are no lower than midsummer, and at properties close to the ski area, they can even be considerably higher. **High season** is regarded as running from Christmas to mid-April and from mid-June to mid-October; **low season** is mid-April to mid-June and mid-October to Christmas.

There are no real **budget** options near the plaza, but the *Snowmansion* hostel, on the road to the Ski Valley to the north, offers bare-bones bunks or simple rooms. Otherwise, chain motels line Hwy-68 south of town, while three or four amusingly adobe-styled **motels** on Kit Carson Road just east of the plaza provide quieter alternatives; call in at the visitor center first to pick up any discount coupons they may have. For a few dollars more, you can avail yourself of atmospheric **B&B** inns – Taos has one of the most extensive selections in the entire Southwest – or luxury **hotels**.

Agencies that reserve lodging in advance include Taos Central Reservations (☎505/758-9767 or 1-800/821-2437, ⓦwww.taoscentralreservations.com) and the Taos Association of B&B Inns (☎505/758-7301 or 1-800/939-2215, ⓦwww.taos-bandb-inns.com).

The best places to **camp** in the vicinity are the nine summer-only campgrounds in **Carson National Forest** (☎505/758-6200, ⓦwww.fs.fed.us/r3/carson), reached by following Kit Carson Road east until it becomes Hwy-64.

Hostels, motels, and hotels

Abominable Snowmansion Hostel/HI-Taos
Taos Ski Valley Rd, Arroyo Seco ☎505/776-8298,
⊛www.abominablesnowmansion.com. Membership is not required at this pleasant, friendly
HI-AYH hostel-cum-ski lodge. It's on a very tight
curve in the road as you enter Arroyo Seco village
on Hwy-150 up to the Ski Valley, five miles north
of downtown. Office hours are daily 8–11am &
4–10pm, so don't arrive at midday. Dorm beds
$15 in summer, $22 in winter, when rates include
breakfast; teepees, and camping space out back;
bargain private rooms and cabins come with and
without en-suite facilities. ❶/❷

Best Western Kachina Lodge de Taos 413
Paseo del Pueblo Norte ☎505/758-2275 or 1-
800/522-4462, ⊛www.kachinalodge.com. Large,
tasteful, family-oriented motel at the Taos Pueblo,
with lots of Southwestern art, a good restaurant, a
pool, live music, and nightly Pueblo dance performances in summer. ❺

El Monte Lodge 317 Kit Carson Rd ☎505/758-
3171 or 1-800/828-8267. Rural 1930s motel
half a mile east of the plaza, with comfortable
en-suite accommodation in a complex of adobe
cottages. ❹

El Pueblo Lodge 412 Paseo del Pueblo Norte
☎505/758-8700 or 1-800/433-9612, ⊛www
.elpueblolodge.com. Southwestern-themed motel,
half a mile north of downtown near the Taos
Pueblo; 1-, 2-, and 3-bedroom condos also available. Rooms ❹, condos ❽–❾

🏃 **Historic Taos Inn** 125 Paseo del Pueblo
Norte ☎505/758-2233 or 1-888/519-8267,
⊛www.taosinn.com. Gorgeous central Taos landmark, where several ancient adobes were welded
together to create an atmospheric and very Southwestern hotel. Each of the 36 rooms plays some
variation on the Pueblo theme; the *kiva* fireplaces
are just for show, but a real fire burns downstairs,
in the cozy, convivial lobby area that, in the 1930s,
used to be an open-air courtyard. Both the excellent *Doc Martin's* restaurant (see p.192) and the
Adobe Bar are packed nightly. ❹–❽

Indian Hills Inn 233 Paseo del Pueblo Sur
☎505/758-4293 or 1-800/444-2346, ⊛www
.taosnet.com/indianhillsinn. The only cheap-ish
highway motel within walking distance of the
plaza; if you're sensitive to noise, be sure to get a
room well away from the street. ❹

La Fonda de Taos, 108 South Plaza; ☎505/758-
2211 or 1-800/833-2211, ⊛www.hotellafonda
.com. Vintage 1930s hotel on the plaza that has
been totally modernized to hold 24 luxurious suites,
with Southwestern furnishings and tiled bathrooms.

The lobby even holds a gallery of D. H. Lawrence
paintings (see p.184). Low season ❻, high ❼

Sagebrush Inn 1508 Paseo del Pueblo Sur
☎505/758-2254 or 1-800/428-3626, ⊛www
.sagebrushinn.com. Attractive three-story adobe
inn, well south of the center near Ranchos de Taos,
which was briefly home to Georgia O'Keeffe and
is filled with Southwestern arts and crafts. Of the
hundred guestrooms, the standard ones are ordinary, but there are some nice well-priced suites,
plus swimming and tennis, a full cooked breakfast,
and live country music in the lobby bar nightly.
Rooms ❹, suites ❻

Taos Super 8 Motel 1347 S Hwy 68 ☎505/758-
1088 or 1-800/800-8000, ⊛www.super8.com.
Among the least expensive of the franchise motels
that line Hwy-68 south of town, this one makes
a half-hearted attempt to look adobe. Low ❸,
high ❹

B&Bs

Casa de las Chimeneas 405 Cordoba Lane
☎505/758-4777 or 1-877/758-4777 ⊛www
.visit-taos.com. Luxurious eight-room B&B, set in
adobe-walled gardens a couple of blocks southeast
of the plaza, with a fitness room and spa. ❽

La Doña Luz 114 Kit Carson Rd ☎505/758-4874
or 1-800/758-9187, ⊛www.ladonaluz.com.
Hispanic-flavored rooms of differing standards in
a peaceful adobe a very short walk east of the
plaza. ❹–❽

Laughing Horse Inn 729 Paseo del Pueblo Norte
☎505/758-8350 or 1-800/776-0161, ⊛www
.laughinghorseinn.com. 1887 *hacienda*, half a mile
north of the plaza, that later became a print shop
and is now a B&B inn. Ten bedrooms share three
bathrooms, and there's also a penthouse suite, plus
a Jacuzzi, psychic readings, and free mountain
bikes. Rooms ❹, suite ❼

🏃 **Mabel Dodge Luhan House** 240 Morada
Lane ☎505/751-9686 or 1-800/846-2235,
⊛www.mabeldodgeluhan.com. Gorgeous 200-
year-old adobe B&B complex, not far northeast
of the plaza off Kit Carson Lane, where the lovely
guestrooms are named in honor of former guests
such as Willa Cather and Ansel Adams. Two rooms,
including the light-filled solarium, share a bathroom
painted by D.H. Lawrence; the cheaper lodge annex
has more modern fittings. The inn regularly plays
host to creative workshops run by writer Natalie
Goldberg among others. ❺

Old Taos Guesthouse 1028 Witt Rd ☎505/758-
5448 or 1-800/758-5448, ⊛www.oldtaos.com.
Vintage adobe *hacienda*, a couple of miles west
of the plaza, now restored as a spacious B&B
complex. Each of the nine rooms offers different

facilities – all have private bath and handcarved furniture, some have *kiva* fireplaces – and there's an outdoor hot tub. Two-night minimum stay. ⑤
Salsa del Salto 543 Hwy-150, Arroyo Seco ☏ 505/776-2422 or 1-800/530-3097, Ⓦ www .bandbtaos.com. Welcoming, comfortable B&B set in a converted modern home just beyond Arroyo Seco en route to the ski valley; dramatic picture windows offer great mountain views. All the plush Southwestern-themed rooms have full bathrooms, several have real fireplaces, and the breakfasts are out of this world. ⑤–⑧

Taos Ski Valley

Amizette Inn PO Box 756, Taos Ski Valley, NM 87525 ☏ 505/776-2451 or 1-800/446-8267, Ⓦ www.amizette.com. Small but comfortable ski

lodge, just over a mile down the valley from the lifts, with an indoor hot tub and sweeping views from its verandas. Rates include breakfast. Low season ④, high ⑥
Edelweiss Lodge & Spa PO Box 83, Taos Ski Valley, NM 87525 ☏ 505/737-6900 or 1-800/458-8754, Ⓦ www.edelweisslodgeandspa.com. Intimate, luxurious hotel at the foot of the slopes with its own French restaurant, plus sauna, Jacuzzi, and in-house masseuse. ⑧
Thunderbird Lodge PO Box 87, Taos Ski Valley, NM 87525 ☏ 505/776-2280 or 1-800/776-2279, Ⓦ www.thunderbird-taos.com. Lively ski lodge – south-facing, so sunnier than most – with a quieter chalet across the road. Rates include full board. Low season ⑧, high ⑨

The Town

Downtown Taos still centers on the old Spanish **plaza**, which has been remodeled several times over the years, and migrated slightly eastwards in the process. The tiny square is now ringed by galleries and souvenir stores, and its tree-shaded benches make a pleasant spot from which to watch the world go by. The Stars and Stripes have flown day and night from the flagpole at its heart ever since it was erected by Kit Carson during the Civil War; the nearby bandstand was a gift from Mabel Dodge Luhan.

While there's little to see on the plaza itself, apart from the **D.H. Lawrence paintings** in the *La Fonda* hotel and the murals in the old **Courthouse**, a short walk along the narrow, winding streets that stretch away in all directions will be rewarded with glimpses of Taos as it used to be. The best of the central museums is the **Kit Carson Home**, but the **Millicent Rogers Museum**, a few miles north, holds a superb collection of Native American and Hispanic artworks.

La Fonda

Although the **La Fonda** hotel, on the south side of the plaza, was built in 1937, well after **D.H. Lawrence**'s death, a gallery in the lobby holds a unique collection of paintings by the Nottinghamshire novelist (irregular hours; $3). Bought from his widow Frieda's second husband, most were painted in Italy rather than Taos; one, *The Holy Family*, was his first-ever canvas, and it shows. Apart from one landscape (a "collaboration" with Frieda and their friend Dorothy Brett), they depict sweaty, fleshy wrestlings such as *The Rape of the Sabine Women*.

Discount museum tickets

Under a scheme run by the Museum Association of Taos (Ⓦ www.taosmuseums.org), a **$20 combination ticket**, sold at each museum and valid for a year, buys admission to five Taos museums – the Millicent Rogers Museum, the Blumenschein Home, the Harwood Museum, the Taos Art Museum and Fechin Home, and the Hacienda Martínez.

Native peoples

For travelers to the Southwest, one of the greatest attractions is the chance to experience Native American cultures up close. Visitors from overseas especially, many of whom think of North America as short on history, are often overwhelmed by the rich continuity of the Native American presence. The Southwest holds around fifty diverse Native American reservations, most of which are far removed from clichéd ideas of poverty and degradation, and is also filled with relics of long-vanished times, in the shape of the extraordinary, and often spellbindingly beautiful, homes, architecture, and artifacts left by its earliest inhabitants.

Exploring such sites can provide a compelling focus for a tour; it would take months to see just most important and accessible ancient sites, while many more remain hidden in remote corners of the desert, seen only by the most intrepid adventurers.

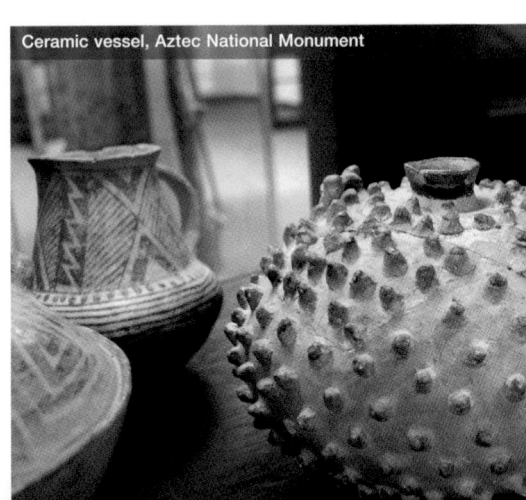

Ceramic vessel, Aztec National Monument

Cliff dwelling, Gila Cliff Dwellings National Monument

Early settlers

The first human beings to reach the Southwest are thought to have been hunters, who up to fourteen thousand years ago, swiftly harried the continent's original "mega-fauna" of mammoths, giant sloth, and the like to extinction. The nomadic hunter-gatherers who followed them were supplanted a little over two thousand years ago by more sedentary cultures that emerged with the arrival of agricultural practices from Mexico. Three main groups came to dominate the Southwest. Prime among them were the **Ancestral Puebloans** – a people archeologists used to call the **Anasazi**, until they realized that the Navajo word meant "enemy ancestors" or "ancient enemies." The Ancestral Puebloans spread across the high country where the modern states of Arizona, New Mexico, Utah, and Colorado meet, now known as the Four Corners region. The **Hohokam** were desert farmers who irrigated the huge valley where modern Phoenix has spread. The **Mogollon** inhabited the high country further east, in what's now eastern Arizona and western New Mexico.

Ancient sites

The Ancestral Puebloans are known for their highly sophisticated culture. By around 1100, many of their communities had taken the form of multi-storied pueblos, in which hundreds of families lived in complexes of contiguous "apartments"; the word "pueblo" comes from the Spanish word for "village." The very largest pueblos, for example those in New Mexico's **Chaco Canyon**, were not so much towns as ceremonial centers, which held small permanent

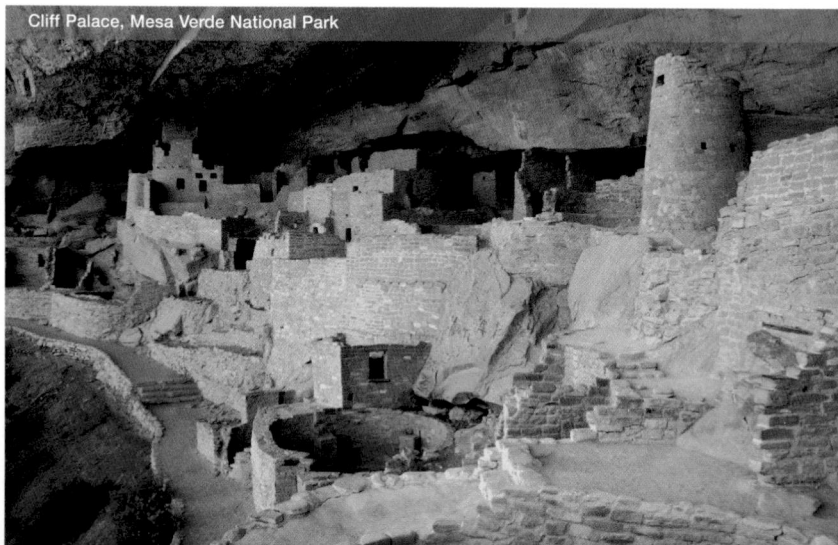

Cliff Palace, Mesa Verde National Park

Wupatki Pueblo, Wupatki National Monument

populations that attracted large numbers of visitors – perhaps pilgrims – for special occasions. By now, the Ancestral Puebloans had acquired considerable astronomical expertise, and sites like Chaco and Arizona's **Wupatki** have been shown to hold significant alignments. At much the same time, certain groups began to construct the astonishing cliff dwellings for which the Ancestral Puebloans are best remembered today.

Many Ancestral Puebloan sites are open to visitors as national monuments. The most famous is **Mesa Verde National Park**, with its "palaces" squeezed like eagles' nests into crevices in soaring canyon walls. Others include **Bandelier National Monument**, where you can climb ladders up to dwellings hollowed out of soft volcanic rock; **Navajo National Monument**, where you can hike or ride horses to the romantic lost cities of Betatakin and Keet Seel; and the ravishing **Canyon de Chelly National Monument**, whose beautiful ancient ruins in a spectacular red-rock canyon are accessible by hikes, horseback rides, and even day-long jeep tours.

A checklist of ancient sites

Among the most significant ancient sites in the Southwest, in the order in which they are described in this book, are:

Betatakin, Arizona. Spectacular ancient pueblo, set into a vast rocky alcove in Navajo National Monument. p.67

Canyon de Chelly, Arizona. Superbly dramatic cliff dwellings in a glowing sandstone canyon that's now owned and farmed by the Navajo. p.75

Hovenweep, Utah. Enigmatic towers poised above a shallow canyon in the heart of the Four Corners. p.90

Mesa Verde, Colorado. Magnificent cliff palaces, high in the canyons of Colorado. p.94

Chaco Canyon, New Mexico. The largest and most sophisticated freestanding pueblos, far out in the desert. p.112

Bandelier National Monument, New Mexico. Large riverside pueblos, and cave-like homes hollowed from volcanic rock. p.160

Gila Cliff Dwellings, New Mexico. Remote agricultural community, in what became an Apache stronghold in the mountains of southern New Mexico. p.245

Wupatki, Arizona. Several small pueblos, built by assorted tribal groups in the aftermath of a volcanic eruption. p.334

Walnut Canyon, Arizona. Numerous canyon-wall homes, hollowed into an isolated promontory above lush Walnut Creek. p.336

Modern-day pueblos

By the time the first Spanish explorers reached the Southwest, in 1539, the Ancestral Puebloans no longer inhabited the Four Corners. Much is made of their supposed "disappearance," but actually there's no mystery as to where they went. They're still here today – in the nineteen pueblos that now line the Rio Grande in **northern New Mexico**, and a handful of communities further west, including the **Zuni** and **Hopi** villages. While there are now fewer pueblos than there used to be – five centuries of wars and disease have seen to that – those that survive retain much of their traditional way of life. Almost all continue to celebrate their feast days with dazzling dances and public ceremonies; if photography wasn't forbidden on such occasions, you'd be so familiar with images of them that you wouldn't need to read about them here. In addition, certain pueblos have barely changed how they look in the last millennium, and have become year-round tourist attractions without compromising their ancient heritage. The prime destinations for travelers who wish to experience Pueblo culture are the amazing "Sky City" of **Ácoma**, perched on a glowing golden mesa, and **Taos**, where twin multi-storied pueblos stand beneath the snow-capped peaks of northern New Mexico.

Rock art

From the Cro-Magnon cave paintings of France to Aboriginal designs in the Australian outback, ancient peoples were creating rock art long before the invention of writing. The deserts of the American Southwest offer perfect conditions for the preservation of ancient art, and the region abounds in both **petroglyphs**, in which images are scratched or chipped into stone surfaces, and **pictographs**, painted with natural dyes and pigments. The single most remarkable site has to be the **Great Gallery**, where Archaic shamen daubed enigmatic, ghost-like figures onto the walls of remote Horseshoe Canyon in Canyonlands National Park. Countless other locations include the so-called "Newspaper Rocks" in Utah and Arizona, carvings in Monument Valley, and painted panels in **Capitol Reef National Park**.

The best-known motif in Ancestral Puebloan rock art, found throughout the Four Corners, is the flute-player **Kokopelli**, whose curving, crested image adorns many a T-shirt and metal sculpture. Archeologists believe that his supposed "hunchback" may in fact be a sack containing seeds, and that Kokopelli was responsible for introducing agriculture to the Southwest.

The rock art tradition continued into very recent times. Thus the Navajo commemorated nineteenth-century Spanish incursions into the **Canyon de Chelly** by painting on the sandstone walls, while for that matter the Spaniards themselves added their own carvings to the remarkable Inscription Rock at New Mexico's **El Morro National Monument**.

DOWNTOWN TAOS

64

Van Vechten-Lineberry Museum Ⓐ

Ⓑ

Fechin Institute

ACCOMMODATION

Best Western Kachina Lodge de Taos	B
Casa de las Chimeneas	I
El Monte Lodge	H
El Pueblo Lodge	A
Historic Taos Inn	C
Indian Hills Inn	G
La Doña Luz	F
La Fonda de Taos	E
Mabel Dodge Luhan House	D

CAFÉS & RESTAURANTS

Apple Tree Restaurant	2
Bent Street Deli & Café	3
Byzantium	5
Caffe Tazza	4
Lambert's of Taos	6
Michael's Kitchen	1

VALVERDE ST

CAMINO DE LA PLACITA

PASEO DEL PUEBLO NORTE

BEDFORD ST

❶

CIVIC PLAZA DRIVE

MARTYR'S LANE

BENT STREET

❷ Governor Bent House and Museum

❸

DON FERNANDO STREET

TERESINA LN

Courthouse

Ⓒ

Ⓓ

PLAZA

Ⓔ

KIT CARSON ROAD

Kit Carson Home and Museum

Ⓕ

❹

MORADA LANE

GUADALUPE PLAZA

RANCHITOS ROAD

DOÑA LUZ

LA PLACITA

LEDOUX STREET

❺

Harwood Museum of Art

Ernest L. Blumenschein Home and Museum

OJITOS ROAD

QUESNEL STREET

PASEO DEL PUEBLO SUR

SILER ROAD

64

Ⓖ

MONTOYA ROAD

N

BURCH AVE

LIEBERT ST

❻

68

LOS PANDOS ROAD

CORDOBA ROAD

Ⓗ

DOLAN ST

Ⓘ

0   200 yds

▼ Ranchos de Taos & Santa Fe

When first exhibited, at London's Warren Gallery in 1929, they were regarded as obscene and banned from further showing in Britain. They now seem tame, though the *Sunday Times'* original verdict remains accurate: "he can do rather less with a paintbrush than a child of seven without any natural flair."

Lawrence's ashes are now held in a memorial chapel north of Taos, as described on p.196; accommodation in *La Fonda* is reviewed on p.183.

The Courthouse and the Harwood Foundation

After much of the north side of the plaza was destroyed by a fire in May 1932, Taos' **Courthouse** was rebuilt in the prevalent Pueblo Revival style. Having ceased to function as a courthouse in 1970, it's a little hard to spot these days, being labeled as both the Mercado and the North Plaza Arts Center. However, if you manage to make your way upstairs without being distracted by the magnificent chocolate shop below, you can admire some fine **murals** depicting the use and misuse of law (no fixed hours; no fee). The four artists responsible, led by Emil Bisttram, a former student of Diego Rivera, were commissioned as part of Franklin Roosevelt's make-work WPA program.

The murals are exhibited under the auspices of the Harwood Foundation, whose **Harwood Museum of Art** is two blocks southwest of the plaza at 238 Ledoux St (Tues–Sat 10am–5pm, Sun noon–5pm; $6, $20 combination ticket). This combines works by twentieth-century Taos artists such as Bert Phillips and woodcarver Patrociño Barelo with *santos* and *retablos* by their nineteenth-century Hispanic counterparts.

Ernest L. Blumenschein Home and Museum

Near the Harwood Museum, the **Ernest L. Blumenschein Home and Museum,** 222 Ledoux St (daily May–Oct 9am–5pm, Nov–April 11am–4pm; $6, $20 combination ticket), preserves the much-restored 1790 house of the co-founder of the Taos Society of Artists. Paintings by Blumenschein, his daughter Helen, and Zuni and Hopi artists such as Fred Kabotie are on display, but the real star is the house itself. Though Taos has grown to obscure its original uninterrupted views, Blumenschein's studio, made gloriously light by its raised ceiling and enlarged windows, still commands a fine prospect of the mountains.

Governor Bent House and Museum

Bent Street, a block north of the plaza, takes its name not from any irregularities but from the first American governor of New Mexico, Charles Bent, whose former home at no. 117 is now the **Governor Bent House and Museum** (daily April–Oct 9.30am–5pm, Nov–March 10am–4pm; $2). The imposition of American rule was resented by Taos' Hispanic and Indian population alike, and Bent was killed here by an angry mob on January 19, 1847. You can still see the hole hacked into the adobe walls through which most of his family attempted to escape; they were captured, but their lives were spared. The rest of the small house serves as a ramshackle museum of frontier Taoseño life, holding Indian artifacts, antiquated rifles, and even an eight-legged lamb.

Kit Carson Home and Museum

Just east of the plaza, across the highway at the end of Taos' sole surviving stretch of wooden boardwalk, is the dusty but evocative adobe home of "mountain man," mason, and part-time US cavalry officer **Kit Carson** (daily 9am–6pm; $5; Ⓦ www .kitcarsonhome.com). Born in Kentucky in 1809, Carson left home to join a wagon train to Missouri in 1826 – a one-cent reward was offered for the return of the teenage runaway – and spent the ensuing winter in Taos. He was to return repeatedly throughout his life, in between escapades like scouting for the 1840s Frémont expeditions and campaigning against the Navajo in the 1860s (see p.592).

Carson bought the house at the heart of today's museum in 1843, upon his marriage to a local woman, Josefa Jaramillo, and it was sold after their deaths in 1868 to support their seven orphaned children. Its current owners, the masons fraternity, have recently chosen to dissociate it from the Museum Association of Taos, and it has therefore been stripped of the bulk of its collection of Wild West memorabilia. All that remains are some mildly interesting press cuttings and photos relating to Carson himself, plus a mock-up of the family's living quarters, complete with *fogón de campaña*, a bell-shaped adobe fireplace.

Taos Art Museum and Fechin Home

Russian artist and woodcarver Nicolai Fechin (1881–1955) made his home in Taos between 1927 and 1933 – almost literally so, in that he sculpted and shaped virtually every inch of the interior. As the **Taos Art Museum and Fechin Home**, it's now open to the public at 227 Paseo del Pueblo Norte, a short way north of the *Historic Taos Inn* (daily except Mon 10am–5pm; $6, $20 combination ticket). Its ornate decorations are in themselves well worth a quick look. Since the recent closure of the nearby Van Vechten-Lineberry Museum, its walls are now adorned with choice pieces by Taos Society of Artists members, including a few lovely Gustave Baumann prints. The house also makes a spectacular setting for regular chamber-music concerts on summer evenings.

Millicent Rogers Museum

Four miles north of the plaza, well past the Taos Pueblo turnoff and reached by a dirt road that angles into a tricky five-way intersection, the **Millicent Rogers Museum** (April–Oct daily 10am–5pm; Nov–March Tues–Sun 10am–5pm; $7. under-17s $2; $20 combination ticket; ⓦ www.millicentrogers.org) is among New Mexico's very finest galleries. Millicent Rogers – a former fashion model who was the granddaughter of a founder of Standard Oil and is said to have been "close" to Cary Grant – lived here until her death in 1953.

The museum focuses on both Native American and Hispanic art and traces how those cultures have been perceived. Its highlight is the family collection of San Ildefonso Pueblo potter **María Martínez**, whose black-on-black ceramics are the most famous (and valuable) Native American artworks of the twentieth century. It also outlines the unbroken thousand-year tradition of Pueblo pottery, from pieces produced by the prehistoric Mimbres and Ancestral Puebloan peoples through Rio Grande works from the fourteenth and fifteenth centuries. Other crafts include turquoise jewelry, Navajo blankets, and some amazing *kachinas* (see p.84), such as a Zuni buffalo *kachina* from 1875, made of hide, fur, and feathers.

The development of Spanish colonial religious art in the New World is shown through an array of rugs, looms, carved wooden furniture, *bultos*, and *retablos*, plus a couple of "**Death Carts**," in which a skeleton holding a bow and arrow, known as Doña Sebastiana, rides in a rickety wooden carriage (see p.175). The earliest relic is a faded representation of *Christ Washing the Feet of the Disciples*, painted on buffalo hide by an unknown Franciscan around 1700.

Taos Pueblo

Tiwa-speaking peoples have lived at **TAOS PUEBLO**, just over two miles north of Taos plaza, for almost a thousand years. While they may have originally arrived from the east, across the plains, they have long been at the forefront of the **Pueblo Indian** cultural tradition, which, as the name implies, can be traced back to the Ancestral Puebloans of the Four Corners. Together with Ácoma (see p.122) and the Hopi mesas (see p.87), the pueblo can claim to be the oldest continuously occupied settlement in the United States. It's also stunningly beautiful, centering on two multistory adobe "apartment blocks" framed beneath the shining forested peak of Taos Mountain.

The northernmost New Mexican pueblo, Taos is among the few not to have been displaced by the coming of the Spaniards in the sixteenth century. Its survival has required a long hard struggle; the pueblo was abandoned for two years in the 1630s, to escape retaliation after the killing of a priest, and it later played a central role in the **Pueblo Revolt** of 1680 (see p.575). When the Spanish subsequently reconquered New Mexico, Taos Pueblo was almost completely destroyed. It revolted again under both Mexican and American rule. In 1837, Taos Indians cut off the head of the Mexican governor of New Mexico and used it as a football, and their leader José Gonzalez briefly usurped the governorship until he was himself executed. Ten years later, they were heavily implicated in the rebellion against Charles Bent (see p.186); when the retaliating US Army besieged and burned the pueblo's church, over 150 women, children, and elderly noncombatants were killed.

In the twentieth century, the pueblo was forced to campaign for the return of the sacred **Blue Lake**, high in the mountains. The source of the Río Pueblo de Taos that flows through the heart of the village, and the focus of an annual three-day pilgrimage, Blue Lake was unexpectedly incorporated into a federal forest reserve in 1906. When Richard Nixon finally handed it back in 1970, it marked the first time that land had ever been returned to Native Americans for religious reasons; access is now forbidden to outsiders.

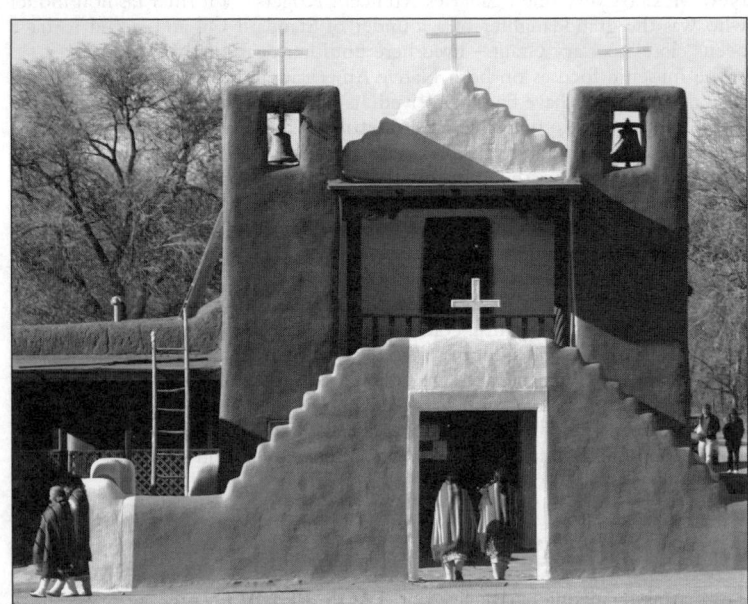

△ San Gerónimo church, Taos Pueblo

Visiting the pueblo

Taos Pueblo is generally open from 8am until 5pm from Monday to Saturday, and between 8.30am and 5pm on Sunday, but it often closes for tribal events such as festivals or funerals and remains closed between mid-February and early April; contact Taos Pueblo Tourism (℡ 505/758-1028, ⊛ www.taospueblo.com) before you visit.

The pueblo can be reached via two approach roads off Hwy-68. One continues north as the highway veers west at the *Best Western Kachina Lodge*, half a mile north of the plaza, while the other branches off at Jackie's Trading Post, another half-mile on. After entering the reservation, they meet and run together to the pueblo plaza, where you pay the **entrance fee** ($10 per person, plus $5 per still or video camera) and park your vehicle. That fee entitles you to join one of the guided **walking tours**, led by Pueblo residents, which leave at regular intervals. While taking a tour may help overcome any awkwardness you might feel, however, it won't take you beyond the limited public areas through which you're free to wander alone.

Visits focus on the two large **adobe complexes** – Hlaauma, the north house, and Hlaukkwima, the south house – that stand to either side of the Río Pueblo de Taos, also known as Red Willow Creek. In their current form, they almost certainly date from the uncertain years that followed the Pueblo Revolt, at the start of the eighteenth century. This architectural design, consisting of individual dwellings stacked like dice and entered via rooftop ladders, was originally adopted for defense and has been abandoned as unnecessary by most other pueblos. At Taos, the homes have been adapted to include ground-level doorways and windows, but their occupants still choose to live without toilets, running water, or electricity. Both the adobe complexes remained fully inhabited until the mid-1970s, but due to the lack of conveniences and the constant tourist intrusion, they now hold a mere ten families between them. The remainder of the reservation's population of three thousand live in newer homes nearby. Several rooms facing the plaza function as **craft shops**, but you can't penetrate any further, and you'll only glimpse the *kivas* (ceremonial chambers), distinguished by their long ladders, from a distance.

Visitors are encouraged to enter, but not photograph the interior of, the pretty little **Church of San Gerónimo** on the edge of the plaza. The latest incarnation of the pueblo's Catholic mission church is decorated inside with murals that feature traditional corn and sun motifs; mass is celebrated every Sunday morning at 7am. Tours also lead across to the ruins of the pueblo's previous church, to the west, which was all but destroyed by the US army in 1847. Its solitary belltower dominates a small dusty cemetery beside the adobe wall that surrounds the entire pueblo. Now just a few feet in height, the wall was originally a defensive fortification that stood twelve feet tall. In the plaza itself, what look like makeshift awnings to shelter parked cars are in fact *ramadas*, wooden racks used for drying corn and chile peppers.

For most of the year, Pueblo life continues with scant regard for visitors, though (camera-less) outsiders are welcome at certain spectacular feast days and dances. Most of these take place in summer; the biggest are the **Corn Dances** (June 13 and 24, July 25 and 26), the **Taos Pueblo Pow Wow** (second weekend in July), and the **Feast of San Gerónimo** (Sept 29 and 30).

Taos Pueblo is one of the many pueblos that rushed to build its own **casino**, three-quarters of a mile northwest of the pueblo itself; it's a relatively small affair, with no accommodation and just a simple restaurant (℡ 505/737-0777, ⊛ www.taosmountaincasino.com). As one unapologetic elder remarked, "poverty was never a part of Pueblo life until the Europeans came."

Ranchos de Taos

The distinct community of **RANCHOS DE TAOS**, which spreads to either side of Hwy-68 three miles southwest of central Taos, was originally an area of Indian farmlands. These were later taken over by the Spanish to grow the crops that fed the townspeople of Taos. Each *rancho* or farm had its own main house, or *hacienda*, and even today Ranchos de Taos retains the feel of a rural village; you can still buy fresh hay for your animals from lots along the highway.

San Francisco de Asis

In Rancho's small unpaved plaza, the mission church of **San Francisco de Asis** turns its broad shoulders, or more accurately its massive adobe buttresses, to the passing traffic on Hwy-68. Built around 1776, it's one of colonial New Mexico's most splendid architectural achievements, with subtly rounded walls and corners disguising its underlying structural strength. Encountering genuine adobe, which crumbles away after heavy rain or snow, can come as a shock after so much fakery elsewhere in the state; the local congregation is obliged to replaster the whole thing yearly.

Though the ever-changing interplay of light and shade across the church's golden exterior has fascinated painters from Georgia O'Keeffe onwards, its **interior** is equally intriguing. Amid a clutter of devotional objects and artworks, a magnificently ornate green-and-red reredos (altarpiece) frames several individual paintings. It was painted by the nineteenth-century *santero* Molleno, who was also responsible for the altarpiece of the Santuario de Chimayó (see p.174). The **plaza** outside – remarkably peaceful considering that the highway is thirty yards away – holds a handful of restaurants and gift stores.

Hacienda Martínez

Two miles west of the highway, roughly halfway between San Francisco de Asis and the downtown plaza on Ranchitos Road, the **Hacienda Martínez** is one of the few Spanish haciendas anywhere to be preserved in something like its original state (daily April–Oct 9am–5pm, Nov–March 10am–4pm; $6, $20 combination ticket). It was built in 1804 by Don Antonio Martínez, an early mayor of Taos who was also the father of Padre Antonio Jose Martínez (see p.175). Within its thick, windowless, adobe walls – the place could be sealed like a fortress against then still-prevalent Indian raids – two dozen rooms are wrapped around two separate patios, holding animal pens and a well. Trade goods of the kind Don Antonio once carried south along the Rio Grande are displayed alongside tools, looms, and simple furnishings of the era, while the rooms farthest from the entrance contain a fine collection of Hispanic religious art.

Taos Ski Valley

Fifteen miles north of Taos, reached via an attractive road that winds up through a narrow gap in the mountains from the village of **Arroyo Seco**, lie the precipitous slopes of **TAOS SKI VALLEY**. Located on the north flank of **Wheeler Peak** – the highest point in New Mexico at 13,161 feet – the runs are usually open to skiers from late November until early April (daily lift tickets late Nov to mid-Dec and late March to early April $28, mid-Dec to late March $57;

information ☎505/776-2291 or 1-866/968-7386, reservations ☎1-800/776-1111, ⓦ www.skitaos.org).

Experts rate Taos one of the most challenging ski resorts in the Rockies – just over half its 72 separate runs, served by seven lifts, are rated for experts only – but the highly rated Ernie Blake Ski School (same telephone numbers) teaches novices aged three and upwards on the nursery slopes. If you've never skied, the **Yellowbird Beginner's Package** is an ideal way to try it out, with lessons, lift tickets, and ski rental costing $75 for one day or $110 for two days. Note that **snowboarding** is not permitted.

The road up into the Ski Valley dead-ends at a massive parking lot that serves several **lodges**, **hotels**, and **condo** blocks, some of which are listed on p.184. There are also a number of cafes, restaurants, and bars, including the casual *Rhoda's* (☎505/776-2005) and the lively *Tim's Stray Dog Cantina* (☎505/776-2894). Most of these accommodation and dining options remain open year-round, but there wouldn't be much point staying in summer.

Eating and drinking

Taos is too small to offer a lot of **nightlife**, but it does have a fine selection of **restaurants** in all price ranges and several **coffeehouses**. If your main priority is to **drink**, the *Adobe Bar* in the *Historic Taos Inn* (see p.183), with its roaring log fire and regular live music, is the coziest spot in town, while *Eske's*, a short way south at 106 Des Georges Lane (☎505/758-1517), is a **brewpub**, open nightly until 10.30pm, that also serves simple stews and snacks.

Coffeehouses

The Bean 900 Paseo del Pueblo Norte ☎505/758-7711, and 1033 Paseo del Pueblo Sur ☎505/758-5123. These serious coffee roasters sell espressos and pastries to a clientele composed largely of forty-somethings, including, at the northern outlet, locals from the nearby pueblo. Mon–Fri 6.30am–6pm, Sat 7am–4pm, Sun 7am–2pm.

Caffe Tazza 122 Kit Carson Rd ☎505/758-8706. Welcoming central café with nice sunlit terrace, serving coffees and light veggie meals to countercultural locals and assorted crazies. Live entertainment most evenings, with anarchic open-mike nights. Free local newspapers. Daily 6.30am–8pm.

Gypsy 360 482 Ski Valley Rd, Arroyo Seco ☎505/776-3166. Unlikely gourmet deli, in a tiny village on the road up to Taos Ski Valley, that offers espresso coffees, pricey but tasty pastries, and sandwiches. Tues, Wed & Sat 8am–4pm, Thurs & Fri 8am–8pm, Sun 9am–8pm.

Island Coffees and Hawaiian Grill 1032 Paseo del Pueblo Sur ☎505/758-7777. Friendly, very inexpensive Hawaiian-themed café near the visitor center, featuring Kona coffee plus noodle dishes, curries, and sandwiches, and cut-rate Internet access. Mon–Sat 11am–9pm.

Restaurants

Apple Tree Restaurant 123 Bent St ☎505/758-1900. Café-style restaurant in an old adobe very close to the plaza, where most entrees on the predominantly New Mexican menu, such as barbecue duck *fajitas* or mango chicken enchiladas, cost $15–20. The courtyard seating is ideal for summer evenings. Mon–Sat 11.30am–3pm & 5–9pm, Sun 11am–9pm.

Bent Street Deli & Cafe 120 Bent St ☎505/758-5787. Airy, partly outdoor place, just north of the plaza; good-value breakfasts, sandwich or pasta lunches, and tasty dinners like shrimp with garlic or organic roast chicken for $15–20. Mon–Sat 8am–9pm.

Byzantium 112 La Placita at Ledoux St ☎505/751-0805. Romantic and classy courtyard restaurant southwest of the plaza, with conventional but flavorful lunches of salads and sandwiches. Much of the dinner menu has a contemporary pan-Asian edge, with *tempura* eel ($15) or duck green curry ($27) alongside the more traditional herb-crusted pork tenderloin ($34) or vegetable pot pie. Mon & Thurs–Sun 5–9.30pm.

Doc Martin's *Historic Taos Inn*, 125 Paseo del Pueblo Norte ☎505/758-1977. Delicious, inventive New Mexican food in romantic old adobe inn, on the main road just east of the plaza. Unusual breakfast options include the $7 Kit Carson (poached eggs on yam biscuits); dinner entrees, such as piñon-crusted salmon or roast chicken, are $17–28. Sunday to Thursday evenings there's a three-course prix-fixe menu that costs around $20, depending on entree. Daily 7.30–11am, 11.30am–2.30pm, & 5.30–9.30pm.

Joseph's Table *La Fonda de Taos*, 108 South Plaza; ☎505/751-4512, ⓦwww .hotellafonda.com. This delightful restaurant, in the historic *La Fonda* hotel, serves wonderful (if rich) food in a lovely setting, with very friendly service. Thanks to a creative use of fabric, the alcoves along one wall have been turned into "love shacks" that resemble tented pavilions, The fabulous parma ham risotto appetizer is $11, while full entrees like a whole roasted duck or lamb shank cost around $30, but you can also order smaller portions from the separate *Joe's Bar* menu, like a buffalo burger for $12. Daily 5.30–10pm, lunch 11.30am–2.30pm May–Aug only.

Lambert's of Taos 309 Paseo del Pueblo Sur ☎505/758-1009. Cozy, low-key restaurant half a mile south of the plaza, with a classy but friendly atmosphere and art on the walls. The cuisine is New American rather than New Mexican, with grilled meat or fish entrees like pepper-crusted duck for

$15–28, and opulent desserts. Daily 5.30–9pm.

Michael's Kitchen 304C Paseo del Pueblo Norte ☎505/758-4178. Inexpensive Mexican and Southwestern dishes in an old adobe kitchen a few blocks north of the plaza, plus fresh-baked pastries, cinnamon rolls, and coffee in the morning. Daily 7am–8.30pm.

Stakeout Grill and Bar 101 Stakeout Drive, Outlaw Hill off Hwy-68 ☎505/758-2042. Well-hidden, unpretentious, and popular dinner-only restaurant in a truly stunning setting, specializing in big, good-value steaks. Only accessible by car, four miles south of Ranchos de Taos, up a dirt track east of the highway. Daily 5–10pm.

Taos Pizza Outback 712 Paseo del Pueblo Norte ☎505/748-3112. Hard-to-find pizzeria tucked behind another building to the left of the highway a mile north of town. It has a welcoming youthful ambience and huge portions of great food – the $9 veggie *calzones* are amazing. Daily 11am–10pm.

Tiwa Kitchen Taos Pueblo ☎505/751-1020. Indian-run restaurant on the road into Taos Pueblo, serving strong chile-flavored stews, traditional *horno*-baked bread, Indian fry bread, and lots of blue corn meal. Daily except Tues, summer 10am–7pm, winter 11am–6pm.

Shopping

If you're **shopping** for souvenirs, Taos may not have Santa Fe's range of stores, or anything like so many upmarket galleries, but it's just as much fun to walk around. Most of the shops on the plaza itself are very predictable, but the area immediately north, toward Bent Street, is more diverting, and there are some genuine oddities elsewhere. As ever, the **museum stores** – especially at the Millicent Rogers Museum – are among the best in town.

Gift stores and galleries

Blue Rain Gallery 117 South Plaza ☎505/751-0066. The very best in Native American arts and crafts, alongside the plaza; unfortunately, the exquisite *kachinas* can run into thousands of dollars.

Coyote Moon 120C Bent St ☎505/758-4437. A riot of color, this is Taos' best selection of Mexican folk art, with plenty of Oaxacan carved animals and Day of the Dead souvenirs.

Dwellings Revisited 10 Bent St ☎505/758-3377. Quirky store where the owners have imported trinkets, oddities, furniture, and folk art from all over the world. Unusual Greek and Indian items sit alongside the more familiar Mexican stuff.

FX-18 140 Kit Carson Rd ☎505/758-8590. Well-chosen crafts and jewelry, plus unusual gifts, a short walk east of the plaza.

Horse Feathers 109B Kit Carson Rd ☎505/758-7457. A great source for all things Western, from Stetson hats and colorful cowboy boots at bargain prices, to off-the-wall antiques.

Taos Artisans Co-op 107A Bent St ☎505/758-1558. Individually styled jewelry, clothing, and sculpture by an assortment of Taoseño artists.

Bookstores

Moby Dickens 124A Bent St ☎505/758-3050. Copious selection of local fiction and history, plus New Age material.

Mystery Ink Bookshop 121 Camino de la Placita ☎505/751-1092. Well-stocked secondhand bookstore a short walk southwest of the plaza, with a particularly fine choice of travel and children's titles.

West of Taos

While the obvious day-trip drive from Taos follows the **Enchanted Circle** to the northeast – see p.196 – a longer and wilder route heads **west** on US-64, across the Rio Grande and over the dramatic **San Juan Mountains**. Branching west off Hwy-68 four miles out of downtown Taos, US-64 reaches the awesome 650-foot-high **Rio Grande Gorge Bridge** seven miles on. Be sure to take the time to park at the end and walk out to the middle; otherwise you'll barely get a glimpse of the narrow chasm as you drive across.

After a magnificent seventy-mile mountain run, punctuated by scenic overlooks, US-64 finally drops into **Chama Valley**. From there, either head south into Georgia O'Keeffe country around **Abiquiu**, or north to **Chama** itself, the base for excursions on New Mexico's best-known **steam railroad**.

Tierra Amarilla

US-64 meets the north–south US-84 in **TIERRA AMARILLA** ("yellow earth"), at the foot of the sheer, furrowed **Brazos Cliffs**. This pastoral village, founded in 1832 when the valley was prone to constant Ute, Apache, and Navajo raids, provides a classic example of how New Mexico's Hispanic population suffered after the American takeover of the territory. In 1860, the US Congress refused to recognize that shared grazing lands belonged to the community as a whole, and instead sold them off to a Yankee landowner from Santa Fe.

Bitter disputes have raged ever since, culminating in an incident commemorated by a defaced roadside marker in the heart of the village. In 1967, a group led by Chicano activist **Reies López Tejerina** (a Texan) seized a nearby campground in the Kit Carson National Forest. Declaring independence from the United States, they burned down Tierra Amarilla's Rio Arriba Courthouse, destroying land-grant records and injuring a policeman and a jailer. The government responded by sending in two hundred military vehicles, including tanks. After a controversial trial, Tejerina was acquitted of any involvement by an Albuquerque court. Although he has long since distanced himself from the campaign, passions still run high – hence the sign reading *TIERRA O MUERTE* ("Land or Death") on the outskirts of town.

While Tierra Amarilla remains the county seat, it has suffered a decline in the last thirty years. Parts are now all but derelict, but the community continues to resist the construction of weekend homes for wealthy outsiders, and the possible development of a ski resort on Brazos Peak. In the nearby village of **LOS OJOS** – the scene of major civil disobedience in 1989 – one cooperative effort to revitalize the local economy has proved a resounding success. **Tierra Wools** maintains local **weaving** traditions by breeding Spanish Churro sheep in the valley, and selling hand-dyed rugs and clothing from the clearly signposted Los Ojos Trading Post (☎505/588-7231 or 1-888/709-0979, ⓦwww.handweavers.com), a mile or so west of US-84.

Chama

Tiny **CHAMA**, set in the meadows at the head of the Chama Valley, a dozen miles north of Tierra Amarilla and a total of 85 miles northwest of Taos, is a former mining camp that has reinvented itself as a base for summer elk hunters and winter skiers.

Chama's major appeal for out-of-state visitors is that the pretty yellow station just below the town center is the western terminus of the narrow-gauge **Cumbres & Toltec Scenic Railroad** (late May to mid-Oct; ☎505/756-2151 or 1-888/286-2737, ⓦwww.cumbrestoltec.com), the highest such railroad in the nation. This exhilarating, if not entirely comfortable, 64-mile steam-train ride crosses the High Brazos mountains into Colorado by way of **Cumbres Pass**, then runs through the deep **Toltec Gorge** and out onto the plains at **Antonito**. Its many movie credits include the opening sequence of 1989's *Indiana Jones and the Last Crusade*. The railroad is such an expensive operation to run that it's frequently in financial jeopardy, so it's well worth checking before you come whether it's still functioning on the advertised schedule. It's not possible to do the entire round-trip by train in one day; passengers either go by van to Antonito and return by train (depart Chama 8.30am; $72), or take the train through the most scenic segment as far as Osier, and pick up a return train there (depart Chama 10am; $59). Make sure you dress warmly; it gets pretty cold up in the mountains.

Practicalities

Chama's **visitor center**, half a mile south of town at the junction of US-64 and Hwy-17 (daily: summer 8am–6pm, winter 8am–5pm; ☎505/756-2235 or 1-800/477-0149, ⓦwww.visitchama.com), can provide details on the whole state, as well as the many **riverfront lodges** along US-64/84 to the south, such as the comfortable *Vista del Rio* (☎505/756-2138 or 1-800/939-9943, ⓦwww.vistadelriolodge.com; ⑤). Back in town, *Gandy Dancer*, 299 Maple St (☎505/756-2191 or 1-800/424-6702, ⓦwww.gandydancerbb.com; ⑥), is a **B&B** in a purple clapboard mansion with seven en-suite rooms; "gandy dancer" was railroad slang for a track laborer. In the heart of town, the colorful *Village Bean Coffee House* (☎505/756-1663) serves good deli lunches. The most convenient place to **camp** is the *Rio Chama RV Campground*, beside the river at the north end of town (☎505/756-2303).

The Cumbres Pass and Antonito, Colorado

North of Chama, **Hwy-17** follows much the same route as the railroad, first climbing far above the single track and then crisscrossing it repeatedly as it makes its way up to the 10,022-foot **Cumbres Pass**. In July 1848, legendary "mountain man" Bill Williams was injured here in a confrontation between the US Army and a combined force of Utes and Apaches.

Beyond the pass, highway and railroad part company, not to meet again until they reach **ANTONITO**, Colorado, fifty miles out of Chama – a dreary, depressing little town that's home to the **Cumbres & Toltec Scenic Railroad** terminus, a reasonable *Narrow Gauge Railroad Inn* (☎719/376-5441 or 1-800/323-9469; ❷) and a few basic cafés.

Dulce

US-64 and US-84 join forces for twelve miles **west of Chama**, then once across the Continental Divide (not at all dramatic at this point), US-64 continues alone for another fifteen miles to **DULCE**, the headquarters of the **Jicarilla Apache Indian Reservation**. Today's three-thousand-plus Jicarilla are descended from separate Apache groups who lived further east, some as Plains nomads in the Cimarron area, and some in adobe villages near the pueblos of the Rio Grande. Their name is often said to come from the little baskets (*jicarillas*) they now sell to tourists, but the Jicarilla themselves suggest that they started making baskets when they were confined to this remote reservation in the nineteenth century, and that the name comes from a Mexican word connected with chocolate.

There's little for tourists to see or do on the Jicarilla reservation, whose economy is based on oil and gas revenues and raising sheep. Dulce itself is just a very sharp dog-leg in the highway, where US-64 is forced to turn south rather than climb onto sheer Archuleta Mesa; after a few miles the road turns west again to head through Vaqueros Canyon and Gobernador Canyon (see p.111). However, the roomy and attractive *Best Western Jicarilla Inn* in Dulce (⊤505/759-3663 or 1-800/742-1938; ❹) is regarded as a model for Indian-owned businesses. It has a good restaurant and offers special deals on train trips from Chama.

The Enchanted Circle

The driving circuit through the Sangre de Cristo range northeast of Taos doesn't quite live up to its tourist-brochure billing as the **Enchanted Circle**, though it does pass a handful of long-abandoned ghost towns amid the mountain scenery. While Oklahomans and Texans flock to the closest **ski slopes** to home, visitors from further afield are more likely to spin off east to the hardbitten frontier town of **Cimarron**.

The Lawrence Ranch

Starting seventeen miles north of Taos on Hwy-222, a rutted, muddy road climbs for five miles east to the **Lawrence Ranch**. The English novelist **D.H. Lawrence** made three six-month visits to Taos in the early 1920s, having been enticed across the Atlantic by Mabel Dodge Luhan (see p.179). Staying at her mountain cabin, then known as Kiowa Ranch, he wrote "there are all kinds of beauty in the world, but for greatness of beauty I have never experienced anything like New Mexico." **Georgia O'Keeffe** was also a guest here, in 1929, when she painted the tree right in front of the main cabin as *The Lawrence Tree*. As seen from below, the painting makes the tree look more like a giant squid; it's usually on display in the Georgia O'Keeffe Museum in Santa Fe.

Lawrence died in France in 1930, but five years later his widow Frieda shipped his ashes back to New Mexico. They now rest in a small **shrine** that enjoys panoramic views of the upper Rio Grande valley, at the top of a zigzag cement footpath cleared through the forest; according to some stories, the ashes were actually poured into a wheelbarrow of cement, to ensure they could never be taken away. Frieda is said to have acquired the ranch from Mabel Dodge Luhan in exchange for the manuscript of *Sons and Lovers* – which Mabel in turn used to pay her psychiatrist – and lived in it until her death in 1956. It now belongs to the University of New Mexico, which holds weekend retreats in the main cabin; only the shrine is accessible to visitors, with no fixed hours or admission fee.

Red River

Half a dozen miles beyond the Lawrence Ranch, as Hwy-522 gathers itself for the final climb into Colorado, **Hwy-38** follows Red River east from **QUESTA**, an ugly little village ravaged by opencast mining. After twelve more attractive riverside miles, it reaches **RED RIVER** itself, a former gold-mining town whose rough-shod timber architecture is more authentic than it looks. Summer visitors hike in the surrounding forests, but Red River is at its busiest during the winter **ski** season, when there's cross-country skiing down in the valley and a downhill resort in the mountains to the south. The emphasis here is primarily on family skiing, with only a few of the 57 runs geared toward either beginners or experts. The season typically lasts from late November until late March, with lift tickets costing $48 per day. For full details contact the information office, which doubles as a central **reservations** service (☎505/754-2223 or 1-800/331-7669, ⓦwww.redrivernm.com).

Red River claims to have more **hotel** rooms than Santa Fe, though it's hard to see where they might be. Appealing options include the *Lodge at Red River*, on W Main St (☎505/754-6280 or 1-800/915-6343; ⑤).

Cimarron

Beyond Red River, Hwy-38 negotiates the 9820-foot **Bobcat Pass** – often closed in winter – then drops by way of the ruins of long-abandoned **Elizabethtown** down to **Eagle Nest**. Just a cluster of cabins and RV parks, Eagle Nest sprang up around a lake formed when the **Cimarron River** was dammed in 1920, and is popular with fishing enthusiasts. US-64 parallels the river to enter impressive **Cimarron Canyon** four miles east, beneath the towering 800-foot **Palisade Cliffs**. This route provided access to Taos for nineteenth-century travelers who split from the Santa Fe Trail's "mountain branch" at **CIMARRON** itself, 24 miles east of Eagle Nest.

Cimarron means "wild" or "untamed," and in its heyday the town was as wild as the West could be. It stood at the heart of the 1.7-million-acre **Maxwell Land Grant**, the largest private landholding in the United States, accumulated by Lucien Bonaparte Maxwell in the years following the American takeover of New Mexico. Maxwell's main business was cattle ranching, but with gold and silver mines booming and busting all over the mountains, Cimarron lured a vast profusion of gamblers, gunfighters, outlaws, and cowboys.

Cimarron's old downtown area stands relatively intact half a mile or so south of the main highway. Its history is lovingly chronicled in the **Old Mill**

Museum (June–Aug Mon–Wed, Fri & Sat 9am–5pm, Sun 1–5pm; May & Sept Sat 9am–5pm, Sun 1–5pm; $3), where visitors can pick up a walking tour map of other nearby relics. The most famous of all is the **St James Hotel** opposite the mill museum, at 17th and Collinson (☎ 505/376-2664 or 1-866/472-5019, Ⓦ www.stjamescimarron.com; ❺). Built by President Lincoln's former White House chef in 1873, it's said to have witnessed 26 murders; names in the guest register include Jesse James and Buffalo Bill, who stayed here while organizing his Wild West Show. It now has its own grand restaurant with a tin ceiling, and a less romantic motel annex.

Angel Fire

The Enchanted Circle loops back to Taos from Eagle Nest along US-64, passing, after ten miles, through the part-**golf**, part-**ski** resort of **ANGEL FIRE** in Moreno Valley, first developed in the late 1960s. Despite recent upgrading, Angel Fire shows few signs of maturing beyond its current brash, unappealing sprawl, though the creature comforts of its centerpiece, the *Angel Fire Resort* itself, cannot be faulted (☎ 505/377-6401 or 1-800/633-7463, Ⓦ www.angelfireresort .com; ❺). As at Red River, the ski slopes are usually active between late November and late March, but here they're considerably more suitable for novices, and a new snowboard park, featuring a slalom course, has also been added. Lift tickets cost $48 per day.

Northeast New Mexico

The "road less traveled" today cuts through the region once regularly traversed by Pueblo Indian traders, pioneers on the **Santa Fe Trail**, and those on transcontinental trains. Now followed by the **I-25** interstate, the traditional route between New Mexico and the plains holds few distractions for those wanting to cover distance in good time. The Wild West town of **Las Vegas** provides a good send-off into New Mexico's **northeast corner**; the Sangre de Cristo mountains gradually recede below the western horizon and the Great Plains begin to unfurl in all their relentless monotony. There's no great reason to stray off the interstate until the Rockies start to loom above **Raton**, a hundred miles on, though with time to spare the detour to **Capulin Volcano** at that point is worth making.

Las Vegas

Seventy-three miles from Santa Fe, the sleepy backwater of **LAS VEGAS**, New Mexico, has more in common with its upstart Nevada namesake than may be immediately obvious. Once a wild, lawless frontier outpost, where almost anything went, it consists of two distinct sections. The **old Plaza** area, above the fertile meadows (*vegas*, in Spanish) that line the Gallinas River, was established in 1835, when Hispanic settlers drove away the Comanche and set about capturing trade on the burgeoning **Santa Fe Trail**. When the **railroad** arrived in 1879, the focus of town shifted across the river to the grid of streets around the new station. Incomers included the legendary **"Doc" Holliday**, who briefly owned a saloon on Center Street before scurrying back to Dodge City to escape a murder charge. In one month alone, Las Vegas witnessed 29 gunshot deaths.

At the end of the nineteenth century, Las Vegas was the principal city in New Mexico, and almost all its buildings still date from the Victorian era. The conspicuous lack of adobe makes it easy to forget you're in the Southwest, but it ranks among the state's most authentic Wild West towns, and while it offers no particular stand-out tourist attractions, it's a real delight to stroll around.

Grand Avenue – the main business drag – and I-25 alike now closely parallel the railroad, leaving the **Plaza** high and dry a mile to the west. Its four-square layout resembles something from the Deep South, though a Victorian bandstand rather than a courthouse stands at its center. The only significant building on the perimeter is the *Plaza Hotel* (see below), but **Bridge Street**, which leads up from the highway, is lined with antiques stores and cafés.

Theodore Roosevelt recruited around forty percent of his volunteer **Rough Riders**, who invaded Cuba in 1898, in Las Vegas. Their exploits, plus the minutiae of local history, are recorded in the free **City Museum**, 727 Grand Ave (Mon–Fri 9am–noon & 1–4pm, Sat 10am–3pm; May–Oct also Sun noon–4pm).

Hwy-518 leads due north from Las Vegas into some of New Mexico's most appealing mountain scenery, and serves as an eighty-mile shortcut to **Taos**. The village of **MORA**, thirty miles out, is the seat of Mora County, a Hispanic farming community that has a population of fewer than five thousand. Mora has been ranked by the *Wall Street Journal* as one of the three poorest counties in the US.

Practicalities

Two Amtrak **trains** pull into Las Vegas each afternoon, from Albuquerque and Chicago. Brochures at the **visitor center**, 513 Sixth St (Mon–Fri 9am–5pm; ☏505/425-8631 or 1-800/832-5947, ⊛www.lasvegasnewmexico.com), detail **walking tours** of town.

The nicest place to **stay** is a restored, antiques-furnished en-suite room at the *Plaza Hotel*, 230 Old Town Plaza (☏505/425-3591 or 1-800/328-1882, ⊛www.plazahotel-nm.com; ❺), which offers substantial discounts for online bookings. Its *Landmark Grill* is Las Vegas' classiest **restaurant**, open daily for all meals. There are also plenty of **motels**, such as the *Super 8*, 2029 N Grand Ave (☏505/425-5288 or 1-800/800-8000, ⊛www.super8.com; ❷), and the *Inn of Las Vegas*, 2401 N Grand Ave (☏505/425-6707; ❸). Local students huddle over lunchtime espressos in the coffeehouse at the back of the Second Time Around bookstore, 131 Bridge St (☏505/454-9501), while the nearby *Rialto*, 141 Bridge St (☏505/454-0037; closed Sat), is more of a traditional diner.

Raton

Appealing little **RATON** is tucked into the foothills of the Rockies around a hundred miles north of Las Vegas on I-25, a mere eight miles south of the Colorado border. Once a way-station on the Santa Fe Trail, it reached its present size after becoming the site of a railroad repair shop in 1880 and can have changed little since then.

Few passengers now bother to dismount from the sleek Amtrak Starliner that pulls into the Santa Fe Depot around noon daily, but an hour or two's stroll in **downtown Raton** can be fun. Photos and oddments in the **Raton Museum**, facing the station at 216 S First St (May–Sept Tues–Sat 9am–5pm; Oct–April Wed–Sat 10am–4pm; free), recall highlights from Raton's first century. Until 1938, the town was dominated by the seven-story *Hotel Swastika*, which then "found it necessary to change its name" to the *Yucca*, and is now a bank.

The *Best Western Sands Motel*, 300 Clayton Rd (℡505/445-2737 or 1-800/780-7234, ⓦwww.bestwestern.com/sandsraton; ❹), is the best hotel in town these days, though you can get a cheaper but perfectly adequate room a few blocks north of the Amtrak station in the *Budget Host Raton*, 136 Canyon Drive (℡505/445-3655 or 1-800/283-4678, ⓦwww.budgethost .com/NewMexicoRaton.html; closed Feb; ❸). Alternatively, keep going twenty miles north to **Trinidad** in Colorado, which makes an equally diverting stop.

Capulin Volcano National Monument

CAPULIN VOLCANO NATIONAL MONUMENT, thirty miles east of Raton on US-64/87 and then three miles north on Hwy-325, preserves the neatest and most symmetrical of a chain of cinder cones that last exploded around ten thousand years ago.

Displays explaining its formation can be examined in the **visitor center** (daily: summer 7.30am–6.30pm; winter 8am–4pm; ℡505/278-2201, ⓦwww.nps.gov/ cavo; $5 per vehicle), but most people drive straight on up the two-mile spiral of road that leads to its summit. Once there, a thousand feet above the surrounding plains, you can **hike** for a mile around the rim, enjoying views to the Sangre de Cristo mountains in the west and Oklahoma to the east, or make the slightly more demanding descent down to the vent where it all began.

FOLSOM, six miles north of the volcano, is renowned in scientific circles as the place where archeologists in the 1920s first identified a type of spear point known as the **Folsom point**. Some were found wedged between the ribs of a species of bison that had been extinct for ten thousand years, proving that Paleo-Indians were here around 9000 BC – much earlier than had previously been thought. Such points have since been found at sites all over the Southwest. The original excavation site at Folsom is not open to the public.

Clayton

The town of **CLAYTON** stands fifty miles on from Capulin in the far north-east corner of the state, just short of both Oklahoma and Texas. Early Spanish explorers named this region the **Llano Estacado**, or "Staked Plains," on the basis that they could only find their way through the high grasslands by hammering a trail of wooden stakes into the ground. Clayton itself was founded when the railroad came through in the 1880s, and it's still hard to imagine that anyone would set out on a journey with this as a destination.

The fenced-in dinosaurs on the lawn of the local **visitor center**, 1003 S First St (Mon–Fri 9am–5pm; ℡505/374-9253, ⓦwww.claytonnewmexico.org) – named "Moonbeam" and "Spike" – are a reference to the dinosaur footprints in the fossilized lakeside mud at **Clayton State Park**, twelve miles north (day use $3, camping $7–11; ☎505/374-8808). As well as rock-bottom **motels** in town, like the *Clayton Motel*, 422 Monroe St (☎505/374-2544, ⓦclaytonmotel.com; ❷), there's a *Super 8* to the south at 1425 US-87 (☎505/374-8127 or 1-800/800-8000, ⓦwww.super8.com; ❸).

Albuquerque and southern New Mexico

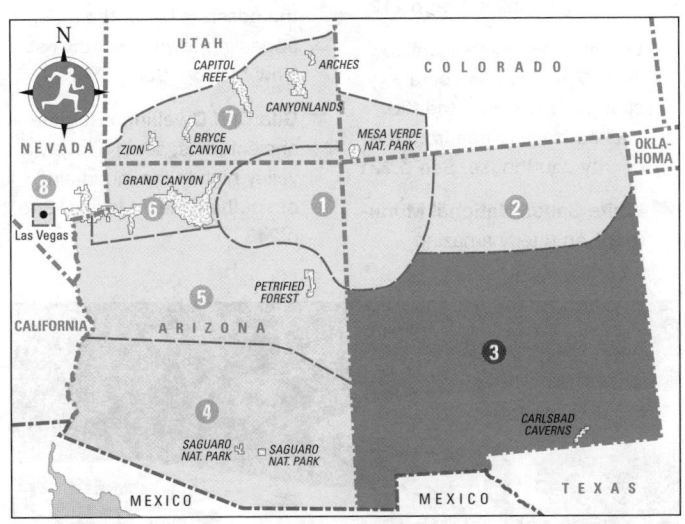

CHAPTER 3 # Highlights

* **Albuquerque International Balloon Festival** It's hard to imagine a more photogenic spectacle than hundreds of colorful hot-air balloons soaring above the Rio Grande on a crisp fall morning. See p.208

* **Indian Pueblo Cultural Center** Albuquerque's premier museum provides a great opportunity to learn about New Mexico's nineteen surviving pueblos. See p.212

* **Lincoln** This quintessential Wild West town has barely changed since Billy the Kid blasted his way free from the county courthouse. See p.221

* **White Sands National Monument** An utterly amazing landscape of pure white sand dunes, lined against the azure sky. See p.229

* **The Underground Lunch Room** A perfect slice of 1950s Americana, this space-age subterranean cafeteria makes a surreal climax to a tour of Carlsbad Caverns. See p.235

* **Silver City** Another wonderful Wild West relic, this mountain retreat from the heat of the desert is by far the most appealing town in southwest New Mexico. See p.243

* **Gila Cliff Dwellings** Remote ancient ruins, set in a lovely valley high in the mountains of southern New Mexico. See p.245

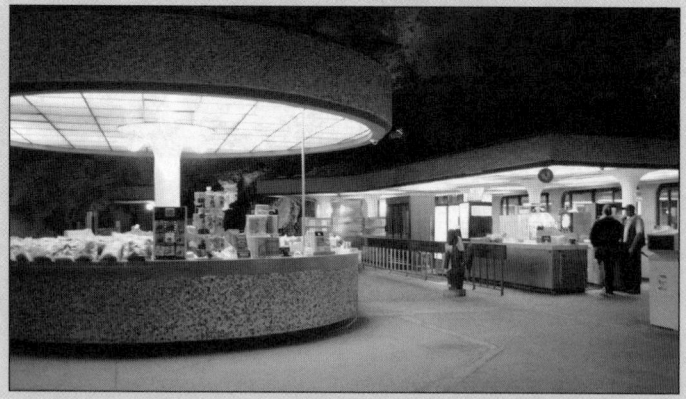

△ Underground Lunch Room, Carlsbad Caverns National Park

Albuquerque and southern New Mexico

C entral and southern New Mexico are not wholly devoid of interest, but it's not surprising that they see fewer visitors than the prime tourist destinations to the north. Despite being the state's largest city, **Albuquerque** holds less to encourage a long stay than Santa Fe or Taos, while few of the towns that lie along the monotonous I-40 highway to the **east**, or in the endless desert expanses to the **south**, are worth going out of your way to see.

Much of the region remained under the domination of the nomadic Apache until well into the nineteenth century. Even Albuquerque was founded long after Santa Fe, while towns such as **Silver City**, **Mesilla**, and **Lincoln** didn't really get going until New Mexico joined the United States in 1846. All three went on to play significant roles in the career of **Billy the Kid**, and all still look today much like the frontier outposts Billy must have known. Together with the pre-Columbian remains of the **Gila Cliff Dwellings** in the remote southwest corner, they're the most appealing historic attractions in the region, but there are also a couple of **geological** wonders. The subterranean labyrinths of **Carlsbad Caverns National Park** lure a million tourists across the plains each year, while the dazzling dunes of **White Sands National Monument** make an extraordinary spectacle against the San Andres Mountains. Top-secret missile tests and bomb blasts give this desolate landscape an added sense of mystery, making its role in popular myth as the site of the notorious **Roswell Incident** a tiny bit more plausible.

ALBUQUERQUE AND SOUTHERN NEW MEXICO

Albuquerque

Sprawling at the heart of New Mexico, where the main east–west road and rail routes cross both the Rio Grande and the old road south to Mexico, **ALBUQUERQUE**, with half a million people, is the state's only major metropolis, even if it isn't the capital. Though many tourists race straight from the airport up to Santa Fe without a thought for Albuquerque, the **"Duke City"** has a good deal going for it. Like Phoenix, it's grown a bit too fast for comfort in the last sixty years, but the original Hispanic settlement is still discernible at its core, and its diverse, cosmopolitan population gives it a rare cultural vibrancy. Even if its architecture is often uninspired, the setting is magnificent, sandwiched between the Rio Grande, lined by stately cottonwoods, and the dramatic, glowing **Sandia Mountains**. Specific highlights for visitors include the intact **Spanish plaza**, the neon-lit **Route 66** frontage of Central Avenue, the fascinating **Indian Pueblo Cultural Center**, and October's **hot-air balloon** extravaganza.

A history of Albuquerque

Three full centuries ago, in 1706, Hispanic colonists founded a new town beside a sweeping curve of the Rio Grande and named it in honor of the Spanish **Duke of Alburquerque**. Albuquerque's earliest surviving adobe buildings, however, still the nucleus of **Old Town**, date from the 1790s, when it occupied a pivotal position on the **Camino Real** – the "Royal Road" from Chihuahua to Santa Fe – which later connected with the **Santa Fe Trail** from the Mississippi. Modern Albuquerque began to grow with the arrival of the railroad in 1880, when its epicenter shuffled a couple of miles east toward the new station. It was around this time that Albuquerque managed to lose its first "r," possibly thanks to a misspelling by a railroad signpainter.

What really transformed Albuquerque was the decentralization of **defense** industries during World War II. Weapons research at **Sandia National Laboratories**, on the giant **Kirtland Air Force Base**, southeast of the city, brought a massive influx of money and jobs. In the 1950s, "Atomic City" was the best-educated city in the nation, in terms of PhDs per capita, and acquired enough federal offices to earn the nickname "Little Washington." It even achieved the dubious distinction of surviving an **H-bomb**: in 1957, a B-36 bomber accidentally dropped a 42,000-pound nuclear device near the air base. Its conventional explosives went off, creating a sizeable crater, but failed to trigger the intended one-megaton thermonuclear blast. Kirtland base these days is effectively a self-contained city, more sealed off than ever from the rest of Albuquerque following the recent spate of terrorist attacks. Manzano Mountain, which is wholly enclosed within its boundaries, is said to be **hollow**, stuffed full of more nuclear weapons than any other site on earth.

Arrival and information

Albuquerque's **International Sunport**, four miles southeast of downtown and New Mexico's principal airport, is served by all major US airlines. All the **rental car** chains have outlets here, while a **taxi** into the center with Yellow

△ National Atomic Museum, Albuquerque

Cab (☎505/247-4888) costs around $10; Airport Shuttle (☎505/765-1234, ⓦwww.airportshuttleabq.com) runs door-to-door shuttles at similar rates. Many hotels and motels also have their own free shuttles. Companies offering bus connections to **Santa Fe** and **Taos** are detailed on p.133 and p.180, respectively.

Both Amtrak and Greyhound are located in an otherwise deserted area, five easy minutes' walk south of downtown. The modern Greyhound **bus terminal**, 300 Second St SW (☎505/243-4435), is used by long-distance east–west services, as well as four daily buses up to Santa Fe ($16) and Taos ($28), and has good-size left-luggage lockers. Two daily Amtrak **trains** – one heading west to Los Angeles, the other east to Chicago – arrive immediately behind the bus depot, at a dilapidated station at 214 First St.

Albuquerque is planning to build a light railway system for local users, to be known as RailRunner; it's hoped that its downtown terminus will incorporate a new Amtrak station. For the moment, the Sun Tran **city bus** network (☎505/843-9200, ⓦwww.cabq.gov/transit) is of more use to commuters than tourists; bus #50 connects the airport with downtown (Mon–Fri 7am–8.30pm, Sat 9am–7pm; $1). However, the **Sun Trolley** circles between downtown and Old Town, Nob Hill, the zoo, and the biological park (same number; daily 7am–7pm; $1).

Information

Free listings magazines and brochures are available from the **visitor center**, adjoining the Albuquerque Convention Center downtown at suite 601, 20 First Plaza NW (Mon–Fri 9am–5pm; ☎505/842-9918 or 1-800/284-2282, ⓦwww .itsatrip.org). Americana enthusiasts will also enjoy their *Historic Route 66* map. Further visitor centers can be found in Old Town, in the Plaza Don Luis on Romero NW (daily: April–Oct 9am–5pm, Nov–March 9.30am–4.30pm), and at the airport (daily 9.30am–8pm). The city's main **post office** is at 1135 Broadway NE (daily 7.30am–6pm).

ALBUQUERQUE AREA

Santa Rosa and Tucumcari

SANDIA MOUNTAINS

Santa Fe

Sandia Peak Tramway

END ROAD

TRAMWAY ROAD

TRAMWAY BLVD

ACADEMY ROAD

PASEO DEL NORTE

SANDIA PUEBLO

ROY

Bien Mur Trading Post

25

Balloon Fiesta Park

ALAMEDA BLVD

JEFFERSON ST

SAN ANTONIO DR

SAN FRANCISCO

MONTGOMERY BLVD

SPAN ROAD

JUAN TABO

MORRIS

EUBANK

MOON

WYOMING

PENNSYLVANIA

COMANCHE ROAD

CANDELARIA ROAD

MENAUL BLVD

INDIAN SCHOOL ROAD

CONSTITUTION

LOMAS BLVD

66

40

CARLISLE

CARLISLE

LOUISIANA

SAN PEDRO DR.

SAN MATEO BLVD

KATHRYN

ZUNI ROAD

CENTRAL AVENUE

Kirtland Air Force Base

Cottonwood Mall

GOLF COURSE ROAD

PARADISE BLVD

N COORS BLVD

EDITH BLVD

SECOND STREET

FOURTH STREET

CHAVEZ/OSUNA ROAD

RIO GRANDE BLVD

Rio Grande

MANTANO RD.

GRIEGOS ROAD

12TH ST

UPTOWN

MIDTOWN

University of New Mexico

NOB HILL

GIRARD

YALE BLVD

GIBSON BLVD

Albuquerque International Sunport

BROADWAY

SECOND STREET

UNIVERSITY BLVD

25

ISLETA BLVD

Indian Pueblo Cultural Center

OLD TOWN

DOWNTOWN

66

TINGLEY DR

COORS ROAD

BRIDGE BLVD

CENTRAL AVENUE

ARENAL ROAD

TOWER ROAD

SAGE ROAD

BLAKE ROAD

RIO BRAVO BLVD

S COORS BLVD

Monument Visitor Center

UNSER BLVD

MANTANO ROAD

ATRISCO DR.

LADERA DRIVE

UNSER BLVD

98TH STREET

40

SCENIC ROAD

GILA ROAD

SQUAW ROAD

UNSER BLVD

Petroglyph National Monument

Acoma and Gallup

N

0   2 miles

3

The balloons of Albuquerque

First held in 1972 as a 50th anniversary stunt for a local radio station, when it featured just thirteen balloons, Albuquerque's annual **International Balloon Fiesta** has grown to become the most important event in world ballooning. By a freak of geography, the **"Albuquerque Box"** offers ideal conditions for balloonists. After takeoff, the prevailing winds consistently blow balloons toward the east, until they clear the top of the Sandia Mountains. Then stronger winds propel them back westwards, making it possible to land more or less where they were launched. As a result, Albuquerque regularly hosts major gas and hot-air ballooning championships, such as the unlikely sounding Coupe de Gordon Bennett.

A photographer's dream, the Balloon Fiesta lasts from the first Saturday until the second Sunday of October. It attracts roughly a thousand balloons and well over a million visitors, so book several months in advance if you need a room, or even a rental car, in early October. The fun focuses on **Balloon Fiesta Park**, half a mile west of I-25 and seven miles north of downtown. Admission costs $6 (under-12s free), with a further $10 for parking. The busiest times are the dawn mass launchings on the four weekend mornings, as well as the "Special Shapes" events, when balloons in shapes ranging from beer bottles to dumptrucks, and dragons to donuts, take to the air. Volunteers are always welcomed to help set the things up, and may be rewarded with a quick flight. For a full festival program, contact ☎505/821-1000 or 1-800/733-9918, ⓦwww.balloonfiesta.com.

Among companies running hot-air balloon flights year round, at typical rates of $140–$180 per person, are Beautiful Balloons (☎505/262-8249 or 1-800/367-6625, ⓦwww.beautifulballoonsco.com), Rainbow Ryders (☎505/823-1111 or 1-800/725-2477, ⓦwww.rainbowryders.com), and World Balloon (☎505/293-6800 or 1-800/351-9588, ⓦwww.worldballoon.com).

Accommodation

The easiest way to find a place to stay in Albuquerque is to cruise the twenty-mile length of **Central Avenue**, the old Route 66, which is lined with the flashing neon signs of dozens of $30-a-night **motels**. Try to have a good look in daylight, to spot those that may turn scary at night. If you want to escape your car for a while, you'll have to pay a little extra to stay in the heart of **Old Town** – which holds few accommodation options – or downtown. Larger convention **hotels** are congregated along the interstates and near the airport – look out for discount coupons in New Mexico's welcome centers – while a handful of **B&Bs** are scattered across the city.

Albuquerque Marriott Pyramid North 5151 San Francisco Rd NE ☎505/821-3333 or 1-800-228-9290, ⓦwww.marriott.com. Gigantic pyramid (stepped not smooth) near exit 232 off I-25 north of town, with a waterfall in the lobby, three restaurants, a fitness center, and over three hundred large rooms, geared especially toward business travelers. ❼

Ambassador Inn 7407 Central Ave NE ☎505/265-1161. There's nothing fancy or exciting about the *Ambassador*, and it's well to the east of the liveliest part of Central Avenue, but for a clean, presentable, ordinary motel room, the price is great. ❷

Aztec Motel 3821 Central Ave NE ☎505/254-1742. Dating from 1931, this small, fake-adobe beauty, featuring a great restored neon sign and festooned with folk art, is the oldest of Albuquerque's Route 66 motels. Most of its guests these days are permanent residents, but it's still a safe and very atmospheric option for tourists, even if the rooms themselves are very basic. ❷

Best Western Insuites Hotel 2400 Yale Blvd SE ☎505/242-7022 or 1-800/780-7234,

@ www.bestwestern.com. Pleasant courtyard motel, quieter than you might expect from its location so close to the airport, and offering a free airport shuttle. ❺

Casas de Sueños 310 Rio Grande Blvd SW ☎ 505/247-4560 or 1-800/665-7002, @ www.casasdesuenos.com. Beautifully furnished, characterful and friendly B&B, very close to Old Town, with themed adobe *casitas* (cottages) and smaller rooms. ❻–❽

Comfort Inn–Airport 2300 Yale Blvd SE ☎ 505/243-2244 or 1-800/221-2222. Good-value motel, served by free shuttles from the airport across the road, and offering complimentary breakfasts. ❹

El Vado Motel 2500 Central Ave SW ☎ 505/243-4594. Vintage adobe Route 66 motel, within easy reach of Old Town. ❷

Hilton Albuquerque 1901 University Blvd NE ☎ 505/884-2500 or 1-800/821-1901, @ www.hilton.com. Midtown high-rise near the intersection of I-40 and I-25. Good rooms, three restaurants, and several busy bars. ❻

La Posada de Albuquerque 125 Second St NW ☎ 505/242-9090 or 1-800/777-5732, @ www.laposada-abq.com. Historic, elegant hotel in a convenient downtown location, built in Mexican style by Conrad Hilton in 1939 – he honeymooned here with Zsa Zsa Gabor. Large, very classy rooms with stylish antique wooden furnishings and openable shutters, a beautiful wood-paneled lobby, and a spacious, atmospheric bar. ❺

Monterey Nonsmokers Motel 2402 Central Ave SW ☎ 505/243-3554 or 1-877/666-8379, @ www.nonsmokersmotel.com. Clean, single-story, fifteen-room motel, two blocks west of Old Town, with pool, laundry, and a strict nonsmoking policy. ❸

Old Town Bed and Breakfast 707 17th St NW ☎ 505/764-9144 or 1-888/900-9144, @ www.inn-new-mexico.com. Friendly, very small-scale B&B in mock-adobe home a couple of blocks from the heart of Old Town. Both of the two guestrooms have private bathrooms, though one is a more extensive suite. ❺/❻

Route 66 Hostel 1012 Central Ave SW ☎ 505/247-1813, @ http://members.aol.com/route66hos/htmlRT66/, @ ctaylor939@aol.com. Albuquerque's only hostel, a friendly place on the outskirts of Old Town, a mile west of downtown, offers dorm beds for $17, kitchen facilities – at times even a free cooked dinner – and very plain but bargain-priced private doubles. Office hours daily 7.30–10.30am & 4–11pm. ❶

The City

Albuquerque consists of several distinct districts, interspersed between anonymous residential areas and threaded through by the twenty-mile artery of **Central Avenue**, the most authentic surviving remnant of the classic Route 66, alive with flashing neon. **Old Town** remains the most interesting area for visitors, with **downtown** two miles to the east and the **university district** and the fashionable **Nob Hill** area beyond that. Further east, the **Sandia Mountains** finally call a halt to the Sunbelt sprawl. The city has begun instead to push west of the Rio Grande, where only **Petroglyph National Monument** holds any interest for tourists.

Old Town

Albuquerque's tree-filled **Old Town Plaza** may lack the cachet of its counterpart in Santa Fe, but it makes an appealing focus for explorations of the old Spanish settlement. After decades of decline, the adobe buildings on all four sides have been restored as souvenir stores and tourist restaurants, with crafts sellers congregating under the porticos on the eastern side. The whole ensemble is still presided over by the twin-towered facade of **San Felipe de Neri church** to the north. Inside the church, the main features are a crucified Christ lying in a glass coffin to the right of the altar and a *retablo* commissioned to celebrate the Bicentennial in 1976.

To get a sense of the city's past, spend an hour or two at the **Albuquerque Museum of Art and History**, a couple of blocks northeast of the plaza at

OLD TOWN

New Mexico Museum of Natural History & Science

National Atomic Museum

Free Parking P

Albuquerque Museum

Tiguex Park

San Felipe de Neri

Rattlesnake Museum

Turquoise Museum

MOUNTAIN ROAD
CHARLEVOIX
SAN FELIPE STREET
ROMERO STREET
SOUTH PLAZA
N PLAZA
OLD TOWN
OLD TOWN ROAD
NINETEENTH STREET
NINETEENTH STREET
MARBLE AVE
SAN PASCALE AVE
LOMAS BLVD
RIO GRANDE BOULEVARD
CENTRAL AVENUE

0 — 100 yds

CENTRAL ALBUQUERQUE

Old Town Plaza (1.1 miles) ▲
Old Town Plaza (1.2 miles) ▲

Galeria Mall

KiMo Theater

Greyhound

Amtrak

GRAND AVENUE
TIJERAS AVENUE
COMMERCIAL
MARTIN LUTHER KING JR BLVD
BROADWAY
FIRST STREET
SECOND STREET
THIRD STREET
FOURTH STREET
FIFTH STREET
SIXTH STREET
SEVENTH STREET
EIGHTH STREET
KELEHER
LOMAS BOULEVARD
ROMA AVENUE
MARQUETTE AVENUE
TIJERAS AVENUE
COPPER AVENUE
CENTRAL AVENUE (ROUTE 66)
GOLD AVENUE
SILVER AVENUE
LEAD AVENUE
COAL AVENUE
FIRST STREET
SECOND STREET
THIRD STREET
FOURTH STREET
FIFTH STREET
SIXTH STREET

0 — 250 yds

ACCOMMODATION

Casas de Sueños	A
La Posada de Albuquerque	B
Route 66 Hostel	C

CAFÉS AND RESTAURANTS

Antiquity	3	La Placita	2
Artichoke Café	4	Red Rock Café	1
Gold Street Caffè	5		

2000 Mountain Rd (daily except Mon 9am–5pm; $4, free Sun 9am–1pm; Ⓦ www.cabq.gov/museum). As well as an impressive array of the armor and weaponry carried by the Spanish conquistadors – though the paucity of local finds means that the exhibits are drawn from sixteenth-century Europe rather than New Mexico – it holds delicate religious artifacts, plus paintings and photos showing Albuquerque through the centuries. There's a lot on the history of weaving along the Rio Grande; Coronado brought five thousand sheep on his expedition here in 1542, which means the region has a longer tradition of sheep-rearing than anywhere else in the United States.

After terrorist attacks around the world made its location within Kirtland Air Force Base inappropriate, the **National Atomic Museum** was moved to new premises at 1905 Mountain Rd NW, across from the Albuquerque Museum (daily 9am–5pm; $5; Ⓦ www.atomicmuseum.com). Until a projected new home is built near the base, visitors can no longer stroll as before amid American fission weapons. Instead, all the exhibits on the history of radiation and nuclear weapons are behind glass. Included are the early discoveries of Madame Curie; newspaper advertisements promoting the health-giving properties of drinking the Radithor brand of radioactive water; and a 1953 *Life* magazine cover reading "*WE ARE IN A LIFE AND DEATH BOMB RACE.*" One of the modern robotic devices on view is the "truck-killing standoff weapon," Fireant. You'll be soothed to learn how much more precise and sophisticated today's weapons are compared to the "primitive city-busting concepts" of the Cold War era, just how safe nuclear waste disposal can be, and a host of other little-known facts. A gift store sells space-age novelties.

Another two blocks east, the **New Mexico Museum of Natural History and Science**, 1801 Mountain Rd NW (daily 9am–5pm; closed Mon in Jan & Sept; $6; Ⓦ www.nmnaturalhistory.org), primarily appeals to kids. Star attractions include full-size animatronic dinosaurs, a simulated volcanic eruption, and a replica of an Ice Age snow cave, plus an engaging, hands-on collection of fossils and dinosaur bones. A Dynamax theater shows the usual limited array of giant-screen movies for an additional charge.

Southeast of the plaza at 202 San Felipe St NW, the bizarre **American International Rattlesnake Museum** has live rattlers on display and rattlesnake curios for sale (Mon–Fri noon–6pm, Sat 10am–6pm, Sun 1–6pm; $3.50; Ⓦ www.rattlesnakes.com). It advertises itself with leaflets that show snakes being handled, but in fact a visit is more likely to consist of walking through a small room at the back of the gift store, where spiders and scorpions as well as snakes are kept in tiny glass cases. Gus' Trading Post, across the highway nearby at 2026 Central Ave SW, stocks a well-priced assortment of Indian crafts and jewelry.

Half a block west of the plaza, in the Old Town Shopping Center at 2107 Central Ave NW, the intriguing little **Turquoise Museum** (Mon–Sat 10am–4pm; $4) looks like just another mall store. Once you step inside, you find that in fact you've entered a fortified bank vault, filled with rare and beautiful turquoise nuggets. The story of worldwide turquoise production is told in copious detail, and there's lots of useful advice on the tricks of the trade; unfortunately, the only way to tell if a piece of turquoise is genuine involves destroying it. Of course, visits end with the chance to buy a few trinkets.

The riverfront

The Rio Grande has shifted its course in the past three hundred years, so there's an unexpectedly low-key gap **west** of Old Town, much of it left undeveloped in deference to the unruly river. Along the wooded eastern riverbank, north of where Central Avenue crosses the river, the **Albuquerque Biological Park** holds two attractions that focus on the natural world.

Not for the squeamish, the **Albuquerque Aquarium** (June–Aug Mon–Fri 9am–5pm, Sat & Sun 9am–6pm; Sept–May daily 9am–5pm; $7; Ⓦwww .cabq.gov/biopark) offers such diverse experiences as eating in a restaurant beside a glass-walled tank filled with live sharks and walking through a tunnel surrounded on all sides by fierce-eyed moray eels. The whole place has been designed with a great eye for aesthetics, with lots of sculpture outside and beautifully lit tanks filled with ethereal, wispy jellyfish within. Across the central plaza, the **Rio Grande Botanic Garden** (same hours, same ticket) consists of two large conservatories – one holding rare plants from the Sonoran and Chihuahua deserts, the other more temperate Mediterranean species – plus a series of formal walled gardens. Disappointingly, the river itself is not visible from either section.

Two miles north of Old Town, by way of Rio Grande Boulevard, the **Rio Grande Nature Center** (daily 8am–5pm; $3 per vehicle; Ⓦwww.rgnc.org) has informative displays describing local wildlife. Two short but pleasant nature trails follow the riverside, feeling far removed from the city.

Indian Pueblo Cultural Center

The **Indian Pueblo Cultural Center**, at 2401 12th St NW, across I-40 a few blocks north of Old Town (Ⓣ505/843-7270 or 1-800/766-4405, Ⓦwww .indianpueblo.org), is a highly informative **museum** (daily 9am–4.30pm; $6) and **crafts market** (daily 9am–5.30pm; free), collectively run by the nineteen New Mexican pueblos. Its horseshoe-shaped design deliberately echoes the architecture of the Ancestral Puebloan city of Pueblo Bonito, in Chaco Canyon.

This is New Mexico's one major museum about Native Americans to be curated by Native Americans, and the displays downstairs, under the banner *Our Land, Our Culture, Our Story*, have a clear and distinct point of view. The shared heritage at the root of Pueblo culture is explained in detail, as is the impact of the Spanish conquistadors. Describing the Pueblo Revolt of 1680 as the "first civil war," it states that by allowing the defeated Spaniards to leave unharmed, the Pueblo peoples "showed them more mercy than they showed us." There's also as good an explanation as you're ever likely to get of a topic Pueblo Indians rarely discuss with outsiders; how indigenous Pueblo religion has managed to coexist with imported Catholicism. Videos illustrate modern Pueblo life, while a separate display case is devoted to each individual Pueblo.

An outstanding selection of pottery and jewelry is sold in the stores upstairs, which you can visit without paying the museum admission fee. A separate **art gallery** hosts changing exhibitions of Native American art. The good-quality *Pueblo Harvest* café on site is reviewed on p.215. On weekends throughout the year, **Pueblo dances** take place in the central courtyard (Oct–March Sat & Sun noon, April–Sept Sat & Sun 11am & 2pm; free).

The National Hispanic Cultural Center

A mile south of Old Town, still on the east side of the river, the Barelas neighborhood traditionally marked the point where the Camino Real trail from Mexico entered Albuquerque. Since 2000, it has been home to the **National Hispanic Cultural Center**, at 1701 Fourth St (daily except Mon 10am–5pm; $3; Ⓦwww.nhccnm.org). Whether you choose to visit this impressive complex of buildings is likely to depend on what's on in its spacious **art gallery**, where stimulating temporary exhibitions complement permanent displays that focus on "Hispanidad," with lots of New Mexican religious iconography. A good **cafe**, *La Fonda del Basque*, serves breakfast and lunch daily.

Downtown

Downtown Albuquerque may be where New Mexico's largest city conducts its daily business, but it holds little that's likely to detain tourists for long; unless you're staying in a hotel nearby, you may bypass it altogether.

The University District

A couple of miles east of downtown, the campus of the **University of New Mexico** stretches along the northern side of Central Avenue. The 26,000-strong student body keeps the southern side of the highway lively around the clock with funky hangouts of all kinds, from bookstores and laundromats to cafés and diners.

Of the six museums on campus, non-academic visitors are most likely to enjoy the **Maxwell Museum of Anthropology** (Tues–Fri 9am–4pm, Sat 10am–4pm; free; ☏505/277-4405, Ⓦwww.unm.edu/~maxwell), which holds a wide range of displays on the Peoples of the Southwest, past and present. There's some fine Mimbres pottery (see p.246), as well as material from Chaco Canyon, while the Ancestors segment traces human evolution from the three-million-year-old Lucy, just 3ft 7in tall, unearthed in Ethiopia.

The Sandia Mountains

The forested 10,500ft peaks of the **Sandia Mountains** tower over Albuquerque to the east; the view from the summit is especially beautiful at and after sunset, when the city lights sparkle below. In summer it's a good 25°F cooler up here than in the valley, while in winter you can go downhill or cross-country **skiing** (mid-Dec to mid-March; lift tickets $35 per day; ☏505/242-9052, Ⓦwww.sandiapeak.com).

The most exciting way to reach the top is by riding the world's longest tramway, the 2.7-mile **Sandia Peak Tramway**, which departs from the end of Tramway Road a dozen miles northeast of town. During the uppermost 1.5 miles of its exhilarating 15-minute climb, not a single support tower interrupts the progress of the cable car (summer daily 9am–9pm; winter Mon & Wed–Sun 9am–8pm, Tues 5–8pm; $8).

If you'd rather **drive** to the top of the mountains, you have to circle around the back and approach from the east, by way of I-40 and the Sandia Crest Scenic Byway – a route described on p.157.

Petroglyph National Monument

Beneath a chain of burned-out cinder cones thrown up by a 150,000-year-old volcanic eruption, a low seventeen-mile escarpment west of the Rio Grande has been designated as the **PETROGLYPH NATIONAL MONUMENT** to protect the area's unusually accessible ancient Native American **rock art**. Apart from the spectacular views of the valley and the Sandia Mountains, there's no great need to go to its **Las Imágenes visitor center** (daily 8am–5pm; ☏505/899-0205, Ⓦwww.nps.gov/petr), reached by crossing the river on I-40 then driving four miles north on Unser Boulevard. Instead, continue to the petroglyphs themselves, another mile north in **Boca Negra Canyon** (same hours; Mon–Fri $1 per vehicle, Sat & Sun $2 per vehicle).

Three short trails off the canyon's one-way loop road lead up to the escarpment, which on close inspection turns out to consist of tumbled black lava boulders; only the half-hour **Mesa Trail** demands any energetic climbing. Most of the crudely scratched images you'll pass, ranging from simple spirals to masked figures and eagles with Bart Simpson hairdos, date from 1300 to 1680 AD. During the eighteenth century, shepherds from the nearby Hispanic settlement of Atrisco added a number of Christian crosses and symbols.

Petroglyph National Monument has for many years been the focus of intense controversy, thanks to repeated campaigns to allow the construction of a new highway through its heart. City boosters argue that the only direction in which Albuquerque can expand any further is westwards, and that the monument is therefore a crucial obstacle to future progress. The snag is, of course, that the whole point of a national monument is to protect an area from development. Albuquerque mayor Martin Chavez announced in 2002 that Unser Boulevard would soon be "aggressively extended" through part of the monument, despite opposition from the nineteen New Mexican pueblos as well as local activists. So far court challenges have prevented that happening, but the issue remains very much alive.

Eating

The chefs of Santa Fe may be trying to redefine Southwestern cuisine, but Albuquerque still knows what it likes – mountainous **Mexican** meals. This is the place to come to grips with what real New Mexican food is all about, with family diners all over the city competing to create the spiciest *chile rellenos*, enchiladas, and *sopaipillas*. If you prefer to stick with the familiar, there are also 25 branches of *McDonald's* and a number of gourmet restaurants where prices are generally well below those in Santa Fe. If you don't mind driving a few miles out of town, further fine dining options within easy reach of Albuquerque include the *Range Cafe* in Bernalillo (see p.155) and *Prairie Star* at nearby Santa Ana Pueblo (see p.166).

Coffeehouses

Gold Street Caffe 218 Gold Ave SW ☎505/765-1633. Oddly formal downtown espresso cafe, offering full breakfasts, and wonderful pastries. Mon–Fri 7am–2pm, Sat & Sun 8am–2pm.

Red Rock Café 308 San Felipe NW ☎505/243-4377. Old Town coffee bar, open for breakfast and lunch daily, with salads and desserts as well as espressos.

Satellite Toys & Coffee 3513 Central Ave NE ☎505/256-0345. University District hangout, marked by the sign of the flying saucer, with the irresistible slogan "serious coffee, silly toys." The toys in question are gifts and novelties rather than playthings; the coffee is all you could ask for. They also serve daily specials like split pea soup; plus, there's some sidewalk seating. Mon–Thurs & Sun 6am–10pm, Fri & Sat 6am–11pm.

Budget restaurants and diners

Duran Central Pharmacy 1815 Central Ave NW ☎505/247-4141. Mexican dining counter attached to a working drugstore, not far from Old Town, with delicious, inexpensive tortillas, enchiladas, and plenty of chile, both green and red. Mon–Fri 9am–6.30pm, Sat 9am–2pm.

Flying Star 3416 Central Ave SE ☎505/255-6633. Lively, crowded Nob Hill café serving eclectic international cuisine to a largely student clientele. Queue at the counter for breakfast specialties, salads, and daily blue plate specials like Vietnamese noodles, pasta pomodoro, or a crab cake sandwich for around $10. No alcohol is served, however. Other branches at 8001 Menaul NE, 4026 Rio Grande NW, 723 Silver SE, and 4501 Juan Tabo NE. Sun–Thurs 6am–11.pm, Fri & Sat 6am–11.30pm.

Frontier 2400 Central Ave SE ☎505/266-0550. Legendary 24-hour diner across from the university, where an unceasing parade of characters chow down on burgers, burritos, and great vegetarian enchiladas.

La Placita 208 San Felipe St NW ☎505/247-2204. Attractive centuries-old adobe hacienda on the Old Town Plaza, where a predominantly tourist crowd enjoys Mexican meals, plus fried chicken or sandwiches, at surprisingly reasonable prices – almost everything costs under $10. There's live Mexican music most evenings, too. Daily 11am–9pm.

Olympia Cafe 2210 Central Ave SE ☎505/242-4890. Good-value Greek and Mediterranean food, including gyros and falafel, that's also available for take-out. Across from the university on Route 66. Mon–Fri 11am–10pm.

Pueblo Harvest Cafe Indian Pueblo Cultural Center, 2401 12th St NW ☎505/843-7270. Indian fry-bread and other Pueblo specialties, plus good guacamole burgers. Mon–Fri 8am–3pm, Sat & Sun 8am–5pm.

66 Diner 1405 Central Ave NE ☎505/247-1421, ⓦ www.66diner.com. Classic Fifties diner near the university, with white-capped waiting staff, a soda fountain, and a lively late-night clientele. Mon–Thurs 11am–11pm, Fri 11am–midnight, Sat 8am–midnight, Sun 8am–10pm.

Sadie's 6230 Fourth St NW ☎505/345-5339. Huge, great-value Mexican restaurant – the stuffed *sopaipillas* are irresistible, as indeed are the margaritas. It's too bright and loud, with giant TV screens, to be romantic, but it's a good place to bring kids. Mon–Sat 11am–10pm, Sun 11am–9pm.

Fine dining

Antiquity 112 Romero St NW ☎505/247-3545. Old Town cottage turned romantic restaurant, serving French cuisine, some of it given a New Mexican twist by a leavening of chile. Entrees typically cost $18–27. Dinner only, nightly from 5pm.

Artichoke Cafe 424 Central Ave SE ☎505/243-0200. Simple but classy restaurant in the heart of downtown, with indoor and outdoor seating and quality art on display. Good, varied menu of California-influenced modern American cuisine; most entrées well under $20. Mon 11am–2.30pm & 5.30–9pm, Tues–Fri 11am–2.30pm & 5.30–10pm, Sat 5.30–10pm, Sun 5–9pm.

High Finance 40 Tramway Rd NE ☎505/243-9742. Pricey seafood and steak restaurant in unparalleled location, at the top of the Sandia Peak Tramway – see p.213 – with eagle's-eye views of the sunset over Albuquerque. Entrees range $15–45. Daily: summer 11am–9pm, winter 11am–8pm.

Gruet Steakhouse at the Monte Vista 3201 Central Ave NE ☎505/256-9463. Upmarket steakhouse, housed in one of Nob Hill's unlikeliest buildings – a restored Art Deco Pueblo Revival fire station. French owners give it a certain continental flair, and naturally a good wine list, but the basic principle is very American – you pay up to $37 for a slab of prime beef, eaten in opulent surroundings. Daily 5–10pm.

Scalo 3500 Central Ave SE ☎505/225-8781. Large, multi-level but nonetheless romantic and stylish Northern Italian restaurant not far from the university, where appetizers like steamed mussels or beef carpaccio cost around $10, entrees such as half a roasted organic chicken are closer to $20, and there's a wide range of pasta and vegetarian options for a little less. Tues–Thurs 11.30am–10pm, Fri 11.30am–11pm, Sat 5–11pm, Sun 5–10pm.

Drinking and nightlife

Most of Albuquerque's best **nightclubs**, theaters, and music venues are concentrated within a couple of blocks along Central Avenue downtown; the spectacularly restored **KiMo Theater** in particular should not be missed. There are also a few **brewpubs** around, while oddly enough, many of the larger chain hotels hold reasonable **bars**. The free weekly *Alibi* magazine (ⓦ www.alibi.com) carries full listings of what's coming up or going down.

The Anodyne 409 Central NW ☎505/244-1820. Downtown's most popular bar offers pool tables, pinball, a good jukebox, and an eclectic mix of customers, from beer guzzlers to martini sippers.

Brewster's Pub 312 Central Ave SW ☎505/247-2533. Raucous downtown bar, where on any night except Monday – reserved for football – you've a good chance of hearing live jazz, Latin, or blues.

Caravan East 7605 Central Ave NE ☎505/265-7877. Enormous honky-tonk, where tenderfeet can do the two-step with throngs of urban cowboys. Two live bands play nightly, with a cover charge of $3 Fri & Sat only, and a free dinner buffet 5–7pm.

Club Rhythm and Blues 3523 Central Ave NE ☎505/256-0849, ⓦ www.clubrb.com. University District bar that plays hosts to Latin, swing, and jazz bands as well as blues acts. Showtime Wed–Sat 9pm.

El Rey Theatre 620 Central Ave SW ℡ 505/243-7546. Live music from salsa to country, and all points in between.

Puccini's Golden West Saloon 620 Central Ave SW ℡ 505/764-2624. Venue of choice for Albuquerque's metal maniacs and host to touring indie bands.

KiMo Theater 423 Central Ave NW ℡ 505/848-1370. Gorgeous city-owned "Pueblo Deco" theater, dating from the late 1920s, which puts on an eclectic program of opera, dance, and theater performances, kids' movie shows, and also regular live bands.

The Launchpad 618 Central Ave SW ℡ 505/764-8887, ⓦ www.launchpadrocks.com. Dance and live music space that showcases touring indie and world music bands; there's also a cluster of pool tables.

Midnight Rodeo 4901 McLeod Rd NE ℡ 505/888-0100. Huge country-music club – the largest in the Southwest – with a great old-fashioned race-track dance-floor, though all the music comes from DJs rather than live bands. Wed–Sat 8pm–2am. Cover $6, Fri & Sat only.

East of Albuquerque

The first twenty miles of I-40's eastward run from Albuquerque are scenic, as the interstate threads its way between the Sandia Mountains. Once through the hills, however, unless you then turn north onto the **Turquoise Trail** toward Santa Fe – see p.156 – you're in for a long hard slog out into the plains. The only place before Texas that might conceivably pique your curiosity is **Fort Sumner**, which played a heart-rending role in Navajo history and also holds the grave of **Billy the Kid**.

Santa Rosa

A hundred unutterably boring miles east of the Sandia Mountains, weary drivers reach their first potential overnight stop. South and west of the interstate, a four-mile stretch of the former Route 66 runs through **SANTA ROSA**. As **Parker Avenue** in the small downtown, and **Will Rogers Drive** further east, it's dotted with diners and motels, but there's little worth going out of your way to see, apart perhaps from the restored classic cars at the **Route 66 Auto Museum**, 2766 Route 66 (daily: May–Aug 8am–8pm, Sept–April 8am–5pm; $5).

Scuba-divers desperate for a wet dip cross the plains to plunge into Santa Rosa's **Blue Hole**, a crystal-clear natural pool that's sixty feet across and eighty feet deep, though to anyone who's seen the ocean it may come as an anticlimax. You'll find it by turning left off Fifth Street, south of the main drag, onto Blue Hole Road. There are operators renting gear in town.

In 1541, the first Spanish expedition into the Southwest is said to have crossed the Pecos River by constructing **Coronado's Bridge**, ten miles south of Santa Rosa on the dead-end Hwy-91. Following the lush riverbanks makes a welcome break from the interstate, and the village of **PUERTO DE LUNA** at road's end is pretty enough, but not a trace of the bridge remains.

Practicalities

Santa Rosa's **visitor center** is at 486 Parker Ave (Mon–Fri 9am–5pm, Sat 9am–1pm; ℡ 505/472-3404 or 1-800/450-7084, ⓦ www.santarosanm.org). Of its dozen or so **motels**, the *Super 8*, 1201 Will Rogers Drive (☎505/472-5388 or 1-800/800-8000, Ⓦwww.super8.com; winter ❷, summer ❸) is large, clean, and comfortable, while the *Best Western Adobe Inn*, 1501 Will Rogers Drive (☎505/472-3446 or 1-800/780-7234; winter ❸, summer ❹) offers high-standard rooms and a pool. The best place to **camp** is Santa Rosa Lake State Park, seven miles north of town on Hwy-91 (☎505/472-3110; $10).

The *Lake City Diner*, downtown at 101 Fourth St (☎505/472-5253), is a spotless **restaurant** straight out of a Norman Rockwell painting. Housed in a converted bank, it was due to change owners as this book went to press, but should continue serving good-value Mediterranean cuisine plus daily specials.

Tucumcari

Sixty miles east of Santa Rosa, **TUCUMCARI** is the definitive Route 66 pit-stop. If you expect its abundant truck stops, diners, and motels to yield a kitsch fascination, you'll be sorely disappointed, but their glittering neon signs make a welcome sight as dusk descends on the plains. No one in their right mind stays two nights in Tucumcari; an hour spent admiring the barbed-wire collection of the **Tucumcari Historical Museum**, 416 S Adams St (June–Aug Mon–Sat 8am–6pm; Sept–May Mon–Fri 8am–5pm; $2.11), should convince you it's time to hit the road again.

Practicalities

Route 66, also known as Tucumcari Boulevard, cuts a broad five-mile swath through town, passing 34 motels along the way, as well as the local **visitor center** at 404 W (Mon–Fri 8am–noon & 1–5pm; ☎505/461-1694, Ⓦwww .tucumcarinm.com). Among the more salubrious places with **rooms** for $40 or under are the classic Route 66 *Blue Swallow* motel, 815 E Route 66 (☎505/461-9849, Ⓦwww.blueswallowmotel.com; ❷), and the *Palomino*, 1215 E Route 66 (☎505/461-3622; ❶). Slightly more upscale options include the *Super 8*, 4001 E Route 66 (☎505/461-4444 or 1-800/800-8000, Ⓦwww.super8.com; ❷), and the *Best Western Discovery Inn*, 200 E Estrella Ave (☎505/461-4884 or 1-800/780-7234; ❹).

As far as **dining** is concerned, the choices are plentiful yet limited; *Del's Family Restaurant*, 1202 E Route 66 (☎505/461-1740; closed Sun), is as good a diner as you're going to find.

Fort Sumner

A 45-mile detour south of I-40 near Santa Rosa brings you to modern **FORT SUMNER**, a small town named after a nineteenth-century Army outpost that stood seven miles southeast, on what's now **Fort Sumner State Monument** (daily 8.30am–5pm; $3; Ⓦwww.nmmonuments.org). The fort was infamous as the headquarters of the **Bosque Redondo Indian reservation**, where nine thousand Navajo and Mescalero Apache captives were incarcerated during the 1860s after being rounded up by General James Carleton and Kit Carson and forced to make their way here on foot in what's remembered as the Long Walk (see p.592). The idea was for the reservation to be self-sufficient and for the Indians to become accustomed to an agricultural lifestyle. In fact, the Pecos

River proved too salty to drink, let alone use for irrigation. In the words of Navajo headman Barboncito:

Whatever we do here causes death. Some work at the *acequias*, take sick, and die; others die with the hoe in their hands; they go to the river to their waists and suddenly disappear; others have been struck and torn to pieces by lightning. A rattlesnake bite here kills us; in our country a rattlesnake before he bites gives warning which enables us to keep out of its way and if bitten, we readily find a cure – here we can find no cure.

The Mescalero escaped in November 1865, only to be chased by Carson and suffer further slaughter. The Navajo remained until General William T Sherman arrived to replace Carleton on May 28, 1868; the treaty that allowed them to return home was signed on June 1. Over three thousand prisoners had died.

A low ridge of adobe bricks on the eastern riverbank is all that remains of the fort the Navajo built for their captors, but the dead are now honored by a large new visitor center-cum-museum, unveiled in 2005 as the **Bosque Redondo Memorial**. It holds detailed exhibits on the whole sorry story, including emotive contemporary photos of soldiers guarding large groups of Native American captives.

After the reservation closed down, the fort and the surrounding land were bought by rancher Lucien Maxwell. **Billy the Kid** was hiding in his son Peter's bedroom here in 1881 when **Pat Garrett** tracked him down and shot him dead. His **grave** is located in the backyard of the **Old Fort Sumner Museum**, a few hundred yards east of the fort (daily 9am–5pm; $3.50). Billy was buried alongside two fellow outlaws, Tom O'Folliard and Charlie Bowdre; all remain imprisoned to this day, as their joint tombstone, poignantly inscribed "*PALS*," is protected from would-be thieves behind steel bars. Originally erected by the film director King Vidor, the tombstone has been stolen so often that participants in an annual festival, held on the second weekend of June, now compete to "steal" an eighty-pound replica, and then throw it as far as possible.

The museum itself holds a jumble of items that may or may not have belonged to Billy, together with displays relating to local history. In that respect, it's indistinguishable from the rival **Billy the Kid Museum**, back in town at 1601 E Sumner Ave (mid-May to mid-Sept daily 8.30am–5pm; mid-Sept to mid-May Mon–Fri 8.30am–5pm, Sun 11am–5pm; $4). The latter museum however is vast, with endless warehouses full of old cars, wagons, typewriters, and other rusty hardware. For the full saga of Billy the Kid, see pp.244–5.

Practicalities

Were you to be trapped by a desert thunderstorm, you might choose to shelter in one of Fort Sumner's otherwise unexciting **motels**, such as the *Coronado*, 309 W Sumner Ave (☎505/355-2466; ❶), or the *Super 8*, 1707 E Sumner Ave (☎505/355-7888 or 1-800/800-8000, ⓦ www.super8.com; ❷). Later on, you'd probably end up eating a cheap Mexican **meal** at *Sadie's*, 510 E Sumner Ave (☎505/355-1461).

Clovis

The midsize railroad and ranching community of **CLOVIS**, on the border with Texas sixty miles east of Fort Sumner and 85 miles southeast of Tucumcari, has twice entered the history books. In 1932, the remains of prehistoric mammoth hunters found at nearby **Blackwater Draw** provided the first firm evidence that humans were present in North America as much as twelve thousand years ago. Although archeologically speaking it was a sensational discovery, the **Blackwater Draw Museum**, en route to **PORTALES** a dozen miles southwest of town on US-70 (summer Mon–Sat 10am–5pm, Sun noon–5pm; winter closed Mon; $2), is not wildly exciting. The excavation site, ten miles east on Hwy-467, is open to visitors in summer (same hours and ticket).

Clovis's other brush with fame came in 1958, when a bespectacled teenager, **Charles "Buddy" Holly**, crossed the state line from Lubbock, Texas, to record a few tunes with his band, the Crickets – *Peggy Sue*, *That'll Be the Day*, and a dozen others. Contact the visitor center in advance (see below) to arrange a tour of Norman Petty's original **studio** – which also gave Roy Orbison his first break – at 1313 W Seventh St. You may even get to meet Buddy's original backing singers.

Practicalities

Clovis's **visitor center** is downtown at 215 N Main St (Mon–Fri 9am–5pm; ☎505/763-3435, ⓦwww.clovisnm.org), near the huge, derelict old *Hotel Clovis*. **Motels** interspersed between the Mexican diners and fast-food specialists along US-60/84 further east include the *Best Western La Vista Inn*, 1516 Mabry Drive (☎505/762-3808 or 1-800/780-7234; ❸), and the *Clovis Inn*, 2922 Mabry Drive (☎505/762-5600 or 1-800/535-3440, ⓦwww.theclovisinn.com; ❷).

Southeast of Albuquerque

Although the Rio Grande Valley, south of Albuquerque – and covered on p.236 onwards – has always held a larger human population, the terrain that lies **southeast** of the city is of far greater scenic and historic appeal. Here you'll find the ancient pueblos of **Salinas National Monument**, the eerie gypsum wastelands of **White Sands**, and the mountain resorts of **Ruidoso** and **Cloudcroft**. Most compelling of all, however, is the rough-hewn frontier town of **Lincoln**. Scene of the bloodiest exploits in the legendary career of **Billy the Kid**, it has remained all but untouched in the century since his death.

Salinas National Monument

The precious salt deposits of **Salinas Valley**, east of the Manzano Mountains around seventy miles southeast of Albuquerque, were regarded by early Spanish colonists as one of New Mexico's greatest treasures. Franciscan missionaries targeted the Pueblo peoples of the valley, erecting massive churches atop their existing settlements, but due to epidemics and Apache raids, the entire region had been abandoned by the time of the Pueblo Revolt of 1680. Three separate ruined pueblos now form **SALINAS NATIONAL MONUMENT**. Each has its own "contact station" (all daily, summer 9am–6pm, winter 9am–5pm; free), and they share a **visitor center** (daily 8am–5pm; free; ☎505/847-2585, Ⓦwww.nps.gov/sapu) in **MOUNTAINAIR**, 36 miles east of I-25 on US-60. Mountainair itself is a small community whose one claim to fame is that fifty years ago it was the "Pinto Bean Capital of the World."

The largest of the Salinas pueblos, **Gran Quivira**, stands on a low hill 26 miles south from Mountainair along Hwy-55. It's the only one where the pueblo itself has been more than minimally excavated, a process which has revealed an impressive 300-room structure complete with hidden *kivas*, built in secret to avoid the wrath of the Spanish priests. The adjoining Mission of San Buenaventura church was probably not yet completed by the time the pueblo was abandoned. Juan de Oñate, who visited Gran Quivira in 1598, reported that its inhabitants painted stripes on their noses.

The main feature of **Quarai**, a mile west of Hwy-55 eight miles north of Mountainair, is the fortress-like stone church of La Purísima Concepción, whose golden walls tower above the rubble-strewn mounds that conceal the pueblo village. At **Abó**, just north of US-60 nine miles west of Mountainair, the church of San Gregorio dominates an even more tantalizing expanse of ruins.

Carrizozo and the Valley of Fires

Fifty miles southeast of Gran Quivira, where US-54 meets US-380, **CARRI-ZOZO** is a parched desert outpost that replaced better-known Lincoln as the seat of Lincoln County in 1909. There's nothing much to it, but it does hold a couple of **motels.** The *Four Winds*, at the crossroads (☎505/648-2356; ❷), has its own restaurant. The *Outpost Bar & Grill* is a rather gloomy saloon at 415 Central Ave (☎505/648-9994) that's renowned for its green chile burgers. The espresso café *Carrizozo Joe's*, 133 Central Ave (☎505/648-5637), serves calzones and sandwiches.

The **Valley of Fires Recreation Area**, four miles northwest (daily dawn–dusk; $3, or $5 per vehicle; ☎505/648-2241), preserves a jet-black river of lava that poured for over forty miles down the Tularosa Valley around 1500 years ago. Though it ranges from four to six miles wide and up to 150 feet deep, the one trail across the lava is less than a mile long. It's so rough underfoot, and so exposed to the sun, that you're unlikely to want to hike any further, but there's a good **campground** alongside ($12). At its southern end, the lava flow abuts the utterly contrasting White Sands National Monument; see p.229.

Three Rivers Petroglyphs

Five miles east of US-54, halfway from Carrizozo to Alamogordo, an extensive if not wildly enthralling collection of pre-Columbian **rock art** now forms the **Three Rivers Petroglyph National Recreation Area** (daily dawn–dusk; $2). Between 1000 and 1400 AD, agricultural Mogollon villagers hacked over twenty thousand petroglyphs into boulders at the foot of the Capitan Mountains, depicting bighorn sheep, stylized masks, and geometric patterns. A representative sample can be admired from a half-mile trail, while a separate, easier trail leads to the remains of three Mogollon dwellings. This area once belonged to Susan Barber, "Cattle Queen of New Mexico" and widow of Alexander McSween, killed in the Lincoln County War (see p.224). She's said to have

Trinity Site

Twice each year, sightseers make a peculiar pilgrimage to the **Trinity Site**, out on the **White Sands Missile Range** in the desert thirty miles west of Carrizozo, where the first **atomic bomb** was detonated at 5.30am on July 16, 1945. Brought by road from Los Alamos (see p.159) in the back of a '42 Plymouth, the bomb, code-named **Fat Man**, was not dropped but placed atop a steel tower. As well as destroying a nearby "doom town" built to study its effects, the blast was strong enough to shatter windows in Silver City, 120 miles west, and to fuse the sands below "Ground Zero" into a thick slab of radioactive green glass known as **trinitite**. It made a crater that was eight feet deep, which was subsequently filled in to minimize radiation.

The Missile Range has witnessed thousands more weapons tests since then, and remains off-limits to nonmilitary personnel except for the first Saturdays of April and October. Visitors on those days can either join a "caravan" of vehicles that sets off from **Alamogordo** at 8am, or enter the range unaccompanied via the **Stallion Gate** (8am–2pm), on US-380 fifty miles west of Carrizozo. You're forbidden to stop or take photos other than at the site itself, or to make political speeches, and urged to resist the temptation to pick up any trinitite you may spot. Not only is it part of a National Historic Landmark, it's radioactive.

For full tour information, contact Alamogordo's visitor center (see p.229). If you'd like to know more about the range itself, drop in at the White Sands Missile Range Museum, described on p.230.

"rode as hard and shot as straight as any man." There's no accommodation in the immediate vicinity.

Capitan

A twenty-mile drive up into the mountains east of Carrizozo brings you to the crossroads known as **CAPITAN**, notable only as the birthplace of a little bear named **Smokey**. Rescued from a forest fire in 1950, the five-month-old Smokey was taken to the National Zoo in Washington DC, where he survived another 26 years and became a national fire prevention symbol. His words of wisdom, seen on anti-fire billboards across the country – "Only YOU Can Prevent Forest Fires" – live on. Smokey's grave is the centerpiece of **Smokey Bear Historical State Park**, which also features exhibits on his life and a short nature trail (daily 9am–5pm; $2; ⓦwww.smokeybearpark.com). Capitan is plagued, incidentally, by a running feud between people who say "Smokey Bear" (good) and willful misfits who insist on "Smokey *the* Bear" (bad).

The *Smokey Bear Restaurant and Motel*, 316 Smokey Bear Blvd (ⓣ505/354-2253 or 1-800/766-5392, ⓦwww.smokeybearmotel.com; ❷) offers basic **accommodation** and dining near the park, while *Rodney's Copa Cabana*, nearby at 321 Smokey Bear Blvd (ⓣ505/354-7637; closed Sun & Mon) serves fancier Mediterranean-influenced food.

Lincoln

Though not strictly speaking a ghost town, tiny **LINCOLN**, twelve miles east of Capitan on Hwy-380, is as perfectly preserved a Wild West settlement as it's possible to imagine. During the late nineteenth century, around 750 people made their home in this cattle-ranching center and Army outpost of **Fort Stanton**, including the legendary outlaw Billy the Kid. Bypassed by the railroads, however, it lost its role as seat of Lincoln County to Carrizozo in 1909; the population soon dwindled to well under a hundred, and time seems to have stood still ever since. No new buildings have joined the venerable false-front structures that line Main Street, and the entire town is now **Lincoln State Monument**, jointly run by the state of New Mexico and Ruidoso's Hubbard Museum of the American West (see p.225). Visitors can stroll its length at any time, while the cheapest way to visit its various historical sites is via a joint admission ticket, sold at each ($6 for all Lincoln sites plus Hubbard Museum, or $3.50 for each individual site; not all sites remain open throughout the winter; ☏505/653-4372, Ⓦwww.nmmonuments.org & Ⓦwww.hubbardmuseum.org).

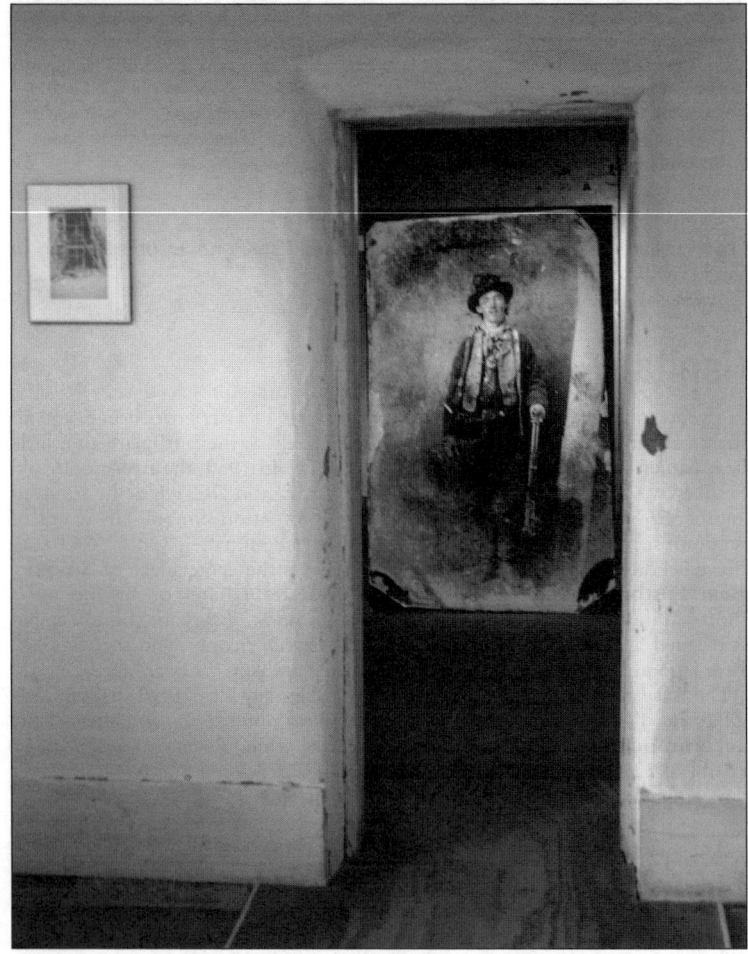

△ Billy the Kid still haunts Lincoln's County Courthouse

The **Historic Lincoln Visitors Center** (daily 8.30am–5pm), toward the east end of town and also known as the Anderson-Freeman Museum, offers the fullest displays on local history, and its short opening video makes a good introduction to Lincoln's complicated story. After exhibits covering Hispanics, cowboys, "Buffalo Soldiers" – the black cavalrymen stationed at Fort Stanton – and Apaches, the museum moves on to the Lincoln County War. Its account of Billy's life is extremely thorough, extending to the coroner's handwritten report on the men shot during his April 1881 escape; none of the artifacts and memorabilia however have been definitively identified as belonging to Billy himself.

Alongside the museum stands Lincoln's oldest building, the **Torreón**. This circular masonry tower may resemble the handiwork of Ancestral Puebloans, but was in fact erected by Hispanic settlers during the 1850s, as a refuge against Apache raids. It's too small to admit visitors; a glance from the street makes it easy to imagine quite how cramped and airless it must have been and speaks volumes about the miserable, unglamorous reality of frontier life.

A few yards further west, the **Tunstall Store** is an extraordinary time capsule (March–Nov daily 9am–5pm). The "mercantile" over which the Lincoln County War was fought – and which passed from the Tunstall to the Dolan factions as a result – must have failed to sell a single item in the ensuing century. It remains stocked with dusty date-expired groceries, plus Victorian storekeeping paraphernalia like weighing scales and cash registers, cases of photos and artifacts, and even Lincoln County's first-ever light bulb, installed in 1914 and allegedly still capable of burning. The wounded Billy the Kid is said to have hidden beneath the floorboards after shooting Sheriff William Brady on the street outside, on April 1, 1878.

After Dolan took over Tunstall's operation, L.G. Murphy's original store, across the road and a hundred yards west, became the **Lincoln County Courthouse** and served as Billy's prison when he was brought back from Mesilla to be hanged (daily 8.30am–5pm). It's hardly surprising that Billy felt he was being railroaded, as evidenced by his increasingly bitter letters to Governor Lew Wallace, displayed upstairs in the actual courtroom where his cell formerly stood. A bullethole at the foot of the stairs shows where he shot Deputy Bell during his famous escape. You can stand at the window through which he then shot Marshal Olinger. Stones in the garden mark where the two men died. That the courthouse is now so old and musty only adds to the atmosphere of it all.

Practicalities

Lincoln doesn't have its own visitor center; call the monument offices for general information. On the first weekend of August, the town fills up and its streets echo with gunfire once again during the three-day **Old Lincoln Days** festival.

Near the courthouse, the *Wortley Hotel* – once owned by Pat Garrett – had to be rebuilt to its original appearance following a fire in the 1930s (☎505/653-4300 or 1-877/967-8539, ⓦwww.wortleyhotel.com; April 28 to mid-Oct only; ④). It now offers seven plain but appealing hotel rooms, furnished with functional Victorian antiques; its dining room serves simple stews and sandwiches at lunchtime only, including the pot roast and mashed potatoes that constituted Marshal Bob Olinger's final meal. If you like a bit more comfort, head to the *Casa de Patrón* (PO Box 27, Lincoln, NM 88338 ☎505/653-4676, ⓦwww .casapatron.com; ⑤), another former store and hideout of Billy the Kid that's now a friendly, romantic B&B, with three en-suite rooms in an 1860 house, two

Billy the Kid and the Lincoln County War

The Hispanic farming community of Las Placitas del Río Bonito, founded during the 1850s, was renamed **Lincoln** in 1869. It became the seat of **Lincoln County**, which occupied a quarter of New Mexico – itself much larger than it is today – and was, at 27,000 square miles, the largest county in the United States. At that time, rival Anglo ranchers and their political allies were competing for economic control throughout the Wild West. What some historians call the **Western Civil War of Incorporation** pitted large cattle-raising conglomerates, federal lawmen, and Republican capitalists against small-scale Democrat ranchers and cowboys. Such tensions were every-where exacerbated by individual antagonisms; Tombstone's **Gunfight at the OK Corral** is a classic example (see p.298).

Lincoln in the 1870s was dominated by a "ring" of men that centered on the mercantile, or store, of **Lawrence G. Murphy**, an Irish former theology student, Freemason, and alcoholic whose business affairs were run by **James J. Dolan**. Their racketeering included rustling cattle from local rancher **John Chisum** to supply beef at knock-down prices to the US Army at nearby Fort Stanton. The arrival of a wealthy 23-year-old Englishman, **John Tunstall** (born in Dalston, east London, in 1853), who opened a rival mercantile in Lincoln with lawyer **Alexander McSween**, triggered the **Lincoln County War**.

On February 18, 1878, Tunstall was murdered on the road to Ruidoso by a posse of Dolan's men. (A plaque on US-70, ten miles east of Ruidoso, now marks the spot.) Among Tunstall's hired hands who witnessed the slaying was the gunslinger history remembers as **Billy the Kid**. Born Henry McCarty in Brooklyn in late 1859, he had been brought west by his mother, who married William Antrim in Santa Fe in 1873. Within a year she had died in Silver City, and young Billy Antrim was cast adrift. A life of petty teenage crime culminated with the shooting in August 1877 of a bullying Irish blacksmith in Fort Grant, Arizona. Now calling himself **Billy Bonney**, the fledgling outlaw fled to Lincoln.

After Tunstall's death, his men formed the **Regulators** and were deputized by the local justice of the peace to seek out his killers. Ten of them, including Billy, killed the two chief culprits in March, then gunned down **Sheriff William Brady**, a Dolan man, on Lincoln's main street on April 1. That July, forty of Dolan's supporters laid siege to the Regulators in the adobe home of Alexander McSween; after five days, they summoned soldiers from Fort Stanton, who trained a Gatling gun on the house and set it ablaze. McSween and three Regulators were killed trying to escape the flames, but Billy and around ten others sprinted to safety.

more in a modern annex, and a couple of individual *casitas*. The *Lincoln Grille*, a tiny shack close to the Torreón, serves simple lunchtime burgers and burritos (☏505/653–4805).

Ruidoso

For visitors from the flatlands of west Texas and Oklahoma – not to mention valley towns like Alamogordo – the hilltop community of **RUIDOSO**, nestling at an altitude of almost 7000 feet amid the forested Sacramento Mountains thirty miles southwest of Lincoln, offers an enticing weekend retreat from the heat of summer. As a result, it's the fastest-growing resort in the Southwest, with motels and mountain lodges lining several miles of the Ruidoso ("Noisy") River. Tourists from further afield, however, may well find it lacking in interest, though it makes a reasonable overnight stop en route to Carlsbad.

Billy spent two years on the run, mostly rustling cattle near Fort Sumner, where he also dealt cards in the saloon of Texan buffalo hunter **Pat Garrett**. In 1880, New Mexico's governor **Lew Wallace** offered an amnesty to all participants in the Lincoln County War who would testify against Dolan. Billy accepted the deal and surrendered, only to escape when he realized that Wallace – then busy writing *Ben Hur* – was not going to keep his word. Later that year, Garrett was elected as sheriff of Lincoln County, on a pledge to recapture Billy (who naturally lobbied for his opponent). Garrett knew exactly where to look. Just before Christmas, after ambushing and killing two of Billy's friends at Fort Sumner, he duly captured Billy himself at nearby Stinking Springs. Reporting his arrest, the *Las Vegas Gazette* made the first-ever reference to "Billy the Kid."

Billy was taken by train to Santa Fe and on to **Mesilla** (see p.241), where he was convicted of Sheriff Brady's murder in the only successful prosecution relating to the Lincoln County War. As he awaited the hangman's noose in Lincoln's courthouse – which was the former Murphy store, its owner James Dolan having by now taken over the Tunstall mercantile down the street – Billy pulled off his most daring **escape**, on April 28, 1881. Taking advantage of a trip to the outhouse, he shot Deputy J.W. Bell with his own gun. Meanwhile, Marshal Bob Olinger, a long-time Dolan ally, was having lunch with a group of prisoners in the *Wortley Hotel*. Hearing the shots, he raced across the street, to be felled by a blast from an upper window. Eyewitness accounts relate how Billy struggled unsuccessfully for an hour to break his shackles, and repeatedly fell off the horse he was attempting to commandeer, watched all the while by a crowd who dared not intervene.

With a $500 reward on his head, Billy fled back to Fort Sumner. Late on the night of July 14, Garrett crept into the bedroom of rancher Pete Maxwell, whose family owned Fort Sumner, to ask if he had seen his friend Billy. Moments earlier, Billy had climbed through the window to find out if Maxwell knew Garrett's whereabouts. Garrett recognized Billy's voice calling out *"quién es?"* (who's there?) and shot him dead.

The next year, Garrett wrote a bestseller, *The Authentic Life of Billy The Kid, the Noted Desperado of the Southwest*. He was not re-elected as sheriff, however, and embarked on a life of wandering that saw him ranching in Texas, a guest of Theodore Roosevelt at the White House, and a customs collector in El Paso, before he was eventually murdered for no apparent reason near Las Cruces in 1908. Strangely enough, the man who shot him, William Brazel, was the uncle of the main "witness" of the Roswell UFO crash in 1947 (see p.231).

Ruidoso's major claim to fame is the **All-American Futurity**, which was, until the 1980s, the world's richest **horse race** of any kind – and with prize money totaling more than $2.5 million, it remains the highest-paying event for quarter horses. (Quarter horses, the world's most popular breed, are so-called because they excel at quarter-mile races.) The race takes place each Labor Day at the **Ruidoso Downs** racetrack, just east of town, as the climax of a 77-day season that runs from late May to early Sept (for a full schedule, see ⓦwww .ruidosodownsracing.com). Also at the track, the **Billy the Kid Casino** offers year-round slot-machine gambling.

All matters equine are celebrated in the **Hubbard Museum of the American West**, alongside the racetrack (daily 10am–5pm; $6; ☎505/378-4142, ⓦwww.hubbardmuseum.org). Outside is the sculpture ensemble of eight life-size galloping horses – *Free Spirits of Noisy Water*. Displays on the natural and human-related history of horses plot their arrival in North America – which was really a return, as horses had become extinct on the continent around 7000

BC – and there's a selection of memorabilia from around the world, such as horse-drawn Russian sleighs, English road coaches, and Wild West stagecoaches. By the time you reach "Anne's Attic," holding collector Anne Stradling's riding trophies and copies of *Black Beauty*, the interest of all but pre-adolescent girls may have been exhausted.

In winter, attention turns to the 12,000ft slopes of **Ski Apache** (☏505/336-4356, ⓦwww.skiapache.com), a downhill ski area northwest of town where lift tickets cost around $54 per day. Though operated by the Mescalero Apache, it's not on tribal land.

Practicalities

The lobby of Ruidoso's **visitor center**, at 720 Sudderth Ave (Mon–Sat 9am–5pm, Sun 1–4pm; ☏505/257-7395 or 1-877/784-3676, ⓦwww.ruidoso .net), remains open even when the office itself is closed, and holds dozens of brochures on local attractions and motels. In addition, an information office alongside the Hubbard Museum (see above; same hours as museum) can provide maps and details on the **Billy the Kid National Scenic Byway** (ⓦwww.billybyway.com).

Despite the large number of **accommodation** options, supply still fails to meet demand on big race days. Among inexpensive options are the *Apache Motel*, 344 Sudderth Ave (☏505/257-2986 or 1-800/426-0616, ⓦwww .ruidoso.net/apache; ❸), and the *Super 8*, beside US-70 at 100 Cliff Drive (☏505/378-8180 or 1-800/800-8000, ⓦwww.super8.com; ❸), which has separate male and female saunas. The ten riverside *Ruidoso Lodge Cabins*, 300 Main Rd (☏505/257-2510 or 1-800/950-2510, ⓦwww.ruidosolodge.com; ❻), provide considerably more comfort and seclusion.

The major local showpiece is the glitzy *Inn of the Mountain Gods*, three miles southwest of town on Carrizo Canyon Road (☏505/257-5141 or 1-800/545-9011, ⓦwww.innofthemountaingods.com; winter ❼, summer ❽). Owned by the Mescalero Apache, and recently totally revamped and expanded to the very highest standards, thanks to its lucrative on-site casino, it offers fine dining, golf, fishing, tennis, and horse riding as well as luxury accommodation. Its premier **restaurant**, *Wendells* (☏505/464-7482), serves hugely meaty and expensive dinners, with steaks costing up to $44. At lunch, fancy burgers and sandwiches run $7–12. The Gathering of Nations buffet offers copious all-you-can-eat spreads at $9.75 for breakfast, $15 for lunch, and $18.50 dinner (summer all meals daily; winter Mon, Tues, Thurs dinner only; Fri lunch and dinner; Sat & Sun all meals).

Other dining possibilities in Ruidoso range from the classy French cuisine of *Le Bistro*, 2800 Sudderth Drive (closed Sun; ☏505/257-0132), to the sandwiches and coffee at the nearby *Books and Beans*, 2501 Sudderth Drive (lunch only, closed Sun; ☏505/630-2326), or the steaks, pasta, and pizzas in *Weber's Grill*, at the *Pub 48* microbrewery, 441 Mechem Drive (☏505/257-9559).

Mescalero Apache Indian reservation

Immediately south of Ruidoso, US-70 runs for around fifteen miles through the highlands of the **Mescalero Apache Indian reservation**. The Mescalero trace their history as a distinct Apache group back to the early eighteenth century, when like the Jicarilla of northern New Mexico (see p.196), they were driven from the plains by the Comanche and turned to a lifestyle partly of farming and partly of raiding Pueblo and Hispanic settlements. In 1862 Kit Carson rounded up some 500 Apaches to be confined with the Navajo at Bosque Redondo (see p.217). The Apache were eventually granted this small reservation in 1873, which was too high to grow or gather many of their traditional foods. The Mescalero were later joined by other Apache refugees, such as those remnants of Geronimo's Chiricahua who chose to return to the Southwest in 1913 from their enforced exile in Oklahoma.

Thanks both to their successful investment in Ski Apache and the revenues from gaming at the *Inn of the Mountain Gods* (see opposite), the Mescalero's tribal economy has greatly strengthened in recent years. Tourists don't get to see much from the highway, and most of the roads leading off it are barred to outsiders. It's well worth driving through the open-range country between Ruidoso and Cloudcroft, however, where wildflowers dot the quasi-Alpine meadows and Apache cowboys gallop in pursuit of their errant cattle.

Cloudcroft

Much smaller and cozier than Ruidoso, the picturesque mountain village of **CLOUDCROFT** – forty miles further south, and almost two thousand feet higher – has been a vacation resort from the word go. It was built in 1898, after a railroad spur was pushed up into the Sacramento Mountains in order to carry timber down to El Paso, and immediately began to attract day-trippers escaping the sweltering valley below. The railroad is long gone and drivers bored by miles of flat straightaways get to twist their way up US-82 from Alamogordo, leaving behind the bare sandstone hills, scattered with creosote bushes, as they penetrate the forested uplands.

Though it lacks any great history or significance, Cloudcroft itself is a pretty little Western community that makes a nice enough place in which to while away an afternoon. The souvenir stores and cafés that line the boardwalk of **Burro Avenue**, one block north of the highway, do seem to be getting a bit more kitschy with each year that passes, which makes **hiking** an increasingly enjoyable alternative to shopping. Cloudcroft stands at the heart of the southern segment of the Lincoln National Forest, which features maintained and waymarked trails of varying lengths. Starting near the west end of town, the **Cloud Climbing Rail Trail** follows the old railroad route for a mile down to a vast ruined trestle which drivers on US-82 may have already noticed. Spectacular views extend right across the valley; it's usually possible to glimpse the White Sands (see p.229) in the form of the thin white line at the foot of the San Andres Mountains on the far side.

Practicalities

Cloudcroft's **visitor center** is housed in a log cabin beside US-82 on the eastern approaches to town (daily 10am–5pm; ☎505/682-2733 or 1-866/874-4447, ⓦwww.cloudcroft.net). For information on this section of Lincoln National Forest, you can also call in at the local ranger station on Chipmunk Avenue (open in summer only, Mon–Fri 8am–5pm; ☎505/682-2251). The rangers are also responsible for several nearby **campgrounds**; the closest to town, about a mile northeast of the center along Hwy-244, is *The Pines* (☎505/682-2551; mid-May to mid-Sept; $8).

Most of the visitors who come to Cloudcroft are here to experience the mountains and rent their own individual **cabin**, even if it's sitting among scores of others. Usually rented for a minimum of two nights, the cabins always have heating and en-suite facilities, while many also offer kitchenettes or extra bedrooms. *Buckhorn Cabins* (☎505/682-2421, ⓦwww.zianet.com/ buckhorn; ❷–❺) is on the highway in the town center – and has a sideline in selling large carved wooden bears – while *Spruce Cabins* (☎505/682-2381, ⓦwww.sprucecabins.com; ❷–❺), and *Tall Timber Cabins*, 1102 Chautaqua Canyon Rd (☎505/682-2301 or 1-888/682-2301, ⓦhttp://home.earthlink .net/~talltimbercabins; ❹) are tucked up in the hills further east. Six miles west of town, perched in the woods down towards Alamogordo, the blue-painted double-decker *Cloudcroft Mountain Park Hostel* (☎505/682-0555, ⓦwww .cloudcrofthostel.com; ❶/❷; cash only) is a smart motel-style **hostel** that offers dorm beds for $17 and private rooms for $30.

South of the highway, a mile up Hwy-130, *The Lodge at Cloudcroft* (PO Box 497, Cloudcroft, NM 88317 ☎505/682-2566 or 1-800/395-6343, ⓦwww .thelodgeresort.com; ❻–❾) ranks among the Southwest's most prestigious **historic hotels**. As well as well-priced B&B rooms, it features some absurdly plush suites and private cottages, and also *Rebecca's*, an attractive continental restaurant with panoramic views. It even has its own golf course, at an elevation of 9000ft.

The choice of **restaurants** in Cloudcroft is relatively limited. The *Front Porch Pizza and Grill* on Burro Avenue (☎505/682-7492) serves espresso coffee as well as pizza, while the *Texas Pit Barbeque*, next to *Buckhorn Cabins* at 211 Hwy-82 (☎505/682-1101), prepares inexpensive barbecued meats.

Alamogordo

Sprawled at the foot of the Sacramento Mountains seventy miles northeast of Las Cruces, **ALAMOGORDO** is, like Los Alamos, a child of the Bomb. Once a quiet ranching center, it has grown since World War II to a town of well over thirty thousand inhabitants, most of whom owe their living to the various military bases and research facilities tucked away in the surrounding deserts. It's a conservative enough place to have held public burnings of the *Harry Potter* books in 2002.

Alamogordo's original central streets remain surprisingly unchanged, but they're now a neglected backwater compared to the frenzy of commercial activity along the five-mile strip of US-54, here known as **White Sands Boulevard**. Given pride of place at the **Tularosa Basin Historical Society Museum**, 1301 N White Sands Blvd (Mon–Sat 10am–4pm; free), an old electric toaster from *Howards Cafe* bears witness to quite how little ever happens around these parts. Other exhibits include a headdress worn by Geronimo and the stuffed head of a grizzly bear.

Any five-story building in Alamogordo would probably be a tourist attraction; that the gleaming glass cube on the hillside east of town holds the **New Mexico Museum of Space History** is gilding the lily (daily 9am–5pm; museum $3, movie theater $6, each additional show $5.25; ⓦwww.spacefame .org). Displays inside trace the history of rocketry from eleventh-century China onwards, covering New-Mexico-based pioneers Robert Goddard (see p.232) and Wernher von Braun (see p.231) – one snap of von Braun's cheery crew sitting astride a V-2 rocket is straight out of *Dr Strangelove* – up to the futuristic Delta Clipper, designed to replace the Space Shuttle and offer the first commercial space flights. A diorama depicts the unfortunate Ham, who became the first chimp in space in 1961 and was trained at Alamogordo by receiving electric shocks or banana-flavored pellets according to which lever he moved. There's also a mock-up Martian landscape – not something it's all that hard to create in New Mexico. The adjoining **Clyde W. Tombaugh Omnimax Theater** shows giant-screen movies and doubles as a state-of-the-art **planetarium**; there's also a "garden" of abandoned rockets outside.

Practicalities

Alamogordo's **visitor center** is alongside the Tularosa Basin museum at 1301 N White Sands Blvd (Mon–Fri 8am–5pm, Sat & Sun 9am–5pm; ☎505/437-6120 or 1-800/826-0294, ⓦwww.alamogordo.com). **Motels** along US-54 range from the *Super 8*, north of town at 3204 N White Sands Blvd (☎505/434-4205 or 1-800/478-8378, ⓦwww.super8.com; ❸) – and directly opposite the huge White Sands Mall (and movie theater) – to the friendly, high-standard *Best Western Desert Aire*, at 1021 S White Sands Blvd (☎505/437-2110 or 1-800/565-1988, ⓦwww.bestwestern.com; ❹), which has an outdoor pool.

As for **food**, it's more fun to head downtown than to eat at the diners along the main highway. *Margo's*, 504 E First St (☎505/437-0689), is a popular Mexican standby, while for a classier evening, *Memories*, 1223 N New York Ave (☎505/437-0077; closed Sun), is a "Continental" restaurant set in a slightly precious, very floral old house, where all the entrées, which include steaks, salmon, and swordfish, cost well under $20 including soup or salad.

White Sands National Monument

The glistening, three-story dunes of **White Sands** fill 275 square miles of the broad Tularosa Basin, between the Sacramento and San Andres mountains. Though its whiteness is beyond dispute, it's not sand but fine **gypsum**, deposited on an ancient seabed 250 million years ago. Anywhere else, the gypsum would have dissolved and been carried off by rivers; here, however, it's trapped in a riverless ring of mountains. The southern portion of this surreal landscape has been set aside as **WHITE SANDS NATIONAL MONUMENT**, entered north of US-70 fourteen miles west of Alamogordo. One of the very few must-sees in southern New Mexico, it also provides a wonderful opportunity for photographers, though the bright light of midday is likely to bleach out your finest efforts.

Beside the highway, the **visitor center** (daily: late May to early Sept 9am–7pm; early Sept to late May 8am–5pm; ☎505/479-6124, ⓦwww.nps.gov/whsa) illustrates the unique bleached life-forms that have adapted to suit this pallid environment. From here, it takes five more miles along the paved portion of **Dunes Drive** (daily: summer 7am–9pm; winter 7am–sunset; $3) before you reach the heart of the dunes. At first, as you drive beyond the entrance station and get your first glimpses of white sand beneath the scrubby vegetation, you may wonder what the fuss is about. Unless you have either an abundance of time or walking difficulties, skip the unenthralling nature trail along the **Interdune Boardwalk**.

A little further along, the plants thin out, and you come to an utterly bizarre world of dazzling white knife-edge ridges and graceful slopes. The drive now loops around a six-mile one-way labyrinth, where the roadway is at times

△ Futuristic picnic shelters at White Sands National Monument

hundreds of yards wide, and then narrows again to a slender channel, as the west winds that constantly replenish the dunes pile sand in your path in luxuriant drifts. Plentiful pull-outs, some of them equipped with fabulous 1950s-style curving picnic shelters, enable you to leave your vehicle and plough through pristine sand to the top of the ridges, which offer long-range mountain views. Slipping and sliding back down again is even better.

There's no developed **campground** at White Sands, but backcountry camping is allowed, by permit only (available at the monument visitor center). Once or twice a year, rangers also lead vehicle convoys up to Lake Lucero, the actual source of the sands; call ahead to see if one is currently scheduled. And note that roughly twice each week, both US-70 and the Dunes Drive **close** for up to two hours while missile tests are underway.

White Sands Missile Range Museum

A couple of miles north of the national monument boundary on the top-security White Sands Missile Range – said to be the largest military installation in the United States – the **White Sands Space Harbor** holds one of the three seven-mile runways where the **Space Shuttle** is able to land. A back-up facility to the regular landing sites in California and Florida, it has only been used once, in 1982. Note that this is *not* the proposed site for Virgin Galactic's commercial spaceflights; see p.240.

For the full story of what goes on here, head for the **White Sands Missile Range Museum**, thirty miles west of the monument en route to Las Cruces, and four miles south of US-70 (Mon–Fri 8am–4pm, Sat & Sun 10am–3pm; free; ☎505/678-8824, ⓦwww.wsmr-history.org). The open-air **Missile Park** alongside offers a chance to inspect "the weapons that won the Cold War and Operation Desert Storm," and displays all the missiles ever tested at White Sands. These date back to "Vengeance Weapon 2," the **V-2** rocket, almost four thousand of which were fired across the English Channel by the Nazis during World War II. After the war, the weapon's designer, Dr Wernher von Braun, directed the firing of sixty more V-2s at White Sands – one went astray and crashed across the border near Ciudad Juarez, Mexico. He moved on to Huntsville, Alabama, in 1950.

The southeast corner

East of the mountains, at the edge of the Great Plains, **southeast New Mexico** has little in common with the rest of the Southwest. It's not quite as dull as it looks, however; all its treasures are tucked away underground, in the shape of the oil and mineral wealth that keeps its economy ticking and the fairytale labyrinth of **Carlsbad Caverns National Park**. Traditionally, Carlsbad used to be the only reason tourists ever strayed this way, but these days a steady influx of pilgrims also make the trek to contemplate the extra-terrestrial wonders of **Roswell**.

Roswell

Fifty-seven miles east of the Wild West town of Lincoln, and seventy-five miles north of the national park at Carlsbad, you'll encounter a history unlike that of any other part of the state. The small ranching town of **ROSWELL** is renowned as the spot near which an **alien spacecraft** supposedly crashlanded on the night of July 4, 1947. The commander of the local air force base authorized a press statement announcing that they had retrieved the wreckage of a flying saucer, which had been taken away for examination. Despite a follow-up denial within a day, claiming that it was in fact a weather balloon – and more recent statements such as President Clinton's categorical assertion that "No, an alien spacecraft did not crash in Roswell, New Mexico, in 1947" – the story of the so-called "**Roswell Incident**" has kept running. As 100,000 *X-Files* fanatics descended upon Roswell in 1997 for a six-day festival to mark the "Incident's" fiftieth anniversary, the US Air Force revealed that the errant balloon had been monitoring the atmosphere for evidence of Soviet nuclear tests. Witnesses were also said to have confused the balloon crash with a series of parachute experiments in 1953, which involved the dropping of dummies from high-altitude planes. UFO theorists, however, remain unconvinced. Incidentally, considerable vagueness surrounds exactly where the crash took place. Since a local entrepreneur bought up one purported site, the original witnesses have started to "remember" that it all happened somewhere else entirely. With TV series such as *Roswell* and *Taken* perpetuating the myth, Roswell's curious tourist boom shows no signs of abating.

Despite its best intentions, and the wishful thinking of the truly weird clientele who drift in from the plains, the central **International UFO Museum**, 114 N Main St (daily 9am–5pm; $2; ☎505/625-9495, ⊛www.iufomrc.org), inadvertently exposes the whole tawdry business as transparent nonsense. Set up by the military press officer responsible for the 1947 announcement, it reveals such gems as the assertion that John F. Kennedy was shot because he was about to reveal the secret, and that Neil Armstrong, astonished at encountering flying saucers on the moon, blurted out "Boy, were they beige!" (You'd have to assume that "big" was the word he was fumbling for.) Murals depict "what might have happened," while the showpiece exhibit is a model of the "**alien autopsy**," said to have taken place at the Wright-Patterson Air Force Base in Dayton, Ohio. Built for the movie *Roswell*, it probably also featured in the grainy "documentary" autopsy footage that created a brief international sensation in 1995. Note also the "fiction" and "non-fiction" sections in the museum bookstore.

By way of contrast, the long-standing **Roswell Museum**, 100 W 11th St (Mon–Sat 9am–5pm, Sun 1–5pm, free), boasts an excellent, multifaceted collection with nary an alien corpse to be seen. Its most sensational section celebrates pioneer rocket scientist **Robert Goddard** (1882–1945), one of whose early experiments prompted the newspaper headline *'Moon Rocket' Man's Test Alarms Whole Countryside*. His entire laboratory has been reconstructed, and an entertaining video shows him wheeling a rudimentary rocket in a wagon to the launch pad, then racing to escape the blast in a model T Ford. Elsewhere, historical artifacts range from armor and pikes brought by Spanish conquistadors, to an Apache Ghost Dancer's shirt and astronaut Harrison Schmitt's spacesuit. There's also a huge, top-quality **art gallery**, displaying Southwestern landscapes by Henriette Wyeth and Peter Hurd as well as a solitary Georgia O'Keeffe, *Ram's Skull With Brown Leaves*.

Practicalities

Roswell's **visitor center**, at 426 N Main St (Mon–Fri 8am–5pm; ☎505/624-0889, ⓦwww.roswellnm.org), is active in promoting the town's annual **UFO Festival**, held on the weekend of July 4 (ⓦwww.uforoswell.com). The finest **motel** in town, the *Best Western Sally Port Inn*, 2000 N Main St (☎505/622-6430 or 1-800/548-5221, ⓦwww.bestwestern.com; ❹), also has a good restaurant; if you just want a place to lay your head, the *Frontier Motel*, 3010 N Main St (☎505/622-1400 or 1-800/678-1401, ⓦwww.frontiermotelroswell.com; ❷), is much cheaper, and has a good pool. The *Cattle Baron*, 1113 N Main St (☎505/622-2465), is a large, good-value **steakhouse** with an extensive salad bar, while *Farley's*, a little further up the hill at 1315 N Main St (☎505/627-1100), is a livelier sci-fi-themed pub and diner that's popular with cadets from the massive New Mexico Military Institute across the street.

Carlsbad

Considering that a million tourists per year pass through **CARLSBAD** en route to Carlsbad Caverns National Park – covered below – the town itself is astonishing in its blandness. A century of ranching and potash-mining has given it a sizeable if characterless downtown area, but the one significant attraction is the **Living Desert State Park**, a couple of miles northwest (daily: summer 8am–8pm, winter 9am–5pm; last admission 1hr 30min before closing; $5). This botanical garden of desert plants doubles as a zoo that houses elk, bear, rattlesnakes, and a prairie dog village.

Carlsbad also possesses the dubious distinction of being home to the **Waste Isolation Pilot Plant**. This subterranean facility, hollowed out from a thick layer of salt two thousand feet below ground level, opened in 1999 as the world's first repository for radioactive waste created during the production of nuclear weapons. It's been marked up to ensure no humans stray down there for at least ten thousand years; you can find more details on Ⓦ www.wipp .energy.gov.

Practicalities

Carlsbad's **visitor center**, at 302 S Canal St (Mon–Fri 8am–5pm; ℡ 505/887-6516 or 1-866/922-9226, Ⓦ www.carlsbadchamber.com), can supply copious lists of local **motels**. The cheap options, like the clean, comfortable *Super 8*, 3817 National Parks Hwy (℡ 505/887-8888 or 1-800/800-8000, Ⓦ www .super8.com; winter ❷, summer ❸), line US-62/180 to the southwest. More central alternatives include the large *Best Western Stevens Inn*, 1829 S Canal St (℡ 505/887-2851 or 1-800/730-2851, Ⓦ www.stevensinn.com; ❹), where rates include a full breakfast at the *Flume Room* **restaurant**. That's as good a place to eat as you're likely to find. In the heart of town, the *Blue House Bakery*, 609 N Canyon St (closed Sun; ℡ 505/628-0555), serves coffee and pastries from 7.30am.

Carlsbad Caverns National Park

CARLSBAD CAVERNS NATIONAL PARK consists of a tract of the Guadalupe Mountains that's so riddled with underground caves and tunnels as to be virtually hollow. Tamed in classic park-service style with concrete trails and electric lighting, this subterranean wonderland is now a walk-in gallery, where tourists come in droves to marvel at its intricate limestone tracery. Before you decide whether to join them, however, be sure to grasp that the park is a *long* way from anywhere else – three hundred miles southeast of Albuquerque and 150 miles northeast of El Paso, Texas.

The Guadalupe Mountains are the remnants of the **Capitan Reef**, a 400-mile-long horseshoe-shaped reef that formed beneath the waters of a primeval ocean. Made up of algae and sponges rather than coral, it was thrust above the plains a mere three million years ago. In the process, cracks were created through which surface moisture has trickled ever since, gnawing at the rock within.

Almost all visitors to the park confine their attention to the main cave, **Carlsbad Cavern** itself, where the summer crowds can get pretty intense. In a strange way, though, that's part of the fun – coming to Carlsbad feels like a real throwback to the great 1950s boom in mass tourism. If you're not convinced, wait until you see the gloriously kitsch Underground Lunchroom.

Arrival and information

The park headquarters is reached by driving twenty miles southwest of the town of Carlsbad on US-62/180, then turning west at **White's City** to climb another seven miles. This narrow, twisting road ends atop the mountains, with sweeping views east across the plains. Part of a complex that includes a restaurant, a gift store, a crèche, and even a kennel, the **visitor center** is the place to pay entrance fees and pick up details of the day's program of tours (daily: summer 8am–7pm, winter 8am–5pm; ℡ 505/785-2232, Ⓦ www.nps.gov/cave).

The standard park fee of $6 for three days covers access to **Carlsbad Cavern** by elevator or on foot; all the national park passes described on p.45 are sold and accepted. For additional fees that range from $7 to $20 you can also join guided tours to otherwise inaccessible parts of the main cavern, or of **Slaughter Canyon Cave**, as detailed on p.236. Some tours require participants to carry flashlights or even to wear kneepads. All tours can be reserved in advance, using Visa or MasterCard, on ☏1-800/967-2283. Note that there's no **camping** at the national park; the nearest campgrounds and motels are at White's City and Carlsbad.

Carlsbad Cavern

The centerpiece of Carlsbad Cavern, the **Big Room**, lies 750 vertical feet below the visitor center – though being inside the mountain, it's also 400ft horizontally from the open air in some places. Measuring up to 1800ft long and 250ft high, it's festooned with stalactites, stalagmites, and countless unnameable shapes of swirling liquid rock. All are a uniform stone gray; the rare touches of color are provided by slight red or brown mineral-rich tinges, improved here and there with gentle pastel lighting. Most visitors take an hour or so to complete the reasonably level trail around its perimeter. Whatever the weather up top – and summer highs exceed 100°F – the temperature down here is always a cool 56°F, so dress warmly.

Direct **elevators** drop to the Big Room from the visitor center (summer first down 8.30am, last up 6.30pm; winter first down 8.30am, last up 4.55pm). They arrive alongside the **Underground Lunchroom**, a vast formation-free side cave paved over in the 1950s to create a diner-cum-souvenir-store that sells indigestible lunches in polystyrene containers, plus Eisenhower-era souvenirs such as giant pencils and Viewmaster reels. To modern eyes, this strange installation seems absurd, but moves to close it down have been stymied by its place in popular affections.

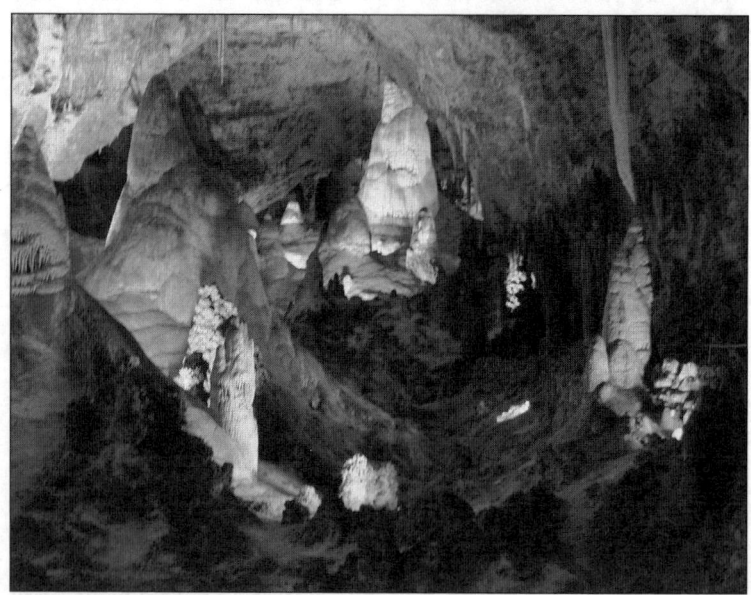

△ Inside the Big Room, Carlsbad Cavern

The bats of Carlsbad

The recesses of Carlsbad Caverns are the summer home of around a million Mexican free-tailed **bats**. Each evening, having slept all day suspended from the ceiling of the imaginatively titled **Bat Cave** – to which there's no public access – they emerge in cloud-like spirals at dusk or a little later, and disperse across the desert in search of delectable insects. Park visitors watch the spectacle from the amphitheater seating that faces the cave mouth, while rangers give a free and informative "Bats aren't as bad as you think" presentation.

It was the bats that first brought the caves to human attention, in the 1890s. Miners employed to dig bat dung or **guano**, which was greatly prized as fertilizer, started to explore what lay beyond the cave mouth. As word of their discoveries spread, sightseers began to arrive. Early visitors were dropped down in buckets and guided through on ropes. The present trail system was constructed after the caverns became a national park in 1930.

To get a better sense of the depth of the cavern, eschew the elevator and **walk** down via the **Natural Entrance Route** (last entry summer 3.30pm, winter 2pm). This steep paved footpath switchbacks into the guano-encrusted maw of the cave, a short way from the visitor center. It takes fifteen minutes to reach the first of the formations and another fifteen to reach the Big Room itself. If you'd like a commentary as you go, $3 buys you a recorded audio tour. All visitors are obliged to ride the elevator back out.

The walk-down trail once meandered through beautiful side caves such as the **King's Palace**, filled with translucent "draperies" of limestone. By the early 1990s formations were being broken at the rate of two thousand per year, so the trails have since been closed to casual visitors. They're now open on guided tours only, which start from the Big Room (daily 10am, 11am, 2pm, & 3pm in summer, diminishing to 10am & 2pm in winter; $8). Additional tours, scheduled in the visitor center, can take you along the **Left Hand Tunnel** route down from the visitor center ($7), or on a much more demanding descent into either **Spider Cave** or the **Hall of the White Giant** (both $20).

The rest of the park

The park's other readily accessible cave is **Slaughter Canyon Cave**, 25 miles southwest of the visitor center. Much less frequented, and much less developed, it can only be explored on two-hour guided tours (late May to mid-Aug daily 10am & 1pm, mid-Aug to late May Sat & Sun 10am; check current schedule on ☎505/785-2232, ⓦwww.nps.gov/cave; $15). To get there, drive five miles south of White's City on US-62/180, then eleven miles west on Hwy-418, and finally hike the steep half-mile up to the cave entrance.

Slaughter Canyon Cave still appears as "New Cave" on some maps, but it's been renamed to avoid confusion since the discovery of **Lechuguilla Cave**. Revealed after cavers cleared a thirty-foot plug of bat dung and rubble in 1986, the astonishing Lechuguilla cave system is not only deeper than Carlsbad Cavern but, at 1600ft, has turned out to be the deepest in the US. Over one hundred miles of tunnels have been mapped so far, but they're so dangerous that Lechuguilla is off-limits to all but the experts. It's expected to remain a "wilderness cave" – even its location is kept secret – so the rest of us will have to content ourselves with the marvelous pictures of its delicate crystalline formations in the visitor center.

White's City

Twenty miles southwest of Carlsbad at the turn-off for Carlsbad Caverns, **WHITE'S CITY** is not a town but a privately owned tourist complex that provides the closest accommodation and camping to the national park. A notorious eyesore, it was opened in 1926 by entrepreneur Charlie White, who cannily anticipated the imminent advent of automobile tourism and bought up the land at this crucial road junction without ever having seen it. The park service has deplored its very existence ever since and has attempted to avoid the same situation arising at parks elsewhere.

All the current components of White's City share the same contact details (17 Carlsbad Caverns Hwy, White's City NM 88268; ☎505/785-2291 or 1-800/228-3767, ⓦwww.whitescity.com). They include the mock-adobe *Best Western Cavern Inn*, on both sides of the highway (❹), which has its own water park for guests; the *White's City RV Park*, which has tent camping space; and the *Velvet Garter Restaurant*.

White's City also boasts the ultratacky **Million Dollar Museum** (daily 7am–8pm; $3), an assortment of decrepit dolls' houses, two-headed snakes, old shoes, arrowheads, the twelfth largest moose ever shot in Wyoming, and even a human corpse, in the nauseating form of a "7000-year-old cliff dwelling baby."

Hobbs

Unless it's on your route home, it's hard to know what impulse might carry you seventy miles east of Carlsbad to **HOBBS**, in New Mexico's far southeastern corner. Surrounded by endless dusty flatlands punctuated only by dementedly bobbing oil-pumps, this 30,000-strong community holds nothing to divert visitors. If you're sure there must be more to it than meets the eye, a handful of cheap motels – such as the *Days Inn*, 211 N Marland Blvd (☎505/397-6541, ⓦwww.daysinn.com; ❸) – will be baffled to accept your custom.

The Rio Grande valley

The 260-mile route between **Albuquerque** and El Paso, Texas at the Mexican border follows one of America's oldest and most romantic trails. For 250 years, the **Camino Real** or "Royal Road" beside the Rio Grande gave the Hispanic colonists of New Mexico their one tenuous link with the outside world, running all the way from Mexico City to Santa Fe. However, the curve of the Rio Grande between **Socorro** and **Las Cruces** was so prone to Apache attacks that travelers on the Camino Real often took a hundred-mile detour behind the mountains that lie east of the river. This route too had its perils – not least a complete lack of water – and became known as the **Jornada del Muerto**, or Dead Man's Route, after Juan de Oñate's chaplain Fray Cristóbal de Salazar died here in the early 1600s. A long litany of subsequent deaths gave it a terrible reputation, and to this day there's no north–south road through the desert. The Camino Real is now paralleled by I-25, a monotonous four-hour drive with little to divert the eye apart from distant views of the mountains to either side. You don't even see much of the river itself, except where it's been dammed to form incongruous turquoise lakes around the town of **Truth or Consequences**. Of the old way-stations en route, only Socorro in the north and **Mesilla** in the south are particularly worth visiting.

Isleta Pueblo

The only New Mexican pueblo south of Albuquerque, **ISLETA PUEBLO** lies just off the interstate a dozen miles from downtown (☎505/869-3111, ⓦwww .isletapueblo.com). The sole survivor of the many pueblos encountered by early Spanish explorers along the lower Rio Grande, it served in the seventeenth century as a refuge where Tiwa peoples gathered to resist the threat of Apache raids. At the time of the Pueblo Revolt, some Isletans accompanied the Spanish retreat southwards to found the pueblo of **Tigua**, outside El Paso, while others fled west to join the Hopi in what's now Arizona. Isleta itself was repopulated in 1718 and remains home to almost four thousand people.

Although the tribal lands mark a verdant interruption amid the dormitory communities that line the interstate's first fifty miles, the reservation is plagued by river-borne pollution from the industries of Albuquerque. Economically, it's dependent on its huge neighbor; a high proportion of Isletans work in the city, and the tribe also runs a 24-hour **casino** (11000 Broadway Blvd SE; ⓦwww .isleta-casino.com), which holds both a gourmet restaurant and an all-you-can-eat buffet, and plans to add a luxury hotel. Every day during daylight hours, visitors have free access to the principal pueblo village – also known as **SHIAW-IBA** – where the main attraction is the white-walled **mission church** of San Agustín de Isleta. In addition, Isleta stages major festivals on August 28 and September 4.

Socorro

Historic **SOCORRO**, eighty miles south of Albuquerque, received its unusual name – "help," in Spanish – from Don Juan de Oñate in 1598, after local Pueblo peoples fed his expeditionary party from their reserves of corn. The first Hispanic settlement was destroyed during the Pueblo Revolt of 1680, whereafter the site was abandoned for over a century. The picturesque **plaza** at its core, a block west of the main road, California Street, and the spruced-up adobe church of **San Miguel,** a couple of blocks north (daily 6am–6pm; free), were rebuilt during the 1820s. Sixty years later, triggered by the arrival of the railroads and the discovery of extensive **silver** deposits nearby, Socorro briefly became New Mexico's largest town. When the silver ran out, so too did most of the population, leaving behind some fine Victorian architecture.

Practicalities

For a self-guided walking tour of Socorro, call in at the **visitor center**, north of the center at 103 Francisco de Avondo (Mon–Fri 8am–5pm, Sat 9am–5pm; ☎505/835-8927, ⓦwww.socorro-nm.com). The most central **budget motel** is the *Sands*, 205 California St NW (☎505/835-1130; ❷); the smarter *Super 8* is further north at 1121 Frontage Rd NW (☎505/835-4626 or 1-800/800-8000, ⓦwww.super8.com; winter ❷, summer ❸). As for **food**, the *Socorro Springs Brewing Company*, 1012 California St (☎505/838-0650), serves calzones and pizzas from its wood-fired oven, along with sandwiches, to go with its home-brewed beers. The atmospheric *Val Verde Steak House*, housed in a former hotel east of the plaza at 203 Manzanares Ave (☎505/835-3380), is open daily for lunch and dinner.

Bosque del Apache Wildlife Refuge

To avoid the encampments at Bosque del Apache (forest of the Apaches), Hispanic colonists crossed the river twenty miles south of Socorro to continue their journey on the Jornada del Muerto trail. This point off Hwy-1 is now the **Bosque del Apache Wildlife Refuge**, the Southwest's most spectacular **bird-watching** site (open daily from 1hr before sunrise to one hour after sunset; visitor center Mon–Fri 7.30am–4pm, Sat & Sun 8am–4.30pm; ☎505/835-1828; ⓦwww.fws.gov/; $3 per vehicle). When migratory birds arrive for the winter, in early December, it can hold as many as twenty thousand sandhill cranes and almost fifty thousand snow geese; even in summer, its riverine marshes and forests are bursting with birds and mammals.

El Camino Real International Heritage Center

The whole story of the Camino Real, which is very much the history of New Mexico as a Spanish colony, is recounted in lavish and fascinating detail at the impressive new **El Camino Real International Heritage Center**, thirty miles south of Socorro, overlooking the Rio Grande from near exit 115 off I-25 (Wed–Mon 8.30am–4.30pm; ☎505/854-3600 ⓦwww.caminorealheritage .org). The trail was the lifeblood of New Mexico, linking Santa Fe with Mexico City, 1500 miles south, and the exhibits are designed to stress ongoing cultural connections. Much smaller-scale trails have been laid out in the immediate vicinity to provide short nature hikes.

Truth or Consequences

Until 1950, the minor spa town seventy miles south of Socorro was appropriately known as **Hot Springs**. Then the radio show *Truth or Consequences* promised that any community prepared to change its name would receive the meager reward of hosting its tenth anniversary edition. Hot Springs prostituted itself for fifteen minutes of fame, and **TRUTH OR CONSEQUENCES** was saddled with the world's worst name – though locals habitually abbreviate it these days to "**T or C**."

Several of the region's **thermal springs** – where Apache warriors such as Geronimo once soaked away the worries of the warpath – are now run as private bathhouses, with prices starting at around $3 for a twenty-minute session. Native American memorabilia, including Mimbres pottery (see p.246), form a prominent part of the historical collection at the **Geronimo Springs Museum**, 211 Main St (Mon–Sat 9am–5pm; $3). You can also learn fascinating snippets about **Ralph Edwards**, presenter of the long-defunct *Truth or Consequences* show, who managed to return each year for the first fifty times the **Truth or Consequences Fiesta** was celebrated, on the first weekend in May. Sadly, however, he died at the age of 92 in 2005.

Practicalities

T or C's small downtown consists of a couple of blocks sandwiched between two busy one-way streets, Broadway and Main Street. The **visitor center** is just off Main Street at 201 Foch St (Mon–Fri 9am–5pm; ☏505/894-3536, ⓦwww .truthorconsequencesnm.net). Most of the better **motels** are well to the north, near interstate exit 79. These include the *Best Western Hot Springs Inn*, 2270 N Date St (☏505/894-6665 or 1-800/780-7234, ⓦwww.bestwestern.com; ❹), where there's a pool and a steakhouse, and the *Super 8*, 2151 N Date St (☏505/894-7888 or 1-800/800-8000, ⓦwww.super8.com; ❸). There are two further options, at either end of the price spectrum. The *Sierra Grande Lodge & Spa*, 501 McAdoo St (☏505/894-6976, ⓦwww.sierragrandelodge.com; ❻–❾), is a gorgeously restored 1920s lodge with luxury rooms and suites and mineral baths, while the lovely *Riverbend Hot Springs* **hostel**, beside the Rio Grande in the heart of town at 100 Austin St (☏505/894-7625, ⓦwww.nmhotsprings .com; ❶–❹), offers $20 dorm beds, private rooms and suites, tent camping, and even individual tepees. The hostel also boasts the town's only heated outdoor pool, as well as spring-fed hot tubs. The dining room at the *Sierra Grande* has to be the best **restaurant** in town, serving contemporary American cuisine at around $20 per entree; *La Cocina*, 280 Date St (☏505/894-6499), is a good Mexican alternative.

Hillsboro

Hwy-152 branches west from I-25 fifteen miles south of T or C, crossing the Mimbres Mountains en route to **Silver City** (see p.243). **HILLSBORO**, less than twenty miles off the interstate in the fertile foothills, is a former gold-mining settlement that has since turned its hand to apple-growing instead, as celebrated in an annual **Apple Festival** held on Labor Day weekend.

Now no more than a village, with a small crop of arts-and-crafts galleries, Hillsboro also boasts the *Enchanted Villa* (PO Box 456, Hillsboro, NM 88042 ☏505/895-5686; ❹), a bright and attractive whitewashed adobe **B&B**. The *Barbershop Cafe*, 200 Main St (☏505/895-5283), is a friendly local **restaurant** that has done well enough to expand from its original little premises in a former barbershop into the large saloon next door.

Hatch

Forty miles south of T or C, along I-25 en route to Las Cruces, tiny **HATCH** is noteworthy only as the home of New Mexico's leading **chile farms**. All year, roadside stalls sell fresh peppers and the dried garlands known as *ristras*, while Labor Day weekend in early September sees a **Chile Festival** (☏505/267-5050,

The Final Frontier

Appropriately enough, given its long-standing association with cutting-edge technology, frontier adventurism, and strange alien spacecraft, New Mexico will become home to the world's first **commercial space flights**. The state government and Virgin Galactic have announced the construction of the **Southwest Regional Spaceport**, which will be built in the empty desert of the Jornada del Muerto, roughly 45 miles northeast of Las Cruces and 25 miles southeast of Truth or Consequences.

The first flights, optimistically scheduled to take place in 2008, will be made by SpaceShipTwo. That's an updated version of the prototype which in 2004 became the first space vehicle to fly to an altitude of over 100km twice within two weeks, thereby claiming the $10 million Ansari X-Prize. Carried aloft by a launch plane, the ship is released and then fires its own rocket engines to reach suborbital space. Amazingly, it uses a combination of nitrous oxide – laughing gas – and solid rubber as fuel. Virgin Galactic is hoping to operate a fleet of five spacecraft, each capable of carrying eight astronauts, and to offer its space voyagers a "five-star destination experience" on the ground as well. The actual flight will last around three hours, culminating in perhaps three minutes of weightlessness; the flight won't orbit the earth. Reservations for US$200,000 tickets are already being accepted; contact Ⓦ www.virgingalactic.com for details. Actress and skincare expert Victoria Principal has commented "I can't wait."

Ⓦ www.hatchchilefest.com) with fiercely competitive chile cook-offs. *Dora's*, 401 E Hall St (Ⓣ 505/267-9294), is renowned for fiery Mexican cuisine.

Las Cruces

Named after "the Crosses" that marked the graves of early travelers killed by the Apache, **LAS CRUCES** is now a major crossroads, where the east–west I-10 meets the north–south I-25. Once a riverside farming community, it has grown beyond recognition and the boom in industrial and military employment has been at the expense of any scenic beauty Las Cruces may once have possessed.

Fifteen miles north of downtown, just south of **RADIUM SPRINGS** on the east bank of the Rio Grande, **Fort Selden State Monument** preserves the ruined adobe walls of a US Army fort built to protect Las Cruces in 1865 (daily 8.30am–5pm; $3; Ⓣ 505/526-8911). The small museum in its visitor center focuses largely on the black troops stationed here in the immediate aftermath of the Civil War, who became known as **Buffalo Soldiers**, and are also commemorated by a bronze statue outside. As the fort was decommissioned in 1891, it basically consists of rounded stumps surrounding its former parade ground, but the place still comes alive on summer weekends during regular re-enactments.

Las Cruces itself however has very little to offer visitors. As New Mexico's second largest city, it boasts a wide array of shops and services, but they're all housed now in the malls that line I-25 to the east, leaving downtown a rather desolate sprawl. Any time you can spare for sightseeing is better spent in neighboring Mesilla.

Practicalities

Las Cruces' downtown **visitor center**, 211 N Water St (Mon–Fri 8am–5pm, Sat 9am–1pm; Ⓣ 505/541-2444, Ⓦ www.lascrucescvb.org), has lists of all the

motels you'd expect. The cream of the crop has to be the *Best Western Mission Inn*, 1765 S Main St ✈ ☎505/524-8591 or 1-800/780-7234; ❸); it may not look all that special from the outside, but the large rooms are surprisingly attractive, featuring lovely Mexican tilework and murals. Rates include a full cooked breakfast. *Lundeen's Inn of the Arts*, 618 S Alameda Blvd (☎505/526-3326 or 1-888/526-3326, ⑩www.innofthearts.com; ❹), is a **B&B inn** where each room is named for regional artists, such as María Martínez or Georgia O'Keeffe, and furnished appropriately.

As for **dining**, the best area is along University Avenue, which marks the northern limits of the New Mexico State University campus at the south end of town near the interstate intersection. *Mix-Pacific Rim*, 1001 E University Ave (☎505/532-2042), specializes in Japanese and Asian cuisine, with a sushi bar, and entrees like Thai green curry priced at anything up to $20. The adjoining *Mix Express* (same phone) serves cheaper takeout. The whole neighborhood is buzzing with student-oriented **coffeehouses**. Just a mile west of the visitor center, the slogan of *Nellie's Cafe*, 1226 W Hadley Ave (☎505/524-9982) – "*Chiles with Attitude*" – tells you what to expect: sublimely spicy Mexican food.

Mesilla

The little-changed Hispanic village of **MESILLA** stands just south of I-10 two miles south of Las Cruces, an easy drive down the Avenida de Mesilla from downtown. When New Mexico passed into American hands in 1846, the Mesilla Valley still belonged to Mexico; Mesilla itself was founded in 1850 by New Mexicans who preferred to remain Mexican. Under the **Gadsden Purchase**, however, signed here in 1853, it passed to the US and soon became one of the Southwest's largest towns, with over eight thousand inhabitants. During the Civil War, Mesilla even served briefly as the Confederate capital of the territory of Arizona, but it went into swift decline when the railroad bypassed it in favor of Las Cruces in 1881.

Mesilla's Old West **plaza** has a real frontier feel to it, even though most of the old adobes that surround it – including the former courthouse where **Billy the Kid** was tried and sentenced to death in 1881 (see p.225) – now house art galleries and souvenir shops. Gift stores stock interesting Southwest souvenirs and jewelry leavened with some much cheaper Mexican crafts, while the Mesilla Book Center has an excellent selection of local literature. Two blocks east at 1875 Boutz Rd, the small **Gadsden Museum** (Mon–Sat 9–11am & 1–5pm, Sun 1–5pm; $2) recounts the town's history and details the events that lead to the Gadsden Purchase.

Practicalities

Mesilla has its own small **visitor center**, east of the plaza where Calle de Santiago meets Hwy-28 (daily 9am–5pm; ☎505/647-9868, ⑩www.oldmesilla .org). The *Mesón de Mesilla*, 1803 Avenida de Mesilla (☎505/525-9212 or 1-800/732-6025, ⑩www.mesondemesilla.com; ❹–❼), is a fifteen-room **B&B**. A five-minute walk east of the plaza, it offers gorgeous mountain views, an outdoor pool, and a top-class dining room. **Restaurants** on the plaza itself include the *Double Eagle* (☎505/523-6700), which has indoor and outdoor seating and serves steaks and salmon as well as burgers, salads, and Mexican dishes for lunch and dinner daily. *La Posta* is a Mexican *cantina* in the former offices of the Butterfield Stage Coach (closed Mon; ☎505/524-3524).

Southwest New Mexico

Most of New Mexico's sparsely populated **southwest corner** – also known as the "**Bootheel**" for the way it steps down into Mexico – consists of open rangeland. Interstate towns like **Deming** and **Lordsburg** are entirely forget-table, though a detour north into the mountains takes you to the mining town of **Silver City** and the ancient **Gila Cliff Dwellings**.

Deming

A bonanza of roadside billboards sixty miles due west of Las Cruces announces your arrival at **DEMING**, a typical desert outpost scattered with motels and diners. Half-hearted attempts at agriculture have left their traces on the land-scape, but the main sign of activity comes from the ever-present swirling dust devils (as the noncommittal billboards beside the interstate would have it, "Dust Storms May Exist"). If you're ready for a break, however, the **Deming Luna Mimbres Museum**, 301 S Silver Ave (Mon–Sat 9am–4pm, Sun 1.30–4pm; $2), has some surprisingly good displays, including cabinets of Mimbres pottery (see p.246) and a great show of minerals and gemstones.

Assuming you have a pickax handy, you're allowed to take away whatever agates, onyx, or geodes you can prise from the arid slopes of **Rock Hound State Park**, ten miles southeast (daily 7.30am–dusk; $5). Any easy pickings have long since been carted away, leaving this as perhaps the most frighteningly boring park in the whole Southwest.

Practicalities

Deming is served by Amtrak **trains** – which call at the central railroad station daily except Friday, in alternate directions but always at around 2.30pm – and more frequent Greyhound **buses**, which use a depot at 300 E Spruce St (☎505/546-3881). The **visitor center**, 800 E Pine St, is at the east end of downtown (Mon–Sat 9am–5pm; ☎505/546-2674 or 1-800/848-4955, Ⓦ www.demingchamber.com). Budget **motels** along the main drag, parallel to the interstate, include a *Super 8*, 1217 W Pine St (☎505/546-0481 or 1-800/800-8000, Ⓦ www.super8.com; ❷), and the central *Anselment's Butterfield Stage*, marked by a flashing neon sign at 309 W Pine St (☎505/544-0011; ❶). The large, renovated *Holiday Inn* at the eastern interstate exit (☎505/546-2661, Ⓦ www.ichotels.com; ❸) is the best of the bunch and has a decent **restaurant**, too. A block south of the main drag at Silver and Spruce, *Joe Perk Coffee Shop* sells smoothies and pastries.

Pancho Villa State Park

Sleepy **COLUMBUS**, thirty miles south of Deming, just north of the Mexican border, is where Mexican revolutionary Pancho Villa led five hundred guerrillas in an attack on the US cavalry on March 9, 1916. "Raid Day" commemo-rates the anniversary each year in **PANCHO VILLA STATE PARK** (daily

8am–5pm; $5). A small museum chronicles the last invasion of the US, and the adjoining sixty-acre desert botanical garden makes a nice place to **camp** (except in summer, when it's baking hot).

If you fancy a *cerveza* or two, the frontier with neighboring **LAS PALO-MAS**, three miles south in Mexico, remains open day or night. Border formalities are minimal, though foreign travelers must be sure to carry their passports.

Silver City

Six thousand feet up in the Mogollon Mountains, **SILVER CITY** stands roughly fifty miles from either of the I-10 towns Deming and Lordsburg. As you drive up from the interstate, however, it's easy not to notice that you're climbing – the region has been so extensively **mined** that many of the hills that once lay to the south of Silver City have now been completely carved away.

Ancient peoples knew this region as a source of top-quality **turquoise**, but the Hispanic settlement of La Cienaga de San Vicente was only founded in 1804, soon after some friendly Apaches showed the Spanish soldier Jose Manuel Carrasco where to find **copper**. The Santa Rita copper mine was repeatedly attacked by the Apache, however, and was abandoned altogether in 1838. Only when **silver** was discovered after the Civil War was the town reestablished, with a new name and a rip-roaring reputation. **Billy the Kid** spent most of his childhood here; according to some stories he committed his first robbery – of a Chinese laundry – in Silver City, and also his first murder.

Things calmed down when the silver ran out, so Silver City today is a somewhat rundown, but nonetheless appealing, Victorian relic, scattered with ornate old buildings. It regularly features in polls of "best small towns in America," and has been voted the third favorite small town in which to retire. The two thousand students of Western New Mexico University, whose campus is on the western edge of downtown, keep things reasonably lively for most of the year, and they're replaced in summer by a large influx of tourists. Copper mining, meanwhile, continues unabated; neighboring Santa Rita, which had become a fully fledged community in its own right and was the birthplace of Apollo 17 astronaut Harrison Schmitt, disappeared into the bowels of an open-pit copper mine in 1966.

Arrival and information

Silver City's **visitor center** is on Hwy-90 as it enters downtown, at 201 N Hudson St (April–Oct Mon–Sat 9am–5pm, Sun noon–4pm; Nov–March Mon–Fri 9am–5pm; ☎505/538-3785 or 1-800/548-9378, ⓦwww.silvercity .org). For information on the town's annual **Blues Festival**, which attracts big names at the end of each May, contact ☎1-888/758-7289 or ⓦwww .mimbresarts.org/bluesfestival.html.

Accommodation

Room rates are surprisingly inexpensive in Silver City, but with most of the **motels** strung along US-180 east of town there's a dearth of options within walking distance of downtown.

Bear Mountain Lodge Bear Mountain Rd ☎505/538-2538 or 1-877/620-2327, ⓦwww .bearmountainlodge.com. A 1920s ranch house four miles northwest of downtown, owned and operated by the Nature Conservancy of New Mexico. The eleven B&B guest rooms include four luxurious suites. On-site naturalists run regular guided tours. ❻

Holiday Inn Express 1103 Superior St ☎505/538-2525, ⓦwww.hiexpress .com/silver-citynm. The best of the chain motels, with a heated spa and free continental breakfasts. ❹

Holiday Motor Hotel 3420 US-180 E ☎505/538-3711 or 1-800/828-8291. Good-value motel rooms on the eastern approaches to town, with a pool and a good Italian restaurant, *Michael's*. ❸

Palace Hotel 106 W Broadway ☎505/388-1811, ⓦwww.zianet.com/palacehotel. Small, nicely restored nineteenth-century hotel, located downtown. Some rooms have showers instead of baths, and they all have historic rather than contemporary fittings, but the ambience – and the rates – are great. ❹

The Town

A massive flood ripped the heart out of downtown Silver City in 1895, washing away its original Main Street. As a result, no buildings survive from the days of **Billy the Kid**; Wild West devotees have to settle instead for inspecting the places where they *used* to be. The former site of Main Street is now occupied by **Big Ditch Park**; stand on its eastern edge, at 11th and Hudson, and you're on the spot where Billy grew up, in a simple one-room cabin. His mother is buried in the town cemetery, on Memory Lane a couple of miles east. After her death, Billy found work as a busboy in the *Star Hotel*, which survives in much-altered form at Broadway and Hudson, but soon turned to crime. The jail where he was imprisoned, and from which he made the first of his many escapes, stood at 304 N Hudson St.

Two good museums explore local history in considerable depth. The **Silver City Museum**, 312 W Broadway (Tues–Fri 9am–4.30pm, Sat & Sun 10am–4pm; free), concentrates on the boom-and-bust mining years, with photos of the frontier era and personal accounts of the vanished community of Santa Rita. It also holds Indian pottery, rugs, and basketry. The emphasis at the **Western New Mexico University Museum**, 12th and Alabama (Mon–Fri 9am–4.30pm, Sat & Sun 10am–4pm; free), is on a remarkable collection of **Mimbres pottery**, tracing its development over a thousand-year period.

Eating

Inexpensive **diners** – not to mention a few hair-raising **bars** – are two-a-penny in the downtown area, but don't expect to find anything more exciting along the highways further out.

Buckhorn Saloon and Opera House 62 Main St, Pinos Altos ☎505/538-9911. Enjoyable Wild West-themed steakhouse in the ghost town of Pinos Altos, seven miles north of Silver City (see below). Open Mon–Sat for dinner only, with live music every night except Tues.

Jalisco Cafe 100 S Bullard St ☎505/388-2060. One of the few options in the heart of downtown, serving Mexican meals daily except Sun.

Shevek and Mi 602 N Bullard St ☎505/534-9168. Bagels and espressos for breakfast, then a full lunch and dinner menu of Mediterranean and, especially, Italian dishes, including seafood, with patio seating in summer. Open for all meals daily.

Red Barn Family Steakhouse 708 Silver Heights Blvd ☎505/538-5666. Exactly what it sounds like: a large steakhouse, painted a lurid red, on Hwy-180 near the Gila turn-off at the eastern end of town. They have their own herd of cows, so the meat is good, and the $6 salad bar is a real bargain.

Into the mountains

North of Silver City, the volcanic **Mogollon** and **Mimbres mountains** are among the remotest wilderness areas in the US. Until the late nineteenth century, they were an Apache stronghold; **Geronimo** was born at the headwaters of the Gila River and returned throughout his free adult life. Before that, they were home to the **Mogollon** peoples, and the main reason to make the fifty-mile dead-end trip into the mountains on **Hwy-15** these days is to see the dramatic Mogollon ruins of the **Gila Cliff Dwellings National Monument**.

Hwy-15 is, however, a beautiful drive in its own right, albeit a slow one. It's never especially steep, let alone dangerous, but the twists and turns seem endless. Potential stops along the way include **Pinos Altos** – a fun little semi-ghost town in the woods just a few miles out of Silver City. It's home to one or two businesses such as the *Buckhorn Saloon* (see above) – and the **Vista Viewpoint** above the Gila River near the far end. Most of this region belongs to the **Gila National Forest**; if you know what you're doing, it offers magnificent opportunities for wilderness adventure.

Gila Cliff Dwellings National Monument

Occupied for just a brief moment in history, between 1270 and 1300 AD, the Mogollon pueblo now preserved as the **GILA CLIFF DWELLINGS NATIONAL MONUMENT** is southern New Mexico's most spectacular archeological site. While not on the scale of the Ancestral Puebloan "cities" of the Four Corners region – see Chapter One – it's also much less visited, and you may well be lucky enough to have the place to yourself. To modern eyes, ancient Southwestern peoples often seem to have chosen to live in inhospitable places, but here there's no such problem. The dwellings are tucked into sheltered south-facing recesses along the wall of a shallow canyon, just a couple of hundred feet above a perennial creek and thus in earshot of running water and the constant rustle of small game. "Gila," incidentally, is pronounced "heela" and comes from an Apache word meaning mountain.

Even when there's no traffic, driving the full fifty miles from Silver City can take two hours. You won't have time to see the monument if you set off from Silver City later than 4pm in summer, or 2pm in winter. If you're coming from the east, Hwy-35, which branches off Hwy-152 fifty miles west of I-25, is not so slow or mountainous, but it's still a hell of a long drive. Either way, the final eight miles up to the monument follow the broad valley of the Gila River, with the **visitor center** poised near the confluence of its Middle and West forks. This is the place to pay the entrance fee of $3 per person or $10 per family (daily: summer 8am–5pm; winter 8am–4.30pm; ☎505/536-9461, ⓦ www.nps.gov/gicl).

The **trail** to the dwellings (daily: summer 8am–6pm; winter 9am–4pm) starts a mile further on, crossing the Gila on a long footbridge. Only once you've followed the creek for half a mile do you get your first glimpse of the pueblo. What from below looks like three separate caves turns out after you climb the hillside to be a single, deep, long alcove with three entrances. Each entrance was sealed with stones and mortar, but behind them lay around forty interconnected rooms, sharing a communal – and presumably very dark – plaza at the rear. As the trail leads into and through the complex, keep an eye out for the pictographs that mark certain dwellings, as well as a granary that still holds a desiccated cache of tiny corn.

Practicalities

The monument maintains a small, free **campground** beside the Gila River, equipped with running water in summer only. There's another pretty campground eight miles south, at the *Gila Hot Springs Vacation Center* (☎505/536-9551, 🕸www .gilahotspringsranch.com; ❹). Tent camping costs a mere $3, and there are also RV hookups and a couple of pretty comfortable, large rental units at bargain rates. The owners offer hunting and horseback trips into the mountains.

There are also a couple of **accommodation** options on Hwy-35, both set in appealing natural surroundings. One stands immediately east of the intersection of Hwy-35 and Hwy-15, seventeen miles south of the monument, in the shape of the motel-like *Grey Feathers Lodge and Restaurant* (☎505/536-3206, 🕸www .greyfeathers.com; rooms ❸, suites ❹), where the restaurant is open for lunch and dinner daily except Tuesdays. Another seventeen miles further southeast, or eleven miles up Hwy-35 from Hwy-152, the *Pueblo on the Mimbres Bed & Breakfast* (☎505/536-9391, 🕸www.puebloonthemimbres.com; ❻) offers three separate Western-themed B&B units, with full kitchen and shared indoor and outdoor seating areas.

The Mogollon and the Mimbres

Archeologists identify the three major cultures of the prehistoric Southwest as the **Ancestral Puebloans** of the Colorado Plateau, the **Hohokam** of the Salt River Valley around modern Phoenix, and the **Mogollon**, based in the **Mogollon mountains** of what's now southwest New Mexico. Thanks to their proximity to Mexico, Mogollon peoples were the first to acquire both **agriculture** – in the shape of corn and squash, around 1200 BC – and **pottery** – around 200 AD.

At its peak, between 100 AD and 1300 AD, the Mogollon culture extended well into modern Arizona and Mexican Chihuahua. Its heartland, however, remained the **Gila** and **Mimbres** rivers, north and east of modern Silver City. The Mogollon sub-group known as the **Classic Mimbres** culture is considered to represent the ancient Southwest's finest artistic flowering. Above all, the Mimbres people – their name comes from the Spanish for "willows" – were superb **potters**. While the intricate stylized borders of their plates and bowls are typical of many pueblo peoples, their vivid naturalistic images of birds, insects, and animals are quite extraordinary. Usually executed in black on white, they also hint at a complex mythology; some show bees or rabbits juxtaposed with strange humanoid creatures, others are what may be prototype *kachina* figures (see p.84), and there are even scenes of decapitation suggesting human sacrifice.

The Mimbres culture reached its apogee around 1100 AD, with around five thousand people farming beside the Mimbres River. As well as a dozen or so walled villages, each of which held up to 200 rooms, they occupied several smaller, more isolated settlements. Depictions of fish that live only in the Pacific would suggest they traveled extensively, but there's little evidence of trade. No Mimbres ceramics have been discovered elsewhere, and it's believed that the finest bowls were created for specific individuals at birth, used in ceremonies throughout their lifetime, and finally **buried** with them. The bowl would be inverted over the head of the corpse, always with a "**kill hole**" punched through it which according to modern Pueblo Indians released its "spirit" to accompany that of the deceased. As a result, undamaged Mimbres bowls are extremely rare, and Mimbres pottery in general is so valuable that the few known Mimbres sites have been extensively looted, rendering the detective work of archeology almost impossible. As far as anyone can tell, the Mimbres stopped producing pottery around 1150 AD, and left the valley soon afterwards, possibly because overuse had depleted its soil.

Lordsburg

Sixty miles down the interstate from Deming, 44 miles southwest of Silver City, and just twenty miles short of Arizona, **LORDSBURG** is southwest New Mexico's last gasp. John Wayne went to a lot of trouble to get here in *Stagecoach*, but the desultory strip of gas stations and motels today makes you wonder why he bothered. Far more redolent of the Old West is **SHAKESPEARE**, two miles south, a privately owned **ghost town** that's only open for infrequent guided tours (March–Dec only, on the second Sat & Sun of each month, plus occasional other weekends, 10am–2pm; $3; ☏505/542-9034, ⓦwww.shakespeareghosttown.com). If you go at any other time, there's no access to the site and nothing to see.

Practicalities

The **New Mexico Welcome Center**, south of the interstate at the west end of town (daily 8am–5pm; ☏505/542-8149), is the best place to pick up information on Lordsburg and the region. If you need a **bed**, the few blocks south of I-10 on Main Street hold much better options than the dismal mom-and-pop motels on Motel Drive, with a reasonable *Super 8*, 110 E Maple St (☏505/542-8882 or 1-800/800-8000, ⓦwww.super8.com; ❷), and a big *Holiday Inn Express*, 1408 S Main St (☏505/542-3666, ⓦwww.hiexpress.com; ❸), with large rooms. *Kranberry's*, opposite at 1405 S Main St (☏505/542-9400), is the best of a humdrum crop of **diners**, and serves a tasty $7 green chile stew.

Phoenix and
southern Arizona

CHAPTER 4 **Highlights**

❋ **The Heard Museum** Arizona's finest collection of Native American artifacts, including hundreds of superb Hopi *kachinas*. See p.260

❋ **Desert Botanical Garden** A tremendous assortment of fascinating desert plants thrives in the heat of the Valley of the Sun. See p.262

❋ **Hotel Congress** Downtown Tucson's hippest hangout; not just a hotel and a hostel, but also a great café and nightclub. See p.267

❋ **Saguaro National Park** There's nowhere quite like it; hordes of towering multi-armed saguaro cactuses march across the desert hills of Tucson. See p.281

❋ **San Xavier del Bac** The spectacular "White Dove of the Desert" has to be the Southwest's most beautiful mission church. See p.286

❋ **Tombstone** From the OK Corral to *Big Nose Kate's*, Tombstone is an irresistible throwback to the wildest days of the West. See p.296

❋ **Bisbee** Atmospheric old mining town that has reinvented itself as a cozy, arty, mountain hideaway for overheated Arizonans. See p.300

❋ **Chiricahua National Monument** Apaches such as Geronimo and Cochise once hid among the weird rock formations of this remote mountain fastness. See p.302

△ Shady Dell RV Park, Bisbee

Phoenix and southern Arizona

Despite every conceivable geographic and climatic disadvantage, ninety percent of Arizonans live in **Southern Arizona**, mainly concentrated in **Phoenix** and **Tucson**. Not only does Southern Arizona for the most part lack the compelling scenery of the state's northern half, it also lacks the **water** to support either city. However, although the very existence of Phoenix and Tucson defies normal logic, they have accrued sufficient political leverage to persuade the federal government to spend ever larger amounts of money on vast canal projects to meet their needs.

Phoenix in particular can be seen as the bloated spider at the center of the web, sucking the juices from the rest of the state. By far the largest city in Arizona, it holds only minimal appeal for tourists. **Tucson** at least has a spark of life, thanks to its long and fascinating history; it started out as a Mexican frontier outpost, and is still surrounded by relics of the Spanish missionary era such as the churches of **San Xavier del Bac** and **Tumacácori**. It's also at ease with its desert surroundings, accessible in **Saguaro National Park** and the **Arizona-Sonora Desert Museum**. Beyond Tucson, **southeast Arizona** is the one area of southern Arizona where the landscapes can truly be said to rival those of the Colorado Plateau. As well as intriguing flora and fauna, its "sky islands" hold a number of evocative Wild West sites, including **Tombstone**, now an entertaining if slightly tacky theme park of a town, and the mining settlement of **Bisbee**.

Phoenix's fragile grip on reality is highlighted by the fact that it was built on the ruins of a long-lost desert civilization. Until 1350 AD, the valleys of southern Arizona were home to the **Hohokam** people and crisscrossed by a sophisticated network of irrigation canals. It's thought that the Hohokam eventually overreached themselves, depleting the land too much for their way of life to endure. Their name means "people who have vanished" in the language of the **'O'odham** (once known as the Pima and the Papago) who later took their place. The 'O'odham now occupy vast reservations in southwest Arizona, while their old enemies, the **Apache**, dominate the mountains to the east.

PHOENIX AND SOUTHERN ARIZONA

NEW MEXICO

Alpine

Clifton

Morenci

Lordsburg

Fort Bowie

Bowie

Apache Pass

Willcox

Chiricahua Nat. Mon.

Douglas

Agua Prieta

Cochise

Safford

Benson

Tombstone

Bisbee

San Carlos Indian Reservation

Peridot

Aravaipa Canyon

Huachuca City

Sierra Vista

Coronado Nat. Memorial

Sonoita

Patagonia

Nogales

Fort Apache Ind. Res.

Salt River

Claypool

Globe

Miami

Superior

Biosphere 2

Oracle

Tucson

SAGUARO NAT. PARK

Kartchner Caverns

Madera Canyon

Green Valley

Nogales

Payson

Tonto Nat. Mon.

Roosevelt

Tortilla Flat

APACHE TRAIL

Apache Junction

Florence

Coolidge

Picacho

SAGUARO NAT. PARK

Tubac

TUMACACORI NAT. HIST. PARK

San Xavier Ind. Res.

Fort McDowell Ind. Res.

Flagstaff

Tempe

Mesa

Salt River Ind. Res.

Scottsdale

Casa Grande

Quijotoa

Sells

M E X I C O

Prescott

Wickenburg

Phoenix

Gila River Ind. Res.

Gila Bend

Papago Indian Reservation

Quartzsite

Gila River

Ajo

Why

Organ Pipe Cactus Nat. Mon.

N

Blythe

Ehrenberg

Colorado River

Yuma

Imperial Dam

San Luis Río Colorado

Golfo de California

CALIFORNIA

Los Angeles

San Diego

25 miles

0

Phoenix

When it began life in the 1860s, **PHOENIX** must have seemed like a good idea. The sweltering little farming town stood in the heart of the **Salt River Valley**, which measures forty miles east to west and twenty miles north to south, with a ready-made irrigation system left by ancient Indians and plenty of room to expand. Within a century, however, Phoenix had turned into what writer Edward Abbey called "the blob that is eating Arizona," acquiring as it did so the money and political clout to defy all notions of common sense and continue its growth. Today, Arizona's capital has filled the entire valley and is the eighth largest city in the US. Well over a million people live within the city boundaries, and almost three million people inhabit the twenty separate incorporated cities (such as Scottsdale) that together make up the metropolitan area. The state's financial and industrial epicenter may be just getting into its stride; boosters claim the megalopolis will one day stretch 150 miles, from Wickenburg to Tucson. Note that although the entire Phoenix area is known colloquially as the **Valley of the Sun**, the term has no official meaning.

The city's phenomenal rise was originally fueled by its image as a healthy oasis, where the desert had been tamed and transformed into a suburban idyll. While retirees still flock to enclaves such as **Sun City**, however, Phoenix now has a deserved reputation as the most unpleasant city in the Southwest – Las Vegas with no casinos, or LA with no beach. Its endless sprawl has long since covered the "golden fields of ripened grain" described in one 1940s guidebook and swallowed a host of neighboring communities, such as **Scottsdale**, **Tempe**, and **Mesa**, while the TB and asthma sufferers who came to the valley's sanatoriums would now choke on its polluted air. Above all, Phoenix is **hot**; between June and August daytime highs average over 100°F, making it one of the world's hottest cities outside the Middle East.

Phoenix epitomizes the Western maxim that "water flows uphill to money," with a history that revolves around its maneuverings to obtain ever more water, from ever further afield. Despite dams and diversions, the drainage of the Salt River soon proved insufficient, so, absurdly enough, the city is now dependent on aqueducts that cross the deserts from the Colorado River. Since the 1980s, when Phoenicians used a profligate 250 gallons of water per person per day, a note of realism has crept in, and it's no longer legal to adorn your latest real-estate development with an artificial lake. The obsession with liquid remains, though: pedestrians clutch bottled water in the street, and you can't fill your gas tank without the digitized gas pump telling you, "Wow it's hot. Wouldn't a cold drink taste good?"

In winter, when temperatures rarely drop below 65°F, **tourists** from colder climes still arrive in Phoenix in large numbers. They pay vast sums to warm their bones in the luxury resorts and spas, concentrated especially in Scottsdale, that are the modern equivalent of the 1930s dude ranches. Unlike golf, tennis, and shopping at one of the city's plentiful upscale malls, **sightseeing** rarely ranks high on the agenda – which is just as well, since there's a good deal of truth in the charge laid by Phoenix's older arch-rival, Tucson, that the city is sorely lacking in culture and history. Apart from the **Heard Museum**'s excellent Native American displays, the cactuses at the **Desert Botanical Garden**, and Frank Lloyd Wright's architecture studio at **Taliesin West**, Phoenix is short of must-see attractions. In fact, if you're on a touring vacation, you'd miss little if you bypassed it altogether.

A history of Phoenix

Although no American settled in the Salt River Valley until **1865**, when John Smith began supplying hay to Camp McDowell, thirty miles northeast, it was

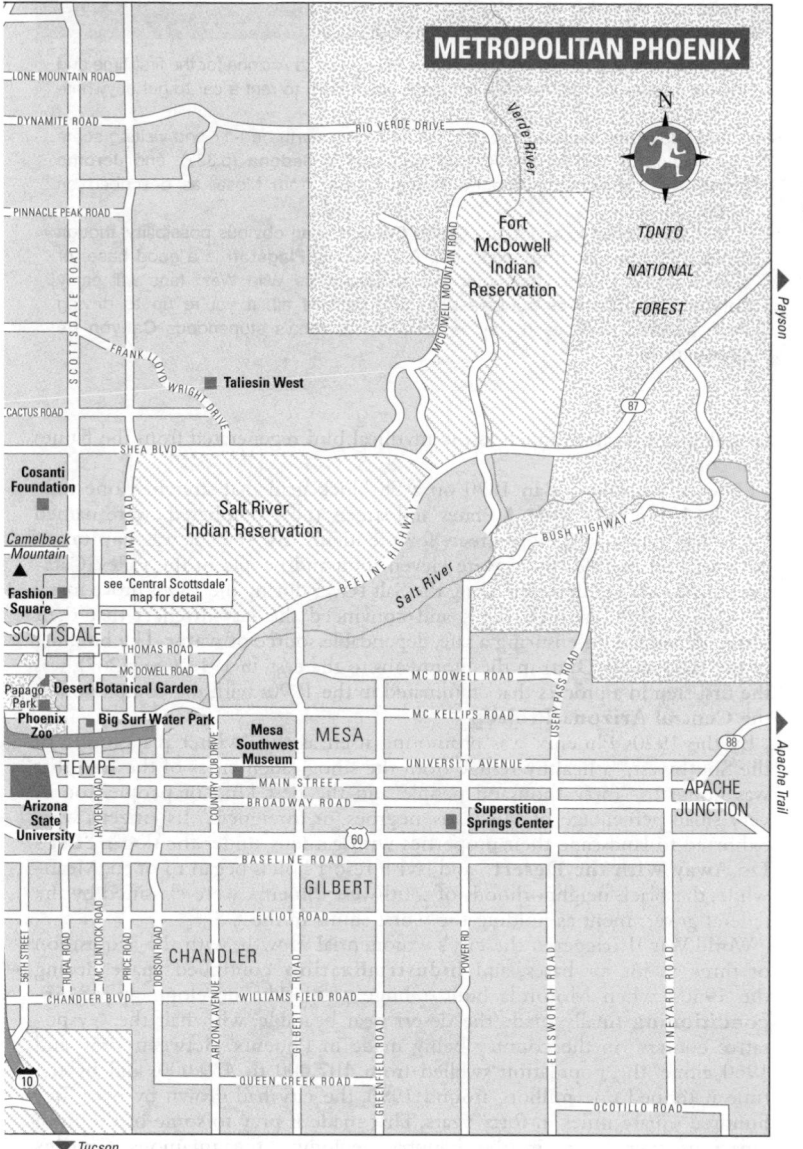

clear to all that the valley had once supported a large population. Traces still remained of over three hundred miles of **canals** – up to fifteen feet wide, ten feet deep, and twenty miles long – dug by the ancient **Hohokam** people (see p.569). Confederate deserter Jack Swilling cleared one such canal in 1867 and thereby established **Phoenix**. The infant city was named by British adventurer "Lord" Darrel Duppa, who saw it as rising from the ashes of the

If a family visit or business trip to Phoenix brings you to Arizona for the first time and you'd like to see a little more of the state, you'll have to rent a car to get anywhere interesting.

Great **day-trips** include driving a hundred miles north on I-17 and visiting some combination of **Montezuma Castle** (see p.347), **Sedona** (p.337), and **Jerome** (p.345), or following the **Apache Trail** northeast from Mesa, as described on p.266.

With a **weekend** to spare, the **Grand Canyon** is an obvious possibility, though it is a 450-mile round-trip excursion. Alternatively, **Flagstaff** is a good base for several lesser known attractions (see p.326), while Wild West fans will enjoy **Tombstone**, 180 miles southeast (p.296). Best of all, if you're up to driving three hundred miles each way, is northeast Arizona's stupendous **Canyon de Chelly** (p.75).

Hohokam civilization much as the mythical bird regenerated from the flames that consumed it.

Phoenix was laid out in 1870 on a 98-block grid that stretched one mile long by half a mile wide. Avenues and streets (now numbered) were named for Indian tribes, and cross streets for presidents. By 1889 it was **capital** of Arizona, and in 1890 there were eleven thousand people in the valley. Catastrophic floods and droughts along the Salt River during the 1890s drove many farmers to abandon their fields and convinced the city-dwellers that their future depended on ensuring a safe, dependable source of **water**. The building of the **Roosevelt Dam** in the mountains to the east, in 1911 (see p.267), was the first step in a process that culminated in the 1990s with the completion of the **Central Arizona Project**.

By the 1920s Phoenix was promoting itself as the "winter playground of the Southwest," a healthy refuge from the smog-laden cities of the East that was home to "forty thousand people and the best kind of people, too. A very small percentage of Mexicans, negroes, or foreigners." Its citizens were exhorted to landscape their properties with gardens, under the slogan "**Let's Do Away With the Desert**," and lavish resort hotels began to open. Meanwhile, the black neighborhoods of southwest Phoenix were classified by the federal government as holding the worst slums in the US.

World War II triggered the city's exponential growth, with the acquisition of three major air bases, and **industrialization** continued apace during the 1950s, when Motorola built a huge plant. The development of **air-conditioning** finally made the desert heat bearable, with half the "evaporative coolers" in the country being made in Phoenix. Between 1950 and 1960 alone, the population swelled from 107,000 to 439,000, and by the time it topped one million, around 1990, the city had grown by over four hundred square miles in forty years. That made it prey to some of the most rapacious speculators in the country, including the infamous **Charles Keating**, among whose projects were the no-expense-spared *Phoenician Resort* and the "masterplanned community" of Estrella. Keating's arrest and ruin in 1989 coincided with the bankruptcy of ten of Arizona's eleven Savings and Loans. Eight years later, in a scandal similar to those in 1989, state governor **J. Fyfe Symington** was forced to resign after being convicted of fraud in his intricate dealings with downtown developments such as the Mercado Mall.

Arrival and getting around

Sky Harbor International Airport (☎602/273-3300, ⓦwww.phxskyharbor .com), three miles east of downtown, receives flights from all over the US and even direct from Europe. All the major **rental car** chains, listed on p.42, are represented. Phoenix is such a vast city, and one so utterly dependent on car travel, that it's much easier to drive than to use public transport – though you shouldn't underestimate the sheer length of time it takes to get from one side of the city to the other. "Red Line" **buses** on the Valley Metro system (☎602/253-5000, ⓦwww.valleymetro.org/transit/) connect the airport with downtown daily, plus Tempe and Mesa on weekdays, but it's easier to take a door-to-door **shuttle bus**, at around $10 for downtown destinations and more like $20 for Scottsdale, with SuperShuttle (☎602/244-9000 or 1-800/258-3826, ⓦwww .supershuttle.com). Arizona Shuttle Services runs south to **Tucson**, every hour on the half-hour (daily 6.30am–11.30pm; one-way $29, round-trip $40 with 7-day advance reservation; ☎520/795-6771 or 1-800/888-2749, ⓦwww .arizonashuttle.com); the Sedona–Phoenix Shuttle (one-way $45; ☎928/282-2066 or 1-800/448-7988 in AZ, ⓦwww.sedona-phoenix-shuttle.com), runs eight daily services to **Sedona**; Open Road Tours runs five daily services up to **Flagstaff** (one-way $42, round-trip $76; ☎928/226-8060 or 1-877/226-8060, ⓦwww.openroadtours.com); and Shuttle "U" connects with **Prescott** (one-way $28, round-trip $48; ☎928/442-1000 or 1-800/304-6114, ⓦwww .shuttleu.com).

Amtrak **trains** no longer serve Phoenix, though there are bus connections timed to coincide with services to the stations at Tucson (see p.274) and Flagstaff (p.327). Greyhound **buses** arrive at 2115 E Buckeye Rd (☎602/389-4200 or 1-800/231-2222), close to the airport. **Getting around** without a car is far from ideal – it can take hours to cross town – but it's not impossible. Valley Metro's commuter bus routes charge $1.25 per ride; pick up a schedule at the downtown terminal, at First and Washington. Tourists are more likely to use the purple DASH buses, which ply between the Arizona Center and the Capitol downtown (Mon–Fri 6.30am–5.30pm; shorter downtown loop continues until 11pm; free). For a **cab**, call Checker Cab (☎602/257-1818) or Ace Taxi (☎602/254-1999). Contact Gray Line (☎602/437-3484 or 1-800/777-3484, ⓦwww.graylinearizona.com) for details of **city** and **regional tours**.

Information

Phoenix's main **visitor center** is downtown at 50 N Second St, at Adams (Mon–Fri 8am–5pm; ☎602/254-6500 or 1-877/225-5749, ⓦwww .phoenixcvb.com); there's also an office at 2404 E Camelback Rd, at the northeast corner of the Biltmore Fashion Park (Mon–Fri 10am–9pm, Sat 10am–6pm, Sun noon–6pm; ☎602/955-1963). **Scottsdale** has its own visitor center at 4343 N Scottsdale Rd (Mon–Fri 8am–5.30pm; ☎480/421-1004 or 1-800/782-1117, ⓦwww.scottsdalecvb.com); **Tempe** has one at 51 W Third St (Mon–Fri 8am–5pm; ☎480/894-8158 or 1-800/283-6734, ⓦwww .tempecvb.com); as does **Mesa**, at 120 N Center St (Mon–Fri 8am–5pm; ☎480/827-4700, ⓦwww.mesacvb.com).

The main **post office** is at 4949 E Van Buren St, though the branch at 522 N Central Ave (Mon–Fri 8am–6pm, Sat 9am–4pm) is more convenient to downtown. Scottsdale's post office is the Scottsdale Hopi Station, 8790 E Via de Ventura (Mon–Fri 8am–6pm, Sat 9am–4pm).

Accommodation

Metropolitan Phoenix is so huge that it's worth paying a bit extra to ensure that your **accommodation** is near the places you want to visit. Oddly enough, **downtown Phoenix** is not one of the more expensive areas, with cheap motels lining the somewhat rundown West Van Buren Street a few blocks north of the center. Room rates are considerably more expensive in **winter**, when snowbirds from all over the US fill the upscale **resorts** of Scottsdale in particular. If you're driving in from elsewhere in the Southwest, you can save significantly by picking up discount lodging coupons at state welcome centers, while courtesy phones at the baggage claim area in Sky Harbor airport enable you to call around for rates. In addition, the main city website for city visitors, Ⓦwww.phoenixcvb.com, has a good accommodation booking facility.

ACCOMMODATION
Budget Lodge Motel **B**
Metcalf House Hostel **A**
San Carlos **C**
RESTAURANTS
Alice Cooper'stown **4**
Carly's Bistro **1**
Pizzeria Bianco **3**
Sam's Cafe **2**

DOWNTOWN PHOENIX

0   800 yds

Central Phoenix

Arizona Biltmore Resort & Spa 2400 E Missouri Ave ☎ 602/955-6600 or 1-800/950-0086, ⓦ www.arizonabiltmore.com. Extraordinarily lavish 500-room resort, built under the influence of Frank Lloyd Wright in the 1930s and still retaining its Art Deco trimmings despite subsequent renovations. It is showing its age, however, and many guests resent the extra charges for almost everything; even self-parking costs $7 per night. Two golf courses, three restaurants, plus tennis and spa. June–Sept ❽, Oct–May ❾

Best Western Bell Hotel 17211 N Black Canyon Hwy ☎ 602/993-8300 or 1-800/780-7234; ⓦ www.bestwestern.com. Smart, well-priced motel, just off I-17 well north of downtown. Summer ❹, winter ❺

Budget Lodge Motel 402 W Van Buren St ☎ 602/254-7247. Reasonably attractive rooms at very attractive rates, in an unexciting motel setting – not far from the center, but you'll feel safer if you drive rather than walk here. ❷

Hotel San Carlos 202 N Central Ave ☎ 602/253-4121 or 1-866/253-4121, ⓦ www.hotelsancarlos .com. Historic, deliberately old-fashioned and very central 1920s hotel, with tasteful, good-value rooms, a nice café, and a rooftop swimming pool; it's liable to be noisier than its modern counterparts, however. ❼

Metcalf House Hostel, 1026 N Ninth St above Roosevelt St ☎ 602/254-9803, http://home.earth-link.net/~phxhostel/. Dorm beds at $15 for HI/AYH members, $18 non-members, in a slightly rundown location in a residential district, 15min walk north of the Arizona Center. No phone reservations, but space is usually available in the ten-bed men's dorm and six-bed women's dorm. No curfew, plus use of kitchen and laundry. Check in 5–10pm, or, usually but not always, 7–10am. ❶

Quality Suites 3101 N 32nd St ☎ 602/956-4900 or 1-800/950-1688. Spacious, good-value kitchenette suites, arrayed around a central pool, in a dull neighborhood where you're nonetheless well poised for both central Phoenix and Scottsdale. Summer ❸, winter ❺

Super 8 Phoenix Airport 3401 E Van Buren St ☎ 602/244-1627 or 1-800/800-8000, ⓦ www .super8.com. Dependable chain motel, a mile north of the airport, with free shuttle connection; there are seven other *Super8*s in the Phoenix area. ❺

Scottsdale

Days Inn Scottsdale Fashion Square Resort 4710 N Scottsdale Rd ☎ 480/947-5411 or 1-800/325-2525, ⓦ www.scottsdaledaysinn.com. Though not all that prepossessing, this two-story motel, immediately north of Fashion Square Mall – just stroll across the street – has perfectly acceptable rooms, plus an outdoor pool with bar and beach volleyball court, and can be a real bargain. Summer ❸, winter ❺

Motel 6 On Camelback 6848 E Camelback Rd ☎ 480/946-2280 or 1-800/466-8356, ⓦ www .motel6.com. Cut-price lodgings are few and far between in Scottsdale, so this budget motel, just off I-17 close to downtown, is well worth considering. ❸

The Phoenician 6000 E Camelback Rd ☎ 480/941-8200 or 1-800/888-8234, ⓦ www.thephoenician .com. Gorgeous 250-acre resort, spread out at the base of Camelback Mountain at the northern end of Scottsdale and offering every conceivable luxury, with golf course, waterfalls, and lush gardens as well as lavish rooms and restaurants. ❾

Scottsdale Pima Inn & Suites 7330 N Pima Rd ☎ 480/948-3800 or 1-800/344-0262. Relatively inexpensive motel, a few miles northwest of central Scottsdale but offering free local shuttles, with comfortable conventional rooms and pricier suites. Summer ❸, winter ❹

Tempe

Fiesta Inn 2100 S Priest Drive ☎ 480/967-1441 or 1-800/528-6481, ⓦ www.fiestainnresort.com. Old-style resort, not quite as plush as its Scottsdale counterparts but not as expensive either, offering large rooms plus two restaurants, pool, tennis, and spa. Summer ❺, winter ❽

Sleep Inn Airport 2621 S 47th Pl ☎ 480/967-7100 or 1-800/631-3054, ⓦ www.sleepinn.com. Above-average chain motel, three miles south of the airport but served by 24hr free shuttles; breakfast and internet access are free. ❹

Tempe Mission Palms Hotel 60 E Fifth St ☎ 480/894-1400 or 1-800/547-8705, ⓦ www .missionpalms.com. Very comfortable Southwestern-themed hotel in Tempe's revitalized Mill Avenue district, with a rooftop swimming pool. Good value in summer, but pricier in winter. Summer ❻, winter ❾

Tempe Super 8 Motel 1020 E Apache Blvd ☎ 480/967-8891 or 1-800/800-8000, ⓦ www .super8.com. Chain motel, within half a mile of the university and five miles of the airport. Summer ❷, winter ❹

Mesa

Arizona Golf Resort 425 S Power Rd ☎ 480/832-3202 or 1-800/528-8282, ⓦ www.azgolfresort.com. Pleasant rooms and suites in individual *casitas*, primarily intended for golfers using the adjoining course, but also handy for forays into the mountains to the east. Summer ❺, winter ❼

Motel 6 630 W Main St ☎ 480/969-8111 or 1-800/466-8356, ⊛ www.motel6.com. The most central of Mesa's three *Motel 6*s; there are three more in Tempe. All offer dull double rooms at budget rates. ❷

Super 8 Mesa 6733 E Main St ☎ 480/981-6181 or 1-800/800-8000, ⊛ www.super8.com. Budget chain motel to the east of central Mesa, en route toward the Apache Trail. Summer ❷, winter ❹

❹ Central Phoenix

Downtown Phoenix – defined as the few blocks east and west of Central Avenue and north and south of **Washington Street** – is too hot and too spread out to walk around in any comfort. Nominally it's still the headquarters of "Arizona Inc," but the major corporate offices and institutions are now scattered throughout the Valley of the Sun. Nonetheless, determined efforts are currently being made to regenerate and revitalize the area; around three billion dollars have been pumped into assorted construction projects, and a ninety-block district has even been rebranded with a new name – **Copper Square**. The major components of the plan are two massive side-by-side sports stadiums, the **America West Arena** and the **Bank One Ballpark**, home respectively to basketball's Phoenix Suns and baseball's Arizona Diamondbacks. Adjoining the two is the one significant downtown **mall**, the **Arizona Center**, on Van Buren Street between Third and Fifth.

What little remains of Phoenix's nineteenth-century architecture now constitutes **Heritage Square**, a couple of blocks southeast of the Arizona Center at 115 N Sixth St. It preserves a quaint assortment of Victorian homes converted into tea rooms and toy museums. You can get a better impression of the early days at the **Phoenix Museum of History**, across the street at 105 N Fifth St (Tues–Sat 10am–5pm; $6; ☎ 602/253-2734; ⊛ www.pmoh.org), which starts with a "calendar stick" used by Pima Indians and features the city's first jail – a rock with a chain attached – as well as early town plans and a steam-powered bicycle.

Immediately south, at 600 E Washington St, the **Arizona Science Center** (daily 10am–5pm; adults $9, children 3–12 $7; ☎ 602/716-2000; ⊛ www .azscience.org) ranks as Arizona's second-favorite tourist attraction, welcoming barely fewer visitors each year than the Grand Canyon. Aimed primarily at children, it's a hands-on museum of learning games and interactive gimmicks that centers on a giant-screen movie theater.

Twenty sun-baked blocks west, at 1700 W Washington St, the sparkling copper dome of the disused **Arizona State Capitol** dominates the low-level sprawl. Documents in the dull, dry **museum** within do little to bring the state's political history to life (Mon–Fri 8am–5pm; free; ☎ 602/542-4675).

Two more significant attractions lie a mile or so north of downtown (and north of I-10, though you won't see the interstate as it burrows beneath Central Avenue). Thanks to extensive recent remodeling, the **Phoenix Art Museum**, 1625 N Central Ave (Tues, Wed, & Fri–Sun 10am–5pm, Thurs 10am–9pm; adults $9, children 6–17 $3; free Thurs; ☎ 602/257-1222; ⊛ www.phxart.org), has plenty of space to display its permanent collection, which includes paintings by Georgia O'Keeffe and Rufino Tamayo, as well as *de rigueur* Western art by Charles M. Russell and Frederic Remington and some middleweight Old Masters, while also maintaining its reputation for controversial temporary exhibitions. A top-quality giftshop stocks Mexican crafts items and jazzy modern ceramics.

Three blocks north of the Art Museum, the **Heard Museum**, 2301 N Central Ave (daily 9.30am–5pm; $10; children 6–12 $3; ☎ 602/252-8848;

@ www.heard.org), has been greatly enlarged in the last few years, while still showcasing the lovely old buildings in which it was originally founded. Unfortunately the displays themselves seem to have been somewhat "dumbed down," perhaps in the hope of holding the attention of the many school groups that come here. Nonetheless, for first-time visitors to the region it offers a good introduction to the culture of the **Native Americans** of the Southwest, and their arts and crafts in particular. There's a special emphasis on the Hohokam, with plenty of artifacts from the large town, now known as "La Ciudad," which occupied the site of modern Phoenix during the twelfth century. Elsewhere, the superb pottery collection includes stunning Mimbres bowls (see p.246), a parrot-headed and -tailed Salado jar from 1350 AD, clay dolls made by the Quechan and Mohave peoples as souvenirs for nineteenth-century railroad passengers, and modern Hopi ceramics. You'll also find a complete Navajo *hogan* (see p.80), some fine old Havasupai baskets, Apache beadwork, and painted buffalo-skin shields from New Mexican pueblos. Best of all are the Hopi **kachina dolls** – see p.84 – four hundred of which were donated by arch-conservative Arizona senator Barry Goldwater.

Scottsdale

Having grown to house well over 200,000 people and stretch almost twenty miles from north to south, the town of **SCOTTSDALE**, founded ten miles northeast of Phoenix in the 1880s, is a remarkable success story in its own right. Despite being almost wholly subsumed into the metropolitan maw, it has carved itself an eccentric double niche as both the city's most chic destination, home to opulent resorts and designer-led malls, and its most determinedly "Western" quarter.

Southeast of **Camelback Mountain** and the grand **Scottsdale Fashion Square** mall, downtown Scottsdale focuses on a few pleasant blocks of sidewalk cafés and souvenir stores. West of Scottsdale Road counts as the **Main Street Arts and Antiques District**; to the east, **Old Town** plays the Wild West theme for all it's worth. At 7374 E Second St, the **Scottsdale Museum of Contemporary Art** (Tues, Wed, Fri, & Sat 10am–5pm, Thurs 10am–8pm, Sun noon–5pm; $7, free Thurs; @480/994-2787 @ www.scottsdalearts.org) is a showcase for stimulating modern art, hosting changing temporary exhibitions rather than a permanent collection.

Whatever its general appearance may suggest, Phoenix has managed to attract some visionary designers. Notable among them is **Frank Lloyd Wright**, who came to the city to work on the *Biltmore Hotel* and returned to spend the winter for most of the 25 years before his death in 1959. His studio, **Taliesin West** – located at 114th Street and Frank Lloyd Wright Boulevard, at Scottsdale's far northeastern edge – is now an architecture school and a working design studio, with multimedia exhibits of the man's life and work (Oct–May daily 10am–4pm, June & Sept daily 9am–4pm, July & Aug Mon & Thurs–Sun 9am–4pm; ☎480/860-2700; ⓦwww.franklloydwright.org). It can only be seen on guided visits; at very regular intervals, increasing to more than one every half-hour between February and mid-April, you can join either an hour-long "Panorama Tour" ($18) or a ninety-minute "Insight Tour" ($22), which grants access to Wright's private living area; call in advance for schedules of occasional longer explorations. Seventy years after Wright first came here, this is still a splendidly isolated spot, and it's one where his trademark "organic architecture" makes perfect sense. Wright and his students camped out and assessed the terrain long before building any permanent structures, and the complex blends seamlessly into the desert. The expertise and enthusiasm of the guides makes the experience well worth the price.

Another less well known architectural attraction is the **Cosanti Foundation**, four miles southwest at 6433 Doubletree Ranch Rd (daily 9am–5pm; $1 donation; ☎480/948-6145 or 1-800/752-3187, ⓦwww.arcosanti.org). The buildings here, designed by **Paolo Soleri**, an Italian-born former student of Wright, and constructed out of rammed earth and concrete, have a similar organic feel to Taliesin. Crafts workshops cast bells and bronzes, and a small museum shows drawings and models of Soleri's life work: the planned community of **Arcosanti**, described on p.349. Mr Solari generously invites women aged 21 to 41 to pose nude for him, for no additional charge.

In **Papago Park** at the south end of Scottsdale, the fascinating **Desert Botanical Garden**, 1201 North Galvin Parkway (daily: May–Sept 7am–8pm; Oct–April 8am–8pm; adults $10, ages 3–12 $4; ☎480/941-1225; ⓦwww.dbg .org), is filled with an amazing array of cactuses and desert flora from around the world. Prime specimens include spineless "totem pole" cactuses from the Galápagos Islands and "living stone" plants from South Africa that at a glance you'd never suspect were alive. Separate enclaves are devoted to **butterflies** – seen at their best in August and September – and to **hummingbirds**, of which Arizona boasts fifteen indigenous species.

Nearby, the **Phoenix Zoo** (daily: June–Sept 7am–2pm; Oct–May 9am–5pm; adults $14, ages 3–12 $6; ☎602/273-1341; ⓦwww.phoenixzoo.org) offers four monkey islands, some giant Galápagos tortoises, and a half-hour ride on a Safari Train. At the **Big Surf water park**, not far east at 1500 N McClintock Ave (May–Sept only, Mon–Sat 10am–6pm, Sun 11am–7pm; adults $19, ages 4–11 $15), you can ride five-foot waves or careen down multistory waterslides into a giant freshwater lagoon.

Tempe

Contemporary Phoenix's major success story has been the transformation of the community of **TEMPE** into the liveliest and most dynamic portion of the Valley of the Sun. It lies south of Scottsdale, across I-60, and around six miles east of downtown Phoenix, As the site of **Arizona State University**, it's home to around fifty thousand students, and they keep the cafés, clubs, stores and restaurants of the red-brick **Mill Avenue** constantly buzzing. Several minor museums and galleries are dotted across the college campus, immediately east, while a couple of blocks north the Salt River has been dammed and its surroundings landscaped to create an appealing park, the **Tempe Town Lake**. For an overview of local history – Tempe started out as a ferry post for travelers crossing the Salt River – call in at the spruced-up **Tempe Historical Museum** at 809 E Southern Ave (Mon–Thurs & Sat 10am–5pm, Sun 1–5pm; free; ☎480/350-5100).

Mesa

Built on the site of the Mormon settlement of Fort Utah, which lasted for three years from 1877, **MESA**, east of Tempe, is now Arizona's third-largest city. Covering more than a hundred square miles, it has a population of well over 400,000. Hidden among its endless broad boulevards are twenty golf courses, several large malls, some of Phoenix's most affordable residential districts, and dozens of cheap motels. With the Superstition Mountains rising to the east, it's not a bad base for passing visitors.

As well as displays on dinosaurs and the Hohokam, the enjoyable **Mesa Southwest Museum**, 53 N MacDonald St (Tues–Sat 10am–5pm, Sun 1–5pm; $6), features a reconstruction of a block of Mesa's Main Street as it looked a century ago. There's also a mock-up of the legendary Lost Dutchman Mine (see p.266), still sought by several expeditions each year.

Eating

Unless you're prepared to pay resort prices, it's hard to find a good **restaurant** in Phoenix with very much atmosphere. Apart from a block or two in central Scottsdale, and Tempe's lively Mill Avenue, no areas of the metropolis are small enough to walk around while you look for a place to eat, but if you're happy to drive, neighborhood diners – especially Mexican – can still be found, and the major thoroughfares are the usual fast-food heaven.

Central Phoenix

Alice Cooper'stown 101 E Jackson St ☎602/253-7337, ⓦ www.alicecooperstown.com. Barbecue restaurant-cum-sports bar, owned by the rock star and located alongside downtown's America West Arena. The food's better than you'd expect, and the atmosphere is fun, with waiters in full Alice make-up. Sun–Thurs 11am–10pm, Fri & Sat 11am–11pm.

Carly's Bistro 128 E Roosevelt St ☎602/262-2759. Pleasant, relaxing bistro near downtown art galleries, serving healthy Mediterranean sandwiches, salads and light meals, and offering regular live music. Mon 11am–3pm, Tues 11am–3pm & 5–10pm, Wed & Thurs 11am–3pm & 5pm–midnight, Fri & Sat 11am–3pm & 5pm–2am.

Durant's 2611 N Central Ave ☎602/264-5967, ⓦ www.durantsaz.com. This old-style downtown restaurant is a venerable institution for Arizona's elite, specializing in rich all-American food such as oysters Rockefeller and, especially, steaks; if you can down the 48-oz Porterhouse, your name gets added to a plaque on the wall. Mon–Thurs 11am–10pm, Fri 11am–1am, Sat 5pm–1am, Sun 4.30pm–midnight.

Greektown Restaurant 8519 N Seventh St ☎602/674-8881, ⓦ www.greektownrestaurant .com. Quintessential Greek restaurant, serving perfectly prepared moussaka, dolmades (stuffed vine leaves), and lamb *kleftiko*, plus *retsina*, *ouzo* and of course a *bouzouki* soundtrack. Open for lunch and dinner daily.

Rosita's Place 2310 E McDowell Rd ☎602/244-9779. Veteran Mexican restaurant, offering a full menu of inexpensive south-of-the-border delights in colorful surroundings. Mon–Fri 10am–10pm, Sat 9am–11pm, Sun 8am–10pm.

Pizzeria Bianco Heritage Square, 623 E Adams St ☏ 602/258-8300. High-quality pizzas in a very convenient downtown location; no wonder it's so popular. Tues–Sat 5–10pm.

Sam's Cafe Arizona Center, 455 N Third St ☏ 602/252-3545, ⓦ www.canyoncafe.com. Hectic downtown mall joint, with patio seating, that's nonetheless a great place to enjoy either modern Southwestern cuisine (or as the menu calls it, Sam-Mex) or classic Mexican dishes (Mex-Mex). As an appetizer, the $13 Coyote Sampler is irresistible; few full entrees cost that much. (There's another branch in the Biltmore Fashion Park, at 24th and Camelback; ☏ 602/954-7100.) Sun–Wed 11am–9pm, Thurs–Sat 11am–10pm.

Scottsdale

Bandera 3821 N Scottsdale Rd ☏ 480/994-3524. Chicken cooked in the wood-burning oven is the specialty in this busy, inexpensive rotisserie on the southeast edge of downtown, though other meats and fish are almost as good. Sun–Thurs 4.30–10pm, Fri & Sat 5–11pm.

Binkley's 6920 E Cave Creek Rd ☏ 480/437-1072, ⓦ www.binkleysrestaurant.com. This expensive but utterly sublime restaurant regularly wins accolades as the finest in Phoenix, combining the best of classic French and contemporary American cuisine. The one snag is that it's a twenty-mile drive north of downtown Scottsdale. Typical entrees like soy braised veal short ribs cost $30–35, while tasting menus start at $50. Daily except Mon 5–10.30pm.

Cowboy Ciao 7133 E Stetson Drive at Sixth ☏ 480/946-3111, ⓦ www.cowboyciao.com. Appropriately enough, considering a decor that blends an Old West roadhouse with an Italian feel, this hip downtown option serves "modern American food with global influences." At lunchtime, burgers cost $8–12 and a barbecue venison sandwich $14; the $12 "Stetson" chopped salad is also available in the evening, when a slow-cooked pork shank is $26 and the elk strip loin $32. Mon–Thurs 11.30am–2.30pm & 5–10pm, Fri & Sat 11.30am–2.30pm & 5–11pm, Sun 10.30am–2.30pm & 5–10pm.

El Chorro Lodge 5550 E Lincoln Drive ☏ 480/948-5170, ⓦ www.elchorro.com. Spacious, classy lodge that's been catering to Phoenix sophisticates since 1937; dine al fresco in summer, or by the cozy fireside in winter. Half a dozen oysters cost $14, while entrees range from $14 burgers up to the $31 prime rib, with the trademark chicken livers at $17. Open for dinner daily, and for lunch Oct–May only, daily except Sat.

Malee's on Main 7131 E Main St ☏ 480/947-6042, ⓦ www.maleesthaibistro.com. Somewhat inconspicuous but very popular and dependably good Thai place downtown, serving all the usual items – pad thai noodles, chicken green curry – at reasonable prices. There's another branch at the mall Desert Ridge Marketplace. Mon–Wed 11.30am–2.30pm & 5–9pm, Thurs & Fri 11.30am–10pm, Sat noon–10pm, Sun 5–9pm.

Roaring Fork 4800 N Scottsdale Rd ☏ 480/947-0795, ⓦ www.roaringfork.com. Contemporary but unfussy Southwestern cuisine at reasonable prices from an award-winning chef, with fried chicken for $16.50, or duck breast with onion jam $24.50. Mon–Sat 5–10pm, Sun 5–9pm.

Tempe

Coffee Plantation 680 S Mill Ave ☏ 480/829-7878. Downtown coffeehouse that's forever crammed with over-excited students, and has spawned ten more outlets across the valley. Daily 6am–midnight.

House of Tricks 114 E Seventh St ☏ 480/968-1114, ⓦ www.houseoftricks.com. Tiny modern-American place in the University district, named for chefs Robin and Robert Trick, with lots of vegetarian options. Dinner entrées range from $20 for pasta with shrimp up to $29 for rack of lamb. Daily except Sun 11am–10pm.

Monti's La Casa Vieja 3 W First St ☏ 480/967-7594, ⓦ www.montis.com. Tempe's oldest adobe house, built beside the Salt River ferry landing in 1873, is now an atmospheric Western-themed diner, serving a conventional steak-and-chicken menu at extraordinarily low prices. Sun–Thurs 11am–10pm, Sat & Sun 11am–11pm.

Ra 411 S Mill Ave ☏ 480/303-9800, ⓦ www.rasushi.com. Lively, trendy Japanese restaurant in the heart of downtown Tempe, where you can get baked green mussels for $7, two soft-shell crabs for around $10, and a full bowl of noodles for under $15, while sushi hand rolls cost around $10 and sushi platters are under $20. Also at 3815 N Scottsdale Rd in Scottsdale. Daily 11am–11pm.

Mesa

The Landmark Restaurant 809 W Main St ☏ 480/962-4652, ⓦ www.landmarkrestaurant.com. Classic mid-American diner housed in a former Mormon church, serving hearty baked and roasted meats for $12–20, including a trip to the excellent salad bar. Mon–Sat 11am–9pm, Sun 11am–7pm.

The Seafood Market 1910 S Gilbert Rd ☏ 480/890-0435. A feast of fresh fish, flown in from all over the world and prepared simply at reasonable prices. Also at 1356 W. Southern Ave (☏ 480/890-0435). Daily 11.30am–9pm.

Nightlife, entertainment, and sports

In recent years, Phoenix's **nightlife** seems to have been losing some of its Western identity; the cowboy dance halls have been closing down, while Tempe and Scottsdale have respectively cultivated an alt-rock, college crowd and a glitzier clubbing scene. For a rundown of what's happening musically, pick up the free weekly *New Times* (Ⓦwww.phoenixnewtimes.com) in local music or bookstores, or check out the bars and clubs listed below.

Both the **Phoenix Symphony Hall**, 225 E Adams St (☎602/495-1999; Ⓦwww.phoenixsymphony.org), and the **Scottsdale Center for the Performing Arts**, 7380 E Second St (☎480/994-2787, Ⓦwww.scottsdalearts.org), adjacent to the Museum of Contemporary Art, put on classical music, theater, and ballet. The **Arizona Diamondbacks** – winners of the World Series in 2001 – have been playing major league baseball beneath the retractable roof of the Bank One Ballpark at 401 E Jefferson St since 1998 (☎602/514-8400, Ⓦwww.azdiamondbacks.com), while the **Phoenix Suns** play NBA basketball at the America West Arena, 201 E Jefferson St (☎602/379-7900, Ⓦwww.suns.com), and football's **Arizona Cardinals** are based at the university's Sun Devil Stadium (☎602/379-0102, Ⓦwww.azcardinals.com).

Bash on Ash 230 W Fifth St, Tempe ☎480/966-5600, Ⓦwww.bashonash.com. Live music venue that's part of a sports bar in the heart of Tempe, featuring reggae, rock, soul, or salsa nightly except Mon.

Char's Has the Blues 4631 N Seventh Ave, Phoenix ☎602/230-0205, Ⓦwww.charshastheblues.com. Phoenix's longest-standing blues venue, set in a small house just south of Camelback Road, offers live music nightly.

e4 4282 N Drinkwater Blvd, Scottsdale ☎480/970-3325, Ⓦwww.e4-az.com. The city's hottest new dance club is a massive, eye-popping affair, designed around the elements of air, earth, fire and water, and holding a Vegas-style "ultra-lounge" downstairs as well as the *Liquid* dance club with cascading waterfalls. Tues & Wed 9pm-2am, Thurs & Fri 5pm-2am, Sat 6pm-2am. Cover $5 Wed & Thurs, $10 Fri & Sat.

Last Exit Bar & Grill 1425 W Southern Ave, Tempe ☎480/557-6656, Ⓦwww.lastexitlive.com. Rock-oriented live music venue in an unpromising mall, where acts range from country-rock to local punks. Mon–Fri 3pm–2am, Sat & Sun 5pm–2am.

Marquee Theatre 730 N Mill Ave, Tempe ☎480/829-0607, Ⓦwww.luckymanonline.com. The best venue to see big-name touring acts, with an open floor rather than seating, and good beer.

Rhythm Room 1019 E Indian School Rd, Phoenix ☎602/265-4842, Ⓦwww.rhythmroom.com. Top-notch blues and jazz acts perform live in an intimate atmosphere, with good barbecue to help things along. Sun–Thurs 8pm–1am, Fri & Sat 8pm–2am.

Shopping

With the city's great outdoors being too hot and sprawling to take for more than a few minutes at a time, you'll probably find yourself looking for a nice cool **mall** at some point.

The biggest of the lot – in the whole Southwest, for that matter – is the **Metrocenter**, just east of I-17 at 9617 Metro Parkway, nine miles north of downtown. The central mall building holds all the usual outlets, plus five large department stores, while countless more stores and restaurants line the oval ring road around it. When you tire of shopping, try the Desert Storm rollercoaster in **Castles'n'Coasters** alongside (June–Aug Fri 5–11pm, Sat noon–11pm, Sun 5–9pm; Sept–May Sun–Thurs 10am–10pm, Fri & Sat 10am–midnight; $24 or pay per ride; ☎602/997-7575, Ⓦwww.castlesncoasters.com).

The **Biltmore Fashion Park**, north of Camelback Road at 24th Street, halfway between downtown Phoenix and Scottsdale, concentrates on designer names and has a giant *Borders* bookstore, while the **Scottsdale Fashion Square**, further east at 7000 E Camelback Rd, is (slightly) more affordable. Also in Scottsdale, a couple of miles north, the smaller **Borgata** mall is notable for its extraordinary mock-Italian architecture, while the **Main Street Arts and Antiques District** is full of pricey galleries, largely specializing in Southwestern and cowboy art. Tempe's **Arizona Mills** mall offers the valley's best discount shopping. Finally, the downtown **Arizona Center** (see p.260) is a bit short on interesting shops but is at least livening the place up a little with its 24-screen movie theater and busy restaurants.

East of Phoenix

Almost two hundred miles of mountainous terrain stands between Phoenix and New Mexico to the east, much of it belonging to two huge Apache reservations. Although sweltering Phoenicians spend summer weekends in hill towns such as Payson and Pinetop to the northeast (both covered in Chapter Five), there's little to detain ordinary tourists on the long drive east.

US-60 and US-70 are the quickest routes to New Mexico, but if you want a quick escape from the desert heat, head instead up the **Apache Trail** into the **Superstition Mountains**. An enduring Arizona legend makes these the site of the **Lost Dutchman Mine**. Two German prospectors, Jacob Waltz and Jacob Weiser, supposedly discovered rich deposits of gold around 1870 and turned up repeatedly in the town of Florence bearing priceless nuggets. Before his death in Phoenix in 1890, Waltz is said to have murdered not only Weiser but another seven men who tried to shadow him back to the motherlode. Ever since, countless expeditions have attempted to follow his deathbed directions to the mine – guarded, according to different accounts, by pygmies or a never-discovered group of Apaches – and an estimated thirty gold-seekers are rumored to have lost their lives.

The Apache Trail

The closest accessible wilderness to central Phoenix lies along **Hwy-88**, which climbs northeast into the Superstition Mountains from Apache Junction, almost twenty miles east of Mesa and a good thirty miles from downtown Phoenix. This fifty-mile highway was constructed in 1904 to provide a direct route to the site of the Roosevelt Dam, then being built at the confluence of Tonto Creek and Salt River. After the dam's completion in 1911, it was renamed **The Apache Trail** by the Southern Pacific Railroad in a bid to drum up tourists, and became a popular scenic drive. It's still a long, slow haul, tortuous enough to take around two hours end to end.

Just four miles up from Apache Junction, as the cactus-studded foothills start to rise, ramshackle **Goldfield Ghost Town** provides an appealing photo opportunity, complete with discarded mine machinery and a street of

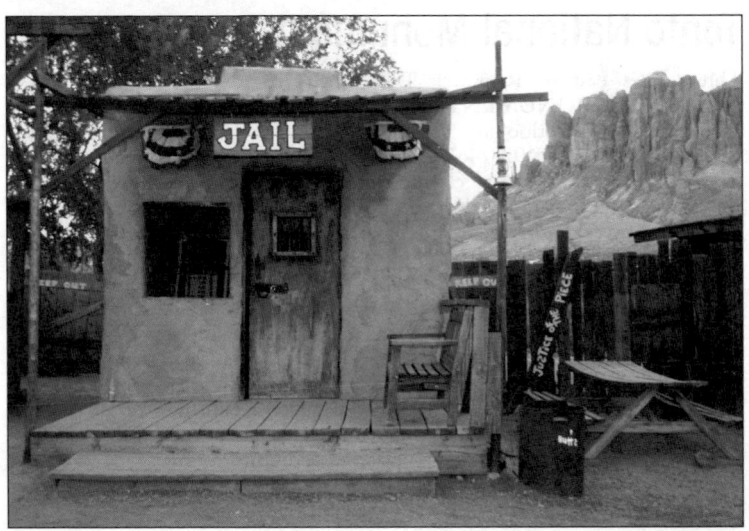

△ Town jail, Tortilla Flat

tumbledown timber-frame stores (daily 10am–5pm; ☎480/983-0333, ⓦwww
.goldfieldghosttown.com). Much of what you see is either fake or brought
here from somewhere else, but it's all quite atmospheric. **Activities** such as
descents into mine shafts, and train rides cost from around $5 per person, and
the various on-site businesses also have details of pricier jeep tours, horse rides
or even helicopter flights in the vicinity. Alternatively, you can pick up a snack
or a meal at the *Coffee Cantina and Bakery* (4650 N Mammoth Mine Rd;
☎480/983-8777) or the *Mammoth Steak House* (☎480/983-6402).

Many day-trippers go no further up the Apache Trail than **Canyon Lake**, fifteen
miles along. Created by a more recent dam, but nonetheless old enough to look as
though it belongs amid the scrubby surrounding hills, it's a bit too narrow to satisfy
pleasure-boaters, who find themselves having to turn around every time they get
up a bit of speed. However, if you're happy to take it easy, a lunch or dinner cruise
on *Dolly's Steamboat* (☎480/827-9144; ⓦwww.dollysteamboat.com) is an enjoyable way to pass a couple of hours. Cruises run daily at noon and 2pm, costing $17
for adults ($9.50 ages 6–12), or $32 with lunch; twilight dinner cruises cost $50
($32 for children). Reservations are required for lunch and dinner.

TORTILLA FLAT, at the east end of the lake, is not so much a town as
a hundred-yard stretch of boardwalk with an Old West flavor that holds the
souvenir-filled County Store, the *Dutchman's Inn* diner, and the *Superstition
Saloon*, all operated by the same management (☎480/984-1776; ⓦwww
.tortillaflataz.com). Named for the nearby flat-topped boulders, Tortilla Flat
has no connection with the Steinbeck novella.

Beyond Tortilla Flat, the mountains finally start to get serious, while Hwy-88
responds by turning to gravel. After a few hair-raising hairpin bends, with stom-
ach-lurching views across the saguaro-studded canyons, it returns to undulating
gently along beside the river. An optional detour drops down to **Apache Lake**,
another busy boating and picnicking spot. Keep going to reach **Roosevelt
Dam** itself, which was recently raised and strengthened to cope with Phoenix's
bottomless thirst for water.

Tonto National Monument

Three miles east of Roosevelt Dam, the **cliff dwellings** of **TONTO NATIONAL MONUMENT** (daily 8am–5pm; $3 per person) stand high above Hwy-88, overlooking Theodore Roosevelt Lake. From the **visitor center** (same hours; ☎928/467-2241; ⓦ www.nps.gov/tont), a very steep trail, which shuts an hour before closing time, climbs half a mile upwards. Not a walk to schedule for the middle of a summer's day, it leads to the remarkably complete **Lower Ruin**, set in a deep alcove near the top of the rocky ridge, with great saguaro cactuses standing sentinel.

This large pueblo was built in the mid-fourteenth century by a people now known as the **Salado** Indians, who are regarded as less sophisticated than the Ancestral Puebloans to the north. Their masonry is much cruder, using lumps of rock that had fallen from the cliff face and were then thickly plastered with mud that still bears thousands of ancient fingerprints. Visitors can walk right through several rooms of the ruin, some of which retain their original beams and saguaro-rib ceilings. "Shelves" and storage niches are tucked into the cave walls, as well as notches that once supported additional rooms.

Between November and April only, rangers lead guided hikes to the **Upper Ruin**, reached by a separate trail up the next ridge along.

Globe

Hwy-88 rejoins US-60, the direct route east from Phoenix, thirty miles on from Tonto National Monument, just outside **GLOBE**. This still-functional mining town sprang into being in the 1880s, when a twelve-mile strip of land on which a globe of pure silver had just been discovered was stripped from the Apache reservation; since the silver and gold ran out, the community has made its living from copper.

The central few blocks of downtown Globe still hold several brick-built Victorian-era structures, though the claim that these include "the West's oldest Woolworth's" betrays quite how little there is of any great interest. On the northern outskirts, the small **Gila County Historical Museum**, 1330 N Broad St (Mon–Fri 10am–4pm; free), explores local history in punitive detail.

That Native American occupation of the region predated the Apache is shown by the ruins of **Besh-Ba-Gowah**, a mile southeast of town, which were home first to the Hohokam and later to the Salado; their modern Apache name is said to mean "metal-its-house." Visitors can enter reconstructed living quarters and a *kiva* (daily 9am–5pm; $3).

If you like your Wild West to be utterly unvarnished and unromantic, head a mile or two west of Globe to the twin communities of **CLAYPOOL** and **MIAMI**. All but engulfed by monstrous mountains of copper-mine tailings, these flyblown towns are packed with gun stores, all-day saloons, and pick-up trucks, and are certainly not a vacation destination to be chosen in preference to Miami, Florida.

Practicalities

Globe's **visitor center** stands in front of the county museum on Hwy-88, at 1360 N Broad St (Oct–April Mon–Fri 8am–5pm, Sat & Sun 10am–4pm; May–Sept Mon–Fri 8am–5pm; ☎928/425-4495 or 1-800/804-5623,

@ www.globemiamichamber.com). Of the dozen or so **motels**, the restored, vintage *El Rey*, 1201 E Ash St (☎928/425-4427; ❷), and the *Ember*, 1105 N Broad St (☎928/425-5736; ❷), which has a pool, offer the best value. Downtown **cafés** include the Mexican bakery *La Luz del Dia*, 304 N Broad St (☎928/425-8400), where the burritos are made with fresh tortillas, while *Java Junction*, at Broad and Center (closed Sun; ☎928/402-8926), serves coffee and sandwiches. On the third weekend in October, Native Americans from all over the Southwest pour in for the three-day **Apache Days** fair.

Superior

Fifteen miles southwest of Miami on US-60 – or, if you're driving up from Phoenix, forty miles east of the start of the Apache Trail – another former silver-mining town, **SUPERIOR**, is now noteworthy as the site of the **Boyce Thompson Arboretum** (daily 8am–5pm; $7.50, ages 5–12 $3; ☎520/689-2811, @ www.ag.arizona.edu/bta). This landscaped public garden spreads through two parallel canyons, and focuses on desert plants from around the world. Cactuses are of course abundant, but there are also spectacular oddities like the towering boojum tree from Baja California. A brisk walk along the main hiking trail takes around an hour, though you could spend much longer exploring additional side trails like the themed "Plants of the Bible" walk. The fall colors are usually at their best during the last two weeks of November and the first week of December.

A mile or so east of the arboretum, **Buckboard City** is a mock-up Western steak-and-barbecue restaurant that also runs the adjoining **"World's Smallest Museum,"** basically a shed filled with all sorts of little oddities, weird trinkets, and old farming equipment (daily 8am–2pm; donations; ☎520/689-5800, @ www.worldssmallestmuseum.com).

San Carlos Indian Reservation

The two-million-acre **SAN CARLOS INDIAN RESERVATION**, which extends a hundred miles east and north of Globe, was created by President Grant in 1872 to protect the **Apache** from such outrages as the Camp Grant massacre of 1871 (see p.270). In the words of one tribal member, the reservation was "the worst place in all the great territory stolen from the Apache. If anybody ever lived there permanently, no Apache knew of it. The heat was terrible. The insects were terrible. The water was terrible."

Around eight thousand Apache now live on the reservation, which offers few activities for tourists apart from sailing or fishing on **San Carlos Lake**, twenty miles east of Globe, or **camping** beside it at *Soda Canyon Point* (☎928/475-2756; $5). The original reservation town of **San Carlos** was drowned – despite strong Apache opposition – when the lake arose behind the new Coolidge Dam in 1930, whereupon the community previously known as **Rice**, ten miles north, was simply renamed San Carlos. Today, the settlement is just an administrative center; if you want to learn more about the Apache, take time to study the displays on their religion and history at the **San Carlos Apache Cultural Center** in **Peridot**, on US-70 nearby (@ www.sancarlosapache.com; Mon–Fri 9am–5pm; $3).

Aravaipa Canyon

One of the most notorious tragedies in the whole sorry tale of Anglo-Apache relations took place in the deceptively beautiful **ARAVAIPA CANYON**, just below the southern boundary of the San Carlos reservation. In 1871, when it was home to a semipermanent Apache encampment under the nominal protection of the US Army, 144 women and children were slaughtered in the **Camp Grant massacre**. Their killers, an unholy party of Tucson vigilantes who called themselves the Committee of Public Safety, consisted of a hundred Tohono 'O'odham, fifty Hispanics, and six Anglos. For more on the so-called "Tucson Ring" who lay behind it, see p. 274.

Reached along a well-maintained eleven-mile dirt road that heads east from Hwy-77 fifty miles south of Globe, Aravaipa Canyon is now a **wilderness area** managed by the federal government and the Arizona Nature Conservancy. The terrain ranges from sun-drenched hillsides covered with saguaros to the deep-red gorge carved by Aravaipa Creek – a rare perennial desert stream – and lined by giant cottonwoods. Visitors keen to experience the desert in its wild state need to come prepared; the canyon has no trails, no established campgrounds, and no signs, and is home to rattlesnakes and scorpions. Only fifty people can enter the thirty-square-mile wilderness at any one time; obtain a **permit** ($5 per day, with a maximum two-night stay) from the Bureau of Land Management, 711 Fourteenth Ave, Safford AZ 85546 (☎928/428-4040).

Safford

The farming community of **SAFFORD**, 77 miles southeast of Globe, is the only sizeable town north of I-10 in southeast Arizona. There's no significant reason to visit, but if you're ready to stop for the night, it holds around a dozen motels, such as the *Econo Lodge*, 225 E Thatcher Blvd (☎928/348-0011; Ⓦwww.econolodge.com; ❷), as well as a pleasant **B&B**, *Olney House*, 1104 S Central Ave (☎928/428-5118 or 1-800/814-5118; Ⓦwww.olneyhouse .com; ❹).

Morenci

At its southern end, the **Coronado Trail Scenic Road** – described on p.321 – twists its way down past a vast tiered pit, where the Gila Mountains still yield 175,000 tons of copper a day. **MORENCI**, at the bottom, is a modern-looking company town that was built in the 1960s to replace a predecessor swallowed up by the mine, and is absolutely dominated by the Phelps Dodge company. The *Morenci Motel and Restaurant* (☎928/865-4111; ❸), perched on a knoll opposite the Phelps Dodge Mercantile Company Store, serves as the starting point for two-hour bus tours of the open-pit mine (Fri & Sat 8.30am & 1pm; $8; ☎1-877/646-8687, Ⓦwww.phelpsdodge.com/community-envi ronment).

A few miles further on, the older town of **CLIFTON** has become seriously rundown and is too derelict to be worth a stop.

From Phoenix to Tucson

The hundred-mile sprint from Phoenix to Tucson along the **I-10** interstate is one of Arizona's less inspiring drives, though it is at least over quite quickly. The main interruption en route is the molar-shaped promontory of **Picacho Peak**, at the base of which the roadside stall of the Rooster Cogburn Ostrich Farm is as good a place to stretch your legs, and possibly buy a feather duster, as any (daily except Wed 9am–5.30pm; ☏520/466-3658 ⓦwww.roostercogburn .com). If you don't mind taking a slightly more circuitous route, however, it's possible to break the journey at a couple of equally unlikely and enigmatic structures – ancient **Casa Grande** and ultra-modern **Biosphere 2**.

Casa Grande Ruins National Monument

On the outskirts of **Coolidge**, fifteen miles east of interstate exit 185, or twenty miles north of exit 210, **CASA GRANDE RUINS NATIONAL MONUMENT** preserves the most substantial surviving example of the architecture of the **Hohokam** people (daily 8am–5pm; $5 per person; ☏520/723-3172; ⓦwww.nps.gov/cagr). It shares its name – Spanish for "Great House" – but little else, with the I-10 pit stop of Casa Grande, thirty miles southwest, and the much larger ancient site of Casas Grandes, far south in northern Mexico.

The Casa Grande itself is a four-story building, made of the concrete-like natural stone known as caliche, that was completed in the early fourteenth century. Spanish priest Father Eusebio Kino passed this way in 1694 – by which time the site had been abandoned for three centuries – and described the main structure as being "as large as a castle" and surrounded by thirteen smaller houses and many ruins. It was clear to him that "in ancient times there had been a city here." The house stood at the center of a walled compound in the floodplain of the **Gila River**, where the villagers used a well-developed network of canals to grow crops, harvested fruit from saguaro cactuses, and traded for shells and macaws with peoples from the south. It's now protected beneath a spiderlike canopy; visitors can enter the compound but not the structure itself. The exact purpose of the Casa Grande is unknown, though in view of the fact that windows and niches in the walls are aligned with key moments in the cycles of both the sun and moon, archeologists speculate that it was an astronomical observatory that doubled as a fortress in case of attack. Comprehensive displays in the visitor center explain the history in great detail.

Biosphere 2

Hwy-89 heads southeast from the small farming community of **FLORENCE**, ten miles east of Casa Grande monument, to meet **Hwy-77** roughly thirty miles north of Tucson. Turning east toward Oracle at this point gives tourists the chance to catch up with the latest developments in the extraordinary science-fiction saga of **BIOSPHERE 2**, at mile-marker 96.5 on Hwy-77 (daily 9am–4pm; $20, ages 6–12 $13; ☏520/838-6200; ⓦwww.bio2.edu).

When it was completed, in 1991, this vast complex of Plexiglas pyramids was trumpeted by its developers and widely publicized around the world as a major laboratory for experiments in applied environmental science. Containing five separate "**biomes**," or self-contained ecosystems – rainforest, marsh, savannah, desert, and a 25-foot-deep ocean – it was designed as a miniature working model of Biosphere 1, planet Earth itself, and stocked like a real-life Noah's ark with almost four thousand species of plants and animals. Investigative journalists soon revealed, however, that it was staffed largely by ex-actors from an obscure experimental theater group, the "Theater of All Possibilities," assembled by a certain John Allen, or "Johnny Dolphin," at the Synergia Ranch outside Santa Fe, in the hope of colonizing Mars and thus escaping the impending nuclear holocaust on Earth. A hundred million dollars' worth of support from Texas oil tycoon Ed Bass got this farfetched scheme off the ground, and top academics were recruited to add a veneer of respectability.

Eight "Biospherians" were sealed into Biosphere 2 in September 1991, their "mission" being to survive in isolation for two full years. This they more or less did, although emergency oxygen twice had to be pumped in as carbon dioxide levels rose, and one member briefly exited for medical treatment (and was seen returning with a suspiciously full bag of belongings). They grew 88 percent of their own food, and lost 13.65 percent of their body weight. Much of what transpired was replete with irony; hungry Biospherians soon found themselves planting bananas and papayas in what they had resolved would be the inviolate wilderness of the rainforest and destroying parts of the desert to boost oxygen, while the ocean proved impossible to keep clean. As for their fellow inhabitants, the African bush babies caught the hummingbirds, and the only birds to survive were unwanted sparrows that snuck in during construction. "Crazy ants" killed all the pollinating insects, so the Biospherians were reduced to the tedious task of pollinating all their plants by hand.

By the time the next crew moved in, conditions at Biosphere 2 had degenerated into farce. Two of the original crew, who had been acrimoniously fired, came back to the Biosphere's seals from the outside, thus aborting the second mission after just six months; they later sued and won compensation for their dismissal.

In its brief heyday, Biosphere 2 was one of Arizona's most popular tourist destinations. Now that no one is locked inside, however, the crowds have dwindled, and Biosphere 2 seems to have become a historical attraction, focused more towards the past than the future. While Ed Bass has maintained his involvement, a liaison with **Columbia University** has been abandoned, and the whole complex is casting to find a new owner who might have some use for it. Even so, the standard two-and-a-half-hour guided tours are still worth taking. Most of that time is spent peering into the greenhouses hoping to spot any sign of life larger than an ant, and marveling at the fact that, whatever you may have assumed, Biosphere 2 is not solar powered but depends on an external natural-gas power plant. Tunnels take you down beneath the "Coral Biome"; the guides insist it isn't an aquarium, but it doesn't half look like one. Only 100,000 gallons of it is authentic ocean water, trucked from the Pacific; the other 650,000 gallons were fresh water, to which a powder known as "Instant Ocean" has been added. Visitors are also allowed into the Biospherians' futuristic living quarters, tacked like a space capsule onto the back of the main block, where they appear to have suffered no privations whatsoever. For an extra $10 you can join a "World of Discovery" tour, which takes you right inside the greenhouses and offers close-up views of the massive "lung" that enables the whole thing to breathe.

The all-day *Cañada del Oro* café serves good **meals** on an appealing terrace.

Tucson

TUCSON has been southern Arizona's leading city for over two hundred years, during which time it has lived under five separate flags. Spreading across a mountain-ringed basin at the northern limits of the **Sonoran Desert**, its 900,000-plus inhabitants pride themselves on being more cosmopolitan, cultured, and liberal than those of its upstart rival Phoenix. Like Phoenix, the "Old Pueblo" has grown way past the point where the flow of the region's rivers, such as the Santa Cruz, is sufficient to quench its thirst. All are now dry sandy washes for most of the year, though flash floods still rage through the cross-town culverts after summer thunderstorms. However, unlike Phoenix, Tucson embraces rather than denies the desert, eschewing lawns and fountains in favor of directing visitors toward the authentic landscapes of **Sabino Canyon** and the **Arizona-Sonora Desert Museum** and the cactus-strewn hillsides of **Saguaro National Park**.

By Southwestern standards, Tucson (pronounced *too-sonn*) is a diverse, attractive, and lively city, home to the 35,000 energetic students of the **University of Arizona** as well as a large recent influx of retirees, and strongly influenced by its long association with Mexico, a mere sixty miles south. Although it suffers from the same Sunbelt sprawl as Albuquerque and Phoenix, it still has a compact and recognizably historic center – currently undergoing a multi-million-dollar reconstruction and rebranding as **Rio Nuevo** – some good parks and museums, affordable accommodation and enjoyable restaurants, and even a pretty good nightlife.

A history of Tucson

The valley of the Santa Cruz had already been inhabited for many centuries by the time Spanish priest Eusebio Kino passed through in 1700 and visited the

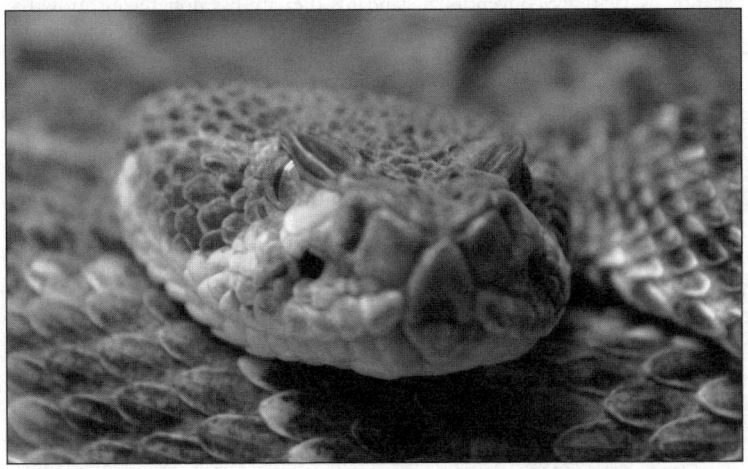

△ Rattlesnake at Tucson's Arizona-Sonora Desert Museum

Pima Indian settlement of *Stjukshon*, or "dark spring." Recent archeological excavations, undertaken west of downtown as part of the Rio Nuevo project, have even led to claims that this may be the oldest inhabited site in North America. In 1776, under the direction of **Hugo O'Conor**, one of the Catholic "Wild Geese" who had fled English-controlled Ireland to fight for Spain, the Spanish relocated their main Arizonan fortress here from Tubac (see p.289). That forty-mile move northwards brought them closer to **Apache** territory, and the energies of the Hispanic and Pima citizens of **San Agustín de Tucson** were largely devoted to resisting Apache raids and sieges. The severed heads of Apache warriors were displayed as trophies on the city walls.

When Tucson was sold to the US government as part of the **Gadsden Purchase** of 1854, the incoming Anglos were generally welcomed as a stabilizing presence. Not only did most of the valley's Mexican farmers remain in Arizona, but they were joined by more of their former compatriots. Soon, however, travelers were describing Tucson as "a place of resort for traders, speculators, gamblers, horse-thieves and vagrant politicians…a paradise of devils."

Although the **Confederates** who occupied southern Arizona in 1862 were swiftly driven away by Union forces from California, suspicions of lingering Confederate sympathies ensured that Tucson was passed over as capital of the new Territory. Conflict with the Apache continued, and a vigilante force of Mexicans, Anglos, and 'O'odham Indians from Tucson was responsible for the notorious **Camp Grant massacre** of 144 Apaches in Aravaipa Canyon in 1871 (see p.270). US Army commanders came to believe that a shadowy "**Tucson Ring**" of businessmen was consistently provoking the Apache in order to profit from the resultant military spending.

The end of the Apache Wars in the 1880s coincided with the coming of the transcontinental **railroad** and the reorientation of the commerce of Tucson along east–west routes. Its role as an entrepôt for trade with Mexico rapidly declined, and the Mexican merchants who had been its wealthiest citizens were driven out of business. Ever since, Mexican laborers have streamed back and forth across the border as the economy expands and contracts, but Tucson has become ever more American. Outstripped by Phoenix during the 1920s, and home to under forty thousand people (in an area of just nine square miles) as recently as 1940, by conventional standards the city has nonetheless grown at a phenomenal rate.

Arrival, information, and city tours

Tucson International Airport, eight miles south of downtown (☎520/573-8100), receives flights from all over the Southwest, but as far as long-distance services are concerned it very much plays second fiddle to Phoenix. It's connected to central Tucson by the slow Sun Tran **bus** #11 or #6 ($1) and the $15 shuttle vans of Arizona Stagecoach (☎520/889-1000, ⓦwww.azstagecoach.com). For **taxi** service, call Allstate Cab (☎520/798-1111) or Yellow Cab (☎520/624-6611).

The Amtrak station, downtown at 400 E Toole Ave, is served by three **trains** weekly in each direction between Los Angeles and points east; connecting Amtrak buses run north to Phoenix. Greyhound **buses** also stop very centrally, at 2 S Fourth Ave (☎520/792-3475 or 1-800/231-2222). Arizona Shuttle Services runs a daily shuttle-van service between Tucson and **Phoenix**'s Sky Harbor airport, with hourly departures, on the hour (daily 6.30am–11.30pm;

METROPOLITAN TUCSON

ACCOMMODATION

Arizona Inn	F
Casa Tierra	D
Catalina Park Inn	G
EconoLodge	J
Flamingo Hotel & Super 8 Downtown	E
Holiday Inn Palo Verde	K
JW Marriot Starr Pass Resort	I
Lodge on the Desert	H
Loews Ventana Canyon Resort	B
Tanque Verde Ranch	C
Westward Look Resort	A

Downtown accommodation and restaurants are marked on the 'Downtown Tucson' map

EATING

Blue Willow	4
Cafe Terra Cotta	1
Cuvee World Bistro	7
J Bar	2
Kingfisher	5
Pastiche Modern Eatery	3
Raging Sage	6
Safehouse Coffeehouse	8

see 'Downtown Tucson' map for detail

0   3 miles

one-way $29, round-trip $40 with 7-day advance reservation; ☎520/795-6671 or 1-800/888-2749, ⓦwww.arizonashuttle.com).

Most of downtown can be explored on foot, but on weekends you can ride the **Old Pueblo Trolley** (Fri 6–10pm, Sat noon–midnight, Sun noon–6pm; $1 per trip or $2.50 all day; ☎520/792-1802; ⓦwww.oldpueblotrolley.org) from Fourth Avenue out to the university, a mile east of the center.

Tucson's downtown **visitor center**, in the garishly painted little La Placita development at 100 S Church Ave (Mon–Fri 8am–5pm, Sat & Sun 9am–4pm; ☎520/624-1817 or 1-800/638-8350; ⓦwww.visittucson.org), has free maps and information. North of the university, Tucson Map & Flag Center, 3239 N First Ave (☎520/887-4234; ⓦwww.mapsmithus.com), stocks Arizona's best selection of maps and local guides. The main **post office** is at 141 S Sixth Ave.

Walking tours of downtown leave from the Sosa-Carillo-Frémont House, 151 S Granada Ave (Thurs & Sat 10am; $10; ☎520/622-0956), while Gray Line (☎520/622-8811 or 1-800/276-1528; ⓦwww.graylinearizona.com) offer $45 **city tours** by bus. Both Gray Line and Great Western Tours (☎520/572-1660; ⓦwww.gwtours.net) can also take you further afield, including to San Xavier Mission ($35), Nogales ($65–85), or Tombstone and Bisbee ($105).

Accommodation

Tucson offers a broader range of **accommodation** than Phoenix, with plenty of reasonably priced **hotels** and **motels** downtown as well as some atmospheric B&Bs both in the historic center and out in the surrounding desert. It also has its fair share of **resorts**, which can be every bit as expensive as their counterparts in Phoenix (if, as a rule, much less stuffy), and **dude ranches**. Once again, rates drop when the mercury rises, and some places are open only in the peak winter and spring seasons.

Hostels and B&Bs

Casa Tierra 11155 W Calle Pima ☎520/578-3058 or 1-866/254-0006, ⓦwww.casatierratucson.com. Secluded, four-room desert-edge B&B near the Arizona-Sonora Desert Museum, modeled on an adobe hacienda, and with an outdoor spa. Summer ❼, winter ❽

Catalina Park Inn 309 East First St ☎520/792-4541 or 1-800/792-4885, ⓦwww.catalinaparkinn .com. A beautiful yet not overly fussy six-room historic B&B across from a quiet park. Within walking distance of the university and happening Fourth Avenue. Closed early July to early Sept. Summer ❺, winter ❻

El Presidio Inn 297 N Main Ave ☎520/623-6151 or 1-800/349-6151. Four tastefully furnished Spanish colonial suites in historic downtown adobe B&B, with spacious wraparound veranda. ❻

Hotel Congress 311 E Congress St ☎520/622-8848 or 1-800/722-8848, ⓦwww.hotelcongress.com. Central, bohemian hotel, an easy walk from Amtrak and Greyhound, with vintage Art Deco furnishings. In the 1930s, bank-robber Dillinger was arrested here after pleading for his strangely heavy luggage to be rescued from a blaze on the third floor; now it offers $20 hostel beds for HI/AYH members (no reservations) and forty plain en-suite guest rooms, with vintage radios rather than TVs. With the *Cup Café* (see p.284) and Club Congress (see p.285) downstairs, this is one of the hottest spots in town, with loud music and dancing at night. ❶/❹

Roadrunner Hostel 346 E Twelfth St ☎520/628-4709, ⓦwww.roadrunnerhostel.com. Small and very central independent hostel in a downtown home, offering space in six-bed dorms for $20 per night or $120 per week, and private rooms for $38, plus Internet access. Free pickup from Amtrak and Greyhound. ❶

Hotels and motels

Econo Lodge 3020 S Sixth Ave ☎520/623-5881 or 1-800/553-2666, ⓦwww.econolodge.com. With its pleasant rooms and well-maintained pool, this inexpensive motel, west of the airport, represents the best value you're likely to find close to downtown. ❸

Flamingo Hotel 1300 N Stone Ave ☎520/770-1910 or 1-800/300-3533, ⓦ www.flamingohoteltucson .com. Despite recent renovations, this Western-themed motel remains at heart a plain budget option, but it does have a pool and spa, and stands barely a mile north of downtown Tucson. ❸

Holiday Inn Palo Verde 4550 South Palo Verde Blvd ☎1-520/746 1161 or 0870/400-9670, ⓦ www.ichotelsgroup.com. Six-story, Southwest-ern-styled hotel with reasonable rooms and a nice pool, located roughly halfway between the airport – served by free shuttles – and downtown. Summer ❹, winter ❺

Super 8 Downtown 1248 N Stone Ave ☎520/622-6446 or 1-800/800-8000, ⓦ www .super8.com. Adequate chain motel, a mile north-west of the university not far from downtown. Summer ❷, winter ❸

Ranches and resorts

Arizona Inn 2200 E Elm St ☎520/325-1541 or 1-800/933-1093, ⓦ www.arizonainn.com. Elegant desert oasis that's been a winter favorite for numerous presidents, Rockefellers, and the Duke and Duchess of Windsor, but with just 86 rooms it remains surprisingly unstuffy and not all that expensive in low season. Rates include gourmet breakfast. Summer ❼, winter ❾

Lodge on the Desert 306 N Alvernon Way ☎520/325-3366 or 1-800/456-5634, ⓦ www .lodgeonthedesert.com. 1930s adobe resort a couple of miles east of downtown, tastefully restored to resemble a Mexican hacienda, with large, comfortable rooms, and a good restaurant. Summer ❺, winter ❽

Loews Ventana Canyon Resort 7000 N Resort Drive ☎520/299-2020 or 1-800/235-6397, ⓦ www.loewshotels.com. Grand red-brick resort, reaching majestically across a hundred acres at the foot of the Santa Catalina mountains northeast of the city, with its own on-site waterfall. Four restau-rants, two golf courses, plus tennis and spa, and the desert on your doorstep. Summer ❽, winter ❾

Tanque Verde Ranch 14301 E Speedway Blvd ☎520/296-6275 or 1-800/234-3833, ⓦ www .tanqueverderanch.com. Arizona's most authentic dude ranch, an irresistibly romantic 400-acre spread adjoining Saguaro National Park twenty miles east of downtown. The accommodations in individual *casitas* are luxurious and the stable is home to more than a hundred horses. Rates include all meals and a full program of rides, from early-morning cowboy cookouts to all-day pack trips; there's also tennis, swimming, and hiking. ❾

JW Marriott Starr Pass Resort 3800 W Starr Pass Blvd ☎520/792-3500 or 1-800/228-9290, ⓦ www.jwmarriottstarrpass.com. Huge luxury resort, perched in the mountains around six miles west of downtown, and offering six-hundred guest rooms, plus 27 holes of golf, half a dozen restau-rants, and a full service spa. ❾

Westward Look Resort 245 E Ina Rd ☎520/297-1151 or 1-800/722-2500, ⓦ www.westwardlook .com. Plush resort, in attractive landscaped grounds north of the city, that retains its atmos-pheric 1912 core but has been modernized and expanded to hold almost 250 extra-large rooms and suites in very private low-slung *casitas*. The emphasis on physical fitness, and tennis in particu-lar, doesn't preclude having a top-quality restau-rant. Summer ❻, winter ❽

Downtown Tucson

Downtown Tucson, which centers on the area where the east–west Congress Street and Broadway Boulevard cross the north–south Stone Avenue, is largely characterized by undistinguished modern architecture, though the 1928 **Pima County Courthouse** on Church is an eclectic mix of Southwestern and Moorish influences. The adobe fortress of San Agustín de Tucson occupied what's now the four-block **El Presidio Historic District**, a couple of blocks northwest. None of its original structures is still standing, but several of their nineteenth-century successors, dating from the period when Tucson passed into American hands, have been restored as cafés, art galleries, and B&Bs.

Access to much of El Presidio is controlled by the **Tucson Museum of Art**, alongside at 140 N Main Ave (Tues–Sat 10am–4pm, Sun noon–4pm; $8, under-13s free; free first Sun of month; ⓦ www.tucsonarts.com). The main building, where a large gallery spirals down into the basement, is used for changing exhibitions of modern painting and sculpture, and the gift shop stocks some interesting contemporary crafts. An adjoining adobe, the Palice Pavilion, holds an excellent collection of pre-Columbian artifacts, including ceramics with extraordinarily life-like faces produced from 100 BC onwards by the Mochica culture of northern Peru, textiles from the later Peruvian Chancay culture, and gold from Colombia and Costa Rica. Mexican artifacts range from masks and effigies created by the ancient Olmec and Mixtec peoples, to eighteenth-century religious pieces and nineteenth-century oil-on-tin family portraits. The oldest house in the complex, **La Casa Cordova** at 175 N Meyer Ave (same hours), contains displays on the city's Mexican heritage. **Walking tours** of the district leave from the museum's tree-shaded courtyard (Oct–April only, Tues–Thurs & Sat 11am; free with museum admission).

Three blocks south, engulfed by the Tucson Convention Center complex, the solitary adobe **Sosa-Carrillo-Frémont House** (Wed–Sat 10am–4pm; free) is the sole survivor of a neighborhood torn down during the 1960s in the name of urban renewal. Built for merchant Leopoldo Carrillo in 1858, it was briefly rented by former explorer John C. Frémont when he was governor of Arizona in 1878. Though much restored, it offers a vivid sense of the more civilized side of frontier life, from the high-quality furniture and the saguaro-rib ceilings to the fig-tree-shaded rear courtyard gardens.

Still within walking distance, **Cushing Street**, three more blocks south, marks the start of the **Barrio Histórico**. The city's 1880s business district holds plenty of century-old adobes, but its most notable landmark is the sidewalk shrine of **El Tiradito**, "the castaway." Said to mark where a young man was killed by his father-in-law for committing adultery with his mother-in-law, and was buried where he fell, it's famous as the **Wishing Shrine**. Light a candle that burns through the night, and your prayers will be answered.

The University district

The other main area of interest in central Tucson is the **University of Arizona**, which spreads between Sixth Street and Speedway Boulevard a mile east of downtown. Park Avenue, on its western flank, is lined with funky cafés and stores that cater to students.

On campus, the highlight is the two-part **Arizona State Museum** at 1013 E University Blvd (Mon–Sat 10am–5pm, Sun noon–5pm; $3; ☎520/621-6302; Ⓦwww.statemuseum.arizona.edu). Its southern wing concentrates on archeology, with a diorama of a mammoth hunt and an exhibit on cave-dwellers, plus pottery and a macaw skull unearthed during university-sponsored excavations at the abandoned Hopi site of Homolovi (see p.325). The remodeled north wing is more innovative, housing the fascinating **Paths of Life** exhibition, which illuminates the history and beliefs of all the major Native American peoples of the Southwest.

Just to the north, at 1030 North Olive Rd, the **Center for Creative Photography** holds one of the world's finest photography archives (Mon–Fri 9am–5pm, Sat-Sun noon–5pm; $2 suggested donation; ☎520/621-7968; Ⓦwww.creativephotography.org). Ansel Adams left his personal negatives, prints, and journals to the university on condition that they be available to the public, and his collection has since been complemented by photographs from all eras. Temporary exhibitions can only show a tiny selection, however, and the archive is primarily intended for serious scholars. Next door, the eclectic

DOWNTOWN TUCSON

EATING
Cafe A La C'art 1
Cafe Poca Cosa 2

ACCOMMODATION
El Presidio Inn A
Hotel Congress B
Roadrunner Hostel C

UA Museum of Art (Tues–Fri 9am–5pm, Sun noon–4pm; free; ☎520/621-7567; ⓦhttp://artmuseum.arizona.edu) has some morbid Spanish *retablos*, Old Masters, and a strong modern collection including Picasso, O'Keeffe, and Warhol, as well as some fine cubist sculpture by Jacques Lipchitz.

The **Arizona Historical Society Museum**, across Park Avenue at 949 E Second St (Mon–Sat 10am–4pm; $5, under-12s free; ☎520/628-5774;

@www.arizonahistoricalsociety.org), surveys the history of southern Arizona with a mocked-up replica of a mine tunnel, and an exhibit covering the legendary "Soiled Doves" who worked in the brothels of the Wild West. There's also a good display on the archeological excavations connected with the Rio Nuevo project. If it's specifically the history of Tucson itself that interests you, it's worth also calling in at the museum's downtown offshoot, at 140 N Stone Ave (Mon–Fri 10am–4pm; $3).

Northern Tucson and the Santa Catalina Mountains

Metropolitan Tucson's northern boundary is formed by the natural barrier of the **Santa Catalina Mountains**, whose bare, dusty slopes are eventually crowned with pine forests. At the edge of the mountains, eight miles north of downtown, **Tohono Chul Park**, a block west of Oracle Road at Ina Road, is a former private estate that has been converted into a desert garden (daily 8am–sunset, last admission 5pm; $5; @www.tohonochulpark.org). The name means "desert corner" in the Tohono 'O'odham language, and it's now filled with yucca, prickly pear, and other cactuses, and a-flutter with hummingbirds. The park's *Tohono Chul Tea Room* is reviewed on p.284.

For an enjoyable taste of the mountains, head to **Sabino Canyon**, at the far end of Sabino Canyon Road in the Coronado National Forest, ten miles northeast of downtown (daily dawn–dusk; free, but parking $5; ☎520/749-2861). The canyon was cut into the lower reaches of Mount Lemmon by Sabino Creek, which manages to flow for up to eleven months of the year, and is lined by green vegetation. Assorted trails lace into the hills from the four-mile riverbank road – barred to private vehicles, but served by jump-on, jump-off **tram rides** ($7.50) – which is popular with early-morning joggers.

The 9157ft summit of **Mount Lemmon**, which towers above Sabino Canyon, is a two-day hike beyond the canyon or a one-hour drive on the **Mount Lemmon Highway**. After branching off Tanque Verde Road, an eastward continuation of Grant Road, a few miles east of the Sabino Canyon turnoff, this winds for 25 slow miles up the mountain, with countless panoramic viewpoints to either side.

Eastern Tucson

The main attraction in eastern Tucson has to be the eastern segment of Saguaro National Park, covered on p.283. While you're on that side of town, it's well worth stopping off to admire the extraordinary array of vintage and modern aircraft displayed at the **Pima Air & Space Museum**, 6200 E Valencia Rd (daily 9am–5pm; Nov–May adults $12, ages 6–12 $8; June–Oct adults $10, ages 6–12 $6; ☎520/574-0462, @www.pimaair.org). Some of the exhibits, like the Wright Brothers' 1903 Flyer and the Apollo capsule, are replicas, but the great majority are the real deal, including plenty of World War II bombers, the prototype helicopters, and the superfast X-15 fighter. The whole place is so huge you may well prefer to pay $4 extra to tour it by tram. If traveling via I-10, take the Valencia Road exit and travel two miles east.

Western Tucson

Twelve miles west of the university on Speedway Boulevard, en route to Saguaro, **Old Tucson Studios**, 201 S Kinney Rd (daily 10am–6pm; $15, under-12s $9.50; ☎520/883-0100; ⓦwww.oldtucson.com), is an entertaining if contrived Wild West theme park. Its focus is a movie-set mock-up of the "Old Pueblo" that was constructed for the 1939 western *Arizona* and has been used for TV shows and movies up to such recent productions as *Tombstone* and *Geronimo*. Visitors can ride a stagecoach or a coal-fired steam train and watch gunfights on Main Street or a bawdy music-hall show in the saloon. Since Old Tucson had to be almost entirely rebuilt after being gutted by fire in 1995, it's now even more spurious than ever. Kids love it all the same.

Part zoo, part garden, the much more worthwhile **Arizona-Sonora Desert Museum** stands two miles further west in Tucson Mountain Park (daily: June–Aug Sun–Fri 7.30am–5pm, Sat 7.30am–10pm; March–May & Sept 7.30am–5pm; Oct–Feb 8.30am–5pm; adults $9, ages 6–12 $2 May–Oct; adults $12, ages 6–12 $4 Nov–April; ☎520/883-1380; ⓦwww.desertmuseum.org). Gallery displays in the museum proper explain regional geology and history, and a series of dioramas is filled with tarantulas, rattlesnakes, and other creepy-crawlers. In enclosures along the loop path beyond – a hot walk in high summer – bighorn sheep, mountain lions, jaguars, and other seldom-seen desert denizens prowl in credible simulations of their natural habitats, and a colony of impish prairie dogs goes about its impenetrable business. Hawks and bald eagles fly about their own large aviary, thankfully separated from the greenhouse full of hummingbirds. Spectacular displays by free-flying Harris hawks are scheduled most afternoons. The museum also serves as an animal rescue center: almost all the animals you see were injured in some way before ending up here and would be unable to survive on their own. The outdoor terrace of the museum's *Ironwood Tree* restaurant makes a great stop-off for a light lunch; it also has a good coffee bar.

Saguaro National Park

Flanking Tucson to either side, the two sections of **SAGUARO NATIONAL PARK** offer visitors a rare and enthralling opportunity to stroll through strange desert "forests" of monumental, multilimbed **saguaro** (pronounced *sa-wah-row*) **cactuses**. Both tend to be seen on short forays from the city; in summer, it's far too hot to do more than pose for photographs, dwarfed beneath some especially eccentric specimen, and there is in any case no lodging, or even permanent campground, in either segment.

Saguaros prefer sloping foothills, which offer a little run-off after rain, to level desert, so both sections include rugged mountain tracts. Most of the **Rincon Mountain District** in the east, which became a national monument in 1933, is much higher, and the one road only penetrates its low-lying fringes. It was joined in 1961 by the **Tucson Mountain District** in the west, which incorporates the world's densest stand of saguaro. The two together were upgraded to national park status in 1994.

Backcountry camping in the park is by permit only; contact park rangers for details.

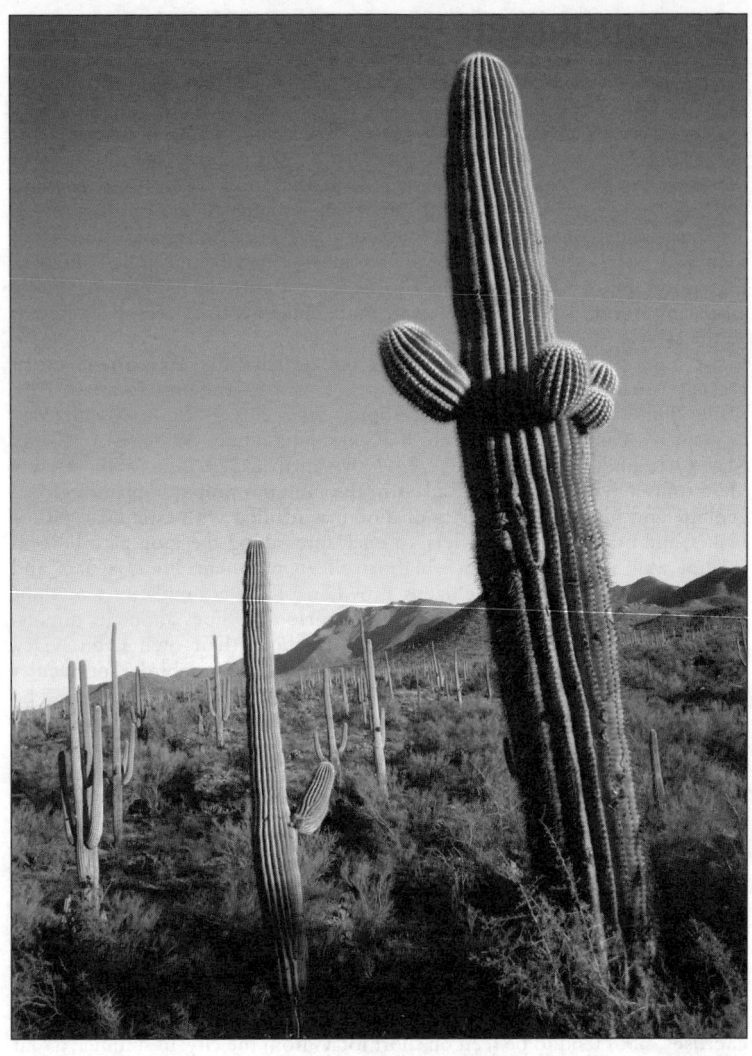

△ Mighty saguaros at Saguaro National Park

The western park: Tucson Mountain District

The **Tucson Mountain District** of Saguaro National Park is located around fifteen miles west of downtown Tucson, on the far side, logically enough, of the Tucson Mountains. The Red Hills **visitor center** (daily 8am–5pm; ℡520/733-5158, Ⓦwww.nps.gov/sagu), where the park admission fee of $10 is levied (good also for entrance to the eastern park during the same week), stands two miles along Kinney Road from the Desert Museum. Another 1.5 miles further

As the mighty, multi-armed **saguaro cactus** is unique to the Sonoran Desert, and Tucson stands near the desert's northeastern extremity, the Tucson region is one of very few places in the Wild West where saguaro grow. Whatever you may have seen in the movies, you can drive a long way in Arizona without seeing a saguaro; the thrill when you finally encounter a thousand at once is deeply satisfying.

Each saguaro can grow up to fifty feet tall and weigh up to eight tons, but it reaches that size at the slowest of rates. A teenage cactus is a foot high, a fifty-year-old more like seven feet. At 75, it sprouts the first of what may amount to forty "arms," and it only reaches its full height at around 150, with perhaps another fifty years to go before it dies. Its roots radiate as much as a hundred feet in all directions, barely three inches below the surface, and can draw enough water from one rainstorm to last the plant for two years.

Each year from the age of thirty onwards, between late April and June, a saguaro grows up to a hundred white flowers, each of which blossoms for a single night and dies by the next afternoon. In its lifetime, each saguaro produces as many as forty million seeds, though few, if any, are likely to germinate and thrive. It's also home to an intricate community of birds, insects, mammals, and reptiles. Woodpeckers and owls burrow holes into the trunk for their nests, which the cactus heals over with hardened "scar tissue" to create permanent hollows. The **Tohono 'O'odham** Indians traditionally cut away these depressions for use as bowls; they also mashed the saguaro's succulent crimson fruit to make jam, syrup, and even wine, and used its long, wood-like ribs to construct dwellings and fences.

on, turn right off the highway to start the six-mile **Bajada Loop Drive**, which although not fully paved is always passable to ordinary vehicles, and leads through a wonderland of weird saguaro, offering plentiful short hiking trails and photo opportunities. Although you can join the road at either of its two intersections, which are less than half a mile apart, its central mile or so is one-way, so the only way to complete a full loop is by starting at the south.

The easiest walk, the **Desert Discovery Nature Trail**, sets off just before the one-way section. It follows a small gully before climbing onto a low brow for sweeping westward views, with abundant saguaro all around; in principle it's around half a mile long, though it's up to you to choose how far you want to walk before you turn back. If you've only time for one hike in the park, however, the best plan is to head further along the road and walk at **Signal Hill** instead, ideally timing your arrival to enjoy its magnificent sunset panoramas. You'll know you're not the first to pass this way; boulders at the top are marked with Hohokam petroglyphs. True gluttons for punishment can follow the longer **Hugh Norris Trail** up a ridge to the 4687ft summit of Wasson Peak.

Branching onto Golden Gate Road from the northeastern limit of the loop drive brings you in around five miles to Picture Rocks Road, which joins **Ina Road** a few more miles along and thus makes an alternative route back to northern Tucson.

The eastern park: Rincon Mountain District

To reach the eastern section of Saguaro National Park, the **Rincon Mountain District**, drive seventeen miles east of downtown Tucson along first Broadway Boulevard and then Old Spanish Trail. The **admission fee** of $10 per vehicle is collected at the **visitor center** at the end of the road (daily 8am–5pm; ☏520/733-5153, ⓦ www.nps.gov/sagu); national park passes are both sold and accepted.

Although short trails such as the quarter-mile **Desert Ecology Trail** lead off the eight-mile **Cactus Forest Drive** (daily: April–Oct 7am–7pm; Nov–March 7am–5pm), this area of the park is less immediately rewarding for casual visitors than its western counterpart. Instead, most of those who make their way here come specifically to hike far from the road, up into the mountains. The saguaro cactuses thin out almost as soon as you start climbing the **Tanque Verde Ridge Trail**, which leads in due course to a hundred-mile network of remote footpaths through thickly forested canyons. All six of the district's wilderness campgrounds are only accessible on foot or by horse, and can only be used if you pay $6 per night for a permit. Water is seasonally available – check with the rangers – but will almost certainly need to be treated before you can drink it.

Eating

Though downtown Tucson's **restaurants** close early – it's hard to find anything open after 9pm – the city has a fine selection of them. Mexican joints and cowboy-style Wild West steakhouses abound in the central districts, while fancier restaurants congregate further north in the Foothills, and especially in the resort hotels.

Coffeehouses

Cup Cafe *Hotel Congress*, 311 E Congress St ☎520/798-1618. Jazzy downtown café, straight out of the 1930s but updated to include an espresso bar, that makes a good breakfast rendezvous. Sun–Thurs 7–10pm, Fri & Sat 7am–11pm.
Raging Sage 2458 N Campbell Ave ☎520/320-5203. Lively, pricey, family-run coffeehouse; the smell alone is irresistible. Daily 7am–5pm.
Safehouse Coffeehouse 4024 E Speedway Blvd ☎520/318-3090. Relaxed local coffeehouse, with excellent coffee and a good range of snacks. Daily 7am–8pm.

Cafés and diners

Blue Willow 2616 N Campbell Ave ☎520/327-7577. Tasty, fruity breakfasts and light lunches and dinners, served on a pleasant garden patio. Mon–Fri 7am–9pm, Sat & Sun 8am–9pm.
Café à la C'Art Tucson Museum of Art, 150 N Main Ave ☎520/628-8533. With such a good café in the art museum courtyard, serving sandwiches, salads and daily specials, there's no need to look further afield. Mon–Fri 11am–3pm.
Cafe Poca Cosa 120 E Pennington St ☎520/622-6400. Popular and stylish downtown café that serves tasty but inexpensive Mexican – or to be more precise, Sonoran – cuisine with a great deal of contemporary Southwestern flair. Typical highlights on the short blackboard menu include shredded beef, or cod with clams. Lunch entrées are under $10; at dinner they're more like $19. Daily except Sun for lunch and dinner.

Tohono Chul Tea Room Tohono Chul Park, 7366 N Paseo del Norte ☎520/797-1222, ⓦwww .tohonochulpark.org. Attractive adobe café in small desert park (see p.280) on the northern fringes of town that's ideal for breakfast, a light lunch, or a scones-and-jam afternoon tea. Daily 8am–5pm.

Restaurants

Cafe Terra Cotta 3500 Sunrise Drive ☎520/577-8100, ⓦwww.cafeterracotta.com. Inventive Southwestern cuisine, a long way north of downtown in the Foothills. The menu ranges from gourmet pizzas cooked in a wood-burning oven to meats grilled with chiles, with typical entrees priced around $20. Sun–Thurs 11.30am–9.30pm, Fri & Sat 11.30am–10.30pm.
Cuvee World Bistro 3352 E Speedway Blvd ☎520/881-7577, ⓦwww.cuveebistro.com. The eclectic menu at this playfully opulent yet casual bistro samples pretty much any tasty world cuisine. All entrees, from crispy sea bass to mahogany roasted duck, are priced at under $20, and there's live music at weekends. Mon–Thurs 11am–10pm, Fri 11am–midnight, Sat 4.30pm–midnight.
J-Bar *Westin La Paloma Resort*, 3770 E Sunrise Drive ☎520/615-6100, ⓦwww.janos.com. Terrific southwest-Mex cuisine by Tucson's nationally acclaimed chef Janos Wilder at half the price of his upscale restaurant, *Janos*, next door – thus his Yucatan plantain-crusted chicken with green curry costs just $14.50. That and the view make it work the trip north to the Foothills. Mon–Sat 5–9.30pm.

Kingfisher 2564 E Grant Rd ☎ 520/323-7739, ⓦ www.kingfisherbarandgrill.com. Upmarket restaurant that serves seafood – from Maine lobsters and Maryland soft-shell crabs to Oregon oysters – with an eclectic mix of American cooking styles from Cajun to New Pacific. Most entrées are priced under $20, and strict meat-eaters can opt instead for barbecue chicken or ribs. The reduced late-night menu can be a life-saver. Mon–Fri 11am–midnight, Sat & Sun 5pm–midnight.

Pastiche Modern Eatery 3025 N Campbell Ave ☎ 520/325-3333, ⓦ www.pasticheme.com. Like Cuvee, this is another somewhat postmodern restaurant, offering foods from all over the world in a slightly cooler, hipper atmosphere. Prices are a little higher, with the cioppino seafood stew at $21 and various beef dishes at $25, but at both lunch and dinner entrees are available in smaller "bistro" portions. Mon–Fri 11.30am–midnight, Sat & Sun 4.30pm–midnight.

Ventana Room Loews Ventana Canyon Resort, 7000 N Resort Drive ☎ 520/615-5494, ⓦ www .ventanaroom.com. Showcase resort dining room, commanding a panoramic view from the northern Foothills. Continental-style grilled meats and fish from $28 per entrée, or go for the prix fixe menus from $75. Tues–Thurs 6–9pm, Fri & Sat 6–10pm.

Entertainment and nightlife

Tucson **nightlife** focuses on Congress Street downtown, with its gaggle of arty cafés and nightclubs; most venues double as bars or restaurants. A handful of student places can be found near the university, and there are half a dozen country and western saloons on the outskirts of town. For a full rundown, check the listings in the free *Tucson Weekly* (ⓦ www.tucsonweekly.com). The Tucson Convention Center Music Hall, 260 S Church Ave (☎ 520/791-4266), features orchestral concerts, opera, and ballet, while the city's prime **theater** venue is the Temple of Music and Art, 330 S Scott Ave (☎ 520/622-2823). The Tucson Jazz Society (☎ 520/903-1265, ⓦ www.tucsonjazz .org) promotes jazz gigs all over town.

Cactus Moon 5470 E Broadway ☎ 520/748-0049. As befits the Western decor, country music is normally the order of the day at this large dance hall-cum-bar, though Wed is hip-hop night and attracts a college crowd. Wed–Sun 5pm–2am. Cover $5, free on Thurs & Sun.

Club Congress Hotel Congress, 311 E Congress St ☎ 520/622-8848. Hectic, trendy, late-opening bar with live music, including some surprisingly big names, a couple of nights each week. Cover typically $3–5.

Gentle Ben's Brewing Co 865 E University Blvd ☎ 520/624-4177, ⓦ www.gentlebens.com. Microbrewery, regularly packed with students, serving simple food.

IBT's 616 N Fourth Ave ☎ 520/882-3053, ⓦ www .ibts.net. Tucson's premier gay downtown dance club features contemporary DJs most nights and also puts on drag acts and revue. Daily noon–2am.

Kon Tiki Lounge 4625 E Broadway ☎ 520/323 7193. Tiki bar with fun South-Seas theme and killer cocktails. Daily except Sun 11am–1am.

The Rialto Theatre 318 E Congress St ☎ 520/740-1000, ⓦ www.rialtotheatre.com. 1920s vaudeville theater that's reopened as Tucson's hottest venue for touring bands.

South to Mexico: the Mission Trail

The tract of southern Arizona that lies between Tucson and the Mexican border was the first part of the state to be settled by the Spanish, and it remained

Arizona's most populous region until well into the nineteenth century. The Spanish called this area **Pimería Alta**, and its scattering of **mission churches** and abandoned forts still testify to their efforts to Christianize its **Pima** inhabitants from 1692 onwards. Epidemics and Apache raids meant that of the early towns, only Tucson grew to any size, but as recently as 1870, the Pima were still Arizona's largest ethnic group.

Twelve thousand Pima – now known as the **Akimel 'O'odham** – survive on the **San Xavier Reservation** a few miles south of Tucson. The magnificent church of San Xavier – the "White Dove of the Desert" – is the prime attraction for modern travelers who drive the 65 miles down to Mexico on the **I-19** interstate, but the artistic community at **Tubac**, and the atmospheric border town of **Nogales**, help to make for an entertaining international day-trip.

San Xavier del Bac

Even today, the white-plastered walls and towers of **San Xavier del Bac**, the best-preserved mission church in the United States, seem like a dazzling desert mirage. How much more dramatic they must have been two centuries ago, when to Christian missionaries and Apache warriors alike they symbolized the Spanish quest to subdue and convert the native peoples of the Southwest.

Located a mere nine miles south of downtown Tucson, just west of I-19, the church stands on the eastern fringes of the arid San Xavier Reservation. It was founded by the Jesuit **Father Eusebio Kino** in 1700, beside the Santa Cruz River and next to the Pima village of W:ak ("where the water emerges"),

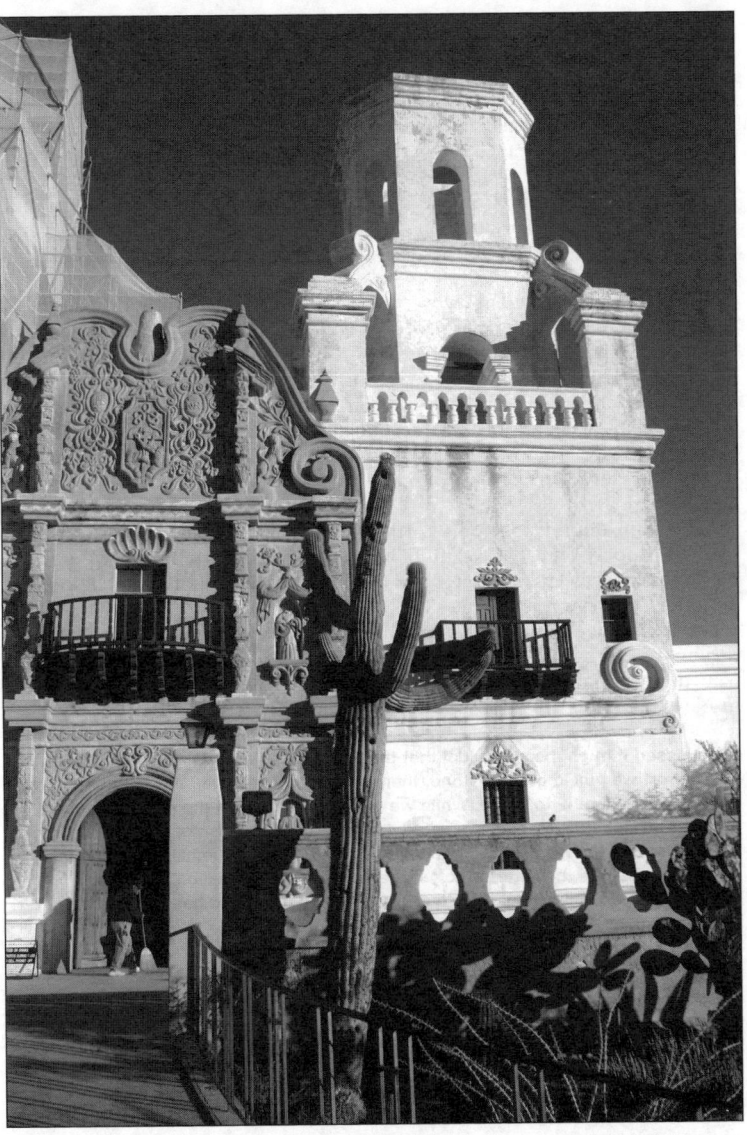

△ Mission church at San Xavier del Bac

which soon became Bac. Kino's church was destroyed by Apaches in 1767; what survives is its replacement, built for the Franciscans between 1783 and 1797. No one knows the name of the architect responsible for its Spanish Baroque, even Moorish lines – it consists almost entirely of domes and arches, making only minimal use of timber – let alone the 'O'odham craftsmen who embellished its every feature. The whole structure, inside and out, was restored during the

1990s to its original resplendence under the supervision of experts from the Vatican.

Although the church attracts a constant stream of tourists (daily 9am–6pm; donation), the ideal time to come is on Sunday morning, when masses at 8am, 11am, and 12.30pm pack in the parishioners from the reservation. As you approach the main entrance across the dusty plaza, with saguaro cactuses to the right and ocotillo to the left, take a moment to appreciate its ornate facade. On the top level, a cat squats on the spiral flourish to the right, eyeing a mouse in the corresponding position on the left. The tower on the right was never completed, possibly to avoid the need to pay a levy to the authorities back in Mexico.

Inside the church, the left alcove holds a recumbent, articulated statue of **St Francis Xavier**, covered with metal *milagros* – images of healed body parts – and photographs of children. Devout Catholics are permitted to lean in and lift his head. The approach to the main altar is guarded by two naive gilt-headed lions, representing the royal lions of León and Castille in Spain. The altar itself holds a telling example of the intermingling of Catholicism with traditional beliefs; the gilded monstrance used to exhibit the host during communion incorporates a wickerwork surround bearing the 'O'odham "man in the maze" design.

Still within the mission walls, to the right of the church, a small **museum** (Mon–Fri noon–4pm, Sat & Sun 8.30am–4.30pm; donation) displays a gigantic illuminated sheepskin psalter and photos of other remote churches on the Tohono 'O'odham reservation.

The little hillock immediately to the east is now topped by a replica of the shrine of Saint Bernadette at Lourdes, France. Juan Mateo Manje, who accompanied Father Kino to W:ak, described finding a white stone on top of this hill in November 1699:

We guessed it might be some idol that the heathen Indians worshipped, so with great effort we pulled out the stone, thereby exposing a large hole. At the time, we did not know what it could be. While we were coming down the hill, a great and furious hurricane developed. We could scarcely walk because of the terrific windstorm. None of the Indians had gone with us to the top of the hill; but when the furious wind arose they started to yell, saying in sort of rebellion, "Vbiriqui cupioca," which meant that the House of the Wind (god) had been opened.

The major **feast days** at San Xavier Mission are those of St Francis of Assisi, on October 4, and St Francis Xavier, December 3.

The Titan Missile Museum

Another sixteen miles south of San Xavier, the **Titan Missile Museum** (daily 9am–5pm; $8.50) focuses on an underground silo that, until November 1982, held two Titan II nuclear missiles. Each was primed and ready to fire at a choice of three specific targets, as much as five thousand miles away; what those targets were remains classified even today, but they never changed during the 22 years that the site was operational. A total of 54 such missiles were deployed at 27 separate locations, in Arizona, California, and Arkansas, but this is the only site to have survived the end of the Cold War. One of its missiles is actually still down there – no longer primed, of course – and can be examined close up on hour-long subterranean **guided tours**.

The whole installation was designed to remain functional in the event of a nuclear war. The vast sliding door of the silo was capable of opening through eight feet of post-holocaust debris, while the crew could live beneath the surface for up to thirty days, and the whole place could even operate on two 28-volt batteries in case of electrical outage. Tours culminate in the control room, still scattered with top-secret manuals, where two keys had to be turned simultaneously in order to fire the missile.

As you might imagine, inspecting colossal rocket launchers and other military hardware seems to be very much a "guy thing." Casual visitors who take the tours may well run out of steam before the excitable gun nuts in the crowd find the time to draw breath.

Tubac

TUBAC, fifty miles south of San Xavier, was the first permanent Spanish settlement in what is now Arizona, founded in 1752 as a **presidio** or fortress to guard against repetitions of the previous year's Pima Revolt against the Jesuits. In 1775, its commander, Juan Bautista de Anza, launched the expedition that established **San Francisco** in California, but Tubac declined after 1776, when its garrison was shifted to the new city of Tucson. For the next century, it was alternately abandoned and resettled as Apache raids permitted; in the 1850s, it even spent a brief period as a **Mormon** outpost.

Following World War II, Tubac redefined itself as an **arts colony**. In recent years it's been so successful that it's grown beyond recognition, the broad streets in its central core now paved and filled with galleries and boutiques that have joined the longer-established folk-art stores. The surrounding fields regularly disappear under yet more real-estate developments. The **Tubac Center of the Arts**, 9 Plaza Rd, holds exhibitions by local artists (mid-April to mid-May and Sept to mid-Nov Tues–Sat 10am–4.30pm, Sun 1–4.30pm; mid-Nov to mid-April Mon–Sat 10am–4.30pm, Sun 1–4.30pm; free; ⓦ www.tubacarts.org).

Although the foundations of the original adobe fortress now lie beneath an earthen mound in the **Tubac Presidio State Historic Park** (daily 8am–5pm; $2), they can be admired from a cool underground viewing gallery. The large museum alongside contains pieces from all periods of Tubac's long history, including some beautiful naive *retablos*, the press that was used to print Arizona's first newspaper, *The Weekly Arizonan*, in March 1859, and a crucifix depicting the black "Christo Negro" – a Native American Christ. On Sundays between October and March, from 1pm until 4pm, costumed locals re-enact the daily life of the eighteenth-century presidio.

Practicalities

For information on Tubac, call in at the state park or the local **visitor center**, in the small mall on Plaza Road, the main road into town (Mon–Fri 10am–5pm, Sat & Sun 10am–2pm; ☏ 520/398-2704, ⓦ www.tubacaz.com). Each year, in early February, the town hosts the weeklong **Festival of the Arts**. The nicest of the **B&B**s in the old center is the *Tubac Country Inn*, a small blue wooden house at 13 Burruel St (☏ 520/398-3178, ⓦ www.tubaccountryinn.com; closed Aug; ⑥), with five en-suite rooms.

The *Tubac Deli & Coffee Company*, 6 Plaza Rd (daily 6.30am–5.30pm; ☏ 520/398-3330), is a friendly, busy coffeehouse and snack place across from the visitor center. For a fuller meal, head for the *Border House Bistro*, nearby at 12

Plaza Rd (Tues–Sat 11am–3pm & 5pm–9pm, Sun 11am–3pm; ☎520/398/8999) which serves good pizzas as well as meat and seafood entrees.

Tumacácori National Historical Park

A **Spanish mission** founded by Father Kino in 1691, before its more celebrated neighbor at San Xavier (see p.286), is now the focus of the **TUMACÁCORI NATIONAL HISTORICAL PARK**, three miles south of Tubac and nineteen miles north of the border (daily 8am–5pm; $3 per person; ☎520/398-2341; ⓦwww.nps.gov/tuma). Like San Xavier, the church here was built at the end of the eighteenth century, but Tumacácori soon proved unable to withstand Apache raids, and was abandoned in 1848, five years before the region passed into US control.

It's now an evocative ruin, topped by a restored whitewashed dome but home only to the birds that fly down from the Patagonia Mountains. Behind its weatherbeaten red-tinged facade, the plaster has crumbled from the interior walls to reveal bare adobe bricks. A few traces of a mural can still be discerned in the raised sanctuary, but little remains of the priests' living quarters alongside.

△ Banner, Tumacácori National Historical Park

A fascinating **museum** holds a replica of a banner carried by missionaries; one side depicts the Madonna and Child, the other shows an Indian burning in hell. Opposite the gate, the *Tumacácori Restaurant* serves Mexican and Greek specialties as well as deli sandwiches.

Nogales, Arizona and Nogales, Mexico

Twenty miles south of Tumacácori, an hour from Tucson, sits the largest of the Arizonan–Mexican border towns, **NOGALES** – in effect two towns, one in the US and one across the border in Mexico. Known jointly as *Ambos Nogales* (both Nogales), they were founded in 1880 to handle the frontier formalities necessary on the main route between their two countries, and still see vast quantities of freight traffic daily. A total of almost four million vehicles pass through the checkpoints each year, while an astonishing 6.7 million people enter from Mexico on foot. Tourists, too, head south from Arizona in considerable numbers, though with cheap Mexican crafts now so widely available in the US, the day-trippers these days tend to be looking for cut-price medicines rather than rugs or hammocks.

There's nothing in particular to see on either side of the border, though the contrast between the sedate, ordered streets of the American town and the jumbled whitewashed houses clinging to the slopes in Mexico hits you as soon as you come in sight. Nogales, Arizona – the birthplace of iconoclastic jazz great **Charles Mingus** – is a dreary little community, while Nogales, Mexico is basically a lively, large-scale street market. If you do plan to set off south, pick up a **tourist visa** just beyond the border crossing. Then take a taxi (around $8) a couple of miles to the **long-distance bus station**, from which regular buses head to **Hermosillo**, **Guaymas** on the Pacific (a good overnight stop), and **Los Mochis**, the start of the Copper Canyon Railroad. There's talk of establishing a **rail** connection with Guaymas in the near future, which might well encourage an even greater volume of tourism.

Practicalities

Nogales' **visitor center** is at 123 W Kino Park at the north end of town (winter Mon–Fri 8am–5pm; summer Mon–Fri 8am–1pm & 2–5pm; ☎520/287-3685, ⓦwww.nogaleschamber.com). Hourly direct **buses** to Tucson are operated by Citizens/Gray Line Bus, 35 N Terrace Ave ($10; ☎520/287-5628). **Crossing the border** is straightforward, as Mexican visas are only required of travelers heading more than 21km south of the border. US citizens should, however, ideally carry their passports or birth certificates – drivers' licenses are not always sufficient – while foreign visitors should check that their visa status entitles them to re-enter the US; if you're on or eligible for the Visa Waiver Scheme (see p.32), you're fine. Make sure your car rental company doesn't restrict you from driving across the border. There's no need to **change money**; US dollars are freely accepted by stores and businesses in Mexico.

None of the Arizona-side **motels** stands within a mile of the border; the closest is the *Best Western Siesta Motel*, 673 N Grand Ave (☎520/287-4671; ❸), while the cluster near the interstate three miles out includes the smart hundred-room *Holiday Inn Express*, 850 W Shell Rd (☎520/281-0123 or 1-800/465-4329; ❹).

Most visitors prefer to **eat** in Mexico, where abundant cafés and diners line the busy central streets. Classier dining is offered by the unusual *La Roca*, hollowed into the rocky hillside just east of the railroad, a couple of blocks from the border at Calle Elias 91, where a full seafood meal still costs well under $20. The best restaurant on the Arizona side is the Italian *Bella Mia*, 204 W Mariposa Rd ($520/761-3535).

Sonoita Valley and Patagonia

A longer but even more attractive route back from Nogales to Tucson avoids the interstate by following highways 82 and 83 northeast from Nogales through the lush **Sonoita Valley**, in the craggy mountains of the Coronado National Forest.

Thanks to the **Patagonia–Sonoita Creek Sanctuary** (April–Sept Wed–Sun 6.30am–4pm; Oct–March Wed–Sun 7.30am–4pm; $5; $520/394-2000), the appealing little Wild West mining and cattle-ranching town of **PATAGONIA**, twenty miles up from Nogales, now attracts weekend crowds of **birdwatchers**. Located at the far southwestern end of a mile-long dirt road that leads off Fourth Street, this dense riverbank stand of oaks and cottonwoods is home to an amazing range of songbirds and raptors, including finches and flycatchers, kingbirds and kestrels, and woodpeckers and cardinals. With all of this colorful collection to choose from, the sighting that is most prized by twitchers from all over the world is a drab little specimen called the northern beardless tyrannulet.

Twelve miles north of Patagonia, **SONOITA** itself is a wide-open desert crossroads, lined with a few false-front stores, at the point where Hwy-83 veers northwest to rejoin I-10 two miles east of Saguaro National Park, while Hwy-82 cuts east toward Tombstone, 35 miles away (see p.296).

Practicalities

Welcoming little **B&B**s in Patagonia include the three-room *Duquesne House*, a century-old adobe boarding house at 357 Duquesne Ave ($520/394-2732, @www.patagoniaaz.com/duquesne_house.html; ❹), while the *Stage Stop Inn*, 303 W McKeown Ave ($520/394-2211 or 1-800/923-2211 in AZ, @www .thestagestopinn.com; ❹), is a convenient modern **hotel**, built in the 1970s as a set for Western movies, which has its own restaurant. *Gathering Grounds*, nearby at 319 W McKeown Ave (Sun–Thurs 7am–5pm, Fri & Sat 7am–9pm; $520/394-2097), is handy for a lunchtime snack of deli sandwiches, pastries, and coffee.

Sonoita holds further accommodation options, like the eighteen-room, cowboy-themed *Sonoita Inn* at the crossroads ($520/455-5935 or 1-800/696-1006, @www.sonoitainn.com; ❺). Just west of town at 3280 Hwy-82, *Cafe Sonoita* (Wed & Thurs 5–8pm, Fri & Sat 11am–2.30pm & 5–8pm; $520/455-5278) has earned a high local reputation for its creative cuisine and high-quality food, with succulent barbecued ribs or pan-seared trout for around $10, and some fancier specialties.

The southeast corner

Although the **I-10** interstate somehow manages to plot a dull and monotonous course across **southeast Arizona**, the rugged territory to the south holds some of the state's most spectacular scenery and memorable historic sites. The much-mythologized Wild West outpost of **Tombstone** is the best known and does its best to entertain the hordes of cowboy fanatics who troop this way, but the mining town of **Bisbee** is in many ways a more evocative relic of frontier times. Tourism in the region has been given a major boost by the opening of **Kartchner Caverns**, which has transformed previously quiet interstate towns such as nearby **Benson**.

Further east, the **Chiricahua Mountains** witnessed the final saga of Native American resistance to federal encroachment, in the 1880s guerrilla campaign of Geronimo's **Apaches**. This mountain range is merely one of around a dozen separate ranges that soar from the deserts, known as "**sky islands**" because each wilderness harbors its own unique ecosystem of plants, birds, and animals.

Benson

About forty miles southeast of Tucson on I-10, sleepy little **BENSON** shook itself awake at the end of the twentieth century to cope with the influx of visitors to Kartchner Caverns. Whereas tourists on their way to Tombstone had long passed through without making any great impact on the town's economy, there's now been a considerable upturn in overnight stays. There's nothing much to do in Benson itself, other than head a couple of miles north, up Ocotillo Avenue, to the Singing Wind **bookshop** (℡520/586-2425), which consists of a farmhouse that's bursting with volumes about Southwestern history and culture.

Practicalities

Benson's **visitor center** is at 249 E Fourth St (Mon–Fri 10am–5pm, Sat 1–5pm; ℡520/586-2842, ⓦwww.bensonchamberaz.com). The town now boasts its very own crop of near-identical chain **motels**, including a *Super 8*, 855 N Ocotillo Ave (℡520/586-1530 or 1-800/800-8000; ❸), and a classier *Holiday Inn Express*, 630 South Village Loop (℡520/586-8800 or 1-888/263-2283; ❹). Four miles southeast of town, the *Skywatcher's Inn* is an absolute one-of-a-kind **B&B** (℡520/615-3886; ⓦwww.skywatchersinn.com; ❺). Located on a hilltop next to the private Vega-Bray **astronomical observatory**, it offers guests (for an additional fee) the chance to have exclusive use of the observatory equipment, including high-power telescopes and even a planetarium.

Back in town, the *Horseshoe Cafe*, 154 E Fourth St (℡520/586-3303), is a quintessential Western **diner**, bedecked with Stetson hats and horseshoes, with a mini-Wurlitzer jukebox on each table.

Kartchner Caverns

Arizona's newest state park, **Kartchner Caverns** – signposted to the west off both Hwy-90 and Hwy-80 seven miles south of Benson – was finally unveiled in 1999. It was much trumpeted in advance as being certain to become one of the state's premier tourist attractions, mainly because the caves, unlike counterparts such as Carlsbad Caverns in New Mexico, are very unusual in being "live." That means they're still being hollowed out of the Whetstone Mountains by each new dose of rainfall, and that the formations within are still growing.

However, it has to be said that while the caves may be an exciting novelty for local residents, they're not really worth traveling across the country – let alone the world – to see, and with a visit for a family of four costing at least $60, they're also wildly overpriced.

Kartchner Caverns were discovered in 1974 by local cavers Gary Tenen and Randy Tufts, who were investigating a strange-smelling hole in the mountainside and squeezed their way into what turned out to be a vast open space. Eventually the two explorers mapped out the total subterranean complex at over two miles long, with around 13,000 feet of passageways. They told no one of their discovery until 1987, when together with the Kartchner family who owned the land, they invited the Arizona state authorities to buy the caverns as a prospective park. It took a further twelve years, and $28 million, to prepare them for display, with constant monitoring to ensure that the formations were not damaged by either construction work or the effects of artificial lighting.

Admission to the park costs $5 per vehicle, but the only way to see the caves themselves is on one of the two distinct **guided tours** detailed below. Overall numbers are very carefully controlled, and heavy demand from Tucson-area residents means that during busy periods all tours may be booked several months ahead. Try to reserve as far in advance as possible, by phone or online (Mon–Fri 8am–5pm; T 520/586-2283, W www.azstateparks.com). You have to pay the full fee by credit card when you book; the fees are not refundable, though it is possible to change the precise time of your tour. If you're hoping to turn up without a reservation, call on your chosen day to see how likely you are to get in; this is a long way to come on a wild goose chase, though if you fail to get in, you can at least content yourself with the displays in the large **Discovery Center** instead (daily 7.30am–6pm).

The shorter of the two available tours, the **Rotunda/Throne Room** tour, follows a narrow, switchbacking cement trail of a third of a mile through the caverns' two upper "rooms" (adults $19, ages 7–13 $10). It lasts for something over an hour, including a tram ride to the cave entrance and 45 minutes spent underground. Among the formations en route are precarious stalactites (the ones that dangle from the ceiling) and towering stalagmites (which rise from the floor) – to add to the confusion, there's also a 21ft hollow soda straw, a combination of both that stretches from floor to ceiling. However, the most spectacular feature is the striated **coloring** of the cavern walls, created by eons of unseen flooding and illuminated by the dramatic sound-and-light show with which the tour culminates.

The longer **Big Room** tour delves deeper into the cave system, and requires visitors to pass through no fewer than six separate airlock doors to keep humidity at the necessary level (mid-Oct to mid-April only; adults $23, ages 7–13 $13). It takes ninety or more minutes, and goes into a little more technical detail, while showcasing unusual wet formations such as a bizarre "fried egg."

The Amerind Foundation Museum

If you choose to continue east from Benson on I-10, the one point of interest on the barren run to New Mexico comes 25 miles later (about 65 miles from Tucson), in the shape of the excellent **Amerind Foundation Museum** (daily except Mon 10am–4pm; $3; T 520/586-3666, W www.amerind.org). This privately run anthropological museum is in the remote Texas Canyon, a mile southeast of exit 318 halfway between Benson and Willcox. Not that you'll see anything as vulgar as a roadside billboard to announce its presence: it's a rather highbrow affair, with the declared ambition to "increase the world's knowledge of ancient man by excavation and collection." Displays cover native cultures from North, Central, and Southern America, but specialize in the Southwest, featuring fine Apache, Navajo, and Hopi crafts, plus older pieces from the Mimbres and Hohokam peoples, and a gallery of Western art. While not on par with museums in Flagstaff, Phoenix, or Santa Fe, it's worth an hour or two of your time if you're passing this way.

Sierra Vista

After a visit to Benson or the caverns, heading 25 miles south on Hwy-90 brings you to **SIERRA VISTA**, a characterless modern town that has grown in tandem with the Army base at **Fort Huachuca**. Once home to detachments of Apache scouts and Buffalo Soldiers, and one of the few nineteenth-century military outposts to survive into the modern era, the fort still employs over thirteen thousand people, now working on high-tech electronic early-warning systems and the like. Its oldest buildings house two museums, the **Fort Huachuca Museum**, which holds disappointing displays on the fort's early years, and the more entertaining **US Army Intelligence Museum** (both Mon–Fri 9am–4pm, Sat & Sun 1–4pm; $2 donation).

A much more enjoyable hour or two can be spent at the **Ramsey Canyon Preserve**, squeezed into a slender gorge in the Huachuca Mountains, off Hwy-92 seven miles south (March–Oct daily 8am–5pm, Nov–Feb daily 9am–4pm; $5; ☎520/378-2785, ⓦwww.nature.org). Owned by the Nature Conservancy, this well-watered spot is dedicated to safeguarding local wildlife in general, but the main reason everyone comes here is for its mind-boggling summer array of colorful **hummingbirds**, which reach their peak population in August. Guided walking tours tour the preserve between March and October only. Be warned that there's not much room for cars here; the 23 parking spaces are first-come, first-served, so there's a risk you'll be turned away.

Practicalities

Plenty of **motels** in town cater to visiting service families and nature-lovers. The *Windemere Hotel*, 2047 S Hwy-92 (☎520/459-5900 or 1-800/825-4656, ⓦwww .windemerehotel.com; ❹), is the newest and largest; the *Super 8*, 100 Fab Ave (☎520/459-5380 or 1-800/800-8000, ⓦwww.super8.com; ❸), among the most reasonably priced. Just outside the preserve, seven miles south, the *Ramsey Canyon Inn*, 31 Ramsey Canyon Rd (☎520/378-3010, ⓦwww.ramseycanyoninn.com; ❼), is a plush six-room **B&B** where a battery of sugar-water feeders attracts countless hummingbirds in summer.

Coronado National Memorial

Tucked into the southernmost notch of the Huachuca Mountains, five miles off Hwy-92, twenty miles from Sierra Vista, **CORONADO NATIONAL MEMORIAL** commemorates the approximate spot where in May 1540 the expedition of **Francisco Vásquez de Coronado** first entered what is now the United States (see p.572). A short video and some interesting displays in the

visitor center (daily 8am–5pm; free; ☎520/366-5515) explain the history, but the memorial basically exists to offer a selection of scenic **hiking trails**.

The best short hike climbs south from **Montezuma Pass**, the highest point along the washboard dirt road west of the visitor center. The 0.4-mile **Coronado Peak Trail** culminates in huge views in all directions, and especially to the pyramidal Mexican mountains across the border. Heading north from the same trailhead, you can hike for twenty miles up the western flank of the Huachucas. If the weather's good enough – check with rangers – ordinary vehicles can continue west on unpaved roads all the way to **Nogales** (see p.291), fifty miles distant beyond the Patagonia Mountains.

Tombstone

Perhaps the most famous town in the Wild West, **TOMBSTONE** lies 22 miles south of I-10 on US-80, 67 miles southeast of Tucson. More than a century has passed since its mining days came to an end, but "The Town Too Tough to Die" clings to an afterlife as a tourist theme park. With its dusty streets, wooden sidewalks, and swinging saloon doors, it's surprisingly unchanged. Most adults, however, have seen too many inauthentic replicas and movie recreations for even the real thing to retain much appeal, and so Tombstone is reduced to trying to divert kids with tacky dioramas and daily shoot-outs. Much more commercialized than its counterpart in New Mexico, Lincoln (see p.221), to be honest, it's also more fun.

When **Edward Schieffelin** began prospecting in the Dragoon Mountains in 1877, he was told by soldiers stationed nearby that all he'd find would be his own tombstone. Hence the name of the town that rose from the desert when he made Arizona's largest **silver** strike, in March 1878. Schieffelin sold his stake for $500,000, but the mine produced $30 million in the next seven years, and by 1880 Tombstone was home to over ten thousand people. Drifters arrived from the played-out gold fields of Canada and Australia, and gamblers came in from

△ Stagecoach, Tombstone

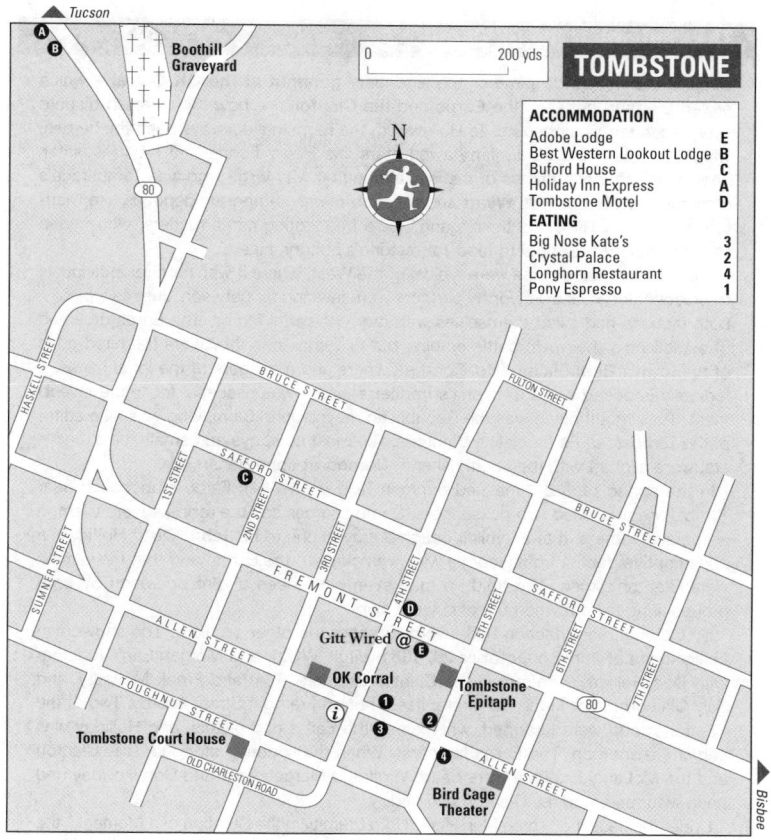

**Boothill
Graveyard**

| | 0 | 200 yds | **TOMBSTONE** |

N

ACCOMMODATION
Adobe Lodge   E
Best Western Lookout Lodge   B
Buford House   C
Holiday Inn Express   A
Tombstone Motel   D
EATING
Big Nose Kate's   3
Crystal Palace   2
Longhorn Restaurant   4
Pony Espresso   1

BRUCE STREET

FULTON STREET

SAFFORD STREET

HASKELL STREET

1ST STREET

2ND STREET

3RD STREET

4TH STREET

FREMONT STREET

BRUCE STREET

SAFFORD STREET

SUMNER STREET

ALLEN STREET

Gitt Wired @

OK Corral

Tombstone
Epitaph

5TH STREET

6TH STREET

7TH STREET

80

TOUGHNUT STREET

Tombstone Court House

OLD CHARLESTON ROAD

Bird Cage
Theater

ALLEN STREET

▶ *Bisbee*

Dodge City, only for the mine to hit water 500 feet below ground in 1886 and be flooded beyond repair.

The Town

Most of the buildings that fill modern Tombstone's simple grid date from the early 1880s. Decaying wagons are parked on the street corners, and signs along the boardwalks mark the sites of famous shoot-outs. **Gunslingers**, too, still pace the streets and snarl at each other, though the prey they're stalking these days are the tourists themselves. Whenever they've rounded up enough customers, usually at around $4 per head, a group of opponents gun each other down on some appropriate vacant lot. With three or so groups usually in town at any one time, there's seldom long to wait. During **Helldorado Days**, held on the third weekend of each October, you can hardly move for corpses.

Although the real gunfight at the OK Corral in fact took place on Fremont Street, the **OK Corral** itself remains the major attraction for visitors, hosting its only daily gunfight at 2pm (daily 8.30am–5pm; $5; ⓦ www.ok-corral .com). As you enter the corral building, on Allen Street between Third and Fourth, the first thing you see is the hearse used to take the victims away.

The gunfight at the OK Corral

Despite the worldwide fame of the legendary **gunfight at the OK Corral** – which ended the feud between the **Earps** and the **Clantons** – how the clannish dispute ever began remains obscure. To Hollywood, the Earps have always been the heroes, with Wyatt Earp played by firm-jawed stars like Henry Fonda and Kevin Costner. They were, after all, officers of the law, although it was **Virgil** who was Tombstone's marshal, and his brothers **Wyatt** and **Morgan** merely temporary deputies. Ike Clanton, his brother Billy, and their "gang" were freebooting cattle rustlers, who raided Mexican ranches for beef to feed Tombstone's hungry miners.

Such family-based clans were typical of the West, where it was hard for individuals to prosper alone but trustworthy partners were few and far between. Just as typically, both factions had allied themselves with more powerful forces. The Earps dreamed of establishing their own cattle empire, but in Tombstone they were the hired guns of the town's **Republican** elite. For the owners and managers of the local mines, a federally imposed end to Arizona's frontier anarchy was essential for future investment. Their mouthpiece was the Republican mayor, John Clum, who was also editor of the *Tombstone Epitaph*. The Clantons, like most cowboys and small-scale ranchers, were aligned with the county sheriff, **Democrat** John Behan.

In the spring of 1881, masked gunmen held up a Wells Fargo stagecoach near Tombstone and killed two passengers. Some sources say the robbers were Clanton associates; others, that a familiar cough betrayed one to be **John "Doc" Holliday**, a consumptive dentist from Georgia who was close to the Earps, and that the victims were Clanton's men. The hold-up may even have been a joint operation by both groups, who fell out when the plan went awry.

By October, each faction had sworn to shoot the other on sight. The showdown finally came at 2pm on **October 26, 1881**. Virgil, Wyatt, and Morgan Earp, together with Doc Holliday, confronted the Clanton brothers, Tom and Frank McLaury, and Billy Claiborne, not in the OK Corral itself, but on Fremont Street nearby. Two of the Clanton group were unarmed, whereas all the Earps had pistols, and Holliday was carrying a shotgun. The Earps fired first. When the shooting stopped, Billy Clanton and the McLaury brothers were dead; Virgil and Morgan Earp and Doc Holliday had been wounded, and Ike Clanton had fled.

Under the headline "Three Men Hurled Into Eternity in the Duration of a Moment," the next day's *Tombstone Epitaph* reported that "the feeling among our best citizens is that the Marshal was entirely justifiable." However, Wyatt and Holliday were charged with murder and were held in jail before being acquitted toward the end of November.

In March 1882, Morgan Earp was killed by a shot fired through the window as he played billiards in Tombstone's *Campbell & Hatch* saloon. Three days later, Wyatt Earp shot the chief suspect, Clanton associate Frank Stilwell, in Tucson. He's said to have killed two more of the Clanton gang that summer before leaving Tombstone for good, with his surviving brothers. Warrants were issued for his arrest, but the governor of Colorado refused to authorize his extradition to Arizona on the grounds that he faced lynching if he returned to Tombstone. Instead, Wyatt Earp moved to Los Angeles, where he was lionized by early moviemakers, and died in 1929. Tombstone's Episcopalian minister at the time of the shoot-out – Endicott Peabody – went on to be Franklin Roosevelt's White House chaplain.

In the second of two baking-hot adobe-walled courtyards beyond, crude dummies show the supposed locations of the Earps and the Clantons, in complete contradiction to contemporary reports of the fight. In the original studio of photographer C.S. Fly alongside, which displays his pictures of Geronimo and other Apache warriors, you can pose for your own souvenir photo or tintype (Thurs–Mon 10am–5pm; $25). Nearby, you can also visit the room from which Big Nose Kate, Doc Holliday's girlfriend, is said to have witnessed the shootings.

On Fifth Avenue between Allen and Fremont streets, you can wander into the former offices of the **Tombstone Epitaph** newspaper (daily 9.30–5pm; free) to see a small exhibition on its founding editor, John Clum, who was present with Fly when Geronimo was captured in 1877. A block further along Allen Street, the **Bird Cage Theater** (daily 8am–6pm; $5) was Tombstone's leading venue for entertainment of all kinds. Seven "bird cages," much like theater boxes but curtained off and said to have been used by prostitutes, hang from either side of the main hall. Those on the left were frequented by the Earps and their cronies, while the ones on the right were the preserve of Sheriff Behan and the Clantons. The theater now holds a motley collection of curiosities, including a revolting foot-long "merman" from China and another ornate hearse, while downstairs you can see the old gaming tables and bordello rooms.

Tombstone's role as the seat of Cochise County – before it was supplanted by Bisbee – is recalled at the **Tombstone Courthouse State Historic Park**, at Third and Toughnut (daily 8am–5pm; $2.50). Among displays on the Apache and early outlaws, the sheriff's office here holds the coroner's report on John Heith, a robber lynched in 1884 by a Bisbee mob: "I find that the deceased died of emphysema of the lungs which might have been caused by strangulation, self-inflicted or otherwise." Upstairs, you can watch a video reenactment of a notorious 1897 murder trial in the former courtroom, and get a view of the gallows in the high-walled yard outside.

Boothill Graveyard, half a mile north on US-80, closed in May 1884, having been filled by 276 burials. In keeping with the souvenir store that now guards the entrance, several of the graves bear dubious jokey epitaphs, and country music is piped from concealed speakers, but you can see where the losers at the OK Corral still rest in peace (daily 7.30am–6pm; free).

Practicalities

Tombstone's **visitor center** is at Allen and Fourth (daily 10am–4pm; ☎520/457-9317 or 1-888/457-3929, ⓦwww.tombstone.org), while the Territorial Book Trader (☎520/457-3170), at the same intersection, has a fine stock of books on local history.

Very central, standard **motels** include the *Tombstone Motel*, 502 E Fremont St (☎520/457-3478 or 1-888/455-3478; ⓦwww.tombstonemotel.com; ❹), and the *Adobe Lodge*, a misnomer of a place across the street at 505 Fremont St (☎520/457-2241 or 1-888/457-2241; ❹). A mile north on US-80 you'll find two classier mountain-view alternatives, the *Best Western Lookout Lodge* (☎520/457-2223 or 1-877/652-6772; ⓦwww.tombstone1880.com/bwlook outlodge; summer ❹, winter ❺), and the *Holiday Inn Express* (☎520/457-9507 or 1-800/465-4329; ⓦwww.holidayinntombstone.com; summer ❹, winter ❺). The *Buford House* is an antique-filled **B&B** at 113 E Safford Street that's not particularly fancy but perfectly acceptable for a night's lodging; two guestrooms share a bath, the other is en-suite (☎520/457-3969; ⓔbufordhouse@yahoo .com; ❹).

Among old-style **saloons** serving steaks and beer in as raucous an atmosphere as they can manage are the very fancy *Big Nose Kate's* at 417 E Allen St (☎520/457-3107), where the waitresses wear period costume, country music musicians entertain most afternoons, and you can still join an ongoing card game; the plainer *Crystal Palace* at Fifth and Allen; and the *Longhorn Restaurant*, diagonally opposite at 501 Allen St (☎520/457-3405). *Pony Espresso*, 424 Allen St (☎520/457-3648), serves espresso coffees, pastries, and deli sandwiches.

Bisbee

Crammed into a narrow gorge 25 miles south of Tombstone, the town of **BISBEE** is rivaled only by Jerome, near Sedona (p.345) as Arizona's most atmospheric Victorian relic. Like Jerome, its fortunes were built on a century of mining mundane, dependable **copper** from the surrounding mountains, rather than a few ephemeral years of gold and silver. Its solid brick buildings still stand as an enduring testament to the days when Bisbee's population of twenty thousand outstripped both Phoenix and Tucson to make it the largest city between New Orleans and San Francisco.

George Warren first discovered copper in Mule Pass Gulch, the site of modern Bisbee, in 1877. So little did he value his claim that he lost it in a fit of drunken bravado, betting he could outrun a man on horseback. The Copper Queen and Phelps Dodge companies soon moved in, then amalgamated rather than face a legal battle over which owned a vast ore body found between their two mines.

The most notorious incident in local history came at the height of World War I, when demand for copper was at its peak. On July 12, 1917, two weeks into a miners' strike, a story in the *Bisbee Daily Review* under the headline "All Women and Children Keep Off Streets Today" announced the formation of a 2200-strong posse to arrest "strange men." In the so-called **Bisbee Deportation**, 1286 alleged members of the International Workers of the World – the "**Wobblies**" – were packed into railroad boxcars and dumped in the desert near Columbus, New Mexico. Following a national outcry, Bisbee's Sheriff Wheeler was tried for kidnapping in 1920, but the charges were dropped.

Phelps Dodge finally closed down its Bisbee operations in 1975, having extracted over six billion dollars' worth of metals. As the miners moved away, however, artists and retirees moved in, preserving Bisbee's original architecture while turning it into a thriving, friendly little community that caters to tourists without being overwhelmed by them.

Walking Bisbee's narrow central streets, lined with galleries and antiques stores, is a pleasure in itself, though you may grow weary of climbing the high staircases built by the WPA during the 1930s. If you'd like to know more about local history, it's well worth calling in at the **Bisbee Mining and Historical Museum**, 5 Copper Queen Plaza (daily 10am–4pm; adults $4, under-17s $1). You can also tour the actual mines, with Queen Mine Tours, 111 Arizona St (☎520/432-2071). Hour-long **underground tours** of the Queen Mine leave daily at 9am, 10.30am, noon, 2pm, & 3.30pm (adults $12, ages 4–15 $5), while **van tours** of the opencast Lavender Pit, a massive hole that ended up swallowing many of Bisbee's earliest homes, set off at 10.30am, noon, 2pm, & 3.30pm ($7 all ages).

Practicalities

Bisbee's **visitor center**, at 2 Copper Queen Plaza (Mon–Fri 9am–5pm, Sat & Sun 10am–4pm; ☎520/432-3554 or 1-866/224-7233, ⓦ www.discoverbisbee .com), has details of **B&Bs** like the *Inn@Castle Rock*, an imposing former boarding house at 112 Tombstone Canyon (☎520/432-4449 or 1-800/566-4449, ⓦ www.theinn.org; ❹), where none of the fifteen guestrooms has phone or TV; and the quirky *School House Inn*, a mile or two further out in a converted school at 818 Tombstone Canyon (☎520/432-2996 or 1-800/537-4333; ❹). A grander alternative is the venerable *Copper Queen Hotel*, in the heart of town at 11 Howell Ave (☎520/432-2216 or 1-800/247-5829 in AZ,

Ⓦwww.copperqueen.com; Jan–April ❻, May–Dec ❺), which has a plush bar and a good restaurant with terrace seating; the only drawback is the antiquated plumbing. And there's some truly unique accommodation on the southern outskirts of town, just beyond the Lavender Pit, in the shape of the beautifully restored, irresistibly kitsch 1950s trailers for rent at the *Shady Dell RV Park*, 1 Douglas Rd (Ⓣ520/432-3567, Ⓦwww.theshadydell.com; ❷–❻). This is not a place to bring your own RV, but a great opportunity to sample how a Southwest road trip used to be. *Dot's Diner* alongside (Ⓣ520/432-1112) serves authentic Fifties fare.

Once-notorious **Brewery Gulch**, which runs north from Main Street, still holds a handful of spit-and-sawdust saloons and diners, while the less atmospheric **Copper Queen Plaza** mall to the south has its own brewpub and espresso café. Nearby, *Café Cornucopia*, 14 Main St (Ⓣ520/432-4820; Wed–Sun 10am–5pm) serves good, simple salads, sandwiches and smoothies, or you can get a much fancier four-course meal for around $20 at the trendy modern *Café Roka*, 35 Main St (Ⓣ520/432-5153; Wed–Sat 5–9pm)

Douglas

As you'll see from the endless tailings that spill from the canyons to the south, room to build in or near Bisbee was extremely limited. In 1900, therefore, a new town was constructed 25 miles to the east, to hold a smelter that processed copper from Bisbee's mines. Nestled against the Mexican border, **DOUGLAS** was equally dependent upon the world demand for copper. Although Douglas has diversified into ranching and industry, the relocation of Phelps Dodge following a bitter strike at the end of the 1980s has left the town's economy too depressed for it to make an appealing stop for tourists. Illegal trade with the much larger city of **AGUA PRIETA** across the border – home to almost 100,000 people – is a major source of income. In one recent case, a drug smuggler with houses in both towns hired surveyors and laborers to dig a deep tunnel between the two, and then had them executed to preserve his secret.

After the US instigated a major national crackdown in 1994, Douglas supplanted El Paso and San Diego as the number-one port of entry for **illegal immigrants** from Mexico. In one month alone, the 275 agents of the Border Patrol stationed in Douglas arrested 61,000 such entrants – a rate of almost one hundred per hour, but nonetheless a small proportion of those who attempt the crossing. Security has tightened considerably since 2001, and if proposals approved by Congress in 2005 come to fruition, the wall that currently separates Douglas from Agua Prieta may become simply part of a much longer extended wall running from California to Texas. Meanwhile, the town is racked by controversy, with unauthorized vigilante patrols pursuing illegal migrants while church and humanitarian groups mount their own programs to find and aid distressed wanderers in the desert, and cut down on the average 250 deaths from dehydration per year.

As for legal border traffic, cars and pedestrians alike cross into Mexico at the foot of Pan American Avenue, a mile or so southwest of downtown Douglas; US citizens don't need to carry passports, but it makes sense to do so. With its whitewashed adobe homes and churches, Agua Prieta is a considerably more attractive place to stroll around than Douglas, and offers plenty of opportunities to eat spicy Sonoran food and buy cheap souvenirs.

Practicalities

Douglas has a **visitor center** at 345 Sixteenth St (Mon–Fri 8am–5pm, Sat 8am–1pm; ☎520/364-4927, ⓦwww.douglasaz.gov). The only building of any distinction in town is the 160-room *Gadsden Hotel*, 1046 G Ave (☎520/364-4481, ⓦwww.hotelgadsden.com; ❸–❺), which opened in 1907 and still boasts an extraordinarily opulent lobby with a white marble staircase leading to a 42ft Tiffany glass window. The guest **accommodation** is not nearly so classy, but both its *Saddle and Spur Lounge* and *El Conquistador* **restaurant**, which serves reasonable meals for under $10, have a real frontier-town air about them. A few more downmarket motels are scattered along Hwy-80 to the east.

Chiricahua National Monument

Stretching northeast of Douglas toward New Mexico, the **Chiricahua Mountains** were renowned in the nineteenth century as the homeland and stronghold of the **Chiricahua Apache**. Led by such legendary warriors as **Cochise** and **Geronimo**, the Chiricahua – the name means "land of wild turkeys" – were the last Native Americans to hold out against the US Army. The 25-year **Apache Wars** began at Apache Pass in 1861, when Cochise met Lt. George Bascom under a flag of truce, and was falsely accused of kidnapping a twelve-year-old boy. He escaped into the mountains, but his brother and two nephews were hanged, precipitating a vicious cycle of raids and killings that only ended with Geronimo's fourth and final surrender in 1886.

Had the small Chiricahua band not fought so long and hard, they might still be permitted to live on the **Chiricahua reservation**, which measured 55 miles on each side and occupied the entire southeastern corner of Arizona. Established during a period of relative peace in 1872, it was disbanded in 1876, when the Chiricahua were forcibly decamped to join their distant cousins on the San Carlos Reservation to the north. No visible sign of the Apache presence remains, but the

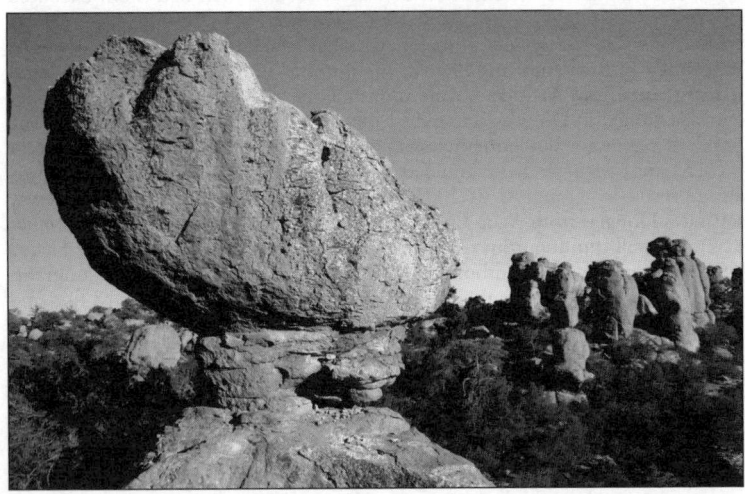

△ Rock formations at Chiricahua National Monument

core of the former reservation now constitutes **CHIRICAHUA NATIONAL MONUMENT**, entered off Hwy-186 27 miles southeast of Willcox. The monument was designated not so much to commemorate the Apache, however, as to protect the bizarre **rock formations** created in the 27 million years since colossal volcanic eruptions covered the landscape with a 2000ft coating of dark rhyolite rock. That layer has now cracked and fragmented into strange towers and columns of stacked and balanced stones, a bewildering maze that always defeated Army attempts to pursue the Apache into the mountains.

Chiricahua National Monument is not as spectacular as the desert canyons of Utah, which is presumably why the 1994 movie *Geronimo*, for all its much-vaunted authenticity, was filmed in Moab. However, this remote fastness preserves a tract of barely touched wilderness that conjures up haunting images of the Wild West, and it's also a sanctuary for rare animals and birds. These include a colony of thick-billed **parrots**, once common here and reintroduced in 1986.

Just one paved road – the eight-mile **Bonita Canyon Drive** – penetrates, but does not cross, the mountains, and stays open 24 hours. From the monument entrance it runs for two miles to the **visitor center** (daily 8am–5pm; T 520/824-3560; W www.nps.gov/chir; $5 per person), then follows Bonita Canyon east before climbing south to reach **Massai Point**, 6870ft up. This high vantage point looks out over the main concentration of rocky pinnacles, in **Echo Canyon** and **Heart of Rocks**; trails drop from the parking lot to circle the promontory below.

Only if you have a few hours to spare, however, does Massai Point make a good spot from which to start **hiking** in the monument; it is possible to walk down into the labyrinth from here, but then you're faced with either a long climb to get back out again, or a one-way walk of at least four miles to reach the visitor center. For a shorter and less demanding stroll, set off instead along **Echo Canyon Trail**, which starts half a mile or so back down the road. This level footpath leads in roughly ten minutes to some dramatic formations, with the option of turning back as soon as you've had your fill. The highest peak in the monument at 7310ft, **Sugarloaf Mountain** can be climbed on a separate mile-long trail, but it's a much less rewarding hike.

To make things a little easier, a **hikers' shuttle** bus, which you can reserve a day in advance, leaves the visitor center daily at 8.30am to reach both the Echo Canyon and Massai Point trailheads. No food, gas, or lodging is available in the monument, and overnight backpacking is forbidden, but you can **camp** year-round at the small *Bonita Canyon Campground* (first-come, first-served; $8). Alternatively, the *Sunglow Ranch* is a 400-acre **guest ranch** just south of the monument at 14066 S Sunglow Rd, Pearce (T 520/824-3344 or 1-866/786-4569; W www.sunglowranch.com; •), which holds three luxurious guest *casitas* of varying sizes; the plushest has two bedrooms and bathrooms and a cozy fireplace area. Rates include dinner at the on-site *Sunglow Café*.

Fort Bowie

The ruins of **FORT BOWIE** (daily 8am–5pm; free), the original focus of the Chiricahua Reservation and now a national historic site, lie just beyond the northern boundary of Chiricahua National Monument. They're reached by a demanding but exhilarating 1.5 mile trail that starts on the north side of **Apache Pass**, a total of 22 miles from the monument visitor center or, if you're coming from the north, thirteen miles from the somewhat desolate I-10 pitstop of **Bowie**.

Apache Pass today is an insignificant back route. The central nine miles of the **Apache Pass Road** across it are not even paved, though other than during periods of heavy rain they're usually passable to ordinary vehicles. This low saddle between the Dos Cabezas and Chiricahua mountains is currently over-grown with mesquite bushes, but when the Apache were here it ran through clear, open grassland, and its perennial natural **springs** were a vital resource. Those same springs, however, made it a crucial way station for the **Butterfield Overland Mail**, which started regular runs through Apache Pass in 1857, as part of a 25-day, 2800-mile service between St Louis and San Francisco. At first, local Apaches were cooperative, but after the Bascom Affair of 1861 (see p.302), the US Army established a permanent military presence at the pass.

Visitors to Fort Bowie should allow at least two and a half hours for the round-trip hike. The first significant relic along the trail comes after half a mile, in the shape of the stone walls of the **Apache Pass Stage Station**, built in 1858. Shortly after crossing the old stage route, now just a narrow furrow in the soil, you reach the **cemetery** where Little Robe, the son of Geronimo who died at the age of two, lies alongside several US soldiers. Not far beyond, the trail reaches the glorious lush creek that flows from **Apache Spring** – the source of all the trouble, but now the preserve of a myriad of playful coatis and bobcats.

There are no views to speak of as you climb; instead, the **fort** itself sits in a deep, broad bowl, ringed by mountains and dominated by a granite knob known as **Helen's Dome**. All that survives of the large complex are the rounded, sun-baked stumps of its adobe walls, though a flag still flutters above the parade ground, and there's a visitor center nearby to provide much-needed shade and water. An optional, slightly longer route back continues up the adjacent hillside – finally enabling you to appreciate that this really was a good vantage point on which to build – before circling down to the trailhead. En route, you step over the geological fault responsible for creating the springs, which instantly transforms the surrounding vegetation from yucca and flowering cactuses (on limestone) to beargrass (on granite).

Willcox

Only one significant community interrupts I-10 in its ninety-mile run east from Benson to the New Mexican border: **WILLCOX**, 36 miles out from Benson and ten miles east of the point where US-191 south from Safford (see p.270) meets the interstate. In its small but atmospheric downtown area, the **Chiricahua Regional Museum**, 127 E Maley St (Mon–Sat 10am–4pm; $2 donation), is a storefront that holds informative displays on both Cochise and Geronimo.

Practicalities

Willcox's Chamber of Commerce runs a **visitor center** at 1500 N Circle I Rd, close to exit 340 off the interstate (Mon–Sat 9am–5pm, Sun 9–11am; ☏520/384-2272 or 1-800/200-2272, Ⓦwww.willcoxchamber.com). Chain **motels** nearby include a *Super 8*, 1500 W Fort Grant Rd (☏520/384-0888 or 1-800/800-8000, Ⓦwww.super8.com; ❸). Back in town, *Rodney's* is a friendly hole-in-the-wall **barbecue** place at 118 N Railroad Ave (☏520/384-6317;

closed Mon), while the *Claim Jumper* espresso café is just along the street, opposite the railroad depot.

Southwest Arizona

Two interstates, **I-8** and **I-10**, run west across central and southern Arizona toward California, 35 miles apart near Phoenix and more than twice that by the time they reach the state line. There's virtually nothing of interest in these vast desert plains, apart perhaps from the strange prototype military airplanes glimpsed above the Barry M. Goldwater Air Force Range, which stretches south from I-8 to Mexico. A long detour south will take you to the wild terrain of **Organ Pipe Cactus National Monument**, but the only town you might conceivably want to visit is **Yuma**, a venerable river crossing on the far southwest border with California, whose mundane present fails to live up to its wild past.

Papago Indian Reservation

The high country to the east of Tucson, known as **Papaguería** to the Spanish, is now dominated by the **PAPAGO INDIAN RESERVATION**. One of three related groups who together call themselves the '**O'odham** – "The People" – the Papago are now known as the **Tohono 'O'odham**, which means "desert people." Unlike the Pima, or Akimel 'O'odham, the "river people" who lived in permanent villages, the Tohono 'O'odham were traditionally "two-villagers," who divided their time between a summer "field" village in the valleys and a winter "well" village near a spring in the foothills. Apart from the mission at San Xavier del Bac, described on p.286, the 'O'odham are best known these days for the music they call *waila*, derived from Mexican accordion and polka music, which may be more familiar as "**chicken scratch**."

Eighteen thousand Tohono 'O'odham now live on the reservation, which was established in 1916. They share it with the less numerous **Hia C–ed 'O'odham**, formerly known as the Sand Papago – desert nomads who in 1976 accepted $26 million as compensation for the loss of the lands now enclosed by Organ Pipe Cactus National Monument and the Barry Goldwater Air Force Base.

For tourists, the only reward in driving the hundred-mile-width of the reservation, which starts 25 miles out of Tucson on **Hwy-86**, is its sheer sense of desolation. The only signs of human occupation are a handful of roadside buildings at **Sells**, the administrative headquarters 56 miles southwest of Tucson, and **Quijotoa**, another 23 miles northwest.

Organ Pipe Cactus National Monument

Hwy-86 ends at **Hwy-85**, fifty miles south of Gila Bend, at a Y-shaped intersection that has over the years acquired the formal name of **WHY**.

A twenty-mile detour south from here through the straight, flat **Sonoyta Valley**, between the jagged ridge of the dry Ajo Mountains to the east and the lower Puerto Blanco Mountains to the west, climbs in due course to reach **ORGAN PIPE CACTUS NATIONAL MONUMENT**, right on the Mexican border.

Located at the heart of the Sonoran Desert, the five-hundred-square-mile monument is a treasure-trove of rare desert plants and animals, but focuses especially on the **organ pipe**, found almost nowhere else in the United States. Where the saguaro stands alone, the organ pipe grows in clusters of tubular "pipes," thrusting up from a shared central root system. The $5 per vehicle monument **entrance fee** is payable only if you leave the main road. From the **visitor center**, just west of the highway (daily 8am–5pm; ☎520/387-6849; ⊛www.nps.gov/orpi), two separate **scenic drives** loop off into the mountains. Both are unpaved and steep, but generally passable for ordinary vehicles; the 21-mile **Ajo Mountain Drive** takes around two hours to complete, the 53-mile **Puerto Blanco Drive** at least half a day. This remote area is so prone to illegal border crossings that it receives virtually constant attention from security forces; roads including the scenic drives are often closed altogether for significant periods, and even when they're not, the presence of border patrols may make you feel too uncomfortable to linger long.

In summer, **hiking** anything more than the hundred-yard nature trail at the visitor center would be far too grueling to consider, but between October and April, you might feel more inclined to walk several short trails that lead further afield. The cooler months are also the only time when the **campground** (first-come, first-served; $10), a mile south of the visitor center, is likely to fill up.

Ajo

Ten miles north of Why, **AJO** is a former copper-mining town that belies its ugly outskirts – the huge open-pit mine to the south is a hideous spectacle – by having a tidy and attractive Spanish-style plaza at its core. Hispanic settlers were digging for copper by 1750; they named the town in honor of the garlic (*ajo*) that grows wild in the hills nearby.

Since Phelps Dodge closed the mine in 1984, after a bitter year-long strike, Ajo has defied the sceptics and clung to life by attracting a steady trickle of tourists and retirees. There's a welcoming bustle about its grassy plaza, surrounded by palm trees and holding two whitewashed Spanish-colonial churches, even if the streets behind hold little of interest.

Practicalities

Two clean, simple **motels** stand on either side of the highway a couple of miles north of town. The *Marine Resort* is tucked behind a screen of cactuses at 1966 N Hwy-85 (☎520/387-7626, ⊛www.marinemotel.com; summer ❷, winter ❸), while *La Siesta* is on the west side, a little further along at 2561 N Hwy-85 (☎520/387-6569; summer ❷, winter ❸). Back in town, the *Guest House Inn*, 3 Guesthouse Rd (☎520/387-6133; ⊛www.guesthouseinn.biz; ❺), is a comfortable **B&B** with four en-suite rooms. The *Copper Kettle* on the plaza, at 23 Plaza St (☎520/387-7000), is the best **restaurant**, serving mainly Mexican dishes.

Gila Bend

At the intersection of Hwy-85 and I-8, **GILA BEND** is a minor farming community whose hopes of prosperity were dashed when the early twentieth-century spate of dam-building all but dried up the Gila River. What little local history is available to be celebrated is recorded in the tiny **museum** that adjoins its rudimentary **visitor center** at 644 W Pima St (daily 8am–4pm; ☎520/683-2002).

While not a destination in itself, Gila Bend has the widest selection of **motels** in almost two hundred miles of interstate, with some rundown options offering rooms for little more than $20. The *Best Western Space Age Lodge*, 401 E Pima St (☎520/683-2273 or 1-866/683-7722, ⓦwww.bestwesternspaceagelodge.com; ➍), however, is a dramatic Fifties relic, where the Sputnik motif extends to a giant neon flying saucer sign. Unfortunately, its adjoining coffeeshop, which featured huge murals of the lunar landings both inside and out, was ignited by a stray spark in 1998; it has since been rebuilt, but in much less compelling style.

Twenty miles west of Gila Bend, the petroglyphs of the **Painted Rock Mountains** are said to mark the boundary between the traditional territories of the Maricopa and Yuma Indians.

Yuma

With a population of 81,000, the sheer size of **YUMA**, a hundred miles west of Gila Bend, surprises most visitors – its numbered streets start a full fifty miles out from the center. The city ranks among the state's oldest communities. Commanding the confluence of the Gila and Colorado rivers, the site's significance was recognized as early as 1540, when **Hernando de Alarcón**, in charge of the naval wing of Coronado's pioneering expedition (see p.572), sailed past its high bluffs. It later became the major river crossing for California-bound travelers, though Spanish attempts to establish a permanent mission settlement were destroyed by the **Yuma Revolt** of 1781, when **Quechan** Indians (known to the Spaniards as the Yuma) massacred over 150 settlers during Mass.

At the height of California's **Gold Rush**, sixty thousand passengers in a single year paid $2 each to be ferried across the Colorado at **Yuma Crossing**. This lucrative trade was at first controlled by the Quechan, but freebooting entrepreneurs wrested it out of their hands, with the US Army at Fort Yuma on hand to stifle Indian resistance. (A phenomenally bloodthirsty account of the struggle appears in Cormac McCarthy's novel *Blood Meridian*; see p.603.) Known initially as Colorado City, and later Arizona City, Yuma took on its current name in 1873, by which time it was experiencing a gold rush of its own.

Now that intricate hydraulic engineering has tamed the Colorado – one canal feeding California's Imperial Valley actually siphons beneath the river – it would take a major dam-burst to cause a repeat of the river's formerly devastating floods. As seen in 1993, for example, when it inundated Yuma's riverfront to a depth of six feet, the Gila remains as dangerous as ever. In theory, Arizona could use its share of the Colorado's water to irrigate the land around Yuma and create a rival to nearby **Imperial Valley**, one of the world's richest farming areas; instead, although Yuma's economy is indeed largely founded on agriculture, the vast bulk of the water is channeled across the desert to Phoenix and Tucson at astronomical expense.

Yuma is not a vacation destination in the usual sense, but its warm, dry winters, when temperatures seldom drop below the mid-70°s F, have made it a goal for hordes of "**snowbirds**" who keep an astonishing 72 local RV and trailer parks busy. During summer, on the other hand, when you can expect daytime highs of over 110°F Yuma is too much of an inferno for anyone to linger very long.

Arrival and information

Although it can offer a certain amount of useful brochures and other information, much of Yuma's **visitor center**, in the oldest part of downtown at 377 S Main St (May–Oct Mon–Fri 9am–5pm, Sat 9am–2pm; Nov–April Mon–Fri 9am–6pm, Sat 9am–4pm, Sun 10am–1pm; ☎928/783-0071 or 1-800/293-0071; ⓦwww.visityuma.com) is devoted to local opportunities for square dancing. Amtrak **trains** from LA to Tucson stop nearby at 291 Gila St, at hideously unsocial hours, while Greyhound **buses** run from 170 E 17th Place (☎928/783-4403) to Phoenix, Tucson, and San Diego.

Yuma River Tours (☎928/783-4400; ⓦwww.yumarivertours.com) runs various **Colorado cruises** from Fisher's Landing, 32 miles upstream from Yuma, including trips on jet boats (five-hour $55, seven-hour $75, both starting at 9.30am daily) and a replica sternwheeler (three-hour, $35, 10am daily).

Accommodation

As well as a plethora of RV parks, the "business loop" that parallels the interstate for around six miles through the heart of Yuma holds dozens of **hotels** and **motels**, with plusher chains along its east–west segment on **32nd Street**, and old-fashioned budget options on the north–south **Fourth Avenue** closer to the river.

Best Western Coronado Motor Hotel 233 Fourth Ave ☎928/783-4453 or 1-877/234-5567, ⓦwww.bwcoronado.com. Veteran central motel, built in appealing Mission Revival style and nicely updated, within easy walking distance of downtown. ❹

Hotel Lee 390 S Main St ☎928/726-6336. Antique-furnished, old-fashioned and not fully modernized downtown hotel, where not all the rooms have en-suite baths. ❷

Super 8 1688 S Riley Ave ☎928/782-2000 or 1-800/800-8000, ⓦwww.super8.com. Dependable chain motel, not far from downtown at interstate exit 2. ❸

Yuma Cabaña 2151 S Fourth Ave ☎928/783-8311 or 1-800/874-0811, ⓦwww.yumacabana.com. Traditional roadside motel, with a lovely old neon sign, a couple of miles up from the river. Clean, quiet, and very good value. ❷

The town

Yuma is not an attractive town; it's much too large to explore on foot, and offers neither a significant historic downtown core nor, for the moment at any rate, attractive public spaces beside the river. Instead, the best place to get a feel for the town's tempestuous past is the **Yuma Territorial Prison State Historic Park**, set high above the Colorado a few blocks east of downtown (daily 8am–5pm; $4). Built in 1876 and known as the "Hell Hole of Arizona," this was the state's principal prison for 33 years. The restored wooden guard tower outside gives great views of the green-lined river meandering in from the north; this spot originally marked the precise confluence of the two rivers, but as the Colorado's flow has dwindled, the meeting point has shifted five miles further upstream. The "Ocean to Ocean" bridge here was built in 1915, not only superseding the ferry but also completing the southernmost uninterrupted transcontinental railroad route.

Inside the prison compound's adobe walls, built by the earliest inmates, fascinating displays tell the stories of its three thousand prisoners. These ranged from teenage burglars to Harvard lawyers and included nine Mormon polygamists, several Mexican revolutionaries, and a handful of women, such as the colorful Pearl Hart, who served five years for committing Arizona's last stagecoach robbery in 1899. You can also enter several cells, many of which were occupied by homeless migrants during the 1930s. Each held six bunks, apart from the pitch-black "dark cell," where unruly prisoners, such as women spotted "flirting," were punished with spells in isolation.

The entire riverfront at Yuma is gradually being transformed into **Yuma Crossing State Historical Park**, which will extend from the prison to the former Quartermaster Depot on Fourth Avenue near the river bridge. So far, only the depot and its grounds have been opened (daily 9am–5pm; $4). All of Yuma's supplies originally reached the town via a fifty-mile river journey from the ocean via Port Isabel on the Gulf of California; the depot still holds two of the three warehouses where the Colorado paddle steamers used to moor. Various ancient wagons, carriages, and even trains have been stabled indoors or set out to pasture on the lawns, but unless transportation history is really your thing, it's not a desperately exciting experience.

Yuma's most unusual attraction has to be the **Saihati Camel Farm**, roughly four miles south of town on Ave 1E (tours Oct–May Mon–Sat 10am & 2pm, by reservation; $3; ☎928/627-2553). Until you get within smelling distance, it's a fiendishly difficult spot to find: Avenue 1E only starts on the south side of the airport, and even then it's a dirt road at first. Furthermore, the farm gates only open briefly, at the exact time of the tours. Assuming you do manage to get in, you'll be able to inspect a large herd of slobbery, drooling dromedaries, bred here for circuses and zoos – there's no camel riding here – plus a cross-section of other wildlife such as ostriches, water buffalo, and Watusi cattle.

Finally, many visitors like to take a day-trip south into **Mexico**, whether to little **Algodones**, across from California a mere ten miles east, or to the much larger city of **San Luis**, 23 miles south. Both offer the usual array of souvenir stores and restaurants, together with cut-price drugstores.

Eating

Yuma is not a place to expect memorable **eating**, though cruising up and down Main Street will take you past every fast-food option imaginable.

The Coffee Bean 2450 S Fourth Ave ☎928/317-0284. Friendly little coffee-and-pastries joint on the main drag.

The Crossing 2690 S Fourth Ave ☎928/726-5551. One of the more upscale diners on the climb up from the Colorado, with inexpensive steak and seafood served daily for lunch and dinner.

Garden Cafe 248 S Madison Ave ☎928/783-1491. Tasteful café with indoor and outdoor seating, behind a small free museum of pioneer life, that's open for breakfast and lunch only and serves salads, sandwiches, and espresso coffees. Closed Mon & June–Sept.

Lutes Casino 221 Main St ☎928/782-2192. This downtown landmark may look like a dull old barn from the outside, but inside it's bursting with quirky oddities and paraphernalia, and does a brisk trade in surprisingly tasty hamburgers. There's no gambling, but plenty of pool and domino players. Mon–Thurs 9am–8pm, Fri & Sat 9am–9pm, Sun 9am–6pm.

River City Grill 600 W Third St ☎928/782-7988. This bright "international" restaurant is Yuma's most fashionable hangout, serving an eclectic and relatively expensive menu that concentrates heavily on Asian-influenced seafood options like Thai crab cakes or seared *ahi*. Outdoor dining available. Mon–Fri 11.30am–2pm & 5–10pm, Sat & Sun 5–10pm.

North from Yuma: Quartzsite

North of Yuma, three **wildlife refuges** – the Kofa, Cibola, and Imperial – line the Colorado River. Established to protect herds of mule deer and bighorn sheep as well as migratory Canadian geese, the parks aren't really designed for human visitors and are virtually inaccessible without a four-wheel-drive vehicle.

Granted that you'd rather not get caught up in the tank battles staged by the army in its **Yuma Proving Grounds**, there's nowhere to stop on the main north–south highway, **US-95**, until you reach **QUARTZSITE**, eighty miles out of Yuma.

With the Colorado now twenty miles to the west, Quartzsite is even bleaker and drier than Yuma and has a nominal population of around two thousand, but it, too, experiences a major winter influx of snowbirds. Literally hundreds of thousands of RV-owners descend on this desert outpost between early January and mid-February each year, ostensibly to bargain for precious, semi-precious, and merely pretty stones, but also to ride out the coldest months with like-minded fellow retirees.

In Quartzsite's dusty **cemetery**, north of the main drag in the heart of town, a pyramidal monument topped by a brass camel commemorates one of the odder episodes in Southwestern history. Inscribed "The last camp of **Hi Jolly**, born somewhere in Syria about 1828, died Quartzsite December 16 1902," it marks the grave of Haiji Ali, who arrived at Indianola, Texas, in February 1856, in charge of 33 **camels** that had been requisitioned by the then Secretary of War, Jefferson Davis. The idea was to see if they might prove suitable for use as beasts of burden; while they adapted well to the desert, army mule handlers and cowboys lacked the patience or inclination to care for them properly, and the experiment petered out during the Civil War. "Hi Jolly" became just another prospector; the abandoned camels continued to breed in the wild into the first years of the twentieth century. To this day, it remains against the law to shoot a camel in Arizona.

Despite its endless expanse of RV parks, Quartzsite has just four tiny and flyblown **motels**, with fewer than ten rooms each.

Parker

Quartzsite's winter crowds spill over to **PARKER**, beside the river 35 miles north. The main activity here is boating on the placid waters downstream of the **Parker Dam**, a Depression-era project designed to divert Colorado water to the thirsty cities of southern California. Arizona's then-governor, Benjamin Moer, was so indignant at losing precious state resources that he sent a detachment of the Arizona National Guard – six men in a boat, nicknamed the Arizona Navy – to halt the dam's construction in 1934. Such differences were soon resolved, however, and since 1985 the dam has also provided water for the **Central Arizona Project**, whose 336 miles of aqueducts stretch as far as Phoenix and Tucson. Almost twenty miles out of Parker, it's the deepest dam in the world, dug 235 feet into the riverbed. Jet-skiers glide up to its base for a closer look, and it can also be seen on free self-guided **tours** (daily 7.30am–4pm).

Before serving as the headquarters for the building of the dam, Parker started life in 1905 as the principal settlement on the **Colorado River Indian Reservation**. Not far from the dam, clearly signposted from Hwy-95, visitors can examine prehistoric rock art, or **intaglios**, made by "carving" the darker top layer of rock away from the desert floor, to reveal lighter layers of sand beneath (daily 8am–sundown; $3). The figures are so huge (up to 160ft) that it's hard to tell what you're looking at, but gaze long enough and you can discern a four-legged animal, and a human and spiral design.

The most appealing **place to stay** in the heart of Parker is the vaguely Moor-ish *Holiday Kasbah Motel*, not far from the California border at 604 California Ave (℡928/669-2133; Sun–Thurs ❷, Fri & Sat ❸). Overlooking the Colorado just under two miles northwest of town, the *Bluewater Resort & Casino*, 11300 Resort Drive (℡928/669-7000 or 1-888/243-3360, ⓦwww.bluewaterfun .com; Sun–Thurs ❷, Fri & Sat ❻) is a huge casino resort, owned by the Colo-rado River Indians, that has its own indoor water park.

Flagstaff and central Arizona

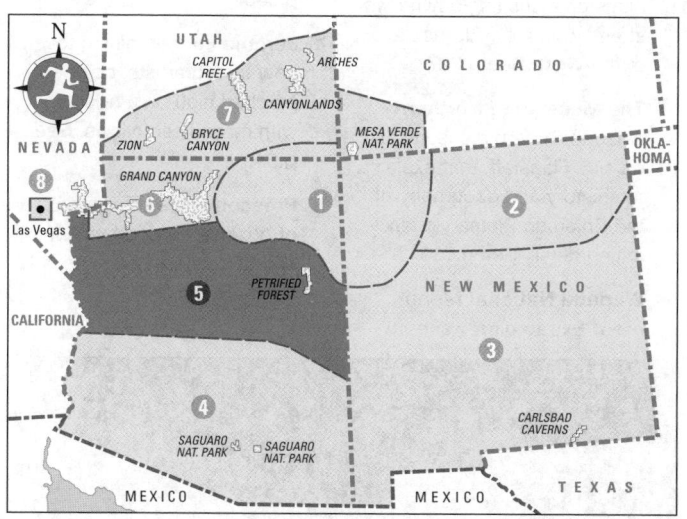

CHAPTER 5

Highlights

✻ **La Posada** Glorious old restored hotel, straight from the plush days of trans-continental rail travel, that's a great reason to spend a night in Winslow. See p.325

✻ **Downtown Flagstaff** Flanking both sides of Route 66 and the Santa Fe Railroad, Flagstaff's bustling downtown streets abound with the flavor of the West. See p.327

✻ **The Museum of Northern Arizona** Superb museum, just outside Flagstaff, that explains the history and geography of the Colorado Plateau in fascinating detail. See p.330

✻ **Wupatki National Monument** Extraordinary site northeast of Flagstaff, where the ancient Sinagua people raised multi-story pueblos out of the desert floor. See p.334

✻ **Verde Canyon Railroad** Take a delightful half-day train ride into the wilderness of little-known Verde Canyon. See p.345

✻ **Jerome** Former mining town, now turned artists' colony, perched high on a hillside with magnificent views. See p.345

✻ **Prescott** Once the capital of Arizona, Prescott remains one of its most charming little towns See p.349

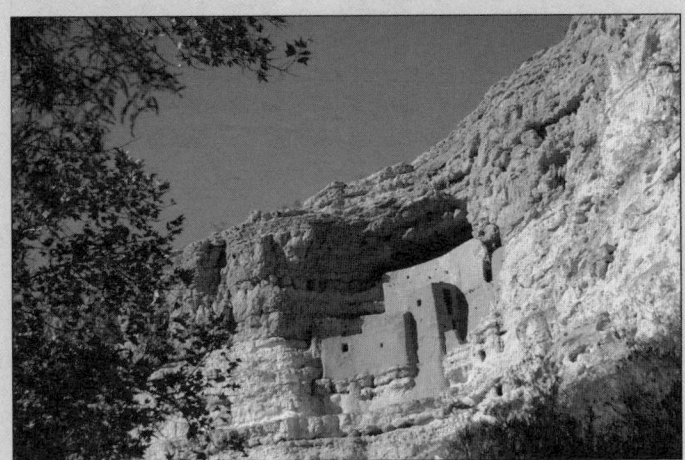

△ Montezuma Castle National Monument

5

Flagstaff and central Arizona

T he state's northernmost hundred miles, from the rugged Navajo and Hopi reservations across to the Grand Canyon, is impassable to east–west traffic. Providing a neatly drawn corridor beneath this tract is the **I-40** and parts of the legendary **Route 66.** Before either road was pushed through, it was the Santa Fe Railroad that cut across the state; and before the railroad arrived, not much more than a century ago, there were no significant Anglo settlements in the region at all.

Even today, only **Flagstaff** of the I-40 towns amounts to much more than an overnight pit stop. No doubt the contrast with the deserts to the east makes Flagstaff, set in the world's largest stand of sweet-smelling ponderosa **pine forest**, one of the Southwest's most characterful and charming towns. It also makes a great base for visits not only to the Grand Canyon (detailed in Chapter Six) but to the dramatic ancient sites of **Wupatki** and **Walnut Canyon** and the superbly positioned New Age mecca of **Sedona**.

The highlight of the long drive between Flagstaff and New Mexico is **Petrified Forest National Park**, where giant fossilized remains lie strewn like matchsticks across the eerie desert badlands. To the west, the road to California is less inspiring, so it makes sense to detour south by way of the historic hilltop mining town of **Jerome** and pristine Victorian **Prescott** or, further west, to take a timewarp spin along Route 66 to the ghost town of **Oatman**.

East of Flagstaff

During its 150-mile run west from the New Mexican border to Flagstaff, **I-40** passes few towns of any size, let alone of any interest. The **landscape,** however, while barren in the extreme, is consistently beautiful, with double rainbows reaching across the desert plain and fiery dawns blazing along the horizon. The

FLAGSTAFF AND CENTRAL ARIZONA

most accessible section of this **Painted Desert** lies within **Petrified Forest National Park**, which makes an intriguing half-day detour.

For many, this relentless desolation is exactly what they came to see; few join the locals in escaping south to the cool uplands of the **White Mountains**.

Chambers

Arizona's easternmost I-40 town – **CHAMBERS**, 25 miles in from New Mexico – is also where you'll hit the interstate as you drive south from Ganado (see p.81) or Canyon de Chelly. It's not so much a town as a speck on the windscreen, consisting of three gas stations, each with its own small grocery, and the *Chieftain* motel (☎928/688-2754; ❹), which has a restaurant.

Petrified Forest National Park

Straddling the interstate 25 miles east of Holbrook, **PETRIFIED FOREST NATIONAL PARK** kills two birds with one stone. While its chief purpose is to protect a prehistoric "forest" of fossilized trees, south of I-40, it also stretches north to include some of the most picturesque stretches of the **Painted Desert**, an ill-defined area of multicolored badlands that covers much of northeast Arizona. Its blue-tinged clays and crumbling sands support little vegetation or life of any kind, and continue to erode at a fearsome rate. Each year, more and more lithified logs are exposed to view, lying in haphazard profusion on the barren slopes. Petrified wood is not in fact all that rare, but its sheer abundance here is extraordinary; the wood-bearing layer, which is also rich in dinosaur bones and other fossils, extends for three hundred feet beneath the ground.

The gigantic trees of Petrified Forest, drawn from long-extinct species such as *Auracarioxylon*, *Woodworthia*, and *Schilderia*, date back 225 million years. This

△ A train passes through Petrified Forest National Park

is not, however, the site of a genuine forest. Its mighty trunks are horizontal, not vertical; they didn't grow here, they accumulated as a vast log jam in an ancient river. Settling onto the riverbed, they were buried by layers of silt and ash, which drastically slowed the processes of decay. Bit by bit, silica seeped in and replaced the original wood cells, then crystallized into quartz.

Cross-sections of petrified wood, cut through with diamond saws and then polished, look stunning; prize specimens are displayed in the park's two visitor centers, and lesser examples of all sizes, gathered outside the park, are sold in commercial outlets nearby. As seen on the ground from trails along the park's **27-mile Scenic Drive**, however, the trees themselves are not always all that exciting. Segmented, crumbling, and very dark, when all's said and done they can just seem like a bunch of logs lying in the sand, even if they are stone logs. The best viewing comes in late afternoon, when the setting sun brings out rich red and orange hues.

Petrified Forest became a national park when large-scale **pilfering** threatened to deplete its stocks of wood altogether. A similar park in the Dakotas had to close in the 1930s after visitors carried off all its fossil treasures, and even today an estimated twelve tons of rock disappears from the Petrified Forest each year. In theory, rangers can search your vehicle as you leave and impose heavy fines on anyone caught with a pocketful of petrified wood-chips. They rarely bother, however, preferring the subtler approach of displaying letters in the visitor centers from repentant rock thieves who have been punished by the loss of hair, health, pets, or progeny.

Arrival and information

Although the main road through the park crosses I-40, there's no access to or from the interstate at that point. Instead, the park has two separate entrances, at the north and south ends of its scenic drive. Which one you use will depend on how much time you can spare, and which way you're heading. If you're coming from New Mexico, turn north off the interstate at exit 311, 22 miles west of Chambers, and within a mile you'll come to the **Painted Desert Visitor Center** (daily: summer 7am–7pm, winter 8am–5pm; ☎928/524-6228, Ⓦwww.nps.gov/pefo). If you're heading east and only have time for a quick look, you can use that same entrance, but if you want to see the entire park it makes more sense to leave I-40 at Holbrook (see p.320) and take US-180 for twenty miles southeast to the southern entrance, near the **Rainbow Forest Museum** (daily 8am–5pm).

Displays at both visitor centers explain the geology of the park and forest. The **admission fee** of $10 per vehicle, or $5 for motorcyclists, cyclists, and pedestrians, is levied at roadside kiosks nearby, where you can also buy National Parks passes.

You can pick up simple snacks at the Rainbow Forest Museum, but the Painted Desert Visitor Center holds most of the park's few facilities, including a *Fred Harvey* **restaurant** that serves overpriced café meals all day, a large gift store, and a gas station. Note that there are no **lodges** or **campgrounds** in the park; the only way to spend a night here is by camping in the backcountry, with a free permit issued at the visitor center.

Seeing the park

Petrified Forest effectively divides into three sections, with an area rich in ancient Indian remains separating the desert in the north from the forest in the south. To see its full range, you have to complete the entire 27-mile scenic drive, but there's no need to stop at every one of the overlooks along the way.

Assuming you enter the park in the north, beyond the Painted Desert Visitor Center, you'll find that you're soon skirting the edge of a giant mesa, which drops away northwards to reveal long-range views across the **Painted Desert** itself. At different times of day, the undulating expanse of clay-topped mounds takes on different colors, with an emphasis on blueish shades of gray and reddish shades of brown. It's best admired through the panoramic windows of the **Painted Desert Inn** (daily 8am–4pm), a mile or two along. This defunct adobe hotel, now being restored as a museum, holds Mexican-style murals of Hopi pilgrimages and dances, painted by Hopi artist Fred Kabotie in 1948. A stone slab bears a thirteenth-century petroglyph depiction of a fierce-clawed mountain lion. From the promontory behind the inn, **Kachina Point**, backcountry **trails** drop down into the Painted Desert Wilderness. Walking these is the only way to appreciate the scale of the place, but even the shortest hike involves a hot climb back up again.

After six miles of similar overlooks, the road crosses first the interstate, and then, in quick succession, the Santa Fe Railroad and the broad but usually dry Puerco River. At the **Puerco Indian Ruin**, just beyond, a short trail leads around a small, partially excavated pueblo, abandoned in 1300 AD by its Ancestral Puebloan inhabitants. Patches of black desert varnish on nearby rocks show some well-preserved petroglyphs, including one you'd swear depicted a stork bringing a baby.

A little further along, a bunch of bigger petroglyph-covered boulders – known collectively, like many such sites, as **Newspaper Rock** – lie at the foot of a rocky incline. Closer access is forbidden, but free binoculars allow you to peer at the indistinct scribbles. In time, some resolve themselves into male and female figures.

By the time you've passed the bizarre pyramidal hillocks of the **Teepees**, you've finally reached the **Petrified Forest**. At roadside halts from here on, rough concrete walkways have been laid over the terrain – and often over the tree trunks themselves – to enable visitors to ramble through the larger concentrations of logs. At **Blue Mesa**, certain tree-trunks are raised on muddy "pedestals" above the surrounding desert, though the most photogenic of all fell from its perch in 2005; at **Agate Bridge**, one even spans a little gully.

The park's busiest trail, the **Long Logs Walk** near the southern entrance, is so popular that its

5

parking lot is closed in the mornings, and hikers have to walk an additional few hundred yards up from the Rainbow Forest Museum. Here at the edge of the desert, a little grass manages to survive, which somehow makes the half-mile main trail especially surreal. The large, shattered logs – which when alive resembled ponderosa pines – are simply strewn across the grasslands, with not another stone or rock in sight. A side trail leads in another half mile to a knoll holding the remains of a seven-hundred-year-old Indian pueblo constructed entirely from petrified wood. **Agate House** might sound amazing, but, thanks perhaps to its rather clumsy restoration, it's oddly banal.

When the Long Logs Walk looks busy, the **Crystal Forest** trail, five miles north, makes a good alternative.

Holbrook

From 1886 to 1900, **HOLBROOK**, halfway between Gallup and Flagstaff, was the rowdy headquarters of the "Hashknife" cattle outfit, the third largest in the country. Not much seems to have happened since, but traffic on Route 66 and I-40 has kept Holbrook ticking.

Unless you're ready to stop for the night, there's no great reason to stray off the interstate, though a romantic patch of Route 66 frontage survives along **Navajo Boulevard**, squeezed between the Little Colorado River and the railroad to the south, and the interstate to the north. The **Old West Museum**, housed in the former courthouse at 100 E Arizona St (Mon–Fri 8am–6pm, Sat & Sun 8am–5pm; free), is an appealing small-town melange of Ancestral Puebloan pots, fading photographs, and dioramas of Wild West shootouts.

Practicalities

Holbrook's **visitor center** is in the museum (same hours; ☎928/524-6558 or 1-800/524-2459, ⓦwww.azjournal.com). By far the most unusual place to **stay** is the *Wigwam Motel*, 811 W Hopi Drive (☎928/524-3048, ⓦwww .galerie-kokopelli.com/wigwam; ❷), a Route 66 relic in which each room is a miniature teepee of white concrete. There's also a *Super 8*, up the hill north of the interstate at 1989 E Navajo Blvd (☎928/524-2871 or 1-800/800-8000, ⓦwww.super8.com; winter ❷, summer ❸), with a Basha's supermarket nearby and a dozen other chain motels.

The best **restaurant** in Holbrook is the self-explanatory *Mesa Italiana*, 2318 Navajo Blvd (☎928/524-6696). The *Butterfield Stage Co*, 609 W Hopi Drive (☎928/524-3447), open for lunch and dinner in summer, and dinner only in winter, serves espresso coffees as well as steaks.

The White Mountains and the Mogollon Rim

Although the spellbinding northern Arizonan desert appears to stretch away forever to either side of I-40, the southern limit of the Colorado Plateau is in fact just beneath the horizon to the south – the 2000ft escarpment of the **Mogollon Rim**, curving two hundred miles from west to east and extending well into New Mexico. As you head south from I-40, it feels as though you're heading into the back of beyond, but you're soon within a hundred miles of the megalopolis of **Phoenix**.

For sweltering city-dwellers, the highland forests – especially in the **White Mountains**, near **Show Low** – make ideal targets for weekend breaks. Visitors from beyond the Southwest rarely stray this way, and unless you're looking to hunt, fish, or, in winter, ski, the only point in doing so is if you want to get to **southern Arizona** without passing through Phoenix. While none of the Mogollon Rim towns amounts to more than the sum of its dreary parts, they do at least offer an abundance of motels. Both roads south, **US-60** and **US-191**, are exhilarating drives, passing through untamed mountainous terrain that evokes the early days of the Wild West.

Springerville and Eagar

The easternmost White Mountain towns, **SPRINGERVILLE** and neighboring **EAGAR**, stand near the edge of the plains in **Round Valley**, just a few miles west of New Mexico. Their only significance is as base camps for trips into the mountains, which you'll encounter a couple of miles south on US-191, or ten miles west on Hwy-260, on the far side of the innocuous Little Colorado River.

Springerville's **visitor center**, 318 E Main St (Mon–Sat 9am–5pm; ☎928/333-2656, ⓦwww.springerville.com), can provide details of nearby attractions. It also holds a tiny museum devoted to **Casa Malpais**, a partially underground pueblo built by the Mogollon people, and organizes up to three daily guided tours of the site, costing $5. The best value among half a dozen **motels** is the plain but friendly *Super 8*, Hwy-60 on the north side of Springerville (☎928/333-2655 or 1-800/800-8000, ⓦwww.super8.com; winter ❷, summer ❸). As for **restaurants**, the *Safire*, 411 Main St (☎928/333-4512), serves meats and beers to match any hunter's appetite.

Coronado Trail Scenic Road

South of Springerville, US-191 is designated as the **Coronado Trail Scenic Road**, though it doesn't so much follow the route taken by Francisco de Coronado in 1540 – see p.572 – as vaguely parallel it. It's such a tortuous high-mountain highway that driving all the way to **Clifton**, 120 miles south (see p.270), can take up to four hours, but so long as you fill up on gas first you're sure to enjoy it.

Alpine, 25 miles south of Springerville, is the only village to interrupt the pine woods and it's here that US-180 branches off east into New Mexico. Just a tiny T-junction in a meadow, Alpine is said to be the chilliest spot in Arizona. It holds a handful of motels, including the *Sportsman's Lodge* near the intersection (☎928/339-4576 or 1-888/202-1033, ⓔsportsmans@cybertrails.com; ❸), and *Tal-Wi-Wi Lodge*, three miles north (☎928/339-4319 or 1-800/476-2695, ⓦwww.talwiwilodge.com; ❹).

Beyond Alpine, US-191 is liable to be closed by snow between mid-December and mid-March. When it's open, roadside trailheads, used mainly by hunters, make it possible to hike into the **Apache-Sitgreaves National Forest**, which also holds several rudimentary campgrounds (call ☎928/339-4384 for details). The most scenic spot is the **Blue Vista** pull-out, in the twistiest stretch of road twenty miles south of Alpine, which commands sweeping views of the misty mountains. It lies just south of the **Hannagan Meadow** clearing, where the big red-timber *Hannagan Meadow Lodge* (☎928/339-4370 or 1-800/547-1416, ⓦwww.hannaganmeadow.com; ❹) rents out rooms and cabins in summer and holds a reasonable restaurant.

Show Low

SHOW LOW, fifty miles south of Holbrook on Hwy-77 and 43 miles west of Springerville on US-60, is the largest town on the Mogollon Rim. It stands on the site of a 100,000-acre ranch, whose co-founders played cards in 1876 to decide who should get to keep it. With the game all square, one invited the other to "show low and take the ranch"; his rival drew the deuce of clubs and duly took possession. He went on to sell the ranch to the Mormon church, which built a small settlement before selling it on again.

In June 2002, Show Low hit the national headlines when it was threatened by Arizona's worst-ever **wildfire**. Started by an out-of-work Apache firefighter hoping to join a fire crew, the **Rodeo Fire** raged up from the southwest, blotting out the sun before its progress was finally halted just half a mile south of town. As you pass through on US-60 today, however, you see surprisingly little evidence of the destruction; the worst damage lies along Hwy-260 to the west.

Show Low is basically a strip of motels and diners ranged along US-60, or **Deuce of Clubs Avenue**. For a full list, stop by the **visitor center**, 951 W Deuce of Clubs Ave (Mon–Fri 9am–5pm, Sat & Sun 9am–3pm; ☎928/537-2326 or 1-888/746-9569, ⓦwww.showlowchamberofcommerce .com). Inexpensive places to stay include the *Super 8*, 1941 E Deuce of Clubs Ave (☎928/537-7694 or 1-800/800-8000; winter ❷, summer ❸). No matter how hard you look, there's nowhere distinctive to **eat**, so you might as well settle for a pizza at the run-of-the-mill *Pat's Place*, 981 E Deuce of Clubs Ave (☎928/537-2337).

Pinetop and Lakeside

Half a dozen miles southeast of Show Low, and a thousand feet higher, the Mormon communities of **PINETOP** and **LAKESIDE** have long since merged into a single amorphous entity. Set deep in the woods, they're a marginally more attractive proposition than Show Low – despite being more visibly scarred by the Rodeo Fire – though once again you have to bring your own entertainment.

The joint **visitor center**, 674 E White Mountain Blvd (summer Mon–Fri 8.30am–5pm, Sat & Sun 9am–3pm; winter Mon–Fri 9am–5pm; ☎928/367-4290 or 1-800/573-4031), has details of stables, fishing lakes, and sporting facilities. There are some pricey luxury ranches around, but if you're just passing through, either the *Blue Ridge Motel*, 2012 E White Mountain Blvd (☎928/367-0758; winter ❷, summer ❸), or the *Best Western Inn of Pinetop*, 404 E White Mountain Blvd (☎928/367-6667 or 1-800/937-8376, ⓦwww.bestwestern .com; winter ❹, summer ❺), should match your needs. The best **restaurants** around, both of which open for dinner only, are *Charlie Clark's Steak House*, 1701 E White Mountain Blvd at Penrod Ave (☎928/367-4900), which has a mesquite grill, and the *Christmas Tree*, south of central Lakeside at 455 Woodland Rd (closed Mon & Tues; ☎928/367-3107), which has outdoor seating.

Fort Apache Indian Reservation

One reason why the mountains of eastern Arizona are not better known is that a large proportion of the central massif still belongs to the **Apache**. As a study of the intricacies of the Apache Wars soon reveals, the Apache are not a single "tribe" in the way outsiders like to imagine; there are two separate but contiguous reservations here. The **FORT APACHE INDIAN RESERVATION**, which starts just a mile or two out of Pinetop and Show Low, stretches south to the Salt and Black rivers; beyond it the **San Carlos Indian Reservation** extends for another hundred miles past Globe.

The Fort Apache Reservation has suffered severely from the Rodeo Fire, which burned a vast tract of the ponderosa pine forest on which its economy depends. Its principal communities were largely unaffected, however. The reservation's headquarters is in the town of **WHITERIVER**, cupped in a mile-high valley twenty miles south of Pinetop and home to the *White Mountain Apache Motel & Restaurant* (T928/338-4927; ❸). What few visitors make it this far, however, are drawn a few miles further southwest, to **FORT APACHE** itself, at the confluence of the North and East forks of the White River. This US Army outpost was founded in 1870 to support the campaigns of General Crook, who was allied with the White Mountain Apache but wanted to keep an eye on them nonetheless. Several buildings survive in reasonable condition and hold displays on the period (Mon–Fri 8am–5pm, Sat 9am–noon; $3). The **tourist office** nearby (Mon–Fri 8am–4.30pm, Sat 8–10.30am; T928/338-1230 or 1-877/338-9629, W www.wmat.nsn.us) can direct you toward crafts stores and other sites.

Two much more contemporary attractions form the backbone of the reservation's tourist trade. The **Hon-Dah Resort Casino** (T928/369-0299 or 1-800/929-8744, W www.hon-dah.com; Sun–Thurs ❺, Fri & Sat ❻), at the junction of highways 260 and 73 three miles southeast of Pinetop, is a 24-hour gaming facility with its own attached hotel, restaurant, and pool. Arizona's most popular **ski resort**, the **Sunrise Park Resort** (T928/735-7669 or 1-800/772-7669, W www.sunriseskipark.com; Sun–Thurs ❸, Fri & Sat ❻), is thirty miles east via Hwy-273, a short spur south of Hwy-260. The 65 runs (including ones for snowboarders) are open generally between November and March. Lift tickets cost $41.

Hwy-60, the only north–south road across the reservation, is also the most direct route between northeast Arizona and Tucson. All of the 87-mile run from Show Low to **Globe** (see p.268) is awe-inspiring, bearing few traces of the 2002 blaze, but the most dramatic moment comes roughly fifty miles along, where it takes five miles of switchbacks for the highway to get to the bottom of gaping **Salt River Canyon**.

Payson

Until 1959, **PAYSON**, ninety miles west of Show Low on Hwy-260, was a sleepy cowboy town that had started out in a gold-rush frenzy and then relaxed into a lifestyle where the yearly round of ranching was punctuated only by the odd rodeo. Then the paving of Hwy-87 placed Payson within two hours' drive of Phoenix, eighty miles southwest. Ever since then, it has been a mountain retreat whose population doubles or triples at weekends, as urban refugees flock to their second homes or at least rent cabins in the forest.

On first glance, Payson, if not exactly appealing, is at least mildly impressive, but somehow as you drive down its long, broad streets, passing representatives of every national fast-food and lodging chain, you never seem to find a compelling reason to stop. Follow the signs for "historic Main Street" and it's a fairly sorry story; you can see that this is a prosperous community with plenty of new residential developments, but its former central thoroughfare, now bypassed by the highway, is desultory and rundown.

Payson's **visitor center**, at 100 W Main St (Mon–Fri 8am–5pm, Sat & Sun

10am–2pm; ☎928/474-4515 or 1-800/672-9766, ⓦwww.rimcountrychamber .com), can supply details of the town's many **motels**. Among the most attractive options is the large *Majestic Mountain Inn*, 602 E Hwy-260 (☎928/474-0185 or 1-800/408-2442, ⓦwww.majesticmountaininn.com; ❹), which holds some luxurious suites as well as more ordinary standard rooms.

None of Payson's **restaurants** is all that exceptional. Weekenders from Phoenix tend to dine Italian-style at *Cucina Paradiso*, 512 N Beeline Hwy (☎928/464-6500). You can pick up coffee and pastries at *Bagels, Brew and More*, in the Ponderosa Village development at 219 E Hwy-260 (☎928/472-2435).

Tonto Natural Bridge

The world's widest and longest (but not quite highest) **travertine bridge,** formed from minerals deposited by constantly flowing springs, is preserved in **TONTO NATURAL BRIDGE STATE PARK**, fifteen miles north of Payson on Hwy-87 (daily: May–Aug 8am–7pm, April, Sept & Oct 8am–6pm, Nov–March 9am–5pm; ☎928/476-4202; ⓦwww.azparks.gov; $5 per vehicle). In 1877, a Scottish gold prospector, David Gowan, supposedly hid in a cave inside the bridge as he fled the Apaches who used the surrounding meadows as a summer camp. He stayed and built a cabin nearby. When a description of the natural wonder bridge appeared in an English newspaper in 1896, David Goodfellow spotted the name of his long-lost uncle and wrote to Gowan, who offered him the site. Goodfellow's ten-room lodge no longer accepts guests but still serves as the park's giftshop and visitor center (same hours).

The bridge itself, reached by a network of short trails, doesn't really live up to the build-up. Spanning a gully that's roughly 150ft wide, it's more of a tunnel, or a dank cave with openings at both ends. With effort, you can scramble down to a boardwalk at the base, but you can't go through it.

Pine and Strawberry

It must have taken the Mormon settlers who established a village in the forest, five miles north of Tonto Bridge, all of five seconds to hit on a name – **PINE**. Together with its neighbor and contemporary, **STRAWBERRY**, it's not a place you'd go far out of your way to visit, but both of these tiny hamlets make very pleasant overnight stops if you're lost in the woods. Pine's *High Country Inn* rents out a couple of nice **cabins** (☎928/476-2150; ❸) and adjoins the friendly *Last Tortilla* **restaurant**, while a little further along Hwy-87, the *Frontier Deli* (☎928/476-3705) does good light lunches.

Winslow

Back on I-40, thirty miles west of Holbrook and 56 miles east of Flagstaff, **WINSLOW** is another Route 66 town that's kept alive by transcontinental truckers. It's also the closest the interstate comes to the Hopi mesas (see p.83), which jut from the desert across sixty miles of butte-studded wilderness to the north.

Winslow was founded as a railroad stop in 1882, not far from the recently established Mormon community of **Brigham City**, now lying derelict a mile northeast. If you only know of it thanks to the line about "standin' on the corner in Winslow, Arizona," in the Eagles' *Take It Easy*, you'll be glad there's an official **Standin' on the Corner Park** at Kinsley Ave and Second, where you

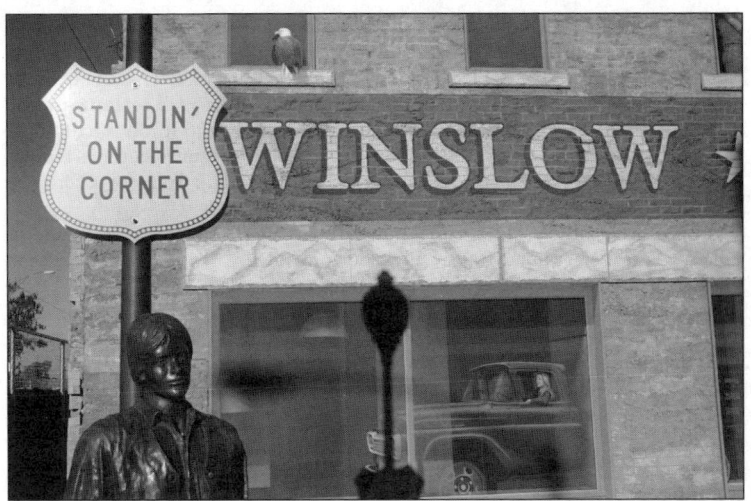

△ Winslow's Standin' On The Corner Park

can have your photo taken with a bronze statue of a guitar-toting hitchhiker. Such genuine history as the town has witnessed is recalled in the diverting **Old Trails Museum**, nearby at 212 Kinsley Ave (Nov–March Tues, Thurs, & Sat 1–5pm; April–Oct Tues–Sat 1–5pm; free).

Three miles northeast of town, **Homolovi Ruins State Park** (daily 8am–5pm; $5 per vehicle; ☎928/289-4106) holds four pueblo villages and hundreds of lesser sites that were occupied by the Hisatsinom people – the ancestors of today's **Hopi** – until perhaps the fourteenth century. Most remain unexcavated, though archeologists are usually hard at work between June and July, when visitors are welcome to join them.

Practicalities

Winslow's Amtrak station still welcomes one daily **train** west to Flagstaff and one east to Albuquerque. Greyhound **buses** along I-40 stop at 1000 E Third St. The local **visitor center** is near I-40 exit 253, at 300 W North Rd (Mon–Fri 8am–5pm; ☎928/289-2434, ⓦwww.winslowarizona.org).

Winslow's grandest **accommodation** option, *La Posada*, 303 E Second St (♣ ☎928/289-4366, ⓦwww.laposada.org; ❺), is such a totally magnificent place that it's worth going a very long way out of your way to spend a night here. It was originally designed during the late 1920s by Mary Jane Colter of Grand Canyon fame (see p.369), though she invented an entire fictional history of its former life as a Spanish hacienda. The last and greatest of the railroad hotels built for the Fred Harvey company, it closed in 1959 when the railroads had been superseded by private cars. In 1999, however, it reopened, restored as a true labor of love by a small group of enthusiasts who proclaim "we are not hoteliers – for us this is about art." Dazzlingly colourful modernist canvases by one of them, Tina Mion, bedeck the public spaces, but the whole place is so enormous that there's also plenty of the earthy Southwestern style you might expect. The surrounding gardens are a delight too, while doors from the lobby lead straight to the old railroad platform. Best of all are the guest rooms, where the fixtures and fittings, and especially the tiling, feel like a real throwback to the heyday of transcontinental travel. All are named for illustrious former visitors ranging from Clark Gable to Roddy McDowell, and have en-suite baths or even whirlpool tubs, but they're without phones. The *Posada's* **restaurant**, the *Turquoise Room* (☎928/289-2888), serves all meals daily, and it too is irresistible in terms both of its decor and contemporary Southwestern cuisine. Dinner entrées can cost well over $20, but it's in a different league from anywhere else along a hundred-mile stretch of highway.

Most of the other, older **motels** in town are now pretty decrepit, so unless you're determined to pay rock-bottom rates you'd do better to head a little further west to either the *Best Western Adobe Inn*, 1701 N Park Drive (☎928/289-4638 or 1-800/937-8376; ❹), or the *Super 8*, 1916 W Third St (☎928/289-4606 or 1-800/800-8000, ⓦwww.super8.com; winter ❷, summer ❸). The pick of the all-day **diners** is the *Falcon Restaurant*, 1113 E Third St (☎928/289-2342), while the best **campground** is at Homolovi Ruins (see p.325), where water is available in summer only.

Meteor Crater

Around 22,000 years ago, a meteorite slammed into northern Arizona, blasting a huge hole, nearly a mile across and over five hundred feet deep, into the scrubby plateau. The site of that impact, **METEOR CRATER** (daily: late May to early Sept 7am–7pm, early Sept to late May 8am–5pm; $12, under-18s $6; ☎1-800/289-5898, ⓦwww.meteorcrater.com) can now be reached by a six-mile spur road that heads south of the interstate eighteen miles west of Winslow and 38 miles east of Flagstaff.

Though the staff dress up in mock Park Service uniforms, Meteor Crater is privately owned and operated and frankly offers poor value for money. A modern gallery beside the parking lot holds the unimaginative **Astronauts Hall of Fame**, which commemorates the fact that the first men on the moon were trained on the cavity's otherworldly surface (some skeptics claim that they faked their entire mission here). Walkways from there climb to the lip of the abyss, where you'll probably find that there's a limit to how long you can spend staring at a featureless hole in the ground. Hour-long guided walking tours set off hourly from 9.15am to 2.15pm, but you can't hike into the actual crater.

Flagstaff

Northern Arizona's liveliest and most attractive town, **FLAGSTAFF**, occupies a superbly dramatic location beneath the San Francisco Peaks, halfway between New Mexico and California. Straddling the I-40 and I-17 interstates, it's a major waystation for tourists en route to the Grand Canyon, just eighty miles northwest, but it's also a worthwhile destination in its own right.

Downtown, where barely a building rises more than three stories, oozes

Wild West charm. Its main thoroughfare, Santa Fe Avenue, used to be **Route 66**, while before that it was the pioneer trail west. A stroll around its central few blocks is gloriously evocative of the past, though these days the diners and saloons are interspersed with outfitter stores and coffee bars, and the local cowboys and Indians share the sidewalks with liberal-minded students from Northern Arizona University. Just to add to the atmosphere, the tracks of the Santa Fe Railroad still divide downtown in two, so life in Flagstaff remains punctuated both day and night by the mournful wail of passing trains.

Flagstaff's first settlers arrived in 1876, lured from Boston by widely publicized accounts of mineral wealth and fertile land. Although they soon moved on, disappointed, toward Prescott, they stayed long enough to celebrate the centenary of American independence by flying the Stars and Stripes from a towering pine tree. This flagpole became a familiar landmark on the route west, and as the town grew it inevitably became known as Flagstaff. Right from the start, it was a cosmopolitan place, with a strong black and Hispanic population working in the (originally Mormon-owned) lumber mills and in the cattle industry, and Navajo and Hopi heading in from the nearby reservations to trade.

Modern Flagstaff, with a population of a little over fifty thousand, makes an ideal base for travelers. As well as the abundant hotels, restaurants, bars and shops within easy walking distance of downtown, outlets of the national food and lodging chains line the interstates slightly further afield, and budget travelers too are well catered for by hostels and student diners. There are also a couple of good museums nearby, together with some wonderful scenery and ancient sites in the close vicinity. Just one word of warning: the altitude here is almost seven thousand feet, which means the nights may well be colder than you're expecting. It can even snow in July.

Arrival, information, and getting around

Though the Santa Fe Railroad is still busy with freight, Amtrak's daily **Southwest Chief** between Chicago and Los Angeles is now the only passenger **train** that stops at Flagstaff's venerable wooden stationhouse, in the heart of town. In summer, the eastbound service leaves at 5.01am for Albuquerque and the westbound at 8.57pm for Los Angeles; winter times are one hour later.

Open Road Tours & Transportation (☏928/226-8060 or 1-877/226-8060, ⓦwww.openroadtours.com), based at the Amtrak station, runs twice-daily **bus service** via Williams to the Grand Canyon. The first bus leaves Flagstaff at 8.30am, the second at 3pm; the one-way fare is $27 for adults, and $19 for children 11 and under. Open Road also offers tours to Sedona and Monument Valley and around Flagstaff itself, as well as five daily **buses** between Flagstaff and **Phoenix** ($39). As detailed below, two local hostels, the *DuBeau* and the *Grand Canyon*, can arrange inexpensive excursions to the Grand Canyon and Sedona. Greyhound, a few blocks south of downtown at 399 S Malpais Lane (☏928/774-4573 or 1-800/231-2222), runs four daily buses to Phoenix and also heads east toward Albuquerque and west to Las Vegas, LA, San Diego, and San Francisco.

Flagstaff's helpful **visitor center** occupies half of the Amtrak stationhouse at 1 E Route 66 (Mon–Sat 8am–5pm, Sun 9am–4pm; ☏928/774-9541 or 1-800/842-7293, ⓦwww.flagstaffarizona.org). Even when it's not staffed, the building remains open for rail passengers, so visitors can still pick up brochures and **discount coupons** for local motels. You'll also find a courtesy phone in

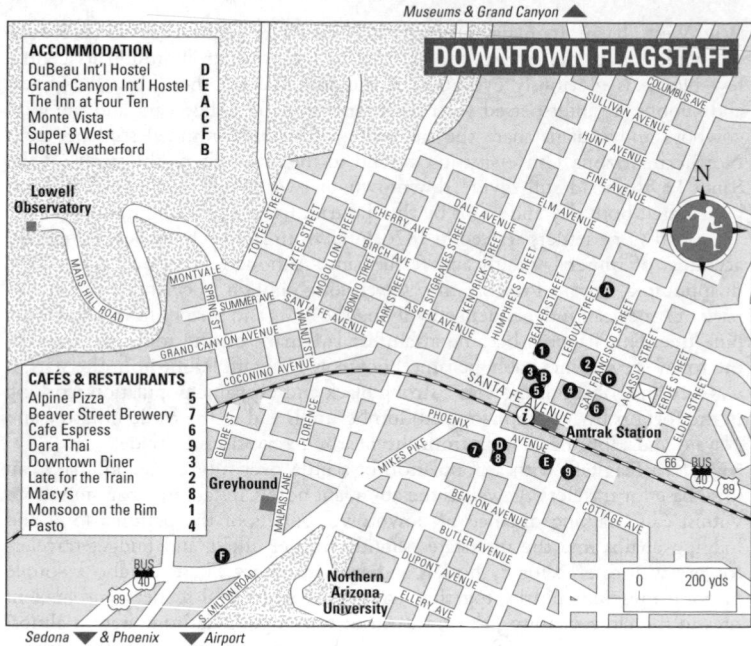

Museums & Grand Canyon ▲

DOWNTOWN FLAGSTAFF

ACCOMMODATION
DuBeau Int'l Hostel — D
Grand Canyon Int'l Hostel — E
The Inn at Four Ten — A
Monte Vista — C
Super 8 West — F
Hotel Weatherford — B

Lowell Observatory

N

CAFÉS & RESTAURANTS
Alpine Pizza — 5
Beaver Street Brewery — 7
Cafe Espress — 6
Dara Thai — 9
Downtown Diner — 3
Late for the Train — 2
Macy's — 8
Monsoon on the Rim — 1
Pasto — 4

Amtrak Station

Greyhound

Northern Arizona University

0   200 yds

Sedona ▼ & Phoenix   ▼ Airport

the Amtrak lobby for making hotel and hostel reservations (daily 8am–5pm).

The least expensive **car rental** agency is Budget, 175 W Aspen Ave (☏928/813-0156); Avis, Hertz, Enterprise, and National also have outlets. Absolute Bikes, 18 N San Francisco St (open daily; ☏928/779-5969, ⓦ www.absolutebikes.net), rents **mountain bikes** at $35 for the first day and $20 for subsequent days, while Arizona Mountain Bike Tours (☏928/779-4161 or 1-800/277-7985) runs local and regional **cycling tours**. Perhaps the best of several local **outfitters** offering equipment for outdoor activities and backpacking expeditions is Aspen Sports, 15 N San Francisco St (☏928/779-1935 or 1-800/771-1935).

Accommodation

As Flagstaff is considerably more than just another interstate pit stop, its dozens of **motels** and **B&Bs** get away with charging higher rates than its I-40 neighbors. They're still not bad value, however, and **budget** travelers can choose between two hostels, as well as a historic hotel that offers hostel-style dorm beds as well as private rooms. Most of the major chain motels are clustered well to the east, along Butler Avenue and Lucky Lane, but staying close to downtown is much more fun. It's worth knowing that if you do manage to find a room where the lonesome whistle of freight trains doesn't wake you up in the night, it's unlikely to be anywhere near Flagstaff.

If you arrive without a reservation, use the free **courtesy phones** in the visitor center (see above) to compare options. Above all, plan ahead on summer weekends, when the town is likely to be booked solid.

The best local **campground** lies three miles south on US-89A, at *Fort Tuthill*

County Park (May–Sept; ☎928/774-3464), though Flagstaff also holds the year-round Flagstaff/Grand Canyon KOA at 5803 N AZ-89A (☎928/526-9926 or 1-800/562-3524, ⊛www.koa.com/az/flagstaff).

DuBeau International Hostel 19 W Phoenix Ave ☎928/774-6731 or 1-800/398-7112, ⊛www

.dubeauhostel.com. Welcoming independent hostel just south of the tracks, whose appealingly converted en-suite motel rooms serve as four-person dorms at $18 per bed or private doubles at $38 Sun–Thurs or $41 Fri & Sat. Internet access is available, and breakfast is free, but the common areas can get noisy at times. The *DuBeau* offers the same program of tours as its sister property, the *Grand Canyon International Hostel* (see below). Closed Nov–Feb. ❶/❷

Grand Canyon International Hostel 19 S San Francisco St ☎928/779-9421 or 1-888/442-2696, ⊛www.grandcanyonhostel.com. Independent hostel, under the same friendly management as the similar nearby *DuBeau*, that offers dorm beds at $18 in summer or $16 in winter and six private rooms priced at $32–39, depending on the season and day of the week. Provides tours to the Grand Canyon (Mon, Wed, Fri & Sat, plus Tues in summer only; $55) and Sedona (Thurs & Sun; $25), as well as car rental discounts. ❶/❷

Holiday Inn 2320 E Lucky Lane ☎928/714-1000, ⊛www.holidayinnflagstaff.com. Large motel in a rather characterless area just off the interstate, with a handful of nearby diners. Winter ❹, summer ❺

Hotel Weatherford 23 N Leroux St ☎928/779-1919, ⊛www.weatherfordhotel.com. Attractive old downtown hotel, with elegant wooden fittings, which bit by bit is restoring its fading rooms to offer tasteful, basic accommodation, without telephones or TVs. The upstairs lounge offers Wild West ambience, but can make for a noisy night. ❹

The Inn at Four Ten 410 N Leroux St ☎928/774-0088 or 1-800/774-

2008, ⊛www.inn410.com. Bright ranch home operating as a luxurious antique-furnished B&B; all nine rooms are en suite, most with fireplaces and three with whirlpool tubs. On summer evenings, the porch and patio make welcoming, convivial retreats. ❼

Little America 2515 E Butler Ave ☎928/779-7900 or 1-800/865-1399, ⊛www.flagstaff .littleamerica.com. Large motel-cum-resort near the interstate, where the 1950s-style ambience conceals a higher standard of accommodation than you might expect. Good pool. ❺

Monte Vista 100 N San Francisco St ☎928/779-6971 or 1-800/545-3068, ⊛www.hotelmontevista .com. Attractive landmark 1920s hotel in the heart of downtown. The assorted restored rooms, with and without attached bathrooms, are named for celebrity guests, from Bob Hope to Michael Stipe. Many of the guests are young international travelers, drawn by the local nightlife, including the hotel's own bar (see p.332). Weekend rates rise by as much as $20. ❸–❺

Super 8 Motel 3725 N Kasper Ave ☎928/526-0818 or 1-888/324-9131, ⊛www.dknhotels.com. Decent budget motel four miles east of downtown, right where Route 66 joins US-89. Winter ❸, summer ❹

Super 8 West 602 W Route 66; ☎928/774-4581 or 1-800/654-4667, ⊛www.dknhotels.com. Attractive chain motel centered on an enclosed swimming pool, adjacent to a Barnes & Noble bookstore less than a mile southwest of downtown, just past the US-89 turnoff toward Sedona. Winter ❸, summer ❹

The Town

Flagstaff's little-changed **downtown** stretches for a few red-brick blocks north of the railroad. Filled with cafés, bars, and stores selling Route 66 souvenirs and Native American crafts, as well as outfitters specializing in tents, clothing, and all sorts of contraptions for outdoor adventures, it's a fun place to wander around, even if it holds no significant tourist attractions. Although the visitor center maps out walking tours, few specific buildings are especially historic; by the time you've browsed a few bookstores, downed a few coffees, and peeped into the old *Weatherford* and *Monte Vista* hotels, you may well be ready to move on. Your most lasting impression is likely to be of the magnificent volcanic **San**

Francisco Peaks, rising smoothly from the plains on the northern horizon, and topped by a jagged ridge.

Museum of Northern Arizona

The exceptional **Museum of Northern Arizona**, three miles northwest of downtown on US-180 (daily 9am–5pm; $5, under-18s $2; ☎928/774-5213, ⓦwww.musnaz.org), rivals Phoenix's Heard Museum as the best museum in the state, and makes an essential first stop for any visitor to the Colorado Plateau. Although it covers local geology, geography, flora and fauna – and can help you come to grips with the various theories that attempt to explain the origins of the Grand Canyon – its main emphasis is on documenting **Native American** life. It provides an excellent run-through of the Ancestral Puebloan past and contemporary Navajo, Havasupai, Zuni, and Hopi cultures, with the overview in the initial gallery followed by further rooms devoted to pots, rugs, *kachina* dolls, and silver and turquoise jewelry. There are also temporary shows of local (not always Native American) arts and crafts, a well-stocked bookstore, and a **nature trail** that runs through the small piñon-fringed canyon outside.

Ever since it was established, in 1928, the museum has actively encouraged the development of traditional and even new skills among Native American craftworkers. The exquisite inlaid silver jewelry now made by the Hopi, for example, is the result of a museum-backed program to find work for Hopi servicemen returning from World War II. During its annual Native American Marketplaces, every item is for sale; the **Hopi** show takes place on the weekend closest to July 4, and the **Navajo** one at the start of August.

For details of **Museum of Northern Arizona Ventures**, an extensive program of tours and expeditions, which include multi-day Grand Canyon trips, see p.31 or check on the museum's website.

The Pioneer Museum

Alongside US-180, a little closer to town than the Museum of Northern Arizona, an impressive steam train guards the **Pioneer Museum** (Mon–Sat 9am–5pm; donation; ☎928/774-6272, ⓦwww.arizonahistoricalsociety.org). Run by the Arizona Historical Society, and housed in what was once the county hospital, the museum holds a random but reasonably entertaining assortment of objects and images from old Flagstaff.

Sharing the same grounds, the **Coconino Center for the Arts** is a gallery and concert hall specializing in works by local artists, while just behind it the co-operatively run **Art Barn** (daily 9am–5pm) sells a wide selection of crafts.

Lowell Observatory

Flagstaff's **Lowell Observatory**, located in the pine forest atop Mars Hill, a mile west of downtown, is famous as the place where the existence of the planet Pluto was first confirmed. Many of the necessary calculations were performed by Dr Percival Lowell, who founded the observatory in 1894 and also deluded himself that he'd discovered canals on Mars. Lowell died in 1916 – he's buried in a small domed mausoleum of blue glass on the hilltop – and the ninth planet was eventually spotted in 1930 by Clyde Tombaugh.

From the **visitor center** (daily: May–Oct 9am–5pm, Feb–March noon–5pm; $5, under-18s $2; ☎928/774-3358, ⓦwww.lowell.edu), where only very technically minded visitors are likely to get much joy from playing with computers or watching explanatory videos, the **Pluto Walk** footpath climbs up to the tiny original observatory. Signs tick off the relative positions of the planets; if it kept going on the same scale, it would have to extend over six hundred miles, beyond Boise, Idaho, to show the position of the nearest star, Alpha Centauri.

Astronomy remains a passion in Flagstaff, and the town has won awards for minimizing night-time light pollution. The observatory reopens most evenings for after-dark **stargazing sessions** (June–Aug Mon–Sat 8pm; Sept–May Wed, Fri & Sat 7.30pm; no additional charge).

Eating

Central Flagstaff is surprisingly short of high-end **restaurants** but more than compensates for that with its lively assortment of both old-style Western **diners** and eclectic **budget** options. Thanks to all those students, the area around San Francisco Street, both north and south of the tracks, is filled with vegetarian cafés and espresso bars.

Alpine Pizza 7 N Leroux St ℡928/779-4109. Raucous downtown student hangout, with decent pizzas and lots of different beers. Mon–Sat 11.30am–2pm & 5–11pm, Sun 5–11pm.

Black Bart's 2760 E Butler Ave ℡928/779-3142. Enjoyable Western-themed steakhouse, across from *Little America* on the east edge of town, with a waitstaff that sings and dances onstage between servings of barbecued steak, ribs, and chicken ($18–26). Daily 5–10pm.

Café Espress 16 N San Francisco St ℡928/774-0541. Great vegetarian breakfasts, then salads, sandwiches, and veggie specials for the rest of the day, plus espresso. Mon, Tues & Sun 7am–3pm, Wed–Sat 7am–9pm.

Charly's Pub & Grill *Hotel Weatherford*, 23 N Leroux St ℡928/779-1919. Café-restaurant in a classy Western setting, serving good, inexpensive meals accompanied by live music (cocktail piano at lunch, bands at night). Sun–Thurs 7am–10pm, Fri & Sat 7am–1pm.

Dara Thai 14 S San Francisco St ℡928/774-0047. Large Thai place just south of the tracks, where the service is great and a plate of delicious pad Thai noodles costs just $7 at lunch, $9 at dinner. Mon–Sat 11am–10pm, Sun noon–9pm.

Downtown Diner 7 E Aspen Ave ℡928/774-3492. Classic Route 66 diner a block north of the main drag, featuring leatherette booths and hefty burgers and sandwiches. Mon–Sat 7am–9pm, Sun noon–8pm.

Late for the Train 107 N San Francisco St ℡928/779-5975. Little coffee bar opposite the *Monte Vista* hotel that serves excellent house-roasted coffee and pastries to a slightly older, literary crowd. Mon–Thurs 6am–6pm, Fri 6am–10pm, Sat 7am–10pm, Sun 7am–5pm.

Macy's European Coffee House & Bakery 14 S Beaver St ℡928/774-2243. Not merely superb coffee, but heavenly pastries to go with it, in a chaotic but friendly, student-oriented atmosphere. Substantial vegetarian dishes include black bean pizza and even couscous for breakfast. You'll also find free wireless Internet and an adjacent coin laundry. Daily 6am–10pm.

Monsoon on the Rim 6 E Aspen Ave ℡928/226-8844. This pan-Asian, sushi-centered restaurant, with huge plate-glass windows in a modern mall-like development in the heart of town, clearly has more to do with the new West than the Old West. While pretty good rather than wonderful, the food is surprisingly cheap, with most of the Thai and Chinese options priced under $10, and the people-watching is fun. Daily 11.30am–9pm.

Pasto 19 E Aspen Ave ℡928/779-1937. Downtown Italian joint, with pasta specials and chicken, shrimp, and vegetarian entrees for $14–19. Mon–Thurs & Sun 11.30am–2.30pm & 5–9pm, Fri & Sat 11.30am–2.30pm & 5–9.30pm.

Nightlife

Milling with international travelers in summer and students the rest of the year, Flagstaff is the liveliest **nightspot** between Las Vegas and Santa Fe. Wander a block or two to either side of San Francisco Street downtown, and you can't go wrong. Besides the *Monte Vista Lounge*, hotel bars that feature live music include both the *Exchange Pub* and the upstairs *Zane Grey Ballroom* at the *Weatherford*.

Beaver Street Brewery & Whistle Stop Café
11 S Beaver St ☎928/779-0079. Popular micro-brewery that also serves inventive and inexpensive food, with an outdoor summer barbecue in the beer garden. Daily 11.30am–midnight.

Flagstaff Brewing Company 16 E I-40 ☎928/773-1442. Bustling downtown pub, with outdoor seating, big windows, and live music Wed–Sat.

The Mad Italian 101 S San Francisco St ☎928/779-1820. Highly sociable downtown bar with several pool tables.

Monte Vista Lounge *Monte Vista*, 100 N San Francisco St ☎928/779-6971. Hip little bar and dance club in the basement of a venerable old hotel, with DJs on weekdays and live music of all kinds on weekends.

The Museum Club 3404 E Route 66 ☎928/526-9434, ⓦwww.museumclub.com. A real oddity, this log-cabin taxidermy museum, popularly known as "The Zoo," somehow transmogrified into a classic Route 66 roadhouse, saloon, and country music venue that's a second home to hordes of dancing cowboys. Open daily noon–1am. Call ☎928/774-4444 for free shuttle service to and from your motel.

Around Flagstaff

The area around Flagstaff is extraordinarily rich in natural and archeological wonders, with three national monuments – **Sunset Crater**, **Wupatki**, and **Walnut Canyon** – within 25 miles, and the **San Francisco Peaks** overshadowing them all. All are generally seen as day-trips from Flagstaff; only Sunset Crater of the monuments has even a campground.

The San Francisco Peaks

The **San Francisco Volcanic Field**, north of Flagstaff, consists of around four hundred distinct volcanic cones, which have appeared over the past two million years. During that time, the region has also been covered by glacial ice on three separate occasions, shaving around three thousand feet off the top of the volcanoes.

The serrated **SAN FRANCISCO PEAKS**, visible from downtown Flagstaff, are the remnants of a single mountain; their highest point today, at 12,643 feet, is the summit of **Mount Humphreys**. They were named by Spanish missionaries in honor of St Francis of Assisi, though the Hopi already knew them as *Nuvatukya'ovi*, the home of the *kachina* spirits, and to the Navajo this was *Dook'o'ooslíid*, one of the four sacred mountains. Seen from afar, topped by a semipermanent layer of clouds, it's obvious why the Hopi and Navajo regarded them as the source of life-giving rain. Ironically, it's because they were sacred to both native groups that they now belong to neither; federal law dictates that Native American reservations can only include lands of which a tribe can prove it has "exclusive use." The Hopi in particular still make annual pilgrimages on foot from their mesas, 65 miles east, to shrines hidden in the mountains.

Around Flagstaff map showing: Grand Canyon, Cameron, Page, Valle, Grand Canyon Railway, Red Lake, Williams, Wupatki Nat. Mon., Wukoki Ruin, Wupatki Ruins, SAN FRANCISCO PEAKS, Sunset Crater Nat. Mon., Mt. Humphreys (12643ft), Arizona Snowbowl, Mt. Elden (9299ft), Sunset Crater (8100ft), Winona, Flagstaff, Walnut Canyon Nat. Mon., Winslow, OAK CREEK CANYON, Slide Rock State Park, Mormon Lake, Meteor Crater (8100ft), Verde Canyon Railroad, Sedona, Tuzigoot Nat. Mon., Clarkdale, Oak Creek, Prescott, Jerome, Cottonwood, Mingus Mtn, Montezuma Well, Montezuma Castle Nat. Mon., Camp Verde, Phoenix

Arizona Snowbowl

Considering that the San Francisco Mountain, which has not erupted for 220,000 years, is dormant rather than extinct, the time may come when the gods decide that Flagstaff's own **ski resort**, the **Arizona Snowbowl**, is a desecration no longer to be tolerated. For the moment, it survives, nestling between Mount Humphreys and Mount Agassiz at the end of a seven-mile spur road north of US-180, and featuring ski runs such as "Boo-Boo" and "Bambi." There's not enough water up here to make artificial snow – an early name for the peaks was the **Sierra Sinagua**, or "waterless range" – so the season typically runs from mid-December through early April. That may change if the Forest Service is permitted to make snow here using treated wastewater from Flagstaff's municipal sewage system; Hopi and Navajo tribal leaders consider the plan a violation of sacred lands.

The *Ski Lift Lodge* provides both food and cabin lodgings (☎928/774-0729, or 1-800/472-3599 from Ariz. and Calif. only; Mon–Thurs & Sun ❹, Fri & Sat ❺), while lift tickets cost $44 for a full day (9am–4pm) or $36 for the

afternoon. For more skiing information, call ☎928/779-1951 or visit ⓦwww
.arizonasnowbowl.com.

In summer, the longest of the Snowbowl's five chairlifts, which climbs to
within a few hundred feet of the 12,350ft summit of Mount Agassiz, remains
open as the **Scenic Skyride** (mid-May to mid-Sept daily 10am–4pm, mid-
Sept to mid-Oct Fri–Sun 10am–4pm; $10 adults, $6 under age 13). To protect
the fragile vegetation, onward hiking is prohibited, but you'll find plenty of
other day-use **trails** in these mountains, most of which are also open to mountain bikers. One switchbacks to the summit of Mount Humphreys for seventy-
mile views to the Grand Canyon and beyond.

Sunset Crater National Monument

The focus of **SUNSET CRATER VOLCANO NATIONAL MONU-
MENT**, three miles down a side road that heads east off US-89 twelve miles
north of Flagstaff, is the youngest of the San Francisco volcanoes. Its most recent
eruption, in 1065 AD, had a profound impact on the local population and economy. Thick deposits of ash for miles around opened up previously infertile land
to cultivation, accelerating – if not triggering – a land rush that threw different
Native American cultures into contact and competition for the first time.

John Wesley Powell named Sunset Crater for its multicolored cone, which
swells from a black base through reds and oranges to a yellow-tinged crest.
Unfortunately, however, its shifting cinders are too unstable to allow hikers to
climb up to the rim. Instead, the one-mile **Lava Flow Trail** at its base offers a
close-up look at the jagged black lava that streamed out across the desert, and
the steeper one-mile **Lenox Crater Trail** ascends a lesser cone nearby.

All is explained in the **visitor center** near the start of the road (daily
8am–5pm; ☎928/526-0502, ⓦwww.nps.gov/sucr) opposite the forest service's
Bonito **campground** (late May to mid-Oct; $10; ☎928/527-0866). The monu-
ment admission fee of $3 per person also covers entry to Wupatki.

Wupatki National Monument

A dozen miles north of Sunset Crater, a cluster of several distinct and exceptionally well-preserved ancient ruins, dramatically poised between the volcanoes and
the desert, jointly constitute **WUPATKI NATIONAL MONUMENT**. They
appear to testify to a period in which different tribal groups lived side by side in
harmony. At some time after the Sunset Crater eruption – though not necessarily because of it, as archeologists formerly believed – the Sinagua people already
present here, who surely witnessed the explosion, were joined by many others,
including the Ancestral Puebloans and the Hohokam. When the rich new soil
had been exhausted, around 150 years later, they all moved on once more.

Although the first of the five separate pueblo complexes you see as you
approach from Sunset Crater is Wukoki (see opposite), to get the most out of
your visit it's best to start at the monument's excellent **visitor center**, slightly
further along the highway (daily: summer 8am–7pm, winter 8am–5pm; admission $3, including Sunset Crater; ☎928/679-2365, ⓦwww.nps.gov/wupa).
This holds informative displays on the history and culture of the Sinagua and
their neighbors, placing them firmly with the context of the traditional migration story of their modern descendants, the Hopi.

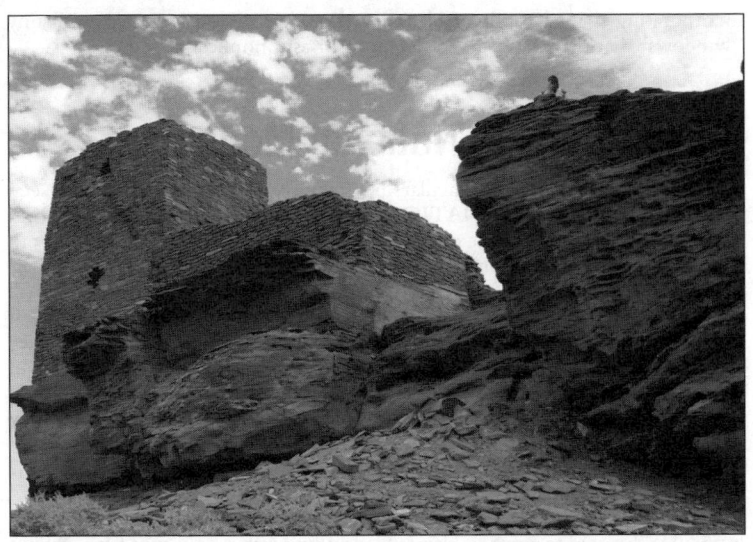

△ Wukoki Pueblo, Wupatki National Monument

A paved loop trail leads down from the visitor center to the main three-story, hundred-room pueblo block of **Wupatki** ("long cut house") itself, molded once again to a sandstone hillock and thereby concealing a number of natural caves. The site's most intriguing features, however, lie a little further along. First comes what seems to be an amphitheater, a walled circular plaza whose purpose remains unknown. Beyond it is an oval **ball court**, the northernmost such court ever found. Similar arenas throughout central America were used for a game – part ritual, part sport – in which players tried to propel a rubber ball through a stone hoop high on a wall, using their knees and elbows alone, much like modern basketball (except that the losers were sacrificed at the end). Alongside the ball court, cracks in the ground have created a natural **blow-hole**, through which air is either sucked or blown depending on pressure and temperature. The audible "breathing" of the earth made this a sacred shrine for Wupatki's ancient inhabitants.

Wukoki, which stands at the end of its own 2.5-mile spur road, takes its name from a modern Hopi word meaning "big house." Reminiscent of the castle-like structures at Hovenweep in southern Utah, it's located within sight of a procession of rounded cinder cones, but was probably positioned for its commanding prospect of the Painted Desert to the north and east. Windows in its central tower, which is molded to the contours of a red-rock outcrop, and built with bricks of the same material, look out in all directions; archeologists believe some are precisely aligned to monitor the position of the sunrise at significant moments in the annual calendar. With the Little Colorado River a full five miles distant, the pueblo's inhabitants must have been desperately short of water.

The loop road past Sunset Crater and Wupatki rejoins US-89 twenty miles south of Cameron (see p.400). Outcrops along its final few miles hold more pueblos, such as one known for obvious reasons as **The Citadel**, perched on and fully occupying a hilltop. While its interior, which appears to hold a large circular *kiva*, remains unexcavated, much of its outer wall is still standing, incorporating striped bands of black lava boulders. It too is dotted with tiny "windows" that may have served defensive or astronomical purposes.

Walnut Canyon National Monument

Another Sinagua site, as spectacular in its own way as Wupatki, can be seen at **WALNUT CANYON NATIONAL MONUMENT**, just south of I-40 ten miles east of Flagstaff. It can also be reached by driving eight miles out from downtown Flagstaff on Route 66. Between 1125 and 1250 AD, this shallow canyon was home to a thriving Sinagua community, who lived in small family groups rather than in communal pueblos. Literally hundreds of their **cliff dwellings** still nestle beneath overhangs in the sides of the canyon. They simply walled off alcoves where softer strata of rock had eroded away, and put up partitions to make separate rooms. No single dwelling is on the same scale as at Wupatki, and only a handful are accessible to visitors, but cumulatively they make for an impressive spectacle.

A large scenic window in the **visitor center** (daily: June–Aug 8am–6pm; March–May & Sept–Nov 8am–5pm; Dec–Feb 9am–5pm; $5; ☎928/526-3367, Ⓦwww.nps.gov/waca) gives an excellent overall view. **Walnut Creek** itself, long since diverted to provide Flagstaff's drinking water, now runs very dry, but you can still see how fertile this valley must have been when the Sinagua first arrived. Trees cling to the porous rock to shade the ancient dwellings, and the vegetation thickens down to a valley floor dense with black walnut and oak.

Only visitors who arrive more than an hour before closing time can set off down the mile-long **Island Loop Trail**; as the dwellings are at their most photogenic in late afternoon, that calls for careful timing. Having dropped steeply down from the visitor center, the trail crosses a narrow causeway to an isthmus of rock high above a gooseneck of the creek. Once there, you can go inside a few Sinagua homes; note the T-shaped doorways, which could only be entered headfirst, and the ceilings blackened by the smoke of generations of fires. Petroglyphs have been found in the other ruins visible on all sides, but none remains on the trail.

The main purpose of the separate **Rim Trail**, which follows the edge of the canyon, is to provide a less strenuous walk. It leads to a picnic area and to some surface ruins (in the dissimilar pueblo style, consisting of large clusters of rooms), though you could keep going to turn this into a lengthy hike. There is no accommodation, and only minimal snack food available at the canyon.

Between June and August each year, rangers lead two- to three-hour **guided hikes** to lesser-known and otherwise inaccessible sites within the monument (Tues, Sat & Sun at 10am; call to confirm).

South of Flagstaff

US-89A threads its way south from Flagstaff down **Oak Creek Canyon** to emerge after 28 miles at **Sedona**, on the threshold of the extraordinary **Red**

Rock Country. Up from the valley rise giant mesas and buttes of stark red sandstone, where Zane Grey set a number of his Wild West adventures. The boom-and-bust mining town of **Jerome** looks down from a mountainside to the south. Hwy 260 links both US-89A and I-17 and the haunting Sinagua ruins of **Tuzigoot** and **Montezuma Castle**.

Oak Creek Canyon

Local claims that **OAK CREEK CANYON**, the largest of several slender chasms that cut into the 2000ft escarpment of the **Mogollon Rim**, is a serious rival to the Grand Canyon are somewhat exaggerated. However, you *can* drive right through it, and with its sheer walls striped in vivid horizontal bands of color, its sparkling streams and densely wooded glens, and its facilities for camping, eating, and general playing around, this would be an unmissable attraction anywhere else in the world.

Lookout Point, its northern end, appears suddenly a dozen forested miles south of Flagstaff on US-89A. Native American craft stalls surround the parking lot, and several overlooks within easy walking distance command prospects of the narrow gorge below. The road then switchbacks sharply down to run alongside **Oak Creek** itself. The lowest level in the rocks to either side, often obscured by maples, cedars, oaks, and pine, is the bright-red Supai sandstone. Above that, layers of white sandstone, buff limestone, and finally black basalt testify to a geological history which has fluctuated from harsh desert to sea bottom. Temperatures are cool enough to make fishing, picnicking, and hiking expeditions welcome escapes.

Seven miles before Hwy-89A reaches Sedona, **Slide Rock State Park** is a natural water chute, where you can swim and slide across smooth boulders set in the river bed (daily: March to mid-May 8am–6pm; mid-May to mid-Oct 8am–7pm; mid-Oct to Feb 8am–5pm; ⓦwww.azstateparks.com; $8 per vehicle in winter, $10 in summer). The absence of still water in Oak Creek means that it's almost insect-free.

Practicalities

The canyon floor is quite narrow and has been heavily developed with leisure facilities, though at least careful landscaping makes most of these inconspicuous. The loveliest place to **stay** of all has to be a cabin at *Garland's Oak Creek Lodge*, reached by crossing a small ford in the river half a mile north of Slide Rock (April to mid-Nov; closed Sun; ☎928/282-3343, ⓦwww.garlandslodge .com; ❽). Rates include breakfast and dinner in the top-quality dining room. More affordable, and more likely to be available, are the well-equipped log huts at *Don Hoel's Cabins*, a couple of miles further north (☎928/282-3560 or 1-800/292-4635, ⓦwww.hoels.com; ❻). **Campgrounds** at river and road level include *Pine Flat* (reservations ☎1-877/444-6777, ⓦwww.reserveusa.com), and the first-come, first-served *Bootlegger* (both mid-May to Sept; $16).

Sedona

There's no disputing the fact that the New Age resort of **SEDONA** enjoys a magnificent setting, amid some definitive Southwestern canyon scenery. Sadly,

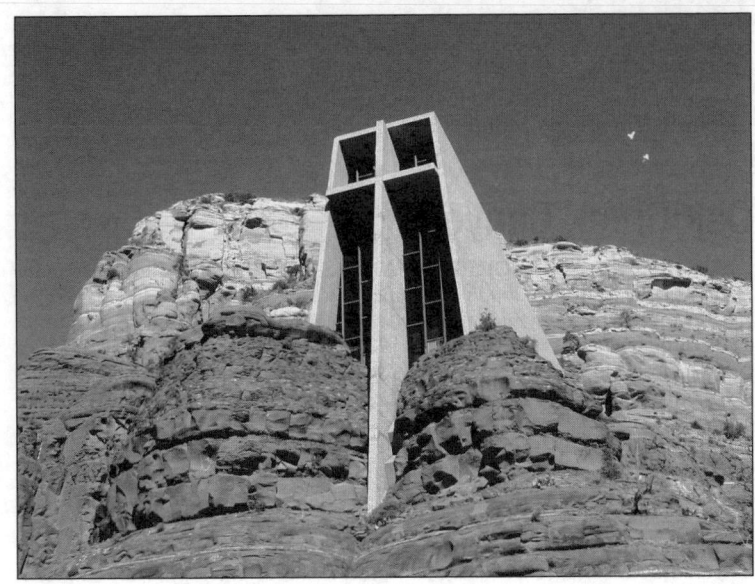

△ Shrine of the Red Rocks, Sedona

however, the town itself adds nothing to the beauty of its surroundings. In fact, it's a real mess, with several miles of ugly red-brick sprawl interrupted by the occasional mock-historical mall monstrosity. Some visitors, particularly Europeans, experience a strong negative reaction, feeling the landscape has been sullied by over-development. Many American travelers, on the other hand, absolutely love it for its combination of luxurious accommodations and fancy restaurants, and its almost limitless opportunities for active outdoor vacationing. In particular, artists, healers, and wealthy retirees have flocked here in the last few decades, hailing it as "the next Santa Fe." Whether you love it or hate it may depend on whether you share their wide-eyed awe for angels, crystals, and all matters mystical – and whether you're prepared to pay over-the-odds prices for the privilege of joining them. Whatever your attitude, Sedona is still a fascinating place to visit, where even the most hard-nosed commercial operation can seem a front for the real business of holding earnest conversations about the state of each other's psyches. Established in 1902 by Theodore Schnebly and named after his wife, Sedona remained a small farming settlement for most of the twentieth century, unmarked on most maps. German surrealist painter **Max Ernst** moved here in the 1940s – the bizarre backdrops of his later canvases seem less surreal once you've seen where they were painted – and Hollywood moviemakers filmed in the area from the 1950s onwards. Elvis Presley came here to shoot his 27th movie, *Stay Away Joe*, in 1967. Sedona's big break came in 1981, however, when Page Bryant, author and psychic, "channeled" the information that Sedona is in fact "the heart *chakra* of the planet." Since pinpointing her first **vortex** – a point at which, it is claimed, psychic and electromagnetic energies can be channeled for personal and planetary harmony – the town has achieved its own personal growth and blossomed as a focus for New Age practitioners of all kinds. Huge crowds came to Sedona in 1987 for the "Harmonic Convergence," paying up to $75 for a seat on Bell Rock at the time when it was

SEDONA

Boynton Canyon ▲

Oak Creek Canyon & Flagstaff ▲

N

CEDAR ST.

89A

JORDAN ROAD

VANDREN ROAD

APPLE AVE.

Ⓐ

Ⓑ

Ⓒ

Sedona Arts Center
'The Barn'

ANDANTE DRIVE

HARMONY DRIVE

MOUNTAIN SHADOWS DRIVE

POSSE GROUND ROAD

SUNSET PASS RD

GODKNIN LN

COFFEEPOT DR

DRY CREEK ROAD

SOUTHWEST DR.

The 'Y'

①

ⓘ

Ⓓ

SCHNEBLY HILL RD

WHITE BEAR RD

Ⓕ

②

⑥

④

⑤

③

Ⓔ

KALLOF PL

NORTHVIEW RD

VIEW DRIVE

Tlaquepaque
Shopping Center

⑦

BRISTLECONE PINES RD

ARROYO PINON DR

THUNDERBIRD DR.

SHELBY STREET

SUNSET DRIVE

BREWER ROAD

FOOTHILLS DR.

AIRPORT ROAD

RACQUE RD

89A

Jerome ◄

✈ Sedona
Airport

Oak Creek

179

CHAPEL ROAD

Chapel of the
Holy Cross
✚

Phoenix ▼

RED ROCK LOOP ROAD

0   800 yds

ACCOMMODATION
Best Western Arroyo Roble Motel	**B**
L'Auberge de Sedona	**D**
Los Abrogados Lodge	**C**
Matterhorn Lodge	**A**
Quality Inn King's Ransom	**F**
Sedona Motel	**E**

CAFÉS & RESTAURANTS
Coffee Pot Restaurant	**2**
Dahl & Diluca	**5**
El Rincon	**7**
Fournos	**6**
Heartline	**3**
Mago Cafe	**1**
Thai Spices	**4**

supposed to launch itself to the galaxy of Andromeda. (Dissatisfied customers are said to have included one gentleman who brought his mouth organ, under the impression that it was a harmonica convergence.)

Arrival and information

Sedona is 28 miles south of Flagstaff on Hwy-89A and 120 miles north of Phoenix. It centers on the intersection known as the "**Y**," above Oak Creek, where Hwy-89A branches southwest toward Cottonwood and Prescott, and Hwy-179 continues by way of the village of Oak Creek to meet I-17, fourteen miles south. This road system is utterly unable to cope with the current level of visitation, incidentally; expect bumper-to-bumper traffic on weekends.

Just north of the "Y," in the area known as **uptown** – the one part of Sedona where the stores and businesses are close enough together to make walking a possibility – the **visitor center**, at Hwy-89A and Forest Road, has full listings of lodgings and tour operators (Mon–Sat 8.30am–5pm, Sun 9am–3pm; ☎928/282-7722 or 1-800/288-7336; Ⓦwww.visitsedona.com or Ⓦwww.sedonachamber.com).

The Sedona–Phoenix Shuttle (☎928/282-2066 or 1-800/448-7988 in AZ, Ⓦwww.sedona-phoenix-shuttle.com), an eight-daily **bus** service between Sedona and Phoenix Airport, costs $45 one way.

For a quick overview of the area, pick up either of the two different 55-minute **tours** run by the Sedona Trolley (daily 10am–5pm; hourly tours, $10; ☎928/282-5400, Ⓦwww.sedonatrolley.com) at the visitor center. Companies that rent **bikes** include Bike & Bean, 6020 Hwy-179 (☎928/284-0210, Ⓦwww.bike-bean.com), which has its own espresso bar. Sedona Jeep and Car Rentals (☎928/282-8700, Ⓦwww.sedonajeeprentals.com), can provide **4WD** vehicles.

Accommodation

Sedona is an expensive place to **stay**, and apart from the immediate area of the "Y," it's too spread out to walk around in the evening. It no longer has a hostel, so if you're watching your budget, you can get better deals nearby at Cottonwood, Jerome, and Camp Verde (see pp.344, 346, & 348); if you don't mind spending well over $100, however, Sedona has some extremely fancy options, including around twenty upscale **B&Bs** and several full-service **resorts**. **Agencies** specializing in local accommodations include Sedona Central Reservations (☎928/282-1518 or 1-800/445-4128, Ⓦwww.sedonacentralreservations.com) and Sedona B&B Guild (☎928/204-1942 or 1-800/915-4442, Ⓦwww.bbsedona.net).

Best Western Arroyo Roble Motel 400 N US-89A ☎928/282-4001 or 1-800/773-3662, Ⓦwww.bestwesternsedona.com. This comfortable multi-tiered motel, stacked up above Oak Creek not far north of uptown Sedona, has recently added a separate deluxe wing, Arroyo Roble North. Winter ❺, summer ❻

The Canyon Wren 6425 N US-89A ☎928/282-6900 or 1-800/437-9736, Ⓦwww.canyonwrencabins.com. Individual two-person cabins, each with a whirlpool tub, six miles north of Sedona in Oak Creek Canyon. ❼

Cathedral Rock Lodge 61 W Los Amigos Lane ☎928/282-7608 or 1-800/352-9149,

Ⓦwww.cathedralrocklodge.com. Small, friendly B&B-cum-New-Age retreat in spacious grounds on the Red Rock Loop Road, with two double rooms, a suite, and a separate cabin – and a resident reiki practitioner. ❼

Cozy Cactus B&B 80 Canyon Circle Drive ☎928/284-0082 or 1-800/788-2082, Ⓦwww.cozycactus.com. Ranch house B&B at the edge of the woods near the foot of Castle Rock, offering five themed, en-suite double rooms. ❼–❾

Enchantment Resort 525 Boynton Canyon Rd ☎928/282-2900 or 1-800/826-4180, Ⓦwww.enchantmentresort.com. Extremely luxurious resort, equipped with four pools and seven tennis courts, that has taken over ravishing Boynton Canyon eight miles west of town. Accommodation is in fully equipped one- and two-bedroom adobe *casitas*. ⑨

L'Auberge de Sedona 301 L'Auberge Lane ☎928/282-1661 or 1-800/272-6777, ⊛www.lauberge.com. Plush two-part resort in the heart of the town, with fancy if somewhat incongruous French-themed motel rooms at road level looking out onto the red rocks, and a cable-car connection to the individual guest cottages ranged along the tranquil banks of Oak Creek below. ⑦–⑧

Los Abrigados Lodge 270 N US-89A ☎928/282-7125 or 1-800/695-4161, ⊛www.ilxresorts.com. Freshly renovated, central motel just north of the "Y," which offers some of the best-value rooms in town – not amazingly well equipped, but perfectly adequate, and offering good views. ⑤

Matterhorn Inn 230 Apple Ave ☎928/282-7176 or 1-800/372-8207, ⊛www.matterhorninn.com. Central motel, on the right as you come into town on Hwy-89A from the north, with two tiers of rooms that face across to the red rocks. Winter ④, summer ⑤

Quality Inn King's Ransom 771 Hwy-179 ☎928/282-7151 or 1-800/228-5151, ⊛www.sedona.net/hotel/ransom. Predictable upper-range motel, a mile or so south of town, with rather small rooms – most with balconies – but a nice garden and a reasonable restaurant. Winter ④, summer ⑤

Sedona Motel 218 Hwy-179 ☎928/282-7187. Small motel, amazingly inexpensive by local standards, in an ideal and attractive location close to the "Y" uptown. ④

Exploring Sedona

Sedona itself has little to detain sightseers, though strolling the two or so blocks that count as **uptown**, just north of the "Y," is pleasant enough. Even above the roar of the traffic, you can usually still hear the synchronized chirruping of the crickets in **Oak Creek** down below, while your eyes are repeatedly drawn to the superb red rocks that tower above the banal buildings along Hwy-89A. A little way south of the "Y," on Hwy-179, **Tlaquepaque Shopping Center** is a very upscale mall, modeled on a Mexican village near Guadalajara, that offers Sedona's most distinctive (and expensive) shopping.

The prevailing pay-no-taxes ethos of Sedona's ardent libertarians has ensured that few of the side roads off the main highways are paved. That dovetails neatly, of course, with the booming business in off-road tours, as listed on p.342. Nonetheless, a lot of the best scenery is visible from the highway, and in any case many of the jeep roads are perfectly passable in ordinary vehicles. So long as you're happy to remain in ignorance as to which rocks are really electromagnetic tuning forks vibrating in harmony with Alpha Centauri, there's no great need to take a commercial tour.

The major problem is **parking**. The National Forest Service requires anyone parking in the forests around Sedona – which means anyone using the majority of roadside pullouts in the vicinity, even for the briefest of halts – to buy a **Red Rock Pass**, which costs $5 for a day, $15 for a week, or $20 for a year. The passes are sold in local visitor centers, stores, motels and B&Bs, and also by vending machines in several parking lots. Golden Age, Golden Access, and Golden Eagle passes (see p.45) are accepted in lieu of a Red Rock Pass; if you have a National Parks Pass, you can buy a $15 hologram upgrade. Just to complicate matters further, four popular scenic spots – Banjo Bill, Grasshopper Point, Red Rock Crossing (site of Crescent Moon Ranch), and Call O' The Canyon (trailhead for the West Fork Trail) – are on private land, and charge their own fees of up to $7, but it is possible to buy a Red Rock Grand Pass for $40 that includes those areas as well.

The closest **vortex** to town is on **Airport Mesa**. Turn left up Airport Road from Hwy-89A as you head west, about a mile past the "Y," and the vortex is at the junction of the second and third peaks, just after the cattle grid. Further up, beyond the precarious airport, the **Shrine of the Red Rocks** looks out across the entire valley.

Dozens of Sedona-based operators compete to offer close encounters with Red Rock Country. The most popular option is a **jeep tour**, but you can also take scenic **flights** – in balloons, airplanes, or helicopters – ride on **horseback**, or trek with a llama. There's also a choice between a traditional tour, on which you'll see formations such as "Snoopy" and "Garfield," and a New Age **vision quest**, in which the same rock may be a "sacred energy area" or a "beacon vortex." Some guides even eschew vehicles altogether, in favor of taking you on a **spiritual journey** instead.

Arizona Helicopter Adventures ☏928/282-0904 or 1-800/282-5141, ⓦwww .arizonahelicopteradventures.com. Chopper flights, from the 12min Red Rock RoundUp ($38) to the 30min Sedona Deluxe ($138).

Earth Wisdom Jeep Tours ☏928/282-4714 or 1-800/482-4714, ⓦwww .earthwisdomtours.com. Choose either sightseeing or insighting – "more than ordinary tours, these are journeys . . . in the way of our Native American friends . . . learn of the ancestral secrets of the Medicine Wheel" – for $48 up to $125.

Legends of Sedona Ranch ☏928/282-6826 or 1-800/848-7728. "Where horses are free . . . but rides ain't"; 1hr $54, 2hr $75.

Mystic Tours with Rahelio ☏928/282-6735, ⓦwww.rahelio.com. Since he "received guidance from the Star people," Rahelio has been offering "vortex empowerments" at $50 for 2hr, $70 for 3hr.

Northern Light Balloon Expeditions ☏928/282-2274 or 1-800/230-6222, ⓦwww .northernlightballoon.com. Relatively unspiritual balloon trips from $180, with champagne picnics.

Pink Jeep Tours (☏928/282-5000 or 1-800/873-3662, ⓦwww.pinkjeep.com). You can't miss this lot in uptown Sedona. Quite exceptionally garish "4-wheelin' vehicles" crunch around in off-road tours lasting 1hr 30min up to 4hr, at $45 to $102 per person.

Red Rock Biplane Tours ☏928/204-5939 or 1-888/866-7433, ⓦwww.sedonaairtours .com. Quick flights over Sedona in an open-cockpit biplane. 20min for $89, longer tours by arrangement.

Sedona Heart Center ☏928/282-2733 or 1-800/943-3266, ⓦwww.sedonaretreats .com. Tour the vortex sites; "use the earth energies for personal transformation." 3hr tour $75, 5hr with lunch $130.

Sedona Red Rock Jeep Tours ☏928/282-6826 or 1-800/848-7728, ⓦwww .redrockjeep.com. Jeep trips from 1hr ($39) up to the 3hr 30min Ultimate ($99). Not only do you get to bomb around the desert, you can "focus on the need to offer love and healing to our earth, as well as each other," and participate in a traditional "smudging" ceremony. Also horseback and hiking tours.

Sedona Spirit Journeys ☏928/282-8966 or 1-866/982-8966, ⓦwww .sedonaspiritjourneys.com. Share time at a vortex with a reiki master; 3hr for $75.

Spirit Steps ☏928/282-4562 or 1-800/728-4562, ⓦwww.spiritsteps.com. "Join other provocative pilgrims from around the world" for drumming ceremonies ($20 per hour) or the Cosmic Wheel of Destiny (up to $90 including vortex tour).

Touch the Southwest ☏928/213-9085 or 1-888/244-5256, ⓦwww.touchthesouthwest .com. "Luxury Wilderness Experiences" with gourmet picnic lunches from $250, both in the immediate vicinity and as far afield as Monument Valley.

Trail Horse Adventures ☏928/282-7252 or 1-800/723-3538, ⓦwww.trailhorseadven tures.com. Horseback trips, largely geared around eating (in traditional cowboy style); 3hr rides in the vicinity of Red Rock State Park for $110, full-day rides for $205, and multi-day customized expeditions at $315 per day.

Three and four miles further along Hwy-89A, two successive turnings to the left mark the Upper and Lower sections of the seven-mile **Red Rock Loop Road**, all of which is paved barring a bumpy but not too difficult mile or so in the middle. Its prime attraction is reached via a spur road a couple of miles down Lower Red Rock Loop Road. **Red Rock State Park** (daily: summer 8am–6pm; winter 8am–5pm; ⓦ www.azstateparks.com; $6 per vehicle or $1 per person) may be the obvious name for a park in the Sedona area, but it's not in fact the best place to see red rocks. Instead it preserves a sweeping curve of **Oak Creek**, both of whose banks at this point used to belong to a private ranch. The riparian environment thus survives reasonably intact – its flora and fauna are explained in the prominent, well-equipped **visitor center** (same hours), which holds stuffed hawks and owls and some live fish in tanks – and can be explored on an assortment of short trails. Two miles from the highway on Upper Red Rock Loop Road, the site known as **Red Rock Crossing** is a small picnic area beside a picturesque ford in Oak Creek that has featured in many movies (daily 9am–8pm; $5 winter, $7 summer). **Cathedral Rock**, which stands on the far side of the stream and used to be called Courthouse Rock, is another vortex.

Dry Creek Road, which heads north off Hwy-89 a mile closer to town, runs north past **Capitol Butte** to reach **Boynton Canyon**. The presence of the lavish *Enchantment Resort* has spoiled some of the magic of Boynton Canyon itself – which has its own vortex – but several neighboring canyons are still perfect for short desert hikes. The resort office can provide trail maps showing the locations of Sinagua ruins in **Red Canyon**, or point the way to **Doe Mesa** or **Loy Butte Canyon**, both of which offer great views of the whole Sedona valley.

South from the "Y," Hwy-179 is soon barreling through the Coconino National Forest. Turn left as soon as you cross Oak Creek, onto the unpaved **Schnebly Hill Road**, to enjoy the area's most spectacular scenic drive. In summer, the road remains open all the way to I-17, twelve rough miles east. Alternatively, continue south for three miles and then take Chapel Road to the left, which soon brings you to the **Chapel of the Holy Cross**. This tall and very narrow concrete chapel, whose facade is shaped like a massive cross, is squeezed into a cleft in the red cliffs (daily 9am–5pm). Another two miles down the highway, **Bell Rock**, on the east as you enter the village of Oak Creek, is Sedona's fourth major vortex.

Eating

Sedona is bursting with expensive Southwestern-style **restaurants**, not all of which are particularly good, and still has a smattering of old-fashioned diners. There's a shortage of places where you can just sit and watch the world go by over a coffee and a sandwich; most of its cafés are twee little places intended mainly to entice tourists into pastel-trimmed gift stores.

Coffee Pot Restaurant 2050 W Hwy-89A ⓣ928/282-6626. Sedona's largest, oldest diner – named for a nearby rock formation – open daily from 6am until late, has a sports lounge, a hundred kinds of omelets, and all the burgers, Mexican dishes, and fried specials you could hope for.

Dahl and DiLuca 2321 W Hwy-89A ⓣ928/282-5219. Northern Italian food served in a romantic mock-up of a Tuscan villa; entrées can cost as much as $27, but you can dine well for much less. Dinner only, daily 5–9.30pm.

El Rincon Tlaquepaque Shopping Center, Hwy-179 ⓣ928/282-4648. Authentic Mexican food in classy surroundings, with entrées costing up to $19 and indoor and outdoor seating. Mon & Sun 11am –5pm, Tues–Sat 11am–9pm.

Fournos 3000 W Hwy-89A ⓣ928/282-3331. Lovely little Greek restaurant, offering traditional dishes with all the right ingredients – feta cheese,

kalamata olives and so on. Open Thurs–Sat, when dinner is served at 6pm & 8pm, and Sun for brunch at noon; reservations required, no credit cards.
Heartline 1610 W Hwy-89A ☎928/282-0785. Tasteful white-table-linen restaurant, with an attractive garden courtyard, that serves determinedly healthy – though not exclusively vegetarian – Southwestern cuisine. Open for lunch daily except Tues & Wed, and dinner daily.
Mago Cafe 207A N Hwy-89A ☎928/204-1600. Very central coffeehouse, near the visitor center and above the *Worm* bookstore, serving organic coffee and oriental teas, and wholesome meals like tomato gnocchi or steamed dumplings as well as juices and pastries, to be enjoyed on a pleasant terrace. Summer daily 8am–8pm, winter daily 8am–6pm.

Thai Spices 2986 W Hwy-89A ☎928/282-0599. West of downtown, near the road out to Boynton Canyon; tasty, healthy Thai food, with meat or seafood green or red curries or pad thai noodles for under $10, plus vegetarian and even macrobiotic choices. Open for dinner daily, plus lunch on weekdays.
Yavapai Restaurant *Enchantment Resort*, 525 Boynton Canyon Rd ☎928/204-6000. Showcase resort restaurant, serving top-class Southwestern cuisine at up to $40 per entrée; plenty of beans and chile to go with the freshest meats and fish. Open Mon–Sat for all meals, Sun brunch only, 10.20am–2.30pm.

Cottonwood

Describing **COTTONWOOD**, eighteen miles southwest of Sedona in the heart of the Verde Valley, the 1930s WPA guide to Arizona wrote, "Familiar figures in the town are the cowboys from the range and the prospector or 'desert rat' who wanders in from his camp in the mountains to break the monotony of his lonely life." Today's Cottonwood is not nearly so romantic, though it has grown much larger thanks to an influx of retirees. It's not really even the same place, as the former downtown is stranded a couple of miles north of Hwy-89A, now lined by modern strip development.

Cottonwood does, however, make an inexpensive base for trips to Sedona and Jerome, and its old main street still possesses a certain charm. Tucked around a flower-filled courtyard, the *Sundial Motel*, 1034 N Main St (☎928/634-8031; ❷), is a pretty – albeit pretty basic – old-style motel, while latterday desert rats break the monotony with a coffee or snack at the friendly *Old Town Cafe* nearby, housed in a small gallery at 1025A N Main St (closed Mon; ☎928/634-5980). If you prefer dependable chain lodgings, the *Best Western Cottonwood Inn* is on Hwy-89A at 993 S Main St (☎928/634-5575 or 1-800/350-0025; ⓦwww .bestwesterncottonwoodinn.com; winter ❸, summer ❹).

Tuzigoot National Monument

At the start of the fourteenth century, the Verde Valley held around fifty major pueblo sites, occupied by the ancient native American people now known as the **Sinagua**. One of the largest, which now constitutes **TUZIGOOT NATIONAL MONUMENT**, perches on a hillock across the Verde River from **Clarkdale**, three miles northwest of Cottonwood.

The ground floor alone had 86 rooms and shows signs of repeated additions; with fifteen more rooms on the upper level, it may have been home to some 225 people. Some archeologists think it was a final enclave, where the Sinagua gathered against encroaching drought before abandoning the area early in the fifteenth century. Artifacts at the **visitor center**, where you pay your entrance fee (daily: summer 8am–6pm, winter 8am–5pm; $3; ☎928/634-5564, ⓦwww .nps.gov/tuzi), include turquoise mosaics and shell jewelry.

Unfortunately, Tuzigoot is one of the least satisfying such sites in the Southwest. When it was restored as part of a 1930s make-work program, a little too much work was done, and its authenticity was all but destroyed by laying a broad cement trail over, across, and through the pueblo. Furthermore, while the river, lined with cottonwoods, still flows past the pueblo, the "fields" below are just a sickly orange mass of tailings from the nearby copper mines.

Verde Canyon Railroad

Although Clarkdale itself is an unremarkable little place, it does serve as the starting point for Arizona's most scenic vintage **train ride**. The **Verde Canyon Railroad** operates 25-mile round-trip excursions year-round, along the otherwise inaccessible Verde Canyon as far as Perkinsville, with plenty of dramatic red-rock scenery and archeological ruins en route. Call ahead for precise schedules, and note that the actual trains are powered by diesel engines, not steam ($55, ages 2–12 $35; ☎928/639-0010 or 1-800/293-7245, ⓦwww.verdecanyonrr.com).

Jerome

The former mining town of **JEROME**, once the fourth largest community in Arizona, stands high above the Verde Valley on Hwy-89A. It's conspicuous from quite a distance; not only is an enormous letter "J" etched deep into the hillside above it, but a large chunk of that hillside is missing altogether, having been blown apart for **opencast copper mining**. This land abounds in mineral wealth – thick veins of copper are interspersed with gold and silver, and an endless supply of limestone is still extracted for cement – but serious exploitation only started in 1876. The **United Verde** mine was partly financed by New Yorker Eugene Jerome (a cousin of Winston Churchill's mother, Jennie Jerome), who insisted that the new town bear his name. The United Verde has been called "the richest mine ever owned by an individual"; it made William Clark $100 million, and by 1953 had produced enough copper to give a thirteen-pound lump to every person on earth. Until the tortuous highway was built, the only way up to Jerome was the rail line that corkscrewed down from the mine to the world's largest copper smelter, at Clarkdale.

With its disproportionate population of young males, Jerome was known as a hard-drinking, hard-living town. The young **Pancho Villa** started out in life by supplying its drinking water, using a relay of two hundred burros, and for a brief period the International Workers of the World (the "**Wobblies**") were a strong presence; several hundred miners and "outside agitators" were literally railroaded out of town in July 1917 and dumped unceremoniously in the remote deserts of southwest Arizona.

Harsh economic realities have always determined local fortunes. Plenty of copper remains in the earth; although the Depression hit hard, the mine was only closed in the early 1950s, when cheap imported copper made it uneconomic to continue, and there's every possibility that as prices rise, it will reopen. To keep the mineral rights from reverting to the state, the present owners are obliged to keep on researching and prospecting; in fact, they do more than they have to, and reportedly find enough gold to cover their expenses.

As recently as the 1970s, Jerome was a **ghost town** in which it was possible to turn up and move into an empty house. Many of those who did so are still here, making a living from arts and crafts, and the town itself has made a dramatic recovery. The fact that it's now solely geared towards the needs of visitors makes it something of a tourist trap, but is nonetheless fascinating to explore.

Arrival and information

On paper, Hwy-89A is a direct through route between **Sedona**, thirty miles northeast of Jerome, and **Prescott**, thirty miles southwest, but the formidable **Mingus Mountain** makes reaching Jerome a slow business. Coming from Cottonwood, it's a painstaking switchback climb; if you approach from Prescott, you're descending into Jerome, with gorgeous views of the valley spread out below.

Hwy-89A branches in two in the heart of town, where a one-way system takes westbound traffic along **Hull Avenue** and eastbound along **Main Street**. The local **visitor center** is at 310 N Hull Ave (Mon–Fri 10am–4pm, Sat & Sun 11am–3pm; ☎928/634-2900, ⓦ www.jeromechamber.com), and there's also a **cybercafé**, the *Reynard*, at 115 Jerome Ave (summer daily 7am–3pm, winter Mon & Tues 7am–2pm, Sat & Sun 7am–3pm; ☎928/634-3230, ⓦ www.cafe-reynard.com), which sells snacks and sandwiches.

Accommodation

There's no room to build **motels** on Jerome's uncertain slopes, so accommodation is restricted to a couple of turn-of-the-century hotels and a few former homes that have been converted into **B&Bs**.

Connor Hotel 164 Main St ☎928/634-5006 or 1-800/523-3554, ⓦ www.connorhotel.com. Small central hotel, offering twelve attractive antique-furnished rooms, each with a tasteful tiled private bathroom, above the *Spirit Room* bar, which gets busy on weekends. ❺

Ghost City Inn 541 N Main St ☎928/634-4678 or 1-888/634-4678, ⓦ www.ghostcityinn.com. Century-old house, at the entrance to town as you come up from Cottonwood, with huge views from its wooden verandah. Each of the six guest rooms has a different theme; some are resolutely Western, others more flowery, but all have en-suite bathrooms. ❺–❻

Mile High Inn & Grill 309 N Main St ☎928/634-5094 or 1-800/634-5094, ⓦ www.innatjerome .com. B&B hotel in the heart of town, where each of the seven rooms has a different theme, ranging from French provincial to Victorian to "Lariat and Lace." All but two rooms have en-suite facilities. The adjoining *Grill* serves simple meals. ❹

Jerome Grand Hotel 200 Hill St ☎928/634-8200 or 1-888/817-6788, ⓦ www.jeromegrandhotel .com. Restored Spanish Mission hotel, housed in a former hospital that spills down five stories from the highest point in town; the views are fabulous, but the accommodation merely evokes bygone days rather than being particularly luxurious. There's also a good on-site restaurant; see opposite. ❻

Surgeon's House B&B 101 Hill St ☎928/639-1452 or 1-800/639-1452, ⓦ www.surgeonshouse .com. Smart, upmarket B&B, set in lovely gardens and enjoying dramatic views from the top of town; four plush, en-suite rooms. ❻–❼

The Town

Thanks to the steep angle of the hillside, Jerome's streets are effectively stacked one on top of the other, and its stone houses – it was far too expensive to haul timber up here – tend to have two stories at the front and four or five at the back. Under the repeated concussion of over two hundred miles of tunnels being blasted into the mountainside, the whole town used to slip downhill at the rate of five inches per year; the **Sliding Jail** on Hull Avenue came to rest 225 feet from where it was built (it's still there, but it's not open to the public).

Built for mine owner "Rawhide Jimmy" Douglas in 1917, the **Douglas Mansion**, on Mine Museum Road below town, is now open as **Jerome State Historic Park** (daily 8am–5pm; $3). Given the sweeping views over the valley, it can be hard to concentrate on the displays that detail the history and workings of the mines and the lifestyles of the bosses.

Up in town, the **Mine Museum** is housed beneath the pressed-tin ceiling of the former *Fashion Saloon* at 200 N Main St (daily 9am–4.30pm; $2). Its amateurish but enjoyable collection of oddities include paintings that record different eras in mining, a chicken-wire stretcher once used for accident victims, and the primitive calculator used to calculate the United Verde Copper Company's payroll.

Many of the **shops** only stock souvenirs, but there are some interesting **crafts** showrooms around, such as the Knapp Gallery at 408 Lower Main Street, and Made in Jerome Pottery, higher up opposite the post office. The Jerome Artists Cooperative Gallery at 502 Lower Main Street is a very mixed bag of all the town has to offer, with some real bargain prices, while the House of Joy, 416 Hull Avenue, entertainingly specializes in relics of bordellos, brothels and all matters burlesque.

Eating and drinking

Day-trippers tend to fill Jerome's tearooms and snackbars at lunchtime – especially on weekends – but come the evening you can still get a faint sense of its riproaring past.

The Asylum *Jerome Grand Hotel*, 200 Hill St ☎ 928/639-3197, ⓦ www.theasylum.biz. Jokey, "fun" restaurant that makes the most of its dramatic, quirky setting in a former hospital, but nonetheless serves excellent Southwestern cuisine. All that plus a fabulous wine list and astonishing views – what more could you ask for? Dinner entrees range $18–28; lunch salads and sandwiches cost more like $10. Daily 11am–3pm & 5–9pm.

English Kitchen 119 Jerome Ave ☎ 928/634-2132. Built in 1899, this claims to be Arizona's oldest restaurant. Under Chinese ownership, it was an opium den; later the Wobblies held meetings downstairs. Now it's open for breakfast and lunch Tues–Sun, with salads and sandwiches for under $10, and its terrace offers a commanding view of the valley.

Flatiron Cafe 416 N Main St ☎ 928/634-2733. Small, friendly joint where the town's two one-way roads meet. Espresso coffees, scrambled-egg breakfasts, and fancy salad-and-sandwich lunches for around $7. Mon, Tues & Fri–Sun 8.30am–3pm, Wed & Thurs 8.30am–11.30am.

Jerome Brewery 111 N Main St ☎ 928/634-8477. Busy microbrewery that serves inexpensive pizzas and deli sandwiches in addition to home-brewed beer and espresso coffee.

Paul & Jerry's Saloon 206 N Main St ☎ 928/634-2603. Old-style saloon dating from 1889, with glorious ornate pool tables and a fine old bar with period trimmings. Open daily.

Spirit Room *Connor Hotel*, 164 Main St ☎ 928/634-5006. Large, very atmospheric old saloon below a restored hotel, which puts on live music on weekends and Scrabble on Wednesdays.

Montezuma Castle National Monument

Toward the east end of the Verde Valley, two dramatic ancient sites jointly constitute **MONTEZUMA CASTLE NATIONAL MONUMENT**. Roughly five miles apart, each now stands a short way east of I-17, around forty miles south of Flagstaff and twenty miles southeast of Sedona.

The northernmost of the two, **Montezuma Well**, is a natural lake that measures 368 feet across by 55 feet deep. Set like a volcanic crater into a small hill, it was formed when the roof of an underground cave collapsed 11,000 years ago. It's still fed by a spring that produces a phenomenal 1.9 million gallons of warm water per day, naturally heated to a constant 75°F. You can't wade in but there is a rough path next to it.

Not surprisingly, the well was sacred to Native Americans; the **Yavapai** people (see p.392) say that this was where they emerged into the world. The **Hohokam** are thought to have moved here around 600 AD and were the first to divert its water for irrigation, while the **Sinagua** replaced them in 1125 AD. Traces of ruined Sinagua pueblos can be discerned on the hilltop, reached by a five-minute walk from the parking lot, and a more complete **cliff dwelling** is set into the inner crater wall. It's now inaccessible, though you get a good view from the foot of the staircase that leads down to the lakeside. A couple more dwellings stand at ground level here, next to the hole or "swallet" through which the water spills out of the lake and flows through the hillside to join Beaver Creek outside. No fee is charged to visitors.

Five miles south in an idyllic setting above Beaver Creek, **Montezuma Castle** itself is a superbly preserved Sinagua **cliff dwelling** from the same era. Filling an alcove in the hillside with a wall of pink adobe and originally reached by three separate ladders from the valley floor, its five stories taper up to fit the contours of the rock. Apparently, the sycamore beams are still in place, and the fingerprints of the masons are still visible on the bricks, but visitors are not permitted to climb up.

The ruins of a much larger, though now much less photogenic, dwelling "next door" were exposed to view by a fire in about 1400 AD. Once again you can't go inside, but the exposed honeycomb of holes in the limestone rock show that it had around 45 rooms, as well as little "cupboards" recessed into the walls. It may have housed as many as a hundred people, as opposed to thirty or so in the castle.

Displays on the Sinagua in the **visitor center** at the castle, where you pay your entry fee (daily: summer 8am–7pm; winter 8am–5pm; $3; ☏928/567-3322, ⓦwww.nps.gov/moca), are stylish and modern, if not all that detailed. The collection includes a macaw skeleton, which suggests trade with the Mexican civilizations thousands of miles to the south. There is, however, no connection with the Aztec ruler Montezuma, though the well is said to appear on a deerskin map that belonged to Cortes himself.

Camp Verde

The scrappy little town of **CAMP VERDE**, a mile or so east of I-17 and another two miles south of Montezuma Castle, is noteworthy principally as the site of **Fort Verde**. Built in 1871 to succeed a neighboring fort established in 1865, it served as headquarters for General George Crook's campaign against the Tonto Apaches. Crook failed to grasp the fact that the Yavapai and the Apache were separate peoples, but his massacre of the Yavapai at Skeleton Cave convinced the Apache to surrender. Both groups were rounded onto a reservation at Camp Verde and later marched east to the San Carlos Reservation. Some ultimately returned, and a few pockets of land are now set aside for Yavapai-Apache joint use. The **Cliff Castle Casino**, run by the Yavapai-Apache Nation, is popular with Phoenix gamblers.

Fort Verde was damaged by fire in 1881 and decommissioned ten years later. The four crumbling adobe buildings that remain are now the **Fort Verde State Historic Park** (daily 8am–4.30pm; $2), with an interesting museum in the commanding officer's house and a few more exhibits – stuffed birds, old wheel-chairs, fearsome medical instruments – in the former doctor's quarters. The fort was never walled (the Apaches preferred to ambush soldiers in the mountains than attack defensive positions), so it bears little resemblance to movie depictions of Wild West military outposts.

Practicalities

Alongside the Cliff Castle Casino, just off I-17 at exit 289, is a large modern **hotel**. Rooms at the *Lodge at Cliff Castle*, 333 Middle Verde Rd (☎928/567-6611 or 1-800/524-6343, ⓦwww.cliffcastle.com; ❺), are of a pretty high standard, while hotel and casino between them hold nine alternative places to eat.

The hotel also serves as the base for Native Visions Tours (☎928/567-0205, ⓦwww.yavapai-apache-tourism.com), which offers **van trips** to the nearby national monuments ($20 for either section of Montezuma Castle, $35 for both, and $50 for Tuzigoot as well) and also **horse rides** in the Verde Valley ($29 for 1hr up to $75 for 4hr).

Arcosanti

Two miles east of the interstate at **Cordes Junction**, 25 miles south of Camp Verde, the space-age project known as **ARCOSANTI** has been gradually rising from the rim of a beautiful high desert canyon since 1970. Designed to be (someday) a self-sufficient community of five thousand people, Arcosanti is the clearest embodiment of **Arcology**, an ideal blend of architecture and ecology created and still overseen by Italian architect **Paolo Soleri**, a former student of Frank Lloyd Wright. His bell foundry at Cosanti, near Phoenix, is described on p.262.

Though far from any sizeable settlement, Arcosanti is intended as a model of future urban environments. Part construction site, part theme park, with buildings shaped to maximize the benefit of the sun's energy, it can be seen on hour-long guided tours (daily 9am–5pm; tours hourly 10am–4pm except noon; $8 donation; ☎520/632-6217, ⓦwww.arcosanti.org). If you like what you see, you can also sign up for one of the month-long workshops and help out with the construction. A spacious **café** serves healthy and tasty meals, and you can stay in the on-site **motel** for as little as $35 for a basic double room. It's often booked up by groups, so be sure to reserve well in advance. In summer, Arcosanti also hosts a very popular series of outdoor **concerts**.

Prescott

The neat little Victorian town of **PRESCOTT** makes an unlikely sight in the Arizona wilderness, a hundred miles north of Phoenix by way of I-17 and Hwy-69 (which branches off the interstate at Cordes Junction). In 1863, when President Lincoln acceded to pressure from mining interests and granted Arizona territorial status, he chose to establish a new capital well away from Tucson, the obvious choice, which he saw as a hotbed of Confederate sympathizers. His first pick, **Fort Whipple**, was replaced in 1864 when gold was discovered near Prescott, which became the site of both fort and capital. It was named in honor of William H. Prescott, the author of the classic *A History of the Conquest of Mexico*, but Prescott himself never visited the town.

Although Tucson duly supplanted it as capital within three years, Prescott survived, with cattle ranchers joining the gold miners to make it the rowdiest, hardest-drinking town within a hundred miles. Those days are long gone, however, and while Prescott refused to die, it hasn't grown either.

Still centering on its venerable courthouse square, it's a charming little town with a real Wild West flavor. Few out-of-state visitors seem to find their way here, as it's not on any obvious sightseeing itinerary, but it makes a rewarding overnight stop, and thanks to Phoenix residents who come to escape the summer heat, it has a thriving infrastructure of hotels and restaurants.

Arrival and information

Coconino/Yavapai Shuttle **buses** connect Prescott with **Flagstaff** (2 daily Mon–Fri, 1 on Sat; $25 one-way, $40 round-trip; ☎928/775-8929 or 1-888/440-8929), while Shuttle "U" runs here from Phoenix's Sky Harbor Airport ($28 one-way, $48 round-trip; ☎928/442-1000 or 1-800/304-6114, Ⓦwww.shuttleu.com). The local **visitor center** stands at 117 W Goodwin St on Courthouse Plaza (Mon–Fri 9am–5pm, Sat & Sun 10am–2pm; ☎928/445-2000 or 1-800/266-7534, Ⓦwww.prescott.org).

Accommodation

For a small town, Prescott holds an ideal range of **accommodation** options. As well as a handful of historic **hotels** around the main square, restored to differing levels of comfort, there are several small-scale **B&Bs** in Victorian homes in the surrounding streets – contact Ⓦwww.prescott-bed-breakfast.org for full listings. The usual array of chain motels can be found on the fringes, but it would be a shame to stay too far from the center.

Briar Wreath Inn 232 S Arizona St ☎928/778-6048 or 1-877/778-6048, Ⓦwww.briarwreath .com. Quaint century-old house run as a four-room B&B, where each nicely furnished room offers a surprising amount of space and light. ⑥

Hassayampa Inn 122 E Gurley St ☎928/778-9434 or 1-800/322-1927, Ⓦwww.hassayampainn .com. Grand 1920s hotel just off the square, owned by the same people as *La Fonda* in Santa Fe, offering very comfortable, individually styled guest rooms and plenty of Art Deco flourishes amid its overall Southwestern them. The *Peacock Room* serves upscale, expensive Continental cuisine. **❼**

Hotel St Michael 205 W Gurley St ☎928/776-1999 or 1-800/678-3757, ⓦwww.hotelstmichael.net. Atmospheric old downtown hotel – some say it's haunted – with a wide range of inexpensive rooms, all en-suite, plus its own coffee bar and mall of antique and specialty stores. Rates are cheaper on weekdays. Winter **❸**, summer **❹**

Super 8 1105 E Sheldon St ☎928/776-1282 or 1-800/800-8000. Chain motel on the eastern edge of town, as you approach from the interstate. **❸**

The Town

Downtown Prescott is centered by the kind of **Courthouse Square** you'd expect to find in the Deep South, not the Wild West. Apart from the Courthouse itself, its central feature is the **Rough Rider Memorial Monument**, a bronze equestrian statue that commemorates William Owen "Buckey" O'Neill. While mayor of Prescott, this frontier character recruited many of Theodore Roosevelt's Rough Riders in 1898 and was killed in Cuba at the Battle of San Juan Hill. A colorful timeline set into the concrete footpath nearby traces events in local history, from a visit by the Spanish explorer Espejo in 1581 up to the opening of the airport's "Automated Flight Service Station" in 1985. Especially on summer weekends, the square plays host to regular community events and arts fairs.

The best place to get a feel for Prescott's past is the **Sharlot Hall Museum**, a short walk west of the center at 415 W Gurley St (Mon–Sat 10am–4pm, Sun noon–4pm; $5; ⓦwww.sharlot.org). Sharlot Hall herself arrived in Prescott with her pioneer parents in 1882, at the age of twelve, and went on to become the official historian of Arizona. She also put together the nucleus of this collection, which has expanded since her death to fill a dozen buildings and an entire city block. In the modern headquarters at the heart of the complex, you can admire the attractive flapper-esque gown of copper worn by Hall when she took Arizona's three electoral college votes to Washington DC to participate in the election of Calvin Coolidge in 1925. Structures nearby include the 1864 Governor's Mansion and the similar Fort Misery, built that same year and said to be Arizona's oldest log cabin. Fort Misery became Arizona's first law office and courthouse as well as a church, general store, and boarding house.

The main museum, in the **Sharlot Hall Building**, covers the town's early history and also explores the travails of the local Yavapai, tracing their story from baskets, bows, and arrows up to their current ownership of two casinos and the luxurious Prescott Resort and Conference Center. The most popular section of all is the **Transportation Building**, which holds a gorgeous Wells Fargo stagecoach, painted red with yellow wheels, which was in use – and was held up by bandits – in Tombstone in 1881.

Eating and drinking

The streets on and around Prescott's Courthouse Square hold a plethora of places where you can **eat** and **drink** at reasonable prices. The best concentration of **bars** can be found on Montezuma Street on its western side, in the block once known as **Whiskey Row**.

1291/2 1291/2 N Cortez St ☎928/443-9292. Styling itself "An American Jazz Grille", this sophisticated restaurant serves classic upper-crust American cuisine such as steaks for around $23 or balsamic calves' liver for $17. There's live jazz nightly except Mon.

Mon–Fri 11am–2pm & 5–10pm, Sat & Sun 5–10pm.

Gurley Street Grill 230 W Gurley St ☎928/445-3388. Large and extremely popular restaurant, just downhill west of the center, whose several separate dining rooms manage to cater to almost every taste, style, and budget, from foreign tourists to students on dates to farmers celebrating their wedding anniversaries. The menu includes chicken, ribs, and steaks, as well as pizzas, pasta specials, and stir-fries, all prepared to above-average standards. Open daily from 11am until late.

Kendall's 113 S Cortez St ☎ 928/778-3658. Good old-fashioned all-American diner, doling out huge burgers and big scoops of ice cream. Mon–Sat 11am–8pm, Sun 11am–6pm.

Palace Saloon 120 S Montezuma St ☎ 928/442-9208. This majestic old saloon, complete with double swinging doors, was originally the centerpiece of Whiskey Row. While still a genuine Western bar, it now also serves lunchtime salads and burgers as well as full meaty dinners. Sun–Thurs 11am–3pm & 4.30–9.30pm, Fri & Sat 11am–3pm & 4.30–10.30pm.

Sweet Tart 125 N Cortez St ☎ 928/443-8587. Attractive French-style bakery a block north of the square, serving sandwiches, salads, and, above all, delicious raspberry, blueberry and lemon tarts – to name but a few. Mon–Sat 8am–6pm, Sun 8am–2pm.

Wickenburg

WICKENBURG, sixty miles southwest of Prescott and the same distance northwest of downtown Phoenix, is another former mining and ranching town now kept humming by tourism. It's only a little higher, and a little cooler, than Phoenix, so the main visitor season is in winter, between November and April.

Wickenburg stands beside the **Hassayampa River**, whose Apache name, meaning "river that runs upside down," refers to the fact that it often flows underground. This spot marks the "pumpkin patch" where Prussian prospector Henry Wickenburg built a mill in 1864 to process the gold he'd discovered in the Vulture Mountains, fifteen miles south. Though it yielded substantial quantities of gold, the **Vulture Mine** was seldom profitable thanks to geological peculiarities and its general inaccessibility. After years of passing from hand to hand, it finally closed down in 1942. By then, however, Wickenburg had established a successful sideline running **dude ranches**, at which well-heeled Easterners could dabble with the Wild West lifestyle for a few carefree days.

In general, Wickenburg is a spruce and prosperous-looking place, with little sense of a desert outpost, though the wooden sidewalks and false-front stores along **Frontier Street** in the heart of town must look much as they did in Wickenburg's heyday. You can still see the mesquite tree that served as the original town "jail"; miscreants were simply chained to its trunk. Local history is recalled at the **Desert Caballeros Western Museum**, 21 N Frontier St (Mon–Sat 10am–5pm, Sun noon–4pm; closed Mon in July & Aug; $7.50; ⓦ www.westernmuseum.org), which features a recreated 1900s street scene as well as paintings by Remington and Russell, lots of sculptures of noble native American warriors, several little dioramas, masses of spurs and bits and hats and chaps, and all the barbed-wire you could eat.

Three miles south, the **Hassayampa River Preserve** (mid-May to mid-Sept Fri–Sun 8am–5pm; mid-Sept to mid-May Wed–Sun 8am–5pm; $5 donation; ⓦ www.nature.org) marks a spot where the river bubbles from its sandy streambed to irrigate a lush stretch of woodland that's home to innumerable bird species.

The **Vulture Mine** itself can also be visited (May–July Sat & Sun 8am–4pm, Sept–April daily 8am–4pm, closed Aug; $7). Its long-abandoned workings rear up from the streets of the well-preserved ghost town of **Vulture City**. Stick to the walking trail as you wander round; the various buildings, which include a blacksmith's shop and the mine's head office, are not as sturdy as they appear.

Practicalities

Wickenburg's **visitor center** is housed in the former railroad station at 216 N Frontier St (summer Mon–Fri 9am–5pm; winter Mon–Fri 9am–5pm, Sat 9am–2pm, Sun 10am–3pm; ☏928/684-5479 or 1-800/942-5242, ⓦwww.wickenburgchamber.com).

Only one working cattle ranch now accepts paying guests, the *Flying E Ranch*, 2801 W Wickenburg Way (Nov–April only; ☏928/684-2690 or 1-888/684-2650, ⓦwww.flyingeranch.com; ⑨), where rates include all meals but not riding. *Rancho de los Caballeros*, at 1551 S Vulture Mine Rd, is a purpose-built luxury resort, complete with its own golf course and stables (mid-Oct to mid-May; ☏928/684-5484 or 1-800/684-5030, ⓦwww.sunc.com; ⑨). Of conventional **motels**, the *Best Western Rancho Grande*, 293 E Wickenburg Way (☏928/684-5445 or 1-800/854-7235, ⓦwww.bwranchogrande.com; ④), is the most attractive, part genuine adobe and part Spanish colonial mock-up, while the *Super 8*, 975 N Tegner Ave (☏928/684-0808 or 1-800/800-8000, ⓦwww.super8.com; ③), is a budget alternative. For a slap-up ranch-style **meal**, head out to *Charley's Steakhouse*, 1187 W Wickenburg Way (☏928/684-2413; closed Mon & June to mid-Oct; dinner only); the *House of Berlin*, 169 E Wickenburg Way (closed Mon; ☏928/684-5044), serves German and other European specialties.

Joshua Forest Parkway

Northwest of Wickenburg, US-93 runs for 108 dramatic miles across some of Arizona's wildest and most scenic mountains, to meet I-40 twenty miles east of Kingman (see p.357). If you're heading up from Phoenix, this slow two-lane highway serves as a reminder of just how much of the state remains given over to wilderness. Apart from the hamlet of **NOTHING** – which might sound enticing on the map, but really is nothing, other than the home base of a towing company that rescues unfortunate stranded motorists – there's almost no sign of human life along the way. Instead, the vegetation provides the main source of interest, with saguaro and ocotillo **cactuses** scattered across the slopes of the impressive rocky outcrops. Above all, these eastern fringes of the Mojave Desert are one of the few places in Arizona where you'll encounter an abundance of **joshua trees** – hence the road's official designation as the **Joshua Forest Parkway**.

West of Flagstaff

Though the two hundred miles of I-40 that run **west from Flagstaff** to California are kept busy by traffic heading to, from, and between the Grand Canyon and Las Vegas, few of the towns along the way are especially interesting in themselves. However, most became reliant on tourism during the heyday of **Route 66**, and driving through any one of them can bring on a frisson of that era's romance.

If you have the time to indulge your 1950s fantasies, then take the 120-mile side trip on the longest surviving section of what John Steinbeck called the

"**Mother Road**," which starts at **Seligman**, loops back down to **Kingman**, and then crosses some wild and mountainous country to the ghost town of **Oatman**. Otherwise, it makes little difference where or even if you choose to take a break from the interstate.

Williams

Although Flagstaff is generally regarded as the obvious base for visitors to the Grand Canyon's South Rim, **WILLIAMS**, 32 miles west, is in fact the closest interstate town to the national park. While it can't boast half the charm or pizzazz of its neighbor, it's a nice enough little place, filled with Route 66-era motels and diners and retaining a certain individuality despite the constant stream of tourists. Its setting helps, cupped in a high grassy valley amid pine-covered hills; the largest peak is the 9264-foot **Bill Williams Mountain** to the south, which was named for pioneer trapper and "mountain man" Bill Williams (1787–1849), and gave its name in turn to the town, founded thirty years after his death.

Like Flagstaff, Williams originally based both its architecture and its economy on the ponderosas of the surrounding forests. Ever since 1901, however, when the Santa Fe Railroad first connected it with the canyon rim, sixty miles due north, Williams has lived off tourism. Though the railroad went out of business in 1968, it reopened in 1989 as the **Grand Canyon Railway**, promoted as a fun ride rather than a serious means of transportation. Most people who spend the night in Williams are here to take the morning train up to the canyon.

Arrival and information

Amtrak's *Southwest Chief* **train** calls in at **Williams Junction**, three miles east of town, twice daily, heading east at 4.20am and west at 9.33pm. The *Grand Canyon Railway Hotel* (see below) runs free connecting shuttle buses into town.

Full schedules and prices for the **Grand Canyon Railway** (☎928/773-1976 or 1-800/843-8724, ⓦwww.thetrain.com), which sets off daily at 10am from the **Williams Depot** in the center of town, appear on p.371.

Williams' **visitor center**, near the railroad depot at 200 W Railroad Ave (summer daily 8am–6.30pm, winter daily 8am–5pm; ☎928/635-4061 or 1-800/863-0546), hands out all the usual brochures, including details of a town walking tour and driving tours in the Kaibab National Forest, and doubles as an entertaining **museum** of neighborhood history.

Marvelous Marv's Tours run daily **guided van tours** of the South Rim from Williams, with the $85 adult rate including admission to the park (☎928/635-4061 or 1-800/655-4948; ⓦwww.marvelousmarv.com).

Accommodation

Although the large *Grand Canyon Railway Hotel* ranks as Williams' leading **accommodation** option, there are plenty of alternatives around. The main downtown streets are lined with vintage motels as well as the odd B&B, while the national chains congregate nearer the interstate exits at either end of town, and the *Red Lake Hostel* to the north caters for budget travelers.

If you're **camping**, you can choose between two *KOA* campgrounds – *Circle Pines*, three miles east (☎928/635-2626), and *Grand Canyon*, five miles north (☎928/635-2307 or 1-800/562-5771; closed Nov–Feb) – or ask at the Chalender

△ Pies at Williams' *Pine Country Restaurant*

Ranger Station, 501 W Route 66 (☎928/635-2676), for details of secluded summer-only mountain sites in the Kaibab National Forest.

Best Value Inn 1001 W Route 66 ☎928/635-2202. Small Japanese-owned motel, just west of the junction where the separate spurs of Route 66 rejoin; a cut above most budget options, with its own pool and spa. Winter ❸, summer ❹
Best Western Inn of Williams 2600 W Route 66 ☎928/635-4400 or 1-800/635-4445. Spacious,

well-equipped motel-resort, with a pool and hot tub, perched near I-40 exit 161 at the west end of town. Winter ❹, summer ❻
Grand Canyon Railway Hotel 1 Fray Marcos Blvd ☎928/635-4010 or 1-800/843-8724, ⊛www .thetrain.com. The Grand Canyon Railway's flagship hotel originally opened in 1908 as the *Fray*

Marcos; since rebuilt and renamed, it lacks much character, though the large open lobby is a pleasant enough place to sit, and there's also an indoor pool, spa, and saloon. All rooms provide two queen beds. Mid-Oct to mid-March ⑤, mid-March to mid-Oct ⑦

Mountain Side Inn 642 E Route 66 ☏ 928/635-4431 or 1-800/462-9381. Large, comfortable motel, set back from the road at the east end of town, with an outdoor pool and even some surprising giraffes in the lobby. Winter ③, summer ⑤

Red Garter Bed & Bakery 137 W Railroad Ave ☏ 928/635-1484 or 1-800/328-1484, ⊚ www .redgarter.com. Plush four-room B&B in a former downtown bordello, serving fresh-baked breakfasts from its own downstairs bakery. Closed mid-Dec to mid-Feb. ⑤

Red Lake Hostel AZ-64 ☏ 928/635-4753 or 1-800/581-4753, ⊚ redlake@azaccess.com. Adjoining a Mustang gas station at a lonely curve on AZ-64 nine miles north of town, this bright red converted motel offers rudimentary accommodation; $12 for a dorm bed, or $22 for a private room. Also offers tent and RV camping. ①/②

Super 8 911 W Route 66 ☏ 928/635-4045 or 1-800/800-8000. Standard chain motel – the more central of Williams' two *Super 8*s – not far west of downtown. The interior hallways are rather faded, but the rooms are fine, and there's an indoor pool. Winter ②, summer ④

Travelodge 430 E Route 66 ☏ 928/635-2651 or 1-800/578-7878. Reliable, clean downtown motel, with a pool and hot tub. Winter ③, summer ④

The Town

Williams holds a definite romantic appeal as the very last town on the old **Route 66** to have been bypassed by the I-40 interstate. Until October 13, 1984, when Bobby Troup of *(Get Your Kicks On) Route 66* fame fronted a closing ceremony, the only stoplight on the interstate between Chicago and Los Angeles stood outside the Williams visitor center.

Much of the former Route 66 frontage remains barely changed, with several quirky antiques stores selling both vintage memorabilia and Native American crafts and jewelry. However, while it's fun to explore the central blocks along the two main one-way streets – Route 66, running west to east, is paralleled by the east–west **Railroad Avenue** – an hour's evening or morning stroll is probably enough; Williams is not really a place to spend the day.

For rail enthusiasts, the Williams Depot holds the slowly expanding **Grand Canyon Railway Museum** (daily 7.30am–5.30pm; free). As well as masses of old photos, including some great hand-tinted ones, it's bursting with vintage tools and implements, with cases of ancient arm-rests and window catches. In due course, they hope to unveil a 650-foot model of the whole rail route up to the canyon.

Highlights of Williams' annual calendar are **Rendezvous Days**, on Memorial Day weekend in late May, when locals dress up as pioneer "buckskinners," and the Labor Day **rodeo**.

Eating

The **restaurant** selection in Williams is frankly disappointing. A few places conjure up the feel of its Route 66 heyday, but there's nowhere that serves interesting food.

Grand Canyon Coffee & Café 125 W Route 66 ☏ 928/635-1255. Tiny downtown café that serves espressos, juices, and pastries throughout the day, then switches to simple Asian dishes such as Korean barbecue in the evenings. Mon–Fri 8am–8pm, Sat 8am–2pm.

Max & Thelma's Williams Depot ☏ 928/635-8970. Named for the owners of the Grand Canyon Railway, *Max & Thelma's* is an adequate but dull

family restaurant aimed at speedily satisfying hungry tour groups. All-you-can-eat buffets are available at every meal – breakfast is $9, lunch $11, and dinner $14 – and you can also order predictable à la carte options. Daily 6.30am–9pm.

Pancho McGillicuddy's 141 W Railroad Ave ☏ 928/635-4150. Popular but very average Mexican cantina, housed in an attractive tin-ceilinged building downtown, with its own authentic-looking saloon. The usual south-of-the border standards, like *flautas, tostadas, tamales,* or *carnitas,* cost under $10, while three mixed platters go for $14; also serves steaks and grills. Daily 7am–10pm.

Pine Country Restaurant 107 N Grand Canyon Blvd ☎928/635-9718. Traditional central diner with friendly waitstaff, where the predictable fare is actually pretty good, and the homemade pies are irresistible. Daily 5.30am–9pm.

Ash Fork

The ranching community of **ASH FORK**, stretched along a brief curving fragment of Route 66 north of the interstate another twenty miles west of Williams, is smaller, less picturesque and far less involved in catering to travelers. By this point I-40 has pulled clear of the forests, and downtown Ash Fork is characterized by buildings constructed with the yellowish local sandstone rather than timber.

The major **motel** chains haven't bothered to set up shop in Ash Fork, but there are still a few homespun alternatives, including the large, pink *Ash Fork Inn,* at the west end of town near I-40 exit 144 (☎928/637-2514; ❷). There's also a *KOA* **campground** at 783 Old Route 66 (☎928/637-2521), and a couple of basic diners in the thick of what few things Ash Fork has to its name.

Seligman

Starting a few miles west of Ash Fork, the old Route 66 parallels its modern replacement at a discreet distance for the twenty or so miles to **SELIGMAN**. This dusty desert halt now feels more than a little stranded, a mile or two north of the interstate, but if you're in the mood to be seduced by its kitsch diners and drive-ins, it makes a mildly diverting stop in a long day's drive. Every business in town strives to outdo the others with eye-catching displays – mannequins of Elvis and Marilyn waving from oddball parked vehicles and the like – and the passing traffic is worth watching too, with all kinds of vintage roadsters making their pilgrimages along the "Mother Road."

You might even choose to follow Route 66's original course as it curves northwards, through a dozen fading villages and part of the **Hualapai reservation** (see p.398), and back south to Kingman. That's a total drive of 88 miles, as opposed to the dreary 65-mile run west on I-40. It also provides access to **Havasu Canyon**, in the depths of the Grand Canyon, which as described on p.391 is one of the Southwest's least-known marvels.

Seligman offers the only **accommodation** along the I-40 stretch between Ash Fork and Kingman, though motels like the *Historic Route 66,* 500 W Route 66 (☎928/422-3204; ❸), and the *Canyon Lodge,* 114 E Route 66 (☎928/422-3255; ❷), are all indifferently indistinguishable. The wackiest of the local **diners** has to be *Delgadillo's Snow Cap* at 301 E Route 66 (☎928/422-3291), where every malt or burger comes with a side order of outrageous puns and put-ons. If you're just looking for a square meal, the *Copper Cart,* in the former railroad station (☎928/422-3241), serves a standard all-American menu.

Kingman

With a population of over thirty thousand, **KINGMAN**, 65 miles on from Seligman and thirty miles short of California, ranks second to Flagstaff among

Arizona's I-40 towns. As all traffic between Phoenix or the Grand Canyon and **Las Vegas** – a mere hundred miles northwest on US-93 – is obliged to pass this way, Kingman also welcomes enough tourists to keep thirty or more motels busy year-round. The best that can be said for it, however, is that it's not particularly ugly – with the exception of the long sprawl beside the railroad tracks north of the interstate – and it's not lifeless. Apart from that, it's a humdrum pit stop with a slight tinge of Route-66 quaintness.

Kingman's main street, curving alongside the railroad tracks, is named in honor of native son **Andy Devine**, the actor who drove the eponymous *Stagecoach* in John Ford's 1939 movie. As the town's promotional brochure puts it, "there must be somebody who hasn't heard of Andy Devine, but that person sure doesn't live in Kingman." His career, the culture and basketwork of the Hualapai, and sundry other unlikely components of Mohave County's heritage, are explored in the **Mohave Museum of History & Arts**, 400 W Beale St (Mon–Fri 10am–5pm, Sat & Sun 1–5pm; $3, under-13s free; ℡928/753-3195). The year 1939, incidentally, was a big one for Kingman: Carole Lombard and Clark Gable were married here on March 29.

Arrival and information

Kingman's large **Powerhouse visitor center** stands at the western edge of downtown, at 120 W Andy Devine Ave (daily 9am–6pm; ℡928/753-6106); as well as the usual brochures, it displays and sells lots of Route 66 memorabilia. The old station in the center of town still welcomes Amtrak **trains** between Flagstaff and LA, but only at unearthly hours of the night, while regular Greyhound **buses**, between Phoenix and Las Vegas as well as east–west, use a terminal up near the interstate at 3264 E Andy Devine Ave (℡928/757-8400).

Accommodation

Granted that you're unlikely to spend more than one night in Kingman – or linger very long in the morning, either – its range of ordinary but inexpensive **motels** should easily meet your needs. There's also beautiful **camping** in the hills five miles southeast of town, in the county-run **Hualapai Mountain Park** (℡928/757-3859), which also holds the *Hualapai Mountain Lodge Resort* (℡928/757-3545; closed Mon; ❹).

Brunswick 315 E Andy Devine Ave ℡928/718-1800 or 1-888/559-1800, ⓦwww.hotel-brunswick.com. This century-old "historical boutique hotel" is downtown Kingman's most characterful lodging, with antique-styled rooms that range from a basic, single-bedded cowboy or cowgirl option, with shared bathroom, to lavish suites. Triple-paned windows keep noise from the nearby railroad to a minimum. All rates include breakfast. ❷–❻
Quality Inn Kingman 1400 E Andy Devine Ave ℡928/753-4747 or 1-800/228-5151. Standard motel a half-mile from downtown, with small but

adequate rooms, that offers a bit of character via a strong Route 66 theme, including a retro breakfast room and outdoor vintage gas pumps. ❸
Ramblin' Rose 1001 E Andy Devine Ave ℡928/753-5541. Appealing, spruced-up independent motel just east of downtown that provides some of Kingman's best budget rooms. ❷
Super 8 3401 E Andy Devine Ave ℡928/757-4808 or 1-800/800-8000. Reliable, inexpensive chain motel well east of town, just north of I-40 exit 53. Winter ❷, summer ❹

Eating

Most of the **restaurants** in Kingman play on the Route 66 angle in some form or other. It's all too spread out for you to wander around comparing menus, but hop in your car and you'll find something.

Dambar & Steakhouse 1960 E Andy Devine Ave ☎ 928/753-3523. Atop the hill, this is a classic Western steakhouse, all sawdust and bare timber, serving grilled and barbecued ribs and chicken, as well as massive steaks. All entrees come in under $20 at dinner and more like $10 at lunch. Mon–Thurs & Sun 11am–10pm, Fri & Sat 11am–11pm.

Hubb's Café *Brunswick*, 315 E Andy Devine Ave ☎ 928/718-1800. The *Brunswick*'s attractively restored dinner-only dining room prepares an eclectic menu of international cuisine, from rich Continental sauces to spicy Asian curries, as well as American standards. Few entrees cost over $20. Mon–Sat 5–9pm.

Mr D'z Route 66 Diner 105 E Andy Devine Ave ☎ 928/718-0066. Across from the visitor center, this loving recreation of a classic Route 66 roadhouse is bursting with memorabilia, neon, and lurid molded trimmings. On the menu are good burgers and shakes, malts and floats, and fries with everything. Tues–Sun 10am–5pm.

Old Town Coffeehouse 616 E Beale St ☎ 928/753-2244. Slightly chintzy café on the eastern fringes of downtown, where you can enjoy espressos, soups, and sandwiches on a small outdoor patio. Mon–Fri 7am–4pm, Sat 8am–5pm.

Chloride

Fifteen miles northwest of Kingman, as US-93 tears through the flat, prosaically named **Detrital Valley** toward Las Vegas, a paved road climbs away into the mountains to the right. Its goal is the former silver mining center of **CHLORIDE**, four miles up, which was established in 1864 and boasts Arizona's oldest still-functional post office. As well as silver, vast quantities of gold, copper, lead, and turquoise were also extracted from the roadless **Cerbat Mountains** beyond, but Chloride these days lives by its wits, exploiting its ramshackle Wild West appearance to attract tourists. You may be encouraged to drive another couple of miles down a dirt road to see the local **murals**, painted onto huge boulders during the 1960s by artist Roy Purcell; his semi-psychedelic meanderings aren't hard to find, but neither are they really worth the bother.

Some of Chloride's erstwhile neighbors – such as **Cerbat** and **Mineral Park** – have become genuine **ghost towns**. In Chloride itself, the epicenter of the visitor industry is *Shep's* (☎ 928/565-4251 or 1-877/565-4251, Ⓦ www .shepsminersinn.com; ❷), an antiques store that doubles as a **B&B**.

Bullhead City and Laughlin

While both the old Route 66 and the interstate head southwest from Kingman, Hwy-68 barrels due west for thirty miles to **BULLHEAD CITY** on the Colorado River. Built as a work camp for the construction of nearby Davis Dam, Bullhead City somehow survived the dam's completion in 1953 and is prospering these days due to its proximity to the casinos of **LAUGHLIN**, Nevada, just across the river.

In terms of temperature, **Bullhead** is the hottest town in the US, exceeding 120°F day after day each summer. In most other respects, however, it's not the least bit hot. Thirty thousand people now live along a ten-mile riverfront stretch of Hwy-95; why on earth you'd join them, even for a night, is hard to imagine.

Not that **Laughlin** is much better, despite the endless hype of its tourist authorities. If you've never been to Las Vegas, you may well be impressed by the sheer size of the dozen or so glittering **casinos** that jostle for position beside the Colorado. They lack the panache of their Vegas counterparts, however, as well as the will to cater to anyone other than hardened gamblers. The only real reason to come here is that **accommodation** rates are so cheap, though it is also fun to take a **paddle-wheeler cruise** on the Colorado, costing about $10 for a little over an hour, from either the *Riverside Resort* or the *Edgewater Hotel*. You might also like to bear in mind that three motorcyclists were killed when a huge gang fight between the Mongols and the Hell's Angels broke out in *Harrah's* in late April 2002, as bikers congregated for the annual five-day **River Run**.

Practicalities

Tri State Super Shuttle (☎928/704-9000 or 1-800/801-8687, ⓦwww.tristatesupershuttle.com) runs daily **bus services** between Bullhead City, Laughlin, and Las Vegas, for around $45 one way.

Laughlin's **visitor center**, across from the *Riverside* at 1555 S Casino Drive (daily 8am–4.30pm; ☎702/298-3321 or 1-800/452-8445, ⓦwww.visitlaughlin.com), offers free courtesy phone connections to all Laughlin hotels; it's actually operated by the Las Vegas Convention & Visitors Authority, so it carries full information on Las Vegas as well.

At least eight casinos in Laughlin offer well over a thousand **rooms** each, with weekday rates that can drop well below $30 per room. The oldest, which traces its ancestry all the way back to an eight-room motel that opened in 1966 but has consistently kept pace with the rest, is *Don Laughlin's Riverside Resort Hotel*, 1650 S Casino Drive (☎702/298-2535 or 1-800/227-3849, ⓦwww.riversideresort .com; Mon–Thurs & Sun ❷, Fri & Sat ❸). Neighbors include the counterfeit Mississippi steamboat that is the *Colorado Belle*, 2100 S Casino Drive (☎702/298-4000 or 1-866/352-3553, ⓦwww.coloradobelle.com; Mon–Thurs & Sun ❶, Fri & Sat ❸); the sleeker *Edgewater Hotel*, 2020 S Casino Drive (☎702/298-2453 or 1-800/677-4837, ⓦwww.edgewater-casino.com; Mon–Thurs & Sun ❶, Fri & Sat ❷); the spruced-up, railroad-themed *Ramada Express*, 2121 S Casino Drive (☎702/298-4200 or 1-800/243-6846, ⓦwww.ramadaexpress.com; Mon–Thurs & Sun ❶, Fri & Sat ❸); and the top-of-the-range *Golden Nugget*, 2300 S Casino Drive (☎702/298-7222 or 1-800/955-7278, ⓦwww.gnlaughlin.com; Mon–Thurs & Sun ❷, Fri & Sat ❸), with *Joe's Crab Shack* for dinner and clubbing at *Tarzan's*. Each of the casinos holds its array of **restaurants** – there are ten in the *Colorado Belle* alone – ranging from buffet joints whose all-you-can-eat specials start at under $5, to steakhouses and dimly lit Italian schmoozeries. It's really not worth eating anywhere other than in the casino in which you're staying, however – it takes a long time to walk from one to the next, and you'll only find the same bland choices you had before you set off.

Oatman

If you're in no great hurry to get to California from Kingman, following Route 66 over the **Black Mountains** is much more enjoyable than skirting south then west on I-40. While **Needles**, California, is only fifty miles away on the "Mother Road," however – as opposed to 64 on the interstate – it's a long, slow drive, and you need to be confident that your vehicle can handle tricky mountain bends.

The eastern approaches to the mountains, at the edge of the Sacramento Valley, are guarded by a splendid solitary rock pinnacle that served as a beacon to early travelers. Following a laborious climb up to a gap between the peaks, the road twists down the far side and eventually enters **OATMAN**. This former gold-mining community, which was established in 1906 and went bust in 1942, is one of Arizona's most appealing **ghost towns**; a second career as an all-purpose movie backdrop and tourist stop-off has ensured that it's never truly been abandoned. The streets are still roamed by semi-wild burros descended from animals left by the miners; stores sell carrots, the only food you're allowed to offer them.

Gift and craft stores now occupy most of the false-front structures along Oatman's raised wooden boardwalk, with snacks available at *Olive Oatman's Restaurant and Saloon* and the *Route 66 Deli and Espresso Shop*. The *1902 Oatman Hotel* (☎928/768-4408; ❷) – a restored adobe that was in fact rebuilt after a fire in 1920 – still rents out basic **rooms**, including the one where Clark Gable and Carole Lombard spent their wedding night in 1939 (see p.358).

Lake Havasu City

Forty miles southwest of Kingman on I-40, ten miles from the California border, a twenty-mile detour south on Hwy-95 brings you to the most incongruous sight of the Southwestern deserts. At **LAKE HAVASU CITY**, the old gray stones of **London Bridge** reach out across the stagnant waters of the dammed Colorado River.

Californian chainsaw manufacturer **Robert P. McCulloch** moved his factory to this unlikely spot – occupied by a disused military airstrip – in 1964, so he could try out his new sideline in outboard motors on Lake Havasu. Three years later, he heard Johnny Carson mention that London Bridge was up for sale; in the words of the nursery rhyme, it really was falling down, unable to cope with all those newfangled automobiles. McCulloch bought it for $2,460,000, and painstakingly shipped ten thousand numbered blocks of granite across the Atlantic. Lacking anything for the bridge to span, he dug a channel that turned a riverbank promontory into the island of **Pittsburg Point**. Despite the jibes that McCulloch thought he was buying London's picturesque Tower Bridge – the turreted one that opens in the middle – his investment in London Bridge, merely the latest in a long line of London Bridges and dating only from 1831, paid off handsomely. The bridge now ranks second among Arizona's tourist attractions, after the Grand Canyon, and Lake Havasu City has become a major vacation resort and retirement center, with a population of thirty thousand. For its part, London Bridge is listed in the *Guinness Book of Records* as the largest antique ever sold.

That said, it's not often you see anything quite as **boring** in Arizona as London Bridge; unless you've never seen a bridge before, it's one to miss. Lake Havasu City is one of those places with an undeniable attraction for the parched urbanites of cities such as Phoenix, who flock to fish on the lake or charge up and down in motorboats and on jet skis, but it holds minimal appeal for travelers from further afield. Be warned that between March and June, it's almost permanently filled with students on **Spring Break**, drinking and partying around the clock.

Only when you cross the bridge onto the island, and then look back, do you appreciate how large Lake Havasu City has grown, sprawling up the gentle slope away from the river. Most of those broad hillside streets are lined with condo blocks and minor malls; the only place tourists bother to visit is the **English Village**, a mock-Tudor shopping mall, which also holds a handful of riverview restaurants, at the base of the bridge. Out on the island, if you head south from the bridge past the *Island Inn Resort*, you'll soon come to **London Bridge**

Beach. The "beach" is more grit than sand, and few people swim from it. With its bizarre fringe of date palms, however, and its panorama of weird desert buttes and the Chemehuevi Mountains, it does at least linger in the memory.

Practicalities

The local **visitor center** at 420 English Village can tell you anything you want to know about Lake Havasu (daily 10am–4pm; ☎928/453-3444 or 1-800/242-8278, ⓦwww.golakehavasu.com). Several operators offer short **river cruises** from the quayside of the English Village, charging around $15 for an hour-long trip focusing on the bridge, or $25 for a two-hour excursion to see rock formations upriver, and **jet ski** rentals are also widely available at about $40 per hour.

Lake Havasu City has a good 25 or so **motels**, though relatively few are immediately obvious from Hwy-95. They range from the perfectly adequate *Bridgeview Motel*, 101 London Bridge Rd (☎928/855-5559; ❷), by way of the more appealing *Island Inn Hotel*, 1300 W McCulloch Blvd (☎928/680-0606 or 1-800/243-9955; winter ❸, summer ❹), to the extravagant riverfront *London Bridge Resort*, 1477 Queen's Bay Rd (☎928/855-0888 or 1-866/330-9231, ⓦwww.londonbridgeresort.com; winter ❹, summer ❼), where the lobby is all but filled by a gilt replica stagecoach. Note that rates are usually higher on weekends than on weekdays.

For a night out, the districts at either end of London Bridge are your best bet. The *City of London Arms* (☎928/855-8782) is a lively pub in the English Village on the mainland, while the *Mudshark Brewing Co*, not far south at 210 Swanson Ave (☎928/453-2981), is a slightly more upscale brewpub with better beer. *Shugrue's* (☎928/453-1400), across the bridge in the Island Fashion Mall, serves good fresh fish – even sushi – as well as salads and pasta.

The Grand Canyon

CHAPTER 6

Highlights

❋ **El Tovar Hotel** The jewel of Grand Canyon Village, this historic hotel provides the South Rim's best food and lodging. See p.379

❋ **Shoshone Point** Little-known viewpoint, accessible only on foot, that feels a world away from all the other South Rim overlooks. See p.382

❋ **Desert View Watchtower** Circular mock-Puebloan tower, blending into the rocks at the east end of the South Rim, that provides stunning canyon views. See p.384

❋ **The Bright Angel Trail** Deservedly the most popular hiking trail within the park; a superb introduction to life below the rim. See p.387

❋ **The South Kaibab Trail** This hair-raising descent to the canyon floor offers the finest day-hikes in the park. See p.389

❋ **Havasu Falls** Astonishing, lush turquoise waterfalls buried deep within the canyon on the Havasupai reservation. See p.396

❋ **The North Rim Campground** The most spacious and least crowded of the national-park campgrounds. See p.406

❋ **Cape Royal** The perfect vantage point from which to appreciate the overall shape of the canyon. See p.407

❋ **Toroweap Point** The remotest canyon overlook within the national park offers unique views into the Inner Gorge. See p.410

△ Shoshone Point, South Rim

6

The Grand Canyon

Although almost five million people come to see the **GRAND CANYON OF THE COLORADO** every year, it seems to remain beyond the grasp of the human imagination. No photograph, no set of statistics, can prepare you for such vastness. At more than one mile deep, it's an inconceivable abyss; varying from four to eighteen miles wide, it's an endless expanse of bewildering shapes and colors, glaring desert brightness and impenetrable shadow, stark promontories and soaring, never-to-be-climbed sandstone pinnacles. While no one is disappointed with their first stunning sight of the chasm, visitors often find themselves struggling to understand what can appear as a remote and impassive spectacle. They race frantically from viewpoint to viewpoint, constantly imagining that the next one will be the "best," the place from which the whole thing will finally make sense. The secret to transcending that initial frantic excitement is to slow down, to appreciate whatever small portion of the canyon may be displayed in front of you at any one moment, and to allow enough time for the bigger picture to develop. And visiting the Grand Canyon need not be an entirely passive experience. In addition to touring the various **overlooks** along each rim, all of which offer views that shift and change unceasingly from dawn to dusk, you can **hike** down into the depths; ride down on a **mule**; hover above the canyon in a **helicopter**; raft through the **whitewater rapids** of the river itself; spend a night at **Phantom Ranch** on the canyon floor; or swim beneath the waterfalls of the idyllic **Havasupai reservation**.

Mapping and defining precisely what constitutes the "Grand Canyon" has always been controversial; **Grand Canyon National Park** covers a relatively small proportion of the greater Grand Canyon area. Only in the past thirty years has it included the full 277-mile length of the Colorado River from Lees Ferry in the east to Grand Wash Cliffs near Lake Mead in the west, and even now it's restricted for most of that way to the narrow strip of the inner gorge. Ranchers whose animals graze in the federal forests to either side, mining companies eager to exploit the mineral wealth hidden in the ancient rocks, engineers seeking to divert the river to feed the deserts of southern Arizona, and Native Americans who have lived in the canyon since long before the first Europeans reached North America, have combined to minimize the size of the park.

Admission to Grand Canyon National Park, valid for seven days on either rim, costs $25 for one private, noncommercial vehicle and all its passengers, or $10 per pedestrian or cyclist. All the park-service **passes** detailed on p.45 are both valid and sold.

For an even more detailed account of the entire Grand Canyon region, see the **Rough Guide to the Grand Canyon**, also by Greg Ward.

The vast majority of visitors arrive at the **South Rim** – it's much easier to get to, there are far more facilities (mainly at **Grand Canyon Village**, inside the park), and it's open all year round. Another lodge and campground are located at the **North Rim**, which by virtue of its isolation can be a lot more atmospheric, but at one thousand feet higher this entire area is usually closed by snow from mid-October until mid-May. Few people visit both rims on a single trip; to get from one to the other demands either a three-day hike down one side of the canyon and up the other, or a 215-mile drive. On both rims, the main activity consists of gazing over the gorge from lookouts placed at strategic intervals along the canyon-edge roads. Whereas in the 1920s the average visitor stayed for two or three weeks, these days it's more like two or three hours – of which forty minutes are spent actually looking at the canyon.

Assuming that you're visiting the Grand Canyon as part of a longer Southwest itinerary, you'll be wondering whether you "should" visit both rims, or which rim is "better." It really depends on how much time you have, and what time of year it is. Wilderness enthusiasts who love to be alone with nature tend to find the summer crowds at the South Rim unbearable, but even there it's possible to escape the throng, and there's great scope for day-hiking. The North Rim is convenient to Zion and Bryce parks and northeast Arizona and has nicer accommodation options. It's probably best to choose whichever rim fits in with your planned route, and not to feel you ought to see the other one as well.

A history of the Grand Canyon

It may look forbidding, but the Grand Canyon is not a dead place. All sorts of desert **wildlife** survive here – sheep and rabbits, eagles and vultures, mountain lions, and, of course, spiders, scorpions, and snakes. The earliest signs of any **human** presence are twig figurines of animals, found hidden in caves in the canyon walls. Dated to around 2000 BC, they were probably created to ensure successful hunting. Remains of later dwellings built by the **Ancestral Puebloans** are scattered throughout the canyon – the most accessible to modern visitors is Tusayan Ruin (see p.383). A separate tribal group, the **Havasupai** (see p.392), are thought to have arrived around 1300 AD.

In 1540 – less than twenty years after Cortés conquered the Aztecs of Mexico – the first **Spaniards** reached the Southwest. At the Hopi mesas, a detachment of Francisco Vázquez de Coronado's company were told of a great river not far to the west, inhabited by people with very large bodies (presumably the Havasupai, who tend to be significantly bigger than the Hopi). A small party, led by García López de Cárdenas, was despatched to investigate. Their Hopi guides led them to a spot somewhere near Grandview Point, but chose not to reveal the trails down to the river. The Spaniards spent three days on the South Rim, only appreciating the scale of the canyon after an abortive attempt to reach the river. They identified the Colorado as being the Tizón or "Firebrand" River, up which a simultaneous naval expedition was attempting to sail (it managed 225 miles, reaching what's now the site of the Hoover Dam).

When jurisdiction over the Grand Canyon passed from Mexico to the United States in 1850, it had never been surveyed and did not even have a fixed **name**. To the Havasupai, it was *Wikatata* ("Rough Rim"); Spanish maps showed it as *Río Muy Grande* ("Very Big River"); and trappers and prospectors knew it as the Big Cañon. The name Grand Canyon, first used on a map in 1868, was popularized by the one-armed Civil War veteran **John Wesley Powell**, whose expeditions along the fearsome and uncharted Colorado, in 1869 and 1871–72 – see p.497 – captured public imagination.

The formation of the Grand Canyon

Although the Grand Canyon could be called the world's clearest geological textbook, scientists continue to argue over how to read the story written in the stone. Layer upon layer of different rocks, readily distinguished by color, and each with its own fossil record, recede down into the canyon and back through time, until the river bed lays bare some of the oldest exposed rocks on earth. Almost all of the successive strata of sandstone and limestone were deposited during periods when the entire region was submerged beneath shallow primeval seas. The bottom layer, the two-billion-year-old **Vishnu Schist**, is so ancient that it contains no fossils; it dates back to the Precambrian era, when life had barely begun.

That same tale of sedimentation, of course, holds true for much of the planet. What until five million years ago was an unremarkable landscape was transformed into the Grand Canyon thanks to two major factors. First of all, the chronic shortage of rain in this desert area prevented the development of vegetation to bind the brittle surface together. Secondly, there was the fast-flowing **Colorado River**, cascading down from the Rocky Mountains with a gradient over 25 times steeper than the Mississippi. In full flood, charged with mighty boulders, it can blast deep crevices into the earth.

However, a crucial mystery remains. The Colorado Plateau is not flat at this point; it's an enormous hill, known to the Paiute Indians as the **Kaibab**, or mountain with no peak, which slopes southwards from a ridge that runs roughly a dozen miles north of the North Rim. Thus the Colorado has eaten away a chunk of the hillside, around a third of the way up the southern slope – which explains why the North Rim is a thousand feet higher than the South. Why, or how, the Colorado River cuts straight through that hill, rather than flowing around it, has long taxed the imaginations of geologists. The hypothesis currently in favor, "**stream piracy**," suggests that until five million years ago, the river did indeed skirt the Kaibab – though what precise course it followed is open to speculation – but was then "captured" by another river and began to flow through it instead. That may have occurred when a powerful stream, at the head of its own canyon, eventually cut so far back that it breached the barrier that separated it from the Colorado. The Colorado would then rush through, abandoning its own course and usurping this alternative channel.

Crudely speaking, while the Colorado is responsible for the **depth** of the canyon – and continues to scour its way ever deeper – it did little to create its **width**, which owes more to both flash-flooding along its tributary streams and to extreme cycles of heat and cold acting on exposed rock faces. Vast slabs of stone are chiseled away when water that trickles into cracks in the earth later freezes and expands, thereby sculpting the fantastic pyramids and mesas that tower above the central gorge. Some layers of rock are much harder than others; thus the solid Tapeats Sandstone of the **Tonto Platform**, a mile-wide shelf above the river that runs through most of the national park, was left behind when the weaker Bright Angel Shale above it eroded away. Because the general slope of the Kaibab runs from north to south, rain that falls north of the canyon flows down toward the gorge, while rainfall to the south flows away. As a result, the **North Rim** is deeply cut by tributaries and pushed back further from the Colorado, while the lower **South Rim** is much more regular.

The most striking features were named for their supposed resemblance to the great temples of India and China – **Brahma Temple**, **Shiva Temple**, **Vishnu Temple**, and so on – by Clarence Dutton, a student of comparative religion who wrote the first Geological Survey report on the canyon in 1881. The tradition was followed by later cartographers such as François Matthes, who named **Krishna Shrine** and **Walhalla Plateau**.

As the Grand Canyon was being recognized as the most extraordinary natural wonder in the US, American settlers arrived in the vicinity in ever greater numbers. Tensions have arisen ever since between this new permanent population, determined to survive in such an unforgiving environment, and visitors hoping to find unspoiled wilderness. Broadly speaking, **logging** and **grazing** interests have retained control of the plateau forests, while in the canyon itself most attempts at **mining** were defeated by the difficulty of the terrain, and **tourism** soon proved a far more lucrative proposition.

When the **railroad** first crossed northern Arizona in 1882, visitors were taken by stagecoach from the nearest station to the Grand Canyon, at **Peach Springs**, to stay at the *Diamond Creek Hotel* by the river. With the growth of the timber towns to the east, that soon declined; by the 1890s, **Flagstaff** was the main terminus, connected with the canyon by three weekly stages. The railroad reached the canyon itself, via a branch line from **Williams,** in September 1901. That triggered the growth of **Grand Canyon Village**, built under the auspices of the Fred Harvey Company, a subsidiary of the Santa Fe Railroad, and dependent on water carried in 120 miles by rail from Del Rio. The company's grand *El Tovar Hotel* – still the showpiece canyon-edge lodging – opened in January 1905, and its early marketing strategies influence the experience of Canyon visitors to this day. Following an internal memo to "get some Indians to the Canyon at once," the Hopi House souvenir store was built, modeled on the Pueblo village of Old Oraibi (see p.87) and staffed with Hopi craftspeople. Similarly, Navajo weavers were exhorted to produce rugs to suit tourist tastes, using previously unfavored "earth" colors such as brown. Pseudo-Pueblo architecture became the dominant theme, with a single architect, **Mary Jane Colter**, designing such structures as Hermit's Rest (1914), the Desert View Watchtower (1932; see p.384), and *Bright Angel Lodge* (1935).

Late nineteenth-century proposals to create a **Grand Canyon National Park** aroused vigorous local opposition. In due course, however, naturalist **John Muir** – who had earlier championed Yosemite Valley in California and declared the Grand Canyon to be "unearthly . . . as if you had found it after death, on some other star" – found a powerful ally in President **Theodore Roosevelt**. Only entitled to protect sites of historical, rather than geological, interest, Roosevelt used the pretext of preserving Ancestral Puebloan ruins to proclaim Grand Canyon National Monument in 1908. Having failed to persuade the Supreme Court to overrule the president, Arizonan politicians finally came round to the idea after Arizona achieved statehood in 1912. Even then, by the time the boundaries of the Grand Canyon National Park were fixed in 1919, they had trimmed away large tracts of grazing land. The new park covered around 1000 square miles and included just 56 miles of the actual canyon.

Meanwhile, tourism to the South Rim had not stood still. **Ralph Cameron** had been accumulating bogus mining claims along the South Rim since 1890, which enabled him to charge a toll of $1 to riders using the Bright Angel Trail. In 1905, he built his own hotel alongside the railroad terminal, thereby forcing the Fred Harvey Company to relocate the station out of sight of the upstart rival. Cameron continued to be a thorn in the side of the new national park. Elected to the US Senate in 1920, he spent a few years hacking at its budget before his mining claims were eventually invalidated. His presence had by then spurred the development of the **Kaibab Trail**, stretching from rim to rim of the canyon by way of the Kaibab suspension footbridge (see p.388). Plans to pave that route never materialized, but a small enlargement of the park in 1927 permitted the construction of a road east to Desert View, which with the completion in 1928 of the Navajo Bridge across Marble Canyon reduced the previous 600-mile drive between the rims to a more feasible 215 miles.

In the early years of the national park, the role of the park system in protecting the environment had yet to be defined, and techniques of **wildlife** management were in their infancy. Bitter rivalry over grazing lands pitted the park service against the forest service, while the decision to eliminate mountain lions on the North Rim during the 1920s resulted in ecological disaster. Free from predators, the deer population boomed from 4000 to 100,000, stripped the Kaibab Plateau bare, then starved to death en masse.

The first **automobile** arrived at the Canyon in 1902, despite running out of gas twenty miles short. By 1926, more visitors were coming by car than by train, and Flagstaff was once again the major point of access. Advance reservations for both mule rides and lodging have been necessary since 1938; annual visitor numbers first exceeded a million in 1956, and ran at over five million through most of the 1990s. Anticipating that visitation would continue to increase at an exponential rate, the park service drew up plans to build a huge new tourism complex close to the South Rim, to be known as **"Canyon Forest Village,"** and also a **light rail** network. However, for reasons no one is able to explain, numbers then dropped back down below five million, and the political will to make major changes seems to have disappeared.

Green activists horrified by the damming of Glen Canyon (see p.482) forced the abandonment of proposals to dam the Colorado within the park itself during the 1960s, but created new problems by arguing for building coal-burning power stations instead. Pollution from the Navajo Generating Station near Page, which was completed in 1976, remained barely controlled until 1999, when scrubbers were installed under the provisions of the federal Clean Air Act. Commercial logging and mining were finally banned from the park when its boundaries were redrawn and enlarged in 1975. With the exception of the Indian reservations, the Grand Canyon is now run exclusively for the benefit of visitors, though maximizing their enjoyment while minimizing their environmental impact is an all but impossible task.

The South Rim

When someone casually mentions visiting the "Grand Canyon," it's almost certainly the **South Rim** to which they're referring. To be more precise, it's the thirty-mile stretch of the South Rim that's served by a paved road; and most specifically of all, it's **Grand Canyon Village**, the small canyon-edge community, sandwiched between the pine forest and the rim, that holds the park's **lodges**, **restaurants**, and **visitor center**.

The reason nine out of every ten canyon visitors come here is not, however, because this is a uniquely wonderful spot from which to see the canyon. In terms of views, it's as good a place to start as any – every visit begins with an eager rush to catch that first breathtaking glimpse of the abyss – but really Grand Canyon Village just happens to be where the canyon's tourist facilities have been concentrated ever since the arrival of the railroad a century ago.

By the time the millennium approached – and despite the emergence of **Tusayan**, just outside the park, as a rival accommodation center – it was looking as though the village could no longer take the strain. An ambitious scheme was therefore drawn up under which visitors would explore the South Rim using a new **light rail** network rather than their own vehicles. As described above, however, visitor numbers suddenly began to drop instead, and it seems increasingly unlikely that the plan will ever be fully implemented. As a result, the park remains in a strange state of limbo. All that's really happened is the construction of the large open-air **Canyon View Information Plaza**, located well away from the village center, and not beside the rim either. That looks great, but as you're supposed to drive into the village and then catch a bus back to the plaza, it's done nothing to relieve traffic congestion, and it doesn't even meet the basic requirement of making an easy first stop.

On a more positive note, the canyon is as majestic as ever, to be admired from countless differing vantage points, not only within the village but also along the eight-mile **Hermit Road** to the west and the 23-mile **Desert View Drive** to the east. The facilities in the village are of a pretty high standard, and generally well priced; the village itself is also a lot more attractive than you might imagine, and once the day-trippers have gone it rarely feels as crowded as the horror stories might suggest.

Getting to the South Rim

The South Rim is separated from I-40 by the sixty-mile expanse of the **Coconino Plateau**, which is covered by the largest **ponderosa pine forest** in the world. Crossing this undramatic landscape, you get no sense of the impending abyss until you reach the very edge of the canyon.

The vast majority of visitors reach Tusayan via either **Williams** (52 miles south; see p.354) or **Flagstaff** (75 miles southeast; see p.326), both on I-40. Flagstaff is served by Amtrak trains, while a separate **rail** service connects Williams with the canyon itself. If you're traveling by **road**, AZ-64 from Williams, also known as the Bushmaster Memorial Highway, joins US-180 from Flagstaff at **Valle**, thirty miles south of the canyon itself. The route from Flagstaff, by way of the San Francisco Peaks (see p.332), is the more scenic of the two, and it's also the one followed by most commercial **buses**. It's also possible to drive to Grand Canyon Village from the east, by turning onto AZ-64 from US-89 at Cameron (see p.400).

There are direct **flights** to Tusayan from Las Vegas and other points in the Southwest.

By train

Amtrak **trains** come no closer to the South Rim than the stations at **Flagstaff** and **Williams**. In summer, westbound services, originating in Chicago, arrive at Flagstaff at 8.51pm and Williams Junction at 9.33pm daily, while eastbound trains, which start in LA, call at Williams Junction at 4.20am and Flagstaff at 4.56am daily. Times in winter are one hour later. Bus connections are detailed below.

Trains on the restored **Grand Canyon Railway** (☏928/773-1976 or 1-800/843-8724, ⊛www.thetrain.com) run for 64 miles from a separate station in the heart of **Williams** to the picturesque station at Grand Canyon Village. The railway is a tourist attraction in its own right, with passengers riding in historic cars of varying levels of comfort and entertained throughout the day by Wild West shoot-outs, hold-ups, pistol-packing marshals, singing conductors, and the like. The scenery en route – part desert scrubland, part pine forest – is far from spectacular, and you never actually see the canyon from the train, but it's still a fun and atmospheric way to visit the park without having to drive. Services operate all year, leaving Williams daily at 10am and arriving back at 5.45pm, though only in summer is the train pulled by **steam engines**. Round-trip fares range from $60 in Coach Class ($35 for ages 11–16, $25 ages 2–10) up to $155 (under-17s $130) in the Luxury Parlor Car. No Amtrak passes of any kind are accepted, and, unless you have a national park pass, an additional fee of $8 is charged for park admission.

By bus

Open Road Tours and Transportation (℡928/226-8060 or 1-877/226-8060, Ⓦwww.openroadtours.com) runs two **bus services** each day from the Amtrak station in **Flagstaff**, via the Grand Canyon Railroad Depot in **Williams**, to the IMAX movie theater in **Tusayan**, and the **Maswik Transportation Center** in Grand Canyon Village. The first service leaves Flagstaff at 8.30am daily, calling at Williams at 9am and reaching Maswik at 10.15am; the second leaves Flagstaff at 3pm and Williams at 3.30pm, reaching Maswik at 4.45pm. Return services leave Maswik at 10.45am and 5.45pm, arriving at Williams at noon and 7pm respectively, and Flagstaff at 12.30pm and 7.30pm. Tickets cost $25 each way from Flagstaff for adults, or $20 from Williams, and $17 or $15 respectively for accompanied under-12s.

Companies that operate **one-day tours** to the Canyon from Flagstaff and Williams are listed on p.327 and p.354 respectively.

By air

The small **airport** at Tusayan – six miles from the South Rim, just outside the park boundary, and used primarily by "flight-seeing" tour companies (see p.374) – also welcomes scheduled services and excursions, especially from **Las Vegas**. Unlike the tours, these flights do not pass directly above the park, but they still give good views. Standard fares tend to be in the region of $150 one way and $250 round trip, but special offers can cost as little as $60 and $100, respectively. The major Vegas operators are Scenic Airlines (℡702/638-3300 or 1-800/634-6801, Ⓦwww.scenic.com), and Air Vegas (℡928/638-9351, 702/736-3599 or 1-800/255-7474, Ⓦwww.airvegas.com).

Arrival and information

While you'd think the obvious first port of call when you arrive at the South Rim would be **Canyon View Information Plaza** (daily: May to mid-Oct 8am–6pm, mid-Oct to April 8am–5pm; ℡928/638-7888, Ⓦwww.nps.gov/grca), it can be impossible in midsummer to park anywhere near it. In fact, so long as you have the park's **free newspaper**, *The Guide*, it's not essential to call in at the visitor center. *The Guide* is handed out when admission is paid at the two **entrance stations** on AZ-64 (one's just north of Tusayan, the other a mile east of Desert View) and is also available in all the lodges.

As well as listing current opening hours and shuttle-bus schedules, *The Guide* carries a full program of **park activities** such as ranger talks and guided hikes. On a typical day in high season, around fifteen such talks or hikes are likely to be taking place, at venues ranging from shuttle bus stops and overlooks to the visitor center or the canyon rim in the village. All are free of charge, and well worth attending.

In addition to the plaza, further **information desks** can be found at Kolb Studio (see p.378), Yavapai Observation Station (see p.378), Tusayan Museum (see p.383), and Desert View (see p.384). For details of the **Backcountry Office**, which issues permits for backpacking and camping in the canyon, see p.387.

Most of these places, as well as several of the lodges and souvenir stores, sell a wide range of **books** about the canyon, including the comprehensive *Rough Guide: Grand Canyon* as well as guides to the various hiking trails. None of the free **maps** on offer is adequate for backcountry hiking, so invest in the detailed hiking maps produced by Earthwalk Press (*Bright Angel Trail*; $3.95) or National Geographic–Trails Illustrated (*Grand Canyon National Park*; $9.95). For even greater resolution, get hold of the appropriate **US Geological Survey** quadrant map, each of which covers a square measuring seven miles by seven (☎1-888/275-8747, ⓦ www.usgs.gov). Orders cost $4 per map plus $5 postage.

Getting around the South Rim

Grand Canyon Village is always accessible to private vehicles and so, too, is the road **east** from the village to Desert View. Both the road **west** from the village to Hermit's Rest, however, and the short access road to **Yaki Point**, east of Mather Point, are only open during the months of December, January, and February. You're almost certain, therefore, to find yourself needing to use one of the park's three free **shuttle bus** routes.

The first of these, the **Village Route**, loops between Grand Canyon Village and the information plaza, also stopping at *Maswik* and *Yavapai* lodges and the campground, from an hour before sunrise until 11pm in summer, 10pm otherwise. The second, the **Kaibab Trail Route**, connects the information plaza with Yaki Point, from an hour before sunrise until an hour after sunset. A quicker early-morning **Hikers Shuttle** service runs direct to Yaki Point from *Bright Angel Lodge* and the Backcountry Information Center; see *The Guide* for current hours. Finally, from March until November, buses follow the eight-mile **Hermit's Rest Route** road west of the village to eight different canyon overlooks, again from before sunrise until after sunset. You can get on and off as often as you choose. **Bus tours** of the park offered for a fee are detailed on p.374, while a 24-hour **taxi** service can be reached on ☎928/638-2822.

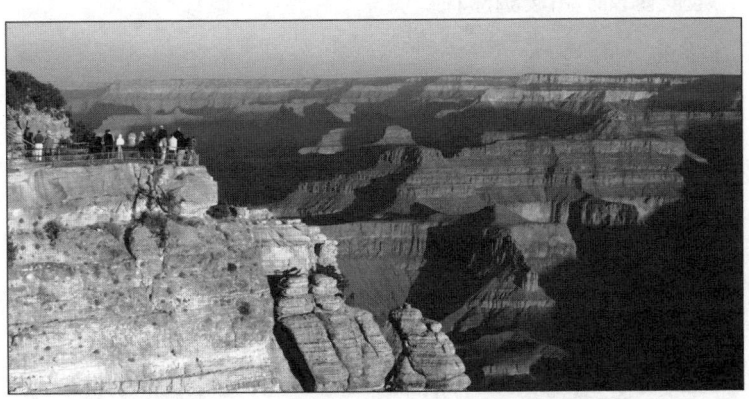

△ Mather Point, South Rim

Park bus tours

For schedules and reservations for guided South Rim **bus tours**, contact the "transportation desk" in any lodge, or call ☎928/638-2631. The **Desert View Tour**, a 52-mile, 4hr round-trip along the East Rim, stops at Yavapai Observation Station and Lipan Point, as well as at Desert View at the far end, and costs $29. The 2hr **Hermit's Rest Tour**, west of the village along the same route as the free Hermit's Rest shuttle bus (see p.373), costs $16.75. Shorter **Sunrise** and **Sunset** tours head east and west of the village respectively, with an adult fare of $12.75. Adults can take any two tours, not necessarily on the same day, for $35, while accompanied children under the age of 17 travel free.

Horse riding

Apache Stables (☎928/638-2891, ⓦwww.apachestables.com), based at *Moqui Lodge* in Tusayan (which is itself permanently closed), charges $30.50 for a one-hour trail ride through the Kaibab Forest, and $55.50 for two hours, and in the evening offers campfire rides on horseback for $40.50, or by wagon for $12.50. To see the canyon itself, you have to take the 4hr East Rim ride, costing $95.50.

Mule rides

Places on the **mule rides** down the Bright Angel Trail are limited, so it's best to make a reservation, on ☎928/638-2631, as far in advance as possible. One-day round-trips as far as Plateau Point cost $136, including lunch, while overnight trips to Phantom Ranch, including accommodation and all meals, cost $366 for one person, $651 for two. Two-night rides, available mid-November to March only, cost $514 for one, $865 for two. If you arrive without a reservation, join the waiting list at the Transportation Desk at *Bright Angel Lodge* and turn up there at 6am on the morning you want to ride; there are normally a few last-minute cancellations.

Grand Canyon Field Institute

The **Grand Canyon Field Institute** offers an extensive program of well-priced, expert-led guided tours and hikes in and around the canyon. Different tours, some of which are restricted to women only, specialize in geology, history, natural history, photography, wilderness techniques, and other topics. Most involve camping and backpacking, others include lodge accommodation or even llama trekking; all are graded according to the difficulty of any hiking involved. Typical prices range from $375 for a three-night hike down to Indian Garden to $535 for a four-night rim-to-rim backpack. For full details, access ⓦwww.grandcanyon.org/fieldinstitute or call ☎928/638-2485 or 1-866/471-4435.

Flight-seeing tours

For safety reasons and to diminish the barrage of **noise** within the park, strict **regulations** surround flights above the national park. Airplanes and helicopters have to fly at different altitudes; no one is allowed to fly below the level of the rim; and 75 percent of the park, including the airspace above the South Rim lookouts and the central rim-to-rim "Corridor," is completely off-limits.

Helicopter companies based at Tusayan include **Papillon** (☎928/638-2419 or 1-800/528-2418, ⓦwww.papillon.com) and **Maverick** (☎928/638-2622 or 1-800/962-3869, ⓦwww.maverickhelicopter.com). They typically fly three standard routes: a half-hour western tour, straight across the canyon and back a few miles west of the village, for around $100 per adult ($70 per child); a forty-minute eastern tour, flying along the rim as far as the confluence of the Colorado and Little Colorado rivers, for roughly $145 ($100); and a fifty-minute loop trip that combines the two by flying across the forest of the North Rim, for perhaps $170 ($120). In addition, Papillon also run the amazing $455 day-trips to the Havasupai reservation, as described on p.394.

The main **airplane** or "fixed-wing" tour operators at Tusayan are **Air Grand Canyon** (☎928/638-2686 or 1-800/247-4726, ⊛www.airgrandcanyon.com) and **Grand Canyon Airlines** (☎928/638-2359 or 1-866/235-9422, ⊛www.grandcanyonairlines .com). Such tours can cover much greater distances than helicopter companies, but are obliged to fly at least one thousand feet above rim level, and thus tend not to offer quite such good views. Fixed-wing tour prices are lower, ranging from $75 per adult ($45 per child) for a half-hour up to about $175 ($95) for ninety minutes.

Whitewater rafting

As the park service only allows about twenty thousand people to float through the canyon of the Colorado River each year, and there's a waiting list of around nine years for permission to do so in your own boat, places on commercial whitewater rafting trips tend to be reserved as much as a year in advance. These vary in length from three days to three weeks, with the main choice being whether to cut the 300-mile voyage from Lees Ferry to Diamond Creek in half by leaving or joining the expedition at Phantom Ranch. An estimated 161 sets of rapids interrupt the full route.

Lobbyists for the industry have so far defeated park plans to ban motorized rafts, so you can also choose between a quieter, slower oar-powered trip or a motorized expedition; both tend to cost around $225 per person, per day. A list of authorized operators, most of whom offer trips of both kinds and of varying lengths, appears below; you can also find the current list online at ⊛www.nps.gov/grca/river/river_concessioners.htm.

No **one-day** rafting trips are available within Grand Canyon National Park. There are two alternatives, however, one at either end of the canyon. Wilderness River Adventures offer one-day **trips** that start immediately below **Glen Canyon Dam** and take out at **Lees Ferry** ($62; ☎928/645-3296 or 1-800/992-8022; ⊛www.riveradventures .com), while further west, the tribal-run Hualapai River Runners arrange pricey one-day trips on the Hualapai reservation, starting at Diamond Creek ($280; ☎928/769-2219 or 1-888/255-9550, ⊛www.destinationgrandcanyon.com).

Arizona Raft Adventures ☎1-800/786-7238 or 928/526-8200, ⊛www.azraft.com

Arizona River Runners ☎1-800/477-7238 or 602/867-4866, ⊛www.raftarizona.com

Canyon Explorations ☎1-800/654-0723 or 928/774-4559, ⊛www .canyonexplorations.com

Canyoneers ☎1-800/525-0924 or 928/526-0924, ⊛www.canyoneers.com

Colorado River & Trail Expeditions ☎1-800/253-7328 or 801/261-1789, ⊛www .crateinc.com

Diamond River Adventures ☎1-800/343-3121 or 928/645-8866, ⊛www.diamondriver .com

Grand Canyon Expeditions ☎1-800/544-2691 or 435/644-2691, ⊛www.gcex.com

Hatch River Expeditions ☎1-800/433-8966 or 435/789-3813, ⊛www .hatchriverexpeditions.com

Moki Mac River Expeditions ☎1-800/284-7280 or 801/268-6667, ⊛www.mokimac .com

O.A.R.S. ☎1-800/346-6277 or 209/736-2924, ⊛www.oars.com

Outdoors Unlimited ☎1-800/637-7238 or 928/526-4546, ⊛www .outdoorsunlimited.com

Tour West; ☎1-800/453-9107 or 801/225-0755, ⊛www.twriver.com.

Western River Expeditions ☎1-800/453-7450 or 801/942-6669, ⊛www.westernriver .com

Wilderness River Adventures ☎1-800/992-8022 or 928/645-3296, ⊛www .riveradventures.com

Grand Canyon Village and around

For almost a century after the *El Tovar Hotel* opened in 1905, at the heart of what became **GRAND CANYON VILLAGE**, most South Rim visitors got their first glimpse of the canyon from the rim-edge footpath alongside the hotel. Now that the information plaza has opened two miles east, your initiation may well come at **Mather Point** instead. That's no cause for regret; the sweeping canyonscape visible from there is far more comprehensive than any from the village.

Mather Point faces northeastwards, toward Bright Angel Canyon on the far side, which is the route followed by the North Kaibab Trail down from the North Rim (see p.408). Two other rim-to-river trails can be spotted closer at hand. To the east, the South Kaibab Trail zigzags down from Yaki Point, while the further west of the two visible stretches of the Colorado River marks the point where it's reached by the Bright Angel Trail. From there, the trail heads east to Phantom Ranch, which is also visible, nestling close to the other tiny patch of river.

Turn left and walk west for ten minutes from Mather Point to reach **Yavapai Point**, where as well as similar long-range views that now take in two different segments of the river, you'll find the **Yavapai Observation Station** (daily: hours vary from 8am–8pm in summer down to 8am–5pm in winter; free), which holds illuminating displays on how the canyon may have been formed. A further ten minutes' walk west brings you within sight of the village.

Grand Canyon Village ranges along the inner curve of a recess that dips as it cuts back into the South Rim. As a result, from the paved, railed terrace that follows the rim for the length of the village you can only see straight across the canyon. Down below, the Bright Angel Trail threads through the oasis of Indian Gardens before disappearing into a deep crevice, while another long trail leads across the flat, pale-green Tonto Platform to Plateau Point. Although the mighty walls of the Inner Gorge – the granite chasm that holds the Colorado – are visible on the far side, you can't see their full 1300ft depth, and the river remains out of sight at the bottom. *Grand Canyon Lodge,* on the North Rim, is visible however, though you're only likely to spot it after dark, when the lights come on.

The original early twentieth-century core of Grand Canyon Village, consisting of self-consciously rugged log-and-boulder buildings such as the *El Tovar* hotel and the Kolb photographic studio, has since been joined by a plethora of less attractive but stylistically similar structures; the whole place is carefully laid out to avoid seeming too crowded. Tucked away in the woods across the road, well back from the canyon, lie several more lodges, stores, restaurants, and the campground, together with the well-hidden residential area used by park employees.

Seven miles from Grand Canyon Village, a mile south of the park entrance, **TUSAYAN** is an unattractive strip-mall of a town that holds nothing beyond an IMAX cinema which continuously runs a mildly entertaining 35-minute movie on the canyon (daily: March–Oct 8.30am–9.30pm, Nov–Feb 10.30am–6.30pm; $10, $7 under-12s).

Accommodation

Roughly two thousand **guest rooms** are available close to the South Rim: half of them in and around **Grand Canyon Village**, and a further thousand in Tusayan (see above). Given the choice, the best place to stay has to be on the very lip of the canyon, but very few rooms indeed enjoy canyon views, and they tend to be booked as much as two years in advance. In fact, for most of the summer it's very unusual for any same-day bookings to be available in

SOUTH RIM: GRAND CANYON VILLAGE

Tusayan

Williams

Desert View

Hermit's Rest

0 — 500 yds

GRAND CANYON PARKWAY

N

64

180

MARKET PLAZA RD

Mather Campground

CENTER ROAD

Clinic

Laundry/Showers

Market Plaza

Trailer Village

Yavapai Lodge

Park Headquarters

Shrine of the Ages

Verkamps Curios

Maswik Transportation Center

Backcountry Information Center

Thunderbird Lodge

Maswik Lodge

Train Depot

Hopi House

El Tovar Hotel

Kachina Lodge

Kolb Studio

Lookout Studio

Bright Angel Lodge

Trailview Overlook

Mather Amphitheater

Canyon View Information Plaza

South Kaibab Trailhead

Yaki Point

Cedar Ridge

Cedar Mesa

O'Neill Butte

SOUTH KAIBAB TRAIL

Mather Point

Museum

Grandeur Point

Yavapai Point

RIM TRAIL

BRIGHT ANGEL TRAIL

TONTO TRAIL

Indian Garden Campground

The Battleship

Maricopa Point

Powell Point

Hopi Point

Mohave Point

Mojave Point

Phantom Ranch & Bright Angel Campground

Feet
0
3200
4400
5600
6880
8000

the park. While the more basic in-park lodges, away from the rim, still make more convenient bases than Tusayan, the hotels in Tusayan do tend to be more modern and better equipped. On the other hand, some of the rates available inside the park represent extraordinarily good value.

All accommodation options within Grand Canyon National Park are run by **Xanterra**. For all **reservations** for lodges or RV camping at Grand Canyon Village, and for Phantom Ranch, contact Xanterra Parks & Resorts (same-day ☎928/638-2631, advance 303/297-2757 or 1-888/297-2757, ⓦwww.grandcanyonlodges.com).

If you are stuck, other possibilities include **Cameron** (see p.400), **Flagstaff** (p.326), and **Williams** (p.354), the latter two of which hold the closest **hostels** to the park.

In Grand Canyon Village

Bright Angel Lodge Individual "rustic" but comfortable log cabins, clustered around an imposing 1935 lodge that also holds some more basic rooms, many of which share bathrooms. Best of all is the Bucky O'Neill Suite, which has two front doors opening right onto the rim. Lodge rooms and historic cabins ❸, Rim Cabins ❻, Bucky O'Neill Suite ❾

El Tovar Hotel Log-built canyon-edge hotel, named for an early Spanish explorer, that has since 1905 exuded both rough-hewn charm and elegant sophistication. Only three suites enjoy extensive canyon views; the rest of the 78 tasteful rooms come in two sizes, but almost all hold only one bed. Standard ❼, larger ❽, suites ❾

Kachina Lodge Anonymous but perfectly adequate motel-style rooms in a low two-story block, near the rim and run in conjunction with *El Tovar*. A few upstairs rooms offer canyon views. ❼

Maswik Lodge Larger complex, a few minutes' walk from the rim at the southwest end of the village. Two distinct blocks of motel-style rooms – *Maswik North* is considerably nicer than the small, cramped *Maswik South* – plus basic summer-only cabins, some of which sleep up to four guests. Cabins and *Maswik South* ❺, Maswik North ❻

Thunderbird Lodge Long, low, box-like lodge that shares the lobby of, and is run with, *Bright Angel Lodge*. Well-equipped if characterless rooms, separated by twenty yards of grass from the canyon edge; a few have views. ❼

Yavapai Lodge 350 reasonable rooms in two quiet motel-type buildings, well back from the rim in the woods near the visitor center. By far the most likely lodge to have availability at short notice, *Yavapai* closes either partially or completely according to demand in low season. ❻

In Tusayan

Best Western Grand Canyon Squire Inn PO Box 130, Grand Canyon, AZ 86023 ☎928/638-2681 or 1-800/622-6966, ⓦwww.grandcanyonsquire.com. Tusayan's most lavish option, with outdoor pool, indoor spa, and bowling alley. Spacious and comfortable, if not all that characterful. ❻

The Grand Hotel PO Box 3319, Grand Canyon, AZ 86023 ☎928/638-3333, ⓦwww.gcanyon.com. Smart modern hotel; the rooms themselves are no better than elsewhere, but there's a nice indoor pool, and it's also home to the *Canyon Star* restaurant (see below). ❼

Red Feather Lodge PO Box 1460, Grand Canyon, AZ 86023 ☎928/638-2414 or 1-800/538-2345, ⓦwww.redfeatherlodge.com. This long-established motel was joined a few years ago by a large new hotel block; they share a pool, the rates aren't bad, and the newer rooms are of a reasonably high standard. Motel ❺, hotel ❻

Seven Mile Lodge PO Box 56, Grand Canyon, AZ 86023 ☎928/638-2291. Tusayan's last little roadside motel; very plain and unadorned and the least expensive option around. No reservations are accepted; rooms are simply given out from 9am daily. Despite the slight premium charged for housing three or four guests in the same room, it's still great value for groups of (close) friends. ❹

Eating and drinking

There's a reasonably wide choice of places to **eat** in Grand Canyon Village, and the prices in the budget cafeterias are not bad considering the canyon's remoteness and lack of water. Summer crowding can lead to endless queueing, however, and it's worth bringing at least some food with you. A few stores – notably the

Canyon Village Marketplace, which has a pretty good **deli counter** (summer daily 7am–6pm, otherwise daily 8am–5pm) – sell basic supplies. As for Tusayan, in addition to the places listed below it also holds several fast-food options.

Both the *Bright Angel* and the *El Tovar* have atmospheric, traditional **bars** open until 11pm nightly, while *Maswik Lodge* has a "sports lounge" with big-screen TV.

Arizona Steakhouse *Bright Angel Lodge*. Informal, good-quality restaurant, only a few yards from the rim but with no views to speak of, specializing in conventional meat and seafood entrées costing $12–24. No reservations accepted, so you may have to wait two hours or more. Daily 11.30am–3pm (summer only) & 4.30–10pm. Closed early Jan to mid-Feb.

Bright Angel Restaurant *Bright Angel Lodge*. Straightforward, windowless diner that serves pretty much anything you might want, from snacks and salads for under $10 to steaks at around $16. No reservations, daily 6.30am–10pm.

Canyon Star *Grand Hotel*, Tusayan ☏ 928/638-3333. Large, attractive hotel restaurant, where dinner is a choice between "hardy ranch fare," like $27 steaks or $16 barbecue ribs, or lighter salads and fish dishes for $15–17. Lunchtime salads, sandwiches, and Mexican staples mostly cost under $10. Also hosts "Native American Experience" dances at 6.30pm and 8pm nightly. Daily 7–10am, 11am–2pm, & 5–9pm.

Coronado Room *Best Western Grand Canyon Squire Inn*, Tusayan ☏ 928/638-2681. Smart dinner-only dining room that serves both all-American

entrées such as prime rib or filet mignon for around $24, and "Southwest favorites" like *fajitas* and *chimichangas* for $17. Daily 5–10pm.

El Tovar *El Tovar Hotel* ☏ 928/638-2631 ext 6432. Grand, classy, and expensive dining room, looking out over the canyon; reservations are accepted for dinner only and tend to be grabbed days in advance. The food itself is very rich, especially at dinner, when almost all entrées, such as braised lamb shank or salmon tostada, cost well over $20. Appetizers are a bit more imaginative, with barbecued sea scallops at $11 and *Clesan-du-Klish*, or Navajo blue-corn tamales, at $9. Breakfast is the most affordable option. Daily 6.30am–10pm.

Maswik Cafeteria *Maswik Lodge*. Self-service fast food, with separate Mexican and Italian sections as well as burgers and standard plate lunches. Breakfast can come in under $5, but lunch and dinner entrées are closer to $10. Daily 6am–10pm.

Yavapai Cafeteria *Yavapai Lodge*. Large cafeteria that's slightly preferable to the *Maswik*'s for its salad bar and fried chicken and slightly lower prices for burgers and daily specials. Summer daily 6am–9pm, spring and fall daily 7am–8pm, shorter hours and probable closures in low season.

Camping on and around the South Rim

Tent and RV camping (without hookups) is available at the park service's year-round **Mather Campground**, south of the main road through Grand Canyon Village. Sites for up to two vehicles and six people cost $15 per night between April and November, when reservations, which are strongly recommended, can be made up to five months in advance through Spherix (same-day ☏ 928/638-2611; advance 1-800/365-2267 or, from outside the US, ☏ 301/722-1257), or online at ⓦ www.reservations.nps.gov. No reservations are accepted between December and March, when sites are first-come, first-served, and the fee drops to $10 per night. The adjacent **Trailer Village** consists exclusively of RV sites with hookups, costing $22 per site per night for two people, plus $2 extra for each additional adult; reservations on ☏ 303/297-2757 or ⓦ www.grandcanyonlodges.com. In summer, additional first-come, first-served, camping sites, without hookups, are on offer 25 miles east of Grand Canyon Village at the **Desert View Campground** (mid-May to mid-Oct; no reservations; $10).

Outside the park, there's a commercial campground, **Camper Village** (☏ 928/638-2887; ⓦ www.grandcanyonentrance.com; some RV hookups; $18–23), in **Tusayan**, while the Kaibab National Forest runs the minimally equipped, first-come, first-served, **Ten-X Campground** (mid-April to Sept; no hookups or showers; $10 per night), two miles south. Twenty miles further south, in Valle, the family-oriented **Flintstone's Bedrock City** (mid-March to Oct; ☏ 928/635-2600; $13 tents, $17 RV hookups) has its own prehistoric theme park plus a simple store and snack bar.

Other in-park facilities

Bank In Market Plaza, with a 24hr ATM machine. Mon–Thurs 9am–5pm, Fri 9am–6pm.

Camping equipment Can be bought or rented at the Canyon Village Marketplace. Daily: summer 7am–8.30pm, spring & fall 8am–8pm, winter 8am–7pm.

Disabled travelers The *Accessibility Guide*, available at all visitor centers and lodges, provides full accessibility details; for further information, call ☏928/638-2631 or look online at ⓦ www.nps .gov/grca. At either park entrance station, you can request a permit to park at the Canyon View Information Plaza. Once there, you can obtain a further permit enabling you to drive on Hermit Road. Although most shuttle buses cannot accommodate wheelchairs, you can ask for an accessible bus by calling ☏928/638-0591 two days in advance.

Gas The closest gas stations to the South Rim are in Tusayan and at Desert View.

Internet access Public computers are at *Bright Angel Lodge*, *Kachina Lodge*, *Maswik Lodge*, *Yavapai Lodge* and Camper Services, as well as at *Jennifer's Bakery* in Tusayan.

Laundromat Near *Mather Campground*. Daily: summer 6am–11pm, spring and fall 7am–9pm, winter 8am–6pm.

Medical help Call ☏911 for emergencies; ☏928/638-2551 for the village clinic (daily 8am–6pm; emergencies only at other times); ☏928/638-2460 for the pharmacy; and ☏928/638-2395 for dentist.

Post office In the Market Plaza. Mon–Fri 9am–4.30pm, Sat 11am–1pm; lobby, with stamp machines, daily 5am–10pm.

Showers Coin-operated showers, available to all visitors, are located in the laundromat building. Daily: summer 6am–11pm; spring and fall 7am–9pm; winter 8am–6pm.

Hermit Road

The eight-mile, dead-end scenic drive officially known as **Hermit Road** – but also familiar to many visitors as the **West Rim Drive** – starts a hundred yards west of *Bright Angel Lodge*, just as Grand Canyon Village peters out. Offering a succession of very different but consistently impressive canyon panoramas, it's the most obvious, and most enjoyable, half-day sightseeing trip from the village. As the only vehicles allowed access in summer are the free Hermit's Rest Route **shuttle buses**, detailed on p.373, the Xanterra bus tours, and those displaying disabled permits, it also makes a welcome escape from the crowds and traffic elsewhere along the rim.

While for most of its length the road runs within a few yards of the canyon, it's paralleled, as ever, by the **Rim Trail**, even closer to the edge. No one walks the entire eight miles, but since you can get on and off the bus at any of eight designated stops, the ideal way to explore is to combine shuttle bus rides with stretches of **walking**. Traveling the full length of Hermit Road without ever getting off the bus takes about ninety minutes. To allow time for a couple of short hikes, and a stop at Hermit's Rest, give yourself perhaps three hours. Alternatively, you need never get on a bus at all; the four-mile round-trip hike from the village to Hopi Point, for example, takes under two hours. And finally, **cycling** is permitted year-round.

The first two viewpoints along the way, known as **Trailview I** and **II**, let prospective Bright Angel Trail hikers (see p.387) see exactly what they're in for, with its red-dirt switchbacks clearly etched against the canyon walls below. After just over a mile, as you round the corner to pass out of sight of Grand Canyon Village, the railed, rocky overlook at **Maricopa Point** commands an almost 360° view, though only the tiniest sliver of the churning Colorado is visible. This is a prime spot for identifying the majestic buttes on the far side of the river, such as the Brahma and Zoroaster "temples," each with its capping layer of hard red sandstone.

Beyond Maricopa, road and trail alike detour inland around a high fence, festooned with solemn radiation warnings. In the heart of this enclosure stands the hulking headframe of the **Orphan Mine**, which started out mining copper in 1893 but became America's largest uranium producer in the 1950s. Production stopped in 1969, and the mine was acquired by the park in 1988. There are still significant uranium deposits in the vicinity, however; by no coincidence, they're located in areas that remain outside the protection of the park. At the far end, **Powell Point** marks the spot where the park was officially dedicated on April 30, 1920, and holds a memorial to the crews of John Wesley Powell's two Colorado expeditions (see p.497).

Beneath the curved terrace at **Hopi Point**, two miles out from the village and the busiest of the western viewpoints, several distinct stretches of the Colorado are exposed to view. The most dramatic lies immediately below Plateau Point (see p.388), the last few yards of the trail to which are also visible. It's hard to believe that the river is 350ft wide down there, lying at the foot of gnarled and impossibly ancient walls of black schist, streaked through with vertical pink faults. To the west, the river threads its tortuous way toward the ocean between interleaved spurs of red rock, and a maze of lesser canyons twists among the mighty buttes.

Road and trail curve gracefully west of Hopi Point for three-quarters of a mile, tracing the lip of a lesser basin sometimes known as **The Inferno**, to reach **Mohave Point**, a large railed promontory from which the long-range vista remains substantially unchanged.

Pima Point is four miles further on, beyond another sheer-walled recess known as **The Abyss**. The river is by now less than two miles from the South Rim – look almost straight down to admire the three-quarter-mile Granite Rapid – but from the far bank it's another twelve labyrinthine miles to the North Rim.

Hermit Road ends slightly over a mile beyond Pima Point, at the **Hermit's Rest** way station, appealingly laid out in 1914 to evoke the dwelling of some imaginary canyon prospector, which sells gifts and simple snacks (daily: summer 8am–7.30pm; otherwise 9am–sunset). **Hermit Trail**, abandoned by the Santa Fe Railroad in 1931 but still popular with inner-canyon hikers (see p.390), starts a short way further along.

Desert View Drive

Desert View Drive runs for 23 miles east from Mather Point to Desert View itself, just inside the park's eastern boundary. Since threats to restrict all the parking lots enroute to shuttle and tour buses have yet to be implemented, the drive is the one part of the South Rim open year-round for self-guided driving tours. Allow two hours at the very least to get to the end and back.

The first lookout along the way, **Yaki Point**, is accessible in your own vehicle only between December and February, though as detailed on p.373 it's served year-round by free shuttle buses. Just two miles east of Yavapai Point, it commands much the same trans-canyon views as its neighbor. The most prominent of several inner-canyon trails on show is the **South Kaibab Trail** (see p.389), which starts its quickfire descent to Phantom Ranch from its own separate parking lot nearby. From the main overlook, you can spot it far below, switchbacking down an exposed scree slope of red rock between two buttes. If you scramble out onto the rocks beyond the viewpoint, you'll have clearer views down to the trail's principal staging post, O'Neill Butte.

Of all the awesome spectacles along the South Rim, few can match the sight of a fully grown **California condor** soaring on the canyon updrafts. These magnificent birds, with a wingspan of more than nine feet and a lifespan of up to sixty years, were reintroduced to Arizona in 1996. They can frequently be seen hovering above Grand Canyon Village, or perching just below the rim.

The birds were native to the canyon, and indeed to most of North America, for thousands of years, but their population was dwindling long before the first Europeans arrived. The last condor in the Grand Canyon area was recorded as nesting near Lees Ferry in the 1890s, while a solitary bird was seen circling Williams in 1924. During the 1980s, the last remaining 22 individuals of the species were trapped in California. A captive breeding program reintroduced the birds first in California, and subsequently in northern Arizona.

At the Arizona release site, located on the Vermilion Cliffs fifty miles northeast of the South Rim – see p.402 – scientists take great pains to keep contact between condors and humans to a minimum, so the birds don't learn to associate humans with food. Condors are very inquisitive creatures, however, and to the delight of tourists almost all the Arizona birds spend much of their time near the village. Project workers and park rangers attempt to discourage them from approaching too close and leave animal carcasses out for them in remote places. These natural scavengers also manage to find carrion by themselves.

Progress has been slow but definite. Around fifty free-flying, but tagged and monitored condors now live in the Grand Canyon, and they've started laying eggs, though no baby condor has yet grown to maturity. Nonetheless, hopes are high that a viable population will soon be established. For the latest news, call in at park visitor centers, or contact the Peregrine Fund (☎928/355-2270, ⊛www.peregrinefund.org).

Shoshone Point, a couple of miles east of Yaki Point, is the least-known and least-visited of the South Rim viewpoints, for the simple reason that it's only accessible on **foot**, along an easy one-mile trail from Desert View Drive. It's an absolute gem of a place, offering beautiful views along with an unparalleled sense of peace and privacy. The trail to Shoshone Point begins from an unpaved parking lot 1.4 miles east of the turn-off to Yaki Point; look for a yellow metal gate barring a dirt road, and a brown park notice reading "Site Use by Permit Only." The sign is there because the park service deliberately does not publicize Shoshone Point to casual visitors, preferring to make it available in summer for weddings and other private gatherings. However, there's no system for issuing permits to casual hikers. Instead, you're simply asked to respect the privacy of any group that may be out there, and not to hike out at all if there are a lot of cars at the parking lot. The point itself is truly spectacular. A solitary pale hoodoo marks the tip of its slender neck, while the sublime views range along the full panoply of the North Rim.

Eight miles east of Yaki Point, a total of twelve miles out from the village, **Grandview Point** is thought to have been where Europeans first saw the Grand Canyon, in 1540 (see p.367). It's suggested that their Hopi guides deliberately led them to a spot from which no trails were visible, to make the canyon appear even more impassable. Grandview was also the place where Grand Canyon tourism first took off, after prospector Peter Berry constructed the Grandview Trail down to his Last Chance copper mine in 1892, and visitors began to gravitate to the site. In terms of views, it's inarguably superior to Grand Canyon Village. The Colorado makes a broad and langorous entrance off to the east before disappearing westwards into the stunning sandstone labyrinth, while down below the twin prongs of **Horseshoe Mesa** reach out toward the North Rim.

Tusayan Ruin, ten miles further east, in the forest just south of the highway (and not to be confused with modern Tusayan), is what remains of a genuine **Ancestral Puebloan pueblo**. One of two thousand such sites identified in the Grand Canyon area so far, it may not be comparable in scale to relics found elsewhere in the Southwest, but its very existence enabled President Theodore Roosevelt to accord National Monument status to the entire Grand Canyon (see p.369). Only low stone walls survive of the original complex of buildings, thought to have been occupied for perhaps 25 years by a group of up to thirty people, around 1185 AD. A small museum (daily 9am–5pm; free) holds displays on the contemporary Navajo and Hopi peoples, as well as 4000-year-old twig figurines and Ancestral Puebloan pottery found nearby.

Desert View, 25 miles east of Grand Canyon Village, is the last viewpoint along Desert View Drive. As Hwy-64, however, the road continues another 34 miles to meet US-89 at Cameron (see p.400), so Desert View also provides visitors approaching from the east with their *first* opportunity to see what all the fuss is about. To the north, four miles distant, the Colorado River can be seen approaching its sudden westward turn. Just north of its last visible curve lies the confluence of the Colorado and Little Colorado rivers. A short way up the Little Colorado from the confluence lies the legendary *sipapu*, the hole through which the Hopi believe that human beings first entered this, the Fourth World (see p.567). You won't find this natural dome, topped by a permanent spring, marked on any map; only the Hopi are allowed access, or even know where it is. Over to the west, by contrast, the Colorado disappears deep into the Inner Gorge, engulfed on all sides by buttes and mesas, temples, shrines, and tabernacles.

The stark cliffs known as the **Palisades of the Desert** delineate the South Rim, while above them the pallid plains of the **Marble Plateau** stretch to the horizon, beneath an overwhelming sky. Sixty-five million years ago, this entire landscape was buried beneath an additional four or five thousand feet of sandstone. Thanks to erosion, all that remains are a few tiny vestiges, such as reddish **Cedar Mountain,** a mile or two back from the rim.

Rather than the canyon itself, however, what immediately draws the eye is the remarkable structure perched at its very lip – the cylindrical **Desert View Watchtower**, built by Mary Jane Colter in 1932, and held together by a solid framework of steel and cement beneath its Ancestral Puebloan-style masonry exterior. Stairs from the gift store at its base (daily 8am–7pm) climb through three successive circular chambers, decorated with authentic murals by the Hopi artist Fred Kabotie, as well as reproduction petroglyphs. Nearby stand an **information center** and bookstore (daily: summer 9am–7pm; spring and fall 9am–6pm; winter 9am–5pm); a **general store** (daily 9am–5pm); a **gas station** (summer daily 9am–6pm, winter daily 9am–5pm); and a gift store-cum-**snack bar** (daily 7.30am–6pm). The **Desert View Campground** (see p.380) is located at the end of a short spur road from the gas station.

South Rim hikes: into the canyon

Hiking any of the trails that descend into the Grand Canyon offers something more than just another view of the same thing. Instead you pass through a

CENTRAL CANYON OVERLOOKS & TRAILS

▲ Jacob Lake

NORTH RIM

T5

T4
Uncle Jim
Point

Sublime
Point

T1

T2

T3

Bright Angel
Point

Widforss
Point

Manu
Temple

Cottonwood
Campground

Shiva
Temple

Buddha
Temple

Deva
Temple

Tower
of Ra

Horus
Temple

Isis Temple

Brahma
Temple

Crystal Rapid

T8

Cheops
Pyramid

Zoroaster
Temple

Boucher Rapid

T3

Colorado River

Granite Rapid

Plateau
Point

Phantom
Ranch

T21

T9

T12

T13

T14

Granite Gorge

Mohave
Point

Hopi
Point

Powell
Point

T12

Pima
Point

T11

Indian Garden
Campground

T15

T13

Yaki
Point

T12

Hermit's
Rest

The Abyss

T10

Grand
Canyon
Village

Mather
Point

Shoshone
Point

Mather
Campground

64

SOUTH RIM

180

TRAILS

Widforss Trail	**T1**	Hermit Trail	**T11**
Transept Trail	**T2**	Tonto Trail	**T12**
North Kaibab Trail	**T3**	Bright Angel Trail	**T13**
Uncle Jim Trail	**T4**	River Trail	**T14**
Ken Patrick Trail	**T5**	South Kaibab Trail	**T15**
Cliff Spring Trail	**T6**	Grandview Trail	**T16**
Cape Final Trail	**T7**	Tonto East Trail	**T17**
Tonto West Trail	**T8**	New Hance Trail	**T18**
Boucher Trail	**T9**	Tanner Trail	**T19**
Dripping Springs		Beamer Trail	**T20**
Trail	**T10**	Clear Creek Trail	**T21**

Tusayan

▼ Williams & Flagstaff

sequence of utterly different landscapes, each with its own distinct climate, wildlife, and topography. However, while the canyon can offer a wonderful wilderness experience, it's essential to remember that it can be a hostile and very unforgiving environment, grueling even for expert hikers.

Park rangers have one simple message for all would-be hikers: **Don't try to hike to the river and back in one day**. It might not look far on the map, but

6

THE GRAND CANYON | South Rim hikes: into the canyon

384

Cameron ▼

it's harder than running a marathon. Several hikers each year die in the attempt, and several hundred more receive emergency medical treatment. If you do want to reach the Colorado, it's best to reserve campgrounds for two nights, so you have a day to recover before the trek out.

The South Rim is 7000 feet above sea level, an altitude which for most people is fatiguing in itself. Furthermore, all hikes start with a long, steep

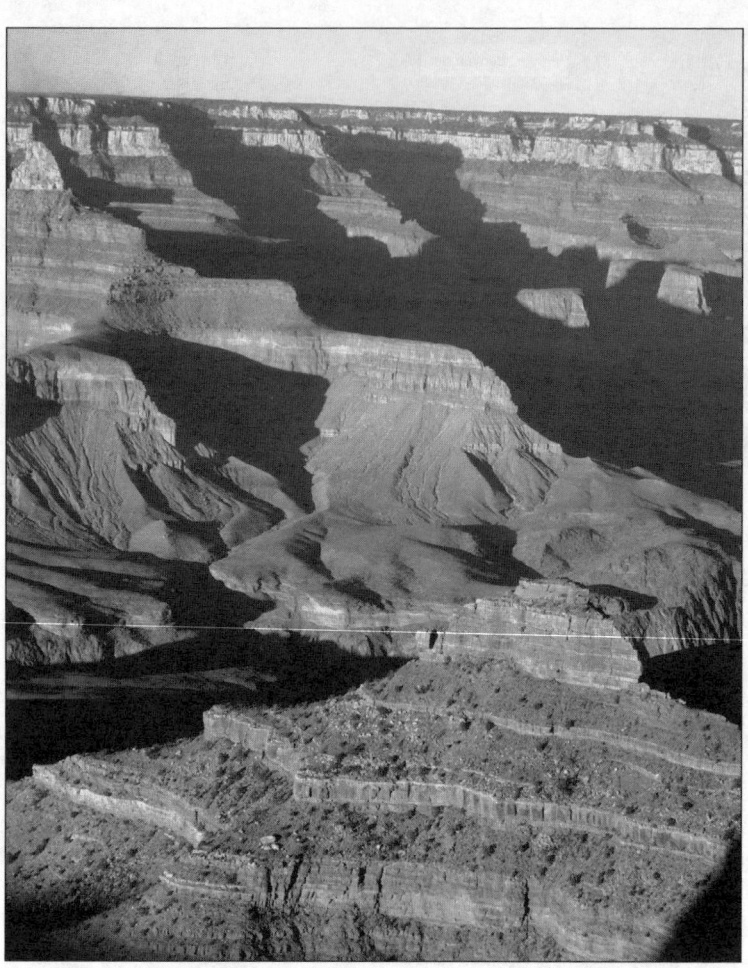

△ Sunset at the South Rim

descent – which can come as a shock to the knees – and unless you camp overnight you'll have to climb all the way back up again when you're hotter and wearier. As a rule of thumb, keep track of how much time you spend hiking down and allow twice that much to get back up again. Average summer temperatures inside the canyon exceed 100°F; to hike for eight hours in that sort of heat, you have to drink an incredible thirty pints of water. Always carry at least a quart per person – and much more if there are no water sources along your chosen trail. You must have food as well, as drinking large quantities without also eating can cause water intoxication. Ideally, the best seasons to hike are spring and fall.

Eight major trails lead into the canyon from the South Rim, but most either start from inaccessible places or are in poor condition. Traffic is heaviest on the **Bright Angel** and **South Kaibab** trails, the two "**Corridor Trails**" that link up in the gorge to lead to Phantom Ranch. They can be combined with the North Kaibab Trail to form a continuous route between the South and North rims. If you do want to hike from rim to rim, bear in mind that Transcanyon Shuttle runs from one to the other, so you can get back where you started (see p.406). The Corridor trails also offer the best **day-hikes** in the canyon; down the Bright Angel Trail as far **Indian Garden**, or at most out to **Plateau Point**, and down the South Kaibab Trail to **Cedar Ridge**.

The Bright Angel Trail

By far the busiest inner-canyon route – with mules as well as hikers – the **Bright Angel Trail** starts in Grand Canyon Village, alongside the wooden shack that once served as the Kolb photographic studio. An old Havasupai route, it was improved by miners a century ago, and then operated as a toll trail when the mines failed to prosper.

Although the side canyon immediately below the village makes access to the Tonto Platform relatively straightforward, it's still a long, hard climb. Most **day-hikers** content themselves with walking to either of the two resthouses in the first three miles, but with an early start you should be able to manage the round trip of nine miles to Indian Garden, or even twelve miles to Plateau Point. In summer, you can obtain water along the trail and only need to carry one quart of water per person; in winter, when there is none, you should carry two. Only try to reach the river – 7.8 miles from the trailhead, with Phantom Ranch almost two miles beyond that – if you've reserved a campsite for the night.

The trail begins with a long, exposed set of switchbacks down the dry, rocky hillside, which changes in color from pale pink to sheer red. There are two short tunnels in its first mile. After another mile, you start to see more wildlife around – deer, rodents, and the ubiquitous ravens – while rock surfaces at various points along the way hold a few pictographs, all but obscured by graffiti. Basic **resthouses**, built in the 1930s, are located after 1.6 and 3.1 miles. Both have water in summer (May–Sept) and emergency phones, but only the 1.6-mile one has restrooms.

Backcountry camping

Backcountry camping below the canyon rim is by permit only, with permits costing $10, plus $5 per person per night. Applications are accepted in person, by mail (PO Box 129, Grand Canyon, AZ 86023), or by fax (℉928/638-2125), but not by email or phone. Full details can be found online at ⊛www.nps.gov/grca/backcountry, or in the park's free *Backcountry Trip Planner* newspaper.

All applications have to specify an exact **itinerary**, detailing where you'll spend each night – either named campgrounds or the wider-ranging "Use Areas" coded on official park maps, also available online. Between March and mid-November, there's a limit on the most popular trails of two nights per party per campsite.

Mailed or **faxed** applications are accepted for dates until the end of the fourth complete month after they're submitted; thus if you're planning a trip in the peak month of July, you'd better mail your application on March 1. To apply **in person**, turn up at either the **Backcountry Information Center**, in the Maswik Transportation Center near *Maswik Lodge* in Grand Canyon Village (daily 8am–noon & 1–5pm; ℡928/638-7875 Mon–Fri 1–5pm only), or at the **North Rim Backcountry Office**, a quarter-mile north of the *North Rim Campground* (daily 8am–noon & 1–5pm; ℡928/638-7868). Even in peak season, your chances of a **last-minute cancellation** are pretty good. Your name is added to a waiting list, and each morning at 8am that day's cancellations are reassigned – though you have to be there on the spot to get one.

Beyond the second resthouse, a set of switchbacks known as **Jacob's Ladder** carry you down the sheer Redwall cliff, a major obstacle throughout almost the entire canyon. Then, finally, the trail starts to level out, and the vegetation gets greener, with a scattering of yellow- and red-blossomed cacti to either side. Soon you hear the astonishing sound of trickling water in Garden Creek, lined by dazzling green trees.

The spring at **Indian Garden**, 4.6 miles from the rim, is the reason this trail exists. Native peoples really did have a garden here, originally planted in prehistoric times and continuously used by the Havasupai from around 1300 AD until the nineteenth century. Now this unexpected little oasis holds a ranger station, restrooms, separate camping and day-use areas, and a staging post for mules.

Plateau Point

From Indian Garden, the Bright Angel Trail continues to the river (see below), while the **Tonto Trail** runs both east and west along the flat, arid Tonto Platform. A spur trail off the Tonto Trail – reached by heading left at Indian Garden, crossing Garden Creek, and then turning right at an obvious intersection three-quarters of a mile along – threads its way out to **Plateau Point**, a superb overlook above the Inner Gorge from which it is not possible to descend any further. Constructed to give day-tripping mule riders a view of the river, this trail also makes an ideal route for hikers, who should allow at least eight hours for the full day-hike from the rim and back. The desert landscape, barren even by inner-canyon standards, is spectacular, with agave and yucca plants shooting up from the sandy soil, and the mighty red buttes and mesas of the canyon now framed against the blue sky.

Shortly after you get your first awesome glimpse of the black tumbling walls of the gorge, the trail comes to an end. Precariously perched on the rocky outcrops, you can see a long stretch of the dark-green Colorado, though both the bridges and Phantom Ranch lie out of sight around the next promontory to the east. With binoculars, you can just make out the buildings back at the top of the rim, six miles away.

Devil's Corkscrew and the Colorado River

The continuation of the Bright Angel Trail beyond Indian Garden first drops through the fertile margins of Garden Creek, then switchbacks down the **Devil's Corkscrew**, hacked into the rock during the 1930s to create a shortcut to the river. Once beside the Colorado, dwarfed beneath thousand-foot walls of dark-gray granite, it undulates through sand dunes scattered with yucca and prickly pear.

Hikers can cross the river around a mile along, using the 1960s **Silver Bridge**; mules, which quite sensibly balk at the prospect of seeing the river between its slats, have to continue a little further. The 400ft **suspension bridge** they prefer was set in place in 1928, hanging from twin cables that were carried down the Kaibab Trail on the shoulders of 42 Havasupai. Not far away on the other side – though you'll have to cross Bright Angel Creek twice to reach it – is **Bright Angel Campground**, with **Phantom Ranch** a short distance up beyond.

The temperature at river level tends to be around 20°F higher than on the South Rim, and there's significantly less rainfall. The **ecology** down here has changed since Glen Canyon Dam was completed in the mid-1960s (see p.482). Previously, up to a million tons of earth and rock hurtled past Phantom Ranch each day. Now it's more like 40,000; trees that would previously have been swept away are establishing themselves, and fish that were perfectly adapted to such conditions are now becoming extinct.

Phantom Ranch

Bright Angel Creek, which flows down Bright Angel Canyon from the North Rim to meet the Colorado below Grand Canyon Village, was named by John Wesley Powell in 1869. His journals record, "We discover a stream entering from the north, a clear beautiful creek coming down through a gorgeous red canyon." The name was chosen to contrast with the muddy Dirty Devil River, upstream in Utah, and identified a small **Ancestral Puebloan ruin** that's still visible today.

This confluence now marks the only place where inner-canyon hikers and mule riders can not only cross the Colorado River but also camp and even sleep in a real bed at the bottom of the canyon. **Phantom Ranch**, beside Bright Angel Creek, consists of assorted cabins, corrals, and outbuildings clustered around a central lodge; all stand amid huge cottonwoods and fruit orchards planted early in the twentieth century to shade a group of tents known as Rust's Camp. Renamed Roosevelt's Camp after a visit by Theodore Roosevelt in 1913, that was replaced by Phantom Ranch in 1922, designed as a dude ranch by Mary Jane Colter.

First call on the fully equipped individual **cabins** (❹) goes to riders on the **mule trips** detailed on p.374, but they're also let to hikers when available, which is more likely in winter. Otherwise, hikers can get beds for just over $30 per night in one of the four ten-bunk, single-sex **dormitories** (❷) – two for men and two for women – with bedding, showers, towels, and soap provided. **Reservations** are essential; as for the South and North Rim lodges, they're handled by Xanterra Parks & Resorts (☎303/297-2757 or 1-888/297-2757, ⓦwww.grandcanyonlodges.com). **Cancellations** are handed out first-come, first-served, at the *Bright Angel Lodge* early each morning. All supplies reach *Phantom Ranch* the same way you do, so family-style **meals** in its **restaurant** are expensive, a minimum of $17.50 for breakfast and up to $32 for dinner.

All **camping** at the beautiful *Bright Angel Campground*, a little closer to the Colorado, is by **permit** only, as detailed on p.387. Do not hike down without a reservation.

South Kaibab Trail

The **South Kaibab Trail**, the most direct route from the South Rim to Phantom Ranch, is never as busy as the Bright Angel Trail. And no wonder – taking just six miles to drop to the river, it's an even steeper haul, and the trailhead lies roughly three miles east of the information plaza. If you plan to combine the Bright Angel and South Kaibab trails in hiking to and from Phantom Ranch, be sure to make the Kaibab the one you go *down*. Even if you can only spare the time for a short day-hike, however, you'll be rewarded by superb views.

The trail starts by descending slightly west of **Yaki Point**, but once past the end of the promontory it runs along the top of **Cedar Ridge**. This high crest surveys a thirty-mile stretch of the canyon in both directions and also faces straight up Bright Angel Canyon toward the North Rim. In the absence of any water en route, most hikers turn back after 1.5 miles. If you keep going, down a precipitous and very exposed slope, you meet the **Tonto Trail**, 4.4 miles down. A long, if level, trek east enables backpackers to connect with the Grandview Trail (see p.390) but the obvious way to go is west. At a spot known as the **Tipoff**, a few hundred yards along, you're poised to plunge down into the Inner Gorge. The river, and the 1928 suspension bridge that leads to Phantom Ranch, are little more than a mile away. Alternatively, continue on the Tonto Trail for four miles to **Indian Garden** (see opposite), and climb back up to the village from there.

△ South Kaibab Trail, South Rim

Grandview Trail

The **Grandview Trail**, down from the parking lot at Grandview Point (see p.383), was built during the 1890s to aid copper mining on **Horseshoe Mesa**, which remains littered with abandoned mine workings. Although it's possible, by connecting with other trails, to use the Grandview to find your way down to the Tonto Platform and thus eventually to the Colorado, it's not itself a rim-to-river route. Instead, the hike down to the mesa and back has become one of the most popular **day-hikes** in the park. That doesn't mean it's easy, however; now officially "unmaintained," it's a very demanding trail. Several of its switch-backs were constructed by inserting metal rods deep into the canyon wall, then covering them with juniper logs, stones, and dirt. At times it can be a little hair-raising, but it has stayed surprisingly sturdy for over a century. Reckon on six hours for the whole round trip.

Hermit Trail

Named in honor of Louis Boucher, a nineteenth-century prospector, the **Hermit Trail** is another unmaintained trail that dates from the days when the obstreperous Ralph Cameron controlled access to most of the prime rim-edge sites (see p.369). Built in 1912 by Fred Harvey for mule riders from the *El Tovar* and abandoned in 1931, much of its engineering remains in good shape. Once more, it's used mainly by solitary types, setting off on long backcountry camping expeditions away from the crowds.

From the Hermit's Rest parking lot at the end of West Rim Drive (see p.381), the trail drops into a side canyon, then switchbacks into Hermit Gorge and slowly descends a high rock wall far above Hermit Creek. A detour less than two miles along allows for the popular day-hike to **Dripping Spring**, which is not recommended for anyone with a fear of heights. Alternatively, if you press on, rockfalls tend to make for slow progress, but the resthouse at **Santa Maria**

Spring, 2.3 miles down from the trailhead, is a lovely day-hike destination. Beyond that, views of the Inner Gorge eventually start to open up. The *Hermit Camp* is not far west of the junction with the Tonto Trail, 7.7 miles along. Turning right (north) shortly before the campground brings you to the Colorado itself, just under nine miles from the trailhead, at **Hermit Rapid**, where the wave-like surge of the river can reach over twenty feet high.

The Havasupai reservation

Havasu Canyon, one of the most spellbindingly beautiful places in the entire Southwest, nestles deep in the Grand Canyon a mere 35 miles west of the park headquarters. The only approach is from the southwest, however, so it's a road trip of almost two hundred miles; once you leave the interstate, the last ninety miles are across the endless Coconino Plateau. You must have reserved a spot of the campground to overnight in the canyon; do not entertain the thought of hiking down and out in a single day.

Those visitors who brave the eight-mile desert hike down into the canyon are rewarded by a stunning oasis of turquoise waterfalls and lush vegetation, a Shangri-La that has been home for centuries beyond record to the same small group of Native Americans. They're here thanks to a geological fluke; although the canyon receives only nine inches of rain each year, all the water that falls for three thousand square miles around funnels down into this one narrow gorge, to create the year-round torrent of Havasu Stream.

Havasu Canyon forms the heart of the **Havasupai reservation**, said by a 1930s anthropologist to be "the only spot in the United States where native culture has remained in anything like its pristine condition." Since then, tourism has become the mainstay of the tribal economy, but visitor numbers are kept deliberately low, at about 35,000 per year. Suggestions of building a road – or even a tramway – down into the canyon have always been rejected, to minimize the impact on the traditional way of life. Instead, the five hundred or so Havasupai earn their keep by ferrying nonhikers up and down the trail on horses and pack mules, and by operating a thriving **campground** beside the stream as well as a comfortable lodge in the village of **Supai**. Although visitors should not expect sweeping views of the Grand Canyon itself – or to have much interaction with the tribal members – for spectacular desert scenery and sheer romance, the Havasupai reservation is beyond compare.

Getting to the reservation

The only way to reach the Havasupai reservation by road is from I-40, turning off at **Seligman** (see p.357), if you're coming from Flagstaff or Grand Canyon Village, or at **Kingman** (see p.357) from Las Vegas or California. Stock up with food, water, and gas when you leave the interstate, then follow Hwy-66 – the

The **Havasupai** – the "people of the blue-green water" – can trace their occupation of Havasu Canyon back at least as far as 1300 AD. The word **"Pai"** means people and refers to a Yuman-speaking group that reached the Southwest via California well over a thousand years ago. They soon quarreled, splitting to form the **Hualapai** ("People of the Tall Pines") of northwest Arizona, and the **Yavapai** ("Almost-People," who no longer quite deserved to be regarded as people) who settled along the Colorado further south. The Hualapai established close links with Pueblo groups such as the Hopi and Zuni, from whom they eventually acquired the art of raising sheep and horses, as well as the seeds and skills to grow such crops as peaches. Until the Havasupai were allocated their own reservation toward the end of the nineteenth century, they regarded themselves not as a separate "tribe" but as just another band of Hualapai.

Although the Havasupai took their name from the turquoise river that watered their fields, they only lived on the canyon floor in summer, in houses of hide-covered branches. In winter, the canyon made a cold, miserable home, lacking big game and wood for fuel and receiving as little as five hours of sunlight per day. Instead, the Havasupai moved up onto the plateau to hunt deer, elk, and antelope, using artificial water holes to lure them closer. Their territory extended beyond the San Francisco Peaks (near modern Flagstaff) and took in the region now occupied by Grand Canyon Village.

In the summer of 1776, as the Declaration of Independence was being signed in Philadelphia, the Havasupai welcomed their first white visitor. **Father Francisco Tomás Garcés**, a missionary from San Xavier del Bac near Tucson, was greeted by five days of feasting. Describing the Grand Canyon as a "calaboose of cliffs and canyons," he dubbed it the Puerto de Bucareli in honor of the Viceroy who had despatched him; more enduringly, he was the first to name the Río Colorado. Meanwhile, as Garcés explored the canyon, the rest of his expedition blazed a trail to California, where they founded San Francisco.

The Havasupai then remained undisturbed for a further eighty years, before Anglo prospectors and surveyors began to enter the region. Conflict arose in 1866, when to encourage the spread of the railroads Congress granted the Atlantic and Pacific Railroad company ownership of swathes of land adjoining its tracks across northern Arizona. Native resistance soon escalated into **war**, and the defeated Hualapai spent several years confined to a reservation near Ehrenberg on the Colorado. Because the Havasupai did not participate in the fighting, they were allowed to remain in their traditional territory. In negotiations over the extent of a permanent Havasupai reservation, the US government was as usual only prepared to acknowledge Native American "ownership" of land that held permanent settlements and cultivated fields. Areas used for hunting, gathering, or even grazing, especially if use was shared by more than one band, were never included in reservations. Fearful of being deported themselves, the Havasupai settled in 1882 for a tiny 518-acre plot at the bottom of Havasu Canyon. Restricted to a fraction of

only surviving segment of **Route 66** not to have been superseded by newer roads – to the poorly marked intersection with **Arrowhead Hwy-18**, six miles east of **Peach Springs** (see p.398).

Hwy-18 runs for its entire 56-mile length with barely a building in sight, across bare sagebrush desert interrupted by patches of thick ponderosa forest. Despite maps to the contrary, it's paved throughout, and there's no possibility of losing your way. Eventually, the road starts to wind down through burgeoning canyonlands, coming to an end at the large plateau known as **Hualapai Hilltop**. Although this is no more than a small cluster of dilapidated shacks, their former range, they were obliged to farm what little land they were granted as intensively as possible.

A century of hardship was to follow, during which the Havasupai repeatedly petitioned to have their reservation enlarged. Suffering great spiritual uncertainty, both the Havasupai and Hualapai took part in the **Ghost Dance** movement in the 1890s, when Native Americans throughout the West joined in trance-like rituals designed to ensure that white men would vanish from the land and the old ways would return. The Havasupai also briefly adopted the rain-making *kachina* dances of the Hopi (see p.585), until a catastrophic **flood** on January 1, 1910 destroyed their village, which then stood half a mile from its current site.

At first, the creation of **Grand Canyon National Park** placed yet more restrictions on Havasupai use of traditional lands. One early supervisor avowed that the "Grand Canyon should be preserved for the everlasting pleasure and instruction of our intelligent citizens as well as those from foreign countries; I therefore deem it just and necessary to keep the wild and inappreciable Indians from off the Reserve." Although Coconino National Forest takes its name from the Hopi word for the Havasupai, tribal members could only graze animals there by annual permit. The Havasupai survived largely through disobeying whatever unenforceable regulations outsiders sought to impose, continuing to spend their winters up on the plateau. Many Havasupai in due course found jobs in Grand Canyon Village, while tourism to Havasu Canyon itself became an important element in the tribal economy.

After endless legal battles – and a lobbying campaign to persuade environmentalist groups that Native Americans could look after wilderness lands every bit as well as the Park Service – the Havasupai finally won their struggle in 1975. Almost 200,000 acres were added to the reservation, the largest tract of land ever returned to Native Americans. It came only just in time; almost immediately, the Grand Canyon region experienced a boom in **uranium** mining, with over 3500 claims filed in the Arizona Strip during the ensuing decade.

In 1988, Energy Fuels Nuclear was granted rights to develop a uranium mine to be known as **Canyon Mine**, at a site outside the reservation, close to **Red Butte** in the Kaibab National Forest, which is sacred to the Havasupai as *Mat Taav Tijundva*. Despite fears that it could contaminate Havasu Stream, Havasu Canyon, and ultimately the Colorado itself, federal courts blocked Havasupai attempts to stop the mine. The mine was built but never went into operation, thanks to a drop in prices caused by the worldwide glut of uranium. It now belongs to the International Uranium Corporation, which continues to deny suggestions that the mine might be about to be reactivated, while nonetheless insisting that the low price of uranium is the only factor holding it back.

The other major threat facing the Havasupai is that any future tourist development at the South Rim – along the lines of the stalled "Canyon Forest Village" scheme (see p.370) – would be liable to deplete the water table for hundreds of miles around. That could mean that Havasu Stream might finally run dry.

there are usually far more vehicles parked here than you might anticipate for such a remote spot.

Hualapai Hilltop commands a long view of the white-walled **Hualapai Canyon**, cutting into the tablelands as it stretches off to the north. From the end of the parking lot, the Hualapai Trail to Supai zigzags steeply down the hillside to the right and can then be seen threading its way across the valley floor below. Do not attempt to go down unless you have already reserved accommodation.

Hikers are free to set off whenever they choose. If you prefer to **ride** down on either horse or mule, make a reservation at the same time that you book your accommodation. The mule train leaves the hilltop at some point between 10am and noon; if you arrive any later than noon, you won't be able to ride down, and you'll lose both your reservation and your deposit. To ride as far as the **village** costs $70 per person one-way and $120 round-trip, and should be arranged with the management of the lodge (☎928/448-2111); riding to the **campground** costs $75 one-way, $150 round-trip, and is arranged by the **Havasupai Tourist Enterprise** (☎928/448-2121 or 2141, ⓦwww.havasupaitribe.com). Riders' baggage weighing over ten pounds has to be carried separately – people share the cost of one animal that can carry up to four packs, again for $70 one-way, $120 round-trip – and many hikers also arrange to have their bags carried.

A **helicopter shuttle** service also operates between Hualapai Hilltop and Supai village. In recent years, it's been active between 10am and 1pm on Thurs, Fri, Sat and Sun between mid-March and October, and on Fri & Sun only between November and mid-March. Passengers are carried on a first-come, first-served basis, without any advance reservations, for a one-way fare of around $85. Call the Havasupai Tourist Enterprise to check whether the service is currently operational.

The trail to Supai

Apart from its initial switchbacks, the **Hualapai Trail** is not especially difficult. It is, however, a long eight-mile walk, with no shade for the first three miles and no reliable water source until very near the end. Allow around three hours to reach Supai village (and four or more to come back up again), and be sure to carry all the food and water you will need for a day in the desert.

Havasupai Tours and Excursions

An expensive but undeniably wonderful way to see Havasu Canyon if you're short on time is to take a **one-day helicopter trip** from **Tusayan**, just outside Grand Canyon Village on the South Rim, with **Papillon Grand Canyon Helicopters** (adults $455, under-12s $435; ☎928/638-2419 or 1-800/528-2418, ⓦwww.papillon.com). While your flight from Tusayan won't take you over the main body of the Grand Canyon, the descent down into Havasupai through assorted side canyons is an exhilarating adventure. Once you're on the ground, you can either ride horseback to Havasu Falls and back, or hike; either way, there's time to linger by the various falls. Meals are not included. When lodge accommodation is available, it's also possible stay overnight and fly back the next day.

In addition, various organizations offer guided expeditions to the Havasupai Reservation. Especially recommended is the **Grand Canyon Field Institute** (see p.374), which typically runs three four-day hiking and camping tours each summer, one of which is reserved for women only, for a fee of around $525 (☎928/638-2485 or 1-866/471-4435, ⓦwww.grandcanyon.org/fieldinstitute).

Some commercial operators promise a more luxurious experience. **Arizona Outback Adventures** (☎480/945-2881 or 1-866/455-1601, ⓦwww.azoutbackadventures .com) offers three-, four- and five-day trips with accommodation at their own private "Base Camp." Various options, including hiking and/or helicopter transport, cost from $1375 up to $1635. **Discovery Treks** (☎520/404-1151 or 1-888/256-8731, ⓦwww .discoverytreks.com) arranges three-day trips with a choice of hiking, horseback riding and helicopter rides, and camping or staying in the lodge. Prices range from around $900 upwards.

The route is very obvious and kept busy throughout the day with small supply trains of mules and horses. Once on the valley floor, it follows the bed of a dry wash between red-rock walls that slowly but inexorably climb to form a deep, narrow canyon. The sand underfoot is so thick that it shifts at every step, but the potential for flash floods is clear from the much-scoured rocks to either side. Mighty boulders occasionally all but block the path, while solitary cottonwoods reach up toward the thin strip of sky overhead.

After almost seven miles, the trail reaches the intersection where Havasu Canyon comes in from the right; until 1910, this was the site of Supai village (see below). Do not continue straight ahead into Cataract Canyon at this point – it took three weeks to find a dehydrated camper who did so in 1975. Bear left instead, at a dense cluster of small trees. The sound of rushing water soon signals the emergence of Havasu Stream from hidden crevices in the rock, and before long it's flowing through the parched landscape in all its blue-green splendor.

Not far beyond, you cross a low rise to be confronted by the meadow that holds the modern village, and the two red-rock pillars that watch over Supai from the high canyon wall on the far side. Known as the **Wigleeva**, these twin sentinels are regarded as the guardian spirits of the Havasupai.

Supai

Though located in a superb natural setting – a wide flat clearing surrounded on all sides by forbidding walls of red sandstone – the village of **SUPAI** is not in itself attractive. The Havasupai were only obliged to build a year-round settlement down in the canyon after losing their lands on the plateau above (see p.392), and this site was their second choice after the first proved prone to flooding. It too has suffered repeated damage from floods, including four major inundations over the past decade. It therefore consists of just a scattering of basic timber-frame houses and prefabricated cabins. The name itself is also a flimsy fabrication; "Supai" is a meaningless abbreviation of "Havasupai," invented by the US Post Office.

Once the Hualapai Trail, running alongside a line of irrigation ditches, has shepherded you into the village, the first building you come to holds the tribal **registration office**. Only campers need to pay the $30 reservation **entrance fee** here; for lodge guests, it's added to their bill. A back room holds a small **museum** (daily 7am–7pm; $1), with a random but reasonably interesting assortment of early twentieth-century photographs and newspaper cuttings. Although the Havasupai are famous for crafts such as basketmaking, ancient artifacts have become too expensive for the museum to afford; instead, the finest old Havasupai baskets to be seen in Arizona are in the Heard Museum in Phoenix (see p.260).

Fifty yards further on, beyond the only post office in the US still to receive its mail by pack mule, lies Supai's dusty, wind-blown **plaza**. Benches outside the village's one **grocery store** form its main social center, where the older Havasupai gather each evening. The younger set, together with a vast popula-tion of dogs, are more likely to be found on the terrace of the **café**, opposite. Once past that, the trail skirts the edge of the village school, then branches off left down toward the campground. Visitors are forbidden to wander away from the main trail into the farm lands around the village.

Practicalities

All visitors, whether planning to camp or stay in the lodge, should make advance reservations by calling either **Havasupai Tourist Enterprises** (☎928/448-2121 or 2141, ⓦwww.havasupaitribe.com) or the lodge. Space is at a premium in summer, and is often fully reserved several months in advance. All prices on the Havasupai Reservation are subject to an additional five percent **tribal sales tax**.

Havasupai Lodge (☎928/448-2111 or 448-2201, ⓔlodge@havasupaitribe .com; ❼) is located slightly apart from things on the edge of the village, close to the canyon wall behind the school. It's a simple two-story structure, much like a typical national park lodge, where the reasonable motel-style rooms are without phones or TVs. All sleep four people.

The *Lodge* has a pleasant little garden, but the only place to get a **meal** in Supai is at the *Tribal Cafe* (daily: hours vary from 6am–7pm in summer down to 8am–5pm in winter; ☎928/448-2981). Here the food is far from exciting, with fried breakfasts, and a lunch or dinner of beef stew, Indian fry-bread, or burritos; pretty much everything seems to cost $7, or more if you want grated cheese on top. The grocery store has a limited selection of processed items, all carried in by mule and priced accordingly.

Spending a night at the **campground** – see below – costs $12 per person.

Below Supai

All the **waterfalls** for which the Havasupai reservation is famous lie further down the canyon beyond Supai. The riverbed immediately below the village is forever being reshaped by flash floods and fresh erosion, and the first set of falls you come to, **Navajo Falls**, tend to look different from one day to the next. About a mile and a half into your descent from the village, you'll probably hear it thundering from the left. Clearings in the undergrowth at regular intervals should enable you to see their foaming white tumbling, but these days it's seldom possible to approach them any closer. The falls were named for Chief Navajo, who led the Havasupai at the time the reservation was first established and died in 1900.

Havasu Falls

The trail beyond Navajo Falls soon reaches the stupendous double cascade of **Havasu Falls**. First seen from an overlook more or less level with the top, this is an absolutely breathtaking sight. The stream foams white as it hurtles over a 150ft cliff, to crash into shallow terraces filled with perfectly clear turquoise water. The rock formations all around are formed from water-deposited limestone known as **travertine** – the same stuff that creates the stalactites of Carlsbad Caverns and clogs the inside of domestic kettles. It's the light travertine coating on the riverbed that gives the water its astonishing blue-green glow. Be sure not to walk barefoot on it, however; travertine is horrendously sharp stuff.

In the days when it was known to the park service as **Bridal Veil Falls**, Havasu Falls used to be a long broad expanse of water, which explains the solidified sheets and curtains of travertine that run right across its wide brim. Then a flash flood punched out a notch right in the center, through which the falls now gush to either side of a small outcrop that's knitted together by a frail cottonwood sapling. Side trails off the main path lead down to an idyllic shaded "beach" beside the largest, deepest pool, where the ceaseless roar makes conversation difficult, but swimming is all but irresistible. On the far side of the natural travertine dams that divide the various terraces – partially reconstructed after the 1993 flood, using artificial groynes that are now buried beneath new deposits – picnic tables stand in a cottonwood grove at a side canyon's mouth.

It's possible to take a short **horseback tour** from Supai village down to Havasu Falls, at a cost of $60; for reservations, contact Havasupai Tourist Enterprise (see p.394).

The campground

A short distance beyond Havasu Falls, two miles down from Supai village, you finally reach the Havasu **campground**, set in an especially narrow and high-walled segment of the canyon. Although this site was once a tribal burial ground, it was only added to the reservation in 1975, having originally been considered to be too rich in mineral deposits to be left to the Indians.

The campground stretches for almost a mile, with tents pitched in clearings in the woods to either side of the stream. Facilities are primitive in the extreme, with no showers or campfires, but it's a wonderful spot, with treatable drinking water provided by fresh springs in the canyon wall. Although villagers are barred from the area in summer by tribal edict, groups of horses stand tethered at the entrance, waiting to carry campers back up the hill.

Mooney Falls and the Colorado River

Havasu campground is brought to an abrupt end by the 200ft **Mooney Falls**. This natural barrier was long regarded as virtually impassable; its modern name comes from an unfortunate prospector who fell to his death here in 1880, after a rope snagged as he was being lowered to the bottom. Colorful stories that he dangled for three days before the rope broke are untrue, but it did take many months before his companions managed to retrieve his body, which lay by then beneath a coating of limestone.

The trail to the bottom is still difficult today. You can scramble down the travertine ledges to reach the two successive tunnels made by Mooney's cohorts that drop through the cliff face. Next you'll come to a sheer section that was blasted away in the flood of 1993 and now consists of a vertical series of footholds, aided by an iron chain fixed into the rock. The prospect of having to climb back up is terrifying enough to make many hikers to turn back at this point; if you press on, there are also two steep ladders to contend with. Assuming you do make it to the bottom, the pools and swimming holes at the foot of the falls are once again gorgeous.

A long day-hike from the campground continues on for three miles to **Beaver Falls**, a quick-fire set of rapids that's as far as the Havasupai recommend any visitors should try to go. Negotiating an onwards route involves climbing up to and along a high ledge, after which it takes four more miles before you eventually reach the Colorado itself. Quite possibly, you'd be greeted by river-runners who preferred to get here the easy way, shooting 157 miles of whitewater from Lees Ferry (see p.401).

The Hualapai reservation: the "West Rim"

Immediately west of the Havasupai reservation, and also inhabited by descendants of the Pai people, the **Hualapai Indian reservation** spreads across almost a million acres, bounded to the north by a 108-mile stretch of the Colorado River.

The only town, **PEACH SPRINGS**, 35 miles northwest of **Seligman** on Route 66 (see p.357), is home to just under a thousand of the total Hualapai population of around 1500. It's no more than a straggle of buildings along the highway, of which the most prominent is the shiny, modern *Hualapai Lodge*, which holds sixty good-sized motel bedrooms and a reasonable restaurant (T1-888/255-9550 or 928/769-2230, Wwww.destinationgrandcanyon.com; April–Oct ❺, Nov–March ❹). The **Hualapai Office of Tourism** in the lodge (Mon–Fri 9am–5pm; same phone) serves as the headquarters for one-day **rafting trips** on the Colorado (departs daily mid-March to mid-Oct at 8am; $280).

Grand Canyon West

A cluster of overlooks above the Hualapai's river frontage, fifty miles northwest of Peach Springs, are promoted as **Grand Canyon West**, or the "**West Rim**" of the Grand Canyon – a canny piece of marketing aimed at Las Vegas's 35 million annual tourists. This is the closest spot to Las Vegas where it's possible to see the canyon, and most of its visitors are day-trippers who don't realize they're not seeing the canyon at its best. As it starts to peter out, the canyon here lacks the colossal depth and width of its central section, and it holds none of the towering mesas, buttes, and temples so conspicuous from the South or North Rim viewpoints. Even so, the so-called West Rim still makes a tremendous spectacle. The Hualapai are currently trying to maximize the commercial potential of their canyon-edge lands. They've announced such ambitious plans that it's hard to say what will truly materialize, but they've clearly attracted a great deal of investment, and the infrastructure is rapidly being transformed.

Several companies offer day-trip **air** tours **from Las Vegas** to the rudimentary airstrip alongside the West Rim headquarters. Papillon Grand Canyon Helicopters (T928/699-3993 or 1-800/528-2418, Wwww.papillon.com), Maverick Helicopter Tours (T702/261-0007 or 1-888/261-4414, Wwww.maverickhelicopter .com) and Sundance Helicopters (T702/736-0606 or 1-800/653-1881, Wwww .helicoptour.com) provide **helicopter** tours starting at around $230, while **fixed-wing** operators, using small airplanes, include *Scenic Airlines* (T702/638-3200 or 1-800/634-6801, Wwww.scenic.com), who charge $249 with a basic bus tour, or $379 with a helicopter flight into the canyon.

The best **driving** routes approach Grand Canyon West not via Peach Springs, but along paved roads from the west and the south. The busiest of the pair, **Pierce Ferry Road**, heads east from **US-93** thirty miles north of Kingman and forty miles south of the Hoover Dam. The new welcome center on Pierce Ferry Road serves as a **park-and-ride** for those wanting to spare their own vehicle the 14-mile unpaved drive on Diamond Bar Road. The bus shuttle costs $5-10 for a round-trip fare; the schedule varies throughout the year and reservations are recommended (T 1-877/716-9378).

To continue driving on your own, from US-93 follow Pierce Ferry Road for twenty-eight miles then turn right (east) onto **Diamond Bar Road**. After a rocky, fourteen-mile climb through foothills scattered with Joshua trees and up the Grand Wash Cliffs, you enter the Hualapai reservation, and reach the airstrip and headquarters for Grand Canyon West five miles later. Alternatively, you can take the forty-mile **Stockton Hill Road** due north from central Kingman to join Pierce Ferry Road. At that point, it's still 26 miles to Grand Canyon West. All visitors to Grand Canyon West report to a small single-story building to the right of the highway, a few hundred yards short of the rim. This serves as the **terminal** for both the airstrip across the road and the helicopter launch-pad right outside, and also the **tribal headquarters** for tours and permits. To reach the two main viewpoints, further down the road, you have to join a **bus tour** from here. If you've flown in, some package will already be included in the overall price you've paid; otherwise, the various permutations and possibilities are outlined in the **Grand Canyon West Tours** box (below).

Eagle Point, a short distance from the terminal, is not on the rim, but faces a narrow, unnamed side canyon whose cliff face bears an uncanny resemblance to a massive eagle with its wings outstretched. This will be the setting for the **Skywalk**, a horseshoe-shaped glass-bottomed walkway that has the potential to become one of the world's most famous tourist attractions. Visitors will be asked to pay approximately $25 for the thrill of walking out over the sheer 4000-foot drop, which is not directly above the Colorado. In addition to this dramatic cantilevered bridge, a modern visitor center with a high-end restaurant and movie theater will be finished by the end of 2006.

At the dead end of the road, two miles from the terminal, the unfortunately named **Guano Point** surveys long stretches of the Colorado in both directions. Though the Grand Canyon looks as if it could go on forever, in fact it comes to an end not far beyond the next bend in the river to the west, where it bisects the Grand Wash Cliffs.

The Colorado River

No hiking trail connects Grand Canyon West with the Colorado River below, but many visitors take the four-minute helicopter ride down from the terminal. The flight in itself is a major adventure, and it's also a real thrill to find yourself walking down by the river in the depths of the inner gorge.

A short footpath leads down from the landing site to the river's edge, where wooden jetties act as the base for the pontoons and jet boats that sweep visitors out for a quick swirl on the river. The adjoining beach is the terminus

Grand Canyon West Tours

The following basic tour packages are offered at Grand Canyon West (☏ 1-877/716-9378, ⓦ www.destinationgrandcanyon.com).

Earth ($29). Bus tour to Eagle Point and Guano Point; no meal included.

The Spirit ($50). Everything on the Earth tour, plus a hike at Guano Point; a photo opportunity with Hualapai tribal members; a Wagon Wheel ride or Wild West show; and either a buffet at Guano Point or a barbecue cook-out.

Explorer ($109). Everything on the Spirit tour, plus either a hummer tour or a horse-back ride. Extra components can be added to any tour**, such as the** Skywalk ($25), a **horseback ride** ($59 or $79), **Hummer tour** ($59 or $79), and **helicopter package** (with hummer tour, jet boat or float trip on Colorado River, $149–$169). All prices are subject to an additional seven percent **tribal tax**.

for the Hualapai's one-day rafting trips, detailed on p.398; participants fly out from here.

The road between the rims

Although the South and North rims stand just eleven miles apart, the shortest driving route between them takes 215 miles and at least four hours. Note that most of this rim-to-rim route is on the Navajo Indian Reservation, which unlike the state of Arizona, observes daylight savings time. This means that for six months of the year, clocks at any establishment enroute are set one hour later than at the Grand Canyon. Starting from Grand Canyon Village, you have to follow first Desert View Drive and then AZ-64 east until you meet US-89 at **Cameron**. Head north to cross **Marble Canyon** on Navajo Bridge, after which you'll be driving west on US-89A to **Jacob Lake**. Here you'll take AZ-67 44 miles south to the North Rim.

Although there are very few towns along the way, the scenery is seldom less than spectacular. Beyond Desert View, AZ-64 runs close to the gorge of the **Little Colorado**; Navajo trinket stalls are dotted along the roadside and at a couple of overlooks, around ten miles west of Cameron.

Cameron

Tiny **CAMERON**, which amounts to little more than a handful of buildings, lies a mile or so north of the intersection of AZ-64 and US-89, on the south side of the suspension bridge spanning the Little Colorado River.

The **Cameron Trading Post** here, established in 1911, stocks a huge array of Southwest arts and crafts, from mass-produced trinkets and jeans to genuine Hopi *kachinas* and museum-quality Navajo rugs. While busy with tourists in summer, it remains at heart a trading center for the Navajo Nation, with some of its business still conducted by barter. In addition, beautifully landscaped gardens surround a large **motel** complex (☎602/679-2231 or 1-877/221-6090, ⓦ www.camerontradingpost .com; March–May ④, June to mid-Oct ⑤, mid-Oct to Feb ③), where all the rooms are smart, and those on the upper floors have large balconies that look out across the Little Colorado. There's also **RV** parking for $15. A pleasant **dining room** with tin ceiling and large fireplace serves all meals, though the food itself is nothing special (daily: summer 6am–10pm; otherwise 7am–9.30pm).

There's further accommodation at **GRAY MOUNTAIN**, ten miles south of Cameron, in the motel-like *Anasazi Inn* (☎928/679-2214 or 1-800/678-2214, ⓦ www.anasaziinn.com; ③), with a restaurant and outdoor pool.

Marble Canyon and Navajo Bridge

Fifteen miles north of Cameron, US-160 branches off northeast toward Monument Valley and Colorado via **Tuba City** (which also has motels; see p.65).

Continuing north, after another forty miles of emptiness US-89 climbs away up the mesa to the right, heading for Page and Glen Canyon Dam (see p.481). US-89A, however, presses on at the foot of the **Echo Cliffs**, to reach **Navajo Bridge** after a further fifteen miles.

There are in fact two Navajo Bridges. The original, which opened in 1929, is now reserved for pedestrians only; a wider facsimile opened 150ft downstream in 1995. The Colorado at this point cuts through the chasm of **Marble Canyon** – it's such a narrow interruption in the vast flat plains that you can't tell it's there until you're right on top of it.

On the west bank, the **Navajo Bridge Interpretive Center** (daily April–Sept 8am–5pm, closed Oct–March; restrooms always open; ℡928/608-6404, Ⓦwww.nps.gov/glca) holds some hair-raising photos of Navajo steelworkers at work on the 1995 bridge, plus displays and literature about the Glen Canyon region. A little further on, *Marble Canyon Lodge* (℡928/355-2225 or 1-800/726-1789; ❹) has more than fifty conventional motel-style rooms; it can also arrange river and fishing trips. In the atmospheric *Lodge* itself, there's an adequate but unexciting **restaurant** that's open for all meals daily, with a 6am start to feed the crowds of river-runners.

Lees Ferry

Before the construction of Navajo Bridge, ferries struggled across the river at **LEES FERRY**, six miles north. Mormon elder Jacob Hamblin was guided to this remote spot – the only place within hundreds of miles to offer easy land access to both banks of the Colorado – by Naraguts, a Paiute, in 1858.

Thirteen years later, **John Doyle Lee** was sent here to set up a ferry service to help Mormon missionaries en route south into Arizona. Lee was on the run after the **Mountain Meadows Massacre** in Utah in 1857, when a wagon train of would-be settlers was slaughtered by an armed white band clumsily disguised

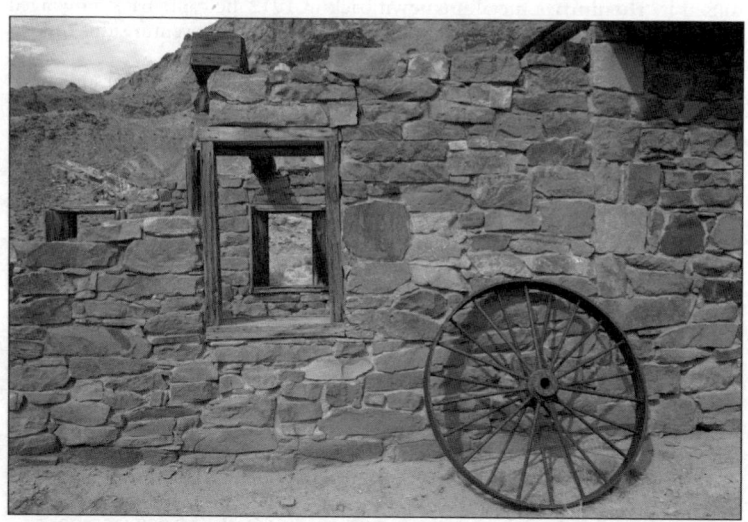

△ Lees Ferry Fort, Lees Ferry

as Indians, Lee among them. Though eventually executed, Lee remains a hero to some Mormons (a plaque at Navajo Bridge calls him "a man of great faith, sound judgment, and indomitable courage"); those who have read Mark Twain's account of the massacre in *Roughing It* may disagree. He was finally arrested in 1874 and executed in 1877, but his (seventeenth) wife Emma remained here, at the place they knew as **Lonely Dell**. Determined not to honor Lee, Congress passed a special act to remove the apostrophe from what used to be "Lee's Ferry."

The ferry service was always perilous, with the boats in constant danger of being swept downstream, and was finally abandoned after a fatal accident in June 1928. A crucial piece of equipment needed to finish the bridge on the left bank was stranded on the right bank; the only way to get it across was to take it eight hundred miles by road, via Las Vegas.

The reason you can get down to the water at Lees Ferry is because it marks the confluence of the Paria River with the Colorado; **Paria River Beach**, at the foot of the gently sloping road from Marble Canyon, is the official start of the Grand Canyon. To the south, the broad Colorado picks up speed as it squeezes into Marble Canyon. A few hundred yards north, across the Paria, you come to a large parking lot and launching ramp, which is where **whitewater rafting** expeditions set off into the Grand Canyon – the first point where boats can get out again is at Diamond Creek, twelve days away by muscle power. A fairly basic **campground** ($10; ☎928/355-2334) is located nearby.

From the far end of the lot, a trail leads within a couple of hundred yards to the sturdy **Lees Ferry Fort**, erected in 1874 as defense against Navajo attacks that never materialized. The most prominent remains here date from an abortive experiment by **Charles H. Spencer**, who set out in 1910 to mine **gold** from the slopes above Lees Ferry. His precipitous **Spencer Trail** still switchbacks up the cliffs – though its poor condition means that it's closed to hikers – while the boiler of his abandoned **steamboat** lies rusting in the Colorado. What stymied Spencer's endeavor was that something kept clogging his amalgamators. Amazingly enough, when he found out fifty years later that the problem was caused by **rhenium**, a metal unknown back in 1912, he came back, now aged over ninety, and embarked on another unsuccessful mining venture, this time in pursuit of rhenium itself.

John Lee lived not at the ferry site, but in the much more congenial surroundings of the **Lonely Dell Ranch**, nestled in a fertile curve of the Paria River around half a mile up from the confluence. His original **log cabin** stands not far beyond a replanted approximation of his **orchards**, rich with apple, plum, and peach trees. For serious backpackers, this marks the end of an epic four- to six-day hike that traces the full length of the **Paria Canyon**, starting at the White House trailhead off AZ-89 between Kanab and Page (see p.447).

The Vermilion Cliffs

West of Marble Canyon, US-89A curves beneath the southernmost section of the **Vermilion Cliffs**. These soaring sandstone walls glow a magnificent red at sunrise and sunset, but the road itself is featureless. Only a couple of small **motels** offer any incentive to get out of your car. Both *Lees Ferry Lodge* (☎928/355-2231 or 1-800/451-2231, Ⓦwww.leesferrylodge.com; ❸) – three miles west of Marble Canyon, and smaller and slightly lower-priced than the *Marble Canyon Lodge* (see p.401) – and the *Cliff Dweller's Lodge* (☎928/355-2261 or

1-800/962-9755, Ⓦwww.leesferry.com; ❹), half a dozen miles beyond, have their own stores and restaurants.

Once past the southernmost promontory of the cliffs, the highway is free to run as straight as an arrow across the broad sagebrush desert. Just under forty miles from the river, it hits the Kaibab Mountains and climbs through thick forest for the final eleven miles to Jacob Lake.

Jacob Lake and DeMotte Park

The crossroads community of **JACOB LAKE**, deep in the pine forest 44 miles north of the North Rim, looks more like a Canadian logging camp than anything you'd expect to find in Arizona. In winter, when AZ-67 down to the Grand Canyon is closed by snow, Jacob Lake goes into hibernation; in summer, however, it makes a good living from the constant stream of tourists.

The *Jacob Lake Inn*, a sprawling but welcoming complex of timber-frame buildings at the road junction, stays open all year round (Ⓣ928/643-7232, Ⓦwww .jacoblake.com). As well as its simple **motel** rooms (❻) and log cabins (❺), it incorporates some pricier family units capable of sleeping up to six (❻), plus a gas station, a general store, an old-fashioned diner counter, and a restaurant where chicken, trout, or steak entrees cost $10–15. Alongside it, the Forest Service's **Kaibab Plateau Visitor Center** has information on the surrounding area (daily 8am–5pm; Ⓣ928/643-7298, Ⓦwww.fs.fed.us/r3/kai) and is responsible for the lovely *Jacob Lake Campground*, on US-89A just west of the intersection, where facilities cater to **tent campers** only (mid-May to Oct; Ⓣ928/643-7395).

Jacob Lake is named for Jacob Hamblin, a Mormon missionary to the Paiutes and Navajo. The Mormons made little use of the forests to the south, however, apart from grazing their cattle in the large meadow-like clearings along the road to the canyon. One of these, **DEMOTTE PARK**, 27 miles from Jacob Lake, is now the site of the *Kaibab Lodge* (mid-May to mid-Oct only; Ⓣ928/638-2389 in summer, 928/526-0924 in winter, or 1-800/525-0924, Ⓦwww.kaibablodge .com), which offers two kinds of cabin – characterful older ones with bare wooden floors (❺), and a few slightly more expensive ones with motel-style trimmings (❻) – plus a simple restaurant open for breakfast and dinner daily. The park entrance is another five miles down the road, with visitor facilities nine miles beyond that.

The North Rim

Higher, bleaker, and much more remote than the South Rim, the **North Rim** of the Grand Canyon is accessible to travelers for less than half the year. Once **AZ-67,** the only road in, has been blocked by the first major snowfall of the winter, the area remains closed until the following spring. Although that first snow used to arrive toward the end of October, locals report that in several recent years the area has received a mere fraction of its official average annual snowfall of 140 inches, and the road has been known to close as late as December 9. The one accommodation option on the North Rim, *Grand Canyon Lodge*, continues to operate on a more rigid schedule, opening during the second week of May and closing on October 15. After it closes, the park itself remains open until the snow comes, but no food, gas, or lodging other than camping is available, and visitors must be prepared to leave at a moment's notice.

Even in peak season, the North Rim offers a sense of splendid isolation, and it receives less than a tenth as many visitors as the South Rim. While that doesn't mean you'll have the place to yourself, it can still make you feel as though you're venturing into unexplored wilderness. The canyon itself is significantly different on this side of the Colorado. Erosion is much more active; twice as much rain falls; and it freezes more often. As the Kaibab Plateau slopes south, the water flows toward the rim, which it has cut twice as far back from the river, meaning that the North Rim is far more indented with massive side canyons. The basic experience of visiting, however, is the same, with a cluster of venerable park-service buildings at **Bright Angel Point**, where the main highway reaches the canyon, and another rim-edge road where drivers can take their pick from additional lookouts.

North Rim practicalities

Visitor activity on the North Rim focuses on the glorified log cabin known as **Grand Canyon Lodge**, perched above the canyon at **Bright Angel Point**. As you approach the lodge complex, the park **visitor center** is the first building on the left (daily May to mid-Oct 8am–6pm; ☎928/638-7864, ⓦwww.nps .gov/grca). **Guest rooms** are not in the main lodge building but in individual cabins and larger motel-style blocks. Each of the well-appointed Western Cabins (ⓖ) has a full-size bathroom and a porch and can sleep up to four people; a mere four offer canyon views, the only North Rim accommodation options to do so, and tend to be booked up to two years in advance. The more spartan Frontier Cabins (ⓢ) can accommodate three guests each and have smaller bathrooms, while the similar Pioneer Cabins (ⓖ) have two separate bedrooms. In addition, a couple of two-story blocks located furthest from the lodge hold twenty motel rooms apiece (ⓢ), each with a queen bed and private bathroom. Only the Frontier cabins and the motel rooms have telephones. **Reservations** for all are essential and are once again handled by Xanterra (same-day ☎928/638-2611, advance ☎303/297-2757 or 1-888/297-2757, ⓦwww.grandcanyonnorthrim.com). Cancellations are frequently available at short notice, so keep calling if you can't get a room or the precise kind of room you want.

Inside the main building, the magnificent **Dining Room** with rough hewn wood and stone walls is open daily for all meals (☎928/638-2612 ext 160; dinner reservations essential, well in advance); the prices aren't bad, and the food is better than in the **snack bar**, entered separately from the driveway. The *Lodge* also holds a **saloon** and **espresso bar**, but its best feature is the **viewing lounge** downstairs, with an array of comfortable armchairs facing vast picture windows.

A little over a mile north, the very pleasant **North Rim Campground** holds 87 car-camping sites ($15), spaced out through the forest. Although all are often reserved in advance, through Spherix (same-day ☎928/638-2611, advance ☎1-800/365-2267 or, from outside the US, ☎301/722-1257, ⓦwww.reservations.nps.gov), additional room is always available for

THE NORTH RIM

THE GRAND CANYON | North Rim practicalities

6

Legend: Canyon rim

Feet
8000
6800
5600
4400
3200
0

0   2 miles

*Map labels:*

DeMotte Park & Jacob Lake

Point Imperial

Nankoweap Creek

POINT IMPERIAL ROAD

FULLER CANYON ROAD

67

KEN PATRICK TRAIL

WIDFORSS TRAIL

North Rim Campground

UNCLE JIM TRAIL

Vista Encantada

Roosevelt Point

Uncle Jim Point

Roaring Springs Canyon

NORTH KAIBAB TRAIL

TRANSEPT TRAIL

WALHALLA PLATEAU

Bright Angel Point

Roaring Springs

The Transept

CAPE ROYAL SCENIC DRIVE

Phantom Ranch & Colorado River

NORTH KAIBAB TRAIL

Cottonwood Campground

Ribbon Falls

Bright Angel Canyon

Deva Temple

Cheyava Falls

Walhalla Glades

Brahma Temple

Clear Creek

Thor Temple

CAPE FINAL TRAIL

Cape Final

Pueblo

CLIFF SPRING TRAIL

Walhalla Overlook

Angels Window

Phantom Ranch

Zoroaster Temple

CLEAR CREEK TRAIL

Clear Creek

Wotans Throne

Cape Royal

Freya Castle

CLEAR CREEK TRAIL

backpackers, bicyclists, and others traveling without their own vehicles, who pay $4 per person.

Although there are ranger talks, there are no organized sightseeing tours currently available at the North Rim, and there's no equivalent to the viewpoint shuttle buses that operate along the South Rim. The only long-distance public transportation is provided by the Transcanyon Shuttle (☎602/638-2820), whose van service to the **South Rim** leaves from outside *Grand Canyon Lodge* at 7am daily. Having reached the South Rim at noon, it departs again at 1.30pm, and arrives back at the North Rim at 6.30pm. A one-way trip costs $65, and the round trip $110, or $50 and $90 respectively for under-13s; no credit cards are accepted.

Ask at the information desk for details of **mule rides** (1hr $30, half-day $55, full-day canyon expeditions $105; ☏ 435/679-8665, ⓦ www.canyonrides.com).

Other North Rim facilities

Camping equipment Can be bought at the General Store, opposite *North Rim Campground*.

Camping permits The North Rim Backcountry Office is just over a mile up the highway from *Grand Canyon Lodge*, not far north of the campground. Daily 8am–noon & 1–5pm; ☏ 928/638-7868.

Gas Near *North Rim Campground* (daily 7am–7pm).

Laundromat and showers Near *North Rim Campground*. Showers $1.25. Daily 7am–9pm.

Medical help There is no health clinic on the North Rim. Call ☏ 911 for emergencies.

Post Office In *Grand Canyon Lodge* (Mon–Fri 8–11am & 11.30am–4pm, Sat 8am–1pm).

Bright Angel Point

A short paved trail leads off left of *Grand Canyon Lodge* to the very tip of **Bright Angel Point**. In places, the trail fills the full width of the slender spit of land, with sheer drops to either side. After four hundred level yards, you reach the sanctuary of a railed viewing area, looking out across the canyon. Because the North Rim is a thousand feet higher than the South, the views stretch far beyond the South Rim to the plateaus of Arizona and the San Francisco Peaks, but it's hard to spot a sign of life at Grand Canyon Village, eleven miles distant. As usual, the Colorado is too deeply buried in the canyon to be seen; if you hear the sound of rushing water, it's coming from **Roaring Springs**, much closer to hand, which supply all the water used by the park on both rims.

To either side, trees somehow cling to the near-vertical red ridges, while high buttes in the canyon proper reach almost to the level of the rims; most prominent of all is the neat-capped **Brahma Temple** straight ahead, framed between two lesser specimens.

Cape Royal Scenic Drive

Apart from Bright Angel Point, all the **canyon overlooks** along the North Rim are ranged along the eastern edge of the **Walhalla Plateau**, a considerable drive from *Grand Canyon Lodge*. This long, high headland, to the east of Bright Angel Point, is reached by turning east onto **Fuller Canyon Road**, three miles north of the *Lodge*. Five miles along, you come to a junction where **Point Imperial Road** branches off to the left, while **Cape Royal Road** winds off into the cool dense woods to the right.

Even if your time is limited, it's well worth making your way right to the end of Cape Royal Road – fifteen miles from the junction – to **Cape Royal**. From the unremarkable parking lot at the end of the highway, an even, paved footpath leads first of all to the **Angels Window**, a natural archway just below the top of a rocky spur. As you approach, you can look down through it all the way to the Colorado River. An extremely narrow railed pathway that detours off the main trail a little further along leads onto the top of the "window," for views across to the flatlands of the Navajo reservation. Two broad, green-trimmed stretches of the river are visible from this point, including the foaming Unkar Creek Rapid.

Views from **Cape Royal** itself, a couple of hundred yards further along the main trail, extend much farther west, though the intervening ridge immediately west obscures Bright Angel Point. The canyon is much narrower here, so flat-topped **Cedar Mountain** is very conspicuous, standing out just above the South Rim.

Other possible halts along Cape Royal Road include the **Walhalla Overlook**, a mile or so back from the end of the road, where a very short forest trail ends at the foundation walls of a small **Ancestral Puebloan dwelling place**. **Roosevelt Point**, about halfway between Walhalla and Fuller Canyon Road, looks across Marble Canyon toward the Echo Cliffs.

Point Imperial

Turn left at the intersection of Fuller Canyon and Cape Royal roads (see above) for a gradual three-mile climb to **Point Imperial**. Although at 8803ft this is the highest spot along either rim of the entire canyon, to reach the actual overlook you have to descend a short distance from the parking lot. A long red sandy ridge pokes out just below the viewing area, with a stark butte at the end, while to the right is the thickly wooded ridge that ends at Cape Royal. Looking down, the landscape is as dry as dust, a labyrinth of spurs and buttes in which it's virtually impossible to guess which is the main gorge of the Colorado.

The plateau of the Navajo reservation on the far side is almost three thousand feet lower, so it spreads for miles at your feet, pierced by further chasms and gorges. To the southeast, the Little Colorado emerges from its own canyon to join the main onward rush of the Colorado.

North Rim hikes

Hikers on the North Rim of the Grand Canyon should take the same precautions – and be as aware of their physical capabilities – as their counterparts on the South Rim (see p.384). There tends to be less scope for getting into difficulties here, however, as almost all the North Rim trails suitable for day-hiking stay on top of the plateau. On the only route that descends into the canyon itself, the **North Kaibab Trail**, hiking to the river and back in a single day is completely out of the question – it's a 28-mile round-trip with a 6000ft change in elevation.

The North Kaibab Trail

Some version of the **North Kaibab Trail**, following Bright Angel Creek down to the Colorado, has been in use for over a thousand years. Its current route, which starts by descending through Roaring Springs Canyon from a roadside trailhead two miles north of *Grand Canyon Lodge*, was established in the late 1920s. Parking at the trailhead is limited, but a limited, early-morning **hiker shuttle** service leaves *Grand Canyon Lodge* at 5.20am and 7.20am daily, costing $5 for the first person in each group, plus $2 per additional passenger.

When planning a day-hike on the North Kaibab, it's easy to be overambitious; the mileages may not seem that great, but the gradient is steep from the word go. Many people go no further than the **Coconino Overlook**, just 1.4 miles down through the fir forests, a high rocky vantage point from which you can

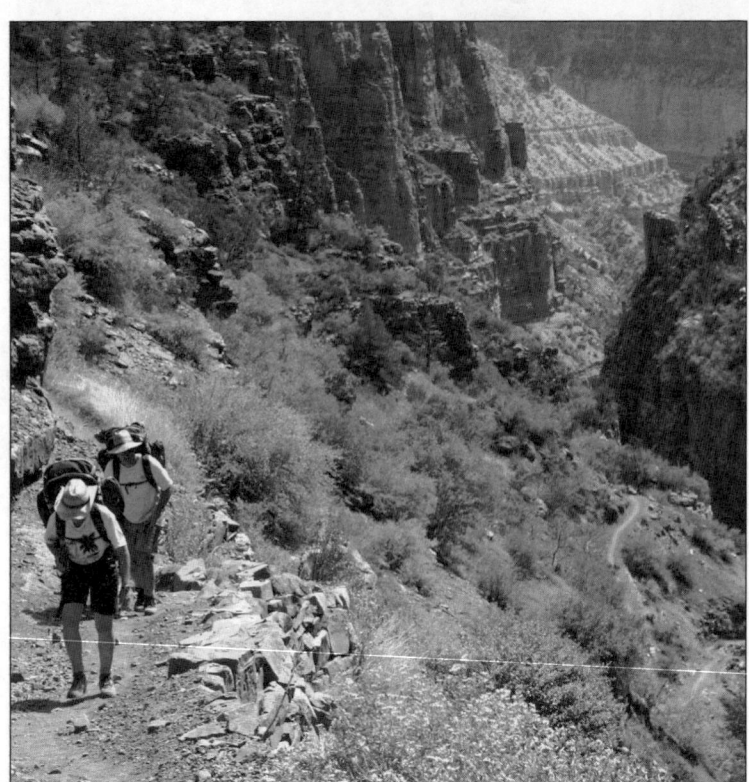

△ Hikers on the North Kaibab Trail

see the junction of Roaring Springs and Bright Angel canyons. The gorgeous waterfalls at **Roaring Springs** come after another 3.6 miles, during which the trail burrows through the **Supai Tunnel**, crosses the suspended **Redwall Bridge**, and makes some spectacular cliffside traverses. Water from the springs is pumped up to the *Lodge* and also piped over to the South Rim, but there's enough left over to tend the "gardens" downstream that were originally planted by the Ancestral Puebloans.

The well-shaded **Cottonwood Campground**, 2.5 miles beyond the springs, is a major way-station for transcanyon hikers. The highlight of the final seven-mile segment to **Phantom Ranch** (see p.389) is the lacy **Ribbon Falls**, reached via a short spur trail a mile past the campground.

Rim-edge trails

The ten-mile **Ken Patrick Trail**, the best canyon-edge trail near Bright Angel Point, alternates dramatic views with stretches of dense forest as it leads from the North Kaibab Trailhead all the way to Point Imperial. The four-mile **Uncle Jim Trail** branches off it to reach a viewpoint that overlooks the North Kaibab Trail, while the **Widforss Trail** heads the other way, west from the inland end of Bright Angel Point out to the tip of the next headland along.

The Arizona Strip

By any logic, you'd expect the **Arizona Strip** – the anomalous area that's sandwiched between the North Rim of the Grand Canyon and the Utah state line – to belong to Utah rather than Arizona. In 1864, Mormon leader Brigham Young called on Congress to grant the Mormons all territory that lay within two degrees of latitude of either side of the Colorado; the boundary was drawn instead along the 37th parallel, and that remains the Utah–Arizona border. Repeated attempts to incorporate the Strip into Utah failed, largely because this remote region became a stronghold of renegade Mormons who didn't accept their church's reversal of doctrine on multiple marriage (see p.583). Effective isolation from the state authorities of both Utah and Arizona suited these die-hard polygamists just fine.

Virtually no roads cross the Strip, and those that do hold just a few tiny, secretive, and often semi-derelict hamlets. Although you have to pass this way in order to complete a full tour around the Grand Canyon, the majority of visitors tend to race the distance between the Grand Canyon and the national parks of southern Utah. Few are aware that they're missing perhaps the most spectacular section of Grand Canyon National Park: the **Tuweep** district, home to two stunning overlooks at **Toroweap Point** that provide a rare opportunity to see the canyon's innermost core.

Fredonia

As Hwy 67 north of Jacob Lake drops off the edge of the Kaibab Plateau, you get tremendous views across southern Utah. Tier upon tier of cliffs rise one behind the other into the distance, making it abundantly clear why the entire region is known to geologists as the **Grand Staircase**. First comes the red sandstone of the Vermilion Cliffs, the formation pierced by Zion Canyon (see p.425); next are the White Cliffs, which form the Kolob Canyons district of Zion National Park; and beyond them, forty miles away, stand the softer Pink Cliffs, sculpted into the hoodoos of Bryce Canyon (see p.450).

The largest town on the Arizona Strip, **FREDONIA**, stands thirty miles northwest of Jacob Lake. With the bigger and much more interesting community of **Kanab** a mere seven miles north, across the Utah border (see p.443), it's hard to see why anyone would choose to spend the night here, but Fredonia does hold a few small **motels**. Options include the very plain log-built *Crazy Jug*, 465 S Main St (℡928/643-7752; ❷), and the ivy-covered *Grand Canyon*, 175 S Main St (℡928/643-7646; ❷). The very helpful modern **welcome center**, on the east side of US-89A close to the state line at the north end of town (℡928/643-7241; Mon–Sat 9am–5pm), is the best place to get advice on the Strip's backcountry routes, and to buy the necessary maps.

Pipe Spring National Monument

Thirteen miles west of Fredonia, just off AZ-389, **Pipe Spring National Monument** (daily 8am–5pm; ℡928/643-7105, ⓦwww.nps.gov/pisp; $5) marks the site of one of the very few water sources on the Arizona Strip. Not surprisingly, ownership of this precious spring has been much contested; a Mormon rancher, Dr James Whitmore, appropriated it from the Paiutes in 1863 and was killed three years later by a party of Paiute and Navajo raiders. The Mormons subsequently enclosed the spring in a fort, known as

Winsor Castle after its first superintendent. They retained control until it was declared a national monument in the 1920s, as much because it stood halfway between the Grand Canyon and Zion national parks as for any intrinsic interest.

Pipe Spring now stands adjacent to the Kaibab Paiute Indian reservation. The buildings remain in good condition and serve as a rather unenthralling museum of early ranching life, of most appeal to students of Mormon history.

Colorado City

AZ-389 continues northwest from Pipe Spring and serves as the most direct route from the North Rim to the I-15 interstate that connects Las Vegas and Salt Lake City. A mile or so before it reaches Utah, a spur road to the right runs up to the staunchly traditional Mormon community of **COLORADO CITY**. Set beneath the towering bluffs of the Vermilion Cliffs, this is a surreal-looking place, laid out with a small grid of extremely broad streets that see very few cars but plenty of gingham pinafores.

Colorado City was the subject of furious political controversy in 2005. Newspaper exposés revealed it as the virtual fiefdom of a small group of polygamists. Until his death in 2002, the octogenarian self-styled "Prophet" Rulon Jeffs was its effective ruler. Not only did he assign the town's young women, often in their early teens, as brides to his middle-aged and already multiply-married cronies – and conduct the wedding ceremonies himself – but he also presided over a system in which the local young men were run out of town as they came of age so they could not rival their elders. Rulon's son Warren, who succeeded him as Prophet and is said to have "inherited" around sixty of his wives, fled town in 2004, and currently figures on the FBI's "Ten Most Wanted" list. If you visit, everyone will assume you're a journalist hoping to write a sensational article, and you'll find no encouragement to linger.

Toroweap

The Arizona Strip holds one tremendous prize for visitors prepared to venture off the paved highways: **Toroweap Point**, the only place where you can drive to the very lip of the canyon's Inner Gorge and peer down sheer 3000ft cliffs to the Colorado River. As the crow flies, it's slightly under sixty miles west of Bright Angel Point, but by road it's almost 150 miles, and even a fleeting visit requires at least six hours of laborious driving on gravel roads.

There are two main routes: the eastern **Sunshine Route**, which starts by following **BLM road 109** south from AZ-389 seven miles west of **Fredonia** and then runs for 61 miles southwest, and remains open all year, and the more scenic but longer western **Main Street Route**, which takes a total of ninety miles from the heart of **St George**, Utah, but is closed by snow in winter. Both roads are generally passable in ordinary vehicles; if 4WD is necessary at all, it will be for the last few miles only. Be sure to inquire locally about driving conditions before you set off; carry all the food, water, and gas you might need and pack a spare tire and emergency repair kit.

Both routes eventually converge to enter the **Tuweep Area** of Grand Canyon National Park. Five very rough miles on, a free, **primitive campground** holds ten first-come, first-served sites. The road comes to a halt a mile after that at a wide, rocky hilltop known as the **Toroweap Overlook**, which at 4600ft is the lowest viewpoint within the national park. The view here may lack the usual buttes and pyramids or labyrinthine spurs and mesas, but tiptoe to the southern

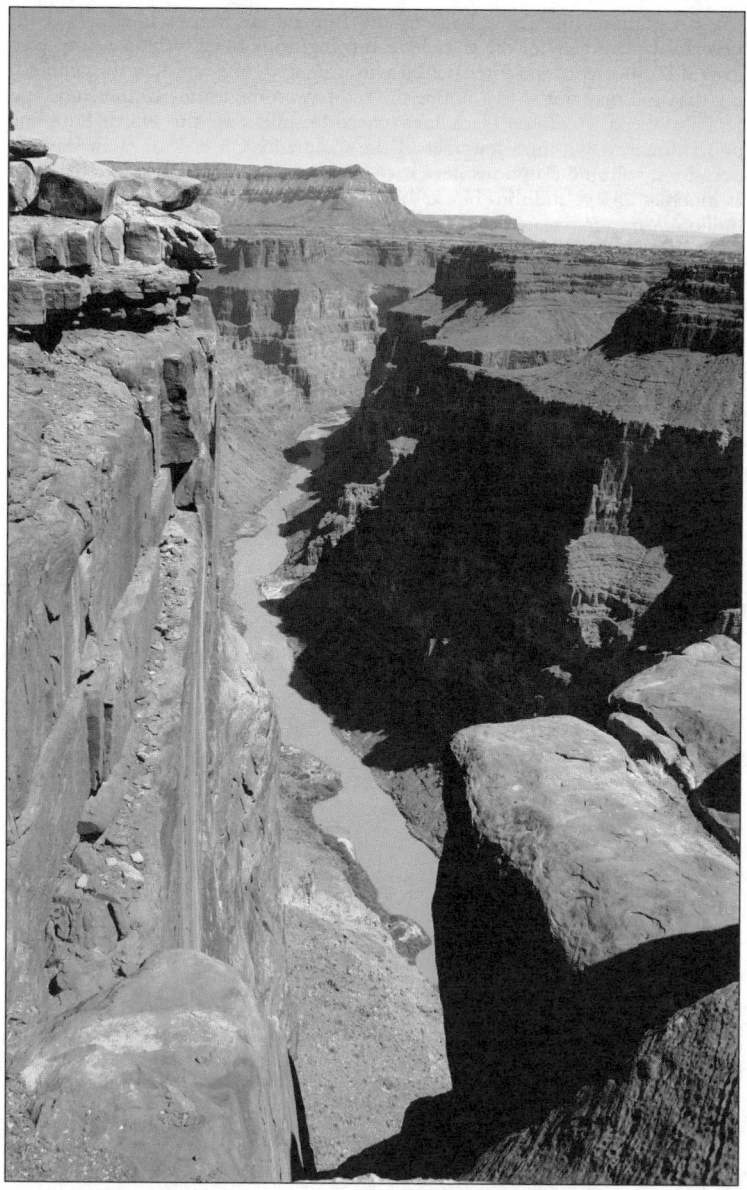

△ The Inner Gorge, as seen from Toroweap Overlook

edge of the parking lot, and the ground suddenly drops 3000ft from your feet. Though you can see the river approaching from the east and flowing away to the west, it's so directly below that you may have to lie full length and peep over the edge to see it right here.

A five-minute hike west leads to the stupendous west-facing **Lava Falls Overlook**. The view of the river here, turning from green to blue as it recedes toward the horizon, and interspersed with mighty white rapids, is so spellbinding that you may not at first notice the most awesome feature of the landscape. Straight ahead, a colossal black **lava cascade** spills over the North Rim and pours down to within a few feet of the Colorado. On at least eight separate occasions, volcanic eruptions here have filled the Grand Canyon to a depth of as much as 2330ft and thus blocked the Colorado. The largest flow, around 1.2 million years ago, created the long-vanished Prospect Dam, which backed the river up to form a lake that stretched all the way east to Lees Ferry. It took an estimated 23 years to fill to the brim; then the Colorado burst over the top and, eventually, wore the dam entirely away.

Southern Utah

CHAPTER 7

Highlights

* **Zion Canyon** Whether you admire it from the roadside, or hike up its soaring walls, Zion is pure magic. **See p.425**

* **Bryce Canyon** Towering incandescent sandstone hoodoos make this one of the most extraordinary-looking places on earth. **See p.450**

* **Calf Creek Falls** An easy trail leads to a magnificent water-fall that's the gem of Grand Staircase-Escalante National Monument. **See p.468**

* **The Great Gallery** Eerie ancient pictographs, hidden deep in a remote section of Canyonlands National Park. **See p.506**

* **Delicate Arch** The hike up to this free-standing natural arch is the crowning glory of a visit to Arches National Park. **See p.515**

* **Rafting in Canyonlands** Penetrate the mysterious wilderness at the heart of Utah on float trips down the Green or Colorado rivers. **See p.524**

* **Muley Point** Though not in a national park, this seldom visited viewpoint is perhaps the finest in all of Utah. **See p.535**

* **Goosenecks State Reserve** The convolutions of the San Juan River near Monument Valley have to be seen to be believed. **See p.535**

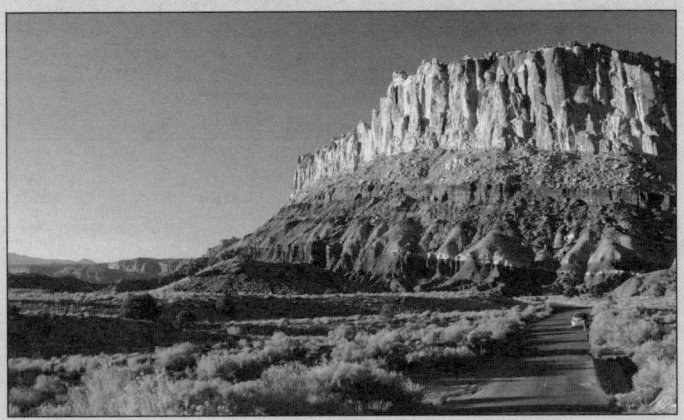

△ Scenic Drive, Capitol Reef National Park

Southern Utah

S**outhern Utah** represents a peculiar combination of the mind-boggling and the mundane. Its **scenery** is stupendous, a stunning geological freakshow where the earth is ripped bare to expose cliffs and canyons of every imaginable color, unseen rivers gouge mighty furrows into endless desert plateaus, and strange sandstone towers thrust from the sagebrush. The tiny **Mormon towns** scattered across this epic landscape, on the other hand, are almost without exception boring in the extreme. Each has its cluster of characterless motels and dull-as-ditchwater diners; they're not unfriendly places, but finding ways to while away your evenings can be a supreme test of the imagination.

Most visitors therefore spend as much time as possible **outdoors**. Southern Utah has the greatest concentration of **national parks** in the US; in fact there have been serious proposals for the entire area to become one vast national park. The five parks that currently exist are not necessarily the most beautiful or spectacular spots in the state – their boundaries are the result of devious behind-the-scenes wrangling, and exclude lands prized by the ranching and mining conglomerates. Taken together, however, they make an ideal focus for a first tour of Utah, each with its own well-maintained infrastructure of hiking trails and scenic overlooks.

In southwest Utah, **Zion National Park** centers on an awe-inspiring and richly fertile canyon, backed by barren highlands of sun-scorched white sandstone, while **Bryce Canyon** is a roaring inferno of flame-like orange pinnacles. Over to the east, **Arches** holds an eroded desertscape of graceful red-rock fins and spurs, all on a more manageable scale than the astonishing hundred-mile vistas of neighboring **Canyonlands**. Both lie within easy reach of **Moab**, a disheveled former mining town that has become Utah's hippest destination. The fifth park, **Capitol Reef**, stretches down the massive rainbow-tinted Waterpocket Fold in the middle of the region, pierced by slender, ravishing canyons.

Lesser-known but equally dramatic wildernesses include **Dead Horse Point** and **Muley Point**, on the eastern side of the state, and the vast new **Grand Staircase–Escalante National Monument** to the west. The most spellbinding wonder of them all, **Glen Canyon**, has been drowned since the 1960s beneath **Lake Powell**, an elongated reservoir whose turquoise waters, lapping

The time in Utah is one hour later than Nevada all year round, and one hour later than Arizona from April to October; from November to March, it's the same hours as Arizona.

SOUTHERN UTAH

0   25 miles

▲ Salt Lake City

Fillmore

FREMONT
INDIAN
STATE PARK

Richfield

Sevier

Loa

Bicknell

Beaver

Junction

U   T   A   H

N

AQUARIUS
PLATEAU

HELL'S
BACKBONE
ROAD

Escalante

Parowan

Panguitch

Cedar
City

Brian
Head

Cedar Breaks
Nat. Mon.

Hatch

Tropic

Cannonville

KAIPAROWITS
PLATEAU

Mountain
Meadows
Massacre
Site

Kolob
Canyons

Bryce
Canyon
Nat.
Park

KODACHROME
BASIN
STATE PARK

Grand
Staircase-
Escalante
National
Monument

Pine Valley

Zion
Nat.
Park

Glendale

Snow
Canyon

Virgin

Orderville

Hurricane

Springdale

Mt. Carmel
Junction

St. George

Coral Pink
Sand Dunes

Kanab

Glen Canyon Dam

Colorado City

Fredonia

Wahweap

Virgin River

Pipe Spring
Nat. Mon.

Vermilion
Cliffs
National
Monument

Lees
Ferry

Horseshoe
Bend

▲ Las Vegas

Kaibab-Paiute
Indian Reservation

A   R   I   Z   O   N   A

Jacob Lake

Grand
Canyon-
Parashant
National
Monument

GRAND CANYON
NATIONAL PARK

closed in winter

GRAND
CANYON
NAT. PARK

Flagstaff ▼

desultorily against the red desert rocks, are a playground for houseboaters and
jet-skiers.

The defining topographical feature of southwest Utah is the **Grand Staircase**. Named by pioneer river-runner John Wesley Powell, it consists of a series
of plateaus, stacked tier upon tier, that climb from the North Rim of the Grand
Canyon. The **Chocolate Cliffs**, near the border with Arizona, are followed

by the dazzling **Vermilion Cliffs**, then the **White Cliffs** – a 2000ft wall of Navajo Sandstone, best seen at Zion Canyon – the **Grey Cliffs**, and finally the **Pink Cliffs** of Bryce Canyon. Although it took a billion years of sedimentation for these rocks to form, the staircase itself has only been created in the last twelve million years, by the general upthrust of the **Colorado Plateau**, which stretches away to the east.

The southwest corridor

That the far southwestern corner is now the most accessible and densely populated area of southern Utah makes it easy to forget how forbidding it seemed to early explorers. In October 1776, close to modern Cedar City, fathers Domínguez and Escalante despaired of finding their way to California and headed back toward Santa Fe. Not until 1830 did the **Old Spanish Trail** establish a permanent route west, and it was another twenty years before Brigham Young ordered Mormon settlers to establish a string of towns at the foot of the **Hurricane Cliffs**.

The largest of those towns, **St George** and **Cedar City** (covered on p.439), stand fifty miles apart on I-15, the busy interstate that links Las Vegas with Salt Lake City. Both now depend on tourism for their livelihood – catering especially to visitors of Zion National Park – despite lacking any great appeal themselves.

St George

Spreading beneath a long sandstone escarpment, nine miles north of the Arizona state line, the venerable Mormon town of **ST GEORGE** is southern

Utah's major population center. Its broad thoroughfares and sturdy well-spaced homes may hold little over fifty thousand inhabitants, but that's double the 1990 figure and five times that of 1970. Most of the newcomers are retirees from elsewhere in the Southwest, attracted by the mildness of the winters at this low elevation of just 2880ft. They've done little to change the essential character of St George, however, which may be cosmopolitan by Utah standards but anywhere else would seem like a conservative country backwater, albeit with a surprising number of motels. Year after year, the town sprawls another few hundred meters further alongside the interstate, with another mall or two to mark its latest limits.

St George was named not for England's dragon-slaying patron but for a Latter-Day saint. Apostle George A. Smith hand-picked the 309 families who were sent to establish a colony here in 1861. The plan was to make Utah self-sufficient in **cotton**, supplies of which were threatened by the Civil War; thus this appropriately southern region became known as "**Utah's Dixie.**"

The cotton-growing era ended when cotton from the Deep South reappeared after the war, made cheaper than ever by the coming of the railroads. St George, however, quietly prospered through growing other crops, and became the winter refuge of Brigham Young and other aging Mormon elders. Young's much-restored adobe **Winter Home** still stands at 200 North 100 West, complete with contemporary furnishings and artifacts (daily 9am–7pm; free).

The gleaming white **Mormon Temple**, 440 South 300 East, was the only LDS temple to be completed during Brigham Young's lifetime. Half fortress, half cathedral, it was a defiant statement that the settlers were here to stay. Young presided over its dedication shortly before his death in 1877, and it remains a powerful symbol to all Mormons. As with all Mormon temples, non-Mormons can't go inside; there is a visitor center (daily 9am–9pm; free), however, where the staff may well be so eager to convert you that the problem might be getting out rather than getting in. If you're sufficiently captivated, ask about guided tours of the smaller red-brick Mormon **Tabernacle** on Main Street, of similar vintage and modeled on the meeting houses of New England.

Note that, as described on p.411, St George is also the starting point for the ninety-mile dirt-road drive along the so-called "Main Street Route" to the remote but wonderful Grand Canyon overlook at **Toroweap Point.**

Arrival and information

Travelers driving up I-15 can call in at the **Utah Visitor Center**, just inside the state line (daily: summer 8am–9pm; winter 8am–5pm; ☎435/673-4542, ⓦwww.utah.com). More localized information on St George itself is available from the town **visitor center**, in the Dixie Center at 1835 Convention Center Blvd, near I-15 exit 8 (Mon–Sat 9am–5pm; ☎435/634-5747 or 1-800/869-6635, ⓦwww.stgeorgechamber.com, ⓦwww.utahsdixie.com or ⓦwww.utahszionandbryce.com).

Greyhound **buses** between Las Vegas and Salt Lake City stop outside *McDonald's* at 1235 S Bluff St, while the St George Shuttle connects with Las Vegas nine times daily (☎435/628-8320 or 1-800/933-8320, ⓦwww.stgshuttle.com; $30). Skywest Airlines (☎1-800/453-9417, ⓦwww.skywest.com) operates daily **flights** to Salt Lake City and Los Angeles from an airport perched on the mesa high above town to the west.

Red Rock Shuttle (☎435/635-9104 or 1-888/404-8687, ⓦwww .redrockshuttle.com) offers one-day **bus tours** and shuttle trips to Zion ($80), Bryce ($99) and the Grand Canyon ($99), while Southern Utah Scenic Tours

(☎435/867-8690 or 1-888/404-8687, ⓦwww.utahscenictours.com) runs multi-day trips through southern Utah. **Mountain bikes** can be rented from Red Rock Bicycle, 190 S Main St (☎435/674-3185, ⓦwww.redrockbicycle .com).

Accommodation

In principle, finding a **room** in St George should be no problem. At last count, the town had 39 motels – most of them along the main drag, St George Boulevard – as well as several B&Bs tucked away on the back streets. On busy summer weekends, however, everything fills up early, and there's enough traffic on the interstate year-round for room rates to remain pretty constant. Watch out, too, for the sudden influx of students on Spring Break, in late March. The best place to **camp** nearby is Snow Canyon; see opposite.

Best Western Coral Hills 125 E St George Blvd ☎435/673-4844 or 1-800/542-7733, ⓦwww .coralhills.com. Very central *Best Western* property, quite large but still characterful, and boasting two pools. ❹
Claridge Inn 1187 S Bluff St ☎435/673-7222 or 1-800/367-3790. Modern, inexpensive motel southwest of the center, close to exit 8 off I-15; all rooms are non-smoking, most have two queen beds. Sun–Thurs ❷, Fri & Sat ❸
Dixie Palm Motel 185 E St George Blvd ☎435/673-3531. The cheapest motel in town, but not the worst. Some rooms have showers not

baths, and there's no pool, but the price and central location may make up for that. ❷
Sands Motel 581 E St George Blvd ☎435/673-3501 or 1-877/673-5681, Ⓔsandsmotel1@hotmail.com. Appealingly old-fashioned budget motel, with a decent pool. ❷
Seven Wives Inn 217 North 100 West ☎435/628-3737 or 1-800/600-3737, ⓦwww.sevenwivesinn .com. Two neighboring historic houses in central St George, one built for a sevenfold polygamist, run jointly as a comfortable, period-furnished B&B inn. All rooms are en-suite, with TVs and phones. ❺–❽

Eating

Dining out in St George tends to be a question of which highway steakhouse or fast-food outlet catches your eye; there's plenty of choice, but not much excitement. The only area you might stroll around looking for a restaurant is right in the center, where the small, slightly faded **Ancestor Square** mall holds a handful of lively options.

Bear Paw Coffee Company 75 N Main St ☎435/634-0126. St George's best espresso café also serves full rich breakfasts and good smoothies and juices. Open for breakfast and lunch daily.
Painted Pony Ancestor Square, 2 W St George Blvd ☎435/634-1700. Fresh, mildly ambitious restaurant in the heart of town that sets out to serve contemporary Southwestern cuisine at reasonable prices, and is as romantic an option as St George has to offer. Entrees cost up to $25, and they have a full liquor license. Open daily for lunch and dinner.
Pizza Factory Ancestor Square, 1 W St George Blvd ☎435/628-1234. This friendly pizza-and-pasta

joint seems to be inexorably taking over its neighbors in Ancestor Square; its terrace makes a nice spot for a light lunch, and things get lively later on, even though no alcohol is served. Closed Sun.
Sullivan's Rococo 511 S Airport Rd ☎435/628-3671. Upmarket steakhouse, poised on the bluff west of town, where half the customers have come for the panoramic views and the other half for the liquor license. Steak, ribs, and seafood entrées cost up to $35 in the evening, but lunchtime sandwiches are under $10. Lunch Mon–Fri, dinner daily.

Snow Canyon State Park

One of Utah's most attractive state parks, focused on a classic red-rock canyon, lies within ten minutes' drive of downtown St George. Don't expect to see snow in **SNOW CANYON STATE PARK**; it was named for two of St George's leading pioneers, Lorenzo and Erastus Snow. Instead, its most distinctive feature is the layer of jet-black lava that flakes off the tops of its sun-baked sandstone pinnacles, left by a volcanic eruption some 10,000 years ago.

The park's six-mile **scenic drive**, which remains open day and night, drops left from Hwy-18 seven miles north of St George, shortly beyond a viewpoint that looks out across most of the canyon. Winding down past a succession of overlooks and rounded monoliths, it reaches the **park headquarters** after a couple of miles. There's no visitor center, but this is the place to pay the $5-per-vehicle entrance fee and pick up hiking details. It's also the site of the pleasant, shaded 36-space *Shivwits* **campground** (☎435/628-2255 or 1-800/322-3770; $14). Reservations are recommended in spring and fall, but things get quieter during the hottest months.

The **Hidden Pinyon Trail**, an excellent hour-long (1.5-mile) round-trip hike, starts a hundred yards further on. After cutting between the craggy - outcrops into a peaceful meadow, it zigzags up and over a ridge to enter a heavily eroded landscape reminiscent of Canyonlands' Needles District (see p.507). Vegetation en route includes Utah junipers, creosote bushes, and assorted cactuses.

If it's too hot to hike, pull off another two miles on instead, where a cluster of lurid **red sand dunes** threatens to drift across the road. Kids especially will enjoy sliding down the slopes, which had a bit part in *Butch Cassidy and the Sundance Kid*. The dunes also doubled for central Asia in Howard Hughes' movie *The Conqueror*, which starred John Wayne as Genghis Khan. It was filmed in 1954, when the Nevada Test Site, just ninety miles west, was at its busiest; Wayne, Hughes, and three-quarters of the cast probably died from cancers caused by fall-out from the nuclear explosions.

Leaving the park at its southern end enables you to complete a 24-mile loop back to St George, but if you want to press on north, double back when you've had enough of the scenic drive.

Pine Valley

Sixteen miles north of Snow Canyon State Park, a dead-end right turning off Hwy-18 leads for ten miles into **PINE VALLEY**. By the time you reach the valley's eponymous village, you're at 6500ft, so Pine Valley serves as a summer retreat for the sweltering citizens of St George. Travelers from further afield may well feel that this gentle Alpine landscape is not what they came to Utah to see, but it's undeniably pretty. There's basic **accommodation** in the *Pine Valley Lodge* (☎435/574-2544, ⊛http://go-utah.com/pine-valley-resort; ❹), and a steakhouse nearby, plus a handful of small forest-service **campgrounds** – and plentiful hiking trails – in the **Dixie National Forest** beyond.

The road to Zion

The main road to Zion National Park, **Hwy-9**, which heads east from the I-15 interstate seven miles northeast of St George, makes a lovely thirty-mile drive. None of the pioneer villages along the way is especially exciting, but the scenery is great, with the cottonwood-fringed Virgin River to the south and gigantic sandstone cliffs to the north. Be warned that you have to pay the admission fee to Zion if you want continue east beyond the park on Hwy-9.

Hurricane

The westernmost town along Hwy-9 is **HURRICANE**, ten miles off the interstate at the junction with Hwy-59. While not actually on the Virgin River, it's connected to it by a seven-mile canal, conceived in 1863 but not completed until 1906. Only then was the town site settled, and it's still much the same agricultural community a hundred years on.

With the recent spurt in tourism, however, Hurricane's early timber-frame homes have been joined by a number of **motels**, including two options on the hilltop west of town, the *Days Inn*, 40 North 2600 West (☎435/635-0500 or 1-800/325-2525, 🅦www.daysinn.com; ❷), and the *Comfort Inn Zion*, 43 N Sky Mountain Blvd (☎435/635-3500 or 1-800/635-3577, 🅦www.comfortinnzion .com; ❸).

Southeast from Hurricane, Hwy-59 takes twenty miles to reach the Arizona border, marked by the traditional Mormon community of **Colorado City** (see p.410). The **North Rim** of the Grand Canyon is another hundred miles beyond (see p.404).

Virgin, Rockville, and Grafton

You'll probably barely notice **VIRGIN**, seven miles east of Hurricane – close to the foot of the **Kolob Terrace Road** north into the Zion backcountry, described on p.437 onwards – and notorious for having introduced a law making gun ownership compulsory. The same goes for **ROCKVILLE**, ten miles beyond Virgin. In fact, it's hard to keep your eyes on the road at all as you come closer to the wonders of Zion. Rockville is nevertheless a pretty little town, with several small-scale **B&Bs** along its tree-lined central avenue, such as the nonsmoking *Hummingbird Inn*, 37 W Main St (☎435/772-3632 or 1-800/964-2473, 🅦www .infowest.com/hummingbird; ❹), where all four rooms have private baths.

If you can spare the time, follow Bridge Road south across the river from Rockville, turn right onto an unpaved track, and in five minutes you'll reach the photogenic little **ghost town** of **GRAFTON**. Mormon farmers abandoned the struggle against floods and Indians around 1900, but residents of Rockville have kept an eye on it ever since. It's also been touched up by Hollywood crews shooting movies like *Butch Cassidy and the Sundance Kid*; this is where Paul Newman rode a bicycle to the tune of *Raindrops Keep Falling On My Head*.

Just beyond Rockville, Hwy-9 veers north at the confluence of the North and East forks of the Virgin River, and heads for the maw of Zion Canyon.

Springdale

SPRINGDALE, the last town before Zion, spreads along a leafy three-mile stretch of the Virgin River just south of the park entrance. Rounding the final corner into town gives you your first stupendous view of Zion Canyon itself. Settled at the same time as the canyon, in the early 1860s (see p.429), Springdale is now devoted almost exclusively to pampering tourists.

With its clashing and totally discordant architecture, Springdale is a classic national-park gateway community, but it's still somehow very appealing. Here and there green fields nestle right up to the highway – some even hold grazing cattle – while the occasional imposing private home interrupts the succession of motels, inns, and restaurants. The whole ensemble is dwarfed into insignificance by the magnificent canyon walls that loom on either side of the river. By the time you've driven up and down the only road, **Zion Park Boulevard**, a couple of times, you'll have seen everything Springdale has to offer, but this lively, friendly community makes by far the nicest base in southwest Utah, and spending three or four nights here is no hardship whatsoever.

Arrival and information

Springdale has its own **visitor center**, at 118 Zion Park Blvd (Mon–Fri 9am–5pm; ℡435/772-3757 or 1-888/518-7070, Ⓦwww.zionpark.com), but for information on Zion you'd do better to go straight to the park (see p.428). You can also learn more about Zion by watching **Treasure of the Gods** at the giant-screen Zion Canyon Theatre, 145 Zion Park Blvd (daily: April–Oct 11am–8pm, Nov–March Tues–Sat 1–6pm; $10; ℡435/772-2400 or 1-888/256-2456, Ⓦwww.zioncanyontheatre.com).

Zion Cycles, at 868 Zion Park Blvd (℡435/772-0400, Ⓦwww.zioncycles.com), offers **bike rental**, while the Zion Adventure Company, based near the Tanner Amphitheater at 36 Lion Blvd (℡435/772-1001, Ⓦwww.zionadventures.com), rents gear and runs a shuttle-van service for prospective Narrows hikers (see p.435), and also offers **guided hikes** (from $50 per day per person) and **canyoneering**, though park regulations mean that such tours can only be outside park boundaries.

Accommodation

As Zion Park Boulevard runs straight between the burgeoning canyon walls toward the park, all the **motels** and **B&Bs** along the way offer the same attractive views. A couple of new properties appear each year, so except at the height of summer you should have no difficulty finding a room to suit your budget. Compared to the rest of southern Utah, standards are exceptionally high.

For details of staying at the in-park *Zion Lodge*, and of **camping** in Zion, see p.430. In Springdale, the shaded *Zion Canyon Campground*, half a mile outside the park at 479 Zion Park Blvd (℡435/772-3237, Ⓦwww.zioncamp.com), offers year-round tent **camping** ($20) and RV hookups ($24), and has its own laundry and pizzeria.

Best Western Zion Park Inn 1215 Zion Park Blvd ℡435/772-3200 or 1-800/934-7275; Ⓦwww .zionparkinn.com. Modern convention-style hotel at Springdale's southern end, offering spacious rooms with panoramic windows and a heated swimming pool. Winter ❹, summer ❻

Cliffrose Lodge & Gardens 281 Zion Park Blvd ℡435/772-3234 or 1-800/243-8824, Ⓦwww. cliffroselodge.com. The closest motel to the park makes a pretty place to stay, with separate units spreading down the hillside to the cottonwoods that line the Virgin River. It also has its own pool and wild gardens. Winter ❹, summer ❼

Desert Pearl Inn 707 Zion Park Blvd ℡435/772-8888 or 1-888/828-0898, Ⓦwww.desertpearl.com. Extremely stylish riverside hotel, offering 71 very arty rooms, with high ceilings, wooden floors, huge windows and balconies, and facing a lovely turquoise pool plus hot tubs. Winter ❻, summer ❼

El Rio Lodge 995 Zion Park Blvd ℡435/772-3205 or 1-888/772-3205, Ⓦwww.elriolodge.com. Small, very friendly, spotless, and cozy mom'n'pop motel, in walking distance of several restaurants. The rooms aren't fancy, but they're great value. ❸

Harvest House 29 Canyon View Drive ℡435/772-3880 or 1-800/719-7501, Ⓦwww .harvesthouse.net. Classy, non-smoking B&B in modern home, tucked beneath the sandstone cliffs. Four en-suite rooms, an outdoor hot tub, and gourmet breakfasts. ❻

Terrace Brook Lodge 990 Zion Park Blvd 435/772-3932 or 1-800/342-6779. This old-fashioned and not especially attractive motel enjoys the same great views as the rest, while its rooms are totally acceptable if all you need is a comfortable place to sleep. Winter ❸, summer ❹

Eating

Springdale lacks the national chains, offering instead a refreshing choice of individually styled **restaurants**. If you prefer a light breakfast, there are also a couple of **espresso cafés** just before the park entrance.

Bit & Spur Restaurant & Saloon 1212 Zion Park Blvd ☎ 435/772-3498. Hectic dinner-only Mexican restaurant and bar, across from *Zion Park Inn* at the south end of town, where the food has a creative edge – try the Zuni stew, made with pork, corn, and delicious vegetables, or the pumpkin and yam tamales – and the margaritas are top-notch. From the outdoor patio, you can watch the moon rise over the mountains. Daily 5–10pm.

Mean Bean Coffee House 932 Zion Park Blvd ☎ 435/772-0654. Small, friendly espresso bar in the heart of town that's a morning rendezvous for energetic locals; the raised outdoor seating area makes a wonderful place to greet the day. Daily 6.30am–5pm.

Oscar's 948 Zion Park Blvd ☎ 435/772-3232. Funky, good-value Mexican café, with outdoor patio, just off the main road facing the *Mean Bean*. Pancakes and burritos for breakfast, hot and cold lunchtime sandwiches for $7–8, and a full dinner menu of burgers for $7–10, or enchiladas, quesadillas and the like for more like $15. Daily 8am–10pm.

Spotted Dog Cafe *Flanigan's Inn*, 428 Zion Park Blvd ☎ 435/772-3244. High-quality traditional restaurant, at the park end of town, that's much larger than it looks – the open-air patio is just the tip of the iceberg. Dinner entrees such as braised lamb shank or rabbit have a zesty, continental feel, and cost $15–24, while the home-made breakfast granola is fabulous. Daily 7–11.30am & 5–10pm.

Switchback Grille 1149 Zion Park Blvd ☎ 435/772-3700. Clean, bright, but rather pedestrian restaurant at the south end of town, aimed at tour groups using the adjacent *Zion Park Inn*, and offering a panoramic dining room plus patio seating. Wood-fired pizzas or standard meat and fish dishes like smoked ribs and spit-roasted chicken, at above average but not extortionate prices, plus inexpensive lunchtime burgers and sandwiches. Daily 7am–2.30pm & 5–9.30pm.

Tsunami Juice and Java 180 Zion Park Blvd ☎ 435/772-3818. Small, but convenient and well-priced café immediately outside the park entrance, with smoothies, espressos, and bulging $7 wraps served hot or cold. Daily 8am–8pm.

Zion National Park

With its soaring cliffs, riverine forests, and cascading waterfalls, **ZION NATIONAL PARK** is the most conventionally beautiful of Utah's parks. On first glance it's also the least "Southwestern," in that its centerpiece, **Zion Canyon**, is a lush oasis that feels far removed from the otherworldly desolation of Canyonlands or the downright weirdness of Bryce. Like California's Yosemite Valley, it's a spectacular gorge, squeezed between mighty walls of rock and echoing to the sound of running water. Also like Yosemite, it's prone to becoming crowded in summer, though the long-standing traffic problems have largely been solved by the introduction of an efficient seasonal shuttle-bus system.

Too many visitors see Zion Canyon as a quick half-day detour off the interstate, as they race between Las Vegas (158 miles southwest) and Salt Lake City (320 miles northeast). Beautiful though the **Scenic Drive** through the canyon may be, Zion deserves much more of your time than that. Even the shortest **hiking trail** within the canyon can help you escape the crowds, while a day-hike will take you away from the deceptive verdure of the valley and up onto the high-desert tablelands beyond. In addition, two less-used roads – **Kolob Canyons Road** and the **Kolob Terrace Road** – lead into remoter sections of the park.

With elevations varying from under 4000ft at the visitor center to almost 9000ft at Kolob Peak, Zion is home to a bewildering array of **flora and fauna**. Its vegetation ranges from the cottonwoods and box elders along the Virgin River to the ponderosa pines and stunted piñons that cling to the high sandstone mesas. Desert flowers and cactuses provide unexpected flashes of color in the uplands, as do darting hummingbirds. Animals include the bank beaver (so named because it doesn't build dams) and the generally retiring Western rattlesnake. Mountain lions have been reintroduced since a disastrous experiment of the 1930s, when their extermination allowed the deer population first to explode and then all but perish in a terrible famine brought on by overgrazing.

Summer is by far the busiest **season**. That's despite temperatures in excess of 100°F, and the violent thunderstorms, concentrated in August and a week or so to either side, that bring most of Zion's scant fifteen inches of annual rainfall. If you can, come in April or May to see the spring flowers bloom – though the mosquitoes are also at their peak – or in September and October, to enjoy the fall colors along the river. The park remains open throughout the winter, but daytime highs drop below 40°F in January, while the nights tend to be freezing from November to March.

Zion Canyon

It has taken thirteen million years for the North Fork of the **Virgin River** to carve **Zion Canyon** into the southern edge of the Markagunt Plateau. For

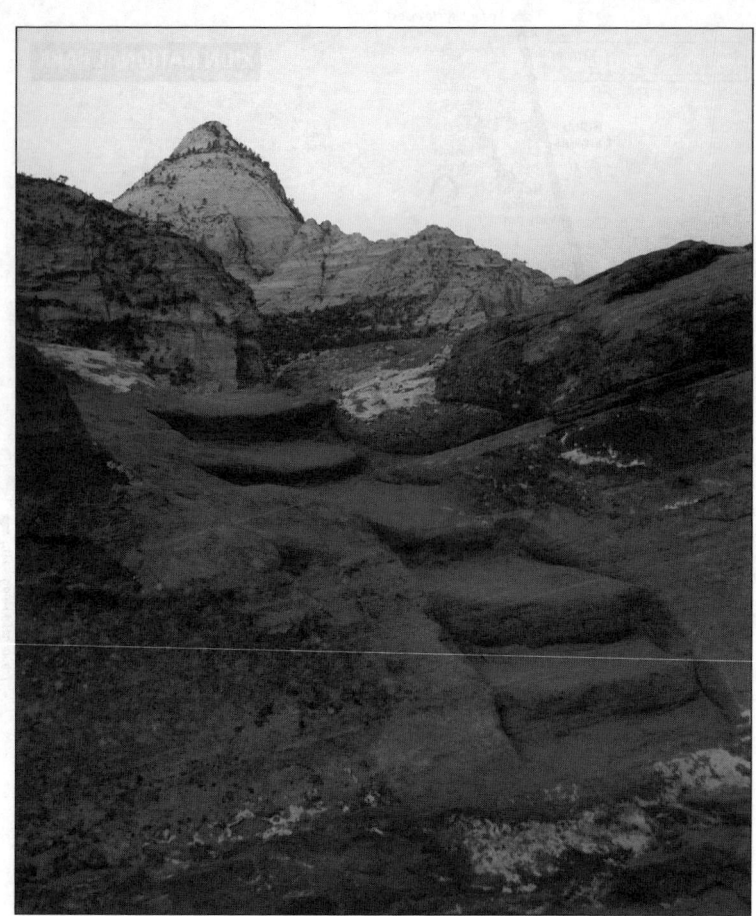

△ Dawn on the Canyon Overlook Trail, Zion National Park

most of the year, the Virgin meanders placidly along the valley floor, en route to the Colorado. After summer thunderstorms, however, run-off from the mesatops is channeled down into the canyon, turning it into a torrent that carries as much as 600,000 cubic yards of rock and sand – a good-sized city block – in a single day. Each winter, the canyon walls grow further apart, as water that seeps through the porous sandstone turns to ice and shears mighty chunks off the cliffs.

As you approach from the south, it's abundantly clear that the **Markagunt Plateau** – one of the seven high plateaus that make up the Colorado Plateau in southern Utah, and named for a Paiute word meaning "highland of trees" – constitutes the next rung of the **Grand Staircase** (see p.409). Zion Canyon serves as a handy cross-section to display the different layers of rock. At the lowest level, around the South Entrance, the thick red **Vermilion Cliffs** rise from a barely discernible bed of the even older and darker Moenave and Kayenta formations. These strata were deposited at the bottom of swampy seas around 200 million years ago, while the 2000ft walls of the canyon itself are composed of rusty **Navajo Sandstone**, once a mass of drifting sand dunes.

The first of the colossal peaks that crown the chasm look down from either side of the South Entrance. The **West Temple** is one of two similar mountains here whose summits consist of neat little box-shaped mesas crowned with pine trees, while the **Watchman** stands guard to the east. At this point, the walls are well over a mile apart; officially the canyon doesn't begin for another few miles, but within just ten miles north it dwindles to a mere twenty feet wide.

Most visitors assume Mormon settlers gave Zion's pinnacles and promontories their portentous names – the **Court of the Patriarchs**, the **Great White Throne**, **Angel's Landing**, and so on – but in fact they were coined by a Methodist minister who visited in 1916.

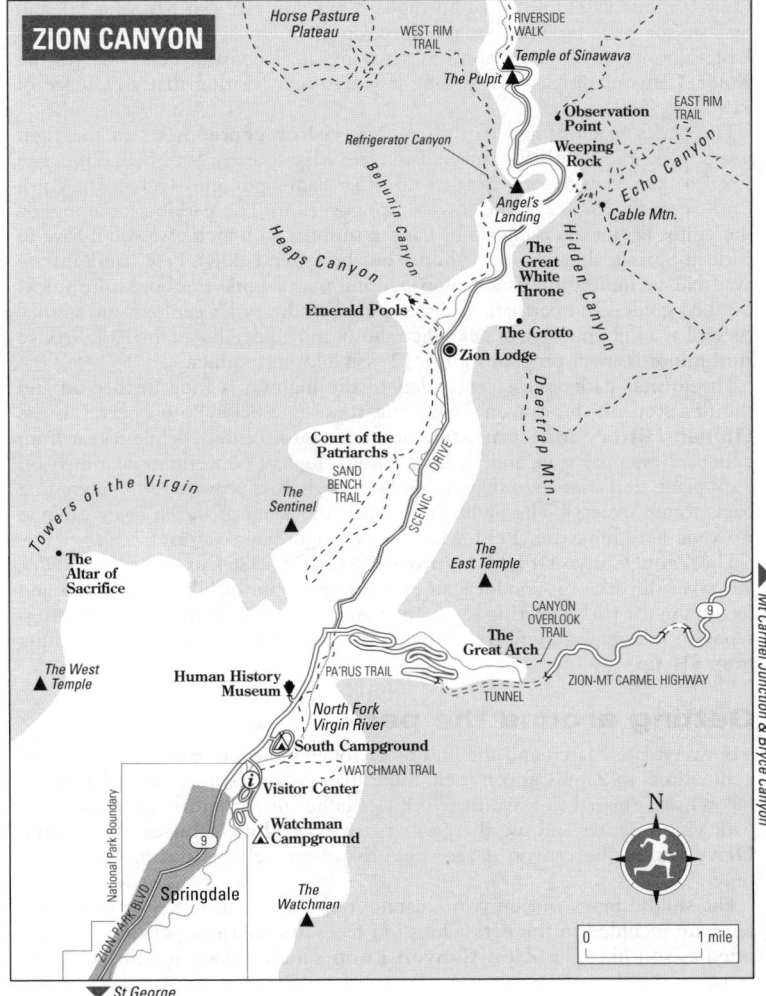

Getting to Zion Canyon

Zion Canyon is 43 miles northeast of St George and sixty miles south of Cedar City, reached by following **Hwy-9** beside the Virgin River for thirty miles east of I-15. Not far beyond the park's South Entrance, just north of Springdale (see p.422), Hwy-9 finally abandons the river, tunneling its way out of the canyon and continuing east to meet US-89. Bryce Canyon, often seen in conjunction with Zion, is a total of 86 miles northeast.

Arrival and information

The **admission charge** for Zion National Park, valid in all sections of the park for seven days, is $20 per vehicle, or $10 for motorcyclists, cyclists, and pedestrians. All nationwide passes, including the National Parks pass (see p.45), are both sold and accepted. Most visitors pay at the South Entrance kiosks on Hwy-9 immediately north of Springdale, but you can also pay your fee and pick up the basic brochures at the kiosk on the highway that marks the park's East Entrance (daily 8am–5pm). A separate, smaller visitor center serves the Kolob Canyons district (see p.438); if you're only visiting that area, a fee of $10 is payable.

The park's spacious and partly open-air **visitor center** is set to the right just beyond the South Entrance (daily: late May to early Sept 8am–7pm, late April to late May & early Sept to mid-Oct 8am–6pm; mid-Oct to late April 8am–5pm; ☎435/772-3256, ⓦwww.nps.gov/zion). The parking lot alongside the visitor center often fills up by 9am in summer, in which case you'll have to park in Springdale and ride a shuttle bus here (see below). Free handouts are available, including the park newspaper and maps, while the bookstore stocks detailed guides, and permanent displays explain the park's geology and history. As well as a full timetable of talks, slide shows and guided hikes, the Park Service runs Junior Ranger programs for 6–12-year-olds in summer.

The former park visitor center, left of the highway a little further on and the first stop on the canyon shuttle bus route (see below), now serves as the **Human History Museum** (same hours as visitor center). While it's far from being an essential stop, and its large photo displays concentrate as much on local plants and animals as they do on humans, it does provide some interesting background material. The highlight is a little mock-up of a *Zion Lodge* cabin as it would have looked in 1930, when an overnight stay cost just $7.50.

The **Zion Canyon Field Institute** (☎435/772-3264 or 1-800/635-3959, ⓦwww.zionpark.org) conducts an extensive program of hikes, excursions and lectures in the park, covering topics that range from reptiles to basketry, photography to solar energy. Full-day classes cost around $80, shorter jaunts anything from $10 up.

Getting around the park

Between late March and the end of October – precise dates vary each year – all visitors to Zion Canyon itself, other than guests staying at *Zion Lodge* (see below), are obliged to leave their vehicles either in Springdale or at the main park visitor center and use the park's network of **shuttle buses**. The **Scenic Drive** within the canyon is accessible to private vehicles during the winter only.

The shuttle buses run on two separate loops. Both are free – or rather, the fares are included in the park admission fee – and you can get on and off as often as you like. The **Zion Canyon Loop** shuttle, which remains active all

A history of Zion Canyon

Zion Canyon may seem like an oasis in the Utah wilderness, but it has never held much of a **human** population. Its earliest inhabitants were probably seminomadic hunter-gatherers, who from 500 AD onwards grew rudimentary crops beside the Virgin River. Known to archeologists as the **Virgin Anasazi**, they are regarded as less sophisticated cousins of the Ancestral Puebloan groups to the east; living in small bands, they never built the "cliff palaces" or pueblos for which their neighbors are renowned. By 1250 AD, drought had driven them out of Zion, leaving isolated pictographs on the canyon walls to serve as their only monument.

During the centuries that followed, **Paiute Indians** migrated seasonally throughout southern Utah, harvesting the few resources the desert could offer. They saw Zion, however, as the abode of Wai-no-Pits, the evil one, who cursed them with disease, and Kainesava, the God of Fire, whose lightning blazed from its high peaks. When the young **Mormon missionary** Nephi Johnson arrived in 1858 to explore the Upper Virgin River, the Paiute would lead him no further than Oak Creek, at the entrance to the canyon.

Isaac Behunin, who set up a log cabin in 1862 where *Zion Lodge* now stands, dubbed the canyon **"Little Zion"** in the hope that it would be a place of refuge for beleaguered Mormons. Some of his fellow farmers were soon taking things too easy; Brigham Young thundered that their indulgence in tobacco and wine made the name **"Not Zion"** more appropriate. In the long run, Zion Canyon proved too narrow to support efficient farming, and its main commercial role was simply as a route through which timber sawn on the high mesas could be shipped out to the plains. Between 1900 and 1930, logs lowered from "Cable Mountain" built the fine homes of such towns as St George.

John Wesley Powell's second Colorado expedition in 1872 (see p.497) had brought the scenery of Zion to national attention, under the Paiute name of "Mukuntuweap Canyon." The canyon itself was set aside in 1909 as Mukuntuweap National Monument; a larger area became Zion National Park in 1919, and the Kolob Canyons district was added in 1956.

In its first full year, 1920, the park attracted fewer than four thousand visitors. Trails and campgrounds remain little changed since their construction during the 1930s, but as visitor numbers climbed to current levels of almost three million per year, Zion began to show the strain. In an attempt to reduce wear and tear, a federally funded system of shuttle buses was introduced in 2000 (as detailed opposite), and private vehicles were banned from using the Scenic Drive in summer.

year round but is only compulsory between late March and October, runs between the visitor center and the end of the Scenic Drive, with nine stops including *Zion Lodge*. It operates between 5.45am and 11pm from late May until early September, between 6.45am and 10pm in spring and fall, and from dawn until sometime after dusk in winter. The **Springdale Loop** connects Springdale and the visitor center, with nine stops en route, between 5.30am and 11.15pm in summer, and 6.30am and 10.15pm in spring and fall, but closes down in the winter. Note that there's a short walk between the different shuttle bus systems at the visitor center; the Springdale buses actually stop just outside the park, so passengers have to pass through entrance gates on foot (where they pay the park fee as well) in order to reach the visitor center and the canyon buses.

Hwy-9, the east–west route through the park, remains open all year. However, vehicles measuring over 7ft 10in wide or 11ft 4in high – which includes virtually all RVs – pay $15 on top of the usual park fees to use the **Zion–Mount**

Carmel tunnel (see opposite). From early April until mid-September, they can only do so between 8am and 8pm; hours vary for the rest of the year. Cyclists are forbidden to ride through the tunnel altogether, but park rangers can arrange for bicycles to be transported by other vehicles.

Zion Canyon practicalities

The only **food** and **lodging** available within the canyon is at *Zion Lodge*, an appealing if often overcrowded complex of low-slung wooden buildings set amid well-shaded lawns a couple of miles up the Scenic Drive. **Reservations** for its motel-style rooms (mid-March to Nov ❼, Dec to mid-March ❺), more characterful cabins (mid-March to Nov ❼, Dec to mid-March Sun–Thurs ❺, Fri & Sat ❻), and larger suites (mid-March to Nov ❼, Dec to mid-March ❻), are handled by Xanterra Parks & Resorts (reservations ☏303/297-2757, 1-888/297-2757, Ⓦ www.xanterra.com or Ⓦ www.zionlodge.com; property phone ☏435/772-3213). The lodge remains open all year, but to get a room in summer you need to call several months in advance.

Whether or not you stay at the lodge, it's well worth stopping to eat in its bright, cool, upstairs **dining room** (☏435/772-7760). The river views will probably linger longer in your mind than its standard breakfasts (daily: summer 6.30–10am, winter 7–10am) and lunches (daily: summer 11.30am–2.30pm, winter 11am–2pm), both costing $7–8. Dinners are slightly more sophisticated (daily: summer 5–9pm, winter 5–8pm), featuring entrées such as steak or trout for $16–20. A snack shop near the main entrance (daily: summer 7am–9pm, winter 8am–7pm) serves burgers, sodas, and ice cream.

It's also possible to arrange **horseback rides** from the lodge (March–Oct; 3hr rides at 9am & 1.30pm daily, $55, minimum age 8; four 1hr rides daily, $30, minimum age 7; ☏435/679-8665; Ⓦ www.canyonrides.com).

Camping

The **Watchman** and **South campgrounds**, which hold around four hundred sites between them, are close to the visitor center. South, which oddly enough is north of the visitor center, is first-come, first-served, and is open between mid-March and October only, while Watchman, to the south, stays open year round and accepts advance reservations between mid-March and October only (☏1-800/365-2267 or Ⓦ http://reservations.nps.gov). Basic sites at either cost $16 per night, or $8 with a Golden Age or Golden Access pass, while Watchman also offers sites with electricity for $18, and riverside sites for $20. Arrive early in summer, when they tend to fill by noon daily.

To camp in the **backcountry**, pick up the necessary hiking **permits**, and a copy of the *Zion Backcountry Planner*, from visitor centers, as detailed on p.428. **Commercial campgrounds** nearby include *Zion Canyon Campground* in Springdale (see p.423), and the less appealing *Mukuntuweep Campground* (☏435/648-3011, Ⓦ www.xpressweb.com/zionpark) just outside the East Entrance, where there's also a café and a gas station.

Zion Canyon by road

Whether you access Zion Canyon using the park shuttle buses, or visit in winter when you're free to use your own vehicle, your first impressions of the place are going to be garnered from the highway. The main road, **Hwy-9**, passes plenty of dramatic formations as it climbs east toward Bryce, but Zion's most memorable monoliths are ranged on either side of the dead-end **Scenic Drive**, which runs for six miles north alongside the Virgin River.

The Scenic Drive

For half a mile north of the visitor center, Hwy-9 follows the west bank of the river. The highest of the peaks to the left, collectively known as the **Towers of the Virgin**, is the **Altar of Sacrifice**, named somewhat gruesomely for the blood-like streaks of rust that seem to flow from its flat crest.

The highway doglegs right to cross the river just beyond its confluence with **Pine Creek**. Guarded by the **Sentinel** to the west and the **East Temple** to the east, this marks the start of Zion Canyon proper. It's also the site of the Canyon Junction shuttle stop, and the northern trailhead of the **Pa'rus Trail** (see p.433). The **Scenic Drive** branches left on the far side of the bridge, while Hwy-9 heads on east (see below).

From here on north the canyon is so narrow, and the walls so steep, that there's barely room to squeeze in a road. Erosion is continuing as fast as ever, and a 200-yard segment of the Scenic Drive had to be rebuilt after a landslide in 1995. The first major roadside pull-out comes after 1.7 miles, facing the **Court of the Patriarchs**, where peaks named for Abraham, Isaac, and Joseph stand arrayed around a small canyon west of the river. A mile further on you reach the meadows of **Zion Lodge** (see opposite). In the height of summer, the crowds here can be overwhelming, but for most of the year it's a pleasant, shady place to break the day, and it's also the trailhead for the popular **Emerald Pools Trail** (see p.433).

Zion Canyon's one designated picnic spot is the **Grotto**, less than a mile beyond the lodge near the foot of the **West Rim Trail** (see p.433). To one side stands **Red Arch Mountain**, named for a natural archway created in 1880 when a vast chunk of the mountain suddenly collapsed and obliterated a newly planted cornfield. To the other is the long western flank of the **Great White Throne**, which from this angle looks neither white nor especially dramatic.

During the next mile the road passes the trailhead for **Weeping Rock** (see p.436) and the **East Rim Trail** (see p.436), as well as a number of unnamed pull-outs where paths lead down to the river. The best views of all come just under five miles from the start of the Drive, as it completes its long curve around the "Big Bend" in the river. The lookout here faces the northern aspect of the Great White Throne, framed between the slender neck of **Angels' Landing** (see p.434) to the right and the pipe-like formations of the **Organ** to the left. Glowing at sunset, the throne is utterly majestic.

A mile or so on, the Scenic Drive – and the shuttle-bus route – comes to an end at a large parking lot that marks the start of the mile-long hike toward the Narrows along the **Riverside Walk** (see p.434). This general area is known as the **Temple of Sinawava**, after a wolfish deity of the Paiute Indians; the most prominent single rock is the **Pulpit**, standing alone near the west bank of the river.

The Zion–Mount Carmel Highway

The side canyon formed by Pine Creek, half a mile north of the visitor center (see p.428), makes it possible for Hwy-9 to continue east, a route known as the **Zion–Mount Carmel Highway**. At first it heads straight for the **East Temple** – like its larger twin, topped by a forested mesa – but it's soon forced to start tacking its way up the hillside. At the eastern end of each extravagant switchback comes a better view of the enormous **Great Arch** at the head of the canyon. Measuring 720ft wide by 580ft high, this is not in fact an arch at all, but simply a deep alcove, or what's known as a "blind arch."

Finally the highway burrows into the rock, entering the first and longer of two remarkable **tunnels** blasted through the canyon walls in the late 1920s.

Five "windows" punctuate its one-mile length to allow air and light into the passageway, but you can't stop to admire the views. Traffic regulations for the tunnels are summarized on p.430. All the rubble from the excavation was allowed to tumble into Pine Creek far below; the river may seem innocuous, but it cleared the whole lot away in the space of a single year.

Easily seen on the enjoyable **Canyon Overlook Trail** (see p.437), the hot dry plateau beyond the eastern end of the main tunnel feels far removed from the lushness of Zion. These pale, smoothly undulating rocks, capped here and there by strange beehives and hoodoos, are the lithified remains of ancient sand dunes. One huge specimen, crisscrossed with stress lines from eons of erosion and resembling some long-abandoned pyramid, is known as the **Checkerboard Mesa**. It looms south of the highway at a clearly marked turnoff around five miles beyond the second tunnel, just a quarter of a mile short of the park's East Entrance. For accounts of Mount Carmel, Kanab, and points east, see p.443 onwards.

Hiking in Zion Canyon

Every visitor to Zion Canyon should **hike** at least one of its many clearly marked and signposted trails. However, almost all trails except the short Riverside Walk require a stiff climb away from the canyon floor, and with summer temperatures in excess of 100°F and elevations of well over 6000ft, it's all too easy to overdo things. Carry plenty of food and drink, and don't imagine that because you have no trouble walking five miles at home you can do it here, straight up a cliff. Water is available on most trails – although not until around five miles along the West or East Rim trails – but must be purified before use. For more detailed advice on desert hiking, see Basics.

As for specific **routes**, it makes sense to avoid the sun by hiking the east side of the canyon in the morning and the west in the afternoon. If you're reasonably fit and have just one day, the best combination is probably an hour or two along the **Riverside Walk** and a longer climb either to **Angels Landing** on the West Rim Trail or **Hidden Canyon** on the East Rim Trail.

All the trails detailed below set off from either Hwy-9 or the Scenic Drive, but some of the longer ones leave the canyon altogether and end up on backcountry dirt roads. If you're planning a one-way hike, look at the **shuttle board** in the visitor center, to see if you can swap vehicles with hikers coming in the opposite direction. Both *Zion Lodge* and the Zion Adventure Company (see p.423) also operate commercial **hiker shuttle services**.

Hiking **permits** are required for all overnight trips, and all hikes that require technical equipment, most obviously the **Zion Narrows** (see p.435). They cost $10 for one or two people, $15 for three to seven, and $20 for eight up to the group maximum of twelve. You can pick them up at any visitor center the day before you hike, and reserve in advance via the park website.

Watchman Trail

Just inside the South Entrance, a right turning leads across the river to the *Watchman* campground (see p.430) and the start of the **Watchman Trail**. This steep mile-long climb switchbacks up a side canyon below Bridge Mountain, then heads back south to loop around a flat promontory below the Watchman itself. Thankfully, it doesn't go right to the top, but its views up the canyon, as well as across to the West Temple and back down to Springdale, tucked among the trees, are a good way to get your bearings when you first arrive. Until around 10am, the canyon walls keep most of the route in shade; later on, it's liable to be baking hot. Allow around two hours to complete the entire two-mile round-trip hike.

Pa'rus Trail

The gentle, paved **Pa'rus Trail**, also open to cyclists, repeatedly criss-crosses the Virgin River on a two-mile route that connects the two campgrounds either side of the visitor center with the shuttle bus stop at Canyon Junction. While it lacks the glamour or rewarding destination of other, more demanding trails in the park, it's a truly delightful stroll, especially enjoyable around sunset at the end of a hard day.

Emerald Pools Trail

The **Emerald Pools Trail**, which starts conveniently from *Zion Lodge*, is every bit as pretty as the name implies. It's also suitable for walkers of all levels, as the lowest of the three pools can be seen on a gentle round-trip stroll of little more than a mile, while the highest makes a good objective for a more energetic hike.

On the far side of the footbridge that crosses the Virgin River from the lodge, the pink-paved trail to the right is the direct route to the **lower pool**. After an easy climb through the forest, with views straight up the main canyon, it cuts left into Heaps Canyon, and soon reaches a huge overhang of red rock, streaked black by deposits from a broad cascade of water. The almost constant flow collects in pools that tend be a muddy red rather than an emerald green; the overhang is deep enough for the trail to circle inside them, running behind the waterfall.

From this point, the trail becomes confusing, with several alternative routes and countless "trails of use" made by lost or blundering hikers. If you're pressed for time, head back the way you came; alternatively, continue straight ahead, along the shelf on the canyon wall, and in just over half a mile you'll drop back to cross the river at the Grotto picnic area, half a mile north of *Zion Lodge*.

Most hikers head instead for the **higher pools**, by following a narrow path through a cleft in the gigantic split boulder to the left. Having first doubled back to the top of the waterfall, where the stream bubbles out of the woods to spill across a lip of slickrock, take the spur trail to the right on the far side.

A hot, hard climb of not much more than five minutes is rewarded by a delightfully cool seep-fed pool at the foot of the monumental outer walls of the canyon. Climbing any higher is out of the question, but this is a good place to linger, with a small sandy "beach" and plenty of shade. Once back on the main trail, head right while still above the main falls to complete a loop back to the lodge, which should take a total of two to three hours.

Angel's Landing and the West Rim Trail

Serious hikers and backpackers rate the **West Rim Trail** as Zion's most compelling challenge. Even if you have nothing to prove, its views and variety make it well worth attempting, but it's not to be undertaken lightly. The first couple of miles involve a grueling 1500ft climb out of Zion Canyon, while to reach the obvious day-hike destination, **Angel's Landing** – a five-mile round-trip from the valley floor that takes a good four hours – you have to brave a terrifying knife-edge ridge.

The trail starts across the river from the Grotto picnic area, half a mile north of the lodge. As it winds ever more steeply toward the sheer canyon wall, it starts to seem that no onward route could possibly exist, but in the end it switchbacks several times and cuts back into a crack in the rock. Unless you've made a very early start, you'll have been out in the sun for a long time by now, and the cool shade of this narrow crevice – **Refrigerator Canyon** – comes as a merciful relief.

However, things soon get worse; beyond the brief flat stretch of the canyon you're confronted by a severe set of switchbacks known as **Walter's Wiggles**. Constructed during the 1920s and named for the park's then-superintendent, these serve as a ladder up what would otherwise be an impassable cliff. At the top lies **Scout Lookout**, a tranquil patch of sand with views up and down Zion Canyon and a population of scavenging chipmunks that feast on the remains of countless well-earned picnics.

Daredevil day-hikers are invariably drawn to the spur trail from Scout Lookout to **Angel's Landing**. What you're letting yourself in for is obvious from the outset; the trail sets off along the top of the steep promontory straight ahead, with awesome drop-offs to either side, and only token stretches of metal chain offer the illusion of security. If you think you're the brave one, take a look to see if there are any climbers scaling the sheer rock face on your left. Your goal is a knee-shaking half-mile on, with a quarter-mile drop to the canyon floor at your feet and the Great White Throne towering a further thousand feet above you on the far side of the river.

Beyond Scout Lookout, the West Rim Trail climbs steadily out of the canyon. After crossing an expanse of slickrock, perilously close to the rim, it descends into a spectacular high-country valley. This is another side of Zion altogether, rimmed with white cliffs, "checkerboarded" by the erosive formation known as cross-bed hatching, and scattered with rounded outcrops of layered sandstone. For a couple of miles, the trail picks its way gingerly across the valley and up the far side, twice crossing streambeds that even when not visibly flowing nurture forest glades. Finally it runs into the monumental wall of red sandstone that marks the head of **Behunin Canyon**, a huge side canyon off Zion Canyon (itself by now way out of view). Doubling back, it clings to the cliff face on a long exposed switchback that comes out on top of **Horse Pasture Plateau**.

Just to set foot on Horse Pasture Plateau is a stiff target for a day-hike from the floor of Zion Canyon, a total round-trip of something over eleven miles. In the full heat of summer even that would be too much to take on, but the trail continues north for another ten miles, to **Lava Point** off the Kolob Terrace Road (see p.437), with plenty of optional scenic detours en route. This is Zion's most popular backpacking trip, usually done as a two-day expedition, starting from Lava Point and working down, and camping near the southern edge of Horse Pasture Plateau. As with any such overnight hike, a backcountry camping permit is required; see p.430.

Riverside Walk

Not least because it involves no climbing, the mile-long **Riverside Walk** at the end of the Scenic Drive is Zion's best-loved trail. Having watched the canyon walls converge ever closer, the urge to find out what happens beyond the end of the road is irresistible. You may well have more company than you'd prefer, but the views from the gentle paved footpath are too beautiful for that to matter. While it's easy enough to complete the round-trip in under an hour, you'll enjoy it more if you allow much longer.

Walls of deep red sandstone soar to either side of the river, which is flanked by shimmering cottonwoods that turn a rich gold in the fall. There are even patches of low-lying "desert swamp," where bullfrogs bellow in the rushes and willows thrust from the mud.

Riverside Walk used to be known as the "Gateway to the Narrows Trail," as it ends where the Virgin emerges from **the Narrows**, overlooked by the mighty **Mountain of Mystery**. For eight miles upstream from this sandy little beach, the river fills the entire gorge, often less than twenty feet wide and channeled

Hiking the Zion Narrows

Hiking the Zion Narrows – the slender gorge through which the Virgin River enters Zion Canyon from the north – has acquired the reputation of being the thing every Zion visitor simply must do. Don't believe the hype. It's a very demanding **wilderness experience**, much more suitable for devotees of extreme sports than for casual hikers.

A ravishing "slot canyon" squeezed between mighty sandstone cliffs and interspersed with fertile grottoes, the Narrows is undeniably spectacular. However, you can only trek its full length by following the river downstream from a remote trailhead that's only accessible in a **four-wheel-drive vehicle**. For at least ten of the sixteen-mile hike from there, you can expect to be wading thigh- or even shoulder-deep in **cold, fast-flowing water**, struggling with every step to find a foothold on the slippery rounded boulders that form the streambed. While it's just possible to complete the whole hike in a single, grueling day – the average **hiking time** is twelve hours – it's more realistic to plan to camp overnight along the way. Specialist **equipment** is essential, in the form of waterproof, super-grip footwear, neoprene socks, and a walking stick or two, complemented in the cooler months by a drysuit. It's not a question of whether, but of how often, you'll fall over, so you'll also need zip-lock plastic bags for everything you carry, and since the water isn't drinkable, you'll have to lug a load of that along too. Though it doesn't have the same kudos among the adventure-sports fraternity, you can also sample the Narrows as a **day-hike** by pushing your way upstream, against the current, from the end of the Riverside Walk, and turning back when you've had enough. However, you'll still need all the gear – don't even dream of setting off without it.

For anything beyond a short day-hike, you have to have a **permit** to hike the Narrows, as detailed on p.430. The park service issues a maximum of eighty such permits per day, of which around half can be reserved in advance, while the rest are available first-come, first-served the day before. Making a reservation does not necessarily mean you'll actually be allowed to hike; the Narrows is always liable to be closed due to flash floods or wildfires. In principle, the **best times to hike** are either in June or from September until early October. July and August see frequent thunderstorms, so the risk of flash floods is at its highest. In addition, the road to the trailhead is often closed altogether between December and April.

The Narrows is just one among many wonderful hikes on offer in the park, most of which don't require nearly so much planning, expertise, or expense. According to park rangers, its current popularity is largely because it's so heavily promoted by commercial companies. As the Narrows lie inside the national park, operators can't offer guided trips, but they do rent **equipment** and run **shuttle services**. In Springfield, both Zion Adventure Company, 36 Lion Blvd (☎435/772-1001, ⓦwww.zionadventures .com), and Zion Rock and Mountain Guides, 1458 Zion Park Blvd (☎435/772-3303, ⓦwww.zionrockguides.com), charge around $16 for one day, or $25 overnight, for the basic summer package of boots, socks and staff, while between October and May, when you need a drysuit as well, it costs $35 for one day, $55 overnight. Both also run shuttles to the trailhead at Chamberlain's Ranch, leaving daily at 6am and 9am in summer, and less frequently at other times, for $25. If you have your own 4WD vehicle, you can get there by turning left 1.7 miles east of the East Entrance (just east of milepost 46 on Hwy-9), and then following North Fork Road, which in due course becomes a rough dirt track, for around seventeen miles north. The total thirty-mile drive from Zion Canyon takes about ninety minutes.

between vertical cliffs almost a thousand feet high. As explained in the box on p.435, it's possible to wade upstream, against the current, to see the Narrows for yourself, while if you arrive towards sunset, you'll also doubtless encounter plenty of exhausted backpackers who have hiked here sixteen miles downstream, from Chamberlain's Ranch.

Weeping Rock

One of the easiest short walks in Zion Canyon – and thus prone to be overcrowded in summer – is the half-mile round-trip hike to **Weeping Rock**. Eaten away from the canyon wall by a perennial spring, this damp alcove is filled with ferns and tiny flowers; while it comes as a surprise in the desert, however, it's not as beautiful as you may be led to expect. The paved trail up starts from the parking lot at the mouth of Echo Canyon, halfway between *Zion Lodge* and the end of the road.

Hidden Canyon and the East Rim Trail

Rewarding hikes of almost any length can be enjoyed by taking the **East Rim Trail**, which sets off from the Weeping Rock trailhead (see above) but branches right rather than left on the far side of Echo Canyon Creek. Only backpackers who camp overnight on the mesa-top attempt its full 10.5-mile length, and they normally prefer to start from the far end, near the park's East Entrance. However, the strenuous two-mile climb out of Zion Canyon is its most exhilarating segment, and offers several spur trails for day-hikers.

After half an hour of ascending along a cement pathway, enjoying ever-improving views of Weeping Rock, the East Rim Trail reaches a stiff set of switchbacks. By the time you reach the top of those, you've climbed about half a mile up the face of Cable Mountain, but you're still only halfway up to the mesa. A stone bench here makes a good place to ponder the decision whether to keep on going, or head instead for **Hidden Canyon**, a "hanging canyon" that has yet to cut its way down to the floor of Zion. A good goal for a half-day hike, it's a three-mile, three-hour roundtrip from the Scenic Drive. To reach it, follow a spur trail for a further half-mile on, beyond a brief stretch of forest and a hair-raising segment, clinging to a wall of rock, which is enough to deter most would-be canyoneers. The broad "lip" of the canyon, perched 700ft above Zion, turns into a waterfall after heavy rain, while the rounded holes scoured into the slickrock fill with water and life. Strictly speaking, the trail ends here; it's just about feasible to press on into the canyon, but only expert rock climbers have any hope of approaching its head.

If Hidden Canyon sounds too intimidating, you may prefer to keep on switchbacking up the East Rim Trail beyond the Hidden Canyon turnoff. A mile or so further on, deep in wafer-thin Echo Canyon – a so-called "slot canyon" with beautiful walls – the **East Mesa Trail** climbs steeply off to the left. A two-mile walk through the woods on top of the plateau brings you to **Observation Point**, which commands views all the way down Zion Canyon. The massive cliffs of Cable Mountain and the Great White Throne stare you full in the face, while Angels Landing towers proudly on the far side. To be on the safe side, allow six hours for the full seven-mile round-trip hike this far, though you may find you do it in less.

Assuming you stay on the **East Rim Trail** rather than taking the East Mesa Trail, it takes a good mile or more to drag yourself up out of Echo Canyon, and there may be streams to negotiate en route. Atop the mesa, walking becomes much easier, as the trails simply follow former logging roads. **Stave Spring**, the only perennial water source on the East Rim Trail, is roughly halfway between

Zion Canyon, five miles west, and the East Entrance, slightly further southeast. Overnight campers can head southwest at this point, along a trail that soon forks to the summits of **Cable Mountain** – where you can take a closer look at the century-old workings that hauled timber down into Zion (see p.429) – or Deertrap Mountain. Either hike is a six-mile detour from Stave Spring.

Canyon Overlook Trail

Alongside the ranger station at the eastern end of the long tunnel on the Zion–Mount Carmel highway (see p.431), steps cut into the rock mark the start of the **Canyon Overlook Trail**. So long as you don't mind edging along the brink of a precipice – at one point the trail consists of wooden planks braced against the cliff-face – this offers a fascinating variety of terrain in the space of just half a mile. It's also the only trail described in this section for which the trailhead is accessible in your own vehicle year-round – though there's so little parking, opposite the trailhead, that you may find that makes little difference anyway. The scenery en route ranges from fern-filled grottoes fed by seeping water to a bare slickrock mesa topped by tiny hoodoos. An informative booklet, usually available at the trailhead, explains the flora and fauna you may spot.

The trail ends at a railed viewing area at the head of Pine Creek Canyon; you can't see it, but you're directly above the Great Arch. Only one of the tunnel's five "windows" is visible in the rock wall to your left, but the road emerges below to zigzag into the valley. Straight ahead of you is the west wall of Zion Canyon; a helpful sign labels the peaks ranged along the far side of the river, from the ruddy tree-capped West Temple to the paler Sentinel. Walking the full length of the trail and returning to the road typically takes around an hour, though you could scurry it in half that.

Kolob Terrace Road

The only road access to the central uplands of Zion National Park is along **Kolob Terrace Road**, which branches inconspicuously north from Hwy-9 at the hamlet of **Virgin**, fifteen miles west of the park's South Entrance (see p.422). Especially in its earlier stages, it's a dramatic drive, deservedly proclaimed a Scenic Byway, but unless you have a high-clearance 4WD vehicle, you won't manage the full 43 miles to meet I-15 just south of Cedar City. Ordinary cars have to turn back after just over twenty miles, so only long-distance hikers or tourists with a spare afternoon to kill tend to come this way. In addition, the entire road is closed to all traffic in winter.

The road starts by climbing through a dry desert valley, dotted with pine trees, heading for two pyramidal mountains that dwarf the cliffs on the horizon. It dips repeatedly in and out of the park boundaries, reaching Zion after just over seven miles, only to exit almost immediately. As it next re-enters the park, you get superb views north across **Hop Valley** to the russet and white pinnacle of **Burnt Mountain**. Keen backpackers can hike to Kolob Arch from here along the **Hop Valley Trail**, but it's not as easy as it looks; you have to plow through thick sand for most of the way, so the fifteen-mile hike is even more difficult than the route described overleaf.

Soon after you leave the park yet again, twenty miles up from the highway, a dirt road to the right leads 1.7 miles to **Lava Point**, back within the park. As well as being the trailhead for the West Rim Trail, which takes fourteen miles to drop down into Zion Canyon (see p.433), this is a superb vantage point in its own right. Poised four thousand feet higher than the visitor center, it overlooks a panorama that stretches north to Cedar Breaks and southeast to the Kaibab Mountains, with the monoliths of Zion Canyon mere incidental details in the foreground. There's a **picnic area** and a free, first-come, first-served, six-site primitive **campground** with no water nearby (June to mid-Oct only).

Kolob Terrace Road is paved for just under two miles beyond the Lava Point turnoff, passing a village of pastel cabins before it turns to dirt for the last mile to **Kolob Reservoir**. Locals flock to this drab little lake to cool off and play with their boats, but it holds no great interest for tourists. To reach I-15 to the north, you have to continue about 20 more miles over dirt on Kolob Terrace Road.

Kolob Canyons

Located just off I-15, twenty miles south of Cedar City, the **Kolob Canyons** have formed part of Zion National Park since 1956. Although easier to reach than Zion Canyon, they remain far less famous and receive far fewer visitors. In all honesty, neither are they as immediately impressive as Zion Canyon, and you'll only get the most out of the area if you can spare the time and energy to **hike**. If you stay in your car, you can drive to the end of the five-mile road, admire the view of the red-rock canyons, and be back on the interstate within the hour, wondering what the fuss is about.

Information on the Kolob Canyons can be picked up from the small **visitor center** at exit 40 off I-15 (daily: late April to mid-Oct 8am–5pm, mid-Oct to late April 8am–4.30pm; ℡435/586-9548). As well as providing free hiking advice, rangers also allot 24 numbered backcountry **campsites** ($5). No gas or food is available.

Beyond the visitor center, **Kolob Canyons Road** twists alongside Taylor Creek and then up through Lee Pass, with countless trailheads and roadside viewpoints en route. It ends at a parking lot that faces across the riverbed to a succession of narrow, red-walled **"finger" canyons** cut into the west rim of the Markagunt Plateau. Each was carved by a separate tiny stream; one, Hanging Valley, is interrupted by a sheer 1500ft cliff, stranding an isolated patch of thick forest far above the valley floor. In the distance, you may just be able to make out the West Temple, above Zion Canyon.

Footpaths on the far side of the lot lead to a picnic spot in the woods. From here, the half-mile **Timber Creek Overlook** trail runs through low trees along the top of the ridge, to end at a rocky promontory with views over the endless rolling forests.

Hiking the Kolob Canyons

The two main **hiking trails** in the Kolob Canyons leave from earlier along Kolob Canyons Road. Starting two miles from the visitor center, **Taylor Creek Trail** follows the Middle Fork of Taylor Creek on a five-mile round-trip to **Double Arch Alcove**, passing long-abandoned cabins built by early home-steaders en route. The trail grows progressively less and less distinct before it culminates by climbing into the lush hollow in the canyon wall that lies beneath the Double Arch itself. The entire round-trip from the trailhead takes around four hours.

The **Kolob Arch Trail**, which ranks among Zion's very finest trails, leads down from Lees Pass along the drainage of Timber Creek. At fourteen miles for the round-trip, however, it only makes an appropriate day-hike for confident, experienced desert hikers. It can be muddy going at times, but at least there's usually plenty of water en route (though it must be purified before drinking). The first couple of miles, heading south, feature superb close-up views of the finger canyons; you then veer east to meet **La Verkin Creek** just above a waterfall. The goal for most hikers is **Kolob Arch**, seven miles along, which may or may not be the world's longest natural rock span. Like Landscape Arch, in Arches National Park (see p.516), it's approximately 300ft across; no one agrees how to measure arches any more precisely, so they're generally considered equals. Camping somewhere nearby (by prior arrangement at the visitor center) makes for a less grueling hike and gives you the option of exploring the remote regions that lie farther along La Verkin Creek.

North from Zion

Although taking Hwy-18 due north of St George leads you through an interesting stretch of mountainous high country (see p.379), the most direct route from St George to Cedar City is to follow the interstate northeast. In the course of fifty miles, I-15 climbs three thousand feet, passing between the Pine Valley Mountains to the west and the Hurricane Cliffs to the east.

Fifteen miles northeast of St George, a spur road to the left leads to the ghost town of **SILVER REEF**. Silver mining never came any easier than here, the only spot in the West where silver was found mixed in with ordinary sandstone. It took two decades, the 1880s and 1890s, to scour the hills bare of metal, during which time Silver Reef reveled in a reputation for very un-Mormon hell-raising. Relics of the era, together with a scale model of the town, can be admired in the **Silver Reef Museum**, 3200 Wells Fargo Rd (Mon–Sat 10am–4pm; $4). Only stunted walls remain of the town itself, however, and few visitors can summon up the energy on a red-hot Utah summer's day to find them of any interest.

There's even less to see at the site of **FORT HARMONY**, another eighteen miles north, just beyond the turnoff for the **Kolob Canyons** district of Zion National Park, and fifteen miles south of Cedar City. **John D. Lee**, of Mountain Meadows fame, established a fortified outpost to guard this high pass in 1852. It was finally abandoned ten years later, after torrential rain caused its earthen walls to cave in, killing two of Lee's children.

Cedar City

CEDAR CITY, 53 miles northeast of St George and now half its size, has a similar history to its upstart rival. It, too, was founded in Mormon Utah's precarious early years, as part of the church's bid for self-sufficiency. The Mormons urgently needed **iron**, so when scouting parties discovered iron ore in southern Utah, the *Deseret News* published an appeal in July 1850 for "fifty or so good effective men, with teams and waggons" to establish an **Iron Mission**.

Cedar City was established in November 1851, between the iron in the hills to the west and the coal deposits of Coal Creek Canyon to the east. Most of its first inhabitants were British miners; they succeeded in smelting iron within a year, but the venture ultimately failed and was abandoned in October 1858. Since then, ore mined in the area has been shipped out for processing.

The Cedar City story is told in full at **Iron Mission State Park**, on the main highway a mile or so north of downtown (daily: June to early Sept 9am–7pm; early Sept to May 9am–5pm; $5 per vehicle or $2 per person). Apart from rusty nuggets, the warehouse-like museum is filled with nineteenth-century horse-drawn vehicles, including wagons, sleighs, and hearses (one of which bears the slogan "Why walk around half dead when we can bury you for just $22?"). There's also a small and somewhat dull display of Native American artifacts, plus some homespun craft items – crocheted doilies and the odd carved pieces of vertebra, and 380 individually tagged samples of barbed wire. Several more wagons are parked in sheds at the back, if you feel up to braving the heat.

Otherwise, there's little to see in Cedar City. It's not a place you're likely to want to tour on foot, despite the lure of historical markers detailing the former locations of the town's social hall, hospital, brick yard, and flour mill.

Tourists do arrive in droves during the summer, however, drawn by the annual **Utah Shakespeare Festival**, a semi-professional event organized by Southern Utah State University since 1962. Running from late June until the first weekend of September, and then again from the last week of September through to the end of October, it usually features nine or so productions, with three or four Shakespeare plays among assorted other classics. Two theaters are used, the most prestigious being the Adams Memorial Shakespearean Theater, a replica of London's original Globe, and tickets range from $16 to $46 (reservations on ☎435/586-7878 or 1-800/752-9849; ⓦwww.bard.org).

Arrival and information

Cedar City's large **visitor center** stands next to Iron Mission State Park at 581 N Main St (summer Mon–Fri 8am–7pm, Sat 9am–1pm; winter Mon–Fri 8am–5pm; ☎435/586-5124 or 1-800/354-4849; ⓦwww.scenicsouthernutah .com or ⓦwww.cedarcity.org); that isn't construction debris outside, but huge boulders of natural ferrous rock.

Greyhound **buses** call at 1744 Royal Hunte Drive, while the airport on the northwest fringes of town is used by Skywest Airlines (☎1-800/453-9417, ⓦwww.skywest.com) for **flights** to and from Salt Lake City.

Accommodation

While Cedar City doesn't have quite the range of **accommodation** to match St George, around twenty motels and hotels line up along Main Street, including several right in the heart of town. Rooms are liable to be booked well in advance for the Shakespeare festival.

There's a large *KOA* **campground** at 1121 N Main St (☎435/586-9872); for more seclusion head for the public sites that start around a dozen miles east of town, along Hwy-14 toward Cedar Breaks (see opposite). For full details, call in at the **Dixie National Forest Ranger Station**, 82 North 100 East (☎435/865-3200).

Best Western El Rey Inn 80 S Main St ☎435/586-6518 or 1-800/688-6518, ⓦwww .bwelrey.com. Very central *Best Western* hotel – one of the first ever – an easy walk away from the Festival events, with rooms of all sizes, plus pool, sauna, and spa. ❸–❻
Best Western Town and Country Inn 189 N Main St ☎435/586-9900 or 1-800/493-0062,

ⓦwww.bwtowncountry.com. Large, smart, and very central option, this time with *two* pools and spas and some luxury suites. ❹
Big Yellow Inn 234 South 300 West ☎435/586-0960, ⓦwww.bigyellowinn.com. Very grand, pastel-yellow Georgian Revival house that offers eleven luxurious B&B rooms, all with en-suite facilities and plush antique furnishings and fancy bed

On location in the Southwest

Many travelers are inspired to visit the Southwest not by some in-depth National Geographic documentary or picture-spread, but by its scene-stealing appearance in the backdrop of a Hollywood film. The region's dramatic desert scenery makes it the perfect destination to embark on a road trip a la Thelma and Louise or to recreate a mock shootout from a well-known Western. Of course to really experience the often surreal landscapes, it's best to get out of your car and make your way on foot; the ten national parks scattered about provide excellent opportunities to scout locations and put yourself in a starring role.

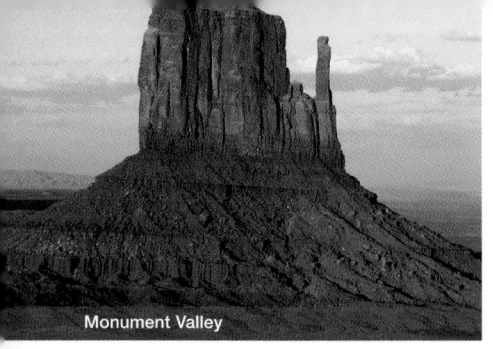
Monument Valley

The open road

In a land where public transport is totally inadequate to meet the needs of visitors, planning your own **road trip** is not only a romantic adventure but also a practical necessity. And you can create a truly superb itinerary simply by following in the footsteps – or road tracks – of the movie crews: your vehicle of choice might be an open-top convertible as seen in the ultimate female buddy-adventure, *Thelma and Louise* (1991), or a king-of-the-road Harley-Davidson motorcycle, made famous in *Easy Rider* (1969). Thelma and Louise spent most of their time in southeast Utah, cruising beneath the sandstone formations of Arches National Park and making their climactic leap at what's now known as **Thelma and Louise Point** in Canyonlands, just below Dead Horse Point State Park (the film had viewers believe they'd reached the Grand Canyon). The hog-ridin' hippies of *Easy Rider*, on the other hand, smoked grass in **Monument Valley**, picked up a hitchhiker on US-89 near Flagstaff, and hung out at Taos Pueblo before continuing on their way to New Orleans.

San Juan Skyway

Scenic drives

The most famous road trip in the United States has to be **Route 66**, which crosses northern New Mexico and Arizona. Its fading neon signs, rundown motels, and dusty diners are certainly evocative of bygone days, but in terms of scenic beauty, the Southwest holds plenty of more appealing driving routes. Here are five favorites, one for each state in the region:

Hwy-12 Southern Utah. Between two national parks, Hwy-12 skirts the top of remote Grand Staircase-Escalante National Monument. p.461

San Juan Skyway Southwest Colorado. Make a lofty loop through the Rockies' mining towns and ski resorts. p.103

Road between the Rims Arizona. There's no quick way through a gaping chasm. A 215-mile drive connects the Grand Canyon's North and South rims. p.400

High Road Northern New Mexico. On your way between Santa Fe and Taos, cut through the Sangre de Cristo Mountains for views of the Rio Grande Valley. p.174

The Strip Nevada. It may only be a six-mile trawl, but it's worth renting a convertible to get an eyeful of the casinos-cum-amusement parks in Las Vegas. p.548

The Wild West

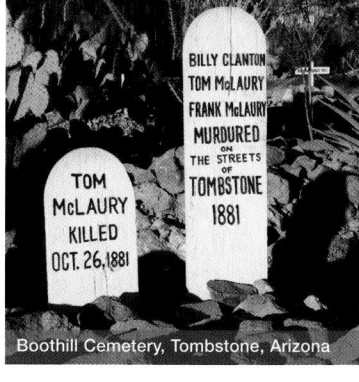

Boothill Cemetery, Tombstone, Arizona

The Southwest also, of course, makes a quintessential setting for **Westerns**. Thanks to its magnificent buttes and stark silhouettes, **Monument Valley**, on the Utah/Arizona border, has become the definitive Western movie location. Director John Ford first popularized the valley in *Stagecoach* (1939) and went on to shoot six more movies there, including *The Searchers* (1956). Films that took advantage of similar backdrops there are *The Eiger Sanction* (1975), *Back to the Future III* (1989), and *Forrest Gump* (1994).

Scriptwriters have an easy time borrowing dramatic material from the real-life gunfights and jailbreaks of the late nineteenth-century Southwest. Billy the Kid, Doc Holliday, and Wyatt Earp all stalked its streets, and towns like **Tombstone**, Arizona – immortalized in such movies as *Gunfight at the OK Corral* (1957) and the later, more satisfying *Tombstone* (1994) – makes a memorable destination for movie buffs, especially since Tombstone continues to play up its Wild West history. **Lincoln**, New Mexico preserves the buildings in which the events of *Pat Garrett and Billy the Kid* (1973) unfolded, but the film was actually shot in northern Mexico. The story of those rather more lovable outlaws, *Butch Cassidy and the Sundance Kid* (1969), was filmed near **Zion National Park** in Utah, though Paul Newman and Robert Redford carried out their daring train robbery on the Durango & Silverton Railroad in southwest Colorado.

The dusty trail

If you're hunting for the perfect location for your own road movie, some of the finest and least spoiled landscapes in the Southwest are found in the region's ten **national parks**; touring them is a sure-fire way to see the desert at its most spectacular. Arizona's three parks include the awesome Grand Canyon, Petrified Forest, and the cactus–studded hills of Saguaro, outside Tucson. Mesa Verde, which focuses on extraordinary ancient "cliff dwellings" set high on remote canyon walls, is in southwest Colorado, while Carlsbad Caverns is hidden beneath a mountain in desolate southeastern New Mexico. Southern Utah is such a wonderland of bizarre sandstone formations that it arguably deserves to become a single vast national park. It holds an amazing five – Zion, Bryce Canyon, Capitol Reef, Canyonlands, and Arches.

West Rim Trail, Zion National Park

However hooked on driving you may be, to act out those Wild West fantasies you can't beat venturing out **on foot**. The parks offer a perfect opportunity to experience the thrill of hiking in genuine wilderness while minimizing the risk of becoming lost or injured. Almost all hold networks of marked and maintained trails that access

Otherworldly settings

Something otherworldly about the Southwestern landscape lends itself to **science fiction** movies. The opening scenes of the original *Planet of the Apes* (1967) were filmed at Lake Powell while its waters were still rising in Glen Canyon, thus recording a doomed and drowning world, while White Sands National Monument stood in for David Bowie's waterless home planet in *The Man Who Fell to Earth* (1976). Utah's Goblin Valley State Park was a hostile alien desertscape in *Galaxy Quest* (1999), where the strangely shaped hoodoos came alive to terrify the hapless interlopers. The desiccated, eons-old deserts of the Southwest can represent the **remote past** as well. In *The Greatest Story Ever Told* (1965), Max von Sydow as Jesus delivered the Sermon on the Mount to a crowd of Moab extras at Green River Overlook in Canyonlands National Park.

Goblin Valley State Park

their most scenic areas, on which it's nonetheless possible to escape the crowds and face real physical challenges. (The exceptions are Mesa Verde, where access to the "cliff palaces" is carefully controlled, and Carlsbad, where the caverns are explored via underground pathways).

Several factors mean that a hike in the Southwest may well be **more demanding** than any you've done before. There's the summer **heat**, often in excess of 100°F; the lack of water; and the **altitude**, which on the Colorado Plateau is more than a mile above sea level. Add to this the unfamiliar, topsy-turvy nature of canyon hiking, in which the hardest part of a day-hike may come at the end, when you have to climb back up to your starting point. Talk to the rangers in each park before attempting any long trails, and be sure to read the advice in the "Health" section of the *Basics* chapter in this book.

National park hikes

Here's a Top Ten of the best national-park hikes in the Southwest, in ascending order of length.

Mesa Arch Trail, Canyonlands	one hour	p.502
Canyon Overlook Trail, Zion	one hour	p.437
Navajo Loop Trail, Bryce Canyon	two hours	p.455
Delicate Arch Trail, Arches	two hours	p.515
Hickman Bridge Trail, Capitol Reef	two hours	p.479
Horseshoe Canyon, Canyonlands	five hours	p.505
Chesler Park Loop Trail, Canyonlands	one day	p.510
North Kaibab Trail to Rainbow Falls, Grand Canyon	one day	p.408
West Rim Trail, Zion	one day	p.433
South Kaibab/Bright Angel trails, Grand Canyon	two days	p.387 & p.389

throws; five cheaper rooms are offered in the less imposing Victorian home across the street. **⑤–⑦**
Super 8 145 North 1550 West ☎ 435/586-8880 or 1-800/800-8000, ⓦ www.super8.com. Reliable budget motel, with little seasonal variation in price. Well out of town, west of I-15 at exit 59. **③**

Willow Glen Inn 3308 N Bulldog Rd ☎ 435/586-3275, ⓦ www.willowgleninn.com. Farm-set B&B, five miles northwest of downtown, near exit 62 off I-15. Rooms with and without bath in main house, and some luxurious suites in garden cottages. **④–⑧**

Eating

A quick-fire succession of chain diners and fast-food outlets punctuates the main highway through Cedar City. For alternatives with more character, head for the student-oriented places near the university, in the blocks immediately southwest of downtown.

Godfather's Pizza 241 N Main St ☎ 435/586-1111. Fills the spruced-up former railroad station opposite the visitor center, serving good pizzas in all sizes ($9–24) plus all-you-can-eat lunch and dinner buffets. Mon–Thurs 11am–10pm, Fri & Sat 11am–11pm.
The Grind Coffee House 19 N Main St ☎ 435/867-5333. Busy, very central local rendez-vous, serving pastries and sandwiches as well as coffee. Closed Sun.
Lefty's Hideout Mexican Cafe 2107 N Main St ☎ 435/586-4741. Lively, moderately priced

dinner-only Mexican option, a fair way north of downtown, with a sideline in chunky steaks, and an open-air veranda that's a midsummer night's dream of a spot for a margarita.
Sullivan's Cafe 301 S Main St ☎ 435/586-6761. Popular breakfast place, a cornucopia of eggs and pancakes, that also has the more expensive *Sulli's Steakhouse* upstairs, a fully-fledged (and liquor-licensed) steak and seafood restaurant. Open for all meals daily.

Cedar Breaks National Monument

Cedar City stands at an elevation of 5800ft, but the densely wooded plateau to the east rises a further five thousand feet. **Hwy-14**, the most direct route to Bryce Canyon, climbs steadily onto the plateau from the narrow gorge east of town. The scenery along the way is rarely short of spectacular, with views that stretch south to encompass all of Zion National Park.

Around fifteen miles along, shortly after the highway enters the **Dixie National Forest**, you can't fail to spot the pink, white, and orange rocks of **CEDAR BREAKS NATIONAL MONUMENT**, immediately below the forest that tops the high ridge to your left. Cedar Breaks is a sort of pocket version of Bryce Canyon (see p.450), where erosive forces have scooped a natural amphitheater into the hillside and filled it with brilliantly colored limestone formations. While it lacks Bryce's opportunities for hiking, it's well worth seeing if you're in the area.

The road through the monument, **Hwy-148**, which branches north from Hwy-14 nineteen miles out of Cedar City – is usually snowbound between late October and mid-May. When it's clear, you can choose between four similar cliff-edge viewpoints. The southernmost, **Point Supreme**, is the best, with pinnacles rising from the orange canyon floor at your feet and sweeping views to the south and west. The small **visitor center** just behind is only staffed in summer (May–Sept daily 8am–6pm; ☎ 435/586-9451, ⓦ www.nps.gov/cebr); if you make it here in spring or fall, you can visit without paying the usual $4-per-person fee. Overnight temperatures only rise high enough to make the adjoining **campground** ($12) an appealing proposition between July and September.

You can hike for short distances along the rim at both Point Supreme and **Chessmen Ridge**, a mile or so north, but no trails descend into the formations.

Panguitch Lake and Brian Head

Near the northern end of Cedar Breaks, Hwy–148 meets Hwy-143 where it turns sharply east toward Panguitch (see p.449). If you're heading for Bryce, it makes little difference in terms of mileage or scenery whether you continue this way or return to Hwy-14. **PANGUITCH LAKE**, in the heart of the forest halfway to US-89, appeals mainly to local trout fishermen, though the **campground** at *Panguitch Lake Resort* ($8; ☎435/676-2657) is nice enough.

Alternatively, keep going north on Hwy-143 and you'll come to tiny **BRIAN HEAD** within a couple of miles. Utah's highest town, at 9700ft, it remains accessible year-round from the north, via a steep fifteen-mile climb from Parowan. It's the site of southern Utah's only **downhill ski resort** (mid-Nov to May; lift tickets around $40 per day; information on ☎435/677-2035, ⓦwww .brianhead.com). Despite offering slopes to suit all levels of competence – and the closest skiing to Las Vegas – Brian Head is not exactly thriving, so don't expect a heady whirl of post-piste partying. In summer, it verges on being a ghost town, but makes a peaceful overnight stop.

In the largest **hotel** – the year-round *Cedar Breaks Lodge*, at 223 Hunter Ridge Drive (☎435/677-3000 or 1-888/282-3327, ⓦwww.cedarbreakslodge.com; summer ❺, winter ❻), where all 200 rooms have whirlpool baths – the *Cedar Breaks Cafe* serves good-value meals, while dinner at the *Double Black Diamond Steak House* costs at least $20. Most of the smaller condo complexes nearby, a few of which have their own restaurants, only open in ski season. The *Bump and Grind* at 259 S Hwy-143 (☎435/677-3111) is a convenient spot for coffee and a sandwich.

East from Zion: US-89

As soon as you leave Zion National Park via its eastern entrance (see p.432), you're out in flat, open ranching country. Eleven nondescript miles further on, Hwy-9 meets **US-89** at Mount Carmel Junction. Turn **north** from here, and once across a mountainous ridge you'll find yourself driving up the broad **Long Valley**, where the **Sevier River** cuts between the Markagunt and Paunsaugunt plateaus. After just over forty pretty but uneventful miles, punctuated by the occasional tiny Mormon settlement, you can choose between keeping straight on toward Salt Lake City or veering east toward Bryce Canyon and the other national parks.

The only real point in heading **south** on US-89 is to reach Arizona, with the North Rim of the Grand Canyon (see p.404) almost exactly a hundred miles away. A century ago, when Mormons from Arizona would come this way to be married in the temple at St George, this route was known as the **Honeymoon Trail**. The largest town along the highway, **Kanab**, retains a strong Mormon identity, but it also has a genuine back-of-beyond frontier feel to it and makes the best overnight stop in the vicinity.

Mount Carmel Junction and Mount Carmel

The eastward progress of Hwy-9 stops when a north–south wall of red cliffs rears up on the far side of the Virgin River. It's a bucolic spot, with cottonwoods lining the river and horses grazing in the meadows to the north. Unless you're ready to stop for the night, however, there's little reason to get out of the car.

MOUNT CARMEL JUNCTION, where Hwy-9 intersects with US-89, consists of a couple of fairly upscale and reliable **motels**, both with licensed **restaurants**. The *Best Western East Zion Thunderbird Lodge* (℡435/648-2203 or 1-888/848-6358, www.zionnational-park.com; winter ❸, summer ❺), which boasts a pool, spa, and even half a golf course, has a considerable edge over the much plainer *Golden Hills* (℡435/648-2268 or 1-800/648-2268, www.goldenhillsmotel.com; winter ❷, summer ❸).

In the parent community of **MOUNT CARMEL**, a mile or two north, the summer-only *Mount Carmel Motel* (℡435/648-2323, www.visiteastzion.info/mtcarmel.html; ❶) offers half a dozen rooms and an unappealing RV site.

Coral Pink Sand Dunes State Park

Few areas in the Southwest conform so exactly to the popular notion of a desert – graceful dunes of fine sand, their parallel crests sweeping toward the horizon – as **CORAL PINK SAND DUNES STATE PARK** (daily 24hrs; $5 per vehicle; ℡435/648-2800). This pseudo-Saharan landscape, a dozen miles south of Mount Carmel Junction, is reached by two separate paved roads that leave US-89 four and nine miles southeast of town respectively.

The only dune field in the Colorado Plateau lies at the foot of a seven-mile bluff of the Vermilion Cliffs, which here unusually face the northwest. Its sand grains are eroded from Navajo sandstone, which itself was originally deposited in the form of dunes.

Hikers who launch themselves from the boardwalk near the entrance station usually find that a few minutes of wading knee-deep in sand sates their *Lawrence of Arabia* fantasies. However, in marked contrast to Utah's federal parks, **off-road vehicles** are positively encouraged. The park was created in response to campaigns by local off-road enthusiasts, and plays host to countless formal and informal **dune buggy races**, most notably each July 4.

The well-shaded **campground** ($14; for summer-only reservations, costing $5 extra, call ℡1-800/322-3770) remains open all year, though it only has water in summer. Spending a night here offers the enticing prospect of seeing not only kangaroo rats but, more to the point, the snakes that prey on them. The tiny rats are named for their squatting postures, and the snakes are not a danger to humans.

Kanab

Until new roads were pushed through the region in the 1950s, **KANAB**, seventeen miles southeast of Mount Carmel Junction and just two miles north of the Arizona state line, was renowned as perhaps the most inaccessible town in the US. Now it's a significant tourist halt simply by virtue of its position halfway between the Grand Canyon, eighty miles southeast, and Bryce Canyon, 83 miles northeast.

Kanab started life in 1864 as **Fort Kanab**, a frontier outpost so prone to Indian attacks that it was abandoned after just two years. Jacob Hamblin founded the town itself in 1870 as a God-fearing ranching community with a sideline in harboring Mormons who fell afoul of the federal government, among them several perpetrators of the Mountain Meadows Massacre. Pulp novelist Zane Grey later cultivated that lawless image, setting many of his Westerns nearby. Kanab's rugged surroundings also drew Western film greats, from Tom Mix, who filmed *Deadwood Coach* here in 1924, to Clint Eastwood, who swept into town with *The Outlaw Josey Wales* in 1976. The town soon earned the nickname "Utah's Little Hollywood."

While ranching has long been in decline in southern Utah, Kanab's citizens would still much prefer to wrest their living from the earth. Though ranching still takes place, the biggest payday came in the late 1950s, when the town served as the construction base for the **Glen Canyon Dam**. During the eighteen months it took to upgrade the 72-mile dirt road to the damsite, not to mention build the new town of Page, Arizona, locals scurried to grab their share of the 200 million federal dollars pumped into the project. In November 1958, the workers decamped for Page, and the boom was over.

Since then, Kanab has pinned its hopes on the prospect of large-scale coal mining on the **Kaiparowits Plateau** to the northeast. The environmentalists and national politicians who thwarted such plans in the 1970s were burned in effigy on the streets of Kanab – victims included "green" actor Robert Redford, which may explain why fewer movies are filmed here these days – while the town closed down in protest for an hour in October 1996 when President Clinton's declaration of Grand Staircase–Escalante National Monument precluded that possibility forever.

Kanab has thus been left to survive by catering for tourists, which it does with reasonably good grace. US-89 is lined with an above-par assortment of motels and restaurants, with the greatest concentration where it briefly doglegs to run east–west along **Center Street**. A few blocks south, US-89 proper branches off east toward Page, while US-89A continues south into Arizona. For an account of **Fredonia**, seven miles south, and the route to the Grand Canyon, see p.409.

Apart from a few large Western-themed souvenir stores, such as Denny's Wigwam, opposite *Parry Lodge* at 78 E Center St (☎435/644-2452), there's almost nothing to do in Kanab, though hikers may enjoy the views from the **Squaw Trail**, which climbs the escarpment just north of town.

Information and tours

Kanab's large **visitor center** – slogan: "The Greatest Earth on Show" – stands just south of Center Street at 78 S 100 East (March–Oct Mon–Fri 9am–7pm, Sat & Sun 9am–5pm; Nov–Feb Mon–Fri 9am–5pm; ☎435/644-5033 or 1-800/733-5263, ⊛www.kaneutah.com). Interesting displays relate the story of the town's filmmaking past. The separate **BLM** visitor center, 745 E Hwy-89 (mid-March to mid-Nov 8am–4.30pm, daily mid-Nov to mid-March Mon–Fri 8am–4.30pm; ☎435/644-4680, ⊛www.ut.blm.gov), provides information on nearby public lands, including Grand Staircase–Escalante National Monument, as well as up-to-date details on driving conditions.

Several local companies offer one- or multi-day **tours** of the backcountry. Operators include Canyon Rim Adventures (☎435/644-8512 or 1-800/897-9633,

(@ www.canyonrimadventures.com), whose camping, biking, and/or backpacking trips run $575 and up for three days, and Canyon Country Out-Back Tours (T 435/644-3807 or 1-888/783-3807, @ www.ccobtours.com), which offers 4WD tours to nearby slot canyons ($25 per person per hour) and an excursion down to Toroweap (a six-hour day that costs $300 for two people; see p.410).

Accommodation

Kanab holds a number of good-value budget **motels**, so don't feel compelled to pay extra for a fancier name. All are within easy walking distance of downtown, but since there's no reason to go there, that makes little difference.

Aiken's Lodge – National 9 Inn 74 W Center St T 435/644-2625 or 1-800/790-0380, @ www .aikenslodge.com. This low-slung and not desperately aesthetic option is nonetheless the ideal budget motel: crisp and clean, right in the heart of town, and with its own pool. ❸

Holiday Inn Express 815 E AZ-99 T 435/644-8888 or 1-800/574-4061, @ www.hikanabutah .com. Large new motel, perched atop a bluff on the eastern edge of town. Somewhat isolated but offers the highest standard of rooms in Kanab, plus a free breakfast bar. Winter ❹, summer ❺

Parry Lodge 89 E Center St T 435/644-2601 or 1-800/748-4104, F 644-2605, @ www.parrylodge .com. Opened in 1931, Kanab's oldest motel has an undeniable air of romance. Photos of celebrity guests festoon the lobby and restaurant, while nameplates identify the rooms in which they slept; you can even bathe in John Wayne's extra-large bathtub. *Parry's* isn't *that* great, though, even if you can get room service from the restaurant; some of the newer rooms are dingy and noisy. Rates include a full cooked breakfast. Winter ❸, summer ❹

Shilo Inn 296 W 100 North T 435/644-2562 or 1-800/222-2244, @ www.shiloinns.com/utah/kanab. Large, presentable motel at the north end of town.

Some rooms have kitchens, and there's a breakfast buffet, pool, and spa. Winter ❸, summer ❹

Super 8 70 S 200 West T 435/644-5500 or 1-800/800-8000, F 644-5576. Dependable budget motel in a quiet zone a block south of Center Street, with a large pool and hot tub. Winter ❷, summer ❹

USA Hostels Grand Canyon 143 E 100 South T 435/644-5554 or 1-877/205-7136, @ www .usahostels.com. Although its name is misleading, considering the canyon lies 83 miles away in a different state, this is a friendly, straightforward hostel, housed in a small, primary-colors-painted converted motel a block east of the highway near the visitor center. Dorm rooms for men, women, and couples, each with a shower and priced at $15 per bed; one private room at $32. There's also a kitchen, library, and laundry.

Victorian Charm Inn 190 N Hwy-89 T 435/644-8660 or 1-800/738-9643, @ www .victoriancharminn.com. More of an inn than a B&B, this huge, new, purpose-built Victorian-style house holds twenty luxurious guest rooms, each with its own hot tub and fireplace. It's all very comfortable and tasteful, and makes a personalized alternative to a top-end motel – but you have to pay $7 extra for a cooked rather than a continental breakfast. ❻

Eating

Around twenty **restaurants** cling to the edge of the highway as it passes through Kanab. One or two make the effort to be distinctive, while the others rest safe in the knowledge that however bad they may be, there's precious little choice for a hundred miles in any direction.

Four Seasons Fifties-Style Restaurant 36 N 300 West T 435/644-2415. Fun mock-'50s diner, with a 10¢ jukebox and a menu of burgers, sandwiches, and fried meats, with nothing stronger than copious malts and shakes to wash them down. Closes 7pm in winter.

Houston's Trails' End 32 E Center St T 435/644-2488, @ www.houstons.net. Western-themed family diner, serving chicken-fried steaks, ribs, fish,

and fried breakfasts. Open daily for all meals, but closed mid-Nov to mid-March.

Nedra's Too 310 S 100 East T 435/644-2030. Informal local hangout at the junction of US-89 and US-89A on the south side of town, with a sister restaurant in Fredonia (see p.409). The unifying factor of the Mexican/American menu is the fryer; even the ice cream comes deep-fried. Open daily for all meals.

Parry Lodge 89 E Center St ☎435/644-2601. Attractive dining room where the menu occasionally hints at the healthy, in the form of dishes like poached salmon; unlike most places in Kanab, it has a license to sell alcohol. Open for all meals in summer, breakfast and dinner only in spring and fall, and closed Nov–March.

Rocking V Café 97 W Center St ☎435/644-8001. This valiant and largely successful bid to improve Kanab's culinary reputation is housed in a former bank, one of the town's oldest buildings. Classic French and Italian dishes for dinner at around $15 per entrée; cheaper, lighter lunches. Open daily for lunch and dinner.

East of Kanab: US-89 and Paria Canyon

US-89, which heads due east out of central Kanab, curves northwards into the southern reaches of Grand Staircase-Escalante National Monument (see p.457) as it makes its spectacular 73-mile run to **Page**, Arizona (see p.481). Though not as popular with visitors as the broadly parallel US-89A further south, which allows access to the North Rim of the Grand Canyon, it's still a dramatic drive and has its own potential diversions in the shape of the old **Pahreah** township and the hikes into **Coyote Buttes** and **Paria Canyon**.

Exploring these or any other areas off the highway requires you to drive down dirt roads that become very treacherous in bad weather, while even the shortest hike leads swiftly into remote backcountry. It is therefore essential to pick up detailed, current advice on conditions, either at the BLM office in Kanab or at the BLM's **Paria Contact Station**, 43 miles east (March to mid-Nov daily 8am–5pm; no phone).

Pahreah

Around 35 miles east of Kanab, close to the northernmost point along US-89's sweep through Grand Staircase-Escalante National Monument, an obelisk on the north side of the highway commemorates the founding of the town of **Pahreah** nearby, by Peter Shirts, in 1865. Though initially threatened by Indian raids, Pahreah managed to keep going as a farming community until the 1930s, when it was finally abandoned after repeated floods.

A dirt road leads down from the obelisk toward the actual town site, dropping steeply through some truly stunning badlands, where the rounded hillocks and cliffs alike are striped with gray and bluish clays as well as red sandstone. Four miles down it passes what little remains of the **Paria Movie Set**, used from the early 1960s until *The Outlaw Josey Wales* in 1976. The set was dismantled in 1999 after flood damage rendered it unsafe, and now just two very new-looking reconstructions flank the road. Beyond that lies the genuine old town cemetery, while the **Paria River** itself is 5.6 miles from the highway. The whole area is so overgrown with tamarisk and young cottonwood trees that it's all but impossible to find a trace of the settlement, but it's a remote and attractive enough spot to spend a few minutes looking.

Coyote Buttes

Five miles on from Pahreah, between mile posts 25 and 26, a conspicuous but unmarked dirt road leads south from the highway, along a high ridge, toward the **Coyote Buttes** area. Since 2000, this has formed part of **Vermilion Cliffs National Monument**, but despite that enhanced status it remains relatively untrampled by human feet. Its guardians, the BLM, are so determined to keep it that way that hiking is rigidly controlled. Day-hikers who stay within the upper reaches of Wire Pass, Buckskin Gulch, and Paria Canyon do not require **permits**, though they still must pay $5 per person per day. For overnight stays in those areas, and for day-hikes as well as overnight backpacking trips further afield, permits are essential – and with just twenty issued per day for the whole region, ten of them for Coyote Buttes North and ten for Coyote Buttes South, they're very hard to come by. **Reservations** can be made up to four months in advance, and once again cost $5 per person per day either at a BLM office in the area, via the Arizona Strip Interpretive Association (ASIA) on ☎435/688-3246, or online at ⓦwww.blm.gov/az/paria. On the first day of each month, permits become available for the fourth month ahead; thus March 1 is the date on which June permits are first sold. It's not unusual for all permits to sell out within an hour.

What everyone is so eager to see is a rock formation known as **The Wave**, an extraordinary, disorienting ripple of sculpted sandstone atop a hard-to-find prominence known as **Top Rock**, just south of the Arizona–Utah state line in the north section of the buttes. As there's no fixed trail, you'll need good advice to complete the seven-mile round-trip hike in a single day. The BLM requests that specific instructions not be published, in order to discourage unauthorized or poorly equipped hikers; if you're lucky enough to get the necessary reservation, they'll provide you with a detailed map. Both the Coyote Buttes and Buckskin Gulch routes start from the **Wire Pass Trailhead**, reached by leaving US-89 between mile markers 25 and 26 and just over eight miles south into the wilderness. The closest BLM office, the **Paria Contact Station** (daily 8.30am–4.15pm), is four miles east of the highway turnoff; if you're approaching from Page, remember it's an hour later here in Utah than it is in Arizona.

Paria Canyon

The same restrictions on backpacker permits described for Coyote Buttes above also apply to hikers intending to make the four- to six-day trek down **Paria Canyon,** which ends at the start of the Grand Canyon at Lees Ferry, Arizona (see p.402). While it's possible to access the route by first hiking down Buckskin Gulch from the Wire Pass Trailhead mentioned above, most hikers start at the **White House Trailhead**, two miles south of US-89 just east of the Paria Contact Station (see above). A basic campground near the trailhead charges $5 per night.

North from Mount Carmel: Orderville

If instead of heading south from Mount Carmel (see p.443) via Kanab, as described in the preceding pages, you turn north on US-89, you'll arrive at **ORDERVILLE** within four miles. From 1875 onwards, this now-negligible settlement was the longest-lasting of several experiments in communitarian living organized by the **United Order**, a Mormon group that believed all property should be held in common. Each family had its own cabin inside a stockade, but meals were eaten en masse, and each adult member of the group received a standard rate of pay, at $1.50 per day for men and 75¢ for women, as credit at the village store; money left unspent was returned to the pool. In 1886, when Orderville's children were drifting away in search of better-paid work, their parents gave up and shared out their assets.

Besides two gas stations and two rock shops, Orderville has a couple of shabby motels, but neither is worth recommending.

Glendale

Five miles beyond Orderville, the almost equally insignificant hamlet of **GLENDALE** nestles amid a cluster of apple orchards. A white clapboard house that looks much like the rest – complete with a large upstairs veranda – serves as the *Smith Hotel*, 295 N Main St, (☎435/648-2156 or 1-800/528-3558, ⊛www.historicsmithhotel.com; ❸), with seven very pleasant en-suite B&B rooms. Alongside, the *Buffalo Bistro*, 305 N Main St (closed Tues; ☎435/648-2778), serves well-prepared steaks and burgers for lunch and dinner, with fresh vegetables and great desserts.

Hatch

Long Valley steadily dries out north of Glendale, so travelers from Cedar City who pick up US-89 at the east end of Hwy-14 – see p.442 – encounter further upland forests rather than farmland.

At 7000ft up, little **HATCH**, 25 miles on, makes a cool overnight stop in summer, but that's the only time its handful of motels are at all busy. The *Riverside Resort & RV Park*, a mile north of town at 594 N Hwy-89 (☎435/735-4223 or 1-800/824-5651, ⊛www.riversideresort-utah.com; ❸–❺), has a dozen surprisingly nice rooms and suites, plus **camping** facilities for $16 per night, while the somewhat smarter *Bryce–Zion Midway Resort*, 244 S Hwy-89 (☎435/735-4199 or 1-888/299-3531; ❹), offers a choice of cabins or ordinary motel rooms, and also a decent **restaurant** serving the usual steak, chicken, and pasta dishes.

Red Canyon and the road to Bryce

The only road in a hundred miles that manages to climb through the wild country east of US-89 is **Hwy-12**, which was blasted into the rocks ten miles north of Hatch to provide a route to **Bryce Canyon** and beyond. Another seven miles' drive from the intersection of Hwy-12 and US-89 brings you to the town of Panguitch (see opposite), though there's some accommodation right at the intersection of US-89 and Hwy-12. *Harold's Place* (closed Nov to April; ☎435/676-2350, ⊛www.haroldsplace.net; ❸) offers twenty log cabins, two of which sleep six people. The same management has taken over and refurbished the motel rooms at the adjoining *Bryce Junction Inn* (☎435/676-8886; ❸).

Hwy-12 climbs away from US-89 by way of **Red Canyon**. For information on this small precursor of the joys ahead, call in at the Dixie National Forest **visitor center** (☎435/676-8815), a few miles along on the left. This parking lot marks the start of the short Pink Ledges **hiking trail**; longer trails leave from the Forest Service's *Red Canyon* **campground** ($8, no showers; ☎435/865-3700), half a mile further on. Immediately beyond that, the highway tunnels through two artificial red-rock arches, before topping out on top of the Paunsaugunt Plateau, with another ten miles to go before Bryce.

Panguitch

The spruce, squeaky-clean and oddly endearing Mormon town of **PANGUITCH** – 24 miles from Bryce, and fifty from Mount Carmel Junction – was established in 1864 and named for no good reason after the Paiute term for "Big Fish." After an uncertain start (it, like many of its neighbors, was abandoned in the face of Indian attacks), Panguitch prospered. It became, and remains, the largest town along the Upper Sevier Valley. That was originally due in part to the brick factory responsible for the distinguished brick homes that still adorn its streets, but Panguitch today depends heavily on tourism for its bread and butter. It's a bit too chilly to linger in the off-season, but in summer, the pumps at the eight local gas stations rarely stop spinning (one, Todd's Truck Stop, stays open 24hrs), and twenty-odd budget motels and restaurants are kept busy.

Panguitch's **visitor center**, at 55 S Main St (daily May–Oct 9am–5pm; ☏435/676-1160 or 1-800/444-6869, Ⓦwww.brycecanyoncountry.com), doles out details of a **walking tour** of the town's historic homes. You'd have to be more than a little weird, however, to spend your morning doing that rather than setting off into the wondrous deserts on your doorstep.

Accommodation

An invisible network seems to connect Panguitch's many **motels**, meaning their rates can vary minute by minute according to demand. Broadly speaking, however, peak season runs from late spring to early fall, and you should be able to find a seriously inexpensive room at most other times. A few winter skiers choose to stay here rather than in Brian Head (see p.442).

Adobe Sands Motel 390 N Main Street ☏435/676-8874 or 1-800/497-9261, Ⓦwww .adobesands.com. It's just as well this budget motel is closed in winter, considering its basic furnishings, but it's a bargain in the warmer months. May–Oct only, ❷
Best Western New Western Motel 180 E Center St ☏435/676-8876 or 1-800/780-7234, Ⓦwww .bestwestern.com. Panguitch's largest motel spreads across both sides of Center Street and has an outdoor pool. Winter ❸, summer ❹
Marianna Inn Motel 699 N Main St ☏435/676-8844 or 1-800/331-7407, Ⓦwww.mariannainn .com. Scrupulously clean, well-run budget motel on the northern edge of town, near several restaurants. Units have one to four beds. Winter ❷, summer ❺
Panguitch Inn 50 N Main St ☏435/676-8871 or 1-800/331-7407, Ⓦwww.panguitchinn.com. Restored inn in the very heart of town, operated by the same management as the *Marianna Inn*, open April–Oct only and offering good clean rooms at low rates and a huge covered parking area. Spring and fall ❷, summer ❹
Red Brick Inn 161 N 100 West ☏435/676-2141 or 1-866/733-2745, Ⓦwww.redbrickinnutah .com. Family-run B&B set in an attractive 1920s Dutch Colonial townhouse, and offering six rooms and two larger suites, plus a hot tub. ❺–❽

Eating

Panguitch does hold half a dozen or so **restaurants**, though it feels more like there's just one restaurant that's repeated at fifty-yard intervals along the highway. If you just want a sanguitch, there's a *Subway* opposite the *Flying M*.

Cowboy's Smokehouse Bar-B-Q 95 N Main St ☏435/676-8030. Feast on moderately priced barbecued meats and huge fruit pies under the impassive gaze of generations of stuffed elk heads, in a grand old Victorian-era edifice in the heart of town. Open Mon–Sat for lunch and dinner.
Flying M 580 N Main St ☏435/676-8008. Large place at the north end of town, which serves stacks of breakfast pancakes and inexpensive diner-style

meals later in the day. It prides itself on pretty good home-cooking specials like fried chicken and turkey pot pie. Open daily for all meals.

Grandma Tina's Spaghetti House 523 N Main St ☎ 435/676-2377. As well as the pasta the name implies, including vegetarian options,

this reasonably priced Italian diner, open for all mails daily, also serves a mean espresso. Closed Mon–Wed in winter.

Joy's Country Corner Cafe 80 N Main St ☎ 435/676-8851. Predictable family diner, right in the heart of town. Daily 7am–9pm.

Bryce Canyon National Park

Few more freakish landscapes can exist than those confined within **BRYCE CANYON NATIONAL PARK**. From the park's rim road, visitors gaze down upon a throng of red, yellow, and orange pinnacles of rock, eating like the flames of a forest fire into the thickly wooded plateau. You can hike down into the inferno and thread your way between the top-heavy towers, to explore a barren desert that's aglow with almost psychedelic colors.

Paiute Indians, who hunted in the vicinity for many generations, had an elegantly precise word for the landscape: *Unkatimpe-wa-Wince-Pockich*, "red rocks standing like men in a bowl-shaped recess." The current name comes from the Mormon settler **Ebenezer Bryce**, who established a short-lived homestead nearby in 1874 and memorably declared that it was "a helluva place to lose a cow." In fact, however, "Bryce's Canyon" is not a canyon at all but a row of crescent-shaped amphitheaters, hollowed into a twenty-mile stretch along the eastern edge of the **Paunsaugunt Plateau**. At up to 9000ft above sea level, this marks the final and most spectacular rung of the Grand Staircase's ascent of southern Utah (see p.409). Between sixty and forty million years ago, the **Pink Cliffs** were deposited in layers of varying thickness and strength on the beds of shallow lakes. Some are limestone, some siltstone; all were dyed and stained with combinations of red, white, orange, blue, or yellow by different concentrations of minerals, especially iron.

Conditions at Bryce are perfect for rapid erosion, with ice forming overnight and thawing in the morning over 200 times per year. Water seeps into cracks in the ground, then expands as it freezes, to wedge the cracks ever wider. Spurs emerge from the cliff-face as it recedes, then dwindle to slender fins and eventually break into separate standing columns. When the topmost rock of a column is hard enough, lower levels erode away beneath it at a much faster rate. A mighty boulder left precariously perched on a tall, narrow pillar is known as a **hoodoo**. At Bryce, thousands upon thousands of hoodoos are crammed into each successive amphitheater, to form a menagerie of multihued, contorted stone shapes. The best known, and most precarious, is **Thor's Hammer**, near Sunset Point.

Since it became a national park in the 1920s – with its irregular boundaries designed to minimize the impact on local ranchers – Bryce Canyon has deservedly ranked as a must-see attraction for any visitor to Utah. If you're at all stretched for time, however, this is one park that you can realistically hope to see in the space of a single day, or even an afternoon. Just be sure that you do at least get out of your car and **hike** into the technicolor ravines – far more vivid than the Grand Canyon, as well as much more human in scale. Most visitors pass through between June and August, but the park is, if anything, even more inspiring in the stillness of winter, when the hoodoos rear their heads from a blanket of **snow**.

Getting to Bryce

Bryce Canyon is around a two hours' drive (86 miles northeast) from Zion Canyon, and something over three hours from Capitol Reef, 120 miles further northeast. The only approach is along **Hwy-12**, which runs within the northern boundaries of the park on its way across southwest Utah. However, you won't see the rock formations – or be liable for the entrance fee – unless you turn south off the main highway thirteen miles east of US-89 (a total of twenty miles southeast of Panguitch), or eight miles northwest of Tropic (see p.456). **Hwy-63** reaches the park entrance station after a further three miles, then traces the rim of the Paunsaugunt Plateau for eighteen miles before coming to a dead end at Rainbow Point.

No public **buses** serve Bryce, but, to no fixed schedule, charter and sightseeing flights from elsewhere in the Southwest land at **Bryce Canyon Airport** on Hwy-12; call ☏ 435/834-5239 for current details. Oddly enough, this is one of the oldest airports in the US, with pine-log hangars built by the WPA in the 1930s. Once on the ground, rent a car from, or join a tour with, Bryce Canyon Scenic Tours (see below).

Finally, keen **hikers** should note that it's possible to avoid the crowds by walking into the park from **Tropic** (see p.456).

Arrival and information

The **entrance fee** to Bryce, payable at kiosks on the park boundary on Hwy-63, is $20 per vehicle, per week; all the national park passes detailed on p.45 are both sold and accepted. Although the park introduced a **free shuttle bus** system in 2000 to reduce traffic congestion, visitors can still drive to all the scenic overlooks year round. Shuttle services have dwindled to the point where buses only run between the last week of May and the first week of September, on one route. Between 9am and 6pm daily, that connects the *Ruby's Inn* complex, just south of the intersection of Hwy-12 and Hwy-63, with the overlooks in Bryce Amphitheater. If that's as far as you want to go – and for most people, even enthusiastic hikers, it's entirely sufficient – then there's no reason to use your own car. If you want to get as far south as Rainbow Point, however, there's no longer a bus service.

The logical first stop for drivers and shuttle passengers alike is the **visitor center**, a short way beyond the park entrance (daily: mid-June to mid-Sept 8am–8pm, May to mid-June and mid-Sept to Oct 8am–6pm, Nov–April 8am–4.30pm; ☏ 435/834-5322, ⓦ www.nps.gov/brca). A valuable source of information on current weather and hiking conditions, this is also the place to pick up backcountry permits (see p.453).

Bryce Canyon Scenic Tours (☏ 435/834-5200 or 1-800/432-5383, ⓦ www .brycetours.com), based at *Ruby's Inn*, runs two-hour **driving tours** of the park (daily: April–Oct regular departures 10am–3pm, Nov–March 10.30am only; $26), as well as sunrise and sunset "champagne tours" (timings vary; $36). They also offer **ATV** – dune buggy – excursions amid red-rock scenery near but not in the park (1hr $29, 3hr $69, all-day $159). Canyon Trail Rides, contactable via the desk at *Bryce Canyon Lodge* (☎435/679-8665; ⒲www.canyonrides.com), arranges **horseback rides** into the canyon (2hr rides starting at 9am & 2pm, $40; half-day rides at 8am & 1pm, $55), as does Scenic Rim Trail Rides, based at *Ruby's* (☎435/679-8761 or 1-800/679-5859; ⒲www.brycecanyonhorseback .com), at similar prices.

Flight-seeing companies based at Bryce Canyon Airport and other nearby spots include Aladdin Air (☎435/834-5555 or 1-800/914-3215) and Bryce Canyon Helicopters (contact via *Ruby's Inn* on ☎435/834-5341, or call ☎1-800/979-5050), whose rates start at $70 for a seventeen-minute flight.

Bryce Canyon practicalities

Accommodation within the park itself is restricted to the venerable Bryce Canyon Lodge, located one hundred yards from the rim between Sunrise and Sunset points, and open between April and October only. This stone-and-timber affair, furnished in its original 1920s style, offers a handful of luxurious suites (**⑦**), a row or two of rough-hewn but very comfortable individual cabins (**⑦**), and about seventy relatively ordinary motel rooms (**⑥**). All have en-suite bathrooms but no TVs, and tend to be reserved several months in advance, through Xanterra Parks & Resorts (reservations ☎303/297-2757 or 1-888/297-2757, ⒲www.xanterra.com or ⒲www.brycecanyonlodge.com; direct line to property ☎435/834-5361).

The main lobby of the *Lodge* holds a fascinating large-scale relief model of the park and leads to several souvenir stores as well as a good-quality **dining room**, open to the public for all meals. Lunchtime quesadillas, burgers, and the like are priced at under $10, and richer dinner entrées like prime rib or pork osso bucco typically cost $16–22. Dinner reservations are mandatory, on ☎435/834-5361.

A few minutes' walk away, slightly north of Sunrise Point, the **General Store** stocks basic groceries, snacks, and camping equipment and holds a laundromat and public showers.

Motels near the park

Bryce Canyon Lodge can only hold a tiny proportion of Bryce's summer influx, and is closed altogether in winter. However, half a dozen alternative options loiter just outside the park along highways 12 and 63; the cluster at the intersection is loosely known as **Pink Cliffs Village**, though there's no village to speak of. All remain open year-round, with considerably reduced rates in winter, and have their own unenthralling restaurants. Otherwise, the nearby towns of **Panguitch** (see p.449) and **Tropic** (p.456) both offer a range of motels.

Bryce Canyon Pines PO Box 43, Bryce, UT 84764 ☎435/834-5441 or 1-800/892-7923, ⒲www .brycecanyonmotel.com. Reasonable if anonymous motel, three miles west on Hwy-12, with a strangely shallow swimming pool in a separate shed. Winter **②**, summer **④**

Bryce Canyon Resort 13500 E Hwy-12, Bryce, UT 84764 ☎435/834-5351 or 1-866/834-0043, ⒲www.brycecanyonresort.com. Simple budget motel at the intersection in Pink Cliffs Village, three miles from the park entrance, with basic summer-only cabins and somewhat more comfortable rooms.

Cabins mid-April to mid-Oct **③**; rooms Nov–April **③**, May & Oct **④**, June–Sept **⑤**

Bryce View Lodge PO Box 640002, Bryce, UT 84764 ☎435/834-5180 or 1-888/279-2304, ⒲www.bryceviewlodge.com. Large, modern, and misleadingly named motel (there are no views), opposite *Ruby's* on Hwy-63 and run by the same management. The rooms are of a pretty high standard for the price. Mid-Oct to mid-May **③**, mid-May to mid-Oct **③**

Foster's Star Route, Panguitch, UT 84759 ☎435/834-5227, ⒲www.fostersmotel.com. Cheap but very shabby motel, just under two miles west of the park turnoff on Hwy-12. Winter ❷, summer ❸

Ruby's Inn PO Box 1, Bryce, UT 84764 ☎ 435/834-5341 or 1-866/866-6616, ⓦ www.rubysinn.com. Large motel complex – something of an eyesore, if truth be told – a mile or so outside the park on Hwy-63. Fifty of the 368 rooms feature whirlpool baths, and there's a heated indoor swim-ming pool, plus a full program of tours. Paying extra to be housed in the main lodge, rather than one of the outlying sections, only makes sense in the depths of winter. The food in the dining room is consistently atrocious. Nov to mid-March ❸, mid-March to mid-May & last two weeks of Oct ❹, last two weeks of May & first two weeks of Oct ❺, June–Sept ❻

Camping

Both of the in-park **campgrounds** cost $10 per night; in summer, all 216 sites tend to be filled by early afternoon. The *North Campground*, which remains open all year, stretches alongside the Rim Trail a short walk from the visitor center. It accepts reservations for the period between mid-May and September only, for an additional charge of $9 (☎ 1-877/444-6777, ⓦ www.reserveusa.com). *Sunset Campground*, a mile or so south, across the highway from the lodge near Sunset Point, operates between May and mid-October, on a first-come, first-served basis. Neither campground offers RV hookups, and the closest showers are by the General Store.

Backcountry campers can choose from several designated sites, all south of Bryce Point below the rim and well away from the main trails. Pick up a $5 permit at the visitor center, and take lots of water.

The nearest **commercial campground** to the park is the slightly more deluxe area adjoining *Ruby's Inn*, a mile north (see above; also ⓦ www.brycecanyoncampgrounds.com; $17.50 per site), which also caters to RVs. If your heart is set on a night in the woods, head instead for the roadside campground at **Red Canyon**, ten miles west on Hwy-12 (see p.448).

Seeing the park

Most visitor activity at Bryce is concentrated around **Bryce Amphitheater**, the largest and most accessible of the indentations in the Pink Cliffs. Whether you park your own car off the loop road that leaves Hwy-63 half a mile south of the visitor center, or get dropped off by the shuttle bus, a brief walk will bring you to the brink of the crescent-shaped depression.

Where along the Rim Trail you get your first blast of the incandescent rocks makes little difference. Of the two official overlooks, around five hundred yards apart, **Sunrise Point** to the north gets slightly less of the tour-bus crowds than **Sunset Point** to the south. Neither name is particularly appropriate; both face east, so you won't see the sun set, while the best place to catch the dawn is **Bryce Point**, a mile or so further south. Here at the southernmost tip of the amphitheater, you can look back west as the first rays of the sun strike the toy soldiers below. Although dawn and dusk are the prime times to **take photos** at Bryce, the views to the east and north are astonishing at any time of day, ranging as much as a hundred miles to encompass the Aquarius Plateau and the Henry Mountains.

Beyond Bryce Amphitheater, Hwy-63 – also known as the **Scenic Drive** – meanders south for another fifteen miles. It's a slow drive, passing a succession of substantially similar viewpoints; no one stops at them all, though each has its merits. Look out in particular for the **Natural Bridge**, which spans a steep gully approximately halfway along the route. Suspended far above

BRYCE CANYON NATIONAL PARK

Panguitch & Zion

Tropic & Escalante (33 miles)

Ruby's Inn
Bryce View Lodge

DIXIE NATIONAL FOREST

Visitor Center
Fairyland Point

Pink Cliffs

Fairyland Canyon

Tropic Valley

Tropic (1 mile)

Paunsaugunt Plateau

Sunrise Point
Sunset Point

RIM TRAIL

Bryce Canyon

Inspiration Point

Bryce Point

see inset below

Paria View

Swamp Canyon

SWAMP CANYON CONNECTING TRAIL

WHITEMAN CONNECTING TRAIL

UNDER-THE-RIM-TRAIL
(BRYCE POINT TO RAINBOW POINT)

N

Fairview Point
Piracy Point

Natural Bridge

Agua Canyon

Ponderosa Point

0   3 miles

Rainbow Point

Yovimpa Point

BRISTLECONE LOOP TRAIL

RIGGS SPRING LOOP TRAIL

(i) Visitor Center

FAIRYLAND LOOP TRAIL

0   1 mile

North

QUEENS GARDEN TRAIL

Sunrise Point

Lodge

Queen's Garden

Thor's Hammer

Sunset Point

Sunset

NAVAJO LOOP TRAIL

PEEKABOO LOOP TRAIL

Silent City

Wall St.

Inspiration Point

RIM TRAIL

Bryce Point

the forest, it doesn't cross running water, so technically it's not a bridge but an 85ft arch.

Hwy-63 climbs steadily as it continues south, until finally the ridge it's following narrows to a slender neck, and the road is forced to end at the highest viewpoint of all, **Rainbow Point**. Both this and nearby **Yovimpa Point** command sweeping views south, to Navajo Mountain and the Kaibab forest that fringes the Grand Canyon.

As you leave the park, bear in mind that **Fairyland Point**, reached via a separate turnoff north of the visitor center, is one of Bryce's quietest yet most scenic viewpoints.

Hiking

The **Rim Trail** follows the lip of the plateau for just over five miles, skirting Bryce Amphitheater between Sunrise and Sunset points, and extending both north and south. Die-hard backpackers can continue beyond its southern limit, at Bryce Point, all the way to Rainbow Point, 22.6 miles on, along the **Under-the-Rim Trail** (which has designated camping spots). By far the most popular trails in the park, however, are those that drop into **Bryce Amphitheater** itself. With several alternative routes to the bottom, and a choice of connections once you're there, you can tailor a hike to suit whatever time you have, from a couple of hours to a full day.

The basic experience is much the same whichever trail you take. The rock stratum that has eroded to form the hoodoos, just below the rim, averages from 300 to 500ft thick, so hiking consists of descending between them until you reach the flatter pine forest beyond, walking through the woods, and then climbing back up again. At an elevation of almost two miles, even a brief hike involves considerable effort; you'll need good footwear and plenty of water.

For a concentrated burst of Bryce at its best, the **Navajo Loop Trail** is ideal. The shortest and busiest trail of all, it plummets abruptly from Sunset Point into a group of formations known as the **Silent City**, then circles back up to complete a hike of 1.4 miles. Allow two hours to enjoy the whole roundtrip without exhausting yourself in the process. Taking the trail's steeper right-hand branch as you set off makes for an easier hike, and also brings you, by way of a precipitous set of switchbacks, straight into the cool crevice of **Wall Street**. In places, this awe-inspiring gulf of orange rock is less than twenty feet wide, but it's too deep for the 800-year-old Douglas firs that grow from its sandy floor to poke their heads above the cliffs.

Beyond Wall Street, you swiftly reach a small sandy wash. The return leg of the Navajo Loop Trail starts a short way to the left and follows a slightly gentler incline back to Sunset Point, passing **Thor's Hammer** and other humongous hoodoos en route. Alternatively, continue northwards on the level footpath just above the wash, pausing perhaps to rest in the shade of the pines and junipers. The basin known as the **Queen's Garden** is somewhere over a mile along. Named for an almost translucent fin that's topped by a rocky pile bearing a vague resemblance to Queen Victoria, it's connected by a mile-long trail up the hillside to **Sunrise Point**. During its climb, the path cuts repeatedly through limestone fins and spurs, with each tunnel framing yet another irresistible photograph. Most of the horseback expeditions in the park – see p.452 – pass this way. Dwarfed beneath the ludicrous, multicolored spires and turrets, the horses make an especially surreal spectacle.

East of Bryce

By continuing east from Bryce Canyon, you're leaving civilization firmly behind. This central region of southern Utah is almost entirely given over to wilderness, and there's barely time to draw breath after Bryce before you plunge into Grand Staircase–Escalante National Monument. A few tiny communities cling to the fringes, however, and **Tropic** offers a few creature comforts as you brace yourself for what lies ahead.

Tropic

The first community east of Bryce along Hwy-12 is **TROPIC**, eight miles from the park turnoff. Among the migrants from Panguitch who settled this tiny hamlet in the 1880s – naming it for its allegedly superior climate – was Ebenezer Bryce himself (see p.450). His restored log cabin is now the center-piece of the *Pioneer Village* motel.

Tropic may turn its back on the flamboyance of Bryce Canyon, ranged along the ridge above it, but it has little appeal of its own; the main street consists of a row of motels and fast-food joints, and strolling around the center is unreward-ing. However, the unmarked road that leads west from Bryce's log cabin reaches the park boundary in a couple of miles, from where it's a further two-mile hike up to the main formations.

Accommodation

You don't gain much by staying in Tropic rather than the motels closer to the park, but it does have quite a reasonable range of **accommodation**. None of the motels expects you to hang around during the day; they don't have pools, for example.

Bryce Canyon Inn 21 N Main St ☎435/679-8502 or 1-800/592-1468, ⊛www.brycecanyoninn .com. Standard motel rooms, plus 18 large new log cabins, available in summer only. Rooms ❹, cabins March–Oct only ❺.

Bryce Pioneer Village 80 St Main S; ☎435/679-8546 or 1-800/222-0381, ⊛www.bpvillage .com. Complex of dull but adequate motel rooms, with showers not baths, and more atmospheric individual cabins, transplanted from the park and equipped with two double beds as well as either baths or showers. ❸–❹

Bryce Point B&B 61 North 400 West ☎435/679-8629 or 1-888/200-4211, ⊛www.brycepointbb.com. Cheerful family-run B&B attached to a private house; all of the five large rooms have picture windows facing Bryce Canyon, plus their own baths and TVs, and there's also a shared deck with hot tub. ❹

Bryce Valley Inn 199 N Main St ☎435/679-8811 or 1-866/679-8811, ⊛www.brycevalleyinn.com.

Plain, large motel, with a (poor) on-site restaurant and a souvenir shop. Mid-Oct to April ❸, May to mid-Oct ❹

Buffalo Sage B&B Hwy-12, ☎435/679-8443 or 1-866/232-5711, ⊛www.buffalosage.com. Modern, purpose-built B&B perched on a bluff at the northwest end of town and enjoying great views from a wraparound deck. Four comfortable, en-suite, nonsmoking rooms. ❺

Doug's Place Country Inn 141 N Main St ☎435/679-8600 or 1-800/993-6847, ⊛www .dougsplace.net. Conspicuous modern motel beside a gas station in the heart of town, with its own store and diner. Nov–March ❸, April–Oct ❺

Grand Staircase Inn 105 N Kodachrome Drive, Cannonville ☎435/679-8400 or 1-877/472-6346, ⊛www.grandstaircaseinn.com. Simple but adequate highway motel five miles south of Tropic, attached to a grocery store and gas station. Oct to mid-June ❸, mid-June to Sept ❹

Eating

No one would make a special trip to eat in Tropic's limited array of restaurants, but once you're here it's not worth driving anywhere else either.

Doug's Place 141 N Main St ☎ 435/679-8632. Bustling diner attached to a large convenience store, which gets really busy at breakfast time and doesn't make all that romantic a rendezvous for dinner.

The Pizza Place Hwy-12 ☎ 435/679-8888. Quick, functional pizza joint, which also does take-outs and deliveries.

Kodachrome Basin State Park

At the village of Cannonville, five miles south of Tropic, Hwy-12 veers east across the Paria River. If you choose to continue south along Paria Valley instead, on Cottonwood Canyon Road, the pavement runs out after eight more miles at **KODACHROME BASIN STATE PARK**. This assortment of contorted rocky columns, tucked beneath the cliffs that climb to Kaiparowits Peak, was named by a *National Geographic* photographer in 1948 in honor of the latest Kodak film; he felt the area's existing name of Thorny Pasture was too prosaic.

By the standards of Utah's national parks, however, Kodachrome Basin is not especially worth making an effort to see. Its main focus is a unique geological phenomenon, not found anywhere else on earth: its 67 **sand pipes**. Each of these misshapen pillars was formed as an underground geyser, created by an earthquake, which was then blocked with tough calcite sediment. When the softer rock that surrounded them eroded away, they were left towering as high as 150ft above the scrubby plain.

After paying the $5-per-vehicle day-use **fee** at the park entrance station (open 24 hrs, ☎ 435/679-8562), follow the road for a couple of miles to the left to reach the park's attractive **campground** ($14; reserve on ☎ 1-800/322-3770). Various trailheads along the way mark the start of short hikes among the formations. Alternatively, the unpaved road that forks right from the entrance station ends after a little over a mile at the trailhead for **Shakespeare Arch**. A pleasant quarter-mile walk brings you to a small high natural arch, named for the park manager who first noticed its existence in 1976, from where you can get good views across the valley to the Pink Cliffs of Bryce Canyon. To arrange a **horseback ride** through the park, contact Scenic Safaris in Cannonville (☎ 435/679-8536).

Grand Staircase–Escalante National Monument

Brought into being by a controversial and unexpected presidential decree in 1996, **GRAND STAIRCASE-ESCALANTE NATIONAL MONU-MENT** is, at 1.9 million acres, the largest US national monument outside

Alaska. Though its staggering landscape unquestionably merits such recognition, it's not so much a homogenous entity as the final piece in a jigsaw puzzle, placing the leftover lands between Bryce, Capitol Reef, the Dixie National Forest, and the Glen Canyon National Recreation Area under federal control. From the Aquarius Plateau in the north (the highest segment of the Colorado Plateau, constituting the top rung of the "staircase") to Lake Powell in the south, only the farming valleys around towns such as Tropic, Escalante, and Boulder remain in private ownership.

Although **Hwy-12** dips in and out of its northern flanks, **US-89** runs briefly through its southern extremities, and the rudimentary **Burr Trail** leads into Capitol Reef from its eastern end (see p.477), no paved roads cross this magnificent wilderness. True, a handful of dirt tracks provides limited access to the backcountry, but even they don't begin to penetrate the extraordinary canyon country at its heart, and all are in any case swiftly rendered impassable by poor weather conditions. What's more, there's only one maintained hiking trail in the whole huge expanse.

While certain issues concerning the monument's future remain to be settled, it was created specifically in order to "maintain the unspoiled nature" of the region, rather than "develop" it for tourism. Grand Staircase–Escalante was the first national park or monument to be administered not by the National Park Service but by the Bureau of Land Management. No new paved roads are going to be built, and all administrative and tourist facilities will be constructed in existing towns, with **Escalante** itself as the prime beneficiary.

The immediate effect of the monument's proclamation was to boost local tourism by fifty percent. Of the million visitors who now pass this way each year, however, many still arrive with little idea of what to do other than simply

The first proposal to create **Escalante National Monument** was submitted to Franklin Roosevelt in 1940 by Secretary of the Interior Harold Ickes. Its boundaries would have enclosed 4.5 million acres, stretching from Lees Ferry as far as Moab and Green River, and taken in 280 miles of the Colorado River, 150 miles of the Green River, and 70 miles of the San Juan. That vast area was then crossed by just one road, and no bridge spanned the Colorado.

In principle, Roosevelt saw himself as an environmentalist, but the greenery of the Hudson River Valley was far more to his taste than the red rocks of the West. In the face of vociferous Mormon opposition in Utah, not to mention the coming of war, the idea was quietly dropped.

When Canyonlands National Park was created in the early 1960s (see p.498), it included only a small proportion of Ickes' suggested tract. Glen Canyon on the Colorado River was by now submerged beneath Lake Powell (see p.482), while the **Kaiparowits Plateau**, which stretches south of Escalante all the way to the lake, remained outside federal protection. That was thanks to pressure from economic interests in southern Utah, acutely aware that what they call Fifty-Mile Mountain stands on top of the world's largest known deposits of **coal**.

Plans to mine the Kaiparowits Plateau have been the focus of repeated rumors and campaigns for well over fifty years. The closest any came to fruition was in the 1970s, when the Southern California Edison Company announced its intention to open a 6000-acre mine, complete with a network of new roads and an on-site electricity generating plant. Controversy over the scheme pitted its supporters, the so-called **Sagebrush Rebels** – an informal but powerful grouping of Utah's Mormon-dominated business elite, plus the workers whose livelihoods were at stake – against environmentalists from across the nation. Although the abandonment of the project in 1976 was largely due to a slackening of demand for electricity in California, communities such as Kanab (see p.444), desperate for jobs, took out their anger by burning effigies of green activists in the streets.

In 1980, a study commissioned by Congress showed that almost 400,000 acres on the Kaiparowits Plateau had already been logged to clear the way for mines. Much of that timber was processed at a mill in Escalante, and when green opposition resulted in a moratorium on tree-felling, Escalante too witnessed its own share of public "hangings." During those years, any stranger with license plates from the notoriously tree-hugging state of California could expect a frosty welcome in the diners of Hwy-12.

Hopes that mining money might revitalize the economy of Escalante rose once more in the mid-1990s, with the news that a Dutch conglomerate was considering strip-mining the Kaiparowits. By now, however, many observers felt that the pro-mining lobby had become merely a vociferous minority, and President Clinton decided that a grand gesture designed to appeal to environmentalists in every state was more important than appeasing the business community in Utah. On September 18, 1996 – little more than a month before his re-election for his second term – he therefore took the stage at the Grand Canyon to declare the creation of the **Grand Staircase–Escalante National Monument**.

Utah legislators promptly condemned it as "the mother of all land grabs" and "a monumental blunder – pun intended," while the ropes came out once again, this time to "hang" both Clinton and his Interior Secretary Bruce Babbitt. However, the move was welcomed in the rest of the nation, and now that the die has been cast, even Escalante seems to have accepted it.

After years of insisting that they'd rather be farming, logging, and mining than running motels, the predominantly Mormon local population does at least seem to have been guaranteed a secure economic future, even if it's not quite the one they anticipated.

drive the hundred-mile stretch of **Hwy-12** between Bryce Canyon and Capitol Reef. Only completed in 1980, thanks to the difficulty of the terrain and the lack of towns en route, this is indisputably the most scenic of all southern Utah's fifteen or so designated "Scenic Byways." No driver could fail to be awed by the highway's ever-changing panoply of red-rock canyons, crystal-clear rivers, and shimmering oases. It's a shame, however, that in the absence of easily accessible information as to what lies beyond the road, most visitors have, until recently, remained firmly in their cars.

The **Escalante River**, which drains this whole region, was the last river to be named, let alone explored, in the continental US, and to this day most maps show the area as a vast blank. As government agencies, commercial publishers and local businesses compete to fill the information gap, however, the back roads and trails are starting to bustle with venturesome tourists. Visitors now tend to stay two or three nights rather than just one, spending perhaps one day exploring rugged **Hole-in-the-Rock Road**, which holds some remarkable **slot canyons**, and another in and around delightful **Calf Creek**. For backpackers, the options are all but infinite, though the sandstone bridges and arches on the lower reaches of **Coyote Gulch** and the Escalante River itself are the prime attraction.

Information

There is no **admission fee** for Grand Staircase–Escalante National Monument. Much the best place to obtain up-to-date information on the public lands both in and around the monument is the state-of-the-art, wind- and solar-powered multi-agency **visitor center** on Hwy-12 at the west end of **Escalante** (mid-March to Oct daily 7.30am–5.30pm; Nov to mid-March Mon–Fri 8am–4.30pm; ☏435/826-5499). The helpful staff here are happy to suggest detailed hiking or mountain-biking itineraries and issue free permits for **backcountry camping**. You can also pick up information from the **BLM** visitor center in Kanab (see p.444), or **online** at ⓦ www.ut.blm.gov/monument. Trails Illustrated/ National Geographic publishes an excellent "Canyons of the Escalante" topographical **map** of the region.

Skutumpah and Cottonwood Canyon roads

Two long, lonely, mostly dirt roads cut north–south trajectories through the western end of Grand Staircase–Escalante, branching off from the paved road to Kodachrome Basin (see p.457). In principle, both can be traveled in ordinary, two-wheel-drive vehicles, but be sure to check current conditions with rangers before setting off. Even slightly adverse weather can make the going impossible, while in winter the roads will almost certainly be not only impassable, but potential death-traps. Unless you have 4WD, don't base your itinerary on the assumption you'll be able to get through.

Skutumpah Road, the better maintained of the two, starts three miles south of Cannonville and takes 52 miles to reach US-89, nine miles east of Kanab. Both the first sixteen and the last sixteen of those miles are paved (the latter part as Johnson Canyon Road), but that still leaves twenty difficult unpaved miles, as the road picks its way across **Bull Valley Gorge** and through the **White Cliffs**. One of the best hikes comes early on, before the terrain becomes difficult, in the shape of a five-mile round-trip stroll though the narrows of **Willis Creek**. From the **trailhead**, six miles down Skutumpah Road, it only takes a few minutes' walking before canyon walls begin to climb to either side of the wash, and they swiftly close in to stand just a few feet apart.

Much of **Cottonwood Canyon Road**, which heads east from Kodachrome Basin, runs across bare **slickrock**. Its graded gravel surface becomes extremely dangerous after rain, but during drier periods, it's well worth continuing for ten miles beyond the park to see the intricate double **Grosvenor Arch**. At that point, the road turns south, to meet **US-89** thirty miles on, roughly half-way between Kanab and Page. En route it threads its way between the dark pyramidal fins of the **Cockscomb**, a bizarre geological oddity resembling the armor-plated back of a stegosaurus that forms the boundary between the Grand Staircase and the Kaiparowits Plateau.

Escalante

Hwy-12 climbs northeast from Cannonville, passing through the speck that is **Henrieville** and then ascending the clay cliffs known as "The Blues." Once atop the cliffs you're confronted by the unexpected sight of the high but fertile **Upper Valley**, kept well watered by snowmelt from the Aquarius Plateau.

A group of Mormon militiamen who pursued Indian raiders through the Upper Valley in 1866 noted the potential of the meadowland beyond, and dubbed the region "Potato Valley" in honor of its abundant wild sweet potatoes. Within ten years, acting on their own initiative rather than Church pressure, several returned to establish a ranching and farming community. They called it **ESCALANTE**, on the suggestion of a passing member of John Wesley Powell's second expedition, despite the fact that the Spanish explorer-priest Fray Silvestre de Escalante (see p.577) never came within a hundred miles of here.

Life was harsh during Escalante's early years; the pioneers spent their first winter, 1875–76, huddled in primitive dugouts. Then came a period of deceptive ease, as their sheep and cattle multiplied on the open range. By 1910, however, it was becoming apparent that the native grasses on which they grazed were not growing back. The land has never recovered, and Escalante has remained frozen at much the same size and appearance ever since.

Escalante is a neat enough little town, with its main street gently sloping down from west to east and a couple of blocks of four-square brick and timber homes to either side. It's also a screamingly dull place to spend the night, though the wilderness that stretches away in every direction more than makes up for that.

If you do find yourself here in the daytime, **Escalante State Park**, beside an artificial lake a mile northwest of town, holds Utah's largest concentration of **petrified wood** ($5 day-use fee; information on ☎435/826-4466). Two short but very steep trails lead through a miniature "forest" of lithified logs, and there's a fully-equipped **campground** ($14; call ☎1-800/322-3770 for reservations). It has to be said, however, that it takes a lot of effort before you see anything, and even then it doesn't hold a candle to Arizona's Petrified Forest National Park (see p.317).

Information

A summer–only kiosk at 100 E Main St (mid-May to mid-Sept daily 10am–6pm; ☎435/826-4810), next to the *Padre Motel*, handles inquiries about Escalante itself. For information on hiking and camping in the surrounding region, head for the **visitor center** of the Grand Staircase–Escalante National Monument, at 755 W Main St (see p.461).

Accommodation

Escalante's half-dozen tiny **motels** are comprehensively outclassed by the more sizeable *Prospector Inn*. Public **campgrounds** nearby include those at Escalante State Park (see opposite) and Calf Creek (see p.468).

Bunkhouse Motel Escalante Outfitters, 310 W Main St ☎ 435/826-4266, ⓦ www.escalanteoutfitters .com. Hikers' and campers' supply store where each of the seven attractive little log cabins out back has heating but no water, phone, or TV. They share use of a bathhouse. There's also tent and RV camping. ❸

Canyons Bed & Breakfast 15 South 100 East ☎ 435/826-4747 or 1-866/526-5667 ⓦ www .canyonsbnb.com. Behind this ordinary-looking townhouse you'll find three attractive en-suite guest rooms, each with its own little patio. Rates include a high-quality organic breakfast. ❺

Circle D Motel 475 W Main St ☎ 435/826-4297, ⓦ www.utahcanyons.com/circled.htm. Basic old-style motel, perched at the west end of town, where identical units share a long wooden veranda; ask for one of the newer rooms. ❷–❹

Escalante's Grand Staircase B&B 280 W Main St ☎ 435/826-4890, ⓦ www.escalantebnb.com. B&B-cum-motel, with five simple but bright and cheerful rooms, that also rents out mountain bikes. ❹

Prospector Inn 380 W Main St ☎ 435/826-4653, ⓦ www.prospectorinn.com. Escalante's largest and most modern motel, the first in town to boast a second story, offers spacious, comfortable twin-bedded rooms. Its unique policy of not changing its room rates all year round makes it a real bargain in summer. ❸

Rainbow Country B&B 586 East 300 South ☎ 435/826-4567 or 1-800/252-8824, ⓦ www .color-country.net/~rainbow/. Small, friendly B&B; comfortable en-suite rooms share use of a hot tub, a large common room, and a mountain-view veranda. Local tours available. ❸

Eating

Restaurants struggle to survive in Escalante, so it holds just a handful of nondescript diners, where it's hard to stretch a night on the town much beyond twelve and a half minutes.

Circle D Restaurant 425 W Main St ☎ 435/826-4550. Dull diner/steakhouse, with a Mexican flavor and a few vegetarian alternatives. Open for all meals daily in summer but closed for much of the winter.

Esca-Latte Escalante Outfitters, 310 W Main St ☎ 435/826-4266. Small-scale espresso bar in outfitters' store, which serves light snacks and pizzas as well as coffee and smoothies, and has the only liquor store in a 160-mile stretch of highway. Summer only, daily 8am–10pm.

Golden Loop Cafe 39 W Main St ☎ 435/826-4433. Typical small-town diner, smack in the middle of downtown Escalante.

Prospector Restaurant 400 West 50 North ☎ 435/826-4658. Formerly a gourmet restaurant, this is now just a very ordinary diner, tucked away from the highway behind the (unconnected) *Prospector Inn*. Mexican specialties such as quesadillas or a combo plate for around $8, and steaks and ribs for up to $16. Open daily for all meals, all year.

Hell's Backbone

While Hwy-12 is by far the quickest route between Escalante and Boulder, summer thrill-seekers can choose instead to take a two-hour, forty-mile trip across the top of the Aquarius Plateau, along the old "Upper Road." Turn north on the 300 East block in Escalante, and the paved **Forest Road 153** heads up Pine Creek Canyon, to reach the appealing mountain-set **Posey Lake** fourteen miles on.

Turn east at the lake, onto Hell's Backbone Road, and the fun begins. Having crawled up the flanks of the 10,000ft Roger Peak, this dirt track teeters along the slender ridge known as **Hell's Backbone**, with sheer drops down to Sand Creek on one side and Death Hollow on the other. The best views come at the hair-raising bridge halfway along. The bizarrely named **Box-Death Hollow Wilderness** far below can only be penetrated on foot and is southern Utah's most difficult hiking region. Tracing its full length necessitates eighteen miles of wading in ice-cold water and takes between four and seven days; don't even consider setting off without first talking to the rangers at the visitor center in Escalante.

For the last ten miles, as it descends through the woods to Boulder, Hell's Backbone Road is paved, but the backcountry section is usually closed by snow between October and late May.

Hole-in-the-Rock Road

These days, **Hole-in-the-Rock Road**, which turns south from Hwy-12 five miles east of Escalante – just beyond a scenic turnout heralding Grand Staircase–Escalante National Monument – is emphatically a dead end. More than fifty slow, hard miles from the highway, its progress is halted by a landslide of tumbled boulders, high above the waters of Lake Powell. When it was created, however, over a century ago, it was intended to become the most direct route across southern Utah.

In November 1879, the 230 Mormon pioneers of the **San Juan Mission** gathered outside Escalante. Intent on reaching their new home, almost two hundred miles east, they were convinced they'd find a shortcut along the uncharted east flank of the Kaiparowits Plateau and across the Colorado. Even when confronted with the abyss of Glen Canyon, their faith saw them through. In the space of six weeks, they dynamited a narrow slit in a fifty-foot cliff – the **Hole-in-the-Rock** – until it was wide enough to squeeze through. Despite snow and ice, they then used ropes to lower 83 wagons down a precipitous "road" that descended 1800ft to the river in less than three-quarters of a mile. Once there, they ferried the whole lot across the Colorado on makeshift rafts, and then repeated the entire process to escape the canyon on the far side. A mere hundred more miles of desert brought them to the townsite of **Bluff** – see p.536 – which they established on April 6, 1880. All 230 members of the party had lived through the trek, and they'd been joined by three babies born en route.

Hole-in-the-Rock Road has never been paved, but its first forty miles are passable for ordinary vehicles for most of the year, and it now constitutes the most popular route into Grand Staircase–Escalante National Monument. It's a long, slow drive, however – expect to take a good three hours to get as far as Dance Hall Rock and back, and be sure to carry water and emergency supplies – and despite the build-up it's not nearly as dramatic as Hwy-12. The reason to make the effort is to enjoy the various **hiking trails** that branch away from it, of which the best for day-trippers is the loop down to the Peek-A-Boo and Spooky **slot canyons**. Staff at the visitor center in Escalante (see p.461) can provide leaflets and simple maps, but if you're planning anything substantial, equip yourself with a proper topographical map.

Devils Garden

For its first five miles, Hole-in-the-Rock Road crosses mundane, level ranching country. It then climbs to reveal a first glimpse of the red rocks of Escalante

Canyon away to the east, and the surface changes from gravel to mud. As you continue across a sagebrush-strewn plateau, there's no real incentive to get out of your car before **Devils Garden**, twelve miles along. Designated as the one official picnic area en route, this small valley, set below the highway to the west, is scattered with clusters of rounded, clay-ish hoodoos and arches, reminiscent of those at Goblin Valley State Park (see p.493). Countless trails and footpaths weave among the excrescences; none leads anywhere in particular, but it's a great place for a game of hide-and-seek.

In winter, after the snow has set in – which is usually sometime in December, Hole-in-the-Rock Road is normally blocked beyond Devils Garden.

The Slot Canyons of Dry Fork

Apart from crossing the occasional bouncy, sandy wash, Hole-in-the-Rock Road remains relatively uneventful as you continue beyond Devils Garden. Now and then, vistas of the color country open up, and 24 miles along you begin to see rounded slickrock domes perched above the canyon. Just as the thought of what lies to the east is becoming seriously frustrating, however, you finally get the chance to see what's down there.

Head east on **Dry Fork Road**, 26 miles (or somewhere over 45 minutes) along Hole-in-the-Rock Road, and after five hair-raising minutes you'll come to a makeshift parking lot on the edge of a shallow canyon. A steep, sandy, and rather hard-to-follow trail takes roughly twenty minutes to switchback down from here into the Dry Fork of Coyote Gulch, where you'll find a couple of Utah's most accessible **slot canyons**. Scoured by fierce desert storms, these kind of impossibly slender and delicate canyons have become hugely popular tourist destinations in the last few years, mainly because they look so utterly gorgeous in photographs. In real life, they're breathtaking; but be warned that they're also very dangerous. If there's the slightest threat of rain anywhere nearby, don't go in – and as if that warning weren't enough, bear in mind that they're also home to midget rattlesnakes.

The first of the pair, **Peek-a-Boo Gulch**, is the gem. Although it's facing you as soon you reach the canyon floor, you might not recognize it. It's *not* the sandy-bottomed canyon heading off to your left, which may be narrow but isn't quite narrow enough to count as a "slot." Peek-A-Boo instead is on the far side, with its mouth at first glance appearing to be blocked by a "chimney" of slickrock. Just to enter it, you have to haul yourself up a couple of chest-high ledges, and they serve as a foretaste of several more to come. Exploring is irresistible, however, as each twist and turn reveals some new arch, bridge, or tunnel to scramble through or over. The walls to either side are never all that high, and it doesn't take long to get all the way through, but the elegant swirls and patterns in the storm-gouged rock make it a constant delight.

Spooky Gulch, which lies another fifteen minutes' walk down Dry Fork, is by contrast downright intimidating. It starts narrow and just keeps on getting narrower, growing darker as it does so. To keep going at all, you have to crawl early on beneath a big fallen boulder, and after that it becomes a very tight squeeze indeed. Soon it's only possible to walk sideways, with serious pressure on your rib cage and back, and a sandpaper-like rasping at your clothes.

Another slot canyon, **Brimstone Gulch**, lies further still along Dry Fork. However, penetrating it is only possible using technical climbing gear, and even to reach it you have to negotiate a huge boulder that's very difficult indeed to get back up again.

Coyote Gulch

Shortly after Dry Fork, the surface of Hole-in-the-Rock Road becomes sandier and more uneven, and progress is that much slower. A mile or so after the solitary finger of **Chimney Rock** first appears on the edge of the mesa, and a total of 33.5 miles from the highway, a parking lot on the right signals your arrival at **Hurricane Wash**. This is the starting point for the monument's single most popular **backpacking** route, the three- to four-day round-trip hike down through **Coyote Gulch** to the Escalante River. If you plan to attempt it, it's essential to have someone at the monument visitor center in Escalante (see p.461) talk you through the route before you set off.

Strictly speaking, the trail proper begins a quarter of a mile down a dirt track to the left of Hole-in-the-Rock Road, but even if your vehicle can get that far, there probably won't be space to park. From there, it's five miles' walk along the sandy but ever-narrowing bed of Hurricane Wash before you reach Coyote Gulch, and then a further eight miles until that meets the Escalante in turn.

Coyote Gulch itself is a spellbinding creek, cutting through a slickrock canyon that's lined with gorgeous sandstone bridges and arches, and punctuated by dramatic waterfalls. Most of it actually lies within the Glen Canyon National Recreational Area, but this is the only way you can reach it on land. When Lake Powell is at its maximum high-water level, the lake extends all the way up the canyon of the Escalante to its confluence with Coyote Gulch, which means there's no scope for hikers for hikers to see, let alone explore, the Escalante River itself. However, in recent years, as described on p.480, the lake waters have remained considerably lower than that. In early 2006, for example, when the surface of the lake was at 3600 feet, a full eight miles of the Escalante River were exposed below the Coyote Gulch confluence, making it possible to hike to long-submerged side canyons as well as beside the river.

Starting from Hurricane Wash, there isn't time to hike to any of the significant features of Coyote Gulch and back in the space of a single day. However, it is possible to snatch a glimpse on a **day-hike** from the end of **Forty-Mile Ridge**, an almost pure-sand "road" that leaves Hole-in-the-Rock Road another couple of miles further on. The first snag is that if you don't have 4WD, you'll probably only be able to drive the first five miles of Forty-Mile Ridge, and thus face an extra two-mile hike to reach the trailhead at its far end. The second snag is that the trail itself enters Coyote Gulch, two miles along, through the **Crack In The Wall**, an incredibly tight squeeze between sandstone boulders perched above a towering cliff that is every bit as alarming as its name suggests. And the final snag: it's much more difficult coming back the other way, so never climb down unless you're certain you can climb up again.

Assuming you can cope with these obstacles, the rewards are tremendous. Before you drop down into the gulch, you cross some fabulous slickrock slopes with colossal views out over the wilderness. Once there, Cliff Arch, Coyote Natural Bridge, and the huge Jacob Hamblin Arch all lie within reach.

Dance Hall Rock

Under normal conditions, two-wheel-drive vehicles should go no further along Hole-in-the-Rock Road than **Dance Hall Rock**, a mile beyond Forty-Mile Ridge and 36 miles from the highway. The 1879 Mormon party (see p.464) camped alongside this superb natural amphitheater while they worked out how to get across the Colorado, creating evening entertainment to keep up their spirits. An easy walk from the roadway enables you to tread the same stage, and it's also worth exploring the rolling slickrock hills that lie immediately behind.

In a couple of places, natural tanks have been scooped deep into the rock, each sheltering a solitary tree on its sandy floor.

The Hole-in-the-Rock

Beyond Dance Hall Rock, the gravel surface gives way to bare slickrock, only negotiable in high-clearance vehicles. The original **Hole-in-the-Rock** lies just past the last parking lot, fifteen miles on. Keen hikers can scramble over the rocks that block it and pick their way down to the lake, which depending on its current level, obliterates some or all of the lowermost thousand feet of the pioneers' primitive pathway.

The Upper Escalante River

While driving Hole-in-the-Rock Road certainly offers the thrill of venturing into the back of beyond, several wonderful hikes start from right alongside Hwy-12. If your time is at all limited and you'd rather spend it on the trails than behind the wheel, there's a lot to be said for staying on the main road until it reaches the **Escalante River**. The first sighting of the Escalante system comes from a roadside lookout at an extravagant curve five miles on from the Hole-in-the-Rock turnoff.

Immediately below the lookout, perched on a rocky eminence near mile marker 74, the solitary *Kiva Coffeehouse* provides an ideal opportunity to get your bearings (April–Oct daily except Tues 8.30am–4.30pm; closed Nov–March; ☏435/826-4550, ⊛www.kivacoffeehouse.com; ❼). Through panoramic windows or from the flowery patio, you can enjoy fabulous views along the river while enjoying simple snacks such as granola, sandwiches or enchiladas. A separate cottage nearby holds two guest rooms, named Sunset and Sunrise for obvious reasons, which rent for $150 per night, or $100 per night for stays of three nights or more.

From here, it takes five more miles for the highway to drop down to the river itself, which it crosses on a low bridge that's designed to allow floodwaters to flow harmlessly over. Immediately on the far side, a parking lot serves as the trailhead for exhilarating hikes both up- and downstream.

It would be possible to make this the starting point for major **backpacking** trips in either direction. The town of Escalante is around two days' walk upstream, while Lake Powell lies at least ten days' hike away downstream. Fortunately, however, intriguing natural features much closer at hand serve as obvious **day-hike** destinations. Whichever way you go, trailside notices announce "Yup, You Gotta Get Wet," so be prepared to ford the river several times. The great thing is, if you're just going a short distance there's no great need to keep pulling your boots on and off – the riverbank is sandy enough to walk barefoot. That said, the whole concept loses its appeal in winter, when the river itself is liable to freeze right over.

Upstream: Escalante Natural Bridge

The shorter of the two potential day-hikes from Hwy-12 heads **upstream** for just 1.6 miles, as far as **Escalante Natural Bridge**. Having started by following the river away from the highway bridge, you're soon obliged to wade over to its south bank. The canyon here is broad and open, and the trail gentle. Once you've crossed the river four times, meaning that you're now back on its northern side, you'll see the bridge open up on its southern wall. Although it's 100ft wide and 130ft high, it spans a mere trickle, dribbling down from a little side canyon.

Downstream: Maverick Bridge and Phipps Arch

The trail **downstream** from Hwy-12, accessed by walking beneath the road bridge and then crossing a footbridge over Calf Creek, is slightly heavier going. Much of the valley floor remains in the hands of private farmers, so it takes a bit of scrambling and dodging to stay outside their fences, but it's still a lovely walk.

The best day-hike in this direction is twice as long as its upstream equivalent, at nearly seven miles for the round trip. The route leaves the Escalante 1.6 miles along, heading south into sandy **Phipps Wash**. There are no signs or marked trail, so look for footprints and carry a good map. After another half mile, you'll see two prominent knobs of Navajo sandstone rising from the top of the canyon wall to your right. A hundred yards before you reach the larger of the two, head right again, up a sandy slope into a side canyon. One hundred yards along, you'll have to pick your way onto a ledge on your left to avoid a deep sink hole; another hundred yards after that, you'll come to **Maverick Bridge**, spanning the wash in front of another round cavity.

Back on Phipps Wash, keep going south for half a mile until another side canyon opens up to your left. Now things get difficult; to reach the stark, mesa-top **Phipps Arch**, you have to scramble up a steep slickrock ledge, and there's no way of knowing whether you've got the right one until you're up there. The views are so good it doesn't really matter, in the end, but make sure you keep track of how to get down again.

Calf Creek Falls

A mile or so north of the Escalante River bridge on Hwy-12, and a total of sixteen miles from Escalante, look out on your left for the parking lot at **Calf Creek**. There's a nice little **campground** right here, with minimal facilities ($7 per night), but most visitors simply come for the day to enjoy the magnificent six-mile round-trip walk to the 125ft **Lower Calf Creek Falls**. Summer sun and deep sand can make it more effort than you might expect, but in principle it's a day-hike to rank with the very best Utah has to offer; this would be a lovely canyon hike even if it didn't culminate with the falls. A day-use fee of $2 is charged, and the round-trip hike to Calf Creek Falls and back takes between three and four hours.

The clearly marked trail heads upstream between the high red walls of Calf Creek Canyon, following a perennial creek, interrupted at intervals by beaver ponds, that feeds a lush riparian environment. Fremont pictographs along the way testify to a long-standing human presence. It takes around ninety minutes to reach the falls themselves, which are absolutely stupendous. Spilling over the pouting lip of a crevice in the center of a vast sandstone amphitheater, they spread over a mossy slope of golden stone, iridescent with permanent rainbows. The water that collects in the pool below is utterly freezing and is fringed by a shaded beach where you can rest before you hike back out again.

The **Upper Calf Creek Falls** do exist, but you can't reach them from here. Instead, you start from a trailhead another six miles along Hwy-12, and make your way for a mile across exposed open slickrock in search of the stream. The slope can seem intimidating, but with good boots it's not too hard, and the views

△ Calf Creek Falls

are amazing. Eventually, the trail forks, with one strand going to the top of the 50ft falls, and the other to the bottom, where once again a lovely pool awaits.

Boulder

BOULDER, thirty miles beyond Escalante, is not so much a town as a group of farms scattered across a pleasant high-mountain valley. Cattle ranching in this remote spot started in 1889, but it was another fifty years before it was connected by road with the outside world, and in that time it acquired a reputation as Utah's own little Shangri-La. Now that it's just another stop on the highway, what magic it may once have had has largely gone.

As the western terminus of the controversial **Burr Trail** – see p.477 – Boulder makes an ideal launching point for explorations into the backcountry of Capitol Reef, but few visitors spend much time in the valley itself. On a shallow knoll beside Hwy-12 in the heart of town, the small **Anasazi State Park** holds the excavated and partly reconstructed remains of an ancient Indian pueblo (daily: mid-May to mid-Sept 8am–6pm; mid-Sept to mid-May 9am–5pm; $5 per vehicle, or $3 per person). Its 83 rooms were occupied by the Kayenta Anasazi, a subgroup of the peoples now generally known as the Ancestral Puebloans, from 1129 AD until 1169 AD, when the whole complex was destroyed by fire. A six-room replica at the end of the short ruins trail illustrates their daily life, which revolved around farming along Boulder Creek.

Practicalities

Boulder offers pretty minimal facilities for visitors, though the modern *Boulder Mountain Lodge*, where Hwy-12 meets the Burr Trail (☎435/335-7460 or 1-800/556-3446, Ⓦwww.boulder-utah.com; ⑤), has twenty comfortable rooms and a reasonable restaurant. There's an **information kiosk**, open erratic hours in season, outside the *Burr Trail Grill* diner nearby (☎435/335-7432).

Otherwise, *Pole's Place*, opposite the state park at 465 N Hwy-12 (☎435/335-7422 or 1-800/730-7422, Ⓦwww.boulderutah.com/polesplace; closed Dec–Feb; ③), is a **motel** with its own café and store. The least expensive rooms don't have a bathroom but access to a locked bathroom cabin outdoors. The *Circle Cliffs Motel* nearby at 205 N Hwy-12 (☎435/335-7353, Ⓔcircle@boulderutah.com; ②–③) is in fact a pink-painted family house that offers three far-from-fancy guestrooms. The best place to **eat** in town lies a short distance along the Burr Trail, in the spotless form of the spruce, timber-built *Boulder Mesa Restaurant*, 155 E Burr Trail Rd (☎435/335-7447), which is open daily for all meals, until 8pm. Everything from cooked breakfasts and smoothies to sandwiches, burgers, and fried chicken is meticulously prepared and presented, and the prices are low.

North to Capitol Reef

Although Hwy-12 leaves Grand Staircase–Escalante for good as it heads north of Boulder, the scenery remains every bit as sublime. The 35-mile link between Boulder and Torrey is the highway's newest section, and takes around an hour to drive. This eastern segment of the Aquarius Plateau is also known as **Boulder Mountain** or Boulder Top. Once Hwy-12 has climbed out of Boulder Valley, a succession of roadside lookouts survey fabulous vistas to the east, across a sea of gold and red sandstone outcrops to the Waterpocket Fold and beyond.

Primitive Forest Service **campgrounds** en route, costing $9 per night, include those at **Oak Creek**, fifteen miles along, and a little further on at **Pleasant Creek**, where a ranger station can provide full details.

Torrey

Poised at the intersection of highways 12 and 24, eleven miles west of Capitol Reef National Park, **TORREY** has thrown its lot in firmly with the tourist trade. As a result, it has quietly prospered while so many of its neighbors have faltered, though it still consists of little more than one tree-lined central avenue plus a handful of slightly stark brick motels on a ridge to the west, all surrounded by golden meadows grazed by contented cows. However, for visitors who see their evenings as opportunities to meet other travelers, Torrey is the most exciting prospect for at least a hundred miles.

In summer, you can pick up local **information** from a hut (open irregular hours) in the forecourt of the gas station that faces the highway intersection.

Accommodation

Torrey holds several hundred **motel** rooms, with rates that range across the full spectrum. If you'd rather **camp**, there are a few private campgrounds in town, but the public sites along Hwy-12 (see opposite) or in the national park (see p.474) are far more attractive.

Austin's Chuck Wagon Motel 12 W Main St ☎ 435/425-3335 or 1-800/863-3288, ⓦ www .austinschuckwagonmotel.com. Well-kept two-story "log cabin" motel, beside a tiny church in the town center. Closed in winter. March & Nov ❸, April–Oct ❹

Best Western Capitol Reef Resort 2600 E Hwy-24 ☎ 435/425-3761 or 1-888/610-9600, ⓦ www.bestwestern.com/capitolreefresort. Well-equipped modern motel-style hotel, three miles east of Torrey, with great views and a good pool. Nov–March ❸, April–Oct ❺

Capitol Reef Inn & Cafe 360 W Main St ☎ 435/425-3271, ⓦ www.capitolreefinn.com. Long-established but crisply maintained little motel, just off the highway in the heart of town, looking south to Boulder Mountain. On-site restaurant (see below) and small bookstore. ❸

Rim Rock Inn 2523 E Hwy-24 ☎ 435/425-3398 or 1-888/447-4676, ⓦ www.therimrock.net. New, wood-built hotel, across the highway from the *Best Western* three miles east of Torrey, and offering cheaper rooms and a better restaurant. March & Nov ❸, April–Oct ❹

Sand Creek RV Park, Hostel & Bunkhouse 540 W Main St ☎ 435/425-3577 or 1-877/425-3578, ⓦ www.sandcreekrv.com. Thriving little complex across from *Café Diablo* not far from the highway intersection, which offers RV facilities from $16; camping for $11; dorm beds in the large wooden bunkhouse for $10 ($12 if you need bedlinen); a couple of inexpensive private cabins for $28; and a coffee bar that serves chai and smoothies. Closed mid-Oct to March. ❶

Skyridge B&B 950 E Hwy-24 ☎ 435/425-3222 or 1-800/448-6990, ⓦ www.skyridgeinn.com. Six nonsmoking en-suite B&B rooms – three of which have hot tubs – in tasteful, imaginatively furnished modern home with expansive grounds. It's on the way toward central Torrey from the intersection of highways 12 and 24. ❻

Wonderland Inn PO Box 750067 ☎ 435/425-3775 or 1-877/854-0184, ⓦ www.capitolreefwonderland .com. With an attractive perch on a bluff just above the highway intersection, these motel-style buildings have a separate covered pool and a humdrum restaurant. Look for the best rates online. Winter ❸, summer ❹

Eating

Whether it's the pressure of competition or just a little local pride, the **restaurants** and **diners** of Torrey make considerably more effort to please than you may have come to expect of southern Utah.

Brink's Burgers Drive-In 165 E Main St ☎ 435/425-3710. Summer-only burger bar; a slap-up feed that's a notch or two above the usual standard. Daily 11am–9pm, closed in winter.

Café Diablo 599 W Main St ☎ 435/425-3070. Surprisingly inventive dinner-only restaurant, offering a slight Southwestern twist to meats and fish, and even "free-range rattlesnake patties," served with aioli. Open mid-April to Oct only, daily 5–10pm.

Capitol Reef Inn & Cafe 360 W Main St ☎ 435/425-3271. Bright café that serves some of Torrey's best food, using fresh ingredients like just-caught local trout. The amazing ten-vegetable salad can form part of a real vegetarian feast, and there are sumptuous banana pies to follow. Avoid the coffee, though. Open April–Oct only, daily 7am–9pm.

Rim Rock Inn 2523 E Hwy-24 ☎ 435/425-3398. Dinner-only hotel restaurant that serves better food than its rustic log-cabin decor might suggest. The $16 chicken *molé* is recommended, while the menu ranges from cheaper burgers and pasta dishes up to $29 steaks. Daily 5.30–9pm.

Robbers Roost 185 W Main St ☎ 435/425-3265. Rustic central bookstore, complete with hammocks and a wooden deck, that's an invaluable resource for information on the parklands, and also serves great coffee. Mon–Thurs 9am–6pm, Fri 9am–8pm, Sat 9am–7.30pm, Sun 9am–5pm.

7

Capitol Reef National Park

CAPITOL REEF NATIONAL PARK, the second largest of Utah's five national parks, is also the least visited. Life might be different if it bore the name originally proposed by locals – **Wayne Wonderland**, this being Wayne County. As it is, that word "reef" seems to confuse visitors. It refers to the fact that the hundred-mile rock wall thrust up by the **Waterpocket Fold** presented an almost impenetrable obstacle to nineteenth-century travelers, who therefore likened it to a reef on the ocean. Add the resemblance of the rounded "knobs" of white sandstone that top its central section to the dome of the US Capitol in Washington, and you have "Capitol Reef."

Apart from the unusual name, Capitol Reef is very much of a piece with the Southwest's other national parks. Within its 378 square miles lie hidden canyons, verdant valleys, and strange rock formations whose colors are drawn from an extravagant palette of golds and greens, reds and whites. Despite stretching for over a hundred miles north to south, the park is often less than ten miles wide. The one east–west highway, **Hwy-24**, crosses it in under twenty miles, following the gorge of the Fremont River. It's an impressive drive, but that's nothing rare in southern Utah, and unless you time your arrival from the west to coincide with the daily magnificent sunset, you could easily pass straight through.

Only if you take the time to explore will you get a sense of the magic of the place, and why it fully deserves its national-park status.

Even a couple of hours is enough to admire the western cliffs from the dead-end **Scenic Drive**, south of the park headquarters at **Fruita**. Given half a day or more, you could venture all the way south to Lake Powell on the unpaved **Notom–Bullfrog Road**, tracing the eastern flank of the Waterpocket Fold, or loop back westward via the **Burr Trail**, halfway along. With **hiking trails** of all lengths and levels setting off into the wilderness, it would be easy to spend a week in this one park.

The best **seasons** to visit Capitol Reef are spring, when the fruit trees blossom and the wild flowers bloom, or fall, when the crowds have gone, the cottonwoods change color, and hiking conditions are at their peak. Midsummer temperatures can reach 100°F, and August in particular is prone to flash-flooding, but so long as you set your sights appropriately low – say, to lazing on your back in the orchards, eating fresh fruit – a summer visit is not such a bad idea.

The geology of Capitol Reef

The **Waterpocket Fold**, which slopes from north to south for the full hundred-mile length of Capitol Reef National Park, is what geologists call a **monocline**, created when layers of sedimentary rock buckled under pressure roughly sixty million years ago. Within the last ten million years, it has in turn been lifted a mile or so above sea level by the general raising of the Colorado Plateau. Most of the original fold has long since eroded away; the reef itself is just the rump. Its western face consists of a long, jagged cliff of hard rock; it rises more gently from the east, in multicolored waves of sandstone that the Navajo called the "Land of the Sleeping Rainbow."

Here and there, the fold is pierced right through by deeply incised canyons. Often hundreds of feet deep but less than twenty feet wide, these slender gorges were mostly blocked by fallen rocks until Mormon pioneers cleared a way through. After summer thunderstorms, rainwater can cascade through the canyons in fearsome flash floods. At other times, it collects in depressions worn into the rock – the "**waterpockets**" for which the whole mighty edifice is named.

A history of Capitol Reef

Although traces of human occupation date back ten thousand years, the first known inhabitants of the Capitol Reef region were the **Fremont Anasazi**. This Ancestral Puebloan subgroup farmed along the valley of the Fremont River from 700 AD until 1300 AD, when changes in the climate forced them to move on. Archeologists distinguish them from their more sophisticated cousins to the southeast by the fact that they lived in pit houses dug into the hillsides, rather than in brick houses, and didn't keep domesticated dogs or turkeys. The most enduring signs of their presence are the intriguing **petroglyphs** still to be seen on the canyon walls.

After many centuries when only the occasional Paiute hunter passed this way, a small group of Mormons established a permanent settlement beside the Fremont River in 1878. The orchards they planted transformed the landscape, and when the post office insisted they gave their community a proper name, a few years later, **Fruita** seemed the perfect choice. The population of the fledgling town never rose above fifty, however, and it was soon suggested that the region had more future as a park than a home. The immediate vicinity of Fruita became Capitol Reef National Monument in 1937, and that was upgraded to national park status when it was enlarged to include the entire Waterpocket Fold in 1971. Former Fruita townspeople and their heirs are still entitled to graze cattle within the park, but ranching is slowly being phased out.

Arrival and information

The defunct village of **Fruita**, at the heart of the park, ranges for a mile or so around the intersection of Hwy-24 and the Scenic Drive, eleven miles east of Torrey. Bryce Canyon is 120 miles southwest, the I-70 town of Green River a hundred miles northeast; no **public transport** passes this way.

The **visitor center**, right at the road junction (daily: summer 8am–7pm, spring & fall 8am–5pm, winter 8am–4.30pm; ☏435/425-3791, ⓦwww.nps.gov/care), holds the usual exhibits, and stocks free handouts on all aspects of local geology and history. For information on facilities in the surrounding area, contact Capitol

Reef Country Travel Council (☎435/425-3365 or 1-800/858-7951, 🌐www .capitolreef.org).

Only visitors who embark on the Scenic Drive, south of the visitor center and campground, are liable for the **admission fee** of $5 per vehicle. All the nationwide passes detailed on p.45 are both sold and accepted.

There are no motels or lodges inside the park; the closest **accommodation** is in Torrey (see p.471). Torrey is also the place to rent a **bike** (Pedal Pusher, 151 W Main St, ☎435/425-3378 or 1-800/896-5773) or to arrange a **4WD**, **hiking** or **horseback** tour of the park (Hondoo Rivers & Trails; ☎435/425-3519 or 1-800/332-2696, 🌐www.hondoo.com). Wild Hare Expeditions, based at 116 W Main St in Torrey (☎435/425-3999 or 1-888/304-4273, 🌐http://sandstone .color-country.net/~thehare/), organizes **guided hiking** expeditions, from a couple of hours at $20 per person up to multiday trips at around $150 per night, and also runs jeep tours.

Camping

All three **campgrounds** in Capitol Reef are first-come, first-served and do not take reservations. By far the largest and most popular is the **Fruita Campground** ($10), which makes a good overnight stop even if you never see the rest of the park. Set amid the orchards, a mile south of the visitor center, it remains open all year, but has no showers and in winter can be without water altogether.

Both the **backcountry** campgrounds – much smaller and more primitive, and free – are 35 miles from the visitor center. **Cedar Mesa** is 22.5 miles south of Hwy-24 along the Notom–Bullfrog Road, while **Cathedral Valley** is 25 miles north of Hwy-24 along either the Hartnet Road (which requires you to ford the Fremont River) or the **Caineville Wash Road**. To camp elsewhere in the backcountry, you must obtain a free permit from the visitor center.

Driving through the park

At its simplest, driving through Capitol Reef on **Hwy-24** takes well under half an hour. However much of a hurry you may be in, it's worth pausing once or twice en route. Rather than a token pit stop at the visitor center, try taking a five-minute hike from one of the clearly marked trailheads.

The first of these lies a short distance south of the highway, roughly three quarters of the way from Torrey to the visitor center. The brief climb to **Gooseneck Point** is rewarded with a 500ft view down into the canyon of Sulphur Creek, an "entrenched meander" that once curved across a flat floodplain but has been etched deep into solid rock by the uplifting of the Colorado Plateau. If you're impressed, be sure to visit the even more stupendously sinuous gorge at Goosenecks State Reserve, in southeast Utah; see p.535. Reached by walking around ten minutes along a different trail from the same parking lot, **Sunset Point** is as the name implies a fabulous vantage point to watch the cliffs glow gold and red as the sun goes down.

Hwy-24 passes the visitor center on the right a couple of miles further along, though the huge, fluted red-rock butte known as the **Castle** to the left is bound to catch your eye first. Whether you fork right to join the Scenic Drive, or continue on the main highway, you'll reach the heart of the village of **FRUITA** within a few hundred yards, where Sulphur Creek meets the **Fremont River**.

CAPITOL REEF NATIONAL PARK

= = = = 4WD vehicles only

= = = = Dirt Road

Cathedral Valley Junction

Cathedral Valley

HARTNET ROAD

FISHLAKE

NATIONAL

FOREST

Waterpocket Fold

Cathedral Valley

Caineville Wash

RIVER FORD ROAD

Chimney Rock
The Castle
Old Fruita Schoolhouse
Petroglyphs
Hickman Bridge
Capitol Dome

Torrey

Sulphur Creek

24

Gooseneck Point
Park Headquarters

Fremont River

12

Fruita

Grand Wash

Behunin Cabin

Egyptian Temple

Golden Throne

Capitol Gorge

Notom

Caineville
(4600ft)

24

Hanksville

see inset map
for detail

DIXIE

NATIONAL

FOREST

Boulder Mountain

Waterpocket Fold

NOTOM-BULLFROG ROAD

Torrey

24

The Castle

Navajo
Knobs

School-
house

RIM OVERLOOK-
NAVAJO KNOBS
TRAIL

FREMONT
CULTURE WALK

Hickman
Bridge

HICKMAN
BRIDGE TRAIL

Capitol
Dome

Fremont
River

24

Hanksville

Sulphur
Creek

Fremont
River

Fruita

Cassidy
Arch

Grand Wash

GRAND WASH
TRAIL

The Narrows

FREMONT
RIVER TRAIL

Fern's Nipple
7067 ft

Scenic Drive

GOLDEN THRONE
TRAIL

Golden Throne
6489 ft

The Tanks

FREMONT
GORGE
OVERLOOK
TRAIL

Egyptian
Temple

Capitol Gorge

Pioneer Register

0   2 miles

Cedar Mesa

Henry Mountains

Circle Cliffs

BURR TRAIL ROAD

Strike Valley

Waterpocket Fold

Miller Twist Canyon

Boulder

Calf
Creek
Falls

12

Calf Creek

Circle Cliffs

GRAND STAIRCASE-ESCALANTE
NATIONAL MONUMENT

Escalante River

Escalante and Bryce Canyon

Bullfrog

Devils
Garden

N

0   5 miles

You may want to peep into Fruita's former **schoolhouse**, just north of the highway. Built in 1896, it hasn't had a pupil since 1941; park rangers, not a Mormon schoolmarm, keep it spick-and-span.

The village's old **orchards**, however, are Capitol Reef's crowning glory. A waxy, luxuriant green against the towering red cliffs, they hold almost three thousand trees planted by the pioneers. The cherries and peaches **blossom** in the first half of April, the apples slightly later, while the **harvest** lasts from the second half of June until well into October. So long as you stay in the orchards, you can eat as much fruit as you like; you only pay for what you take away.

A short distance further down the highway beyond the schoolhouse, the **Fremont Culture Walk** is an easy amble along a raised boardwalk that leads beside a canyon wall crammed with ancient **petroglyphs**. As well as stylized representations of goats and Bighorn sheep, some show how the Fremont people (see p.473) may have seen themselves – unless of course these strange helmeted figures, with triangular bodies and massive shields, really did come from other planets.

Hwy-24 crosses the Fremont two miles east of the visitor center, near the start of the longer **Hickman Bridge Trail** (see p.479). Only beyond this point does **Capitol Dome**, high above the north bank another half-mile ahead, resolve itself into a dome; so far you've seen it from the side, as a slender fin. By now Fremont Canyon is at its deepest, and it's joined within the next couple of miles by **Chimney Rock Canyon** from the north and **Grand Wash** from the south (see p.478). A mile past Grand Wash stands the sandstone cabin of one of Fruita's earliest settlers, **Elijah Behunin**, with the eastern boundary of the park another 2.5 miles down the road.

The Scenic Drive

Other than Hwy-24, the only paved road in Capitol Reef is the **Scenic Drive**, which parallels the golden cliffs of the Waterpocket Fold for twelve miles south from the visitor center. The first couple of miles lead through Fruita, where a cluster of restored barns and houses serve as homes for park employees, while overnight visitors camp out in the orchards.

Beyond the village, and the fee station where your $5 admission charge is collected, the road undulates through the desert, dipping into dry sandy washes and then climbing scrubby rolling hillocks. Successive individual pinnacles, such as **Fern's Nipple** and the **Egyptian Temple**, line the crest of the red-rock battlements to the east. Until Hwy-24 was pushed through the Fremont Canyon in 1962, this unlikely route was southern Utah's main east–west thoroughfare. It now ends at a large parking lot, facing a crack in the cliffs that marks the start of **Capitol Gorge**. For a century, traffic squeezed its way between the narrow walls beyond, but now the gravel continuation known as the Capitol Gorge Road peters out just over two miles in. Hikers however can keep going on foot, to see the Pioneer Register where early wagon-drivers carved their names (see p.478).

The Notom–Bullfrog Road

If you'd rather survey the Waterpocket Fold from the comfort of your car than sweat it out on foot, the long drive south along the **Notom–Bullfrog Road** is Capitol Reef's best option. Just be sure to stock up on gas and water; you'll have to drive at least seventy miles to find any facilities.

The road leaves Hwy-24 nine miles east of the visitor center, not far outside the park. Only its first four miles are paved, as far as the tiny but well-irrigated settlement of **NOTOM**, now home to perhaps half a dozen ranchers. Thereafter, its rough surface repeatedly ripples into a "washboard" as it follows a dry-as-dust bench above Sandy Creek, with the eerie badlands of the Waterpocket Fold to the west and the volcanic **Henry Mountains** to the east.

Ordinary vehicles should have no problem negotiating the full length of the Notom–Bullfrog Road, which re-enters the park twenty miles along and then leaves it again in the southeast corner fifteen miles on. Seventy miles from the highway, after a final 25-mile segment where you find yourself constantly stopping to swoon at the turquoise expanse of Lake Powell on the southern horizon, you come to the modern marina at **Bullfrog** (see p.490).

The Burr Trail

These days, most drivers who set off south on the Notom–Bullfrog Road don't make it to Bullfrog but complete a loop around the Waterpocket Fold by branching onto the **Burr Trail**. This is the only road actually to cross the fold, rather than slice through it, and it does so by means of a fearsome set of switchbacks that climb west from the Notom–Bullfrog Road, roughly halfway down.

The Burr Trail began life as a rutted wagon trail, which was upgraded by uranium prospectors in the 1940s and 1950s. The four miles within the national park are still unpaved, but the remaining thirty, running west to Boulder on Hwy-24, were paved during the late 1980s. Wilderness advocates argued that increased road use would irreparably damage one of Utah's least-spoiled regions; Garfield County authorities, keen to grab a piece of the Capitol Reef action from their neighbors in Wayne County, went ahead anyway. From their point of view, they were just in time; the area has since been incorporated into the Grand Staircase–Escalante National Monument, which will probably preclude further road construction.

If all that leaves you feeling too guilty to take the Burr Trail, you're missing out. The panorama that unfolds as you ascend the switchbacks and head west is out of this world. Looking back across the Notom–Bullfrog Road, you see the top of Swap Mesa – whose coal deposits may well be the next target of the mining companies – and the stark Henry Mountains. Just past the topmost ridge, the Upper and Lower sections of **Muley Twist Canyon** stretch to north and south through the heart of the Fold. Both make excellent multiday backpacking expeditions, starting from near the highway. As you leave the park and enter the national monument (where the pavement begins), an extraordinary procession of reefs marches south, with the white canyons of the Waterpocket Fold in the foreground and four or five craggy red cliff-faces beyond, leading on to Lake Powell.

The oval plain just west of the park, ringed by the Circle Cliffs, was described by the nineteenth-century geologist Clarence Dutton as "a spot which is about as desolate as any on earth." The Burr Trail leaves it by way of the deep **Long Canyon**, then struggles on to reach Hwy-24 immediately south of Boulder (see p.469).

Cathedral Valley

Capitol Reef's least accessible section is **Cathedral Valley**, north of Hwy 24. Like the Notom–Bullfrog Road, it parallels the eastern side of the Waterpocket Fold, but the territory here is much more forbidding than the sagebrush plain to the south. In among the heavily eroded red, blue, and gray hills lie deep canyons and primeval gardens, populated by strange stone monoliths. Unless you have your own 4WD or high-clearance vehicle, you'll only see it by joining one of the 4WD tours mentioned on p.474.

Two roads run north into the backcountry from Hwy-24, 11.5 and 18.6 miles east of the visitor center. The first, **River Ford Road**, traverses the Fremont River by means of a crude ford a few hundred yards along. If you're planning a loop drive, come this way first – it's not safe to cross when the water's more than a couple of feet deep, and you wouldn't want to find that out at the end of a sixty-mile drive. The second route, the **Caineville Wash Road**, meets the first – by now Hartnet Road – at the far end of Cathedral Valley. Several more dirt roads leave the park at this northern extremity, connecting with I-70 to the north or joining Hwy-72 above Loa to the west.

Hiking in Capitol Reef

You probably won't drive far in Capitol Reef before you feel the backcountry starting to beckon. Choosing which of the many, mostly short, **trails** to hike is largely a matter of whether you feel up to climbing; only a few, such as the walks through the Capitol Gorge or Grand Wash, remain on level ground, while the rest demand mountain-goat-style scrambling up the slickrock.

If you do choose to stick to the canyon floors, bear in mind the danger of **flash floods** after rain, and try not to pause anywhere where there's no clear escape route.

Grand Wash

The busiest Capitol Reef trail connects the Scenic Drive with Hwy-24, by way of the gravelly bed of the **Grand Wash**. Both trailheads are roughly four miles from the visitor center, one at the end of the unpaved Grand Wash Road, which leaves the Scenic Drive a mile past Fruita, and the other on the south bank of the highway a mile or two beyond Capitol Dome.

As a one-way walk, the **Grand Wash trail** is just over two miles long and takes around an hour, but unless you arrange a pick-up at the far end you'll have to double back. In the half-mile stretch known as **The Narrows**, the vertiginous 800ft canyon walls close in to a mere sixteen feet apart. **Butch Cassidy** and his gang are said to have used the tangle of side canyons that lead off Grand Wash as hideouts, but there's no evidence that Butch ever saw **Cassidy Arch**, reached by a short steep climb from near the southeast end of the trail.

Capitol Gorge

The **Capitol Gorge trail**, reached by driving the full length of the Scenic Drive, is every bit as claustrophobic as the Grand Wash. It's a short and easy walk, providing you spare yourself an extra 4.6-mile round-trip by parking not at the foot of the Scenic Drive but at the end of the gravel road beyond, which is where you'll find the trailhead.

In the space of a mile, the trail inches all the way through a crack in the Waterpocket Fold, though hikers have to turn back when they reach the private land on the far side. From 1871 onwards, this "**Blue Dugway**" was a major trans-Utah thoroughfare, as the painstaking inscriptions on the **Pioneer Register**, carved into the canyon wall halfway along, will testify.

A couple of twists of the canyon past the Register, side canyons start to open up to both left and right. Not far along, after two or so sets, a sign on the left reads "Tanks 0.2." Climb up the cairned trail here and within a few hundred yards you'll come to a succession of circular clifftop "tanks." Early travelers would break off from the laborious haul through the gorge, in the hope of finding fresh water in such clifftop "**waterpockets**."

A separate two-mile (one-hour) trail from the Capitol Gorge trailhead launches itself straight up the hillside to the north. The slickrock flatlands that cap the Waterpocket Fold enjoy huge views to Boulder Mountain in the east and the Henry Mountains in the west. The dominant feature up here, however, is the glowing Navajo-sandstone butte of the **Golden Throne**, at the foot of which the trail ends.

Hickman Bridge

The **Hickman Bridge Trail** may not be the easiest of Hwy-24's roadside trails – the Fremont Culture Walk, detailed on p.476, is far less demanding – but it makes a supremely rewarding two-mile, two-hour hike. Setting off along the north bank of the Fremont River, two miles east of the visitor center, it meanders briefly through the cottonwoods before climbing a brisk stairway out of the canyon to the shadeless heights up top.

Once you've marveled at Capitol Dome, off to the east, fork left at the junction ahead. Pockmarked black boulders strewn on all sides, incongruous against the red, pink, and cream sandstone, testify to ancient lava flows. Three-quarters of a mile along, the path loops around and through the arching span of **Hickman Bridge**. A hundred feet high, a hundred feet wide, it's a genuine natural bridge, worn through the rock by a side channel eager to reach the Fremont below. The rocky chaos beneath somehow complements the grace of the bridge itself.

Taking the right rather than the left fork at the junction lets you in for a nine-mile round-trip on the **Rim Overlook Trail**. Highlights include a towering overview of the orchards of Fruita, and the **Navajo Knobs** at its furthermost point.

Lake Powell

Until the early 1960s, it was all but impossible to travel between southwest and southeast Utah. In the unseen heart of the endless desert, the mighty Colorado River churned its way toward the Pacific through a succession of yawning canyons. Here and there boatmen might ferry the occasional passenger across, and a few adventurous souls even rafted down the river itself, but there was no highway for two hundred miles north of Arizona.

Now the Colorado has gone, submerged beneath the huge, docile **Lake Powell**. For many people – especially those who knew the sublime **Glen Canyon** that it destroyed – the new lake is a loathsome abomination. Many more see it as a thing of beauty, and Lake Powell has become Utah's number-one tourist attraction, drawing around four million visitors per year – by tradition, over half a million on Labor Day alone – and matched in popularity in the Southwest only by the Grand Canyon. It is, undeniably, an extraordinary spectacle, its turquoise waters rippling against its stark red-rock rim and cradling islands that once were buttes and mesas. No one could ever mistake this for a

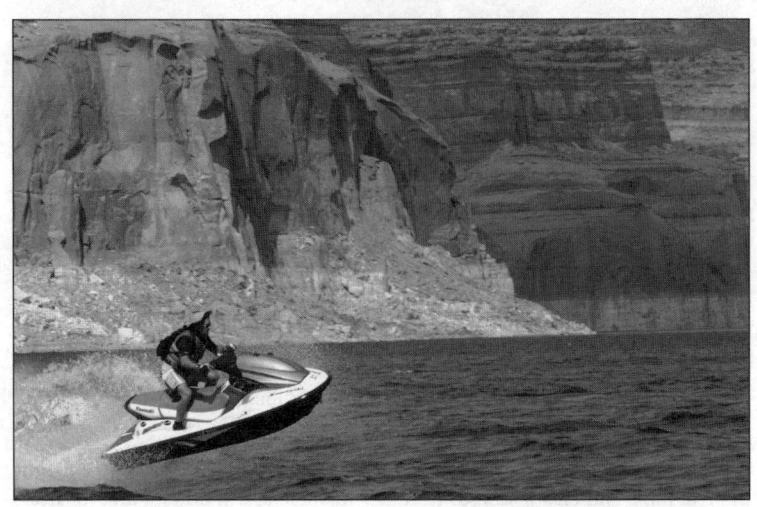

△ Jet-skiing on Lake Powell

natural landscape, however, and you don't have to be an out-and-out environmentalist to be disturbed by the transformation of America's last great wilderness into a playground. The concessionaires of the **Glen Canyon National Recreational Area** invite you to "think of Lake Powell as a 160,000-acre bathtub and consider our boats, floats, boards, and tubes as your toys." Beyond the unappealing rhetoric, there's some truth in what they say; granted that the lake exists, if you're going to come here at all, the best way to enjoy your visit is to get out on the water.

Lake Powell's success as a wet'n'wild theme park has been a surprise spin-off from its real purpose. Glen Canyon Dam was constructed to regulate the flow of water along the Colorado River. Half is kept back to irrigate the deserts of the plateau, while the rest gushes through its turbines, generating electricity as it goes, and makes for Arizona and California. Demand is so precisely monitored that the level of the lake fluctuates according to whether it's dinnertime in Phoenix. Hence its closest resemblance to a bathtub – the scummy dirty-bath tidemark that sullies the sandstone around its edge.

The whole vast system cost $300 million to build. When full, Lake Powell is 550ft deep at the dam and holds enough water to cover all of Arizona five inches deep. It stretches back up 186 miles of the Colorado River and 72 miles of the San Juan River, as well as inundating 96 side canyons formed by rivers such as the Escalante and the Dirty Devil. The total shoreline of 1960 miles is longer than the entire US Pacific coast. Despite the searing sun, the lake is officially claimed to lose a mere 2.5 percent of its volume each year to evaporation.

The fullest the lake has ever been was in 1983, when water flowed over the top of the dam, and an emergency release had to be instigated. As recently as 1999, the level was just four feet below the maximum, but drought set in from 2000 onwards, and by the spring of 2005 the waters had dropped 146 feet. That was enough for Glen Canyon to begin to reappear, and backpackers flocked to marvel at such long-submerged wonders as the Cathedral in the Desert. The lower reaches of the Escalante River sprang back to life; in their five years above the lake level, banks became host to twenty-foot high trees, while the thick layer of sediment deposited on the lake bed was being steadily washed away. As this book went to press, however, rains had brought the lake 50ft higher.

Six **marinas** have been built thus far around Lake Powell, of which five are accessible by road. Two are south of the state line in Arizona: the largest, **Wahweap**, lies just west of the dam itself and the purpose-built town of **Page**, while the newest, **Antelope Point**, is on Navajo land immediately east of Page. The remaining four are in Utah. **Bullfrog** and **Hall's Crossing** are roughly two thirds of the way northeast up the lake from the dam, and are connected by a ferry service that makes it possible to drive between Capitol Reef National Park and Natural Bridges National Monument. **Hite** is in theory at the northeast limit of the lake, though the recent drop in water levels has left it stranded high and dry, and it's not currently in operation. The sixth and final marina, **Dangling Rope**, is a refueling station that can only be reached by boat.

There's surprisingly little accommodation on land; it's assumed you'll want to join the armada out on the water, either in your own vessel or in a rented **houseboat**. For a quick taste, you can join a **guided tour** at either Wahweap or Bullfrog – the trips to **Rainbow Bridge** are by far the most popular – or take the **ferry** service that plies between Bullfrog and Hall's Crossing.

Page

Home to almost ten thousand people, **PAGE** – which is actually just south of the state line in Arizona but is the only town of any size on the periphery of Lake Powell – is now the largest community in a 720-mile stretch of the Colorado River. Before Glen Canyon Dam was constructed four miles west, this all but barren mesa belonged to the Navajo Nation. Thanks to a small spring, however, it made the best site to house the dam's workforce. The Navajo agreed to swap it for a similar-sized chunk of desert between Bluff and Hatch in southeast Utah, a new road was blasted through the Echo Cliffs, and the town was born on Thanksgiving Day 1958.

At first, Page seemed destined to wither away once the dam was completed. Ironically, it gained a new lease of life when Congress decided that instead of building more dams, the Southwest could meet its power needs by burning coal instead. The **Navajo Generating Station**, which creates electricity using coal from Black Mesa and pumps water from Lake Powell to Phoenix, went up four miles southeast of town, and has kept Page in work ever since.

Arrival and information

The helpful staff at Page's **visitor center**, 608 Elm St (Mon–Fri 8am–5pm; ☎928/645-2741 or 1-888/261-7243, ⓦwww.pagelakepowellchamber.org), offer advice on local amenities and attractions, while brochures are also available at the Powell Memorial Museum (see p.484). Several other offices in town that purport to be information centers are in fact tour operators offering trips to Antelope Canyon (see p.485).

No scheduled buses or flights serve Page, though charter airlines do occasionally fly into the local **airport**, a mile east of town on AZ-98. Grand Circle Shuttle (☎928/645-6806, ⓦwww.grandcircleshuttle.com) runs a local **taxi** and shuttle service, charging $50 per person for the ride to or from Flagstaff.

Lake Powell: controversy and compromise

The western half of the United States would sustain a population greater than that of our whole country today if the waters that now run to waste were saved and used for irrigation.

President Theodore Roosevelt, State of the Union address, 1901

The twentieth-century growth of the American West was largely the story of the "taming" of the **Colorado River**. If the Colorado were to run dry, Los Angeles, Las Vegas, and Phoenix would die, and the exodus from the Southwest would dwarf anything from the Dustbowl era.

In terms of volume, the Colorado does not rank among the top 25 rivers in the US. However, the sheer aggression with which it hurtles from 13,000ft up in the Rockies makes it the fastest and fiercest of them all. That's why it's responsible for so many magnificent canyons; and that's also why civil engineers can't bear to leave it alone. They yearn to harness its energy with hydroelectric dams and divert its flow to irrigate the desert instead of rushing uselessly to the sea.

Early in the twentieth century, the sparsely populated southwestern states began to fear that southern California's ever-increasing thirst might one day drain them dry. The **Colorado River Compact**, signed in 1922, divided the river between an **Upper Basin**, consisting of Utah, Wyoming, Colorado, and New Mexico, and a **Lower Basin** – Arizona, Nevada, and California. Each basin was to receive 7.5 million acre-feet of the estimated annual flow of 16.8 million, with the dregs left over for Mexico. This was the first of fifteen such agreements in fifty years, largely because the estimates were wrong; the correct figure is more like 13.9 million acre-feet.

The task of distributing the water fell to a new federal agency, the **Bureau of Reclamation**, and the main tool at its disposal was the **dam**. Its engineers saw their mission as being to reshape the West, to "reclaim" it to the way it ought to be. They began in 1935, by damming Black Canyon, on the doorstep of California, with what came to be known as the **Hoover Dam** (see p.555). That project inspired a spree of dam-building, in the US and all over world. Though critics argued the American dams were supplying far more hydroelectric power than the nation could possibly need, it was all absorbed soon enough into feeding the war effort and fueling the economic boom of the 1950s. According to the Bureau of Reclamation, yet more dams were required. Its plans for the Colorado Plateau were clear from the subtitle of one report: *A Natural Menace Becomes A Natural Resource*. Proposals included damming the Green River in northwest Colorado, the San Juan in New Mexico, and the Colorado itself in both Bridge Canyon in Arizona and Utah's Glen Canyon.

Almost a century earlier, in 1869, John Wesley Powell had been entranced by the idyllic canyon that lay below the confluence of the Green and Colorado rivers: "A curious ensemble of wonderful features – carved walls, royal arches, glens, alcove gulches, mounds, and monuments . . . . We decide to call it **Glen Canyon**." Those few river-runners who had seen it since knew it as a cool, tranquil haven, bursting with luxuriant vegetation and desert wildlife, and a far cry from the cataract-filled canyons both up- and downstream. Theirs were lone voices in the wilderness, however; too little known to have been granted federal protection, Glen Canyon's remoteness was to work against it.

As a campaigning force, the environmental movement was in its infancy in the 1950s, and its strategy concentrated on defending national parks at all costs. The Green River dam-site being within Dinosaur National Monument, **David Brower**, the executive director of the Sierra Club, argued before a Congressional committee that damming Glen Canyon was a far better idea – in fact he originally endorsed the construction of a dam in the Grand Canyon *on condition* that a dam was built at Glen Canyon as well. He felt that only if the Glen Canyon dam was built could he be sure the one in Dinosaur never would be. Conservationists prided themselves on a job well done when it was eventually decided to dam the Green River outside Dinosaur, at Flaming Gorge to the northwest, and to go ahead with damming Glen Canyon. The one concession to "the abominable nature lovers," as one Utah senator termed them, was that water would not be allowed to encroach upon Rainbow Bridge National Monument.

The first blast at the dam-site was detonated on a signal from President Eisenhower in September 1956. Meanwhile, with Glen Canyon doomed but not yet drowned, archeologists, artists, and photographers set out to chronicle its disappearing treasures. These included the glowing, fern-dripping alcove known as the **Cathedral in the Desert** – described in Eliot Porter's bestselling *The Place No One Knew* as "the single most spectacular place I ever visited" – and the **Crossing of the Fathers**, where the Spanish priests Domínguez and Escalante forded the river in 1776. Floyd Dominy, the gung-ho head of the Bureau of Reclamation, preferred to dwell on the future, writing in the glossy coffee-table volume *Lake Powell, Jewel of the Colorado* that "like a string of pearls, ten modern recreation areas will line Lake Powell's shores."

The Colorado River was brought to a halt on January 21, 1963. That same day, President Kennedy's Secretary of the Interior, Stewart Udall – the great-grandson of John D. Lee, of Lees Ferry (see p.401) – announced plans to build two further dams within the Grand Canyon. By now, the Sierra Club had realized its mistake; and it promptly made another. This time it argued for building coal-burning power stations instead of hydroelectric dams. The Navajo Nation, imagining that nuclear power might soon render its mineral resources worthless, decided to cash in by permitting the strip-mining of Black Mesa (see p.68), and the hideously polluting Navajo Generating Station was constructed outside Page.

It took seventeen more years – and a Supreme Court decision that said Congress could ignore its own previous rulings and allow the lake to lap against Rainbow Bridge – before Lake Powell was filled to the brim, on June 22, 1980. David Brower, who left the Sierra Club to found Friends of the Earth in 1969, was by now describing his support for Glen Canyon Dam as "the greatest sin I have ever committed." Shortly before his death, in 2000, the 87-year-old "Archdruid" hosted a "Day of Action Against Dams" at the dam site, during which he called once again for Lake Powell to be drained so the canyon could regenerate: "watching Nature heal the Glen will be one of the great dramas on Earth." One of the original arguments for the dam had been that the Colorado's phenomenal load of silt would otherwise fill **Lake Mead**, behind the Hoover Dam, within a few years; Brower argued that the floodgates at Glen Canyon should remain open until that really does happen, perhaps two hundred years from now. Other activists would go much further. The central fantasy of Edward Abbey's *The Monkey-Wrench Gang* involved dynamiting the dam, and Abbey was among the demonstrators who in 1981 signaled the birth of the **Earth First!** movement by suspending a 300ft strip of plastic down its face to simulate an almighty crack. To some extent, though, the argument has been won; no major dam has been built since the 1960s, and the general consensus is that Glen Canyon Dam will be the last.

The debate over the future of Lake Powell was given an extra spin by the **droughts** of the early twenty-first century (see p.480), which threatened to restore Glen Canyon by default, and demonstrated how rapidly flora and fauna could re-establish themselves. Some argued that global warming was responsible, and that the lake would never refill; others countered that this latest dry spell was typical of the region's long-term weather patterns, and showed precisely why the dam was built in the first place. In any case, drought may be a natural phenomenon, but the level of the lake is dictated by political decisions, and specifically the amount of water released to the Lower Basin states. In January 2006, prompted in part by the drought, the seven t

continued overleaf

Colorado River states proposed a new system for implementing the Colorado River Compact. The plan calls for the levels of Lake Powell and Lake Mead to operate in tandem, and for Lake Powell to hold onto more water during dry years but have a slightly lower "normal" at other times.

Proposals to destroy the dam are surrounded by greater political acrimony than ever. The scheme has been adopted as national Sierra Club policy, but it's opposed by the club's Utah chapter. Each year since 2000, Utah's congressional delegation has attached a rider to the Department of the Interior's annual appropriations bill specifically prohibiting it from spending any money to "study or implement any plan to drain Lake Powell." For the latest news and opinions, take a look at the websites of the pro-draining Glen Canyon Institute (ⓦ www.drainit.org) and the anti-environmentalist Friends of Lake Powell (ⓦ www.lakepowell.org).

Accommodation

While no one would choose to spend much time in Page itself, Lake Powell is enough of an attraction to keep its **motels** busy for most of the year and allow them to hike their rates higher than you might expect.

Best Western Arizonainn 716 Rim View Drive ⓣ 928/645-2466 or 1-800/826-2718, ⓦ www .bestwestern.com. Standard upmarket motel on the outskirts of Page, commanding a massive desert panorama from the poolside. ❺

Best Western at Lake Powell 208 N Lake Powell Blvd ⓣ 928/645-5988 or 1-888/794-2888, ⓦ www.bestwestern.com. Large, good-value motel perched above downtown Page, with a pool. ❹

Courtyard by Marriott 600 Clubhouse Drive ⓣ 928/645-5000 or 1-800/851-3855, ⓦ www .courtyard.com/pgacy. Page's most incongruous splash of luxury – a 153-room resort, complete

with golf course – is below the mesa in view of the dam. ❺

Holiday Inn Express 751 S Navajo Drive ⓣ 928/645-9000 or 1-800/465-4329, ⓦ www .holiday-inn.com. Good quality chain motel, with a pool and free continental breakfast. ❺

Uncle Bill's Place 117 Eighth Ave ⓣ 928/645-1224 or 1-888/359-0945, ⓦ www.canyon-country .com/unclebill. This small, friendly old-fashioned motel in Page's original residential district offers B&B suites, with one- and two-bedroom en suite options as well as kitchenette apartments that share a bathroom, at very reasonable prices. ❷–❻

Downtown Page

The view as you descend toward Page is utterly surreal. The three power plant chimneys stand silhouetted amid sandstone outcrops, while lines of pylons march off across the desert and the misty hump of Navajo Mountain rises in the distance. As you approach, the waters of Lake Powell emerge from the haze, with drowned buttes poking their heads here and there above the surface.

Page itself, on the other hand, resembles a dull suburban mall writ large; if it has a redeeming feature, you'll have a hard time finding it. Permanent structures have replaced most of its original trailer homes, but the only sight of any interest is the **John Wesley Powell Memorial Museum**, 6 N Lake Powell Blvd (Mon–Fri 9am–5pm; $5; ⓦ www.powellmuseum.org). In addition to charting the exploits of the first man to raft down the Colorado (see p.497), the museum celebrates later river runners and also recounts Page's own brief history. It also holds a locally excavated plesiosaur fossil and an amazing collection of fluorescent rocks. The museum can make reservations for local boat trips and tours.

Antelope Canyon

A couple of miles southeast of Page on AZ-98, mile marker 299 marks the trailhead for **Antelope Canyon**, Arizona's most famous **slot canyon**. The canyon actually comprises two separate sections, on either side of the highway, and both are on Navajo land.

Immediately north of the highway, **Lower Antelope Canyon** achieved worldwide notoriety in 1997, when the tragic deaths of eleven hikers in a flash flood proved just how dangerous such places can be. Nevertheless, they're also

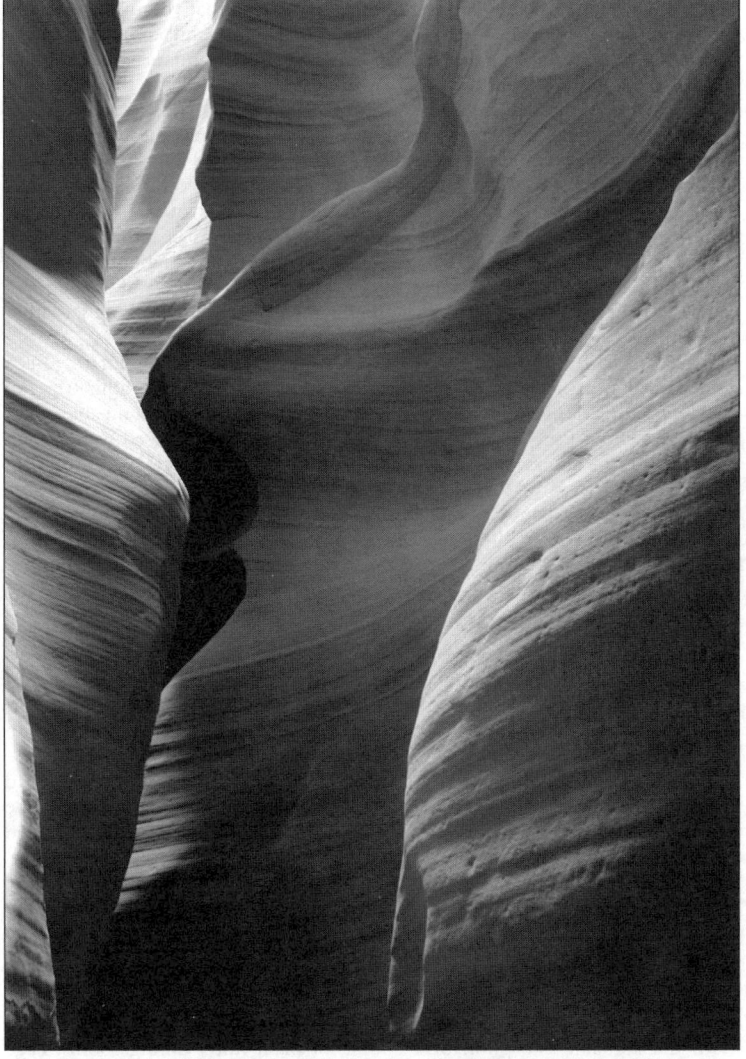

△ Sculpted sandstone at Antelope Canyon

irresistibly, astonishingly beautiful. In the last few years, the Navajo have realized what an invaluable tourism asset Antelope Canyon represents, and they now control all access (May–Oct daily 8am–5pm; ☎928/698-3347, ⓦwww.navajonationparks.org/htm/antelopecanyon.htm).

In summer, tourists can visit both sections of the canyon simply by turning up at the parking lot. However, not only is there a $6 entry fee, but you also have to pay an outrageous $13 for a "guide" service that consists either of pointing you to the entrance of Lower Antelope or driving you in a shuttle van down to **Upper Antelope Canyon**, a matter of perhaps two miles.

You're deposited just outside a slender, unprepossessing crack in a red sandstone wall. Stepping inside is like entering both a cathedral, in that you find yourself in a majestic chamber adorned with delicate glowing colors, and a pinball machine, in that you can just imagine that any second some mighty and unavoidable boulder will come thundering down the narrow passageway. Walking the full length of the canyon and back takes barely twenty minutes, even with frequent pauses to admire the interlacing fins of multihued rock that swirl overhead, in places to a height of 120ft. A flash flood is capable of filling the slot to the brim with water and spilling over the top; once such a flood recedes, on the other hand, it leaves the canyon floor scrubbed bare of its usual eight-foot layer of fine soft sand.

Be warned that while Antelope Canyon is every bit as beautiful as photos suggest, it offers little of the wilderness feel of other desert highlights. It's both short and narrow enough to feel *very* crowded at busy times, and as the main priority for all visitors is to take photographs, it can feel like a working set rather than a place to contemplate beauty.

Given the high cost of an unaccompanied visit, you may prefer to join a guided **tour** from Page that typically costs about $25 for a one-hour trip and up to $35 for a longer photography tour. Several competing companies have offices in central Page. Highly recommended for his personalized small-group excursions is the affable, self-styled Chief Tsosie of Grand Circle Adventures, 48 S Lake Powell Blvd (☎928/645-5594, ⓦwww.antelopeslotcanyontours.com), who also leads day-trips to lesser-known canyons and overlooks, while Overland Canyon Tours, 697 N Navajo Drive (☎928/608-4072 or 1-800/684-4072, ⓦwww.overlandcanyontours.com), offers extended trips into the backcountry.

Horseshoe Bend

An easy self-guided hike not far south of Page leads to an amazing view of **Horseshoe Bend**, where the Colorado River makes an extravagant 180-degree turn in the depths of Marble Canyon, roughly halfway through its short course between Glen Canyon Dam and the official start of the Grand Canyon at Lees Ferry.

To reach the overlook, drive south on US-89 and turn west on the dirt road just past mile marker 545, exactly 2.6 miles south of the Wal-Mart in Page. The road leads to a parking lot at the foot of a small sandy hill. Climb the railed path to the top of that hill, then down another 0.4 mile to the lip of the gorge. The river itself is only visible from the very edge, which is unrailed, windy, and pretty hair-raising. The huge curving sweep far below barely fits into the widest-angled lens. Be sure to carry water and allow about an hour for the exposed round-trip hike.

Eating

With the arguable exception of a couple of plain hotel dining rooms, Page offers a pretty poor choice of restaurants; a *KFC* across from the visitor center

△ Horseshoe Bend on the Colorado River

is as good a bet as anything else. In Dam Plaza, *Beans Gourmet Coffee House*, 644 N Navajo Drive (℡928/645-6858), serves espressos and light snacks, while the adjacent *Gunsmoke Saloon* offers beer and live country music nightly.

Bella Napoli 809 N Navajo Drive ℡928/645-2706. All-you-can-eat Italian buffets (soup, salad, pizza, and pasta) for lunch ($7) and dinner ($10), plus a full menu. Daily 11am–2pm & 5pm onward.

Dam Bar & Grille 644 N Navajo Drive ℡928/645-2161. Themed diner and bar, appealingly designed to echo the days when Page was populated solely by dam-building hard-hats.

Steak and pasta entrées for around $15. Daily 3–11pm.

Peppers Restaurant *Courtyard by Marriott*, 600 Clubhouse Drive ℡928/645-5000. Upscale but not especially expensive hotel restaurant on the way to town as you approach from the dam. Varied if not wildly exciting menu ranges through salads, pasta, sandwiches, and dinner specials. Open daily for all meals.

Glen Canyon Dam

Glen Canyon Dam plugs **Marble Canyon** (see p.400) not at its narrowest point, but at its northern end, just downstream from Wahweap Creek. As US-89 crosses Glen Canyon Bridge four miles outside of Page, the vast curve of the dam is to the north, while Marble Canyon drops 700ft below you.

There's no stopping on the bridge, so if you want a better look, call in at the ultramodern **Carl Hayden Visitor Center** (daily: Oct–April 8am–5pm, May–Sept 7am–7pm; ℡928/608-6404; Ⓦwww.nps.gov/glca) on the west bank, which doubles as the main source of information on the **Glen Canyon National Recreational Area**. Security concerns have meant that **free tours** of the actual dam have been suspended for most of the time since September 11, 2001. If they're running when you turn up, allow half an hour to drop via two elevators first to the walkway along the top, and then a further 500ft to the generating station at the bottom. Beneath the roar of the 1.3-million kilowatt turbines, a digital counter steadily ticks off the billions of dollars earned thus far by the sale of power.

Just before the bridge, a spur road on the east bank tunnels down through the cliffs to the river; rafters use it as an access point for the gloriously lazy fifteen-mile **float trip** down to Lees Ferry. There's no white water along the way, and strictly speaking you never enter the Grand Canyon, but it's still a very pleasant drift between imposing high-canyon cliffs. The trips are run by Wilderness River Adventures, 57 S Lake Powell Blvd, Page (daily: 11.15am mid-March to mid-May and mid-September through May, 7.30am or 1pm June to mid-September; $62 adults, $52 age 12 and under). Water and sodas are provided, but you're expected to bring your own picnic lunch.

Wahweap

Unlike Page, **WAHWEAP**, a couple of miles west of Glen Canyon Dam, has never become a town. Lake Powell's principal **marina** has, however, grown steadily since it was established in 1963, coordinating most of the boat rental and tour business and also offering several hundred motel rooms.

To the fury of the federal authorities, the first man to appreciate Wahweap's potential did so long before the dam was ever built. Art Greene, the owner of the *Marble Canyon Lodge* (see p.401), ran boat trips upriver to Rainbow Bridge from the 1940s onwards; when he got wind of plans to dam Glen Canyon, he shrewdly leased the land at the mouth of Wahweap Creek at a knockdown rate. Knowing it made the perfect site for a marina, Greene refused to budge, and wound up making a killing as official concessionaire.

Practicalities

Only half the rooms in the plush *Lake Powell Resort* (☎928/645-2433 or 1-800/528-6154, ⓦwww.lakepowell.com; Nov–April ⑤, May–Oct ⑦) overlook Lake Powell. Its *Rainbow Room* restaurant, however, provides huge lakeside windows and serves good food daily for all meals, with prices kept relatively low to cater to the many tour groups that pass through. The same management also operates an adjacent first-come, first-served **campground** ($18), as well as an **RV park** (April–Oct $26, Nov–March $18).

Boat tours from Wahweap

In addition to the **Rainbow Bridge** trips detailed below, Lake Powell Resorts and Marinas (see box opposite) run boat tours from Wahweap that range from a one-hour paddlewheeler trip (daily June to early Sept; $15 adults, $12 under age 13) to ninety-minute Antelope Canyon excursions ($33 adults, $26 under age 12) and a dinner cruise (daily May–Sept; $67).

Rainbow Bridge National Monument

Millions of tourists have Lake Powell to thank for providing effortless access to the **world's largest natural bridge**, the magnificent **RAINBOW BRIDGE NATIONAL MONUMENT**. The Navajo, seeing this formerly sacred site swarming with visitors, are far less enthusiastic, though at least the height of

To rent a **houseboat** on Lake Powell, contact Lake Powell Resorts and Marinas (☎928/645-2433 or 1-800/528-6154, ⓦwww.visitlakepowell.com). Between mid-May and mid-October, the smallest Explorer houseboat, capable of sleeping six, costs $1360 for three days or $2205 for a week, while rates for the luxury ten-berth Admiral class of boat are well over double. For the rest of the year, prices drop by around forty percent.

Any number of **package deals**, offering different combinations of time spent on houseboats, in the marina lodges and on guided tours, are also available.

Many houseboat users like to **camp** overnight onshore; National Recreation Area (NRA) regulations insist that anyone who camps within a mile of the lake must carry and use portable toilets.

7

Glen Canyon Dam, and thus the level of the lake, was mandated to ensure that Rainbow Bridge was not drowned – unlike the nearby and equally revered confluence of the Colorado and San Juan rivers.

Both the Navajo and the Paiute knew of Rainbow Bridge before the first university-sponsored expedition reached it in 1909. Within a year, it was declared a national monument, but it remained far off any beaten track until the coming of Lake Powell. The bridge now lies a couple of miles down Forbidding Canyon, a side canyon located just around fifty miles by water from the dam.

Tours from **Wahweap** are operated all year round by Lake Powell Resorts and Marinas (April–Oct daily 8am & 10am, Nov–March Sat 9am; adults $115, under-13s $80; ☎928/645-2433 or 1-800/528-6154, ⓦwww.visitlakepowell .com). These schedules are open to considerable variation, as the length of the trip depends on the level of the lake. What used to be a half-day excursion has become an eight-hour one in recent years because certain deep-water channels are no longer navigable. It's possible that the waters may rise again sufficiently for the tour boats to make two round-trips in a single day. For much of the year, the tours are fully booked well in advance; make sure to reserve a seat on a boat before you finalize your itinerary.

Even with the water low, Lake Powell remains a broad expanse, spread beneath a huge sky. When you reach Forbidding Canyon, on the other hand, you enter another world; it's a beautiful high-walled slot canyon that twists mysteriously away from the lake proper. Eventually, the tour boats moor at a floating jetty, the precise location of which varies. A walk from here that may be over a mile leads to the astonishing sandstone gateway of the bridge, climbing nearly 300ft high. It's also almost 300ft wide, with Navajo Mountain visible through its superbly smooth curve. The upper section, including the forty-foot-thick span, is composed of Navajo sandstone, while the base belongs to the harder Kayenta formation, not so easily cut by flowing water. When the lake is full, the bridge spans open water, but these days the former streambed is usually dry. What were once waterfalls nearby have also been exposed; what a spot this must have been. The Park Service asks visitors to consider not walking right up to, or beneath, the bridge itself, out of respect for Navajo spiritual traditions.

With a great deal more difficulty, Rainbow Bridge can also be reached on **foot**. Two fourteen-mile trails start respectively 38 and 42 miles up Arrowhead Hwy-16, which runs north from Hwy-98 from a junction 57 miles southeast of Page. They loop to either side of Navajo Mountain, before joining for the last half-mile. This hike should only be attempted by experienced canyoneers, all of whom must obtain **permits**, costing $5, plus $5 per person per night,

from the Navajo Nation Parks & Recreation Dept (☎928/871-6647, ⓦwww
.navajonationparks.org). The website of the Glen Canyon Natural History
Association (ⓦwww.glencanyonnha.org) provides up-to-date details on the
two alternative routes.

Bullfrog

The marina at **BULLFROG** is slapped atop the slickrock on the west side of
Lake Powell, seventy miles upstream from Wahweap, or seventy miles southeast
of Capitol Reef National Park on the Notom–Bullfrog Road (see p.472). It's
the focus of a small community that now proudly boasts its own high school,
as well as a Glen Canyon NRA **visitor center**, open in summer only (March
Sat & Sun 8am–5pm, April–Oct daily 8am–5pm; ☎435/684-7400; ⓦwww
.nps.gov/glca).

A houseboat on stilts above the road serves as a sign for the *Defiance House
Lodge* (☎435/684-3000 or 1-800/528-6154, ⓦwww.visitlakepowell.com;
April–Oct ⑥, Nov–March ⑤). The best place to enjoy the big lake views from
this pricey mesa-top **motel** is its *Anasazi* restaurant, even though the food
itself is indifferent. The park concessionaires also have some fully furnished
but deeply unatmospheric **housekeeping units** (similar to trailers) for rent
(April–Oct ❼, Nov–March ⑥). A year-round first-come, first-served **campground** charges $18 per night (☎435/684-3000).

All boat tours from both Bullfrog and Hall's Crossing have been suspended
since the lake level dropped. The best way to find whether they've been
resumed is by contacting the Powell museum in Page, which formerly served as
a reservations agent (see p.484; ⓦwww.powellmuseum.org)

Hall's Crossing

HALL'S CROSSING, on the east shore of Lake Powell, now plays second
fiddle to its larger neighbor Bullfrog to the west. As the name suggests, it was the
base of a river ferry operator long before the lake existed. **Charles Hall** started
out by building his own boat at Hole-in-the-Rock, 35 miles downstream (see
p.467), in 1870. Business there was so bad that he moved here in 1881, only

The Lake Powell Ferry

The ferry crossing between **Bullfrog** and **Hall's Crossing** takes 25 minutes. Up-to-
date schedules can found on ⓦwww.nps.gov/glca/ferry.htm, but in recent years the
timetable has run as follows:

	From Hall's Crossing	**From Bullfrog**
mid-April to Oct	8am, 10am, noon, 2pm, & 4pm	9am, 11am, 1pm, 3pm, & 5pm
Nov to mid-April	8am, 10am, noon, & 2pm	9am, 11am, 1pm, & 3pm

Fares: Foot passengers $4, ages 5–11 $2, under-5 and over-64 free; bicycles $6,
motorcycles $8, ordinary cars $16. Increased rates for larger vehicles.
Ferry service is frequently suspended for repairs in winter; contact Glen Canyon
visitor centers for current information.

to give up altogether when the transcontinental railroad rendered his service redundant. Hall charged $5 per wagon and 75¢ per passenger; the going rate these days for a family car is $16 (see box opposite).

The GNRA Ranger Station above Hall's Crossing marina is rarely staffed; call ☎1-800/582-4351 in emergencies. **Accommodation** possibilities are limited to housekeeping units in a glorified trailer park (phone number and rates as for Bullfrog), or an $18-per-night first-come, first-served **campground** (☎435/684-7000). If you're looking for a **meal**, you can either take your pick from a small assortment of Twinkies on sale at the local gas station, or a marginally wider range of groceries at the marina store. There's nothing at all at the **ferry ramp**, just over a mile beyond the marina.

When they finally get around to colonizing Mars, the first settlement should look much like the airstrip on top of the bare red mesa that rises above Hall's Crossing. Hwy-276 to the east makes an exhilarating drive, dropping down the **Clay Cliffs** with views across the red plains to Monument Valley, and running for forty empty miles to meet Hwy-95 near Natural Bridges (see p.532).

Ticaboo

Hwy-276 sets off bravely into the desert northwest of Bullfrog, passing a series of unlikely looking warehouses used to store boats during the winter. Twelve miles up, well past the turning to Notom (see p.476) and only a few miles short of the red-tinged peak that marks the southernmost point of the Henry Mountains, the grandiose resort development of **TICABOO** stands to the left of the highway.

An optimistic venture that still hasn't quite paid off, Ticaboo consists of the comfortable *Ticaboo Lodge* (☎435/788-2110 or 1-877/842-2267, ⓦ www.ticaboo .com; Nov to mid-April ❸, mid-April to Oct ❺); a Conoco gas station; and the *Horny Toad Lounge*, which serves steak and pasta dinners daily in summer and opens as a bar only on winter weekends.

Hite

The northernmost of Lake Powell's marinas, at **HITE**, is reached via **Hwy-95**, which branches off Hwy-24 halfway between Capitol Reef and I-70 to run for 122 miles southeast to Blanding. The only highway to cross the Colorado between the Glen Canyon Dam and Moab, Hwy-95's most dramatic segment is the twenty-mile stretch as it approaches the river from the west, rattling along beside the North Wash.

At the mouth of the North Wash canyon, the highway climbs to the wind-swept hilltop that holds **Hite Overlook**. You'll almost certainly be confronted here by the fact that while Hite remains accessible by road, it's no longer on the lake. An ongoing drought let Lake Powell recede out of sight several years ago; it's just possible the waters will have returned by the time you read this, but don't bet on it.

Hite has always felt like something of a God-forsaken spot, and even more so these days that it's lake-forsaken as well. Signboards at the overlook point out the site of the short-lived gold-mining town of **Hite** itself, which flourished for thirty years from 1883. Though it's currently back in the open air again, after forty years underwater, it's totally obliterated by sediment.

Once past the overlook, Hwy-95 loops north to cross first the Dirty Devil River and then the Colorado. Reaching the ramshackle **Hite Marina** itself involves a detour of a couple of miles on the far side. At the time of writing, no boats could reach Hite, so all the marina facilities were shut. There's still a small gas station and a grocery store, and it's even possible to rent a **housekeeping unit** (same phone number and rates as for Bullfrog), though that would be a seriously bad idea. There's also primitive camping alongside the marina if you absolutely have to spend the night (☏435/684-7400).

Between Capitol Reef and Canyonlands

No direct route crosses the tract of craggy sandstone and eroded clay that stretches for a hundred miles east of Capitol Reef. Travelers making the circuit of Utah's parks are obliged to make a giant detour to the north or south, either crossing Lake Powell at Hite or taking **Hwy-24** up to meet I-70 and then looping back down to Moab – a total drive of around 150 miles.

The scenery along Hwy-24 is consistently awesome, beginning with the **badlands** twenty miles beyond Capitol Reef, where the 1500ft **Factory Butte** rises above corrugated humps of grayish-blue clay reminiscent of Arizona's Painted Desert (see p.319). Only small sections of the backcountry are at all accessible, however, and the town of **Green River** on the interstate is the only town of any size the whole way to Moab.

Hanksville

Forty miles from the Capitol Reef visitor center, Hwy-24 turns sharply north toward the interstate, while Hwy-95 runs south toward Lake Powell. The tiny farming community of **HANKSVILLE** stands at the intersection, a few miles south of the confluence where the Fremont and Muddy rivers join to form the Dirty Devil.

Hanksville is only a dot on the map, but with the next dot a good fifty miles away in any direction, it draws in enough weary drivers to keep it ticking. The most appealing overnight options are a couple of **B&Bs**: the friendly, three-room *Joy's*, 296 S Center St (☏435/542-3252; ❸; closed Nov–March) is open to couples only, and *Fern's Place*, 99 East 100 North (☏435/542-3251; ❷), resembles a tiny motel, consisting of a cluster of simple but reasonably comfortable blue cottages. There's also a large commercial **campground**, the *Red Rock*, at 226 East 100 North (March–Nov, $12; ☏435/542-3235 or 1-800/452-4971), which has a decent restaurant. Otherwise your choice is restricted to a handful of small family-run **motels**; most are rundown, but the *Whispering Sands*, 140 S Hwy-95 (☏435/542-3238, ⓦwww.hanksville.com/whisperingsands/motel.htm; ❸), is OK. Straight opposite it, poised on a low bluff close to the intersection, *Blondie's Eatery*, 3 N Hwy-95 (☎435/542-3255), is better than it looks, serving steak and eggs for around $7.

A couple of solitary structures also interrupt the badlands west of Hanksville. The *Caineville Cove Inn*, at mile marker 99 on Hwy-24 (☎435/456-9900; ❸), is a small but comfortable motel with a swimming pool, while the *Luna Mesa Oasis*, two miles on at mile marker 101 (☎435/456-9122; ❶/❷), is an inexpensive Mexican restaurant that also offers tent camping ($12) plus three teepees and three motel rooms.

Goblin Valley State Park

Utah's quirkiest park, **GOBLIN VALLEY STATE PARK**, nestles at the foot of the San Rafael Reef, a short distance west of Hwy-24 just over twenty miles

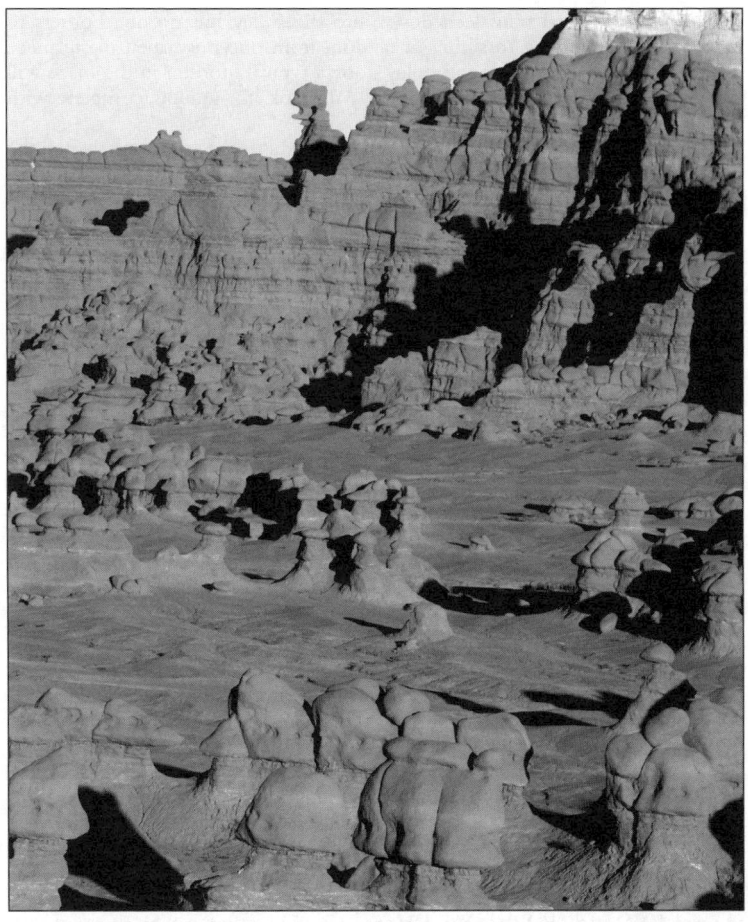

△ Goblin Valley State Park

north of Hanksville. This small patch of barren desert became a park for the simple reason that its clay-like rock formations are **funny**. The man who first noticed them, in the 1940s, called it Mushroom Valley, but "goblin" is as good a name as any. In the 1999 movie *Galaxy Quest*, a sci-fi spoof, Goblin Valley doubles believably as an alien planet, and its rocks come to life in a fabulous computer-generated sequence.

To reach the park, branch west from Hwy-24 near mile post 137 – which is half a mile north of the dirt road that leads to the **Horseshoe Canyon** subsection of Canyonlands National Park; see p.504 – and drive for five miles along Temple Mountain Road, then turn south onto a seven-mile paved spur road. Past the entrance kiosk ($5 day-use fee, open 24 hours; ☎435/564-3633), the road ends beside a sheltered overlook, poised above a slim valley whose sandy floor is completely devoid of vegetation. It's filled instead with parallel fins of pale Entrada sandstone, each topped by a ridge that's indented with weird eroded figures. Some hoodoos also stand alone, while larger buttes and columns loom around the periphery.

A couple of formal trails lead down into the valley, but no one bothers to follow them, preferring to slither at random from one misshapen masterpiece to the next. Once you're on the valley floor, a typical monster in the maze will rise a few feet over your head; some really do look like goblins, complete with eyes and ears.

Away from the main valley, but still engulfed by stunted sandstone sprites, the park has a well-equipped **campground** with running water, toilets and showers, open year-round ($14; reservations on ☎1-800/322-3770).

The San Rafael Swell

The **San Rafael Swell**, fronted by the "reef" that soars immediately northwest of Goblin Valley, is one of southern Utah's least known but most tantalizing wilderness areas. With so many named, mapped and tamed parklands available to explore in the region, for such instant and abundant rewards, few out-of-state visitors have time to add this difficult, mountainous terrain to their itineraries. A glimpse of it from I-70, as the interstate plunges east down its craggy foothills toward Green River, usually has to suffice.

In the past, the main deterrent to casual sightseeing was that most of the swell was only safely accessible in a 4WD vehicle – hence its popularity with fans of off-road vehicles (ORVs). Now Emery County has upgraded a significant number of dirt roads – quite possibly in order to forestall any further attempt to give the region official wilderness protection (in 2002 Utah Governor Mike Leavitt asked President Bush to consider designating a 620,000-acre San Rafael National Monument, but county voters rejected the notion in a nonbinding referendum). In the meanwhile, local tourist authorities have produced lavish color booklets and maps detailing possible driving tours. Assuming that you're driving an ordinary two-wheel-drive vehicle, it's still essential to enquire locally, ideally at the Green River visitor center or Goblin Valley, before attempting to explore on your own. Conditions vary month to month; many roads become impassable every winter, and are only fit for conventional use in early summer, when the damage wrought during the preceding harsh winter has been repaired.

A couple of highlights are detailed below; others, for which you're more likely to need 4WD, include **Little Wild Horse Canyon**, a slot canyon that cuts into the reef roughly seven sandy miles west of Goblin Valley, and the swell's highest point, the **San Rafael Knob**, a four-hour round-trip hike from the end of Copper Globe Road, which heads south from I-70 at exit 114.

Black Dragon Canyon

No part of the San Rafael Swell is easier to see than spectacular **Black Dragon Canyon**, which lies immediately north of I-70 three miles west of Hwy-24, and a total of seventeen miles west of Green River. You can only approach it from the interstate's westbound lane. Pull directly off the highway just past milepost 147, and go through the gate, closing it behind you. Drive straight ahead for a mile on a dirt road, ignoring a possible west turn, then follow the sign west, and park when you feel the road surface deteriorate. From there, a short walk leads into the towering, golden-walled canyon itself. The prime goal here is a group of dramatic Barrier Canyon-style **pictographs** (see p.505), on the north side around a quarter-mile along. If that's all you have time for, you can easily be back on the interstate within an hour of leaving it.

Alternatively, with a good map, it's possible to make a full day of it by hiking the full length of the canyon, which is barely two miles long, then climbing north over a pass and back down again to meet the San Rafael River, which will lead you back to where you left your car. That demanding fifteen-mile loop will take at least seven hours to complete.

Heart of Sinbad Road

The 24-mile **Heart of Sinbad Road** runs from the end of Temple Mountain Road – the spur road off Hwy-24 that leads to Goblin Valley (see opposite) – up to exit 131 off I-70, 33 miles west of Green River. Although it's unpaved, it's usually good enough for ordinary vehicles, and it provides access to many remote and fascinating areas of the San Rafael Swell. There's no room here to describe them all; pick up a brochure in Green River and choose for yourself.

Green River

Hwy-24 joins I-70 44 miles north of Hanksville, just as the interstate completes a dramatic descent from the uplands of the San Rafael Swell to slope gently east through a landscape of soaring buttes. Within a few miles, a ribbon of green vegetation becomes visible ahead, cutting through the desert at the bottom of a long broad valley – the line of the **Green River**. To the north stand the forbidding **Uintah Mountains**, while to the south the stream burrows into a labyrinth of twisting canyons, so this is the best place to ford the river for hundreds of miles.

The town of **GREEN RIVER** has long straddled crucial cross-country routes. For east–west travelers, it remains the major way-station between Colorado and Utah, while river-runners from John Wesley Powell onwards have launched themselves south from here toward the Colorado. The first bridge was built to serve the Denver & Rio Grande Railroad in 1883.

While Green River is a welcome oasis, however – fertile enough to be considered the "melon-growing capital of east Utah" – it still amounts to little more than a strip of motels, gas stations, and fast-food outlets. Given a sensible reluctance to erect permanent structures too close to the river, there's a gap where you might expect downtown to be; most of the built-up strip lies to the west.

The east bank of the river, however, is noteworthy as the site of the modern and very well laid-out **John Wesley Powell River History Museum**, at 885 E Main St (April–Oct daily 8am–8pm, Nov–March Tues–Sat 9am–4pm; $2; Ⓦwww.jwprhm.com). This recounts the epic journeys of the Canyonlands region's first true explorer, whose second voyage started at Green River on May 22, 1871. Powell made that trip partly because he lost the notes from his first, so the second time around he ensured that his every movement was fully recorded, in photos that now make marvellously evocative viewing. A twenty-minute multimedia show and several rooms of exhibits cover developments in river navigation since then, ranging through several turn-of-the-century steamers – none managed more than a handful of voyages – up to the army-surplus rubber inflatables that triggered the postwar boom in whitewater rafting. Spare a moment to glance out of the panoramic windows, and you'll see that the river here is not green at all, but a dark muddy brown.

South of Main Street, sandwiched between the river's west bank, the railroad tracks, and Green River Boulevard, a cluster of fine old cottonwoods marks the attractive waterfront **Green River State Park**. This makes a good spot to break your journey with a picnic, and also holds the area's nicest **campground** (day use $5, camping $14; Ⓣ435/564-3633; for summer reservations, costing $5 extra, call Ⓣ1-800/322-3770).

Arrival and information

The Powell museum at 885 E Main St doubles as Green River's friendly **visitor center** (hours as above; Ⓣ435/564-3526 or 1-800/635-6622, Ⓦwww.greenriver-utah.com), which can advise you on driving local backcountry roads. Amtrak's *California Zephyr* calls at the train station at 250 S Broadway daily, heading east toward Denver at 8.19am and west toward Salt Lake City at 5.59pm, while Greyhound **buses** between Denver and points west stop at the *Rodeway Inn*, 525 E Main St.

Companies running **rafting trips** from Green River include Moki Mac River Expeditions (Ⓣ435/564-3361 or 1-800/284-7280; Ⓦwww.mokimac.com) and Holiday Expeditions (Ⓣ801/564-3273 or 1-800/624-6323; Ⓦwww.bikeraft.com). Every Memorial Day, hundreds of boats set out on weekend-long convoy trips that cruise down to the Colorado confluence and then chug back upriver to Moab.

Accommodation

Although Green River is not much of a destination in its own right, it has around five hundred **motel** rooms. They tend to fill by early evening in summer, partly with the overspill from Moab and partly with long-distance interstate travelers. The best camping in town is at Green River State Park (see above).

Best Western River Terrace 880 E Main St Ⓣ435/564-3401 or 1-800/780-7234, Ⓦwww.bestwestern.com. High-quality option, often filled by tour groups, with a pool, river views, and adjacent restaurant. Winter ❹, summer ❺

Book Cliff Lodge 395 E Main St Ⓣ435/564-3406 or 1-800/493-4699, Ⓦwww.bookclifflodge.com. Low, sprawling complex, set back from the highway west of the river, and holding 100 basic motel rooms, souvenir stores,

a gas station, and a crazy golf course. Winter ❷, summer ❹

Holiday Inn Express 963 E Main St Ⓣ435/564-4439 or 1-800/465-4329, Ⓦwww.ichotelsgroup.com. Crisp, clean chain motel, next door to the museum and visitor center, with an indoor pool, laundry, and free breakfast. ❹

Super 8 1248 E Main St Ⓣ435/564-8888 or 1-800/800-8000, www.super8.com. Reliable, budget motel, perched on a slight elevation at the east end of town. Winter ❷, summer ❹

Until **John Wesley Powell** led the first expedition to float down the full length of the Green and Colorado rivers, the Colorado Plateau was a vast blank at the heart of maps of the American West. No one knew how the mountains and waterways of the region fitted together, or whether falls larger than Niagara might prevent river traffic completely.

Powell was born in Ohio in 1834, the son of a traveling preacher, and spent his youth making solo forays along the Ohio, Mississippi, and Illinois rivers. He lost his right arm fighting for the Union at Shiloh, where he formed a lasting friendship with the future president Ulysses Grant. Once the Civil War was over, the veteran major headed west, and decided to explore the Colorado Plateau at his own expense.

Powell, his brother Walter, and eight frontier types who volunteered to serve as an unpaid crew set off from Green River, Wyoming, on **May 24, 1869**. They had four flat-bottomed wooden boats, purpose-built in Chicago; Powell was lashed to an upright wooden chair in the leading vessel. Not long after entering the Uintah Mountains, by way of **Flaming Gorge**, they were reduced to three boats, when one was smashed to smithereens in Lodore Canyon. They then whisked through Green River, Utah, and plunged into the desert, encountering their biggest challenge so far in the shape of **Cataract Canyon**, soon after the Green met the Grand to form the Colorado. Wherever possible, they carried their boats around the fiercest rapids, and with prodigious energy Powell repeatedly climbed out of the canyon to get his bearings. After several terrifying days, they burst out of the gorge, for an idyllic period of respite in **Glen Canyon**.

Three members of the party became demoralized in the depths of the **Grand Canyon**, when the blackness of the walls to either side seemed to presage further ferocious rapids ahead. They decided to hike their way out, only to be murdered mysteriously – some say by suspicious Mormons, others by Shivwits Indians. Powell, however, made it through the remainder of the canyon with unexpected ease; it took him merely one more day before he arrived at the **Grand Wash Cliffs**, at the confluence of the Colorado and Virgin rivers (now beneath Lake Mead) on August 30. Two of his crew continued all the way to the Pacific, but Powell and his brother left the river, after almost a hundred days afloat.

Now a national celebrity, Powell returned for a better-funded and much more leisurely trip two years later. Starting this time from Green River, Utah, he documented his experiences in much greater detail, and used them as the basis of a bestselling book. During the voyage, he left the canyon at every opportunity, and even returned to Washington DC for the winter, while his crew holed up in Kanab.

In later years, Powell became director of the Smithsonian Institution's **Bureau of Ethnology** in Washington, DC, and of the **US Geologic Survey**. His forceful opinions as to how the federal government should administer the limited resources of the West – and especially its water – are now regarded as prophetic. Refusing to accept the then-current adage that "rain follows the plow," he argued that state boundaries should be drawn along natural watersheds, to prevent water issues from bedeviling the region's political future. It was his advocacy of federally funded water projects that led the bureaucrats to name **Lake Powell** in his honor, but one can't help imagining that Powell himself would prefer Glen Canyon as it was in the beginning.

Eating

As well as the usual fast-food places and a couple of local cafés, a handful of Green River's motels have their own restaurants.

The Green River

But for political shenanigans in the 1920s, the **Green River** might rank among the most famous rivers in the world. It starts by flowing north to loop around the Wind River Mountains of central Wyoming, then heads south into Utah, briefly ducks into the northwest corner of Colorado, and then crosses Utah to meet the Colorado River after a 730-mile journey.

Until 1859, when Captain J. N. Mancomb discovered the confluence deep in the heart of the canyonlands, no one knew that the Green River flowed into the Colorado, although the Green had first been identified by Fray Alonzo de Posada in 1686 as the boundary between the territories of the Ute and the Comanche. The **Colorado River** had been named by the Spanish founder of New Mexico, Juan de Oñate, in 1606, while French trappers in what's now Colorado state stumbled across what they named the **Grand River** perhaps a century later.

The trouble is, at the confluence the Colorado has flowed a mere 430 miles from the Rockies of central Colorado. As geographical convention dictates that the principal course of a river is its longest, the Green River should be regarded as the main course of the Colorado River, and their entire combined course should bear the same name. Either the Green should become the Colorado, or the Colorado below the confluence should become the Green – in which case the Grand Canyon should arguably be called the Green Canyon, which doesn't bear thinking about.

The news that the "Colorado River" did not originate in Colorado, as had always been assumed, mortified Colorado's legislators. When apportioning its waters became a major issue in the 1920s (see p.482), they simply defied convention and renamed the Grand the Colorado, which fortunately dovetailed with a vote in conservative Utah against changing the name of the Green River.

Ben's Cafe 115 E Main St ☏ 435/564-3352. Friendly if grungy diner toward the west end of town, where almost nothing on the menu costs over $10. Open daily for all meals.

Green River Coffee Co 22 S Broadway ☏ 435/564-3411. Lively local coffee bar, just south of the main drag a mile or so west of the river. Mon–Thurs 6am–2pm, Fri–Sun 6am–5pm.

Tamarisk Restaurant 870 E Main St ☏ 435/564-8109. Brisk, busy restaurant, overlooking the river opposite the museum; the menu is wide-ranging and cheap, with most full dinners costing under $10, but the salad bar is atrocious. Open daily for breakfast, lunch, and dinner.

West Winds Restaurant 545 E Main St ☏ 435/564-8240. A 24-hour licensed diner, near the river's west bank, where breakfast is available non-stop, and burgers, sandwiches, steaks, and Mexican dishes are served until 2am.

Canyonlands National Park

CANYONLANDS NATIONAL PARK, the largest and most magnificent of Utah's national parks, is as hard to define as it is to map. Its closest equivalent, the Grand Canyon, is simply an almighty crack in an otherwise relatively flat plain; the Canyonlands area is a bewildering tangle of canyons, plateaus, fissures, and faults, scattered with buttes and monoliths, pierced by arches and caverns, and penetrated only by a paltry handful of dead-end roads.

The 527 square miles of the park are just the core of a much larger wilderness that stretches to the horizon in every direction. To nineteenth-century explorers, this was the epitome of useless desolation; only since uranium prospectors blazed crude trails across the trackless wastes in the 1950s has it become at all widely known. Even after Canyonlands park was created in 1964, it took a couple of decades before tourists arrived in appreciable numbers.

Canyonlands focuses upon the Y-shaped confluence of the Green and Colorado rivers, buried deep in the desert forty miles southwest of Moab. There's only one spot from which you can see the rivers meet, however, and that's a five-mile hike from the nearest road. With no way to get down to the rivers, let alone cross them, the park therefore splits into three major sections. The **Needles**, east of the Colorado, is a red-rock wonderland of sandstone pinnacles and hidden meadows that's a favorite with hardy hikers and 4WD enthusiasts, while the **Maze**, west of both the Colorado and the Green, is a virtually inaccessible labyrinth of tortuous, waterless canyons that presents a stiff challenge even to expert climbers and backpackers. In the wedge of the "Y" between the two, the high, dry mesa of the **Island In The Sky** commands astonishing views across the whole park and beyond, to be seen from several overlooks that can easily be toured by car. Getting from any one of these sections to the others involves a drive of at least a hundred miles. Both the Needles and the Island In The Sky are reached via long approach roads that leave US-191 north and south of Moab respectively; the Maze is an endless jolting ride on dirt tracks from either Hwy-24 or the town of Green River.

The **rivers** themselves count as Canyonlands' fourth major component. A **rafting** expedition from Moab, with the operators detailed on p.524, is the best way to experience the eerie stillness of the deep canyons, at once exhilarating and supremely restful. However, since there's no way out before Lake Powell, you'll need to set aside several days, and several hundred dollars – and be prepared to face the awesome power of **Cataract Canyon**, just beyond the

Canyonlands fees and permits

For full information on Canyonlands National Park, see the official website at ⓦwww.nps.gov/cany. The **entry fee** of $10 per vehicle, $5 for cyclists or hikers, is valid for seven days in all sections of the park. All the usual passes (see p.45) are sold and accepted.

Only limited numbers of visitors are allowed to spend a night or more in the backcountry, and all such groups are required to have **permits**. **Backpacking** permits, covering a maximum party of seven persons in the Needles and Island In The Sky districts, or five persons in the Maze, cost $15. Permits for **four-wheel-drive** or **mountain biking** expeditions that involve backcountry camping, issued for groups of up to three vehicles with a total of fifteen people in the Island In The Sky, ten in the Needles, or nine in the Maze, are $30. **Day-use** permits, costing $5, are also required for bikes and 4WD vehicles that enter Horse or Lavender canyons in the Needles district.

Though not compulsory, **reservations** are essential for the most popular areas, especially in the peak seasons of spring and fall. They must be purchased at least two weeks in advance, and are issued for dates throughout each calendar year from the second Monday of July in the previous year. Permits must be picked up in person – with every member of the group present – from the appropriate park visitor center, at least one hour before it closes.

For application forms and full details of the park's complex regulations, visit or write to the **National Park Service Reservations Office**, 2282 S West Resource Blvd, Moab UT 84532-8000 (fax ⓕ435/259-4285); call ⓣ435/259-4351 (Mon–Fri 8am–4pm); contact a park visitor center; or see the website above.

The geology of Canyonlands

In a land with so little water, the sheer *effort* that went into creating the splendor of Canyonlands is almost impossible to conceive. As you look out from the park's highest point, atop the Island in the Sky, the cliffs drop away a thousand feet, with the rivers a thousand feet below that. For a hundred miles to the south, successive plateaus, benches, and tablelands diminish into the distance, studded with the occasional butte. And yet twelve million years ago, this entire landscape was one vast plain, level with where you're standing. Bit by bit, at the rate of two inches every thousand years, the topsoil has crumbled to silt and been carried away by the rivers. Most of it was deposited at the edge of the Pacific, but these days it's gradually filling up Lake Powell instead.

Canyonlands was not literally carved by the rivers, however. Both the Green and the Colorado began life as gentle streams that ran across the plains. In the last twelve million years, as the Colorado Plateau pushed its way up, they have remained in their original courses, ever more deeply entrenched into the earth. Meanwhile, ice produced in a ceaseless cycle of freezes and thaws has chiseled away at the rocks that surround them, tumbling boulders into the water to be swept away.

Canyonlands is unique in that it rests on a mile-thick bed of **salt**, which was deposited on the bottom of an ancient sea three hundred million years ago and now fills the **Paradox Basin**. That salt was covered by subsequent layers of sediment, themselves interspersed with further deposits of salt. Under the pressure of thousands of feet of harder rock, the salt layers are squeezed like toothpaste until they flow far underground, then bubble up toward the surface. As they do so, they push up fins and spurs of rock that crack and split to create phenomena such as the Needles, or they may hit ground water and dissolve, leaving gaping caverns behind.

confluence, which contains some of the most intense whitewater rapids in the US.

Finally, there's one last subsection of the park: **Horseshoe Canyon** in the west, which was added in 1971 to preserve the Southwest's finest collection of ancient **rock art**.

Canyonlands is not a place that lends itself to a short visit. With no lodging and little camping in the park, and no loop road to whisk you through it, it takes a full day to have even a cursory look at a single segment. If you're among the many visitors who find the conditions too grueling to spend much time out of your car – summer temperatures regularly exceed 100°F, and most trails have no water and little shade – then the Island In The Sky is the most immediately rewarding option. On the other hand, if you fancy a long day-hike you'd do better to set off into the Needles.

The largest selection of **motels** near Canyonlands is in Moab (see p.521), while park **campgrounds** are detailed on p.502, 503, 509 and p.510. A full list of operators who run **tours** into the Canyonlands backcountry appears on p.524.

The Island In The Sky

It's not obvious from most maps, but like the Colorado River confluence over which it looms, the mesa known as the **Island In The Sky** is itself shaped like a "Y." After a steady climb of around 25 miles, **Hwy-313**, which heads southwest from US-191 eight miles north of Moab, enters the park across the slender **Neck** that forms the right-hand fork of the Y. It then branches to the

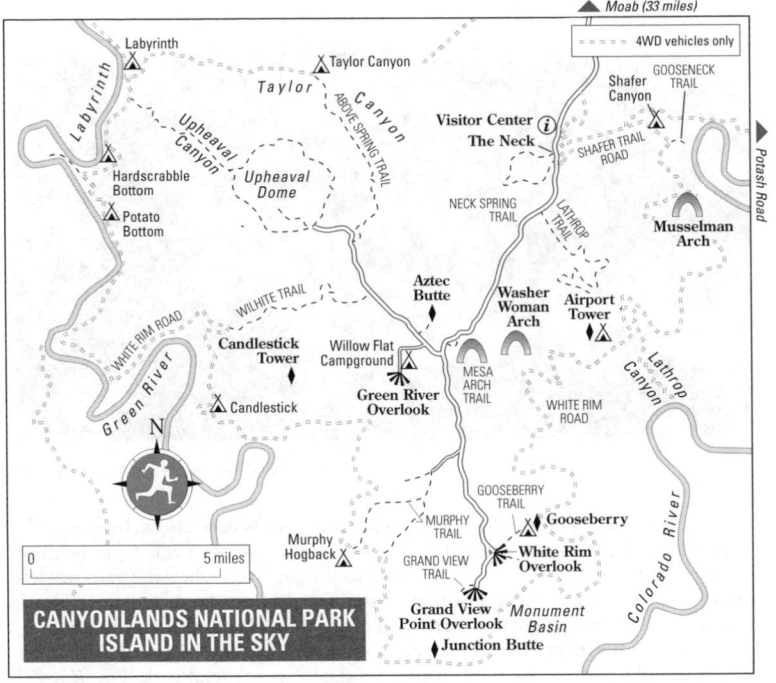

CANYONLANDS NATIONAL PARK ISLAND IN THE SKY

northwest, to run as far as the crater of **Upheaval Dome**, and to the south, where it ends at the overwhelming **Grand View Point**.

Most visitors to the Island In The Sky content themselves with driving from one overlook to the next. Some also walk one or two of the short, easy trails that cross its thin capping of Kayenta sandstone, to gaze over the brink of the sheer Wingate cliffs that hold it up. It is also possible, however – either in a sturdy 4WD vehicle, or by some very strenuous hiking – to make your way down to the pale plateau of the **White Rim**, prominent a thousand feet below.

Note that whatever certain inaccurate maps may suggest, ordinary vehicles **cannot** reach the Island In The Sky from Moab by way of Hwy-279, the Potash Road.

Dead Horse Point State Park

Shortly before you reach the national-park boundary, twenty miles in from US-191, a turning to the east leads in four miles to the smaller but equally breathtaking **Dead Horse Point State Park**. This miniature version of the Island In The Sky stands at the tip of another narrow mesa, poised two thousand feet above a stupendous "gooseneck" loop in the Colorado. Off to the east, the turquoise evaporation ponds of Moab's potash plant (see p.526) make a garish contrast with the red rocks, while the Anticline Overlook (see p.527) stands guard above the far side of Meander Canyon.

Dead Horse Point's **visitor center**, two miles short of the main overlook, incorporates a **Desert Museum** of human and natural history (daily: summer 8am–6pm; winter 8am–5pm; ☏435/259-2614). Displays here explain the park's

△ Colorado River from Dead Horse Point State Park

name: nineteenth-century cowboys used the mesa as a natural corral, herding wild horses behind the piñon fence that blocked its ninety-foot neck. One band of horses is said to have been too scared to cross the gap even when the gate was left open, and perished of thirst. For that matter, Dead Horse Point remains a death trap for unwary pet **dogs**; the current record is three drop-offs in a month.

Day-use of the park costs $7 – and remember that any National Parks pass you may hold will not be valid, as this is a state not a federal park. The *Kayenta* **campground** ($14; reservations mid-March to mid-Oct only, costing $5 extra, on ☎1-800/322-3770) makes an excellent alternative if there's no room in Canyonlands, though it doesn't offer showers.

Island In The Sky Visitor Center

A couple of miles south of the turnoff to Dead Horse Point, and a mile or so in from the entrance to Canyonlands National Park, the modern **visitor center** for the Island In The Sky district stands to the right of the highway (daily: mid-March to late Oct 8am–6pm, late Oct to mid-March 8am–4.30pm; ☎435/259-4712, ⓦwww.nps.gov/cany/island). Rangers have full details on road and trail conditions as well as campsite availability.

Mesa Arch Trail

Four miles past the visitor center, just short of the fork in the road, the **Mesa Arch Trail** is the Island In The Sky's best short hike. It's more of a walkway than a trail really, cemented for its full length and equipped with occasional stairways. During a mile-long loop around the mesa-top hillocks, it runs right to the rim of the abyss, where long, shallow **Mesa Arch** frames an extraordinary view of the La Sal Mountains, 35 miles northeast. Admiring Washer Woman Arch and Monster Tower, closer at hand, it would be easy to stumble right through the gap – there's no barrier.

Grand View Point Overlook

Grand View Point Overlook, at the southern end of the road, is the Island In The Sky's definitive vantage point, and a real agoraphobe's nightmare. It commands a hundred-mile prospect of layer upon layer of naked sandstone, here stacked thousands of feet high, there fractured into bottomless canyons.

The most conspicuous feature is the plateau formed by the **White Rim** layer, a thousand feet below, whose faint smattering of grass is crisscrossed by abandoned mining trails and ends at the White Rim itself. That peters out in the mass of white-capped red-rock pillars known as **Monument Basin**, where the **Totem Pole** may be 305ft tall but looks the size of a pencil. Neither river can be seen; the Colorado River is tucked out of sight another thousand feet down, while the equivalent canyon of the Green River is hidden by the twin buttes to the west. Everything is, however, mirrored by an identical chaos on the far side, rising toward the snow-capped peaks of the **Abajo Mountains**, forty miles south.

A stroll along the **Grand View Trail**, a two-mile roundtrip that heads across a lovely level shelf just below and to the right of the overlook, enables you to contemplate the whole jigsaw puzzle from countless additional angles. Every now and then, you may spot the silhouette of the Needles, far to the south.

By the middle of each day, the entire landscape takes on a hazy pallor; for the best **photographs**, you'd ideally be at the national-park overlooks early in the morning, and Dead Horse Point at sunset.

Green River Overlook and Willow Flat campground

A couple of hundred yards north of the fork in the park road, a paved 1.2-mile spur road leads to the **Green River Overlook**, which is itself freshly paved and railed. The clearer, flatter expanse of the White Rim that spreads below is pierced by the green-trimmed meandering course of the river itself, as it flows through placid **Stillwater Canyon**. At this very spot, in the Biblical epic *The Greatest Story Ever Told*, Max von Sydow (aka Jesus) delivered the Sermon on the Mount to an audience of Moab Rotarians bedecked in false beards and tea towels.

The Island In The Sky's only developed **campground**, the waterless, twelve-site, first-come first-served *Willow Flat* ($5), is just back from the overlook. Contact the visitor center for current availability (see opposite).

Upheaval Dome

The northern end of the park road, five miles up from the fork, comes at the geological oddity of **Upheaval Dome**. This jagged 1500ft-deep crater is a highlight of park air tours (see p.525), but from close up, at the end of the steep ten-minute climb from the parking lot, it's something of a disappointment. Elaborate theories that explained the prongs of pale stone bursting from its darkest depths as the product of undulating subterranean salt have recently been abandoned in favor of the simpler notion of a sixty-million-year-old **meteor strike**.

Over the Edge: the White Rim Road

The reason the Island In The Sky is accessible at all, and that crude dirt tracks strike off into the wilderness almost everywhere you look, is that this region was a prime target for the freelance **uranium prospectors** of the 1950s (see p.518). They knew that uranium is often found in the gray-green rocks of the **Chinle formation**, which here forms the talus slopes found at the bottom of the Wingate-sandstone cliffs, not far above the White Rim.

The rough-and-ready hundred-mile **White Rim Road**, scraped out by would-be miners at the base of the cliffs, is now most often explored on three- or four-day **4WD expeditions**, with overnight stops at various primitive campgrounds en route (by permit only; see p.499). Only the hair-raising **Shafer Trail Road**, which drops from just south of the visitor center, connects the mesa-top with the White Rim; otherwise drivers join the White Rim Road by means of the **Potash Road** from Moab (see p.523), or along **Mineral Bottom Road**, which runs west from Hwy-313 a couple of miles north of the Dead Horse Point turnoff. None of these routes should be attempted in ordinary vehicles.

Hikers can, however, clamber between the Island In The Sky and the White Rim along various trails. All are too demanding for a round-trip day-hike down to the White Rim – let alone to either river – to be a good idea. Register with the Park Service before you set off on a multi-day trip. Options include the **Lathrop Trail**, an utterly exhausting nine-mile route that makes it all the way to the Colorado, passing close to abandoned but potentially toxic uranium mines; the **Upheaval Canyon Trail**, which drops down to the Green River from the far side of Upheaval Dome; and the **Shafer Trail Road** itself.

Horseshoe Canyon

Remote **Horseshoe Canyon**, a detached chunk of Canyonlands National Park located well northwest of its main body, is home to the most extraordinary **rock art** to be found anywhere in North America. No one now knows the meaning of the mysterious, haunting figures that line the sandstone walls of the **Great Gallery**; although to the modern eye they suggest an astonishing sophistication, they are among the **oldest** such images to survive.

Even if you're not a rock-art enthusiast, the six-mile round-trip **hike** down to the gallery – there's no road access – is one of Utah's most beautiful. With either forty miles of dirt road to negotiate south of Green River, or 32 miles southeast from Hwy-24, before the trail even starts, few visitors come this way, so you may well get the gorgeous red-rock canyon, rustling with wildlife, to yourself.

The San Rafael Desert: the road to Horseshoe Canyon and the Maze

Unless the weather has been dreadful – check at the Green River visitor center (see p.496) for current conditions – ordinary vehicles should have no problem driving to Horseshoe Canyon. Of the two alternative routes, the one that starts from **Green River** is more convenient if you want to sleep in a motel the night before, but it's marginally more likely to be impassable. Assuming it's clear, follow signs for the airport from the center of town until you cross the railroad tracks. Once the surface has turned to gravel, fork left at a BLM sign pointing toward the San Rafael River.

After an initial flat section, the road pushes through painted-desert badlands formed by the fossil-rich Morrison Formation, and then winds down to a glorious panorama of Monument Valley-style buttes. It crosses the **San Rafael River** on a rickety wooden bridge after nineteen miles, then climbs again to offer views that stretch to the Henry Mountains in the west and the La Sals in the east.

Just over forty miles south of Green River, beyond **Antelope Valley** – home to one of Utah's few surviving herds of pronghorn antelope – an easily missed spur road branches off to the east. The **Horseshoe Canyon trailhead** is at its far end, at the edge of the plateau two miles along.

As the road veers west, a junction 5.5 miles past the Horseshoe Canyon turnoff marks the start of the 21-mile drive south to **Hans Flat Ranger Station**, the main point of access for the Maze (see p.506). Keep going west, and a total of 32 miles from Horseshoe Canyon – at best, around an hour's driving – you'll finally meet **Hwy-24**, just south of Goblin Valley (see p.494). This last stretch crosses Sweetwater Reef before dropping into the **San Rafael Desert**, where it insinuates itself between two impressive buttes known as Little Flat Top and Big Flat Top.

Note that if you're heading east from Capitol Reef, it's much quicker to reverse the route described above; just be sure you have enough gas.

The hike to the canyon

Between April and October, rangers lead six-hour **guided hikes** into Horseshoe Canyon, starting at 9am on Sat & Sun; call ☏435/259-2652 to check.

The rock art of Horseshoe Canyon

At the time it was first studied, Horseshoe Canyon was called **Barrier Canyon**, and that name still defines the style of art for which it's famous. Such art is characterized by anthropomorphic figures, roughly life-sized but tending to be weirdly elongated, and often lacking both arms and legs. Those that have eyes have large round ones, or simply empty sockets, and many seem draped in stylized robes; for most visitors to this lonely desert backwater, the cumulative effect is to suggest ghosts or spirits from another, different time.

While spear points found in Horseshoe Canyon date back as much as twelve thousand years, archeologists believe that the pictographs were produced by people of the **Archaic** culture, which flourished between 7500 BC and 500 AD. At the start of that period, the climate was much wetter, and the canyon held lakes, ponds, and plentiful game. When conditions dried out, it was briefly abandoned, but then reoccupied.

Life was now far more difficult, and **shamanistic rituals** were increasingly used in the attempt to ensure successful hunting. These involved the creation first of clay statuettes, from 5000 BC onwards, and later of figurines made out of split willow-twigs, which have been found here and in the Grand Canyon (see p.366). Many represent what seem to be deities or shamans as well as animals; and the pictographs of the Great Gallery are thought to depict those same entities.

As for **technique**, the Great Gallery is very literally rock art. To produce the paint, different colored rocks were ground up, dissolved in water, and bonded with saliva produced by chewing seeds. The red is hematite, heavy with rust; the white is gypsum or chalk; even the blue comes from a local stratum. Some figures were produced with brushes, others by blowing or flicking paint at a stencil. Archeologists have recently discovered that the digital manipulation of photographs of the images, using computer programs like Photoshop, enables them not only to reveal faded colors but even discern different layers, and thus see how specific figures were changed and redrawn over the centuries.

Experts estimate the gallery to be anything from 1600 to 6000 years old. Carbon-dating tests that suggested extreme antiquity have recently been discounted, but certain sites do seem to have been rendered inaccessible by rockfalls that occurred a very long time ago indeed. All that's certain is that none dates from later than 400 AD, when the Archaic people acquired the bow and arrow – not shown in any of the Great Gallery images – and began to transform into the **Fremont** culture. Fremont art, as seen elsewhere in Utah as well as here in Horseshoe Canyon, has its own very distinct style.

Otherwise, it's easy enough to make the trek on your own, but be sure to allow at least five hours for the round-trip; start early, or sit out the midday sun down in the canyon.

The route picks its way down from the trailhead described above, marked by cairns as it crosses patches of deep sand alternating with slickrock. Once you reach the bottom, which takes perhaps half an hour, follow the dry sandy wash to your right. Stay initially on the left bank of the wash, and after something under ten minutes you should spot the first rock-art site, the **High Gallery**, above the talus on the left wall of the canyon. It's not easy to see detail here, though, so you'll soon be ready to press on.

All the remaining sites are across the wash on the right wall. The first, the **Horseshoe Shelter**, nestles beneath an overhanging cliff a hundred yards further on. When Harvard archeologists excavated this site in 1930, it held several rooms; all that remains is a vivid band of **pictographs** in the palest stratum of the rock, which was above the roofs of the shelters and is thus now out of reach. The animals, squiggles, and triangular figures – many with strange protuberances on their heads – date from the Fremont era, but the scattering of ghostly footless figures are in the earlier Barrier Canyon style.

Another twenty minutes' walk on, beyond several twists and turns in the canyon walls, it's well worth climbing up into a massive pale sandstone alcove where a red-and-white band of rock holds another small collection of pictographs.

Eventually, after twenty minutes more, you round the final bend to be confronted by the **Great Gallery**, suddenly apparent beneath a lesser overhang. It's a breathtaking moment. Framed between the cottonwoods, a long row of dark, hollow-eyed, other-worldly entities stands stark against the pale rock. Though the details grow clearer the closer you get, somehow a sense of vast, alien distance remains.

Apart from a couple of well-shaded stone benches, there are no facilities for visitors. Look out, however, for two army-issue metal boxes, marked PLEASE OPEN ME: one holds a set of powerful binoculars, the other copies of relevant academic papers.

No **camping** is permitted in Horseshoe Canyon itself, but there's a basic site beside the parking lot at the trailhead.

The Maze

The name of Canyonlands' **Maze** district is no exaggeration. This brainteaser of convoluted canyons and barren desert washes, west of the Green and Colorado rivers, must be the least explored region of the United States. If you're determined to get away from it all, the Maze is the place for you; getting back to it all when you've finished is more of a problem.

Somewhere in the heart of the Maze is the legendary **Robbers Roost**, a canyon fastness used as a hideout by nineteenth-century cattle rustlers and bandits such as **Butch Cassidy** and his Wild Bunch. They'd escape the long arm of the law by riding the Outlaw Trail up from the Green River near Mineral Bottom; lacking their familiarity with the terrain, pursuing posses had no choice but to turn back defeated. No roads entered the region until uranium prospectors bulldozed their way in during the 1950s.

Even today, you'll need a high-clearance 4WD vehicle to get any further than **Hans Flat Ranger Station**, also referred to as the **Maze Visitor Center** (daily 8am–4.30pm; ☎435/259-2652, ⓦwww.nps.gov/cany/maze), which stands 21 miles south of the road through the San Rafael Desert to Horseshoe Canyon, described on p.504. That makes it 46 miles east of Hwy-24 and 66 miles south of Green River. An even worse sixty-mile dirt track also runs south, to connect it with Hite on Lake Powell. Technically the ranger station is in Glen Canyon National Recreation Area, but it's the main source of information for hikers and drivers setting off into the Maze.

The **jeep roads** beyond Hans Flat take another twenty or thirty miles to jostle and switchback into the actual Maze. There are two main routes in, one ending at the **Maze Overlook**, and the other at **Doll House Butte**, which marks the far end of the **Land of Standing Rocks**, above the west bank of Cataract Canyon and straight across from the Needles.

Having come this far, most backpackers launch themselves into the wilderness for days or weeks at a time. There are few formal trails, but favored destinations include **Pictograph Canyon**, not far beneath the Maze Overlook, where Barrier Canyon-style pictographs (see box on p.505) seem to record the moment when the Archaic people first acquired the skills of agriculture. However, unless you're extremely self-sufficient, a workhorse when it comes to carrying vast quantities of water, and a fearless, fully equipped rock-climber, you're never going to see them.

The Needles

Thanks to its intricate tracery of backcountry trails that offer the chance to engage with the landscape as opposed to merely marveling from a distance, the **Needles** district is Canyonlands National Park's most satisfying segment for hikers, bikers, and 4WD drivers. While it has its share of long-range vistas – including the park's only **Confluence Overlook** – the Needles is noted primarily for its namesake thickets of candy-striped **sandstone pillars**. Clustered on scrubby rock outcrops, concealing pockets of incongruous grassland, these intriguing formations can be explored on brief forays or multiday backpacking expeditions.

The **Needles** area is a very long way from civilization, at the far end of the stunning **Hwy-211**, a total of 75 miles from Moab and fifty from Monticello. If you're planning a number of successive day-hikes, it makes sense to camp overnight in the park, so reserve a spot at *Squaw Flat* or in one of the backcountry sites as soon as you know you're coming (see p.499). Note incidentally that, confusingly enough, the **Needles Overlook** is not in the national park at all, but in the BLM's Canyon Rims area; see p.527.

Ordinary mortals, as opposed to obsessive canyoneers, should also be warned that even casual **hiking** in the Needles area may well be the hardest thing you've ever done. Carry a good map and a *lot* of water, stick to the trails, and above all be very careful how far you climb – it's much easier to go up than it is to come down, and you run the risk of getting "rim-rocked."

The road to the Needles: Squaw Flats Scenic Byway

The 35-mile **Hwy-211** – also known as the **Squaw Flats Scenic Byway** – heads west of US-191 forty miles south of Moab. You can't miss the turning; it's marked by a colossal butte immediately opposite, which, if you happen to be hungry, may well seem to resemble a giant brioche.

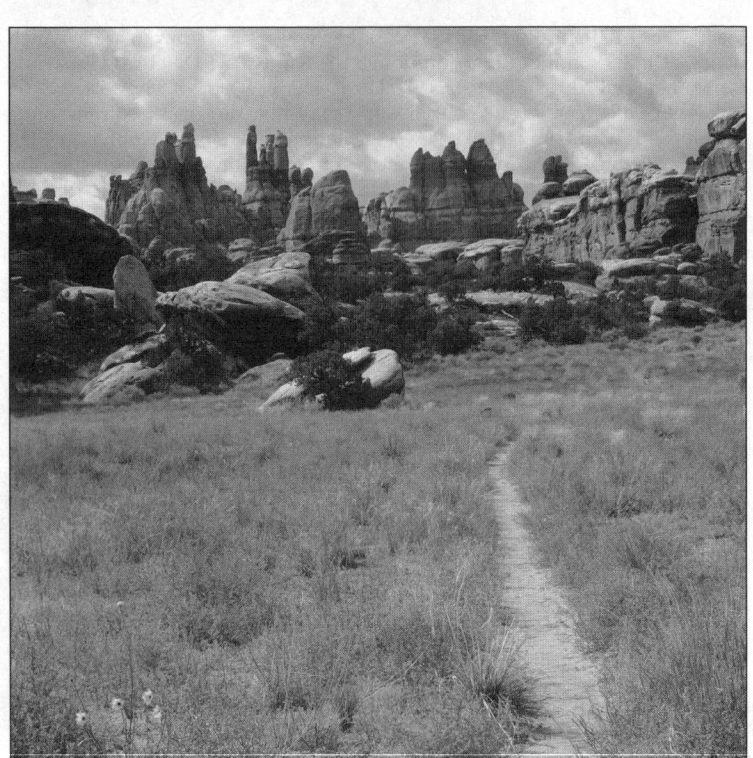

△ Needles along the Chesler Park Loop Trail

As it winds lazily into the park, between cottonwood-lined **Indian Creek** stream and canyon walls of rich red sandstone, and overlooked by the twin castellated **Sixshooter Peaks**, the byway seems to carry you back a century, into the unspoiled Wild West. Much of the route lies through open grazing country, making this one of the few spots in the Southwest where you're still likely to see genuine **cowboys** riding the range. The Dugout Ranch, halfway along, was established in 1885, and later amalgamated with its neighbors to form the Indian Creek Cattle Company, Utah's largest cattle outfit.

Newspaper Rock

Newspaper Rock Recreation Site, next to Hwy-211 twelve miles west of US-191, preserves a panel of black desert varnish that's inscribed, like some prehistoric newspaper, with literally hundreds of **petroglyphs**. Ancient peoples clearly recognized this as a perfect site for creating conspicuous and enduring images, sheltered by a protective rock lintel beneath a hillock at a narrow bend in the valley immediately north of the Abajo Mountains. As well as abstract designs, the images include helmeted human figures, buffalo, and bighorn sheep, plus lots of six-toed footprints and what look like bear pawprints. Some are probably symbols left by clans who performed particular ceremonies here, or simply passed by. With the obvious exception of recent graffiti, it's hard to say when they were executed, but you have to suspect that most are not in fact all that old; nineteenth-century Ute are thought to be responsible for the mounted riders, shown hunting with bows and arrows.

The riverside woods across the road from the rock hold a lovely if basic **campground**, free but waterless. A short way further west, Hwy-211 meets the mountain road from Monticello that's described on p.528.

The Needles Outpost

Up a short spur road just outside the park boundary, the privately owned **Needles Outpost** (March–Nov, daily 8am–7pm; ☏435/979-4007, ⓦwww .canyonlandsneedlesoutpost.com) is a summer-only grocery store and gas station that has its own small **campground** ($15). Showers cost $3 extra, or $7 if you're not staying overnight.

Driving into the Needles

Rangers at the **Needles visitor center**, a mile inside the park (daily: mid-March to late Oct 8am–6pm, late Oct to mid-March 8am–4.30pm; ☏435/259-4711, ⓦwww.nps.gov/cany/needles), can provide up-to-date hiking information, with a handy model of the whole park to make things clearer. They issue 34 **backpacking permits** per night, each for a group of up to seven people; in high season, if you don't have a reservation (see p.499) the chances are none will be available. Day-hikers don't need permits.

Roughly three miles along from the visitor center, a left turning leads to the first-come first-served *Squaw Flat* **campground**, where space is at an absolute premium in spring and fall ($10). Ordinary vehicles can continue beyond the campground, on an uneven dirt road, for three more miles to **Elephant Hill**.

The main park road presses on past the Squaw Flat turnoff for another four miles, ending where the **Big Spring Canyon Overlook** confronts an array of mushroom-shaped hoodoos. Of the short hiking trails along the way, the half-mile **Pothole Point Trail** is an easy stroll to the top of the roadside ridge, while the longer 2.5-mile **Slickrock Trail** provides an enjoyable orientation to the region, following a cairn-marked footpath from one sandstone knoll to the next, each with its own long-distance mountain-and-mesa views.

The Chesler Park Loop Trail

Chesler Park, the high grassy meadow whose stubby sandstone pinnacles gave the Needles its name, makes a great destination for a long day-hike. Simply to reach it requires a six-mile round-trip trek from Elephant Hill, or a ten-mile one from Squaw Flat campground, while looping around the "park" itself adds another five miles. As a result, you should allow seven hours for the complete hike from Elephant Hill, and even longer if you start from Squaw Flat.

As you climb across the cairned stretches of slickrock that rise from both Elephant Hill and Squaw Flat, look north for sweeping views to the Island In The Sky, with the White Rim neatly etched beneath it. The two trails meet half an hour up from Elephant Hill, then dip west to cross the wash that runs through **Elephant Canyon** – it may look dry, but there's usually water flowing far beneath the sand – before the final ascent to Chesler Park.

For the most part, the **Chesler Park Loop Trail** undulates around the edge of the 600-acre clearing, on the slopes below the red-and-white barber-pole Needles. On the eastern flank, however, it runs straight across the lavender-tinted grassland, while in the far southwestern corner it disappears into an extraordinary mini-canyon whose blackened walls are seldom as much as three feet apart. This claustrophobic segment, almost a mile long and known as the **Joint Trail**, is the highlight of the trip. A ledge perched above its eastern end, a 500ft detour off the main trail, provides a superb overview of Chesler Park. Through a gap to the west, the gigantic Doll House Butte (see p.507), across the Colorado River, can also be glimpsed. Note that if you have a 4WD vehicle, you can join the Chesler Park Loop near the Joint Trail, and walk the loop alone as a five-mile hike.

As an alternative to circling Chesler Park, consider following the spur trail that branches south along Elephant Canyon. It takes just over three miles of steady climbing to reach **Druid Arch**, named for its resemblance to the rough-hewn monuments of Stonehenge.

Several more trails can be used to connect Chesler Park and Elephant Canyon with Squaw Flat, including routes through **Squaw Canyon** and the upper reaches of **Big Spring Canyon**. Backcountry **camping** is, however, only allowed at specific sites along the jeep road that runs west and north of Chesler Park, of which the closest to the main trails is at Devils Kitchen Camp – and you'd be lucky to get one of the necessary permits (see p.499).

The Confluence Overlook Trail

According to writer Edward Abbey, the local business community only agreed to the creation of Canyonlands park in 1964 on the understanding that its different parts would be linked by a loop drive, of which the focus would be the **Confluence Overlook**. It was even anticipated that this would be the site of a Junction Dam, which would create an even larger lake than Lake Powell. In the absence of either road or dam, however, the demanding eleven-mile round-trip hike from **Big Spring Canyon Overlook**, which takes a good seven hours, remains the only way to see the spot where the Green River meets the Colorado.

The trail starts with a steep drop down into Big Spring Canyon, then laboriously climbs out again. After twenty exhausting minutes you emerge through a natural portal between two huge nodules to be greeted by long-distance views of the red-rock wilderness ahead – and cool shade closer at hand. A short metal ladder brings you out onto a level plateau, but you're soon descending again into **Elephant Canyon**, at this point several miles north of, and considerably broader than, the segment near Chesler Park (see opposite). Each time you climb back onto the slickrock mesa-top, new views open up, either south to the Needles or north to Junction Butte beneath the Island In The Sky.

Clambering from rock to rock beyond Elephant Canyon, you pass through several lifeless valleys known as **grabens**, from the German for "ditches." Thought to be a mere 55,000 years old, these were created when shifting underground salt beds caused landslides. At times, the scrambling is hard going, and you have to haul yourself up onto head-high ledges, but it always stops short of actual rock climbing. Finally, after a half-mile section of jeep road – 4WD drivers can get this far via a nine-mile drive from Elephant Hill – you teeter out to the edge of the plateau and see the confluence for the first time.

A thousand feet below the **Confluence Overlook**, the Green River flows in from the west, and the Colorado from the northeast. They're never the same color. Sometimes the Green really is a pale green, and the Colorado almost red, tinted with dissolved red sandstone; at other times the Green is more of a yellow, and the Colorado a muddy chocolate. In any case, the two hues remain distinct for the first mile or two after the rivers combine, intermeshing like a zipper as they flow parallel but separate toward the fearsome Cataract Canyon.

Arches National Park

ARCHES NATIONAL PARK seems to have become the national park for people who aren't quite sure whether they like national parks. It's not too hard to get to, just five miles out of Moab; it's not too big, with just twenty miles of paved roads; and it has a catchy name, to tell you what to expect. Nearly a million visitors a year drive in, tick off however many arches they feel they have time for, and drive on to their next destination.

Thanks to *Desert Solitaire*, **Edward Abbey's** lyrical evocation of his year as an Arches ranger, the park is also dear to the hearts of environmentalists and wilderness enthusiasts. The irony is that when Abbey was here, during the 1950s, there was no road into the body of the park, and the only way to explore it was to blaze your own trails. Now you can cruise round in a couple of hours, and barely step out of your vehicle.

For all that, Arches remains very much worth visiting. The **Colorado River** here is literally peripheral, running unseen along the park's southern boundary. The emphasis instead is on the stark, strangely disjointed **sandstone scenery** of the higher ground to the north. As at Canyonlands, these rocks rest on an unstable layer of salt. Salt Valley, which slopes down across the park toward the Colorado, was formed by the collapse of an underground salt dome. That massive subsidence left high ridges to either side, which cracked along vertical fault lines to create long parallel "fins" of orange-pink Entrada sandstone.

Over the eons, water collects in pores in the fins and scours them into potholes; piece by piece, the stone flakes away, until a hole is worn right through. Estimates of how many such "**arches**" the park holds vary from the eighty or so named on maps to the official count of over two thousand. No one has bothered to define whether a "window" is a type of arch or just another word for one, but it's agreed that an arch or window has to be at least three feet wide. Both are distinct from "bridges," which span running water.

As far as Edward Abbey was concerned, the arches themselves were a "small and inessential" feature of the park's landscape. Unless you're a real obsessive – in which case, you can buy specialist arch-and-bridge magazines – the appeal of hunting down arch after arch soon palls. The park's short, straightforward **hiking trails** are enjoyable enough in their own right, however, so you're bound to see a good number of arches along the way. **Delicate Arch** is by far the most impressive, in that it's a free-standing crescent of rock. Most of the rest are just holes, though **Landscape Arch** is such a big one it would be a shame not to see it.

Apart from one solitary cabin, testament to a failed attempt at cattle ranching, very few traces of human occupation remain in this forbidding desert. It became a national monument after the Klondike Bluffs area was found by a wandering prospector in the 1920s, and was enlarged into a national park in 1971.

Most visitors now arrive in **mid-summer**, despite blazing temperatures that can reach 110°F. Hiking conditions are much more bearable in spring – when the wild flowers blossom – or fall.

Arrival and information

Arches National Park has just one **entrance**, located east of US-191 just over two miles across the Colorado River from Moab. The **admission charge**, valid for seven days, is $10 per vehicle, or $5 for motorcyclists, cyclists, and pedestrians. All the passes detailed on p.45 are sold and accepted.

The park's very fancy new **visitor center** opened in 2005 (daily: early March to late Oct 7.30am–6.30pm, late Oct to early March 8am–4.30pm; ☎435/719-2299, ⓦwww.nps.gov/arch). It stands at the base of a long, tall escarpment, formed by the Moab Fault, that conceals the bulk of the park from the highway. While it's bursting with the latest technology, with interactive touch-screen computers to help plan your itinerary, its huge model arches are much more show than tell, and there's little information of any substance to be found. Rangers however issue backcountry permits (see p.514), and provide advice on hiking conditions.

Of **park regulations** you'll need to know, the most important is that each **parking lot** along the road is designed to hold a specific number of vehicles, to limit the number of hikers on any one trail. Park illegally, and there's a $25 on-the-spot fine. No vehicles, or bikes, are allowed on the trails, but there are a few **4WD** roads.

ARCHES NATIONAL PARK

DEVILS GARDEN
Dark Angel
KLONDIKE BLUFFS
Double O Arch
Landscape Arch
Devils Garden Trailhead
Broken Arch
Sand Dune Arch
Salt Valley
FIERY FURNACE
Fiery Furnace Viewpoint
Salt Valley Overlook
Wolfe Ranch
Delicate Arch
Delicate Arch Viewpoint
Panorama Point
Balanced Rock
Cove of Caves
Double Arch
Turret Arch
North Window
South Window
THE WINDOWS SECTION
Petrified Dunes Viewpoint
COURTHOUSE TOWERS
Courthouse Towers Viewpoint
La Sal Mountains Viewpoint
PARK AVENUE
Visitor Center
Colorado River
Jackson Canyon
Negro Bill Canyon
Moab
POTASH ROAD

= = = = 4WD vehicles only

0   2 miles

Camping

Rangers at the visitor center will know whether there's room at Arches' only **campground**, at the far end of the road across from the **Devil's Garden** trailhead ($10; no showers). The campground remains open all year; 24 of its 52 sites are always first-come first-served, and throughout the summer, all are usually taken by early morning. The remaining 28 can be reserved between March and October only, at least four and at most 240 days in advance (☎518/885-3639 or 1-877/444-6777, ⓦ www.reserveusa.com). The nearest **motels** are in Moab; see p.519.

So long as you pick up a free **permit** at the visitor center, you can camp anywhere in the **backcountry** that's out of sight of roads, trails, and named arches. In practice, Arches sees little overnight backpacking, as most people do all the hiking they want within a day.

Park Avenue and Courthouse Towers

Beyond the visitor center, the park road begins its eighteen-mile journey north to Devil's Garden with a steep climb up the cliffs, offering views across to Moab. A parking lot at the top, a mile along, marks the start of the simple one-mile walk down **Park Avenue**. The trail follows the rocky bed of a dry wash, named for the "skyscrapers" that top the high ridges to either side. It ends amid a group of chunky monoliths known as the **Courthouse Towers**; any arches there may once have been have long since fallen.

Unless you arrange to be met at the northern of its two trailheads, you'll have to walk Park Avenue as a two-mile round-trip. The road in between the two passes the **La Sal Mountains Viewpoint**, which offers the first glimpse of the peaks to the east.

The Windows Section

In the heart of the park, almost ten miles up from the visitor center, the fifty-foot **Balanced Rock** rests precariously on its slanted pedestal. Immediately beyond, a spur road to the right leads in three miles to the **Windows Section**. Several fine arches can be admired from the parking lot at the end, the largest in the park, which is also the starting point for a couple of very popular short trails.

North and South Windows

The busy one-mile loop trail to the North and South Windows ambles gently upwards for a couple of hundred yards toward **North Window**, the only one of the pair that's visible from the road. Take the steeper spur trail that leads right up to it, gaze through, and you'll appreciate why the word "window" is so appropriate. So far the gaping aperture has framed only blue sky, but now a magnificent desert panorama comes into view.

South Window is just a few yards away, though you have to rejoin the main trail and round one last pinnacle to see it properly. You can't climb right up to it, though a much rougher trail continues around the back and leads eventually back to the parking lot. Alternatively, you'll have noticed by now that the lone fin across the main trail is pierced by **Turret Arch**. Wander over there, then look back for a shot of the two windows side by side – a pair of dazzling blue eyes, separated by a bulbous snub nose.

Double Arch

A shorter, half-mile trail leads from further around the Windows parking lot to **Double Arch**, where the roof of a wedge-shaped arch has fallen in to create either a skylight, or two separate arches, depending on your point of view. On the far side, the **Cove of Caves** is packed with incipient future arches, burrowing into the cliffs.

Delicate Arch

As befits the state's single most remarkable natural phenomenon, **Delicate Arch** has become a symbol of Utah. Oddly enough, its sturdy bow-legged form, familiar from automobile license plates and millions of tourist brochures, is not in fact all that delicate. It was originally called "Landscape Arch," for the view of the La Sal Mountains it so neatly frames, and only swapped names with what is now Landscape Arch (see p.516) due to a mapmaker's mistake.

A side road toward Delicate Arch leaves the park road shortly beyond **Panorama Point**. The arch itself can only be reached via the grueling **Delicate Arch Trail**, which leads up from Wolfe Ranch 1.2 miles along. If you lack the time or energy for that, you can see it from afar from the **Delicate Arch Viewpoint**, at the end of a level hundred-yard trail that begins a mile further on. For **photographs**, Delicate Arch Viewpoint is best in early morning, while the Delicate Arch Trail is better in the afternoon.

The Delicate Arch Trail

The **Delicate Arch Trail** may be just 1.5 miles long, but the three-mile round-trip to the arch and back involves a steep climb across bare slickrock that can take the wind out of the hardiest hiker's sails; it's worth allowing a good two hours to enjoy it without rushing. The trail starts just short of **Wolfe Ranch**, where Civil War veteran John Wolfe built a cabin in 1906, using cedar and cottonwood logs hauled seven miles from the Colorado. His cattle had by then been denuding the nearby slopes for almost twenty years; when sheep-farmers began to graze their animals on this impoverished soil as well, Wolfe gave up and moved back to Ohio.

Beyond the cabin, a footbridge crosses the shallow perennial **Salt Wash**, and the trail begins its determined ascent. Considering that fewer than ten inches of rain fall here each year, the terrain is surprisingly varied, from the scrubby riverbanks, choked with tamarisk, by way of a small-scale piñon-juniper forest, up to the naked rock three-quarters of a mile up. An alcove off to the left, just below the hill top, cherishes "**hanging gardens**" of rushes and even orchids, fed by a spring that stains the rocks.

It's easy to lose the sparsely cairned trail at the top of the mesa; the trick is to follow a narrow ledge in the rock that leads around the back of a high fin. Suddenly, from a viewing area neatly fenced off by a natural rock parapet, you're confronted by the full glory of **Delicate Arch**. Standing in superb isolation on the high lip of a canyon, it looks taller than its 45 feet. Quite how much closer you dare to approach depends on your confidence walking across the steeply inclined slickrock. There's no physical reason to stop you from standing right under it; lots of people do.

Delicate Arch is deservedly the most popular place in the park from which to see the **sunset**. Be sure to arrive at the trailhead at least an hour before the sun is due to go down, and longer in busy periods, when parking is at a premium. The sumptuous red glow of the arch deepens right until the final moment, so it's worth staying up there as long as you can – which means you'll be glad of a **flashlight** for the hike back down again.

The Fiery Furnace

An uninspiring overlook three miles on from the Wolfe Ranch turnoff gives little idea of the labyrinthine complexity of the **Fiery Furnace**. Named not for any exceptional heat but for its golden late-afternoon glow, this warren of high-walled dead-end gullies and parallel fins is so disorientating, and so fragile, that you're strongly advised to enter it on a ranger-led **guided hike**. These take place daily in high season at 10am and 4pm, and at 10am and 2pm in spring and fall. Numbers are restricted, so you should register at the visitor center as soon as you arrive, and pay the **fee** of $8 for adults, $4 for ages six to twelve. The hikes don't involve walking all that far – most of the time is spent standing still, while the ranger explains the various rock formations and signs of life along the way – but they're fascinating if you're at all interested in learning more about the desert. Alternatively, it is possible to hike into the Furnace without a guide, but once again you need to register at the visitor center, and pay $1 for adults, $1 for ages six to twelve. No backcountry camping is permitted.

The Devil's Garden

The park's largest concentration of arches is found in the **Devil's Garden**, beyond the far end of the road eighteen miles up from the visitor center. The prime target here is the 300ft **Landscape Arch**, reached by a graveled, reasonably level one-mile trail. This slender span is so frail that hikers are not allowed up to or through the arch itself; as mentioned on p.515, what's now Landscape Arch was originally Delicate Arch, and vice versa. A sixty-foot-long slab dropped off it in 1991, and lesser rockfalls happen all the time. Arch aficionados will probably still be debating whether this or Kolob Arch in Zion National Park (see p.439) is the world's longest arch when it finally disintegrates. Landscape Arch is incidentally much harder to photograph than Delicate Arch, especially when the sun is right behind it in the afternoon; for best results, come here as early in the day as you can.

If your appetite for high-desert hiking has been whetted, press on beyond Landscape Arch on a trail that immediately becomes far cruder. After another mile – during which one hundred-yard section obliges you to totter along the top of a narrow sandstone fin – you round a corner to see **Double O Arch** on the skyline. At first, only its large upper oval is visible; as you approach, you'll see the much smaller ring beneath it as well. The pallid alkali wastelands that stretch away to the east were once prime uranium territory, and one heavily polluted section is still known as the "**Poison Strip**."

The four-mile round-trip hike to Double O Arch also leads past half a dozen other named arches and assorted minor pinpricks and peepholes. Real gluttons for punishment can turn it into a seven-mile loop, by circling back on the Primitive Loop Trail, but that route is every bit as demanding as its name implies.

Moab

Boom-and-bust cycles are a recurring theme in Western history, but few communities can have experienced quite such a rollercoaster ride as **MOAB**.

Within the last sixty years, it has gone from an insignificant backwater in the 1940s to being celebrated as "The Richest Town in the USA" by *McCalls* magazine in the 1950s, only to become what one journalist called "one of the most economically depressed towns in Utah" by 1986, and then find itself transformed, almost against its will, into the Southwest's number-one adventure-vacation destination.

Through it all, Moab has never been a large town – the population still hasn't reached ten thousand – and neither is it, in itself, a particularly attractive one. The **setting** is what matters. With two national parks on its doorstep, plus millions more acres of public land, Moab is an ideal base for **outdoors enthusiasts**. The first to turn up were **jeep** drivers, taking advantage of the remote dirt roads cleared by the uranium prospectors. Then the **whitewater rafting** companies moved in, and the town swiftly became a mecca for **mountain bikers** too, lured by the legendary **Slickrock Bike Trail**. These days, Moab is almost literally bursting, all year, with legions of lycra-clad holidaymakers from all over the world.

Perhaps the main reason Moab has grown so fast is that out-of-state visitors tend to find Utah's rural communities so irredeemably boring. As soon as Moab emerged from the pack, it became a beacon in the desert, attracting tourists ecstatic to find a town that stayed up after dark. Moab amounts to little more than a few miles of motels, restaurants, and bars, but that's enough to make it the only southern Utah town where you can stay for a week and still feel that you haven't seen everything, and everyone, a dozen times.

A history of Moab

Moab stands just south of the Colorado River, at the north end of a long valley created by the collapse of an underground salt dome. Because a similar valley slopes down to the river on its northern side, it's the best place to cross the Colorado in all of Utah. Ute Indians passed this way for generations, but the site was first recorded by Juan de Rivera in 1765, and a ferry service later helped travelers on the **Old Spanish Trail**. The **Elk Mountain Mission**, set up in 1855, had to be abandoned after Indian attacks, but Mormon pioneers returned in the 1870s to establish a farming settlement. They named it for the biblical wilderness of Moab, located at the edge of Zion.

Until Charlie Steen discovered **uranium** in 1952 – the first of a series of major finds in the region – the biggest thing ever to hit Moab was when **Butch Cassidy** hijacked the Colorado ferry on his way home from a bank job. The uranium boom lasted well into the 1970s, but as it dwindled, the local political scene turned very sour. Moab was a major focus of the **Sagebrush Rebellion** (see p.460), which pitted mine-owners and Utah businessmen, together with their fearful workforce, against the burgeoning national coalition of **environmentalists** and the federal government that seemed to support them. Grand County commissioners repeatedly defied federal legislation by smashing bulldozers into neighboring **Negro Bill Canyon** – named for a local character and administered by the BLM – in the hope of opening it and other protected wilderness areas for mineral exploitation.

While they may have won the bitter **Bulldozer Wars** – Ronald Reagan came to power proclaiming that he too was a "Sagebrush Rebel" – Utah's conservatives were no match for the world economy. The uranium market crashed in 1980, thanks partly to the accident at Three Mile Island in 1979 and partly to

Charlie Steen: the Uranium King

In the early 1950s, as the Cold War gathered steam and nuclear power stations seemed to hold infinite promise, the US government was desperate to locate a reliable domestic source of **uranium**. The Atomic Energy Commission therefore offered a $10,000 reward to anyone who discovered a mineable uranium deposit – even on public land – and guaranteed to buy whatever it produced for the next ten years.

Freelance prospectors converged on the Colorado Plateau, where uranium had been found and mined as early as 1912. Their war-surplus jeeps piled with provisions, they set off into Utah's uncharted backcountry, waving their Geiger counters at whatever likely-looking rocks might catch their eyes. Most knew which strata offered the best odds, and searched for places along the cliffs and canyon walls where they might be exposed.

Charlie Steen, a geologist from Texas, was mocked for insisting that he could find uranium by **drilling**. He would project the angle of the canyonlands' crazily tilted slopes deep underground, and calculate where the precious mineral might have accumulated atop layers of harder rock. Concentrating his efforts on the **Lisbon Valley**, thirty miles southeast of Moab, he staked out countless claims and gave each a Spanish name.

In July 1952, the 31-year-old Steen broke his last drill bit in a 200ft bore on the **Mi Vida** ("my life") claim. Driving back to his trailer home in despair, he pulled into a gas station in Cisco, Utah. The attendant offered to test the final plug of rock on the bed of Steen's pick-up; his Geiger counter went straight off the scale.

Following his $60-million strike, Steen opened a processing mill in Moab that became Grand County's largest employer. As the **"Uranium King,"** he built himself a hilltop mansion above town and threw a lavish annual party for all its citizens. He had his own plane, in which he'd circle above Moab at night since TV reception was better at that altitude, and he was even a celebrity guest on *I Love Lucy*. In quick succession, he was elected to the Utah senate, then resigned after failing to change the state's liquor laws. Selling Mi Vida, he moved to Nevada, only to fritter his entire fortune away, losing $250,000, for example, on a pickle factory.

By the early 1970s, Steen was back in Utah, once more searching the canyon country as a penniless prospector. This time he traveled in disguise under a false name, in order both to avoid media attention and to protect any discoveries he might make. Success eluded him, however, and he eventually conceded defeat and moved to Colorado, where he still lives. He has recently been reported as suffering from Alzheimer's Disease, while his sons are suing each other in the hope of discovering whether any of the Mi Vida millions still exist, and if so, who owns them.

the discovery of vast deposits of high-grade uranium in Canada in 1980. At the same time, the bottom also fell out of oil, coal, and potash. Unemployment in Moab rocketed, and the population dwindled.

The wilderness devotees who saw the region's future as resting with **tourism** now seized the chance to prove their case. They succeeded beyond their wildest dreams; out of nowhere, Moab became the West's hottest new destination, the desert equivalent of chic mountain hideaways like Aspen and Telluride in Colorado.

Sadly, almost everyone agrees that things have now gone too far. Most of the old-timers have left, driven out by rising real-estate prices and none too keen to swap mining for motel clerking at a third of the wages. Low-impact ecotourism seemed a real possibility when only the select few had even heard of Moab, but the canyonlands now seem to be taking as hard a battering from the fat-tire brigade as they ever did from the mining conglomerates. Just to make matters worse, the price of uranium is finally rising once again, and there are constant rumors that Utah is about to experience another uranium boom.

Getting to Moab

No scheduled **buses** connect Moab with the outside world, but Bighorn Express (℡801/746-2417 or 1-888/655-7433, ⓦwww.bighornexpress.com) runs a daily **shuttle service** between Salt Lake City and Moab ($56 one-way), via Green River and continuing on to Monticello, while the nearest Amtrak station is at Green River.

Salmon Air offers daily **flights** to **Canyonlands Airport**, twenty miles north of Moab on US-91, from Salt Lake City (Mon–Fri twice daily, Sat & Sun once daily; $114 one-way; ℡435/259-0566, 1-800/448-3413; ⓦwww.salmonair .com). Arriving passengers can take a $15 **taxi** ride into town with Coyote Shuttle (℡435/259-8656, ⓦwww.coyoteshuttle.com) or Roadrunner Shuttle (℡435/259-9402, ⓦwww.roadrunnershuttle.com), both of which also provide shuttle services for bikers, rafters, and hikers.

Information

The superb **visitor center** for Moab and Grand County stands right in the heart of town at Center and Main (daily: March to mid-May & late Sept to Oct 8am–8pm; mid-May to late Sept 8am–9pm; Nov–Feb 9am–noon & 1–5pm; ℡435/259-8825 or 1-800/635-6622; ⓦwww.discovermoab.com). As well as stacks of information on Moab itself, it carries brochures and maps for the nearby parks and public lands; almost all the information can also be found on, and downloaded from, the website.

Other good sources for news and information include Moab's **coffeeshops** (see p.522) and the excellent Back of Beyond **bookstore**, 83 N Main St (℡435/259-5154), all of which should have copies of the free *Canyon Country Zephyr* (ⓦwww.canyoncountryzephyr.com), which keeps a critical eye on local goings-on. Detailed topographical **maps** can be picked up from TI Maps, across from the visitor center at 29 E Center St (℡435/259-5529).

The high spots of Moab's calendar are the **Jeep Safari** (ⓦwww.rr4w.com) at Easter and the **Moab Halloween Bike Fest** (formerly known as the Fat Tire festival; ⓦwww.moabbikefest.com) in late October.

Accommodation

If you've already been in Utah for a while when you reach Moab, the glittering neon signs of **motels** like the *Greenwell* and the *Landmark* will come as a big surprise. At last count, there were over thirty motels in town, but every one of the 1500-plus rooms is taken on many nights between mid-March and October, so **reservations** are strongly recommended. If you arrive without having booked anything, call in first at the visitor center, where the free *TravelHost* guide contains useful discount coupons. In winter, **room rates** can drop as

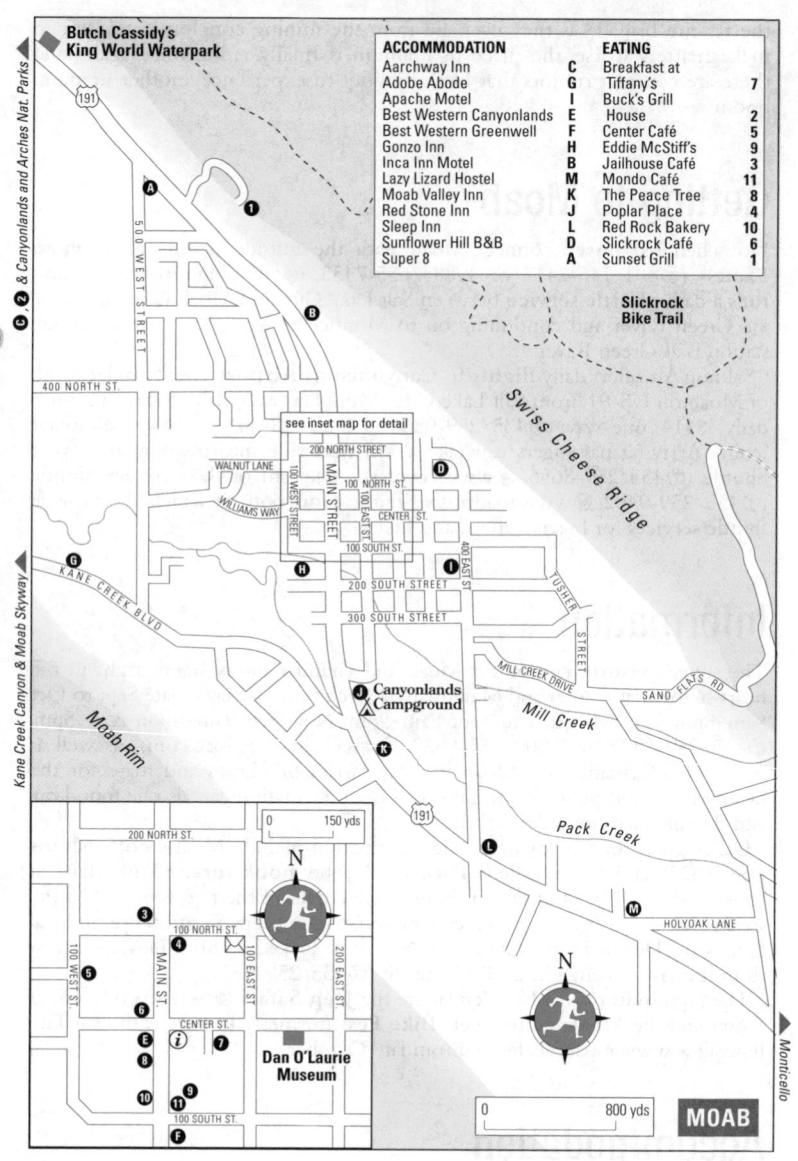

ACCOMMODATION		EATING	
Aarchway Inn	C	Breakfast at	
Adobe Abode	G	Tiffany's	7
Apache Motel	I	Buck's Grill	
Best Western Canyonlands	F	House	2
Best Western Greenwell	E	Center Café	5
Gonzo Inn	H	Eddie McStiff's	9
Inca Inn Motel	B	Jailhouse Café	3
Lazy Lizard Hostel	M	Mondo Café	11
Moab Valley Inn	K	The Peace Tree	8
Red Stone Inn	J	Poplar Place	4
Sleep Inn	L	Red Rock Bakery	10
Sunflower Hill B&B	D	Slickrock Café	6
Super 8	A	Sunset Grill	1

Slickrock Bike Trail

Swiss Cheese Ridge

Butch Cassidy's King World Waterpark

191

500 WEST STREET

400 NORTH ST.

see inset map for detail

200 NORTH STREET

WALNUT LANE

100 WEST STREET

MAIN STREET

100 N. ST.

100 EAST ST.

WILLIAMS WAY

CENTER ST.

100 SOUTH ST.

KANE CREEK BLVD

200 SOUTH STREET

300 SOUTH STREET

400 EAST ST.

TUSHER STREET

MILL CREEK DRIVE

SAND FLATS RD

Moab Rim

Canyonlands Campground

Mill Creek

191

Pack Creek

HOLYOAK LANE

200 NORTH ST.

0   150 yds

N

100 NORTH ST.

100 WEST ST.

MAIN ST.

100 EAST ST.

200 EAST ST.

CENTER ST.

Dan O'Laurie Museum

100 SOUTH ST.

N

0   800 yds

MOAB

low as $35 per night, but you'd be lucky to find anything much below $75 in high season.

Moab's dozen commercial **campgrounds** can be a godsend, considering the dearth of sites in the national parks – Canyonlands options are described on p.502, p.503 and p.509, and the one in Arches on p.513 – but they do tend to be dominated by family parties.

Hotels, motels, and hostels

Aarchway Inn 1551 N Hwy-191 ☎435/259-2599 or 1-800/341-9359, ⊛www.aarchwayinn.com. Large, well-equipped motel with a nice pool, not far from the Colorado River at the north end of town. **⑤**

Apache Motel 166 South 400 East ☎435/259-5727 or 1-800/228-6882, ⊛www.apachemotel.net. Long-established, two-story traditional motel on a quiet back street east of the center. John Wayne stayed here while filming *Rio Bravo* in the nearby canyons. Winter **②**, summer **④**

Best Western Canyonlands Inn 16 S Main St ☎435/259-2300 or 1-800/780-7234, ⊛www.canyonlandsinn.com. Standard, dependable *Best Western*, across from the visitor center. Winter **④**, summer **⑥**

Best Western Greenwell Inn 105 S Main St ☎435/259-6151 or 1-800/780-7234, ⊛www.bestwesternmoab.com. Central, modern hotel that offers spacious good-value rooms, with tasteful furnishings and fittings, and often microwaves; ask for a room away from the highway. Winter **②**, summer **⑥**

Gonzo Inn 100 West 200 South ☎435/259-2515 or 1-800/791-4044, ⊛www.gonzoinn.com. Luxurious if rather self-consciously "hip" 43-room inn – or "funky place to crash," if you prefer. Complete with kitsch retro furnishings, gecko door handles, quirky artwork, outdoor pool, spa, and in-house espresso bar. **⑦**

Inca Inn Motel 570 N Main St ☎435/259-7261 or 1-866/462-2466, ⊛www.incainn.com. Clean, minimally equipped but adequate budget motel. Closed Dec–Feb. **③**

Lazy Lizard International Hostel 1213 S Hwy-191 ☎435/259-6057, ⊛www.lazylizardhostel.com. Amiable, very laid-back private hostel, well south of the center (just beyond a bowling alley), with $9 beds in six-person dorms, $6 campsites, private room at $24 for two, and private cabins, ranging from $27 for one person up to $47 for six, plus a hot tub, kitchen, and Internet access. No membership necessary. **①**

Moab Valley Inn 711 S Main St ☎435/259-4419 or 1-800/831-6622, ⊛www.moabvalleyinn.com. Modern, large, and well-equipped motel at the south end of downtown, with indoor and outdoor pools and hot tub. Nov–Feb **④**, March–Oct **⑤**

Pack Creek Ranch PO Box 1270, Moab UT 84532 ☎435/259-5505 or 1-888/679-6622, ⊛www.packcreekranch.com. Large guest ranch, with individual cabins and cottages capable of holding from two to eight guests, plus assorted pools and tubs, twenty miles southeast of town, just off the lower reaches of the La Sal Mountain Loop Road

(see p.526). Trail rides on horseback available April–Oct. **⑤–⑧**

Red Cliffs Lodge Mile 14, Hwy-128 ☎435/259-2002 or 1-866/812-2002, ⊛www.redcliffslodge.com. Luxury resort occupying a beautifully verdant location beside the Colorado sixteen miles northeast of town. As well as seventy Western-themed suites, it holds two restaurants, stables, a large pool, and even a winery. **⑧**

Red Stone Inn 535 S Main St ☎435/259-3500 or 1-800/772-1972, ⊛www.moabredstone.com. Bargain-rate recently built motel, a few blocks south of the center. Winter **②**, summer **④**

Sleep Inn 1051 S Main St ☎435/259-4655 or 1-877/424-6423, ⊛www.moab-utah.com/sleepinn. Comfortable chain motel, with a pool and an indoor spa, whose location a mile south of downtown means it offers highly competitive rates. Winter **③**, summer **④**

Super 8 889 N Main St ☎435/259-8868 or 1-800/800-8000, ⊛www.super8.com. Moab's largest motel, decorated in *Super 8*'s normal drab colors but offering good value for money, at the north end of town not far from the Colorado. Winter **②**, summer **④**

B&Bs

Adobe Abode 778 W Kane Creek Blvd ☎435/259-7716, ⊛www.adobeabodemoab.com. This attractive, low-slung, Southwestern-Pueblo-style home feels like it's way out in the desert, despite being just a few hundred yards from downtown Moab. All its six B&B rooms are comfortable and tastefully furnished, and the breakfasts are superb. **⑥**

Castle Valley Inn 424 Amber Lane, Castle Valley ☎435/259-6012, ⊛www.castlevalleyinn.com. Large, beautifully furnished B&B, set in spacious grounds in magnificent Castle Valley, twenty miles east of town (see p.526). Five en-suite rooms and three separate bungalows; dinner served five nights weekly. **⑥–⑧**

Sunflower Hill B&B 185 North 300 East ☎435/259-2974 or 1-800/662-2786, ⊛www.sunflowerhill.com. Antique-furnished former farmhouse, now a 12-room B&B, away from the bustle on a dead-end side street. All units are en suite, some are in separate cottages, and there's a pool. Winter **⑥**, summer **⑦**

Campgrounds

Canyonlands Campground 555 S Main St ☎435/259-6848 or 1-800/522-6848, ⊛www.canyonlandsrv.com. Large, year-round site in the heart of town, catering mainly to RVs but equipped with tent sites at around $19 per night.

Sand Flats Recreation Area 1924 S Roadrunner Hill ☎ 435/259-6111, ⓦ www.blm.gov/utah/moab/campgrounds.html. Barely developed BLM campground, intended primarily for mountain bikers and costing $8 per night, along the top of the mesa to the east of town near the Slickrock Bike Trail.

Slickrock Campground 1301 N-Hwy 191 ☎ 435/259-7660 or 1-800/448-8873, ⓦ www.slickrockcampground.com. Moab's biggest site, a mile north of town, but it's a pleasant enough and well-shaded spot, charging $18 per tent per night, and offering a wide range of amenities including a pool and hot tub, plus a store.

The Town

Main Street, the broad five-mile section of **US-191** that sweeps through the center of Moab, is lined with all the gas stations, diners, motels, and other businesses that you'd expect. For two blocks north and south of **Center Street**, which crosses it at the visitor center in the middle, window-shopping pedestrians stroll the sidewalk and browse the menus. Elsewhere, everybody drives or cycles. Squeezed between Swiss Cheese Ridge to the east and the Moab Rim to the west, the town has little room to expand, but you can still see a few pioneer homes, and the occasional apple orchard, if you venture down the side streets.

Local history is enjoyably recalled at the **Dan O'Laurie Museum**, also known as the Canyon Country Museum, at 118 E Center St (summer Mon–Sat 1–8pm; winter Mon–Thurs 3–7pm, Fri & Sat 1–7pm; free). Displays start with a mammoth tusk dredged from the Colorado and the replica of an ancient petroglyph claimed to show the "Moab mastodon." The usual small-town assortment follows, ranging from an Ancestral Puebloan basket to Moab's first telephone switchboard, plus plenty of souvenirs from the uranium days. A **gallery** upstairs holds separate exhibitions of contemporary art.

On a hot summer's day, you might prefer a quick wallow at **Butch Cassidy's King World Waterpark** (mid-April to mid-Sept daily 10am–10pm; adults $14, under-13s $12). This complex of water slides and swimming pools is tucked into a side canyon at the north end of town, said to have been used as a hideout by the Wild Bunch.

Eating

While Moab has yet to acquire the range of **restaurants** you might find in a major resort, it offers by far the greatest choice in southern Utah, and for once most places make a serious effort to cater to **vegetarians**. Full menus appear in the *Moab Menu Guide*, available free at local motels (ⓦ www.moabhappenings.com/menuguide.htm). There's also no problem getting a **drink** – Moab even has two pubs and its own winery – while **coffee bars** are springing up all over town. Several bike shops have espresso counters for early-morning customers.

Amid much local controversy, certain restaurateurs, arguing that foreign visitors seem unfamiliar with the American custom of **tipping**, have taken to adding a fifteen percent service charge to all checks. Be sure you don't end up paying twice.

Breakfast at Tiffany's 90 E Center St ☎ 435/259-2553. Very friendly and inexpensive little café housed in a quirky 1950s antiques store across the parking lot from the visitor center, and decked out in retro furnishings. Delicious breakfasts – orange

cinnamon challah French toast or waffles – and lunchtime snacks. Summer daily 7am–3pm, winter Mon–Fri 7.30am–2pm, Sat & Sun 7.30am–noon.

🏃 **Buck's Grill House** 1393 N Hwy-191 ☎ 435/259-5201. Belying its stockade-like exterior, this "American Western Food" joint is actually a sophisticated and highly recommended affair, serving rich, classy Southwestern food, such as game hen or pork ribs, at very reasonable prices. No entree costs over $20, few over $15. Open for dinner nightly, from 5.30pm.

Center Cafe 60 North 100 West ☎435/259-4295. This gourmet restaurant serves contemporary American cuisine with a Pacific twist. Entrées, costing from $20 to $32, range from Asian seared tuna to pan-roasted lamb or grilled tenderloin with polenta. Open for dinner nightly, from 5.30pm.

Desert Bistro 1266 N Main St ☎435/259-0756. This expensive but top-notch restaurant is probably Moab's best option for a romantic evening out. Set in a ranch home with a patio that's perfect for summer nights, it offers a modern Mediterranean-influenced bistro menu, on which entrees like venison medallions or smoked rabbit agnolotti cost up to $35. Open daily for dinner, from 5.30pm.

Eddie McStiff's 57 S Main St ☎435/259-2337. Central pub, next to the visitor center, which has some interesting beers, including raspberry and blueberry. The restaurant serves a varied menu, with inexpensive salads, fancy Southwestern pizzas (with toppings like sundried tomatoes and jalapeño peppers) from $9, plus pasta and steak dinners, but the service can leave a lot to be desired. Open daily for lunch and dinner.

Jailhouse Cafe 101 N Main St ☎435/259-3900. Very popular central café, open for moderately priced breakfasts only. There's indoor and outdoor seating year round, and great specials like ginger pancakes and eggs Benedict, for around $8. Mon–Fri 7am–noon, Sat & Sun 7am–1pm.

Mondo Cafe 59 S Main St ☎435/259-5551. Groovy daytime hangout next to *Eddie McStiff's*, serving espresso coffees plus inexpensive waffles, paninis, pastries, and sandwiches. Daily 6.30am–6pm.

The Peace Tree 20 S Main St ☎435/259-8503. Very central juice bar and café that serves good sandwiches, wraps, and smoothies to take out or eat on the small outdoor patio. Daily 8am–6.30pm.

The Poplar Place First North and Main St ☎435/259-6018. Friendly, classy adobe bar, serving draft beers and good pizzas. Daily 11.30am–11pm.

Red Rock Bakery & Net Cafe 74 S Main St ☎435/259-5941. Small café-bakery opposite the visitor center, which also offers Internet access from a back room. Daily 7am until dusk.

Slickrock Cafe 5 N Main St ☎435/259-8004. Central, modern café that gives every meal of the day a Southwestern flavor. Omelettes, burritos, burgers, and sandwiches earlier on, and some good chicken and pasta entrées for $11–17 in the evening. Daily 7am until late.

Sunset Grill 900 N Hwy-191 ☎435/259-7146. Charlie Steen's luxury hilltop home (see p.518) is now one of Moab's classiest restaurants, with tasty meat, seafood, and pasta entrées for $16–21, great desserts, and stunning views across the valley. The tortuous if short approach road from the north end of town (lit at night) means it's no place to drink and drive. Open for dinner only, Mon–Sat 5pm until late.

Around Moab

Although most visitors head straight for the national parks, several lesser-known areas in the Moab region are well worth exploring. Both upstream and downstream, minor roads run alongside the **Colorado River**, while the **La Sal Mountains** to the east make a snowy contrast to the aridity of the desert.

The Potash Road

The dead-end **Potash Road**, Hwy-279, which doubles back southwest along the Colorado's west bank from just north of the bridge on US-191, passes a number of intriguing **rock art** sites and provides a great close-up view of the river. In this stretch the Colorado is broad and lazy, tinted the same reddish brown as the Navajo sandstone cliffs that tower above it. These cliffs are often busy with **rock climbers**; if you're interested in renting equipment or joining a guided climb, contact Pagan Mountaineering (☎435/259-1117, ⓦwww .paganmountaineering.com).

Seven miles down the road, you reach a group of **petroglyphs** a dozen feet up on the canyon wall to the right. Scraped into the dark "desert varnish" by

Adventure travel in Moab

As southern Utah's main center for wilderness activities, Moab is filled with companies that specialize in guiding and equipping adventurous travelers. The visitor center can provide full lists of tour operators and rental outlets, plus free maps and route suggestions for bikers and 4WD drivers; you'll find it online at ⓦwww.discovermoab .com/tour.htm. Another list, with hyperlinks to most operators, appears on the National Park Service website at ⓦwww.nps.gov/cany/guided.htm.

Colorado River trips

Virtually everyone who goes **rafting** on the Colorado River does so with one of Moab's **river-running operators**. All those listed below offer motorized one-day trips for $40–50, plus half-day tasters for $30–40; most also offer multi-day expeditions and day-trip combinations such as jeep-and-raft or horse-and-raft.

Shorter trips start northwest of Moab, near Fisher Towers, and arrive near town in the afternoon; many companies give passengers the chance to float quieter stretches in two-person kayaks. While there are enough stretches of small-scale whitewater to whet the appetites of first-timers, a little romance is lost by the fact that the road runs alongside the river for much of the way. **Longer** (2–7-day) trips head through Cataract Canyon and other wild Canyonlands spots. **Oar-powered rafts** are slower but much quieter, and less expensive than motorboat trips. Expect to pay anything from $750 up to $1400 for a five-day trip, depending on whether you're prepared to lift a finger to help.

Mountain biking

While the Moab area is ideally suited to **mountain-bike touring**, only experienced riders should attempt its most famous route, the **Slickrock Bike Trail**. Originally laid out as a motorbike trail in 1969, this challenging ten-mile loop explores the sandstone knobs east of Moab, skirting the rim of Negro Bill Canyon with views to the La Sal Mountains and the Colorado River. Following the white dotted line around this exposed expanse of lithified red dunes, up steep inclines and along narrow ledges,

Adrift Adventures ☎ 435/259-8594, 1-800/874-4483 ⓦwww.adrift.net
Canyon Voyages ☎ 435/259-6007, 1-800/733-6007 ⓦwww.canyonvoyages.com
Canyonlands by Night & Day ☎ 435/259-2628, 1-800/394-9978 ⓦwww.canyonlandsbynight.com
Canyonlands Field Institute ☎ 435/259-7750, 1-800/860-5262 ⓦwww.canyonlandsfieldinst.org
Dreamride ☎ 435/259-6419, 1-888/662-2882 ⓦwww.mountainbiketours.com
Moab Adventure Center ☎ 435/259-7019, 1-888/622-4097 ⓦwww.moabadventurecenter.com
Moab Cyclery ☎ 435/259-7423, 1-800/559-1978 ⓦwww.moabcyclery.com
Navtec Expeditions ☎ 435/259-7983, 1-800/833-1278 ⓦwww.navtec.com
O.A.R.S. Canyonlands Tours ☎ 435/259-5865, 1-800/342-5938 ⓦwww.oarsutah.com
Pack Creek Ranch ☎ 435/259-5505, 1-888/679-6622 ⓦwww.packcreekranch.com
Poison Spider Bicycles ☎ 435/259-7882, 1-800/635-1792 ⓦwww.poisonspiderbicycles.com
Rim Tours ☎ 435/259-5223, 1-800/626-7335 ⓦwww.rimtours.com
Sherri Griffith Expeditions ☎ 435/259-8229, 1-800/332-2439 ⓦwww.griffithexp.com
Slickrock 4x4 Rentals ☎ 435/259-5678 www.moab-utah.com/jeep/jeep.html
Tag-a-Long Expeditions ☎ 435/259-8946, 1-800/453-3292 ⓦwww.tagalong.com
Western Spirit Cycling ☎ 435/259-8732, 1-800/845-2453 ⓦwww.westernspirit.com
Worldwide River Expeditions ☎ 435/259-7515, 1-800/231-2769 ⓦwww.worldwideriver.com

takes at least four hours. Be sure to allow enough daylight, and carry two gallons of water – far more than you can take in bike bottles alone.

To reach the trail, which lies within the **Sand Flats Recreation Area**, climb Salt Flats Road up from Millcreek Drive, which branches off 400 East Street four blocks south of Center Street. There's a fee of $5 per vehicle or $2 per person. Several companies in Moab offer a shuttle service to carry cyclists up to this and other trails; call Roadrunner Shuttle (☎435/259-9402, ⊛www.roadrunnershuttle.com) or Coyote Shuttle (☎435/259-8656, ⊛www.coyoteshuttle.com).

If you're looking for an easier ride, you may prefer to try the red-rock side canyons east and west of Moab, such as **Kane Creek**. Several of the operators listed below offer excellent guided biking trips into Canyonlands National Park.

Jeep tours and rentals
The dirt roads that crisscross the backcountry on all sides of Moab – most created by 1950s uranium prospectors – make perfect goals for **4WD** explorations. The roads described on p.523 onwards are good for half-day trips, while obvious destinations further afield include the Island In The Sky and Needles districts of Canyonlands. Jeep **rental** rates are in the region of $100 per day; guided tours cost from $50 per person for half a day up to around $100 for a full day.

Scenic flights
From Canyonlands Airport (see p.519), **Redtail Aviation** (☎435/259-7421 or 1-800/842-9251; ⊛www.redtailaviation.com), **Slickrock Air Guides** (☎435/259-6216 or 1-866/259-1626; ⊛www.slickrockairguides.com), and **Mountain Flying Service** (Sept–April only; ☎435/260-0062; ⊛www.flyglacierbay.com/moab) run unforgettable flights over Canyonlands and beyond, at rates of $100–125 per person per hour. **Arches Helicopters Filming Services** (☎435/259-4637; ⊛www.moab-utah .com/arches/helicopter.html) are rather more expensive, at around $250 for a two-hour flight.

River Tours	River Rentals	Jeep Tours	Jeep Rentals	Bike Tours	Bike Rentals	Horses	Guided Hikes
•		•				•	•
•	•	•		•			•
•	•	•					
•		•					•
				•	•		•
•		•		•		•	•
				•		•	•
•	•						
•		•					
						•	
				•	•		
				•	•		
•							
			•				
•	•	•		•			
					•		
•							

Fremont Indians, some time between 700 and 1300 AD, they depict animals and anthropomorphic figures, including a chain of linked humans resembling paper dolls.

A mile further on, two mounted metal tubes tucked among the roadside bushes point to a group of barely discernible **dinosaur tracks**. More petroglyphs can also be seen, this time higher on the cliffs. The signposted **Jug Handle Arch**, seven miles on, is not all that spectacular, while a smaller and even less enthralling arch is located on the western flank of the same side canyon.

Just past the arches, seventeen miles from US-191, the valley floor widens. The road officially ends here, at the ugly green plant where Moab Salt produces salt and **potash** (potassium carbonate), accompanied by billowing clouds of white smoke. It is possible to drive on, but how much further you go probably depends on whether you own the vehicle you're driving. The surface is paved for another 1.3 miles, while 1.7 bumpy miles beyond that you get your first glimpse of the 23 vinyl-lined **evaporation ponds** where the potash is prepared. Dyed a lurid bluish-turquoise to speed evaporation, they're a real eyesore, clearly visible from Dead Horse Point far above (see p.501).

Only **4WD** vehicles can continue past the ponds and the nearby boat-launch ramp. *Thelma and Louise* freeze-framed their way into the final credits from the mesa-top a few miles further up, and in due course the Potash Road meets up with the White Rim Road in Canyonlands (see p.501).

Castle Valley and the La Sal Mountains

Turning northeast off US-191 just south of the bridge takes you onto **Hwy-128**, which follows the Colorado's east bank for 35 miles, then crosses the river to meet **I-70** ten miles further up. In summer, this superbly scenic section of the river is busy with one-day rafting trips, which can be watched from several roadside lookouts. Roughly twenty miles along, the three-pronged red butte of **Fisher Towers** rises to the right of the road. These were originally named "Fissure Towers"; there was no "Fisher."

For an excellent sixty-mile **loop trip** back to Moab – which takes something over two hours to complete in summer, and is usually closed by snow between November and April – turn right, southeast, fifteen miles along the river road, onto Castle Valley Road. **Castle Valley** is a verdant cleft that boasts some quintessentially Western scenery, with red sandstone walls and buttes such as the **Priest and Nuns** to the east and high dark hills to the west. At its far southern end, eleven miles along, another right turn sets you climbing up the volcanic 10,000ft **La Sal Mountains**. A handful of narrow squeezes and hairpins later, you reach a vantage point commanding views across the Colorado to Arches and Canyonlands. Beyond that, the road runs through the high mountain landscape of the **Manti–La Sal National Forest**, which becomes a feast of color in late fall. A few campgrounds are tucked into the woods, but you won't see another building before the road eventually drops back toward Moab Valley.

It's equally easy to drive this loop in the opposite direction – for morning starts, drive south from Moab to keep the sun behind you for most of the way.

Hole N" The Rock

The peculiarly punctuated **Hole N" The Rock**, 15 miles south of Moab on US-191 (daily 9am–6pm; $4.50), is a classic piece of 1950s Americana. Having started out with a roadside diner at the foot of a cliff, Albert Christensen and his wife Gladys ended up hollowing an entire home deep into the red sandstone. Albert was a dreadful taxidermist – his unfortunate donkey Henry has to be seen to be believed – and painter – cross-eyed Christs a specialty – but his cool, well-lit house is a masterpiece. He died in 1957, without completing the spiral staircase that was planned to lead 65ft up to a roof-top patio. In the fine tradition of the jewelry that Gladys made from broken beer bottles, the gift store is stocked with home-spun souvenirs. Don't confuse the Hole N" The Rock with the Hole-in-the-Rock pioneer river crossing near Escalante, incidentally; see p.467.

Canyon Rims Recreation Area

The vast and almost completely empty mesa, west of US-191, that separates Moab from the Needles district of Canyonlands National Park (see p.507), is largely taken up by the BLM-run **Canyon Rims Recreation Area**. Not much recreation goes on up here, although it has the usual 4WD-only roads and a scattering of hiking trails; there are also two basic year-round **campgrounds**, *Hatch Point* near the far end, and *Windwhistle* closer to the highway (water available at both mid-April to mid-Oct only; $10; ☏435/259-6111).

Only consider visiting the two main overlooks if you have a lot of time to spare – it involves a two-and-a-half-hour detour from the highway – or if you're not going to get to the Needles district, in which case the **Needles Overlook** provides a (relatively) quick overview that's as dramatic as any in Canyonlands itself.

The Needles Overlook

The paved road into the Canyon Rims Recreation Area leaves US-191 32 miles south of Moab. Its dreary 22-mile course westwards comes to an abrupt halt at the windswept **Needles Overlook**, where a short railed footpath gives eagle's-eye views across the canyonlands. Specific landmarks are hard to pick out amid the orange sandstone ledges that spread below, but looking south you should spot the twin **Sixshooter Peaks** and Hwy-211 winding alongside Indian Creek toward the Needles district (see p.507). Further west, the Needles themselves poke from the hillocks, while the Colorado loops its way from the north toward its confluence with the Green River.

The Anticline Overlook

Fifteen miles in from US-191, or seven miles short of the Needles Overlook, forking right onto an even, broad gravel road commits you to the 25-minute drive across the tumbleweed-strewn sagebrush desert to the **Anticline Overlook**. You probably won't pass another vehicle before the final parking lot, from which a five-minute walk leads to a high promontory that faces the potash evaporation ponds (see opposite) and **Dead Horse Point** across the Colorado.

Some people call this the Anti-climax Overlook, disappointed to realize that they've driven almost all the way back to Moab. As you'll see if you follow the fence around the headland, only **Kane Creek Canyon** – where the creek is the tiniest of green slivers in the red wasteland – intervenes. You'll almost certainly hear motorbikes scrambling across the slickrock of the Moab Rim on the far side. To the northeast, silhouetted above a brief stretch of the Colorado, you also get a remarkable view of the fins of **Arches National Park**, where the line of sight passes straight through the South Window.

Southeast Utah

It may lack big-name national parks, but Utah's **southeast corner** is every bit as scenic as the neighboring regions. The desert here is so unforgiving that only a handful of widely separated settlements cling to life, and large tracts remain entirely without roads.

Culturally as well as geographically, southeast Utah has much in common with the Four Corners area covered in Chapter One. The **Ancestral Puebloans** were here in force, as countless abandoned pueblos can testify. They're thought to have moved off to the south and east around 1250 AD, but even now almost half the population of **San Juan County**, which covers the bulk of the region and is larger than several states, is Native American. A few are Utes, but most are **Navajo**, many of them descended from families who hid here during the 1860s to escape the Long Walk (see p.592).

The first **Mormons** to reach this far-flung corner were the Hole-in-the-Rock pioneers (see p.464), who established **Bluff** in 1880 and went on to found **Blanding** and **Monticello** as well. All those towns make viable bases, but the real attraction, as ever, is the landscape, with hikers heading for **Natural Bridges National Monument**, more ambitious backpackers for **Grand Gulch**, and drivers rattling across the desert to the unbelievable **Muley Point**, **Goosenecks State Reserve**, and the **Valley of the Gods**.

Monticello

The first fifty miles of US-191 south of Moab are so desolate that it comes as a major shock, on climbing some straggling foothills, to find yourself confronted by plowed green fields. To Mormon pioneers, this terrain resembled Thomas Jefferson's country home in Virginia – hence the name of **MONTICELLO** (pronounced "monti-sello"), six miles further on. Farming has never been all that easy here, however, and the economy has only recently been put on a steadier footing by the growth of tourism.

The normal route to the Needles District of Canyonlands, fifty miles northwest, is to take Hwy-211 west from US-191, roughly 22 miles north of town. In summer, it's also possible to take a very different approach, through the volcanic **Abajo Mountains**, which rise west of town to over 11,000ft. The road up, from the west end of 200 South, is pretty straightforward and passes through some lovely quasi-Alpine meadows where you may spot browsing deer. You then veer north and drop down a much rougher track, to meet Hwy-211 near Newspaper Rock (see p.508).

To the east of Monticello, US-491 (which previously achieved infamy as **US-666**; see p.108) heads off to Colorado through what looks like a segment of the Great Plains that has wandered astray, complete with grain silos and fields of wheat and beans.

Arrival and information

While Monticello is not on any scheduled bus route, and the vast majority of visitors simply drive through, Bighorn Express (℡801/328-9920 or 1-888/655-7433, ⓦwww.bighornexpress.com) offers a **shuttle service** to and from Moab and Salt Lake City. Information on the town, and on the parks and public lands in the vicinity, can be picked up from the multi-agency **visitor center**, in San Juan County Courthouse at 117 S Main St (April–Oct Mon–Fri 8am–5pm, Sat & Sun 10am–5pm; Nov–March Mon–Fri 8am–5pm; ☎ 435/587-3235 or 1-800/574-4386; ⊛ www.southeastutah.org).

Accommodation

Monticello is not nearly as lively a place to spend the night as Moab, but it does have a reasonable set of **motels** to choose from.

Best Western Wayside Inn 197 E Central Ave ☎ 435/587-2261 or 1-800/633-9700, ⊛ www .bestwestern.com. Comfortable upscale motel, with pool and spa, a few yards down US-491 toward Colorado. Winter ❸, summer ❹
Canyonlands Motor Inn 197 N Main St ☎ 435/587-2266 or 1-800/952-6212. Run-of-the-mill roadside motel, on the north side of town; adequate rooms at reasonable rates. Winter ❷, summer ❸
Days Inn 549 N Main St ☎ 435/587-2458 or 1-800/325-2525, ⊛ www.daysinn.com. The biggest,

smartest motel around, on the brow of the hill at the north end of town. Winter ❸, summer ❹
Go West Inn 649 N Main St ☎ 435/587-2489. Monticello's northernmost motel, recently converted from a *Super 8*, offers a pool, clean rooms, and friendly managers. Winter ❷, summer ❹
Triangle H Motel 164 E Central Ave ☎ 435/587-2274 or 1-800/657-6622. Neat, unexciting, but inexpensive single-story motel, with some two-bedroom units. Winter ❷, summer ❸

Eating

Like any self-respecting farming town, Monticello abounds in wholesome if unexciting **diners**, plus a few fast-food outlets.

MD Ranch Cookhouse 380 S Main St ☎ 435/587-3299. Attractive timber-built restaurant, with heavy wooden furniture and an attached gift store, that's a bright, efficient oasis in such a quiet town. Grilled breakfasts and sandwich lunches are available, but the real *raison d'etre* is to serve big steak dinners, like the $17 New York steak, served with "Them Taters," an extraordinary concoction cooked in a Dutch Oven and containing mushroom soup, chiles, and bacon. They also have

fish, shrimp, ribs, and veggie burgers. Live music Fri & Sat.
The Peace Tree 518 N Main St ☎ 435/587-2601. Espresso coffees, smoothies, and fresh pastries from 8am, on the open-air terrace of a gift store. Closed Wed in Oct & April, closed completely Dec–March.
Wagon Wheel Pizza 164 S Main St ☎ 435/587-2766. Home-made pizzas of all sizes and one shape, plus deli sandwiches.

Blanding

BLANDING, just over twenty miles southwest of Monticello, was established as "Grayson" in 1905, when a new irrigation channel brought water to this site from the Abajo Mountains. In 1915, **Thomas Bicknell**, an East Coast millionaire, offered to give a library to any Utah town that would change its name to his own. Two jumped in; Thurber, near Torrey, became Bicknell, while Grayson took his wife's maiden name, Blanding. Each got a new library, though it's said they didn't get as many books as they'd expected.

Having skirted the Abajos, US-191 runs due west as it enters Blanding, and at the four-way stop in the center of town, makes a sharp dogleg turn south. That brief pause is as much time as most travelers give Blanding, whose broad avenues seldom seem to display much sign of life. However, head north at the central junction, then west, and you'll come to the interesting

Edge of the Cedars State Park, 660 West 400 North (daily: mid-April to mid-Sept 8am–7pm; mid-Sept to mid-April 9am–5pm; $6 per vehicle or $2 per person; ☎435/678-2238). An excellent museum here, primarily an educational resource for local kids, holds displays that range from the Ancestral Puebloans to the Anglos. In a town with a notorious reputation for illegal pottery-hunting by profit-seeking amateurs – known locally as "Moki poachers" – it emphasizes the role and techniques of proper archeology. Some of the Ancestral Puebloan artifacts are truly remarkable, including pots and pendants, stylish wooden plates, and a complete loom dated to around 1150 AD. Outside, a footpath leads around a pueblo occupied between 700 and 1220 AD. In the one section to have been excavated, visitors can climb down a ladder into a musty, haunting *kiva*. Signs point out that all the buildings face south, probably to maximize sunlight, whereas Navajo dwellings always face east.

Several blocks further south, the **Nations of the Four Corners Cultural Center**, 707 West 500 South (open 24hr; free), is a small park holding reconstructions of a Navajo *hogan*, a Ute teepee, a Mormon cabin, and an Hispanic hacienda. It occasionally hosts cultural events on summer evenings.

Arrival and information

Blanding's local **visitor center** is just off the highway at the north end of town, at 12 N Grayson Parkway (Mon–Fri 8am–5pm; ☎435/678-3662; Ⓦwww.blandingutah.org). The town is not served by any form of public transportation.

Accommodation

Traffic between Lake Powell to the west and Moab to the north keeps Blanding's **motels** busy enough in summer, but they're not a very inspiring bunch.

Best Western Gateway Inn 88 E Center St ☎435/678-2278 or 1-866/921-2279. Blanding's smartest motel; dependable standards, if far from enthralling. Winter ❸, summer ❹

Cliff Palace 132 S Main St ☎435/678-2264 or 1-800/553-8093. Small, slightly rundown 1960s motel that advertises itself with the slogan "Watching Your Pennies? Stay At The Cliff Palace." ❷

Comfort Inn 711 S Main St ☎435/678-3271 or 1-877/424-6423, Ⓦwww.comfortinn.com. Characterless chain motel well south of the center, with an indoor pool and complimentary continental breakfasts. Winter ❸, summer ❹

Four Corners Inn 141 E Center St ☎435/678-3257 or 1-800/574-3150, Ⓦwww.fourcornersinn.com.

Large, modern, two-story motel, just after the highway doglegs to the right, with some kitchenettes and free continental breakfasts. Winter ❸, summer ❹

Rogers House 412 S Main St ☎435/678-3932 or 1-800/355-3932, Ⓦwww.rogershouse.com. This former family home, complete with white picket fence, now offers five comfortable, antiques-furnished B&B rooms and sumptuous breakfasts. ❹

Super 8 755 S Main St ☎435/678-3880 or 1-877/888-8981, Ⓦwww.super8.com. Spick-and-span chain motel at the south end of town, with a strict nonsmoking policy. Winter ❸, summer ❹

Eating

Eating in Blanding is indeed bland eating.

Homestead Steak House 121 E Center St ☎435/678-3456. Ribs, burgers, chicken, and steaks, served for lunch and dinner in the throbbing epicenter of downtown Blanding.

Old Tymer 735 S Main St ☎435/678-2122. Conventional tourist diner, between the *Comfort Inn* and the *Super 8* at the south end of town. Open daily for all meals.

West of Blanding

A mile or so south of Blanding, at a junction marked only by a solitary gas station, **Hwy-95** heads west from US-191, to embark on a magnificent 120-mile trans-Utah journey to Hanksville. Until it was completed in 1976 – which is why it's also known as the **Bicentennial Highway** – east–west travel was effectively barred by the massive monocline of **Comb Ridge**, ten miles west of Blanding. To the Navajo, this thousand-foot wall of red rock, which stretches over eighty miles from north to south, was the backbone of the earth, as well as one of four "arrowheads" protecting their homeland. To Mormon pioneers, it was a definitive "reef" (see p.472). To the modern highway builders, it was an obstacle they simply had to blast their way through.

No towns interrupt Hwy-95 apart from the speck that is **Hite**, 87 miles along at Lake Powell (see p.491). Several side canyons off Hwy-95 bear traces of an Ancestral Puebloan presence, while the cattle ranchers who tried their hands here a century ago were later succeeded by uranium miners in the 1950s.

The Butler Wash Ruins

Ten miles west of the highway intersection, a short spur road climbs west of Hwy-95 to the parking lot for the **Butler Wash Ruins**, a stimulating Ancestral Puebloan site that's located on BLM land (24hr; free). A ten-minute hike, much of it up steep bare rock, leads to an overlook into a side canyon just short of the crest of Comb Ridge. The ruins are located in the topmost of three natural rock alcoves; a long stone ledge to the left leads down to the fertile wash where the inhabitants farmed. Archeologists see them as combining elements from what are usually regarded as distinct subgroups of the Ancestral Puebloans, in that the complex includes one Kayenta-style square *kiva* and three Mesa Verde-style round *kivas*.

Comb Ridge

Immediately beyond Butler Wash, Hwy-95 picks its way down the intense red wall of **Comb Ridge** to a cottonwood-rich valley, watered by **Comb Wash**. Confronted by the ridge on their endless journey east, the Hole-in-the-Rock party decided to head south at this point, which explains why they ended up at Bluff (see p.536). Don't copy them, however; a tempting dirt road does branch south from the highway beside the stream, with a nice little campground a short way along, but it soon succumbs to deep drifts of sand no ordinary vehicle could hope to overcome.

Mule Canyon

Roughly seven miles west of Comb Wash, after Hwy-95 has climbed laboriously back up onto the plateau, a dirt road to the north, signed for Texas Flat, leads to two separate trailheads for **Mule Canyon**. The northern sides of each of this shallow canyon's two forks hold several small but well-preserved Ancestral Puebloan **cliff dwellings**. Both forks are around six miles long, but the most interesting ruins are roughly one mile and three miles along the South Fork, so a six-mile day-hike is enough for most visitors. In itself, it's not a difficult walk, but as few hikers pass this way it's important to be prepared for all eventualities. For current advice, ask at the Kane Gulch Ranger Station (see p.534).

A separate paved turnoff, half a mile along from the Texas Flat road, leads in a few yards to **Mule Canyon Ruin**, a partly restored Ancestral Puebloan pueblo that dates from around 1000 AD. This small site, a bit too near the highway to be very evocative, is similar to Boulder's Anasazi State Park (see p.470). Its most conspicuous features – a round *kiva* that has been roofed over for preservation, and a two-story masonry tower – are connected by an underground tunnel, perhaps used for surprise appearances during religious ceremonies.

Through the Bear's Ears

Before Hwy-95 was constructed, the main road west of Blanding – and the principal access to Natural Bridges (see below) – was a dirt track that climbed across the southern fringes of the Abajo Mountains. In reasonable weather, ordinary vehicles can still follow this attractive route, by turning north from Hwy-95 seven miles from the intersection. The 32-mile detour takes well over an hour.

After a cool, pleasant drive through the mountain-top woodlands, the road crosses a razorback ridge above Arch Canyon and then descends between two rounded outcrops known as the **Bear's Ears**. This prominent landmark is regarded by the Navajo as the embodiment of a bear, guarding the northern limits of their territory. The road eventually switchbacks down a sheer red cliff to join the approach road that leads into Natural Bridges.

Natural Bridges National Monument

Three of the world's largest natural bridges span the streambeds of the small, unspectacular White and Armstrong canyons, which cut through the white sandstone of **Cedar Mesa** southwest of the Abajo Mountains. **NATURAL BRIDGES NATIONAL MONUMENT** was the loneliest of spots when prospector Cass Hite stumbled across it in the 1880s, and remained all but inaccessible when it was made Utah's first federal park in 1908. Now, however, it can be easily accessed by a four-mile spur road off Hwy-95, forty miles west of Blanding.

Originally dubbed Edwin, Augusta, and Caroline, the bridges were given Hopi names when it was realized that much of the rock art found on the canyon walls represented Hopi clan symbols. It's thought this was one of the many places that the Ancestral Puebloan ancestors of the Hopi passed through during their migrations, departing around 1270 AD after a stay of perhaps six hundred years.

Each bridge can be seen from overlooks along the one-way, nine-mile **Bridge View Drive** that loops through the monument. With considerably more effort, you can clamber down into the canyons for closer inspection, and also follow the stream from one to the next for a potential hike of up to nine miles.

Practicalities

Admission to Natural Bridges costs $6 per vehicle or $3 per person; the gates to the loop drive are open from dawn until dusk daily. The **visitor center** – which is solar-powered, being so far from any other source of energy – stocks free trail guides and other background material (daily: March–Oct 8am–5.30pm; Nov–Feb 9am–4.30pm; ☏435/692-1234, ⓦwww.nps.gov/nabr). Excellent displays and scale models explain how the bridges were formed, pointing out that natural bridges occur throughout the US, from West Virginia to Illinois. The visitor center holds the only public **payphone** in the 122 miles

△ Owachomo Bridge, Natural Bridges National Monument

between Hanksville and Blanding, and is also the only source of water for the first-come first-served **campground** nearby ($10).

The closest **motel** to the monument, the isolated *Fry Canyon Lodge*, twenty miles west on Hwy-95, has been forced to close indefinitely by the lowering level of Lake Powell; it's just possible that it will have reopened, if the waters have risen, by the time you read this (☏435/259-5334; ⓦwww.frycanyon.com). As things stand, however, the nearest places to stay are in Blanding.

Bridge View Drive

The first and largest bridge, **Sipapu Bridge**, was named for the "hole" through which the Hopi emerged into this world. Standing at 220ft high by 268ft wide, it is surpassed only by Rainbow Bridge (see p.488). Although the roadside overlook provides a good straight-on view as it thrusts from a tangle of rocks, you'll only really appreciate Sipapu's size if you hike down from the trailhead half a mile further on. This is the most difficult trail in the monument, involving three short ladders, two metal staircases, and a couple of stretches of slickrock with steep drop-offs. The best photos come from a ledge halfway down; by the time you're amid the trees directly beneath it, it's too big to fit in most viewfinders.

The next parking lot on the road is the start of a half-mile mesa-top trail that leads to a vantage point above **Horsecollar Ruin**. This small Ancestral Puebloan site, tucked into an alcove low on the canyon walls, is not visible from below.

Even after a 4000-ton rockfall in 1992, **Kachina Bridge**, the next stop, is much thicker than Sipapu, being more of a tunnel beneath a broad span of desert-varnish-stained sandstone. Seen from the overlook, it's far less distinct, with rocks rather than sunlight visible through the gap. On the trail down, railings guide you across the slickrock, and there's a crude staircase made from sandstone slabs. The stream at the bottom is lined by splendid cottonwoods, while pictographs near the base of the bridge resemble the *kachinas* of Hopi religion (see p.84).

Natural bridges are short-lived phenomena. Even the oldest in the monument – **Owachomo**, two miles beyond Kachina by road – is a mere 5000 years old, and it's unlikely to last much longer. Though 180ft across, it tapers to just nine feet thick. It now stands slightly to one side of the streambed of Armstrong Canyon, reached by an easy half-mile round-trip hike down from the overlook. *Owachomo* means "flat-rock mound," a reference to the hummock at the left end of the span.

The **streambed trail** that connects the three bridges makes a delightful walk, meandering along the sandy wash beneath the trees. However, unless you double back, returning to your starting point involves a long hike across the mesa top, which is not as flat as you'd imagine and offers very little shade; allow five hours for the full 8.6-mile walk. One idea would be to start from Owachomo or Kachina and hike back toward Sipapu, hoping you'll meet up with someone who can give you a ride back to your vehicle.

Grand Gulch Primitive Area

If you share a passion for archeology with the stamina for long-distance hiking, an expedition into the **GRAND GULCH PRIMITIVE AREA**, south of Natural Bridges, can make you feel like a real-life Indiana Jones. Every twist and turn of this deep, dramatic gorge seems to be filled with relics of its thousand-year occupation by the Ancestral Puebloans, although they abandoned the canyon six centuries before it was named by the Hole-in-the-Rock pioneers.

Grand Gulch gouges across Cedar Mesa for just over fifty miles, dropping 2700ft to meet the San Juan River. There's no access for vehicles; the only path in starts from **Kane Gulch Ranger Station** (March to mid-Nov, daily 8am–noon; no phone), five miles south of the point where Hwy-261 leaves Hwy-95, two miles east of the Natural Bridges turnoff. Typical backpacking expeditions last as long as a week, and you can only camp overnight in the gulch with an $8 permit, obtainable up to six months in advance from the San Juan Resource Area office in Monticello's visitor center (see p.529; ☎435/587-1532). So long as your group consists of fewer than eight people, you should be able to pick up a permit at the ranger station on the day you set off. In any case, register there before you set off, even if you're just day-hiking, for which a fee of $2 is levied.

The trail begins by dropping steadily down Kane Gulch, a side canyon that deepens as it goes, and joins Grand Gulch proper four miles along. **Junction Ruin** here, the largest ruin in the canyon system, makes a popular day-hike destination, though **Turkey Pen Ruin**, at 4.7 miles, and **Stimper Arch** just beyond, are also within round-trip reach. If you're making a longer trip, it's possible to leave Grand Gulch via **Bullet Canyon** to the east – in which case a total hike of 23 miles brings you back to Hwy-261 roughly seven miles south of the ranger station – or **Collins Canyon** to the west further along – a 38-mile hike that ends at a dirt road south of Hwy-276. For either of those routes, you'll need a car shuttle to get back to your vehicle, but that's probably easier to arrange than fixing for someone to meet you by boat on the San Juan, which is the only way out if you hike all the way to the end of Grand Gulch. Most visitors find it simpler just to double back at some point en route.

Kane Gulch Ranger Station can also provide details on day-hikes that head **east** from Hwy-261, into remote side canyons on Cedar Mesa. Road conditions are often treacherous, so don't set off without obtaining up-to-the-minute advice.

Muley Point

South of Kane Gulch, Hwy-261 crosses Cedar Mesa for its remaining seventeen miles. Before you take the plunge on the **Moki Dugway**, **MULEY POINT**, exactly five miles west of its top along a red-dirt road, is an absolute must-see. Note that the turnoff is signposted, but the sign is only conspicuous if you're coming from the north, and that the lesser viewpoint 3.9 miles along is not Muley Point.

When they finally get around to declaring all of southern Utah to be one vast national park, Muley Point will surely be the centerpiece. Quite simply, these are among the most stupendous views in the world (though they're at their finest in the morning, when the sun is behind you). You're now at the southernmost tip of Cedar Mesa and the eastern extremity of Glen Canyon National Recreational Area. Far below, the San Juan River goosenecks its way west, while the Navajo Nation stretches off on the far side. Features on the horizon include Monument Valley in all its glory, the Sleeping Ute in Colorado, Navajo Mountain, and the cliffs above the west shore of Lake Powell.

The Moki Dugway

Hwy-261 doesn't stand on ceremony when it needs to get down off Cedar Mesa; it just plummets over the edge. The **MOKI DUGWAY**, which drops 1100ft in little more than two miles, is an exhilarating switchback ride, much of it still on a "washboard" strip of gravel, although it feels a whole lot safer now that most of its many hairpin bends are paved. This ancient trail was originally improved by mining companies during the 1950s; you'll just have to hope you don't meet a truck-load of uranium coming the other way. If you have the nerve, the pullouts for vehicles to pass make great viewpoints, but it's best to do all your sightseeing at the top. Soon after the pavement resumes at the bottom of the Moki Dugway, another dirt road marks the western end of the **Valley of the Gods**; see p.537.

Goosenecks State Reserve

Just before Hwy-261 meets US-163, six miles from the foot of the Moki Dugway and five miles north of Mexican Hat, the inconspicuous **Hwy-316** branches off to the west, to end 3.5 miles along at the extraordinary **GOOSE-NECKS STATE RESERVE**. Although the railed viewing area here stands a thousand feet below Cedar Mesa, the **San Juan River** is still another thousand feet down.

The river is an amazing sight, looping between huge pyramidal buttes in a textbook example of what geologists call an "entrenched meander." Its serpentine coils – once meanders on a muddy plain, later fixed in stone by the uplifting of the Colorado Plateau – are so extravagant that it flows six miles while advancing little more than one mile west. Above the distant sliver of riverbank greenery, alternate layers of gray limestone and red sandstone stripe the cliffs, while Monument Valley once again stands out on the skyline.

Goosenecks State Reserve has no visitor center and no opening hours, and charges no fee.

Bluff

BLUFF, 23 miles south of Blanding (see p.529) on US-191, is a pretty little riverside settlement whose somewhat humdrum existence belies the extraordinary efforts its founders made to get here. The 230 **Hole-in-the-Rock** pioneers who reached this site on April 6, 1880 had trekked right across the heart of Utah, literally blasting their way through the canyons of the Colorado; for the full story, see p.464.

Once they arrived, they settled down to a life of ranching and agriculture, made difficult by the San Juan River's propensity to flood. The back streets still hold a dozen or so of their original sturdy homes, making Bluff the least spoiled, most authentic town in the region. Its setting is consistently stunning, from the red-rock pinnacles known as the **Navajo Twins**, which mark the mouth of the narrow **Cow Canyon** gorge through which US-191 drops in from the north, to the cottonwoods that line the San Juan River, glinting against the sheer red bluff that rises on the far side. **Ancestral Puebloan** remains abound, including petroglyphs along Hwy-163 to the east, and the unexcavated mound, thought to conceal a buried pueblo, beside the town cemetery on a hillock just north of the center.

Information and tours

Bluff doesn't have its own **visitor center**, though you can pick up local information online at Ⓦwww.southeastutah.org. In late October, it plays host to the three-day **Utah Navajo Fair**.

The town is a center for **river-running** on the San Juan, with rafts putting in at **Sand Island Recreation Area**, three miles west. The chief local operator, Wild Rivers Expeditions (Ⓣ435/672-2244 or 1-800/422-7654, Ⓦwww.riversandruins .com), runs one-day float trips to Mexican Hat (adults $125, under-13s $75), plus a range of longer voyages. In addition, **Far Out Expeditions** (Ⓣ435/672-2294, Ⓦwww.faroutexpeditions.com) runs all-day 4WD tours of Monument Valley, for around $130per person, and half-day trips to canyons and archeological sites closer at hand.

Accommodation

Bluff may not be the fanciest place in the world, but its genuine small-town feel makes it a nicer prospect than any of its neighbors. It's also a handy overnight stop for **Hovenweep National Monument**, forty miles northwest; see Chapter One, p.89.

Calf Canyon B&B Seventh East at Black Locust Ⓣ435/672-2470 or 1-888/922-2470. Spacious three-room B&B , set in an imposing Victorian family home, on the northeast side of town. Closed Nov–March. ⑤

Desert Rose Inn 701 W US-191 Ⓣ435/672-2303 or 1-888/475-7673, Ⓦwww.desertroseinn.com. New timber-built motel at the west end of town, with thirty attractively designed and well-furnished rooms plus individual cabins of similar standard. Nov–Feb ③, March–Aug ④, Sept & Oct ⑤.

Far Out Guest House 700 East & Mulberry Ⓣ435/672-2294, Ⓦwww.faroutexpeditions.com. Historic home that holds two guestrooms, each of which has six beds and can be either rented out on a bed-by-bed basis, in which case a dorm bed costs around $15, or as a private room ($69). Most visitors are here to take one of Far Out's tours, detailed above. ①–④

Kokopelli Inn PO Box 27, US-191 Ⓣ435/672-2322 or 1-800/541-8854 Ⓦwww.kokoinn.com. Friendly, quiet roadside motel, adjoining a gas station and grocery with a deli counter. Winter ②, summer ③

Recapture Lodge PO Box 309, US-191 Ⓣ435/672-2281, Ⓦwww.bluffutah.org/ recapturelodge@aol.com. Pleasantly rural wooden motel, reaching back toward the river, plus a few rooms in two old pioneer homes. For groups, the owners can arrange area tours, including Monument Valley expeditions and llama treks. ③

Eating

Despite its size, Bluff has a good range of **restaurants**, though they're a bit too spread out to walk from one to the next comparing menus.

Cottonwood Steakhouse US-191 ☎435/672-2282. Open-air barbecue at the west end of town, with wooden tables arranged around a giant cottonwood. A great place to enjoy beer and steaks beneath the stars; the steaks are priced at up to $22, and the menu's a bit short if you're not a beef-eater. One corner of the pseudo-Western stockade serves as Fort Crapper (the toilets). Dinner only, from 5pm in spring and fall, 6pm in summer. Closed mid-Oct to Feb.

Cow Canyon Trading Post Hwy-163 ☎435/672-2208. Former trading post, where Hwy-163 leaves US-161 and heads for Colorado, that is now an imaginative and moderately priced local restaurant. If you've had your fill of Navajo tacos, this is the place to sample a Navajo quiche. A traditional lamb stew costs $11. Usually open in summer only, Thurs–Mon 6–9pm.

Twin Rocks Cafe Navajo Twins Drive ☎435/672-2341. Glass-fronted diner, set against the rocks north of town, just west of US-191. Breakfast bagels and muffins, then salads and sandwiches, and chicken or fajita dinners for around $10. The adjoining *Trading Post* is well worth exploring. Summer daily 7am–10pm, winter Mon–Sat 8am–9pm.

The Valley of the Gods

Bluff is very much at the edge of the desert; driving west you soon descend the southern end of **Comb Ridge** (see p.531) into vintage red-rock badlands, with the buttes of Monument Valley silhouetted above the horizon.

Similar, smaller-scale monoliths can be toured closer at hand, with no restrictions or admission fees, in the **VALLEY OF THE GODS**. This "garden" of isolated sandstone columns – said by the Navajo to be petrified warriors – holds no fixed hiking trails. Drivers can see it all from a winding **seventeen-mile dirt road**, which leaves US-163 on the far side of Lime Creek, roughly eighteen miles west of Bluff, and meets Hwy-261 near the foot of the Moki Dugway (see p.535), 10.6 miles northwest of Mexican Hat.

It's a rough road, which becomes impassable when wet, but so long as you don't mind a few bangs on the bottom as you cross dry stony washes you should be able to make it in a rental car. The east side holds the best of the "monuments," and the most difficult terrain, but there's something to be said for driving in from the west, which offers great views all the way along.

The only building en route is the *Valley of the Gods B&B* (☎970/749-1164; Ⓦwww.zippitydodah.com/vog; ⑤), which squats in superb isolation half a mile in from the west. All of its four rooms have baths, dinner is served by prior arrangement, and the owners can also fix backcountry **tours**.

Mexican Hat

MEXICAN HAT, the last stop in southeastern Utah before the start of the Navajo Indian reservation across the San Juan River, is an appealingly dusty outpost that has never amounted to the status of a town. It first sprang into being in 1901, following false reports that gold had been discovered nearby, and was kept going by a genuine oil strike in 1908 and the uranium boom of the 1950s. For tourists, it now makes a convenient base for **Monument Valley**, twenty miles south (see p.69).

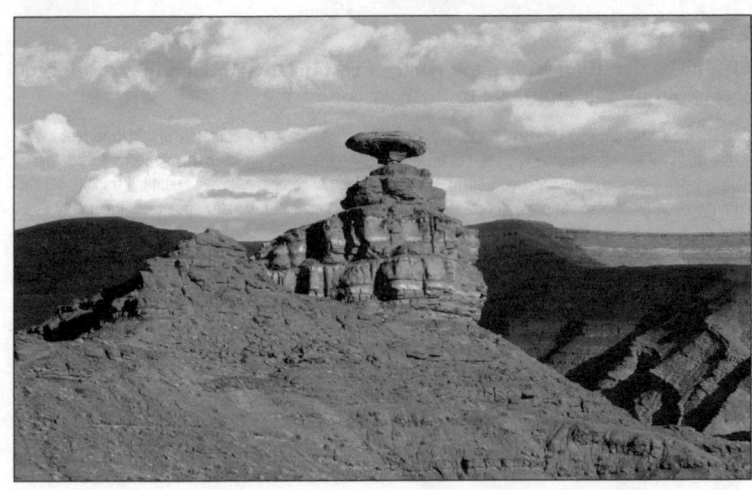

△ Mexican Hat Rock

Mexican Hat Rock, the sandstone sombrero for which the settlement was named, looks down on the San Juan a mile north. The highway passes a few hundred yards west, but a gravel road permits closer inspection. It's at its best in the afternoon, when the sun strikes the amazing zigzag striations of the gray and white cliffs across the river. This pattern, known as the **Navajo Blanket**, is said to show the skin markings of a giant bullsnake that lives in the river below, and carved out the "goosenecks" to the west (see p.535).

Practicalities

All of Mexican Hat's four **motels**, except the budget *Canyonlands*, have their own inexpensive restaurants and stores and are substantially the same. There are virtually no other buildings around.

Canyonlands Motel PO Box 310187, US-163, Mexican Hat, UT 84531 ☎ 435/683-2230. Very basic ten-room motel, on the higher side of the highway next to the Texaco gas station, and open in summer only. ❷

Hat Rock Inn PO Box 310337, US-163, Mexican Hat, UT 84531 ☎ 435/683-2221. Modern, timber-built motel, 100 yards up from the river, with good quality rooms and its own Mexican restaurant, the *Hat Rock Café*. Current renovations are scheduled to include construction of a pool and the provision of river access. Winter ❸, summer ❹

Mexican Hat Lodge PO Box 310175, US-163, Mexican Hat, UT 84531 ☎ 435/683-2222, ⓦ www.mexicanhat.net. Mexican Hat's northernmost motel, with a pool and a nice open-air steakhouse. Nov–April ❷, May–Oct ❹

San Juan Inn & Trading Post PO Box 310276, US-163, Mexican Hat, UT 84531 ☎ 435/683-2220 or 1-800/447-2022. Solid, long-established motel perched fifty feet above the north bank of the San Juan, beside the highway bridge. The *Olde Bridge Bar and Grill* serves a full menu from 7am daily, ranging from Navajo tacos to steaks, plus cold beers. ❸

Las Vegas

CHAPTER 8

Highlights

✳ **Luxor** Bursting with Egyptian motifs and attractions, this giant, smoked-glass pyramid is irresistible for all ages. See p.550

✳ **New York–New York** A loving recreation of the Big Apple in the heart of the Big Cheese. See p.551

✳ **The Forum** "Living statues" and fake sky make the mall at *Caesars* fun even for determined small spenders. See p.552

✳ **Grand Canal** *The Venetian*, centering on the irresistibly absurd Grand Canal, holds more to see and do than any other casino. See p.553

✳ **Big Shot** The city's craziest thrill ride: Free-fall from the top of the *Stratosphere*. See p.554

✳ **The Buffet at Bellagio** Quantity and quality; you pay a bit extra, but *Bellagio*'s buffet is out of this world. See p.556

✳ **Ghostbar** The hub of Las Vegas's nightlife in the twenty-first century, a new-breed "ultra-lounge" with fabulous views. See p.559

✳ **Lance Burton** Las Vegas's most engaging magician wows family audiences nightly at the *Monte Carlo*. See p.561

✳ **Cirque du Soleil** With O at *Bellagio*, Mystère at *TI*, Kà at the *MGM Grand*, and more besides, the Canadian troupe dominates Las Vegas's entertainment scene. See p.561

△ New York–New York

8

Las Vegas

> Little emphasis is placed on the gambling clubs and divorce facilities – though they are attractions to many visitors – and much is being done to build up the cultural attractions. No cheap and easily parodied slogans have been adopted to publicize the city, no attempt has been made to introduce pseudo-romantic architectural themes or to give artificial glamour or gaiety. Las Vegas is itself – natural and therefore very appealing to people with a wide variety of interests.
>
> *WPA Guidebook to Nevada*, 1940

Shimmering from the desert haze of Nevada like a latter-day El Dorado, **LAS VEGAS** is the most dynamic, spectacular city on earth. At the start of the twentieth century, it didn't even exist; now it's home to over one million people, with enough newcomers arriving all the time to need a new school every month. Boasting fourteen of the world's twenty largest hotels, it's a monument to architectural exuberance, whose flamboyant, no-expense-spared **casinos** lure in thirty-seven million tourists each year.

Las Vegas has been stockpiling superlatives since the 1950s, but never rests on its laurels for a moment. First-time visitors tend to expect the city to be a repository of kitsch, but the casino owners are far too canny to be sentimental about the old days. Yes, there are a few Elvis impersonators around, but what characterizes the city far more is its endless quest for **novelty**. Long before they lose their sparkle, yesterday's showpieces are blasted into rubble, to make way for ever more extravagant replacements. A few years ago, when the fashion was for fantasy, Arthurian castles and Egyptian pyramids mushroomed along the legendary Strip; now Vegas demands nothing less than entire cities, and holds pocket versions of New York, Paris, Monte Carlo, and Venice.

While Las Vegas has certainly cleaned up its act since the early days of Mob domination, there's little truth in the notion that it's become a **family** destination. Neither is it as consistently **cheap** as it used to be. It's still possible to find good, inexpensive rooms, and the all-you-can-eat buffets offer unbeatable value, but the casino owners have finally discovered that high-rollers happy to lose hundreds of dollars per night don't mind paying premium prices to eat at top-quality restaurants, while the latest developments are budgeting room rates of more like $300 than $30 per night.

Your first hours in Las Vegas are like entering another world, where the religion is luck, the language is money, and time is measured by revolutions of a

---

For an exhaustive account of Las Vegas, see the separate **Rough Guide Directions: Las Vegas**, also by Greg Ward.

roulette wheel. Once you're acclimatized, the whole spectacle can be absolutely exhilarating – assuming you haven't pinned your hopes, and your savings, on the pursuit of a fortune. Even so, while Las Vegas is an unmissable destination, it's also one that palls for most visitors after a couple of (hectic) days.

If you've come solely to gamble, there's not much to say beyond the fact that all the casinos are free and open 24 hours per day, with acres of floor space packed with ways to lose money: **million-dollar slots**, video **poker**, **blackjack**, **craps**, **roulette** wheels, and much, much more. The casinos will just love it if you try to play a system; with the odds stacked against you, your best hope of a large win is to bet your entire stake on one single play, and then stop, win or lose.

⑧ A history of Las Vegas

Las Vegas has a shorter history than almost any other city in the world. The only US city founded in the twentieth century to boast over a million inhabitants, it's also the only one that has consistently prioritized the need to attract visitors over the quality of life of its own residents.

The name *Las Vegas* – Spanish for "the meadows" – originally applied to a group of natural springs that from 1829 onwards served as a way-station for travelers on the Old Spanish Trail. For the rest of the nineteenth century, the Paiute Indians shared the region with a handful of Mormon ranchers, and the valley had a population of just thirty in 1900. Things changed in 1905, with the completion of the now-defunct rail link between Salt Lake City and Los Angeles. Las Vegas itself was founded on May 15 that year, when the railroads auctioned off lots around what's now Fremont Street.

Ironically, Nevada was the first state to outlaw gambling, in 1909, but it was made legal once more in 1931, and the workers who built the nearby Hoover Dam flocked to Vegas to bet away their pay-packets. Providing abundant cheap electricity and water, the dam amounted to a massive federal subsidy for the infant city. Hotel-casinos such as the daring 65-room *El Rancho* began to appear in the early 1940s, but the Midwest Mafia were the first to appreciate the potential for profit. Mobster Bugsy Siegel raised $7 million to open the *Flamingo* on the Strip in December 1946; early losses forced him to close again in January, and although he swiftly managed to reopen in March, his erstwhile partners were dissatisfied enough with their returns to have him murdered in LA in June.

By the 1950s, Las Vegas was booming. The military had arrived – mushroom clouds from **A-bomb tests** in the deserts were visible from the city, and visitors would drive out with picnics to get a better view – and so too had big guns like **Frank Sinatra**, who debuted at the *Desert Inn* in 1951, and **Liberace**, who received $50,000 to open the *Riviera* in 1955. As the stars gravitated toward the Vegas honeypot, nightclubs across America went out of business, and the city became the nation's undisputed live-entertainment capital.

The beginning of the end for Mob rule in Vegas came in 1966, after reclusive airline tycoon **Howard Hughes** sold TWA for $500 million and moved into the *Desert Inn*. When the owners tired of his nongambling ways, he simply bought the hotel, and his clean-cut image encouraged other entrepreneurs to follow suit. **Elvis** arrived a little later; the young rock'n'roller had bombed at the *New Frontier* in 1956, but started a triumphant five-year stint as a karate-kicking lounge lizard at the *International* (now the *Las Vegas Hilton*) in 1969.

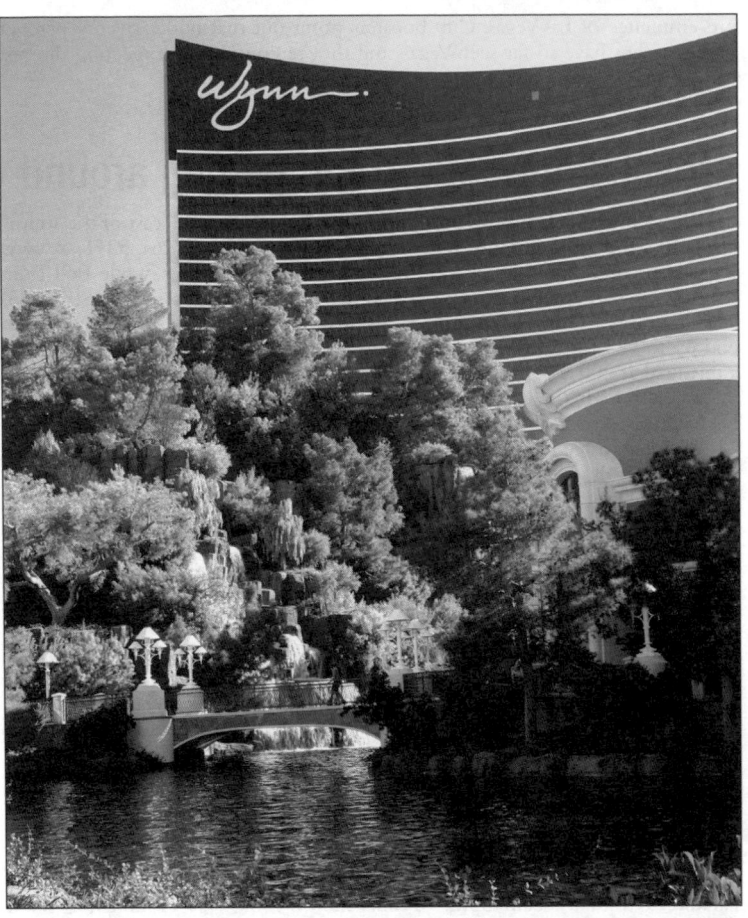

△ Wynn Las Vegas

Endless federal swoops and stings drove the Mob out of sight by the 1980s, in time for Vegas to reinvent itself on a surge of junk-bond megadollars. The success of Steve Wynn's *Mirage* in enticing a new generation of visitors, from 1989 onwards, spawned a host of imitators. A spate of casino building saw *Excalibur* and the *MGM Grand* followed first by *Luxor* and *New York–New York* and then, as the millennium approached, by the opulent quartet of *Bellagio, Mandalay Bay, The Venetian*, and *Paris*. The 21st century, however, started with shockwaves. Unsuccessful investments elsewhere forced Steve Wynn to sell *Bellagio* and the *Mirage* to the MGM group; the new *Aladdin* swiftly went bankrupt; and the tragedy of September 11, 2001, hit the Las Vegas economy hard.

And yet, once again, Las Vegas has bounced back, with *The Venetian* after an uncertain start going from strength to strength as the flagship for all that the city does best, and Wynn himself opening his biggest casino yet, *Wynn Las Vegas*, on the site of the old *Desert Inn*. Beneath the glitz, **gambling** remains the bedrock, and the spread of casinos elsewhere in the US has done nothing to dent the pre-eminence of Las Vegas. City boosters point out that under twenty percent of Americans have so far seen Vegas, and they're confidently expecting the rest to turn up any day now.

Arrival, information, and getting around

Las Vegas's busy **McCarran International Airport** is a mile east of the southern end of the Strip, and four miles from downtown (☎702/261-5211, ⓦwww .mccarran.com). Some hotels run free shuttle buses for guests, while Bell Trans (☎702/739-7990, ⓦwww.bell-trans.com) runs **minibuses** to the Strip ($5) and downtown ($6), and a **cab** to the Strip costs from $15 for the southern end up to $25 for casinos further north. Greyhound's long-distance **buses** use a terminal at 200 S Main St downtown, but Amtrak **trains** no longer serve Las Vegas – although a new high-speed service between LA and Las Vegas has long been rumored to be coming soon.

If you plan to see more of Vegas than the Strip – and even there, it's too hot in summer to walk more than a couple of blocks in the daytime – a **car** is invaluable. All the rental companies listed on p.42 have outlets at the airport. **Public transport** does exist, however. The **Las Vegas Monorail**, unveiled in 2004, runs along the eastern side of the Strip from the *MGM Grand* to the *Sahara*, making a business-traveler-friendly off-Strip detour via the Convention Center and the *Hilton* (daily 6am–2am; single trip $3, 1-day pass $10, 10-ride pass $20; ☎702/699-8299, www.lvmonorail.com). However, the Monorail doesn't connect the Strip to either the airport or downtown, so it's more of a handy, high-priced extra than a much-needed lifeline – and for short hops along the Strip it can easily be slower than walking, because the actual stations tend to be located at the back of the casinos. Separate, free monorail systems also link *Mandalay Bay* with *Excalibur* via *Luxor*, and the *Mirage* with *TI*.

In addition, the oak-veneered streetcars of the **Las Vegas Strip Trolley** (☎702/382-1404) ply the Strip between *Mandalay Bay* and the *Stratosphere*, for a flat fare of $1.65. CAT **buses** (☎702/228-7433, ⓦwww.catride.com) serve the whole city; #301 and #302 connect the Strip to downtown ($2).

Although there is a **visitor center** at the vast Convention Center, 3150 Paradise Rd (daily 8am–5pm; ☎702/892-0711 or 877/VISIT-LV, ⓦwww .vegasfreedom.com), at half a mile east of the Strip it's too far to reach on foot, and its brochures hold little that you can't find more easily elsewhere. The casino where you're staying, for example, will almost certainly hold racks of brochures, plus a booking desk that can make reservations for shows, tours and the like. The **website** of the Las Vegas Convention & Visitors Authority (ⓦwww.lasvegas24hours.com) is packed with information on lodging, activities, transportation and tours, while every issue of the daily newspaper *Las Vegas Review-Journal* has a four-page guide to the city.

There can be no easier city in which to **change money**: the casinos gladly convert almost any currency, and their walls are festooned with every conceivable ATM machine.

Accommodation

Although Las Vegas has well over 135,000 motel and hotel rooms (almost all hitched to casinos), it's best to book accommodation ahead if you're on a tight

Second only to making your fortune as a reason to visit Las Vegas is the prospect of **getting married**. Over a hundred thousand weddings are performed here each year, many so informal that bride and groom just wind down the window of their car during the ceremony. Long before the Britney Spears fiasco, a Vegas wedding was a byword for tongue-in-cheek chic. What's more surprising, however, is that most marriages are deeply formal affairs. Both the casinos and a horde of independent wedding chapels compete to offer elaborate ceremonies with all the traditional trimmings, from white gowns and black limousines to garters and boutonnieres. Especially busy days include New Year's Eve, which gives American couples the right to file a joint tax return for the preceding year, and Valentine's Day.

You don't have to be a local resident, American, or take a blood test to get wed here. Assuming you're both at least eighteen years old and carrying picture ID– and not already married – simply turn up at the Clark County Marriage License Bureau, downtown at 200 S Third St (Mon–Thurs 8am–midnight, and continuously from Fri 8am to Sun midnight; ☎702/455-4415, ⊛www.accessclarkcounty.com/clerk/Marriage_Information), and buy a marriage license for $55 cash. You can then walk over to the Clark County Court House at 309 S Third St (daily 8am–10pm), and be married by the Commissioner for Civil Marriages.

If you want a little more ceremony than that, wedding chapels claim to charge as little as $55 for basic ceremonies, but at that sort of rate even the minister is an "extra" costing an additional $45. Reckon on paying at least $150 for the bare minimum, which is liable to be as romantic a process as checking in at a hotel, and to take about as long. The full deluxe service ranges up to whatever you can afford. Novelty options include pledging your eternal loyalty on the deck of the *USS Enterprise* at the Hilton (☎702/697-8750); floating on a gondola in *The Venetian*'s Grand Canal (☎702/414-4253); or cavorting in medieval costume at *Excalibur* (☎702/597-7278); or beside your helicopter at the bottom of the Grand Canyon (Papillon; ☎702/736-7243).

Graceland Wedding Chapel 619 S Las Vegas Blvd ☎702/382-0091 or 1-800/824-5732, ⊛www.gracelandchapel.com. Home of the King – an Elvis impersonator will act as best man, give the bride away, or serenade you, but unfortunately he can't perform the service.

Little Chapel of the Flowers 1717 Las Vegas Blvd S ☎702/735-4331 or 800/843-2410, ⊛www.littlechapel.com. Weddings at this rather twee, traditional establishment, featuring two antiques-furnished chapels, range upwards from $195. For $1195 you get a helicopter ride to the Grand Canyon thrown in, while for $4995 you can be married on a yacht on Lake Mead.

Little Church of the West 4617 Las Vegas Blvd S ☎702/739-7971 or 1-800/821-2452, ⊛www.littlechurchlv.com. Once part of the *Last Frontier* casino, this fifty-year-old chapel is on the National Register of Historic Places, and has moved progressively down the Strip to its current site south of *Mandalay Bay*. Among the more peaceful and quiet places to exchange your Vegas vows – if that's really what you want.

Little White Chapel 1301 S Las Vegas Blvd ☎702/382-5943 or 1-800/545-8111, ⊛www.alittlewhitechapel.com. Where Bruce Willis and Demi Moore married each other, Michael Jordan and Joan Collins married other people, and Britney Spears married Jason Alexander in January 2004. Open all day every day, with ceremonies in the roofed-over driveway (or "Tunnel of Love") for those in a major hurry.

budget or arriving on Friday or Saturday; upwards of 200,000 people descend upon the city every weekend. Whatever you may have heard, Las Vegas hotels no longer offer incredibly cheap deals at the drop of a hat; with occupancy rates averaging ninety percent year-round, they don't need to. It is true that serious gamblers can get their accommodation free, but to count as "serious" you'd have to commit yourself to gambling several thousand dollars, which is a pretty strange definition of "free."

Precise **room rates** are entirely dictated by supply and demand. Even if you stay in the same room for several consecutive days, you'll be charged a different rate for each day, depending not only on the day of the week but also which conventions or events may be happening in town and the hotel's general level of business. Whatever rate you're quoted, it's always worth trying a little negotiation; you may get a discount if you're attending a convention or if you belong to a motoring organization such as the AAA or the British AA. The only surefire way to get a cut-price room, however, is to **visit during the week** rather than on the weekend. Rates everywhere rise enormously on Friday or Saturday; expect to pay perhaps $30 to $50 extra per night in a lower-end property, more like $100 extra in the big-name casinos. On top of that, many hotels won't accept Saturday arrivals. **Room taxes** add an additional eleven percent downtown, nine percent elsewhere.

The **Las Vegas Convention & Visitors Authority** offers an availability and reservations service on ☎1-877/847-4858. It's also worth trying both general **online reservations** websites, such as ⓦwww.expedia.com and ⓦwww.travelocitycom, and local specialists like Las Vegas Hotel Reservation Center (☎702/873-8041 or 1-800/394-7750, ⓦwww.lasvegashotel.com).

The Strip

Aladdin Resort and Casino 3667 Las Vegas Blvd S ☎702/785-5555 or 1-877/333-9474, ⓦwww.aladdincasino.com. The financially troubled *Aladdin* may well have been rebranded as *Planet Hollywood* by the time you visit, but hopefully it will remain much more user-friendly than most of its giant neighbors. Each of its 2600 spacious rooms is within easy reach of an elevator, with separate bath and shower, while the dining and shopping are first class. Mon–Thurs & Sun ⑤, Fri & Sat ⑦

Bellagio Resort & Casino 3600 Las Vegas Blvd S ☎702/693-7111 or 1-888/987-6667, ⓦwww.bellagio.com. The very top end of the spectrum. Extremely luxurious rooms, superb pool complex, and the best restaurants in town. You can, however, live the high life in other Vegas casinos for half the price. Mon–Thurs & Sun ⑦, Fri & Sat ⑨

Caesars Palace 3570 Las Vegas Blvd S ☎702/731-7222 or 1-800/634-6661, ⓦwww.caesarspalace.com. *Caesars*' older rooms still burst with pseudo-Roman splendor, while those in the newer Tower are more conventionally elegant; paying as little as $10 extra can get you a suite with a four-poster bed. It's just a shame the place is such a colossal, baffling labyrinth. Mon–Thurs & Sun ⑥, Fri & Sat ⑧

Circus Circus Hotel/Casino 2880 Las Vegas Blvd S ☎702/734-0410 or 1-800/444-2472, ⓦwww.circuscircus.com. *Excalibur*'s one serious rival for family appeal; kids love the theme park and circus acts, adults love the low room rates. Rooms in the motel-like Manor section at the back are pretty grim; pay a little more to stay in one of the Towers instead. Mon–Thurs & Sun ③, Fri & Sat ④

Excalibur Hotel & Casino 3850 Las Vegas Blvd S ☎702/597-7700 or 1-800/937-7777, ⓦwww.excaliburcasino.com. The 4000 rooms in this fantastically garish fake castle don't reflect the property's theme and are nothing special. Few have views to speak of – many face in rather than out – and they have showers, not baths. What's more, the whole place tends to be uncomfortably crowded. Mon–Thurs & Sun ③, Fri & Sat ⑥

Flamingo 3555 Las Vegas Blvd S ☎702/733-3111 or 1-800/732-2111, ⓦwww.flamingolasvegas.com. Bugsy Siegel's *Flamingo* is not quite in Vegas's premier league, but it offers 4000 well-appointed rooms and a great tropical-themed pool complex, complete with real flamingos. Mon–Thurs & Sun ⑤, Fri & Sat ⑦

Imperial Palace 3535 Las Vegas Blvd S ☎702/731-3311 or 1-800/634-6441, ⓦwww.imperialpalace.com. One of the best-value options in the heart of the Strip. Standard rooms are adequate if not exciting, while the irresistible "luv tub" suites, at about $30 extra, offer huge beds, even bigger sunken baths, and mirrors everywhere you can imagine. Mon–Thurs & Sun ③, Fri & Sat ⑥

Luxor Las Vegas 3900 Las Vegas Blvd S ☏ 702/262-4102 or 1-888/777-0188, ⓦ www.luxor.com. Vast, smoked-glass pyramid, in which all two thousand rooms face outwards, with tremendous views – and they're much larger than usual. Unlike the extra two thousand rooms in the newer tower next door, however, most have showers, not baths. Mon–Thurs & Sun ❹, Fri & Sat ❻

Mandalay Bay Resort & Casino 3950 Las Vegas Blvd S ☏ 702/632-7777 or 1-888/632-7000, ⓦ www.mandalaybay.com. This upscale, young-adult playground is a long way south of the central Strip, but all its luxurious rooms have both bath and walk-in shower, and there's a spectacular wave pool. Mon–Thurs & Sun ❻, Fri & Sat ❽

MGM Grand Hotel/Casino 3799 Las Vegas Blvd S ☏ 702/891-1111 or 1-800/929-1111, ⓦ www.mgmgrand.com. Waiting for any kind of service, especially check-in, at the largest hotel in the US – 5005 rooms and counting – can be horrendous, but you get a great standard of accommodation for the price. Mon–Thurs & Sun ❺, Fri & Sat ❼

Mirage 3400 Las Vegas Blvd S ☏ 702/791-7111 or 800/627-6667, ⓦ www.mirage.com. The glitzy *Mirage* is not the market leader it used to be, and its smallish rooms are paired with even smaller bathrooms. Even so, the public areas downstairs remain impressive, the pool complex is nicely laid out, and the weekday rates for one of Las Vegas's most prestigious addresses aren't at all bad. Sun–Thurs ❻, Fri & Sat ❽

New York–New York Hotel & Casino 3790 Las Vegas Blvd S ☏ 702/740-6050 or 1-800/693-6763, ⓦ www.nynyhotelcasino.com. Thanks to sheer attention to detail, this is the most exuberantly enjoyable casino on the Strip – and it's small enough that you're not always shuffling down endless corridors. The rooms are very nice, if a bit cramped, and filled with Art Deco flourishes. Mon–Thurs & Sun ❺, Fri & Sat ❼

Paris–Las Vegas 3655 Las Vegas Blvd S ☏ 702/946-7000 or 1-877/796-2096, ⓦ www.parislasvegas.com. If not the absolute pinnacle of luxury, rooms and services at the flamboyant *Paris* are still pretty good, and for location, views, and ambience it more than holds its own. Mon–Thurs & Sun ❻, Fri & Sat ❽

Sahara Hotel & Casino 2535 Las Vegas Blvd S ☏ 702/737-2111 or 1-888/696-2121, ⓦ www.saharavegas.com. Garish Moroccan-themed rooms in the finest Vegas tradition, though quite a trek from the best parts of the Strip. Mon–Thurs & Sun ❹, Fri & Sat ❺

Stratosphere Hotel & Casino 2000 Las Vegas Blvd S ☏ 702/380-7777 or 1-800/998-6937, ⓦ www.stratospherehotel.com. Despite its very unfashionable location at the far north end of the Strip, the *Stratosphere* has survived thanks to low rates and a steady flow of budget tour groups. No accommodation is in the hundred-story tower, so don't expect amazing views, just large, plain, but good-value rooms, more likely than most to offer last-minute availability. Mon–Thurs & Sun ❷, Fri & Sat ❹

TI 3300 Las Vegas Blvd S ☏ 702/894-7111 or 1-800/288-7206, ⓦ www.treasureisland.com. Formerly known as *Treasure Island*, and no longer geared toward families, *TI* remains a fun and convenient place to stay, though the rooms themselves are relatively small. Mon–Thurs & Sun ❺, Fri & Sat ❼

The Venetian 3355 Las Vegas Blvd S ☏ 702/414-1000 or 1-888/883-6423, ⓦ www.venetian.com. The Strip's best-value luxury hotel. Even the standard rooms are split-level suites, offering gorgeous antique-style canopied beds, plus roomy living rooms, marble bathrooms with walk-in showers, and a mind-blowing array of shops and restaurants at hand. Mon–Thurs & Sun ❽, Fri & Sat ❾

Wynn Las Vegas 3131 Las Vegas Blvd S ☏ 702/770-7000 or 1-888/320-7123, ⓦ www.wynnlasvegas.com. Steve Wynn has once again rewritten the Strip's definition of luxury, but the very stylish rooms, most of which offer great views of the "Lake of Dreams," do of course come at a substantial price. Mon–Thurs & Sun ❽, Fri & Sat ❾

Downtown and off the Strip

California Hotel & Casino 12 Ogden Ave at First St ☏ 702/385-1222 or 1-800/634-6255, ⓦ www.thecal.com. Most of the guests in this mid-range, downtown casino are Hawaiians playing it safe with the Hawaiian food and drink that dominate the bars and restaurants. The actual rooms are plain but adequate. Mon–Thurs & Sun ❸, Fri & Sat ❹

El Cortez Hotel & Casino 600 E Fremont St, ☏ 702/385-5200 or 1-800/634-6703, ⓦ www.elcortezhotelcasino.com. Veteran downtown casino, where the cut-price rooms in the main building are better than the dismal gaming area might suggest. The mini-suites in the new tower are really good value, while the rudimentary bargain-basement accommodation in *Ogden House* across the street costs just $18 for a double room with bathroom. Hotel rooms ②

Golden Gate Hotel and Casino 1 E Fremont St ☎702/385-1906 or 1-800/426-1906, ⓦwww .goldengatecasino.net. The oldest joint downtown, founded in 1906, when Las Vegas was just a year old. With a hundred retro-furnished rooms, it's tiny by Vegas standards, and slightly lower-key than its Fremont Street neighbors. Mon–Thurs & Sun ②, Fri & Sat ④

Hard Rock Hotel & Casino 4475 Paradise Rd ☎702/693-5000 or 1-800/473-7625, ⓦwww .hardrockhotel.com. Over a mile east of the Strip, "the world's only rock'n'roll casino" can't match Las Vegas's showcase giants for size or splendor. Instead, it's a relatively intimate and even chic alternative, with above-average rooms – the French windows actually open – high-class restaurants, a fabulous pool, and the odd big-name rock gig. Mon–Thurs & Sun ⑥, Fri & Sat ⑧

Las Vegas International Hostel 1322 E Fremont St ☎702/385-1150 or 1-800/550-8958, ⓦwww .usahostels.com. Former *Best Western* motel, in a slightly forbidding neighborhood ten blocks east of downtown. It's much the better of the city's two independent hostels, with dorm beds from $13 and private double rooms from $38. Rates include free breakfast; cheap dinners are also available. There's also a heated swimming pool. The friendly staff arrange city and national-park tours, including a weekly clubbing night. ①/②

Main Street Station 200 N Main St at Ogden ☎702/387-1896 or 1-800/465-0711, ⓦwww. mainstreetcasino.com. Downtown's best-value option, two blocks from Fremont Street, with four hundred large guest rooms plus a brewpub and good restaurants. Ask for a room on the south side, rather than right next to the freeway. Mon–Thurs & Sun ③, Fri & Sat ⑤

Palms 4321 W Flamingo Rd ☎702/942-7777 or 1-866/942-7777, ⓦwww.palms.com. Although it ranks among the hottest newer casinos in town, thanks to some very fancy nightclubs and restaurants and a strong celebrity quota, *Palms* is primarily a fun place for those who will never make it past the velvet ropes into the exclusive VIP areas. Thus, while the rooms are very comfortable, you may not feel it's worth paying premium rates for the inconvenient location a mile west of the Strip. Mon–Thurs & Sun ⑤, Fri & Sat ⑦

Rio Suite Hotel & Casino 3700 W Flamingo Rd ☎702/777-7777 or 1-877/752-9746, ⓦwww .playrio.com. Though west of the interstate, the *Rio* makes a serious attempt to rival the Strip giants. The restaurants, bars, and buffets are all excellent; the attempt to give everything a carnival theme is nicely realized; the pool is great; and the rooms are large and luxurious, with floor-to-ceiling windows and great views. The prices are not cheap, however, and the Strip stands half a mile away, along a highway no one would ever dream of walking. Mon–Thurs & Sun ⑥, Fri & Sat ⑧

Sin City Hostel 1208 Las Vegas Blvd S ☎702/385-9955. Bare-bones independent hostel in a dilapidated former motel, in an insalubrious area on the fringes of downtown, not far north of the *Stratosphere*. A dorm bed, or a basic "semi-private" double room costs $17.50 per person. ①

Super 8 4250 Koval Lane ☎702/794-0888 or 1-800/800-8000. The closest of Vegas's three *Super 8*s to the Strip – though it's a very hot ten minutes' walk in summer – offers three hundred rooms, a pool, its own little casino, and a reasonable restaurant. For dedicated bargain-hunters only. Mon–Thurs & Sun ②, Fri & Sat ④

The City

Though the Las Vegas sprawl measures fifteen miles wide by fifteen miles long, most tourists stick to the six-mile stretch of **Las Vegas Boulevard** that includes both the **downtown** area, slightly southeast of the intersection of I-15 and US-95, and the **Strip**, home to the major casinos. In between lie two somewhat seedy miles of gas stations, fast-food drive-ins, and wedding chapels, while the rest of town is largely residential and need barely concern you at all.

The Strip

For its razor-edge finesse in harnessing sheer, magnificent excess to the deadly serious business of making money, there's no place like the **Las Vegas Strip**. It's hard to imagine that Las Vegas was once an ordinary city, and Las Vegas

Boulevard a dusty thoroughfare scattered with the usual edge-of-town motels. After six decades of capitalism run riot, with every new casino-hotel setting out to surpass anything its neighbors ever dreamed of, the Strip seems to be locked into a hyperactive drive for thrills and glamour, forever discarding its latest toy in its frenzy for the next jackpot.

Each casino is a self-contained fantasyland of high camp and genuine excitement. Almost against your will, huge moving walkways sweep you in from the sidewalk; once inside, it can be almost impossible to find your way out. The action keeps going day and night, and in this sealed and windowless environment you rapidly lose track of which is which. Even if you do manage to get back onto the streets during the day, the scorching heat is liable to drive you straight back in again; night is the best time to venture out, when the neon's blazing at its brightest.

Mandalay Bay

The Strip's procession kicks off with the glowing gilded tower of **Mandalay Bay**, which opened in 1999 and boasts a vaguely Burmese theme. Financed through the profits from its neighbors, *Luxor* and *Excalibur*, *Mandalay Bay* is more upmarket than either, and its excellent restaurants and the *House of Blues* music venue keep it lively at night. During the day, all it has to offer the casual sightseer is the **Shark Reef** aquarium, a long walk from the Strip at the back of the property (daily 10am–11pm; $16, under-12s $10). The basic premise there is that you're exploring a steamy, half-submerged temple complex, encountering crocodiles and jellyfish as well, of course, as sharks. It's expensive for how long it takes to see, and all the so-called "coral" on offer is actually a multicolored mix'n'match plastic kit.

Luxor and Excalibur

Standing next door to *Mandalay Bay* is the 36-story pyramid of **Luxor**. From the palm-fringed avenue of sphinxes guarding the entrance, to the reconstruction of Tutankhamun's tomb inside, the whole building plays endless variations upon the theme of Egyptian archeology, and it ranks as a real must-see. In Las Vegas's closest approximation to Disneyland, three separate simulator rides and 3-D movies combine to relate a confusing saga of derring-do that's overpriced at $25. Meanwhile, the most powerful artificial light beam ever created shines up from the pyramid's apex.

Luxor's architect, Veldon Simpson, had previously designed **Excalibur**, immediately north. A less-sophisticated mock-up of a medieval castle, complete with drawbridge, crenellated towers, and a basement stuffed with fairground-style sideshows for the kids, it's usually packed out with low-budget tour groups.

MGM Grand

Excalibur's brief reign as the world's largest hotel, from 1990 to 1993, ended when the five-thousand-room **MGM Grand** – another Simpson creation – opened diagonally across the street. At that time, the *MGM Grand* sold itself on the strength of having its own **theme park**. No match for the parks of Orlando or LA, the park has long since closed down, but the *Grand* is prospering nonetheless, even if it has lost its "world's largest" status to a new complex in Thailand. Turnover in the casino is so phenomenal that when the crowds at the June 1997 Holyfield–Tyson debacle mistook the popping of champagne corks for gunfire and panicked, forcing the gaming tables to close for two hours, the loss was estimated in millions of dollars. In the **Lion Habitat**, a walk-through wooded zoo near the front entrance, real lions lounge around a ruined temple beneath a naturally lit dome. Admission is free (daily 11am–11pm), while for $20 you can have your photo taken with a cute little lion cub (11am–5pm; closed Tues).

New York–New York

Excalibur and the *MGM Grand* are not the only giants facing off across the intersection of Las Vegas Boulevard and Tropicana Avenue, said to be the busiest traffic junction in the US. The northwest corner, diagonally opposite the veteran *Tropicana*, is occupied by an exuberantly meticulous recreation of the Big Apple, **New York–New York**. This miniature Manhattan – built vertically, like the original, in response to space limitations – boasts a skyline featuring twelve separate skyscrapers and is fronted, of course, by the Statue of Liberty. Unusually, the interior is every bit as carefully realized, with a lovely rendition of Central Park at dusk (not perhaps somewhere you'd choose to be in real life). In one respect, it even surpasses New York itself: for $12.50, or $25 all day, you can swoop around the whole thing at 65mph on the hair-raising Manhattan Express **roller coaster**.

Aladdin and Paris

North of the *MGM Grand*, the $1.4-billion **Aladdin** opened in 2000 as Las Vegas's first megacasino of the new millennium, but it really represented the last gasp of the Strip's 1990s construction boom. Beset by funding difficulties from the word go, the resort was tipped into bankruptcy by the 2001 terrorist attacks of September. The Middle Eastern theme didn't exactly help, and the *Aladdin* is expected to be revamped and renamed Planet Hollywood in the very near future. Its gigantic **Desert Passage** shopping mall, and 7000-seat auditorium, will probably survive the transformation intact.

Next door, **Paris** was the 1999 handiwork of the same team of designers as *New York–New York*. With a half-size Eiffel Tower straddling the Arc de

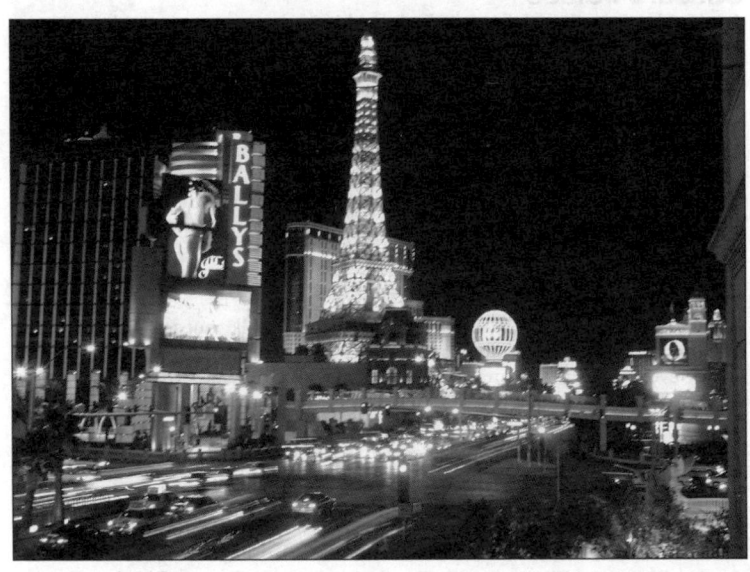

△ The Strip at night

Triomphe and the Opera, it all feels a little compressed, but once again the attention to detail is a joy. There's also a fine assortment of top-notch French restaurants. Elevators soar through the roof of the casino and up to the summit of the Eiffel Tower, for stunning views of the city, at their best after dark (daily 10am–midnight; $9). The tower was cheekily positioned to enjoy a perfect prospect of *Bellagio*, across the Strip.

Bellagio

Steve Wynn, then owner of the *Mirage*, unveiled the *Bellagio* in 1998 as his attempt to build the best hotel in world history. Bellagio is undeniably a breathtaking achievement, but Wynn set himself a pointless and self-defeating task. Traditionally, casino theming is playful – you're not supposed to think that being in *Luxor* is like being in ancient Egypt, just that it's fun to pretend. No longer, however, is it enough to create an illusion: *Bellagio* wants to be somehow more authentic than the original. The trouble is that *Bellagio* is not in Europe; it's in Las Vegas and stuffed full of slot machines (inlaid with jewel-like precision into marble counters, perhaps, but still slot machines). The main hotel block, a stately curve of blue and cream pastels, stands aloof from the Strip behind an eight-acre artificial lake in which hundreds of submerged fountains erupt every half-hour in Busby-Berkeley water-ballets, choreographed with booming music and colored lights.

Otherwise, *Bellagio's* proudest boasts are the **Via Bellagio**, a covered mall of impossibly glamorous designer boutiques, and its opulent **Conservatory**, where a network of flowerbeds beneath a Belle Epoque canopy of copper-framed glass is replanted every few weeks with ornate seasonal displays. When Steve Wynn was bought out by MGM in 2000, he took the permanent collection from his groundbreaking **Bellagio Gallery of Fine Art** with him, so it now hosts changing – and seldom very enthralling – temporary exhibitions (daily 9am–5pm; $15).

Caesars Palace

Across Flamingo Road from *Bellagio* – this is the intersection where rapper Tupac Shakur was gunned down in 1996 – the long-established **Caesars Palace** still encapsulates Las Vegas at its best. Here, the walkway delivers you past grand marble staircases that lead nowhere, and full-size replicas of Michelangelo's *David*, into a vast labyrinth of slots and green baize, peopled by strutting half-naked Roman centurions and Cleopatra-cropped waitresses. Above the stores and restaurants of the extraordinary **Forum**, the blue-domed ceiling dims and glows as it endlessly cycles from dawn to dusk and back again, while the animatronic statues that top its ornate fountains come to life at regular intervals.

The Mirage and TI

Night-time crowds jostle for space on the sidewalk outside the glittering **Mirage**, beyond *Caesars*, to watch the somewhat half-hearted volcano that erupts every fifteen minutes, spewing water and fire into the lagoon below. Although veteran magicians Siegfried and Roy were finally driven into retirement by Roy's near-fatal accident in 2003, their trademark white tigers can still be seen in the *Mirage's* spacious **Secret Garden & Dolphin Habitat** (daily 10am–7pm; $15, under-13s $10).

Next door, a pirate galleon and a British frigate, crewed by actors, continue to do noisy battle outside **TI**, the former *Treasure Island*, though ludicrously enough the sailors these days are no longer gnarled buccaneers but the scantily-clad **Sirens of TI** (every 90min after dark; free). *Treasure Island* used to be pirate-themed throughout, but when MGM took over the Mirage empire in 2000, they abandoned the idea of appealing to children. All *Treasure Island*'s lovingly crafted fripperies have been stripped away, from its huge video arcade and bizarre $400,000 bone chandeliers to the skull motifs that adorned everything from its main sign to the doorhandles.

Elvis-A-Rama

At the corner of *TI,* take Spring Mountain one block west of the Strip to reach the Fashion Show Mall at 3401 Industrial Road. Behind the mall, you can admire (if not step on) the King's very own blue suede shoes at **Elvis-A-Rama** (daily 10am–6pm; $10). As well as boasting a fine array of Elvis memorabilia, the museum puts on hourly impersonator shows.

The Venetian

Across the Strip from *TI,* the facade of another 1999 newcomer, **The Venetian**, includes loving facsimiles of six major Venice buildings, as well as the Rialto Bridge and the Bridge of Sighs. The main emphasis in the casino itself is on the **Grand Canal Shoppes,** reached via a stairwell topped by vivid frescoes copied from yet more Venice originals. The absurd recreation of the **Grand Canal** at the top, complete with gondolas and singing gondoliers ($12.50 a ride), is quintessential Las Vegas, and as such utterly irresistible – for God's sake, it's *upstairs.*

In fall 2001, *The Venetian* opened not just one but two distinct Guggenheim **art museums**, designed in an ultramodern style by Dutch architect Rem Koolhaas. The **Guggenheim Hermitage** (daily 9.30am–8.30pm; $20, under-13s $14.50) aims to provide much-needed funds for St Petersburg's legendary State Hermitage Museum in return for displaying its finest treasures on a six-monthly changing rotation. Exhibitions so far have concentrated on Impressionism and Cubism, with Monet and Picasso well represented. The much larger **Guggenheim Las Vegas**, however, further back on the casino's ground floor, never managed to attract large enough crowds to justify its prime location, and closed its doors early in 2003.

The Venetian also holds an outpost of **Madame Tussaud's** renowned waxwork museum (daily 10am–10pm, some seasonal variation; $23, under-13s $13), which styles itself "Interactive Wax" because visitors can sing karaoke for Simon Cowell or sink a putt with Tiger Woods. The whole experience is ridiculously expensive, its token animatronic showpieces not a patch on the free shows at *Caesars.*

Wynn Las Vegas

Next door to the *Venetian* stands the newest mega-casino of them all, the project into which Steve Wynn sank all the fortune he accrued by building and selling the *Mirage* and *Bellagio.* **Wynn Las Vegas**, which opened in 2005 on the site of the vanished *Desert Inn,* has lived up to its creator's promise that it would be designed to be seen from the inside out. From the Strip, it's largely obscured by an artificial tree-covered mountain; once you find your way inside, you discover that the mountain makes a backdrop for the bizarre, enormous **Lake of Dreams**, an "environmental theater" in which ethereal sculpted figures emerge from a large expanse of water. It's in front of a massive waterfall which continually changes color, as do the trees and the entire mountain.

Circus Circus

The family-oriented **Circus Circus**, nearly a mile north of *Wynn Las Vegas,* uses live circus acts to pull in the punters – a trapeze artist here, a fire-eater there – and also has an indoor theme park, the **Adventuredome** (Mon–Thurs 10am–6pm, Fri & Sat 10am–midnight, Sun 10am–8pm), where you pay separately for each roller coaster or river-ride, or can buy an all-day pass at $22 for anyone over 4ft, $14 for those under.

The Star Trek Experience

Half a mile east of *Circus Circus* at 3000 Paradise Rd, the **Las Vegas Hilton** is home to the **Star Trek Experience** (daily 11am–11pm; $35, under-13s $32), which is roughly equivalent to a high-echelon ride in an LA or Orlando theme park; it's pretty good, but absurdly expensive. Visits start from the Space Quest Casino, a sort of *Enterprise* with slots. The ramp beyond the ticket booths doubles as a queuing area – you can wait as long as two hours on summer weekends – and a "museum," which recounts an episode-by-episode chronology of every *Star Trek* series. It all culminates in two separate twenty-minute shows: *Klingon Encounter* and *Borg Invasion 4-D*, both of which involve you being caught up in alien plots and sent on vomit-inducing motion-simulator rides through deep space. You eventually emerge in a shopping area (which you actually could have reached without paying) where memorabilia prices boldly go to well over $2000 for a customized leather jacket. The adjoining *Quark Bar*, with its deep-space decor and intergalactic cocktails, makes a fun place to recuperate.

The Stratosphere

Sahara Avenue traditionally marked the northern limit of the Strip, but the 1996 opening of the **Stratosphere**, a few blocks north, tried to change that. At 1149ft, the *Stratosphere* is the tallest building west of the Mississippi, and the outdoor deck and indoor viewing chamber in the sphere near the summit offer amazing panoramas across the city ($9). Three utterly demented thrill rides can take you even closer to heaven; the world's highest roller coaster ($4) swirls around the outside of the sphere, X-Scream ($8) dangles passengers over the edge in a precarious gondola, and the ludicrous Big Shot ($8) shunts you to the very top of an additional 160ft spire, from which you free-fall back down again.

Downtown and the Liberace Museum

As the Strip has evolved from strength to strength, **downtown** Las Vegas, the city's original core, has by comparison been neglected. Actually it has never really been a "downtown" in the conventional sense, having never developed a significant infrastructure of stores and other businesses apart from its few compact blocks of lower-key casinos. Long known as "Glitter Gulch," it has however repeatedly attempted to revive itself. The principal sign of that is the **Fremont Street Experience**, in which five entire blocks of the central Fremont Street were roofed over with an open-air mesh. This "Celestial Vault" is studded with over twelve million LED nodules to create a movie screen, choreographed by computer in dazzling nightly displays

Almost all of Las Vegas's off-Strip museums are eminently missable, with one unarguable exception: the **Liberace Museum**, two miles east of the Strip at 1775 E Tropicana Ave (Mon–Sat 10am–5pm, Sun noon–4pm; ☏702/798-5595, ⓦ www.liberace.org; $12). Best remembered for his ruffled shirts and rhinestone-studded coat-tails, the unlikely pop-star (1919–1987) was a classical pianist, yet started his true career tickling the ivories in the rough bars of Milwaukee during the 1940s. A decade later, he was star of his own TV show, being mobbed by screaming adolescents and ruthlessly hounded by the scandal-hungry press. All this is recalled by a yellowing collection of cuttings and family photos, along with electric candelabra, bejeweled quail eggs with inlaid pianos, rhinestone-covered fur coats, glittering cars, and more.

Red Rock Canyon

For a blast of sunlight and fresh air away from the casinos and a sample of some classic Southwestern canyon scenery, head twenty miles west of the Strip along Charleston Boulevard to the **Red Rock Canyon National Conservation Area**. This BLM-run park consists of a cactus-strewn desert basin surrounded by stark red cliffs pierced repeatedly by narrow canyons accessible only on foot.

Red Rock Canyon's **visitor center**, which has displays about the canyon and a viewing window overlooking its main features (daily 8am–4.30pm; ☎702/363-1921, ⓦwww.redrockcanyon.blm.gov), stands at the start of the **Scenic Drive** (daily 7am–dusk; $5 per vehicle). As this thirteen-mile loop road meanders around the edge of the basin, it passes trailheads like the one for the cool, slender **Ice Box Canyon** (a 2.5-mile round-trip hike), and the three-mile **Pine Creek Trail**, which follows a flower-lined creek beyond a ruined former homesite toward a towering, red-capped monolith.

Lake Mead and the Hoover Dam

Many Las Vegas visitors make the pilgrimage to **LAKE MEAD**, the vast reservoir thirty miles southeast of the city that was created by the construction of the Hoover Dam. As with the similarly incongruous Lake Powell (see p.479) it makes a bizarre spectacle – the blue waters a vivid counterpoint to the surrounding desert – but it can get excruciatingly crowded all year round.

Though the Lake Mead National Recreation Area straddles the border between Nevada and Arizona, the best views come from the Nevada side. Even if you don't need details of how to sail, scuba-dive, water-ski, or fish from the marinas along the five-hundred-mile shoreline, call in at the Alan Bible visitor center (daily 8.30am–4.30pm; ☎702/293-8990, ⓦwww.nps.gov/lame), four miles northeast of Boulder City on US-93, to enjoy a sweeping prospect of the whole thing.

Eight miles on, beyond the rocky ridges of the Black Mountains, US-93 reaches the **Hoover Dam** itself. Designed to block the Colorado River and provide low-cost electricity for the cities of the Southwest, it's among the tallest dams ever built (760ft high), and is made of enough concrete to build a two-lane highway from the West Coast to New York. It was completed in 1935, as the first step in the Bureau of Reclamation program that culminated with the Glen Canyon Dam (see p.487). For security reasons, the dam no longer offers extensive behind-the-scenes tours, but you can still ride an elevator to the turbine room at the bottom. Regular half-hour guided tours leave from the **Hoover Dam Visitor Center** on the Nevada side of the river (daily April–Sept 8.30am–5.45pm, Oct–March 9.15am–4.15pm; $10, plus $5 parking; ☎702/293-1824).

For details on day-trips to the Grand Canyon from Las Vegas – or more precisely, to the so-called West Rim, the nearest part of the canyon – see p.398.

8

LAS VEGAS | The City

Eating

As recently as the early 1990s, the **restaurant** scene in Las Vegas was governed by the notion that visitors were not prepared to pay for gourmet food. Casinos laid on both pile-'em-high buffets at knock-down prices and 24-hour coffeeshops offering bargain steak-and-egg deals, but the only quality restaurants were upscale Italian places well away from the Strip. Now, food has to be another element of the entertainment and the major casinos compete to attract superstar chefs to open Vegas outlets. Many tourists now come to the city specifically to dine at several of the best restaurants in the United States, without having to reserve a table months in advance or pay sky-high prices. Which is not to say that fine dining comes cheap in Las Vegas, just that most of the big-name restaurants are less expensive – and less snooty – than they are in their home cities.

The restaurants reviewed below form only a tiny proportion of the total. The choice on the Strip in particular is overwhelming, and you'll almost certainly find a good restaurant to suit your tastes and budget in your own hotel. For that reason, the places reviewed here tend toward the higher end of the spectrum; they're the exceptional ones worth making a special effort to reach. Note, too, that in terms of price or quality, let alone convenience, there are few reasons to venture into the rest of the city; good places do exist away from the Strip and downtown, but the best are right where the tourists are.

Buffets

Almost every casino still features an all-you-can-eat **buffet**, open to guests and nonguests alike for every meal of the week. At its best, the traditional buffet experience is like being granted unrestricted access to the food court in an upmarket mall: you'll get good fast food, but not great cooking. The best such buffets tend to be neither on the Strip nor downtown, but in casinos like the *Rio* and the Stations chain that depend on locals as well as tourists. By contrast, those at the largest Strip casinos, like *Excalibur* and the *MGM Grand*, are often poor pickings. A more recent development, however, has been for high-end casinos like *Bellagio* and *Paris* to raise buffet prices to a level that makes it possible to provide true gourmet feasts.

The Buffet *Bellagio*, 3600 Las Vegas Blvd S ☎702/791-7111. Far and away Las Vegas's best buffet. At 800 items, all prepared fresh in small quantities, the sheer range is extraordinary. At breakfast ($14), in addition to bagels, pastries, and eggs, you can have salmon smoked or baked, fruit fresh or in salads, and omelettes cooked to order. Lunch ($18) can include sushi, cold cuts, dim sum, wild boar ribs, and seared quail, plus fresh-baked focaccia and tasty fruit tarts. At dinner, costing $26 Mon–Thurs & Sun and $34, including champagne, Fri & Sat, the stakes are raised again with the addition of lobster claws, fresh oysters, and venison.

Carnival World Buffet *Rio*, 3700 W Flamingo Rd ☎702/252-7777. The *Rio* uses its buffet as a loss-leader, hoping to lure bargain-hunters west from the Strip; its prices are not what they were, at $13 for breakfast, $15 for lunch, and $23 for dinner, but the value is excellent. The variety

is immense, with Thai, Chinese, Mexican, and Japanese stations, as well as the usual pasta and barbecue.

Fantasy Market Buffet *The Palms*, 4321 W Flamingo Rd ☎702/942-7777. Easy to find and afford, the *Palms'* buffet has rapidly established itself as a local favorite. Food and decor alike are bright and appealing, with a broad spectrum that takes in salads, a little sushi, Mexican and Italian specialties, teriyaki chicken, barbecue beef, and a lot of lovely cakes and pies. Breakfast is $6, lunch $7, and dinner $12, rising to $16 on Fri for the crab legs and prime rib special.

Feast Around The World *Sunset Station*, 1301 W Sunset Rd ☎702/547-7777. Primarily aimed at locals, all the Station casinos offer similarly appealing buffets at unbeatable prices, with a wide range of international cuisines; breakfast is $6, lunch $7, and dinner Sun–Thurs $9, Fri & Sat $13. Friday and Saturday are steak nights.

Garden Court Buffet *Main Street Station*, 200 N Main St ☎702/387-1896. Everything is clean and spruce at downtown's best-value buffet, but it's not all that exciting, despite dishes ranging from fried chicken and corn at "South to Southwest," to tortillas at "Olé," and pork chow mein and oyster tofu at "Pacific Rim." Breakfast is $6, lunch $8, and dinner varies $11–16, depending on each day's specialty; Tuesday is steak, Thursday is filet and scampi, and Friday is seafood.

Le Village Buffet *Paris*, 3655 Las Vegas Blvd S ☎702/967-7000. Rather than incorporating every conceivable cuisine, *Paris*'s buffet showcases only delicious French dishes. The seafood is superb, whether it's the scallops, shrimp, and crab in Sunday's brunch or the Dover sole and rich *bouillabaisse* midweek; roast chicken comes fricasseed, as *coq au vin*, or with mustard; vegetables are superfresh; and there's a full cheese board. Breakfast is $13, lunch $18, and dinner $25.

🏃 **Todai Seafood Buffet** Desert Passage, *Aladdin*, 3663 Las Vegas Blvd S ☎702/892-0021. Not to be confused with the *Aladdin*'s own (adequate but not exceptional) buffet, *Todai* belongs to a California chain specializing in magnificent all-you-can-eat Japanese spreads. It's seafood heaven, with unlimited sushi and sashimi plus hot entrées, noodles, and barbecued and teriyaki meats. Lunch Mon–Fri $15, Sat & Sun $17; dinner Mon–Thurs & Sun $26, Fri & Sat $28.

Restaurants on the Strip

America *New York–New York*, 3790 Las Vegas Blvd S ☎702/740-6451. Cavernous diner, featuring a vast 3-D "map" of the United States that curls down from the ceiling. The menu is staggeringly eclectic, and each item supposedly comes from some specific part of the country, with entrées including Texas barbecue ribs for $14 and New York pizzas for $9–11. At any hour of day or night, there really is something for everyone, and it's all surprisingly good. Daily 24-hours.

Aureole *Mandalay Bay*, 3950 Las Vegas Blvd S ☎702/632-7401, ⊛www.ewinetower.com. Welcome to wine-lover's heaven, where harnessed "wine angels" swoop around a three-story "wine tower" that holds 10,000 bottles, at prices from $36,000 down to $21. New York chef Charlie Palmer's "progressive American cuisine" is every bit as impressive. Choose between a prix-fixe menu on which $85 buys a substantial appetizer and entrée, or the changing $95 "Celebration Menu," which features up to eight smaller courses. Standout dishes, all beautifully presented, include the curry-nut crusted tuna, the halibut topped with a black truffle foam, and the pork chop stuffed with prosciutto and gruyere. Daily, dinner only.

Border Grill *Mandalay Bay*, 3950 Las Vegas Blvd S ☎702/632-7403. At the Strip's finest Mexican restaurant, lunch offerings include sandwiches, like a portabello torta, or a chicken Caesar salad for around $13; dinner is more expensive, with slow-roasted pork *mole* at $19 and a 12oz gaucho steak for $28. In summer, tables spread across a large patio facing *Mandalay Bay*'s spectacular wave pool. Mon–Thurs & Sun 11.30am–10pm, Fri & Sat 11.30am–11pm.

🏃 **Bouchon** Venezia Tower, *The Venetian*, 3355 Las Vegas Blvd S ☎702/414-6200. Despite its sky-high reputation and exclusive setting, Thomas Keller's spacious recreation of a classic French bistro is both friendly and affordable, and sitting outside on the huge piazza is a real joy. Every dish is prepared with perfect precision. A delicious French onion soup costs $8.50 and a roast chicken flavored with onions and garlic costs $22.50. There's also plenty of seafood, like oysters and mussels. Breakfast is a Francophile's dream of croissants, pastries, yogurt and coffee. Open for all meals daily.

Chinois Forum Shops, *Caesars Palace*, 3570 Las Vegas Blvd S ☎702/737-9700. Wolfgang Puck's Asian-fusion restaurant offers café-style terrace seating at the mall level, and a more formal dining room upstairs. The décor is very stylish – all tiles, jade, and turquoise, with running water to aid the *feng shui* – and the food itself is upmarket, nouvelle-tinged Chinese. Appetizers at $7–10 include pork potstickers, while entrees, at $22–31, range from sizzling catfish to roast duck or Shanghai lobster. Good-value, three-course set lunches cost $13–15. Cafe lunch and dinner daily 11.30am–midnight, restaurant daily 6–10.30pm.

🏃 **Commander's Palace** Desert Passage, *Aladdin*, 3663 Las Vegas Blvd S ☎702/892-8272. New Orleans' renowned haute Creole restaurant – repeatedly voted the best restaurant in the US – is formal but friendly, though at $8 for a bowl of gumbo the prices can come as a shock. The menu ranges from classic appetizers like shrimp remoulade ($10.50), through entrées such as pecan-crusted Gulf fish ($29) or veal chop Tchoupitoulas ($39), to bananas Foster for dessert ($7.50). Daily 11.30am–2pm & 6–11pm.

Fat Burger 3765 Las Vegas Blvd S ☎702/736-4733. There's no more to this gleaming, all-American burger joint than meets the eye. Quite simply, you can walk or drive in from the Strip at any time, and get a perfect burger, fries, and shake. Daily 24-hours.

Il Fornaio *New York–New York*, 3790 Las Vegas Blvd S ☎702/650-6500. Rural-Italian restaurant that's the nicest place to enjoy the atmosphere of *New York–New York*, with a high-ceilinged "indoor" dining room plus terrace seating alongside Central Park. Pizzas for around $12, or full meals like mixed antipasto ($9.50) followed by seafood linguini ($19) or rotisserie chicken ($16). The delicious olive breads, pastries, and espresso coffees are also sold in a separate deli nearby. Mon–Thurs & Sun 7am–10pm, Fri & Sat 7am–midnight.

Mon Ami Gabi *Paris*, 3655 Las Vegas Blvd S ☎702/944-4224. The first and the finest major casino restaurant to offer open-air seating right on the Strip has the feel of a proper French pavement bistro. At lunch, try the gloriously authentic onion soup ($7), the mussels ($11), or the thin-cut *steak frites* ($21). Dinner features more expensive steak cuts and fish entrées. Mon–Thurs & Sun 11.30am–3.30pm & 5–11pm, Fri & Sat 11.30am–3.30pm & 5pm–midnight.

Olives *Bellagio*, 3600 Las Vegas Blvd S ☎702/693-8181. *Bellagio*'s best-value gourmet restaurant has a lovely terrace setting, facing the Eiffel Tower across the lake. Even if it is the kind of place that calls a $15 pizza an "individual oven-baked flatbread," the largely Mediterranean menu is uniformly fresh and superb. It's a great spot for lunch, with $10–13 appetizers like beef carpaccio, pasta dishes like butternut squash tortelli ($16), and specials such as barbecued yellow-fin tuna on roasted onion polenta ($21.50). Dinner entrées are pricier, at $28–50. Daily 11am–2.30pm & 5–11.30pm.

Vialé *Roman Plaza*, *Caesars Palace*, 3500 Las Vegas Blvd S ☎702/731-7110. Inexpensive sidewalk Italian trattoria, outdoors on the Strip on *Caesars'* Roman Plaza, that's almost too good to be true. Lunch beneath its black-and-white awnings is an absolute treat, with a burger or warm panini sandwich costing under $10, and a Caesar salad (well you would, wouldn't you?) for $7, or $10 with chicken. The dinner menu offers many of the same salads, plus pasta as both appetizer ($7–9) and entree ($12–17), and more substantial entrees like grilled quail with mascarpone stuffing ($19). Daily 11am–4pm & 5–11pm.

Zefferino *Grand Canal Shoppes*, *The Venetian*, 3355 Las Vegas Blvd S ☎702/414-3500. Though purists might not approve of the intrinsic fakery of the *Venetian* branch of this venerable Genoa restaurant, any Las Vegas aficionado just has to love it. It manages to be both very romantic and yet utterly playful, with its ornate balconies overlooking the Grand Canal. Dinner entrées can be pricey, with a basic ravioli at $26 and fish soup at $45, but the $20 three-course set lunch, served daily except Sundays, is exceptional value. Mon–Sat 11.30am–1am, Sun 10am–2.30pm & 5–11pm.

Restaurants elsewhere

Carluccio's Tivoli Gardens 1775 E Tropicana Ave ☎702/795-3236. Upscale Italian restaurant, two miles east of the Strip, with an irresistible angle – it was designed by Liberace himself, whose museum stands next door. The menu is wide ranging and consistently rich, with pizzas and chicken dishes at $10–12, and linguini with mussels for $14, but it's hard to resist Liberace's own personal favorite, the $9 baked lasagna. Daily except Mon 4.30–10.30pm.

The Coffee Shop *Binion's Horseshoe*, 128 E Fremont St ☎702/382-1600. Deep in the bowels of the *Horseshoe*, it's the round-the-clock Las Vegas coffeeshop of your dreams. The food is American-diner-heaven, with excellent prices for a changing timetable of specials like the all-night steak dinner, which between 11pm and 7am costs just $6 for steak, potato, and salad. Breakfast, which works out better value than most buffets, is served around the clock. Daily 24-hours.

Mr Lucky's 24/7 *Hard Rock Hotel*, 4455 Paradise Rd ☎702/693-5000. With its open kitchen, faux-fur booths, and subdued tan-and-cream paint-job, the *Hard Rock*'s 24-hour coffeeshop is a very stylish joint, and the food is well above average too. As well as all the usual breakfast items, it serves burgers, sandwiches, pizzas, and pasta dishes for $7–12, a 12-oz steak for $18, and milkshakes or microbrews for $5. Daily 24 hours.

Nobu *Hard Rock Hotel*, 4455 Paradise Rd ☎702/693-5090. Las Vegas's chic-est celebrity restaurant, run by Japanese-Peruvian chef Nobu Matsuhisa, as seen in New York, LA, and London. The décor is supremely tasteful, and the food is exquisite, though the temptation to order yet another morsel means the prices tend to rocket before your eyes whether you simply go for the sushi bar, or select from the "special cold dishes" (three tiny oysters for $12, or salmon tartar with caviar at $25). Sushi or sashimi set dinners start at $30, with a "chef's choice" for $65. Daily 6–11.15pm.

Paymon's Mediterranean Cafe and Market Tiffany Square, 4147 S Maryland Pkwy at Flamingo ☎702/731-6030. Simple but highly recommended Middle Eastern restaurant, with attractive Cretan murals, that's Las Vegas's best vegetarian option. Salads and pitta sandwiches cost $7–9, and spinach pie $10, while dips such as hummus or the eggplant-based *baba ganoush* are $5. A mountainous best-of-everything combination plate is just $11. Daily except Sun 11am–9pm.

Bars and clubs

As the perfect fuel to turn a dithering gawker into a diehard gambler, alcohol is very easy to come by in Las Vegas. If you want a drink in a casino, there's no need to look for a bar; instead, a tray-toting waitress will come and find you. All the casinos do have actual **bars** as well, but in terms of enjoying a proper night out, they're just a small part of the picture. The old-fashioned **Las Vegas lounge** has returned in force, whether knowingly retro-styled for twentysomething rockers, glammed up as an "ultra-lounge," or lovingly recreated for older visitors looking to recapture the quieter but still somehow deliciously decadent flavor of the Rat-Pack era.

What's even more striking is that Las Vegas has finally come of age as an international **clubbing** capital. No longer are clubbers considered a breed apart from tourists; instead, the success of nightclubs at hipper casinos like the *Hard Rock* and *Mandalay Bay* has prompted all their major rivals to follow suit, often with spectacular results.

As for **live music**, check newspapers like *City Life* and the *Las Vegas Review Journal* to see who's appearing when you're in town. In general, it'll help if your tastes are rooted in the 1960s or even earlier, but some of the newer breed of casinos are now orienting themselves toward younger audiences.

Bars and lounges

Gaudi Bar *Sunset Station*, 1301 W Sunset Rd, Henderson ☎702/547-7777. Las Vegas's most weird and wonderful casino lounge; a billowing mosaic-encrusted toadstool of a tribute to Spanish architect Gaudi, complete with faux-sky underbelly and best appreciated with the aid of a $4 specialty martini. Daily 24 hrs.

Ghostbar *Palms*, 4321 W Flamingo Rd ☎702/940-7777. Self-proclaimed "ultra-lounge," whose lack of a dance floor, and low music volume, stops it being categorized as a nightclub. Thirty-something hipsters wait to pay the cover charge, then venture out on its cantilevered open-air deck, which has a terrifying Plexiglas floor. Daily 8pm–dawn. Cover Sun–Thurs $10, Fri & Sat $20.

Gordon Biersch Brewery 3987 Paradise Rd ☎702/312-5247. Cavernous, ultratrendy microbrewery a mile east of the Strip, packed with local big spenders (including a *lot* of singles) and featuring fine lagers, reasonable food, live music from swing to reggae, and no slot machines. Mon & Sun 11.30am–midnight, Tues–Sat 11.30am–2am.

Nine Fine Irishmen *New York–New York*, 3790 Las Vegas Blvd S ☎702/740-6463. The affinity between New York and all things Irish finds expression in this two-story wood-paneled pub, shipped over from Ireland and featuring live Irish musicians, singers, and dancers nightly. Sun–Thurs 11am–2.30am, Fri & Sat 11am–3.30am. Cover $5 Wed & Thurs, $10 Fri & Sat.

rumjungle *Mandalay Bay*, 3950 Las Vegas Blvd S ☎702/632-7408. Hybrid bar-restaurant-nightclub where you have to run a gauntlet of go-go dancers and volcanic gas jets just to get in. Leopardskin-clad staff serve a wide array of well-priced cocktails, plus a vast menu of rums. It's too loud to do anything more than watch or join the Latin-tinged action on the (small-ish) dance floor. Mon & Thurs–Sat 5.30pm–4am, Tues & Wed 5.30pm–2am. Cover, for non-diners only, $20.

Tangerine *TI*, 3300 Las Vegas Blvd S ☎702/212-8140. *TI*'s "speakeasy" changes character several times per day. When it opens in daylight, it offers fruit cocktails and Caribbean drumming; later its open-air deck serves as a crowded viewing station for the adjacent *Sirens of TI* show; and from 10.45pm onwards, an indoor stage hosts fifteen-minute burlesque performances every hour. There's also live and DJ music nightly. Tues–Sat 5pm–4am; deck opens 3.30pm. Cover men $20, women $10.

Triple Seven Brewpub *Main Street Station*, 200 N Main St ℡ 702/386-4442. Roomy, high-ceilinged downtown brewpub with poor service but great beers and tasty food. Daily 11am–7am.

Clubs and music venues

The Beach 365 Convention Center Drive ℡ 702/731-1925, @ www.beachlv.com. This round-the-clock multiroom dance club is at heart a permanent Spring Break, attracting a very young crowd to the massive dance floor downstairs and sports bar upstairs. Daily 24-hours. Cover (men only) usually $10.

Flex Lounge 4371 W Charleston Blvd ℡ 702/385-3539. Flamboyant gay club, several miles west of the Strip, with occasional strip shows. Beer flows freely all week, with DJs Wed–Sat, and karaoke on Mon. Daily 24-hours. Cover varies, up to $5.

Gipsy 4605 Paradise Rd ℡ 702/731-1919. High-profile gay dance club, where apart from the free cruise nights on Wednesdays, there's normally some form of live entertainment to justify the $5 post-midnight cover charge, with go-go boys performing Friday, and beer busts most nights. The elaborate lost-city decor attracts young ingenues and local celebs. Daily 10pm–6am.

House of Blues *Mandalay Bay*, 3950 Las Vegas Blvd S ℡ 702/632-7600, @ www.hob.com. The Strip's premier live-music venue, the voodoo-tinged, folk-art-decorated *House of Blues* has a definite but not exclusive emphasis toward blues, R&B, and the like. Typical prices range from around $30 for medium names up to $85 for stars like Aretha Franklin.

The Joint *Hard Rock Hotel*, 4455 Paradise Rd ℡ 702/693-5066. The venue of choice for big-name touring rock acts, not least because its affluent baby-boomer profile enables bands like Aerosmith to charge $180 a throw. Tickets to see the Rolling Stones here in 2002 cost $505 and $1005, but more typically admission for performers such as Elvis Costello or Neil Young ranges between $50 and $100. The cheaper rates are for the much less atmospheric balcony.

Ra *Luxor*, 3900 Las Vegas Blvd S ℡ 702/262-4400. Despite the splendidly camp Egyptian motifs, *Ra* feels like a real city nightclub, booking big-name DJs to cater to a ferociously hip and very glamorous crowd. Cage dancers watch over a changing schedule of special nights. Wed–Sat 10pm–5am. Cover $10 women, $20 men.

Rain *Palms*, 4321 W Flamingo Rd ℡ 702/940-7246. Vast, glitzy, no-expense-spared water-themed 1200-capacity club, featuring spectacular fountains of water and fire. When it's warm enough, the action extends outside into the pool area. Thurs 11pm–5am, $10, Fri & Sat 10pm–5am, $20.

Studio 54 *MGM Grand*, 3799 Las Vegas Blvd S ℡ 702/891-7254. Three-story, four-dance floor recreation of New York's legendary *Studio 54*. Tuesday's EDEN (Erotically Delicious Entertainers' Night) party is the best time to come; the music varies little from night to night, rarely straying from house and other forms of electronica. Tues–Sat 10pm–5am. Cover men only, Tues–Thurs $10, Fri & Sat $20.

Tabú *MGM Grand*, 3799 Las Vegas Blvd S ℡ 702/891-7183. The definitive Las Vegas "ultra-lounge"; not only do go-go girls dance on the tables, but the tables themselves respond to touch by dancing with swirling colors. Expert and beautiful staff mix any cocktail, while despite the lack of a proper dance floor they host themed nights like "Slide" (old school hip hop) on Sundays, or the more general "Dolce Vita" on Thursdays. Tues–Sun 10pm–5am. Cover $20.

Entertainment

There was a time when Las Vegas represented the pinnacle of any show-business career. In the early 1960s, when Frank Sinatra's Rat Pack were shooting the original *Ocean's 11* during the day then singing the night away at the *Sands*, the city could claim to be the capital of the international entertainment industry. Then the world moved on. In the last few years, however, Las Vegas has started to come back into its own. One by one, the cheesy, feathers-and-tassels revues have closed down, to be replaced by surprisingly stimulating, postmodern shows by the likes of the now-ubiquitous **Cirque du Soleil** and the **Blue Man Group**. A new generation of big-name stars are taking up the kind of long-term residencies we all thought had vanished with Elvis. **Celine Dion** and **Elton John** at *Caesars'* huge Colosseum are the most conspicuous, but more are expected to follow.

The Amazing Johnathan *Sahara*, 2535 Las Vegas Blvd S ☏702/737-2111, ⊛www.amazingj .com. The emphasis on the Amazing Johnathan's unbridled craziness might lead you to expect a crude late-night gross-out, but barring the cartoonish violence he directs against his ditzy blonde assistant "Psychic Tanya," Johnathan's a lovable character. He's basically a comedic magician, with the emphasis on the comedy, meaning that he barely completes a trick all evening. That's probably for the best, anyway, as carefully honed patter and hilarious skits like "Bad Karate Theater" make this one of Las Vegas's funniest shows. Daily except Thurs 10pm. $50 & $60.

Blue Man Group *The Venetian*, 3265 Las Vegas Blvd S ☏1-866/641-7469. Enter a strange and unfamiliar world, in which three bald, blue performance artists sell out a 1750-seat theater every night of the week. Don't expect stars, or a plot, or even words; instead, you get synchronized eating of breakfast cereal and live endoscopies on audience members, plus deafening, exhilarating drumming from the Men themselves, and some stunning special effects. It's not for everyone, but breathtaking novelty is at least part of what Las Vegas is all about. Sun–Fri 7pm, Sat 7pm & 10pm. $79–90.

Celine Dion in A New Day *Caesars Palace*, 3570 Las Vegas Blvd S ☏702/731-7865. Celine Dion serves up Las Vegas entertainment on an epic scale in *Caesars*' vast Colosseum. Unless you're a big fan, however – in which case you'll love the amazing sound – what's been dubbed the "Cirque de Celine" may well leave you cold. Celine herself is all but dwarfed on the gigantic stage, while the abundant Cirque du Soleil trimmings seem at odds with the essentially lightweight songs. Seasonal, Wed–Sun 8.30pm, $87.50–225.

Folies Bergere *Tropicana*, 3801 Las Vegas Blvd S ☏702/739-2411. A fixture since 1959, the *Folies Bergere* is the longest-running show in the US. The basic formula remains the same: a mildly "naughty" Parisian revue designed to blow the minds of stout, bearded farmers from Iowa. Showgirls with fixed grins and feathered headdresses – and topless at times during certain performances – high-kick and waltz through a succession of big production numbers. When they take a breather, quick-fire Mexican juggler Wally Eastwood plays the piano with his balls. All the music is recorded. Mon, Wed, Thurs & Sat 7.30pm & 10pm (topless), Tues & Fri 8.30pm (topless); all shows except 7.30pm over-16s only. $45–55.

Kà *MGM Grand*, 3799 Las Vegas Blvd S ☏702/891-7777, ⊛www.ka.com. Las Vegas' fourth Cirque du Soleil production, *Kà*, is an absolute must-see. With a budget of $165 million, and nightly cast of 75 performers and 158 technicians, it's the most expensive theatrical production ever staged anywhere; in fact it's more like a feature film such as *Crouching Tiger, Hidden Dragon*. Though more plot-driven than other Cirque shows, telling a complex saga about two Asian twins – supposedly a boy and a girl, but confusingly played by two women – separated by kidnappers, it's still at heart a succession of truly breathtaking vignettes. The maneuverability of the stage allows for some staggering aerial battles, and there's an astonishing "Wheel of Death" routine. Add in some extraordinary puppetry and sumptuous costumes, plus the artful use of fire and fog, and *Kà* is certain to expand your horizons. Fri–Tues 7pm & 10:30pm. $99, $125, $150.

Lance Burton *Monte Carlo*, 3770 Las Vegas Blvd S ☏702/730-7160. Las Vegas's best family show, featuring the superb and very charming master magician Lance Burton. As well as traditional but very impressive stunts with playing cards, handkerchiefs, and doves, Burton masters large-scale illusions like the disappearance of an airplane and a narrow escape from hanging. Tues & Sat 7pm & 10pm, Wed–Fri 7pm. $66 & $73.

Legends in Concert *Imperial Palace*, 3535 Las Vegas Blvd S ☏702/794-3261. Celebrity-tribute show, with a changing roster that ranges from impersonators of Tina Turner to Rod Stewart. The slick Four Tops are unbeatable, but the surreal recreation of Michael Jackson's *Thriller* is a joy to behold, and a tongue-in-cheek Elvis clowning through *Viva Las Vegas* makes a fitting finale. Check if they're giving away tickets on the sidewalk before you buy. Daily except Sun 7.30pm & 10.30pm. $40–60, including one drink; ages 12 and under $25–45.

Mac King Improv Theater, *Harrah's*, 3475 Las Vegas Blvd S ☏702/369-5111. Magician Mac King's afternoon show represents one of Las Vegas's best entertainment bargains. Mac's an endearingly wide-eyed innocent in a plaid suit who specializes in good old close-up magic, using ropes, cards, torn-up $20 bills and the like. His corny patter leaves plenty of room for good-natured improvised gags at the expense of those unwary audience members he lures up on stage. Tues–Sat 1 & 3pm. $22.

Mystère *TI*, 3300 Las Vegas Blvd S ☏1-800/392-1999. The Cirque du Soleil's original Las Vegas show is such a visual feast that it barely matters whether you see its dreamscape symbolism as profound and meaningful or labored and empty. Seen at first as being too "way-out" for Las Vegas, its success redefined the city's approach to entertainment. Above all, it's a showcase of fabulous circus skills, with tumblers, acrobats, trapeze artists, pole climbers, clowns, and strong men, but no animals apart from fantastic costumed apparitions. Wed–Sat 7.30pm & 10.30pm, Sun 4.30pm & 7.30pm. $95.

🏃 **0** *Bellagio*, 3600 Las Vegas Blvd S ☎702/693-7722. Another Cirque du Soleil triumph, and a remarkable testament to what's possible when the budget is barely an issue. Any part of the stage at any time may be submerged to any depth. One moment a performer walks across a particular spot, the next someone dives headfirst into it from the high wire. From the synchronized

swimmers onwards, the Cirque display their magnificent skills to maximum advantage. Highlights include a colossal trapeze frame draped like a pirate ship and crewed by fearless acrobats and divers, and footmen flying through the air in swirls of velvet drapery. Wed–Sun 7.30pm & 10.30pm. $99–150.

V – the Ultimate Variety Show V Theatre, *Aladdin*, 3667 Las Vegas Blvd S ☎702/932-1818. Old-fashioned but enjoyable revue show that gives assorted singers, comedians, jugglers, and the like a few minutes each to prove their worth. If the hilarious Russ Merlin is on the bill, be sure not to miss it. Daily 7.30pm & 9pm, $29–89.

Contexts

Contexts

A history of the Southwest

What is now the Southwest USA has been home to Native Americans for about twelve thousand years. Around four hundred years ago, they were joined by a small group of Hispanic colonists, who claimed the region for Spain as New Mexico. After over two hundred years of Spanish rule, it passed briefly into the hands of the newly independent nation of Mexico, before being taken over by the United States, which has now held it for around 160 years.

Throughout that long history, the Southwest has been either controlled, or at least heavily influenced, by distant powers. Its best-known ancient peoples, the Ancestral Puebloans and the Hohokam, drew their cultural inspiration from the civilizations of Mexico; the settlers of Santa Fe looked to Madrid and Mexico City for financial and spiritual support; and even the current status of the region owes much to federal funding from Washington.

What makes the history of the Southwest so fascinating is that so many of the different peoples who have migrated into the region are still there, and still inter-reacting with each other. In the words of an anthropologist from Zuni Pueblo, "the Anasazi are alive and well and living in the Rio Grande valley." The Navajo, relative latecomers, form the majority population in the Four Corners region, though they've never displaced the Hopi. Santa Fe remains a visibly Hispanic, Catholic city, while Utah is still seventy percent Mormon, and Phoenix and Las Vegas typify the Anglo impact.

The Paleo Indians

No trace of human beings in the Americas has been dated any earlier than 14,000 years ago, when the true pioneers of North America, nomadic hunter-gatherers from Siberia, first reached Alaska. Thanks to the last ice age, when sea levels were three hundred feet lower than the modern Bering Strait, a "**land-bridge**" – actually a vast plain, measuring six hundred miles north to south – connected Eurasia to America.

At that time, Alaska effectively formed part of Asia rather than North America, being separated by impenetrable glacier fields from Canada and points south. Much like an air lock, the region "opened" in different directions at different times; migrants reaching it from the west, oblivious to the fact that they were leaving Asia, would at first have found their way blocked to the east. Several generations might have passed, and the connection back toward Asia severed before an eastward passage appeared. This migration was almost certainly spurred not by the urge to explore, but the pursuit of large mammal species, especially the mammoth, that had already been harried to extinction throughout almost all of Eurasia. Imagine therefore the glee of the so-called **Paleo Indians** when they finally encountered America's own indigenous "mega-fauna," such as mammoths, mastodons, giant ground sloths, and enormous long-horned bison, all of which had evolved without fear of, or protection against, human predation.

It's intriguing to reflect upon how small the original group of human settlers may have been. If a band of around a hundred individuals entered the virgin continent, they need only have advanced at a rate of eight miles per year, with a population growth of 1.1 percent each year, to fill both North and South America with a total of ten million people within a thousand years.

Between 10,000 BC and 8000 BC, the Southwest was dominated by what archeologists call the **Clovis** culture, whose distinctive flaked-stone spear-points were first identified at Clovis, New Mexico. Living in small groups, constantly on the move, Clovis hunters pursued their prey across large distances. Their weapons have been found poking from the ribs of mammoth skeletons, and they seem to have been such successful killers that they drove the indigenous fauna – which included horses – to extinction.

The Archaic culture

As the large animals died out, early Southwesterners had to adapt and became **hunter-gatherers**. The people of the **Archaic** or **Desert** culture learned where and when particular plants would ripen, and migrated seasonally within relatively restricted areas – often between canyons or valleys and nearby hillsides – in search of fresh food. Hunting for small mammals such as rabbit and deer was still important, however. The development of shamanistic rituals is demonstrated by the clay statuettes and split-twig figurines, depicting what appear to be deities as well as animals, that have been found in remote locations in the Grand Canyon and elsewhere. Few substantial remains of their actual homes survive, however; it's thought they lived in caves wherever possible. The most remarkable manifestation of Archaic culture was the haunting, mysterious rock art of the **Great Gallery** in Canyonlands National Park (see p.505); they also constructed "intaglios," giant earthworks in the shape of enigmatic figures or snakes, in the deserts of southwest Arizona.

The Archaic era was brought to an end by the gradual infiltration of Mexican influences from the south. The first and most crucial was agriculture. **Corn** – in the shape of tiny fingers of maize, much smaller than today's strains – may have been cultivated in the highlands of southern Mexico as early as 5000 BC. The skill of growing it was then passed northwards from group to group, accompanied no doubt by the prayers and rituals necessary to ensure a good harvest, and may have reached southern New Mexico around 1500 BC. However, anthropologists have noted a common reluctance among hunter-gatherers the world over to give up what they regard as a pleasant lifestyle, which offers individuals food in return for comparatively little effort, and lots of free time. Initially the Southwest's low level of farming was more like gardening and served to supplement the traditional. diet Communities only made the transition to intensive agriculture when forced to by increasing population levels.

The Basketmakers

Southwestern peoples embarked on the large-scale cultivation of crops – corn, together with a more recent arrival, **squash** – from around 100 BC onwards. The first such society was confusingly named **Basketmaker II** by early archeologists, who assumed that more primitive "Basketmaker I" sites would subsequently be found. The Basketmakers lived in extended family groups, in shallow **pithouses** – rectangular pits dug two to six feet into the ground, with earth-covered roofs

A separate history of the **Hopi** tribe appears on p.585, and of the **Navajo** and **Apache** peoples on p.590.

that rose above ground level. They hunted using the *atlatl* – a lever-like spear-throwing device used throughout the Americas. Cooking entailed dropping hot rocks into yucca-leaf baskets that had a waterproof lining of pitch. By now they had also domesticated **dogs**, for hunting, and **turkeys**, used mainly for feathers rather than food.

Pottery is thought to have spread from Mexico, by way of the Mimbres region of southwest New Mexico (see p.246), in the first few centuries AD. All pots were made by women, using the technique of hand-coiling, which involves layering successive strips of rolled clay on top of each other and then smoothing them together. The use of fragile ceramic vessels presupposes a relatively sedentary society that's willing to settle down for the benefits the vessels offer. It's much easier to boil **beans** in a pot than a basket, so the Southwest acquired its third great staple food, and basketmaking declined.

By around 500 AD, the so-called **Basketmaker III** culture had emerged. As well as corn, squash, and beans, they grew another Mexican import, **cotton** – originally cultivated mainly for its oil-rich edible seeds – and used **bows and arrows** for the first time. Sizeable **villages** (what the Spanish later called **pueblos**) started to form.

Each village soon focused around one specific pithouse that was larger than the rest, and was probably set aside for public or ritual use. Such buildings are recognizable as the first *kivas* – the ceremonial underground chambers that remain at the heart of Pueblo religion. Each *kiva* was entered from above, via an opening that also served as the smokehole for the central firepit. A bench ran around its circumference, and there were also niches set into the walls where ritual objects may have been placed. A small depression in the floor in front of the firepit, known as the *sipapu*, symbolized the hole through which human beings emerged onto this earth.

The Ancestral Puebloans

By 700 AD, much of the Southwest was populated by the forerunners of the modern Pueblo Indians. This book follows contemporary practice among archeologists and Pueblo Indians by calling these people "**Ancestral Puebloans**" in preference to the previously common term "**Anasazi**." The Hopi in particular object to that name, which comes from a Navajo word meaning "enemy ancestors," and have championed the use of either their own word for "ancestors," **Hisatsinom**, or the more generally applicable "Ancestral Puebloans."

Over the course of six centuries, from 700 AD to 1300 AD, Ancestral Puebloan civilization spread beyond the **Four Corners** region to cover most of what's now northern Arizona and New Mexico, as well as southern Utah and Colorado, reaching as far as the depths of the Grand Canyon and into southern Nevada. At the start of that period, there was a steady increase in the size and sophistication of villages, and also a crucial change. Individuals stopped living in pithouses, and instead built surface structures of mud plastered onto a framework of brushwood – a style known as wattle-and-daub. However, they continued to dig large subterranean *kivas*, which kept the pithouse form but were exclusively designed for communal or ceremonial use. Many such *kivas* could now be accessed not only through the roof, but also via concealed underground tunnels, which may have enabled costumed priests or dancers to make surprise appearances during rituals.

The Ancestral Puebloans were the first North Americans to use looms to weave cotton. In addition to cotton clothes, they made blankets and even socks from yucca leaves interwoven with turkey feathers, and wore yucca sandals. For a time, they seem to have deliberately flattened and broadened their skulls by binding the heads of babies against cradleboards. As you might imagine from their tiny doorways and cramped living quarters, they were on the small side, with women averaging five feet in height and men a few inches more. Life expectancy was thirty or less, although perhaps one in ten reached the age of fifty. Adults were plagued by the twin problems of arthritis, often exacerbated by years of carrying heavy loads, and loss of teeth. Their teeth were worn away by the grit in their food, the result of grinding corn between a hand-tool or *mano* and a flat slab known as a *metate*, both made from sandstone; in the words of a modern Hopi saying, "a person eats a rock in a lifetime." They also had some medical expertise, using cottonwood bark, which contains aspirin's main active ingredient, as a painkiller, and the sap from piñon pines as an all-purpose antiseptic.

The Ancestral Puebloans of the Four Corners reached a cultural peak during the eleventh century. By that time, three main subgroups had emerged – centered on Chaco Canyon in what's now northwest New Mexico, Mesa Verde in southwest Colorado, and the Kayenta region of northeast Arizona – and there were also smaller groups such as the Virgin Anasazi of southern Utah.

The **Chacoans** seem to have been the most sophisticated of all, as witnessed not only by the architectural complexity of the multistory pueblos of Chaco Canyon, but by the fact that the canyon was so unsuited for large-scale occupation that they must have survived by extracting tribute from surrounding regions. A detailed account of the "Chaco Phenomenon" appears on p.114.

The wealth of Chaco demonstrates that by 1050 AD the Southwest was crisscrossed by extensive **trading routes**. In the absence of pack animals, most of the trade was in lightweight ritual or ornamental objects rather than the necessities of life. In exchange for **turquoise** from the mines of Cerrillos (see p.156), which passed from group to group all the way down to the Aztecs in central Mexico, the Ancestral Puebloans received silver and copper goods from Mexico, sea-shells from the Pacific Coast, and the most prized ceremonial objects of all – live **macaws**.

The decline of Chaco, during the first half of the twelfth century, was mirrored by a general decline in the Ancestral Puebloan population. Following a period of instability and mass migrations, however, Ancestral Puebloan civilization had a majestic final flourish in the Four Corners. The thirteenth century – when they constructed "**cliff dwellings**," squeezed dramatically into narrow alcoves high on canyon walls, for which they're now celebrated – was also characterized by the widespread growth of major **towns**. Colorado's Montezuma Valley was typical in holding around eight large pueblo complexes across the valley floor and along neighboring ridges, each home to over a thousand people. The nearby cliff dwellings preserved in **Mesa Verde** National Park (see p.94) were home to a smaller, probably peripheral group; though compellingly beautiful to modern eyes, they represent a relatively minor aspect of Ancestral Puebloan life.

The disappearance of the Ancestral Puebloans

Between 1275 AD and 1300 AD, the Ancestral Puebloans vanished from the entire Four Corners region. Their "**disappearance**" is still widely presented as a great mystery, although the increasing use of the term "Ancestral Puebloans" in preference to "Anasazi" is in itself an indication that that the puzzle has largely been solved. Modern Pueblo peoples are so self-evidently their descendants that it's clear the Ancestral Puebloans migrated away rather than simply dying out. Why they did so is harder to explain. Traditional accounts say that a sustained **drought** forced them to leave, but it has now been demonstrated that such droughts were not uncommon, and that the region remained capable of producing enough food to support them.

It seems more likely that the drought coincided with a period of cultural upheaval. While archeologists argue as to whether individual Ancestral Puebloan cliff dwellings were intended for defense, there's no disputing the fact that the region as a whole was prone to violent conflict at this time. Recent proof of cannibalism in the Montezuma Valley has shattered notions of Ancestral Puebloan society as being utterly peaceful, and isolated groups appear to have banded together in larger settlements for mutual defense.

The influence of the blood-drenched civilizations of ancient Mexico was also at its height. As described on p.84, the *kachina* religion, which centered on supernatural entities that, at this formative stage, closely paralleled the warring deities of the Aztecs, spread rapidly across the Southwest. Recent discoveries at Chaco Canyon, as detailed on p.115, have even suggested to some archeologists that the *kachina* cult was introduced by cannibalistic warrior refugees from the south. Such theories remain very controversial, however. In any case, over time, religious emphasis shifted away from blood and sacrifice toward ceremonies designed to bring rain, and thus corn. The drought of the late thirteenth century may have seemed like the first crucial test of, or judgment upon, those rainmaking powers, and it may be that charismatic religious leaders persuaded their followers that the failure of the harvest was a signal to move on.

In addition, the Ancestral Puebloans had severely depleted their **environment**. The need for fuel and building materials meant that the landscape for many miles around their settlements had been stripped bare; the pueblos of Chaco Canyon, for example, used over 200,000 large wooden beams. Cutting down trees not only made the search for firewood increasingly arduous, but led to the process known as *arroyo*-cutting, whereby, once the trees that held their banks together were removed, previously placid streams became savage torrents that destroyed prime riverside farmland. It may be no coincidence that the Four Corners remained all but deserted until the arrival of the Navajo during the sixteenth century (see p.590); it may have taken that long to recover from overexploitation.

The Hohokam

While the Basketmakers and Ancestral Puebloans held sway further north, the deserts of southern Arizona and northern Mexico were home to the equally sophisticated **Hohokam** civilization. This region was not then so barren as it appears today – much of it was covered with grass until the Spanish allowed their cattle to overgraze – and the Hohokam were primarily **farmers**. They lived not in compact pueblos but in what the Spanish later called *rancherías* – sprawling farming communities, where each separate homestead consisted of a framework of timber, brush-coated with mud. Thousands of such villages, most of which were occupied for many generations, were scattered across the desert, interspersed with larger "towns" that were probably ceremonial and trading centers rather than residential districts. The population was most heavily concentrated in the **Phoenix Basin**, where inhabitants compensated for the lack of rainfall by digging over three hundred miles of irrigation **canals**. Constructed without the use of metal tools, and requiring constant maintenance, these enabled the Hohokam to reap two separate harvests each year. Corn, beans, and squash were once again the staples, but the Hohokam cultivated sixteen distinct plant species, including cotton for trade.

Whether the Hohokam migrated into the region from central Mexico around 300 BC, as some archeologists believe, or simply evolved from indigenous desert peoples, they were clearly heavily influenced by Mexican culture. Each major town had at least one Mexican-style **ballcourt**, where a ritual game with similarities to modern basketball was played with a rubber ball, and a raised-earth **platform mound** – a primitive pyramid – used for religious ceremonies. Like the Ancestral Puebloans, with whom they had little direct contact, the Hohokam traded commodities like cotton and salt for treasured ritual items from the south, such as copper bells, onyx, parrots, and macaws.

During the eleventh century, the Hohokam trading complex known as **Snaketown**, at the confluence of the Gila and Salt rivers, rivaled Chaco as the largest settlement in the Southwest. Though Snaketown then declined, the Phoenix Basin became one of the most densely populated areas in North America, with perhaps eighty thousand inhabitants in the thirteenth century. However, the Hohokam **disappeared** from history at much the same time as the Ancestral Puebloans, around 1350 AD. The very word "Hohokam" means "all used up" in the language of the later **'O'odham** people of southern Arizona (known to the Spanish as the Pima and the Papago), and reflects 'O'odham oral history that the Hohokam drained every possible drop of sustenance from the land. Archeologists agree, suggesting that they damaged the region's delicate ecological balance so extensively that their descendants were reduced to an impoverished subsistence lifestyle. In addition, by the end of the seventeenth century the arrival of European **diseases** such as smallpox, measles, and typhus reduced the population of the Phoenix Basin to less than five thousand.

While no modern Native American group claims direct physical descent from the Hohokam, it's possible to trace certain cultural continuities. The *ranchería* style of dwelling endured until recent times among tribes such as the Yavapai, the Havasupai, and the **'O'odham** themselves. These peoples also follow an individualistic system of belief, without *kachinas* or *kivas*, and depending on shamans rather than priests, that seems to be in line with what little is known about Hohokam religion.

The Mogollon

Archeologists distinguish a third significant group among the pre-Columbian peoples of the Southwest – the **Mogollon**. Contemporaneous with the Ancestral Puebloans and the Hohokam, and sharing elements of both cultures, the Mogollon occupied an extensive area in what's now west-central New Mexico and east-central Arizona. The main geographical feature of the region is the **Mogollon Rim**, a 200-mile long, 2000ft high escarpment that marks the southern limit of the Colorado Plateau. The Mogollon people lived on the cool plateau above the rim, farming the upland meadows and hunting in the adjacent mountains.

Being so close to Mexico, the Mogollon heartland, which focused on the valleys of the **Gila** and **Mimbres** rivers, was probably the first area of the Southwest to acquire the techniques of agriculture and pottery. The Basketmaker phase lasted longer here than in the Four Corners; the Mogollon only stopped building pithouses around the eleventh century, and the few pueblos they constructed, such as the one now preserved as Gila Cliff Dwellings National Monument (see p.245), were on a smaller scale than their Ancestral Puebloan counterparts. In one respect, however, Mogollon culture was unsurpassed – the extraordinary **pottery** produced by the **Classic Mimbres** people, a Mogollon offshoot described in detail on p.246.

Much like the Four Corners, the entire Mogollon region became **depopulated** during the fourteenth century. As the Mogollon peoples had probably been instrumental in introducing the *kachina* religion to the Southwest, it makes sense to suppose that their descendants helped to create modern Pueblo culture. Specific Mogollon-descended pueblos may well have been the hardest hit by the arrival of both the Spaniards and the Apache, however, and if their inhabitants survived at all, they probably fled north as refugees.

The Pueblo world and the Spanish invasion

Although the Ancestral Puebloan era ended with their departure from the Four Corners, their immediate descendants created the Southwest's largest pre-Hispanic communities of all. In particular, the city of **Casas Grandes**, which flourished between 1300 AD and 1400 AD in what's now the northern Mexican state of Chihuahua, consisted of over two thousand rooms and served as a major macaw-breeding center.

However, the most enduring legacy of the Ancestral Puebloans was the emergence of **Pueblo** communities throughout what had until the fourteenth century been relatively uninhabited areas of northern New Mexico. Most of the people of Mesa Verde migrated to the northern reaches of the **Rio Grande** valley, where they founded pueblos such as Taos and Santa Clara; their language, known as Tanoan, evolved into the Tiwa and Tewa languages spoken today. The Chacoans, on the other hand, who spoke the language that became Keresan, moved further south to establish pueblos like Cochiti and Santo Domingo, as well as Ácoma and Zuni to the west.

Other population centers – not so well known today, as they failed to survive the impact of the Spanish – included the **Galisteo Valley**, not far southeast of Santa Fe, which held around a dozen large pueblos; the **Chama Valley**; and the **Tigüex** region near modern Albuquerque.

By the time the Spanish arrived, the Southwest may have held as many as a hundred separate pueblos, with a total population approaching one hundred thousand. New forms of social organization had emerged, and individual pueblos consisted of alliances of either **clans** – each with its own religious or military responsibilities – or **moieties** – the technical term for a society divided into two halves, in which half the pueblo might belong to a *kiva* associated with winter ceremonies, and the other half to one connected with summer. However, pueblos did not have chiefs or leaders in the European sense, and neither was there any tradition of alliances between pueblos. That lack of political unity seriously weakened their ability to resist the

Spanish invaders, who turned their attention northwards after completing the conquest of Mexico.

The coming of the Spaniards

The first Spanish expedition to reach what is now the US, led by **Ponce de León**, sailed up the Atlantic Coast in 1513 and named **Florida**. The next Spanish voyage, in 1528, ended in shipwreck in Tampa Bay, but a junior officer, **Alvar Núñez Cabeza de Vaca**, survived. Together with three shipmates, he spent eight years on an extraordinary transcontinental odyssey. Living with various Native American groups – initially held as slaves, later revered as seers – they made their way across Texas, following the Pecos River and the Rio Grande. It's unlikely that they reached modern New Mexico or Arizona, but while staying in the pueblo of the Jumano tribe, somewhere on the Rio Grande, they heard tales of larger pueblos further north, and in northern Mexico they were given emeralds that had been purchased with parrot feathers from a people who lived to the north.

Cabeza de Vaca's eventual arrival in Mexico City in 1536 created a sensation, and the Viceroy of New Spain resolved to investigate his tales of golden cities deep in the desert. After all, it was still less than twenty years since the Spanish had conquered the inconceivably wealthy civilization of the Aztecs, and subsequent expeditions within New Spain had discovered further riches. One of Cabeza de Vaca's companions had been a black African from Azemmour in Morocco, called **Esteban de Dorantes**. Rather than return to a life of slavery, he volunteered to map the route for a new expedition led by the Franciscan friar **Fray Marcos de Niza**, who had recently witnessed at first hand Pizarro's conquest of the Incas in Peru. In 1539, Esteban set off ahead of Fray Marcos, and followed a long-established native trading route north across the Rio San Pedro into what's now Arizona.

A giant of a man, dressed like a shaman in jewelry and feathers and accompanied by two colossal greyhounds, he amazed the native peoples he encountered, and soon acquired a large entourage. Having arranged to send a signal back to Fray Marcos if he discovered anything to rival the marvels of Mexico, he duly did so as he approached the pueblo of **Zuni** (see p.118). Zuni at this time was a major trading center, where the trail from the south met others from the Pacific Coast to the west and the Rio Grande pueblos to the east. The Zuni villages were nonetheless simply clusters of adobe houses, not cities on the Mexican scale. According to the Zuni, Esteban's demands for tribute were incompatible with his claims to be a medicine man, and they punished his sacrilegious behavior by killing him, cutting him into strips, and distributing his flesh among their neighbors.

Fray Marcos reported that he was in sight of Zuni when he heard of Esteban's death and fled back to Mexico; it seems more probable that he never reached Arizona. Even so, he announced "this land…is the greatest and best of all that have been discovered." Rendering the Zuni name Shi:wona as Cíbola, he called the six Zuni villages the **Seven Cities of Cíbola**, and identified them with the legendary Seven Cities of Antillia. Supposedly founded by seven bishops who had fled westwards across the Atlantic during the Muslim conquest of Spain, around 700 AD, these prosperous Christian communities had long been sought by Spanish explorers.

On February 22, 1540, therefore, a further expedition, led by **Francisco Vásquez de Coronado**, set off into the Southwest from Compostela in northern Mexico. More than three hundred Spanish soldiers, along with hundreds of

Indian "allies" and servants and several thousand horses and cattle, marched up through Arizona and reached Zuni on July 7. In front of the town of Hawikku, the Zuni drew a line of sacred cornmeal along the ground, which they forbade the Spaniards to cross. During the pitched **battle** that ensued – the first ever fought between Europeans and Native Americans – Coronado himself was knocked unconscious, but Spanish weapons prevailed. When the town was taken, its storehouses revealed not gold, but something that by now seemed equally precious – food.

Within two weeks, news of the fall of Zuni spread throughout the Southwest. Coronado made his headquarters in the conquered pueblo and dispatched exploratory parties in all directions. One such, under Pedro de Tovar, forced the "warlike" Hopi pueblos to surrender (see p.586) and reached as far as the **Grand Canyon**; another, commanded by Melchor Díaz, crossed the Colorado further south, and thus penetrated modern **California**. A detachment led by Hernando de Alvarado headed east, passing Ácoma Pueblo – "the greatest stronghold ever seen in the world" – and reaching the pueblos of the Rio Grande.

Meanwhile, emissaries from the Pueblo world were traveling to Zuni. Peaceful overtures from two men from **Cicuyé** (now Pecos National Historical Park; see p.147), known to the Spaniards as **Cacique** (meaning "Governor") and **Bigotes** ("Whiskers"), persuaded Coronado to move his expedition east. They camped for the winter beside the Rio Grande, in a region they called **Tigüex**, and commandeered an entire pueblo as their new base. This may have been Kuaua, now preserved as Coronado State Monument (see p.154) – it's hard to say, because relations with the Tigüex soon degenerated into full-scale war, and in a bloody succession of sieges and massacres, all the Tigüex pueblos were destroyed.

Coronado remained convinced that gold was somewhere to be found. In the spring of 1541, he decamped northeast to Cicuyé, which was a prosperous community where Pueblo peoples traded with nomads from the Plains. In what may well have been a deliberate plot, Cacique and Bigotes introduced him to "**the Turk**," a Pawnee captive, who knew of a city far to the east, **Quivira**, that was rich in gold. Details of the Turk's story suggest that he was familiar with the culture of the Mississippi Indians, but he was probably released by the leaders of Cicuyé in the hope that he'd lead the Spaniards into oblivion on the endless Plains.

In the event, the expedition wandered for three fruitless months across what they called "the domain of the cows," in honor of its vast buffalo herds. From the Llano Estacado or "Staked Plains" of **Texas**, where they drove wooden stakes into the ground to avoid losing their way, they veered northeast into **Kansas**, following the Arkansas River along the route of what later became the Santa Fe Trail. There they did indeed reach a land known as Quivira, but its inhabitants were nomadic and utterly gold-free buffalo-hunters. At that point, Coronado lost patience; the Turk was garrotted and the Spaniards returned to the Rio Grande. Remarkably, at their furthest east Coronado's party may have come within a hundred miles of Hernando de Soto's even more rapacious military expedition, which had marched up from Florida and was at this time exploring west of the Mississippi. Legend has it that one unfortunate Indian band fleeing Coronado's advance blundered into the path of the de Soto group.

After another beleaguered winter in Tigüex, the Coronado expedition embarked on the long journey back to Mexico, leaving behind a handful of (swiftly martyred) missionaries and many of their Mexican-Indian allies. Popular myth has it that Coronado was disgraced on his return home, but while his expedition was certainly seen as a failure, the man himself held important offices in Mexico City for the rest of his life.

The colony of New Mexico

During the fifty years after Coronado's departure, unauthorized Spanish adventurers made occasional forays into the Southwest. Not until 1598, however, was **Don Juan de Oñate** granted royal permission to establish a permanent **colony**. His expedition, consisting of 130 families and two hundred single men, crossed the Rio Grande near modern El Paso on May 1 and took possession of the land under the name of **New Mexico**. The geography of the region remaining unknown, the precise boundaries of the colony were not specified, but broadly speaking it extended from the Colorado River in the west to the Pecos River in the east, and included not only what's now New Mexico, but all of Arizona, plus parts of Utah, Colorado, Nevada, and California. At that time, the name "Mexico" referred only to what we call Mexico City – the modern country of Mexico was known as "New Spain" until 1821 – so "New Mexico" was named in the hope that it would match the riches of the Aztecs.

As Oñate's party traveled north along the river, each pueblo they reached had been hurriedly deserted by its inhabitants, fearful of being captured as slaves. Eventually, at the confluence of the Rio Grande and the Chama River near what's now Española, the settlers took over the pueblo of O'ke, renamed it San Juan, and made it their **capital**. Like Coronado before him, Oñate sent soldiers to all quarters of his new realm in search of gold; and like Coronado he soon found himself at war. After a group commanded by Oñate's nephew was all but wiped out, he launched a full-scale artillery onslaught on Ácoma Pueblo. Over eight hundred Acomans were killed, and eighty male prisoners had their feet chopped off in public ceremonies in the pueblos of the Rio Grande.

By the time Oñate returned to his capital, most of the colonists had given up and returned to Mexico. Oñate himself was recalled to Mexico City in disgrace once Franciscan missionaries reported his cruelty to their superiors. Meanwhile, however, Captain Pérez de Villagrá had trumpeted Oñate's "achievements" in an epic poem, *Historia de Nueva México*. In the face of all the evidence, Villagrá still insisted that New Mexico had the potential to become the greatest kingdom in the Spanish empire, and he was sufficiently believed in Madrid for another attempt at colonization to be launched. **Don Pedro de Peralta** was therefore sent to New Mexico with orders to found a new capital, and the city of **Santa Fe** was duly laid out in 1610.

The early Spanish colonists of New Mexico dreamed of emulating their predecessors in Mexico, who had accumulated both land and wealth in prodigious quantities. However, it soon became clear that New Mexico was the end of the road, with no access to the ocean and no rich neighbors for the Spaniards either to trade with or plunder. Santa Fe never grew into a mighty city, but remained a remote military outpost of crude adobe buildings. Enterprising colonists therefore dispersed up and down the valley of the Rio Grande, appropriating Pueblo farmlands – and often enslaving Pueblo peoples – to create **ranches** on which they raised sheep and corn and planted orchards of peaches, plums, and cherries. **Wheat** was the most significant of the new crops. Unlike the traditional triumvirate of corn, beans, and squash, which must be grown entirely in spring and summer, wheat can be planted in December for harvest in June.

At the same time, **Franciscan missionaries** set out to convert the Pueblo Indians to Catholicism. One or two friars would attach themselves to a specific pueblo, recruit Indian labor to build adobe mission churches, and set about persuading the Pueblos that their *kachina* cults and corn ceremonies were wicked.

Throughout the seventeenth century, the Spanish civil and religious authorities in New Mexico were at loggerheads. The church deplored violence against the Pueblos and yet demanded the eradication of their beliefs; the military governors preferred not to antagonize the Indians unnecessarily, but felt their authority ultimately rested on the sword.

Quite apart from any specific actions, the very presence of the Spaniards utterly disrupted the region. Settled communities like the villages of the Rio Grande were especially vulnerable to **epidemic diseases** such as smallpox, measles, and typhus, which were unknown before the arrival of the Europeans. By 1640, the Pueblo population had dropped from a hundred thousand down to around thirty thousand, and more than half of all pueblos had been abandoned. Existing patterns of **trade** across the Southwest had also been shattered, and the Rio Grande valley became a prime target for Native American raiders who coveted Spanish arms and, above all, **horses**. Tribes such as the Navajo and the Apache – turned from wandering nomads into fearsome mounted warriors, and all too often it was the Pueblo peoples who bore the brunt of their attacks.

The Pueblo Revolt

In 1675, as it became ever more obvious that traditional Pueblo beliefs still endured beneath a veneer of Catholicism, the Spanish arrested 47 Pueblo religious leaders. Three were condemned as "witchdoctors" and hanged at Santa Fe; the rest were publicly horsewhipped. One of these, a man called **Po'pay** from San Juan Pueblo, made his way to Taos Pueblo and turned one of its *kivas* into the center of a campaign of resistance. A date was set for a concerted uprising against the Spanish, and knotted strings were sent out to all the pueblos, with the instruction to untie one knot each night until the last signaled the arrival of the great day. Somehow, the plot was betrayed, so the **Pueblo Revolt** began a day early, on August 9, 1680.

For the first and only time in their history, the Pueblos of the northern Rio Grande, plus their cousins in Ácoma, Zuni, and the Hopi mesas, combined in unison; they were even joined by the Navajo and the Apache. Their anger fell especially upon the missionaries; 21 out of New Mexico's 33 priests were murdered, as were 375 men, women, and children out of a total of 2350 Spanish colonists.

After a ten-day **siege of Santa Fe**, the governor, the garrison, and around one thousand citizens were allowed to retreat south. They were joined en route by the Christianized majority from Isleta Pueblo – the only modern pueblo not to join the attack – and all the Pueblo peoples who lived south of Albuquerque. For the next thirteen years, the refugees remained together at what's now Ciudad Juarez, across the Rio Grande from El Paso. Those Indians who had joined the exodus founded Ysleta del Sur and other pueblos in the neighborhood, while the former colonists, refused permission to continue any further south, awaited an opportunity to return north.

Back in Santa Fe, the doors and windows of the Palace of the Governors had been sealed up and the building turned into a typical multistory pueblo. Po'pay was nominally in control, but the concept of a central political administration was alien to the Pueblos, and the alliance soon fragmented.

Not until 1692 did the Spanish crown appoint a new governor of New Mexico, **Don Diego de Vargas**. His exploratory expedition encountered no opposition when it returned to Santa Fe that September. As a result, he set off again with a party of colonists the following year; this time they had to fight before they could re-enter the city, in December 1693. The return of the Spanish triggered mass migrations throughout the region. Modern Navajo culture originated from the intermingling of the ancestral Navajo with Pueblo refugees during this period. There were further minor insurrections in the years ahead, but the **Reconquest** was completed by 1696.

The eighteenth century

Although Hispanic settlers continued to dominate the region for 150 years after the Pueblo Revolt, New Mexico was always a peripheral part of the Spanish empire. Separated from the rest of New Spain by vast tracts of empty desert, the colonists were obliged to be self-sufficient, and found themselves thrown into alliance with the Pueblo peoples to resist the threat of Ute and Comanche attack. The Spaniards and the Pueblos had much in common; the New Mexican landscape was similar to that of Andalucia in Spain, as indeed were its adobe hamlets or *pueblos*. The Pueblos had long been subsistence farmers who traded for rare luxuries with far-off civilizations to the south, and the Hispanic ranchers slotted into the same pattern. There was little intermarriage, although Pueblo communities came to acquire sizeable populations of *genízaros*, the bastard offspring of captured Plains Indians and their Spanish masters.

In the first half of the eighteenth century, the **French** established their own colony to the east, **Louisiana**. The immediate Spanish response was to set up missions among the Indians of what now became a separate province of New Spain, **Texas**. As the French and Spanish zones of influence expanded, there were armed clashes; thus a combined force of Spaniards and Pueblos was defeated by a French-Pawnee alliance near North Platte, Nebraska, in 1720.

In general, the French coexisted more amicably with Native Americans than did the Spanish; they were predominantly traders, eager to acquire beaver and other furs and not interested in converting Indians to Christianity. Unlike the Spanish, they were also prepared to supply Indians with **guns**. As a result, the Comanche, Ute, and Apache, equipped with the latest European firearms, consistently raided along the Rio Grande at harvest time, seizing crops and livestock, while the Hispanic villagers, inadequately supplied from Mexico, could only offer minimal resistance with their bows and arrows. The colonists financed the occasional retaliatory expedition by selling Indian captives to work as slaves in the silver mines of Mexico, thereby incurring ever greater Indian hostility.

Louisiana having proved no more profitable to France than was New Mexico to Spain, Louis XV of France simply gave it to Spain in 1762. The Mississippi River now formed the Spanish frontier in North America. Determined to resist encroachment by the infant United States, King Carlos III placed the entire region under his direct control from Spain in 1776. However, far too few Hispanic settlers moved in to make any difference, and in 1802, as the Spanish empire weakened, he handed Louisiana back to Napoleon. Carlos' hope that the French would serve as a buffer against the Yankees was misplaced; Napoleon sold his American territories to the US in the following year, in the **Louisiana Purchase**.

At the end of the century, Santa Fe was home to around two thousand Hispanic citizens, while the Pueblo population had dwindled to perhaps nine thousand, in a mere nineteen pueblos.

The settlement of Arizona

Before the Pueblo Revolt, the Spanish presence in New Mexico was confined to the valley of the Rio Grande and the scattered pueblos to the west. Under the names of **Pimería Alta** and **Papaguería**, what's now southern Arizona was left to peoples the Spaniards called the **Pima** and the **Papago**, known today as the **'O'odham**.

Around 1700, however, **Jesuit** missionaries conceived the notion of constructing a chain of missions all the way from New Spain to California, and built churches in a couple of 'O'odham villages. Hispanic ranchers and prospectors also drifted in. In 1736, a Yaqui Indian created a silver-mining camp, a few miles southwest of modern Nogales, called **Arizonac**. The name came either from the 'O'odham *ali shonak*, meaning "small springs," or from the Basque language of Spain, in which *arritza onac* means "valuable rocky places," and *aritz onac* means "good oaks."

After an 'O'odham rebellion killed several Jesuits, the Spanish installed a military garrison at **Tubac** (see p.289) in 1752. This *presidio* (fort) was relocated forty miles north to San Agustín de **Tucson** in 1776. Another Indian revolt in 1781, in which 150 settlers were wiped out during mass at **Yuma**, dashed Spanish hopes of establishing a permanent trail to California, and Tucson, like Santa Fe, came to be seen as a remote and insignificant dead-end town. In 1804, by which time there were around a thousand Spanish colonists in the vicinity, its commander reported, "we have no gold, silver, lead, tin, quicksilver, copper mines, or marble quarries... the only public work here that is truly worthy of this report is the church at **San Xavier del Bac**" (see p.286).

The end of the Hispanic era

The decline in New Mexico's importance to its Spanish rulers was mirrored by increasing contacts with the rest of North America. In the closing years of the eighteenth century, permanent trails were established both west to California – in the form of the **Old Spanish Trail**, painstakingly mapped across Utah by the Franciscan friars **Domínguez** and **Escalante** in 1776 – and east to St Louis, along the **Santa Fe Trail** blazed by French explorer Pedro Vial in 1792. After the Louisiana Purchase, expeditions sponsored by the US government also crossed the Plains, such as **Lewis and Clark**'s trek to the Northwest in 1804 and **Lt. Zebulon Pike**'s incursion into New Mexico in 1807.

Within a few years, the Spanish grip on the New World was finally loosened; following a **revolution** led by General Agustín Iturbide, Mexico became an independent nation in 1821. Although their governors swiftly transferred allegiance to Mexico City, neither New Mexico nor California perceived any advantage in their new status as Mexican territories. As the flow of resources from the south – including the handouts that had started to keep the Apache relatively docile – dwindled to rock-bottom levels, the effect on the New Mexican economy was crippling.

For the authorities in Santa Fe, the only answer seemed to be to increase trade with the US. Traffic along the Santa Fe Trail swiftly turned New Mexico into an entrepôt through which American goods were shipped south into Mexico. No Americans were permitted to live in New Mexico, but freebooting Anglos began to make their way across the Plains to seek their fortunes in the West. Among them were fur-trapping "**mountain men**" such as **Bill Williams** and **Kit Carson**, who made extended forays along the region's rivers in pursuit of beavers (known as "hairy banknotes"). **Taos** became renowned for its annual rendezvous, at which Anglo, Hispanic, and Native American traders gathered far from the authority of any government. Northern New Mexico was now also beyond the reach of the Catholic Church; devout Hispanics kept their faith alive by forming sects such as the **Penitentes** (see p.175) and established a tradition of religious folk art that endures to this day.

Meanwhile, enough Yankee newcomers had flocked into **Texas** to outnumber its loyal Mexican subjects. In 1836, after Texas fought to gain independence from Mexico and then voted for annexation by the US, the president of Mexico attempted to hold onto New Mexico by closing down the Santa Fe Trail. It was too late. The doctrine that it was the United States' "**Manifest Destiny**" to extend across the whole continent led the US government first to try to **buy** New Mexico and California, and then, when negotiations failed, to declare **war** on Mexico in 1846. American economic might was neatly illustrated when the US Army of the West took Santa Fe without a fight, in August 1846; the Mexican governor was simply paid $50,000 to leave, together with his garrison.

Territorial days: New Mexico and Arizona

Under the **Treaty of Guadalupe-Hidalgo**, signed in September 1847 after US soldiers had captured Mexico City, the United States took formal possession of New Mexico, Texas, and California – seen as the real prize – in return for a payment of $18.25 million. New Mexico, which consisted of all those parts of modern New Mexico and Arizona that lie north of the Gila River, plus areas of Nevada and Utah, was generally regarded as an arid, worthless wasteland. General Sherman is said to have jibed that "we had one war with Mexico to take Arizona, and we should have another to make her take it back."

Ironically, only the discovery of **gold** in California in 1847 gave New Mexico any great value to the US – as a route west. Surveyors mapping possible courses for a southern transcontinental railroad soon realized that the best routes lay on the Mexican side of the border. The Mexican government accepted the least extensive of five suggested land deals, and in June 1854, the $10 million **Gadsden Purchase** gave the US what's now southern Arizona, including Tucson, Tubac, and Tumacácori.

Another 25 years were to pass before the railroad reached the Southwest – during that time, **Yuma** on the lower Colorado River burgeoned as a major port – but prospectors trekking to and from California soon began to investigate the region more thoroughly. After gold was found near the confluence of the Gila and Colorado rivers, **miners** fanned out across central Arizona, and reports of rich silver and copper lodes lured ever more migrants in.

Feeling that they had little in common with the Hispanic farming communities of the Rio Grande, the new arrivals argued that the territory was too large to govern as a single unit and should be split in two. Many came originally from the South, and they seized upon the start of the **Civil War** in 1861 to declare the formation of the Confederate Territory of **Arizona**, which consisted of all the Gadsden Purchase lands. Its capital was Mesilla, in what's now New Mexico.

The Confederate cause in the Southwest was short-lived: a Confederate army sent to establish a military presence was turned back by Union forces at **Glorieta Pass** – outside Santa Fe, near modern Pecos – in March 1862. The federal government recognized the existence of Arizona in 1863, but to avoid giving it a built-in Confederate majority drew a north–south boundary rather than an east–west one, and thereby delineated the two modern states.

The Indian wars

In the early years of the Civil War, US Army outposts throughout the Southwest were abandoned when the troops were sent east. That spurred a new era of raiding by the **Apache** and **Navajo**, and the Anglo and Hispanic settlements of southern Arizona in particular became depopulated. By late 1861, there were only two significant non-Native settlements left in Arizona; two hundred citizens remained in Tucson, and a band of miners held out at Patagonia.

However, the Army soon returned in greater strength than ever, resolved to eradicate the Indian "menace" once and for all. As detailed on p.592 onwards, Brigadier General James Carleton and Kit Carson drove the **Navajo** into exile in New Mexico in 1865 – they were soon back in Arizona, but never again posed a military threat – while a long cycle of treaties, betrayals, and guerrilla campaigns wore down **Apache** resistance by 1886.

Towards statehood

The increasing subjugation and confinement of the region's Native American population cleared the way for a large-scale influx of Anglo settlers. During the 1860s, ancient Hohokam canals in the Salt River Valley were cleared to irrigate the new city of **Phoenix**, which swiftly became the capital of Arizona. Mining camps in the mountains, such as **Silver City** in New Mexico and **Tombstone** and **Jerome** in Arizona, turned into fully fledged towns, while massive cattle ranches began to spread across the open desert.

At first, the Anglo newcomers were almost exclusively male and married into Hispanic families. Spanish remained the lingua franca, Catholicism the dominant religion, and silver Mexican pesos the common currency. With the coming of the **railroad**, however, around 1880, things began to change, and the pattern of north–south links was replaced by commerce oriented toward the east and west. The Southwestern economy became increasingly **extractive**, digging up minerals and depleting natural resources for shipment to distant cities. Where Native Americans and Hispanics had farmed for self-sufficiency, the Anglos sought profit. During the 1880s, huge herds of sheep and cattle were introduced to marginal grasslands that swiftly proved incapable of supporting them; well over half a million cattle died in southern Arizona when drought hit in 1893.

Toward the end of the nineteenth century, tensions began to pit both the large-scale mining and cattle-raising concerns, backed by wealthy eastern corporations and the federal government, against individual prospectors and cowboys. These swiftly became so acute, and so recurrent, that some historians speak of a **Western Civil War of Incorporation**. Many legendary Wild West incidents, like the **Gunfight at the OK Corral** in Tombstone, Arizona (see p.297) and the **Lincoln County War** in New Mexico, which brought Billy the Kid into the public eye (see p.224), stemmed more from behind-the-scenes political maneuvering than from the whims of trigger-happy outlaws.

As well as bringing an influx of cowboys, miners, and other adventurers to the Southwest, the railroads also created new industries. Communities such as Flagstaff and Williams sprang up to exploit the vast ponderosa forests of northern Arizona – not least to build the railroads themselves – while the increased accessibility of the Grand Canyon, recently publicized by the voyages of John Wesley Powell (see p.497), meant that the first **tourists** began to arrive.

Meanwhile, in New Mexico, Hispanic villagers looked on helplessly as huge tracts of their lands were parceled out to newly arrived Anglo ranchers. New Mexicans had traditionally owned small plots for individual use and shared all grazing lands in common, but American courts refused to recognize communal land rights. Families who had been farmers, ranchers, and skilled laborers found themselves increasingly obliged to work as unskilled laborers.

To a considerable degree, it was anti-Hispanic Anglo racism that delayed **statehood** for both Arizona and New Mexico. For many years, Republicans in Washington clung to the idea that they should be reunited and admitted as a single state, in the hope that Arizona's larger Anglo population would help to "temper" the Hispanic majority in New Mexico. Arizonans overwhelmingly defeated that proposal in a referendum in 1906 (which passed in New Mexico), and both were finally admitted in 1912 – **New Mexico** in January as the **47th** state, **Arizona** in February as the **48th**, the last of what are now known as the "Lower 48."

Utah in the nineteenth century

Until the nineteenth century, the history of what's now the state of Utah forms a minor adjunct to the story of the Southwest as a whole. Its main Ancestral Puebloan groups, the Virgin and the more nomadic Fremont peoples, abandoned southern Utah around the same time their Four Corners brethren moved away. By the time Spanish explorers such as Domínguez and Escalante began to pass through, in search of a route to California, it had become the domain of Ute and Paiute Indians. An estimated twelve to thirty thousand of them were present in 1850; most had traditionally been farmers, but they had recently acquired horses and were starting to raid travelers on the newly created Old Spanish Trail, which linked Santa Fe to Los Angeles.

The reports of men such as the fur trapper **Jedediah Smith**, who named the Virgin River, and **John C. Frémont**, who mapped much of southwest Utah in the early 1840s, attracted the first permanent white settlers to the region. By far the most important of these were the massed ranks of the Church of Jesus Christ of Latter-Day Saints, known to the outside world as the **Mormons**.

The Mormons

The Mormon church was founded by **Joseph Smith**, who was born to a family of itinerant farmers in Sharon, Vermont, on December 23, 1805. Smith was a farmhand in Palmyra, western New York, when he had his first vision of the **Angel Moroni** in 1823. On his third annual visit, Moroni led him to a set of golden plates hidden in a nearby hillside. Only Smith was ever to see them; concealed behind a curtain in his house, he translated them from the "reformed Egyptian" with the aid of two mysterious devices he called the Urim and the Thummim, and thus dictated the *Book of Mormon*. Harshly described by Mark Twain as "chloroform in print," this revealed that two Israelite families fled

Jerusalem around 600 BC, and sailed east from the Red Sea to the "Promised Land," led by a man named Lehi. His sons later quarreled; Nephi remained loyal and was rewarded by a visit from the risen Christ, while Laman and Lemuel led the dissident, cursed Lamanites, the ancestors of the Native Americans. After a thousand years of conflict, the Lamanites finally defeated the Nephites in a great battle at the hill of Cumorah. The one Nephite survivor – Moroni, son of Mormon – buried the plates close by.

Smith proclaimed his new church on April 6, 1830. He was not unique among contemporary frontier prophets in attracting thousands of followers. His vision of an ordered, communalistic society was clearly rooted in the economic uncertainty of his own life, and struck a deep chord with his peers. To their unconverted "**Gentile**" neighbors, on the other hand, leadership by divine revelation smacked of Catholicism, and like the Catholics the Mormons were suspected of owing their first loyalty to their church and not their country. Their most controversial trait was the practice of **polygamy**, or "celestial marriage." Smith denied this to outsiders, pointing to a passage in the *Book Of Mormon* that called polygamy "abominable." In private, however, he declared his disciples to have a sacred duty to marry and produce children, thereby freeing disembodied spirits from limbo by giving them bodily form. Preaching the salvation of the dead, which said that the dead could be baptized by proxy, he argued that Mormon marriage was different to the "until death do us part" Christian sacrament. Church elders had a duty to establish polygamous, patriarchal families that would endure into the afterlife. Smith also became a Mason, and many of his church's rituals were inspired by Masonic practices.

In the face of constant harassment, Smith moved his family to Kirtland, **Ohio** – where they built their first temple – and then on to **Missouri** in 1838. After bloody clashes between slave-holding Gentiles and the Mormon militia, the Sons of Dan, he was captured and sentenced to death, then allowed to escape by sympathetic guards. The Mormons were next given sanctuary by the governor of **Illinois**, who saw them as hard-working potential citizens, and their new settlement of **Nauvoo** swiftly became the largest city in that state, with a population of 25,000.

In 1844, when Joseph Smith announced that he was running for president, the Latter-Day Saints were being attacked not only by their neighbors but also from within. When a group of antipolygamy dissenters attempted to establish a rival church in Nauvoo and set up their own newspaper, Smith ordered that its presses be destroyed. Together with his brother Hyrum, Smith was arrested and imprisoned in nearby Carthage. A "blackface" mob attacked the jail, and both men were shot.

It was widely assumed that the Mormon Church would disintegrate after Smith's death. However, although one of his sons decamped to Missouri with his own monogamous splinter group, Smith's successor, **Brigham Young**, held the flock together. Young, who was also of Puritan Vermont stock, promised the governor of Illinois in 1845 that the Mormons would abandon Nauvoo the following year, and set about organizing a mass **westward migration**. In the winter of 1846, ten thousand Saints camped near modern Omaha, Nebraska, while Young scouted ahead. Descending the western flank of the Rockies, he declared "This is the place," and in 1847 his followers founded **Salt Lake City**.

At that time, the all-but-empty wilderness claimed by the Mormons as **Deseret** (a Mormon word meaning "honeybee," to denote industry), or the **Great Basin Kingdom**, still belonged to Mexico. As well as what's now Utah, its putative boundaries included almost all of modern Nevada, most of Arizona and southern California, and sizeable chunks of four other present-day states. Mormon dreams of establishing an independent theocracy, outside the United States, were dashed within a year, when the US government annexed the entire region and the Gold Rush wagon trains began to roll west. The Saints therefore petitioned Congress for Deseret to be granted statehood. Suspicious of its religious underpinnings, Congress instead recognized a smaller area as the **Territory of Utah** in 1850, and appointed Brigham Young as its first governor.

Recognizing that individual farmers could make little impact on the uncompromising terrain of the West, the Mormons embarked on a massive communal effort to irrigate the desert. They were joined over the next decade by thousands more converts recruited by missionaries throughout America and Europe, to reach a total by 1860 of over fifty thousand. Fifteen thousand arrived from England alone, of whom three thousand literally walked across America, pushing their belongings in handcarts ahead of them.

During the 1850s, and especially once Young, who felt no further need for diplomacy, had publicly acknowledged the existence of polygamy in 1852, the federal government came to see the Mormons as a significant threat to the Union. The newly formed Republican party – whose presidential candidate in 1856 was John C. Frémont, the veteran Western explorer – railed against slavery and polygamy in equal measure, as "twin relics of barbarism." Congress decided to appoint a new non-Mormon governor of Utah, and sent him west with a detachment of 2500 soldiers, representing one-sixth of the US army. Salt Lake City was temporarily abandoned, but thanks in large part to the secession of the Confederacy, the anticipated Mormon War never quite happened.

When the **Civil War** in the East cut off supplies of commodities such as cotton, Brigham Young redoubled his commitment to making the Mormons **self-sufficient**. Pioneer parties were dispatched to create "missions" throughout the Southwest, but while many of the small farming communities they established still survive – especially in southern Utah, where examples include **Cedar City** and **St George** – they did little to diminish Utah's economic interdependence with the rest of the US. The advent of the railroads and the arrival in Utah of ever-increasing numbers of non-Mormons – especially miners – exacerbated the situation.

As the Mormons set out to "tame" the wilderness, the **Ute** fought back. Reciprocal raids by Utes and whites escalated into the **Black Hawk War**, waged between 1865 and 1867, in which the Utes were eventually worn down and finally confined to reservations in the territory that by now bore their name. In an eerie postscript, the dying Ute leader, Black Hawk, insisted on making a personal tour of all the towns affected by the war, to apologize in person. With Indian resistance broken, the Mormons spread throughout southern Utah. The "**Hole in the Rock**" party (see p.464), for example, made the grueling trek across the central deserts in the winter of 1879–80 to establish the community of **Bluff** in the east. Little now survives from simultaneous Mormon attempts to settle in **northern Arizona**, apart from a few tiny settlements along the Arizona Strip.

Meanwhile the federal authorities renewed their attacks on polygamy. The **Morrill Anti-Bigamy Act** of 1862, which was upheld by the Supreme Court in 1878, subjected polygamists to disenfranchisement and the confiscation of their property; as one federal judge put it, "we want you to throw off the yoke of the Priesthood, to do as we do, and be Americans in deed as well as name." Utah retaliated by giving women the vote, so Mormon women could consolidate the Church's hold on State power; the **Edmonds-Tucker Act** of

1887 hit back, dissolving the Church and confiscating its assets, and once more disenfranchising women.

Brigham Young had died in 1877, and the new Mormon leaders now sensed that they would do better to drop polygamy on their own terms before they were forced to do so. Polygamy was therefore formally renounced in 1890 – although a few thousand dissidents still practice it to this day – and the way was cleared for Utah to become a **state** in **1896**. Mormons were now encouraged to participate in national politics; church authorities even suggested that half should become Democrats and half Republicans.

The modern Southwest

Arizona, New Mexico, and Utah spent most of their first century of statehood battling to secure ever greater quantities of **water**. In the early years, the main objective was to prevent California – already undergoing rapid development – from grabbing the lion's share of the flow of the Colorado River. Later on, cities such as Phoenix fought for federal funds to build grandiose water-diversion schemes. The political machinations behind the construction of the **Hoover Dam** in the 1930s, and the controversial damming of **Glen Canyon** in the 1960s, are chronicled on p.482. Suffice it here to say that with the completion of the **Central Arizona Project** in 1991, John Wesley Powell's nineteenth-century prediction that "All the waters of all the arid lands will eventually be taken from their natural channels" has now all but come true.

While New Mexico at the start of the twentieth century remained much what it had always been – a cluster of farming towns along the Rio Grande Valley – Arizona was prospering on the large-scale exploitation of its mineral wealth. **World War I** saw a leap in copper prices, and in alliance with state politicians the mine-owners easily quashed labor disputes such as the one that led to the **Bisbee Deportation** in 1917 (see p.300). Arizona employers could also take cynical advantage of the vast pool of potential workers just across the border to the south. After the Wall Street Crash of 1929, for example – by which time the state was responsible for half of all US copper production – over 500,000 Mexican laborers, now surplus to requirements, were deported.

Though the **Depression** hit hard across the Southwest, the region also benefited from a massive injection of federal cash, in the form of make-work public projects such as dam- and road-building. **World War II** not only renewed demand for copper and other metals but kick-started the phenomenon of **urbanization** throughout the Southwest. Partly to make them less vulnerable to attack, defense installations were relocated away from the coasts, presenting **Albuquerque** and **Phoenix** in particular with their first major industrial plants, as well as greatly increased numbers of consumers. A former school in **Los Alamos**, New Mexico, was transformed into the laboratory that developed the atomic bomb – hence, some say, the alien crash-landing at **Roswell** in 1947 (see p.231).

After the war, the defense and other industries stayed on, and the ensuing period of mass migration to the Southwest resulted in an extraordinary population boom. Arizona and New Mexico were home to around 500,000 people each in 1940; Arizona's population is now approaching six million, with half that number in the metropolitan Phoenix area alone, while New Mexico has around 1.9 million. Even more striking is the fact that whereas at the start of the twentieth century, Arizona was 84 percent rural, by the end of the century around 90 percent of the population were city-dwellers. **Las Vegas**, Nevada, did not even exist until 1905; it now boasts well over a million inhabitants.

Meanwhile, **southern Utah** has remained sparsely inhabited. Attempts at large-scale ranching in the late 1800s resulted in destructive overgrazing, and the region relied on subsistence farming until the discovery of **uranium** in 1952 (see p.518) triggered a **mining bonanza** that sent prospectors scurrying into every nook and cranny of the wilderness. Local Mormon businessmen of southern Utah lobbied hard for mine and dam projects in the face of growing environmental opposition. Calling themselves the "**Sagebrush Rebels**," they attracted support from then-President Ronald Reagan, but were ultimately defeated as much by the realities of world commodity markets as by the "tree-huggers" they despised. Since the collapse of mining in the early 1980s, **tourism** has finally been appreciated as a major industry, and towns like **Moab**, which formerly reveled in their isolation, have begun to develop facilities for travelers smitten by the lure of the desert.

The Hopi

Nowhere in the Southwest is the continuity between the pre-Hispanic past and the present more apparent than on the three Hopi mesas, on the southern edge of Arizona's Black Mesa. The Hopi have lived here for at least one thousand years, preserving their culture despite repeated incursions from outsiders, and their history is sufficiently distinct to be worth relating as a separate narrative.

For a guide to visiting the Hopi mesas today, and an account of the *kachina* religion, see the section that starts on p.83.

The origin of the Hopi

According to Hopi mythology, this, the **Fourth World**, is inhabited by the righteous people who escaped the destruction of the Third World by climbing a reed through the dome of the sky. They emerged in the depths of the Grand Canyon, through a hole beside the Little Colorado River known as the *sipapu*. There they were greeted by the terrifying but nonetheless kindly disposed deity **Maasaw**, who explained the rules of life in this world and despatched them on migratory journeys to the four points of the compass. Their wanderings ended with a return to the **Sacred Circle** and the establishment of the villages on what are now the Hopi mesas.

Myth and history agree on a picture of the Hopi as a peripatetic people who became ever more sedentary as they learned the techniques of agriculture and pottery. Archeologists and Hopi alike recognize the cultural continuity between the Hopi and the ancient peoples of the Southwest. The Hopi refer to their ancestors as the **Hisatsinom** and have pressed for the use of the term "Ancestral Puebloans" in preference to the more familiar Navajo name **Anasazi**, which means "ancient enemies." There's no doubt that the earliest occupants of the Hopi mesas migrated here from nearby Kayenta Anasazi and Sinagua settlements, but whether they had previously wandered further afield – most obviously, into central America, where the language and beliefs of the **Aztecs** show clear parallels to the Hopi – remains unproven.

The Hopi mesas were probably inhabited from around 700 AD onwards, but the process the Hopi describe as the **"gathering of the clans"** was at its peak between 1100 AD and 1300 AD, and thus coincided with the abandonment of the most famous Ancestral Puebloan sites. One by one, small groups of refugees arrived at the mesas and petitioned those who were already there for land and the right to settle. Each was required to demonstrate what it could offer the rest, with the crucial factor being the ceremonial power to produce rain. After being allowed to stay, each group – in reality, most were probably no more than individual families – was regarded as a separate **clan**.

The Bear clan, said to have come from Mesa Verde, was the first to arrive – which is why it retains precedence to this day – and established the Second Mesa's "mother village," at the foot of the mesa. Originally called Maseeba, this village changed its name to **Shungopavi** when it relocated to the mesa-top several centuries later. Similarly, **Walpi** on First Mesa, when founded by the Snake clan from Hovenweep, stood several hundred yards below its present, highly defensible mesa-top site. **Oraibi**, the "mother village" of Third Mesa, is generally regarded as the oldest of the Hopi villages because it has occupied the same spot since its foundation; beams used in its construction have been dated to 1260 AD, but earlier dwellings may be a century or more older.

By 1275 AD, the three mesas held 35 villages. The Fire, Water, and Coyote clans had come from the cliff dwellings of Keet Seel and Betatakin, now in Navajo National Monument; the Flute clan from Canyon de Chelly; the Rabbit clan from the south, perhaps Casas Grandes in Mexico; and others had streamed in from Chaco Canyon and the Sinagua sites of Wupatki and Walnut Canyon. While each village remained autonomous, this disparate community forged a common culture, adopting its own variation of the *kachina* religion as it spread throughout the pueblos of the Southwest.

The coming of the Spaniards

Hopi prophecies have long predicted the return of *Pahaana*, the "True White Brother" who was separated from the Hopi at an early stage of their migrations. Assuming that he finds the Hopi living lives of purity and righteousness, he will help solve whatever problems they may be facing and lead them in due course into the Fifth World. If the Hopi saw *Pahaana* in the first **Spanish** explorers to reach the mesas, their illusions were soon shattered. A detachment of Coronado's expedition led by Lieutenant Pedro de Tovar arrived in 1540.

Exactly what happened is uncertain. Alerted by the Zuni, the Hopi greeted the party in the fields, signaling that they should not cross a line of sacred cornmeal sprinkled on the earth. According to the official Spanish report, a Franciscan friar, exasperated by the rigmarole, commented, "To tell the truth, I do not know why we came here" – and that was enough to trigger a Spanish onslaught. By the next sentence in the report, the two sides are at peace, and Hopi guides went on to lead a group of Spaniards to the Grand Canyon (see p.367). Some sources suggest that this encounter took place at a village called Kawaika-a, which was completely destroyed by the Spanish.

During that and subsequent sixteenth-century Spanish incursions, the Hopi seem to have taken care to make their lands – which the Spanish called **Tusayan** – appear as valueless as possible. As a result, the Spanish never bothered to leave either a garrison or any settlers in the vicinity. Franciscan **missionaries** did, however, return in 1629 and set about building churches in Awatovi, Shungopavi, and Oraibi. The one at Awatovi was on a similar scale to the San Esteban del Rey mission that still survives at Ácoma (see p.124) and required a similar amount of forced Indian labor; others involved the filling-in and "rededication" of existing *kivas*. The missionaries also brought sheep and cattle to the mesas, so the Hopi were the first people to raise livestock in Arizona.

The Hopi were enthusiastic participants in the **Pueblo Revolt** of 1680, sacking the churches and killing four priests. Fearing a Spanish return, they welcomed Tewa-speaking Pueblo refugees from the Rio Grande, who founded the First Mesa village of Hano. By now, the **Navajo** – whom the Hopi called *Tasavuh* or "head pounders," as they were said to bash in their captives' skulls with a rock – had entered the picture. They too joined the Pueblo Revolt, but were also starting to crowd the Hopi away from their summer farming and grazing lands, and to raid for animals. It was during this unsettled period that the villages of Walpi, Shungopavi, and Mishongnovi moved to occupy fortified positions up on the mesa tops.

After the Spanish reconquered New Mexico, those Hopi who still regarded themselves as Christians gathered in **Awatovi**. When the other Hopi villages realized that the people of Awatovi were willing to invite the missionaries back to stay, they determined to eradicate the Christian menace once and for all. At the end of 1700, the men of Awatovi were betrayed by their headman, who called a predawn meeting in the *kiva*. Warriors from all the other villages pulled up the ladder, rained arrows down on the trapped men, and then set light to the *kiva*; surviving women and children were divvied as booty.

That act of savagery probably spared the Hopi both from internal dissent and missionary interference for the remainder of the Spanish and Mexican era. The mesas were, however, increasingly beleaguered by mounted Navajo and Ute war parties and slave raiders from the south.

The Hopi under the United States

By the time the Southwest was acquired by the United States, during the 1840s (see p.578), the Hopi were desperate for protection from the marauding Navajo. Hopi scouts eagerly participated in General Carleton's 1864 round-up which forced the Navajo on the Long Walk to Bosque Redondo (see p.592).

Within a few years, the Navajo were back, reasserting their control over their former territory and raiding extensively to replenish their herds. Called upon to define who "owned" what land, the US government was inadequate to the task. The very concept of a "tribe" was a federal invention; neither Navajo nor Hopi recognized any overall authority above clan or village level. Moreover, the idea of a reservation only worked if one group or other had exclusive use of an area. Only villages and fields counted as the "possession" of land; hunting grounds were regarded as unoccupied. Because the San Francisco Peaks are sacred to, and used by, both the Navajo and the Hopi, they belong to neither.

The **Moqui Indian reservation**, established in 1882, was a rectangle measuring 70 by 55 miles. It did not even include all the Hopi villages; the hundred Hopi at Moenkopi were excluded, while an estimated three hundred Navajo lived within the boundaries. As was standard, the decree creating the reservation states that it was intended not only for the Hopi but for "such other Indians as the Secretary of the Interior shall settle thereon." The resultant disputes have simmered ever since.

Outsiders now appeared on the mesas in ever-increasing numbers. Mormon and Mennonite **missionaries** came and went, and **anthropologists** stuck their oars in; Jesse Walter Fewkes called the Hopi "the most primitive aborigines of the United States" in 1891. **Tourists** too came by bus and railroad, with two thousand or more turning up for the annual Snake Dances. Turn-of-the-twentieth-century images of Hopi ceremonies make it clear why photography was soon barred altogether; the crowds and cumbersome equipment made it all but impossible to move. Above all, the federal agents of the **Bureau of Indian Affairs** caused the most grief, by such actions as ordering haircuts for all Hopi men, for whom long hair is a sign of initiation, and kidnapping Hopi children to attend distant boarding schools, from 1887 onwards. Nineteen elders who protested against compulsory Christian education were imprisoned on Alcatraz in 1894.

The modern era

At the start of the twentieth century, the Hopi were divided between what outsiders perceived as the "**Friendlies**," who if not well disposed toward the federal government at least felt resistance was futile, and the "**Hostiles**," who sought to defend and preserve the old ways. Their differences in fact had as much to do with tensions between clans and a breakdown in the allocation of resources and land now that Hopi territories were so circumscribed. The split became explicit at **Oraibi**, where the two factions declared themselves unable to co-exist any longer. On September 8, 1906, each lined up behind its leader, with each man's hands on the shoulders of the next, for a "pushing contest." The "Hostiles" were literally pushed out and established their own village of **Hotevilla** nearby.

The dispute at Oraibi politicized the role of each village's ceremonial priest, known as the kikmongwi. When the Hopi were obliged to adopt a Tribal Constitution in 1936, under the provisions of the New Deal Indian Reorganization Act, the *kikmongwis* were automatically appointed as governors of their village. Part of their function was to endorse members elected to the new **Hopi Tribal Council**. Ever since then, however, many *kikmongwis* have refused to recognize the authority of the tribal council and aligned themselves instead with the **Traditionalists**, the heirs of the "Hostiles."

The Traditionalists, who regard themselves as the guardians of all that is truly Hopi (and speak of their opponents as the *pensilhoyam,* or "little pencil people"), have raised awareness of the Hopi throughout the world. Rather than waiting for their savior brother figure *Pahaana* to appear, they have embarked on what they call a "search" for him. The movement started immediately after World War II, when certain Hopi elders announced that following the use of the atomic bomb it was time to reveal teachings and prophecies that were supposed to remain secret until "a gourd of ashes fell from the sky." Since 1948, the Traditionalists have written to every US president, and addressed the United Nations, with a message stressing Hopi sovereignty and religious integrity and the importance of respecting the environment. Among their successes was the recognition of Hopi religion as a "peace religion," which excluded Hopi from military service.

In practical terms, the Traditionalist movement has drawn those who oppose **mineral leasing**. The Hopi Constitution did not allow the tribal council to lease land for mining, yet the council, heavily influenced by the US Secretary of the Interior, did just that in 1961. The ensuing strip mining by the Peabody Company devastated much of the Black Mesa (see p.68). Virtually all of the pitifully poor income that was earned from the leases during the 1960s was invested by the tribal council in an unsuccessful bra factory near Winslow. In the 1980s, the leases were renegotiated on much more favorable terms, including environmental stipulations, and mining became more acceptable to many Hopi. Traditionalists continued to strive through the courts to have the mines closed down, however, and although they didn't succeed, Black Mesa Mine was indeed forced to cease operations in 2006, as a consequence of environmental activism in Nevada.

To some extent, Traditionalist resistance to modernization is based on a refusal to become dependent on external agencies. Thus while Hotevilla forcibly rejected the installation of public utilities, there is little objection to individual use of solar energy.

Meanwhile, the **Navajo–Hopi land dispute** has raged on. By 1958, the ranks of the Navajo living on Hopi lands had swollen to outnumber the Hopi by more than two to one, while the Navajo reservation had completely surrounded the Hopi mesas. Much of the impetus to resolve the problem came from the federal authorities and the mineral companies, who could not commence mining operations until definite title to the land was established. Public sympathies, and court rulings, swayed back and forth for decades. A **Joint Use Area** was established in 1958, to be shared equally between the Hopi and the Navajo, but it soon became evident that 98 percent of it was being used by the Navajo alone. In the 1970s, therefore, separate Hopi and Navajo **Partitioned Lands** were defined, stipulating that Hopi living on the Navajo side of the line relocate, and vice versa. More Navajo than Hopi were affected, and the plight of the **Big Mountain** Navajo in particular, who were given five years to move in 1981, made them a national *cause célèbre*.

The most recent solution, the **Navajo–Hopi Land Dispute Settlement Act**, was signed by then President Clinton in 1996. It allowed Navajo residents of Hopi land to sign 75-year leases, after which ownership will revert to the Hopi. If enough Navajo sign, the Hopi will receive $50 million to buy land elsewhere in northern Arizona (though their water rights will be restricted, which goes against more than a century of Indian policy). Dissident Navajo argue that the problem has simply been postponed for another generation.

The Navajo and the Apache

The best-known Native American peoples in the Southwest – mainly on account of the fierce resistance they put up against the US Army in the nineteenth century – are the **Navajo** and the **Apache**. Both are now largely concentrated in Arizona, though both also occupy parts of New Mexico, and the Navajo Nation also extends into southern Utah. They are also relative newcomers to the region, having moved into their current territories around the time that the Spaniards arrived, and their impact was every bit as devastating as that of the European colonists.

Although the Navajo and the Apache are now distinct peoples, their languages are, with patience, mutually comprehensible, and their paths have only diverged within the last five hundred years. Both are descended from **Athabascan** peoples, whose Asian ancestors crossed into Alaska seven or eight thousand years ago, long after the New World's first migrants. Other Athabascans remained in the north, becoming the **Dene** peoples of Alaska and northwest Canada, and the **Na** of what's now the northwest US, who include the Haid and Tlingit. At some point, however, the ancestral Navajo and Apache migrated south, hauling their possessions on dog-sleds as they pursued bison down the eastern flanks of the Rockies.

Estimates of when they reached their first base in the Southwest – probably on the edge of the Plains, somewhere east of the Rio Grande – range from 575 to 1525 AD, with the most likely date being 1250 to 1300 AD. Like nomads the world over, they traded the fruits of their hunting and gathering, especially buffalo hides, for the agricultural produce of more settled communities like the Rio Grande pueblos. Chroniclers traveling with Coronado's expedition of 1540 (see p.572), the earliest Spanish venture into the Southwest, drew no distinction between the Navajo and the Apache, referring to both as *Querecho*. However, by the time the Spanish returned at the end of the century, the Navajo, who called themselves the *Diné*, had separated off from the Apache, or *Ndee*.

The Navajo

It was once thought that the Navajo' arrival in the Four Corners region was what forced the Ancestral Puebloans to eventually leave at the end of the thirteenth century (see p.568). In fact, however, the Navajo only moved west to occupy the now-empty San Juan Basin well after the Ancestral Puebloans had gone. Some even suggest that it was the Ancestral Puebloans who ejected the Navajo, arguing that when the Chaco Canyon and Mesa Verde communities fragmented and their inhabitants headed east to establish pueblos along the Rio Grande, they displaced the ancestors of today's Navajo from their riverside homes.

During the late sixteenth century, a region centered on Largo Canyon, east of modern Farmington – still the core of Navajo territory – became known as the **Dinétah**, meaning "Among the People." The *Diné* defined their new realm as lying between four **sacred mountains**: Blanca Peak, or *Sis Naajini*, away to the east in Colorado; Hesperus Peak (*Dibé Nitsaa*), also in Colorado but to the north, near modern Durango; Mount Taylor (*Tsoodzil*), further south in New Mexico; and the San Francisco Peaks (*Dook'o'oosliid*) near what is now Flagstaff, Arizona. Legends began to grow up that detailed how First Man and First Woman lived near **Huerfano Mountain**. They found a baby on **Gobernador Knob** whom they named Changing Woman, and she in turn gave birth to the Navajo Twins, Monster Slayer and Child Born for Water.

The Lords of the World

By the 1580s, the Navajo had started to impinge upon the pueblos of Ácoma, Zuni, and Hopi. Their expansion was soon given a huge boost when a permanent Spanish presence enabled them to acquire **horses**. From 1606 onwards, the Navajo embarked on a cycle of raiding Hispanic and Pueblo settlements along the Rio Grande, seizing livestock, new crops, and metal wares. In the Tewa language, spoken in many pueblos, *apache* means "strangers" or "enemies," and *nabaj·* means "big planted fields." The first Spanish mention of the "Apaches de Nabajú" appeared in 1626, and the name was soon truncated to "Navajo."

The Navajo and the Pueblo peoples were not always at war, however, and some Navajo participated in the **Pueblo Revolt** of 1680 (see p.575), which briefly succeeded in expelling the Spanish from the Southwest. When the Spanish returned to reconquer the region a dozen years later, many Pueblo peoples escaped their revenge by retreating to join the Navajo. As detailed on p.111, the culture of the modern Navajo, which anthropologists regard as a hybrid of Athabascan and Pueblo elements, was forged in the remote fortresses known as the **"Pueblitos of Dinétah**," in Largo and Gobernador canyons.

While any explicit Pueblo-Navajo alliance soon foundered, the Navajo had by the eighteenth century acquired such Pueblo skills as pottery and weaving, as well as Pueblo-influenced social and religious structures. Obtaining horses vastly increased their mobility, while their large flocks of **sheep** enabled them to live well on what had previously been considered marginal lands. They therefore expanded westwards to cover a much greater area, occupying most of northeast Arizona and encircling the Hopi.

To the Spanish, the Navajo at this time were Los Dueños del Mundo, the "Lords of the World" – feared horsemen with a solid economic base in their own lands who nonetheless continued to plunder the pueblos at will. For most of the eighteenth century, however, the Navajo and the Hispanic settlers of New Mexico were nominally at peace, united in resisting incursions by the allied **Utes** and **Comanches** of the north. Then the Navajo realized that in fact the Spanish were tacitly encouraging Ute and Comanche raiders, and buying their Navajo captives as slaves. After 1786, when the Spanish signed a formal treaty with the Comanche, they were at constant war with the Navajo.

With conversion to Christianity as an excuse, Navajo women and children were shipped into slavery in Mexico; the Navajo replenished their numbers by carrying off Pueblo villagers. Certain mission settlements had to be abandoned in the face of Navajo attacks. By and large, the Navajo heartlands remained impregnable, although **Lieutenant Narbona**'s party of 1805 penetrated the Canyon de Chelly and massacred over a hundred Navajo (see p.81).

War with the United States

Mexican independence in 1821 did nothing to diminish the conflict, and the Navajo and the Hispanic settlers of New Mexico were still at loggerheads when the US Army marched in and took control of the Southwest in 1846. The Navajo were amazed to find that the American invaders expected them to make peace with their old enemies, on the basis that the New Mexicans were now themselves considered to be Americans.

A major factor in the American failure to sign and keep treaties with the Navajo was the fact that the Navajo were not a single homogenous group. They did not have "chiefs" as the Americans understood the term, let alone a single paramount chief. No Navajo could speak for much more than his immediate family, or felt bound by a pact signed by another without his knowledge or consent. Even so, the Navajo remained broadly at peace with the Americans until a widely respected elder – who, confusingly, had taken the name **Narbona** – was murdered and scalped by US soldiers, under a flag of truce, in 1849. For the next fifteen years, Narbona's son-in-law, **Manuelito**, fought a running war with the US cavalry, based at **Fort Defiance**, near Window Rock. New Mexican slave raiders, meanwhile, continued to steal Navajo children.

In 1863, **General James Carleton** resolved that the Navajo should be removed from their lands altogether, partly so that they might "become an agricultural people and cease to be nomads" and partly to allow New Mexicans to expand beyond the Rio Grande valley and seize whatever agricultural and mineral wealth the *Dinétah* might hold. Aided by veteran scout **Kit Carson**, he launched a scorched-earth campaign that culminated early in 1864 with the destruction of the *hogans*, fields, and peach orchards of the Canyon de Chelly. As the starving Navajo surrendered, they were sent to "Fair Carletonia," the **Bosque Redondo** reservation at Fort Sumner in eastern New Mexico (see p.217).

A total of nine thousand Navajo made the **Long Walk** of 370 miles to Bosque Redondo, where three thousand of them died. The reservation was utterly unsuitable for agriculture; far from being self-supporting, it became a burden on the federal government. Carleton was dismissed, and in 1868, after four years, twelve Navajo leaders – including **Barboncito**, who pleaded "I hope to God you will not ask me to go to any other country except my own" – signed a treaty, popularly remembered as the **"Old Paper,"** that allowed them to return home.

The Navajo Nation

By treating the Navajo as an independent people, the "Old Paper" formed the basis of the Navajo Indian reservation – which the Navajo prefer to call the **Navajo Nation** – as it endures to this day. The original reservation of 1868 was, however, just a small rectangle of northeast Arizona and northwest New Mexico, which included Canyon de Chelly and Shiprock but not Window Rock. Here the survivors of Fort Sumner rejoined those Navajo who had evaded capture in the backcountry; some had hidden near **Navajo Mountain**, and now regarded it too as a sacred peak.

During the twentieth century, the Navajo **population** grew at a phenomenal rate, from 20,000 in 1900 to approaching 350,000 today. Similarly, in over a dozen different transactions, the boundaries of the reservation expanded from six thousand to 27,000 square miles. A formal Navajo **government** was only established in 1923, when the major oil companies needed to find someone who could sign leases allowing them to exploit the reservation's newly discovered oil reserves. The **chapter** system of local administration was set up soon afterwards, and Window Rock became tribal headquarters in 1927.

The most traumatic event of the twentieth century was the 1933 **stock reduction**, when the federal authorities killed off a million sheep and goats

The basis of Navajo society and family life is the clan system. Each Navajo child is said to be born "to" its mother's clan, and born "for" its father's clan. Navajo identify themselves to each other by the clans of their parents, and no one is supposed to marry a member of either their mother's or father's clan. Traditionally, all members of a clan were responsible for each other's crimes or debts.

Originally, there were just four clans, each descended from one of the four pairs of men and women said to have been created in the west by Changing Woman. There are now more like sixty clans, with each new clan having arisen when a woman from another tribe, or another place, has married into the Navajo. While certain clan names identify the descendants of Zuni, Mescalero, Mexican, Ute, and Jemez newcomers, most hark back to specific locations on the reservation, mythical incidents, or other attributes – the Turning Mountain Clan, Salt Clan, the People That Have Fits Clan, the Rock-Extends-into-Water Clan, and so on.

and reduced the total Navajo herd to half a million animals. They argued that over-grazing was washing silt into the Colorado that threatened the new Hoover Dam; the effect was to force a change away from pastoralism toward wage labor.

Since World War II, the Navajo Nation has continued to modernize, acquiring its first paved road in 1947 and the first college ever built on an Indian reservation, Tsaile's Navajo Community College, which opened in 1969. While many families still manage to live a traditional Navajo lifestyle, the exploitation of **mineral** resources has brought the greatest change to the nation. Mines and generating stations have appeared all across the region, often just outside the reservation but still dependent on Indian labor. Many projects have been deeply controversial. The **Four Corners** plant near Farmington has been described as the single worst source of pollution in the United States, while the Peabody Company's strip-mining of **Black Mesa** to feed the **Navajo Generating Station** at Page is widely regarded as an environmental tragedy. In 1979, **Church Rock**, northeast of Gallup, was the scene of the worst contamination in the history of the US nuclear industry, when a dam-burst at the United Nuclear Corporation mill released almost a hundred million gallons of radioactive water and a thousand tons of radioactive mud. In 1975, Tribal Chairman **Peter MacDonald** helped set up the Council of Energy Resource Tribes, which he described as a "domestic OPEC." While the mineral leases of the 1950s and 1960s paid pitifully low returns, more lucrative agreements have now strengthened the Navajo economy. Navajo opposition to the principle of mineral exploitation has also grown however, as its long-term effects become apparent. Many feel that the long-running **Navajo–Hopi land dispute** (see p.589) has been manipulated by federal politicians and mineral companies for their own ends.

Peter MacDonald's efforts to diversify the economic base ranged from computer software companies to *shiitake* mushroom farms, but suspicion that he was feathering his own nest in the process led to a fourteen-year jail sentence in 1989. Although found guilty by a federal court of bribery, corruption, and conspiracy, MacDonald remains popular on the reservation; tribal elections since then have alternated between his opponents and pro-MacDonald factions who have granted him "pardons" not recognized under federal law. Meanwhile, according to official figures from 2005, 48 percent of Navajo are unemployed, and 43 percent live below the poverty level.

The Apache

Around 1600 AD, as the Navajo began to incorporate Pueblo elements and become an entirely distinct people, the **Apache** fragmented into several separate groups. The **Western** Apache occupied the mountains of central Arizona; the **Jicarilla**, regions of northwest New Mexico between the Chama Valley and the Four Corners; and the **Lipan** moved east onto the plains of west Texas. At the same time, in southern New Mexico, the **Mescalero** started to range east of the Rio Grande, while the **Chiricahua** spread west as far as what's now southern Arizona.

These groups were not "tribes" in the way outsiders like to imagine. Apache lived in nomadic, clan-based societies of between thirty and two hundred people, each of which would elect its own "chief." A chief's primary responsibility was to ensure his band got enough food; his authority soon collapsed in the event of failure. Most groups raised a few seasonal crops, but they supported themselves above all by **raiding**, not only against settled Pueblo communities, but against the Navajo, and even each other.

The coming of the Spaniards gave the Apache **horses** for the first time. At first, they stole them solely to eat, but once they learned to ride they swiftly adapted to a regular calendar of raiding the villages of the Rio Grande at harvest time, while allowing them to continue largely unmolested for the rest of the year. It was beneath Apache dignity even to breed their own horses, let alone sheep like the Navajo; they simply stole livestock when they needed it.

The colonists of New Mexico, who remained confined for the whole period of Spanish and Mexican rule to a fragile ribbon of riverside land, called the huge Apache-dominated territories that surrounded them **Apachería**. Since the Apache never united to engage in formal warfare – no Apache war party in history exceeded two hundred warriors – it was impossible to take concerted action against them. In the first half of the eighteenth century, the Apache were nonetheless forced to consolidate into smaller and more mountainous areas, as the even more aggressive mounted **Comanche** warriors swept in across the Plains with ever-increasing regularity.

Later in the eighteenth century, the Spaniards managed to pacify the Apache to some extent by establishing *presidios* or forts that supplied them with food, alcohol, and even guns that were adequate for hunting but not war. When Mexico became independent, however, in 1821, the new administration could no longer afford such subsidies. Instead it placed a bounty of $100 on each Apache scalp – male or female, young or old – that was brought into the *presidios*.

The Apache Wars

To the federal government of the United States, which took over New Mexico in the 1840s, the Apache way of life was an utter anathema. As a group of Mescalero Apache acknowledged to a US Army quartermaster in 1850, "We must steal from somebody… if you will not permit us to rob the Mexicans, we must steal from you or fight you." In total, the Southwest held between six and eight thousand Apache. By far the strongest resistance came from a group of just over a thousand, the **Chiricahua**, led by a chief known as **Cochise**, meaning "Oak."

Conflict between the US Army and the Apache flared into war in 1861, when Cochise agreed to meet Lt. George Bascom in southeast Arizona, and found himself falsely accused of kidnapping a child. Although Cochise managed to escape into the Dragoon Mountains, his brother and two nephews were hanged. Cochise then rampaged across Arizona, killing miners, prospectors, stagecoach passengers, and soldiers wherever he might find them. As Anglos packed up and fled the territory, he imagined he had driven them out forever. What he didn't realize was that his campaign had coincided with the start of the **Civil War**, which meant that all US forces were withdrawn east.

Within a year, the Union army was back, under the leadership of General James Carleton (see p.592). His Apache policy was simple, though directed at first against the Mescalero rather than the Chiricahua: "All Indian men of that tribe are to be killed whenever and wherever you can find them." During the winter of 1862–63, the Mescaleros were rounded onto the **Bosque Redondo** reservation at Fort Sumner in eastern New Mexico, where they were soon joined by the Navajo (see p.217).

In 1862, Cochise's group had linked up with another Chiricahua band, the **Warm Springs** Apache of New Mexico, under the veteran **Mangas Coloradas**. The treacherous murder of Mangas Coloradas the following year, by US soldiers at Pinos Altos, where he had been invited for peace negotiations, hardened Chiricahua resolve even further. Over the next ten years, the US Army spent an estimated $38 million on campaigns that killed a total of a hundred Apache; the Apache meanwhile accounted for over a thousand Americans.

It was during this period that the name of **Geronimo** became widely feared. He was born around 1823 into the Bedonkohe subgroup of the Chiricahua Apache, near the Gila cliff dwellings in New Mexico. Named Goyahkla, meaning "One Who Yawns," he reached adulthood without seeing a white American. After his mother, wife, and three children were killed by Mexican soldiers at Janos in northern Mexico, in March 1851, he sought revenge in repeated raids on Mexico for years to come. Somehow, the Mexican battle-cry to St Jerome, "Gerónimo," became the name he used for the rest of his life. Although he became a respected healer and medicine man, he was never, strictly speaking, a "chief."

In the **Camp Grant Massacre** of 1871, a Tucson-based alliance of Tohono 'O'odham Indians, Hispanics, and Anglos massacred 144 Apache – of whom no more than eight were men – supposedly under the protection of the US Army in Aravaipa Canyon, Arizona (see p.270). A public outcry back East led President Grant to adopt a new policy toward the Apache, under which the **White Mountain** (also known as the Fort Apache Indian Reservation; see p.332) and **San Carlos** (see p.269) **reservations** were established in 1872.

Any Apache who failed to present themselves at the reservations, however, were deemed to be renegades. The task of hunting them down was given to **General George Crook**, who adopted the new scorched-earth strategy of "total war," developed during the Civil War. Employing White Mountain Apache scouts, on the basis that the best person to track an Apache was another Apache, he "overhauled" the Tonto Basin during the winter of 1872–73, killing around five hundred Apache.

Following an uneasy truce, the Chiricahua were granted their own reservation, a small square measuring roughly fifty miles in each direction that centered on what's now Chiricahua National Monument (see p.302). Within three years, however, renewed cross-border raiding after the 1874 death of Cochise caused the reservation to be disbanded. The Chiricahua were moved onto the San Carlos reservation, despite the fact that they traditionally regarded the San Carlos Apache as "Bi-ni-e-Dine," or "brainless people."

In 1877, another Chiricahua leader, **Victorio**, assembled a five-hundred-strong band of Apache from the many different groups who hated life at San

Carlos. A lengthy guerrilla campaign across New Mexico and West Texas resulted in another thousand Anglo deaths before the Chiricahua were driven into Mexico and killed in Chihuahua in October 1880. The few survivors were sold into slavery.

Geronimo, who had not joined Victorio, now became the focus for dissident Apache. During the 1880s, he repeatedly burst out of the reservation and went on the warpath, with a dwindling band of followers each time. The first time was in 1881, when he passed within a few miles of Tombstone and was pursued by Wyatt Earp and his brothers. In 1883, General Crook tracked him down in the Sierra Madre in northern Mexico, and was briefly captured by the Apache before Geronimo chose instead to surrender to him.

Geronimo fled the reservation again in May 1885 and surrendered to Crook once more in Mexico in 1886, on the understanding that he'd be exiled to the eastern United States for not more than two years. Before Crook could get him back to San Carlos, Geronimo got drunk and escaped yet again. Crook resigned his command, to be replaced by **General Nelson Miles**.

The Chiricahua's final five-month guerrilla campaign, in the summer of 1886, pitted a band of 37 Apache, of whom eighteen were warriors, against five thousand soldiers, a quarter of the entire US Army. General Miles eventually managed to contact Geronimo in Mexico, and falsely told him that all the Chiricahua who remained on the reservation had been shipped to Florida. In despair, Geronimo **surrendered** for the fourth and final time in Skeleton Canyon, Arizona on September 3, 1886. The general's lie now became the truth. Geronimo and five hundred Chiricahua – along with the Apache scouts who had fought on the side of the US Army – were indeed sent to **Florida** by rail. Men and women were segregated in separate camps. In time, the Chiricahua were reunited on reservations in first Alabama, and then Oklahoma, but Geronimo never returned to the Southwest. Among many public appearances in his later years, he rode at the head of Teddy Roosevelt's inaugural procession in 1905; he died in 1909.

In 1913, the 261 surviving Chiricahua were allowed to choose between remaining in Oklahoma or joining the Mescalero Apache in New Mexico; around two-thirds made the trip. In addition, it's thought that perhaps ten Chiricahua never were rounded up by the Army and stayed hidden in Mexico; free Apache were reported still to be fighting in the Sierra Madre as late as the 1930s.

The Apache today

A total of around twenty thousand Apache now live in the Southwest. Their largest two reservations are in Arizona: the **Fort Apache** Reservation (see p.322), which has the third highest population of all Native American reservations in the US, and the neighboring **San Carlos** Reservation. The **Jicarilla** still live in northwest New Mexico, concentrated around the settlement of Dulce (see p.195).

Visitors are, however, most likely to come into contact with the **Mescalero** Apache, who share their lands with the descendants of the last Chiricahua in the mountains of southeast New Mexico. Among unlikely ventures here that have brought them a rare degree of economic security are the Ski Apache **ski resort** (see p.226), which the tribe bought for $1.5 million in 1962 and which features the luxurious *Inn of the Mountain Gods* hotel/casino. More controversially, the Mescalero have also signed an agreement permitting the storage of high-level nuclear waste adjacent to the reservation.

Books

The following list is a selection of books that proved most useful, interesting, or entertaining during the research for this guide. A large proportion are only available in the US, and most of those you'd be lucky to find in bookstores anywhere outside the Southwest, though they can usually be obtained online. Unless otherwise specified, all books are published by the same publisher in the US and the UK.

History and archeology

Richard Abanes *One Nation Under Gods* (Four Walls Eight Windows). Polemic but fascinating account of Mormon history from an unyielding Christian perspective, which documents some very murky goings-on during the nineteenth century.

Donald A Barclay, James H Maguire, and Peter Wild (eds) *Into the Wilderness Dream* (University of Utah Press, US only). Gripping collection of Western exploration narratives written between 1500 and 1800; thanks to numerous little-known gems, the best of many such anthologies.

Pedro de Castañeda *The Journey of Coronado* (Dover). An invaluable historic document – the eyewitness journals of a Spaniard who accompanied Coronado into the Southwest in 1540.

Fray Angélico Chávez *My Penitente Land* (Museum of New Mexico Press, US only). Inspirational history of Hispanic New Mexico, written by a Franciscan friar, which stresses the parallels between the New Mexican landscape and pastoral lifestyle – and soul – and both Spain and ancient Palestine.

Richard Flint and Shirley Cushing Flint (eds) *The Coronado Expedition* (University of New Mexico Press, US only). This collection of papers from a 2000 academic conference provides a satisfying and accessible overview of current knowledge about Coronado's epochal expedition.

Franklin Folsom *Indian Uprising on the Rio Grande* (University of New Mexico Press, US only). Short but definitive history of the Pueblo Revolt.

Jack D. Forbes *Apache, Navajo, and Spaniard* (University of Oklahoma Press, US only). A rather unsettling but very thoroughly documented account of frontier conflicts in the seventeenth century, which challenges much received wisdom by suggesting, for example, that the Ancestral Puebloans violently displaced the Navajo along the Rio Grande.

Pat Garrett *The Authentic Life of Billy, the Kid* (University of Oklahoma Press, US only). "I have known the Kid personally since and during the continuance of what was known as the Lincoln County War, up to the moment of his death, of which I was the unfortunate instrument" – irresistible Western history, straight from the horse's mouth.

Rick Hendricks and John P Wilson (eds) *The Navajos in 1705* (University of New Mexico Press, US only). The little-known campaign diary of Spanish soldier Roque Madrid provides the first eyewitness account of the Navajo in the Four Corners.

Paul Horgan *Great River: The Rio Grande in North American History*

(Wesleyan University Press, US only). Horgan's monumental study of New Mexican history makes weighty reading; his more accessible *The Centuries of Santa Fe* (University of New Mexico Press, US only) is a lightly fictionalized set of biographies drawn from different periods of history.

J. Donald Hughes *In The House of Stone and Light* (Grand Canyon Natural History Association, US only). The human history of the Grand Canyon in words and pictures.

John D Lee *Mormonism Unveiled* (Fierra Blanca Publications). In his "Life and Confession," John Lee, of Lees Ferry fame, doesn't quite tell all he knows – like where he buried the gold – but there's a lot of eye-opening material in here.

Clyde A. Milner II, Carol A. O'Connor, Martha A. Sandweiss *The Oxford History of the American West* (Oxford University Press). Fascinating collection of essays on Western history, covering topics ranging from myths and movies to art and religion.

David Grant Noble *New Light on Chaco Canyon* (SAR Press, US only). Accessible and informative overview of the latest research into New Mexico's most important Ancestral Puebloan site.

Stephen Plog *Ancient Peoples of the Southwest* (Thames and Hudson). Much the best single-volume history of the pre-Hispanic Southwest, packed with diagrams and color photographs.

Carroll L. Riley *Rio del Norte* (University of Utah Press, US only).

Fascinating history of the upper Rio Grande valley from prehistoric times up to the Pueblo Revolt.

Carroll L. Riley *The Kachina and the Cross* (University of Utah Press, US only). A comprehensive history of the early relations between Pueblo peoples and Hispanic colonists, highlighting how they grudgingly came to share the land of New Mexico.

Thomas E. Sheridan *Arizona – A History* (University of Arizona Press). Stimulating reassessment of 11,000 years of Arizona history.

Alex Shoumatoff *Legends of the American Desert* (HarperCollins). Comprehensive, anecdotal, and entertaining first-person survey of several centuries of Southwestern history.

Stewart L. Udall *Majestic Journey* (Museum of New Mexico Press, US only). Lively, well-illustrated chronicle of Francisco Coronado's 1540–42 *entrada* into the Southwest, written by a former US Secretary of the Interior, plus an attempt to reconstruct the Spaniard's route.

Richard White *It's Your Misfortune and None of My Own* (University of Oklahoma Press). Dense, authoritative, and all-embracing history of the American West, which debunks the notion of the rugged pioneer by stressing the role of the federal government.

Charles Wilkinson *Fire on the Plateau* (Island Press, US only). This authoritative examination of the recent history of the Colorado Plateau is good on environmental and legal issues, but a bit heavy on personal reminiscence.

Native Americans

Between Sacred Mountains (Sun Tracks & University of Arizona Press). Superb overview of Navajo

history, culture, and politics, written by Navajo teachers and parents as a sourcebook for Navajo students.

Richard O. Clemmer *Roads in the Sky* (Westview). A history of the Hopi, with an emphasis on the twentieth century and the role of prophecy.

Nancy Yaw Davis *The Zuni Enigma* (W. W. Norton). An intriguing if ultimately unconvincing elaboration of the author's theory that a wandering group of Japanese pilgrims joined the Zuni tribe during the thirteenth century.

Angie Debo *Geronimo* (University of Oklahoma Press, US; Pimlico, UK). Gripping full-length biography of the Apache medicine man who led the last Native American uprising against the US Army.

Paula Richardson Fleming & Judith Lynn Luskey *The Shadow Catchers* (Laurence King, UK only, o/p). A history of nineteenth-century photographers of Native Americans, with some stunning images of the Hopi and Navajo.

Basil C. Hedrick, J. Charles Kelley, and Carroll C. Riley (eds) *The Meso-American Southwest* (Southern Illinois University Press, US, o/p). Intriguing essays exploring possible trade, cultural, and religious links between the ancient Southwest and the "high cultures" of Mexico.

Robert H. Keller and Michael F. Turek *American Indians and National Parks* (University of Arizona Press, US only). What happens when the federal park system appropriates land from its former indigenous inhabitants; Mesa Verde, Rainbow Bridge, and the Grand Canyon are among examples considered in detail.

Raymond Friday Locke *The Book of the Navajo* (Mankind, US only). Comprehensive history of the Navajo, from their mythic origins to the present day.

Jerry Mander *In the Absence of the Sacred* (Sierra Club, US only). Stimulating diatribe that pits the endurance of Native American values – with much discussion of the Hopi and Navajo – against the shortcomings of modern technology.

Robert S. McPherson *Sacred Land Sacred View* (Signature Books, US only). Intriguing anthropological account of how the Navajo perceive the Four Corners region.

David Roberts *Once They Moved Like The Wind* (Simon & Schuster). Excellent, fast-moving history of the Apache.

Polly Schaafsma (ed) *Kachinas in the Pueblo World* (University of New Mexico Press, US only). Well-illustrated survey of the *kachina* cult in the Southwest (see p.84).

Stephen Trimble *The People* (SAR Press, US only). Excellent introduction to all the Native American groups of the Southwest, bringing the history up to the late twentieth century via contemporary interviews.

Frank Waters *The Book of the Hopi* (Viking Penguin, US; Penguin, UK). As authoritative an account of Hopi religion as it's possible to find, though it's said that Waters' informants were not themselves initiated into all the secrets of the *kiva*.

Travel

Kenneth A. Brown *The Four Corners* (HarperCollins). Slightly dry but very comprehensive journalist's account of his wanderings in search

of the geology and history of the Four Corners region.

Edward Dolnick *Down The Great Unknown* (Harper Collins). Deft re-telling of the saga of John Wesley Powell's first Grand Canyon voyage that takes great pains to make it all intelligible to modern readers, with the analogies flowing thick and fast.

Colin Fletcher *The Man Who Walked Through Time* (Vintage Books). Enjoyable account by the first man to hike the full length of the Grand Canyon.

Susan Shelby Magoffin *Down the Santa Fe Trail and into Mexico* (University of Nebraska Press, US only). Absorbing first-person account by a trader's wife who reached Santa Fe in August 1846 in time to witness the Yankee takeover of New Mexico.

Melanie McGrath *Motel Nirvana* (Picador, US, o/p; Flamingo, UK). Entertaining account of a British traveler's experiences in the Southwest, with some enjoyable swipes at various New Age nonsenses.

John Wesley Powell *The Exploration of the Colorado River and Its Canyons* (Dover). Powell is said to have adapted the details of his first epic journey down the Colorado

for public consumption, but his journals still make exhilarating reading.

Douglas Preston *Cities of Gold* (University of New Mexico Press, US only). Long but very readable account of a horseback journey in the steps of Coronado, which throws a lot of light on history both ancient and modern.

David Roberts *In Search of the Old Ones* (Touchstone Press). An engaging chronicle of one man's obsession with Southwestern archeology.

Mark Twain *Roughing It* (Penguin). This rollicking account of Twain's peregrinations across the nineteenth-century West may well be the greatest story ever told, though only his account of the Mormons is of much relevance here.

Ted J. Warner (ed) *The Domínguez-Escalante Journal* (University of Utah Press, US only). The extraordinary diary of the two Franciscan friars who crossed Utah in 1776 in search of a new route to California, and came back via the Grand Canyon.

The contemporary Southwest

Atlas of the New West (Norton). Absorbing, well-illustrated compendium of changes and developments in the contemporary West, produced by the Center of the American West at Boulder.

Alan Hess *Viva Las Vegas* (Chronicle). A comprehensive, beautifully illustrated survey of Las Vegas's architectural history, which consistently throws fascinating sidelights on the development of the city.

Shawn Levy *Rat Pack Confidential* (Doubleday, US; Fourth Estate, UK). Enjoyable hymn to the "last great showbiz party," when Las Vegas

prostrated itself at the feet of Frank Sinatra and the boys.

Scott Norris (ed) *Discovered Country* (University of New Mexico Press, US only). Anthology of essays focusing on the impact of tourism on the Southwest, with some interesting material on the repackaging of Native American culture for Anglo consumption.

Debra Rosenthal *At the Heart of the Bomb* (Addison Wesley, US only, o/p). Intriguing reportage of what really goes on in New Mexico's vast defense laboratories.

Hal K. Rothman *Devil's Bargains: Tourism in the Twentieth-Century*

American West (University Press of Kansas, US only). Thought-provoking assessment of how tourism has shaped the modern West, which overturns many a cozy historical myth about places such as Santa Fe and Las Vegas.

Hunter S. Thompson *Fear and Loathing in Las Vegas* (Random, US; Paladin, UK). Classic account of a drug-crazed journalist's lost weekend in early-1970s Vegas; what's really striking is how much further over-the-top Las Vegas has gone since then.

Mike Tronnes (ed) *Literary Las Vegas* (Mainstream Publishing, UK only). Sin City, Nevada, as seen by Tom Wolfe, Joan Didion, Noel Coward, and others.

Mike Weatherford *Cult Vegas* (Huntington Press, US only). Local entertainment columnist runs a loving eye over Las Vegas's music and movie scene; both Elvis and Sinatra get their own chapters.

Chris Wilson *The Myth of Santa Fe* (University of New Mexico Press, US only). Eye-opening and very detailed account of how the Santa Fe known to tourists today is largely a twentieth-century concoction.

Environment and natural history

Edward Abbey *Desert Solitaire* (Ballantine Books, US; Robin Clark Ltd, UK). Abbey's classic evocation of his year as a ranger at Arches National Park was the first of his many volumes championing the wildernesses of the Southwest.

Donald L. Baars *A Traveler's Guide to the Geology of the Colorado Plateau* (University of Utah Press, US only). Among the more readily comprehensible explanations of the geology of the Four Corners.

Philip L. Fradkin *A River No More* (University of California Press). The story of the Colorado River, from John Wesley Powell to the water-management issues of today.

Edward A. Geary *The Proper Edge of the Sky* (University of Utah Press, US only). Loving evocation of the history and topography of southern Utah.

Michael P. Ghiglieri and Thomas M. Myers *Over The Edge: Death in Grand Canyon* (Puma Press, US only). In their bid to account for the demise of every single person known to have died within the Grand

Canyon, the authors transcend the merely morbid to throw fascinating light on every aspect of the canyon's history, and provide masses of useful advice on how to avoid becoming another fatality. The morbid stuff's good, too.

Ed Marston (ed) *Reopening the Western Frontier* (Island Press, US only, o/p). In-depth articles on the changing Southwestern environment from the *High Country News* newspaper; particularly good on southern Utah.

Russel Martin *A Story That Stands Like A Dam* (Henry Holt, US only). Meticulously chronicled indictment of the West's last great dam, which inundated Glen Canyon in the 1960s.

Lisa Michaels *Grand Ambition* (W. W. Norton, US; Hodder & Stoughton, UK). Gripping novelistic reconstruction of a true-life romantic mystery; just what did happen to honeymooners Glen and Bessie Hyde in the winter of 1928, when they tried to become the first couple to row down the Grand Canyon?

Barbara J. Morehouse *A Place Called Grand Canyon* (University of

Arizona Press, US only). Fascinating academic analysis of how the Grand Canyon has been defined and exploited.

John A. Murray *Cinema Southwest* (Northland, US only). A critical, well illustrated overview of the long history of movies filmed in the Southwest, with plenty of location information.

Marc Reisner *Cadillac Desert* (Penguin). The damning saga of the twentieth-century damming of the West.

Raye C. Ringholz *Uranium Frenzy* (University of New Mexico Press, US only). Lively account of the 1950s uranium boom on the Colorado

Plateau, with plenty of hard-hitting material on the health consequences for the miners.

Jeremy Schmidt *Grand Canyon National Park – A Natural History Guide* (Houghton Mifflin). A superb single-volume account of the Grand Canyon's environment, ecology, and geological origins.

Bette L. Stanton *Where God Put The West* (Four Corners Publications, US only). Photo-packed history of moviemaking in Monument Valley and Moab.

Ann Zwinger *Wind in the Rock* (University of Arizona Press). An inveterate canyoneer's account of the natural history of southeast Utah.

Fiction

Edward Abbey *The Monkey Wrench Gang* (Perennial, US; Robin Clark Ltd, UK). Classic wishful thinking from the wilderness advocate, this fast-paced novel centers on plans by environmental saboteurs to destroy the Glen Canyon dam.

Willa Cather *Death Comes for the Archbishop* (Vintage Books, US; Virago, UK). Not as sensational as the title implies, but a magnificent evocation of the landscapes and cultures of nineteenth-century New Mexico. Cather's *The Professor's House* (Vintage) features an extended account of the discovery of Ancestral Puebloan remains on a remote New Mexican mesa.

Clyde Edgerton *Redeye* (Viking Penguin, US; Penguin, UK). Brief, bumptious Western, focusing on the discovery of Ancestral Puebloan cliff dwellings and the aftermath of the Mountain Meadows Massacre.

Natalie Goldberg *Banana Rose* (Bantam, US only). Taos-based creative-writing guru – her *Wild Mind*

(Bantam, US; Rider, UK) and *Writing Down the Bones* (Shambhala Publications) have inspired countless would-be writers – practices what she preaches in this evocative novel, set partly in New Mexico.

Zane Grey *Riders of the Purple Sage* (Penguin). Gloriously purple prose, first published in 1912, from the doyen of Western writers.

Tony Hillerman *A Thief of Time* (HarperCollins, US; Penguin, UK), *The Dark Wind* (HarperCollins, US; Sphere, UK o/p), and several others. Hillerman has written about a dozen entertaining, intricately plotted detective novels set on and around the Navajo Nation, all packed with fascinating detail about Navajo, Hopi, and Zuni culture and beliefs.

Barbara Kingsolver *Pigs in Heaven* (HarperCollins, US; Faber, UK). A magnificent evocation of tensions and realities in the contemporary Southwest, by a Tucson-based writer who ranks among America's finest prose stylists.

Cormac McCarthy *Blood Meridian* (Random, US; Picador, UK). A disturbing portrayal of the West in all its bloody reality – the scenes at Yuma Crossing are horrendous – if a tad macho for some tastes.

N. Scott Momaday *House Made of Dawn Time* (HarperCollins). Pulitzer Prize-winning novel, written by a Kiowa Indian, about the spiritual crisis of a young Pueblo Indian.

John Nichols *The Milagro Beanfield War* (Owl Books, US; Deutsch, UK o/p). Thanks to the Robert Redford movie, this entertaining saga of a water-rights rebellion by dispossessed Hispanic villagers in northern New Mexico is the best-known of Nichols' *New Mexico* trilogy (the others are *The Magic Journey* and *The Nirvana Blues*).

Michael Ondaatje *The Collected Works of Billy the Kid* (Random, US; Picador, UK). Slim volume of poetry and contemporary accounts which add up to an evocative picture of New Mexico's most famous tearaway.

Simon J. Ortiz *Men on the Moon* (University of Arizona Press, US only). Evocative contemporary short stories by an Ácoma Indian poet.

Leslie Marmon Silko *Almanac of the Dead* (Penguin, US only). Epic novel, by a Laguna Pueblo Indian, of a Native American mother searching for her lost child on the fringes of the Tucson underworld; look out also for Silko's *Ceremony*.

Glossary

adobe Construction material, consisting of bricks of mud, sand, and grass or straw, and by extension a building itself; see p.129.

Anasazi Term formerly used for the ancient people of the Four Corners region; see p.567.

anticline Geological term for a dome or ridge shoved upwards by subterranean bulging.

arroyo Flat, often dry desert stream-bed.

backcountry Term used particularly in national parks to signify wilderness areas that cannot be reached by road (as opposed, occasionally, to frontcountry).

atlatl Spear-throwing device – a sort of detachable, lever-like handle that gave extra power and accuracy – used by ancient Native Americans.

bulto or *santo bulto* Carved wooden statue of a saint, characteristic of Hispanic New Mexico.

butte Geological term for a flat-topped outcrop of rock that's taller than it is wide, usually formed by the erosion of a larger mesa.

casita Cottage, now applied mainly to individual guest accommodations in upmarket B&Bs.

cuesta Long sloping mesa terminated by an abrupt bluff.

desert varnish A natural veneer, caused by leaching minerals, that accretes over the centuries on exposed rock faces and makes an ideal surface on which to etch petroglyphs.

genízaros In colonial New Mexico, the mixed-race offspring of captured Plains Indians and their Spanish masters.

graben Geological term, from the German for "ditches," applied to narrow valleys created by the erosion of underground salt beds.

Grand Staircase Topographical feature of southwest Utah, stretching from the Grand Canyon to Bryce Canyon.

Great House Archeological term for a defensively oriented, multistory ancient pueblo with hundreds of rooms, as seen at Chaco Canyon; see p.112.

Great Kiva Archeological term for a *kiva* that was used by an entire community rather than an individual clan or family.

heishi Necklace of threaded disks, usually cut from seashells, as made originally by Ancestral Puebloans and now by Santo Domingo Pueblo.

Hisatsinom The Hopi name for their Ancestral Puebloan forebears.

hogan Navajo dwelling; see p.80.

Hohokam Ancient people of southern Arizona.

hoodoo Natural sandstone formation in which a boulder is left balanced on a slender pillar, as at Bryce Canyon.

kachina (also spelled *katsina*) "Spirit messengers," central to the religions of the Hopi and other Pueblo Indians; see p.84.

kiva Underground chamber used for religious ceremonies by Pueblo Indians, usually located underground; see p.567.

latilla Light pole used in the roof construction of adobe buildings.

LDS Abbreviation to denote the Latter-Day Saints, or Mormons.

mano Handheld stone traditionally used to grind and crush seeds.

mesa From the Spanish for "table"; geological term for a large, broad flat-topped outcrop of rock.

metate Stone slab or trough, used with a *mano* for grinding seeds.

Mimbres Ancient people of southern New Mexico, renowned for their pottery; see p.246.

Moki or **Moqui** The former name for the Hopi people of northern Arizona.

monocline Geological term for an abrupt irregularity in the usual stratification of rocks, often resulting in a dramatic cliff.

Penitentes Catholic sect in nineteenth-century New Mexico; see p.175.

petroglyph Ancient rock-art image carved or pecked into stone.

pictograph Ancient rock-art image painted into stone.

presidio Spanish term for a fortress built during the colonial period.

pueblo Spanish word meaning "village"; applied to ancient Native American dwellings and also to modern Indian communities and peoples.

reef Word applied by early Anglo settlers to such vast natural barriers to their progress across the desert (usually created by monoclines) as Utah's Capitol Reef.

reredos Painted altarpiece, as seen in Hispanic churches at Chimayó (see p.174) and elsewhere.

retablo Kind of Hispanic religious folk art, painted on tin or wood.

ristra Garland of chile peppers, sold as souvenirs in New Mexico.

santo In Hispanic folk art, an image or holy object.

sipapu In Pueblo religion, the hole through which humans reached this earth.

Sinagua Ancient people of central Arizona.

slickrock Pioneer term for smooth, undulating stretches of sandstone, as a rule only slick after rain.

syncline The opposite of an anticline, a syncline is a rock formation created by an underground collapse.

talus Fallen rock debris which accumulates to form slopes at the bases of cliffs and canyon walls.

viga A broad beam of ponderosa or fir, as used by the Ancestral Puebloans in roof construction, and prominent in adobe architecture today.

Travel store

D: Rough Guide **DIRECTIONS** for short breaks

For more information go to www.roughguides.com

For **flying visits**, check out Rough Guide **DIRECTIONS**

It's like having a local friend plan your trip.

"A guide as *direct* as DIRECTIONS is exactly what I need when I'm visiting a city for the first time"
The Independent, UK

Rough Guide DIRECTIONS

Gran Canaria

Focusing on cities, islands and resort regions, Rough Guides **DIRECTIONS** are richly illustrated, with a third of each guide in **full colour**.

US$10.99, CAN$15.99, £6.99

Choose from dozens of worldwide titles, from London to Las Vegas.

BROADEN YOUR HORIZONS

ROUGH GUIDES

Small print and
Index

A Rough Guide to Rough Guides

Published in 1982, the first Rough Guide – to Greece – was a student scheme that became a publishing phenomenon. Mark Ellingham, a recent graduate in English from Bristol University, had been traveling in Greece the previous summer and couldn't find the right guidebook. With a small group of friends he wrote his own guide, combining a highly contemporary, journalistic style with a thoroughly practical approach to travelers' needs.

The immediate success of the book spawned a series that rapidly covered dozens of destinations. And, in addition to impecunious backpackers, Rough Guides soon acquired a much broader and older readership that relished the guides' wit and inquisitiveness as much as their enthusiastic, critical approach and value-for-money ethos.

These days, Rough Guides include recommendations from shoestring to luxury and cover more than 200 destinations around the globe, including almost every country in the Americas and Europe, more than half of Africa and most of Asia and Australasia. Our ever-growing team of authors and photographers is spread all over the world, particularly in Europe, the USA and Australia.

In the early 1990s, Rough Guides branched out of travel, with the publication of Rough Guides to World Music, Classical Music and the Internet. All three have become benchmark titles in their fields, spearheading the publication of a wide range of books under the Rough Guide name.

Including the travel series, Rough Guides now number more than 350 titles, covering: phrasebooks, waterproof maps, music guides from Opera to Heavy Metal, reference works as diverse as Conspiracy Theories and Shakespeare, and popular culture books from iPods to Poker. Rough Guides also produce a series of more than 120 World Music CDs in partnership with World Music Network.

Visit www.roughguides.com to see our latest publications.

Rough Guide travel images are available for commercial licensing at www.roughguidespictures.com

Rough Guide credits

Text editor: Christina Knight
Layout: Ankur Guha
Cartography: Jai Prakash Mishra
Picture editors: Siobhan Donoghue
Production: Aimee Hampson
Proofreader: Stewart Wild
Cover design: Chloë Roberts
Editorial: **London** Kate Berens, Claire Saunders,
Geoff Howard, Ruth Blackmore, Polly Thomas,
Richard Lim, Alison Murchie, Karoline Densley,
Andy Turner, Keith Drew, Edward Aves, Nikki
Birrell, Helen Marsden, Alice Park, Sarah Eno, Joe
Staines, Duncan Clark, Peter Buckley, Matthew
Milton, Tracy Hopkins, David Paul, Lucy White,
Ruth Tidball; **New York** Andrew Rosenberg,
Steven Horak, April Isaacs, AnneLise Sorensen,
Amy Hegarty, Sean Mahoney, Ella Steim
Design & Pictures: **London** Simon Bracken,
Dan May, Diana Jarvis, Mark Thomas, Jj Luck,
Harriet Mills; **Delhi** Madhulita Mohapatra, Umesh
Aggarwal, Ajay Verma, Jessica Subramanian,
Pradeep Thapliyal, Sachin Tanwar, Anita Singh

Production: Sophie Hewat, Katherine Owers
Cartography: **London** Maxine Repath, Ed
Wright, Katie Lloyd-Jones; **Delhi** Rajesh Chhibber,
Ashutosh Bharti, Rajesh Mishra, Animesh Pathak,
Jasbir Sandhu, Karobi Gogoi, Amod Singh,
Alakananda Bhattacharya
Online: **New York** Jennifer Gold, Suzanne Welles,
Kristin Mingrone; **Delhi** Manik Chauhan, Narender
Kumar, Shekhar Jha, Rakesh Kumar, Amit Verma,
Rahul Kumar, Amit Kumar
Marketing & Publicity: **London** Richard Trillo,
Niki Hanmer, Louise Maher, Jess Carter; **New
York** Geoff Colquitt, Megan Kennedy, Katy Ball;
Delhi Reem Khokhar
Custom publishing and foreign rights: Philippa
Hopkins
Manager India: Punita Singh
Series editor: Mark Ellingham
Reference Director: Andrew Lockett
PA to Managing and Publishing Directors:
Megan McIntyre
Publishing Director: Martin Dunford

Publishing information

This fourth edition published October 2006 by
Rough Guides Ltd,
80 Strand, London WC2R 0RL UK
345 Hudson St, 4th Floor,
New York, NY 10014, USA
14 Local Shopping Centre, Panchsheel Park,
New Delhi 110017, India
Distributed by the Penguin Group
Penguin Books Ltd,
80 Strand, London WC2R 0RL
Penguin Putnam, Inc.
375 Hudson Street, NY 10014, USA
Penguin Group (Australia)
250 Camberwell Road, Camberwell,
Victoria 3124, Australia
Penguin Books Canada Ltd,
10 Alcorn Avenue, Toronto, Ontario,
Canada M4V 1E4
Penguin Group (New Zealand)
67 Apollo Drive, Mairangi Bay, Auckland
1310, New Zealand
Cover concept by Peter Dyer.

Typeset in Bembo and Helvetica to an original
design by Henry Iles.
Printed and bound in China
© Greg Ward 2006
No part of this book may be reproduced in any
form without permission from the publisher except
for the quotation of brief passages in reviews.
632pp includes index
A catalogue record for this book is available from
the British Library
ISBN 1-84353-683-8
ISBN 13: 9-78184-353-683-3
The publishers and authors have done their best
to ensure the accuracy and currency of all the
information in **The Rough Guide to Southwest
USA**, however, they can accept no responsibility
for any loss, injury, or inconvenience sustained by
any traveler as a result of information or advice
contained in the guide.

1   3   5   7   9   8   6   4   2

Help us update

We've gone to a lot of effort to ensure that the
fourth edition of **The Rough Guide to Southwest
USA** is accurate and up to date. However, things
change – places get "discovered," opening hours
are notoriously fickle, restaurants and rooms raise
prices or lower standards. If you feel we've got it
wrong or left something out, we'd like to know, and
if you can remember the address, the price, the
time and the phone number, so much the better.
We'll credit all contributions, and send a copy of
the next edition (or any other Rough Guide if you

prefer) for the best letters. Everyone who writes
to us and isn't already a subscriber will receive
a copy of our full-color thrice-yearly newsletter.
Please mark letters: "**Rough Guide to Southwest
USA Update**" and send to: Rough Guides, 80
Strand, London WC2R 0RL, or Rough Guides,
4th Floor, 345 Hudson St, New York, NY 10014.
Or send an email to **mail@roughguides.com**
Have your questions answered and tell others
about your trip at
www.roughguides.atinfopop.com

Acknowledgments

Thanks of course to my wife Sam Cook – here's to a lifetime of road-trips in the Southwest – and to everyone at Rough Guides, including Christina Knight for her scrupulous editing; Steve Horak and Andrew Rosenberg for overseeing the whole thing; Siobhan Donoghue for her work on the pictures; Jai Prakash Mishra for the maps. Thanks, too, to the many people who helped while I was on the road, especially Edie Jarolim,

Steve Lewis in Santa Fe, Bruce Brossman at the Grand Canyon, Kelly Bagley at *La Posada* in Winslow, Justine Mroziak in Las Vegas, Robin Palmer in Springdale, Gina Yager at Grand Canyon West, Hylton and Robert at Papillon, Rosanda Bahe, Brett Brooks, Marian DeLay, Christine Fox, Jeannene Glenn, Keith Herriman, Pam Maisey, Lorraine Moore, and Kimberly Schmitz.

Readers' letters

Thanks to all the readers who have taken the time to write in with comments and suggestions (and apologies if we've inadvertently omitted or misspelt anyone's name):

Amy Bristow, Marthe and Glen Bucci, Fiona Haddon, Dik Hoogmoed, Alan Jowsey, John Kirton, David Lacey, Cathy Layton and Andy Conner, David Newton, John Nilsson, Susan Osborne,

Susan Parry, Valma Rees, Federica Scarpa, Gene Scharf, William Scott, Julia Spiess, Martin Straub, Richard Velleman, Vicki Warthen, and Marion and George Wilson

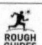

Photo credits

ROUGH GUIDES

SMALL PRINT

Index

Map entries are in color.

INDEX

Map symbols

maps are listed in the full index using colored text

----	Chapter division boundary	⸫	Ruin
-··-··-	International border	⤵	Viewpoint/overlook
--·--·	State border	🏔	Butte
17	Interstate highway	⌒	Cave
89	U.S. highway	▪	Pueblo
12	State highway	⚑	Museum
======	Dirt road/track	✈	Airport
▬▬	Railway	≋	Rapids
- - - -	Footpath	✦	General point of interest
·············	Hiking trail	⊠-⊠	Gate
○—○	Tramway	ⓘ	Tourist office
——	Waterway	⊠	Post office
⤙	Bridge/pass	@	Internet access
⋀⋀	Mountains	◉	Accommodation
▲	Peak	▣	Parking
⌇	Gorge/canyon/cliffs	⊞	Hospital/clinic
⚐	Ski area	▮	Building
⌒	Arch	⊞	Church
⚠	Campsite	⊞	Cemetery
⌂	Lodge	▨	Park/monument
⚑	Waterfall	⧄	Indian reservation